THE PHILISTINES AND OTHER "SEA PEOPLES" IN TEXT AND ARCHAEOLOGY

Society of Biblical Literature

Archaeology and Biblical Studies

Tammi Schneider, Editor

Number 15

The Philistines and Other "Sea Peoples" in Text and Archaeology

THE PHILISTINES AND OTHER "SEA PEOPLES" IN TEXT AND ARCHAEOLOGY

edited by

Ann E. Killebrew and Gunnar Lehmann

Society of Biblical Literature
Atlanta, Georgia

THE PHILISTINES AND OTHER "SEA PEOPLES" IN TEXT AND ARCHAEOLOGY

Library of Congress Cataloging-in-Publication Data

The Philistines and other "sea peoples" in text and archaeology / edited by Ann E. Killebrew and Gunnar Lehmann.

p. cm. — (Society of Biblical Literature Archaeology and biblical studies ; v. 15)

"This volume developed out of a 2001 workshop devoted to the Philistines and other Sea Peoples, which was co-organized by Ann E. Killebrew, Gunnar Lehmann, Michal Artzy, and Rachel Hachlili, and co-sponsored by the University of Haifa and the Ben Gurion University of the Negev"—Introd.

Includes bibliographical references and index.

ISBN 978-1-58983-129-2 (paper binding : acid-free paper)

1. Philistines—Antiquities. 2. Sea Peoples—Mediterranean Region—History. 3. Iron age—Mediterranean Region. 4. Social archaeology—Mediterranean Region—History. 5. Bible. O.T.—History of Biblical events. 6. Mediterranean Region—Antiquities. I. Killebrew, Ann E. II. Lehmann, Gunnar. III. Society of Biblical Literature.

DS90.P55 2013

938'.01—dc23

2012033937

Printed on acid-free, recycled paper conforming to ANSI/NISO Z39.48-1992 (R1997) and ISO 9706:1994 standards for paper permanence.

Contents

The Other "Sea Peoples" in the Levant

Anatolia, the Aegean, and Cyprus

Appendix

When the Past Was New: Moshe Dothan (1919–1999), an Appreciation

*Neil Asher Silberman**

Moshe Dothan was my most important teacher, though he never gave me a written examination and I never attended any course he taught. From 1972 to 1976, I worked as his assistant at the Israel Department of Antiquities and Museums in Jerusalem's Rockefeller Museum, working on the publication of his Ashdod excavations and participating in the beginnings of his ambitious Tel Akko dig. It was a time that now seems so distant. Archaeology in Israel was still living in the warm afterglow of its Yadin-esque heyday; extensive excavations around the Temple Mount and the Jewish Quarter in Jerusalem were still underway. Yet it was also a time of archaeological transition from an era of romantic national celebration to a more complex engagement with the material remains of the past. The study of the Sea Peoples—and of the Philistines in particular—was part of this dramatic transformation. Old-style antiquarianism and the quest for biblical illustration was giving way to a recognition that archaeology could also shed important new light on the nature of ancient ethnic dislocation, cultural interaction, and social change.

As a member of the pioneering generation of Israeli archaeologists, Moshe Dothan was born in Poland and immigrated to Palestine in the late 1930s, exchanging his former surname, Hammer, for a new identity and a new life in the soon-to-be-established Jewish state. After service in a Palestinian unit of the British army during World War II among the ruined modern cities and ancient monuments of Italy (whose impression on him would never be forgotten) and after further service in the 1948 Israel War of Independence, he began his studies at the Hebrew University of Jerusalem under the guidance of Israeli archaeology's founding fathers, E. L. Sukenik, Michael Avi-Yonah, and Benjamin Mazar. His

* Center for Heritage and Society, The University of Massachusetts, Amherst.

Fig. 1: Moshe Dothan (left) discussing stratigraphy at Tel Akko with Yigael Yadin (center) and Steve Rosen (right; photographer: Michal Artzy).

classical gymnasium education in Krakow served him well as he embarked on an archaeological career; it provided him with a solid background in Greek and Latin and a familiarity with a wide range of historical subjects and philosophies. In 1950, he joined the staff of the newly created Israel Department of Antiquities and Museums, gaining valuable field experience and a deep appreciation for rigorous archaeological method during his work with the legendary British archaeologist, P. L. O. Guy. His PhD dissertation on the ancient settlement patterns of the lower Rubin Valley was not only one of the first wide-ranging modern archaeological surveys undertaken in Israel; it also marked the beginning of his continuing interest in coastal archaeology.

In the annals of Sea Peoples scholarship, Moshe Dothan will of course be remembered first and foremost for his excavations at Ashdod. Following his earlier discoveries of Philistine remains at Azor (1958) and at Tel Mor (1959–1960), he embarked on nine seasons of digging at Tel Ashdod between 1962 and 1972, uncovering unprecedented evidence for the character and evolution of Philistine settlement. It is not an exaggeration to say that with this project, the modern understanding of Philistine culture entered a new era, refining and expanding the archaeological framework established by his wife and colleague, Trude, in linking the origins and interactions of Philistine culture with the wider Mediterranean world.

In earlier eras of exploration, the Philistines had been seen as archetypal biblical villains, ethnically linked to the Aegean and historically implicated in a struggle for *Lebensraum* with the emerging Israelite nation. The Aegean-style decorative motifs on Philistine pottery had long been seen as static ethnic markers; the fearsome biblical image of the looming Philistine giant, Goliath, shaped popular perceptions of Philistine culture—far more pervasively than the archaeological evidence. Yet, the Ashdod excavations played an important role in overturning that simplistic perception, shifting the archaeological focus from a stark vision of ethnic invasion to a recognition of the complex economic, cultural, and social changes experienced by the Philistines during their initial settlement and subsequent development on the Canaanite coast.

Indeed, Ashdod's most spectacular finds have become distinctive icons of the modern archaeological understanding of Philistine material culture. The astonishingly abstract cultic figurine nicknamed "Ashdoda"—half offering table, half Aegean-style goddess—clearly showed the creatively composite character of Philistine culture, in its amalgamation of Mycenaean and Bronze Age Near Eastern styles. The inscribed seals from Iron I strata were the first evidence of Philistine literacy. Yet even though their characters *resembled* Cypro-Minoan script, they could not be pinned down to a particular place of origin, further suggesting the hybrid nature of Philistine society. In the higher levels, the famous "Musicians' Stand", the red-burnished "Ashdod Ware", and the city's impressive six-chambered gate (so close in plan and dimensions to the supposed "Solomonic" monuments) demonstrated the gradually strengthening links of the city to the contemporary Levantine cultures of Iron Age II. The Ashdod excavations thus revealed the slow evolution of a complex society, tracing its beginnings as an urban coastal center in the Bronze Age, through its period of distinctive Philistine culture, to its eventual destruction as a petty vassal kingdom under the Assyrian Empire.

Particularly crucial for the modern understanding of the Sea Peoples' initial settlement throughout the entire eastern Mediterranean was the discovery at Ashdod of an initial post-Late Bronze Age stratum containing locally made monochrome Mycenaean IIIC-style pottery types. These distinctively decorated vessels were clearly not offloaded immigrant housewares, but the product of a creative transformation, in which a vague and generalized memory of Mycenaean styles was gradually articulated into distinctive regional variants. Ashdod's Mycenaean IIIC proved to be just one of many versions that were produced in the widely dispersed archipelago of sites across Cyprus and along the coasts of Cilicia and the Levant established by new settlers in the wake of the Late Bronze collapse. In the case of Ashdod, it is now clear that Philistine history and cultural evolution involved far more than just a sudden, violent displacement from a specific Aegean homeland; Dothan's excavations showed it to be a process of complex social adaptation in the cultural cauldron of the Iron Age Levant.

Ashdod was also a new kind of excavation in a very practical sense. Conceived as a joint Israeli-American expedition, sponsored by the Israel Department of Antiquities and Museums, the Pittsburgh Theological Seminary, and Pittsburgh's Carnegie Museum, it brought together archaeologists trained in separate national traditions and field methods to forge a common excavation style. It was also a site where nearly an entire generation of post-Hazor-era Israeli archaeologists received their first extensive field experience. Anticipating the later appeals of Yigael Yadin for passionate amateurs to come join the excavations at Masada, the Ashdod expedition was the first of its kind in Israel to solicit and welcome the participation of enthusiastic volunteers from abroad. No less important were the multi-disciplinary and international scholarly connections; the excavations at Ashdod were the first in Israel to utilize extensive Neutron Activation Analysis for ceramic provenience (specifically of its Mycenaean IIIC wares), and the first to engage in continuous and close dialogue with scholars working on Cyprus on a similar Sea Peoples' phenomenon.

Soon after the completion of the Ashdod excavations, Dothan began his ambitious excavations at Tel Akko (1973–1989), the last major archaeological undertaking of his life. These excavations provided intriguing new data on the nature of the Sea Peoples' process of settlement farther up the coast. Amidst the extensive finds of Hellenistic houses and fortifications, Crusader ruins, Phoenician public buildings, and an imposing Middle Bronze Age rampart, the Akko excavations revealed evidence of the Sea Peoples' presence—in this case, presumably the Shardana, localized in this area by the Onomasticon of Amenope. The discovery of an area of pottery and metal workshops, containing implements for copper smelting, metal working, unbaked vessels, and scattered fragments of yet another variant of Mycenaean IIIC pottery. These finds suggested that the short-lived settlement of Sea People at Akko functioned as a center for craft production at the end of the thirteenth and early-twelfth centuries B.C.E. In subsequent years, Dothan became fascinated by the possible connections of the Shardana with Sardinia—and the hypothesis of post-Late Bronze cultural and possibly economic contact between the Levant and the western Mediterranean suggested by such a link. In 1992, he summed up his insights about the Sea Peoples in a popular book he coauthored with Trude: *People of the Sea: The Search for the Philistines*, presenting the most important discoveries and the general conclusions they had both formulated about the archaeology and history of the Philistines and the other Sea Peoples they had investigated in the course of their careers.

For Moshe Dothan, the past was not a static reality but a dynamic and ever-changing field of research in which new ideas and new theories were not disturbing exceptions but important motivations for serious archaeological work. Over an active career of more than four decades, his contributions extended far beyond the geographical and chronological boundaries of Sea Peoples studies. In his years of surveys and excavations on behalf of the Israel Department of Antiquities and Museums, he had also uncovered the important Chalcolithic site of Horvat Batar, near Beersheva (1952–1954); the seaside Canaanite temple at Nahariya with its silver sea goddess and seven-spouted lamps (1954–1955); the Iron Age desert citadel at Tell el-Qudeirat, identified with Kadesh Barnea (1956); and the late Roman-to-Early Islamic era synagogue at Hammath Tiberias with its spectacular zodiac (1961–1963). The finds from each of these excavations have enriched many subfields of the discipline with rich material for continuing discussion and questions for further research.

In 1972, Dothan was appointed professor of archaeology at the University of Haifa. He served as chairman of the Department of Maritime Studies from 1976 to 1979 and was instrumental in the establishment of the Department of Archaeology where he also served as its departmental head. Yet Moshe was never entirely comfortable in the classroom, presenting lessons from a well-polished syllabus. He was far more at home in the field and at his excavation sites, huddling with his surveyor over sections and top plans or studying assemblages of newly dug pottery. Whether it was the nature of Chalcolithic culture, of Canaanite religion, the expansion of the Iron Age Israelite kingdoms, or the use of pagan imagery by Jews in the Late Roman period, Moshe Dothan contributed abundant evidence for understanding the evolution of human culture in the Land of Israel over the millennia.

As an unforgettable personality and independent thinker, he rarely gained the main spotlight of archaeological celebrity. Yet Moshe Dothan's contribution to the archaeology of Israel in general and of the Sea Peoples and the Philistines in particular was profound. He worked with energy and impatience, under conditions and with resources that few of today's archaeologists would ever attempt. He possessed more creativity, historical scope, and courage to challenge conventional wisdom and to break disciplinary boundaries than many other of his contemporaries who fancied themselves more famous, more erudite, or more rigidly systematic than he. In his life and work, Moshe Dothan embodied the belief that the past is always new, forever awaiting the next discovery or insight that might shatter our preconceptions and change our understanding of human history in surprising and unexpected ways.

That is what he taught me. That is the greatest lesson an archaeologist can ever teach. May this volume on the archaeological search for the Philistines and other Sea Peoples be a tribute to him.

Acknowledgments

The Philistines and Other "Sea Peoples" is the result of the contributions and editorial assistance of numerous individuals. First and foremost, we would like to express our gratitude to all the authors of this mega-volume for their essays, which reflect their expertise and first-hand knowledge of the material culture and texts associated with the Philistines and other Sea Peoples. We thank them for their contributions, and especially for their patience throughout the process of preparing the manuscripts for publication. Special thanks are due to the volume's copy editors, Heather D. Heidrich and Dr. Gabriele Faßbeck. Their meticulous and very professional work was invaluable! This tome is due in no small part to their assistance and input. We would also like to express our sincere appreciation to Dr. Billie Jean Collins, acquisitions editor at the Society of Biblical Literature, for her expert work on the final editing and layout of this especially complex and massive volume. We are also indebted to Professor Tammi J. Schneider, editor of the Archaeology and Biblical Studies series, for her enthusiastic encouragement during the preparation of this book. Lastly, many thanks are due to Dr. Bob Buller, editorial director at the Society of Biblical Literature, for his guidance and advice throughout the process of preparing the manuscripts for publication. This book would not have been possible without the participation, assistance, and contributions of all of you. Thank you!

Ann E. Killebrew and Gunnar Lehmann

Abbreviations

AA	*Archäologischer Anzeiger*
AASOR	Annual of the American Schools of Oriental Research
ABD	*Anchor Bible Dictionary*. Edited by D. N. Freedman. 6 vols. New York, 1992.
ADAJ	*Annual of the Department of Antiquities of Jordan*
AEL	*Ancient Egyptian Literature*. M. Lichtheim. 3 vols. Berkeley, 1973–1980.
AEO	*Ancient Egyptian Onomastica*. A. H. Gardiner. 3 vols. London, 1947.
AJA	*American Journal of Archaeology*
AJBA	*Australian Journal of Biblical Archaeology*
ANET	*Ancient Near Eastern Texts Relating to the Old Testament*. Edited by J. B. Pritchard. 3rd ed. Princeton, 1969.
AnSt	*Anatolian Studies*
AOAT	Alter Orient und Altes Testament
AoF	*Altorientalische Forschungen*
ARAB	*Ancient Records of Assyria and Babylonia*. Daniel David Luckenbill. 2 vols. Chicago, 1926–1927.
ARE	*Ancient Records of Egypt*. Edited by J. H. Breasted. 5 vols. Chicago, 1905–1907. Reprint, New York, 1962.
ASAE	*Annales du service des antiquités de l'Egypte*
ASOR	American Schools of Oriental Research
Atiqot	*'Atiqot*
BA	*Biblical Archaeologist*
BANEA	British Association for Near Eastern Archaeology
BAR	*Biblical Archaeology Review*
BAR	British Archaeological Reports
BASOR	*Bulletin of the American Schools of Oriental Research*
BIES	*Bulletin of the Israel Exploration Society*
BK	*Bibel und Kirche*
BKAT	Biblischer Kommentar, Altes Testament. Edited by M. Noth and H. W. Wolff.
BN	*Biblische Notizen*
CANE	*Civilizations of the Ancient Near East*. Edited by J. M.

	Sasson. 4 vols. New York, 1995.
CRAI	*Comptes rendus de l'Académie des inscriptions et belles-lettres*
CTH	*Catalogue des texts hittites*. Edited by E. Laroche. Paris, 1971.
EA	El-Amarna tablets. According to the edition of J. A. Knudtzon. *Die el-Amarna-Tafeln*. Leipzig, 1908–1915. Reprint, Aalen, 1964. Continued in A. F. Rainey, *El-Amarna Tablets, 359–379*. 2nd revised ed. Kevelaer, 1978.
ErIsr	*Eretz-Israel*
FM	Furumark Motif
FS	Furumark Shape
HO	Handbuch der Orientalistik
IEJ	*Israel Exploration Journal*
IstMitt	*Istanbuler Mitteilungen*
JAOS	*Journal of the American Oriental Society*
JCS	*Journal of Cuneiform Studies*
JEA	*Journal of Egyptian Archaeology*
JEOL	*Jaarbericht van het Vooraziatisch-Egyptisch Gezelschap (Genootschap) Ex oriente lux*
JNES	*Journal of Near Eastern Studies*
JSOT	*Journal for the Study of the Old Testament*
JSOTSup	Journal for the Study of the Old Testament: Supplement Series
KAI	*Kanaanäische und aramäische Inschriften*. H. Donner and W. Röllig. 2nd ed. Wiesbaden: Harrassowitz, 1966–1969.
KBo	*Keilschrifttexte aus Boghazköi*. WVDOG 30, 36, 68–70, 72–73, 77–80, 82–86, 89–90. Leipzig, 1916–
KTU	*Die keilalphabetischen Texte aus Ugarit*. Edited by M. Dietrich, O. Loretz, and J. Sanmartín. AOAT 24. Neukirchen-Vluyn, 1976. 2nd enlarged ed. of *KTU: The Cuneiform Alphabetic Texts from Ugarit, Ras Ibn Hani, and Other Places*. Edited by M. Dietrich, O. Loretz, and J. Sanmartín. Münster, 1995 (= *CTU*).
KUB	*Keilschrifturkunden aus Boghazköi*
MDAIK	*Mitteilungen des Deutschen Archäologischen Instituts, Abteilung Kairo*
MDOG	*Mitteilungen der Deutschen Orient-Gesellschaft*
MVAG	*Mitteilungen der Vorderasiatisch-ägyptischen Gesellschaft*. Vols. 1–44. 1896–1939.
NABU	*Nouvelles assyriologiques brèves et utilitaires*
NEA	*Near Eastern Archaeology*
NEAEHL	*The New Encyclopedia of Archaeological Excavations in the Holy Land*. Edited by E. Stern. 4 vols. Jerusalem, 1993.

OBO	Orbis biblicus et orientalis
OIP	Oriental Institute Publications
OJA	*Oxford Journal of Archaeology*
OLA	Orientalia lovaniensia analecta
OLP	*Orientalia lovaniensia periodica*
Or	*Orientalia* (NS)
PEFQS	*Palestine Exploration Fund Quarterly Statement*
PEQ	*Palestine Exploration Quarterly*
PRU	*Le palais royal d'Ugarit*
Qad	*Qadmoniot*
QDAP	*Quarterly of the Department of Antiquities in Palestine*
RAr	*Revue archéologique*
RB	*Revue biblique*
RDAC	*Report of the Department of Antiquities of Cyprus*
RGG	*Religion in Geschichte und Gegenwart*. Edited by K. Galling. 7 vols. 3rd ed. Tübingen, 1957–1965.
RS	Ras Shamra
SAOC	Studies in Ancient Oriental Civilizations
SBL	Society for Biblical Literature
SCIEM	The Synchronisation of Civilisations of the Eastern Mediterranean in the Second Millennium B.C.
SHCANE	Studies in the History and Culture of the Ancient Near East
SIMA	Studies in Mediterranean Archaeology
SMEA	*Studi Micenei ed Egeo-Anatolici*
TA	*Tel Aviv*
TGI	*Textbuch zur Geschichte Israels*. Edited by K. Galling. 2nd ed. Tübingen, 1968.
TUAT	*Texte aus der Umwelt des alten Testaments*. Edited by O. Kaiser. Gütersloh, 1984–.
TZ	*Theologische Zeitschrift*
UF	*Ugarit-Forschungen*
VAB	Vorderasiatische Bibliothek
VT	*Vetus Testamentum*
VTSup	Supplements to Vetus Testamentum
WMANT	Wissenschaftliche Monographien zum Alten und Neuen Testament
YCS	*Yale Classical Studies*
ZÄS	*Zeitschrift für ägyptische Sprache und Altertumskunde*
ZDPV	*Zeitschrift des deutschen Palästina-Vereins*

Introduction: The World of the Philistines and Other "Sea Peoples"

Ann E. Killebrew and Gunnar Lehmann

This volume developed out of a 2001 workshop devoted to the Philistines and other "Sea Peoples," which was co-organized by Ann E. Killebrew, Gunnar Lehmann, Michal Artzy, and Rachel Hachlili, and cosponsored by the University of Haifa and the Ben Gurion University of the Negev. Both the workshop and this updated publication resulted from a sense of frustration with the unidirectional and overly simplistic interpretations of the Philistine phenomenon that has dominated scholarship during the twentieth century (see, e.g., T. Dothan 1982; T. Dothan and M. Dothan 1992; Yasur-Landau 2010). In an attempt to redress what we consider to be a blinkered approach to the topic, this edited tome assembles a collection of papers that examines the Philistine and the broader "Sea Peoples" phenomenon from a variety of viewpoints and disciplines. First coined in 1881 by the French Egyptologist G. Maspero (1896), the somewhat misleading term "Sea Peoples" encompasses the ethnonyms Lukka, Sherden, Shekelesh, Teresh, Eqwesh, Denyen, Sikil/Tjekker, Weshesh, and Peleset (Philistines).[1] Often considered

1. The modern term "Sea Peoples" refers to peoples that appear in several New Kingdom Egyptian texts as originating from "islands" (tables 1–2; Adams and Cohen, this volume; see, e.g., Drews 1993, 57 for a summary). The use of quotation marks in association with the term "Sea Peoples" in our title is intended to draw attention to the problematic nature of this commonly used term. It is noteworthy that the designation "of the sea" appears only in relation to the Sherden, Shekelesh, and Eqwesh. Subsequently, this term was applied somewhat indiscriminately to several additional ethnonyms, including the Philistines, who are portrayed in their earliest appearance as invaders from the north during the reigns of Merenptah and Ramesses III (see, e.g., Sandars 1978; Redford 1992, 243, n. 14; for a recent review of the primary and secondary literature, see Woudhuizen 2006). Henceforth the term Sea Peoples will appear without quotation marks.

either a catalyst or a consequence resulting from the crisis that struck the eastern Mediterranean at the end of the Late Bronze and early Iron Ages, archaeologists composed a twentieth-century Sea People narrative of migrating populations originating from the west Aegean who had been displaced by the collapse of the Mycenaean palace system and the aftermath of the Trojan War (see, e.g., M. Wood 1996, 210–59). Most infamous among these west Aegean migrating peoples were the Philistines, best known for their negative portrayal in the Bible as a major antagonist of ancient Israel (see tables 1–2; Adams and Cohen, this volume).

Table 1: Egyptian primary sources mentioning Sea Peoples according to specific group (based on Adams and Cohen, this volume).

Sea Peoples Group	**Egyptian Text**	**Ruler/Dynasty**
Denyen (Danuna)	Amarna letters (EA 151)	Amenophis III/IV
Denyen (Danuna)	Medinet Habu	Ramesses III
Denyen (Danuna)	Papyrus Harris	Ramesses III
Denyen (Danuna)	Onomasticon of Amenope	Late 20th–22nd Dynasties
Eqwesh	Great Karnak Inscription	Merenptah
Eqwesh	Athribis Stele	Merenptah
Karkiša	Kadesh Inscription	Ramesses II
Lukka	Amarna letters (EA 38)	Akhenaten
Lukka	Kadesh Inscription	Ramesses II
Lukka	Great Karnak Inscription	Merenptah
Lukka	Onomasticon of Amenope	Late 20th–22nd Dynasties
Peleset (Philistines)	Medinet Habu	Ramesses III
Peleset (Philistines)	Papyrus Harris	Ramesses III
Peleset (Philistines)	Rhetorical Stele (Chapel C at Deir el-Medina)	Ramesses III
Peleset (Philistines)	Onomasticon of Amenope	Late 20th–22nd Dynasties
Peleset (Philistines)	Pedeset Inscription	ca. 900 B.C.E. (?)
Shekelesh	Great Karnak Inscription	Merenptah
Shekelesh	Cairo Column	Merenptah
Shekelesh	Athribis Stele	Merenptah
Shekelesh	Medinet Habu	Ramesses III
Sherden (Shardana)	Amarna letters (EA 81)	Amenophis III/IV
Sherden (Shardana)	Amarna letters (EA 122)	Amenophis III/IV
Sherden (Shardana)	Amarna letters (EA 123)	Amenophis III/IV

Sherden (Shardana)	Stele of Padjesef	19th–22nd Dynasties
Sherden (Shardana)	Kadesh Inscription	Ramesses II
Sherden (Shardana)	Tanis Stele	Ramesses II
Sherden (Shardana)	Papyrus Anastasi I	Ramesses II
Sherden (Shardana)	Great Karnak Inscription	Merenptah
Sherden (Shardana)	Athribis Stele	Merenptah
Sherden (Shardana)	Papyrus Anastasi II	Merenptah
Sherden (Shardana)	Stele of Setemhebu	Late 19th/Early 20th Dynasty
Sherden (Shardana)	Medinet Habu	Ramesses III
Sherden (Shardana)	Papyrus Harris	Ramesses III
Sherden (Shardana)	Papyrus Amiens	20th Dynasty
Sherden (Shardana)	Papyrus Wilbour	Ramesses V
Sherden (Shardana)	Adoption Papyrus	Ramesses IX
Sherden (Shardana)	Papyrus Moscow 169 (Onomasticon Golénischeff)	Early 21st Dynasty
Sherden (Shardana)	Papyrus BM 10326	End of 20th Dynasty
Sherden (Shardana)	Papyrus Turin 2026	End of 20th Dynasty
Sherden (Shardana)	Papyrus BM 10375	End of 20th Dynasty
Sherden (Shardana)	Onomasticon of Amenope	Late 20th–22nd Dynasties
Sherden (Shardana)	Donation Stele	Osorkon II
Teresh	Great Karnak Inscription	Merenptah
Teresh	Athribis Stele	Merenptah
Teresh	Medinet Habu	Ramesses III
Teresh	Rhetorical Stele (Chapel C at Deir el-Medina)	Ramesses III
Tjekker/Sikila(?)	Medinet Habu	Ramesses III
Tjekker/Sikila(?)	Papyrus Harris	Ramesses III
Tjekker/Sikila(?)	Onomasticon of Amenope	Late 20th–22nd Dynasties
Tjekker/Sikila(?)	Report of Wenamun	22nd Dynasty
Weshesh	Medinet Habu	Ramesses III
Weshesh	Papyrus Harris	Ramesses III

Table 2: Egyptian primary sources mentioning Sea Peoples in chronological order (based on Adams and Cohen, this volume).

Dynasty	Pharaoh	Sea People Group	No. of Texts
18th	Amenophis III/IV	Denyen (Danuna)	2
18th	Amenophis IV (Akhenaten)	Lukka	1
18th	Amenophis III/IV	Sherden (Shardana)	3
19th	Ramesses II	Karkiša	1
19th	Ramesses II	Lukka	1
19th	Ramesses II	Sherden (Shardana)	3
19th	Merenptah	Eqwesh	2
19th	Merenptah	Lukka	1
19th	Merenptah	Shekelesh	3
19th	Merenptah	Sherden (Shardana)	3
19th	Merenptah	Teresh	2
Late 19th–Early 20th	—	Sherden (Shardana)	1
19th–22nd	—	Sherden (Shardana)	1
20th	Ramesses III	Denyen (Danuna)	2
20th	Ramesses III	Peleset (Philistines)	3
20th	Ramesses III	Shekelesh	1
20th	Ramesses III	Sherden (Shardana)	2
20th	Ramesses III	Teresh	2
20th	Ramesses III	Tjekker/Sikila(?)	2
20th	Ramesses III	Weshesh	2
20th	Ramesses V	Sherden (Shardana)	1
20th	Ramesses VI	Sherden (Shardana)	1
20th	Ramesses IX	Sherden (Shardana)	1
20th	—	Sherden (Shardana)	1
End of 20th	—	Sherden (Shardana)	2
Late 20th–22nd	—	Denyen (Danuna)	1
Late 20th–22nd	—	Lukka	1
Late 20th–22nd	—	Peleset (Philistines)	1
Late 20th–22nd	—	Sherden (Shardana)	1
Late 20th–22nd	—	Tjekker/Sikila(?)	1
Early 21st	—	Sherden (Shardana)	1

22nd	Osorkon II	Sherden (Shardana)	1
22nd*	—	Peleset (Philistines)	1
22nd	—	Tjekker/Sikila(?)	1

* Pedeset Inscription ca. 900 B.C.E. (?)

In part, this Eurocentric view of events and the processes responsible for the demise of the Late Bronze "Age of Internationalism" can be understood as resulting in part from western-dominated scholarly agendas that were reinforced by political realities in the eastern Mediterranean during the late nineteenth and twentieth centuries (see, e.g., Silberman 1998; Leriou 2002; Killebrew forthcoming a). The focus on classical sites in Greece and biblical locales in the southern Levant and elsewhere in the region resulted in both a distorted and uneven archaeological record for the thirteenth and twelfth centuries B.C.E. In recent decades, new pieces of this jigsaw puzzle have been and continue to be uncovered gradually by excavations in previously underexplored regions of the east Aegean, Turkey, and northern Levant. The resulting data is transforming our understanding of this pivotal period of time. The evidence now points to a vastly more complex system of interactions and multi-directional interconnections between lands bordering the eastern Mediterranean Sea and its islands during the thirteenth through eleventh centuries B.C.E. (see, e.g., Maran 2004; Gilboa 2006–2007; Killebrew 2006–2007; 2010; Bachhuber and Roberts 2009; Venturi 2010; Hitchcock 2011). Our 2001 workshop was organized with the goal of addressing the Philistine and Sea People phenomenon in light of more recent discoveries in the eastern Mediterranean. The present volume is a collection of essays devoted to the texts, material culture, sites, regions, and themes discussed during this workshop and after.

Despite the ever expanding archaeological record, the origins, identity, and material manifestations of the Sea Peoples and their role in the eastern Mediterranean world during the thirteenth and twelfth centuries B.C.E. remain elusive. The textual and archaeological evidence leaves no doubt that the major political powers of this period—the Hittites and Egyptians—experienced a profound crisis during the transition from the Late Bronze to the Iron Age, resulting in the decline or dissolution of these great powers (see, e.g., Liverani 1987; Ward and Joukowsky 1992; Drews 1993; Killebrew 2005, 21–92; forthcoming a; Dickinson 2006, 24–57; Bachhuber and Roberts 2009; Venturi 2010).[2] Symptomatic of

2. Although centralized Hittite imperial control collapsed at the end of the thirteenth century, a Hittite dynasty at Carchemish was still governing northern Syria around 1100 B.C.E. during the period of Tiglath-pileser I (Hawkins 1982, 372–441, 948–55; 1995b, 1295–1307; 2009,

this reconfiguration of the eastern Mediterranean at the end of the Late Bronze Age is the disappearance or interruption of highly specialized Bronze Age writing systems and recording traditions (e.g., Linear B, Hittite cuneiform, Ugaritic, and/or Akkadian) that coincided with the crumbling centralized administrative and economic structures. The resulting localized networks are characterized by decentralized systems, a trend that is reflected in well-defined regional variations in Iron I material culture assemblages. As a result, the eastern Mediterranean region succumbed to a gradual process of political, economic, social, and cultural fragmentation. Corresponding with the deterioration of the Late Bronze Age *ancien régime*, "ethnically" defined groups begin to appear in contemporary and later texts. These include various Sea Peoples groups, most notably the Philistines, as well as later Iron Age peoples such as the Phoenicians, Israelites, Aramaeans, Moabites, and others, whose traditional geographical territories often correspond to regionally defined archaeological assemblages (see, e.g., Liverani 1987; Routledge 2004; Killebrew 2005; 2006; Sader 2010).

The complexity of this period is best illustrated by the diverse fates of Late Bronze Age settlements and regions in the eastern Mediterranean that witnessed both continuity and change. Some sites, such as Mycenae, Hattuša, Troy, Ugarit, Hazor, Megiddo, Lachish, and Ashdod, experienced large-scale destruction during the final century of the Late Bronze or Late Bronze/Iron Age transition. However, it is noteworthy that the dates of these destructions are often separated by decades or even as much as a century. Sometimes a site was resettled soon afterwards or, in some cases, was abandoned for a period of time (e.g., Ugarit, Hazor, and Lachish), either to be followed by a cultural break (i.e., settlement by a different group of people who introduces new cultural traditions [e.g., Ashdod]) or cultural continuity (resettlement by the same cultural group [e.g., Megiddo]). Other locales are characterized by little or no destruction, demonstrating cultural continuity well into the Iron I period. These include a number of sites such as Yarmuth in the Shephelah and Tel Rehov in the northern Jordan Valley. Significantly, the New Kingdom Egyptian stronghold at Beth Shean, another Jordan Valley settlement just north of Tel Rehov, was destroyed in the twelfth century B.C.E. and Egyptian-style material culture disappeared and in its stead local traditions returned. In the northern Levant, Late Bronze Age cultural traditions continued at major inland sites such as Carchemish on the Euphrates River and

---

164–73). Both the textual and archaeological evidence testifies to continued Egyptian influence in the southern Levant through the first half of the twelfth century B.C.E., and possibly as late as the reign of Ramesses VI (Weinstein 1981; 1992; Bietak 1993, 292–306; Killebrew 2005, 51–92; Morris 2005).

along the Phoenician coastline, where cities like Byblos, Sidon, and Tyre survived the disruptions at the end of the Late Bronze Age.

General settlement patterns also present a mixed picture throughout the eastern Mediterranean. The southern Levant, for example, experienced a decline of urban culture during the course of the Late Bronze Age that culminated in the final decades of the Bronze Age. This trend, probably abetted by the exploitation of regions under Egyptian imperial control, is corroborated by textual references to social instability and increased uprooting of Late Bronze Age populations. With the declining fortunes of the Egyptian Empire and the disappearance of imperial Hittite rule, some regions, particularly those along the Levantine coast including key Philistine sites, witnessed a flourishing of urbanization and increase in population. In the northern Levant, the available evidence points to a continuation of urbanism in the region of the so-called Neo-Hittite city-states of northern Syria and southeast Anatolia, such as Carchemish and Malatya. Along the Syro-Lebanese coast, population centers continued to be inhabited (see, e.g., Gonen 1984; Herzog 1997; 2003; Bunimovitz 1989; 1994; 1995; Casana 2003, 233, table 41; Marfoe 1979; 1998; Liverani 2005, 26–29).

Indicators of increasing instability, such as the mention of fugitives and social outcasts, begin to appear already during the course of the Late Bronze Age. These groups, who were particularly troublesome for the Egyptians, rarely appear in Bronze Age texts before 1500 B.C.E., but become a frequent phenomenon during the later centuries of the Late Bronze Age and seem to be an important factor in the formation of early Iron Age societies (see, e.g., Ugaritic texts that address the problems of defections in rural communities [Heltzer 1976, 52–57; Snell 2001]). Outlaws, such as the *ḫabiru/ḫapiru* (*ʿabiru/ʿapiru*), appear to have eluded imperial and local political power and exploitation, the latter expressed by heavy taxation, forced labor, and slavery of subject populations (see, e.g., Naʾaman 1986; Rainey 1995). Late Bronze Age texts describe these groups as armed and residing in marginal areas such as the mountains and the steppe, which were outside the sphere of imperial or city-state influence. These peripheral areas have, throughout history, been ideal locales, particularly during times of increasing instability, from which to stage raids against settled populations in the plains.

Into this complex Late Bronze Age geopolitical context and demographic mix, groups associated with the Sea Peoples appear in New Kingdom Egyptian texts with increasing frequency (tables 1–2; for a summary of the ancient sources, see Adams and Cohen, this volume). These Sea Peoples make their initial appearance in the fourteenth century B.C.E. The Lukka, Sherden, and Danuna were first mentioned during the reigns of Amenophis III and Amenophis IV (Akhenaten), often in the role of mercenaries (tables 1–2; Redford 1992, 246; Moran 1992, Lukka: EA 38:10, Danuna: EA 151:50–55, Sherden: EA 81:16, 122:35, 123:15). The mention of various groups associated with the Sea Peoples reached its apex during the reign of Ramesses III, which includes the earliest references to the Philistines (see table 2).

The origins and identification of the Sea Peoples, especially the Philistines, in the archaeological record continue to be matters of considerable debate (see, e.g., Bunimovitz and Yasur-Landau 1996; Killebrew 2005, 197–246; 2010; this volume; Woudhuizen 2006). The appearance of an Aegean-style material culture, especially Late Helladic (LH) IIIC ("Mycenaean IIIC") pottery, in early Iron I strata at Philistine centers at sites mentioned in the Hebrew Bible (Josh 13:3), located in the southern coastal plain of the modern state of Israel, led to the identification of these artifacts as "Philistine" already a century ago (for a discussion, see T. Dothan and M. Dothan 1992; T. Dothan and Ben-Shlomo, this volume; Killebrew, this volume, and bibliography therein). Perhaps more importantly, and less understood and explored in the scholarly literature, are the broader socio-economic, historical, and environmental processes that gave rise to the Sea Peoples phenomenon.[3]

In the following chapters, the contributors to this volume address questions dealing with the identity, origins, material cultural manifestations, political, socio-economic, and historical processes associated with the Sea People phenomenon. *The Philistines and Other "Sea Peoples"* opens with a tribute to the late Professor Moshe Dothan, excavator of Ashdod and one of the pioneers in Philistine and Sea Peoples studies. The essays are divided into three general sections: studies on the Philistines in their heartland (the southern coastal plain of Israel); aspects of material culture often associated with other Sea People groups in the northern Levant; and selected topics and sites in the Aegean, Anatolia, and Cyprus relevant to our understanding of the Philistines and Sea Peoples in their broader context. An appendix that brings together for the first time a comprehensive listing of primary sources relevant to the Sea Peoples completes this volume.

The Philistines in Text and Archaeology

Itamar Singer's opening essay addresses the historicity of the biblical record. He challenges Israel Finkelstein's view that "the biblical references to the Philistines do not contain any memory of early Iron I events or cultural behavior" (Finkelstein 2002b, 131). In particular, he rejects attempts to re-date biblical accounts of

3. Regarding recent research which indicates a marked climatic change at the end of the Late Bronze Age resulting in drier climatic conditions and its possible implications regarding the date, identity, and origins of the Sea Peoples, see, e.g., Kaniewski et al. 2010; 2011.

the early Philistines to literary production during the seventh century B.C.E., or even later as some have suggested. Singer argues in his chapter for the historicity of the accounts, dating them to Iron Age I through Davidic periods. This view is not only supported by archaeological discoveries at the Philistine "pentapolis cities," but also by epigraphic finds in Cilicia and Syria, especially from Karatepe, Çineköy, and Arsuz/Rhosus (Çambel 1999; Tekoğlu and Lemaire 2000; Dinçol and Dinçol forthcoming), suggesting that the Homeric traditions of Aegean migrations to the region do reflect memories of actual historical processes.

Tristan Barako also tackles the chronological debate surrounding the initial appearance of the Philistines in the southern Levant. In light of the Medinet Habu inscription, the arrival of the Philistines has traditionally been dated to the reign of Ramesses III. Archaeological evidence in the southern Levant indicates conclusively that Egyptian imperial presence persisted well into the twelfth century B.C.E., perhaps as late as the reign of Ramesses VI (ca. 1145–1137 B.C.E.). Proponents of a lower chronology post-date the arrival of the Philistines following the retreat of Twentieth-Dynasty Egypt from Canaan, approximately 50 years later than the "high," or conventional chronology (Finkelstein 1995; 2000). Based on a comparison of the stratigraphic sequences at Tel Mor, a small Egyptian military outpost, and nearby Ashdod, a major Philistine center, Barako persuasively argues in favor of the traditional Iron I chronological sequence, placing the arrival of the Philistines during the reign of Ramesses III.

Ceramics have long been considered the hallmark of the Philistines and their presence. One particular class of Aegean-style pottery, variously termed Mycenaean IIIC, LH IIIC, White Painted Wheelmade or Philistine 1, has traditionally been associated with the appearance of the Philistines in their heartland, Philistia, and with the Sea Peoples in general. This style became popular at the beginning of the Iron Age, appearing at numerous sites in the eastern Mediterranean. Stylistically, it clearly derives from Greek Mycenaean LH IIIB pottery; however, numerous archaeometric studies have proven conclusively that by the twelfth century B.C.E., the production of Mycenaean IIIC was decentralized and the pottery was being locally manufactured throughout the eastern Mediterranean, particularly along the coast (see, e.g., Killebrew, this volume). The Philistine LH IIIC, or Aegean-style, vessels share the principle features of vessel form and decoration, while there are also distinct inter-site variations at Philistine urban centers. Three chapters (T. Dothan and Ben-Shlomo; Mountjoy; and Killebrew) discuss the significance of Mycenaean IIIC pottery and its associated assemblages for our understanding of the identity, dating, and transmission of technological knowledge and style associated with the early Philistines. Trude Dothan and David Ben-Shlomo trace the development of LH IIIC/Mycenaean IIIC:1 in the southern Levant during the twelfth century B.C.E. Tel Miqne-Ekron has provided quantitatively and qualitatively one of the best stratified corpora of LH IIIC pottery in the Levant. The vessels were locally produced at Ekron (Killebrew, this volume) and Penelope Mountjoy (this volume) presents a detailed discussion of the stylistic influences and parallels. She concludes that Philistine pottery shares features with Mainland LH IIIC pottery, but notes that this Aegean-style pottery may well have reached Philistia via Cyprus, Cilicia, and other eastern Aegean regions. Additional sources of inspiration came from the eastern Aegean and Crete, creating a "hybrid" Aegean-style in the southern Levant. Mountjoy assigns the LH IIIC corpus at Ekron to the first phase of LH IIIC Early (Stratum VIIB) and to the second phase of LH IIIC Early (Stratum VIIA). Ann Killebrew's essay goes beyond the typological and explores the technological aspects of Philistine Aegean-style pottery at Ekron, stressing the clear break from previous Late Bronze Age ceramic traditions, and the close technological and typological connections with contemporary Cypriot and Cilician Aegean-style assemblages.

Most scholarly attention has focused on the Aegean-style pottery assemblage. However, many other features of Philistine material culture mark a well-defined break with the preceding Late Bronze Age traditions. Linda Meiberg re-examines lion-headed cups that appear in Philistine and other Iron I coastal sites in the Levant. Earlier scholarship stressed the Aegean origin of this category of objects. However, as Meiberg demonstrates in her chapter, Philistine lion-headed cups can be traced to Anatolian and north Syrian traditions, reflecting the complex transmission of material culture traditions and peoples during this period.

The site of Tell el-Farʿah South, located on the border of the Negev and the coastal plain, has often been associated with Philistine expansion because of the appearance of Bichrome Iron Age and other Aegean-style pottery found in rock-cut chamber tombs. This formed one of the lynch pins to the erroneous theory that associated Egyptian-style clay anthropoid coffins with the Philistines at Tell el-Farʿah South, a New Kingdom Egyptian stronghold, and several other sites where anthropoid coffins coincided with Egyptian imperial presence (see, e.g., Oren 1973, 142–46; Killebrew 2005, 65–67 who provide evidence against this equation). Sabine Laemmel stresses the continuity of local Late Bronze Age traditions and concludes that long-term processes of "socio-economic and cultural change" and outside influences from Cyprus were responsible for the relatively modest amounts of Aegean-style material culture, rather than the presence of actual Philistines at the site.

Tell eṣ-Ṣafi, identified as biblical Gath, has provided unparalleled information regarding the transitional Iron I /Iron II period in Philistia. As outlined by Aren Maeir, Philistine material culture experienced a rapid process of change during the early Iron II period (ca. tenth century B.C.E.). Many of the Aegean-style features disappeared, attesting to a process of acculturation. At the same time, what apparently were especially meaningful cultural expressions, such as the notched scapulae, persevered into the Iron II period. The excavations at Tell eṣ-Ṣafi fill in a key component of Philistine settlement in the southern coastal plain and illustrate their ability both to survive and retain their cultural uniqueness and ethnic identity well into the Iron II period.

In chapter ten, Hermann Michael Niemann analyzes the Philistine–Israelite conflict as presented in the Bible with the aim of reconstructing a history of the Philistines stripped of its biblical ideology. Recognizing that an historical account of the Philistines cannot rely solely on the biblical text, Niemann's contribution integrates geographical, archaeological, epigraphic, iconographic, anthropological, and sociological studies. He proposes that differences between Philistines and Israelites were not solely ideological, but were largely the result of well-documented social and economic differences between populations in the plain and highland dwellers.

The Other "Sea Peoples" in the Levant

Gunnar Lehmann's opening chapter analyzes the repertoire of Aegean-style pottery in the northern Levant, documenting the close typological connection between LH IIIC assemblages in this region and on Cyprus. In Lehmann's opinion, the stratigraphic sequence at Enkomi is key to reconstructing the chronology of these assemblages. He divides the LH IIIC pottery at Enkomi into two groups: 1) the LH IIIC Early and Middle styles (or Mycenaean IIIC:1) and 2) "Granary" Ware and Wavy Line style (end of LH IIIC Middle and LH IIIC Late/Submycenaean), dating the first group to the twelfth century B.C.E. and the second group to the first half of the eleventh century B.C.E. As presented in his chapter, a number of sites in northern Syria have yielded particularly important information on the Late Bronze/Iron Age transition and the early Iron Age. Excavations at Tell Afis and the renewed research in the 'Amuq region provide essential data for the chronology and the material culture of the early Iron Age (Venturi 2007; T. Harrison 2009). A somewhat unexpected and complex picture of continuous Hittite cultural traditions together with new Mediterranean influences is emerging. For example, the persistence into the Iron Age of Luwian hieroglyphs and Hittite artistic traditions at some sites in the 'Amuq Plain and northern Syria, coexisting alongside locally produced Aegean-style material culture, indicate continued affinities with the Hittite past of this region that postdate the influx of new cultural or demographic features (see, e.g., Bonatz 1993). Most surprising is the recent epigraphic discovery that the 'Amuq Plain was referred to as Palistin during the early Iron Age (Hawkins 2009).

Although some of the main excavations on the north Syrian coast have not been fully published, preliminary reports indicate Aegeanizing finds clustering around Ras el-Bassit and Ras Ibn Hani, on the territory of the vanished kingdom of Ugarit (Sherratt, this volume). Some scholars interpret these finds as evidence for settlements of Sea Peoples in the area (Badre 1983; Lagarce and Lagarce 1988; for more literature, see Mazzoni 2000, 34 n. 11; cf. also Sharon 2001, 576–79). Others, however, have expressed doubts that the Sea Peoples settled in northern Syria (i.e., Sherratt, this volume; Caubet 1992, 130; Bonatz 1993, 125–26, 134–35; Venturi 1998, 135; Mazzoni 2000, 34).

In her chapter, Michal Artzy focuses on the other Sea Peoples who are known mainly from Egyptian sources. Based on her excavations at Tel Nami, Tell Abu Hawam, Tel Akko, and the evidence from other sites in the Plain of Akko, Artzy highlights the importance of this region in our understanding of the Sea Peoples phenomenon, which differs from the archaeological evidence unearthed in Philistia. In her opinion, the other Sea Peoples were quite familiar with the eastern Mediterranean littoral and played a key role as economic mercenaries, secondary contractors, and international intermediaries during the final century of the Late Bronze Age. When the geopolitical and economic Bronze Age structures weakened, these groups, or "nomads of the sea," were well positioned to fill the void in a variety of ways, including marauding and other entrepreneurial activities.

Based on the recent excavations at Mycenae and Tiryns in mainland Greece, Elizabeth French proposes that the initial appearance of LH IIIC assemblages in the eastern Mediterranean, which followed destructions of these major Mycenaean centers, should be dated to the LH IIIC Early. As presented in her chapter, Aegean-style material culture makes its debut slightly later in Cilicia and the Levant, near the end of this phase (LH IIIC). Her observations have considerable chronological importance regarding the initial appearance of LH IIIC pottery in Cilicia and Philistia, which she dates well into the twelfth century B.C.E.

Susan Sherratt and Amihai Mazar (with an appendix by Anat Cohen-Weinberger) provide an important chronological basis for non-locally produced LH IIIC Middle pottery unearthed at Beth Shean Level VI, which has been assigned to the Twentieth Dynasty, possibly continuing as late as the reign of Ramesses VI (1143–1136 B.C.E.). They use the classification of their material as "Late Helladic IIIC Middle" with hesitation, since in their view there was no uniform development of *one* LH IIIC style throughout the Aegean and the Levant, but distinct regional developments. As in the case of Beth Shean, the small quantity of LH IIIC has its closest parallels in Cyprus (Enkomi late Level IIIa and probably early Level IIIb) and, as detailed in the petrographic study by Anat Cohen-Weinberger, most likely originated from Cyprus.

As the only site specifically associated with a non-Philistine Sea People group, the *TKR/SKL*, the excavations at Tel Dor are particularly insightful. In contrast to the southern coastal plain of Philistia, where indisputable evidence exists for a significant migration of new group(s) of peoples associated with the Philistines, the Iron I material culture at Dor represents a strong continuity with Late Bronze Canaanite culture. Although new features, such as monochrome pottery, bimetallic knives, and notched scapulae, do appear in modest quantities, in the opinion of Ilan Sharon and Ayelet Gilboa, this does not constitute evidence for the arrival of a new people. Rather the material culture suggests a more nuanced "Cypro-Phoenician dialog" that included a Cypriot and northern Levantine (Syrian) presence at Dor, together with the continuation of an indigenous southern Levantine ("Canaanite") tradition.

Anatolia, the Aegean, and Cyprus

Until renewed research in Cilicia in the 1990s, the archaeology of the Sea Peoples focused on the southern Levant. New excavations and surveys demonstrated that the early Iron Age of Cilicia is closely connected with the appearance of Sea Peoples in the Levant (for a survey of recent research, see French and Gates, this volume). Cilicia, ancient Kizzuwatna during the Late Bronze Age, was annexed by Šuppiluliuma I and remained part of the Hittite Empire for the rest of the Late Bronze Age. The transition from Late Bronze to Iron Age in Cilicia is, thus, connected to the end of the Hittite Empire. In recent research, the decline and fall of the Hittite Empire appears to be a complex and enduring process. As explored by Hermann Genz, internal problems apparently played an important part in the process and foreign invasions or migrations were at best only one of the factors involved.

Due to the paucity of archaeological data, it is difficult to fully understand the settlement hierarchy of Cilicia during the Late Bronze and early Iron Ages. The distribution and character of LH IIIC evidence in Cilicia is fully discussed in the chapter by Elizabeth French (see also Gates 2011, 394 and Sherratt, this volume), whose analysis is greatly aided by the complete publishing of the LH IIIC ceramics from Tarsus, one of the key sites for our understanding of this period in Cilicia (Goldman 1956, 44–59; Slane 1987, 445–65; Mountjoy 2005b; Yalçın 2005). French demonstrates that this Aegean ceramic style appears frequently in Cilicia at a number of sites. Increasingly, recent excavations and surveys are revealing that Aegean-style material culture is more prevalent at sites in Cilicia than in Palestine.

A case in point is the recent excavations at Kinet Höyük in eastern Cilicia where LH IIIC pottery has been recovered. Here, a Hittite town was destroyed in the thirteenth century B.C.E. During the following early Iron Age, a small rural settlement was founded above the destroyed Late Bronze settlement. As cogently presented by Marie-Henriette Gates, the artifactual and faunal evidence of this village reflects a clear break with the preceding Late Bronze Age, marked by the appearance of Aegean-style LH IIIC ceramics.

These recent discoveries shed new light on textual references to the elusive Hypachaioi, or "sub-Achaeans" of Cilicia, mentioned by Herodotus (*Hist.* 7, 91, see also *Peripl. M. Mag.* 186, 1–2 and Strabo, *Geogr.* XIV 5.8, 1–3) as a former name for the Cilicians. The inscriptions found at Çineköy (Tekoğlu and Lemaire 2000) and Arsuz (classical Rhosus) (Dinçol and Dinçol forthcoming) leave little doubt that the Danuna of ancient Adana and their kings trace their ancestry back to Mopsos.[4] These perceived or actual genealogical traditions strengthen the suggestion that Ahhiyawa (or Hiyawa), which is usually understood to refer to a Late Bronze Age entity on mainland Greece (the Achaeans), instead refers to a "Mycenaeanized" state on the Anatolian coast (Finkelberg 2005b, 140–59; Jasink and Marino 2007; Fischer 2010). Additional evidence for the latter interpretation is provided by the identification of Hiyawa with ancient Que in Assyrian sources for Cilicia (Tekoğlu and Lemaire 2000, 982). The relationship between the Achaeans and Cilicia, and how and when they reached Cilicia remains unclear. However, the connection between a Late Bronze Age Mycenaean state or Mycenaeanized state on the coast of Asia Minor and the Danuna of Adana, who trace their ancestry back to Mopsos and appear as one of the Sea Peoples groups mentioned in earlier New Kingdom Egyptian texts, is increasingly likely.

Additional clues regarding the diffusion and development of Aegean-style culture are found in the eastern Aegean. Mario Benzi presents a summary of research on LH IIIC in the southeast Aegean. He discusses the complex development of the ceramics, burials, and Mycenaean traditions in Miletus and the Dodecanese, independent of direct influences from the Greek Mainland. Southeastern Aegean material culture, which flourishes during the LH IIIC Middle phase, represents an individual stylistic development and distinct demographic trends. There are indications of a decline in the following LH IIIC Late period, trends that are still difficult to understand.

Penelope Mountjoy provides a detailed analysis of the stylistic development and distribution of LH IIIB and LH IIIC Early pottery during the Late Bronze/

---

4. Mopsos was, according to Greek myth, the legendary seer and founder of a number of cities in Asia Minor mentioned in Greek myth and was of unclear ethnic origin.

Iron Age transition in the eastern Aegean and western Anatolia. She traces the parallels between the eastern Aegean and the Levant, noting the limited comparisons between the two regions and the challenges presented by the insufficient number of publications. Thus the southeast Aegean fits well into the complex picture of decentralized, regional settlements that exchanged with other similarly organized regions throughout the eastern Mediterranean.

In their stylistic analysis of the earliest Philistine ceramic assemblages, Jeremy Rutter and Susan Sherratt both confirm the close connections between southern Levantine and Cypriot Aegean-style material culture. Rutter identifies the earliest pottery as an advanced stage of LH IIIC Early (or LH IIIC Phases 2–3). He concludes that the LH IIIC pottery of Philistia was derived from Cyprus rather than even partly from the Aegean, which could have far reaching consequences. If the imported Mycenaean IIIC pottery at Beth Shean (e.g., Sherratt and Mazar, this volume) and the locally produced LH IIIC Early ceramics at Philistine sites are closely related to similar LH IIIC assemblages on Cyprus, which clearly predate 1130 B.C.E., this would tend to refute Finkelstein and Ussishkin's low chronology date (post-1130 B.C.E.) for the Philistine migration to Palestine (Finkelstein 1995; 1998).

The archaeological evidence for Cyprus also demonstrates both continuity and change, as indicated by the chronological terminology Late Cypriot IIIA and IIIB, approximately corresponding to the Iron I period on the mainland Levant. As outlined by Maria Iacovou, some settlements are destroyed, others continue, and new settlements are established. The major twelfth-century B.C.E. sites at Enkomi, Hala Sultan Tekke, Kition, and Paphos weathered the disintegration of the great empires, with urbanism, state functions, and copper production remaining intact. Aegean influence was already evident during the fourteenth and thirteenth centuries with the appearance of Mycenaean pottery, which was initially imported, but was later gradually replaced with locally produced Mycenaean-style pottery. This process of Aegeanization continued during the twelfth century, with the appearance of White Painted Wheelmade III pottery (an alternative term for Mycenaean IIIC on Cyprus) and other Aegean-inspired wares. The resulting Aegean-style material culture incorporates Cypriot, Levantine, and both eastern and western Aegean components, a blending of cultural features which has been termed 'creolization' or 'hybridization' (Webster 2001; van Dommelen 2006; Stockhammer 2012). Interpretations differ regarding the significance of the prevalence of Aegean-style material on twelfth-century Cyprus. These include large-scale migration and colonization to more nuanced processes of interaction that take into consideration external and internal stimuli, such as long-term economic migration, creolization, and hybridization, which would typify diverse urban populations (see, e.g., Iacovou 2008a; this volume; Knapp 2008, 249–97; Voskos and Knapp 2008).

This volume closes with reflections on the Sea People phenomenon, particularly as reflected in the ceramic evidence, by Susan Sherratt, who urges us to examine the archaeological, and specifically ceramic, evidence on its own terms, freed of the "tyranny of the text." As she rightly points out, the archaeological record needs to be considered on multiple levels, including site specific and regional contexts as well as a multitude of other less visible factors that may have had an impact on the appearance of Aegean-style ceramics. Following Sherratt's concluding chapter, an appendix by Matthew Adams and Margaret Cohen lists the primary textual sources relevant to groups traditionally associated with the Sea Peoples.

Final Observations

Who, then, were the Sea Peoples (as they are known in modern scholarship), which make their debut in Egyptian New Kingdom texts and are often understood to have served as protagonists in the crisis (or crises) that occurred at the end of the Late Bronze Age? Both the textual and archaeological evidence is largely ambiguous regarding the identity of these peoples. Their identity in the archaeological evidence has focused on the appearance of Aegean-style ceramic assemblages, especially LH IIIC pottery, in the eastern Aegean, on Cyprus, and along the Levantine coast. However other material culture features such as hearths (Lehmann, this volume; Iacovou, this volume), fibulae (Lehmann, this volume; Benzi, this volume; see also Pedde 2000 and Giesen 2001), and detailed studies of Aegean-style loom weights, have also been published (see, e.g., Rahmstorf 2003a–b; 2008; 2011). Objects associated with cultic practices, such as Aegean-style female figurines, notched scapulae, and lion-headed cups (see, e.g., Meiberg, this volume) have also been interpreted as possible material remains of the Sea Peoples. Still, Sherratt is correct in claiming that "take away the [LH IIIC] pottery" and one of the main foundations of attempts to identify the Sea Peoples in the archaeological record will have vanished.

While aspects of the Sea Peoples phenomenon are still not sufficiently studied, what the volume clearly demonstrates is the complexity of economic, political, and cultural multi-directional interactions between lands bordering the eastern Mediterranean during the thirteenth and twelfth centuries B.C.E. These interregional connections begin to unravel at the end of the thirteenth century/early twelfth centuries, particularly affecting the trade routes linking the west Aegean and the Levant, and coinciding with the collapse or retreat of Hittite and

Egyptian imperial influence over the region, which marks the crisis at end of the Late Bronze Age and the assertion of power by local groups freed from centuries of imperialistic exploitation. As in all such situations where there is a breakdown of central control, there are "winners" and "losers," resulting in a complex and multivariate picture. In some instances, as with the Philistine phenomenon, there is clear evidence for the arrival of large numbers of new peoples, bringing with them an Aegean-style material culture with strong Cypriot/Cilician underpinnings that coincides with textual evidence supporting such a scenario. In the northern Levant, Cilicia, and now the ʿAmuq Plain, locally produced Aegean-style material culture also appears in noteworthy quantities at select locales following the collapse of the Hittite Empire. On Cyprus, the transition to a locally produced Aegean-style material culture begins already in the final decades of the thirteenth century, becoming the dominate cultural feature by the twelfth century B.C.E. Likewise locally produced Aegean-style pottery begins to appear in the eastern Aegean during the final decades of the thirteenth century. It is also increasingly clear that, contrary to earlier treatments of the topic, the Sea Peoples were hardly a homogenous population of destitute refugees fleeing the west Aegean eastwards as a result of the breakdown of a politically and economically centralized palace system. Rather, these peoples, categorized under the rubric Sea Peoples, were most likely well acquainted with the eastern littoral of the Mediterranean long before the end of the Bronze Age. They should be understood as enterprising communities that also included displaced or migrating populations, who took advantage of the power vacuum resulting from imperial breakdown and decline during the crisis years. Groups associated with the Sea Peoples were among the "winners" to emerge from the ruins of the Late Bronze Age.

We hope this volume will encourage continued dialogue between scholars working in all regions of the eastern Mediterranean regarding the Sea Peoples phenomenon in its broader and multi-regional context. The processes that led to the demise of the Bronze Age and created new cultural, social, and political structures were complex, and continued over a period of about a century. It is increasingly evident that the Sea Peoples comprised diverse groups of populations that were impacted by the crisis that ended the Age of Internationalism. Based on an interpretation of the textual evidence, these peoples have traditionally been identified in the archaeological record by the appearance of Aegean-style material culture in areas east of its source of inspiration—the west Aegean Mycenaean homeland. The world of the Late Bronze Age did not completely perish. On its partly ruined foundations, emerged a new configuration of diverse cultural identities and Mediterranean connectivity during the early Iron Age, characterized by locally controlled and multidirectional entrepreneurially driven networks, and decentralized political and cultural structures.

Chapter Two

The Philistines in the Bible: A Short Rejoinder to a New Perspective

*Itamar Singer*ז״ל[*]

In a recent article Israel Finkelstein (2002b) challenges traditional views on the early Philistines, claiming that "the biblical references to the Philistines do not contain any memory of early Iron I events or cultural behavior" (Finkelstein 2002b, 131).[1] Most of them are rather "based on the geographical, historical and ideological background of late-monarchic times," even if they may contain some "seeds of early tales" (Finkelstein 2002b, 131). The revision of the so-called Philistine paradigm is a natural sequel of the overall "deconstruction" of the biblical united monarchy in the last decades, and as such, it provides a new stimulus to the prolific debate on the Philistines and the Sea Peoples. Obviously, this short paper does not intend to come to grips with the difficult problems involved in the historical reconstruction of the early monarchic period in Israel, nor with the disputed chronology of the early Iron Age. It will only attempt to briefly challenge Finkelstein's proposal to "deconstruct" the early Philistines as well. In a more gen-

---

* Zikhrono livrakha "of blessed memory."

My lecture on "The Sea Peoples and the Collapse of the Hittite Empire" at the Philistines and Other Sea Peoples workshop organized by Ann E. Killebrew, Gunnar Lehmann, and Michal Artzy in May 2001 was basically a brief review of the evidence presented in Singer 2000a. Therefore, I considered it more expedient to contribute to this new volume on the Sea Peoples another paper, a slightly revised version of a lecture presented at the annual Yohanan Aharoni Memorial Day held at Tel Aviv University on April 10, 2003. This written version was prepared in October 2003 and has not been revised since (except for some biblical references), but I am not aware of new discoveries or publications that would contradict its conclusions. A Hebrew version was published in Singer 2006a.

1. His theory had already been presented in a lecture held at the annual Yohanan Aharoni Memorial Day in March 2001.

eral vein, it will touch upon the intriguing question of how historical memory is preserved in traditional societies with reference to a thought-provoking analogy from a not-too-distant society.

The crucial element in Finkelstein's argument pertains to the political and military terminology employed in the characterization of the biblical Philistines. In his view, these terms lead to the conclusion that what the late authors had in mind were not early Philistine leaders and warriors, but rather seventh-century B.C.E. western Anatolian and Greek mercenaries. Let us briefly discuss these entries and their alleged chronological value, although I should state first off that, to my mind, these issues have only a secondary importance in the dating of the Israelite-Philistine encounter described in the books of Samuel.

The idea that the Cherethites and Pelethites in David's army allude to much later Carian and Cretan mercenaries is not impossible, and, in fact, not entirely new.[2] That the detailed description of Goliath's armor might represent a seventh-century Greek hoplite, augmented by some Assyrian elements (notably the shield bearer), is also not impossible, and in fact, recalls Galling's (1965) concept of a highly eclectic depiction. One should mention in passing, however, that heavy metal armor, not unlike Goliath's, is already known from a Late Bronze Age chamber tomb at Dendra (Åström 1977; see also Drews 1993, 175). Further, while the Homeric parallels for the duel between champions are well known, there are also much earlier examples (Singer 1994, 314, n. 180; Machinist 2000, 59 and n. 34). Actually, the individual fighting of *promakhoi* conforms better to ancient martial traditions than to the hoplite *phalanx* that began to develop in Homer's times (van Wees 1997). We shall return to Homeric historiography later on.

The dating value of the term *seranim/sarnei*, relating only to the Philistine leaders, is also quite shaky. First of all, the connection to Greek *tyrannos*, proposed long ago, is not devoid of difficulties, notable among which is the different initial consonants (Edel 1983). Indeed, alternative etymologies, both Anatolian (Garbini 1991)[3] and Semitic (Edel 1983), have been proposed. And even if one accepts the Greek etymology, which in turn derives from Luwian *tarwanis*, this would hardly provide a firm chronological anchor, since Hieroglyphic Luwian

---

2. See, e.g., Singer 1994, 327: "In one of the passages the word 'Carite' is found in place of 'Cherethites' (2 Sam 20:23). It may be that the author had in mind the Carian mercenaries who served during later periods in the Egyptian and other armies, including that of Judah (2 Kgs 1:4, 19). The substitution finds its explanation not only in the similar spelling but also in the nature of the two groups." Note also that, according to 2 Kgs 11:4, 19, Carian mercenaries served in the Judean army long before the Josianic reform.

3. In fact, Garbini, to whom reference is given in Finkelstein's article, considers the *seren* > *tyrannos* connection as "scarcely defensible on linguistic grounds" (1991, 516), and suggests another Anatolian etymology instead (*ser-* or *sar-* with the suffix *-en* or *-an*).

tarwanis is already attested in tenth-century B.C.E. inscriptions (Hawkins 1995a, 78 with n. 37) and may even go back to late-imperial precursors (Hawkins 1995c, 108–13).

It is difficult to see how Finkelstein's (2002b, 150–52) intricate discussion on "Philistine origins" advances his case for a late dating and it would be too exigent to delve here into the numerous issues involved. Let me just note in passing that the very preservation of the second-millennium B.C.E. term Kaptara in biblical Caphtor, the alleged origin of the Philistines, is suggestive for a long historical memory.[4]

Finally, Finkelstein questions the historicity of Achish, king of Gath, a contemporary of Saul and Solomon. On the evidence of seventh-century *ʾkyš* /Ikausu, king of Ekron, attested in the inscription from Tel Miqne and in Assyrian texts, respectively, he claims that an earlier king bearing the same name never really existed and that the name was simply duplicated in the Davidic narrative for political purposes.[5] As for the change of Ekron into Gath, he offers an intricate explanation connected to the Judahite claim on Ziklag. Here lies the gist of Finkelstein's historical method, linking himself to a celebrated school of thought. The late Achish, more-or-less contemporary with the Deuteronomistic composition, purportedly sheds serious doubts on the very existence of an early Achish who may have ruled three hundred years earlier. I must admit that the logic of this rationale has always escaped me. To me it is tantamount to denying the existence of Jeroboam I on the evidence of Jeroboam II, or of the early Sargon on the evidence of his later namesakes. Since corroborative external evidence is lacking, I simply do not know whether Achish of Gath existed or not, but I would certainly not recruit Achish of Ekron to eliminate his earlier namesake. Perhaps one day

4. For the earliest attestations of Kaptara/Keftiu, see Guichard 1993 and Singer 2000a, 23–24 (with references). The term seems to have broadened its meaning, covering not only Crete but also other parts of the Aegean.

5. Finkelstein (2002b, 134) follows Naveh (1998, 36), who states that the name of the king of Ekron in the seventh century B.C.E. reflected on the name of "the Philistine king(s) of Gath in the narrations of the time of Saul and Solomon." However, contrary to Finkelstein's claim, it is not clear at all that "Naveh indeed identified seventh-century Ikausu of Ekron with biblical Achish of Gath." Rather, he "disregards the historicity of the biblical narratives mentioning Achish of Gath…" (Finkelstein 2002b, 134). I employ in this paper the traditional vocalization of the biblical name, Achish, ignoring Naveh's plausible vocalization as *Akhayus*. The consequences emanating from this vocalization (which is of course related to Homeric *Achaioi* and Hittite *Ahhiyawa*) cannot be discussed here. To the references cited by Naveh one should add now the highly interesting Luwian *Hiyawa*, which in the new bilingual from Çineköy (Tekoğlu and Lemaire 2000) corresponds to Phoenician *Dnnym*! See also Singer 2006b; forthcoming.

some evidence will turn up (at Tell eṣ-Ṣafi?) that may support or invalidate the historicity of this tenth-century Achish, but until then I prefer to remain agnostic.

To conclude this brief overview, I claim that none of the items adduced by Finkelstein has binding chronological value for the dating of the Philistines described in the books of Samuel. I certainly concur with the idea that some of the entries may contain late interpolations, just as Finkelstein (2002b, 155) admits that some episodes may echo layers of earlier realities. But the question is one of proportions: To which historical reality does the backbone of the biblical description conform? To the late-monarchic period, as claimed by Finkelstein, or to the early Iron Age, as maintained by the so-called traditional Philistine paradigm, to which I voluntarily subscribe. In the present context there is no need for more subtle chronological definitions, and, for the sake of a common terminological basis, I will even adopt in this rejoinder Finkelstein's definition of the Iron I, which includes the tenth century B.C.E. (Finkelstein 1996a; 2002b, 141). Thus, the real issue to be debated is whether the text describes circumstances anchored in the first three or the last three centuries of the Iron Age. I will argue for the former, but first, I would like to add a comment on the preservation of historical memory in ancient Israel and elsewhere.

The mainstream of current biblical scholarship tends to accept the premise that the main part of the Deuteronomistic history was composed in Jerusalem in the seventh–early sixth century B.C.E. The more difficult questions concern the sources at the disposal of the late authors and how they were exploited. Most commentators would agree that some written sources must have been kept in the palace or temple library in Jerusalem, probably for educational purposes (see, e.g., Na'aman 1996 with further references).[6] These may have included literary and historical works, notably "the chronicles of the kings of Israel" and "the chronicles of the kings of Judah." Perhaps there were also some royal building inscriptions, such as have been found in neighboring countries, but so far none has been discovered in Israel. These postulated written sources are usually dated no earlier than the eighth century B.C.E. (Na'aman 2002, 216), which still leaves a gap of several centuries between the time of writing and the events described. Orally transmitted

---

6. One must also count with the possibility that some of the coastal city-kingdoms, both Phoenician and Philistine, may have had written sources recording their own traditions. Writing has never disappeared from Phoenicia, and the Philistines presumably brought with them some writing system(s) from their places of origin. The evidence for this is so far quite meager, notably, a small fragment of a clay tablet discovered at Tel Aphek (Singer 2009, see also Singer 1983a, 26). Shortly after their arrival, the Philistines adopted, as did other peoples, the much simpler Canaanite alphabet (Singer 1994, 334–35). Philistine oral traditions, too, would probably have been familiar in Israelite literary circles.

narratives may have filled this large gap, but the haunting question has always been how much credibility should be ascribed to such oral transmissions.

A lot of field work has been done in this domain in the last generations, starting with the ground breaking studies of Halbwachs (1950; 1992), through the investigations of Vansina (1965; 1985) and Tonkin (1992) in Africa, and Parry (1953–1979) and Lord (1960; 1991) in the Balkans, to the seminal studies of Assmann (1992) and Goody (2000). Some of the theories have also been applied to Old Testament studies (e.g., Kirkpatrick 1988; Niditch 1996; Carr 2005), but, as a rule, biblical historiography has mainly been preoccupied with questions relating to written transmission. With regard to the historicity of oral traditions in general, opinions have differed widely among scholars, ranging from total rejection to cautious consideration. However, an important distinction has been made between the evaluation of oral transmission in illiterate societies and in societies which have already mastered the knowledge of writing, like the ancient Near East and the Aegean. The main problem is usually the lack of parallel sources against which the accuracy of the oral traditions may be tested. The situation in the ancient Near East is rather different, as external sources and archaeology provide an occasional glimpse into the society under scrutiny, as in the case of ancient Israel. Still, dependence on the reconstruction of oral traditions is admittedly quite speculative, and most scholars would abstain from resorting to them as a valid source for the trustworthy preservation of historical memory. Nevertheless, I believe that comparative studies with other regions, in which oral transmission has been closely studied, may benefit research into the ancient Near East in general and ancient Israel in particular. The following example may be instructive in demonstrating this.

Homeric historiography has gone through strikingly similar processes as biblical historiography. As even a cursory comparison of the old (Wace and Stubbings 1963) and the new (Morris and Powell 1997) *Companion to Homer* will show, there has been a general tendency to minimize the "historical core" and to concentrate almost exclusively on the realities of Homer's own times in the second half of the eighth century B.C.E.[7] But perhaps the tide may be changing again, due to comparative studies with the Hittite world and to renewed archaeological work at Troy.[8] The so-called Greek Renaissance of the eighth century B.C.E. was primarily aimed at consolidating the heterogeneous population groups

7. See Rutherford's (1999) penetrating review of the *New Companion*.

8. For a recent presentation of the problems and their suggested solutions, see Latacz 2001 and the relevant articles in the catalogue of the German exhibition on Troy (Archäologisches Landesmuseum Baden-Württemberg 2001). For other opinions, see, e.g., the articles gathered in Ulf 2003. For a detailed analysis of ancient residues in the Homeric story and their relevance

of Greece, taking the Mycenaean Heroic Age as the only common term of reference in shaping a collective memory (Finkelberg 2005a). The question remains, however, as in the case of the Deuteronomistic history, how much was retained from that distant past? The problems are similar, but in the case of Homer there are some extraordinary circumstances which should provide better answers concerning the validity of oral transmission. After the disappearance of the Mycenaean script, centuries passed without any attested writing until the adoption of the Phoenician script and its development and widespread usage for the recording of Greek. During these long centuries the ancient traditions could only have been passed on from generation to generation through oral transmission, by storytellers and epic singers (for which see, e.g., Foley 1997; Mackay 1999). No doubt, many traditions were altered or forgotten altogether during this long, practically scriptless period, but fortunately, there is an ancient source that can authenticate the general geo-political background of the Homeric narrative: the Hittite documents.

The basic plot of the *Iliad* recounts the war between a Greek coalition headed by Mycenae and an Asiatic Trojan coalition including participants from Paphlagonia in the north to Lycia in the south.[9] This geo-political map has hardly any relevance to Homer's days, but, on the other hand, it reflects quite accurately the division between the two major powers on either side of the Aegean in the thirteenth century B.C.E., Hatti and Ahhiyawa. Moreover, the latter is exactly the name used by Homer to designate the Greeks, Achaioi, which, after many years of vain controversy, has been definitively proven to reflect Ahhiyawa.[10] Moreover, a Hittite text actually mentions a conflict between Hatti and Ahhiyawa over the city of Wilusa, which can only be Homer's Ilios.[11] Now, how could Homer have invented such an accurate geopolitical background situated half a millennium before his own day? To be sure, the story had been revised time and again

---

to second-millennium B.C.E. western Anatolia, see Starke 1997; for a short summary, see Bryce 1998, 392–404.

9. For the Trojan coalition and its significance, see, recently, Visser 2001 (with further references).

10. For the phonetic correspondence, see Finkelberg 1988. For the history of the controversy, see Bryce 1998, 59–61, with further references.

11. The so-called Tawagalawa Letter, which was addressed to an unnamed king of Ahhiyawa. The reading of the damaged name Wilusa is quite certain, as maintained by Güterbock (1986, 37), a reading that I had occasion to collate and confirm on the original tablet kept in Berlin. To be sure, it is *not* claimed that the conflict mentioned in the Hittite text refers to the very war described by Homer, but that the geo-political circumstances are similar. The same applies to the name of a thirteenth-century king of Wilusa, Alaksandu, nearly homonymous with Homer's prince of Ilios, Alexander-Paris.

and adapted to contemporary needs, but its basic features had been remembered and kept alive in all probability *without* any written transmission. In evaluating the historicity of a story, a distinction should be made between its main structure and its secondary details. In other words, even if Odysseus's boar-tusk helmet were proven to be late, there would still remain the general situation described by Homer, which fits much better the Mycenaean Age than his own times.[12]

The relevance of this analogy to the Philistine-Israelite encounter narrated in the Books of Samuel is obvious. The armament of Goliath, even if shown to contain late elements, should not obscure the overall impression gained from the essential situation described in the story. And this, in my opinion, conforms much better to the Iron Age I than to any subsequent period in Israelite history, including, of course, the late-monarchic period.

The essential plot recounts how the lowland polity of the Philistines, consisting of five city-kingdoms, managed to gradually take over the central highlands, due to military and technological superiority.[13] After their victory at Ebenezer near Aphek, the way was open for the Philistines to demolish the central sanctuary at Shiloh and to advance into the heartland of the Israelite tribal territories. Philistine garrisons were set up in the main centers of the tribal units, at Gibeah of Benjamin and Bethlehem of Judah. A well-organized army, consisting of charioteers, bowmen, and infantrymen, managed to hold this territory for a certain period of time. However, as has been the case in countless historical analogies, the long supply lines and control of this difficult terrain became increasingly difficult to maintain and eventually, Israelite guerrilla attacks pushed the Philistines back to their lowland bases. Like in any national epic, this underlying framework is interlaced with stories of mighty heroism and tragic losses.

Now, to which era does this basic narrative conform better, to the Iron I or the late-monarchic period? By now, it must be clear that archaeology does not supply easy answers and one cannot simply follow the trail of pottery to reconstruct complex historical developments. Yet, even a cautious archaeologist like Finkelstein admits, in his and Silberman's *The Bible Unearthed* that, "while some of the details of these stories are clearly legendary, the geographical descriptions

12. In addition to the Homeric parallel, I cited in my lecture another instructive analogy, further removed in time and space: the *Anglo-Saxon Chronicle*, written during the reign of Alfred the Great in the ninth century C.E. This national epic was also construed on the basis of written and oral sources, the validity of which can at least partly be tested against archaeological evidence. Not surprisingly, a similar array of opinions, ranging from total skepticism to more traditional approaches, characterizes the field of Alfredian history as well. Compare, e.g., Nelson 1999 and Swanton 1996.

13. For a detailed presentation, with references, see Singer 1993; 1994, 322–65.

are quite accurate. More importantly, the gradual spread of the Philistines' distinctive Aegean-inspired decorated pottery into the foothills and as far north as the Jezreel Valley provides evidence for the progressive expansion of the Philistines' influence throughout the country" (Finkelstein and Silberman 2001, 134). But even if one were to disregard this ceramic evidence, which may perhaps be interpreted differently, one would still be left with the unequivocal evidence from (at least)[14] two important sites, Shiloh and Gath, both of which are discussed by Finkelstein.

Shiloh was utterly destroyed in the late Iron I, in the eleventh century B.C.E. according to the traditional dating, or in the tenth century according to Finkelstein's Low Chronology. It never recovered its former status. This proves, according to Finkelstein, that "the biblical memory on the prominence of Shiloh in early Israelite history must echo the importance of the site in the Iron I, no later than the tenth century BCE" (Finkelstein 2002b, 155).

The case of Philistine Gath is no less compelling. It figures as one of the leading cities of the Pentapolis in early accounts, but disappears altogether from late-monarchic accounts and contemporary Assyrian inscriptions (Na'aman 2002, 210–12; Finkelstein 2002b, 137–39). This textual evidence seems to be fully corroborated by the new excavations at Tell eṣ-Ṣafi. The site is continuously occupied until the end of the eighth century B.C.E., with a major destruction in the late-ninth or early-eighth century B.C.E. From the seventh century there are only sparse remains (Maeir 2001, 114; Maeir and Ehrlich 2001, 27; Maeir 2008). Once again, the textual and the archaeological evidence are in full agreement in demonstrating that "the Deuteronomistic Historian's notion of a league of five Philistine states, if historically reliable, can reflect only one period—Iron I" (Finkelstein 2002b, 141). But instead of embracing this simple and obvious solution,[15] Finkelstein is compelled by his own theory to perform a rather complicated *tour de force*, whereby the Deuteronomist would have added Gath to the four Philistine cities known in his own time for propagandistic purposes, namely, to justify Judahite claims on Ziklag (Finkelstein 2002b, 136, 142). Still, he adds that "there may have been a memory that in the distant past, before the emergence of Ekron to prominence, Ziklag was ruled by Gath" (Finkelstein 2002b, 136).

These examples, which could easily be multiplied, all lead to the same simple conclusion: The Deuteronomistic history preserves a relatively accurate memory of the distant past, of a time when the Philistines expanded from their five city-

---

14. A third site mentioned by Finkelstein (2002b, 155) is the border town of Beth-shemesh. However, its case is not unequivocal (see Bunimovitz and Lederman 2001, 146–47).

15. Also supported by the marked continuity in the demarcation of the eastern confines of the Kingdom of Gath, from the Late Bronze to the early Iron Age (Singer 1993, 137–40).

kingdoms northwards and eastwards to the central highlands, or in other words, of the Iron I. But Finkelstein, who is of course aware of this straightforward interpretation of the archaeological evidence, much of which comes from his own extensive field work, prefers to attribute more weight to the putative seventh-century Aegean mercenaries disguised as Goliath or as the Cherethites and Pelethites, perhaps in order to reconcile the evidence on the Philistines with his views on Israelite history and historiography. The biblical narrative obviously contains late anachronisms, but I do not see how the main core of the story could be relevant to a late-monarchic setting, when the balance of power between the protagonists had shifted substantially and the settlement map had changed as well.[16]

Like in countless other national epics throughout the world, the main features of the heroic saga—the description of the crucial struggle against the Philistines, the quintessential "other" who played such a dominant role in the formation of Israelite identity (Machinist 2000, 68–69)—were remembered and cherished throughout the centuries, before being immortalized in the Deuteronomistic history.

---

16. A similar discrepancy has been observed by Na'aman (2002, 216): "It is clear that the history of David's wars with Israel's neighbors reflects a reality that is quite different from that of the seventh—early sixth century B.C.E." However, Na'aman dates the earliest sources used by the Deuteronomist to the first half of the eighth century B.C.E., leaving very little data that may tentatively be assigned to the time of the historical David. In consequence, he suggests "that the detailed history of David, including his wars and achievements, be left in the hands of able writers and novelists ..." (Na'aman 2002, 216).

Chapter Three
Mycenaean IIIC:1 Pottery in Philistia: Four Decades of Research

*Trude Dothan and David Ben-Shlomo**

Philistine pottery was recognized over a hundred years ago and was linked to the material culture of the Philistines during the early Iron Age in Philistia. Trude Dothan's work (1982) summarized the Aegean characteristics of this culture and created a comprehensive framework for it, based on the information available up to the early 1970s. However, the identification of another class of pottery during the late 1960s, the Mycenaean IIIC:1 or Philistine Monochrome, marked a new stage in the research of the Philistine material culture. The appearance of this pottery unquestionably sheds new light on cultural and chronological aspects of the Philistines in particular and on wider issues in the southern Levant of the twelfth century B.C.E. This paper will outline the progress of research on the Mycenaean IIIC:1 pottery in the past four decades from its initial discovery to the present and discuss its implications.

Mycenaean IIIC:1 sherds were first discovered in Area H of Tel Ashdod. During the 1968 season of the excavation, directed by Moshe Dothan, it was realized that a unique class of pottery was present in the earliest levels of the Iron Age I. Though the sherds were of such well-known Philistine forms as bell-shaped bowls and kraters, the fabric and decoration were distinctively different. This ware was similar to Mycenaean IIIC pottery from Sinda (Furumark 1944; 1965) and especially to early twelfth-century Mycenaean IIIC pottery that had just been published from Enkomi (Dikaios 1969–1971). The fabric was very light-colored and well levigated and the decoration was in one color (monochrome), usually dark brown. At first it was suspected that these vessels were imports from

* Trude Dothan, Professor Emeritus of the Hebrew University of Jerusalem and David Ben-Shlomo, Researcher, Hebrew University of Jerusalem. Email: davden187@yahoo.com.

the Aegean or more likely from Cyprus (this was the first impression of several archaeologists expert in Mycenaean and Cypriot pottery as well):

> … at Ashdod we have the clinching evidence that the Philistine potters had with them the Mycenaean IIIC:1 ware which served them as a model and a base for further development. Since Mycenaean IIIC:1 was found at Ashdod in the lowest Philistine stratum, and only in small quantities, it seems likely that it was not imported but brought to Ashdod by the Philistines from their last stopping place. This would mean that at least some of the Philistines came, at least to Ashdod, directly from Cyprus and not later than during the prevalence of the Mycenaean IIIC:1 style.… (M. Dothan 1972, 54)[1]

Following the 1968 season at Ashdod, it was decided to analyze these sherds chemically without delay, in order to determine their provenance. A newly developed technique was used—Neutron Activation Analysis (NAA)—in collaboration with Isodore Perlman and Frank Asaro. The results (Asaro, Perlman, and M. Dothan 1971) showed without doubt that these sherds were not imports, but that their chemical fingerprint fits clay sources from Philistia including clay used for the later Philistine Bichrome Ware. The chemical composition of five Mycenaean IIIC:1 sherds from Ashdod was compared to Mycenaean IIIC pottery from three sites in Cyprus (Enkomi, Palaeopaphos, and Kition) and to Philistine Bichrome pottery from Ashdod. There was a distinct difference in composition between the Ashdod Mycenaean IIIC:1 and the Cypriot examples, especially in the concentration of the element hafnium; the composition of the Mycenaean IIIC:1 sherds fit better the Philistine Bichrome sherds from Ashdod. Although this was not a comprehensive provenance study using typical reference material, it ruled out a Cypriot origin for the Mycenaean IIIC:1 pottery from Ashdod and suggested that it was locally produced. It should be noted that this study was a pioneering one using these techniques, and very few compositional databases of pottery were at hand.

Accordingly, it was understood that this ware, appearing in the initial phase of the Iron I, reflects the manufacture of Mycenaean-like pottery by the newly arrived immigrants to Philistia, utilizing knowledge brought from their homeland:

> We have already seen that the two groups of Tel Ashdod wares (Philistine and MycIIIC1) match each other in chemical profile as well as can be expected.

---

1. It should be noted that in the final section of the 1972 article (based on a paper given during 1969) a paragraph was added describing the new conclusions according to the NAA results (M. Dothan 1972, 56).

> In form, design, and fabric the MycIIIC1 pieces adhere closely to MycIIIC1 wares from other places, particularly with that found on Cyprus. Contrariwise, the Tel Ashdod MycIIIC1 ware looks distinctly different from the local Philistine ware, yet the clays are the same. These latter facts point strongly to particular pottery making techniques (kiln conditions) which are different for the two types of wares. It is logical to ascribe the techniques which produced the MycIIIC1 wares as those traditional for the potters and hence that we are dealing with a recently transplanted people.... (Asaro, Perlman, and M. Dothan 1971, 175)

It was also suggested at that stage by Moshe Dothan that the Mycenaean IIIC:1 pottery represents an earlier (late thirteenth- or early twelfth-century) wave of Sea Peoples arriving to Philistia (T. Dothan and M. Dothan 1992, 162), possibly in relation to the sea battle with the Sea Peoples described in the Medinet Habu reliefs. On the other hand, the Philistine Bichrome pottery reflects the culture of the biblical Philistines settling during the twelfth century B.C.E. Amihai Mazar (1985a) and Trude Dothan (1989; 1998b) suggested a gradual evolution of the Philistine Bichrome pottery from the earlier Mycenaean IIIC:1 pottery.

During the 1968–1969 seasons at Ashdod, Mycenaean IIIC:1 pottery was uncovered in large quantities in Areas H and G. In Area G, located on the acropolis, the stratigraphic context of this material was in the first Iron I city (Stratum XIIIb). In relation to Stratum XIIIb in Area G an important group of about thirty vessels should be noted. This assemblage (Locus 4106), containing mostly simply decorated bell-shaped bowls, was found in a small room, grouped together and lying upside down (M. Dothan and Porath 1993, 54, figs. 12–14). It is possible that this group belongs to a potter's workshop.[2]

During the early 1980s the Tel Miqne-Ekron project was initiated by the Hebrew University of Jerusalem and the W. F. Albright Institute: a joint project headed by Trude Dothan and Seymour Gitin. Fortunately, in the acropolis in Field I a large amount of Mycenaean IIIC:1 pottery was soon discovered in a distinct context overlying the Late Bronze destruction layer (in Stratum VIIB). In addition, several pottery kilns belonging to the same phase were unearthed. This material too was chemically analyzed by the NAA laboratory of the Hebrew University (Gunneweg et al. 1986) and petrographically analyzed by Ann E. Killebrew (1998a; 1999a; this volume). In all of these cases the pottery was found to be locally produced on site. Petrography and the nature of the kilns pointed to distinctive technological features: for example, one of the kilns is rectangular, a shape

2. Concerning the material from Ashdod, the cycle is now complete as the final publication of Area H was published by David Ben-Shlomo (M. Dothan and Ben-Shlomo 2005).

not known in the Levant for kilns in the Late Bronze and Iron Ages (Killebrew 1996a). The Mycenaean IIIC:1 assemblage from Field I at Ekron also exhibits outstanding diversity in both form and decoration, indicating a developed center of production on site.

In the following seasons of the Tel Miqne-Ekron project, Field IV was excavated, where the Mycenaean IIIC:1 pottery was placed within the chronological sequence of the early Iron Age and its spatial distribution within the architectural units was established. Other assemblages of Mycenaean IIIC:1 pottery were discovered in Field X (T. Dothan 1998a) and Field III (currently in analysis).

Some Philistine Bichrome pottery from Tell 'Eitun and other sites was analyzed by petrography in the early 1970s as well (Edelstein and Glass 1973); the results of this very limited study demonstrate to some extent the technological characteristics of the later Philistine pottery.

The accumulated material from Tel Ashdod and Tel Miqne Fields I, IV, and X enables a more comprehensive typological, technological, and chronological description of this pottery. The vast majority of a Mycenaean IIIC:1 pottery assemblage consists of bowls. The most common type is the bell-shaped bowl. Carinated bowls with strap handles are also frequent, while large bowls with horizontal handles are much less numerous. Larger open vessels (kraters and kalathoi) appear in smaller numbers. Other open forms (kylikes, trays, and cups) are infrequent. Closed tablewares and containers such as feeding bottles, strainer-spout jugs, and stirrup jars and jugs are much less common than open forms. Coarseware cooking jugs are widespread in all strata in which Mycenaean IIIC:1 pottery appears. The Canaanite tradition of jugs, juglets, flasks, and storage jars provided more closed tablewares and containers for the population of the site (T. Dothan and Zukerman 2004). The Mycenaean IIIC:1 pottery comprises 40–50 percent of the pottery assemblages of the early-twelfth century in Tel Miqne; in some areas (for instance near the kilns in Field I) the percentage is even higher.

The Mycenaean IIIC:1 ceramic style may be characterized by several features that are common to most of the vessels that it comprises. The vessels are usually carefully formed. The walls of small vessels, such as bowls and stirrup jars, are delicate and thin; the joints between the handles and the body are smoothed. However, alongside the delicate bell-shaped bowls there is a smaller group of vessels with thicker walls and less carefully formed details of form.

Nevertheless, the Mycenaean IIIC:1 assemblage from Ashdod and Ekron is remarkable for its morphological, technological, and decorative diversity. The substantial range of variations in shape, clay composition, and decorative styles clearly indicated that the production of Mycenaean IIIC:1 wares was not standardized, and testifies to the multiplicity of its sources of inspiration (this calls for further compositional and petrographic analysis of this pottery). Moreover, every vessel or group of vessels exhibits a different degree of similarity to its Aegean or Cypriot prototypes. It can be demonstrated clearly that this early Mycenaean IIIC:1 pottery retains a much closer resemblance to the Aegean Mycenaean pottery than the later Philistine Bichrome pottery. However, it seems that the Aegean motifs have a longer life span than the forms, and thus very typical and at times rare Mycenaean IIIC motifs also appear on some Philistine Bichrome vessels.

During the 1980s Mycenaean IIIC:1 pottery was also discovered in Moshe Dothan's excavations at Tel Akko. These sherds were discovered in relation to pottery kilns of the initial Iron I levels (M. Dothan 1989) and may be seen to reflect a settlement of a different group of Sea Peoples in the northern coastal area (possibly the Danuna). It should be noted, though, that the Mycenaean IIIC:1 sherds from Akko are very few and are somewhat different in their appearance from the Mycenaean IIIC:1 pottery from Philistia.

During the past thirty years, Mycenaean IIIC:1 has been reported from several sites along the Lebanese and Syrian coast, such as in Sarepta (Anderson 1988), Ras Ibn Hani (Bounni et al. 1979; du Piêd 2006–2007), possibly Tell Afis (Bonatz 1998), and most recently in the 'Amuq at Tell Ta'yinat (Janeway 2006–2007). This Mycenaean IIIC:1 pottery appears in twelfth-century contexts and is likely to have been locally made and not imported, judging from both its visual appearance and its context (in Sarepta in relation to pottery kilns). Nevertheless, these assemblages have not yet been published in full, nor are any archaeometrical results reported (for an overview of the evidence from the northern Levant, see Lehmann, this volume).

A different phenomenon appearing in northern Israel during the beginning of the Iron Age I is Mycenaean IIIC pottery apparently imported from the Aegean. This pottery appears at Beth Shean (Hankey 1966; Sherratt and Mazar, this volume[3]), Tel Keisan (Balensi 1981), and possibly at Megiddo as well (D'Agata et al. 2005). It should be noted that this pottery differs in appearance from the locally produced Mycenaean IIIC:1 from Philistia and appears in limited forms (such as stirrup jars) and decorative motifs. The imported Mycenaean IIIC of the Iron Age I probably reflects limited commercial connections between the remaining Canaanite or Egyptian-controlled cities of northern Israel and the Aegean and/or Cyprus.

During the 1980s and 1990s, several interpretive studies of the Philistines and the Sea Peoples appeared. This was considered a "hot" subject, possibly due to its potential implications for processual, postprocessual, and cognitive archaeology. The Philistine material culture in general and the Mycenaean IIIC:1

---

3. We wish to thank Prof. A. Mazar for the permission to quote this article.

pottery in particular were a typical case of the "pots and people" question. Initially there was a tendency to view the Philistine material culture, or at least parts of it, as a phenomenon reflecting local processes, not necessarily related to a substantial immigration from the west (e.g., Bunimovitz 1986; Brug 1985; Artzy 1997). Subsequently the trend changed and emphasis was put on immigration processes and phenomena related to them (Bunimovitz 1998; Bunimovitz and Yasur-Landau 1996; T. Dothan 2000; Barako 2000; Oren 2000; Bunimovitz and Faust 2001). However, although various interpretations of the available data were suggested, no new data were offered to support these views and it was apparent that fresh and detailed publications of the Philistine centers were urgently required.

Accordingly, recent years have seen the unearthing of assemblages of Mycenaean IIIC:1 pottery from newly excavated Philistine cities. These include Ashkelon (Stager 1995) and Tell eṣ-Ṣafi/Gath (Maeir and Ehrlich 2001). At the same time, further efforts are being made to publish the assemblages from Ashdod and Tel Miqne-Ekron. It is now clear that this pottery characterizes the Philistine Pentapolis during the first decades of the twelfth century B.C.E., although isolated examples appear in other sites, such as Tel Haror (Oren 1993).

The question of the absolute chronology of the end of the Late Bronze Age and the beginning of the Iron Age has been the focus of several debates in recent years. The appearance and character of the Mycenaean IIIC:1 pottery in Philistia is crucial to this issue. On the one hand it is now clear, according to the results from Ashdod and Ekron, that this pottery postdates the final Late Bronze strata and precedes the Philistine Bichrome pottery. Thus, we have isolated a stratigraphic and cultural horizon of the early Iron Age I. On the other hand, in terms of absolute chronology we do not have enough textual evidence from this period, though according to the available data, this period must be in the first quarter of the twelfth century B.C.E. The Mycenaean IIIC:1 pottery from Philistia is probably contemporary, on both stylistic and stratigraphic grounds, to the Late Helladic IIIC Early in the Aegean and the Late Cypriot IIIA–B in Cyprus. It should be noted that, unlike the Philistine Bichrome pottery, the Mycenaean IIIC:1 has a very limited appearance, probably only in the major Philistine cities. Thus, contemporary strata of southern Palestine (such as Lachish VI, Tel Sera‘ IX, and Aphek X11) lack this pottery. Ussishkin and Finkelstein's (1995; 1998) New and Low Chronology dates the Mycenaean IIIC:1 pottery from Philistia to the late-twelfth century B.C.E., after Ramesses IV. In this view the Philistine Bichrome pottery should be dated even later. This view is based only on limited exposures of Lachish Level VI and Tel Sera‘ Stratum IX and on the assumption that different material cultures cannot coexist in the same area due to ethnic, political, or other divisions. This minimalistic conception is not in accordance with the entire body of data now available from Philistia.

From the cultural point of view, as research advances it seems clearer the Mycenaean IIIC:1 pottery reflects to various degrees the transportation and transformation of Aegean styles of pottery production by people having direct contact with this parent culture. This marks a distinct difference from the situation in the Late Bronze Age, when Aegean and Cypriot pottery was imported to the Levant and occasionally copied by local potters. This contrasts with Susan Sherratt's view (1998 and this volume) that describes the Mycenaean IIIC:1 pottery basically as a continuation of the imitation industry of the Late Bronze Age, which increased due to lack of supply.

It is not yet clear from which location within the Aegean and/or Cyprus the stylistic and technological know-how was brought to Philistia by the immigrants. It seems that most comparisons can be drawn with Cyprus, although a mixture of several origins is also apparent in some cases. Hopefully, with the new and updated research of Mycenaean pottery in the Aegean and Cyprus by Mountjoy (e.g., 1999b and this volume) and others (most recently see, e.g., Deger-Jalkotzy and Zavadil 2007; Deger-Jalkotzy and Bächle 2009), the geographical and chronological links with the Aegean can be refined.

Research of the Mycenaean IIIC:1 pottery in Philistia has now reached an advanced stage. A comprehensive typological and chronological framework has been established (in collaboration with Alexander Zukerman; T. Dothan and Zukerman 2004). David Ben-Shlomo has examined regional production centers within Philistia and their relation to the various fabric appearances of this pottery utilizing typological, chemical, and petrographical methods (2006). Analysis of the spatial distribution of this pottery and its significance is being conducted by Laura Mazow (2005). The aim of all this research is the comprehensive definition of the phenomenon of the Mycenaean IIIC:1 pottery within both the Philistine material culture of the early Iron Age and the wider cultural and chronological horizon of the southern Levant of the twelfth century B.C.E.

Chapter Four
Philistines and Egyptians in Southern Coastal Canaan during the Early Iron Age

*Tristan J. Barako**

Essential to an understanding of the early history of the Philistines is their relationship to Twentieth Dynasty Egypt. Egyptian texts, particularly Papyrus Harris I and the Great Inscription at Medinet Habu, have informed the debate over how and when the Philistines came to be settled in southern coastal Canaan. According to the traditional paradigm, the Egyptians forcibly garrisoned the Philistines in southern Canaan after 1174 B.C.E., which corresponds to the eighth year of Ramesses III's reign.[1] Increasingly over the past dozen years, however, both the circumstances and the date of the Philistines' settlement have been called into question. An assessment of these revisionist theories, on the basis of an examination of both textual and archaeological data, is the subject of this paper.

Egypt's Role in the Philistine Settlement

Textual Evidence

William F. Albright (1930–1931, 58) and Albrecht Alt (1953) first formulated the traditional paradigm, whereby Egypt settled the Philistines in garrisons within Canaan, based primarily on a brief notice contained in Papyrus Harris I, 76.7–8:

---

* Office of the Vice President for Research, Brown University, Providence, RI 02912. I wish to thank Ann Killebrew for the invitation to contribute the following article to this volume. Appreciation is also due to Mario Martin and James Weinstein who made helpful suggestions in terms of bibliography.

1. The Low Chronology, which yields dates of 1182–1151 B.C.E. for the reign of Ramesses

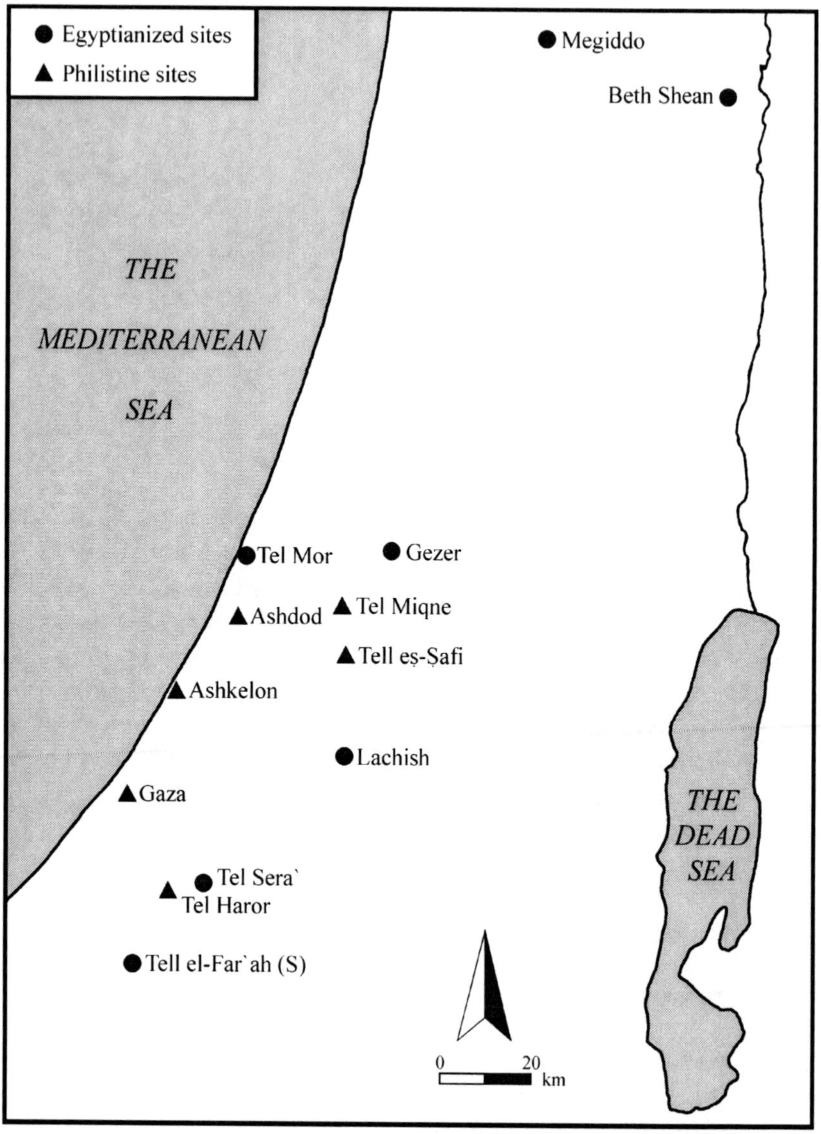

Fig. 1: Egyptianized and Philistine sites in the southern Levant during the twelfth century B.C.E. (drawing adapted from Bietak 1993, fig. 3 and Stager 1995, fig. 2).

> I slew the Denyen in their islands, while the Tjeker and the Philistines were made ashes. The Sherden and the Weshesh of the Sea were made nonexistent, captured all together and brought in captivity to Egypt like the sands of the shore. I settled them in strongholds, bound in my name. (John A. Wilson in *ANET* 262)

From this passage it was assumed that, following their unsuccessful attack on Egypt in the eighth year of Ramesses III's reign, the Philistines were garrisoned in southern Canaan. Once they had grown sufficiently strong and numerous, they then extricated themselves from Egyptian authority.

As a number of scholars have observed, however, there are two fundamental problems with this proposed scenario: 1) Papyrus Harris I does not specify where the Philistines were garrisoned (Singer 1985, 109; Higginbotham 2000, 56); and 2) there is little or no evidence for an Egyptian presence at sites within Philistia during the Twentieth Dynasty (Weinstein 1992, 145; Bietak 1993, 299–300). The majority of texts that describe the disposition of prisoners of war, in fact, favor a location within Egypt (B. Wood 1991, 48; Cifola 1994, 6). For example, in the Rhetorical Stela from Deir el-Medineh, Ramesses III claims to have caused the defeated Libyans and Meshwesh "to cross the Nile streams, (they being) brought to Egypt and being made (to settle) into strongholds by the victorious king" (Peden 1994, 65).

Alternatively, war captives were settled in regions over which Egypt exercised hegemony, as did Ramesses II according to an inscription from the Great Temple at Abu Simbel: "... bringing the land of Nubia to the land of the north, the Asiatics (+*ʿ3mw*) to the land of Nubia ... filling the strongholds, which he built, with the captivity of his mighty sword..." (*ARE* III §457). In either event, to settle one's enemies in the very region those enemies seek to conquer, as the traditional paradigm would have it, makes for poor military strategy (Bietak 1991, 37; Higginbotham 2000, 56).

Archaeological Data

Nor does the archaeological data support the old paradigm (fig. 1). Twelfth-century B.C.E. strata at Canaanite sites, particularly in the northern Negev, inner Shephelah, and interior valleys, have produced an abundance of Egyptian and Egyptianized material culture (e.g., Weinstein 1981, 20; Bietak 1993, figs. 2–3). At Philistine Pentapolis sites, on the other hand, there is an almost complete absence

III, is followed here (Wente and van Siclen 1977). For a more recent assessment of the state of Egyptian absolute chronology, see Kitchen 2000.

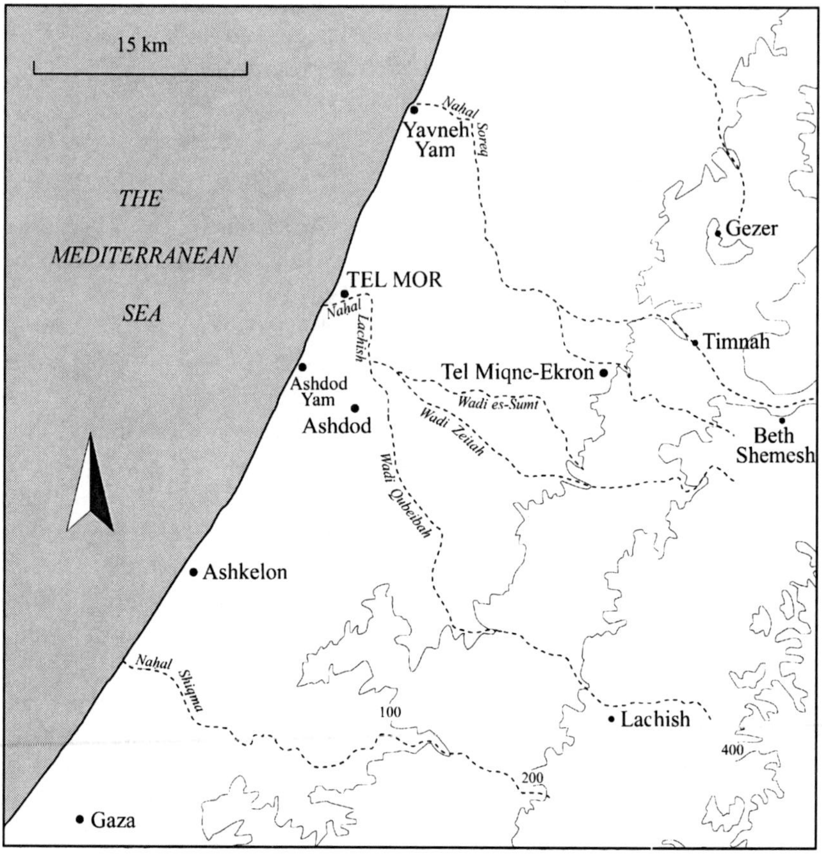

Fig. 2: Map of the southern Levantine coastal region (drawing adapted from T. Dothan 2000, fig. 7.1).

of evidence for an Egyptian presence during the Twentieth Dynasty (Weinstein 1992, 145; Bietak 1993, 299–300; Stager 1995, 344).

The Pentapolis site with the best exposure of twelfth-century B.C.E. strata, which correspond to the period of the initial Philistine settlement, is Tel Miqne-Ekron. In Stratum VIII (= thirteenth century B.C.E.), a limited assemblage of imported Aegyptiaca was found, mostly the type of small luxury items common at Canaanite sites during the Late Bronze Age (e.g., T. Dothan and Gitin 1993, 1052).[2] This apparent lack of Egyptian interest in Tel Miqne is not surprising

2. In terms of Egyptianized pottery, only a couple beer jar fragments were excavated in the preceding Stratum IX (Killebrew 1999a, Ill. II:4:21–22).

given the site's diminutive size: The Late Bronze Age settlement was confined to the 2.5-hectare acropolis in the northeastern corner of the tell. Built on top of a thick destruction level, the Stratum VII settlement, however, encompassed the entire tell, an area of ca. 20 hectares (T. Dothan 1998b, 150–52; but see Killebrew 1996b, 21–27; 1998a; this volume for an alternative interpretation). The sudden appearance of the Philistine material culture, especially considerable quantities of locally produced Mycenaean IIIC:1b (Myc IIIC:1b), characterizes Stratum VII. At the same time, the amount of Egyptian material culture at Tel Miqne decreased. It is surprising that a large site in southern Canaan should produce no evidence for Egyptian presence or interaction at a time when Egypt, reinvigorated by Ramesses III's reign, attempted to regain control of the region.

Ashdod is the only other Pentapolis site where a significant amount of the twelfth-century-B.C.E. settlement has been exposed. As a coastal site along the Via Maris, Ashdod was undoubtedly of interest to New Kingdom Egypt. A large fortified building in use throughout the Late Bronze Age (= Strata XVI–XIV) was excavated in Area G and identified as a "Governor's Residence" or palace (M. Dothan and Porath 1993, 10, 39–49, Plan 7). With this "Residence" the excavators associated an inscribed stone fragment, possibly from a doorjamb, which was found in a later fill context (= Stratum XIIB) from the same area.[3] The inscription reads "Fanbearer on the Kings' Right Hand" (*tꜣỉ hw* [*hr*] *wnmy n nsw*), an honorific accorded only to high officials in the pharaonic court (Kitchen 1993). Egyptianized bowls (M. Dothan and Porath 1993, 45, figs. 10:1; 11:1–6; 8–12), a beer jar (fig. 11:24), and an alabaster vessel (fig. 12:15) were also found in Area G, Stratum XIV.[4] In Stratum XIII, after a partial destruction of Area G, Myc IIIC:1b first appears at Ashdod and Egyptianized material culture virtually disappears.

The destruction levels at Tel Miqne and Ashdod briefly described above constitute further evidence against the traditional paradigm. At both sites, thick layers of ash and burnt mud brick separated the Canaanite (Miqne VIII, Ashdod XIV) from the initial Philistine settlements (Miqne VII, Ashdod XIII). At Tel Miqne the small Canaanite settlement ended in a great conflagration, over which the much larger Philistine city was built (T. Dothan 2000, 147). At Ashdod the clearest sequence comes from Area G, where the Canaanite city ended in an "intense destruction" followed by a settlement of a "different character" marked

---

3. Note also that a surface survey in the area between Ashdod and Tel Mor produced a fragment of a monumental statue of one of Ramesses II's queens (Schulman 1993).

4. At Late Bronze Ashdod, Egyptianized bowls were found also in Areas A (M. Dothan 1971, fig. 1:1), B (M. Dothan and Freedman 1967, fig. 22:1–4), and H (M. Dothan 1971, fig. 81:3). Another beer jar was found in Area H (M. Dothan 1971, fig. 81:14).

by the appearance of significant amounts of Philistine pottery (M. Dothan and Porath 1993, 53, Plan 8). Elsewhere, in Areas A, B, and H, the excavators found ca. 80-centimeter–thick ashy layers covering Stratum XIV (M. Dothan and Freedman 1967, 81; M. Dothan 1971, 158–59, Plan 20).

During the past few years, key transitional strata at Ashkelon are beginning to be revealed. In Grid 38, evidence of Egyptian presence, the probable remains of a fortress similar to Tel Mor and Deir el-Balah, have been uncovered (Master 2005, 339–40; Stager et al. 2008, 256–57). The associated Egyptianized and imported Egyptian pottery suggest a date in the late Nineteenth or early Twentieth Dynasty (Martin 2009). Early Philistine remains rest on top of this structure (Stager 2008, 1580–81). It is worth noting that during the excavations of Garstang and Phythian-Adams at the site, a thick layer of black ash was found separating their Late Bronze (Stage V) from the Iron Age (Stage VI) strata (Phythian-Adams 1923, 63–64, figs. 3–4). Mackenzie observed a similar sequence in the same part of the tell a decade earlier, and tentatively ascribed the destruction and subsequent settlement to the Philistines' arrival (1913, 21, pl. 2). However the current excavations at Ashkelon in Grid 38 have not uncovered signs of a destruction at the end of the Late Bronze Age (Stager 2008, 1580).

Such destruction levels are more the mark of hostile invaders than subdued prisoners of war. The complete absence of evidence for Egyptian involvement in the strata that follow (i.e., Tel Miqne VII, Ashdod XIII) is a further blow to the traditional paradigm. What is more, the majority of New Kingdom inscriptions report that defeated enemies were garrisoned in Egypt. The combined archaeological and textual data, then, strongly suggests that the Philistines settled in southern Canaan by force, probably in opposition to Egypt.

Chronology of the Philistine Settlement

In recent years Israel Finkelstein and David Ussishkin have argued that the date of the Philistine settlement should be lowered by roughly fifty years—that is, to about 1130 B.C.E.[5] Briefly described, their argument is as follows: Because certain sites located near the Philistine Pentapolis contain strata that are clearly datable to the reign of Ramesses III, but have not yielded Philistine pottery, this type of pottery elsewhere must have been produced for the first time after the destruction of these strata. The two key sites mentioned in this regard are Lachish VI

5. See especially Finkelstein 1995 and 2000. Ussishkin was the first to propose the "Low Chronology" based on his excavations at Lachish (1985); however, Finkelstein has been, by far, the more vocal advocate for chronological revision.

and Tel Seraʿ IX. In both these strata Egyptian inscriptions dating to Ramesses III were found (Gilula 1976; Goldwasser 1982, 1984), but no Philistine pottery. On the other hand, neighboring sites generally thought to be contemporaneous, particularly Tel Haror B4–2, did produce both Philistine Monochrome and Bichrome pottery (Oren 1993, 582–83).

The underlying assumption of this argument is that cultural boundaries must be permeable for all types of material culture. A corollary holds that two neighboring sites that do not possess the same full range of material culture cannot be contemporaneous. Amihai Mazar, however, has adduced examples from the archaeology of Syria-Palestine to demonstrate that distinct material cultures have coexisted side by side with little or no interaction (1997b, 158; see also Ben-Tor and Ben-Ami 1998, 31). Furthermore, as pointed out by Shlomo Bunimovitz and Avraham Faust, even intensive interaction between cultures does not necessarily lead to material culture exchange (2001). Indeed, in order to maintain group identity and strengthen solidarity during times of conflict with a neighboring group, people tend not to acquire items emblematic of their rivals.

Case Study: Philistine Ashdod and Egyptian Tel Mor

The excavations at Ashdod and Tel Mor provide a useful archaeological case study for this cultural phenomenon, especially as it pertains to the question of the relationship between Philistines and Egyptians in southern Canaan.[6] As noted above, Ashdod was one of the cities that constituted the Philistine Pentapolis established in the twelfth century B.C.E. on the ruins of a Canaanite settlement. Located six kilometers northwest of Ashdod on the northern bank of the Nahal Lachish (Wadi Sukreir) is the small site of Tel Mor (fig. 2). Throughout most of the Late Bronze Age and into the early Iron Age, Tel Mor functioned primarily as an Egyptian outpost. Indeed, it is likely that Tel Mor corresponds to *Mḫś/ḏ/z* mentioned in New Kingdom texts (M. Dothan 1981b, 151, n. 3; Barako 2007a, 4–5) the name appears as *M<?>ḫś/* in a topographical list of Thutmosis III (Simons 1937, 117); as *Muḫḫazu* (= ^{al}*Mu-u[ḫ]-ḫa-zi*) in EA 298:25 (Moran 1992, 340); and as *M'wḫꜣḏꜣ* in another list dating to the reign of Ramesses II at ʿAmara West (B. Mazar 1975).

Despite the proximity of Tel Mor and Ashdod, their material cultural assemblages were markedly different, particularly during the twelfth century B.C.E. As

6. Moshe Dothan, in whose memory the 2001 international workshop "The Philistines and Other Sea Peoples" was held, excavated both these sites. Through generous funding from the Shelby White–Leon Levy Program for Archaeological Publications, I published Dothan's excavations at Tel Mor (Barako 2007a). For a fuller refutation of the Low Chronology based on the excavations at Ashdod and Tel Mor, see Barako 2007b.

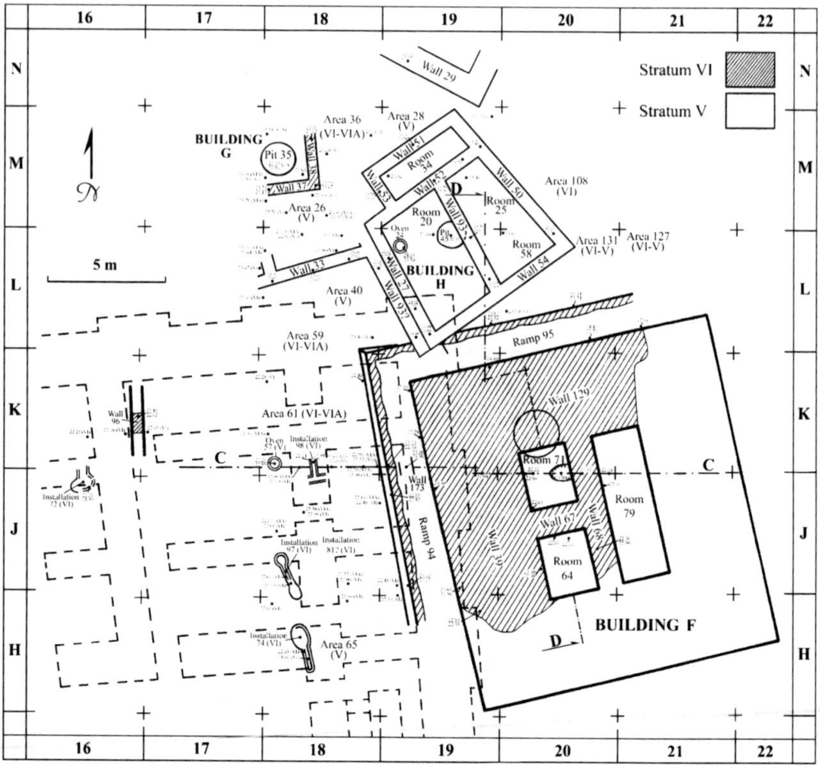

Fig. 3: Tel Mor, Strata IV–V (drawing by I. Dunayevsky).

presently shown, these differences represent another blow to the proposed chronological revision of Finkelstein and Ussishkin.

Ashdod

Even though the sequence at Ashdod has already been outlined above, it bears repeating here. Stratum XIV corresponds to the last Canaanite settlement at Ashdod. At this time Mycenaean and Cypriot pottery was still being imported (e.g., M. Dothan and Porath 1993, 48–49, fig. 12:2–4), and a small amount of Egyptianized pottery was being made at or brought to the site. At the end of the thirteenth century B.C.E., Ashdod was largely destroyed. In Area G, where the best Late Bronze to early Iron Age sequence was preserved, a new settlement (Stratum XIII) was built atop the ruins. More than anything else, the initial appearance of Myc IIIC:1b characterizes Stratum XIII. Noteworthy also are the absences of Mycenaean and Cypriot imports as well as Egyptianized pottery in this stratum.

Tel Mor

A large Egyptian-style building dominated the tiny summit (ca. one dunam) of Tel Mor during the thirteenth century B.C.E. (= Strata VIII–VII; M. Dothan 1993b, 1073; Barako 2007a, 20–26). Egyptianized pottery, mostly bowls and beer jars, comprised approximately 9 percent of the Stratum VII ceramic assemblage (Martin and Barako 2007, Table 4.12). Cypriot and, to a lesser extent, Mycenaean imports appear in small amounts. As with Ashdod, Tel Mor was destroyed at the end of the thirteenth century B.C.E. Above the thick destruction level that covered Stratum VII was a thin layer of wind-blown sand; thus indicating a brief period of abandonment. A smaller fort (Building F) was constructed in Stratum VI above and partially over the large fortress of Stratum VII (fig. 3).

In terms of pottery types, there are no major differences between the assemblages of Strata VII and VI. The amount of Egyptianized pottery, however, nearly doubled from 9 to 15 percent of the total registered sherds in Stratum VI. A small amount of Cypriot pottery was also found in this stratum, such as an intact late White Slip II bowl (Barako 2007a, fig. 5.5:8) and a Base Ring II juglet (Barako 2007a, fig. 5.3:20), the latter is probably a local imitation.

Stratum VI ended in destruction. Numerous whole or almost whole vessels lay smashed on the floors of the fort, particularly in Room 71. On top of these vessels were fallen mud bricks and then more broken pots, which, taken altogether, indicates a second-story collapse. In the following Stratum V, the fort was rebuilt, and a smaller building (H) was constructed to the north of it (fig. 3). Egyptianized pottery still comprised about an eighth of the total assemblage in this stratum. In Room 34 of Building H, an intact Egyptian-style globular cooking jar was found (fig. 4). It is probably a Nile B Egyptian import that dates to the period of the Twentieth Dynasty (David Aston, personal communication). Mycenaean and Cypriot imports, on the other hand, were not found in Stratum V, nor, significantly, was Myc IIIC:1b pottery.

Because there is no mention in the field notes of Stratum V having ended in destruction, it is best to assume that its buildings, particularly the fort, simply fell out of use. In the succeeding strata, the character of the site changed considerably. A single massive building no longer dominated the tell. Instead, the settlement became more open with relatively little architecture. Stratum IV, for example, consists only of a poorly preserved building, the walls of which roughly follow the outline of Building H from the preceding stratum. Virtually no Egyptianized pottery was found in Stratum IV or in any subsequent strata. For the first time, however, small amounts of Philistine Bichrome pottery appeared in Stratum IV. The succeeding Stratum III, which is comprised mostly of pits, contained even more Bichrome.

Fig. 4: Egyptian globular cooking jar from Tel Mor, Stratum V (photograph courtesy of the Israel Antiquities Authority).

Altogether about seventy sherds and whole vessels that may be described as "Philistine" were found at Tel Mor. This type of pottery comprises only 6 percent of the overall assemblage in Strata IV–III, which correspond to the Iron Age I period. The fact that the excavators appear to have collected all decorated body sherds, however, inflates this percentage. Most of the Philistine pottery is the familiar Bichrome with smaller amounts of "Aegean-style" cooking jugs and "Ashdod Ware" [7] present.

7. For a comprehensive analysis of "Ashdod Ware" and a convincing proposal to rename it "Late Philistine Decorated Ware," see Ben-Shlomo, Shai, and Maeir 2004.

Again, there is no locally made Myc IIIC:1b. Only the more notable Philistine sherds/vessels are described here.[8]

A decorated body sherd from a krater may be the earliest piece of Philistine Bichrome at Tel Mor (fig. 5.1). It preserves the tail of a water bird, the quintessential Philistine motif. To the right of the tail are four vertical lines belonging to the triglyph. The now-faded red and black paint was applied on a white slip. According to Trude Dothan, the bird motif is characteristic of the first two phases of Philistine pottery, which correspond to the twelfth and the first half of the eleventh centuries B.C.E. (1982, 198; see, more recently, T. Dothan and Zukerman 2004, 39–40). The water bird motif has been found, for example, on Bichrome kraters at Ashdod in Strata XIII (M. Dothan and Porath 1993, fig. 22) and XII (M. Dothan and Porath 1993, fig. 27:1–2).

The best-preserved example of Philistine Bichrome is from a krater that bears the typical spiral motif on a white wash (fig. 5.2; see also M. Dothan 1960b, pl. III:2). The following features characterize its form: A T-shaped rim that slopes inward; two horizontal loop handles attached to the upper body at an angle; a deep bell-shaped body; and a ring base (not preserved here). Its decoration consists of a red band on the rim and handles, and horizontal red bands that frame the main register located in the upper body. The metopes contain dark-painted spirals facing the same direction with red filling, and the triglyphs are comprised of alternating dark and red, wavy, vertical lines. The closest parallels, in terms of both the vessel's shape and decoration, derive from mid- to late twelfth-century-B.C.E. strata such as Ashdod XI (M. Dothan 1971, figs. 2:6; 86:7), Tel Miqne-Ekron VI (Killebrew 1998a, fig. 12:9), and Tell Qasile XII (A. Mazar 1985b, fig. 13:23 [= Type KR 2b]).

A couple restorable "Aegean-style" cooking jugs were found in a Stratum III pit (fig. 5.3–4). They possess the following morphological attributes: An everted rim; one, or occasionally, two handles that extend from rim to shoulder; a globular-shaped body; and a flat or low ring base. The surface of both is blackened, which is undoubtedly on account of their use as cooking vessels (fig. 6). In Canaan, these jugs frequently appear in strata containing Philistine pottery, both Myc IIIC:1b and Bichrome. They are found at sites on Cyprus during the Late Cypriot IIC and IIIA periods, and in the Aegean region primarily during the Late Helladic IIIC period (for references, see Killebrew 1998a, 397; 1999b). Cooking pots in the Late Bronze Age Canaanite tradition—that is, with everted, triangular-profiled rims—continue to appear in Stratum III as well. Unfortunately, the small

8. For the complete publication of Philistine pottery from Tel Mor, see Barako 2007a, 69–72, fig. 3:32.

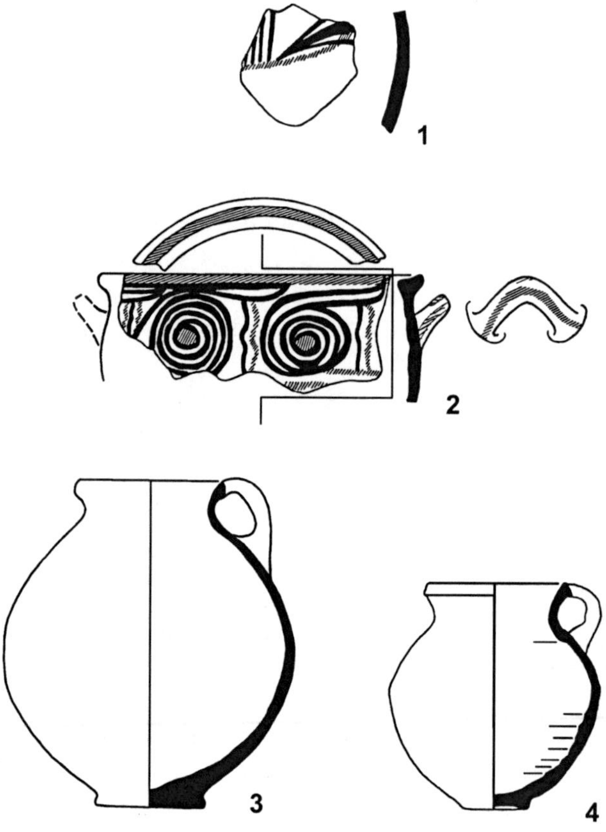

Fig. 5: Philistine pottery from Tel Mor, Strata IV–III.

sample size of cooking pots from this stratum precludes a meaningful statistical analysis of Canaanite versus Philistine types.

The presence at Tel Mor of cooking vessels from three different cultural backgrounds (i.e., Egyptian, Philistine, and Canaanite) merits further comment. Kitchenware is widely held to be an enduring ethnic marker on account of its resistance to change (as opposed to fine ware), and because it is often a part of a family's domestic traditions (e.g., Bunimovitz and Yasur-Landau 1996, 91). Moreover, food preparation was primarily the domain of women in the ancient world (e.g., Watterson 1991, 128–34; King and Stager 2001, 64–65). Thus, the distribution of cooking pots in southern Canaan during the twelfth century B.C.E. may

Table 1: Stratigraphy of Tel Mor and Ashdod compared.

Tel Mor			Ashdod		
Philistine	*Stratum*	*Egyptianized*	*Philistine*	*Stratum*	*Egyptianized*
absent	VII	present (9%)	absent	XIV	present (small amount)
absent	VI	present (15%)	absent	XIV	present (small amount)
absent	V	present (12%)	present (Myc IIIC:1b)	XIII	absent
present (Bichrome)	IV	absent	present (Bichrome)	XII	absent
present (Bichrome)	III	absent	present (Bichrome)	XI	absent

reveal information about the composition, especially in regard to gender, of the various populations present.

During the Nineteenth and Twentieth Dynasties, necked globular jars and large carinated bowls were used as cooking vessels in Egypt, both of which are extremely rare at Canaanite sites. In Canaan the former has been found at Tel Mor (fig. 4) and the latter at Beth Shean (Killebrew 1999a, 148–50, Ill. II:70.3). A very different trend in regard to foreign cooking vessels has been observed at Pentapolis sites. In strata corresponding to the initial Philistine settlement (e.g., Tel Miqne VII), Aegean-style cooking jugs largely supplant Canaanite cooking pots (Killebrew 1999b). There is strong evidence, then, that women were part of the Philistine migration and settlement (Barako 2003); whereas, mostly male administrators and soldiers must have staffed Egyptian garrisons in Canaan. In this case, the imported Nile B cooking jar from Tel Mor is an anomaly.

At first glance the relatively small amount of Philistine pottery present at Tel Mor is surprising, especially given the proximity of Ashdod, which was

Fig. 6: Aegean-style cooking jug from Tel Mor, Stratum III (photograph taken by D. D. Barako).

a major production center for Myc IIIC:1b, Philistine Bichrome, and Ashdod Ware. This dearth is understandable, however, when considered against the backdrop of Tel Mor's settlement history during the Iron I period. In the first half of the twelfth century B.C.E. (= Strata VI–V), which corresponds roughly to the reign of Ramesses III, the site continued to function as an Egyptian outpost. Thus, Egyptianized pottery is plentiful and Myc IIIC:1b altogether absent. After the abandonment of the Stratum V fort (= Building F) in the second half of the twelfth century B.C.E., there was very little architecture on the summit of Tel Mor. Utilitarian pottery, and not luxury wares like Philistine Bichrome and Ashdod Ware, is to be expected at such a poor, relatively minor site.

Synthesis

Based on the initial appearance of Philistine Bichrome, the stratigraphic sequences of Tel Mor and Ashdod match up as shown in table 1. The critical strata are Ashdod XIII and Tel Mor V, both dated by Moshe Dothan to the first half of the twelfth century B.C.E. Ashdod XIII produced significant amounts of Myc IIIC:1b but no Egyptianized pottery; whereas ca. 12 percent of the ceramic assemblage of Tel Mor V was Egyptianized pottery. Myc IIIC:1b does not appear in any stratum at Tel Mor, which appears to have been inhabited continuously throughout the twelfth century B.C.E.

Finkelstein and Ussishkin explain this marked patterning of Egyptianized and Philistine material culture by chronological revision. The evidence from Tel Mor and Ashdod suggests, however, that two nearby sites can be both contemporaneous and possess different material culture assemblages. A more convincing explanation holds that Egypt adopted a policy of containment in response to the Philistines' carving out their homeland from the southern coastal plain. Or, as Manfred Bietak (1993) and Lawrence Stager (1995, 342–44) have argued, a *cordon sanitaire* was established, whereby Egypt maintained outposts (e.g., Tel Mor) at sites directly opposed to Philistine capital cities (e.g., Ashdod).

In support of this view is the dearth of Egyptian and Egyptianized material culture at Pentapolis sites during the time of the Philistine settlement. Under Ramesses III, Egypt attempted to regain control of southern Canaan, an effort reflected in the numerous Egyptian finds that date to the Twentieth Dynasty found at sites in Canaan, but largely outside of Philistia. This apparent lack of Egyptian activity during the Twentieth Dynasty in Philistia is no mere coincidence: The Egyptians were not in Philistia during this period because the Philistines were there instead; and not as garrisoned prisoners-of-war but, rather, as an intrusive population hostile to Egypt. The weight of the evidence from Philistine Pentapolis sites is considerable, and the pattern that emerges cannot be dismissed due to the vagaries of archaeological discovery. It reflects a historical development that offers a more reasonable explanation of the archaeological data than does chronological revision.

Chapter Five
The Mycenaean IIIC Pottery at Tel Miqne-Ekron

*Penelope A. Mountjoy**

Excavations at Tel Miqne have taken place on the acropolis in Field INE (Killebrew 1996b; forthcoming b; Meehl, Dothan and Gitin 2006), in the center of the tell in Field IVNW (Garfinkel, Dothan and Gitin, forthcoming), in the southern part in Field III, and on the western slope in Field XNW (Bierling 1998; see also T. Dothan and Gitin 1993; T. Dothan and Gitin 2008 for a general overview). The material studied here comes from Fields I, IV, and X. It dates to Stratum VII. This stratum can be divided into VIIB (earlier phase) and VIIA (the later phase). Phase VIIB can be further divided into an earlier and a later subphase. The material is grouped together here under the general heading of VII, since almost all of the illustrated pieces belong to VIIA; the few VIIB late pieces included are noted in the Index.[1]

The Shapes

The range of shapes represented is small in comparison to assemblages from the Aegean; some shapes are represented by only one or two examples. Closed shapes comprise the straight-sided alabastron, the large jug, the trefoil-mouthed jug, the

* British School at Athens, Souedias 52, 10676 Athens, Greece. This article was submitted in 2002. Acknowledgements: I thank the directors of the Tel Miqne excavations, T. Dothan and S. Gitin, for permission to study the material and present it here and for much helpful information. My thanks are also due to the excavators, A. E. Killebrew, M. Meehl, and A. Zukerman, for allowing me access to their material and, in particular, to A. E. Killebrew for much helpful discussion. I would also like to thank E. French and P. Warren for useful information based on their unpublished work on the excavations at Mycenae and Knossos respectively.

1. For pottery from Stratum VIIB, see Field INE: T. Dothan, Gitin, and Zukerman 2006, figs.

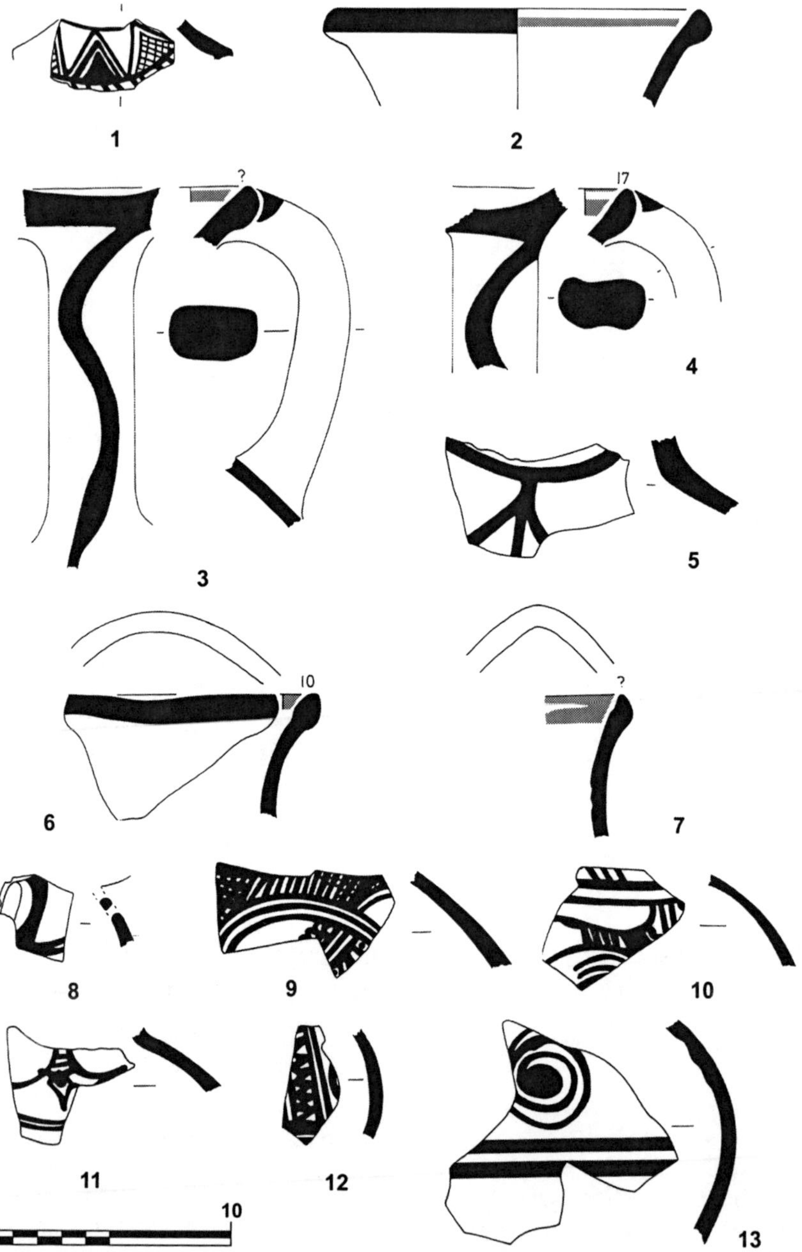

Fig. 1: **1)** straight-sided alabastron FS 96; **2–5)** jug FS 106; **6–7)** trefoil-mouthed jug FS 137; **8–13)** strainer jug FS 155.

strainer jug, the feeding bottle, and the stirrup jar. Sherds, which can be recognized as belonging to one or the other of these shapes, are few, but there are a number of closed body sherds, particularly linear ones, which cannot be more closely assigned. Open shapes include conical bowls, the deep bowl, ring-based krater, kylix, basin, shallow angular bowl, and tray. Conical bowls, both unpainted and linear, are the most common open shape, followed by the deep bowl and krater; the kylix and tray are very rare.

Alabastron, Straight-Sided FS 96 (fig. 1.1)

One sherd belonging to this shape has been recovered. The sloping shoulder is decorated with outlined cross-hatched triangles and an outlined solid triangle. The sides seem to be decorated with diagonal bars.

Jug FS 106 (fig. 1.2–5)

A few rims with a diameter of 12–15 centimeters seem to belong to this shape rather than to the trefoil-mouthed jug FS 137. It is possible that some of these rims belong to amphora FS 69, but that has two vertical handles and there are not many of those present, suggesting that the jug is represented rather than the amphora. For the same reason an assignation of hydria FS 128 can also be ruled out, as its large horizontal side handles do not seem to be present. A further candidate for these rims, narrow-necked jug FS 120, can be excluded since it has a much smaller rim diameter, generally 6–9 centimeters.[2] The jug rims are rounded (fig. 1.2–3) or long oval (fig. 1.4). The handle is large oval. The handles have a medium width wavy line down them, which may start on the righthand side at the top (fig. 1.3–4). Three shoulder fragments, all from Field I, can also be assigned to this shape from their large neck diameter. Two are decorated with a tassel pattern (fig. 1.5). The tassel differs from the contemporary fat Mainland version (Mountjoy 1986, fig. 175:2), but is very similar to those from Enkomi Level IIIA.[3] Such tassels also appear on Crete (Mook and Coulson 1997, 356, fig. 25:91, Phase 2). The tassel does not appear in the earliest IIIC phase at Mycenae or Lefkandi, but in the Tower Phase at Mycenae and Phase 1b at Lefkandi (Mountjoy 1986, 135 and fig. 175). The third sherd (Dothan, Gitin, and Zukerman 2006, fig. 3:17:16)

3:3–10; Field IVNW: Zukerman and Gitin forthcoming, figs. 5:1–10; and Field XNW: T. Dothan 1998a, pls. 1–2.

2. See, e.g., Mountjoy 1986, LH IIIB 101, fig. 122; 125, fig. 152; Mountjoy 1999d, Melos nos. 126–27.

3. See, e.g., Dikaios 1969–1971: Area I Floor V deposit pl. 94:22, Area I Well 3 pl. 109:12–13.

carries the edge of what may be a dot-outlined rosette FM 27; it is attached to the neck band by three vertical bars. The thick section of a fourth fragment, also possibly decorated with FM 27, suggests it too may belong to the large jug.

Trefoil-Mouthed Jug FS 137 (fig. 1.6–7)

All the examples of this shape are made in a coarser fabric. Only rims can be identified (fig. 1.6–7; T. Dothan, Gitin, and Zukerman 2006, figs. 3:17:19; 3:19:7–8; 3:23:18–19); they may be hollow (T. Dothan, Gitin, and Zukerman 2006, fig. 3:27:14) and there are no obvious handles. The shape seems to be linear, but there are no complete examples from Ekron to be sure. It has been termed Form AS 9 by Killebrew (2000, 241–42, fig. 12:3:7–9). Killebrew notes that the shape has a long history in Cyprus in other wares, whereas in the Aegean it does not appear until LH IIIC Middle (advanced), suggesting it comes into the Aegean repertoire from the east (2000, 242). This may well be so, especially as, although the shape has a long history on Cyprus in other wares, it is actually rare in the LC IIIA Mycenaean corpus, which corresponds to LH IIIC Early and Middle on the Greek Mainland.[4] Nor does it seem to be present on Crete during the LM IIIC Early and Middle phases.[5]

Strainer Jug FS 155 (fig. 1.8–13)

Figure 1.8 is a characteristic strainer spout. A number of other sherds can be assigned to this shape, but they could belong to the stirrup jar, which also seems to be elaborately decorated. The sherds seem to have two narrow shoulder bands (fig. 1.10–11), as also occurs on examples from Level IIIA at Enkomi (Dikaios 1969–1971, pls. 75:44; 98:3). Figure 1.9, a large example, is decorated with triple stems belonging to streamers or tongues with cross-hatched and bar fill. Figure 1.11 is decorated on the shoulder with antithetic spiral flanking a lozenge and figure 1.12 is decorated on the belly with antithetic spiral flanking a triglyph with fill of zigzag. Another sherd (fig. 1.10) has antithetic spiral in the belly zone with bars across the loops and the edge of a triple-stemmed tongue/spiral on the shoulder. Figure 1.13 has a large eye spiral, which may also be antithetic. The shape is very popular on Rhodes at Ialysos in LH IIIC Early (Mountjoy 1999d, 1040–43), but it is already present on the Greek Mainland in LH IIIB (Mountjoy 1999d, 138). Thus, it may have reached Ekron via Rhodes.

4. Kling (1989, 150) lists only four examples.

5. I thank P. Warren for information on his excavations at Knossos.

Feeding Bottle FS 162 (fig. 2.14–15)

The shape seems to be rare at Ekron in the Mycenaean phase. It is termed Form AS8 by Killebrew (2000, fig. 12:3:3–6) and described as unpainted or linear (2000, 240). Figure 2.14 has a hollow rim and a small oval basket handle. The handle is decorated with bars which culminate in a circle with reserved center across the top.[6] This feature begins in LH IIIC Early (Mountjoy 1986, fig. 179).[7] The spout of figure 2.15 has a band around the tip and the base of the spout. This band and the base of the spout are LH IIIB features, which continue into LH IIIC Early (Mountjoy 1999d Attica no. 346). In the latter phase spouts decorated with the ray pattern, which becomes so popular in LH IIIC Middle–Late, start to appear (Iakovidis 1969–1970, T.190.698 pl. 58a, T.147.1107 pl. 35b). LH IIIC feeding bottle spouts at Ekron do not seem to have this motif.

Stirrup Jar FS 175 (fig. 2.16–18)

Not enough sherds can be assigned to this shape for any in-depth analysis to be carried out on the material from Level VII. Killebrew classes it as Form AS 11 and also notes that it is rare (2000, 241, 243; fig. 12:3:10). One problem is that sherds may be muddled with those of the strainer-spouted jug FS 155. One vessel (fig. 2.16) depicts a zone of stacked zigzag above a zone of stacked triangles with solid centers. A spout (fig. 2.17) is preserved with the beginning of the adjacent false neck. The latter seems to be of the hollow variety. The spout has vertical stripes down it similar to the ray decoration on the spouts of LH IIIC feeding bottles on the Mainland (see above). It is decorated with a bird with its head turned backwards; the bird has a solid painted body. A false mouth (fig 2.18) also has a hollow neck; it has concentric circles or a spiral on the disc; the top of the disc has a slight cone. The handle of figure 2.18 may have bars down it as one seems to be present at the top.

Lipless Conical Bowl FS 204 (fig. 2.19)

This is a local shape comprising a lipless shallow bowl made in coarse fabric (fig. 2.19). There are many unpainted and linear sherds belonging to this shape. It seems to have replaced not only the LH IIIC one-handled conical bowl FS 242,

6. E.g. Mountjoy 1986, figs. 179, 246.

7. The design on the handle of a LH IIIB vessel from Zygouries seems to be a forerunner (Mountjoy 1999d, Korinthia no. 127).

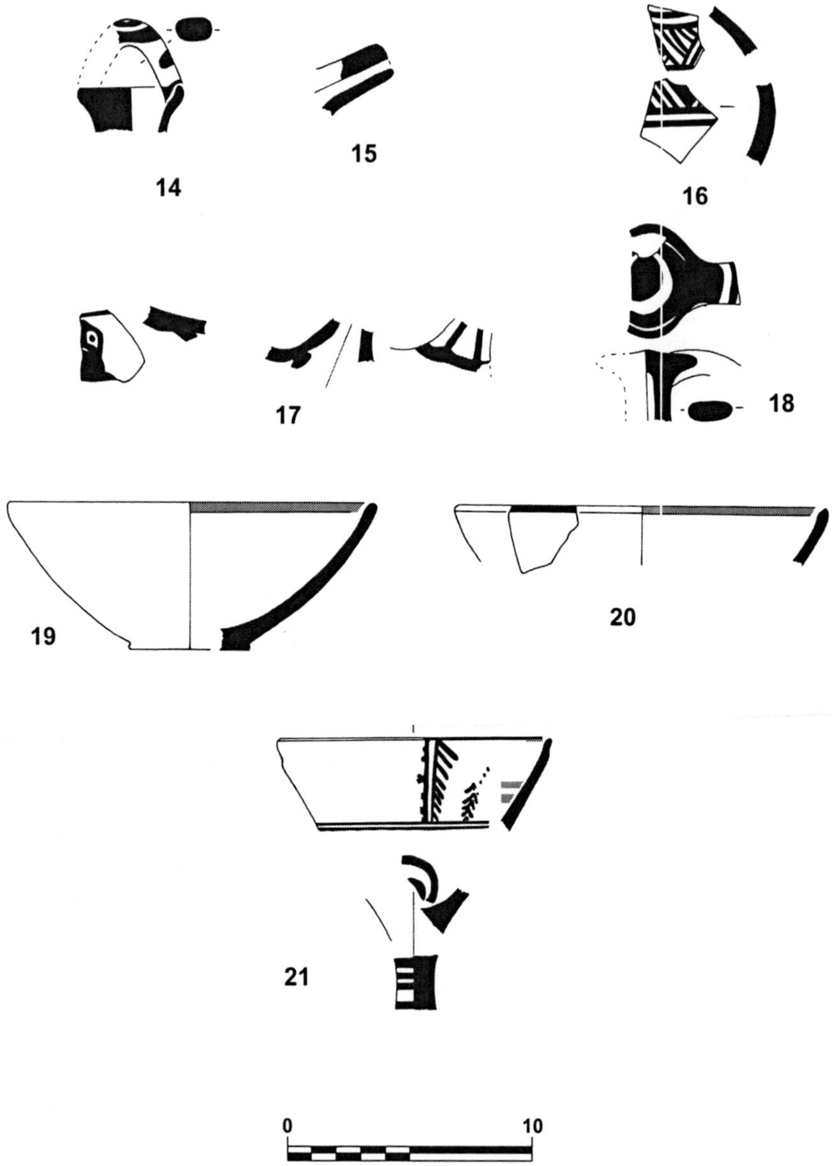

Fig. 2: **14–15**) feeding bottle FS 162; **16–18**) stirrup jar FS 175; **19**) lipless conical bowl; **20**) one-handled conical bowl FS 242; **21**) kylix FS 276.

but also all the varieties of LH IIIC Early linear small bowls found on Cyprus.[8] With the exception of the shallow angular bowl FS 295, these small linear bowls, which are so common on Cyprus, are not found at Ekron.

One-Handled Conical Bowl FS 242 (fig. 2.20)

One linear rim sherd (fig. 2.20) qualifies as this shape. The fabric and paint is that of the well-levigated, hard-fired, locally made Mycenaean pottery. The shape is much deeper than that of the coarser shallow bowl. However, since no obvious handles have been found belonging to this shape, figure 2.20 could be a version of FS 204 made in Mycenaean ware.

Kylix FS 276 (fig. 2.21)

The shape is very rare at Ekron (fig. 2.21). It has a short, shallow upper body above a carination. This is a Minoan form.[9] The stem is very narrow. Decoration consists of fringed triglyph with zigzag fill flanked by chevrons; the base of the bowl seems to have a spiral on the interior.

Krater, Ring-Based FS 282 (figs. 3.22; 4.23–26; 5.27–31)

Only one complete profile can be restored (fig. 3.22). The shape corresponds to Killebrew's Form AS 5 (2000, 237; fig. 12:1:12–13). It is a large globular shape. The rim may be T-shaped (see fig. 4.24), T-shaped and everted (figs. 3.22; 4.23), flaring everted (fig. 5.28), or short everted often with a trough-like depression on the top (figs. 4.25; 5.27). Another variant is a heavy rounded type (fig. 5.31). The rim may have bars across it (fig. 4.24), but this seems to be rare. The upper body may be rounded inturning (figs. 3.22; 4.25), straight (fig. 4.24), or carinated (fig. 5.29). The latter type is rare. Only a few handles are extant. They are set very high on the body and are very short (fig. 3.22). They may be out-turning (fig. 4.25). Handle decoration may consist of multiple splashes (figs. 3.22; 4.24); alternatively there may be the three-splash system found on the Greek Mainland consisting of a splash across each joint and a third along the top of the handle (Mountjoy 1986, fig.189:4, 8), but often at Ekron the central splash is 2-centimeters long

8. See Karageorghis 1974, T. 9 Upper Burial pls. 155–62 for a selection.

9. See the discussion in Hallager 1997, 38–39 with examples figs. 34–35; Hallager and Hallager 2000, pls. 3:84 P0714; 37:77 P0748; and Mook and Coulson 1997, 346, fig. 11:31; 359, fig. 31:136, 139.

Fig. 3: **22)** krater FS 282.

and the side splashes are very thin (fig. 4.25). The base is ring (fig. 3.22). Bases may be unpainted on the interior (fig. 3.22) or have spiral or concentric circles (T. Dothan, Gitin, and Zukerman 2006, fig. 3.11:25); on the exterior they may be banded (fig. 3.22).

Among the linear rims, there is an example (fig. 5.31) with straight-sided inturning upper body with three bands on the exterior rim. Another linear vessel has four medium bands on the belly (Zukerman and Gitin forthcoming, fig. 5:20:1).

Deep Bowl FS 284 (figs. 5.32–8.55)

Only a few complete profiles can be restored (figs. 6.37, 40; 8.50–52). The form is classified as Form AS 4 by Killebrew (2000, 236–39; fig. 12:1:8–11). It is a small globular shape. The rim is usually flaring lipless as on the Greek Mainland, but there is also a pointed variant on both decorated (fig. 6.35–36) and linear examples (fig. 8.50). On this type the lip thins out to a tip instead of remaining a uniform width. Some vases, which may belong to a particular workshop (i.e., the three-stripe workshop), have a turned-out rim (fig. 6.38–39). Another type of rim is everted and found on decorated (fig. 7.47) and linear (fig. 8.53) examples.

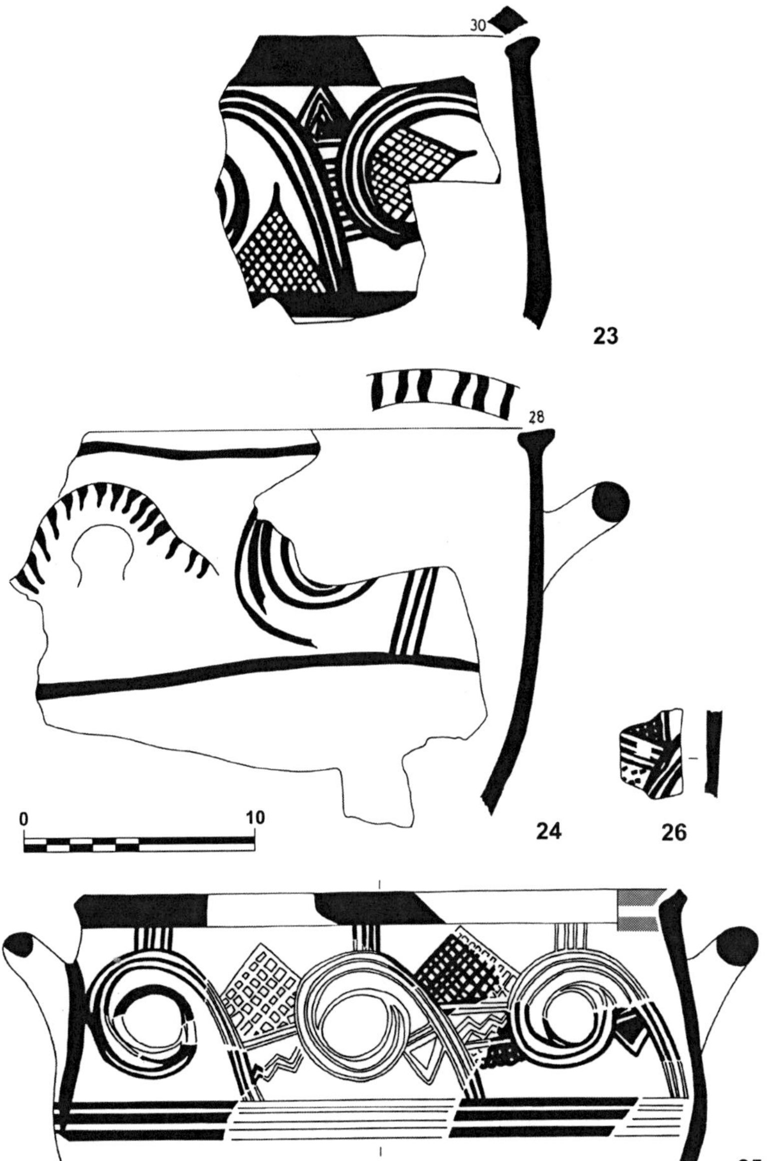

Fig. 4: **23–26**) krater FS 282.

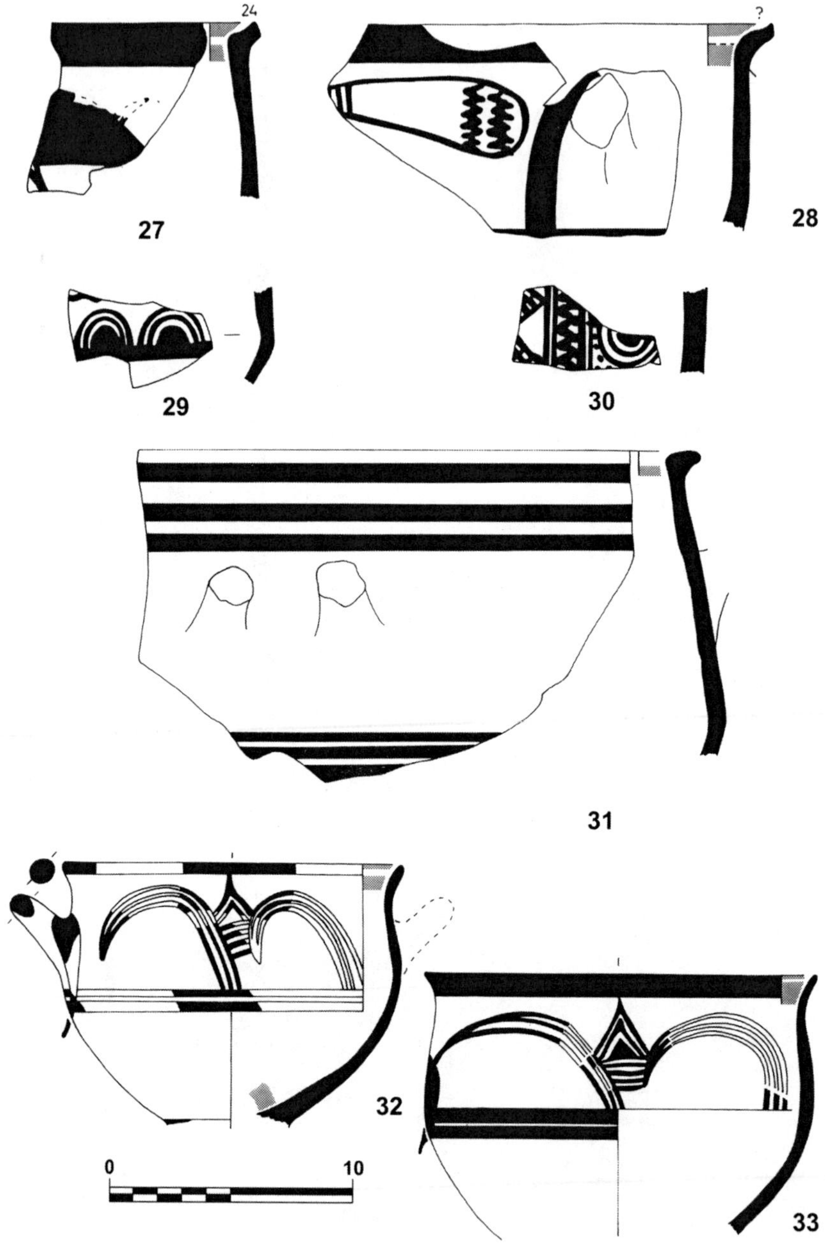

Fig. 5: **27–31**) krater FS 282; **32–33)** deep bowl FS 284.

The body may sometimes be carinated on both decorated (fig. 7.44, 49) and linear (fig. 8.54) examples (T. Dothan and Zukerman 2004, pl. 23:14). The carinated shape bears no relation to the shallow carinated bowl FS 295. Carinated deep bowls appear on the Greek Mainland in the Transitional LH IIIB2–IIIC Early phase, particularly in the south Peloponnese (Mountjoy 1997b, 129, fig. 11 deep bowl Type 3), and may ultimately have a Cretan provenance (Mountjoy 1999a, 511–12 and n. 11; Cretan examples, Hallager and Hallager 2000, pl. 35).

Handles may be high on the body and protruding (figs. 6.37, 40; 8.52) or high and set close to the body (fig. 8.50). Handle decoration may consist of three splashes (fig. 6.41), as on the Greek Mainland, but at Ekron the central splash is generally 2 centimeters long with a neat rounded end (it may have been executed while the wheel was turning; figs. 5.32; 7.42). Handles may also have multiple splashes (fig. 6.37, 40). Alternatively, the handle may be unpainted (fig. 8.51). Bases of decorated deep bowls are ringed and may have concentric circles on the interior (fig. 5.32); the exterior base may be linear (fig. 5.32) or unpainted (fig. 6.37, 40; for a selection of bases, see T. Dothan, Gitin, and Zukerman 2006, fig. 3:16:19–22).

There are large numbers of linear bowls (e.g., T. Dothan, Gitin, and Zukerman 2006, figs. 3:18:4–13; 3:20:6–16; 3:23:1–6, 8; 3:24:4–17; 3:26:14–21). They generally have a single medium band on the rim and two narrow or medium bands on the belly and two interior rim bands (fig. 8.50). Bases are ring with a simple spiral on the interior (fig. 8.51) or raised concave with a simple spiral on the interior (fig. 8.55), or both types may have concentric circles (fig. 8.50); the exterior base is often unpainted (fig. 8.50–52). There may be extra narrow bands on the interior belly (fig. 8.50, 53), a band below an unpainted exterior rim (fig. 8.51), or a second exterior rim band (fig. 7.47; a decorated example).

Basin FS 294 (fig. 8.56–58)

This is a large, broad shallow shape with a heavy strap handle (fig. 8.56). Rim diameters are around 24–30 centimeters (e.g., T. Dothan, Gitin, and Zukerman 2006, figs. 3:18:20–24; 3:27:7–12). The rim may be round everted (fig. 8.56), or flat everted (fig. 8.57), or everted with a trough-like depression on the top similar to that of the kraters (fig. 8.58). There is often a band on the rim and on the belly and two bands on the interior rim. The shape is classified by Killebrew as AS 1 and assigned to FS 296 (Killebrew 2000, 235, 237; fig. 12:1:1–2), but FS 296 is a small shape close in size to FS 295 (Furumark 1941a, 636 FS 296 H.4–6cms). FS 296 is not present at Ekron.

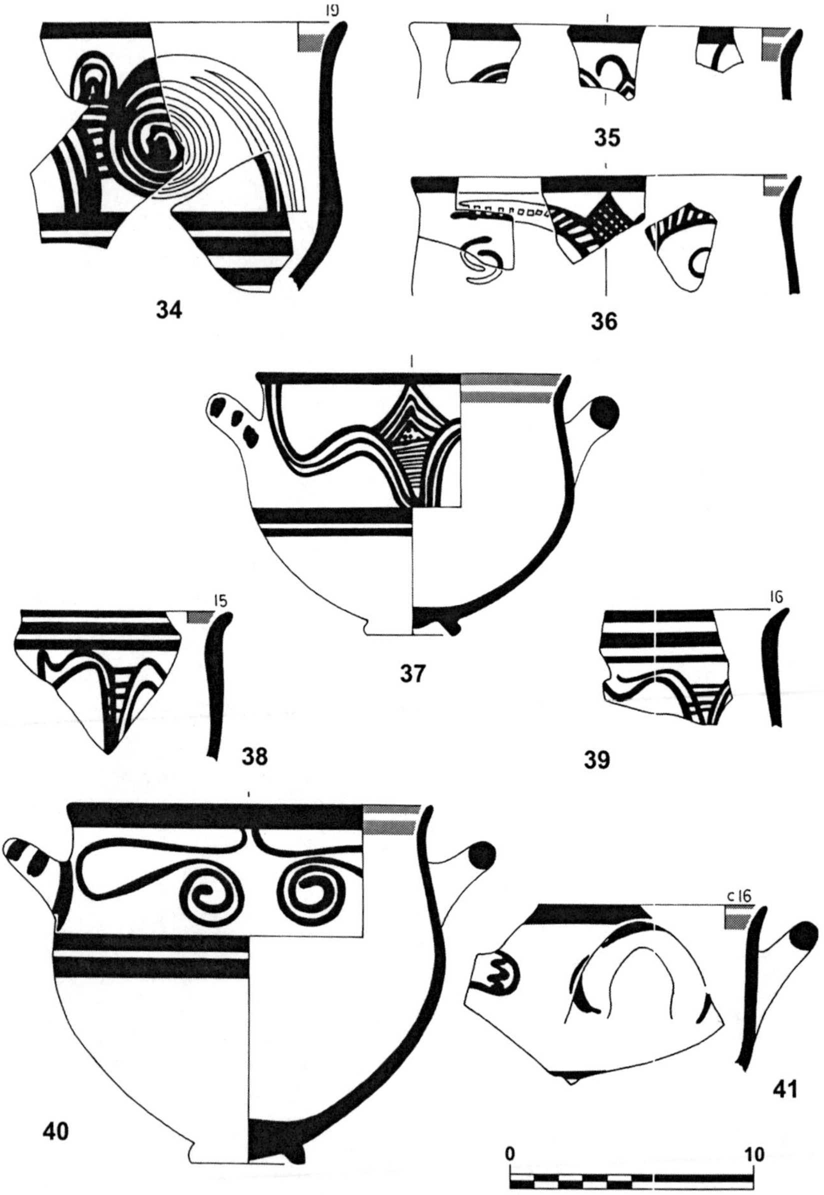

Fig. 6: **34–39**) deep bowl FS 284; **40–41)** deep bowl FS 284.

Shallow Angular Bowl FS 295 (fig. 9.59–61)

The shape corresponds to Killebrew's Form AS 3 (2000, 235, 237; fig. 12:1:4–7). This is a small shape with a conical lower body and deep flaring upper body above the carination; the handle is strap and the base raised concave (fig. 9.59). Most examples are unpainted (fig. 9.59), but there are some linear vessels. Some are linear on the interior only (fig. 9.60), others on interior and exterior (fig. 9.61). The shallow angular bowl first carries linear decoration in LH IIIC Early at Mycenae (Mountjoy 1986, 134 and fig. 197:1). The shallow angular bowl with a similar deep flaring upper body to that of the Ekron vessels is common at Enkomi and Tarsus in both linear and unpainted versions (e.g., Dikaios 1969–1971, pls. 94:10, 21; 95:10; 98:4 and many unpublished sherds; Mountjoy 2005b, 128, fig. 15.372–96 and unpublished).

Tray FS 322 (fig. 9.62)

This is a very rare shape at Ekron. Figure 9.62 is the only example. Killebrew classifies it as Form AS 7 (2000, 240–41; fig. 12:2:7). It has the short straight sides and lipless rim of this shape and the usual double roll handles attached to the side of the vessel. Aegean examples generally have blobs across the handles. On figure 9.62 the blobs have been painted across both rolls, giving the effect of diagonal bars.

The Motifs

The range of motifs is limited. The most common are triple-stemmed motifs, rendered either as tongues, streamers, or spirals. Antithetic spiral is also relatively common with or without a central motif. Narrow zonal motifs, such as wavy lines, joining semicircles, or zigzags, appear.

The most common decorated shapes are the krater and the deep bowl. The most frequent motifs on these shapes are rows of triple-stemmed tongues (figs. 4.23, 25; 5.32–33; krater and deep bowl), rows of double stemmed spirals (fig. 3.22; krater; T. Dothan, Gitin, and Zukerman 2006, fig. 3:21:1; T. Dothan 1998a, pl. 3:8), rows of triple-stemmed spirals (fig. 6.34; deep bowl), and antithetic streamers (fig. 6.35–36; deep bowl). All may have elaborate fill.

The fill linking the stems of tongues or spirals generally consists of triangles sitting on parallel bars. The triangles may be cross-hatched (fig. 4.25), stacked (figs. 4.23; 5.32), stacked with solid center (fig. 5.33), or stacked with cross-hatched center (fig. 4.26). Triangles may have a tail on their apex (fig. 6.35). Alternatively,

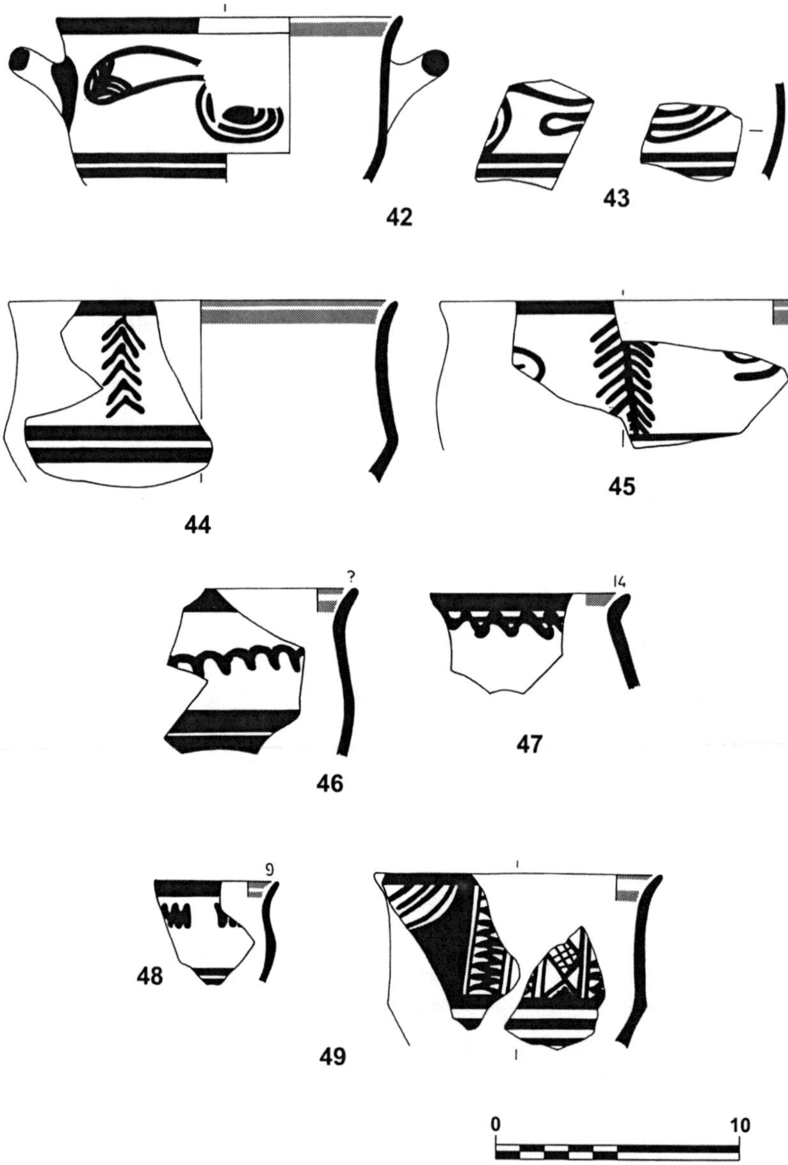

Fig. 7: **42–49**) deep bowl FS 284.

semicircles may sit on parallel bars (fig. 6.34). Additional filling ornament can be attached inside the coils (fig. 4.23) and to the upper belly band (fig. 4.23).

Antithetic streamers are linked by a fill of cross-hatched triangles (fig. 6.36) or dot-filled stacked triangles (fig. 6.37). They appear in the triple-stripe workshop linked by simple bars (fig. 6.38–39). One example has barred streamers (fig. 6.36) similar to those on a deep bowl from Kition Tomb 9 Upper Burial (Karageorghis 1974, pl. 157:138), which probably dates to LH IIIC Early, and on deep bowls from Pylos (Mountjoy 1997b, 126, fig. 9:58; 130, fig. 12:73) dating to the Transitional LH IIIB2–IIIC Early phase. The motif on the Pylian bowls may come from Crete (Mountjoy 1997b, 127).

The best parallels to the antithetic streamers come from Crete (fig. 10). Single, double, and triple-stemmed tri-curved streamers appear in LM IIIC Early (Hallager and Hallager 2000, pl. 35, second row right, third row, fourth row left, pl. 39), particularly on deep bowls and kraters, and may be linked by chevrons, hatched lozenges, or spirals. The streamers are often fringed (Hallager and Hallager 2000, pl. 39 center three vases and bottom left) as they derive from the fringed LM IIIB octopus or flower (Mountjoy 1999a, 513–14). At Ekron the vertical groups of bars linking tongues to rims could have derived from this (fig. 4.25).

The multiple-stemmed tongues and spirals at Ekron may have derived ultimately from the Minoan streamer, but could have come via the east Aegean islands of Kos and Kalymnos, although here the motif has an outlined solid stem (Mountjoy 1999d, fig. 441g) and may be later (it is dated to LH IIIC Middle stylistically as no stratigraphy is preserved [Mountjoy 1999d, 1075]). Here, too, the motif will have derived ultimately from Crete.

The double-stemmed spirals could have come from the east Aegean; this motif is popular, especially in a short-stemmed version, on Kos (Mountjoy 1999d, 1080 and fig. 441e–f [dated stylistically to LH IIIC Middle]) and also present on Kalymnos and at Miletos (Schiering 1959–1960, pl. 14:3 left, Heilmeyer et al. 1988, 25 no. 3 Inv. 316901 in Transitional LH IIIB–IIIC Early or in LH IIIC Early context). These spirals are not common at Ekron but there are examples from Field X (fig. 4.23; Dothan 1998a, pl. 3.8); they also appear at Ashdod (M. Dothan 1972, 55; fig. 1:2, 5). Long triple-stemmed spirals may also have come from the east Aegean, although there they do not have filling ornament (Mountjoy 1999d, Kos no. 99 [dated stylistically to LH IIIC Middle]).

Antithetic streamers do not appear on the Mainland until LH IIIC Middle (Mountjoy 1986, fig. 203) and rows of tongues and multiple stemmed spirals linked by elaborate fill do not appear at all, nor do they appear on Crete.[10]

---

10. I thank P. Warren for this information based on his excavations at Knossos.

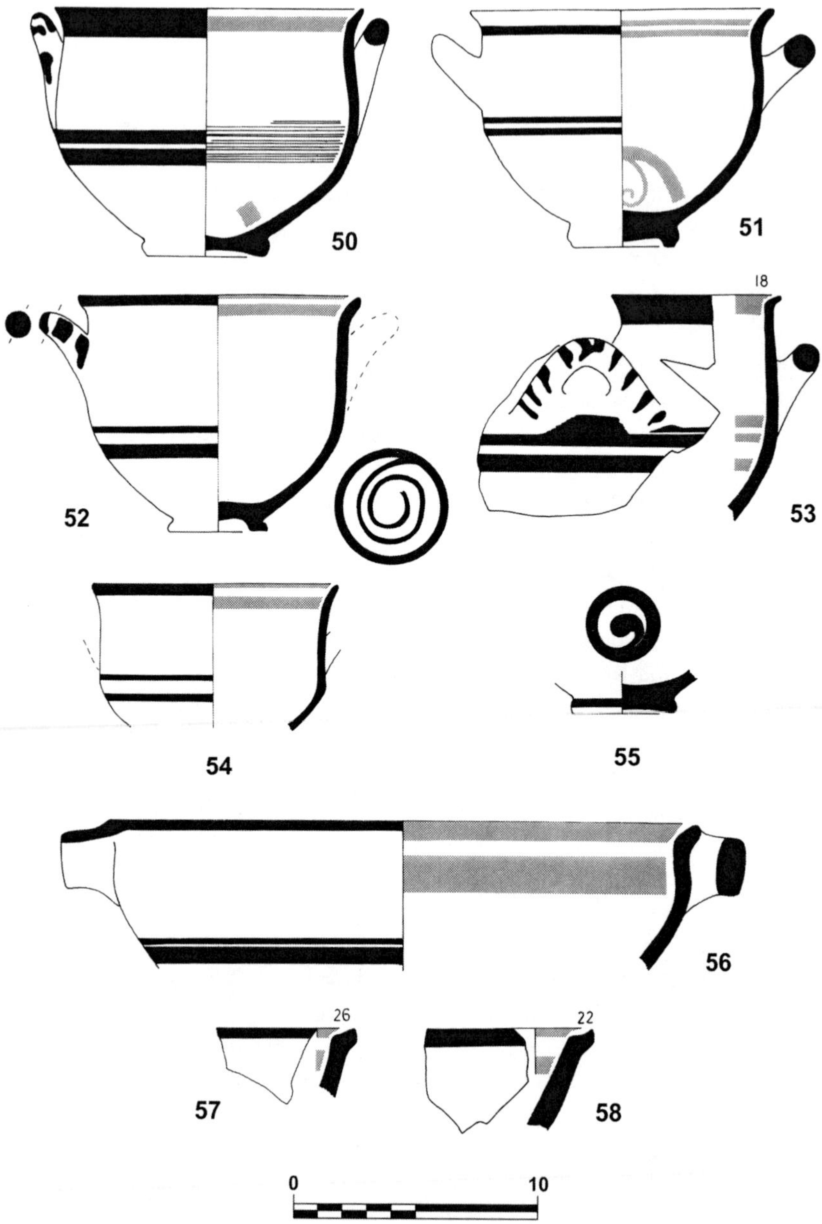

Fig. 8: **50–55**) deep bowl FS 284; **56–58**) basin FS 294.

Multiple stemmed spirals appear on Cyprus (Dikaios 1969–1971, pl. 67:15), but are not common, as are antithetic streamers (e.g., Dikaios 1969–1971, pl. 94:28). The filling motifs used with multiple stems, such as cross-hatched triangles and stacked triangles, do not appear on the Greek Mainland until LH IIIC Middle (advanced)–LH IIIC Late, but have a long history on Rhodes where they are already present in a local style dating to LH IIIA2; they have been adapted from Minoan pottery (Mountjoy 1995a, 21–35).

Paneled patterns occur, particularly on kraters, the triglyphs generally with zigzag fill often embellished by other motifs, such as lozenge chain and dot fringed semicircles with solid center (figs. 5.30; 7.49). Paneled patterns seem to be rare on deep bowls at Ekron. They are found on the Greek Mainland on deep bowls and kraters from LH IIIB1 onwards (Mountjoy 1986, figs. 142:3; 143:1).

Antithetic spirals appear (fig. 6.40). These may have barred loops (fig. 5.28), flanking a lozenge (T. Dothan, Gitin, and Zukerman 2006, fig. 3:16:14, 15), and there may be a vertical zigzag in the loops (figs. 5.28; 6.41) or a chevron (fig. 7.42). There may be no central triglyph (fig. 6.40; T. Dothan, Gitin, and Zukerman 2006, fig. 3:16:10). In figure 7.42, there is a half antithetic spiral set in the center of the side of the vase. Spirals can consist of simple coils (fig. 6.40) or have eye centers (fig. 7.42). Antithetic spirals with no central triglyph or flanking a lozenge are found on Cyprus (Karageorghis and Demas 1988, with no triglyph: pl. 75:600; Dikaios 1969–1971, with lozenge: pls. 78:18; 80:37, 39) and at Tarsus (Goldman 1956, with no triglyph: fig. 330:1305, with lozenge fig. 330:1288, 1289); this type appears at Mycenae during the transition from the first phase of LH IIIC Early to the second.[11] The antithetic spiral motif itself is rare on Crete, being found at Knossos and Phaistos (Popham 1965, 322, figs. 3; 4:9–11 mixed LM IIIC Early sherds from Knossos and Phaistos) and Kastelli (Kanta 1997, 90, fig. 2:21), but ubiquitous on the Greek Mainland especially on deep bowls (Mountjoy 1986, 150–51). It should have come ultimately from the Greek Mainland to the east.

Narrow zonal motifs appear on the deep bowl. They include groups of horizontal zigzag (fig. 7.48), to which there is a parallel from Cyprus (Åström 1998, fig. 20); horizontal wavy line (T. Dothan and Zukerman 2004, pl. 22.9); and inverted joining semicircles (fig. 7.46), similar to examples from Cyprus.[12] There is also an example from Ligori on the Greek Mainland (Mountjoy 1999d, Attica no. 352). Another motif at Ekron, pendent joining semicircles (fig. 7.47), is ubiquitous at Enkomi (e.g., Dikaios 1969–1971, pls. 74:3; 94:16; 97:19 and many

11. I thank E. French for this information.

12. Karageorghis 1974, Tomb 9, pl. 142:69–70 probably belonging to the latest burials in the Lower Burial Layer and therefore dating to Transitional LH IIIB2–IIIC Early; Yon and Caubet 1985, 114, fig. 53:251; Karageorghis and Demas 1988, pl. 253:1954/XII.

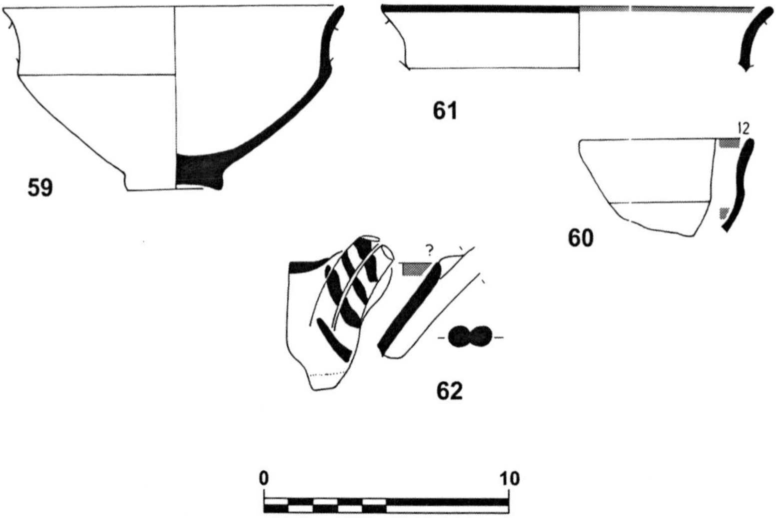

Fig. 9: **59–61**) shallow angular bowl FS 295; **62**) tray FS 322.

unpublished examples); there is one example from Phylakopi (Mountjoy 1999d, Melos no. 151) and one from Tarsus (Mountjoy 2005b, 112, fig. 8.171). This motif does appear on the Greek Mainland, but is rare (Mountjoy 1986, fig. 189:4). The popularity of the motif at Enkomi suggests it may have come from there to Ekron. Several of the Ekron examples are drawn in a quick, cursive fashion giving rise to a scribbled wavy line as in figure 7.47.

Pictorial motifs are present. The bird (fig. 2.17; T. Dothan, Gitin, and Zukerman 2006, figs. 3:17:11; 3:25:3) and the fish (fig. 5.27) appear, both with solid painted bodies. Part of a ship (T. Dothan, Gitin, and Zukerman 2006, fig. 3:27:2) is also present. Birds and fish with solid painted bodies are also found in Anatolia: a lion and a bird at Troy, a ship at Miletos, and a lion at Kazanli.[13]

Other motifs used on the krater include semicircles with solid centers (figs. 3.22; 5.29) or bar fill (fig. 3.22; T. Dothan, Gitin, and Zukerman 2006, fig. 3:25:4), and checker patterns (Zukerman and Gitin forthcoming, fig. 5:20:10).

Other motifs depicted on the deep bowl include herring-bone (fig. 7.45), chevrons (fig. 7.44), vertical zigzag (T. Dothan, Gitin, and Zukerman 2006, fig. 3:19:3), and double-axe (fig. 7.49). One motif is also found on Cyprus: multiple-looped spirals (fig. 7.43), which are present at Enkomi (Dikaios 1969–1971, pls.

13. See Mountjoy 2006 for an overview of Anatolian IIIC pictorial pottery.

110:12 Well 20; 109:5 Well 2). Quirk is used to flank streamers (fig. 6.36) or to flank a central motif acting as a triglyph, such as the herring-bone (fig. 7.45).

Summary

The Mycenaean pottery at Ekron is a hybrid style resulting from the blending of a number of influences. The Greek Mainland may ultimately have been responsible for the presence of the shallow angular bowl FS 295, but it could have reached Ekron via Cyprus or the south Anatolian litoral (Tarsus). The antithetic spiral, paneled decoration, the tassel, and possibly pendent joining semicircles and inverted joining semicircles may also have all come from Mainland Greece. The carinated deep bowl may have come from Mainland Greece, but a Minoan origin cannot be ruled out.

Strainer jugs may have come from the Dodecanese. The shape is already present on the Greek Mainland in LH IIIB, but it is rare there; in contrast it is extremely popular on Rhodes at Ialysos in LH IIIC Early. The double-stemmed spiral may also have come from the east Aegean. It is particularly popular on Kos and also appears on Kalymnos and at Miletos. Cross-hatched and stacked triangles may have come from Rhodes where these motifs have a long history; they appear there in LH IIIA2 in contrast to Mainland Greece where they are current in LH IIIC Middle (advanced)–LH IIIC Late.

The carinated kylix and carinated deep bowl are Cretan manifestations. The antithetic streamer, one of the most important motifs at Ekron, also seems to have a Minoan origin.

There are parallels from Cyprus to the groups of horizontal zigzag, the inverted joining semicircles, the joining semicircles pendent from the rim, and the multiple-looped spirals. The shallow angular bowls with deep upper body are also found on Cyprus and at Tarsus, as also are antithetic spirals flanking a lozenge or with no central triglyph; the latter is found on Cyprus, but does not seem to be very common, at least at Enkomi.

Local developments at Ekron include the trefoil-mouthed jugs, the unpainted and linear small conical bowls, the trough rims on kraters and basins, the high-set handles on kraters and deep bowls, the two-centimeter handle splash on kraters, deep bowls and basins, the fondness for the multiple splash on krater and deep bowl handles, and the rows of linked triple-stemmed tongues and triple-stemmed spirals.

The parallels with Crete date to LM IIIC Early, with the Greek Mainland and Cyprus to Transitional LH IIIB2–IIIC Early and LH IIIC Early, and with the east Aegean to LH IIIC Early. Some of the parallels with Cyprus, which do not

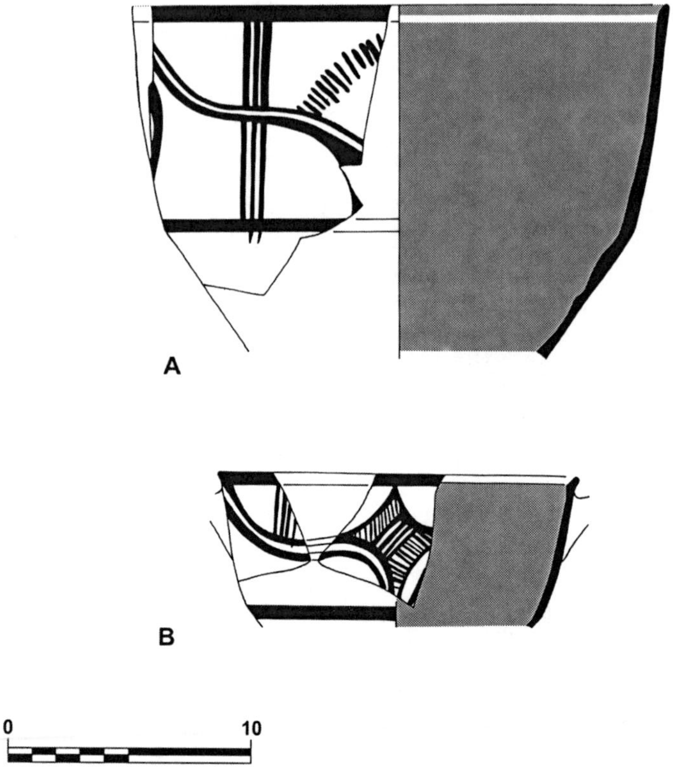

Fig. 10: LM IIIC krater and deep bowl with antithetic streamers after Hallager and Hallager 2000, A=pl. 39.71-P 0733, B=pl. 35.77-P 0121/0141 (+73-P 9295/1034).

appear on the Greek Mainland, may have been transferred directly from Cyprus to Ekron, but others, such as the shallow angular bowl and antithetic spiral with no triglyph or with lozenge, have already appeared on the Greek Mainland and may have ultimately come from there. The pottery from Ekron and on Cyprus at Enkomi is not a direct continuation of that in the destruction levels on the Greek Mainland; nor is it similar to that from the Transitional phase. In Greek Mainland terms it is similar to a well advanced stage of LH IIIC Early.[14] On Cyprus the first phase of LH IIIC Early seems not to be present in the settlement at Enkomi. As noted by Dikaios (1969–1971, 520–21), there seems to be a gap there after the

14. I thank E. French for information on LH IIIC Early at Mycenae based on her recent work.

destruction at the end of LC IIC. At Ekron Stratum VIIB Early should date to the first phase of LH IIIC Early, while the Stratum VIIA material is equivalent to the second phase of LH IIIC Early. The LH IIIC pottery from Enkomi and Ekron is so similar that it suggests a simultaneous appearance from a common source, rather than a gradual infiltration from Cyprus to Ekron.

Index of Pieces Illustrated

Figure 1:
1 Field I: Killebrew forthcoming b, Topsoil 37.6.1.
2 Field I: T. Dothan, Gitin, and Zukerman 2006, fig. 3:25:15.
3 Field I: T. Dothan, Gitin, and Zukerman 2006, fig. 3:17:21.
4 Field I: T. Dothan, Gitin, and Zukerman 2006, fig. 3:19:9.
5 Field I: T. Dothan, Gitin, and Zukerman 2006, fig. 3:19:6.
6 Field I: T. Dothan, Gitin, and Zukerman 2006, fig. 3:21:13.
7 Field I: T. Dothan, Gitin, and Zukerman 2006, fig. 3:23:18.
8 Field I: T. Dothan, Gitin, and Zukerman 2006, fig. 3:11:21.
9 Field I: T. Dothan, Gitin, and Zukerman 2006, fig. 3:17:17.
10 Field I: Killebrew forthcoming b: L4121 4.401.11.
11 Field I: T. Dothan, Gitin, and Zukerman 2006, fig. 3:14:16.
12 Field I: T. Dothan, Gitin, and Zukerman 2006, fig. 3:17:10.
13 Field IV: Zukerman and Gitin forthcoming, fig. 5:22:5.
Figure 2:
14 Field I: Killebrew 1998a, 394, fig. 10:20 (L2152 2.663).
15 Field IV: Zukerman and Gitin forthcoming, fig. 5:22:9.
16 Field I: T. Dothan, Gitin, and Zukerman 2006, fig. 3:21:8.
17 Field I: T. Dothan, Gitin, and Zukerman 2006, fig. 3:17:14.
18 Field I: Killebrew 2000, 241, fig. 12:3:10 (L36081 36.204.2).
19 Field IV: Zukerman and Gitin forthcoming, fig. 5:1:1.
20 Field I: T. Dothan, Gitin, and Zukerman 2006, fig. 3:24:4.
21 Field I: T. Dothan, Gitin, and Zukerman 2006, fig. 3:25:6.
Figure 3:
22 Field X: T. Dothan and Zukerman 2004, fig. 16:1; Mountjoy 2010, fig. 1:1.
Figure 4:
23 Field IV: T. Dothan and Zukerman 2004, fig. 17:2.
24 Field X: T. Dothan 1998a, pl. 1:5 (Stratum VIIB); Mountjoy 2010, fig. 2:4.
25 Field I: T. Dothan, Gitin, and Zukerman 2006, fig. 3:27:1.
26 Field I: Killebrew 1998a, 394; fig. 10:19 (L36081 36.266.34).

Figure 5:

27 Field I: T. Dothan, Gitin, and Zukerman 2006, fig. 3:23:13.

28 Field I: T. Dothan and Zukerman 2004, fig. 17:5; Killebrew forthcoming b, L4117 4.379.34 4.389.6.

29 Field I: T. Dothan, Gitin, and Zukerman 2006, fig. 3:14:15: Mountjoy 2010, 2:6.

30 Field I: T. Dothan, Gitin, and Zukerman 2006, fig. 3:21:10.

31 Field IV: T. Dothan and Zukerman 2004, fig. 17:1.

32 Field IV: T. Dothan and Zukerman 2004, fig. 8:11.

33 Field I: T. Dothan and Zukerman 2004, fig. 8:10; T. Dothan, Gitin, and Zukerman 2006, fig. 3:23:10.

Figure 6:

34 Field IV: T. Dothan and Zukerman 2004, fig. 8:5.

35 Field I: T. Dothan, Gitin, and Zukerman 2006, fig. 3:18:17.

36 Field I: T. Dothan and Zukerman 2004, fig. 8:9; T. Dothan, Gitin, and Zukerman 2006, fig. 3:16:12.

37 Field IV: T. Dothan and Zukerman 2004, fig. 8:7.

38 Field IV: T. Dothan and Zukerman 2004, fig. 8:8 (Stratum VIIB).

39 Field I: Killebrew forthcoming b, L2136 2.567.19.

40 Field IV: T. Dothan and Zukerman 2004, fig. 6:19 (Stratum VIIB).

41 Field I: Killebrew 2000, 237; fig. 12:1:10 (L4117 4.392.1).

Figure 7:

42 Field IV: T. Dothan and Zukerman 2004, fig. 8:1.

43 Field IV: Zukerman and Gitin forthcoming, fig. 5:22:1.

44 Field I: T. Dothan, Gitin, and Zukerman 2006, fig. 3:20:17.

45 Field I: T. Dothan, Gitin, and Zukerman 2006, fig. 3:16:3.

46 Field I: Killebrew 1998a, 394; fig. 10:6 (L36081 36.224.9, 12, 31).

47 Field IV: T. Dothan and Zukerman 2004, fig. 9:3 (Stratum VIIB).

48 Field I: T. Dothan, Gitin, and Zukerman 2006, fig. 3:16:9.

49 Field I: Killebrew 2000, 237; fig.12:1:11 (L37027 37.74.33, 37.88.41, 50, 57).

Figure 8:

50 Field I: Killebrew forthcoming b, L3095 3.493.6; 3.506.15.

51 Field I: Killebrew 2000, 237; fig.12:1:8 (L3100 3.506).

52 Field IV: T. Dothan 2000, 154, fig. 7:7:2.

53 Field IV: T. Dothan and Zukerman 2004, fig. 6:24 (Stratum VIIB).

54 Field IV: T. Dothan and Zukerman 2004, fig. 17:18.

55 Field I: Killebrew forthcoming b, L4122 4.471.8.

56 Field I: T. Dothan, Gitin, and Zukerman 2006, fig. 3:17:3.

57 Field I: Killebrew 1998a, 390, fig. 7:3 (L37027 37.81.1).

58 Field I: Killebrew 1998a, 390, fig. 7:2 (L37027 37.79.3).

Figure 9:

59 Field IV: T. Dothan 2000, 154, fig. 7:7:1.

60 Field IV: IVNW.27.382.33 (Stratum VC) (Zukerman and Gitin forthcoming, fig. 5.8.7).

61 Field IV: T. Dothan and Zukerman 2004, fig. 8:5 (Stratum VIIB).

62 Field I: Killebrew 2000, 241, fig. 12:3:2 (L37027 37.87.1).

Chapter Six

Early Philistine Pottery Technology at Tel Miqne-Ekron: Implications for the Late Bronze–Early Iron Age Transition in the Eastern Mediterranean

*Ann E. Killebrew**

The search for the biblical Philistines has provided previously unanticipated insights into one of the most pivotal periods of time, namely, the demise of the Late Bronze "Age of Internationalism," and the ensuing cultural and political fragmentation of the eastern Mediterranean region. Though clearly not composed during this period of transition and transformation, biblical accounts of the Philistines provide invaluable clues leading to the recovery of their material world. Referred to as the "Peleset" by the Egyptians, the Philistines are one of several invading peoples known from New Kingdom Egyptian texts that are grouped under the modern generic term "Sea Peoples" (see Adams and Cohen, this volume). In an attempt to discover the material remains of the Philistines, archaeological investigations have focused largely on those mounds in the southern coastal plain of Israel and the Gaza Strip that are identified with the five Philistine cities specifically mentioned in the Hebrew Bible—Ekron, Gath, Ashdod, Ashkelon, and Gaza (fig. 1). Early excavations at several of these sites revealed a distinctive Aegean-style bichrome pottery, heralding the appearance of a foreign group who settled at these sites and others in the southern coastal plain (see, e.g., T. Dothan 1982). During subsequent excavations in the later decades of the twentieth century, an earlier type of locally produced decorated Aegean-style pottery was identified by Moshe Dothan during his excavations at Tel Ashdod (Asaro,

* Classics and Ancient Mediterranean Studies, Jewish Studies, and Anthropology, The Pennsylvania State University, University Park, PA. Email: aek11@psu.edu.

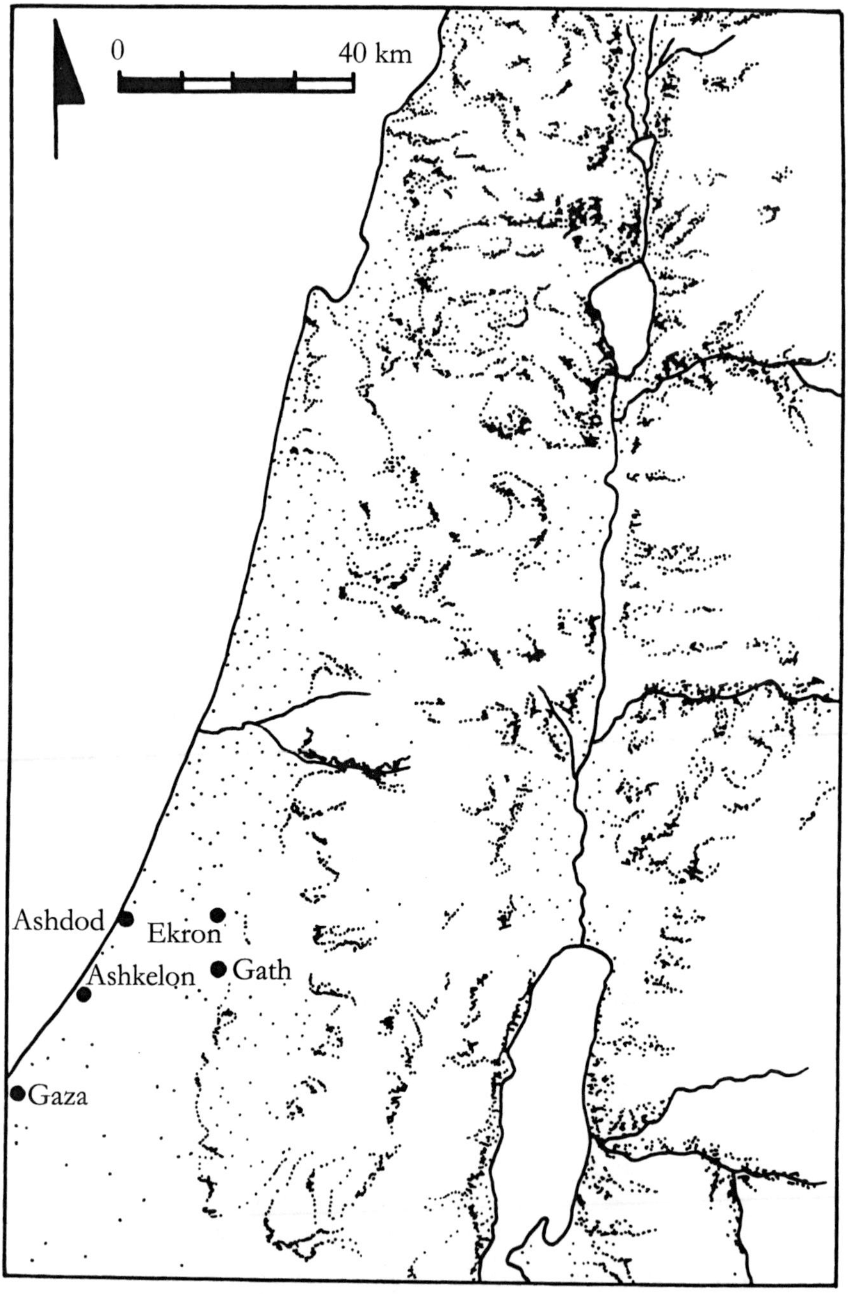

Fig. 1: Location of Tel Miqne-Ekron and other, major early Philistine sites.

Perlman, and M. Dothan 1971; M. Dothan 1979; and T. Dothan and Ben-Shlomo, this volume, for an overview). Initially referred to as Mycenaean IIIC:1b and more recently by the terms Mycenaean IIIC Early and IIIC Middle or "Philistine 1,"[1] this Aegean-style monochrome-decorated ceramic group is sandwiched in strata situated directly above occupation layers dated to the end of the Late Bronze Age, but clearly below strata containing Iron Age bichrome pottery. Following its discovery at Ashdod, similar stratigraphic sequences have been excavated at Tel Miqne-Ekron, Ashkelon, and Gath (Tell eṣ-Ṣafi; see Maeir, this volume), coinciding with large-scale urbanization, most notably at Tel Miqne-Ekron (see, e.g., T. Dothan and Gitin 1993; 2008 for summaries of the evidence). Scholarly consensus today attributes this twelfth-century monochrome-decorated Aegean-style pottery to the earliest stages of Philistine migration and settlement in the southern coastal plain. Several typological studies of this pottery repertoire have been published (e.g., Killebrew 1998a; 2000; T. Dothan and Zukerman 2004; T. Dothan, Gitin, and Zukerman 2006; see Mountjoy, this volume), providing significant insights into Philistine identity, origins, and lifestyle.

Equally distinctive is the sophisticated technology employed in the manufacture of these Aegean-inspired pottery assemblages. The discovery of five twelfth-century B.C.E. pottery kilns in Field INE at Tel Miqne-Ekron, used in the firing of monochrome-decorated and other Aegean-style pottery, is key to our understanding of production of this very distinctive repertoire (see, e.g., Killebrew 1996a; 1998a). In what follows, I briefly summarize the relevant stratigraphic sequence at Tel Miqne-Ekron, including a short overview of the basic ceramic assemblages associated with each major phase, as a prelude to the focus of this chapter—Philistine ceramic technology. The technology employed to produce this distinctive ceramic assemblage is examined with an emphasis on the clay sources, clay recipes, and firing techniques used to produce this pottery at Tel Miqne-Ekron.[2] The Philistine ceramic production sequence is then contextualized and compared with earlier millennia-long indigenous potting techniques

1. For a discussion of various terms used for this Aegean-style pottery in Philistia, see, e.g., Killebrew 1998a, 393–95. Regarding the definition of Mycenaean (or Late Helladic [=LH]) IIIC Early and Middle see, e.g., Mountjoy 1999b and 2007b, and see Vitale 2006 for a critique of Mountjoy's definition of LH IIIC Early. Regarding the use of "Philistine 1" as a term designating locally produced Mycenaean IIIC pottery in Philistia, see T. Dothan, Gitin, and Zukerman 2006.

2. Early Philistine pottery technology was one of the main topics of my dissertation, "Ceramic Craft and Technology during the Late Bronze and early Iron Ages: The Relationship between Pottery Technology, Style, and Cultural Diversity," at the Hebrew University of Jerusalem (Killebrew 1999a). This contribution represents an updated version of my research on this subject, with some of the results published here for the first time. See also Killebrew 1996a; 1996b; 1998a; 1999b.

in the southern Levant. Lastly, I consider the broader regional implications of these results for our understanding of the transition from the Late Bronze to Iron I periods.

Tel Miqne-Ekron Stratigraphic Sequence: Thirteenth–Twelfth Centuries b.c.e.

Tel Miqne-Ekron is a fifty-acre mound in the southern coastal plain of Israel located approximately 20 kilometers inland from the Mediterranean Sea. Excavations conducted at the site from 1981–1996 under the direction of Trude Dothan and Seymour Gitin (1993; 2008 for a summary and extensive bibliographic references) have uncovered remains spanning the Middle Bronze Age through the end of the Iron Age (ca. late-seventh/early-sixth century b.c.e.). The Late Bronze Age settlement at Tel Miqne-Ekron was modest in size (ca. ten acres), confined to the northeastern area of the tell (Gittlen 1992). Three strata of Late Bronze Age occupation were reached during the course of excavations: Strata X–VIII, ranging in date from the fifteenth to early-twelfth centuries b.c.e. Although Stratum VIII (thirteenth–early-twelfth centuries b.c.e.) was discovered in two main fields of excavation in the northeast—INW/SW Summit and INE East Slope—only in Field INE East Slope was a continuous and undisturbed Late Bronze–Iron I (Strata X–V) stratigraphic sequence documented at Tel Miqne-Ekron (Killebrew 1996b, 13–18, 21–27, Meehl, T. Dothan, and Gitin 2006, 27–55). In Field INW/SW on the summit, Stratum VIII was reached but was very disturbed due to extensive later pitting of the area. Stratum VII, dating to the early Iron I, marks the appearance of a dramatically distinct material culture that represents the initial arrival and settlement of the Philistines during the twelfth century. Ekron quickly expanded in size to encompass the entire fifty-acre mound coinciding with the construction of the twelfth-century b.c.e. fortifications. The following description summarizes the findings of this well-stratified Late Bronze IIB–Iron I (Strata VIII–VI) sequence in Field INE, with a focus on Areas INE.4, INE.36, and INE.37 where a series of fire installations were uncovered, several of which have been identified as kilns.

Late Bronze IIB (Stratum VIIIB: Mid-Fourteenth–Thirteenth Centuries b.c.e.) and Transitional Late Bronze/Iron I (Stratum VIIIA: Late Thirteenth Century–ca. 1175/1150 b.c.e.)

In Field INE, Stratum VIIIB (Field Phases 11D–A), formerly designated as Stratum IX (see, e.g., Killebrew 1996b, 14, 23–25; 1998a, 381–83; T. Dothan and Gitin

2008, 1953), was reached in limited areas in several squares: Areas INE.5 (Phases 11C–A), INE.6 (Phases 11D–A), and INE.7 (Phase 11D). Only a very small portion of the Late Bronze IIB settlement at Ekron has been uncovered thus far. The structures appear to be of a domestic and/or industrial nature (for a detailed description, plans, and sections, see Killebrew 1996b, 23–25). On the surfaces associated with this architecture, large quantities of flint debitage and tools, stone weights, slag and copper, and olive pits, perhaps indicative of industrial activities that took place in this area, were found. Noteworthy remains include a complete donkey skull and local pottery typical of the Late Bronze IIB period (Killebrew 1996b, 23–24, pls. 4–7; see Way 2010 regarding second-millennium donkey burials), especially large shallow platter bowls and handled kraters (e.g., table I: vessel no. 12 [fig. 11.6]), which typify the Late Bronze II period.

Phase 11C is characterized by more substantial architectural remains (Killebrew 1996b, 24). A socle wall constructed out of boulders divided the excavated area into two spaces. A nearly complete storage jar decorated with an ibex and palm-tree motif (table IV: vessel no. 57 [fig. 17.1]) rested on one of the surfaces. Phase 11B continues the architectural plan of Phase 11C (Killebrew 1996b, 24–25). Restorable vessels found on top of Surface 5097 include a carinated bowl and a jug characteristic of the Late Bronze IIB (Killebrew 1998a, fig. 1:1, 7–8). Other noteworthy finds are a gypsum vessel, ivory pendant, bead, scarab and faience seals, and a ring—all associated with the simple grave of an articulated skeleton below beaten-earth Surface 6021 (Killebrew 1996b, pls. 5:1–12; 16).

The latest phase of Stratum VIIIB, 11A, was destroyed by a conflagration (Killebrew 1996b, 25). This burnt layer with complete vessels resting on the floors is, in my opinion, contemporary with the massive destruction layer in Field INW/SW on the summit to the west of Field INE.[3] Associated with this destruction in Area INE.5 are a decorated carinated krater, a jug with a trefoil rim, several Canaanite storage jars, a White Slip II bowl, and an imported Cypriot Base Ring II flask (Killebrew 1996b, pl. 6). Although the easternmost extent of Phase 11A was disturbed by the foundations of the Iron I mud-brick city wall, several significant features were preserved in Area INE.6 (Killebrew 1998a, fig. 2). These include a circular, plaster-lined bin (6011) that contained restorable cooking pots with everted triangular-shaped rims (e.g., table III: vessel no. 44 [fig. 15.3]) and an imported Cypriot White Slip II bowl (Killebrew 1998a, fig. 3). These and other

3. But see T. Dothan and Gitin 2008, 1953 who assign this destruction in Field INW/SW Summit to Stratum VIIIA, contemporary with the latest phase (10A) in Field INE East Slope, which was not destroyed by fire. Until the field report for Field INW/SW Summit is published, it will not be possible to resolve the specific relationship between the conflagration in Field INW/SW Summit and Strata VIIIB and VIIIA in Field INE East Slope.

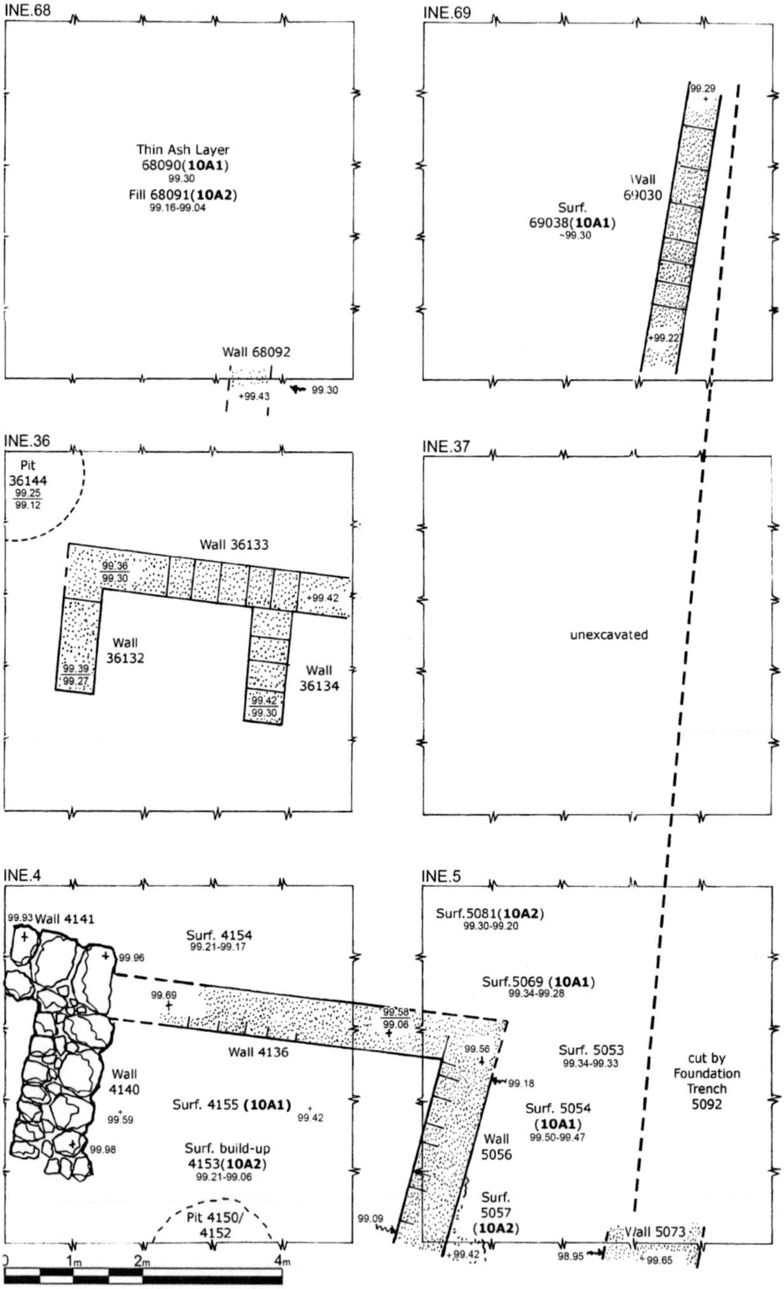

Fig. 2: Plan of Stratum VIIIA, Phase 10A, Subphases A1 and A2 in Field INE, east slope (drawn by J. Rosenberg; courtesy of the Tel Miqne-Ekron Excavation and Publication Project).

vessels recovered from associated surfaces (e.g., table IV: vessel no. 55 [fig. 16]) are typical of Late Bronze IIB thirteenth-century assemblages (see, e.g., Killebrew 1996b, pls. 6–7; 2005, 110–48)

Stratum VIIIA (Phases 10D/C–A), the transitional Late Bronze/early Iron I period (ca. 1200–1175/1150 B.C.E.), comprised a series of superimposed beaten-earth surfaces with an accumulation of occupational debris of more than a meter. This stratum was documented in two excavation areas in Field INE East Slope (sondage: Killebrew 1996b, 26–27, pl. 20 and the northern extension: M. Meehl [Meehl, T. Dothan, and Gitin 2006, 27–29]). The earliest phases, 10D/C and B, were reached only in parts of two squares: INE.5 and INE.36 (Killebrew 1996b, 26, Phases 10D–B plans and sections; Meehl, T. Dothan, and Gitin 2006, 28–29, fig. 3, Phases 10C–B plan and sections). Phases 10D and C comprised several beaten-earth surfaces with clear signs of metal working. These included numerous copper droplets, slag, crucibles, and other artifacts associated with metallurgy resting on beaten-earth surfaces with ash that may be the result of industrial activities. On top of Phase 10C, several additional beaten-earth surfaces covered with thin layers of ash were assigned to the following phase, 10B. The pottery repertoire consists mainly of sherds belonging to undecorated local coarse wares and utilitarian shapes. These included bowls, kraters, cooking pots, and storage jars, vessels that typify the end of the Late Bronze Age and transitional Late Bronze/Iron period (see, e.g., table IV: vessel no. 58, fig. 17.2; Killebrew 1998a, fig. 4:3–11; 1999b, pl. 8:6–11; T. Dothan, Gitin, and Zukerman 2006, 72–74, fig. 3:1–13).

Phase 10A represents the final phase of the Late Bronze/Iron I transition (Killebrew 1996b, 26–27; forthcoming b; Meehl, T. Dothan, and Gitin 2006, 29). Architecturally, it is best represented and defined in Squares INE.4 and INE.5 by E–W mud-brick Wall 4136 that bonds with mud-brick Wall 5056 in Square INE.5 to the east and runs westward up to the eastern face of stone Wall 4140 (fig. 2). Two subphases (A1 and A2) are discernible in several instances (e.g., Surfaces 5054 and 5069 [A1] and Surfaces 5057 and 5081 [A2], fig. 2). Pottery recovered from these surfaces consists mainly of local utilitarian wares in the Late Bronze Age tradition, with only a handful of imported wares (Killebrew 1996b, pl. 8:1–5; 1998a, 381–83, fig. 4:1–5; T. Dothan, Gitin, and Zukerman 2006, 72–74, fig. 3.2:1–24). Mendable sherds belonging to an Anatolian Gray Burnished krater, imported from the region of Troy (Allen 1994), and to a White Painted Wheelmade III bowl from Cyprus comprise the majority of *in situ* Stratum VIIIA (Phase 10A) imported wares (Killebrew 1998a, fig. 4:1, 2).

Noteworthy is the marked decline in imported wares in Stratum VIIIA, especially the dramatic drop in imported Mycenaean pottery from the Greek Mainland and west Aegean. Small quantities of imports from Cyprus continue, together with the appearance of imported pottery from the east Aegean (e.g., Anatolian

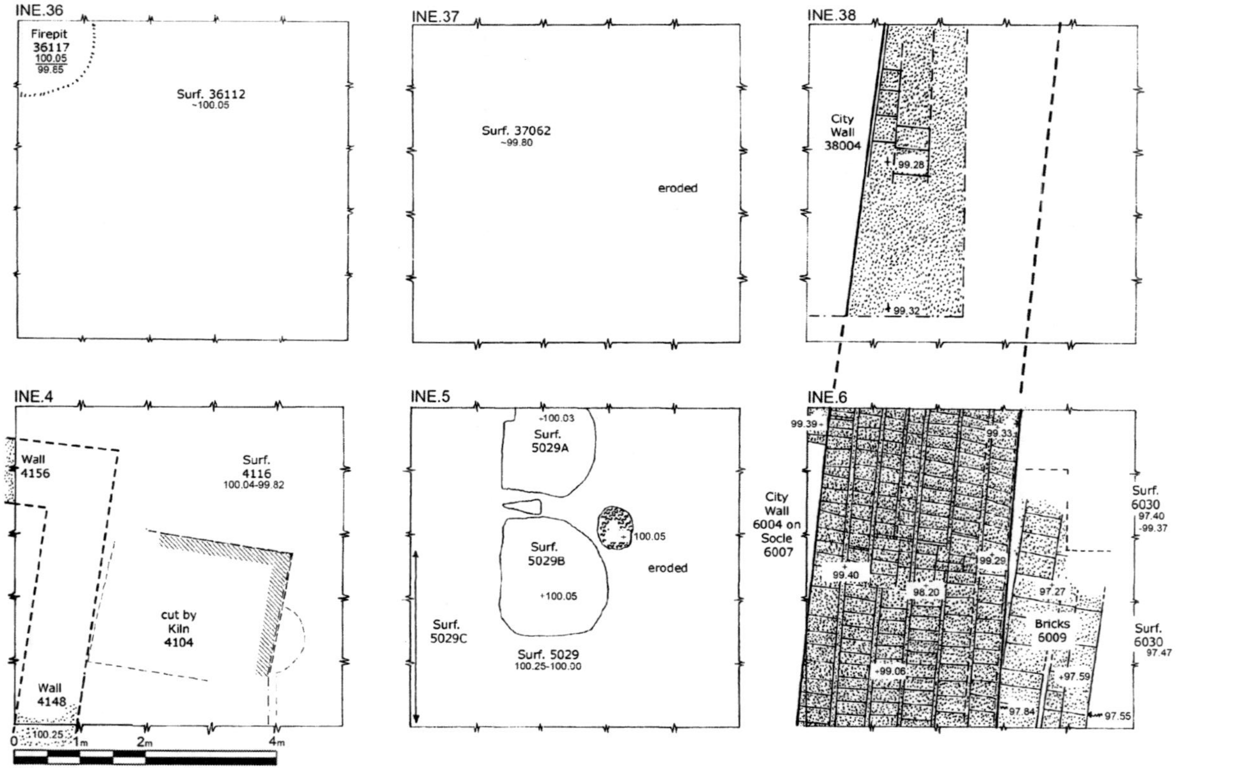

Fig. 3: Plan of Stratum VIIB, Phase 9C, Iron I potters' workshop area in Field INE, east slope (drawn by J. Rosenberg.; courtesy of the Tel Miqne-Ekron Excavation and Publication Project).

Gray Burnished Ware). As political and economic conditions in the eastern Mediterranean deteriorate during the final decades of the Late Bronze Age, ceramic evidence points to a cessation of direct contact with the west Aegean, while limited interaction persists between the southern coastal plain, Cyprus, and the east Aegean. At Tel Miqne-Ekron, the Late Bronze/Iron I occupation in Field INE East (Stratum VIIIA, Phase 10A) did not end with destruction. Rather the subsequent Iron I occupation on the east slope represents a sudden, but apparently nonviolent, transformation from the modest settlement of Stratum VIIIA to the fortified urban center of Stratum VII characterized by an Aegean-style material culture associated with the arrival of the Philistines.

Early Iron I (Stratum VII: ca. Second Half of the Twelfth Century B.C.E.)

Stratum VII, subdivided into VIIB (Phases 9D–C) and VIIA (Phases 9B–A), marks the initial appearance of Aegean-style pottery including the monochrome-decorated ("Philistine 1") fine wares and the beginning of the urbanization process and expansion of Philistine Ekron (Killebrew 1996b, 16–17; 1998a, 383–85; forthcoming b; Meehl, T. Dothan, and Gitin 2006, 29–44; for a general ceramic discussion, see T. Dothan, Gitin, and Zukerman 2006, 74–88). In the earliest subphase of Stratum VIIB (Phase 9D3), a 3.25 meter-wide mud-brick city Wall 6004/38004 was constructed (see Meehl, T. Dothan, and Gitin 2006, 30–31 for a detailed description). The construction of the city wall was followed by the leveling of the area with an artificial fill consisting of crushed burnt mud bricks and debris (Phase 9D2). This fill material was probably obtained via large-scale pitting of the area to the west on the summit (Field INW/SW) that included cutting the massive destruction of the Late Bronze Age Stratum VIIIB settlement (see, however, T. Dothan and Gitin 2008, who assign the destruction to Stratum VIIIA). This distinctive orange layer was apparently intentionally deposited and served as a leveling fill covering the Stratum VIIIA architectural remains. This layer also covered the foundation trench for the construction of the mud-brick city wall, thus indicating a *terminus post quem* date for this Iron I fortification. The orange fill has been excavated in numerous squares on the east slope, including INE.2, INE.4, INE.5, INE.36, INE.37, and INE.68 (Killebrew 1996b, 16; forthcoming b; Meehl, T. Dothan, and Gitin 2006, 31–32). The pottery repertoire from Phase 9D largely continues the Late Bronze Age ceramic tradition (see, e.g., table I: vessel nos. 1 [fig. 11.2], 4, 9–11, 13–14; table III: vessel no. 52). This fill demarcates the beginning of the Iron Age from the previous Stratum VIIIA local Late Bronze cultural horizon and the subsequent appearance of the markedly different Iron I

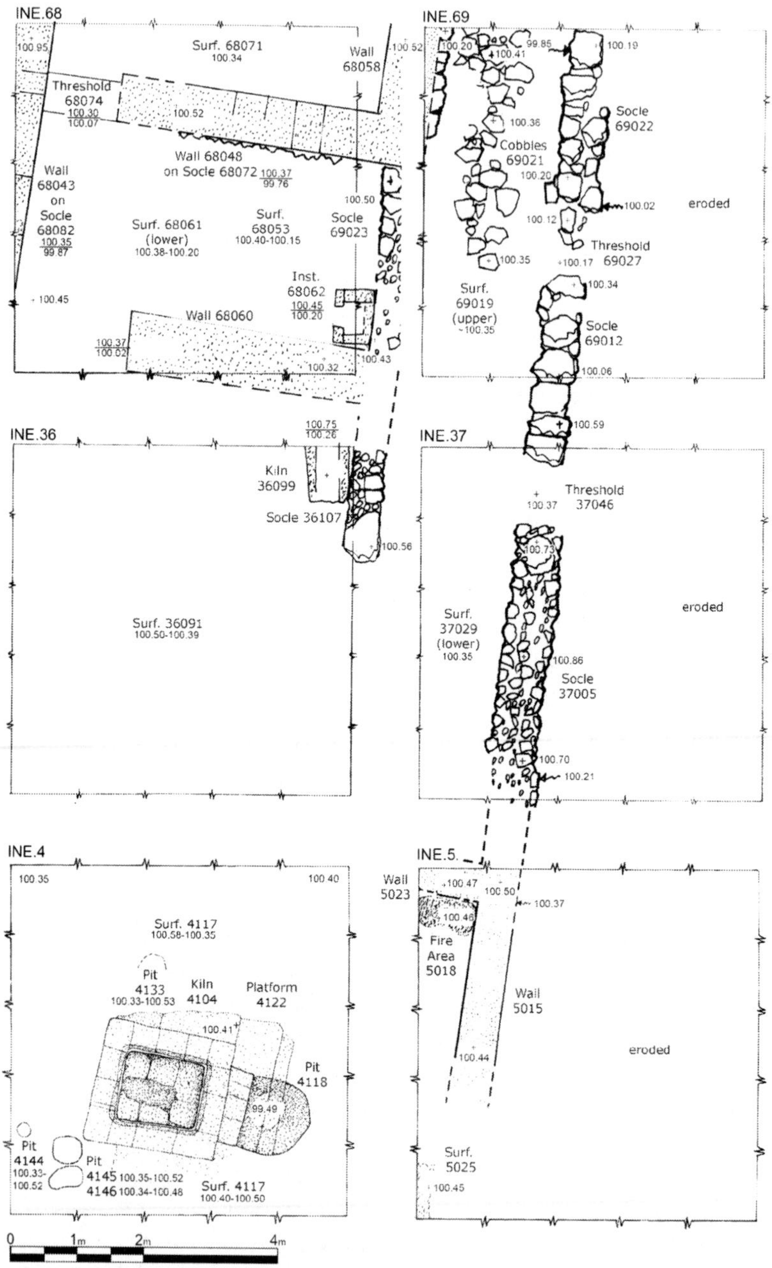

Fig. 4: Plan of Stratum VIIA, Phase 9B, Iron I potters' workshop area in Field INE, east slope (drawn by J. Rosenberg; courtesy of the Tel Miqne-Ekron Excavation and Publication Project).

Aegean-style Philistine material culture assemblage that dominates and defines Stratum VIIA.

The following phase, 9C of Stratum VIIB, is characterized by beaten-earth surfaces (e.g., 4116, 5029, 36112, and 37062) that rest on top of the orange and construction fills of Phase 9D (fig. 3; Meehl, T. Dothan, and Gitin 2006, 33–34, fig. 3.6–9). The ceramic repertoire includes the continuation of the domestic Late Bronze IIB pottery tradition (mainly shallow open bowls, kraters, and Canaanite storage jars) along with the first appearance of several shapes generally dated to the early Iron I, including hemispherical bowls (table I: vessel nos. 2, 3 [fig. 11.4], 4, 5 [fig. 11.5], 6–7, 15 [fig. 11.1]; table III: vessel nos. 43, 51, 54). Small quantities of Aegean-style pottery begin to appear in secure stratigraphic contexts (Killebrew 1998a, 383, fig. 6:1–14; forthcoming b).

Stratum VIIA includes Phases 9B and 9A, each with several subphases (see Meehl, T. Dothan, and Gitin 2006, 34–44 for a detailed description; Killebrew, forthcoming b). The earliest phase, 9B, represents the first major Iron I occupation with rooms, a passageway running parallel to city Wall 6004/38004, and open activity areas that included industrial, domestic, and cultic activities (fig. 4; city Wall 6004/38004 is located to the east of Wall 5015 and Socles 37005 and 69012—see also figs. 3 and 5). All architecture is oriented parallel to and on the same north–south alignment as city Wall 6004/38004. Large quantities of Aegean-style pottery, including monochrome-decorated ("Philistine 1") wares, appear for the first time as well (see table II: vessel nos. 23 [fig. 13.4], 26, 30 [fig. 12.6], 33 [fig. 12.3], 34 [fig. 12.4], table III: vessel no. 47).

This stratum also marks the first appearance of a series of fire installations of varying sizes and complexity spanning Strata VIIA–VI (Killebrew 1996a; Meehl, T. Dothan, and Gitin 2006, 34–49 for an overview of these installations and their context in Strata VIIA–VI). These are all located to the west and inside mud-brick city Wall 6004/38004, forming what appears to be an "industrial zone," and are described below. Five of these have been identified as pottery kilns used in the production of Aegean-style early Philistine pottery, including the monochrome-decorated wares (Killebrew 1996a). An additional three installations may have also served as kilns. All installations date to the Iron I period, that is, the second half of the twelfth century and continuing into the eleventh century B.C.E. All the kilns and most of the fire installations of Strata VIIA and VI are found in adjoining Squares INE.4, INE.5, INE.36, and INE.37, and appear to be situated in a large open courtyard characterized by a series of superimposed beaten-earth surfaces. This open area was flanked by rooms to the north and west, and by the mud-brick city wall to the east. The area to the south of the kilns remains unexcavated.

Kiln 4104, assigned to Stratum VIIA (Phase 9B; fig. 4), was roughly square in shape, measuring 1.4 by 1.1 meters. This installation, the largest and most sophis-

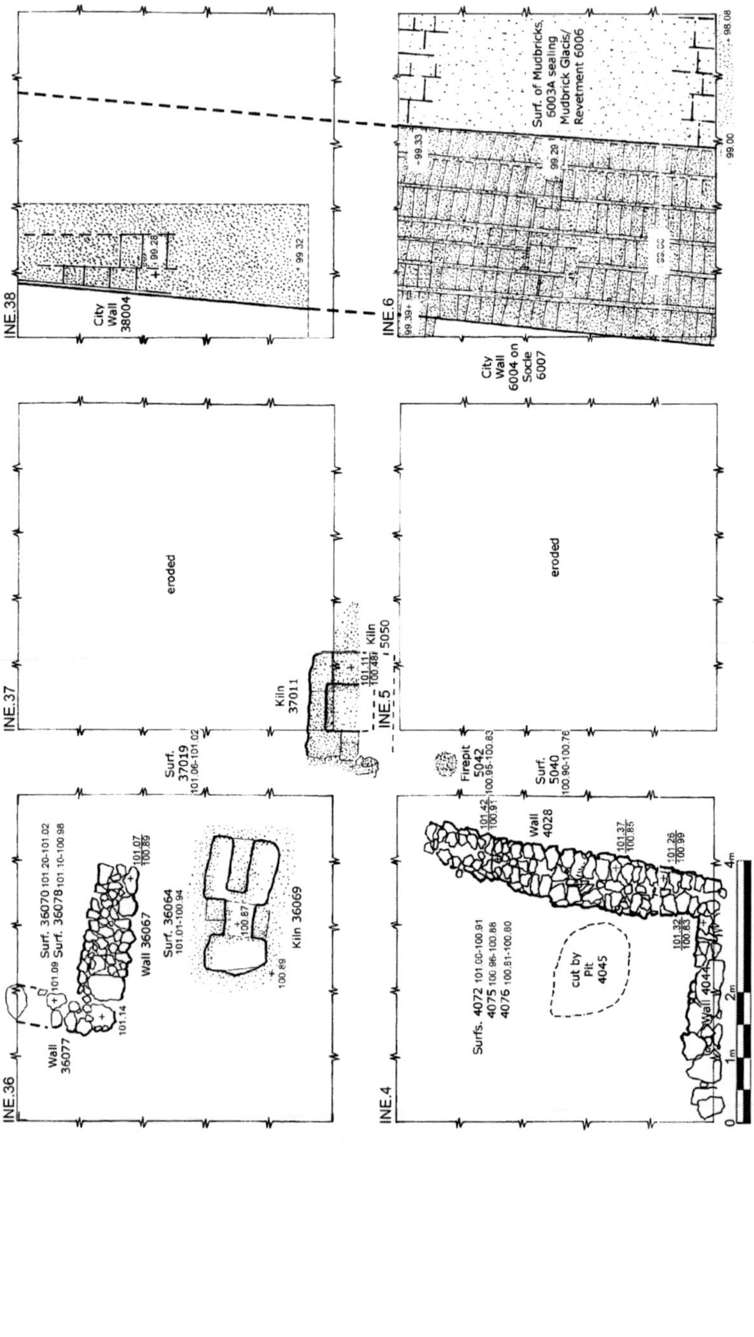

Fig. 5: Plan of Stratum VI, Phase 8C, Iron I potters' workshop area in Field INE, east slope (drawn by J. Rosenberg; courtesy of the Tel Miqne-Ekron Excavation and Publication Project).

ticated kiln excavated at Ekron, included a firing chamber, separated from the lower combustion chamber by a mud-brick platform. The debris inside the firing chamber contained a few Iron I sherds, including Aegean-style monochrome-decorated pottery and several bones. Upon removal of the debris, a relatively well-preserved mud-brick platform, 4103, was revealed that separated the combustion chamber from the firing chamber. A few holes, most likely vents or flues, penetrated the platform, visible in several corners. The platform rested on a massive mud-brick pillar about .50 meters wide, which was attached to the back of the combustion chamber wall. An arched opening in the east wall of the combustion chamber enabled stoking of the fire (Killebrew 1996a, 146). Its use spanned several subphases of 9B (Killebrew, forthcoming b). Three additional fire installations—5018, 36099, and 5049/37045—were in use during several subphases of Stratum VIIA/Phase 9B (see fig. 4 for fire installations labeled as Kilns 36099 and Fire Area 5018; installation 5049/37045 appeared below Kiln 5050/37011). It is suggested that two of these, 36099 and 5049/37045, functioned as kilns (Meehl, T. Dothan, and Gitin 2006, 40, 343, 366).

The final phase of Stratum VIIA, 9A, is the last cultural horizon where decorated Philistine pottery is represented only by monochrome-painted wares, preceding the appearance of bichrome-decorated ("Philistine 2") pottery, which begins to appear in modest amounts only in the following Stratum VI, Phase 8C. The industrial character of this area is evidenced by fire installations 100007 and 100019. Large quantities of Aegean-style pottery dominate the ceramic assemblage in Phase 9A, alongside small numbers of vessels that continue the Late Bronze Age tradition (table II: vessel nos. 21, 25, 27–28, 29 [fig. 12.5], 32 [fig. 12.7]; table III: vessel nos. 40 [fig. 15.5], 46 [fig. 15.6]; table IV: vessel no. 59 [fig. 17.3]; Meehl, T. Dothan, and Gitin 2006, 44, fig. 3.26–27).

Iron IB (Stratum VI: ca. Late-Twelfth Century–First Half of Eleventh Century b.c.e.)

Stratum VI marks the earliest appearance of decorated Aegean-style bichrome pottery alongside monochrome-decorated wares. This stratum is subdivided into three main phases, 8C, 8B, and 8A. Monochrome-decorated ("Philistine 1") ware and other Aegean-style vessels form the majority of Aegean-style pottery recovered from the earliest phase, 8C. Monochrome-decorated pottery continues in Phases 8B and 8A, with increasing percentages of non-Aegean wares (table II: vessel nos. 17 [fig. 13.1], 20 [fig. 12.1], 24 [fig. 12.2], 31 [fig. 12.8]; table III: vessel nos. 42, 48, 49 [fig. 15.1], 50 [fig. 15.2], 53 [fig. 15.4]). Relative percentages of bichrome-decorated pottery gradually increase with each phase of Stratum VI (see, e.g., Meehl, T. Dothan, and Gitin 2006, 44; T. Dothan, Gitin, and Zukerman

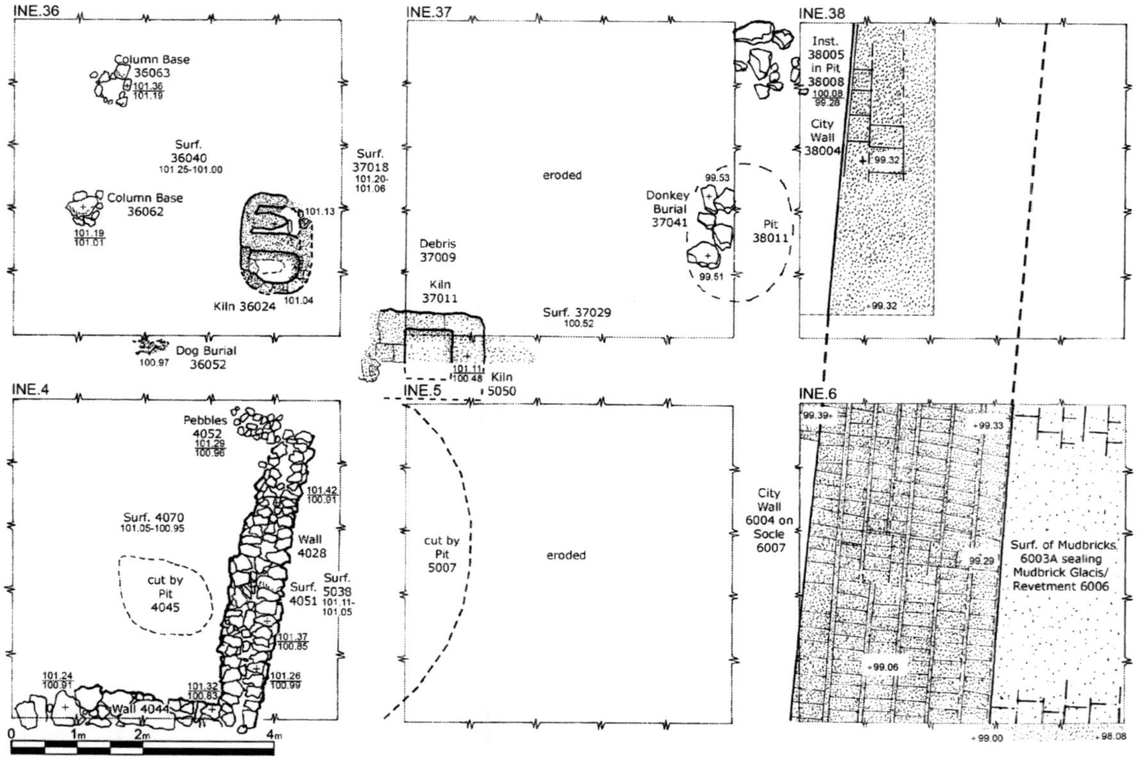

Fig. 6: Plan of Stratum VI, Phase 8B, Iron I potters' workshop area in Field INE, east slope (drawn by J. Rosenberg; courtesy of the Tel Miqne-Ekron Excavation and Publication Project).

2006, 88–91). By Stratum V, bichrome pottery dominates the decorated Aegean-style pottery, coinciding with the disappearance of monochrome Aegean-style wares (table II: vessel no. 36 [fig. 14.2]). The transition from monochrome to bichrome decoration is gradual and represents the development of Aegean-style pottery from the late-twelfth to the early-eleventh century B.C.E. (table II: vessel no. 35 [fig. 14.1]). Stratum VI has traditionally been dated to the second half of the twelfth century (e.g., T. Dothan and Gitin 2008, 1953–54); however, based on my dating of the end of Strata VIIIA to the ca. 1175/1150 and Stratum VII to the second half of the twelfth century, I propose lowering the date of Stratum VI and the initial appearance of bichrome-decorated pottery to the end of the twelfth/early eleventh centuries B.C.E.

Kiln 5050/37011, Kiln 36069, and Firepit 5042 are assigned to Stratum VI, Phases 8C and 8B (figs. 5–6). Kiln 5050/37011 is a small square- to rectangular-shaped fire installation, with a maximum outer width of ca. 1.55 meters. Kiln 5050 was first discovered in 1985 when its southern wall was sectioned during trimming of the northern balk line in Square INE.5, extending into the balk between Squares INE.5 and INE.37 (see Killebrew 1996b, 98–99; forthcoming b). In 1987 the combustion chamber itself was excavated in Area INE.37 and designated as Kiln 37011. Its interior chamber measured ca. .65–.75 meters in width. It is contemporary with Surfaces 5040 and 37019 and with the use of Kiln 36069 and Firepit 5042 of Phase 8C. Kiln 5050/37011 may have continued in use during Phase 8B.

Kiln 36069 is roughly square-shaped, with a mud-brick support against the back wall upon which a platform may have rested (fig. 5). Only the lowest part of the subterranean combustion chamber remains. A smaller pit, L. 36072, connected to the subterranean combustion chamber, probably served as the stoking hole for this kiln and was located to the west. The interior of the combustion chamber measured ca. 1 meter (N–S) by 1 meter (E–W) and ca. .30 meters in depth. A mud-brick pillar, measuring ca. .75 meters by .25 meters in size, was constructed against the inner eastern wall of the combustion chamber and probably supported a mud-brick platform, which was not preserved. Its interior walls were plastered with mud that was fired but not vitrified, indicating a relatively low firing temperature.

Kiln 36024, belonging to the following Phase 8B, was constructed on top of Kiln 36069 and involved several architectural modifications (fig. 6). Upon sectioning through the two kilns, it became clear that these two features represent two separate kilns or two different phases of use. This roughly oval-shaped mud-brick kiln measured ca. 1.5 meters (N–S) by 1.10 meters (E–W). Only the subterranean section of the kiln that served as the combustion chamber was preserved of what was originally most likely a two-chamber kiln. The combus-

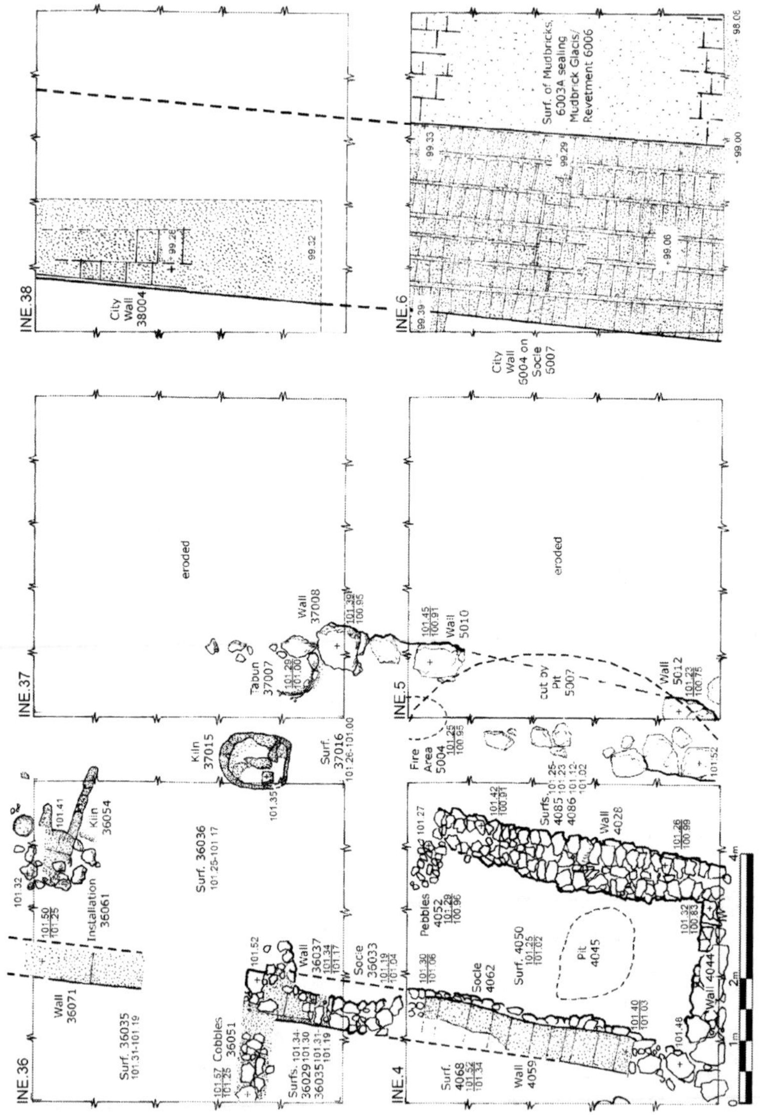

Fig. 7: Plan of Stratum VI, Phase 8A, Iron I potters' workshop area in Field INE, east slope (drawn by J. Rosenberg; courtesy of the Tel Miqne-Ekron Excavation and Publication Project).

tion chamber was divided by an interior wall into two subchambers, each with a mud-brick support constructed against the western wall, presumably to support a platform separating the combustion chamber from the firing chamber that was not preserved (Killebrew 1996a, 148; forthcoming b). It is contemporary with Surface 36040, Column Bases 36062 and 36063, and Dog Burial 36052 excavated below Surface 36040 (fig. 6; regarding the dog burial, see Killebrew and Lev-Tov 2008, 345 and Killebrew, forthcoming b).

The two latest fire installations, 37015 and 36054, are associated with Phase 8A, the final phase of Stratum VI when bichrome pottery dominated the decorated Aegean-style wares (fig. 7). Kiln 37015 is oval-shaped, measuring ca. 1.25 meters (N–S) by .90 meters (E–W) at its maximum dimensions. Remnants were uncovered of an interior pillar that may have supported a platform separating the combustion chamber from the firing chamber. The kiln was constructed out of mud bricks; however, individual bricks were not clearly distinguishable. The width of the kiln walls was ca. .15 meters. Only the subterranean section of the kiln that served as the combustion chamber was preserved. Several fragmentary mud bricks had collapsed into the combustion chamber. Surface 37016 ran up to the outer face of Kiln 37015 and is contemporary with Tabun 37007 and Wall 37008. Due to its close proximity to the top surface of the tell, Kiln 37015 and the features contemporary with it are very fragmentary in nature (Killebrew 1996a, 148; forthcoming b).

The second installation, 36054, is irregular in shape and poorly preserved. It is "U"-shaped measuring ca. 1.10 meters (E–W) by .65 meters (N–S) at its maximum preserved dimensions (fig. 7). The outer walls of the installation, measuring ca. .12 meters in width, were formed by one row of mud bricks standing on their narrow edge. Only one course of bricks was preserved. The mud bricks were fired during the course of the use of the installation; however, due to the lack of vitrification, the firing temperature was not high. Installation 36061 was built against the west end of Kiln 36054. A sunken storage jar base abutted against the kiln's northern face. Kiln 36054 is contemporary with Surface 36036, Installation 36061, Kiln 37015, and Walls 36037 and 36071 (Killebrew 1996a, 148; forthcoming b).

The series of kilns, fire installations, and the ceramic industrial area for the production of Iron I monochrome, bichrome, and undecorated utilitarian Philistine wares coincides with the sudden appearance of an Aegean-style material culture, providing a key piece of evidence for the Philistine puzzle. The plans of Strata VII and VI differ from those of both the preceding and succeeding strata. The excavations in Field INE East Slope revealed that pottery production dominated this area of the Iron I Philistine settlement at Ekron during the course of a century (ca. second half of the twelfth–mid-eleventh centuries B.C.E.). These kilns

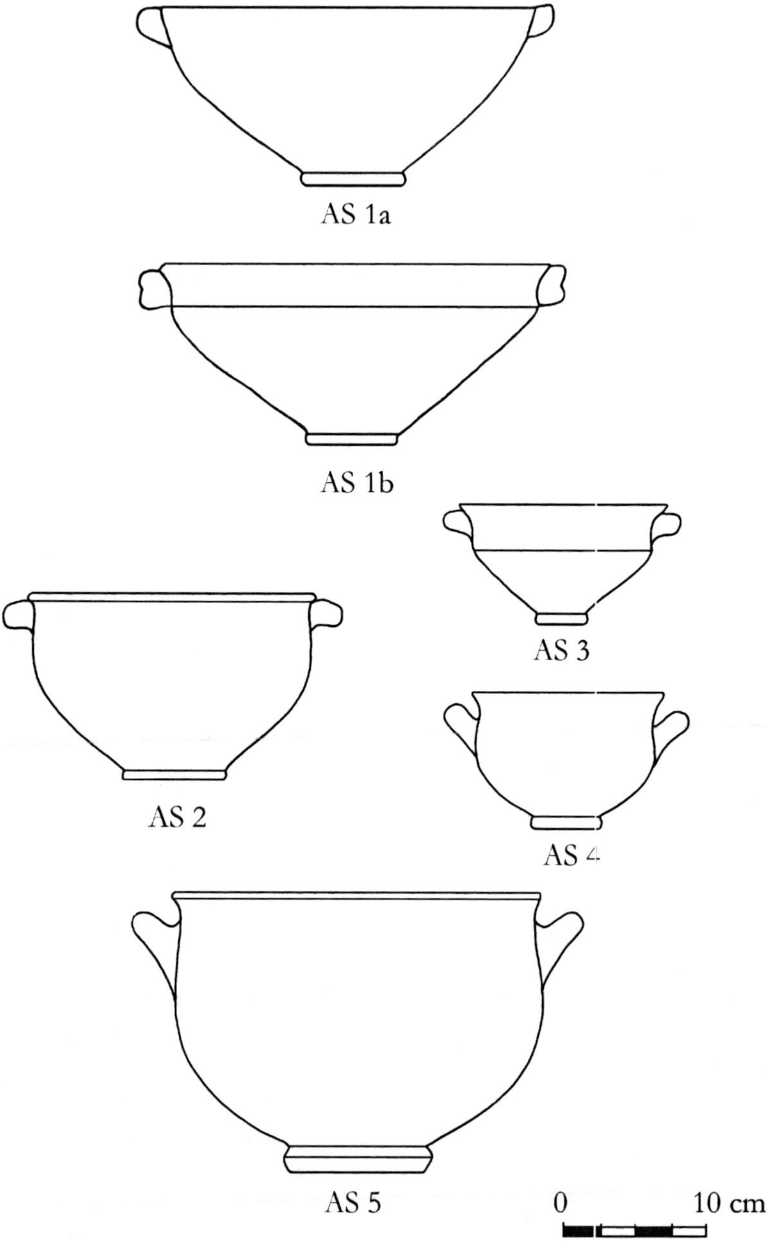

Fig. 8: Philistine pottery forms AS 1–5.

are constructed close to the interior face of the city wall and on the outer edges of the Iron I urban center, a feature typical of industrial areas. It is noteworthy that the area contained no potter's tools, wasters, or raw materials that would suggest a potter's workshop, which may be a result of the continuous habitation and use of this area just inside the Iron I city fortifications. Reflecting other aspects of early Philistine material culture that represent the appearance of new cultural and technological traditions in the twelfth-century southern coastal plain, these kilns represent a break from earlier potting traditions of Canaan (see, e.g., Killebrew 1996a for a discussion of Late Bronze and Iron Age kilns in Canaan). In particular, the square shape of several of the kilns, including the earliest kiln, Kiln 4104, is unusual and lacks any exact parallels. Furthermore, relatively low firing temperatures were maintained inside these installations, which differ from previous potting traditions that require higher temperatures. Both the shape and size of these kilns as well as the firing techniques seem to be especially suited for producing monochrome- and bichrome-decorated wares, which form the focus of this discussion (see below).

Iron I Philistine Pottery Typology

Several detailed discussions of early Iron I Aegean-style Philistine pottery and its associated monochrome-decorated wares produced in the southern coastal plain of Canaan have appeared (e.g., Killebrew 1999a, 168–85; 2000; 2005, 219–30; T. Dothan and Zukerman 2004; Mountjoy, this volume) and the later Iron I development of bichrome-decorated wares (e.g., T. Dothan 1982, 94–218; A. Mazar 1985b; Sharon 2001a; Ben-Shlomo 2006, 25–46). Based primarily on vessel proportion and morphology, I classify the early Iron I Aegean-style Philistine assemblage from Tel Miqne-Ekron according to two basic functional categories that these vessels may have served in antiquity: I) kitchenwares, which include: A) tablewares and B) cooking wares; and II) containers. A third category, varia (III), includes Aegean-style shapes that are rare in the Philistine repertoire. The assemblage comprises monochrome-decorated ("Philistine 1") and undecorated (plain and coarse wares) vessels whose shapes are Aegean- and/or Cypriot-inspired (figs. 8–10; for a detailed treatment of the typology summarized below, see Killebrew 1999a, 168–85).

Category I: Kitchenwares (Bowls): The Aegean-style bowls included in this family (AS 1–4; fig. 8) are all semi-hemispherical to hemispherical in shape, with two horizontal handles, and have no locally produced Canaanite antecedents (Killebrew 2000, 234–39). Bowl AS 1a (fig. 8) is a small semi-hemispherical bowl with two flat horizontal strap handles at the rim or just below it. This bowl type is

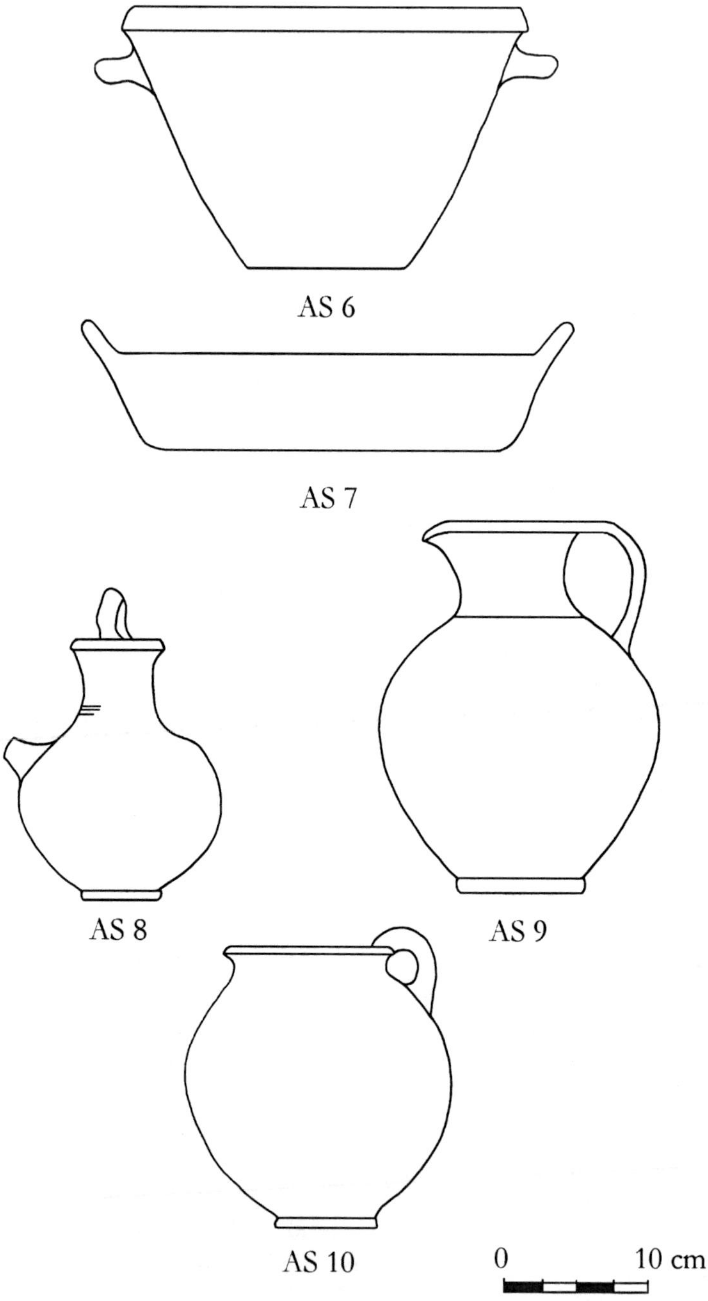

Fig. 9: Philistine pottery forms AS 6–10.

most common and best known from Cyprus (Killebrew 2005, 220, n. 73 for parallels; T. Dothan and Zukerman 2004, 7, Type A). Bowl AS 1b (fig. 8), similar in concept to AS 1a, is distinguished from Bowl AS 1a by its slight carination underneath the horizontal handle (Killebrew 2005, 220, n. 74 for parallels). Bowl AS 2 (fig. 8) is a deeper and rounded version of AS 1, with a more restricted vessel opening and flat horizon strap handles (Killebrew 2005, 220, n. 75 for parallels). Bowl AS 3 (fig. 8; table II: vessel nos. 32 [fig. 12.7], 34 [fig. 12.4], 37) is a carinated semi-hemispherical bowl with horizontal handles. In addition to its popularity in Iron I levels at sites in the southern coastal plain, it is also popular on Cyprus, the southern coast of Anatolia and coastal Syria, and the Aegean (Killebrew 2005, 220, nn. 76–77; see also T. Dothan and Zukerman 2004, 7–8, Type C). Bowl AS 4 (fig. 8; table II: vessel nos. 33 [fig. 12.3], 38) is a hemispherical (bell-shaped) bowl with horizontal handles and ring base. Often termed a skyphos, it is a well-known type in the southern coastal plain, throughout the Aegean, on Cyprus, and at several sites along the eastern Mediterranean coast. The decorative treatment on the bowls from Philistia is very similar to that on bowls from eastern Cyprus and Cilicia; however the shape is first known in the Aegean indicating that Form AS 4 has its antecedents in the Mycenaean world (Killebrew 2000, 236–39; 2005, 220, 222, nn. 78–82 for parallels; T. Dothan and Zukerman 2004, 8–12, Type D).

Category I: Kitchenwares (Kraters): The three basic krater forms, AS 5–7 (figs. 8–9), are distinctly different from the same family of forms known in Canaan during the Late Bronze IIB and Iron IA periods. Krater AS 5 (fig. 8; table II: vessel nos. 19 [fig. 13.2], 20 [fig. 12.1], 24 [fig. 12.2], 29 [fig. 12.5], 35 [fig. 14.1], 39) is a hemispherical krater. In literature relating to the Philistines, this shape is termed a bell-shaped krater (T. Dothan 1982, 106–15). Krater AS 5 equals the larger version of Furumark's Form 80 (Furumark 1941b, 633), or a Deep Rounded Bowl with Horizontal Handles. It is a common shape in the southern coastal plain at sites associated with the Philistines, on Cyprus, and in the Aegean (T. Dothan and Zukerman 2004, 12–16, Type E; Killebrew 2005, 222, nn. 83–86 for parallels). Krater AS 6 (fig. 9; table II: vessel nos. 28, 31 [fig. 12.8]), is an open, straight-walled deep krater-basin with horizontal handles, a slightly everted and thickened rim, and a flat base that rises slightly in the center (see also T. Dothan and Zukerman 2004, 16–21, Form F). The undecorated vessel, often termed a kalathos (Kling 1989, 145–47, fig. 10c), is found with monochrome- and bichrome-decorated Philistine assemblages at Tel Miqne-Ekron and Ashdod. Its closest parallels originate from Cyprus and differ from similar shapes found on the Greek Mainland and west Aegean (Killebrew 2005, 222, nn. 87–88 for parallels). Krater AS 7 (fig. 9) is a shallow krater tray with a slightly everted, straight-sided vessel profile and high horizontal handle. This form is very rare in Philistia (Killebrew 2000, 12.3:2; 2005, 222, n. 89 for parallels; see also T. Dothan and Zukerman 2004, 28, Type L).

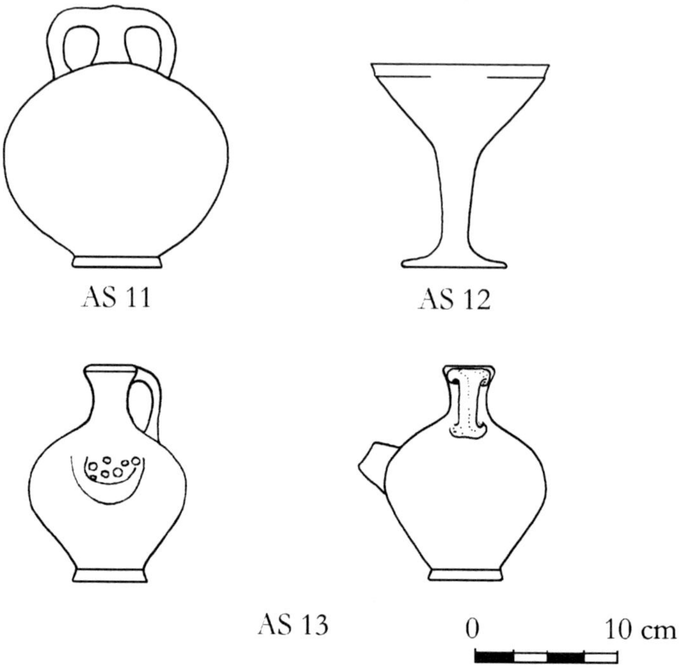

Fig. 10: Philistine pottery forms AS 11–13.

Category I: Kitchenwares (Juglets): Juglet AS 8 (fig. 9) is spouted with globular body profile and a basket handle situated at a right angle to the spout over the opening at the top of the vessel. Examples are known from Tel Miqne-Ekron and Ashdod, on Cyprus, and the eastern Aegean where it is suggested this particular shape first developed (Killebrew 2000, 240; 2005, 222, nn. 90–92 for parallels; T. Dothan and Zukerman 2004, 24–28, Type J).

Category I: Kitchenwares (Jugs): Jug AS 9 (fig. 9; table II: vessel no. 30 [fig. 12.6]) is characterized by its tall concave neck, often with a trefoil mouth. It is usually decorated with painted linear bands at the rim. Several examples are known from Iron I contexts at Tel Miqne-Ekron and Ashdod. Jugs with and without trefoil mouths appear in the Aegean and Cyprus, but it is noteworthy that jugs with a trefoil spout are an eastern embellishment on a Mycenaean form (Killebrew 2000, 242; 2005, 222, nn. 93–96 for parallels; see also T. Dothan and Zukerman 2004, 22, Type H).

Category I: Kitchenwares (Cooking Pots): The Aegean-style Cooking Jug AS 10 (fig. 9; table III: vessel nos. 47–48, 49 [fig. 15.1], 50 [fig. 15.2]), which makes its appearance for the first time at Tel Miqne-Ekron during the early Iron I, marks a total break with a millennium-long Canaanite tradition (Killebrew 1999b; 2000, 242–43; Ben-Shlomo et al. 2008). This cooking pot is characterized by its globular shape and flat base. Generally these closed cooking pots have one vertical handle and, less often, two vertical handles that are attached to the rim and shoulder. The rim is usually a simple or slightly thickened everted rim. Both the single- and double-handled cooking jug is a form well known in Cyprus during the Late Cypriot (LC) IIC and IIIA periods (Killebrew 2005, 222–23, nn. 97–98 for parallels). There is no doubt that the inspiration for this general cooking pot shape is the Aegean; however, already in LC IIC this cooking pot was adopted on Cyprus, increasing in popularity during LC IIIA. Since the closest parallels to these cooking pots are found on Cyprus where they chronologically precede the Philistine examples, it is preferable to see Cyprus and the surrounding region as the direct source for these, while recognizing its earlier Aegean origins (contra T. Dothan and Zukerman 2004, 28–31, Type P, who suggest a direct Aegean source).

Category II: Containers (Specialty Containers): Specialty Container AS 11 (fig. 10), or stirrup jar, is a well-known Aegean shape. It is a small jar with two handles that extend from the top of the closed ("false") neck to the shoulder. Form AS 11 has a long history in the Aegean and on Cyprus (Kling 1989, 161–65), already making its appearance in the locally produced Mycenaean IIIC repertoire in Philistia (see, e.g., Killebrew 2000, fig. 12:3:10; T. Dothan and Zukerman 2004, 28, Type K). It increases in popularity in the later Iron I bichrome assemblage (T. Dothan 1982, 115–25).

Category III (Varia): Several Aegean-style forms, such as the kylix (Form AS 12, fig. 10), appear in very small numbers and are not common shapes in the repertoire of Aegean-style pottery in Philistia (T. Dothan and Zukerman 2004, 22, Type G, fig. 27:2 and see parallels there). The fact that the kylix was one of the most common shapes in the Mycenaean west Aegean pottery repertoire, a tradition that continues into the twelfth century B.C.E. (e.g., see Mountjoy 1999d, 43), provides additional evidence that Philistine Aegean-style pottery did not derive directly from mainland Greece. A second rare form in early Iron I contexts is the strainer jug, Form AS 13 (fig. 10; T. Dothan and Zukerman 2004, 24, Type I, fig. 30:2). This vessel type is known in the Aegean and Cyprus; however, recent excavations indicate that the strainer jug first develops on Cyprus (Killebrew 2005, 225, n. 99 for parallels; contra T. Dothan and Zukerman 2004, 24).

Although Aegean-style pottery forms dominate the earliest Philistine occupation at Tel Miqne-Ekron, especially Stratum VIIA in Field INE, select Late Bronze ceramic types do continue to appear alongside the Iron I Aegean-inspired assemblages. Several of the shapes, known throughout the eastern Mediterranean during the thirteenth century, are produced at multiple pottery workshops in the

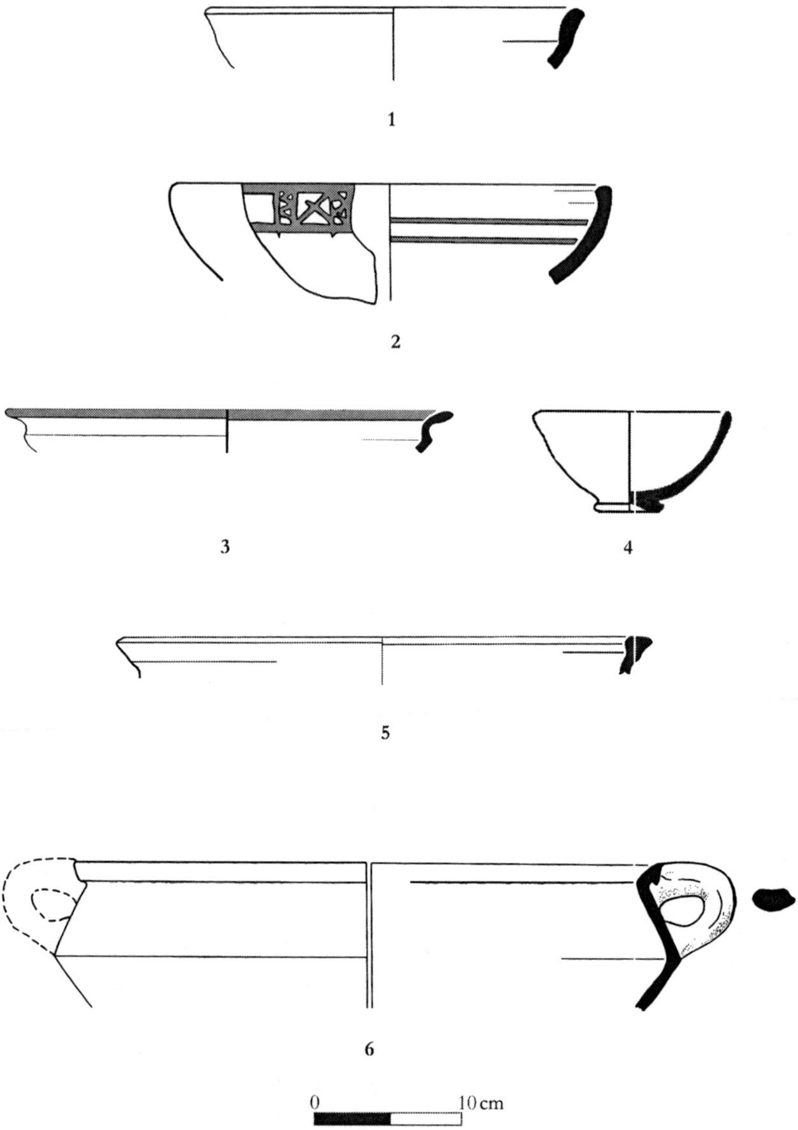

Fig. 11: Late Bronze II and early Iron I Canaanite-style pottery from Tel Miqne-Ekron sampled for petrographic analysis (redrawn by Silvia Krapiwko; see table I for description).

Levant and can be considered an "international" pottery style. The most ubiquitous form is the Canaanite storage jar (Form CA 21: figs. 16–17; Killebrew 2007). Another "international" shape well known in the eastern Mediterranean during the Late Bronze Age is the flask (Form CA 28: table I: vessel no. 7; Killebrew 2005, 125, 127). Two bowls that develop out of the Late Bronze Age Canaanite tradition include the cyma bowl (Form CA 7: table I: vessel nos. 11, 16 [fig. 11.3]) and the hemispherical bowl (Form CA 8: table I: vessel nos. 3 [fig. 11.4], 13). Sherds belonging to Canaanite-style cooking pots (Form CA 18: table III: vessel nos. 41, 43, 44 [fig. 15.3], 45, 52, 53 [fig. 15.4], 54; and Form CA 19: table III: vessel nos. 40 [fig. 15.5], 42, 46 [fig. 15.6], 51) appear in small numbers and could be intrusive. Canaanite-style lamps (Form CA 37), which are also known on Cyprus, occasionally appear (see Killebrew 2005, 132 for a discussion of these Late Bronze Age forms). The types and quantities of Iron I indigenous pottery increase in popularity during the following Strata VI and V and illustrate the process of assimilation, fusion, or "creolization" as it has been termed by various scholars, that is already underway following the first generation of Philistine colonists (for an overview of these issues, see Uziel 2007). The results of this and other typological studies of late thirteenth- and twelfth-century Aegean-style pottery produced in the east Aegean, Cyprus, and the Levant illuminate the complex multi-directional flow of influences that characterize the final centuries of the Bronze Age (see Killebrew 2010 for a detailed discussion; Killebrew and Lehmann, this volume), rather than one-dimensional Euro-centric theories of a unidirectional west Aegean cultural transmission to the east and overly simplistic notions regarding the west Aegean origins of the Philistines (see, e.g., Yasur-Landau 2010).

Philistine Pottery Technology: The technology used in the production of Aegean-style pottery at Philistine sites also represents a clear break with millennia-long potting practices. These changes are evident in all phases of the pottery production sequence, including clay procurement and preparation, formation techniques, and firing temperatures (see Killebrew 1998b, 397–401; 1999a, 187–257; 1999b for the first detailed discussions; see also Ben-Shlomo 2006 for an expanded study that includes later Iron I Philistine pottery technology). The results of a series of petrographic and Neutron Activation Analyses (NAA) of a representative assemblage of the various Tel Miqne-Ekron pottery types and wares best illustrate these technological changes in potting traditions of the local ceramic production at early Philistine sites in the southern coastal plain.[4] These

4. See Killebrew 1999a, 191–218 for a detailed, but previously unpublished, petrographic analysis of Late Bronze and Iron I pottery assemblages in the southern Levant, including locally produced Aegean-style pottery at Tel Miqne-Ekron. Regarding NAA analyses of the Tel Miqne-Ekron assemblage, see Gunneweg et al. 1986 and Asaro, Perlman, and M. Dothan 1971

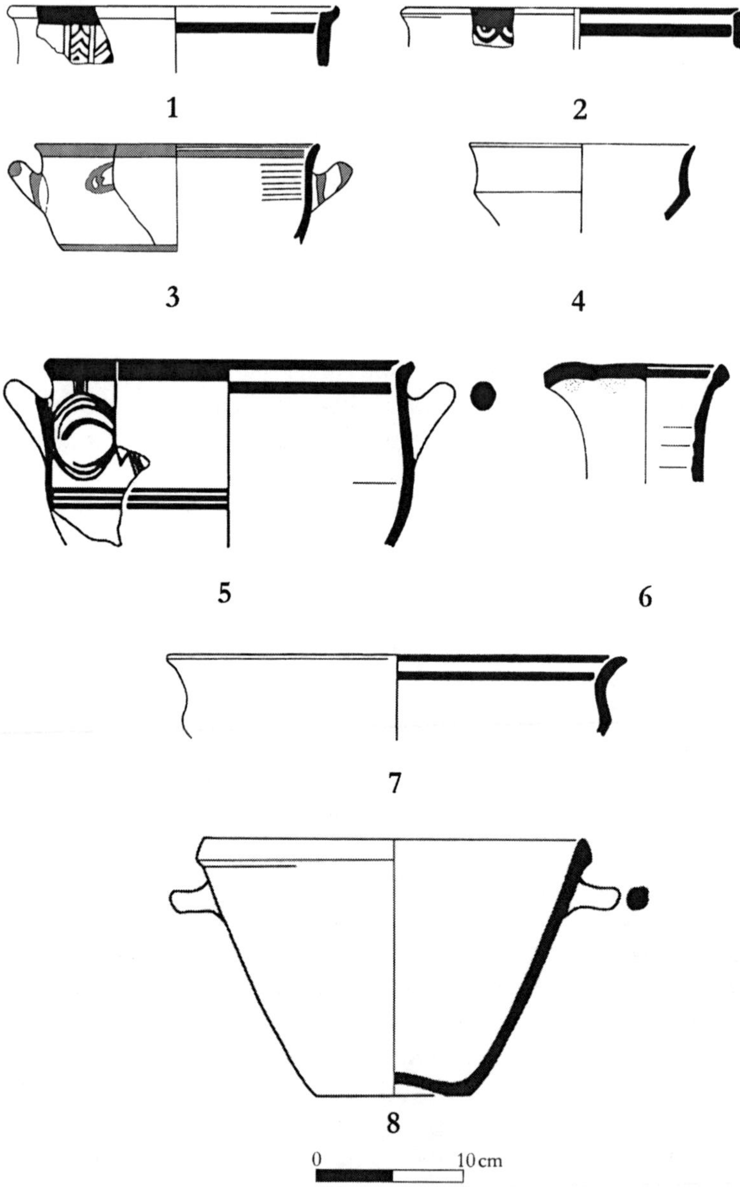

Fig. 12: Early Iron I Aegean-style pottery from Tel Miqne-Ekron sampled for petrographic analysis (redrawn by Silvia Krapiwko; see table II for description).

two approaches, one examining the mineralogical components of the clay and the second measuring chemical trace elements, confirm that the majority of Late Bronze Canaanite-style and Iron I Aegean-style vessels were locally produced by potters who intentionally utilized distinctly different modes of production and clay sources readily available in the general vicinity of Tel Miqne-Ekron (for a summary, see tables I–V; see also Gunneweg et al. 1986 and Killebrew 1999a, 198–206, 220–23).

Geology of the Tel Miqne-Ekron Region: Geographically, Tel Miqne-Ekron is located at the eastern end of the coastal plain, near the western flanks of the Shephelah, and along the southern bank of Nahal Timna, which is a tributary of the Nahal Soreq wadi system (see Killebrew 1999a, 198–201; Master 2003; Ben-Shlomo 2006, 137–43 for a detailed description of Tel Miqne-Ekron and the southern coastal plain). Geologically, there are several difficulties when discussing the region of the western Shephelah and coastal plain. One of the main problems in the geological mapping of the Shephelah is the thick calcareous calcite crust referred to as "nari," a weathered product that develops on porous chalky rocks in semi-arid Mediterranean climates (Buchbinder 1969, 1–2). A second difficulty is the thick layers of quaternary alluvial soil, sand dunes, and kurkar ridges, which characterize the valleys and flat plains of the Shephelah and coastal plain. The accumulation of alluvial soils has been especially rapid in recent history and it has been estimated that since the Byzantine period several meters have accumulated in the vicinity of Tel Miqne-Ekron (Rosen, unpublished report; see also Ben-Shlomo 2006, 138–40 and bibliography therein). Thus the landscape of the area surrounding Ekron has undergone a significant transformation during the millennia following the thirteenth and twelfth centuries B.C.E.

Tel Miqne-Ekron sits on grumusol clay, composed of fine-textured alluvial sediments typical of valley terraces, resting above the Rehovot Formation. The latter is composed of alternating layers of loose Late Pleistocene dune sands and red paleosols. Under the Rehovot Formation, the Ahuzam Conglomerate and the Pleshet Formation form the lower levels of the Pleistocene. The area of the eastern coastal plain includes outcrops of the Pleshet Formation, comprised of calcareous pebbly sandstone, which overlies the Yafo Formation, made up of Pliocene open-sea marls (Buchbinder 1969, 9; Gvirtzman 1969; Gvirtzman et al. 1999). To the east, in the Shephelah, a more homogeneous picture is evident with the lower Zor'a Formation ('Adulam Member), which consists of white chalk and silicified chalk with alternations of flint beds and nodules, overlying the chalky shales of

for the first NAA analyses establishing the local production of "Mycenaean IIIC" in the southern coastal plain. For a description of NAA analyses, see, e.g., Yellin 2007 and bibliography therein.

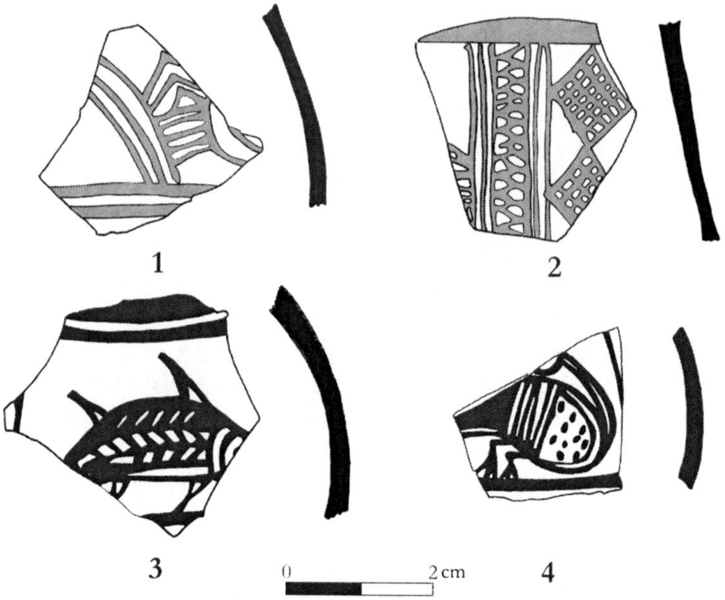

Fig. 13: Early Iron I Aegean-style pottery from Tel Miqne-Ekron sampled for petrographic analysis (redrawn by Silvia Krapiwko; see table II for description).

the Taqiye Formation (Buchbinder 1969, 5). These formations are exposed in the Nahal Soreq region, not far from Miqne-Ekron.

Ancient Clay Sources: Approximately two kilometers west of Tel Miqne-Ekron, a modern quarry is located on the Jerusalem–Beer Sheva road. The sediments revealed in the quarry's section cut were first described by Paul Goldberg during a visit to this site with me (Killebrew 1999a, 200–201). This quarry was used during the British Mandate period for sand quarrying and more recently by Kibbutz Revadim. The quarry sections through approximately 20 meters of sediment accumulation revealed seven main units, described from top to bottom: a brown grumusol layer (Unit 1), a gray-brown soil (Unit 2), a gray-brown soil with calcic horizons (Unit 3), and a red hamra soil (husmas) (Unit 4). Below the hamra soil are two loose sand dune layers (Units 5 and 7) and a reddish-brown hamra and nazzaz layer (Unit 6). The clay in this region can be characterized in general as smectite-rich. An ancient wadi system, which cut through several of these sediments, was also identified and sampled by Goldberg during our visit. Several archaeological sites including a Lower Paleolithic Middle/Late Acheulian one, remnants of an Early Bronze Age settlement, and a Middle Bronze Age cemetery have also been identified in the quarry sections (see Dagan 1982; Marder et

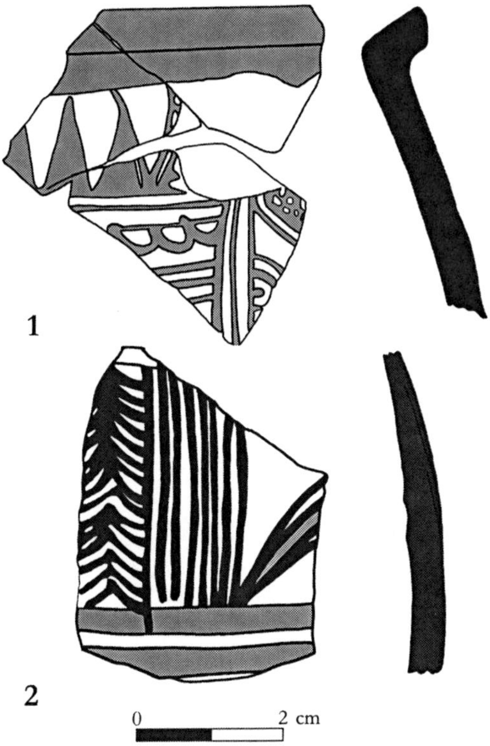

Fig. 14: Early Iron I Aegean-style pottery from Tel Miqne-Ekron sampled for petrographic analysis (redrawn by Silvia Krapiwko; see table II for description).

al. 1999, 22). Most of the Lower Paleolithic archaeological artifacts were found at the approximate contact level between Units 3 and 4, indicating a post-Middle/Late Achuelian date for the deposition of Units 1–3 (see Marder et al. 1999, 25–31 for a detailed description of these units and archaeological findings). Present-day soils are remnants of Mediterranean brown forest soils, water-logged vertisoils near the wadi, and alluvial soils in the valley surrounding the site (Rosen, unpublished report).

Samples were taken from the various units and ancient wadi system (see below). Small amounts of each were formed into cubes and fired at temperatures ranging from 500–800°C and examined under a petrographic microscope. In my petrographic analyses of these sediments and of the Tel Miqne-Ekron Late Bronze and Iron Age pottery assemblages, I employed Naomi Porat's clay classification and approach to petrographic ceramic analysis (1989, esp. 26–31 and fig.

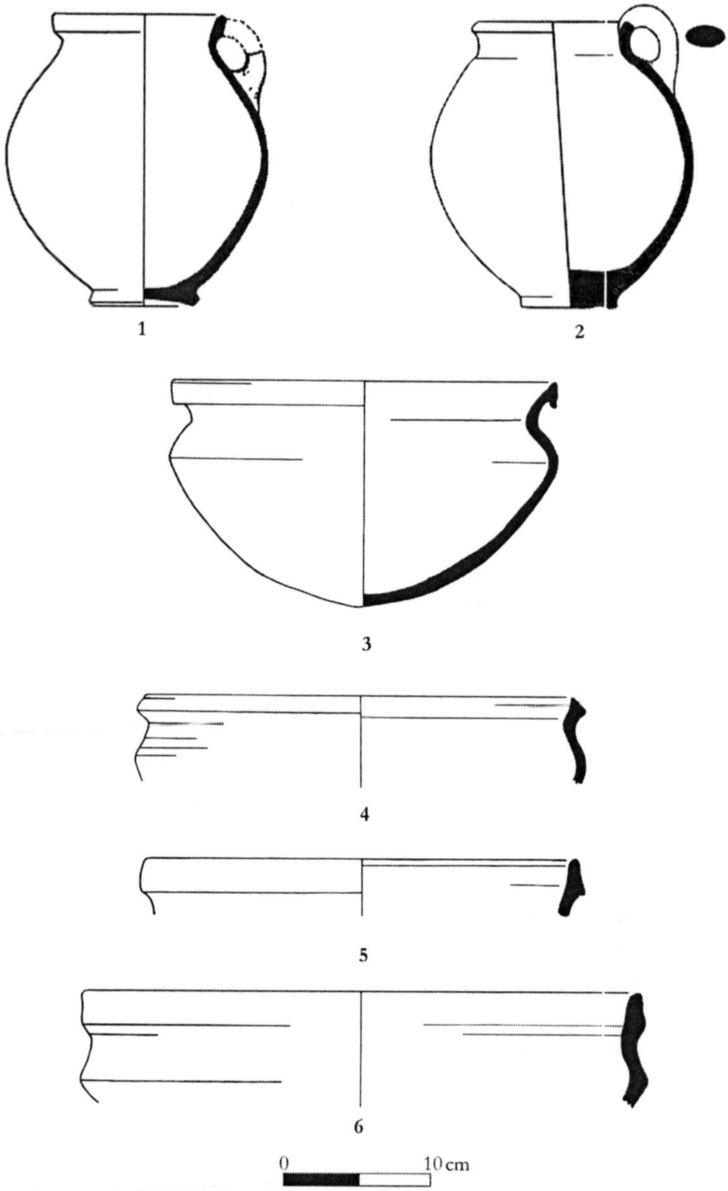

Fig. 15: Late Bronze II and Iron I Canaanite-style and Aegean-style cooking pots sampled for petrographic analysis (redrawn by Silvia Krapiwko; see table III for description).

6:3). Porat divides clays used in pottery production into nine main types: Type 1 is a calcareous clay with microfauna (fossiliferous marl clay) and only rarely silt-sized quartz. Type 2 is a calcareous clay with silt-sized to fine sandy quartz and carbonates (loess clay, usually an eolian or fluvial source, the latter often includes land snails and chert); feldspar and heavy minerals, such as hornblende, epidote, and zircon, are common. Type 3 is a silty, noncalcareous clay. Type 4 is a dolomitic clay. Type 5 is a pure clay. Type 6 is a calcareous clay without microfauna (nonfossiliferous marl clay), where silt-sized quartz is rare. Type 7 is a clay rich in silty iron oxides. Type 8 is a basaltic clay formed from basaltic soils with silty plagioclase and pyroxene (Golan clays). Type 0 is a silty noncalcareous micaceous clay (Nile mud). Types 1–5 can be found in the vicinity of Tel Miqne-Ekron.

The gray-brown sediments from the ancient wadi, similar in composition to Unit 2 in the Revadim Quarry, have moderate quantities of well-sorted silt-sized quartz (ca. 5–10%) and a slightly smaller quantity of sub-rounded fine sandy quartz (5%). It is a calcareous clay that belongs to clay Type 2 (fig. 18). It is similar in composition to Ware Group ME-B, the ware that is most commonly used in the manufacture of locally produced Canaanite-style Late Bronze and Iron I pottery from Tel Miqne-Ekron (see below). The hamra clay of Unit 4 has large quantities of well-sorted subrounded sand-sized quartz (ca. 50%) with smaller quantities of chert and limestone (fig. 19). The matrix is rich in clay-sized particles and can be classified as noncalcareous, belonging to clay Types 3 or 5. It is similar in composition to Ware Group ME-C, a clay that is less commonly used to produce the continuation of Canaanite-style pottery in the Iron I (table V and see below).

During a survey of the region with Naomi Porat of the Geological Survey of Israel and Natan Aidlin of Kibbutz Revadim, no suitable marl clay quarries were visible in the area surrounding Tel Miqne-Ekron. Calcareous marl clays were most commonly used in the production of Aegean-style monochrome-decorated ("Philistine 1") pottery, designated at Tel Miqne-Ekron as Ware Group ME-A (see below). Highly calcareous wares characterize Mycenaean-style decorated pottery in general. One Mycenaean IIIB sherd recovered from Tel Miqne-Ekron was examined under the petrographic microscope (fig. 20; Killebrew 1999a, 205–6). It belongs to a closed vessel formed out of marl clay belonging to clay Type 1, most likely manufactured in Cyprus. This clay lacks temper, but has large amounts of carbonate and foraminifera, some filled with iron—features common in marl clays. Heavy minerals include muscovite and biotite mica, neither of which is common in Israel. The applied slip is clearly visible in the section of the sherd. Similar marl clays are available and could have been procured in the region slightly to the east of Ekron. Local bedrock visible on the surface today includes

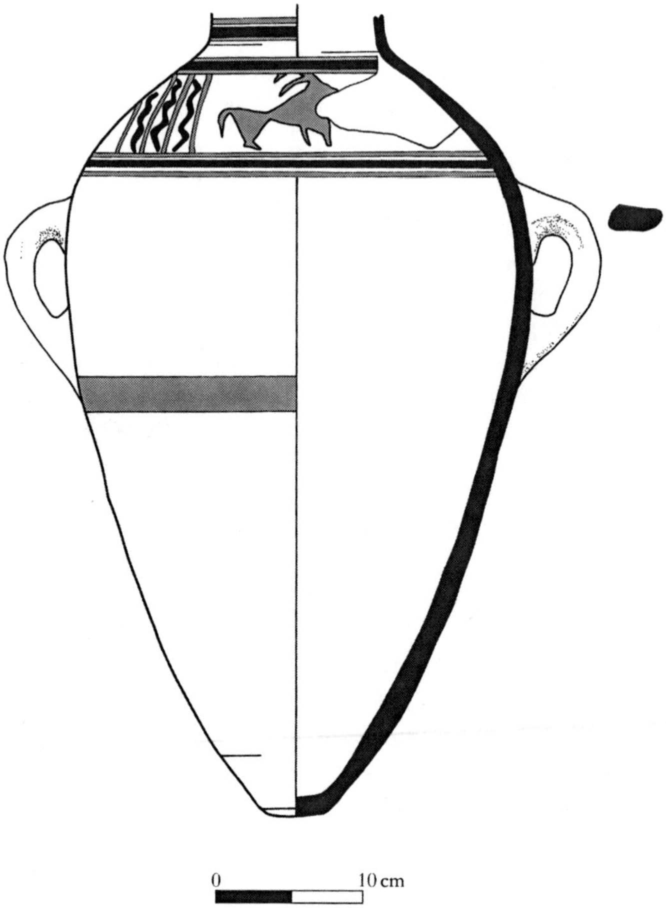

Fig. 16: Late Bronze Age Canaanite-style storage jar sampled for petrographic analysis (redrawn by Silvia Krapiwko; see table IV for description).

Eocene chalk and chalky marl appearing on the outcrops of low hills several hundred meters east of the tell, as well as a few outcrops of Neogene beachrock.

Tel Miqne-Ekron Ware Groups: The Late Bronze II and Iron I pottery at Tel Miqne-Ekron has been divided into five main locally produced ware groups and several subgroups.[5] Groups A, B, and C comprise the vast majority of the wares

5. See also Ben-Shlomo 2006, 189–93, whose petrographic and other archaeometric

used to produce pottery at Tel Miqne-Ekron and are described here. Ware ME-A is a mixture of Porat's clay Types 1 and 2, is characterized by its highly calcareous clay matrix, and is typical of marl clays used to produce imported Mycenaean wares (fig. 20). Ware ME-B belongs to clay Type 2, is similar in composition to the wadi clay sample (fig. 18), and is subdivided into seven possible subgroups based on temper in a silty calcareous clay matrix. Ware ME-C belongs to clay Types 2–5 or 3–5, is similar in composition to local hamra clays (fig. 19), and includes a very large amount of sandy quartz temper in its matrix with smaller quantities of limestone temper. Two ware groups identified at Tel Miqne-Ekron are not of local origin. These include Ware ME-D, which is unusual at Tel Miqne-Ekron and is defined by its matrix, which is assigned to clay Type 3. It includes large rounded pieces of shell. The second is Ware ME-E, a fine-grained calcareous marl clay with large quantities of forminifera, typical of the Taqiye Formation. Large quantities of sand-sized quartz were added to this paste as temper (see tables I–IV).

WARE GROUP MIQNE-EKRON A is subdivided into two sub-types. The first is a highly calcareous clay matrix with very small (ME-A1 [figs. 21–22]) to moderate amounts (ME-A2 [fig. 23]) of sand-sized temper (Killebrew 1999a, 202). ME-A1 (table II: vessel nos. 17 [fig. 13.1], 18, 19 [fig. 13.2], 20 [fig. 12.1], 21, 22 [fig. 13.3], 24 [fig. 12.2], 25–28, 29 [fig. 12.5], 30 [fig. 12.6], 31 [fig. 12.8], 32 [fig. 12.7], 33 [fig. 12.3], 34 [12.4]) is a highly calcareous clay that can be described as a mixture of loess and chalk, either naturally occurring levigated clay combination or a paste specially prepared from these two different clay sources. The matrix consists of extremely little or no temper, with small to moderate quantities of well-sorted silt-sized quartz (ca. 4–10%), occasional pieces of clear round carbonate, mudballs, disintegrated foraminifera, and chalk. Only a few sporadic sub-rounded sandy quartz grains (<1%) are visible. This clay does not belong to the wadi, grumusol, or hamra clays described above. Although the clay source is not identified in the field, this clay naturally occurs in this region and its local origins were previously confirmed by NAA analysis (Gunneweg et al. 1986). All these samples belong to the Aegean-style monochrome-decorated and undecorated wares, both closed and open shapes, and one Iron I storage jar—most of which originate stratigraphically in the earlier Stratum VII phases in Field INE (see table II).

Ware ME-A2 (table II: vessel nos. 35 [fig. 14.1], 36 [fig. 14.2], 37–39) is a highly calcareous clay with moderate amounts of well-sorted silt-sized quartz (4–10%) and is also a mixture of clay Types 1 and 2, but with a larger percent-

---

analyses of the Tel Miqne-Ekron Iron I wares and other Philistine assemblages corroborate my earlier conclusions.

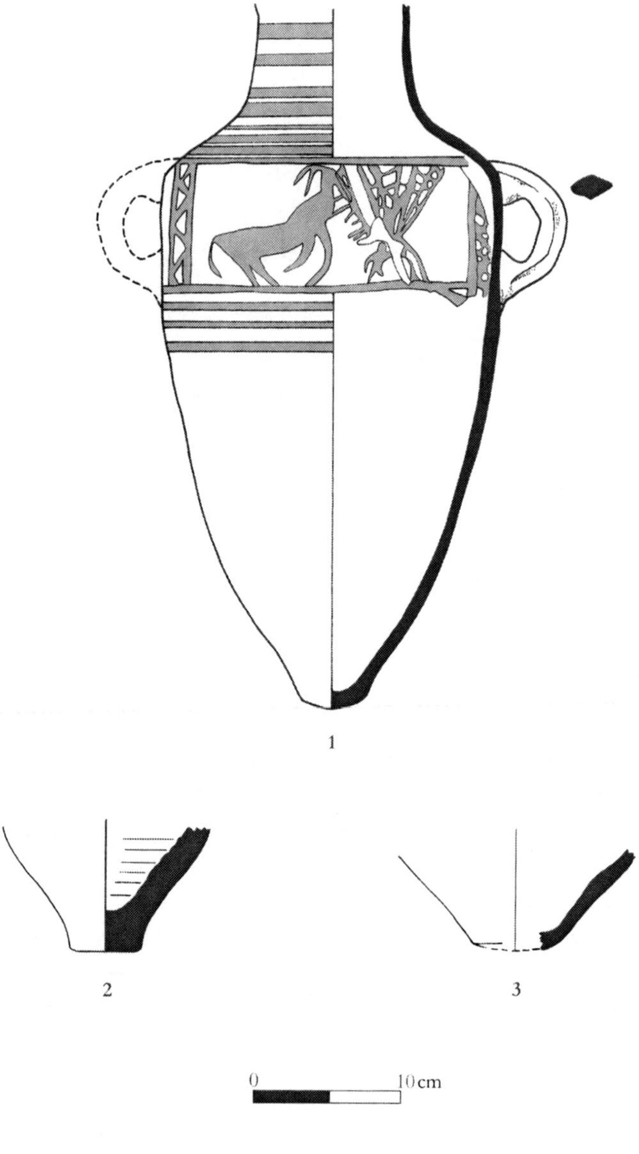

Fig. 17: Late Bronze Age and Early Iron I Canaanite-style storage jars sampled for petrographic analysis (redrawn by Silvia Krapiwko; see table IV for description).

age of loess clay Type 2 in its matrix. It is very similar to ME-A1; however, a moderate amount of well-sorted silt-sized quartz (4–10%) temper appears in the matrix. Mudballs and foraminifera also occur in this ware group. This clay does not belong to the wadi, grumusol, or hamra clays described above and belongs to a clay source not identified in the field, though this clay naturally occurs in this region. The local source of this ware was also previously confirmed by NAA analyses (Gunneweg et al. 1986). All of these samples belong to a stratigraphically later phase of Aegean-style pottery that mainly includes bichrome-decorated pottery and undecorated kraters and bowls (see table II).

WARE GROUP MIQNE-EKRON B is a silty calcareous clay containing some fine, sandy quartz, with different types of temper that have been divided into seven subgroups. It is similar in composition to the Revadim Quarry ancient wadi clay (fig. 18) sampled in the vicinity of Tel Miqne-Ekron (Killebrew 1999a, 203–4). Ware ME-B1 (table I: vessel nos. 1 [fig. 11.2], 2, 3 [fig. 11.4], 4 [fig. 24], 5 [fig. 11.5], 6–11, 12 [fig. 11.6]) is a calcareous clay matrix typical of Ware ME-B and includes small amounts of well-sorted silty quartz (1–3%), feldspar, and foraminifera. Moderate amounts of medium to well-sorted, fine sandy quartz (4–10%) comprise the main temper. Mudballs are sometimes visible. Occasionally signs of straw temper are discernible. This clay is similar to the fluvial wadi clay sampled from the ancient wadi without any additional mineral tempers. This group includes Late Bronze II–early Iron I bowls, kraters, flasks, and storage jars, all in the local Canaanite tradition, and one possible Iron I cooking jug (see tables I and IV).

ME-B2 (table III: vessel nos. 40 [fig. 15.5], 41–43, 44 [fig. 15.3], 45, 46 [fig. 15.6]) has a calcareous clay matrix that is similar to the ancient wadi clay, however with moderate to large quantities of sub-rounded limestone and shell temper (generally > 10%) that were added to the matrix. Pieces of kurkar also appear occasionally. This group consists of Late Bronze II and Iron I cooking pots in the local Canaanite tradition (see table III) with a composition similar to the cooking pot ware from Deir el-Balah (Ware DB-A2: Killebrew 1999a, 209) and to cooking pot ware from the Lachish potters' workshop (Magrill and Middleton 1997, 69; see also Magrill and Middleton 2004).

ME-B3 (table III: vessel nos. 47 [fig. 26], 49 [fig. 15.1], 50 [fig. 15.2]) also is characterized by its calcareous matrix that can be defined as almost a pure loess matrix that includes moderate amounts of well-sorted silty quartz (4–10%). Small amounts of poorly sorted subangular sandy quartz (1–3%) and occasionally straw were added to the matrix. Only Aegean-style Iron I cooking jugs appear in this group.

ME-B4 (table III: vessel no. 51) with its calcareous matrix typical of ME-B wares is distinguished by the appearance of moderate amounts of crushed calcite

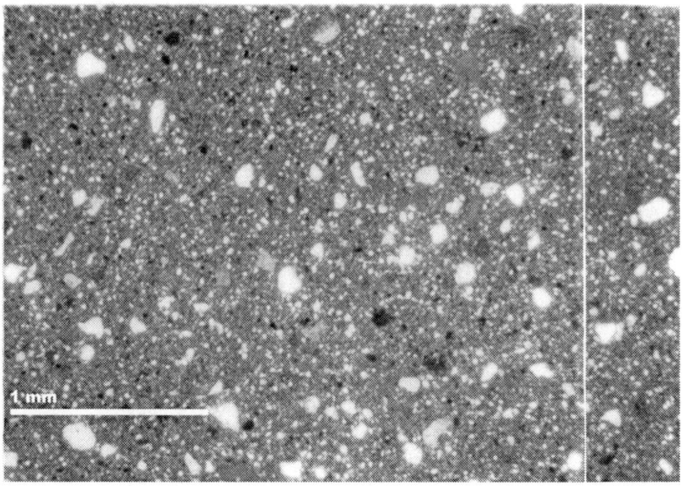

Fig. 18: Photomicrograph of wadi clay sample from Revadim Quarry. Taken with cross-polarized light (XPL). Scale = 1 mm (See table V for description).

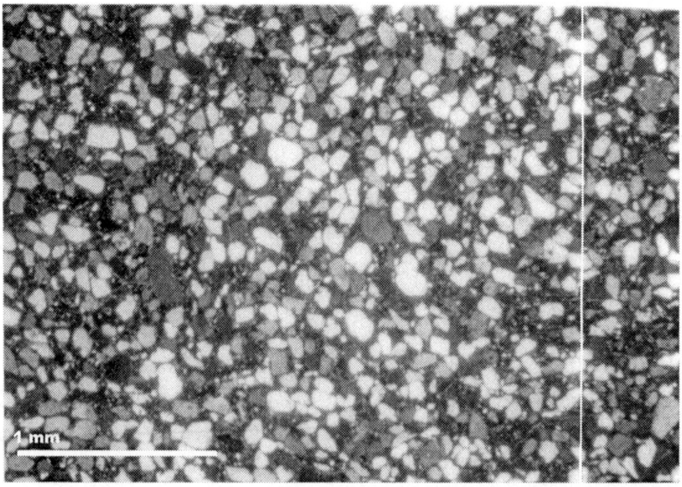

Fig. 19: Photomicrograph of hamra clay sample from Revadim Quarry. Taken with cross-polarized light (XPL). Scale = 1 mm (See table V for description).

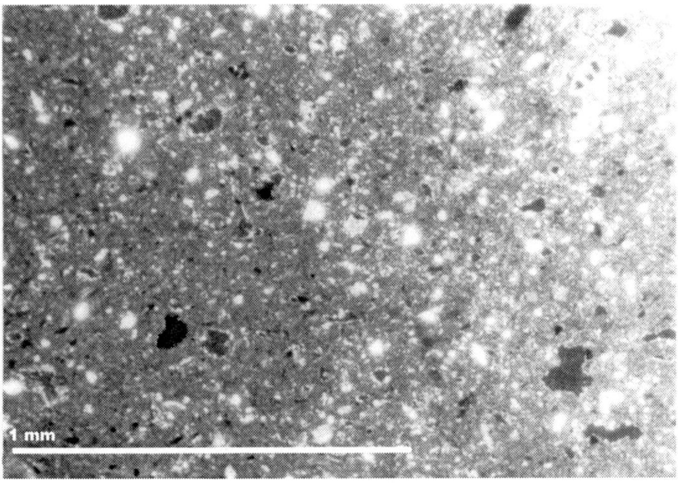

Fig. 20: Photomicrograph of imported Mycenaean IIIB sherd recovered from Tel Miqne-Ekron. A highly calcareous matrix with small amounts of moderate to well-sorted silt-sized quartz. Note foraminifera in upper-right corner. Taken with cross-polarized light (XPL). Scale = 1 mm.

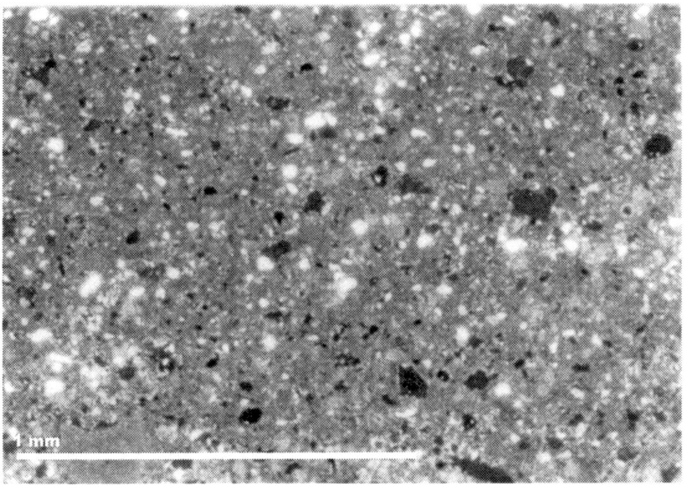

Fig. 21: Photomicrograph of ware group ME-A1 (table II: vessel no. 20: Aegean-style Krater, AS 5 [fig. 12.1]): Detail of ME-A1's fine-grained silty calcareous clay with almost no sand-sized quartz temper (<1%) and moderate amounts of well-sorted silt-sized quartz (4–10%). Note carbonate grain in the bottom left corner. Taken with cross light (XPL). Scale = 1 mm.

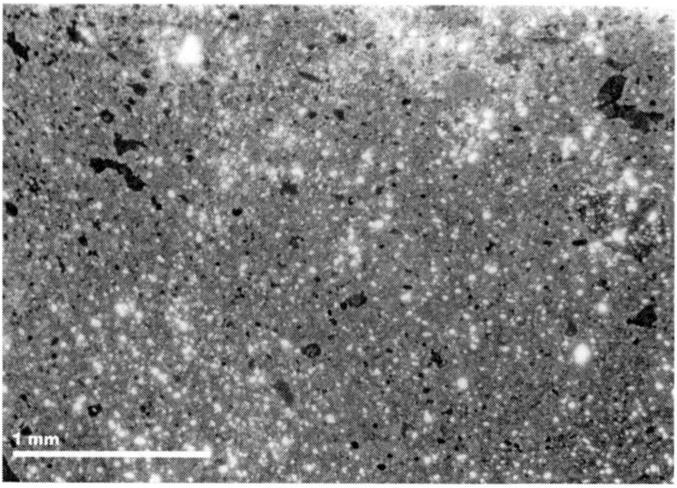

Fig. 22: Photomicrograph of ware group ME-A1 (table II: vessel no. 20: Aegean-style krater, AS 5 [fig. 12.1]). General view of fig. 21. Taken with cross-polarized light (XPL). Scale = 1 mm.

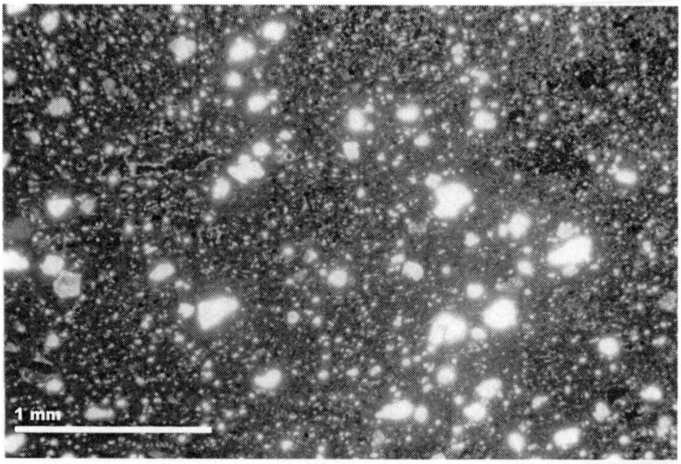

Fig. 23: Photomicrograph of ware group ME-A2 (table II: vessel no. 35: Aegean-style krater, AS 5 [fig. 14.1]): A fine-grained silty calcareous clay with moderate amounts of silt-sized quartz (4–10%) and a small amount of moderately sorted subangular to sub-rounded, relatively large-grained quartz sand (ca. 1–3%). Taken with cross-polarized light (XPL). Scale = 1 mm.

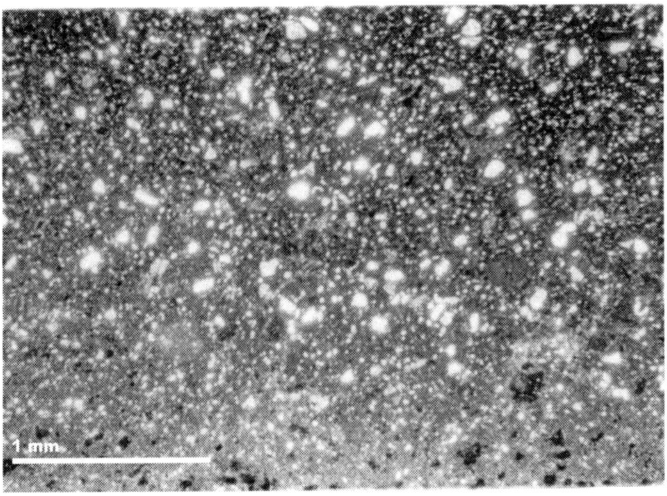

Fig. 24: Photomicrograph of ware group ME-B1 (table I: vessel no. 4: Canaanite-style bowl, CA 2). A fine-grained silty calcareous clay with almost no sand-sized quartz temper (<1%) and moderate amounts of well-sorted silt-sized quartz (4–10%). Taken with cross-polarized light (XPL). Scale = 1 mm.

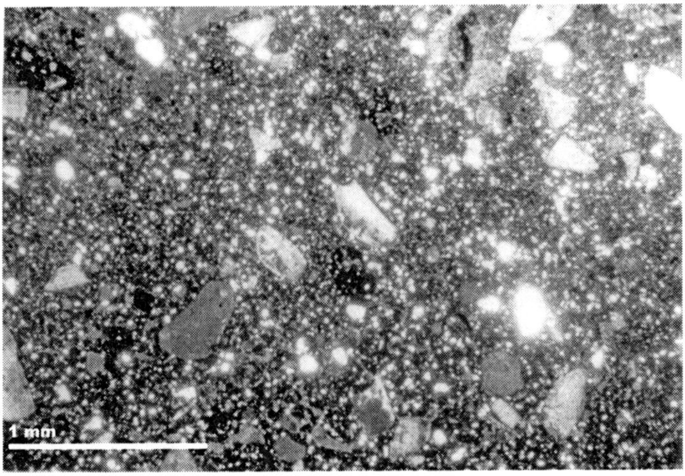

Fig. 25: Photomicrograph of ware group ME-B2 (table III: vessel no. 40: Canaanite-style cooking pot, CA 19a [fig. 15.5]). Calcareous clay with moderate amounts of moderately sorted silt-sized quartz (4–10%), large amounts of rounded shell and/or limestone (>10%), sand-sized kurkar and quartz (4–10%). Taken with cross-polarized light (XPL). Scale = 1 mm.

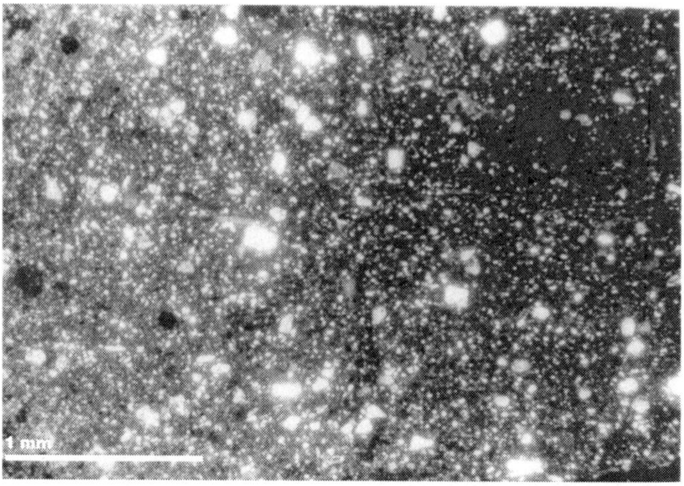

Fig. 26: Photomicrograph of ware group ME-B3 (table III: vessel no. 47: Aegean-style cooking jug, AS 10). Calcareous clay with moderate amounts of well-sorted silt-sized quartz (4–10%), small amounts of poorly sorted subangular sand-sized quartz (1–3%) and occasional rounded shell. Taken with cross-polarized light (XPL). Scale = 1 mm.

Fig. 27: Photomicrograph of ware group ME-C (table III: vessel no. 53: Canaanite-style cooking pot, CA 18d [fig. 15.4]). Non-calcareous matrix (similar to hamra, see fig. 19) with a large amount of well-sorted subrounded to subangular sand-sized quarter (ca. 30%) and a small amount of limestone (1–3%). Taken with cross-polarized light (XPL). Scale = 1 mm.

(4–10%) temper, which is extremely rare in this assemblage. Only one sample, an Iron I cooking pot, belongs to this subgroup.

ME-B5 (table I: vessel no. 13) is a loess clay that is differentiated from the other ME-B wares by the addition of moderate amounts of chalk temper (4–10%). It includes a storage jar and bowls, all from the earliest phases of Stratum VII, immediately preceding the appearance of the Iron I Aegean-style wares.

ME-B6 (table I: vessel nos. 14–15 [fig. 11.1]), with its typical ME-B calcareous matrix that includes forminifera, is not well defined. The outstanding feature of this clay is the large quantities of well-sorted subrounded sand-sized quartz (>10%) temper. Further analyses are necessary in order to define this group, which was used in the production of pottery in the Late Bronze II tradition, more clearly.

ME-B7 comprises a single bichrome krater with a calcareous clay matrix, which is difficult to classify. It includes large quantities of well-sorted silty quartz (10–20%) and moderate amounts of well-sorted sand quartz (4–10%). It is very similar to bichrome Philistine sherds examined from Deir el-Balah (Ware DB-A3, Killebrew 1999a, 203, 209–10).

WARE GROUP MIQNE-EKRON C (table III: vessel nos. 52, 53 [figs. 15.4, 27], 54; Killebrew 1999a, 204–5) comprises vessels characterized by a relatively large amount of well-sorted sub-angular to sub-rounded sand-sized quartz (ca. 30%). Vessel nos. 52 and 53 have a noncalcareous matrix typical of clay Type 3, similar to the hamra sediment in close proximity to the tell. A few shells are also present in the fabric of these two vessels. Limestone and kurkar occasionally appear as temper in the matrix. This group is made up of Iron I cooking pots in the Canaanite tradition (see table III) and possibly in later Iron II assemblages.

WARE GROUP MIQNE-EKRON D (table III: vessel no. 54; Killebrew 1999a, 205) was identified in only one Late Bronze Age-style cooking pot. It is a silty noncalcareous clay, belonging to clay Type 3, and is not locally available. The temper includes large quantities of sandy quartz and large rounded pieces of limestone.

WARE GROUP MIQNE-EKRON E (table IV: vessel nos. 57 [fig. 17.1], 58 [fig. 17.2], 59 [fig. 17.3]; Killebrew 1999a, 205; 2007) is defined by its calcareous marl matrix with large quantities of foraminifera and is similar in composition to the Taqiye Formation marls, designated by Goren (2000) as the Taqiye Marl. The distinguishing feature of this ware is the large amounts of well-sorted sand-sized quartz (>10%) temper that was added to the matrix. Only storage jars appear in this group. This clay type is not evident in the immediate area of the site of Tel Miqne-Ekron; however, as noted by Goren (1995, 52–53; 1996; 2000), the Taqiye Formation is common and exposed in several neighboring regions and is a common pottery ware at nearby Tel Gezer (see also Sugerman 2000, 104–5 and Killebrew 2007, 178).

Concluding Observations

The results from this comparative analysis of the Canaanite-style Late Bronze and Aegean-style Iron I pottery assemblages from Tel Miqne-Ekron reflect the forces at play during the final decades of the Bronze Age that ultimately result in the emergence of new regional and ethnic formations during the twelfth century. The majority of sampled Late Bronze and Iron I vessels belong to two distinct and typologically defined ware groups, ME-A and ME-B, indicating two very different potting traditions. Most of the Late Bronze II and Iron I pottery that can be classified as Canaanite in style, that is, continuing the Late Bronze Age indigenous traditions, were formed out of Ware ME-B from a locally procured clay. Several possible variations of this ware were defined based on temper visible in the matrix. Only a few vessels, mainly storage jars and a very small number of cooking pots, bowls, and kraters were not locally produced. The greatest variety of ware types was evident in storage containers.

Aegean-style vessels from Tel Miqne-Ekron demonstrate a clear break with earlier Late Bronze Age clay procurement strategies and manufacturing traditions. The potters of this assemblage preferred a highly calcareous clay comprising a mixture of loess and chalk for the production of tableware. This ware, ME-A, is confined to Aegean-style monochrome (A1) and bichrome (A2), with a smattering of storage jars dating to the Iron I period. Ware ME-B3, a clean loess clay, lacking temper typically added to Late Bronze II and Iron I Canaanite-style cooking pots, was used for Aegean-style cooking jugs. Aegean-style shapes were produced exclusively on the fast wheel, while a combination of hand and wheel techniques was used by the potters of Canaanite-style forms (Killebrew 1999b, 223–44). Based on the analysis of stable isotopes of carbon and oxygen in carbonates (Nissenbaum and Killebrew 1995), Fourier Transform-Infrared (FTIR) spectrometry analysis (Killebrew 1999b, 223–25), refiring experiments (Killebrew 1999b, 239–41), and lack of vitrification in the Tel Miqne-Ekron pottery kilns, there is also a clear indication that significantly lower firing temperatures were used in the production of Aegean-style monochrome pottery.

As is the case with Late Bronze and Iron I Canaanite-style pottery, Aegean-style monochrome pottery was also produced in a professional workshop setting. However, several technological aspects, such as the carefully prepared clays and highly skilled potters required to produce such fine wares, may indicate that its roots lie in large-scale industrial production. This factory-style mode of manufacture most likely continued earlier Late Helladic Mycenaean pottery traditions that were initially centered in mainland Greece but began to be produced in numerous workshops in the Aegean and eastern Mediterranean already during the latter part of the thirteenth century. That is when these new production centers begin to depart from strictly mainland Greek Mycenaean pottery traditions, with eastern influences observable in west Aegean ceramics, and vice versa, hinting at the multi-directional flow of cultural influences throughout the eastern Mediterranean. Localized variations intensify during the twelfth century (e.g., Mountjoy 1999d; 2009; this volume).

This comparative analysis of the earliest monochrome and undecorated plain wares from Tel Miqne-Ekron, representing only one aspect of the distinct Philistine culture that appears suddenly on the southern coastal plain of Canaan during the twelfth century, is a case study par excellence of the material manifestation of immigration in the archaeological record (see, e.g., Killebrew 2005, for a detailed discussion and bibliography; Killebrew and Lehmann, this volume). Early Philistine pottery at Tel Miqne-Ekron also illustrates the complexity of cultural and technological diffusion that transpired during this transformative period in the eastern Mediterranean. Equally significant, this ceramic investigation illuminates early Philistine ties with Cyprus, Cilicia, and the Aegean, especially the east Aegean, mirroring the gradual breakdown of Late Bronze Age trade connections, the collapse of monopolistic economic systems, and the rise of regional fragmentation that brought the "Age of Internationalism" to an end (see, e.g., Killebrew 1998a; 1999a; 2000; 2005, 230; 2007; Mountjoy, this volume).

Table I: Locally produced Canaanite-style (CA) pottery (tablewares): Selection of sampled ware groups ME-B1, ME-B5, ME-B6, and ME-C. Late Bronze IIB, Transitional LB/Iron I, and Iron I bowls, kraters, and flasks. (See Killebrew 2005,110–38 for a detailed description of Canaanite vessel types referred to in Table I.)

Vessel No. Fig. No.	Registration No. (Vessel Type): Publications	Ware Group (Petrographic No.)	NAA No.: Publication	Locus No.	Stratum (Phase): Date
1 fig. 11.2	INE.5.181/38 (Bowl CA 2): Killebrew 1999a, 228, Ill. III:1:19	ME-B1 (No. 66)	No. 12: Gunneweg et al. 1986, fig. 3:5	Orange Fill 5033	Str. VIIB (9D): 12th c.
2	INE.5.101/1 (Bowl CA 2): Killebrew 1999a, 292	ME-B1 (No. 80)		5027 = Sed. 5006	Str. VIIB (9C): 12th c.
3 fig. 11.4	INE.5.100/1 (Bowl CA 8): Killebrew 1998a, fig. 6:1; 1999a, 296, Ill. III:2:7	ME-B1 (No. 104)	No. 7: Gunneweg et al. 1986, fig. 3:1	Surface 5029	Str. VIIB (9C): 12th c.
4 fig. 24	INE.4.443/16 (Bowl CA 2): Killebrew 1999a, 297, Ills. III:1:8, IV:4:1	ME-B1 (No. 114)		Orange Fill 4131	Str. VIIB (9D): 12th c.
5 fig. 11.5	INE.4.446/4 (Krater CA 10a): Killebrew 1998a, fig. 6:9; 1999a, 299, Ills. II:22:9; III:4:4	ME-B1 (No. 125)		Surface 4116	Str. VIIB (9C): 12th c.
6	INE.5.123/3 (Bowl CA 1): Killebrew 1999a, 299	ME-B1 (No. 126)		5027 = Sed. 5006	Str. VIIB (9C): 12th c.
7	INE.5.135/26 (Flask CA 28): Killebrew 1999a, 299	ME-B1 (No. 128)		Surf. 5029	Str. VIIB (9C): 12th c.

8	INE.4.136/60 (Bowl CA 1): Killebrew 1999a, 300	ME-B1 (No. 131)		Debris 4011E	Mixed
9	INE.4.443/29 (Bowl CA 1): Killebrew 1999a, 300	ME-B1 (No. 132)		Orange Fill 4131	Str. VIIB (9D): 12th c.
10	INE.4.450/6 (Bowl CA 1): Killebrew 1999a, 300	ME-B1 (No. 133)		Orange Fill 4131	Str. VIIB (9D): 12th c.
11	INE.5.168/3 (Bowl CA 7): Killebrew 1999a, 300, Ill. III:2:5	ME-B1 (No. 134)		Orange Fill 5031	Str. VIIB (9D): 12th c.
12 fig. 11.6	INE.6.227/1 (Krater CA 10a): Killebrew 1996b, pl. 4:13; 1999a, 302, Ills. II:4:13; III:4:6	ME-B1 (No. 143)		Surface 6048	Str. VIIIB (11D): 13th c.
13	INE.5.168/1 (Bowl CA 8): Killebrew 1999a, 297, Ill. III:2:9	ME-B5 (No. 118)		Orange Fill 5031	Str. VIIB (9D): 12th c.
14	INE.4.449/4 (Bowl CA 1): Killebrew, 1999a, 299	ME-B6 (No. 112)		Orange Fill 4131	Str. VIIB (9D): 12th c.
15 fig. 11.1	INE.5.137/14 (Bowl CA 1): Killebrew 1999a, 299, Ill. III:1:3	ME-B6 (No. 129)		Surface 5029	Str. VIIB (9C): 12th c.
16 fig. 11.3	INE.3.58/12 (Bowl CA 7): Killebrew 1999a, 291	ME-C (No. 78)	No. 38: Gunneweg et al. 1986, fig. 3:7	Fill 3011	Pre-Str. IV: Mixed Locus

Table II: Locally produced Aegean-style (AS) Iron I pottery (tablewares): Selection of sampled ware groups ME-A1 and ME-A2. Monochrome (Myc. IIIC Early & Middle; "Philistine 1"), bichrome ("Philistine 2"), and undecorated Aegean-style wares. (See Killebrew 2005, 219–26 for a detailed description of Aegean-style vessel types referred to in Table II.)

Vessel No. Fig. No.	Registration No. (Vessel Type): Publications	Ware Group (Petrographic No.)	NAA No.: Publication	Locus No.	Stratum (Phase): Date
17 fig. 13.1	INE.4.88/2 (Krater sherd: Monochrome): Killebrew 1999a, 289	ME-A1 (No. 67)	No. 20: Gunneweg et al. 1986, fig. 1:6	Debris 4036	Str. VI (8A): 12th/11th c.
18	INE.4.133/7 (Krater AS 5?: Monochrome): Killebrew 1999a, 289	ME-A1 (No. 68)	No. 23: Gunneweg et al. 1986, fig. 1:3	Pit 4045	Post Str. VIA (post 8A): 11th c.
19 fig. 13.2	INE.4.80/2 (Krater AS 5?: Monochrome): Killebrew 1999a, 289	ME-A1 (No. 69)	No. 16: Gunneweg et al. 1986: fig. 1:10	Pit 4004	Mixed Locus
20 figs. 12.1, 21, 22	INE.4.128/44 (Krater AS 5: Monochrome): Killebrew 1999a, 289, Ill. IV:2:1, 2	ME-A1 (No. 70)	No. 22: Gunneweg et al. 1986, fig. 1:2	Debris 4036	Str. VIA (8A): 12th/11th c.
21	INE.5.71/4 (Strainer of Jug: Monochrome): Killebrew 1999a, 290	ME-A1 (No. 75)	No. 19: Gunneweg et al. 1986, fig. 1:11	Surface Build-up 5003	Str. VIIA (9A): 12th c.
22 fig. 13.3	INE.4.144/81 (Jug: Monochrome): Killebrew 1999a, 293; T. Dothan and Zukerman 2004, fig. 35:7	ME-A1 (No. 86)	No. 24: Gunneweg et al. 1986, fig. 1:12	Debris 4011A	Mixed Locus

23 fig. 13.4	INE.5.192/23 (Jug: Monochrome): Killebrew 1999a, 293; T. Dothan and Zukerman 2004, fig. 35:8	ME-A1 (No. 93)	No. 32: Gunneweg et al. 1986, fig. 1:13	Sed. Layer 5028	Str. VIIA (9B): 12th c.
24 fig. 12.2	INE.4.88/10 (Krater AS 5: Monochrome): Killebrew 1999a, 294	ME-A1 (No. 97)	No. 21: Gunneweg et al. 1986, fig. 1:1	Debris 4036	Str. VIA (8A): 12th/11th c.
25	INE.5.33/6 (Sherd: Monochrome): Killebrew 1999a, 294	ME-A1 (No. 98)	No. 18: Gunneweg et al. 1986, fig. 1:7	Surface Build-up 5003	Str. VIIA (9A): 12th
26	INE.5.134/6 (Krater AS 5?: Monochrome): Killebrew 1999a, 294	ME-A1 (No. 99)	No. 30: Gunneweg et al. 1986, 8	Sed. Layer 5028	Str. VIIA (9B): 12th c.
27	INE.5.97/11 (Krater AS 5?: Monochrome): Killebrew 1999a, 295	ME-A1 (No. 101):	No. 28: Gunneweg et al. 1986, fig. 1:8	Surface Build-up 5003	Str. VIIA (9A): 12th c.
28	INE.4.339/7 (Kalathos AS 6): Killebrew 1999a, 298	ME-A1 (No. 121)		Surface 4091	Str. VIIA (9A): 12th c.
29 fig. 12.5	INE.37.74/64 (Krater AS 5: Monochrome): Killebrew 1998a, fig. 7:14; 1999a, 303, Ills. II:25:14, III:25:12; T. Dothan and Zukerman 2004, fig. 16:7	ME-A1 (No. 148)		Surface 37027	Str. VIIA (9A): 12th c.

Table II continued.

Vessel No. Fig. No.	Registration No. (Vessel Type): Publications	Ware Group (Petrographic No.)	NAA No.: Publication	Locus No.	Stratum (Phase): Date
30 fig. 12.6	INE.4.379/19 (Jug AS 9: Trefoil with Linear Decoration): Killebrew 1998a, fig. 6:30; 1999a, 303, Ills. II:22:30, III:26:7; T. Dothan and Zukerman 2004, fig. 27:10	ME-A1 (No. 150)		Surface 4117	Str. VIIA (9B): 12th c.
31 fig. 12.8	INE.3.371/28 (Kalathos AS 6): Killebrew 1998a, fig. 12:14; 1999a, 304, Ills. II:28:14, III:26:1, IV:3:1; T. Dothan and Zukerman 2004, fig. 25:4	ME-A1 (No. 152)		Pit 3074	Str. VIA (8A): 12th/11th c.
32 fig. 12.7	INE.37.72/8 (Bowl AS 3): Killebrew 1998a, fig. 7:6; 1999a, 304, Ill. II:25:6	ME-A1 (No. 153)		Surface 37027	Str. VIIA (9A): 12th c.
33 fig. 12.3	INE.4.392/1 (Bowl AS 4: Monochrome): Killebrew 1998a, fig. 6:23; 1999a, 304, Ills. II:22:23, III:25:10	ME-A1 (No. 155)		Surface 4117	Str. VIIA (9B): 12th c.
34 fig. 12.4	INE.4.395/2A (Bowl AS 3): Killebrew 1998a, fig. 6:21; 1999a, 305, Ills. II:22:21, III:25:6	ME-A1 (No. 157)		Surface 4117	Str. VIIA (9B): 12th c.
35 figs. 14.1, 23	INE.4.154/19, 52 (Krater AS 5: Transitional Bichrome): Killebrew 1999a, 290, Ill. IV:3:2	ME-A2 (Nos. 71 and 74)	No. 26 Gunneweg et al. 1986, fig. 1:9	Pit 4045A	Post-Str. VIA (Post-8A): 11th c.

36 fig. 14.2	INE.5.8/3 (Sherd: Bichrome): Killebrew 1999a, 290	ME-A2 (No. 72)	No. 36: Gunneweg et al. 1986, fig. 2:4	Topsoil 5000	Mixed Locus
37	INE.4.59/12 (Bowl AS 3): Killebrew 1999a, 290	ME-A2 (No. 73)	No. 38: Gunneweg et al. 1986, fig. 3:10	Pit 4004	Mixed Locus
38	INE.4.73/2 (Bowl AS 4?: Transitional Bichrome): Killebrew 1999a, 290; T. Dothan and Zukerman 2004, fig. 25:6	ME-A2 (No. 81)	No. 15: Gunneweg et al. 1986, 8	Pit 4004	Mixed Locus
39	Surface (Krater AS 5: Bichrome): Killebrew 1999a, 293	ME-A2 (No. 83)	No. 33: Gunneweg et al. 1986, fig. 2:2	Surface of Tell	Mixed Locus

Table III: Locally produced Canaanite (CA) and Aegean-style (AS) cooking pots. Selection of sampled ware groups ME-B2, ME-B3, ME-C, and ME-D. Late Bronze IIB and Iron I cooking pots and cooking jugs. (See Killebrew 1999b for a detailed description of Late Bronze and Aegean-style cooking pot vessel types referred to in Table III.)

Vessel No. Fig. No.	Registration No. (Vessel Type): Publications	Ware Group (Petrographic No.)	NAA No.: Publication	Locus No.	Stratum (Phase): Date
40 figs. 15.5, 25	INE.5.33/28 (Cooking Pot CA 19a): Killebrew 1999a, 293, Ill. IV:4:2	ME-B2 (No. 87)	No. 39: Gunneweg et al. 1986, fig. 3:12	Surface Build-up 5003	Str. VIIA (9A): 12th c.
41	INE.4.127/2 (Cooking Pot CA 18a): Killebrew 1999a, 296	ME-B2 (No. 107)		Pit 4045	Post Str. VIA (Post 8A): 11th c.
42	INE.4.313/27 (Cooking Pot CA 19a): Killebrew 1999a, 298	ME-B2 (No. 120)		Debris on Surf. 4070A	Str. VIB (8B): 12th/11th c.
43	INE.4.433/5 (Cooking Pot CA 18d): Killebrew 1999a, 298	ME-B2 (No. 123)		Surface Build-up 4116	Str. VIIB: (9C): 12th c.
44 fig. 15.3	INE.6.163 (Cooking Pot CA 18a): Killebrew 1996b, pl. 6:8; 1998a, fig. 3:8; 1999a, 301, Ills. II:9:8; III:7:1; 1999b, fig. 1:1	ME-B2 (No. 139)		Fill from Bin 6011A	Str. VIIIB (11A): 13th c.
45	INE.7.190/52 (Cooking Pot CA 18a): Killebrew 1996b, pl. 2:5; 1999a, 302	ME-B2 (No. 144)		Debris 7037	Post-Str. IX: (Post 12A): 14th c.

46 fig. 15.6	INE.36.244/23 (Cooking Pot CA 19a): Killebrew 1998a, fig. 10:12; 1999a, 304, Ills. II:26:12, III:8:21; 1999b, fig. 2:2	ME-B2 (No. 151)		Surface 36081	Str. VIIA (9A): 12th c.
47 fig. 26	INE.4.413/1 (Cooking Jug AS 10): Killebrew 1999a, 297, Ill. IV:5:1, 2	ME-B3 (No. 113)		Fill 4124	Str. VIIA (9B): 12th c.
48	INE.3.439/5 (Cooking Jug AS 10): Killebrew 1999a, 298	ME-B3 (No. 122)		Install. 3087	Str. VIA (8C/B): 12th/11th c.
49 fig. 15.1	INE.3.439/3 (Jug AS 10): Killebrew 1999a, Ill. III:26:14; 1999b, fig. 3:4	ME-B3 (No. 147)		Install. 3087	Str. VIA (8C/B): 12th/11th c.
50 fig. 15.2	INE.3.376/6 (Cooking Jug AS 10): Killebrew 1998a, fig. 12:15; 1999a, 305, Ills. II:28:15; III:26:11; 1999b, fig. 3:1; T. Dothan and Zukerman 2004, fig. 36:4	ME-B3 (No. 156)		Column Base 3073	Str. VIA (8C-A): 12th/11th c.
51	INE.5.100/8 (Cooking Pot CA 19b): Killebrew 1999a, 297, Ill. III:8:6	ME-B4 (No. 111)		Surface 5029	Str. VIIB (9C): 12th c.
52	INE.4.443/6 (Cooking Pot CA 18d): Killebrew 1999a, 297	ME-C (No. 116)		Orange Fill 4131	Str. VIIB (9D): 12th c.
53 figs. 15.4, 27	INE.3.371/23 (Cooking Pot CA 18d): Killebrew 1998a, fig. 12:19; 1999a, 297, Ills. II:28:18, IV:6:1	ME-C (No. 117)		Pit 3074	Str. VIA (8C): 12th/11th c.
54	INE.5.131/4 (Cooking Pot CA 18a): Killebrew 1999a, 298	ME-D (No. 119)		5027 = Sed. 5006	Str. VIIB (9C): 12th c.

Table IV: Nonlocal and locally produced Late Bronze IIB and Iron I Canaanite-style (CA) storage jars: Ware groups ME-B1, ME-C, and ME-E. (See Killebrew 2007 for a detailed description of Canaanite-style storage jar vessel types and ware groups referred to in Table IV.)

Vessel No. Fig. No.	Registration No. (Vessel Type): Publications	Ware Group (Petrographic No.)	NAA No.: Publication	Locus No.	Stratum (Phase): Date
55 fig. 16	INE.5.275 (Storage Jar CA 21a): Killebrew 1996b, pl. 7:1; 1999a, 302, Ills. II:10; III:9:4	ME-B1 (No. 145)		Surface 5048	Str. VIIIB (11A): 13th c.
56	INE.3.133/1 (Storage Jar): Killebrew 1999a, 295	ME-C (No .102)	No. 2: Gunneweg et al. 1986, fig. 2:10	Surface 3024P	Str. VB (6A): 11th c.
57 fig. 17.1	INE.6.126 (Storage Jar CA 21a): Killebrew 1996b, pl. 5:13; 1998a, fig. 1:13; 1999a, 302, Ills. II:6:13; III:9:3	ME-E (No. 142) Not Local to Miqne-Ekron		Surface 6038	Str. VIIIB (11C): 13th c.
58 fig. 17.2	INE.5.430 (Storage Jar CA 21a): Killebrew 1996b, pl. 8:11; 1998a, fig. 4:11; 1999a, 303, Ill. II:18:11	ME-E (No. 146) Not Local to Miqne-Ekron		Surface 5082	Str. VIIIA (10B): 13th/12th c.
59 fig. 17.3	INE.36.219/75 (Storage Jar CA 21): Killebrew 1998a, fig. 10:23; 1999a, 303, Ills. II:26:23; III:15:20	ME-E (No. 149) Not Local to Miqne-Ekron		Surface 36081	Str. VIIA (9A): 12th c.

Table V: Revadim quarry fired-clay samples

Fig. No.	Quarry Clay & Petrographic Description	Similar to Ware Group	Petrographic No.: Publication
fig. 18	Wadi Clay Sample. Calcareous clay matrix with a moderate amount of well-sorted silt-sized quartz (5–10%) and a slightly smaller quantity of sub-rounded fine sandy quartz (ca. 5%); fired to a temperature of 700°C.	ME-B1	No. 137: Killebrew 1999a, 301; Ill. IV:1:2
fig. 19	Hamra Clay Sample. Non-calcareous clay matrix with a large amount of well-sorted sub-rounded sand-size quartz (>50%) and small quantities of chert, feldspar and limestone; fired to a temperature of 700°C.	ME-C	No. 136: Killebrew 1999a, 301; Ill. IV:1:1

Chapter Seven
Philistine Lion-Headed Cups: Aegean or Anatolian?

*Linda Meiberg**

Several sites in Israel have yielded a type of zoomorphic ceramic vessel whose lower part was molded into the shape of an animal's face that most resembles a lion, or more precisely, a lioness. The faint traces of bichrome decoration preserved in red and black paint, as well as the find contexts for those uncovered in systematic excavations, clearly indicate that these vessels are to be classified within the Philistine cultural sphere. Trude Dothan was the first to study these vessels as a class of object, concluding that they are closely related to lion-headed rhyta from the Bronze Age Aegean world and "seem to be the last echo of a long Mycenaean-Minoan tradition of animal-headed rhyta" (1982, 231). Although these "Philistine lion-headed cups" indeed appear to be closely related to lion-headed rhyta from the Bronze Age Aegean, they lack the essential secondary opening required in this class of vessel through which liquid would need to flow and drain. Uza Zevulun recognized this fact and persuasively argued against using the term "rhyta" when referring to these lion-headed cups (1983–1984; 1987). Nevertheless, the term "rhyta" for these vessels still pervades current literature (Herzog 1993, 483; Kochavi 1993, 1525; Stern 1993a, 358; 1994a, 94; 1995, 84; 1998a, 347–48; 2006, 387, fig. 1a; T. Dothan 1995, 49, fig. 3:10; Maeir and Ehrlich 2001, 29; Maeir 2003b, 242; 2006, 335, however see n. 1, 338) and, following Trude Dothan, many would like to draw parallels between Aegean Bronze Age

* The University of Pennsylvania, Philadelphia, PA 19104. Email: meiberg@sas.penn.edu.
This article is based on the talk I presented at the American Schools of Oriental Research annual meeting in 2005 in Philadelphia. Since the original presentation of this paper, another study has appeared that essentially supports the conclusions reached here (Zuckerman 2008). I am very grateful to my advisors, Philip Betancourt and Robert Koehl, who helped me conceive and develop the ideas presented here.

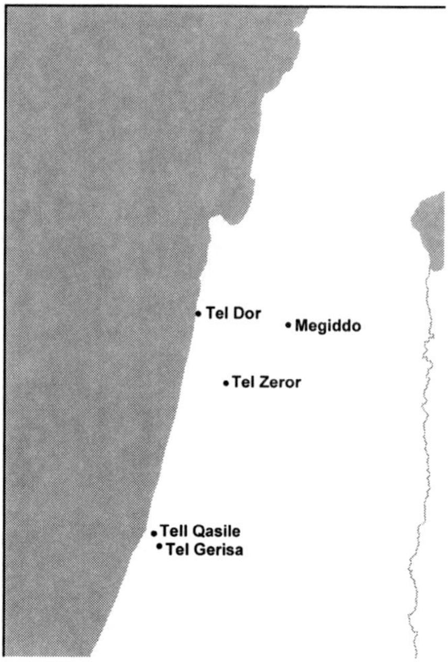

Fig. 1: Map of Israel.

rhyta and these Philistine lion-headed cups in order to infer an Aegean origin for the Philistines (A. Mazar 1980, 102; T. Dothan and Gitin 1990, 28; Barako 2000, 523; Yasur-Landau 2002, 339, 342–43).

This paper, however, will explore another possibility, that Philistine lion-headed cups are more closely related, both morphologically and functionally, to those of Bronze Age Anatolia and northern Syria, where various types of animal-headed cups have been found dating as early as the Old Assyrian Trading Colony period. As such, I will present an alternative view with regard to at least some of those who settled in Philistia and along the southern coastal plain in Israel during the early-twelfth century B.C.E.

Seven sites in Israel have yielded eight lion-headed cups: Tell eṣ-Ṣafi, Tel Dor, Tel Zeror, Megiddo, Tell Qasile, Tel Gerisa, and Tel Miqne-Ekron; each yielded one except for Tell eṣ-Ṣafi, which yielded two (fig. 1).

Tel Zeror is located in the northern part of the Sharon Plain approximately ten kilometers from the coast. The main area of excavation on the tell consists of a settlement that was founded in MB IIA and continued to the Roman period (Kochavi 1993, 1524). Strata XI (mid-twelfth to early-eleventh century B.C.E.) and X (second half of eleventh to mid-tenth century) are dated to the early Iron Age

(Ohata 1970, 12–13). The material culture represented in these two strata attests that the site was occupied by one of the Sea Peoples, possibly the Sikil, who settled at nearby Dor. The cemetery, which is situated 150 meters northwest of the tell, yielded several varying types of graves including nine stone-built cist tombs that are dated by their finds, such as typical Philistine pottery, to Iron Age I (Kochavi 1993, 1524). Included among the finds is a partially restored lion-headed cup whose context within the Iron I cemetery is unclear (Ohata 1970, 72). The cup (fig. 2) was produced in reddish-brown clay. The ears, eyes, nose, and mouth are delicately molded, and a single handle extends from the left temple to the base. Although its surface is badly worn, traces of paint are still discernable and include a checkerboard pattern, a common Philistine motif, framing the preserved right side of the face, as well as black dots on the muzzle suggesting whiskers. No doubt the cup was originally painted all over as shall be seen on other examples (Ohata 1970, 72; T. Dothan 1982, 229).

Tel Dor lies some 20 kilometers north of Tel Zeror. According to Stern, two phases of occupation may be attributed to the Sikil—the earlier represented in Phase 10 in Area G and the later represented in Phase 9 in Area G and Phase 12 in Area B1 (1998a, 348). Area E on the western side of the tell yielded an unstratified fragment of "a decorated lion's head rhyton of the type known from other Philistine sites" (Stern 1993a, 358; 1994a, fig. 48 on left; 1995, 84; 1998a, 347–48). The fragment (fig. 3) preserves only the area around the animal's muzzle. Painted patterns in bichrome decoration include vertical stripes below the mouth and across the bridge of the nose as well as dots suggestive of whiskers.[1]

Megiddo was excavated extensively by the Oriental Institute of the University of Chicago and many of the objects were sent to Chicago for study. Upon examination of the material in storage at the Institute, Benjamin Mazar identified one of the unstratified and unpublished pottery finds as a vessel in the shape of a lion's head (T. Dothan 1982, 229 n. 30). The cup (fig. 4) is fragmented and only the upper part of the head with ears, eyes, and part of the nose survive enough to discern that it was probably a lion (T. Dothan 1982, 229). Since the lower part of the vessel is not preserved, it cannot be stated with any certainty that this was not a rhyton, although this supposition seems unlikely. A single handle extends from the right temple and was probably attached to the cup's lost rim. The ears and eyes are molded and accentuated by red paint while the rest of the cup is densely covered in bichrome geometric motifs. These designs include a net pattern, elongated triangles, alternating triangles, and chevrons. The motifs, especially the net pattern, are characteristic of the Philistine pottery from Megiddo (T. Dothan 1982, 229–31).

1. I am indebted to Ayelet Gilboa for bringing this example to my attention.

Fig. 2: Tel Zeror lion-headed cup (height 12 cm; 67–386; courtesy of the Israel Antiquities Authority).

Tell Qasile is located on the north bank of the Yarkon River about two kilometers east of its estuary. A Philistine city was founded at the site on virgin soil in the twelfth century B.C.E. The earliest strata (XII, XI, and X) are dated to Iron I. Stratum XI in Area C consisted of a temple complex (Building 200) flanked by a spacious courtyard. On the north side of the courtyard was a favissa or pit for cultic offering (A. Mazar 1993b, 1208). It was within this favissa that the only example of a complete Philistine lion-headed cup was found to-date (fig. 5). The vessel was wheel-made as a one-handled cup of reddish-brown clay. Raised plastic decoration was added to the vessel's bottom to emulate the lion's features which were then enhanced with red and black paint. The style of the animal's face

Fig. 3: Tel Dor lion-headed cup (with permission of Ephraim Stern).

Fig. 4: Tel Megiddo lion-headed cup (A 13533; courtesy of the Oriental Institute of the University of Chicago).

departs from the more naturalistic convention seen on the previous cups. The molded features consist of two small ears, elliptical eyes, and a thickened mouth with a projecting tongue, and what appear to be four teeth or fangs. The cheeks are outlined in black and curiously emphasized by a star pattern, while the nose is represented by a long flat ridge decorated with stripes. A bichrome frieze of geometric designs decorates the body of the vessel, including a double-spiral pattern, a hallmark of Philistine pottery (A. Mazar 1980, 101–2).

Tel Gerisa is situated on the banks of the Yarkon River about two kilometers east of Tell Qasile. The few structures and pottery remains belonging to the early Iron Age strata point to this being a small Philistine village near the central city of Qasile (Herzog 1993, 484). Although the Gerisa material has yet to be published,

Fig. 5: Tell Qasile lion-headed cup (length 13.5 cm, height 12.8 cm; with permission of Amihai Mazar).

secondary sources state that a fragmentary lion-headed cup was uncovered in an Iron I stratum (A. Mazar 1980, 102). The fragment consists of the left eye and left cheek as well as nose and mouth (fig. 6). The features are molded and enhanced in red and brownish-black paint. The eye, the bridge of the nose, and the cheek are boldly outlined, and a net pattern is just barely discernable on the cheek. The mouth is slightly open and the tongue hangs out (T. Dothan 1982, 231). Although the depiction is quite schematic, this fragment should also be classified as a Philistine lion-headed cup.

Tel Miqne is located on the eastern border of the southern coastal plain in Philistia proper. The site has been conclusively equated with biblical Ekron, one of the five cities of the Philistine Pentapolis (T. Dothan and Gitin 1990, 24; 1993; T. Dothan 2000, 145). In the early Iron Age, during the first third of the twelfth century B.C.E., the Canaanite settlement ends and elements of a new material culture attributed to the Philistines suddenly appear (T. Dothan 1995, 42; 1998b, 151–52). One of these elements, in Field INE, is a series of superimposed shrines. In Stratum VI, in a disposal area adjacent to the shrine, typical Philistine bichrome pottery, zoomorphic and anthropomorphic figurines, and the fragment of what the excavators have called a "lion-headed rhyton" were uncovered (T. Dothan and Gitin 1993, 1053; T. Dothan 1995, 47–48, fig. 3:10; 1998b, 155, fig. 6). The vessel's molded features include large, bulging eyes consisting of two concentric circles and a protuberance at the top of the forehead running down the bridge of the nose (fig. 7). A long incision colored in red paint just under the nose represents the animal's mouth. Traces of red paint can also be discerned around the rest of the face. The two holes denoting nostrils do not communicate with the interior of the vessel (S. Gitin, personal communication) and, as such, the cup cannot be classified as a rhyton. However, the identification of the cup as lion-headed, albeit uncharacteristic, appears to be justified.

The final two lion-headed cups come from Tell eṣ-Ṣafi, located seven kilometers south of Tel Miqne in Philistia. The site was first excavated in 1899 by Bliss and Macalister. A fragment bearing the facial features of a lion, which no doubt belonged to a lion-headed cup, was apparently "found together with Philistine pottery, but not in a systematic excavation" (T. Dothan 1982, 231) since "the main finds of the excavations were discovered not in the stratigraphic excavation but in an old rubbish dump" (Stern 1993c, 1523). The naturalistic features of the animal (fig. 8), such as its ears, eyes, nose, and mouth were enhanced with filling ornaments in faint traces of red and black paint, including chevrons and horizontal lines. Dots decorate the area below the eyes and suggest whiskers (T. Dothan 1982, 231). Excavations at Tell eṣ-Ṣafi were renewed in the late 1990s by Aren Maeir of Bar-Ilan University. The finds, including the abundant amount of Philistine pottery, would seem to confirm the written sources that the site was biblical

Fig. 6: Tel Gerisa lion-headed cup (with permission of Ze'ev Herzog).

Fig. 7: Tel Miqne-Ekron lion-headed cup (length [top to bottom over the front] 5.6 cm, height [top to bottom over the back] 5.1 cm, width [from the nose to the back] 2.4 cm; with permission of Trude Dothan).

Gath, one of the five cities of the Philistine Pentapolis (Maeir and Ehrlich 2001, 25; Maeir 2003b, 246; 2006, 335). Temporary Stratum 6 in Area A yielded the face of a second lion-headed cup dated by the excavators to late Iron Age I (Maeir 2003b, 242; 2006, 335). As with all of the previous examples, the ears, eyes, nose, and mouth are molded onto the bottom of the vessel (fig. 9). Red and black paint

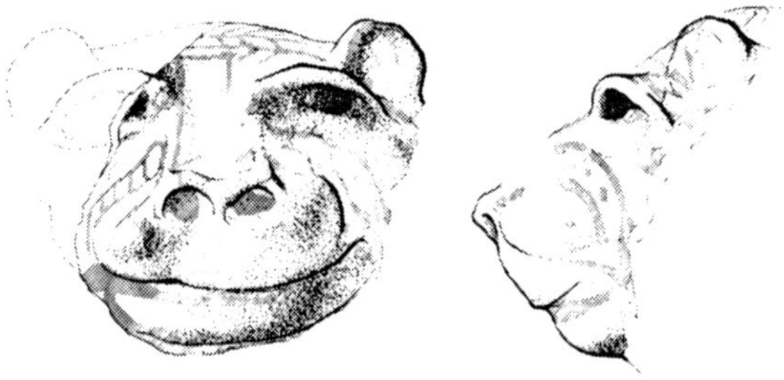

Fig. 8: Tel eṣ-Ṣafi lion-headed cup (height 8.0 cm; 69.9.121; courtesy of the Israel Museum, Jerusalem).

Fig. 9: Tel eṣ-Ṣafi (renewed excavations) lion-headed cup (with permission of Aren Maeir).

was added to enhance the features, including what appear to be whiskers, while a net pattern decorates the bridge of the nose (Maeir 2006, 338).

All of these elements—the molded features, bichrome decoration, and single handle where preserved, as well as find contexts within the early Iron Age—clearly show that all eight[2] of these vessels belong to the same artistic tradition,

2. A complete lion-headed cup was uncovered in 2007 during Israel Antiquities Authority

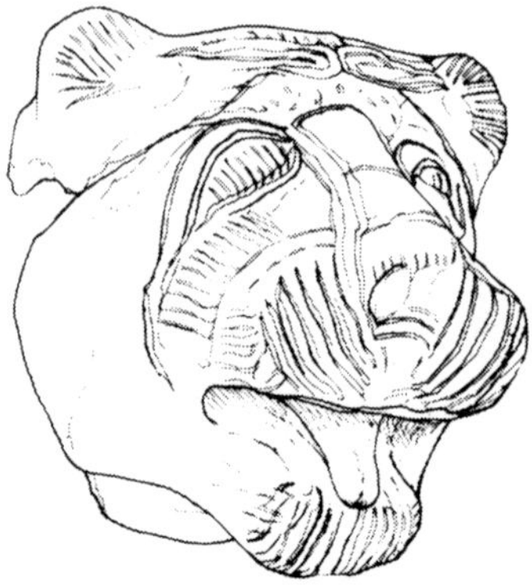

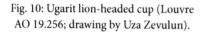

Fig. 10: Ugarit lion-headed cup (Louvre AO 19.256; drawing by Uza Zevulun).

Fig. 11: Ugarit lion-headed cup (height 16.2 cm; RS 16.052; drawing by Uza Zevulun).

which can be attributed to the Philistines or, as in the case of the Tel Zeror and Tel Dor cups, to one of the Sea Peoples.

Uza Zevulun (1987, 104) suggests that the origin of the Philistine lion-headed cups should not be sought in the Aegean world but that it should be viewed as a Syro-Canaanite tradition whose inspiration comes from northern Syria. She cites three Late Bronze examples from Ugarit upon which she draws parallels to the Philistine lion-headed cups (1987, 94–95).[3]

The first was uncovered in the northeastern area of the upper city in a subterranean funerary chamber below one of the houses and dates to the fourteenth century B.C.E. (Schaeffer 1938, 194–96, pl. XIX:1). Only the lion's face has survived while the body of the cup, which once bore a handle, has not (fig. 10). Fashioned in terracotta, the ears, eyes, nose, and mouth were molded. The animal's gaping jaws display its tongue thrust out as on the Qasile and Gerisa examples. Deep and shallow incisions enhance these features, and shorter incisions covering the rest of the face may indicate hair (Zevulun 1987, 96).

---

salvage excavations at the site of Nahal Patish in the northern Negev. An article on the cup by Pirhiya Nahshoni and Linda Meiberg is forthcoming.

3. An example of a lion-headed vessel made of Baltic amber (not ivory as previously thought) was uncovered in the 2002 season of excavations at Qatna in the main chamber of the royal tomb (al-Maqdissi et al. 2003, fig. 12). It has been dated to ca. 1400 B.C.E. and fits nicely in the chronological framework outlined here. I would like to thank Jack Green for bringing this example to my attention.

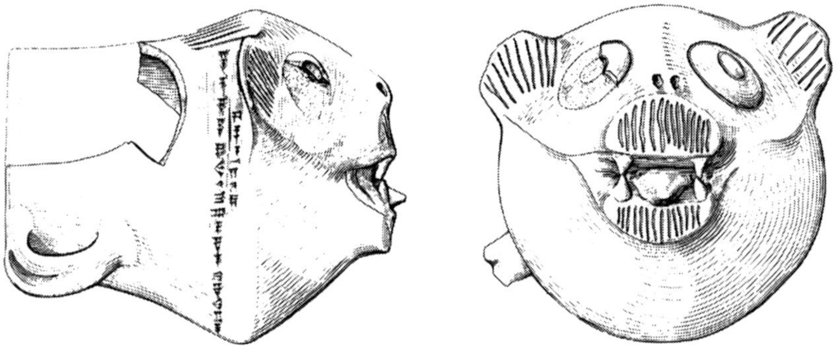

Fig. 12: Ugarit lion-headed cup (height 18.5 cm; RS 25.318; drawing by Uza Zevulun).

According to Yon (1997, 158, pl. 36a), the second lion-headed cup was uncovered in the Royal Palace and was locally fashioned in terracotta. However, she provides no date for the cup while other publications give a range to sometime between the fifteenth to thirteenth centuries B.C.E. (Kohlmeyer and Strommenger 1982, 139; Weiss 1985, 291). Nevertheless, this rather naturalistically rendered example is exceptional (fig. 11). The molded face is enhanced with details indicated by incision including lines suggestive of whiskers clearly visible beneath a barrel-shaped nose. The mouth is open but no tongue is indicated. At one time the almond-shaped eyes must have been inlaid and a single handle is preserved (Yon 1997, 158).

The third lion-headed cup from Ugarit had been "carefully deposited in a small cell built inside a room in a large private house" on the southern edge of the acropolis (Zevulun 1987, 96). The cup, also of terracotta, is dated to the thirteenth century B.C.E. and bears a dedicatory inscription mentioning the "Son of Agap-Sharri" which lends its name to the house (Schaeffer 1978, 149). More significant is the continuation of the inscription, which reads in Ugaritic "lion face," thereby identifying the very vessel on which the inscription is written (Zevulun 1987, 96–97). The facial features of this example are schematically rendered (fig. 12). The ears are pinched flat with incised lines on the inside. The eyes consist of two oval incisions, the smaller of which indicates a pupil. The gaping jaws, enhanced by vertical incisions, display a projecting tongue and two sets of fangs. A single handle is also preserved (Schaeffer 1978, 151–53; Zevulun 1987, 98).

Zevulun, in my opinion, is correct in tracing the influence of the early Iron Age Philistine lion-headed cups to Late Bronze examples from northern Syria rather than to the Aegean world. However, could not the Late Bronze lion-headed cups from Ugarit themselves have their roots in Minoan and Mycenaean proto-

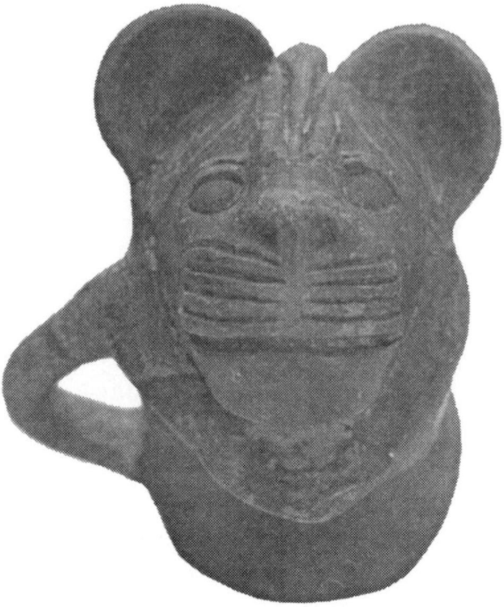

Fig. 13: Kültepe lion-headed cup (height 10.3 cm, width 14.0 cm; with permission of Fikri Kulakoğlu).

types? Many would argue that this indeed must be the case since contemporary examples of animal-headed rhyta, though none of a lion, were imported from the Aegean to Ugarit (Schaeffer 1949, 222–23, fig. 93:5–7) as well as locally reproduced (Schaeffer 1949, 220–21, fig. 92). Although this possibility cannot be ruled out, I propose looking elsewhere, that is, to Anatolia.

Zoomorphic vessels appearing in the shapes of different domestic and wild animals were known to have been produced in workshops at Kültepe-Karum Kanish (T. Özgüç 2002, 122). Excavations of Level Ia yielded an exquisite example of a one-handled lion-headed cup dated by the excavators to ca. 1730 B.C.E. (T. Özgüç 2002, no. 33). Fashioned in terracotta and painted with a red glaze (fig. 13), the head of the cup was skillfully molded to produce delicate, naturalistic features. The face is characterized by large, almond-shaped eyes and a wide flat nose with deep nostrils. The whiskers, mouth, and chin are emphasized by thick incised lines. Although some three centuries separate the Kültepe cup from the Ugarit cup (fig. 11), a comparison of the two speaks for itself.

Less naturalistic examples also exist. The animal-headed cup "found on the slope of Tell Atchana in 1953 by local village farmers," which is now in the Antakya Museum, may very well depict a lion (Yener 2005, 104). The animal's

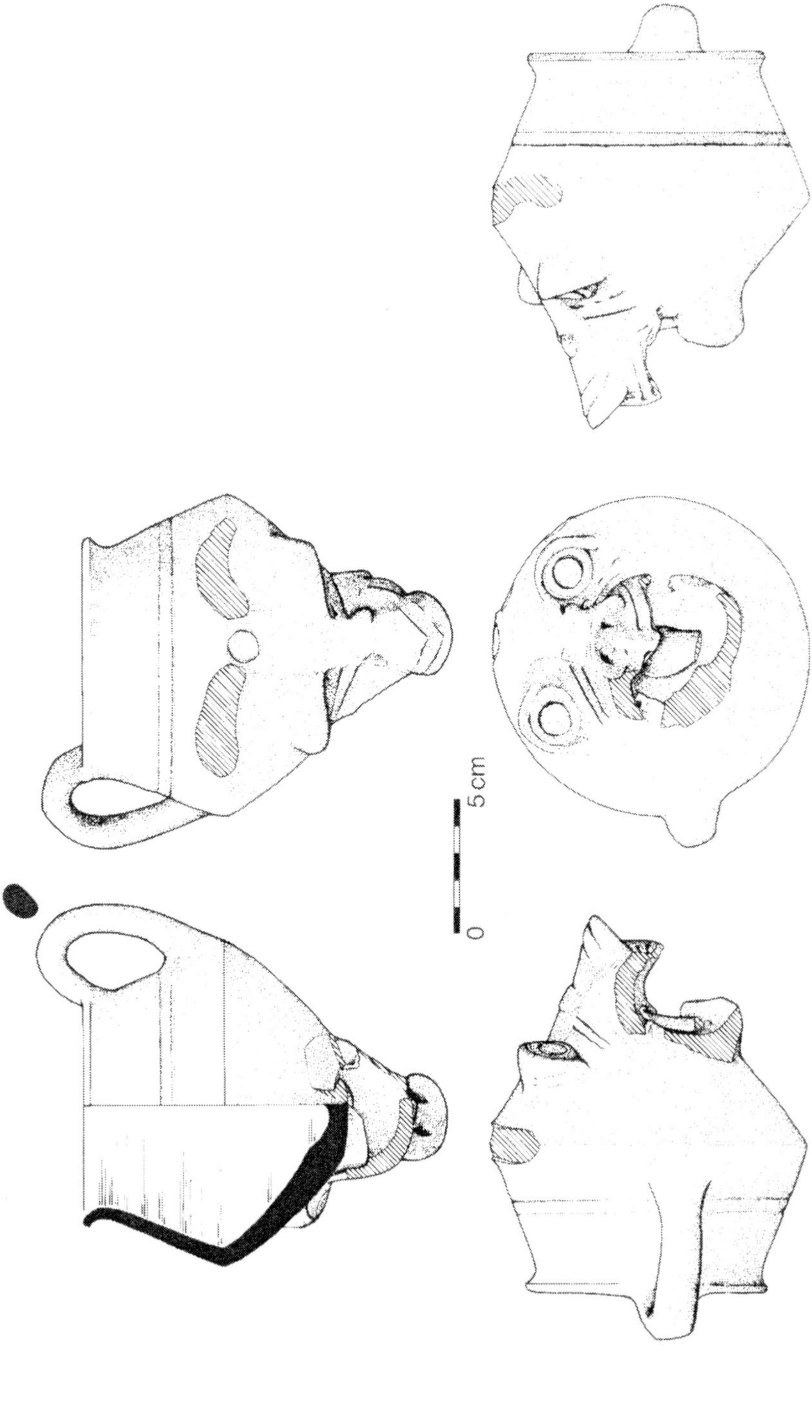

Fig. 14: Tell Atchana lion-headed cup (with permission of Aslihan Yener).

features are rather exaggerated and the lower jaw and ears are missing (fig. 14). However, traces of two incised lines below the molded snout that are still visible seem to denote whiskers. Wheelmade of terracotta with a single handle, it shares similar features with other lion-headed cups such as its gaping mouth and the protruding tongue that is partially preserved (Yener 2005, 104, pl. 8). Based on these stylistic grounds, the cup may be dated to the Old Hittite Kingdom period, approximately the time of Kültepe/Kanish Ia (Yener 2005, pl. 8).

The practice of fashioning drinking vessels into animal-headed cups appears to be a tradition that began in the Middle Bronze Age in Anatolia. For reasons unknown, lion-headed cups seem to be particularly popular. Toward the end of the Middle Bronze, the concept diffused, spreading to the Greek world where it was espoused, but altered by the addition of a secondary aperture to suit the functional requirements of the culture, i.e., the pouring of libations. Animal-headed rhyta from the shaft graves at Mycenae are a prime example of this. At the same time, this practice also spread southwards from Anatolia into northern Syria. Although we are lacking examples of lion-headed cups from the seventeenth and the sixteenth centuries B.C.E., this may simply be due to chances of archaeological discovery. However, the three lion-headed cups from Ugarit as well as the vessel from Qatna, dating from ca. 1500 to ca. 1300 B.C.E., attest to their popularity there.

It is my belief that the lion-headed cups from Philistine contexts belong to this originally Anatolian tradition. At the end of the Bronze Age with the collapse of palatial centers around the eastern Mediterranean basin and great movements of populations, the tradition was brought to Israel by those displaced northern Syrian people who perhaps joined other displaced people already on the move east and south. Once they had settled in the southern Levant and Philistia proper, they carried on their custom to the best that their ancestral memories enabled them to and embraced new elements which they now adopted into their artistic repertoire. As such, Philistine lion-headed cups should not be viewed as "the last echo of a long Mycenaean-Minoan tradition of animal-headed rhyta" (T. Dothan 1982, 231), but as that of an Anatolian one.

Chapter Eight
A Few Tomb Groups from Tell el-Far'ah South

*Sabine Laemmel**

Starting from the premise that political and/or socioeconomical changes in ancient societies are to some extent reflected in contemporary material culture, this paper will examine how the transition from the Late Bronze to the early Iron Age (from the late-thirteenth/early-twelfth to the mid-eleventh centuries B.C.E.) at the southern border of Canaan manifested itself in the material remains from the peripheral site of Tell el-Far'ah South in the Negev. Although the importance of Tell el-Far'ah is relevant to other significant aspects of the region's history and archaeology at that time, such as the relationship between the southern Levant and Egypt, the emphasis here will be placed on the controversial episode of the emergence of the Sea Peoples in the region and what is generally seen as the settlement of foreign populations in the area.

The basis for the present study consists of pottery assemblages from a few tomb groups recovered from the Far'ah cemeteries. Before entering the discussion, however, a short review of these cemeteries is necessary in order to place the tombs and their furnishings within their general context.

---

* Freelance archaeologist. Email: sabinelaemmel@yahoo.fr. This paper was originally prepared for the 2001 workshop on the Philistines and other Sea Peoples, held at the University of Haifa and Ben Gurion University of the Negev. At the time, I was a DPhil candidate at the University of Oxford and this work formed part of my doctoral research. As such, the bibliography in this article may not include all of the most recent literature on the subject (see also Laemmel 2009). I take this opportunity to thank Dr. Susan Sherratt for her comments on the original paper.

The Site and the Cemeteries

The site of Tell el-Far'ah lies about 25 kilometers southeast of Gaza and 26 kilometers west of Beer Sheva on the southern coast of Palestine, at the border of the Negev Desert to the east and the coastal plain, with higher rainfalls to the north and west (Gazit 1996, 9). The tell, situated on the right bank of the Wadi Ghuzzeh (Nahal Besor), was first investigated by W. M. F. Petrie in the course of two seasons of excavations, the first from late fall 1927 to spring 1928 and the second during the winter of 1928–1929 (Petrie 1930; Starkey and Harding 1932; Albright 1929). The settlement itself, on the summit of the mound, yielded evidence for an almost continuous occupation from the Middle Bronze Age to the Roman period and a series of eight graveyards were also identified, scattered around the tell. With the exception of the Cemetery 900,[1] which was cut into the hard marl of the west slope of the Middle Bronze Age defense system, all the cemeteries from Tell el-Far'ah were situated in the surrounding plain on the right bank of the wadi, at a distance varying from about 100 meters to about 350 meters from the edges of the tell (Petrie 1930, pl. 51).

The various cemeteries range in date from the Middle Bronze Age to the Hellenistic period.[2] Some remained in use over a very long period of time, occasionally with significant interruptions, as in the case of the Cemetery 500, where the series of Middle Bronze Age graves (Price Williams 1977) is accompanied by a group of early Iron Age tombs. Out of the eight graveyards, only Cemeteries 900 and 1000 seem to have remained in use over a well delimited and continuous period of time, the former in the final phase of the Late Bronze through very early Iron Age and the latter in the Middle Bronze IIC period. None of the cemeteries displayed any consistency in tomb orientation. The graves were usually arranged in close clusters with later tombs occasionally cutting through earlier ones.

The Middle Bronze II period, which corresponds to the first period of settlement on the tell, is represented by a significant number of graves in the 500 cemetery, all those of Cemetery 1000 and twelve additional ones in Cemetery 700. The Late Bronze I period is only attested by a few graves in Cemetery 600 (Tombs 610–614, 618, 624, and 657). In contrast, the end of the Late Bronze II and early Iron Age (end of the thirteenth–end of the eleventh centuries B.C.E.) are probably

---

1. Petrie named the clusters of tombs he discovered at Tell el-Far'ah Cemetery 100, Cemetery 200, Cemetery 300, etc. This allowed him to allocate successive numbers to individual tombs while tracking to which cemetery each belonged (e.g., Tomb 105 belonged to Cemetery 100 and Tomb 523 to Cemetery 500).

2. For a discussion of the date of the individual cemeteries, see, e.g., McClellan 1975, 176–84; Yisraeli 1993.

the best represented periods within the Tell el-Far'ah graveyards with tombs in every cemetery with the exception of Cemeteries 700 and 1000. In Iron IB and II, continuing into the Persian period, Cemetery 200 developed extensively and tombs were also added in the areas of Cemeteries 800 and 700. Some of the Iron II tombs from Cemeteries 200 and 700 bear witness to the introduction of cremation burials in local funerary customs. Among the burials of the Persian period, Tomb 650, which yielded among other things the frames of a metal couch, a stool, and a fine bronze drinking set (Petrie 1930, 14, pls. 44–46; Iliffe 1935; Yisraeli 1993, 444), is remarkable for its display of wealth. Other graves belonging to the same period in Cemeteries 700 and 800 stand out by virtue of the recurrent presence of metal goods and by the lack of pottery vessels. Finally, only a few tombs, scattered in Cemeteries 100 and 700, may belong to the Hellenistic period, but after that time all eight graveyards apparently fell into disuse.

The Late Bronze II and early Iron Age graves at Tell el-Far'ah reflect a certain variety of tomb types and burial practices. The most common are the pit or shaft graves, which appear in all cemeteries of this period.[3] They consist of simple rectangular pits or shafts dug into the ground or, in the case of the 900 cemetery, into the slope of the abandoned western defense ditch. Those located in the plain were often lined with mud or stones. In most cases, these simple shafts contained only a single individual, though some had two, three, or up to four bodies. Tomb 534, which housed eleven burials, constitutes an exception at Tell el-Far'ah. It is also a simple shaft tomb, but the bodies here were deposited in successive layers. Its upper burial layer held five individuals, laid side by side.

A second well-known and often discussed tomb type at Tell el-Far'ah is the chamber tomb, which appears in Cemeteries 900 and 500. Although they all share the same basic characteristics, these tombs exhibit a variety in shape and structural details. They were simply dug into the flat or sloping ground and were accessed by a sloping or stepped "dromos" opening into the main chamber. In Cemetery 900 the burial chambers are rectangular, rounded, bilobate, or trapezoidal, sometimes with recesses in the walls, while all five chamber tombs of Cemetery 500 are trapezoidal in shape, with an additional small burial chamber at the rear in two cases (Tombs 542 and 552). All the chambers of the Cemetery 500 burials, as well as Tombs 902, 905, and 914 have an irregular depression cut in their center, leaving wide bench-like features along their side ledges. As a rule, the chamber tombs were designed to receive several bodies, which were laid either on benches or the floor in a more or less orderly manner.

Three anthropoid clay sarcophagi were found in chamber Tombs 552, 562 (Petrie 1930, 8, pl. 24), and 935 (Starkey and Harding 1932, 25), although the

3. For Late Bronze Age pit graves, see Gonen 1992, 70, 96–97.

number of individuals they contained at the time of their discovery is unspecified. These sarcophagi appear as large containers with a lid modelled in the shape of a human face. Similar sarcophagi, sometimes containing up to six individuals, were found in association with Late Bronze material at Deir el-Balah (T. Dothan 1979). Other Palestinian anthropoid clay coffins are known from Beth Shean (Oren 1973, 132–50, figs. 78–84) and Lachish (Tufnell 1958, 131–32, pls. 45:1–2, 46). In Jordan, they were found at Pella (Yassine 1975) and, in later contexts, at the Amman citadel (Yassine 1988, 33–46), Sahab (Albright 1932a), and Dhiban in Tomb J3 (Reed 1964, 57–60, pls. 52–53).[4] For some time, these clay coffins were linked to the arrival of Sea Peoples in the Levant, but later research showed that they should be considered as the product of an Egyptian influence in the region.[5]

Unfortunately, little can be said of the burial customs at Tell el-Far'ah. The contextual information recorded by Petrie at the time of the excavations is particularly scant. Only in rare cases did he specify the position or the sex of the bodies, though he seems to have regularly noted when a skeleton was that of a child (easily recognizable by their small size). In effect, a fair number of children's bodies appear in his notes, either sharing the tomb with an adult or in a grave of their own. The number of bodies within a single grave and their position therein can only be specified in the few cases when a drawing of the tomb and its contents was sketched on the back of the tomb card. In his publication (Petrie 1930), only the drawing and general description of the larger chamber tombs appear. These drawings show that, in undisturbed chamber tombs (whether those of the 900 or 500 cemetery), individuals were laid on their backs with their hands joined on their pelvis, or laid straight along their sides (as in Tomb 532) with heads looking up or turned to the side. In the smaller pit-graves, bodies were laid out in a similar manner or in a crouching position. When two or more bodies occupied a single shaft, the remains of the earlier burial(s) were swept aside, or the new body was placed head to foot with the latter.

Considered as a whole, the furnishings found in the Late Bronze and early Iron Age tombs at Tell el-Far'ah illustrate the richness and diversity of the contem-

4. See also Weippert 1988, 366–73.

5. Anthropoid clay coffins were also found in Egypt at the site of Tell Nebesheh, Tell el-Yahudiyeh, Kôm Abu Billou, and Tell el-Dab'a in the Nile Delta (Petrie, Murray, and Griffith 1888, 20–21; Naville and Griffith 1890, 16–17, pls. 12:2, 13, 14:1–2; Leclant 1971, 227, figs. 8–9; Bietak 1984, 139). However, they are also known from other areas of Egypt and its provinces in the New Kingdom. They occur at Gurob (Brunton and Engelbach 1927, 9–17, pl. 18); Riqqeh (Engelbach 1915, 18, pl. 19:1); Rifeh, southwest of Asyut (Petrie 1907, 22, pl. 27B); and at Aniba in Nubia (Steindorff 1937, 72–73, pls. 39–40). A detailed reassessment and analysis of Egyptian clay coffins can be found in Cotelle-Michel 2004. For a discussion of anthropoid coffins in Palestine and their possible origins, see also Gonen 1992, 28–30, with bibliography.

porary material culture and the variety of its influences and origins. No doubt, careful investigation of the funerary assemblages and of the nature of individual artifacts may shed light on the cultural makeup of the inhabitants and its changes over time. One obstacle however, should be kept in mind, namely, that, more than seventy years after Petrie's excavations, the furnishing of many of the tombs cannot be reconstructed with certainty. After it was brought to light, the material from the site and from the tombs was distributed to different museums and institutions (in England, the United States, and Japan) in recompense for helping finance the expedition. Over the years, the collections have been moved from place to place, for example, in London, from the Palestine Exploration Society to the Institute of Archaeology of University College, London. Other assemblages have been brought to one institution from another, as in the case of the Jewish Museum in New York who, in the 1970s, acquired the Tell el-Far'ah tomb groups that had originally been sent to New York University. It is also the case that material has been lost or damaged, such as two tomb groups in Hull, which were destroyed by German bombs in World War II.

Besides the complicated distribution of this material, another and perhaps more acute difficulty inherent in any attempt to reassess the tombs' furnishings lies in the fact that, in many cases, the data published in the excavation reports do not match either the information recorded in the original field notes or what is actually preserved in museums. In light of these difficulties, the safest option is to base any discussion mainly on what remains physically available to be studied. The missing items mentioned either in the tomb cards or in Petrie's notes and records can only be considered as accessory information.

This unsatisfying and somewhat frustrating situation, where original data and information are both incomplete and scant, triggers the need for a rigorous theoretical and methodological framework, which, in other circumstances, might be thought superfluous.

A Few Theoretical Premises

Before proceeding further with the discussion of the material from the tombs, a few remarks should be made on some methodological and mainly theoretical issues that underlie historical and archaeological analyses in general and the interpretation of the troubled period of the twelfth century B.C.E. in the eastern Mediterranean in particular. The foundation for the traditional historical reconstruction of this region and period, including the eruption of a foreign population of Aegean origin and their settlement in southern Canaan, lies essentially in the interpretation of rare contemporary literary sources, which mainly consist of

Egyptian "propaganda" texts (such as the Papyrus Harris I and the Medinet Habu temple reliefs) and in the series of Ugaritic letters exchanged between the rulers and officials of the eastern Mediterranean.[6] In the archaeological record, these events are usually believed to be represented by such things as the presence of destruction layers at a number of sites and by the introduction of new and foreign elements in the local material culture, particularly the pottery. However, the reading of the written records mentioned above, as well as the understanding of their accompanying reliefs, confronts us with two major problems of interpretation.

The reliability of these texts and monuments as historical record has long been questioned, not only because they are scarce and relatively uninformative,[7] but also because their original purpose was likely to be quite different from that of a historical record. As argued by some text specialists, ancient Near Eastern texts and their distinctive rhetoric have actually more to do with ideologies and propaganda than with historical facts, in a modern understanding of the term, and, consequently, the nature of the information they provide cannot be taken at face value.[8] These texts were the product of and produced for a small, unrepresentative and privileged social group and are more likely to reflect the ideological beliefs of the latter than actual events. When overlooking the function of these documents as expressions of ideological or political statements, modern scholars make themselves "the champions (…) of the ancient rulers and the social order that served them" (Baines 1996, 342).

If the validity of this point is relatively widely accepted among texts specialists, who acknowledge the many levels of significance pertaining to ancient textual documents, such cautionary approach has often been neglected in the field of archaeological research, and the archaeological evidence of Late Bronze and early Iron Age Near Eastern sites has often been too readily associated with what the texts say.[9] This approach, which basically consists in adapting material remains to a preconceived historical scenario, has often led to rather confusing situations where things do not always find appropriate explanations because, in this process, the empirical object is too easily deprived of any potential for interpretation, thus preempting any alternative suggestions.

---

6. E.g., Gustav Lehmann 1983.

7. As pointed out by Bauer (1998, 151), this element was already emphasized by Sandars more than three decades ago (1978, 120).

8. These reservations about the value of ancient texts as historical documents do not put into question their potential for the study of the political ideologies (and other sorts of ideologies) of their authors and the cultural contexts in which they lived (Liverani 1988, 55–61).

9. For example, see Niemeyer's conclusions that "there are no doubts about the event (attack of the Sea Peoples on the Levant) having taken place" (Niemeyer 2000, 92).

Instead of considering material culture and the changes therein from the view of a modern-style political history, what needs to be done is to start from the bottom up, by considering the actual physical evidence within its own context and working upwards from there to a wider picture. To this end, the object has to be considered in its own terms, in its multiple intrinsic and interactive aspects, such as its technological, stylistic, functional, and cultural dimensions.

The tendency to adapt material remains to an historical framework is quite frequently encountered in Near Eastern archaeology (including Cypriot archaeology) and that is typically the case of the Mycenaean-style pottery in the Late Bronze and early Iron Age (particularly with reference to the question that is addressed in this volume). On Cyprus, this is well exemplified by the way in which the presence of a locally produced Mycenaean-style pottery, identified in the post-destruction layers of a number of sites such as Enkomi or Kition, was interpreted by the excavators as representing the arrival of groups of Achaean colonists sometime around 1200 B.C.E. (the date proposed for this event may vary significantly depending on the author).[10] However, it has now been shown that much of the archaeological evidence does not really fit into this long-held historical picture. In effect, a number of scholars have demonstrated that pottery imitating Mycenaean shapes and decoration on Cyprus, White-Painted Wheelmade III (WPW III), was not a sudden innovation in LC IIIA, but that it progressively developed in the course of the Late Cypriot IIC period. Moreover, although this pottery class has an undeniable Mycenaean look to it, it also incorporates, from the start, many traditional Cypriot elements that would not make sense in the case of a large-scale invasion of the island. WPW III also appears at sites that otherwise present no signs of intruders, such as Alassa-Pano Mandilaris, for example, which was not destroyed at any time during the LC IIC or LC IIIA (Hadjisavvas 1991). The gradual increase of WPW III noticeable at Cypriot sites over this period is more likely to find a suitable explanation in socioeconomical considerations than in some time-specific political or military event.

10. This pottery appearing in the aftermath of the LC IIC destructions was first called Myc IIIC (1a, 1b, 1c) after Furumark's terminology for Mycenaean pottery, which was later abandoned for its unsuitability in the Aegean, but remained in use in Cyprus and in the Levant (see Kling 1989). Regarding chronology, see Manning et al. 2001 for a series of radiocarbon determinations from a number of Cypriot sites which seems to confirm the traditional date of ca. 1200 B.C.E. for the transition from LC IIC/LC IIIA. (I thank S. Sherratt for pointing out this reference to me.)

The "Sea Peoples" and Mycenaean IIIC

The situation on Cyprus is not without significance for the Levantine mainland, because a similar scenario, featuring violent conquest by foreign populations, is often assumed there. Here as well, the presence of newcomers of notably Aegean origin and commonly identified with the "Sea Peoples" of the Egyptian records[11] was advanced on the basis of destruction horizons at a number of sites, the appearance of a locally made Mycenaean type pottery (here called Myc IIIC),[12] and other changes relating to urbanism, architectural features (e.g., A. Mazar 1991, 97; Noort 1994; T. Dothan 1995; Barako 2000; Strange 2000; Sharon 2001a, 581–82; Killebrew 2005, 197–246), and even dietary customs (Hesse 1986; Hesse and Wapnish 1997; Killebrew and Lev-Tov 2008). However, a closer look at this ceramic material and at the contexts of its occurrences reveals a picture that is not as tidy and straightforward as is usually suggested in the literature. The context of its emergence on the Near Eastern coastland is far from homogenous and seems to reflect much more complex cultural processes than some mass invasions from the west or northwest. The fact that at the Philistine sites of Ashdod and Tel Miqne-Ekron, Myc IIIC appears in post-destruction horizons is systematically emphasized in order to support the invasion theory (but see Killebrew, this volume).[13] However the neat and clear-cut story suggested by the stratigraphy of these two sites, when compared to other contemporary settlements with Myc IIIC pottery, reveals a number of uncertainties which are difficult to explain in a traditional way. Myc IIIC or related wares, although sometimes in limited quantities, have been reported from many sites along the eastern Mediterranean coast. They are mentioned at: Troy (Bittel 1983, 38–39), Tarsus (Goldman 1956, 227–29, figs. 336–337; 1963, fig. 57:74) in the ʿAmuq (Swift 1958, 71–79); at Ras Ibn Hani (Bounni et al. 1978, 246, fig. 28; Bounni et al. 1979, 245–57, figs. 19:11–12, 14, 25:1–2, 7–12; Bounni and Lagarce 1989, 94) and Ras el-Basit in Syria (Courbin 1986–1987, 108–9); Tell Sukas (Riis 1961–1962, 140; 1973, 204–5), Sarepta (Anderson 1988, 273, pls. 28:19, 30:10; Koehl 1985, 44–45, 119–22, figs. 20:192–96, 21:197–99; Herscher 1975, 90–91, fig. 26:4–5), Byblos (Salles 1980,

---

11. Or, as Strange puts it, "There is today an agreement that the Sea Peoples came from the Balkans and the Aegean world, with Cyprus as the last stop on their way before the invasion into the Levant" (Strange 2000, 129).

12. See Asaro, Perlman, and M. Dothan 1971; Gunneweg et al. 1986; Killebrew, this volume.

13. Barako 2000, 520–22; Stone 1995, 14. However at Tel Miqne-Ekron, a one-meter-thick accumulation of occupation debris, comprising four successive floors and architecture, probably indicating some kind of industrial activity, separated the LB II destruction layer from the first levels containing the locally made Myc IIIC in Area INE.5 (Killebrew 1998a, 381–83; 1998b, 163–64; and this volume).

30, 66, pls. 11:2a–b, 7a–c, 10:9), and Tyre (Bikai 1978, 65–66, pl. 39:20) in Lebanon; as well as at Akko (M. Dothan 1981a) and Tell Keisan (Briend and Humbert 1980, 229–30, fig. 56; Balensi 1981, 399–400) in Israel. They also occur at the inland site of Beth Shean, in Lower Stratum VI (James 1966, pl. 49:4; Hankey 1967, 127–28; A. Mazar 1993b, 216; 1997a, 71). In the case of some of these sites, it seems that the Myc IIIC was imported from Cyprus. This is likely so at Beth Shean (A. Mazar 1993b, 216; Sherratt and Mazar, this volume) and certainly so at Tell Keisan (Gunneweg and Perlman 1994). On the other hand, for most of the remaining sites, like Ras el-Basit and Ras Ibn Hani, Akko and Sarepta, it has been argued that Aegeanizing pottery, or at least part of it, was locally produced, just as at Ashdod or Tel Miqne. At Sarepta notably, Myc IIIC was found in an industrial quarter and even inside a pottery kiln in Area II, X.[14] The presence of Aegeanizing ware, similar in character to that found at the two excavated cities of the Pentapolis, was explained by proposing that other Sea Peoples, the Sherden and the Shekelesh, established themselves in some sites on the Syrian coast, more or less contemporaneously with the first settlements of the Philistines in the south. As in the southern Canaanite sites, the settlement process in Syria is thought to have started with the violent destruction of the Late Bronze cities. The light constructions that leaned on the ruined walls of the large buildings of palatial character at Ras el-Basit and Ras Ibn Hani during the Late Bronze Age, and in which Myc IIIC pottery was found, are generally seen as a sign of the arrival of newcomers, who as in southern Canaan started to manufacture the traditional pottery wares of their homeland(s).

With regards to ware definition, several reports, in particular those of Ashdod (e.g., M. Dothan and Porath 1993; M. Dothan and Ben-Shlomo 2005) and Tel Miqne-Ekron (e.g., T. Dothan and Zukerman 2004; Killebrew, this volume; Mountjoy, this volume), have provided good physical descriptions of Myc IIIC, a representative sample of pots appear in line drawings and a few are photographed (though usually in black and white; see also Ben-Shlomo 2006 for a recent overview). These, compared with the description we have from other sites further north, show that Myc IIIC fabrics display a certain degree of variation in aspect and texture.[15] However, a few proposed identifications have been made of Myc IIIC sherds at sites where, according to the dominating historical scenario, they ought not to be. Israel Finkelstein (1998; 2000, 164, with references) and, before him, Bunimovitz and Zimhoni (1993, 111), have mentioned a number of settle-

14. Kiln G. The kilns of Area II, X at Sarepta represent a large and conspicuous industry, lasting from at least the mid-fifteenth to the fifth/fourth centuries B.C.E., see Anderson 1989.

15. A. Mazar for example has expressly emphasized the difficulty of identifying Myc IIIC (A. Mazar in Gitin, Mazar, and Stern 1998, 185).

ments, outside the limits of the Pentapolis, which may have yielded some Myc IIIC Ware. To date, the list of these controversial locations includes Tel Eitun, Tell Jerishe, Tel Haror, Tel Sippor, Gezer, and Tell el-Hesi. Nothing can really be said about the first two sites, because the material identified as Myc IIIC here has not been published. The sherds from Tel Haror come from an apparently mixed context and are so small and so few that they are difficult to ascribe in a conclusive manner to any definite pottery class.[16] However, the remaining sites all yielded a number of two-handled carinated or bell-shaped bowls decorated with plain red or brown painted bands (e.g., Matthers 1989, 61–62, fig. 13; Dever 1986, 202–3, pls. 20:19, 21:19; Biran and Negbi 1966, fig. 6:1–3). Only line drawings of these pieces are available, but their shape, decoration, and description often fit those of some Myc IIIC bowls from Ashdod XIIIb and Tel Miqne-Ekron, which continue to appear side by side with the earliest appearance of Bichrome Ware in the later part of the twelfth and first half of the eleventh century.

The geographically widespread occurrences of Myc IIIC along the Levantine coast, the diversity of its accompanying contextual data, the important stylistic and technological variety of the ware itself (both within and between sites), and its often-cited resemblance to the Cypriot WPW III are all elements pointing to the highly complex nature of this pottery and its transmission. Now, considered in its own terms, the appearance of the Aegean-style Myc IIIC in the early twelfth-century eastern Mediterranean and the other phenomena that are occasionally related to it (destruction layers, changes in urbanism, architecture, foodways, etc.), are quite likely to reflect something rather more complicated than the traditional scenario of Sea Peoples' invasions or mass migrations. The interpretation of Myc IIIC and all that goes with it as the material manifestation of a specific event (or, for that matter, a chain of events) is a daring move, implying that short-term politico-historical shifts have a direct translation to material culture, particularly pottery.[17] In fact, many ethnographic and archaeological studies have clearly shown that changes in material culture (and perhaps particularly in pottery) are slow processes that are liable to be affected by a great variety of factors, mostly relevant to modifications of social makeup, varying modes of cultural interaction, environment, and technological traditions (e.g., McGovern 1986).

---

16. These sherds were found, together with, among others, Philistine Bichrome Ware in a pit that was ascribed to Stratum B4–B2 (Oren 1993, 582–83; Sharon 2001a, 582). During the 2001 workshop, participants were shown these unpublished fragments from Tel Haror by E. Oren, at the Ben Gurion University of the Negev.

17. For examples of direct inconsistencies between pottery models and documented historical facts, see, e.g., Lambrou-Phillipson 1993, 365.

The Graves of Tell el-Far'ah

In the light of these considerations, I would like to present here the ceramic material from twelve tombs at Tell el-Far'ah, which have been selected on the basis of the presence of Aegean-style locally made pottery. The tombs are located in five different cemeteries and the period they cover is long enough to be marked by some degree of change, even in pottery production, which is after all a notably conservative craft (Arnold 1985; Rice 1984).

The first two graves (Tombs 902 and 920) still date from the second part of the thirteenth to the early twelfth centuries. The others (Tombs 105, 126, 525, 542, 562, 608, 615, 828, 834, and 839) belong altogether to a later period from the mid-twelfth to the mid-eleventh centuries, or possibly later,[18] namely, during the period of use of Philistine Bichrome, though here, only two tombs (Tombs 542 and 562) actually contained Bichrome pots. In the two Cemetery 900 graves (902 and 920), a large part of the pottery assemblage belongs to the local Canaanite tradition; these include various types of bowls, large storage jars, pilgrim flasks, lamps, pointed-base jugs and juglets, and mugs in the Late Bronze "Gazelle-and-Bird" ware (figs. 1.2–4, 6; 2.13, 17–18; 3.2, 4).[19] Other shapes, like the flat-based bowls with everted rims (fig. 1.1) reflect, not only from a morphological but also from a technological point of view, the strong Egyptian influence, which, by the second half of the thirteenth century, had been so-to-speak integrated into the local repertoire. Finally, the last group of vessels in Tombs 902 and 920 is composed of local imitations of Mycenaean and Cypriot vessels (figs. 1.7–9, 11–12; 2.14–15; 3.1, 4) to which can be added a few isolated cases of imported traditional Cypriot White Slip and Base Ring Wares (figs. 1.5; 2.16). The Aegean-type pots in these tombs (even the finest among them, like the piriform jar from Tomb 902, fig. 1.12) were probably locally made: the appearance and texture of their clay matches that of the usual local wares. In the Cemetery 900 tombs in general, imitations of Aegean shapes outnumber those of traditional Cypriot vessels, both in quantity and variety, a fact that may leave the modern scholar with the impression that influence from Greece was more important than that from Cyprus at the very end of the Late Bronze Age. However, this conclusion can only make sense if the fact that Cyprus, already during the thirteenth century, was producing large amounts of Aegean-style wares is disregarded; and, as a matter of fact, there is one small juglet from Tomb 902 that relates directly to this phenomenon. This juglet (fig. 1.10) is characterized by a very fine greenish-buff clay and

18. Tombs 126 and 525 may even be dated to the last part of the eleventh century B.C.E.

19. See also Amiran 1969, 139–43, 161–68.

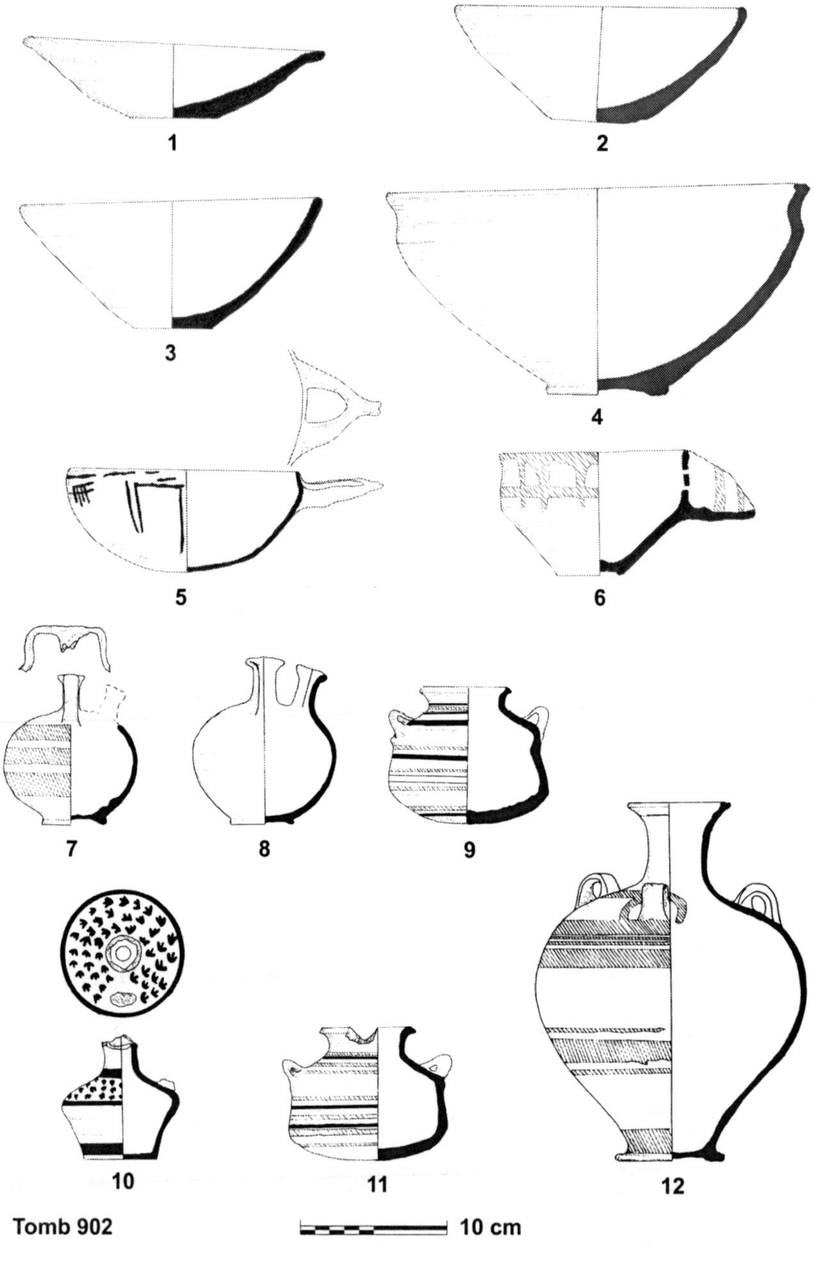

Fig. 1.

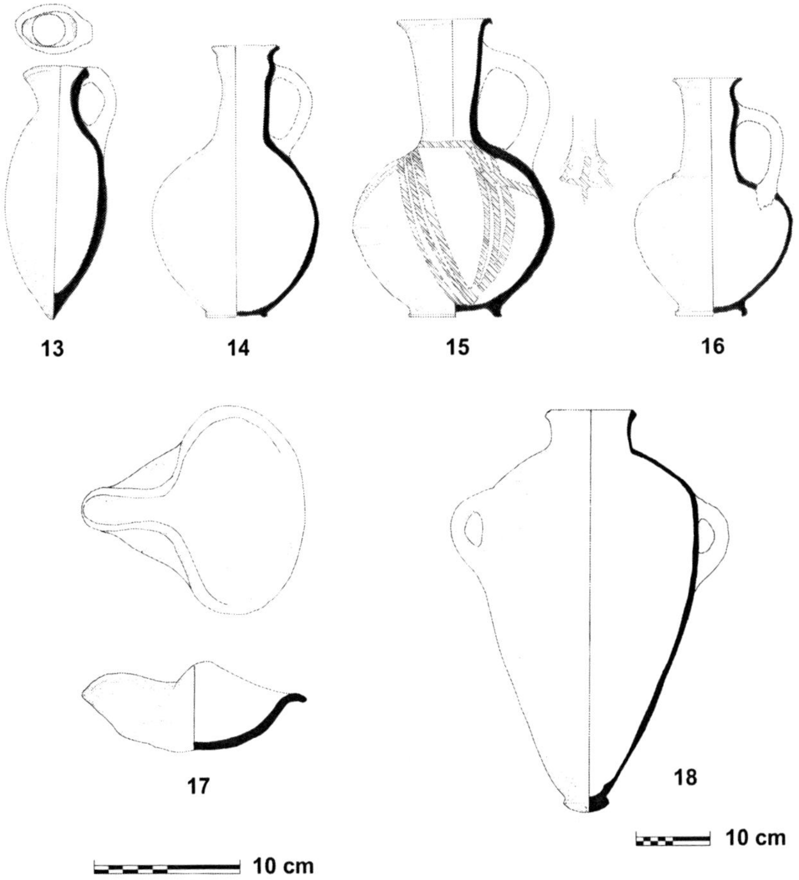

Tomb 902

Fig. 2.

Key to figs. 1 and 2.

1.1	Bowl	University College London (UCL) E.VI.24/2	Fabric: red-orange, buff surface. Inclusions: organic temper.
1.2	Bowl	UCL E.VI.24/1(a)	Fabric: red-orange, buff surface. Inclusions: dark grits, quartz, organic temper.
1.3	Bowl	UCL E.VI.24/1(b)	Fabric: red-orange. Inclusions: quartz, organic temper.

1.4	Large bowl	UCL E.VI.24/3	Fabric: red-orange, buff surface.
1.5	Milk bowl	UCL E.VI.24/4	Fabric: red, light gray slip; gray core. Dark brown paint.
1.6	Strainer bowl	UCL E.VI.24/5	Fabric: red-orange, buff polished surface. Red-orange paint.
1.7	Stirrup jar	UCL E.VI.24/41	Fabric: orange, light buff slip. Red paint.
1.8	Stirrup jar	UCL E.VI.24/10	Fabric: orange-salmon; no core. Inclusions: black and gray grits.
1.9	Pyxis (amphoriskos)	UCL E.VI.24/9(a)	Fabric: orange, buff surface (slip?). Red and dark brown paint.
1.10	Juglet	UCL E.VI.24/11	Fabric: greenish-buff, buff slip; no core. Black, slightly glossy paint.
1.11	Pyxis	UCL E.VI.24/9(b)	Fabric: red-orange, buff surface. Red and dark brown paint.
1.12	Piriform jar	UCL E.VI.24/8	Fabric: buff-orange, buff smoothed slip; no core. Red paint.
2.13	Pointed base juglet	UCL E.VI.24/12	Fabric: red-brown, buff surface.
2.14	Jug	UCL E.VI.24/7(b)	Fabric: orange, salmon-buff surface. Inclusions: limestone, quartz, organic temper.
2.15	Jug	UCL E.VI.24/6	Fabric: orange. Inclusions: white grits, organic temper. Red paint.
2.16	Jug	UCL E.VI.24/7(a)	Fabric: light gray, slightly burnished surface; gray core.
2.17	Lamp	UCL E.VI.24/13(a)	Fabric: orange, buff patches on surface. Black soot inside lamp.
2.18	Storage jar	UCL E.VI.24/14	Fabric: brown.

a slightly lustrous and smooth surface. It has a flat base, incurved conical sides, and a narrow neck. The handle, which is oval in section, and the upper part of the neck are missing. The decoration, realized in a brown-black slightly lustrous paint, consists of horizontal bands around the lower part of the body, a wider band on the carination, and diagonally arranged motifs on the shoulder zone. In spite of its non-canonical appearance in an Aegean context, this vessel would probably be classified as Aegean (at least Aegean-style) by any specialist on the grounds of its technology, shape, and decoration (which are all absolutely foreign to any local traditions), but the best parallels for this object seem to come from Cyprus.[20] It can be compared to a LC IIC bird jug from Kition Bamboula, which, in a larger version, displays a similar shape (except for the beak which is missing) and whose shoulder zone is decorated with a similar motif (Yon and Caubet 1985, fig. 65:299). The shape has another approximate parallel at Enkomi, though with two loop handles (Dikaios 1969–1971, 322, pl. 101:4) and the motif of the shoulder zone is visible on a Myc IIIA:2 bull rhyton from that same site (Dikaios 1969–1971: 330, pl. 110:2–3).

This juglet is probably a Cypriot product, quite likely dating to the LC IIC period, and ascribable to the WPW III pottery class.[21] It may provide an example of a Cypriot-made Aegean-style pot being exported to the Levantine coast as substitute for real Mycenaean pottery and, in any case, suggests that Cypriot influences may have played some role in the development of the locally made Aegean-style Myc IIIC Ware of the early Iron Age.

The remaining ten tombs (105, 126, 525, 542, 562, 608, 615, 828, 834, and 839) discussed in this paper represent a later chronological stage, the latest of the group being probably Tombs 126 and 525. Two of them, Tomb 542, which contained eleven burials, and Tomb 562, which, although disturbed at the time of the discovery, still preserved the remains of two anthropoid clay sarcophagi, may have been first used contemporaneously with the latest interments of Tomb 902 towards the mid-twelfth century B.C.E. or shortly before. However, as attested by the character of the bulk of their furnishings, the majority of the burials in these two tombs date to the second half of the twelfth century and later, probably down to the first part of the eleventh century B.C.E.

Tombs 542 and 562 contained pottery that would not seem out of place in the two Cemetery 900 graves discussed above, and which do not survive long into

20. E.g., see Sherratt and Mazar, this volume, for a discussion of Mycenaean-style vessels produced in Cyprus that appear in the southern Levant.

21. The main objection to a Cypriot attribution is the lustrous appearance of the paint but though most of the Cypriot Mycenaean-style ware is indeed decorated with a matte color, there are exceptions to the rule (e.g., Sherratt 1990a, 111).

the early Iron Age. These are Egyptian-style bowls with bulging sides (fig. 4.8–9), a painted ring-base pyxis (fig. 10.21), and Canaanite storage jars (fig. 8.48)[22] of the typical Late Bronze Age Canaanite type. It is possible that some of the large storage jars in these tombs had already served for a long time in a domestic context before they were placed in the grave, but such a long life seems less likely for the bowls and the pyxis.

However, the major part of the furnishing from these two tombs and from the eight others mentioned above consists of material that is most typical of the early Iron Age, though in many cases with direct Late Bronze antecedents, indicative of a non-negligible degree of cultural continuity. These are the pointed base juglets (Tombs 542, 562, 615, 608: figs. 5.29–32; 10.22–26; 12.5–6; 15.5),[23] the pilgrim flasks (Tombs 542, 562, 834, 828: figs. 6.34–38; 10.16–20; 11.4; 14.2),[24] the lamps (Tombs 542, 562, 834, 828: figs. 5.33; 9.13–15; 11.3; 14.3), the large trefoil-mouth jugs (Tomb 542, fig. 8.45–46), the bowls—cyma-shaped (figs. 9.11–12; 12.3–4; 15.2), hemispherical (figs. 4.7; 9.5, 8), and with inverted rims (figs. 4.1, 3–4, 10; 9.1–4; 12.2),[25] the chalices (Tombs 542, 615, figs. 5.25–26; 12.7),[26] and the strainer jars (Tombs 105, 542, 562, 828: figs. 7.40; 13.3; 14.4).[27] The Iron Age

22. For the development of the Canaanite storage jar, see, e.g., Amiran 1969, 140–42; A. Mazar 1985b, 54–56 and Killebrew 2007 for a detailed discussion and extensive bibliography.

23. One of the juglets from Tomb 562 (fig. 10.25), however, with its conical neck, oval opening, and slender body should be assigned to an earlier date and may be interpreted as an heirloom. Otherwise, various types of pointed base juglets, comparable to the items presented here, appear, for example, at Tel Qasile from Stratum XII to X (A. Mazar 1985b, 70, figs. 11:24, 15:9, 20:9–11).

24. The shape and decoration of these pilgrim flasks have mid-twelfth-century parallels at Tel Qasile Stratum XII (A. Mazar 1985b, 71–72, fig. 11:23), Ashdod (M. Dothan and Porath 1993, figs. 32:11, 15; 41:11, pls. 43:4, 6; 49:3), Deir el-Balah (T. Dothan 1979, ills. 140–41), and Beth Shean, Level VI (James 1966, figs. 52:3, 53:21). However, in the Levant these objects are very common already in the Late Bronze Age from Deir ʿAlla (Franken 1992, figs. 4/24:9–10, 5/18:10, 5/19:14) and Tell es-Saʿidiyeh (Pritchard 1980, 7, figs. 12:2, 13:9, 14:4, 18:2, 27:2, 31:3, 39:6–7, 43:2–3, 56:4) in Jordan to Tel Kazel in Syria (Badre et al. 1994, 327–28, fig. 52:f). They also occur on Cyprus at Kition (Floors III to I) and Hala Sultan Tekke in LC IIB–C contexts (Karageorghis and Demas 1985, 53, pl. 52:499; Åström 1998, fig. 249).

25. Parallels for these types of bowls appear at Tel Qasile, from Stratum XII onwards (A. Mazar 1985b, 33–36, fig. 11:2–4).

26. On the Syro-Palestinian coast chalices occur in both the Late Bronze and Iron Ages. Late Bronze examples are found at Ugarit (Courtois and Courtois 1978, 268–73, figs. 24:21, 25; 25:4; 26:7) and Megiddo, Stratum VI (Loud 1948, pl. 87:5–9). Good parallels for the types shown here are found at Tel Qasile, Stratum XI (A. Mazar 1985b, 48–49, fig. 24:18) as well as further north in Stratum H at Sarepta (Anderson 1988, pl. 25:19).

27. Strainer jars are a new shape of the early Iron Age. At Tel Qasile, they first occur in Stratum XI in the Philistine Bichrome technique (A. Mazar 1985b, 64–67, fig. 24:19) and with

character of this assemblage is also made clear by the total absence of handmade Cypriot imports and their local imitations, the disappearance of local imitations of Aegean Late Bronze shapes and the presence, though in scant quantities, of Philistine Bichrome Ware (Tombs 542, 562; figs. 5.23–24; 7.39–40). The strainer jar of Tomb 105 (fig. 13.3) even provides an example of the early Red Slip technique, where the slip is applied irregularly and lacks burnishing.

One of the distinctive features in this sample of tombs is a series of both decorated and undecorated bowls (in particular figs. 4.13–18; 9.7–9; 11.1–2; 12.1–2; 14.1), which, as far as shape and decoration are concerned, are reminiscent of types found in the early "Sea Peoples'" settlements of Ashdod or Tel Miqne (e.g., M. Dothan and Porath 1993, figs. 14, 16:9; T. Dothan 1998a, pls. 1:1–2, 6:2; Killebrew 1998a, figs. 7:2–10, 10:3, 9; 12:1–6). The bowls in question are middle-sized, bell-shaped with thinned rim and horizontal handles (figs. 4.13, 15–16; 9.7),[28] hemispherical, with or without side handles (figs. 4.17–18; 9.8–9; 12.2) with a "cyma" profile (figs. 12.3–4; 15.2),[29] or small-sized with thin walls and everted rims (figs. 4.14; 11.1–2; 14.1). Their decoration is restricted to red or red-brown matte-painted horizontal bands inside and/or outside and concentric circles and spirals inside the base, generally without the application of any slip or wash. The clay, ranging from red-brown to light beige, is undoubtedly local and although variably refined, always contains the quartz inclusions distinctive to the area. This assemblage relates to a group of Myc IIIC Aegean-style shapes from Ashdod and Tel Miqne-Ekron, made of red-brown clay and decorated with monochrome plain horizontal bands. This type of vessel is well exemplified by the assemblage from the potter's workshop at Ashdod Stratum XIIIb (M. Dothan and Porath 1993, viii–ix), but continued to be manufactured throughout the later twelfth century and into the eleventh. The bowls from Tombs 126 and 525 (fig. 15.1–2) may represent the latest stage of this production. Their late date is indicated by minor morphological details (notably, as suggested by T. Dothan [1982, 98], the small size of the handles), but it finds also confirmation in the accompanying finds (a conical blank seal in Tomb 126 and a Twentieth–Twenty-First Dynasty plaque in Tomb 525). But just like those from Ashdod and Tel Miqne-Ekron, the Aegean-style bowls from Tell el-Far'ah can be compared to some Cypriot WPW

red-slip, basket handle, and black-painted decoration in Stratum X (A. Mazar 1985b, 64, figs. 35:3, 36:1).

28. A similar (undecorated) shape occurs at Tell Kazel Level 5 (Badre et al. 1994, 304, fig. 39:b).

29. An undecorated version of this bowl occurs for example at Tel Sippor in Late Bronze Stratum III (Biran and Negbi 1966, fig. 7:4). This shape is however quite frequent in the Iron Age, in both white and red slip, for example, at Tel Qasile in Strata XII–IX (A. Mazar 1985b, 39–41).

Fig. 3.

Key to fig. 3.

3.1	Piriform jar	UCL E.VI.21/2	Fabric: orange-brown, cream slipped, slight burnish; grayish core. Red paint.
3.2	Mug	UCL E.VI.21/3	Fabric: red brown, cream slipped, slight burnish. Red-brown paint.
3.3	Pyxis (amphoriskos)	UCL E.VI.21/1	Fabric: red-orange, buff polished surface. Red-brown paint.
3.4	Pitcher jug	UCL E.VI.21/4	Fabric: orange-brown, buff surface.

III shapes of the LC IIIA–IIIB period.[30] The bowl from Tomb 105 can be added to this vessel group (fig. 13.1); it has a straight rim decorated with a series of incised lines and a lug-handle to the side. In the Levant similar shapes occur quite commonly in late eleventh- to tenth-century horizons in the Red Slip technique, but the example presented here is not red slipped. The type, however, is found on Cyprus from the LC IIC to the LC IIIB period.[31] The clay of this bowl matches well that of the other local wares, and there is no reason why it should not be considered as a local product.

Like the bowls discussed above, the one-handled jars from Tomb 542 (fig. 7.41–44) also relate to the same early Philistine assemblage that occurs at Tel Miqne-Ekron and Ashdod. They can be compared to the so-called cooking jugs at the latter sites (Killebrew 1998a, 397, figs. 10:13–14, 12:15; 1998b, pl. 16:10;

30. Compare, for example, the assemblages of bowls with linear decoration from Wells F.1241 and 1244 at Hala Sultan Tekke (Åström 1998, figs. 14, 17–18, 39, 41). One of the bowls from Tomb 562 (fig. 9.7) has a good parallel in Maa-Paleokastro Floor II (Karageorghis and Demas 1988, 111, pls. 50, 175: Room 60/3). The bowl from Tomb 615 (fig. 12.2) resembles a bowl from Enkomi Level IIIA (Dikaios 1969–1971, pl. 73:33) and the decoration on another bowl from the same tomb (fig. 12.1) can be compared to that found on a sherd from Maa-Paleokastro Floor II (Karageorghis and Demas 1988, pl. 71:99/1). The bowl (fig. 14.1) from Tomb 828 is similar in shape to a bowl from Kition Floor I (Karageorghis and Demas 1985, 75, pls. 33:1151, 55:1151).

31. At Enkomi, these bowls were classified by Dikaios as Decorated Late Cypriot III (Dikaios 1969–1971, 265, 288, 297, pls. 72:5, 83:3, 84:10, 85:12), but Kling (1989, 136–37, fig. 6:c) included them into her White-Painted Wheelmade class.

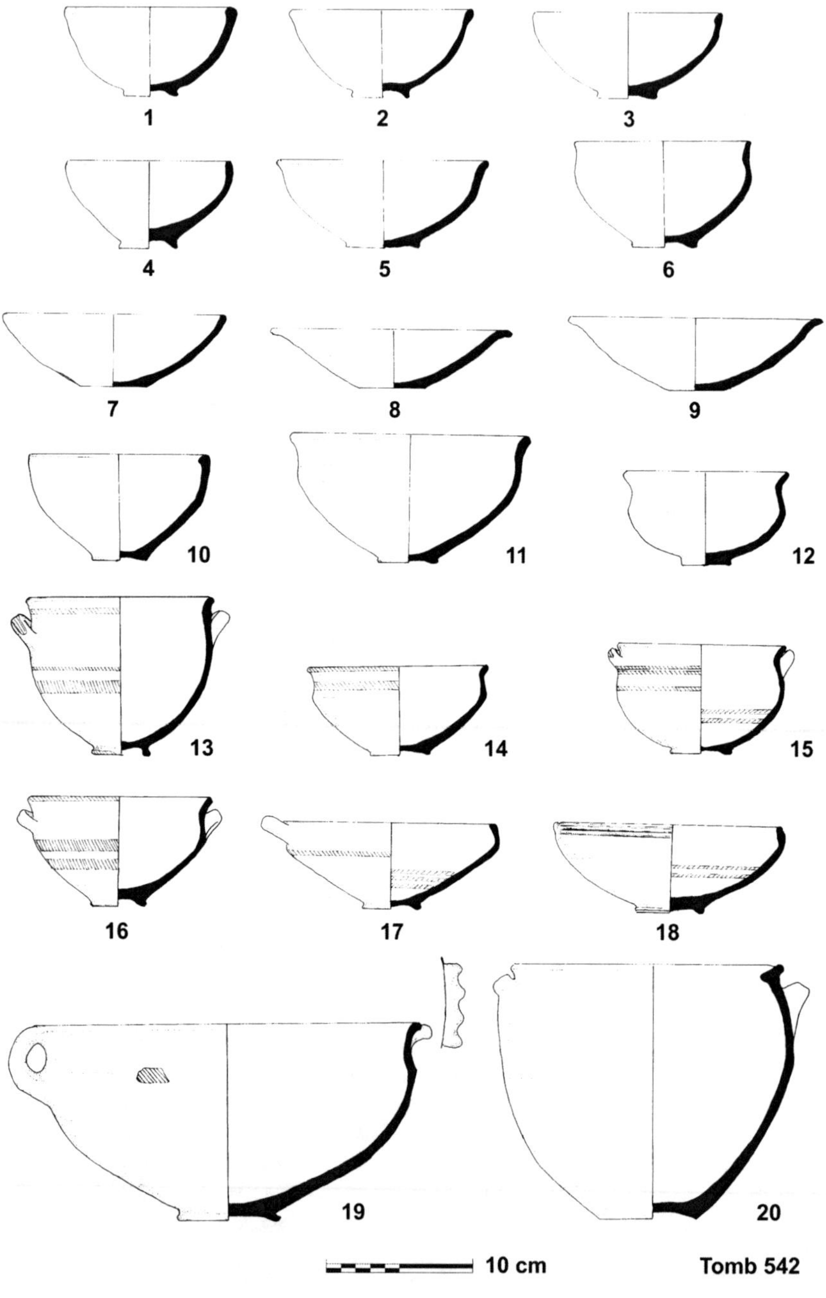

Fig. 4.

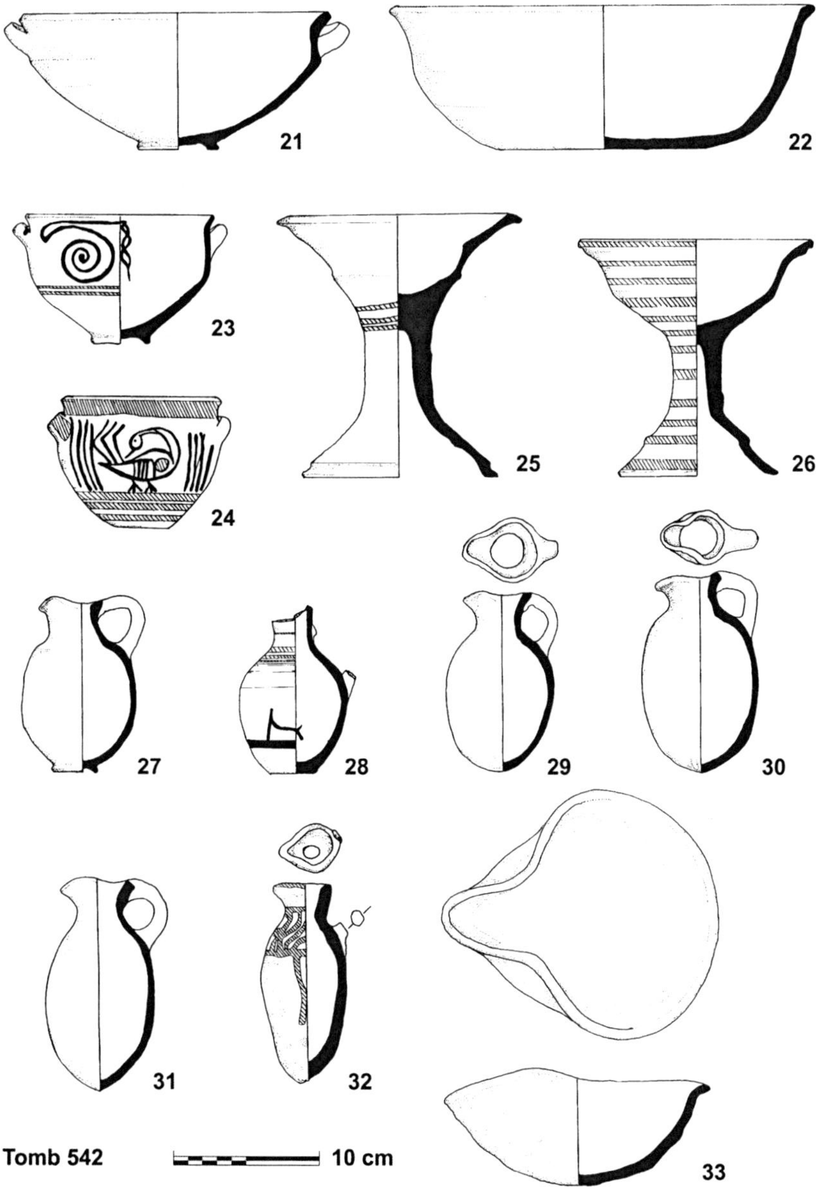

Fig. 5.

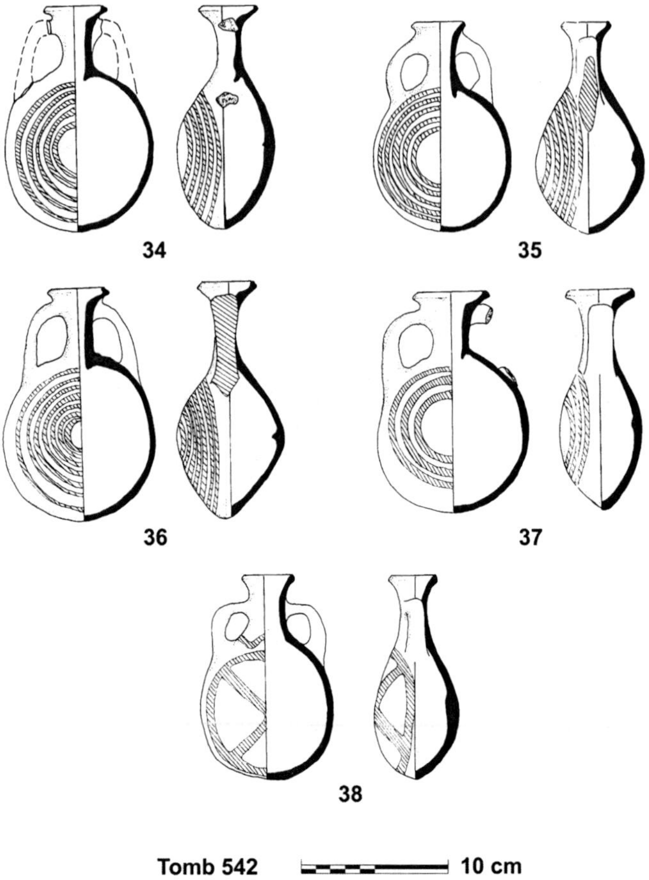

Fig. 6.

1999b, 93–94, fig. 3; M. Dothan and Porath 1993, fig. 15:5; T. Dothan 1998a, pl. 6:7–8), though similar shapes are also found in later Philistine levels, for example at Tel Qasile Stratum X (A. Mazar 1985b, fig. 49:10, 12–13), Ashdod (M. Dothan and Porath 1993, fig. 34:2), and Ashkelon. The resemblance between the Tell el-Far'ah jugs and those from the Philistine sites is further emphasized by their fabric, which is characterized by quartz inclusions, and, often, by the use of straw temper. These pots have no local Late Bronze antecedents in Canaan, and, as far

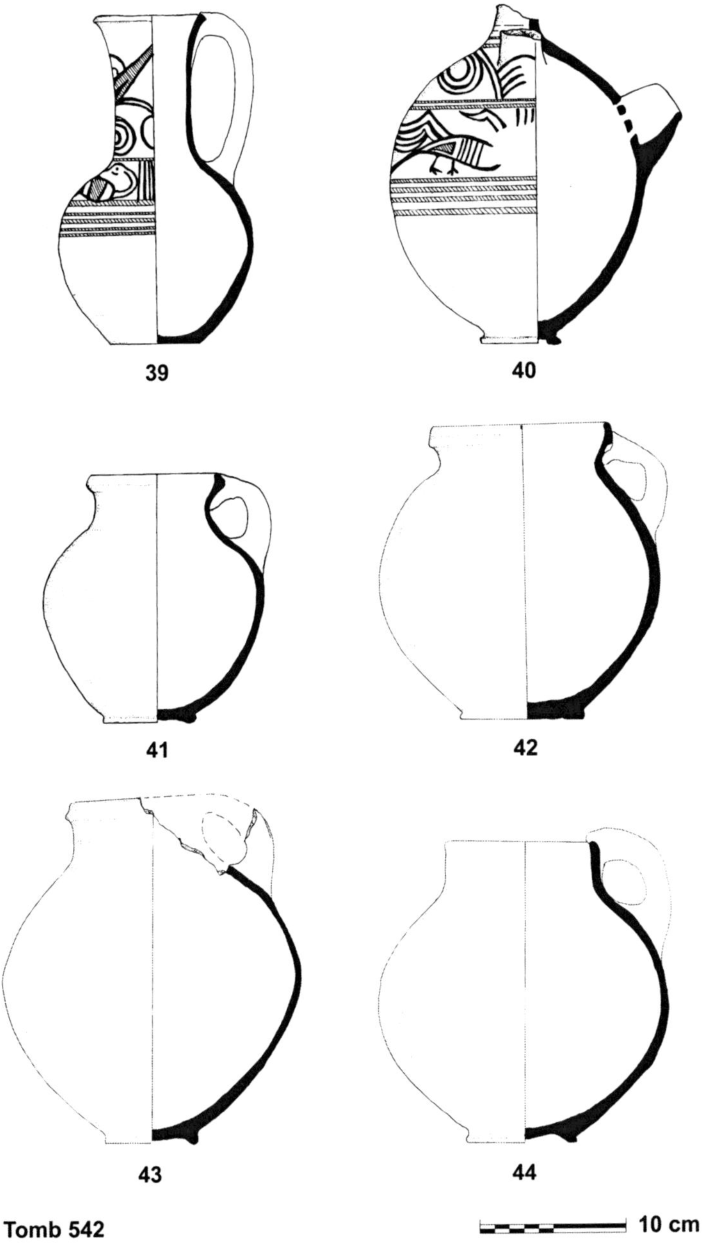
39
40
41
42
43
44
Tomb 542
10 cm

Fig. 7.

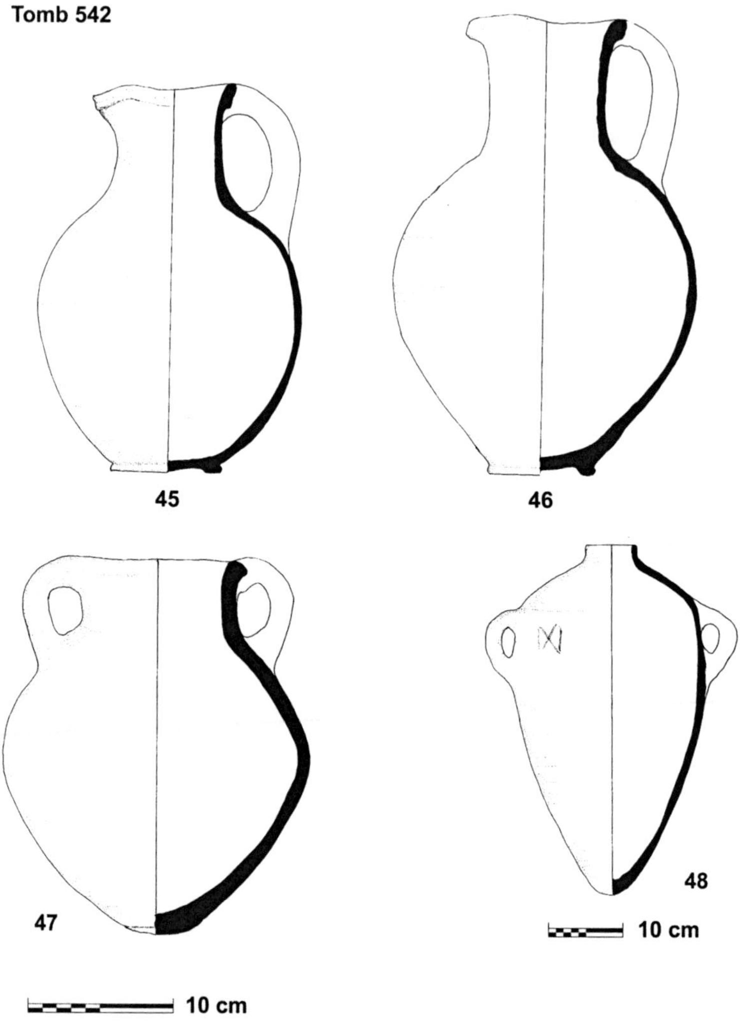

Fig. 8.

as shape is concerned, find their best parallels in LC IIIA–B Cyprus.[32] However, unlike several of the jugs from Tel Miqne and Ashkelon which bear burn marks

32. Similar jugs in Plain White Wheelmade appear at Maa-Palaeokastro Floor II (Karageorghis and Demas 1988, 136, pls. 98:134, 207:134) and Kition Floor III (Karageorghis and Demas 1985, 27, 57, 71, pls. 44:570, 51:688/1, 55:318). They are found also at Pyla-Kokkinokremos,

Key to figs. 4–8.

4.1	Bowl	Rockefeller Museum (RM) I.4303	Fabric: beige, gray-buff surface. Inclusions: sand-quartz, calcite.
4.2	Bowl	RM I.4251	Fabric: dark red-brown. Inclusions: sand quartz.
4.3	Bowl	RM I.4229	Fabric: beige. Inclusions: white grits, sand quartz.
4.4	Bowl	RM I.4277	Fabric: red-orange, gray-buff surface.
4.5	Bowl	RM I.4284	Fabric: gray-buff. Inclusions: organic temper.
4.6	Bowl	RM I.4237	Fabric: red-orange, buff surface. Inclusions: white grits, quartz.
4.7	Bowl	RM I.4285	Fabric: dark red, rose-buff surface. Inclusions: quartz, organic temper.
4.8	Bowl	RM I.4286	Fabric: red-orange; light gray core. Inclusions: white grits, organic temper.
4.9	Bowl	RM I.4275	Fabric: red-orange. Inclusions: calcite, sand quartz, organic temper.
4.10	Bowl	RM I.4253	Fabric: red-orange, buff surface. Inclusions: sand quartz.
4.11	Bowl	RM I.4250	Fabric: red-orange, buff surface.
4.12	Bowl	RM I.4236	Fabric: orange-brown. Inclusions: white and gray grits.
4.13	Bowl	RM I.4287	Fabric: orange. Inclusions: gray grits, quartz.
4.14	Bowl	RM I.4259	Fabric: orange-salmon. Inclusions: gray grits, quartz. Red-orange paint.
4.15	Bowl	RM I.4293	Fabric: red-brown. Inclusions: gray grits, quartz. Red paint.

4.16	Bowl	RM I.4256	Fabric: orange-brown, buff surface. Inclusions: quartz, organic temper. Red paint.
4.17	Bowl	RM I.4272	Fabric: orange-brown, cream slip(?). Inclusions: sand quartz. Red paint.
4.18	Bowl	RM I.4281	Fabric: orange-brown, brown surface. Inclusions: grits, quartz. Red-brown paint.
4.19	Krater	RM I.4273	Fabric: red-brown, buff surface. Inclusions: gray and white grits, sand quartz. Red-brown paint.
4.20	Krater	RM I.4291	Fabric: red-orange, buff patches on surface. Inclusions: white grits, quartz.
5.21	Krater	RM I.4264	Fabric: red-orange, gray-buff surface. Inclusions: sand quartz.
5.22	Large bowl	RM I.4260	Fabric: red-brown. Inclusions: white grits, quartz.
5.23	Bowl	RM I.4271	Fabric: beige, cream slip. Inclusions: gray and white grits. Black and red paint.
5.24	Bowl	RM I.4290	Fabric: red-orange. Inclusions: grits. Black and red paint.
5.25	Chalice	RM I.4280	Fabric: red-orange. Inclusions: gray grits, sand quartz. Red-brown paint.
5.26	Chalice	RM I.4241	Fabric: beige salmon. Inclusions: grits. Red paint.
5.27	Juglet	RM I.4289	Fabric: beige-buff. Inclusions: gray grits, quartz.
5.28	Juglet	RM I.4257	Fabric: whitish. Inclusions: reddish and dark grits. Brown paint.

5.29	Juglet	RM I.4252	Fabric: red-brown. Inclusions: white and gray grits.
5.30	Juglet	RM I.4234	Fabric: red-beige. Inclusions: white grits, sand quartz.
5.31	Juglet	RM I.4228	Fabric: salmon. Inclusions: white grits, organic temper.
5.32	Juglet	RM I.4235	Fabric: red-orange, cream slip. Red-brown paint.
5.33	Lamp	RM I.4230	Fabric: orange-brown, buff surface. Inclusions: dark grits, sand quartz.
6.34	Pilgrim flask	RM I.4279	Fabric: orange-beige. Inclusions: grog, white grits. Red paint.
6.35	Pilgrim flask	RM I.4258	Fabric: red-brown, cream slip. Inclusions: dark grits. Red paint.
6.36	Pilgrim flask	RM I.4254	Fabric: red-orange, salmon surface. Inclusions: white and gray grits. Red paint.
6.37	Pilgrim flask	RM I.4245	Fabric: grayish-red, cream slip. Inclusions: sand quartz. Red paint.
6.38	Pilgrim flask	RM I.4292	Fabric: gray-beige. Inclusions: black grits, quartz. Red-brown paint.
7.39	Jug	RM I.4276	Fabric: red-orange, buff surface. Inclusions: gray grits, quartz. Black and red paint.
7.40	Strainer jug	RM I.4239	Fabric: red-orange, cream slip. Inclusions: gray grits, quartz. Black and red paint.
7.41	Jug	RM I.4246	Fabric: red-brown. Inclusions: dark gray grits, quartz, organic temper. Black soot on lower body.
7.42	Jug	RM I.4265	Fabric: orange-salmon, buff surface.

7.43	Jug	RM I.4295	Fabric: red-brown. Inclusions: quartz, organic temper.
7.44	Jug	RM I.4304	Fabric: brown, buff surface. Inclusions: gray grits, quartz.
8.45	Pitcher jug	RM I.4299	Fabric: red, gray-buff surface. Inclusions: white grits, quartz.
8.46	Pitcher jug	RM I.4301	Fabric: orange-salmon, buff surface. Inclusions: gray grits, quartz.
8.47	Two-handled jar	RM I.4228	Fabric: light gray, buff surface. Inclusions: gray and white grits.
8.48	Storage jar	RM I.4270	Fabric: red-orange, brown surface.

on their external surfaces (Killebrew 1998a, 397; 1998b, 164), the specimens from Tomb 542 at Tell el-Far'ah, with a single exception (fig. 7.41), whose external lower surface was blackened by fire, do not show any evidence for having been actually employed as cooking pots.

Another conspicuous utilitarian shape that appears in the Tell el-Far'ah tombs is the two-handled jar (Tombs 542 and 562; figs. 8.47; 10.27). Although those discussed here were apparently not used for that purpose before being deposited in the grave, one may suppose that they were also originally meant to function as cooking-pots. Like the one-handled cooking-jugs, these jars are attested at Ashdod (M. Dothan and Porath 1993, figs. 23:5–6, 34:7, pl. 43:5) and have parallels on Cyprus in Coarse Wheelmade fabrics, sometimes with a partly fire-blackened exterior.[33]

Finally the last pottery group to be discussed is composed of two isolated foreign imports. The first is a round-mouth Bucchero juglet (fig. 13.2), probably an import from Cyprus. It is decorated with ridges below the rim and at the base of the neck and with incised vertical lines on the body. Bucchero Ware appears

a single-level site from which no Myc IIIC has been reported (Karageorghis and Demas 1984, 37, pls. 20:58, 36:58).

33. At Maa-Palaeokastro Floors I and II (Karageorghis and Demas 1988, 115, 148, pls. 60:692, 109:387, 183:692, 211:387) and, without burn marks, at Kition Area I, Floor I (Karageorghis and Demas 1985, 69, pl. 55:659/1).

on Cyprus in the Late Bronze Age,[34] but this example finds its best parallels at Enkomi or Kition at the end of LC IIIA–Early LC IIIB.[35]

The second import is a Midianite flat base juglet, from Tomb 542 (fig. 5.28) with remains of bichrome (red and black) painted decoration of horizontal bands on the shoulder and neck and the remains of an animal figure(?) on the central panel. It is characterized by rather thick walls and a light buff (almost white) clay with no core and large dark and colored (predominantly reddish) inclusions. Apart from Tomb 542, Midianite Ware at Tell el-Far'ah was also found in the area of Cemetery 900 and on the tell itself, in the same layers as the Philistine Bichrome. It is, however, relatively rare in the Levant. It was notably recorded at Tel Masos (Fritz and Kempinski 1983, pls. 97A, 142:10, 148:11; Kempinski 1993, 988–89) and at the copper mines of Timna (Rothenberg 1972, 109, fig. 32, pls. 48–54, col. pls. 12–14; 1988, 93–94, 100–101, 113–14, pls. 4, 16–18, 106:1, figs. 4–10), where it might have been manufactured.[36]

The general impression left by the pottery finds confirmation in the accompanying small finds assemblage. Some of them show direct continuity with the earlier period. Most of the beads belong to types that already occurred during the Late Bronze Age in the same materials (mainly carnelian and faience, but also limestone, quartz, shell, and gold) and other objects, like the faience pilgrim flask from Tomb 839 (fig. 15.8)[37] and the Bes and Ptah faience amulets (Tombs 126 and 834),[38] point to a persisting Egyptian influence. A slight change from the preceding period can be perceived in the drop in the number of scarabs and plaques (Tomb 542, 562, 615, and 525), most of which seem to date to the Nineteenth–Twentieth Dynasties (as a matter of fact, just like those of Tombs 902 and 920).[39] The difference is also marked by the appearance of a quartz conical seal

34. The earliest Bucchero Ware is related to Base Ring II fabrics and the later types are connected to Black-Slip and Red-Slip Wheelmade (Åström 1972, 425). The repertory of shapes is limited to juglets, jugs, and amphorae.

35. At Enkomi, see French Tombs 1 and 5 (Schaeffer 1952, 161, 232, figs. 66:7, 88:3) and in Level IIIB (Dikaios 1969–1971, 598, pl. 77:2). Compare also with sherds from Kition Floors I–II (Karageorghis and Demas 1985, 60, pl. 29:179/1).

36. For a discussion of the ware's characteristics and its distribution, see Kalsbeek and London 1978. Midianite pottery is mainly dated to the early Iron Age, but according to the context of the Midianite sherd found on the Amman citadel, which included Egyptian "Amarna Blue" Ware, it seems that the production had already started in the Late Bronze (van der Steen 1996, 56).

37. Compare with a fragmentary faience pilgrim flask from Timna (Rothenberg 1988, pl. 21, fig. 37:34) and another from Lachish (Tufnell 1940, pl. 22:56).

38. See also Herrmann 1994, 439–40, no. 599.

39. For scarabs with Baal-Seth iconography from Tomb 542, see Keel 1995, 209, fig. 412,

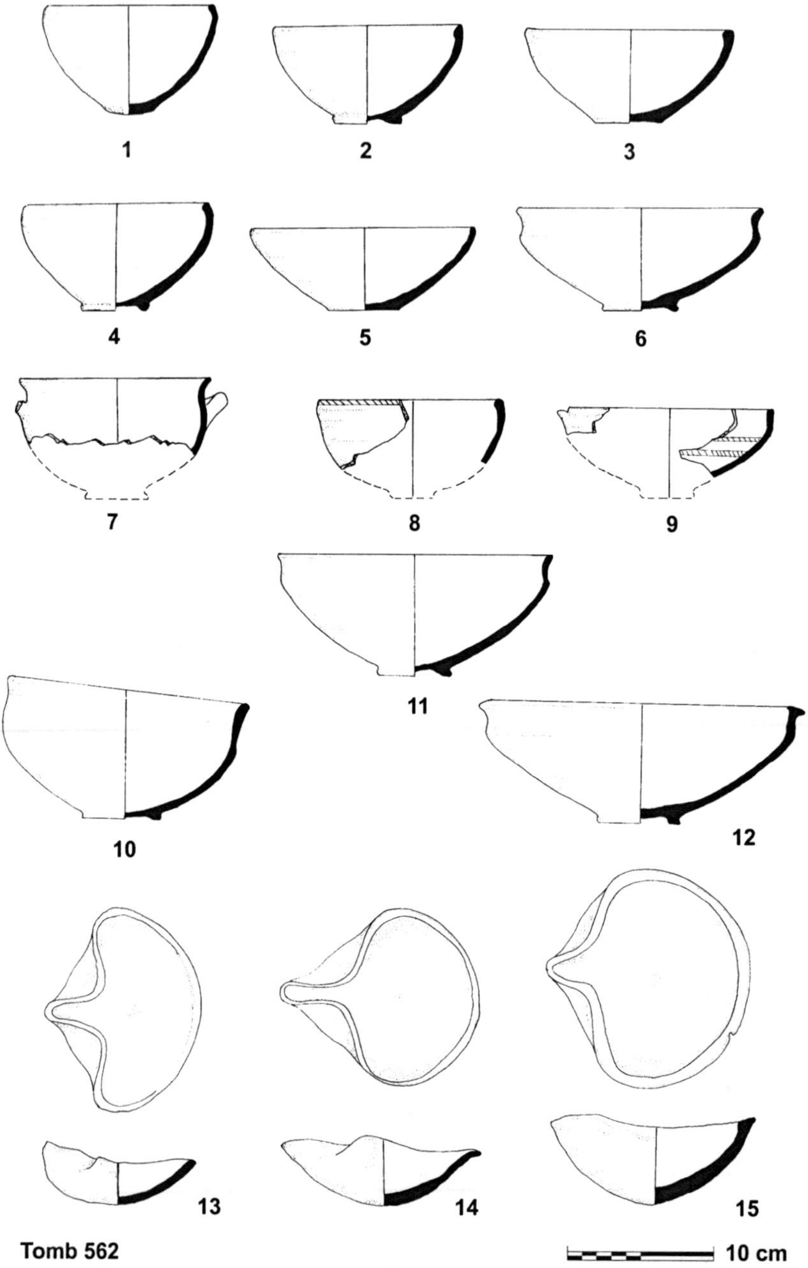

Fig. 9.

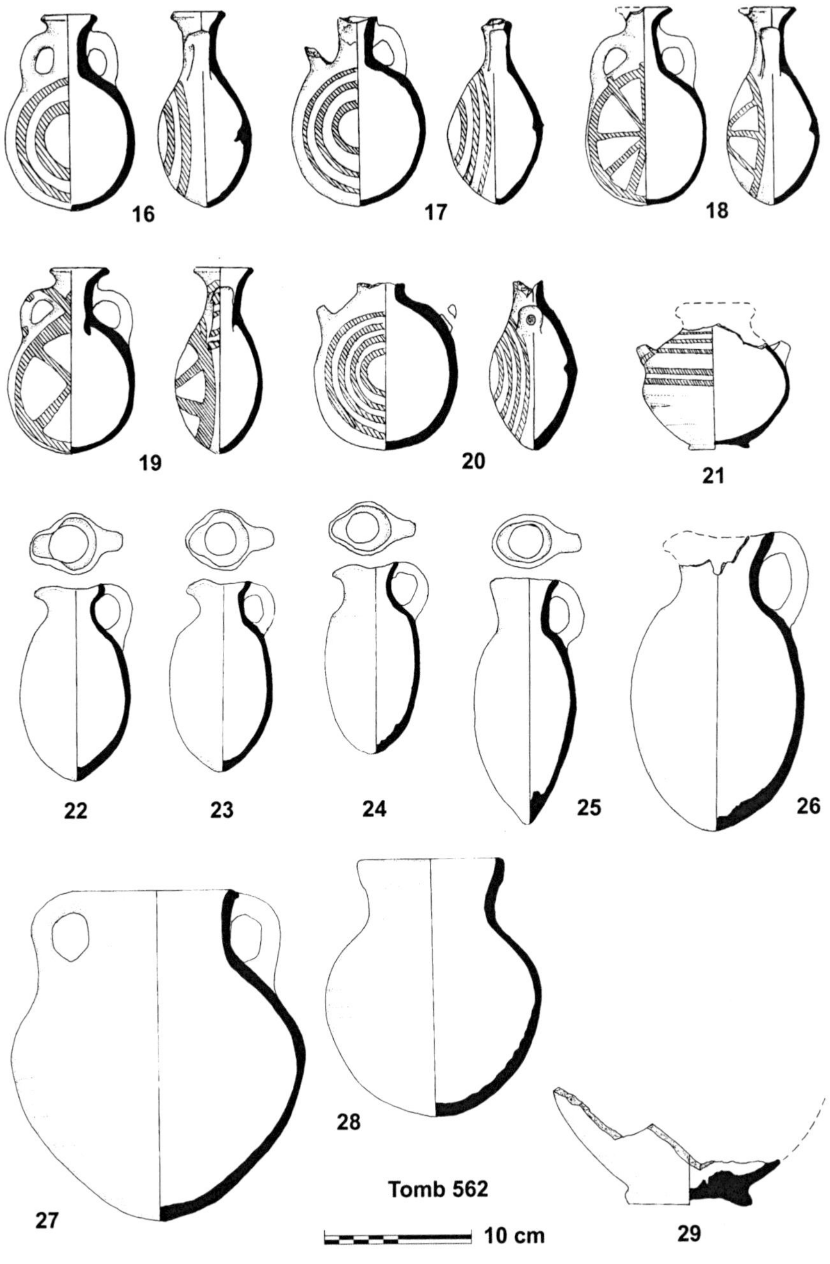

Fig. 10.

Key to figs. 9 and 10.

9.1	Bowl	UCL E.VII.81/5	Fabric: red, buff surface. Inclusions: gray and white grits, quartz.
9.2	Bowl	UCL E.VII.81/2(c)	Fabric: orange-salmon, buff slip. Inclusions: gray and white grits.
9.3	Bowl	UCL E.VII.81/2(a)	Fabric: red-brown. Inclusions: gray grits, quartz.
9.4	Bowl	UCL E.VII.81/2(d)	Fabric: red-brown. Inclusions: large gray minerals, white grits, quartz.
9.5	Bowl	UCL E.VII.81/4	Fabric: orange-salmon. Inclusions: white grits, sand-quartz.
9.6	Bowl	UCL E.VII.81/6	Fabric: red-orange. Inclusions: dark grits, grog (?), quartz.
9.7	Bowl	UCL E.VII.81/9	Fabric: red-orange, pink-buff surface; gray core. Inclusions: gray grits, quartz.
9.8	Bowl	UCL E.VII.81/2(b)	Fabric: red-orange, pink-buff surface. Inclusions: white grits, quartz. Red-brown paint.
9.9	Bowl	UCL E.VII.81/11	Fabric: red-orange; light gray core. Inclusions: gray grits, sand quartz. Red-brown paint.
9.10	Bowl	UCL E.VII.81/8	Fabric: red-orange Inclusions: gray and white grits, quartz.
9.11	Bowl	UCL E.VII.81/8	Fabric: orange-salmon; gray core. Inclusions: gray grits, quartz.
9.12	Bowl	UCL E.VII.81/7	Fabric: beige-brown, gray-buff surface. Inclusions: white and gray grits, sand quartz.

9.13	Lamp	UCL E.VII.81/25(b)	Fabric: orange-salmon. Inclusions: gray grits, grog (?), quartz.
9.14	Lamp	UCL E.VII.81/25(a)	Fabric: red-orange. Inclusions: white grits, sand quartz.
9.15	Lamp	UCL E.VII.81/26	Fabric: red-brown. Inclusions: sand quartz.
10.16	Pilgrim flask	UCL E.VII.81/29	Fabric: red-orange. Inclusions: gray and white grits, shell (?), quartz. Red-brown paint.
10.17	Pilgrim flask	UCL E.VII.81/23(d)	Fabric: red-orange; no core. Inclusions: white grits, large gray minerals, organic temper. Red-brown paint.
10.18	Pilgrim flask	UCL E.VII.81/23(c)	Fabric: beige, cream slip; no core. Inclusions: gray grits. Red-brown paint.
10.19	Pilgrim flask	UCL E.VII.81/23(b)	Fabric: red-orange, cream slip. Inclusions: gray and white grits. Red paint.
10.20	Pilgrim flask	UCL E.VII.81/24	Fabric: orange-brown, buff surface. Inclusions: gray grits, quartz. Red-brown paint.
10.21	Pyxis (amphoriskos)	UCL number not legible	Fabric: red-orange, buff-orange surface; no core. Inclusions: gray grits, quartz. Red-brown paint.
10.22	Juglet	UCL E.VII.81/14(a)	Fabric: orange-salmon, buff surface. Inclusions: dark grits, quartz.
10.23	Juglet	UCL E.VII.81/14(b)	Fabric: red-orange, brown surface. Inclusions: white grits, quartz.
10.24	Juglet	UCL E.VII.81/15	Fabric: light beige, buff surface; no core. Inclusions: gray grits, sand quartz.

10.25	Juglet	UCL E.VII.81/12	Fabric: red-brown; no core. Inclusions: quartz.
10.26	Pitcher jug	UCL E.VII.81/19	Fabric: red-orange; no core. Inclusions: white grits, quartz.
10.27	Two-handled jar	UCL E.VII.81/22	Fabric: red-brown, buff surface. Inclusions: large gray minerals, sand quartz.
10.28	Handless jar	UCL E.VII.81/20	Fabric: red-brown. Inclusions: gray grits, sand quartz, organic temper.
10.29	Jug	UCL number not legible	Fabric: red-brown; gray core. Inclusions: gray and white grits, sand quartz.

from Tomb 126.[40] However, the most conspicuous and probably most significant difference between the early Iron Age graves, such as those sampled here and those of the Late Bronze Age 900 tombs has to do with utilitarian metals (bronze, iron, copper, and alloys). This manifests itself not only in the appearance of iron for both weapons/tools and ornaments (Tomb 542, 562, 839, and 615), a material totally absent from Cemetery 900, but also in a general rise in the number of metal artifacts, in particular of metal vessels, which are extremely rare in the Cemetery 900 tombs.

The sample of graves, ranging in date from within the thirteenth to the second half of the eleventh century B.C.E., exemplifies the gradual change that affected local pottery production during this period with the appearance of the Philistine White Slip and Bichrome technique of decoration and the emergence of the early Red Slip technique. The change is also perceptible in a slight shift in the nature of the clay. Several of the bowls, pilgrim flasks, or juglets dating from the mid-twelfth to the eleventh centuries belong to a single fabric group distinguished by a red-brown to brown beige or buff clay, often with a gritty surface due to the

and also Shuval 1990, 133–34, nos. 20–21. All the scarabs and seals in Tombs 542 and 562 can fit a date in the Nineteenth–Twentieth Dynasties. The plaque from Tomb 525, which bears the cartouche of Tuthmosis III, was dated by O. Keel in the Twentieth–Twenty First Dynasties. For the scarabs from Tomb 920, see Giveon 1985, 44–46, nos. 68–71.

40. The seal from Tomb 126 is blank but the object is morphologically related to a series of Iron I incised seals (Keel 1995, 100).

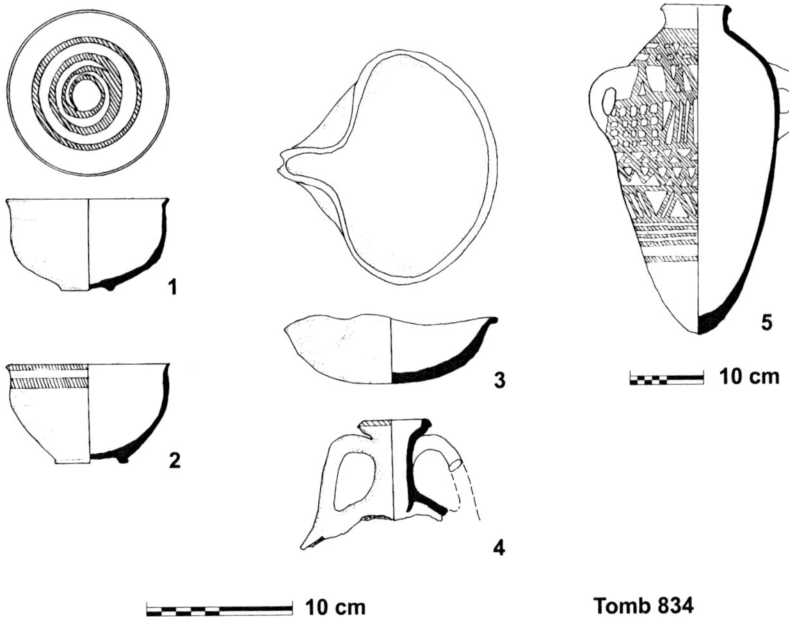

Fig. 11.

Key to fig. 11.

11.1	Bowl	UCL E.VII.7/1	Fabric: red-orange; gray core. Inclusions: gray grits, quartz. Red-brown paint.
11.2	Bowl	RM I.4419	Fabric: light orange, buff surface. Inclusions: white and dark grits, quartz. Red paint.
11.3	Lamp	RM I.4420	Fabric: light orange, buff surface. Inclusions: quartz.
11.4	Pilgrim flask	RM I.4416	Fabric: orange-brown, salmon surface; no core. Inclusions: gray grits, quartz. Red-brown paint.
11.5	Storage jar	RM I.6910	Fabric: orange-brown. Inclusions: large gray minerals, quartz. Red-brown paint.

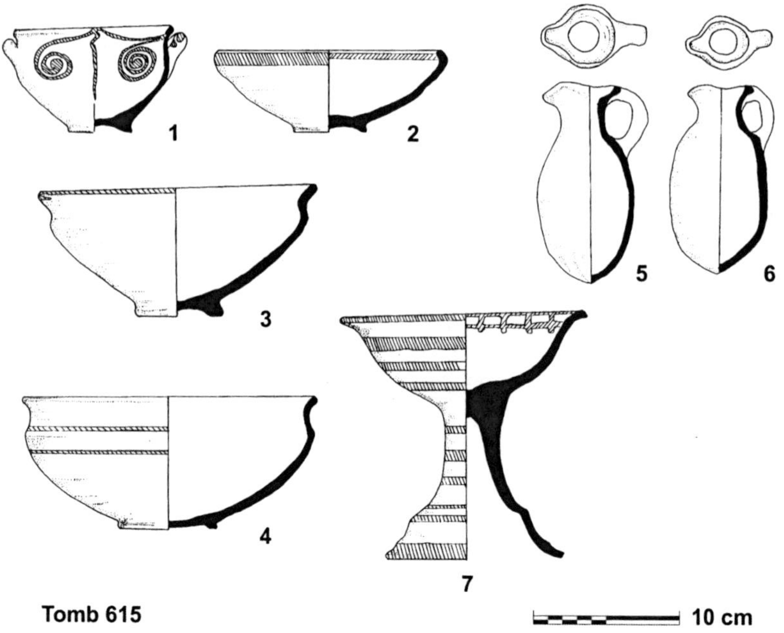

Fig. 12.

Key to fig. 12.

12.1	Bowl	UCL E.VII.12/3	Fabric: red-orange. Inclusions: organic temper on handle. Red-brown paint.
12.2	Bowl	UCL E.VII.12/4	Fabric: red-orange, cream slip. Inclusions: white grits, quartz. Red paint.
12.3	Bowl	UCL E.VII.12/2	Fabric: light salmon, buff slip(?). Inclusions: white grits, quartz. Red-brown paint.
12.4	Bowl	UCL E.VII.12/1	Fabric: brown. Inclusions: gray grits, quartz. Red paint.
12.5	Juglet	UCL E.VII.12/6	Fabric: red-orange. Inclusions: grog, quartz.
12.6	Juglet	UCL E.VII.12/7	Fabric: orange-salmon; gray core. Inclusions: grog(?), quartz, organic temper.

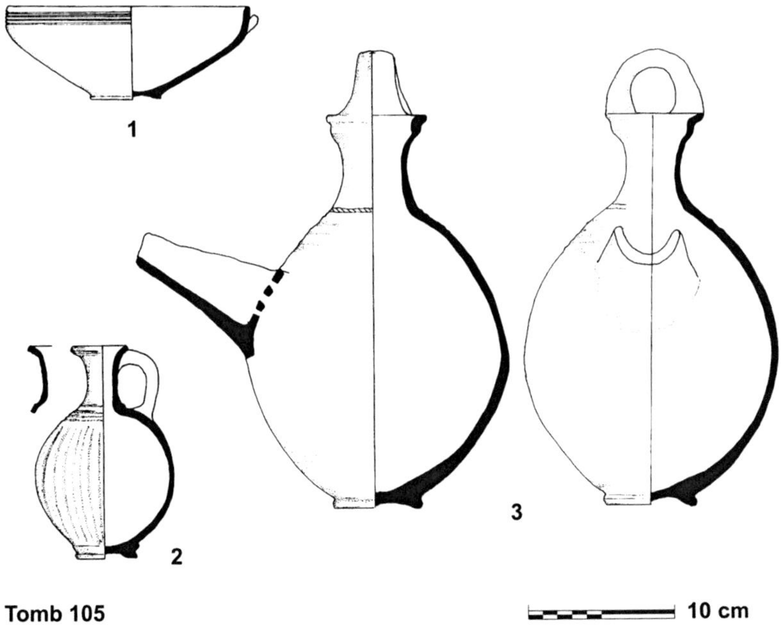

Fig. 13.

12.7	Chalice	UCL E.VII.12/5	Fabric: red-orange, buff surface; no core. Inclusions: gray grits, quartz, organic temper. Red-brown paint.

Key to fig. 13.

13.1	Bowl	UCL E.VII.69/1	Fabric: red-orange. Inclusions: gray and white grits, quartz, organic temper. Remains of red paint.
13.2	Juglet	UCL E.VII.69/2	Fabric: gray; no core. Inclusions: gray grits.
13.3	Strainer jar	UCL E.VII.69/3	Fabric: red-brown, red slip. Inclusions: dark and white grits, quartz. Remains of red slip.

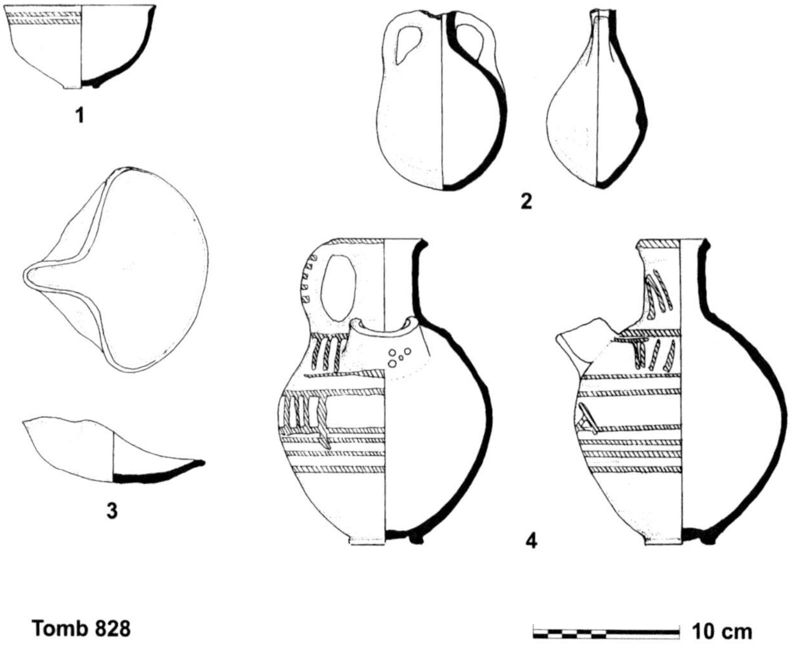

Fig. 14.

Key to fig. 14.

14.1	Bowl	UCL E.VII.2/1	Fabric: brown, buff slip; no core. Inclusions: gray grits. Dark brown paint.
14.2	Pilgrim flask	UCL E.VII.2/2	Fabric: light orange; no core. Inclusions: gray grits.
14.3	Lamp	UCL E.VII.2/4	Fabric: dark orange, buff surface; gray core. Inclusions: gray grits, quartz.
14.4	Strainer jar	UCL E.VII.2/3	Fabric: light beige, cream slip. Inclusions: gray grits, quartz. Red-brown paint.

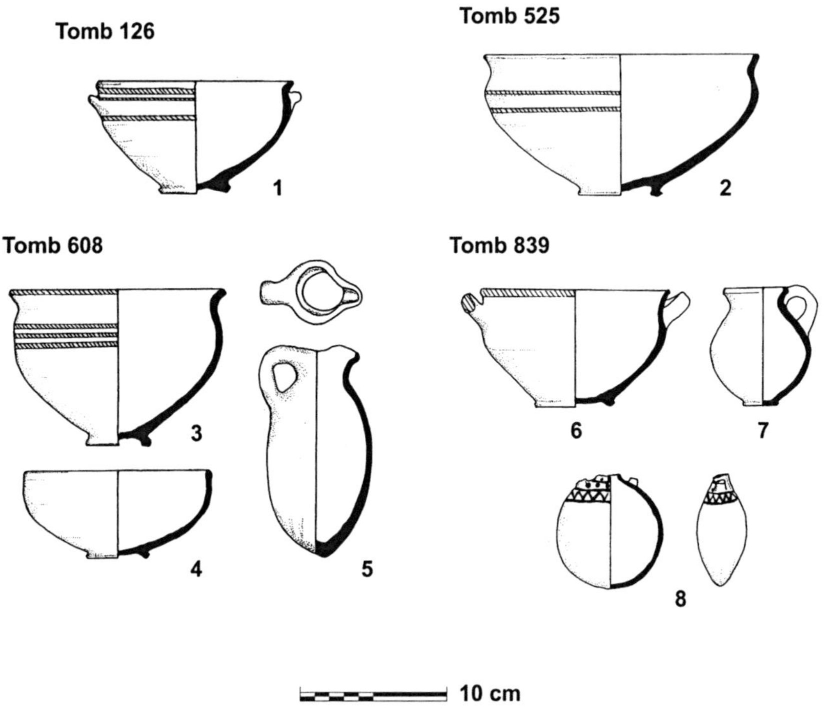

Fig. 15.

Key to fig. 15.

15.1	Bowl	UCL E.VII.70/1	Fabric: light orange, buff surface. Inclusions: quartz. Red paint.
15.2	Bowl	UCL E.VII.55/1	Fabric: red-orange, remains of buff slip(?). Inclusions: gray grits, quartz. Red paint.
15.3	Bowl	UCL E.VII.47/2	Fabric: red-orange, gray-buff surface. Inclusions: dark grits, quartz.
15.4	Bowl	UCL E.VII.47/1	Fabric: red, cream slip; no core. Inclusions: gray and white grits, sand quartz. Red-brown paint.

15.5	Juglet	UCL E.VII.47/3	Fabric: red-brown. Inclusions: gray grits, quartz.
15.6	Bowl	UCL E.VII.6/1	Fabric: red-orange, cream slip. Inclusions: gray grits, quartz. Red paint.
15.7	Juglet	UCL E.VII.6/2	Fabric: orange-brown. Inclusions: gray and white grits, quartz, organic temper.
15.8	Faience pilgrim flask	UCL E.VII.6/3	Blue glazed faience. Black paint.

presence of a fair amount of mineral inclusions, predominantly quartzite (sand quartz). This clay differs from that employed for many vessels of the earlier Cemetery 900 assemblages, which, in spite of the occasional addition of straw or chaff, is often smoother, with fewer mineral inclusions. The tomb material discussed here also represents a certain continuity in both style and technology that goes back all the way to the end of the Late Bronze Age. This can be seen in the Egyptian-style bowls, the lamps, and the storage jars, the appearance of the reddish matte paint used for the decoration, but also in a persisting taste for Cypriot and Aegeanizing stylistic elements, represented by the Cypriot Bucchero juglet[41] and by the locally made Aegean or Cypriot-inspired bowls. A small number of decorative objects, which all refer to a wide eastern Mediterranean cultural sphere, like the drop lunate-shaped earrings[42] and the ivory fittings from Tomb 542,[43] points to the persistence into the early Iron Age of the cultural *koiné* (either in a material or stylistic form) that existed in the Late Bronze eastern Mediterranean.

There are probably many ways to interpret the material presented here, in particular to explain the nature and significance of the twelfth and eleventh century Aegean-type vessels. Considered within a wider context in connection with other sites, it may suggest a picture that is not so straightforward and perhaps less dramatic than usually thought. As stated above, there are few similarities between

41. The imported Bucchero juglet from Tomb 105 is not an isolated example at Tell el-Far'ah. Other specimens, among which may figure local imitations, appear in other tombs at the site.

42. See, e.g., Golani 1996, 25–26.

43. The ivory "pommel" from Tomb 542 has a good parallel at Tyre Stratum XIII–2 (Bikai 1978, pl. 37:10). As for the small ivory disc with engraved rosette, also from Tomb 542, it has a bone parallel, at Kition, Floors I–II (Karageorghis and Demas 1985, 65, pl. 32:948) and an ivory one at Toumba tou Skourou (Vermeule 1974, fig. 62 right).

all the Syro-Palestinian sites that have produced this type of material. Among this diversity, one specific element may emerge as a link between them, namely, the fact that, already during the Late Bronze Age, these sites were in, at least, indirect contact with the Aegean and certainly in close relations with Cyprus.

It has been argued before that imitated Mycenaean ware, either locally produced or imported from Cyprus, could not be considered as precursors of Myc IIIC pottery, but that their similarities only derive from the fact that they both share the same prototypes. However, from a socioeconomic point of view, it would make more sense to consider the Cypro-Aegean imitated wares, Myc IIIC and its successors, as part of a single phenomenon, namely, the emergence of new kinds of goods production and distribution. Similarly, the fact that the appearance of the Myc IIIC style is marked by a functional change in the Mycenaean-type pottery from a dominance of closed containers among the LH IIIB imports and imitations, to the preponderance of drinking vessels, in particular skyphoi and kraters from the twelfth century onwards, should not necessarily be interpreted as the result of fresh influence from the Aegean, let alone as a sign of an Aegean migration. This change may as well be assigned to an influence from Cyprus where open drinking vessels of Mycenaean type (i.e., in WPW III Ware) gradually take over the traditional production of White Slip and Base Ring bowls in the course of the LC IIC and especially the LC IIIA period.[44]

A number of scholars, like Sherratt (this volume), Artzy (1998; see also this volume), and Bauer (1998), have been particularly concerned with the Philistine and other Sea Peoples question and have newly reconsidered the innovations and changes of the transitional period from the Late Bronze to the early Iron Age in the eastern Mediterranean without the usual *a priori* historical interpretation endemic in the archaeology of this area. Sherratt (1998) and, following her argument, Bauer (1998), have suggested considering the Sea Peoples as the main actors in a deep and fundamental shift that took place in the socioeconomic and political structure of the old palace-based economy of the Late Bronze.[45] From the elite-controlled centralized and codified system of exchange that dominated most of the trade in the second millennium B.C.E., they have proposed seeing the emergence of a new type of decentralized, sea-oriented economy that operated on the basis of free private enterprise, in the hands of independent merchants and middlemen that specialized in the manufacture and commerce of substitute elite goods.

44. Already emphasized by Brug (1985, 114).

45. Sherratt (1992; 1994b) also developed this model for Cyprus.

As argued by Sherratt, it is significant that the earliest signs of this phenomenon are detectable on Cyprus, particularly in the southeastern maritime centers of Hala Sultan Tekke, Enkomi, and Kition already during the thirteenth century, first in the form of pottery trade, and particularly Aegean-style wares and increasingly in the circulation of metal goods. Though it originated on Cyprus, this new economic structure, by the early-twelfth century, had certainly spread to other areas of the Levant where it probably posed a direct threat to the economic and political order of the great powers of the time. By then, the peoples that were involved in this system of exchange were of quite diverse origins, some local to the eastern Mediterranean, and others ambitious adventurers coming from further away.[46] Though they were certainly not systematically leaving havoc and destruction in their wake as suggested by the Egyptian records, it might well be that these peoples were not adverse to some pirating activities on land or sea, and perhaps also against each other.

This long-term process of socioeconomic and cultural change certainly had a far-reaching impact on the material culture of the ancient Levant. Somehow it also found its reflection in the outlying border site of Tell el-Far'ah, although it was still under strong Egyptian influence. The underlying Cypriot flavor, distinctive to the Tell el-Far'ah grave assemblages (and grave architecture), starting already in the final phase of the Late Bronze Age and persisting throughout the early Iron Age, though without deeply affecting the continuity of the local traditions, may, in effect, be considered a sign of gradual changes in both trading and production systems. The analysis of the content of the few graves presented here may suggest that the changes observed at the site may have more to do with intensified contacts with Cyprus and with the development of a new type of society than with the traditional view of the Philistine expansion.

---

46. As Sandars (1978) already argued, it is most likely that the "Peoples of the Sea" as they appear in the Medinet Habu texts and reliefs never really constituted distinct ethnic groups. See also Sherratt 1998, 307, n. 32.

Annex: Tomb Characteristics and Furnishings

Tomb 105
(fig. 13)
Tomb type: pit grave.
Burials: 2.
Pottery: 3.
1 bowl; 1 juglet; 1 strainer jar.

Tomb 126
(fig. 15:1; Petrie 1930, pls. 32:170–71, 33:361)
Tomb type: pit grave.
Burials: 1 (child).
Pottery: 2.
2 bowls.
Gold jewelry: 1 earring.
Iron jewelry: 2 anklets.
Beads: 1 string of beads. 21 beads: 15 carnelian; 3 faience (1 flower-shaped disc); 2 shells; 1 gold. 4 pendants: carnelian.
Amulets: 1 faience Ptah.
Seals: 1 quartz conoid pendant seal (blank).

Tomb 525
(fig. 15:2; Petrie 1930, pl. 35:397)
Tomb type: pit grave.
Burials: 3.
Pottery: 4.
1 bowl; 3 juglets (1 of which is a Cypriot Bucchero juglet).
Beads: 2.
Plaque: 1 steatite.

Tomb 542
(figs. 4–8; Petrie 1930, pls. 19, 20, 21:89–91, 22:184–187, 23:1, 3–4, 25)
Tomb type: bench chamber tomb.
Burials: 11 (1 pottery coffin).
Pottery: 87.
34 bowls; 2 chalices; 6 juglets (1 of which is a Midianite juglet); 8 jugs (5 of which are round-mouth, short-neck jugs); 1 pyxis; 1 strainer jar; 16 pilgrim flasks; 6 two-handled jars; 6 storage jars; 5 lamps.
Bronze jewelry: 6 items: 1 bracelet; 5 finger rings.
Iron jewelry: 4 items: 3 bracelets; 1 ring.
Gold jewelry: 2 earrings.
Bead: 1 string of beads. 53 beads: 2 faience; 3 carnelian; 1 clay; 46 shells (5 cowries); 1 flint.
Ivory: 3 fragments (fittings).
Bronze weapons and tools: 1 dagger blade with chain rings; 1 tweezer.

Iron weapons and tools: 1 dagger (iron blade and bronze handle).
Scarabs: 4 (3 steatite; 1 faience).
Others: small silver fragments; animal bones.

Tomb 562
(figs. 9–10; Petrie 1930, pls. 19, 21:94–97, 22:205–209A, 23:5, 7, 25)
Tomb type: bench chamber tomb.
Burials: not indicated (1 pottery coffin).
Pottery: 48.
17 bowls; 5 juglets; 4 jugs; 1 pyxis; 1 strainer jar; 7 pilgrim flasks; 1 two-handled jar; 1 handless jar; 6 storage jars; 5 lamps.
Bronze jewelry: 1 toggle pin.
Beads: 8 beads: carnelian, faience, quartz.
Bronze tools and weapons: 1 dagger (bone handle).
Iron tools and weapons: 1 knife.
Metal vessels: 1 bronze bowl.
Scarabs: 5 (3 steatite; 2 faience).
Seals: 1 conoid (limestone).
Others: 1 limestone whetstone; 1 flint; 1 shell.

Tomb 608
(fig. 15:3–5)
Tomb type: pit grave.
Burials: not indicated.
Pottery: 4.
3 bowls;1 juglet.

Tomb 615
(fig. 12; Petrie 1930, pls. 30:109, 111–12, 31:289, 291–92)
Tomb type: pit grave.
Burials: 3 (2 burials swept aside).
Pottery: 11.
4 bowls; 2 juglets; 2 chalices; 2 storage jars; 1 lamp.
Iron jewelry: 2 finger rings.
Iron tools and weapons: 1 knife with bone handle.
Metal vessels: 1 copper bowl.
Scarabs: 2 (1 steatite; 1 faience).

Tomb 828
(fig. 14)
Tomb type: pit grave.
Burials: 1.
Pottery: 4.
1 bowl; 1 strainer jar; 1 pilgrim flask; 1 lamp.

Tomb 834
(fig. 11; Petrie 1930, pl. 28:834)

Tomb type: pit grave.
Burials: 1.
Pottery: 7.
2 bowls; 1 juglet; 1 round-mouth jug; 1 pilgrim flask; 1 storage jar (decorated); 1 lamp.
Metal vessels: 1 bronze bowl.

Tomb 839
(fig. 15:6–8)
Tomb type: pit grave.
Burials: 1.
Pottery: 3.
2 bowls; 1 round-mouth jug.
Iron jewelry: 1 bracelet.
Others: 1 faience pilgrim flask.

Tomb 902
(figs. 1–2; Petrie 1930, pls. 12:151–180, 13, 16)
Tomb type: bench chamber tomb.
Burials: 9.
Pottery: 31.
12 bowls; 1 strainer bowl; 3 juglets; 3 jugs (Base-Ring and Base-Ring imitations); 1 piriform jar; 3 pyxides; 3 stirrup jars; 1 pilgrim flask; 3 storage jars; 3 lamps.
Bronze jewelry: 4 items: 2 rings; 1 drop-lunate earring; 1 toggle pin.
Beads: 4 strings of beads (1 missing) and 1 isolated bead. 204 beads (the missing string of beads was not examined): 167 carnelian; 24 yellow quartz; 3 faience; 1 red jasper; 1 red-striped stone; 6 clay; 1 glass; 1 black limestone (?); small fragments of glass and faience beads.
Amulets: 1 carnelian Hator head.
Scarabs: 24 (18 steatite; 5 faience; 1 carnelian).
Plaque: 1 (steatite).
Others: 1 stone weight; kohl.

Tomb 920
(fig. 3; Starkey and Harding 1932, pls. 49, 50:41–45)
Tomb type: chamber tomb.
Burials: 1.
Pottery: 5.
1 mug ("Gazelle-and-Bird" ware); 1 jug; 2 pyxides; 1 piriform jar.
Bronze jewelry: 1 ring; 1 earring.
Beads: 1 string of beads. 77 beads: 25 carnelian; 42 faience; 6 yellow quartz; 4 clay.
Amulet: 1 faience udjat eye.
Scarabs: 4 steatite.
Others: faience kohl stick; kohl.

Chapter Nine

Philistia Transforming: Fresh Evidence from Tell eṣ-Ṣafi/Gath on the Transformational Trajectory of the Philistine Culture

*Aren M. Maeir**

Human culture, both in the past and present, has undergone (and is still undergoing) constant processes of change. Defined under the general rubric of "culture change" (see, e.g., Keesing 1973), they are amongst the most fascinating aspects in the study of human culture. Needless to say, within this wide definition, a broad range of processes and trajectories have been identified, both as causes and results. For example, much has been written on the changes caused by the movement of populations from one location to another, whether through migration, immigration, and/or other related processes. Likewise, in a wide range of societies one can see evidence for changes that occur subsequent to the arrival of a new group (and/or influence) in a new location. These processes have been classified in various manners, including acculturation, assimilation, syncretism, creolization, etc. (e.g., Cusick 1998; D'Agata 2000; Gans 1994; Hill 1999; Jennings 1991; Joppke 1999; Wilkie 2000; Webster 2001).

In the last several decades, migration was often not seen as a viable explanatory medium in many archaeological circles. Many questions have been raised as to the traditional interpretations (and purported over- and misuse) of identifying such processes in the archaeological record (see, e.g., Philip 1999) and, at the

* The Institute of Archaeology, Bar Ilan University, Ramat Gan, 52900, Israel. Email: maeira@mail.biu.ac.il.

The text of this article was completed in 2003 (and was not subsequently revised, save for minor corrections inserted before the article went to press). Since then, the excavations at Tell eṣ-Ṣafi/Gath have continued, many publications have appeared. For a more recent summary of the excavations and relevant bibliography, see now Maeir 2008.

same time, inquiring on the theoretical level (often from a somewhat skeptical perspective) to what extent such processes have an actual effect on and/or could be recognized in the archaeological record (e.g., Adams, Van Gerven, and Levy 1978). However, in more recent years, once again, the theoretical underpinnings and cultural manifestations of the influx of new populations is being discussed from a more positive perspective (e.g., Anthony 1990; Burmeister 2000; Chapman and Hamerow 1997; Lucassen and Lucassen 1999; Nichols 1998).

In the following pages I wish to focus on the study of the cultural transformation of what is seen by most scholars to be an excellent example of an immigrant culture, namely, the Philistines of the Levantine Iron Age. In particular, this discussion will be based on fresh evidence from the renewed excavations at Tell eṣ-Ṣafi/Gath.

The Philistine culture, whose primary components seem to have derived from the Aegean region and/or south-central Europe (e.g., T. Dothan 1995; Barako 2000; Killebrew 1998a; 1998b; 2000; Lipiński 1999; *pace*, e.g., Noort 1994; Bauer 1998; Drews 1998; 2000; Sherratt 1998),[1] appeared in the southern Levant during the initial stages of the Iron Age I (ca. post-1200 B.C.E.).[2] Following their arrival in the region, they settled in the southern coastal plain, often referred to as "Philistia" (e.g., Orni and Efrat 1980, 45–46). It is from this point onwards that the Philistine culture begins a unique developmental trajectory. If during the early stages of this culture many aspects displaying foreign traits can be observed (among them Mycenaean IIIC pottery) as the Iron Age unfolds, distinct chances in their cultural assemblage should be seen, with the gradual appearance of more and more local features. Towards the end of the Iron Age, a study of the main attributes of the Philistine material culture indicates that, in fact, it had much in common with the material cultures of other contemporaneous groups in the southern Levant (e.g., Gitin 1989). Nevertheless, the Philistines retained a distinct definition (from an internal and external [T. Dothan 1994], as well as emic and etic perspectives) as a separate cultural entity. Thus, the disappearance of the Philistines as a definable cultural entity occurs only after they are deported by

---

1. It would appear that the varied and quite heterogeneous origins (beyond that of the Aegean cultural realm) of the Philistines are insufficiently stressed in most studies. Nevertheless, this has been noted by several scholars (e.g., Brug 1985, 46–50; R. Harrison 1988; Sweeney and Yasur-Landau 1999; Edelstein and Schreiber 2000; Killebrew 2006–2007; this volume).

2. In this article the chronological framework of the "traditional" higher chronology of the Iron Age (e.g., A. Mazar 1990; 1997b) is followed. Nevertheless, it should be stated that the principal arguments and conclusions hold true if one adheres to the "low" chronology as well (e.g., Finkelstein 1995).

the Babylonians, following Nebuchadnezzar's campaign to Philistia in 603 B.C.E. (Eph'al 1997).

The Philistine culture in general and its developmental trajectory in particular has been the focus of much research. Due to the fact that it is a spatially and temporally well-defined culture, it serves as a prime example for the study of the appearance of a new group in a defined region; the processes of transformation as part of its ongoing contacts with the surrounding cultures; and finally, its disappearance. To a certain extent, the development of the Philistine culture can be seen as an "archaeological laboratory" for the study of culture change.

It has been suggested in the past that the developmental process that the Philistine culture went through should be understood as a process of assimilation (e.g., Kempinski 1986; Bunimovitz 1990), a process in which the Philistines slowly lost their "cultural core." Stone (1995) has convincingly demonstrated that instead, this should be seen as a process of acculturation. In other words, although the Philistine culture did go through a process of change in which many of their original, foreign cultural traits were lost; this was not done in an arbitrary matter. Rather, choice aspects, aspects that were undoubtedly of social, ethnic, and political meaningfulness were retained, perpetuating the Philistine self-definition. Only after the Philistines lost their political independence, following their conquest and exile by the Babylonians, did they assimilate into the Mesopotamian cultures, losing their separate group identification.[3]

To demonstrate the evidence for acculturation, Stone (1995) examined the developmental sequence of the Philistine culture by focusing on two cultural "snapshots." These snapshots represented key elements of the Philistine culture during the early, initial phase, and during the late, terminal phase. From these snapshots it is clear that significant and unique aspects of the Philistine culture were in fact retained throughout the Iron Age.

Despite the seemingly valid arguments that Stone (1995) presents, the fact that only two snapshots (the early and late) were discussed weakens his case. Clearly, if this argument was based on a continuous sequence of such snapshots, especially those pertaining to the intermediate stages of the Philistine culture, it would present a much stronger and lucid argument. But the lack of an "inter-

3. The archaeological evidence from Philistia appears to indicate that most if not all of the Philistine sites were completely destroyed by the Babylonians and subsequently scarcely resettled until the Persian period. At that time, a new population of Phoenician origin settled at these sites (see, e.g., Stern 2001b, 316–19). Thus, it may be assumed that even if small portions of the original Philistine population did in fact remain in Philistia subsequent to the Babylonian destruction and deportation, the numbers were small and negligible, and the Philistine ethnic and cultural self-definition did not survive.

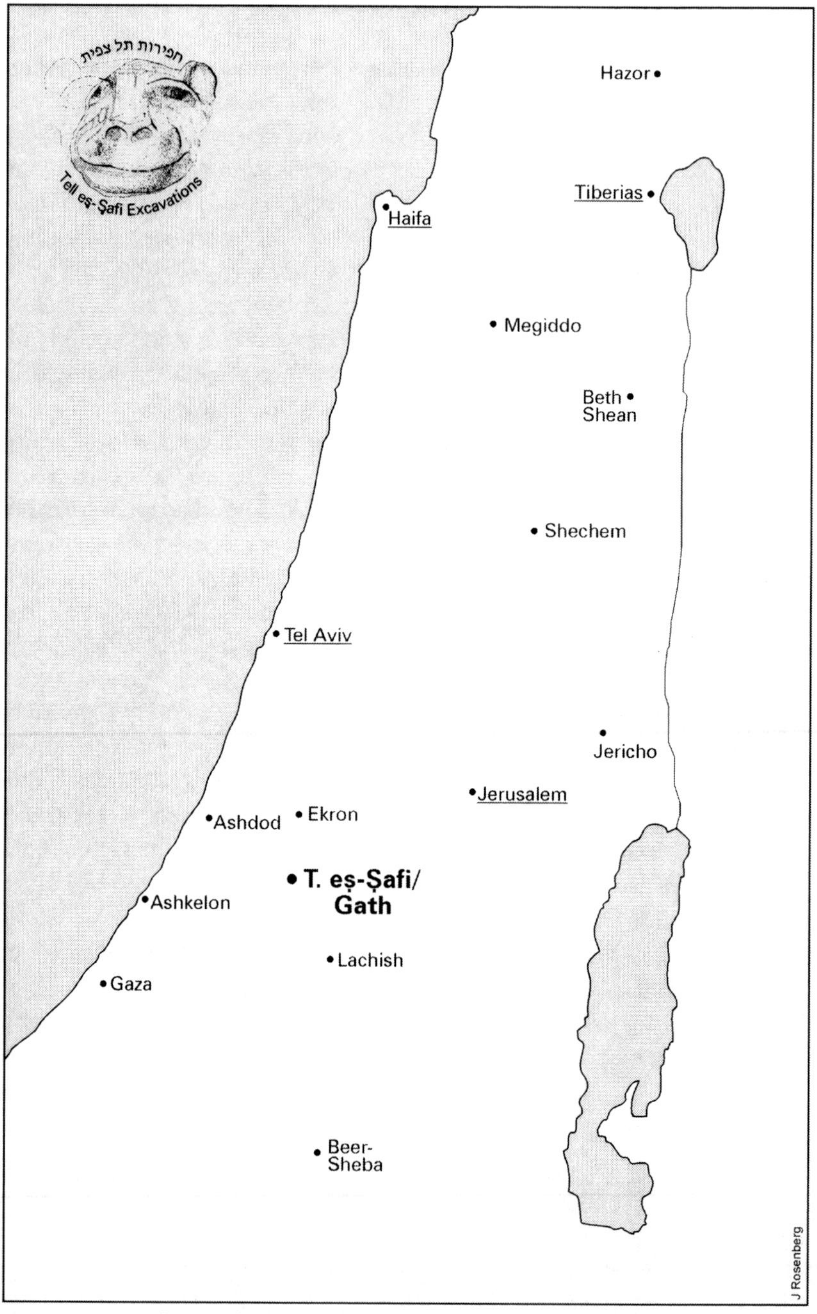

Fig. 1: General map of the southern Levant with the location of Tell eṣ-Ṣafi/Gath and other central sites.

mediate snapshot" is not accidental. When one examines most of the available archaeological data for the study of the Philistine material culture, it is apparent that not all the phases in this sequence are sufficiently known. At most of the Philistine sites (and thus, in most of the scholarly discussion), significant data exists regarding the early stages of the Philistine culture, during the Iron I Age (ca. 1200–1000 B.C.E.). Likewise, there is sufficient information on the final stages of the Philistine culture, during the late Iron Age IIB (from the late-eighth century B.C.E. to the end of the seventh century B.C.E.). But if one looks for data pertaining to the "middle phases," dating from ca. 1000 B.C.E. to the late-eighth century B.C.E., the lack of data is conspicuous. This is the situation at most of the Philistine sites. At Tel Miqne-Ekron, this period is poorly represented (Gitin 1998, 167) as well as at Ashkelon (Stager 1991) and Tel Qasile (A. Mazar 1985b). Although these levels apparently have been excavated at Ashdod (M. Dothan and Porath 1982; 1993), the lack of sufficient stratigraphic control somewhat confounds the discussion of the relevant levels at this site. If one adds to this that contemporary levels are poorly represented at nearby, non-Philistine sites as well (e.g., Lachish [Zimhoni 1997] and Batash [A. Mazar and Panitz-Cohen 2001]), this situation is only more apparent.

In light of the lack of sufficient stratigraphic data on the complete sequence of the Philistine culture, the recent excavations at Tell eṣ-Ṣafi are of importance. In the following pages, the preliminary results on the renewed excavations at this site and their relevance to the understanding of this process of transition will be discussed.

The Site

Tell eṣ-Ṣafi is a multi-period site that is situated on the northeastern border of Philistia with the Judean Shephelah (Rainey 1983), overlooking the Elah Valley (figs. 1–2). Settled continuously from the Chalcolithic period (fifth millennium B.C.E.) until modern times, it is one of the largest, pre-classical sites in the southern Levant (ca. 50 hectares; figs. 3–4). The site is identified by most scholars as "Gath of the Philistines," one of the five major cities of the Philistines (Rainey 1975; Schniedewind 1998; Maeir and Ehrlich 2001).

Since 1996, a long-term archaeological project under my direction (the Tell eṣ-Ṣafi/Gath Archaeological Project) has been underway at the site (Maeir and Boas 1998; 1999; Boas, Maeir, and Schneider 2000; Maeir 2000; 2001; Maeir and Ehrlich 2000; 2001; and see Maeir 2008 for a recent summary and bibliography).[4]

4. The project is directed by the present author. In the 1996 season, it was co-directed with A. Boas and T. Schneider; in the 1997 season A. Boas was co-director; during the 2000–2001

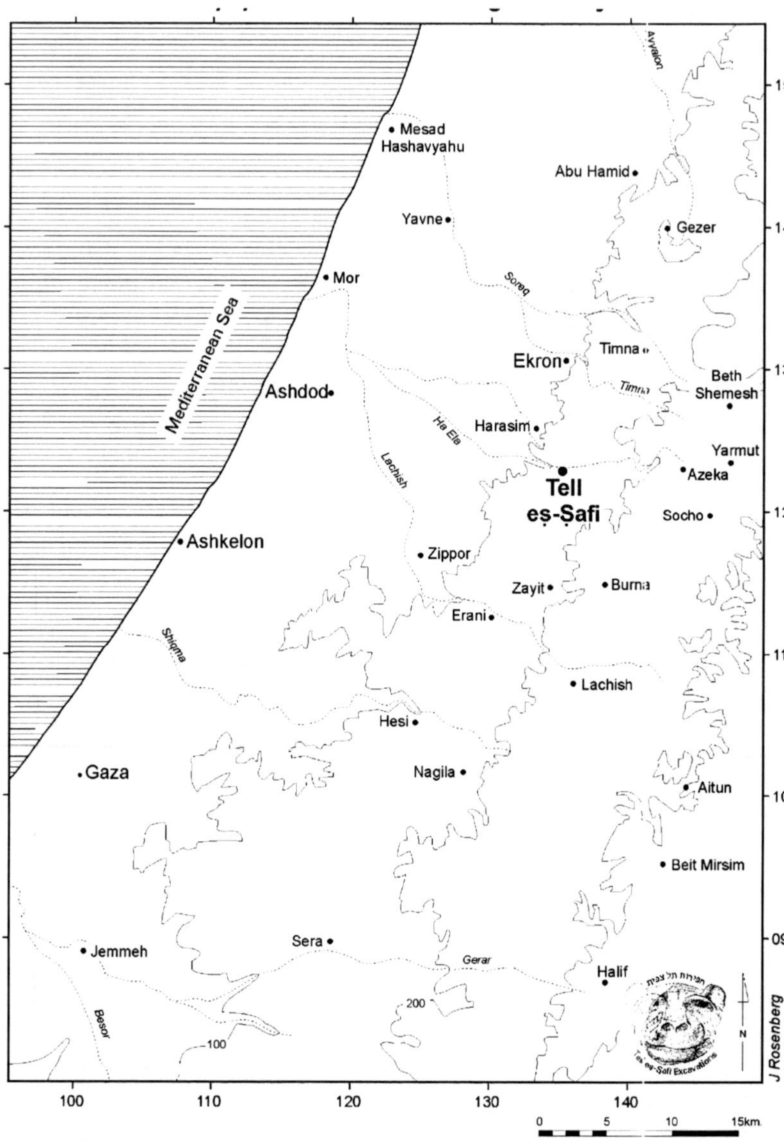

Fig. 2: General map of the southern coastal plain and the Judean Shephelah. Note the location of Tell eṣ-Ṣafi/Gath in relation to other Bronze and Iron Age sites.

During the preliminary surface survey in 1996, the size and periodization of the site was verified, and an attempt was made to locate potential excavation areas (Boas, Maeir, and Schneider 2000), particularly in light of the substantial medieval and modern remains covering extensive parts of the site. Based on the results of the survey, the main areas of excavation were positioned on the eastern slope of the tell in two adjacent terraces (Fields A and E; figs. 3, 5). In addition to exposing, immediately below surface, remains dating to the Late Bronze and Iron Ages, one of the more salient results of the first few seasons was the uncovering of a virtually complete stratigraphic sequence (see table 1), spanning the Late Bronze Age II (ca. thirteenth century B.C.E.) through the Iron Age IIB (ca. late-eighth century B.C.E.). Of particular interest are the impressive remains dating to the post-Iron Age I, pre-Iron Age IIB phases (ca. tenth–ninth centuries B.C.E.), representing the cultural phases which, as mentioned above, are virtually missing at most of the neighboring sites. Although still in a preliminary stage of analysis, the available evidence from Tell eṣ-Ṣafi/Gath offers a unique opportunity to study, in a more sequential manner, the cultural development of the Philistine culture. Albeit, at present, one can hardly claim that this offers a complete and uninterrupted history of the Philistine culture, nevertheless, this new data hopefully provides the beginnings of a "movie" sequence (as opposed to the more restricted "snapshots" mentioned above) of the development and acculturation of the Philistines.

The Evidence

Although Tell eṣ-Ṣafi/Gath was occupied from the fifth millennium B.C.E. onwards, the excavations on the eastern side of the site have revealed stratigraphic evidence of but a portion of this cultural sequence (table 1). In fact, aside from the as-of-yet limited exposure of remains dating to the Early Bronze Age II–III that were discovered in and around the excavations areas, the stratigraphically

seasons C. Ehrlich served as co-director. The core staff of the excavation are (alphabetically): O. Ackemann, R. Avisar, S. Ben-Gedalyah, I. Bordowitz, D. Castel, J. Chadwick, T. Cohen, E. Deutsch, A. Greener, M. Im, J. Johnson, A. Levi, U. Riess, J. Rosenberg, B. Schultz, I. Shai, J. Uziel, A. Zuckerman, and Z. Zwieg. The project website is located at http://www.dig-gath.org. The project has been supported by, among others, The Ihel Foundation, Bar Ilan University; the Krautheimer Chair in Archaeology, Bar Ilan University; the Kushitzky Family Foundation, Bar Ilan University; The Institute for Aegean Prehistory; Mr. Lloyd Cotsen; and the The Yoav Regional Council. This paper was completed while the author was a post-doctoral fellow at the Dibner Institute for the History of Science and Technology, Massachusetts Institute of Technology in 2002–2003.

Table 1: Temporary stratigraphic sequence in Areas A and E at Tell eṣ-Ṣafi/Gath. (All dates B.C.E. unless otherwise indicated.)

Date	Ṣafi Temp. Strata	Ṣafi Area A	Ṣafi Area E	Ṣafi Area C	Event/Note	Miqne	Batash	Ashdod	Ashkelon	Lachish
twentieth century C.E.	1	+			Military Trenching and Agriculture					
Late Modern	2	+			Muslim Burials					
Iron Age IIB—late-eighth century	3	+	-	-	Sennacherib?	II	III	VIII	+	III
Iron Age IIA—late-ninth century	4	+	+	+	Hazael's Conquest?	III?	Gap?	IX (unclear stratigraphy)	?	IV (poorly represented)
Iron Age IIA—tenth century	5	+	-	sherds	Hand Burnishing	IV–III (poorly represented)	IV	X (unclear stratigraphy)	?	V (poorly represented)
Iron Age IB—eleventh century	6	+	-	sherds	Degenerated Philistine Ware	V–IV	V?	XI	+	Gap
Iron Age IA—twelfth century	7	sherds	+	sherds	Bichrome Philistine Ware	VI	V	XII	+	Gap
early Iron Age IA—twelfth century	8	sherds & vessels	sherds	sherds	Mycenaean IIIC	VII	Gap?	XIII	+	VI
Late Bronze IIB—late-thirteenth century	9	sherds	+	sherds	Cypriot, Egyptian, and Mycenaean Imports	VIIIA	VIB	XIV	+	VII (P1)
Late Bronze IIB—thirteenth century	10	sherds	+	-	Cypriot, Egyptian, and Mycenaean Imports	VIIIB	VIA	XV	+	VII
Early Bronze II–III	-	sherds	+	-	Abydos Ware					

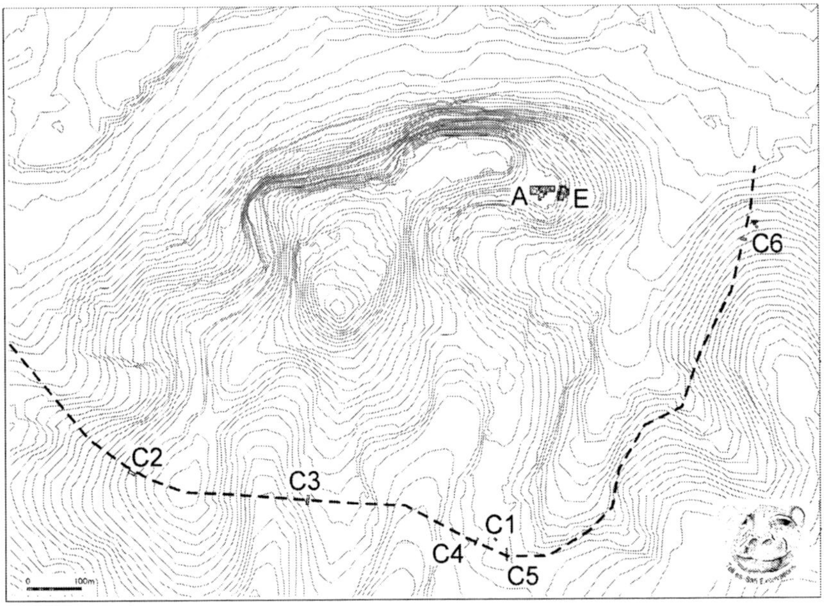

Fig. 3: General plan of Tell eṣ-Ṣafi/Gath with main areas of excavation.

defined finds that have been excavated are, as noted above, limited to a specific time frame within the overall sequence represented at the site, from the end of the Late Bronze Age (ca. thirteenth century B.C.E.) to the early Iron Age IIB (ca. late-eighth century B.C.E.). It should be noted that this stratigraphic sequence was not found in the field in one continuous sequence. Rather, the earlier (Late Bronze and early Iron Age I) were found in the lower terrace (Area E) while the latter phases (later Iron Age I and Iron Age IIA and IIB) were discovered in the upper terrace (Area A). The overall stratigraphic sequence thus represents the combination of the two separate local sequences.

The Late Bronze Age

The finds dating from the Late Bronze Age were discovered in stratigraphic contexts only in the southern side of Area E. Situated immediately below the surface, two levels from this period were revealed, Temporary Strata 10 and 9. The actual extent of exposure was quite limited (only 4–5 squares) and, in some cases, due to the proximity to the present-day surface, the remains were not always well preserved. The earlier stratum was only exposed in a limited way and, in fact, besides

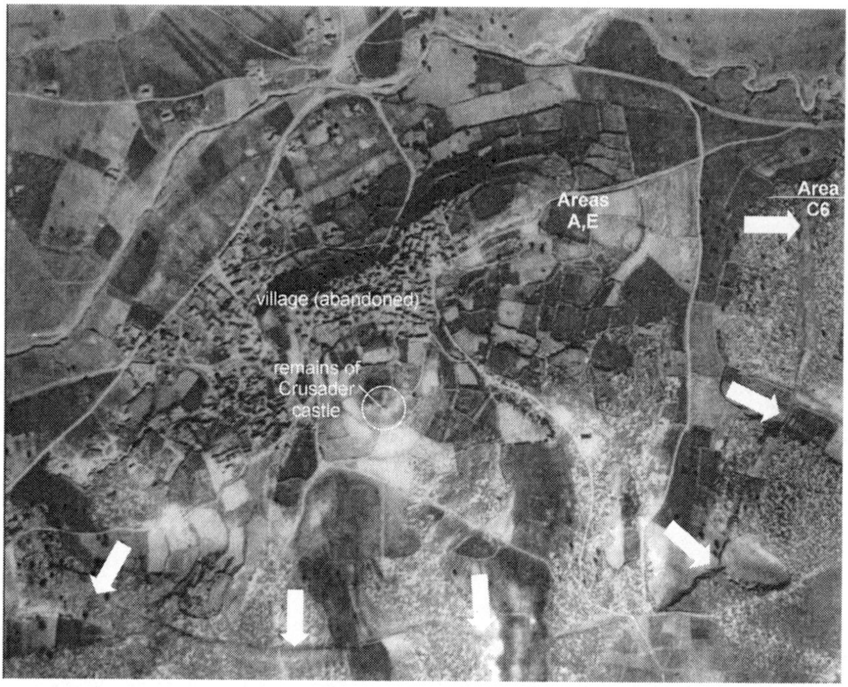

Fig. 4: Aerial view of Tell eṣ-Ṣafi/Gath.

having reached several definable surfaces below Temporary Stratum 9, little can be said of the architectural context of Temporary Stratum 10, save for the fact that finds from the latter part of the Late Bronze were discovered in this level.

The level above this, Temporary Stratum 9, yielded more extensive finds, including portions of several architectural units. Several rather thick and well-built walls were discovered, which may be part of a public-oriented building whose function as of yet is unclear. On the various surfaces related to this level, evidence of destruction was uncovered. This was manifested in large amounts of smashed, but restorable pottery, and telltale signs of burning. Among the finds, one can note a wide repertoire of local Late Bronze Age types, such as "Canaanite" storage jars (fig. 6.7), and cooking pots and various types of bowls (fig. 7), well-paralleled in terminal Late Bronze Age levels at sites in the region (e.g., Lachish [Ussishkin 1985] and Miqne-Ekron [Killebrew 1998a]). Two "lamp-and-bowl" deposits were also found, well known from sundry Late Bronze Age sites in the southern Levant (e.g., Bunimovitz and Zimhoni 1993). Imported pottery from the Late Bronze Age can be mentioned as well, including several types of Cypriot pottery (e.g., Base Ring II and White Slip II; fig. 6.3–4, 6) and fragments of Aegean imports, including a fragment of a Mycenaean IIIB pictorial krater with a chariot decoration.

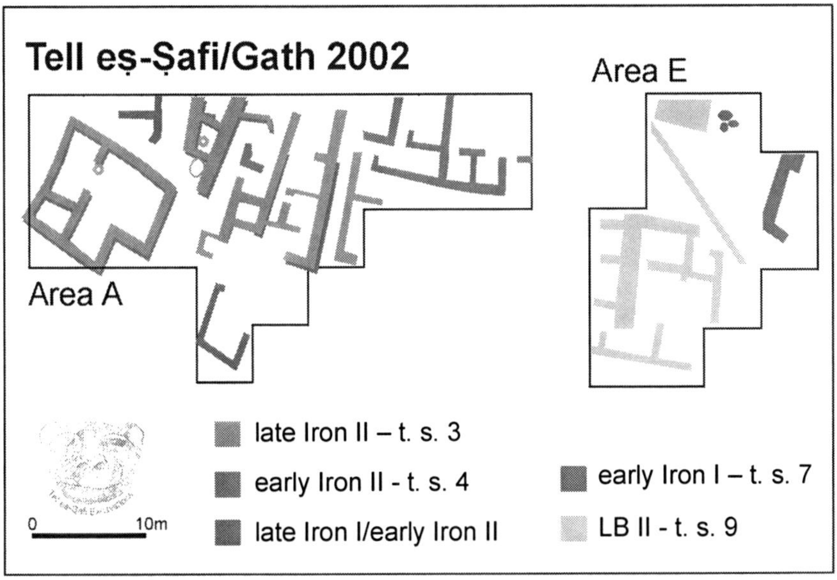

Fig. 5: Schematic plan of the excavations in Areas A and E at Tell eṣ-Ṣafi/Gath. Note the various stratigraphic layers.

Several noteworthy small finds from this stratum can be mentioned. A small selection of Egyptian-style seals derive from this level, apparently of late Nineteenth Dynasty dating (fig. 8.1–2), to which one can add an Eighteenth Dynasty scarab, which was a surface find (fig. 8.3). The two fragmentary figurines were surface finds as well, although they clearly date to the Late Bronze Age. The first (fig. 9.2) is quite common in Palestine during this period (e.g., M. Tadmor 1982, 157, pl. 8); the second (fig. 9.3) is of a type that while very common in northern Syria during the Late Bronze Age, is rarely found in the southern Levant (Conrad 1985; Maeir 2003a). Also from this level can be noted an enigmatic inscribed sherd (fig. 9.1). Although a full decipherment is not yet available, it has been suggested that it is in Egyptian Hieratic.[5]

Overall the finds from this level can be dated to the latter phases of the Late Bronze Age. It should be stressed that in this stratum there was no evidence of finds dating to the initial stages of the Late Bronze Age (e.g., pottery types such

5. I would like to thank D. Sweeney and S. Wimmer for their preliminary observations on this inscription. A more detailed discussion of this inscription, by S. Wimmer, M. Martin, and the present writer has been published in *Egypt and the Levant* 14 (Maeir, Martin, and Wimmer 2005).

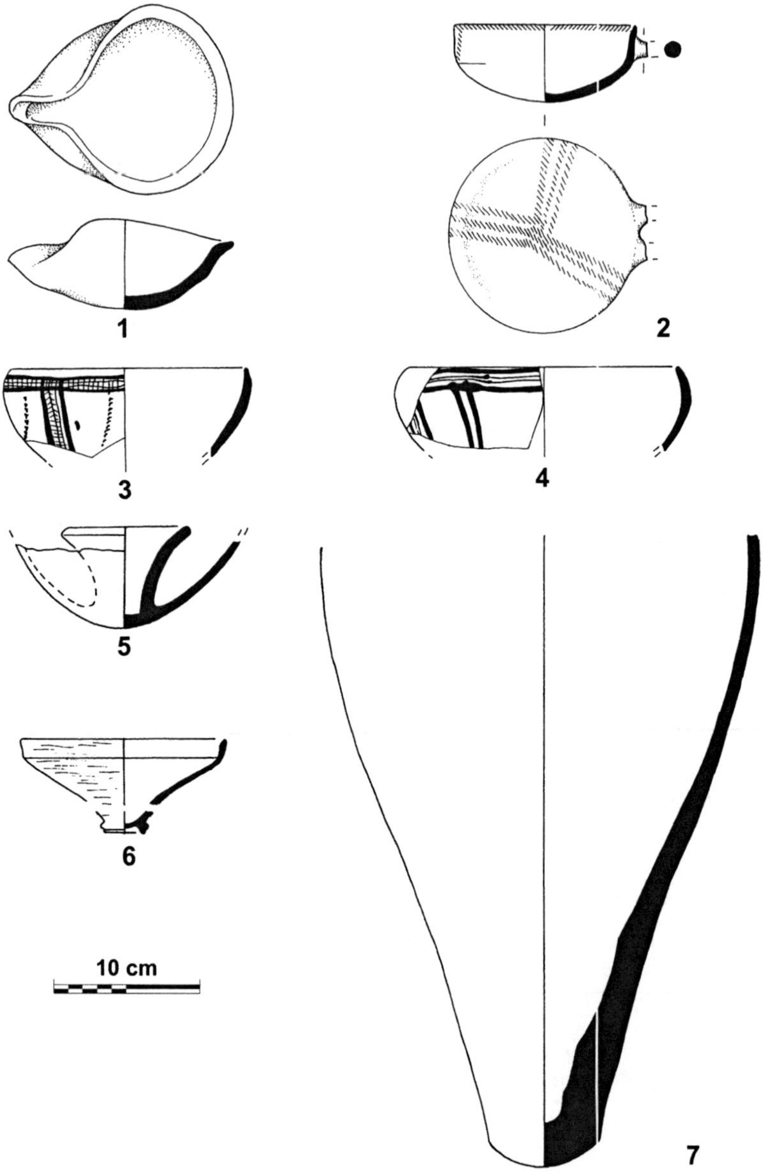

Fig. 6: Selected finds from the Late Bronze II (ca. late-thirteenth century B.C.E.), Temporary Stratum 9.

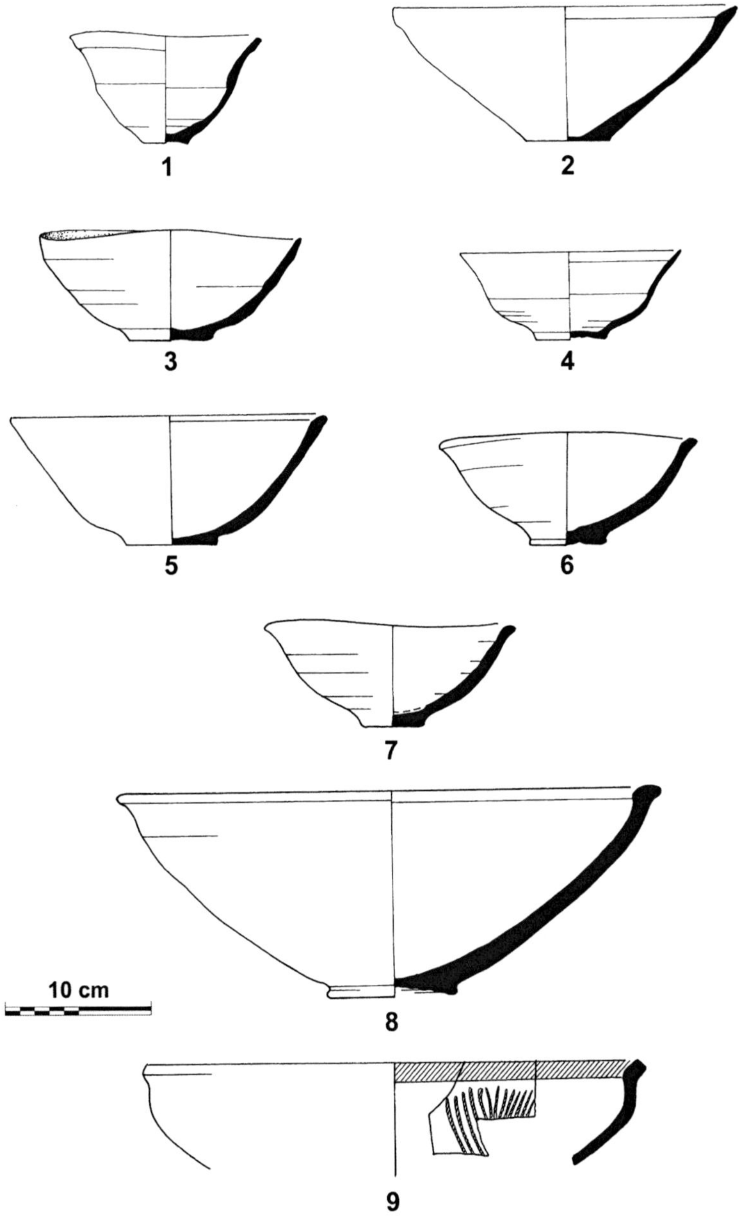

Fig. 7: Selected pottery (bowls and cooking pots) from the Late Bronze Age II (ca. late-thirteenth century B.C.E.), Temporary Stratum 9.

as Bichrome, Base Ring I, White Slip I, Monochrome, etc.) although such pottery (and other finds) were found in the surface survey of the site and in various poorly defined stratigraphic contexts. It appears that this level did not continue to exist into the first half of the twelfth century B.C.E., since there are relatively large amounts of imported pottery, types that cease to appear after the end of the thirteenth century B.C.E. (e.g., Åström 1993). Thus, it would seem that this level can be paralleled with Lachish Stratum VII (and not Stratum VI; e.g., Ussishkin 1985).

The evidence of a destruction seen in this level, as well as the general dating of the finds, appear to support the suggestion that Temporary Stratum 9 is the final phase of the Late Bronze Ginti/Gath, a Canaanite city that is attested in the mid-fourteenth-century B.C.E. el-Amarna archive (for a summary of the references to Gath in the el-Amarna letters, see, e.g., Rainey 1975; Singer 1993, 135–36; Schniedewind 1998). This may represent the final destruction of Canaanite Gath, prior to the settlement of the Philistines at this site during early Iron Age I.

Iron Age I

Based on a comparison to the sequences at other major sites in Philistia (e.g., Ashdod, Ashkelon, and Miqne-Ekron), it is highly likely that following the destruction of the Late Bronze Age city and with the arrival of the Philistines, a new phase of settlement was initiated at Tell eṣ-Ṣafi. At these other sites, this phase is typified by the appearance of new types of pottery (the so-called Mycenaean IIIC pottery) and assorted other components of the material culture (e.g., T. Dothan 1995; 2000; Killebrew 1998a; 1998b; 2000). Although, as of yet, this initial stage of the Philistine settlement at Tell eṣ-Ṣafi/Gath has not been exposed in a stratigraphic context, ceramic evidence has been found. Thus, we have referred to it as Temporary Stratum 8 (see table 1). In both Areas A and E, sherds (and more recently, complete vessels) have been found that can be classified as Mycenaean IIIC types (e.g., fig. 10.1–2).[6] An additional find that may possibly relate to this phase is a pinched cylindrical ceramic object (fig. 11.5), that, although found in an Iron Age IIA context (Temporary Stratum 4), can apparently be identified as a "reel" or "spool"—a loom weight of a type found in the Aegean region and Cyprus during the Late Bronze and early Iron Ages. In recent years, several examples of this unique type of loom weight have been

6. I would like to thank T. Dothan, E. French, P. Mountjoy, J. Rutter, and S. Sherratt for examining selected examples of the Mycenaean IIIC pottery and confirming their identifications.

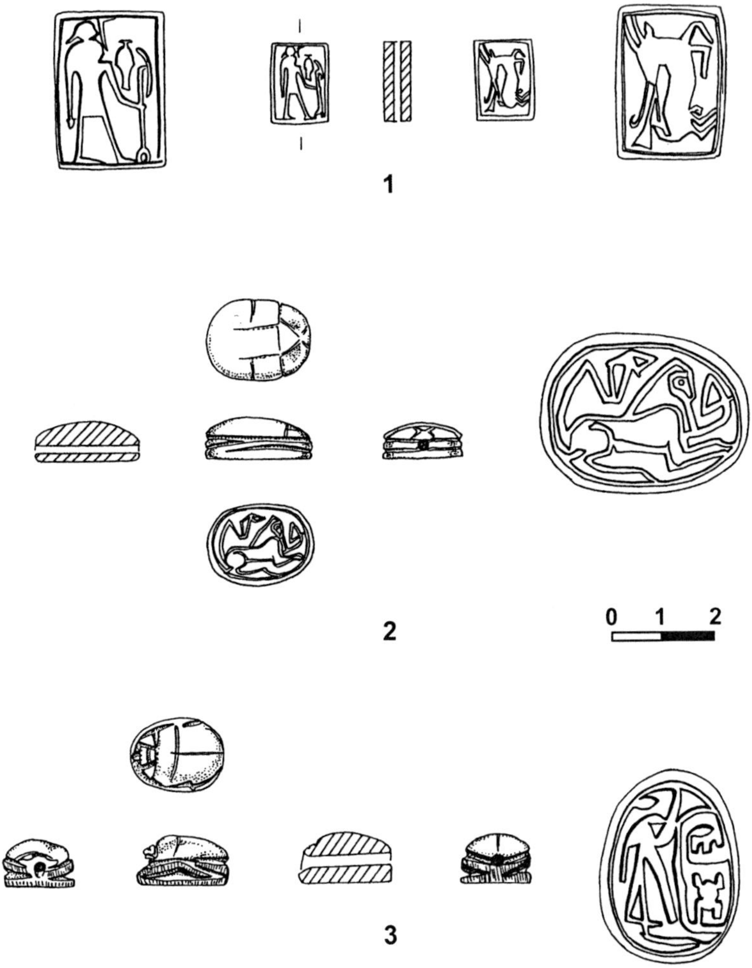

Fig. 8: Selected finds from the Late Bronze II (ca. late-thirteenth century B.C.E.), Temporary Stratum 9.

reported at early Iron Age sites in Philistia (Ashdod, Ashkelon, and Ekron; e.g., Stager 1995, 346; Lass 1994, 32–33; T. Dothan 1995) as well as further afield (e.g., see sites listed in Stager 1995, 346 and now Cecchini 2000, 212). It has been suggested that this should be seen as an example of a unique aspect of the "Sea Peoples" culture, one that was brought with them when they settled in the east,

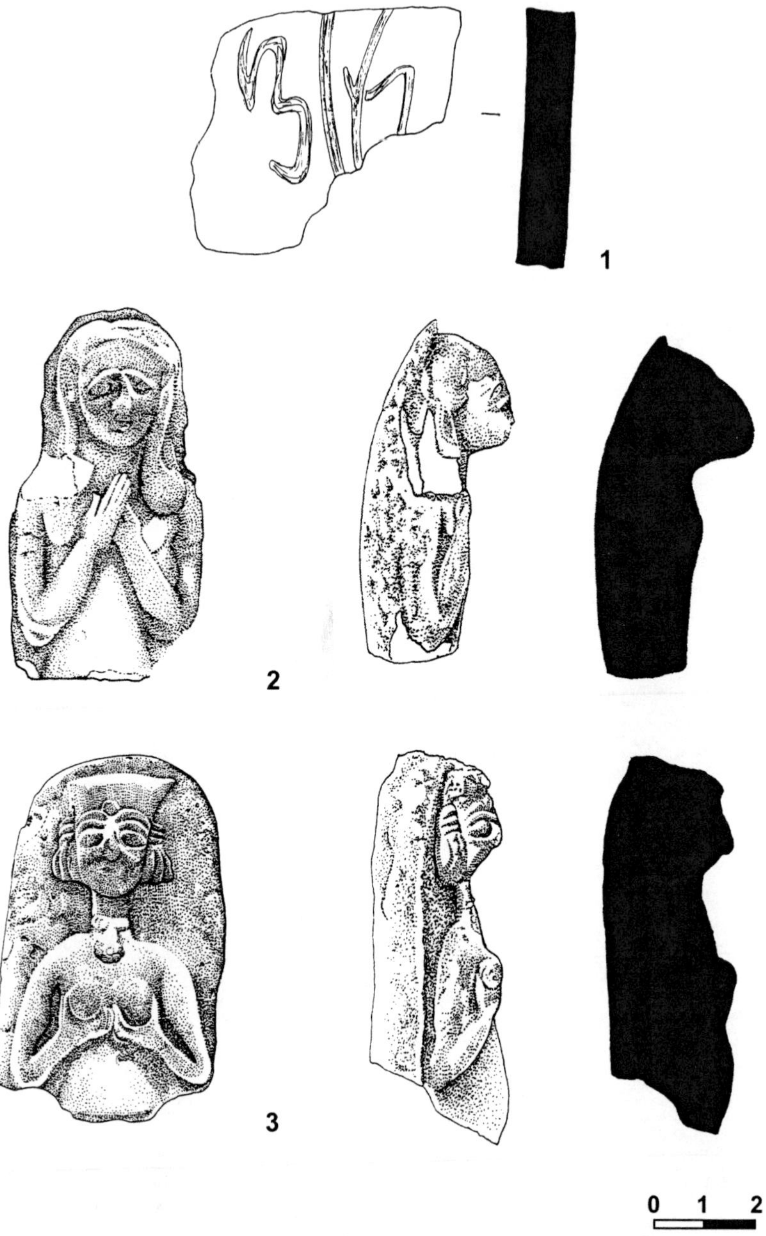

Fig. 9: Selected finds from the Late Bronze II (ca. late-thirteenth century B.C.E.), Temporary Stratum 9.

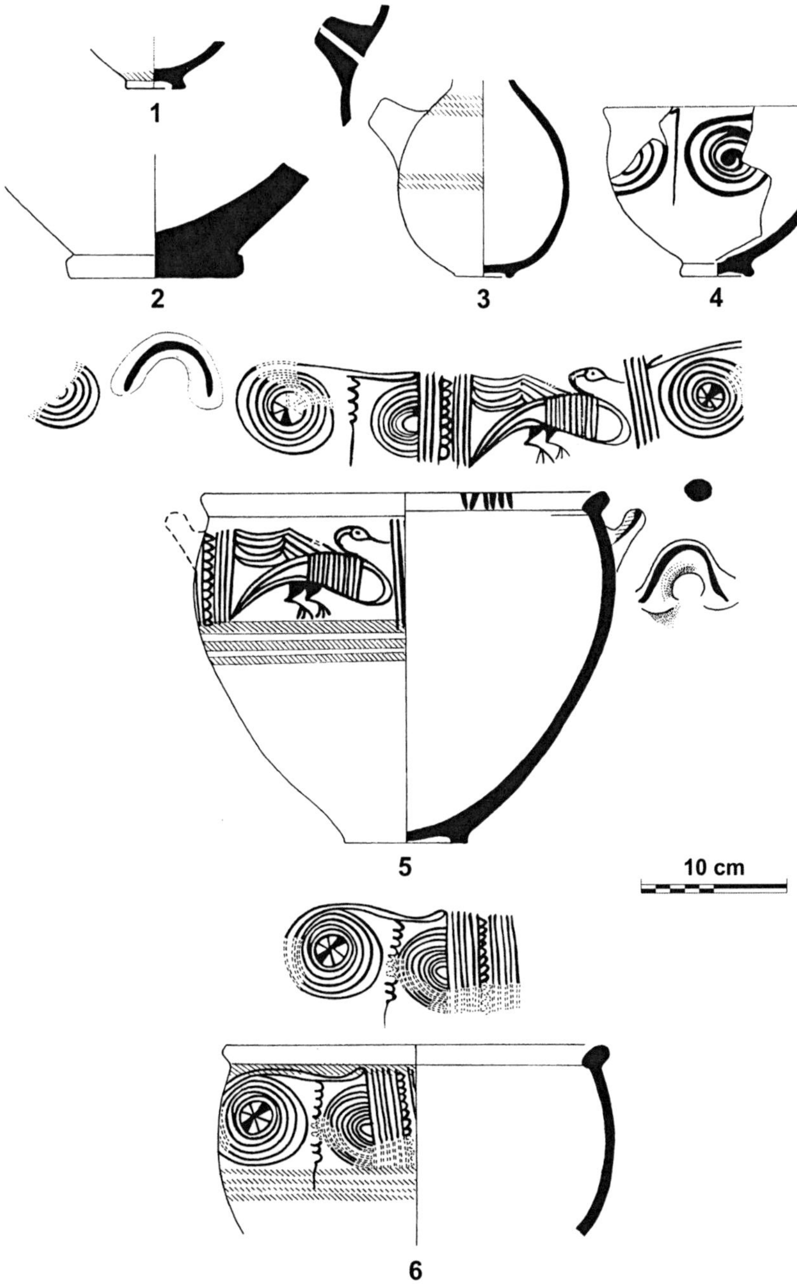

Fig. 10: Selected pottery from Temporary Stratum 8 (no. 1), Temporary Stratum 7 (nos. 5, 6), and Temporary Stratum 6 (nos. 2–4).

but that disappeared soon afterwards. In sites in Philistia this seems to be the case, since all reported examples have come from Iron Age I contexts, and if so, the example from Tell eṣ-Ṣafi/Gath belongs to this cultural horizon. It should be noted that in Syria, such types continue to appear well into the Iron Age II–III (e.g., Cecchini 2000, 212) and this might very well be the case for this example as well.[7] In any case, these finds indicate that in future seasons, stratified evidence of this earliest phase of the Philistine settlement (and the pertinent material culture) will be discovered.

Following this initial phase, the finds from several sites have shown that during the Iron Age I, the Philistine material culture developed in a well-known cultural trajectory. Subsequent to the initial phase typified by the Mycenaean IIIC pottery, three major phases are known, best seen in the developmental sequence of the Philistine decorated pottery (e.g., T. Dothan 1982; see as well A. Mazar 1985a; Stager 1995, 339). The earliest of these phases is characterized by the appearance of the readily identifiable Philistine "Elaborate Bichrome Decoration" (T. Dothan's "Phase I"), in which large percentages of the vessels are decorated with a red and black bichrome decoration on a thick white slip.

Stratigraphic and architectural evidence of this cultural phase was found in the northern part of Area E, while sherds from this phase were abundant in the various levels in Area A.[8] Several surfaces, a bit of architecture, as well as several midden pits containing large amounts of such Philistine Bichrome pottery (and other contemporaneous types) were uncovered (figs. 10.5–6; 12.4; 13). These were found immediately below surface (as with the Late Bronze Age remains which were exposed just to the south of these). The extent of exposure was quite limited and the levels that were directly above and below this phase have not yet been exposed. Thus, the stratigraphic relationship with the other levels in Areas A and E is based on typological grounds. This level has been termed Temporary Stratum 7. In light of the architectural remains and pit-like materials, it appears that this part of the site was within the settled area and it appears that during the early Iron

7. Such objects have been also reported in the Iron Age levels at Qatna, Syria (M. Luciani, personal communication). During the summer of 2001, an Iron Age II site was discovered and excavated just 4 kilometers to the west of Tell eṣ-Ṣafi/Gath. Among the finds were a large number of objects that are virtually identical to well-known types of Iron Age ceramic loom weights, including the pinched type discussed above. Thus, this may provide evidence that this type continued to be used in this region subsequent to the early Iron Age. A cautionary note should be added: If in fact these objects served as loom weights, the contemporaneous appearance of several different types may raise serious queries regarding their accepted chrono-typological definitions (e.g., Friend 1998). I would like to thank the excavator, Y. Israel (of the Israel Antiquities Authority) for graciously showing me the finds and for permission to mention them.

8. As well as in the surface survey of the site.

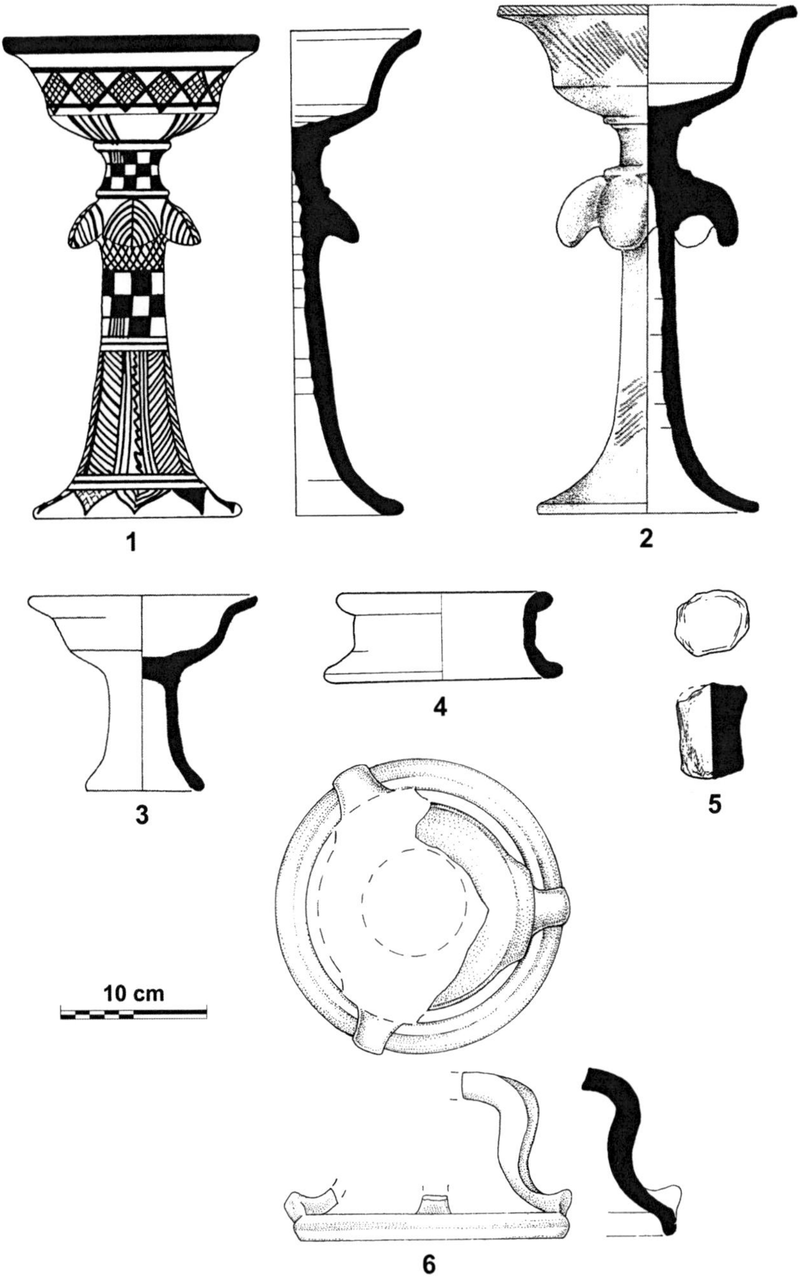

Fig. 11: Selected pottery and other finds from Temporary Stratum 4: 1–3) chalices; 4) pot stand; 5) "reel," "spool," or loom weight; and 6) fenestrated chalice base.

Age I, the site extended well to the east of the summit of the tell and was quite extensive in size.

Without a doubt, further excavations should reveal additional finds from this phase and, most likely, additional internal phasing to this very stage. Due to the large quantities of remains relating to this cultural stage, found both in the present excavations and survey as well as in the earlier work at the site, it is clear that this was a period in which Tell eṣ-Ṣafi/Gath was large and well developed.

Finally, an interesting point regarding the bichrome Philistine decorated pottery should be noted. Although this pottery is well known from other Philistine sites (e.g., T. Dothan 1982), the examples from Tell eṣ-Ṣafi/Gath appear to display a decorative "syntax" unique to the site, somewhat different from that seen at the other Philistine sites.[9]

Iron Age IIA

Temporary Stratum 6

The next phase, Temporary Stratum 6, has been discovered only in Area A in the upper terrace, and, once again, only in a very limited exposure. In several of the, at present, limited probes below the Iron IIA phases (Temporary Stratum 4 and 5, see below), a level was reached which contained typical late Iron I pottery. This included two complete vessels of the "Degenerate Philistine" style (fig. 12.1, 3), as well as sherds and fragmentary vessels typical of this phase (fig. 10.2–4). As of yet, the architectural evidence from this phase is somewhat limited, but several courtyard and street-like surfaces have been defined. Typologically, the pottery

9. An in-depth comparison between the pottery from the major Philistine sites may open up the possibility of distinguishing between the decorated pottery of different Philistine sites, perhaps even enabling the definition of local workshops, "hands," or even "painters." In general, little use has been made of "style-analysis" tools for the definition of the decoration of ceramics from the ancient Levant, despite widespread and, often, quite successful use in both traditional archaeological interpretation (e.g., Cook 1997), in "processual" archaeology (for a summary, see, e.g., Rice 1987, 244–73), and recently even in "post-processual" studies (e.g., Shanks 1999). The classic example of such a study on pottery from the Bronze Age Levant is perhaps Heurtley's (1938), now thoroughly outdated, study of the Late Bronze Bichrome Ware (and his proposed identification of the "Ajjul painter"; cf. Epstein 1966; Artzy 1975; 2001). Although the results of this particular study are hardly relevant today, similar analytic paths should not be abandoned and may provide interesting insights in the future (e.g., Artzy 2002). It can only be hoped that the much larger corpus of decorated pottery groups that exist today (derived from well-excavated and properly published archaeological research), coupled with a more sophisticated use of these and similar tools, will open up new vistas in the study of the decorated pottery groups in the ancient Levant.

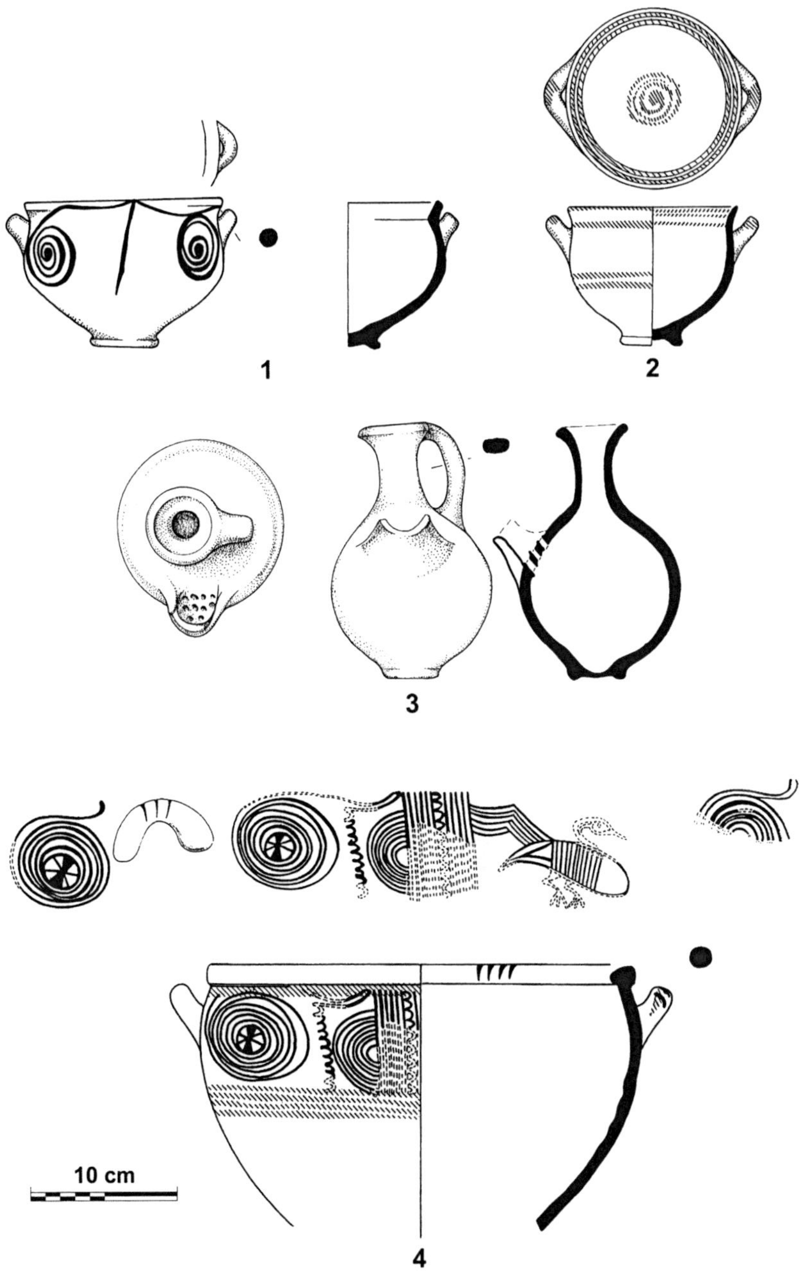

Fig. 12: Selected pottery from Temporary Stratum 8 (no. 2), Temporary Stratum 7 (no. 4), and Temporary Stratum 6 (nos. 1, 3).

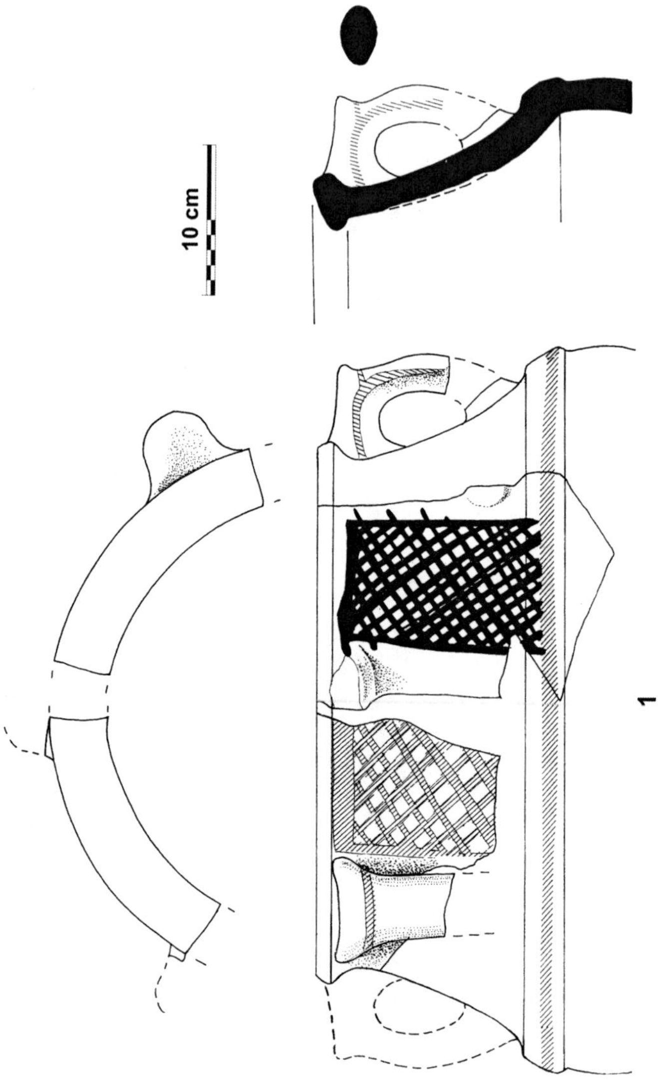

Fig. 13: Pottery from Temporary Stratum 7.

found can be compared to other late Iron I sites in Philistia, such as Miqne-Ekron Stratum IV (T. Dothan 1989, 9–12), Qasile Stratum X (A. Mazar 1985b, 123–27), and Ashdod Stratum XI (e.g., M. Dothan and Porath 1982, 52–53).

Several interesting finds from this level can be noted. Of some interest is the base of a "head cup" (rhyton) in the shape of lion's head (fig. 14). Only the base of the vessel has survived and it appears that it was in secondary use since it seems to have been intentionally and evenly broken off. The well-produced bichrome decoration indicates as well that this vessel derives from an earlier phase. Similar vessels are known from quite a few Philistine and Sea Peoples sites (e.g., T. Dothan 1982, 229–34; A. Mazar 2000, 225; note the somewhat different example found by M. Dayan at Tell eṣ-Ṣafi, T. Dothan 1982, 231–32, fig. 7) and are of apparent ritual and symbolic significance (e.g., A. Mazar 2000, 225).[10] Such head cups have not been found in post-Iron I/early Iron IIa contexts and thus may represent a class of symbolic objects that lose their meaningfulness at a quite early stage of the process of the Philistine cultural transformation (Maeir 2006; see Meiberg, this volume, for a discussion of these rhyta).

An additional find of some interest was discovered in the 2002 season. Deriving from a context which may be of cultic nature (due to the discovery of several "votive"-like vessels), the complete blade of a curved, single-edged iron knife was found (fig. 15a). This knife, whose handle was missing, appears to be one of the well-known "bi-metallic" knives (T. Dothan 2002). It represents a well-known component of the Sea Peoples cultic paraphernalia with apparent connections to the Late Bronze Age south-central European early Urnfield and Balkan cultures (Bouzek 1985, 147).

Temporary Stratum 5

This stratum has been revealed in a relatively limited way by several probes below Temporary Stratum 4. As of yet, the small exposure does not permit one to say much about this level. Nevertheless, the ceramic finds from this level indicate its potential importance in the future. The pottery from this level appears to conform with what would be considered classic Iron Age IIA pottery. This is typified by the appearance of a relatively large percentage of vessels with red-slipped, hand-burnished surface treatment (A. Mazar 1998). Overall, the pottery from this level is quite similar to the Iron Age IIA forms found in the subsequent Temporary Stratum 4 (see discussion below), while being much less analogous to the forms typical of the late Iron Age I (as found in Temporary Stratum 6, see above).

10. Note that possible fragments of several additional "head cups" have been found in the excavations.

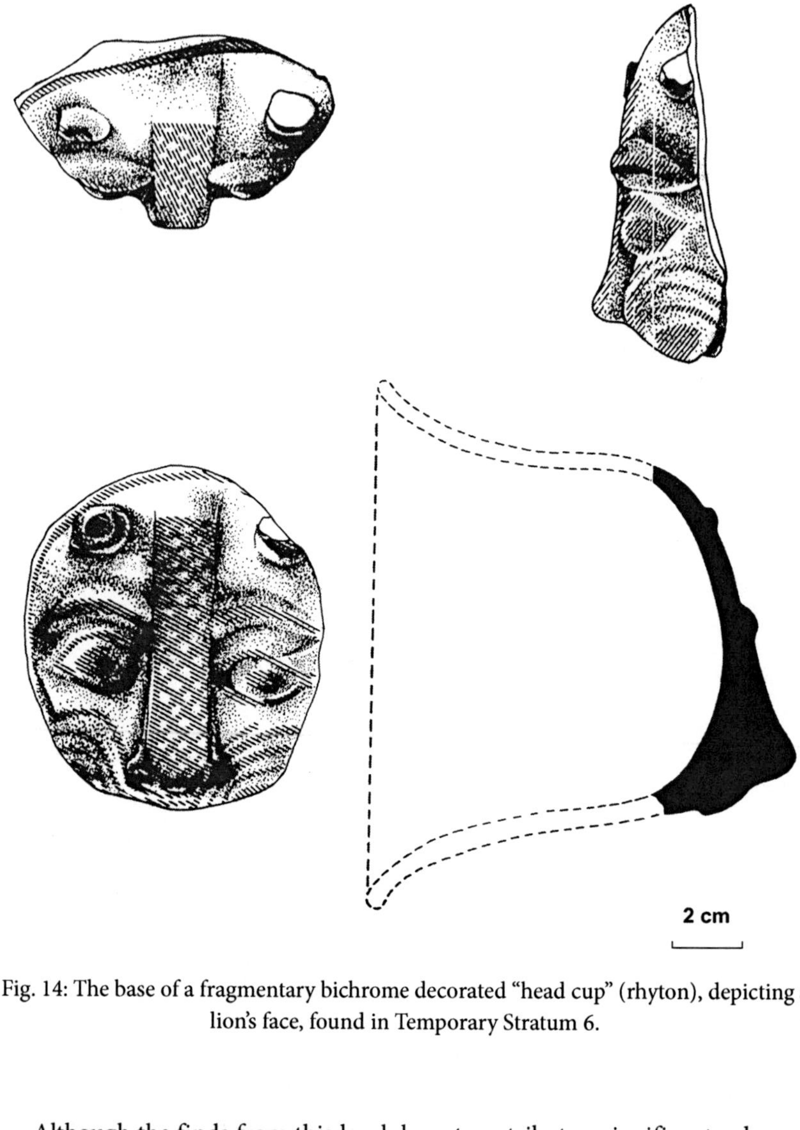

Fig. 14: The base of a fragmentary bichrome decorated "head cup" (rhyton), depicting a lion's face, found in Temporary Stratum 6.

Although the finds from this level do not contribute a significant volume of data relevant to the central question of this study (the process of the Philistine transformation), the limited data do indicate the future potential importance. The very fact that this seems to represent a distinctly recognizable early Iron Age II phase, immediately succeeding the final late Iron Age I phase (Temporary Stratum 6) and preceding the well-documented Iron Age IIA (Temporary Stratum 4), is of cardinal importance. As mentioned above, it is just this phase of the Philistine

Fig. 15a: View of "bi-metallic type" knife *in situ*, Temporary Stratum 6.

Fig. 15b: View of architectural preservation in Temporary Stratum 4. Notice height of preserved walls and remnants of the original plaster adhering to the walls.

cultural trajectory that is so poorly known. A future, more comprehensive view of the assemblage from this stage would most probably indicate which traits of the earlier Philistine culture were already lost in the transition to the Iron Age II and which continued, either to be eventually phased out, or endure until the later phases of the Iron Age. If in fact this does represent a well-defined archaeological phase that can be classified as post-Iron Age I, but prior to the late eighth-century B.C.E. cultural horizon (as with the level above it, Temporary Stratum 4), this will provide important fresh data relevant to the ongoing controversy on the chronology of the Iron Age (e.g., Finkelstein 1995; A. Mazar 1997b).

Temporary Stratum 4

From the very commencement of the excavations, Temporary Stratum 4 has been the most predominant stratum in Area A, in many cases appearing immediately below surface. This stratum is a very well-preserved destruction level with a wide array of finds, providing an excellent representation of the material culture from a chronologically well-defined point. Since, for the most part, there was a limited amount of activity in Area A after this destruction level, the amount of post-depositional destruction processes (such as robber trenching, leveling, etc.) was quite limited and the preservation of the architectural remains and associated finds from this stratum was quite impressive.

As can be seen from the schematic plan (fig. 5), remains from this stratum were found throughout Area A in well-defined stratigraphic contexts. Although in many cases this level was discovered only ten to thirty centimeters below surface, overlaid only by topsoil in several cases, it is mostly covered by either Iron Age IIB (Temporary Stratum 3, see discussion below) or even scantier modern period remains (Temporary Strata 1–2). On the other hand, wherever the excavations have penetrated below this level, the earlier strata described above were exposed. The stratigraphic matrix of the level itself was usually comprised of a debris level, often one meter thick, containing the destruction debris, lying on well-defined surfaces. In this debris level and on the surfaces there was extensive evidence of a conflagration, demonstrated by many burned and charcoaled deposits and finds, collapsed and vitrified bricks and brick walls, and building stones and stone objects that had fractured due to extreme heat. Thus, not only was this level rich in finds, but it was quite easily delineated and differentiated.

Portions of several architectural units have been exposed, although, as of yet, the exact dimensions and overall plans of these buildings cannot be determined. Based on the constructional techniques, some of these edifices appear to be of high quality (evidenced, for example, through the use of large dressed stones) while others appear to have been made using simpler construction techniques. In several cases, the walls of these structures were preserved to a height of over a meter with remains of plaster still adhering to the mud-brick or stone walls (e.g., fig. 15b). In some of the buildings there was evidence of several architectural phases (such as door-blockings, partition walls, etc.), indicating that architecturally this stratum had more than an ephemeral duration.

The finds from this stratum offer a wide and very well-preserved spectrum of material culture at a particular junction in time, due to the character of the destruction process (and the relative lack of severe post-depositional processes). Whether the objects had originally laid on the floors or had fallen from shelves or upper floors, many of these were found in pristine condition. Hundreds of ceramic vessels were recovered (the current estimate is in the region of 500); the overall majority are fully restorable, while quite a few were unbroken. In addition, a relatively wide range of other classes of material remains were discovered, including: small finds of various types; the skeletons of at least two people who had been inadvertently buried in the debris during the destruction; and assorted ecofacts, including archaebotanical and archaeozoological data. Although even a partial review of the finds from this stratum is beyond the scope of this study, a choice group of these finds will be presented.

If one starts from the pottery assemblage, several aspects can be singled out. The assemblage on the whole is extremely varied (fig. 16). Virtually every primary type of vessel is represented, some with many examples, others with fewer. This includes open and closed vessels of all sorts; serving, storage, and food preparation vessels; domestic, cultic, and specialized forms; and local and imported wares. At the same time, the transitional character of the assemblage is noticeable. On the one hand, a few types that are reminiscent of classic late Iron Age I types can be found (e.g., deep bowl [fig. 17.3] and the pyxis [fig. 18.6]). On the other hand, types that can be seen as precursors of later Iron IIB types are found (and in particular, from well-dated assemblages such as Lachish Level III), such as the ridged cooking pots and some of the jars (especially the so-called Pre-LMLK jars, fig. 19.1–2; for an in-depth discussion, see Shai and Maeir 2003).[11] To this one can add that the assemblage is typified by certain attributes traditionally associated with the Iron Age IIA. Thus, a large percentage of the vessels are red-slipped and hand-burnished (e.g., A. Mazar 1998), while wheel burnishing, so typical of the Iron Age IIB, is completely absent. The existence of certain groups, particularly the Cypro-Phoenician Black-on-Red juglets (fig. 18.12–13; e.g., Schreiber 2001) as well as the so-called Ashdod Ware (figs. 20.1–2, 4; 21.1–4),[12]

11. Note as well that there are many jars of similar volumes, indicating production standardization and commercial aptitude.

12. It may be that the Ashdod Ware combines two sets of decorative syntax. Without a doubt, it is highly influenced by the Phoenician pottery styles. On the other hand, it may very

Fig. 16: View of a selection of the pottery assemblage from Temporary Stratum 4.

indicates a post-Iron Age I relative dating. Particular note can be made of the decorated chalices/thymiateria (fig. 11.1–2). Quite a few complete and fragmentary examples of this type have been found and they can be compared to several additional examples that were previously found at Tell eṣ-Ṣafi/Gath (Ornan 1986). While morphologically, these vessels have a long history, continuing, in metal at least, into the Persian period (e.g., Stern 1981, 317–19)[13], the painted decoration

well be that there is a direct, or at least indirect, relationship with the so-called degenerated Philistine style, typical of the late Iron Age I. Perhaps, this family is an example of the fusion of two ceramic traditions. This pottery group clearly warrants further research.

13. Note that Stern 1981 in his discussion of earlier parallels to somewhat similar Persian period vessels mentions and publishes an illustration (Stern 1981, fig. 7:2) of one of these vessels, found at Tell eṣ-Ṣafi/Gath by M. Dayan. He suggests a late-eleventh-century B.C.E. dating for this

is of particular interest. On the one hand, the bichrome red and black painting as well as some of the motifs (e.g., the checkerboard design and hatched lozenges) are reminiscent of the early Philistine decorative traditions (e.g., T. Dothan 1995). On the other hand, the technical application of this decoration is quite unusual. The painted decoration is applied post-firing, a method virtually unknown in Bronze and Iron Age Palestine (for good reason, since it is easily washed off!). One can wonder if this might represent an unsuccessful attempt to imitate the earlier Philistine decorative traditions.

All told, the very fact that this assemblage combines older and newer types, along with transitional ones, safely places this assemblage somewhere between the late Iron Age I and the second half of the eighth century B.C.E. (the latter based on the comparison to assemblages such as Lachish III). More importantly, for the needs of the present study, it represents a "snapshot" of the development of the Philistine culture at a crucial stage—as many of the earlier Iron Age I pottery types were disappearing and the late Iron Age II traditions were beginning to appear.

But this is not only seen in the pottery assemblage. As mentioned above, other components of the material culture of this cultural horizon are well represented, several of which point to the transitional character of this stage. The following examples can be mentioned.

The sphragistic corpus from this level (e.g., fig. 22.2), although not extensive as of yet, is indicative of the same post-Iron I, pre-Iron IIB dating and cultural horizon (e.g., Keel 1990; 1994). Of some interest is the appearance of several notched scapulae (both bovine and caprid) from this level (e.g., fig. 22.1). Such scapulae are a well-known component of the Sea Peoples and Philistine material culture, often associated with cultic activities (e.g., Webb 1985). In fact, it has been suggested that it is one of the imported components of their cultic paraphernalia (e.g., A. Mazar 2000). All previously reported examples from Sea Peoples and/or Philistine contexts are dated to the Iron Age I (including reused examples from later contexts, e.g., Stern 1994b). Thus, the appearance of three such samples from a ninth-century B.C.E. setting provides evidence for the continued use of this symbol-laden item. Note should be made that the scapulae were found in close association with production activities (both olive-related and weaving). Although cultic activities associated with similar production sites are known from later Philistine contexts (e.g., stone altars found in olive oil production facilities in late Iron Age IIB Ekron [e.g., Gitin 1998]), similar scapulae have

and other vessels that had been found at Tell eṣ-Ṣafi/Gath, a dating that can now be revised (to the late-ninth century B.C.E.) in light of the finds from the current excavations.

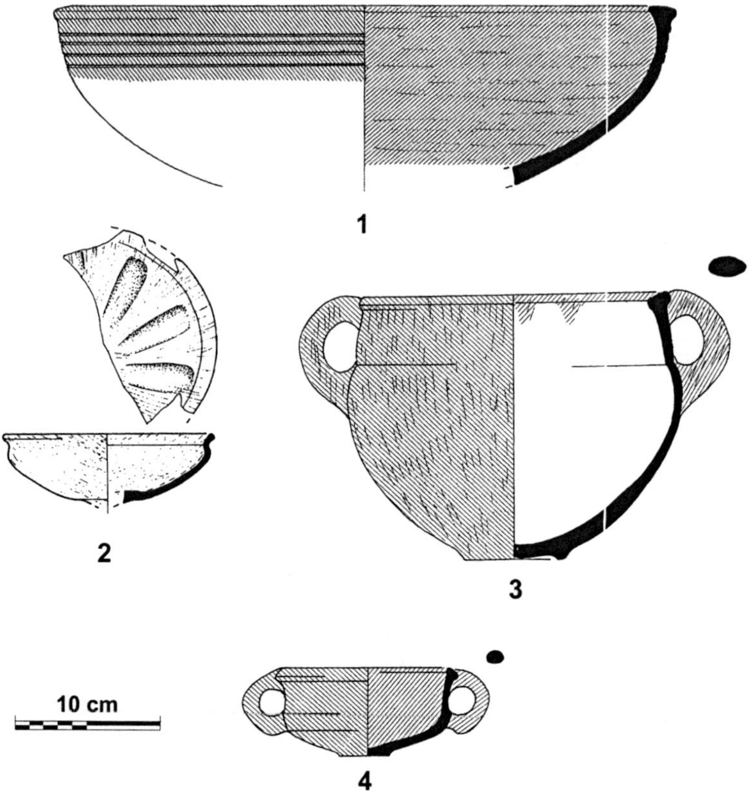

Fig. 17: Selected bowls and kraters from Temporary Stratum 4.

not been found in these later production/cultic contexts. Thus, it would seem that the scapulae represent a "meaningful" item that lost its significance at a relatively late stage (post-ninth century B.C.E.).

The question of writing and language is also of importance. Although far too little is known, there is some evidence indicating that at least some of the Sea Peoples/Philistines brought with them a nonlocal language, most probably of Indo-European origin. Hints of non-Semitic vocabulary and onomastics (e.g., Sapir 1936; Ben-Dov 1976) as well as several enigmatic inscriptions (Franken 1964b; T. Dothan and M. Dothan 1992, 153, pls. 10–11) point to this (for recent summaries, see, e.g., Singer 1994, 335–37; Machinist 2000, 63–64). On the other hand, evidence from the Iron Age IIB demonstrates that at some stage, the Philistines started using the Phoenician language and script, eventually virtually replacing (or at least overshadowing) the earlier, non-Semitic linguistic traditions,

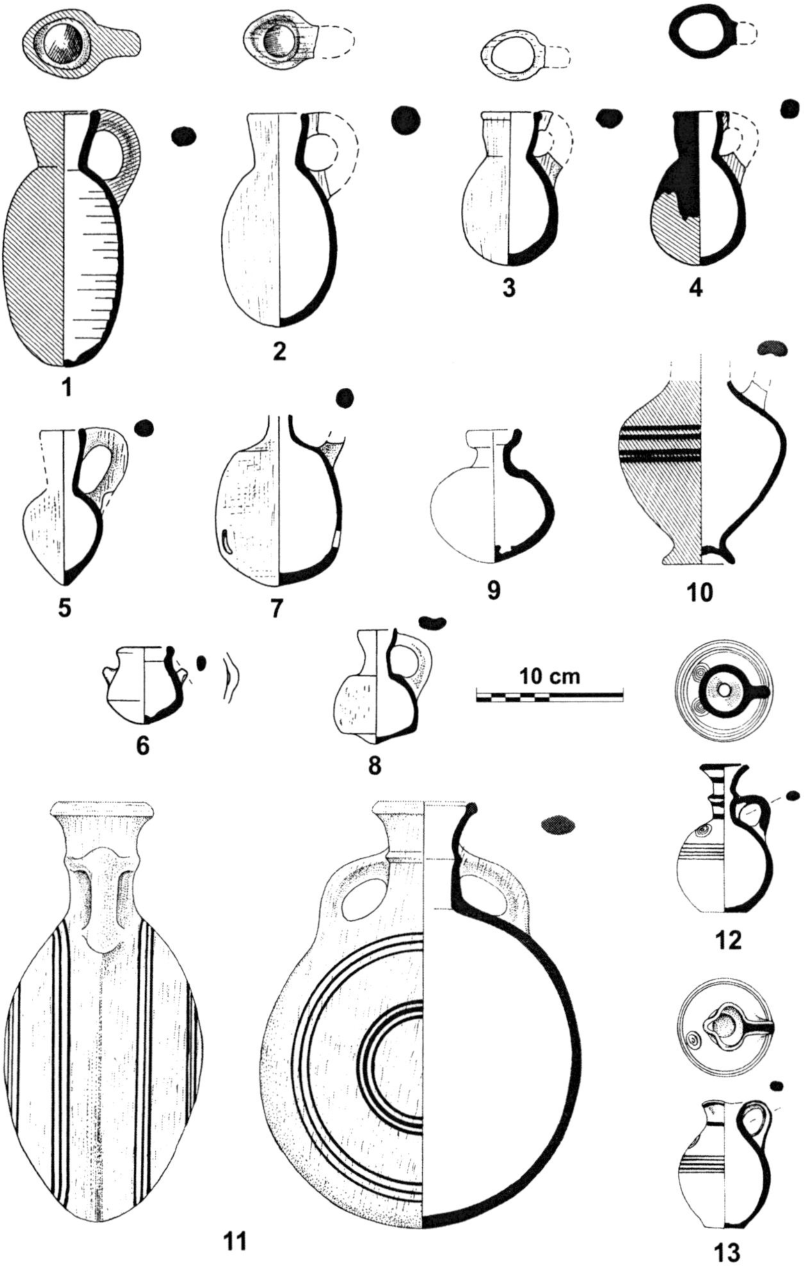

Fig. 18: Selected juglets and a pilgrim flask from Temporary Stratum 4.

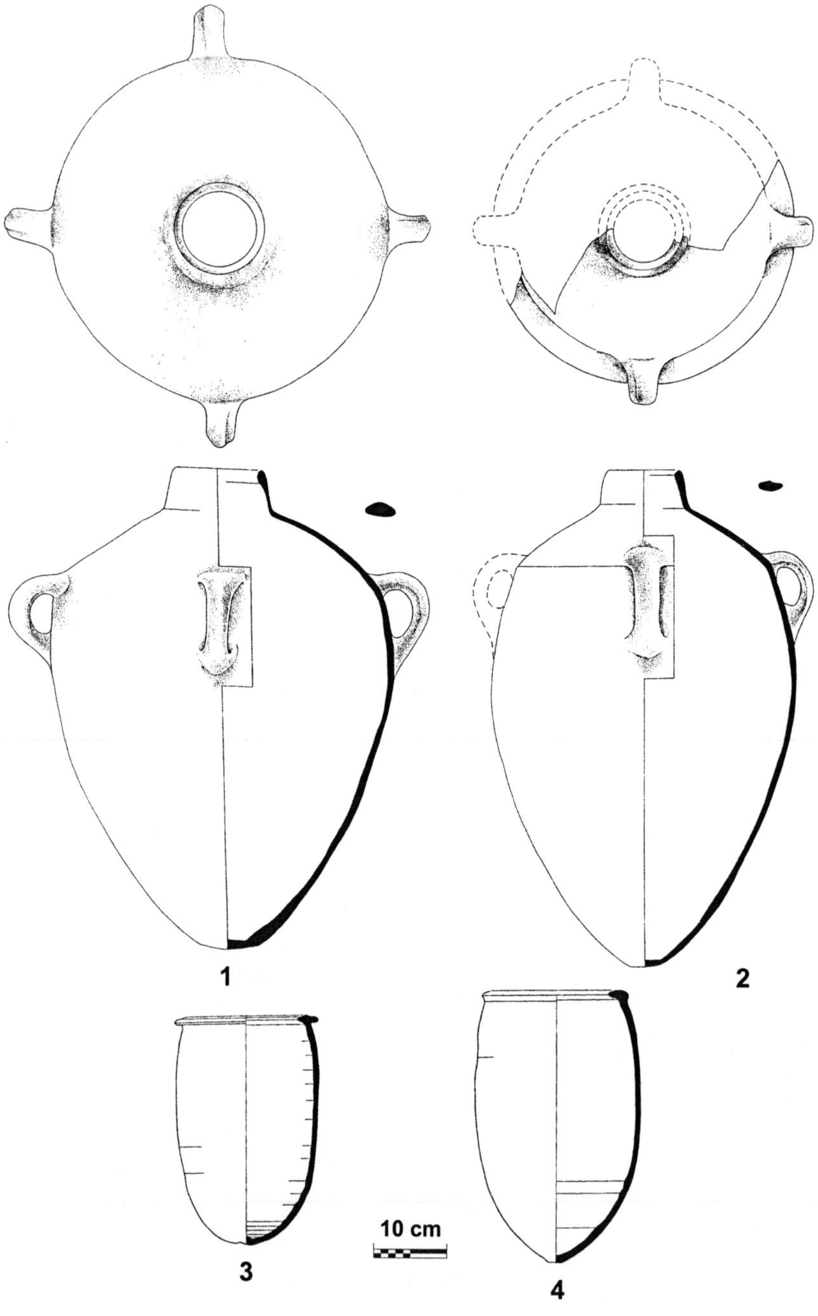

Fig. 19: Selected jars from Temporary Stratum 4.

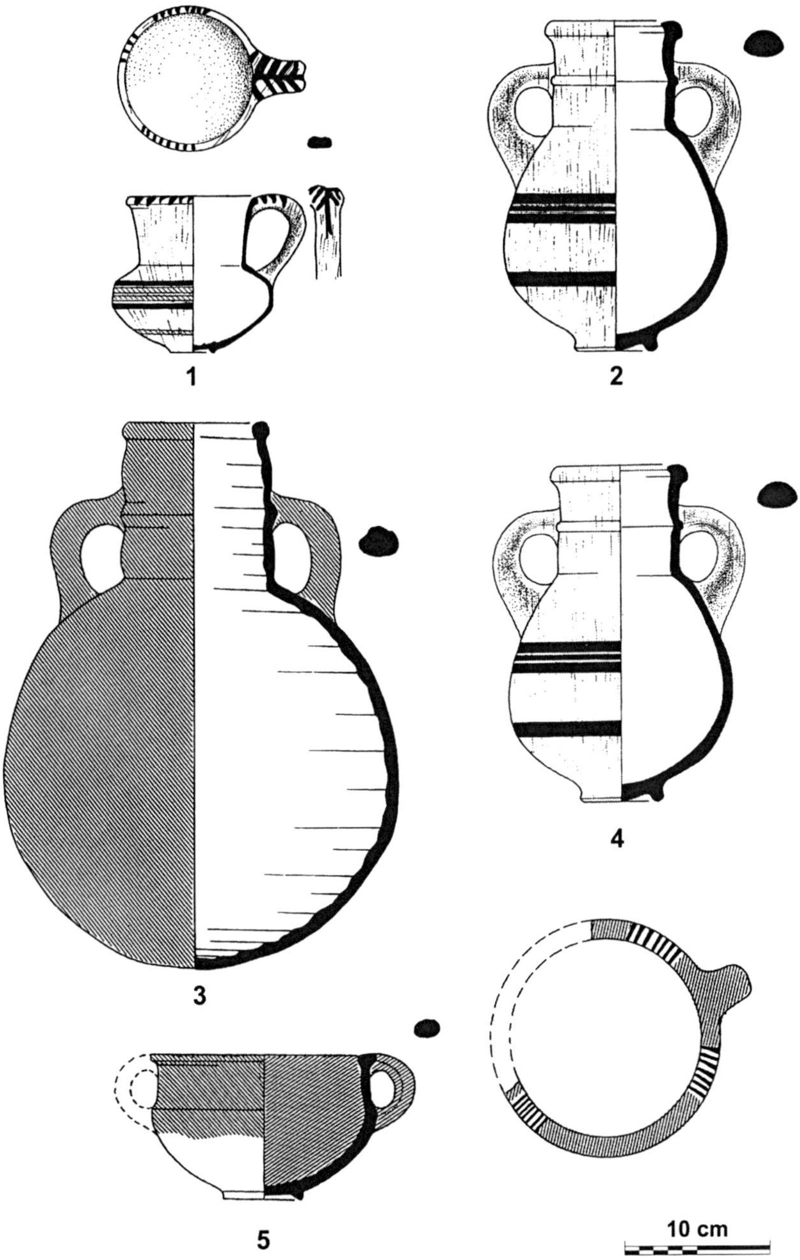

Fig. 20: Selected decorated vessels from Temporary Stratum 4, including the so-called Ashdod Ware (nos. 2, 4).

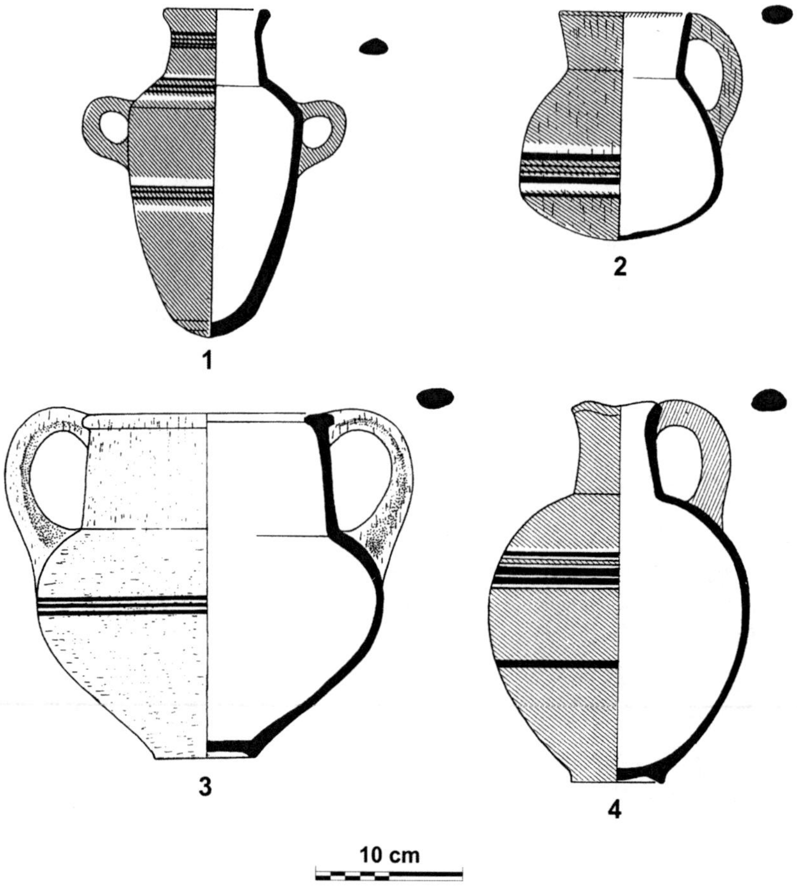

Fig. 21: Selected decorated Ashdod Ware vessels from Temporary Stratum 4.

so much so that the non-Semitic linguistic antecedents are but vaguely hinted at in the Philistine inscriptions of the end of the Iron Age (e.g., Kempinski 1986; Naveh 1985; Gitin, T. Dothan, and Naveh 1997; Demsky 1997; Schäfer-Lichtenberger 2000). The evidence of a full sequence of language(s) and script(s) used in Philistia during the Iron Age is wanting. As noted regarding other classes of material culture, little or no evidence from the "middle stages" is available.[14] In this

14. The "Revadim Seal" is often seen as the earliest evidence for the use of a Semitic alphabet

light, the slowly expanding, if still limited corpus of inscriptions from Iron Age IIA levels at Tell eṣ-Ṣafi/Gath can contribute new insights. From what is currently available it is evident that by the late-ninth century B.C.E. (Temporary Stratum 4), the Phoenician script was in use. A short incised inscription on the body of a storage jar of a clearly local type (fig. 23.2) and several letters incised on jar handles are indicative of this. One can but hope that additional evidence, both in quantity but particularly in a sequential order, will be uncovered in the future.

This destruction level has also provided environmental data. Having implemented a rather comprehensive program for the retrieval of ecofacts from the excavation,[15] a wide range of information on the subsistence and bio-ecology of the site is slowly emerging. As is well known, foodways often serve as excellent indicators of social and ethnic boundaries (e.g., Emberling 1997; Bunimovitz and Yasur-Landau 1996). Not surprisingly, past research has indicated that the Philistines had unique subsistence patterns. Thus, a high level of pork consumption in Philistine society (as opposed to a much lower level in other groups) has been noted (e.g., Hesse and Wapnish 1997; see though Lev-Tov 2000). The appearance of a unique, non-local (and most probably Aegean) cultigen (*Lathyrus sativus*) at Iron Age I Qasile (Kislev and Hopf 1985) is instructive as well.[16] Needless to say, the construction of a broad sequence is imperative. As in other components of the material culture, a relative substantial amount of information is available for the early and later stages of the Philistines, while virtually nothing has been published for the middle stages.

Following preliminary analysis, Temporary Level 4 has yielded a wealth of such information.[17] This includes data on a wide range of cultigens that were in use, of which several can be noted. Extensive evidence for olive cultivation and apparent olive oil production was found, a precursor of the extensive olive-related industry in Iron Age IIB Philistia (e.g., Gitin 1997). Viticulture is attested as well with evidence of both grape seeds and raisins. To this one can add several related

---

for writing in Philistia (e.g., Sass 1983), although it should be kept in mind that this was a surface find, dated solely on epigraphic criteria.

15. This includes large-scale soil-sample retrieval, geomorphological sampling, phytolith analysis, and wet- and dry-sieving of selected contexts.

16. *Lathyrus sp.* pulses have been reported from the late Iron Age destruction of Ashkelon (Weiss and Kislev 2001, 79, table 1). Although, as of yet, their exact identification is not available, if in fact this does indicate that Aegean-oriented *Lathyrus sativus* was in use, this may be evidence of an additional "early" component that continued in the Philistine diet until the very end of the Iron Age, centuries after the Philistines' arrival in Palestine.

17. The archaeobotanical analyses are being conducted by Y. Mahler-Slasky; the archaeozoological analyses are being conducted by L. Kolska Horwitz; and geomorphological analyses are being conducted by O. Ackermann and M. Larkum.

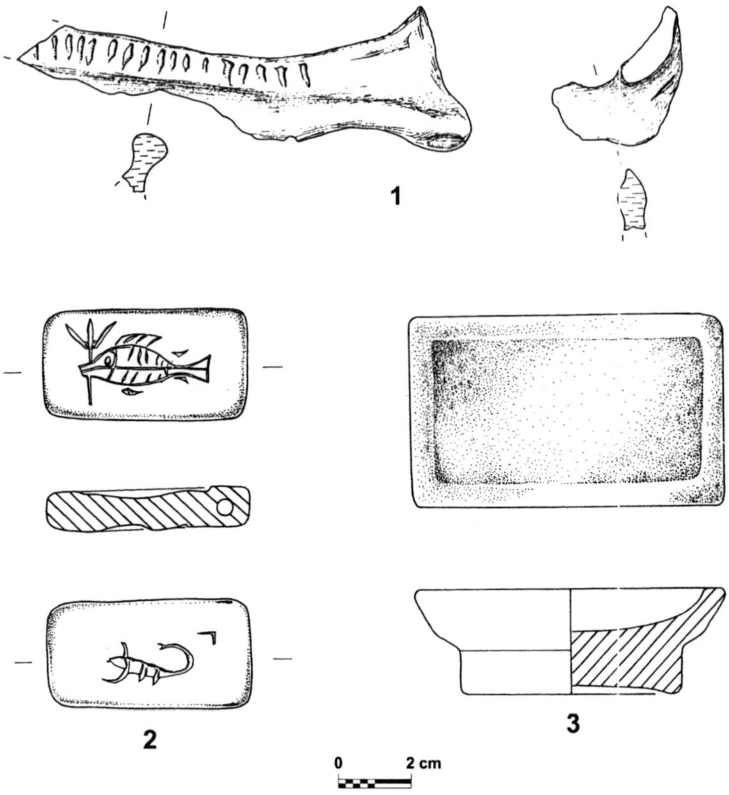

Fig. 22: Selected pottery and other finds from Temporary Stratum 4: 1) incised scapula; 2) incised pendant; and 3) basalt bowl.

finds: what appears to be a small and quite unusual wine (or beer?) press (fig. 24) and numerous kraters (e.g., figs. 25.11; 26.1, 3), bowls (e.g., figs. 25.1–10), and strainers (fig. 27.1), which may very likely have served as components of "wine sets." In light of the apparent importance of viticulture among the Philistines (e.g., Stager 1996, 62*–65*), this may shed light on a rather unknown, but clearly significant component of the Philistine culture.[18] The archaeozoological data, albeit

18. The apparent importance of wine in the early Philistine culture is witnessed through the popularity of "wine sets" (comprised of kraters, skyphoi, and strainer spouted "beer jugs"; e.g., King and Stager 2001, 102). It has been suggested that wine consumption played an important role in the incipient Philistine culture (e.g., Joffe 1999). The finds from the Iron IIA at Tell eṣ-Ṣafi (botanical and ceramic) indicate that wine continued to have an important role at later stages as

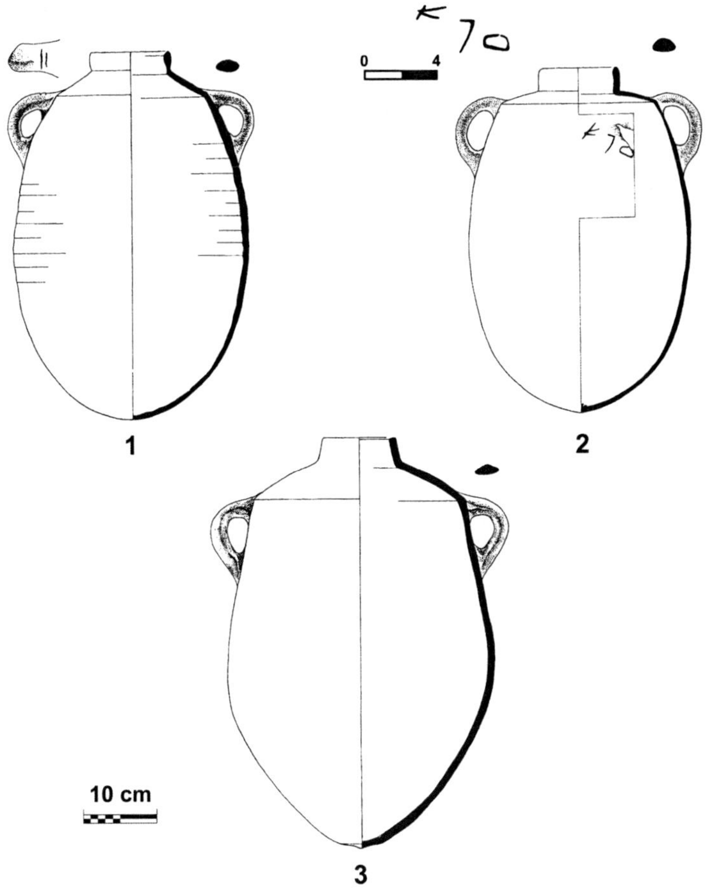

Fig. 23: Selected jars from Temporary Stratum 4. Note the incised inscription on the upper body of no. 2.

only partially analyzed, is tantalizing as well, with apparent evidence of extensive pork consumption in all stages of the Iron Age.

The dating of Temporary Level 4 is quite clear. Although the radiometric dating is as of yet insufficiently robust, the abundant and varied finds from this level

---

well. In the biblical narrative, the very fact that Samson is considered a teetotaler, as opposed to the "wine-guzzling" Philistines, may stress that in Israelite eyes, wine drinking was a significant, identifying component of the Philistine culture.

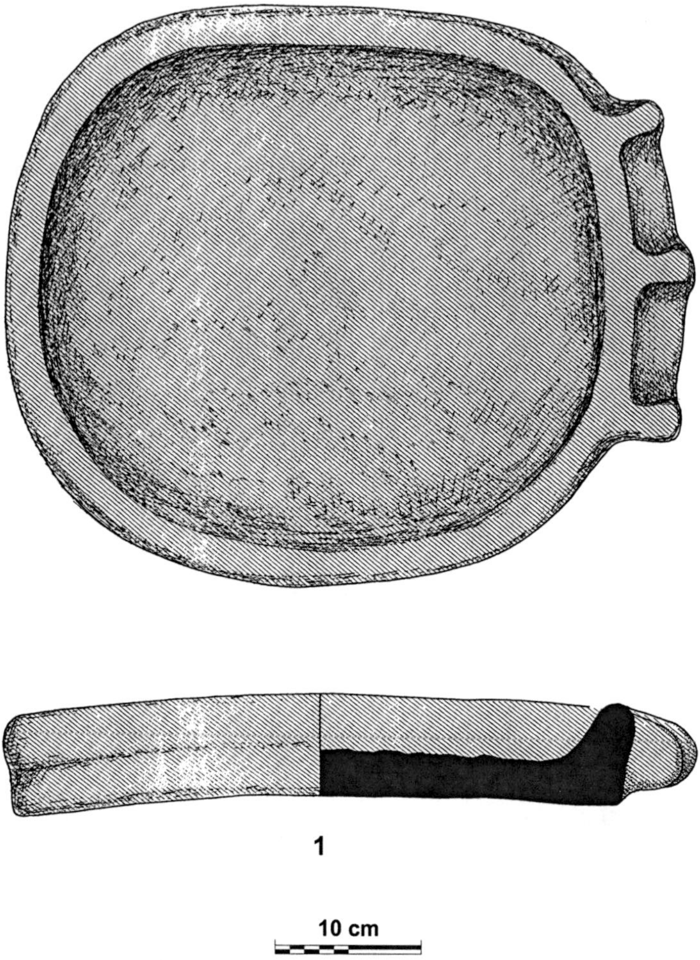

Fig. 24: Burnished production basin from Temporary Stratum 4.

enable a relative, typological dating of the material culture. It is this relative dating that points to a late ninth-/early eighth-century B.C.E. date for this assemblage—on the one hand clearly post-Iron I, but on the other, without a doubt, earlier but not too much earlier than well-dated late eighth-century B.C.E. assemblages.

As noted in the past (Maeir and Ehrlich 2001), a historical context for the site-wide destruction of Tell eṣ-Ṣafi/Gath, Temporary Stratum 4 can be suggested. To start, perhaps one should disqualify some scenarios. At first glance, one might suggest that the most likely candidate for the cause of such an impressive destruction would be the Assyrians, whose military conquests in this region are well known. This explanation is not viable due to the pre-mid-eighth century B.C.E. dating and the lack of relevant finds. Although extensive evidence does exist for later, post-mid-eighth-century B.C.E. Assyrian campaigns in this region (e.g., H. Tadmor 1966), there is no historical evidence for such activity at an earlier stage. Likewise, both at the site and its vicinity there is no material indication of Assyrian related activities.

The biblical narrative provides two possible historical scenarios for this destruction. One reference, 2 Kgs 12:17, relates (providing little detail) that Hazael of Damascus captured Gath, somewhere in the late-ninth century B.C.E. The second, 2 Chr 26:6, informs us that Uzziah, king of Judah, destroyed the walls of Gath during the first half of the eighth century B.C.E.

Due to the constraints of space and without going into extensive details, it is the first of the latter two options (Hazael of Damascus) that is propounded. Hazael, who during the second half of the ninth century B.C.E. was the predominant figure in the geopolitical arena of the Syro-Palestinian littoral (e.g., Lipiński 2000, 377–90), campaigned far and wide throughout the entire region. Had he in fact set his eyes on Philistia,[19] Gath, most likely the largest site in the region, would have been a prime candidate for subjugation.[20]

Additional support for connecting this to an Aramaean siege is found in the large man-made trench that surrounds the site (figs. 3–4). Over two kilometers long and originally more than 5 meters deep and 5 meters wide (figs. 28–30), this feature was apparently a major component of a large-scale siege operation that was carried out against the site. The feature is dated to the Iron Age IIA on the basis of a wide array of archaeological and geomorphological criteria (Ackermann, Bruins, and Maeir 2005). In addition, there is epigraphic evidence for the use of a similar method in the siege of Hadrach (in northern Syria) by Hazael's son, Bir-Hadad, several decades later (e.g., *KAI*, 204–11, #211). Thus, it is highly likely that both the siege works and the site-wide destruction level can be related to the same event—the siege and eventual conquest of Gath by Hazael. As mentioned above, it is evidenced in both the excavations and the survey of the site.[21]

Subsequent to the destruction of Temporary Stratum 4, Tell eṣ-Ṣafi never regained its vitality. Although the site was continuously settled until modern times, it seems to have lost its relative importance, never again to be an urban

---

19. As hinted in the Septuagint, 2 Kgs 13:22.

20. See e.g., Lipiński 2000, 387.

21. The many complete vessels that were illicitly collected at various locations on the site by the late M. Dayan, which are quite typologically similar to the finds from Temporary Stratum 4, serve as additional evidence for such a site-wide destruction (see Ornan 1986).

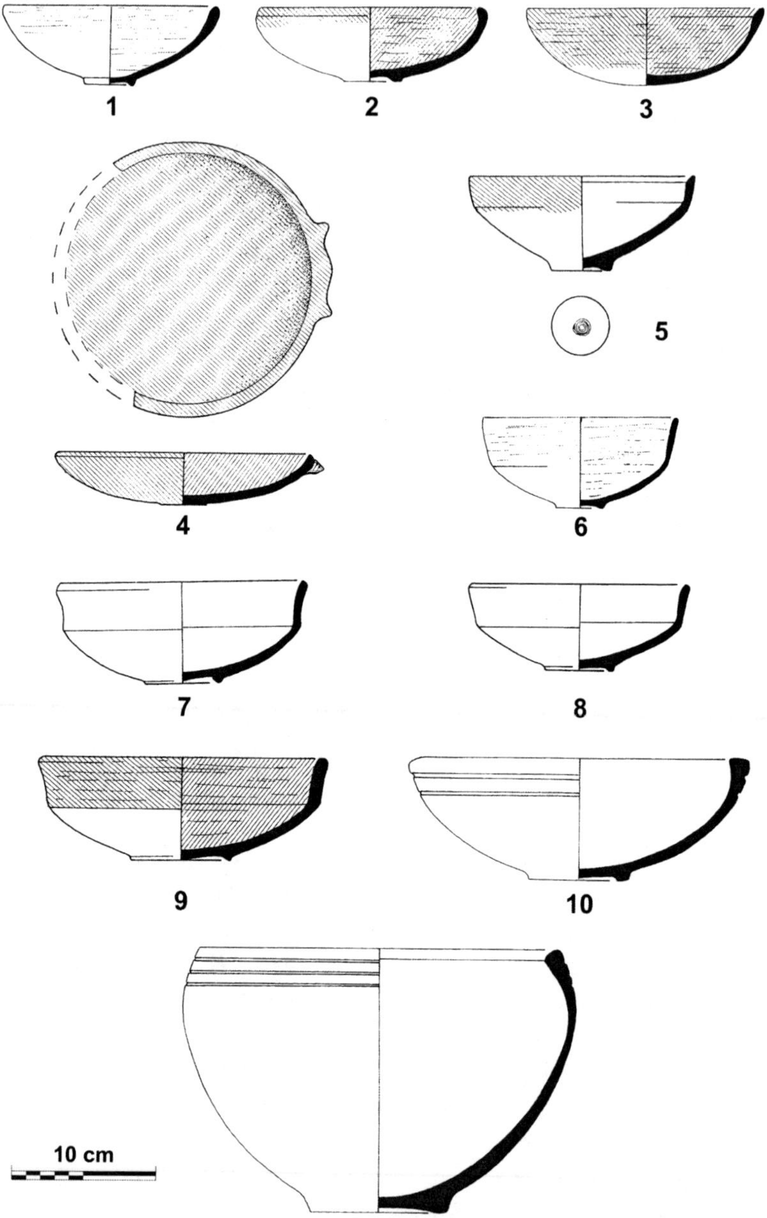

Fig. 25: Selected bowls and kraters from Temporary Stratum 4.

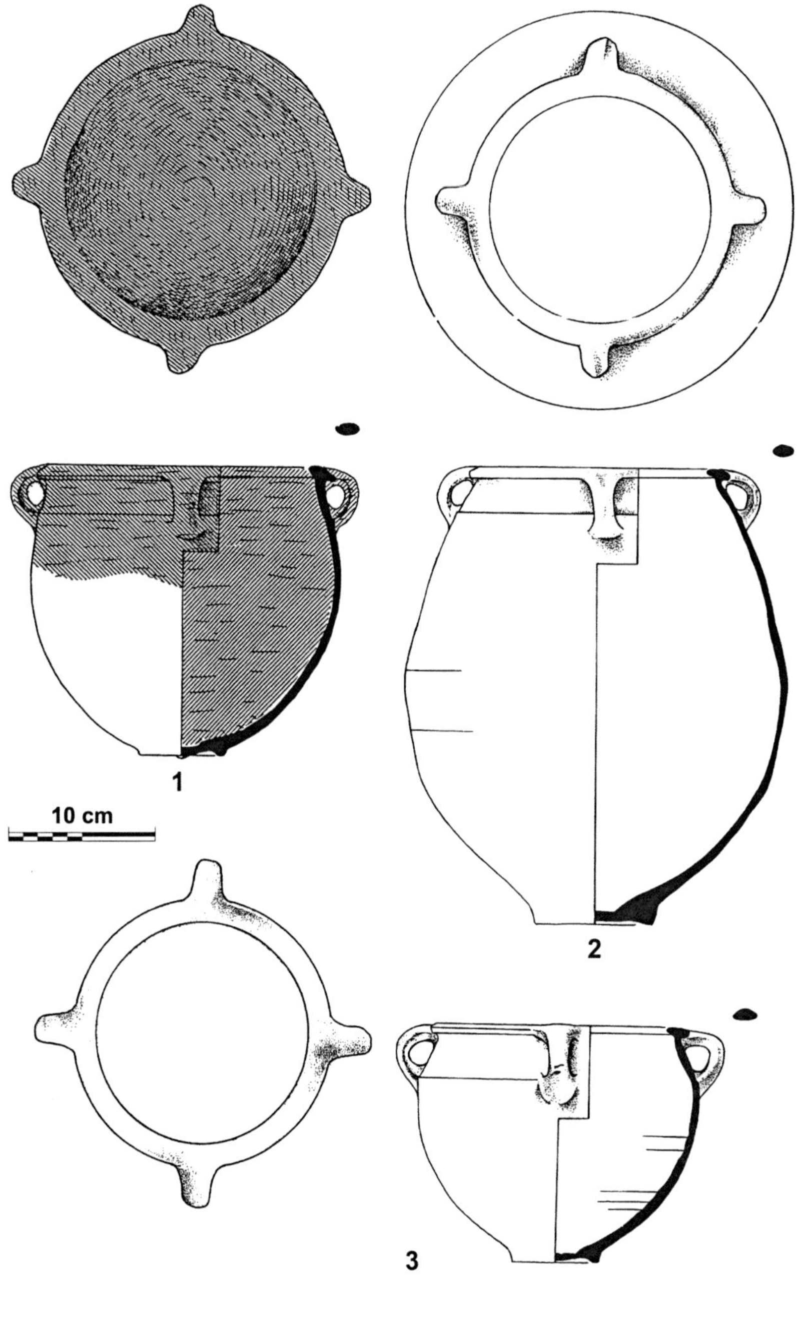

Fig. 26: Selected pottery vessels from Temporary Stratum 4.

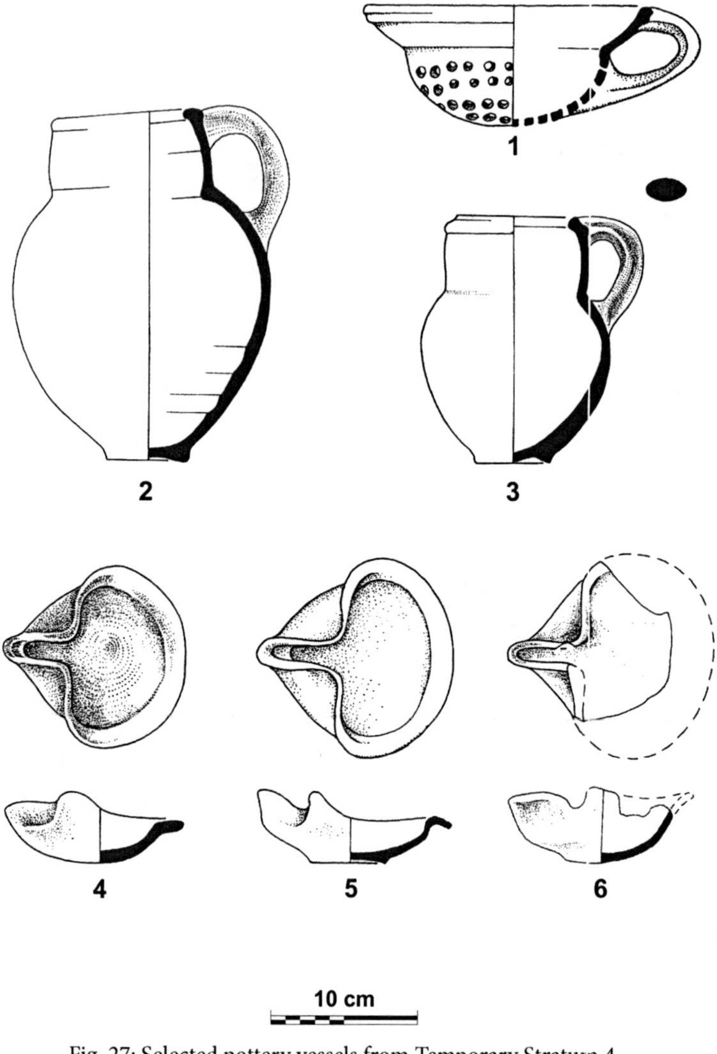

Fig. 27: Selected pottery vessels from Temporary Stratum 4.

entity of any significance. In many ways, post-Temporary Stratum 4 Tell eṣ-Ṣafi undergoes a substantial change.

Post-Temporary Stratum 4

Above Temporary Stratum 4, evidence of a sparsely settled and much more poorly preserved level, Temporary Stratum 3, was discovered. Although only a small number of architectural features and surfaces from this level were discovered, they nevertheless clearly overlaid the underlying Temporary Stratum 4. Thus, Temporary Stratum 3 provides the uppermost capping of the Iron Age stratigraphy in Area A.

Although the remains were not as impressive as in the previous stratum, nevertheless, the material culture of this level facilitated a clear definition of its character. Based on the pottery and small finds (figs. 31–34), it is dated to the late-eighth/early-seventh centuries B.C.E. In stark contrast to the earlier Iron Age levels, which were culturally oriented primarily to the coastal region ("Philistia"), the finds from Temporary Stratum 3 appear to be of a predominantly Judean character. Evidence for this can be seen, for example, in the "Judean, folded-rim" bowls (fig. 32.1) and a Judean, "pinched" pillar figurine (fig. 34; e.g., Kletter 1996, 29, "Type A"). Contemporaneous finds can be noted at Lachish Level III (e.g., Zimhoni 1990) and Batash Stratum II (A. Mazar and Panitz-Cohen 2001, 156–60).

The evidence from this stratum in Area A corresponds with evidence from other parts of the site. In the survey of the tell that was conducted in 1996 and 2001, a relatively small amount of Iron IIB pottery was found and in a limited dispersal. In the earlier British excavations on and near the summit of the tell, evidence of a late eighth-century B.C.E. level was attested, notably evidenced by several LMLK handles and other contemporaneous finds (Bliss and Macalister 1902, p. 121, pl. 56:21; see, e.g., Barkay 1992, n. 39; Barkay and Vaughn 1996, 30–33, n. 4, table 1:1, 3, fig. 1). All told, although the archaeological evidence points to the existence of a late eighth-century B.C.E. settlement on Tell eṣ-Ṣafi/Gath, it was of limited size and importance.[22]

The written evidence suggests a similar picture. Gath is often attested in the biblical narratives that relate to events prior to the mid-eighth century B.C.E. In fact, in these narratives, Gath is mentioned more often than any of the other Philistine cities. But this changes after the mid-eighth century B.C.E. In the "historical books" (2 Kings and Chronicles), there is no mention of Gath at these later stages, while in the late "literary books" (particularly the later prophetic books, such as Jeremiah, Zephaniah, and Zachariah), although the other Philistine cities

22. Evidence of a seventh-century B.C.E. settlement is minimal as well. Although not found in the excavations, a few distinctively seventh-century B.C.E. finds, and in particular, Judean "Rosette" handles (Cahill 1995), where found in the survey of the site. This indicates that the site was settled during this period, albeit in a very limited manner and that it most probably was under Judean influence.

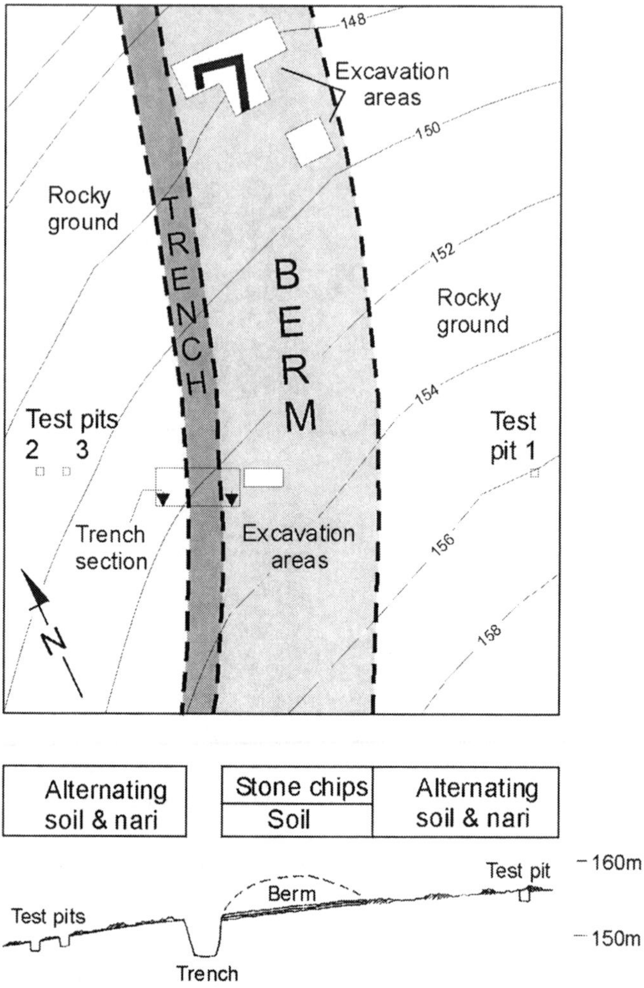

Fig. 28: Plan of the excavation in Area C6. Note the trench and adjacent berm.

are known and castigated, Gath is not mentioned.[23] Similarly, while Gath is mentioned (as an apparent dependent of Ashdod) by Sargon of Assyria in 712 B.C.E.

23. The exceptions to this are: Mic 1:10, where Gath is mentioned, but seemingly an intertextual literary reference to the mention of Gath in David's eulogy of Saul in 2 Sam 1:17 and in Amos 6:2, an apparent allusion to the quite recent destruction of Gath.

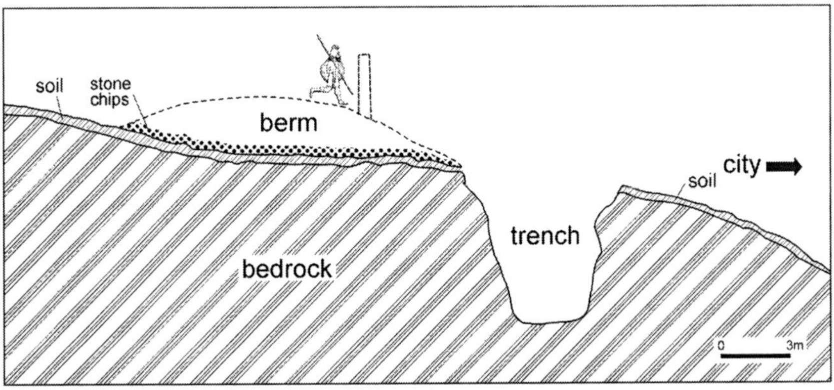

Fig. 29: Cross-section and suggested reconstruction of the excavation of the trench and associated features in Area C6.

(e.g., *ANET*, 287), it does not appear in any of the numerous later Assyrian (or for that matter Babylonian) texts relating to events in this region during the late-eighth, seventh, and early-sixth centuries B.C.E.[24]

It thus appears that following the late ninth-/early eighth-century B.C.E. destruction, various changes occurred at Tell eṣ-Ṣafi/Gath. On the one hand, when the site was resettled, it was under Judean control (at least for significant portions of this time), with a predominantly Judean-style material culture. Simultaneously and subsequently, it loses its previous dominant status and extensive size, and remains as such for the remainder of the Iron Age. Thus, for the purpose of the present study, following the destruction of Temporary Stratum 4, it would not be prudent to relate to the finds at the site as being of Philistine character. And in fact, to properly study the final phases of the Philistines, one must turn to the sites such as Ekron and Ashkelon, where finds relating to these final cultural "snapshots" are abundant (e.g., Gitin 1995; Stager 1996).

24. Note should be made that Na'aman (1974) suggested to reconstruct a reading of Gath in the so-called Azekah inscription, a late eighth-century B.C.E. Assyrian text. This though should be related to with caution since: a) it is only a suggested reconstruction of a missing part in a fragmentary text; b) this reconstruction is not accepted by all (e.g., Galil 1995, 325) and Na'aman himself (1994) has retracted his opinion; and 3) finally, the exact dating of the text is unclear.

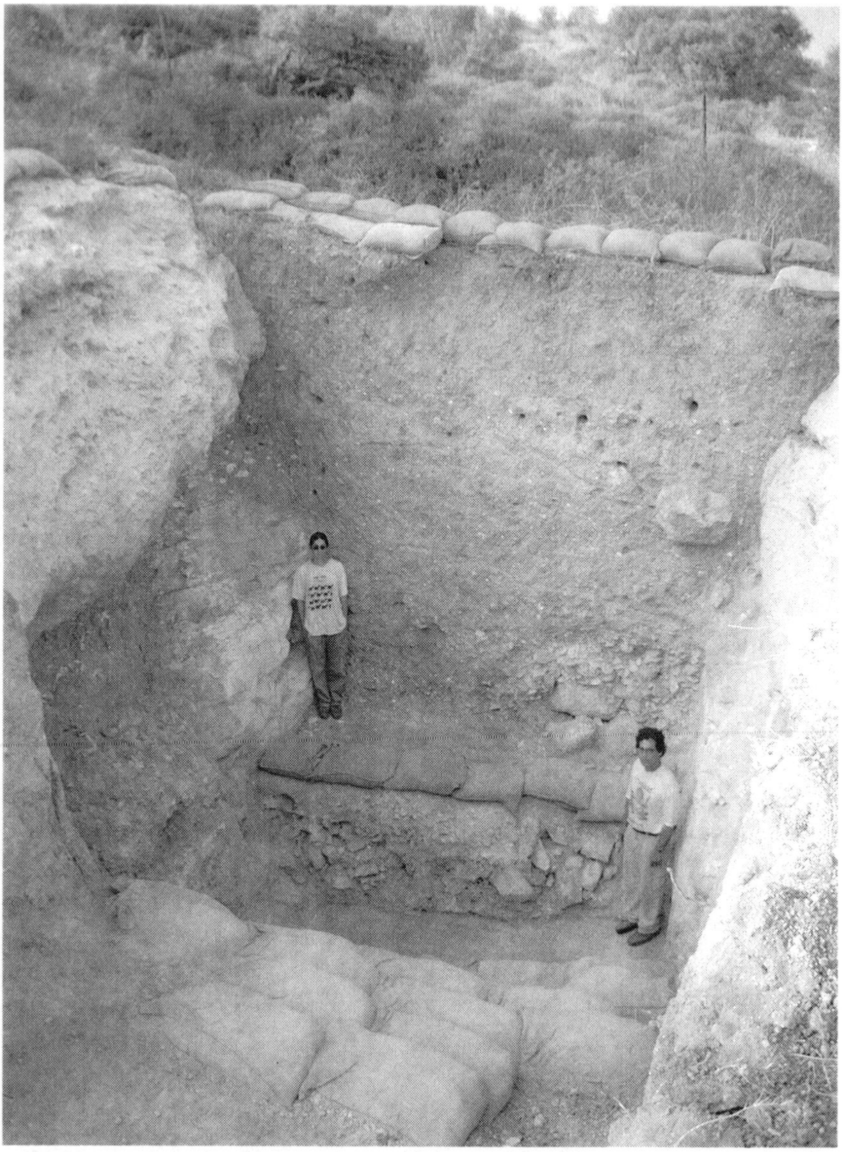

Fig. 30: View of the excavation of the trench in Area C6.

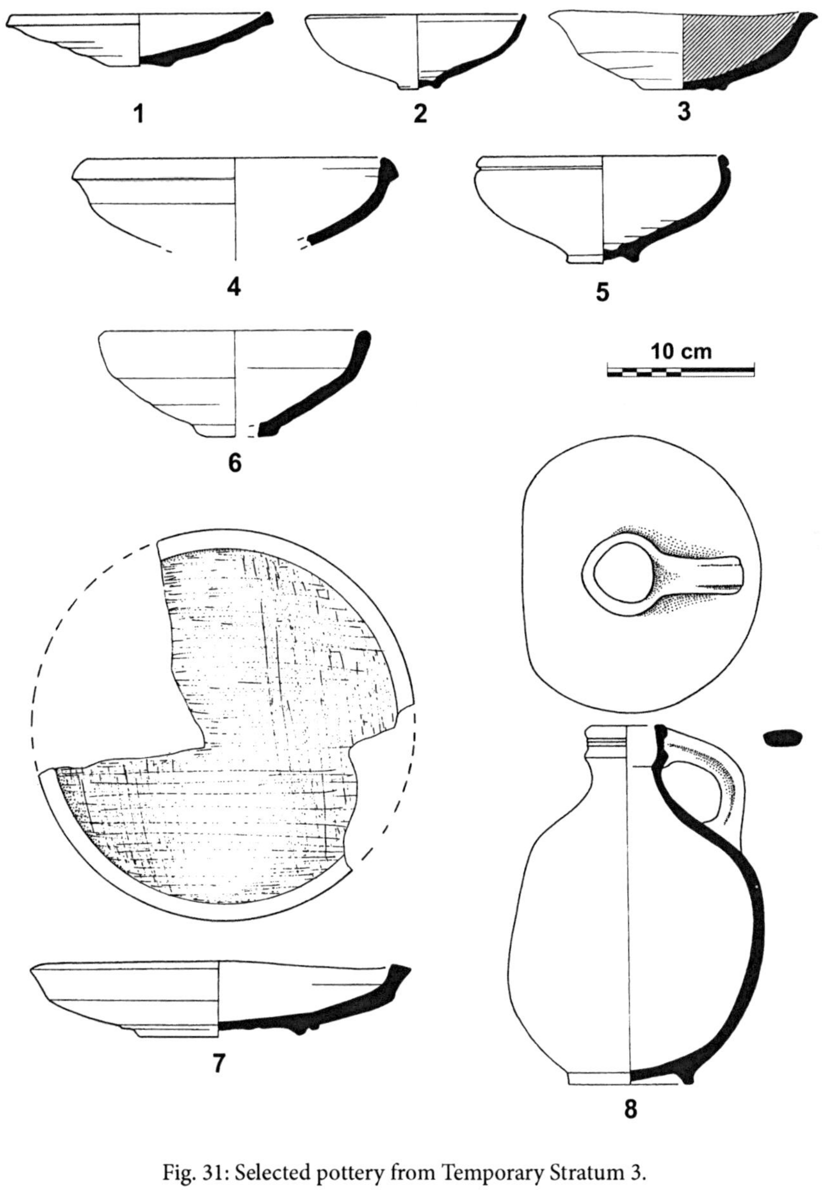

Fig. 31: Selected pottery from Temporary Stratum 3.

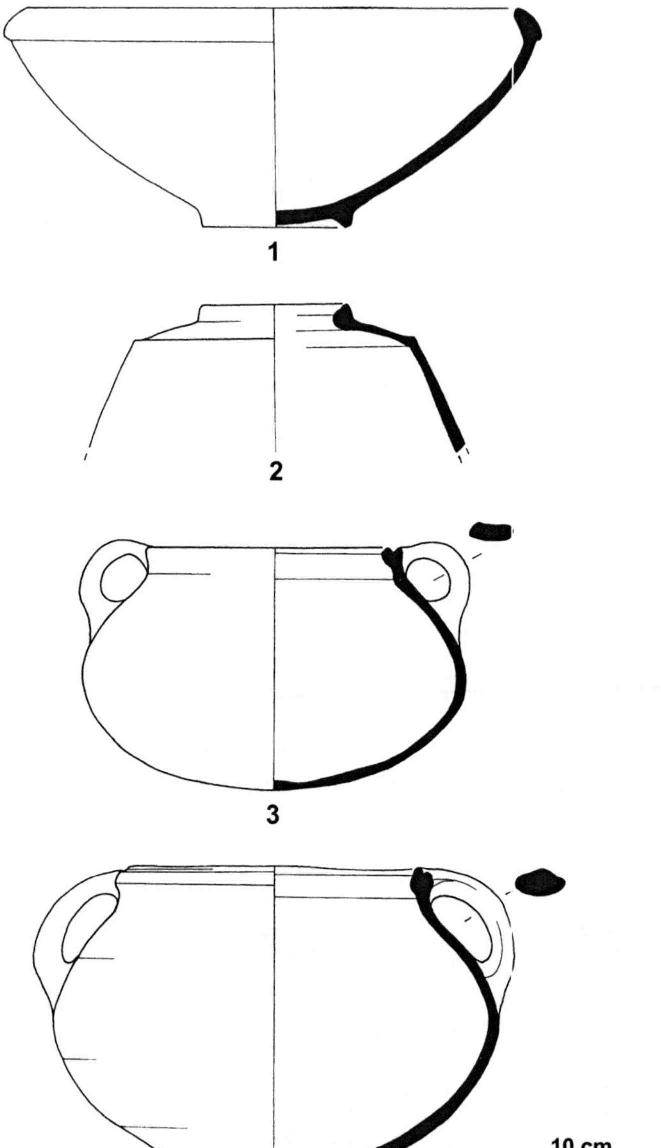

Fig. 32: Selected pottery from Temporary Stratum 3.

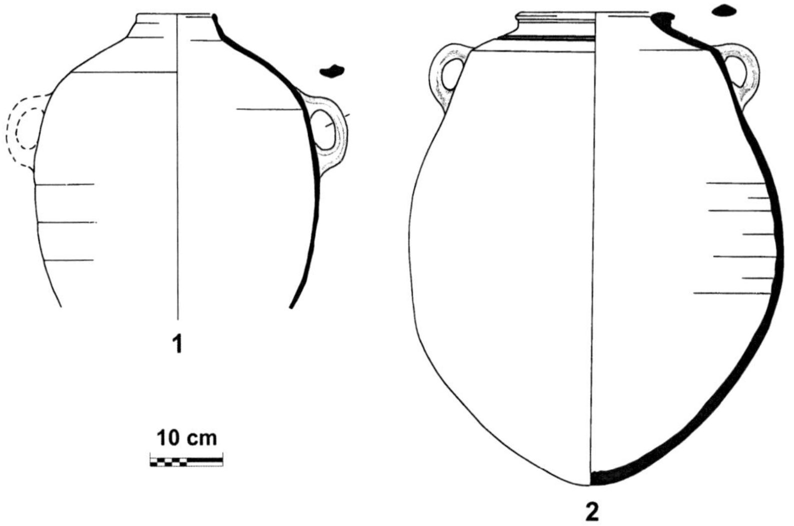

Fig. 33: Selected pottery from Temporary Stratum 3.

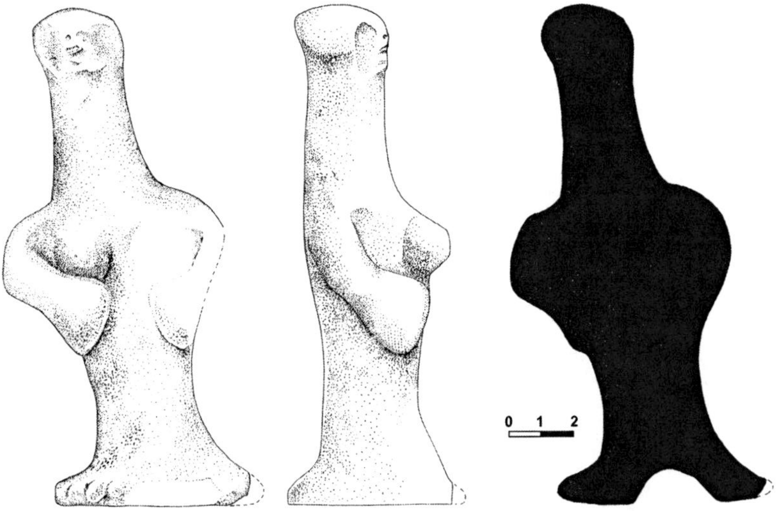

Fig. 34: Figurine from Temporary Stratum 3.

Discussion

In light of the discussion above, one can now return to the questions raised in the beginning of this study. In particular one must ask how does the evidence from Tell eṣ-Ṣafi/Gath shed new light on the understanding of the cultural metamorphosis of Philistine culture?

Although at present the evidence from Tell eṣ-Ṣafi/Gath is far from complete and, in fact, represents but a partial sequence and limited window on the cultural history of the Philistines at this site, nevertheless, some important insights have emerged.

As was presumed, the finds from Tell eṣ-Ṣafi/Gath do start to fill in the lacunas in our knowledge on the transition of the Philistine culture from the end of the Iron Age I until the Iron Age II. Despite the as-of-yet incomplete chronological sequence as well as the fact that the material finds from the various stages are not consistently and evenly represented, the evidence available is highly instructive. From an overview of a rather wide range of cultural finds, the patterns of typological change, the appearance or disappearance of specific materials, classes or types, and, at times, telltale evidence of cultural influences, are all indicative of this.

First and foremost this is seen in the pottery assemblages. In the pottery from the two Iron Age IIA levels (Temporary Strata 4 and 5), the overall feeling is one of deep change and transition. Despite the fact that some continuities of the Iron Age I pottery traditions are felt, this is not the rule. Rather, new shapes and decorative patterns are strongly felt. Thus, the most common surface treatment and decoration, red painting and burnishing, is a new development in the Philistine culture, most likely influenced by Phoenician pottery traditions.[25] Although some degree of continuity from Iron Age I decorative styles may be discerned (such as in the Ashdod Ware and on the decorated chalices), this definitely was not the norm.

The same can be said about most of the other classes of finds. Most of the Iron Age I attributes have disappeared and/or are in the process thereof. It is only the rare and unique classes of objects in which a clear and rather unchanged continuation into the Iron Age IIA is seen. It would appear that this happens only with highly symbol-laden objects such as the notched scapulae. But even then, these very types do not continue to appear in the Iron Age IIB.

25. The appearance of red-burnished decoration can be explained in relation to social changes as well (see A. Faust, personal communication).

Even in language and writing this seems to be the case. Despite the fact that much of the evidence for cultural continuity (and acculturation) between the early and later Philistine culture is seen through aspects related to language (Iron IIB Philistine vocabulary and onomastics), the epigraphic finds currently available from the Iron IIA levels at Tell eṣ-Ṣafi/Gath indicate that the use of Semitic alphabetic writing, and apparently language as well, was widespread.

In light of the above, the overall trend appears to be that during the Iron Age IIA, Philistine culture went through a rather intensive process of change. A large portion of the foreign, mostly "Aegean" components that typified the Iron Age I assemblages are lost (at least those easily discerned from an archaeological perspective). If in fact an accelerated rate of change occurs during the Iron Age IIA, this may hint to the reasons and underlying mechanisms behind this change.

It is during the Iron Age IIA that many polities and ethnic groups undergo an invigorated process of change. Slowly reemerging from the economic sluggishness of the Iron Age I, the various groups in the Levant began to transform profoundly. This process was first felt in Phoenicia during the eleventh century with the evidence of urban culture, settlement diversification, and associated material finds (e.g., Gunnar Lehmann 2001a, 93–94), and the first signs for the renewal of intense international trade (e.g., Bikai 1987; Gilboa 1998). It can be assumed that due to a core-periphery relationship, other groups such as the Philistines soon followed suit, developing economically and politically, while at the same time emulating and developing a dependency and need for various components of Phoenician culture.

Thus, it is suggested that the deep changes that occurred in Philistia during the Iron Age IIA may be highly influenced by these very processes. Philistine culture becomes involved in the international trade slightly later than the Phoenicians (e.g., T. Dothan 1996). At the same time, strong Phoenician influence is felt as in the pottery decoration and in language. Likewise, the appearance of standardized jars, most likely for trade purposes, points in this direction. It is thus hypothesized that due to the pressures of the developing Levantine economy, spearheaded by the Phoenicians, the Philistines emerged from a relatively conservative and, by-and-large, inward looking cultural state of mind, and opened up to the influences of the core Phoenician culture. Thus, the adoption of a Semitic language and writing system may very well not have occurred through a long and gradual process of cultural interaction (e.g., Nichols 1998), but was rather most probably due to short-term economic needs. One may assume that only once the Philistines "fit in" to the local cultural and economic milieu (and could easily interact with it), could they go on actively and intensively to play a role in the ever-expanding Iron Age "world system" (e.g., Gitin 1998).

Nevertheless, the Philistines did retain their cultural uniqueness and social and ethnic identity up until the end of the seventh century B.C.E. It can be suggested that despite the accelerated changes that occurred in the Iron Age IIA, meaningful aspects of the Philistine culture were intentionally and tenaciously retained. Some only lasted briefly (such as the notched scapulae), but others, such as a unique viticulture and some components of language, did survive. And it was most probably these as well as other (at least presently) unknown components that served as the identifying criteria to answer the question "What is a Philistine?"

Thus, although a fully-fledged "movie-sequence" of the development of Philistine culture is not yet available, the new evidence from Tell eṣ-Ṣafi/Gath can provide fresh data, new insights, and additional "snapshots" to better understand these processes.

Chapter Ten
Neighbors and Foes, Rivals and Kin: Philistines, Shepheleans, Judeans between Geography and Economy, History and Theology

*Hermann Michael Niemann**

The methodical consideration of the geographical, ecological, economic, and sociological structures of southern Syria and Palestine is required for reconstructing its historical developments in the first millennium B.C.E. and distinguishing them from the theological presentation in the Bible, which is highly Israel-centered. In light of the area's geography of coastal plain, hill country, and mountain region, and countering the Bible's point of view, this chapter will use the coastal perspective. Viewing the structure of local hierarchy from the coast (Ashdod) toward the eastern border of the coastal plain (Gath/Ekron), and the Shephelah (Timnah) to Beth Shemesh at the western border of core Judah, shows a gradual cultural and economic decrease, apparently from west to east with the Shephelah holding a mediating position. Here, one has to be extremely careful in drawing ethnic and/or political borders.

---

* University of Rostock, Faculty of Theology, Schwaansche Strasse 5, 18055 Rostock, Germany. E-mail: hmn@uni-rostock.de. Dedicated in gratitude to Manfred Weippert (July 6, 2012).

I am grateful to Michal Artzy, Ann E. Killebrew, and Gunnar Lehmann for inviting me to read an early draft of this paper at the international workshop in memory of Prof. Moshe Dothan, May 1–3, 2001, at the University of Haifa and Ben-Gurion University of the Negev, Beer Sheva. I am also grateful to Susan Sherratt, Aren M. Maeir, Amihai Mazar, Itamar Singer, and other participants for substantial discussion and critiques after the lecture, to Philippe Guillaume (Geneva) and Edward Ball (Nottingham) for great care they gave to this text producing a readable English style, to Axel Knauf, as always, for critical remarks, and to Nadja Boeck and Ulrike Purrer for technical assistance. The manuscript has been completed and sent to the editors in February 2002; updated in May 2008 especially in light of the Beth Shemesh, Timnah, and Gath excavation reports published recently.

The Bible portrays the Philistines mostly as Israel's and Judah's wealthy archenemy. However, the idea of a lasting Philistine war (1 Sam 4–2 Sam 5) reflects Davidic royal ideology. The biblical delimitation between a period of Philistine wars followed by a post-Philistine war era and the sharp distinction between Philistines and Israelites/Judeans do not correspond to real conditions, but exaggerate geographical, economic, and social structures because of ideological and theological aims. From the seventh to sixth centuries B.C.E. the designations "Philistines" and "Tyrians/Sidonians" replace and sometimes complement the older pejorative term "Canaanites" for the "rich coastal population" in the Bible. These theological and ethnic demarcations, made in order to stabilize Judean identity, do not reflect historical reality. Daily life was determined rather by different socioeconomic conditions found on the coast, Shephelah, and hill country rather than by ethnic differences.

First Biblical Picture: The "Evil" Philistine

According to the Bible, the Philistines threatened Israel from its very inception.[1] They began to subjugate the Israelite tribes (1 Sam 4–5) until Samuel managed to turn the tide by persuading the people to be faithful to God. Since Samuel's sons proved to be unreliable, Israel longed for a stable institution in order to face the Philistines: Its answer was kingship. Saul was at first successful, but was soon crippled by disobedience. Faithful David finally rid Israel of the menace of its old enemy. In "exilic and post-exilic" times, however, the old enmity reappeared, for example, with the Ashdodites, and the "uncircumcised" were blamed for almost all the evils.

The Other Philistine: Interplay between Geography and History

Research has made significant advances in relating the historical evidence to the biblical text (Niemann 2001; Knauf 2001a). Geography as well as the macrohistorical and micro-historical contexts have been recognized as basic factors conditioning all subsequent social, economic, and political developments. The labels "Philistine," "Israelite," and so forth are no longer taken as clear indicators of ethnicity or nationality.

1. For a thorough, though Israel- and Bible-centered study, see Machinist 2000.

The present analysis is limited to the area between Ashdod and Ashkelon with its eastern hinterland. How was the interaction between the inhabitants of the coast and coastal plain, of the hill country, and of the mountains influenced by the physical geography of their respective regions, and how is this reflected in the biblical texts relating to the seventh through third/second centuries B.C.E.?[2]

Geographical Context

There is a sharp contrast between the coast and its mountainous hinterland (the eastern Judean Desert and the Jordan Valley are not considered here). Between those two areas lies the Shephelah, a region with its own peculiarities, which have not yet been sufficiently recognized, in spite of their importance to the political history of the surrounding areas.

While communication in the hill country was more difficult, the coastal zone of southern Palestine has always been marked by the varying fortunes of international trade passing through the Via Maris. As a positive result, seatrade between Egypt and Mesopotamia from the second millennium B.C.E. fostered the transportation of foodstuffs from both sides of the Jordan towards the coast. This relationship is evidenced by the spread of collared-rim jars (Wengrow 1996; Artzy 1994; 1997), while sub-Mycenaean ceramics indicate the movement of the Sea Peoples from the coast into the interior (Gunnar Lehmann 2001b). Politically, these economic conditions led to the establishment of secondary states which were dependent on the situation in the south (Philistia) or in the north (Phoenicia) (Knauf 2000b, figs. 2–4). As a negative result, the coastal area and its population were the first to be occupied by interregional powers, in order to exploit their wealth, but also their strategic position. In the beginning, the hill country was spared, and we shall see below the special role played by the Shephelah.

Due to their exposed but economically optimal location, the cities of the coast developed more innovative and flexible economies than the inland states. The coastal cities naturally vied for the economic resources of their hinterland. Such attempts at opening up their markets did not necessarily lead to political occupation, although the "exploited" neighbors most likely considered such a movement as aggression and a direct threat.

As the hinterland of the coast, Judah was a mountainous complex of small geographically distinct areas where farmers and pastoralists practiced subsistence farming within a tribal society, sometimes dominated by an urban elite. Since

2. When I am convinced they were produced; see Niemann 1998; Finkelstein and Silberman 2001.

ploughing was restricted to the alluvial valley floors, the raising of small livestock was essential, along with orchard and garden husbandry. The opportunities for demographic increase were limited, but the hill country was a safe haven. Under favorable conditions, the highland tribal or city-state organization could develop into territorial states.[3]

The Shephelah between Coast and Hill Country

The importance and the peculiarities of this region have not yet been fully recognized.[4] The Shephelah forms a hilly area approximately 45 kilometers long north–south and approximately 15 kilometers wide, narrowing towards the south. It is made of eocene limestone, marl, and chalk, thus differentiating it from the cenomanian limestone of the mountain range (Karmon 1983, 201–2). The altitude rarely exceeds 300 meters; the valleys are wide, accessible, and fertile. The Ayalon Valley limits it to the north[5] as does Wadi Shari'a to the south. In the east, the gap between the Judean mountain range and the Shephelah is marked by a "great fosse" or a "great hollow"[6] of senonian chalk. This has always served as a road[7] and the localities that spread along it[8] marked the boundary of the Judean heartland. In the west, the Shephelah grades into the coastal plain. Geologically and geographically, the Shephelah seems to belong to the coast rather than to the hill country. The name Shephelah ("lowland") has obviously been given from the perspective of the highlands (Smith 1931, 144–45). Was it ever given a name from the coastal perspective?[9] The biblical texts always distinguish it from the moun-

3. Samaria (Omri/Ahab and successors); Tirzah (Jeroboam I and successors); Shechem (Lab'ayu); Gibeon (Saul); Jerusalem (Abdi-Heba; House of David); and Hebron (David). Handling foreign affairs cleverly, the Omrides established the first supraregional state, controlling the whole of the highlands between Galilee and the Negev ("from Dan to Beersheba") including Judah as junior partner.

4. But see Smith 1931, 143–71; Baly 1957, 141–47 with fig. 30; Karmon 1983, 201–3; Rainey 1975; 1980; 1983; for the Nahal Ayalon region, see Shavit 2000. Schniedewind (1998) takes the geographic and geopolitical context seriously, but his interpretation is Israel-centered and too dependent on biblical traditions.

5. Smith 1931, 145; cf. Shavit 2000.

6. Smith 1931, 147; Baly 1957, 144; for "moat," see Baly 1957, fig. 30 and his geological map (p. 17).

7. Smith 1931, 147; Baly 1957, 144–45; and Dorsey 1991, 151–53, map 9.

8. Ayalon, Asna, Eshtaol, Zenoach, Tappuach, Adullam, Qeïla, Nezib, Iftah, and Debir.

9. Isa 11:14: "shoulder of the Philistines" seems also to be a name from a hill country (Judean) perspective.

tains, but do not automatically connect/identify it with the coastal area (Deut 1:7; 2 Chr 26:10).

Fertile alluvial valleys with Rendzina soils on the slopes and an average yearly rainfall of 500 millimeters in the north allow ploughing. In contrast, the southern parts, which receive only 250 millimeters of rainfall annually, no longer permit dry farming.[10] Livestock, grainfields, and olive groves are characteristic; wine and oil presses are numerous.[11]

The transverse valleys that cut across the general north–south orientation of the Shephelah were important for commercial and military operations.[12] Smith rightly says that these east–west oriented valleys do not belong to the Shephelah alone because they run from the mountains to the coast, connecting the Judean heartland to the coastal cities. These valleys help us to understand military tactics, from Thutmosis III until 1948 C.E.,[13] but also formed vital trade links:

- Nahal Ayalon from Jafo towards Gezer and Jerusalem;
- Nahal Soreq from Ashdod to Ekron, Timnah, Beth Shemesh, and Jerusalem;
- Nahal Ela from Ashdod, via Gath and Azekah, Libnah, Qeïla, and Adullam as far as Beth Zur and Hebron; and
- Nahal Guvrin from Ashdod and Ashkelon through Gath, Mareschah, and Hebron.[14]

The Shephelah was characterized by its fertility, its proximity to the coastal centers, and roads that provided access to the isolated mountain regions. As a transitional zone, it united production and industry, exchange and logistics.[15]

---

10. Karmon 1983, 201; for the northern part of the Shephelah around Gezer and its agricultural resources, see Shavit 2000.

11. Smith (1931, 148) portrays it poetically: "The sun beats strong, but you see and feel the sea; the high mountains are behind, at night they breathe upon these lower ridges gentle breezes, and the dews are heavy…."

12. Smith 1931, 149; and Baly 1957, 144.

13. Smith 1931, 148. The apparently comfortable wadi openings towards Judah and Jerusalem were not easy to "walk" in times of war, when they were blocked cleverly. Smith (1931, 152–53; Baly 1957, 144–45) points out that while the Shephelah was often occupied militarily, the attacker sometimes failed to hold the mountain region permanently. Na'aman (1991, 40) notices that Egypt was usually only interested in the coast and the valleys.

14. See also, Baly 1957, 146–47 and Rainey 1983, 2. For Wadi Qubeibeh/Nahal Lachish; Wadi el-Hasa/Nahal Adorayim, see also Dorsey 1991, maps 9, 13–14.

15. Cf. Shavit 2000, 201: many beasts of burden around Gezer/Nahal Ayalon!

The Shephelah provided food for the inhabitants of the coast, both for their own subsistence and for export. In the mountains, the eastward trade expansion of the coast was perceived as aggression (Isa 9:12), its commercial and technical superiority as oppressive (1 Sam 13:19–20), and it was opposed with hopeful oracles (Isa 11:14). From the coastal cities' point of view, military operations in the hinterland to maintain order and free trade hardly came under consideration (contra Baly 1957, 144), since both sides benefited from the commercial ties that linked the mountains to the coast. The mountain elite needed outlets for its food surplus and the possibility of obtaining prestige goods. Military intervention or lasting military occupation was therefore only required in times of crisis (cf. Smith 1931, 147).

The highlanders certainly looked on the Shephelah and on the rich coastal cities with envy. They sat at the top of a natural "amphitheatre" (Smith 1931, 143, 147), contemplating the coastal business scene to which they had no access. The inhabitants of the mountains had three options: they could isolate themselves from the Shephelah, settle in it (cf. Lipschits 1999), or cooperate by trading their own products. The Shephelah appeared to the highlanders as a treasury that they gladly would have possessed and despoiled (Josh 15:45–47), and as a glacis against the "greedy"[16] inhabitants of the coastal plain (Philisto-Canaanites).

The Shephelah functions as a glacis on its eastern and western sides, the coastal plain, and the mountains. Although it had enough economic and cultural resources for independence, its position inbetween would have turned it into an intermediary (i.e., a business agent or merchant at best), or a disputed area (i.e., a war theater at worst).[17] Autarchy was conceivable,[18] but the Shephelah was predestined for commercial and cultural exchange[19] between the mountains and the coast, as well as for transport logistics. Indeed, each side would be tempted to lay claim to the Shephelah as its "own" glacis,[20] and local and regional competition would lead to many changes in control.

16. Isa 9:12; 11:14; Baly 1957, 144.

17. Smith 1931, 147: "Riding along the fosse between, I understand why the Shephelah was always debatable land, open equally to Israelite and Philistine, and why the Philistine, who so easily overran the Shephelah, seldom got farther than its eastern border, on which many of his encounters with Israel took place."

18. See Shavit 2000 with figures for population density in the Shephelah and the Ayalon Valley, as compared with Lower Galilee.

19. See Carter 1999, 94, who on the other hand, indicates a particular type of handcraft in the Shephelah.

20. Compare this with the disputed area of Benjamin in the north of Jerusalem: 1 Kgs 15:17–22; Schunck 1963, 169; Lipschits 1999.

The existence of the Shephelah explains differences in the destiny of the regions north and south of the Ayalon Valley. In the north, the absence of a middle zone between the central Palestinian mountains and the coastal plain (Smith 1931, 146–48) had important consequences that should be taken into account when reconstructing the history of Israel and Judah (fig. 1).[21]

From the Coast through the Shephelah into the Hill Country

Ideally, the cities lying between the coast and the mountains should have diminished in size from west to east and should therefore fit into four categories: a) the coast with cities of the first order (Ashdod, Ashkelon, Gaza);[22] b) the coastal periphery with second-order cities (Ekron, Gath); c) the Shephelah's third-order towns (Timnah on the western side, Beth Shemesh on the eastern side); and d) the hill country where localities of the fourth order are to be expected (see table 1). The Philistine cities of Ashdod, Ekron, and Gath, and the Judean capital Jerusalem partially fit this categorization (estimated urban area in hectares):[23]

21. Smith 1931, 149; in the south, the Shephelah, as a buffer zone, effects a relatively harmonious way of life. In the north, the absence of such a buffer zone led to direct confrontation or co-operation between coast and mountains. Mareshah served as a commercial hub for the Shephelah, thus showing that the Shephelah was open both to west and east (Smith 1931, 163). In the time of Lachish IV/III and II, the hill country (Judah) moved its border as far as possible to the west, cf. also Rainey 1980, 194; 1983, 6–7, 11. I guess that Libnah's revolt (2 Kgs 8:22; 2 Chr 21:10) was motivated by the desire to do its own trading. What is the subject and the object in Obadiah 19 is debated. According to Rudolph (1974, 314), the Shephelah will take possession of Philistia; in Wolff's view (1977, 40–41), the Shephelah here is presented as "land of the Philistines" by means of a syndetic addition. In any case, the particular place of the Shephelah between Judah's heartland and (as) the eastern part of Philistia is underlined.

22. There are good reasons not to include Ashkelon and Gaza with Ashdod for the study of the links between coast and hinterland. Ashkelon certainly played a role, but not with Judah: Due to its distance from Judah, among other things, this important commercial center never dealt directly with Judah (Judg 14:19 cannot be safely dated), but always in conjunction with some or all of the other Philistine centers. The same can be said for Gaza: It is mentioned as a distant border post (Judg 6:4; 16; 1 Kgs 5:4; 2 Kgs 18:8) over which Judah had no influence (Judg 1:18). Ashkelon's and Gaza's secondary roles in Judean history appear when one notices that the main contacts go through the Ashdod–Ekron–Gath corridor and the nearby wadis (see fig. 1); note the itinerary of the ark (1 Sam 5–7) and the escape route of the Philistines (1 Sam 17:52, also 2 Sam 5:25).

23. For sources on Ashdod, see Finkelstein and Singer-Avitz 2001; for Ekron, see Gitin 1997; for Gath, see Maeir and Ehrlich 2001; Uziel 2003; Uziel and Maeir 2005; Maeir and Uziel 2007; for Jerusalem, see Knauf 2000b; Finkelstein and Silberman 2001 and Finkelstein 2001. Dates are according to the low chronology: Finkelstein 1995; 1996a; 1996c; Killebrew 1998a; 1998b; 2000; Knauf 2000a; Gunnar Lehmann 2001b.

Table 1: The size of cities lying between the coast and the mountains by century in hectares.

Centuries	Ashdod	Ekron	Gath	Jerusalem
12	7	20	17–23	3
11	7	20	17–23	4
10	1(+X)	4	40–50	5
9	7	4	24	8
8	30	4(+X)	1	12
7	15[24]	20–30	1	>50
6	15	0	0	4

Tel Ashdod lies on the Via Maris, today four kilometers inland, and it had two harbors. The Lachish River was navigable and Ashdod was Judah's closest Mediterranean harbor. It belonged to the heart of the coastal area from which sprang secondary states between 1100 and 700 B.C.E. (Knauf 2000b, 86, fig. 4; cf. 82, fig. 2.). However, Ashdod lagged behind Ashkelon (approximately 40–50 hectares) and Ekron from the twelfth to the ninth centuries B.C.E. In the eighth century, Ashdod reached its zenith with over 30 hectares. After its destruction by Sargon II in 711 B.C.E., its function was partially absorbed by Ashdod-Yam (15 hectares). In addition to circulation of goods, the presence of Judean workers in Ashdod until the Persian period is likely,[25] perhaps through the intermediary of Ekron, with all the human repercussions that such a situation entails.[26] The importance of Ashdod grew after the demise of Ekron (and Gath) after the seventh century. In the Persian era, Ashdod outdid all other lowland towns (Lachish, Gath, and Azekah), and minted its own coins as Ashkelon and Gaza did. Ashdod (cf. Uehlinger 1998) was the westernmost city of the three northern Philisto-Canaanite centers, the closest harbor to Judah, and was coveted (Amos 1:6–8; 3:9) for its riches. This may explain why the short-lived influence of King Uzziah over Ashdod, in the wake of Jeroboam II's glory, was remembered (2 Chr 26:6). The

24. Ashdod-Yam replaced Tel Ashdod in the seventh and sixth centuries B.C.E.

25. Indicated by the stone foundation of a large public building, four large halls (cf. the "residency" in Lachish; housing Persian officials?), Attic ceramics, Persian jewelry, and an Aramaic ostracon of the fifth century B.C.E. (wine delivery by Zebadiah): M. Dothan 1993a, 100; 1992, 481.

26. Commercially beneficial for both sides, but considered negatively from the eastern religious point of view, see Neh 13:23, Zech 9:6–7.

potential integration of Ashdodite Philisto-Canaanites through conversion to Israel's god would have been considered a victory over a superior entity, often envied and admired (Zech 9:6–7, contra Neh 13:23).

After reaching its maximum extent first in the Early Bronze Age II–III (24 hectares) and then again in the Late Bronze Age (27 hectares), Tell eṣ-Ṣafi/Gath (Keel and Küchler 1982, 836–44) expanded into one of the largest Philistine sites in late Iron Age I (23 hectares) and during the tenth (40 or 50 hectares) and the ninth century B.C.E. (max. 24.5 hectares; Uziel 2003; Uziel and Maeir 2005; Maeir and Uziel 2007). After its destruction by Hazael (843–805/798 B.C.E.) at the end of the ninth century B.C.E. (indicated by a siege trench dug on the outer side of the fortifications), Gath remained unimportant, which allowed Ashdod's expansion in the eighth century B.C.E. and Ekron's new growth in the seventh century B.C.E. The destruction level at the end of the ninth (or beginning of the eighth?) century B.C.E. holds many storage jars of the LMLK type, considered by the excavators to be older than the "Hezekiah" LMLK type.[27] In addition to their function concerning the maintenance of the royal military and the administration, the LMLK handles[28] found outside the Judean kingdom may indicate commercial activities of the government with its neighbors.[29] The Philistine Iron Age I ceramics may indicate the extant of the Philistine realm that at first reached as far as Ekron and afterwards Gath (Uziel and Maeir 2005, 58–60) with both places coexisting in Iron Age I (politically unified? closely connected?) but competing in Middle Bronze Age, Late Bronze Age, and Iron Age IIA (Uziel and Maeir 2005, 65–67; Maeir and Uziel 2007; cf. Garfinkel 2007). Did Gath sometimes side politically with Judah against Ekron?[30]

Gath reached its zenith in the tenth–ninth centuries B.C.E. and was subsequently sacked by Hazael of Damascus (2 Kgs 12:18). Was a direct assault on Jerusalem in the hinterland of Gath unnecessary after Hazael's victory over Gath (2 Kgs 12:19)? In the eighth century B.C.E., the diminished Gath belonged to upstart Ashdod,[31] and they were punished together for their revolt against Assyria. If the vague mention in Sennacherib's "Letter to God"[32] can be interpreted thus, Hezekiah may have occupied Gath. Gath therefore allows us to document the following evolution from west to east: a) ceramics spread towards

27. Maeir and Ehrlich 2001, 30; cf. Zimhoni 1997, 221, especially 225–32.

28. Stern 1993c, 1523–24; Maeir and Ehrlich 2001, 30.

29. Niemann 1993, 156–69; Fox 2000, 216, especially 227, 232.

30. Cf. Halpern 2001, 290–94, 302–6, 326–31.

31. Prism fragment from Sargon's eleventh year, see Luckenbill 1926–1927, 2:13–14; cf. Amos 1:8; 6:2.

32. Na'aman 1974, 25–39: Hezekiah occupied Gath and fitted its water system.

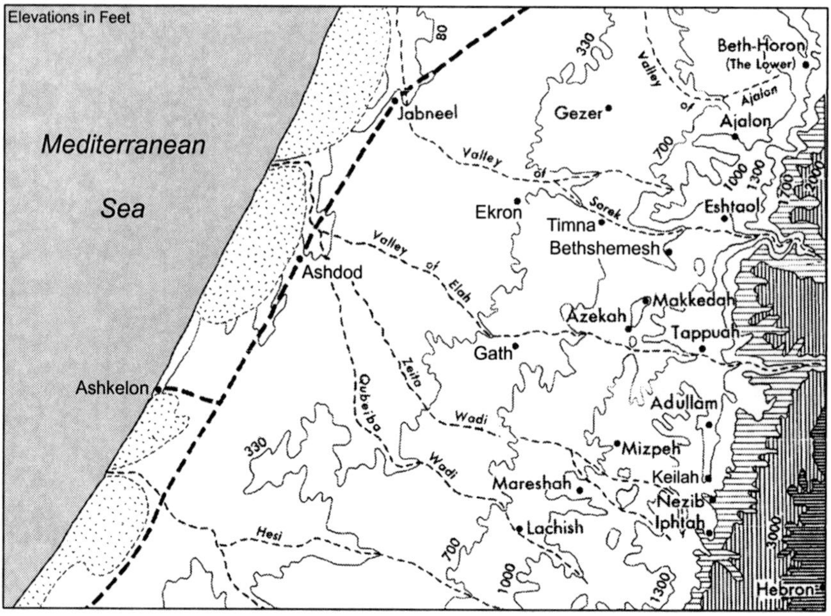

Fig. 1: From the coast through the Shephelah into the hills.

Ekron and Gath (as well as Timnah; Uziel and Maeir 2005, 58–60); b) the LMLK jars have probably a forerunner in the Shephelah (before Hezekiah integrated it into his own administrative system); and c) Hazael's campaign in the coastal zone and his attack on Gath shows that this city was then the hub of the Shephelah, an economically important region. Jerusalem at that time belongs to Gath's hinterland and submits voluntarily (2 Kgs 12:18–19).

Ekron (Tel Miqne/Khirbet el-Muqanna') lay to the east of Ashdod in the eastern margin of the coastal plain and controlled the road that linked Gezer[33] to Ashdod and Ashkelon. Timnah (Tel Batash) was six kilometers to the east of Ekron,[34] and six to seven kilometers further to the southeast was Beth Shemesh on Nahal Soreq where the ascent towards the mountain begins. Like Gath, Ekron[35] lay on the periphery of the area which, between 1000 and 750 B.C.E., sparked state building in the hinterland. In the eleventh to tenth centuries B.C.E.,

33. Gezer lies ca. 11 kilometers northeast of Ekron, towards Gath in the south, it is only 8 kilometers.

34. Eight kilometers south of Gezer, in Nahal Soreq.

35. According to the place name "Unfertile" (Keel and Küchler 1982, 829), its strategic position is more important than its economy.

Ekron covered ca. 20 hectares, shrank in the tenth/ninth to eighth centuries (4 hectares), and recovered in the seventh century to reach 20–30 hectares. Stratum I (Gitin 1997) reveals an "industrial" town of the Assyrian period with at least 115 oil installations, having a yearly capacity of 1,000 tons (= 48,000 jars = 4,800 hectares of orchards), requiring 2,000 workers. This indicates a large production for export, rather than for local needs. Over 600 loom weights reveal that textile production was practiced between the oil seasons.[36] Gitin interprets the horned altars found in each workshop as a sign of the presence of Judean workers at Ekron (although this does not necessarily mean that all the workers were Judeans). Seventh-century Ekron was multicultural with an elite under Assyrian supervision[37] until its destruction at the end of that century.

Ekron's booming activity depended upon two factors: first, its intermediary role in the Shephelah between the coast and the hills, and second, the integration of Syria and then Palestine into the Assyrian Empire, which greatly stimulated local economy in its periphery. From Gaza, Ashkelon, and Ashdod-Yam, the impulse spread inland. Ekron took part in Gaza's revolt at the time of Shalmaneser V's death, and in Ashdod's rebellion against Sargon II. Sargon besieged Ekron in 711 B.C.E. (Khorsabad Inscription) and from then on Ekron learned its lesson. King Padi kept out of the 705–701 revolt (*ANET* 287–88; *TGI* 68). Ekron made the most of its favorable situation, halfway between the Mediterranean harbors and the oil and wool producing hinterland (from 701 B.C.E. including some western parts of the former Judean hill country).[38] In return for its loyalty to the Assyrians, Ekron received a fair share of the eastern part of the Shephelah, which had previously belonged to Judah (H. Tadmor 1966, 86–102, especially 95). The economically unattractive and politically refractory hill country was thus separated from the Shephelah in 701 B.C.E. Ekron concentrated on oil and textile production (Gitin 1997, 87, 91) and Judah set out to stabilize its agriculture.[39] Judah simply

36. Ashkelon exported oil and wine, and imported fish and grain from Egypt, see Gitin 1997, 84.

37. Gitin 1997, 91: One of the largest buildings of Iron Age Palestine came to light in the Ekron excavations, indicating coastal trade links. The building (60 by 30 meters) featured a courtyard, a rectangular sanctuary with eight pillar bases and a 4-meter-wide doorstep, orthostats with graffiti, and an Assyrian rosette; a storeroom with hundreds of 4.75-liter jars (maybe for tax measurement) and 32-liter transport jars, Assyrian, Greek, and other imported ceramics, silver hoards (trade!), and luxury items from southwestern Asia Minor. In the elite complex, near Building 650, fifteen administrative and cultic inscriptions in Phoenician letters, mostly on jar shoulders, provide additional evidence of trade.

38. For the development in the Shephelah and in the Judean mountains, in Gezer, Lachish, and Jerusalem before and after the Assyrian invasion, see Gitin 1997, 82–83.

39. Royal domains in the Buqeʿa, Vered Yeriho, see Gitin 1997, 83–84; Niemann 1993, 160–62 and 127–29.

delivered raw materials and workers to Assyrian Ekron and to the other Philistine centers and harbors, which exported wine and oil, and imported fish and grain from Egypt (Gitin 1997, 84). However, the high cultural level reached by Ekron (Gitin 1997, 85) by the middle of the seventh century B.C.E. came to an end with the demise of the Assyrians. Ekron lost its central function between coast and mountains, and the city was destroyed between 604 and 603 (or 601) B.C.E. by Nebuchadnezzar.

The analysis of the development of Ashdod, Ekron, and Gath in the Iron Age shows that they were never collectively strong or weak simultaneously. On the contrary, they went on competing with each other for economic and political hegemony.[40]

What about the material, cultural, and economic as well as the geopolitical position of Shephelean Timnah between the coastal plain and the Judean hill country? When did the cultural and political influence of the coast reach Timnah[41] and where did it come from? Does the seal found in Stratum V, similar to one found in Ashdod, indicate that Shephelean Timnah was already under Philistine rule (Kelm and Mazar 1995, 92–93, 98; Mazar and Panitz-Cohen 1997, 254)? The weakness of its fortifications can be interpreted as a sign of dependence (Kelm and Mazar 1995, 101–2; Mazar and Panitz-Cohen 1997, 254). Nearby Ekron (7 kilometers) covers 20 hectares, Timnah itself 2.4 hectares (Mazar and Panitz-Cohen 1997, 277). The similarity of the gate arrangements in Stratum IV with that of tenth-century B.C.E. Ekron, as well as the one from Ashdod (Kelm and Mazar 1995, 105; Mazar and Panitz-Cohen 1997, 255), demonstrates the architectural influence that the coast had on locales to the east. Kelm and Mazar interpret Timnah's ceramics as characteristic of the Shephelah. Rather than indicating a Judean-Davidic conquest as the excavators claim,[42] this fact underlines the cultural peculiarities of the region between coast and mountains. The city of Stratum III was conquered possibly in the eighth century B.C.E. by Uzziah, king of Judah (Mazar and Panitz-Cohen 1997, 8, 255; Mazar and Panitz-Cohen 2001, 279–80). Kelm and Mazar rely on a LMLK impression found in Stratum III and on 2 Chr 26:6 and 28:18 to call the modification and reinforcement of the fortifications in the eighth–seventh century B.C.E. (Strata III–II) a "Judaean fort"

40. When Ekron decreased, Ashdod increased and vice versa. Ashdod and Gath complemented each other, but Gath lagged behind Ashdod and Ekron in the (eighth) seventh century (see above). The so-called Philistine Pentapolis was no unified political unit, cf. Niemann 2003.

41. Kelm and Mazar 1995; cf. A. Mazar 1994b.

42. Kelm and Mazar 1995, 110–11, see also Mazar and Panitz-Cohen 1997, 255. They presuppose that the increasing Philistine influence led to a change of rule and that the population was replaced by Philistine immigrants. I do not see any evidence for this.

(Stratum III) (Kelm and Mazar 1995, 120, 131; Mazar and Panitz-Cohen 1997, 255–57; Mazar and Panitz-Cohen 2001, 279–80). In addition to a similar layout of Timnah's city gate and other gates from the tenth to seventh centuries B.C.E. in different regions all over the country, the reconstructed orthogonal city plan of Timnah Strata III–II (compare Tel Qasile Stratum X or Megiddo Stratum III) is different from Judean towns (Mazar and Panitz-Cohen 1997, 256–60). Mazar and Panitz-Cohen call into question that a small town and the small number of its inhabitants (ca. 500–1,000) would be able to erect Timnah's Stratum III fortifications, thus this is an example of the Judean state (1997, 257). However, no lasting Judean control of Timnah is provable. King Ahaz lost it to the Philistines (2 Chr 28:18). Before deciding whether Timnah was independent or under Ekronite or Judean rule during the Assyrian period, one should clarify whether ethnic, political, or economic domination is meant. In a frontier zone, this question is particularly difficult to answer. Kelm and Mazar notice that Timnah's ceramics and metal tools often have no parallels in Judah but resemble those in Ekron and in Ashdod, while the house-type is typical of both Shephelah and mountain areas (Kelm and Mazar 1995, 146). It is not surprising that Timnah displays a mixture of cultural and material influences;[43] archaeology simply reflects Timnah's geographical position in the hilly Shephelah between the coastal plain and the hill country,[44] where influences come from two opposite directions, and where cultural and material developments require some time for dissemination and implantation.[45] The result is that the intermediate area has its own mixed profile[46] and that not every material or cultural change indicates a political integration or change of borders.

---

43. Compare round and square oil-press basins, see Kelm and Mazar 1995, 155–57. The ceramic mix at Timnah reflects the position of the Shephelah between Ashdod, Ekron, and Judah. LMLK jars with rosette impressions do so for the seventh century (164); cf. A. Mazar 1994, 253. The presence of Judean seals and weights (Kelm and Mazar 1995, 169–70), indicates in my opinion that the Shephelah, as an intermediate zone, displays trade and various shifting economic influences without proving political integration. Cf. also Mazar and Panitz-Cohen 2001, 277–83.

44. A. Mazar (1994b, 256) interprets the archaeological evidence along sharp geographical/political boundaries and claims that Timnah belonged either to Judah or to Ekron. In intermediate zones, cultural influences should not too quickly be attributed to political integration.

45. A. Mazar (1994b, 257) shows that in Timnah, Ekron's influence appears mainly in architecture and ceramics, at least in the seventh century B.C.E. (Timnah II and Ekron IB). That Josiah annexed Timnah is unclear or doubtful (see Na'aman 1991), but for a short period Judean influence at the end of the eighth century may be possible: Mazar interprets some ceramics (together with 2 Chr 28:18) in that way.

46. Mazar and Panitz-Cohen 1997, 6, 9, 263; 2001, 277, 279–83. See also Gunnar Lehmann 2001b: the Philistines did not expand far into their hinterland, but they preferred to strengthen their urban base.

In Beth Shemesh, the excavations[47] have reached early Iron phase(s) in the northeastern part of the tell.[48] Another early Iron phase presents distinctive construction methods, for example, the roof supports.[49] In the late-tenth to early-ninth centuries B.C.E. (Bunimovitz and Lederman 2001, 144–47; 2003) or—perhaps more convincing—in the middle or second half of the ninth century or early-eighth century B.C.E. (Finkelstein 2002b, 131–33; Fantalkin 2004), a planned town with a city wall was built, along with commercial storage, public buildings, industrial installations, and a large water-storage system (Bunimovitz and Lederman 2001, 141–47; 2003, 7–20). This level came to a violent end in the Babylonian conquest of the Shephelah and Jerusalem between 604 and 586 B.C.E. (Finkelstein and Na'aman 2004, 68–69; Fantalkin 2004, contra Bunimovitz and Lederman 2003). The excavation confirms the presence of industrial installations, which indicates oil (and textile?) production.[50] But what brought the modification of the roofing techniques between the twelfth and tenth centuries B.C.E.? Some kind of cultural or demographic change? The excavators emphasize the cultural mixture of the excavated remains (Bunimovitz and Lederman 2001, 138–40; Fantalkin 2004, 254). A Proto-Canaanite ostracon from Beth Shemesh (twelfth–eleventh centuries B.C.E.), a draughtboard fragment (Bunimovitz and Lederman 1997, 48, 75), and a fragment of a bowl found in Timnah[51] (both from the tenth to ninth centuries B.C.E.) all bear the same name, *ḥnn* (Hanan). These findings and the name could indicate the presence of a common family or clan in both Beth Shemesh and Timnah (Bunimovitz and Lederman 1997, 48.75), although one should be careful before defining ethnic or political groups on such evidence. Who fortified Beth Shemesh in the ninth B.C.E.? The king of Jerusalem or—why not the local Shephelean inhabitants or both in an act of political and economic collaboration or *Realpolitik* (Fantalkin 2004, 255)? Was Timnah the easternmost "Philisto-Canaanite" town or was it Beth Shemesh (looking from the coastal plain)? Was Beth Shemesh the last Judean settlement in the west (looking from the Judean mountains)? Or—most convincing in my mind—are the inhabitants of Timnah and Beth Shemesh simply Shepheleans, settled between Philisto-Canaanites (Ekron, Gath, etc.) and Judeans of the mountains? Is Jeru-

47. Bunimovitz and Lederman 1997; 1998; 2000; 2001; 2003.

48. For example, in Area A a "patrician house" long room, plastered floor, inner court, upper floor and "gold treasury": Bunimovitz and Lederman 1997, 45.

49. Bunimovitz and Lederman 1997, 45–48; indicating, I believe, the plurality of influences during a transitional period as well as an in-between region of some unincorporated (independent) towns open to any group from both sides interested in this area.

50. Bunimovitz and Lederman 2000, 254–58; 2003; and Fantalkin 2004.

51. Including the name [*B*]*n-ḥnn*, cf. A. Mazar 1994b, 254–55.

salem involved at all in Beth Shemesh and beyond, and to what degree and at what point? The quantity of LMLK handles and handles with private seal impressions confirms the importance of the Beth Shemesh region in the eighth century B.C.E., since higher numbers of handles were discovered only in Jerusalem, Lachish, Ramat Rahel, Gibeon, and Tell en-Nasbeh.[52] Do those jars indicate trade or Judean occupation, economic or political; or do they simply reveal the growing influence of the east? A few identical names on seals (handles) have been found in Beth Shemesh as well as Ramat Rahel and Jerusalem. This may suggest Judean sovereignty over Beth Shemesh, although it is not sure. The place could be (half-) independent, appropriate for its geographical location as well as for its mixed culture. The excavation reports as well as the interpretation of the *ḥnn* (Hanan) inscriptions do not allow us to presume an ethnically and politically clear definition of the site and its inhabitants.[53]

The study of the main towns between the coast and the mountains reveals that: a) political, social, and cultural developments progress at different speeds from the coast to the mountains;[54] b) the mountains stood in the shadow of the coastal plain with its better traffic conditions and more dynamic developments (this position has both negative and positive effects on the highlands); c) the existence of the Shephelah, independent of or as a glacis for one or more of its neighboring zones, is an important factor for historical reconstructions; and d) great caution is required for ethnic attributions and the definition of borders.[55] It is worth investigation in more depth whether the devastation of the Shephelah in 701 B.C.E. and the following period of Manasseh's reign contributed to the rapid development of Jerusalem, which then became the main city of seventh-century B.C.E. southern Palestine (cf. Halpern 1991; Knauf 2005). Coincidentally, a gradual revitalization of the Shephelah took place in the seventh century B.C.E. (Finkelstein 1994; Finkelstein and Na'aman 2004; Fantalkin 2004, 253–58).

52. Thirteen new LMLK handles (previously forty-two) and three new handles with "official ('private') seal impressions" (until then twelve): Bunimovitz and Lederman 1997, 75; 2000, 255–56.

53. Cf. Fantalkin 2004, 254: Beth Shemesh as "a border city"; "... the regional frontiers of material culture ... were blurred due to the pax Assyriaca."

54. Reverse movements in the opposite direction are also possible.

55. Frontier areas like the Shephelah are interaction zones where identity formation, changes and manipulations can be observed. For an interesting example of another in-between region and its mechanisms and dynamics, cf. Bienkowski (2007) describing "the Wadi Arabah as Relationship and Discourse," looking for the landscape as relationship/process, also looking for movements, negotiations, and exchange, where people "have a constantly changing emotional relationship" with the landscape (2007, 411). Bienkowski analyzes structures of "power, domination, and reciprocal relations in the landscape" as well (2007, 417–18).

A Second Biblical Picture: Viewing the Coast with Holy Wrath

How is the relationship between Philistines and Judeans reflected in the Bible since the seventh century B.C.E.? The Philistines are the archenemy in the west.[56] Many substantial texts admire and envy jealously the Philistines and the Phoenicians for their traditional superiority and riches.[57] According to the theologian Ezekiel, wealth leads directly to arrogance.[58] The merchants from the coast are by definition aggressive, hostile, vengeful, greedy, arrogant, and without feelings (Amos 1:6–8, 9–10; Joel 4:4–8; Ezek 25:15–17; Isa 14:28–32). "Canaan" as a category reminiscent of Late Bronze Egyptian colonialism is used to brand Philistines and Phoenicians as "exploiters" and "oppressors" (Zeph 2:4–5; Isa 23:1–18; Gen 10:19; Josh 13:1–6). The occasional geographical descriptions that use the term "Canaan" (Josh 13:1–6; Isa 23:1–18; Jer 25:15–26; 47:1–7; Zech 9:1–7) are also pejorative. The situation is all the more depressing for the hill people since Assyria conquered both the coastal plain and the hills with the former enjoying greater prosperity. Zephaniah 2:1–7 expresses the wish to grow rich from Philistia without doing the necessary and risky work of the (maritime) merchants. The highland shepherds want to occupy the coast but use it only as grazing grounds, a waste of economic potential! For the time being, religious sublimation is the sole consolation offered to face the arrogance and wealth of the coast (Zech 9:1–7).

On the other hand, Ashdod is angered by Jerusalem's moves towards autonomy and isolation (Neh 4:1–2), which tend to curtail the free movement of goods and people, while Neh 13:15–28 considers isolation necessary to bolster Judean identity. Phoenician merchants settle in Jerusalem to boost the economy. Of course, they trade on the Sabbath as do the Jerusalemites and people from Yehud! Although Yehud cannot do without external stimulation and know-how, identity is considered endangered when its inhabitants marry Ashdodite women, as they always did. Economically, Nehemiah's stringent requirements are counterproduc-

---

56. Arameans in the east; Isa 9:12, 1 Macc 3:41.

57. Isa 23:1–18; Jer 25:15–26; 47:1–7; Zeph 2:1–7. Ezek 25:15–17; 26–28 expresses both admiration and envy towards the inaccessible wealth and technological superiority but also a kind of malicious joy about the fall of the rich ones, both stemming from the hurt pride of the weak and poor hinterland which supplies only food and in return for prestige goods and know-how—typical for a third-world state (cf. also Ezek 27:17 from the sixth century B.C.E.).

58. See the prince of Tyre, who claims to be God (Ezek 28). Ezekiel would want Jerusalem to be the "Gateway of the peoples" (Ezek 26:2) but verse 2 really describes Tyre. In reality Jerusalem is far too small and too poor to make Tyre jealous. Jerusalem/Ezekiel is simply projecting onto Tyre its own jealousy, expressing its envy and admiration for the rich coastal city.

tive.[59] Whether or not the resentment was legitimate is irrelevant; what matters here is to notice how much anger is expressed by biblical texts against the coast.

The tendency of prophetic texts to identify Phoenicians and Philistines with Canaanites seems to have prompted other biblical texts to interpret the present in the light of the past, thus affording consolation in hard times by remembering the great victories won by the ancestors over the inhabitants of the coast. After the many campaigns described in 1 Sam 4–2 Sam 5, David remains as the sole war leader (2 Sam 1:1–5:5). This situation was acceptable to the Philistines since David was their vassal, always siding with the winning side. They did not consider that his conquest of Jerusalem (2 Sam 5:6–15) was an attempt to gain independence (Halpern 2001, 315–32) or that it represented a danger for their own security. In fact, David never endangered the Philistines, and 2 Sam 5:17–25 is the first and only time that David is shown fighting the Philistines. This text is really and simply an etiology for the name Baal-Perazim. In a second move, David sets an ambush in the Rephaim Valley, but it is God who beats the Philistines. The last words in 2 Sam 5:25 "He smote the Philistines from Geba to Gezer" do not fit the geographical framework of the Davidic traditions, but match perfectly the Saul narratives and Benjaminite topography.[60] For lack of traditions in the David story recounting any war against the Philistines, one was borrowed from Saul and attributed to David, with the odd result that David fights the Philistines without ever defeating them. In David's time the Philistines vanish from the "theological history-writing" of the Bible.[61] This Davidic "Philistine war silence" should be compared to David's political and geographical position vis-à-vis the Philistines.

David's historical relationship with the Philistines was very different from the theological picture of the Bible. That David ran away from Saul to Gath seems obvious.[62] Knowing that "my enemy's enemy is my friend," Achish of Gath

59. For a different viewpoint, see Mal 2:15–16 contra Neh 13:23.

60. Niemann 1997, 268–69 with n. 38: "The phrase does describe the geographical area from which Saul, in defence of his residence Gibeon (=Geba), might have driven the Philistocanaanites back to their starting point (Gezer)."

61. The "hero list" in 2 Sam 23:6–39 belongs to David's early career under Saul. 2 Sam 8:1 is not a description of a new war campaign against the Philistines but a summary of the (alleged) battles of David. How did David start ruling Jerusalem, how did he evolve from vassal to autocrat? A conquest of Gath by David (1 Chr 18:1) could derive from 2 Sam 8:1 which does not mention Gath (but cf. 2 Sam 21:20–22). The single combats in 2 Sam 21:15–22 (cf. 1 Sam 17) are impossible to date; the concentration of three battles in unidentified Gob, while only one is situated near Gath, is similar to 2 Sam 2:12–17. These fights are not real wars. Cf. below n. 69.

62. Gath is the nearest and thus most referred to Philistine town: Amos 6:2; Mic 1:10; 1 Sam 7:14; 17:52; 1 Sam 5:8–10; 6:17; cf. 1 Sam 21; 27.

trusted David (1 Sam 27:12; 28:1–2) in spite of initial qualms (1 Sam 21:11–16). David was so smart that six hundred (?) Gittite soldiers offered themselves spontaneously and their king did not bat an eyelid![63] David then rallied to himself a Philisto-Canaanite personal guard (Kreti and Pleti), stemming from different origins and specially committed to his person in order to counterbalance the influence of his Gittite contingent. Of course, these are speculations based on the biblical "Saul-David-narrative." What is certain is that David was pacifying Judah and collecting taxes for Achish (more "personal" tax-collecting in 1 Sam 25; official tax-collection in 1 Sam 27) as the leaders of the central Palestinian range had already done with their own mercenaries during the Amarna period. David did exactly what the Philistines wanted him to do; even on his way from Hebron to Jerusalem, David was still under Gath's protection. Achish had no reason to consider David a rebel rather than his vassal, even after his settling in Jerusalem. There, David may have been fairly discreet over his ties with Gath, in order to keep his options open and to make sure he remained on the winning side (cf. 1 Sam 30:26–31). Was there ever a decision to sever David's ties with Gath? Were single combats used to that purpose (2 Sam 21:15–22; 2 Sam 2:12–17; 1 Sam 17)? Whether 2 Sam 5:17–25 was the decisive confrontation between "the Philistines" and David is unclear.[64] Was there a cease-fire agreement that was later interpreted as victory on each side? This would explain the absence of the Philistines in the books of Samuel and Kings. Gath marks Judah's westernmost zone of influence for a long time.[65] The unpromising image of David as a Philistine-Apiru leader is improved by a series of victories over Philistine warriors (1 Sam 17; 2 Sam 21:15–22). The Gittite Apiru henchman becomes the biblical champion over the Philistine.[66] The position of Gath in the Shephelah corridor between coast and mountains also explains, *en passant*, other behavioral patterns.[67]

---

63. 2 Sam 15:18–22; 18:2: were they commissioned by Achish, simultaneously watching for David's actions?

64. Garsiel (2000) shows that the narrator has a good knowledge of the geography and how a battle would make sense, but this does not imply the historicity of the battle, cf. above with n. 61.

65. Mic 1:10; 1 Kgs 2:39–41: in Gath, Shimei's slaves thought to be out of Judah's reach but since relations between Judah and Gath were good, they were caught. Even after great victories (1 Sam 17:52; 2 Sam 5:25b), Israel never ventured further than the Gath–Ekron line.

66. 2 Sam 1:19–25 fits the context of a Benjaminite lament at Ishbaal's court perfectly (cf. Judg 5; Knauf 2005), Jerusalemite/Judahite royal tradition added 2 Sam 1:26–27 and attributed it to David, simultaneously covering up David's "desertion" (1 Sam 29).

67. 1 Chr 7:21 tells of Gittite raids against Ephraim. In 1 Chr 8:13, Ayalon (Benjaminite) attacks Gath. These actions are typical of inbetween zones and cannot be dated. In this geographical middle position Gath had to have battle specialists ready (2 Sam 21:15–22; 2 Sam 15:17–21; 1 Chr 20:6–8; 1 Sam 17).

David accomplished his work of "pacifying" the Judean Mountains, each side interpreting it differently. Inhabitants of the coastal plain begin to cohabitate with those of the mountains, without massive friction.[68] Neither side has any significant superiority over the other. Compared to the previous phase allegedly marked by continuous fighting, this period is marked by a peaceful equilibrium between coast and hill country, except for a few raids (*ghazwa*). However, there was still a difference of cultural, economic, and technical levels between the two areas.[69] The biblical picture of two different regions and phases, of a clear front between the coast and the oppressed and despoiled hill country, and an all-out war followed by a peaceful period, is contradicted by other passages in the Bible itself.[70]

---

68. 2 Chr 26:6–7 tells of a campaign by Uzziah against Gath, Jabne(el), and Ashdod in the first half of the eighth century B.C.E. (Welten 1973, 153–63). It is unclear wether this campaign was more than a simple raid against the Philistines. It is also uncertain whether Uzziah was able to establish military strongholds ("cities") in Philistia as he claims since there is no additional evidence to support this. Historically, a (short-term) campaign by Uzziah as junior partner in the wake of Jeroboam II is not improbable. The biblical context refers to a campaign because of economic interest. Was the surprise coup from 1 Chr 18:1 attributed to David under the influence of 2 Sam 8:1? During Ahaz's reign (741–725 B.C.E.) the situation is reversed (2 Chr 28:18): The Philistines are present in the Shephelah and in the Negev. In the Shephelah, Beth Shemesh, Ayalon, Gederot, Socho, Timnah, and Gimso represent the overlap between Judah and the coast. Their inhabitants do not commit to belonging necessarily to either side: The border was not clearly defined and the merchants of the coastal plain wanted it to be stable and open, as did the commission agents and producers of the Shephelah as well as the producers in the mountains because they were interested in the sales of surplus. The situation was tense (Welten 1973, 174–75) but the merchants needed to calm down and to keep borders open instead of conquering land and spending large amounts of "money" and manpower on military forces and administration. The biblical texts presented here show that both sides coveted the towns of the Shephelah. During the reign of Hezekiah (725–697 B.C.E.), Judah gained the upper hand again. He may have gone as far as Gaza (2 Kgs 18:8), profiting from the Assyrian pressure on the coast: Travelling for negotiations in the context of the rebellion against the Assyrians or simply Judean raids (Hobbs 1985, 253)? In any case, Judah paid a heavy price (*TUAT* I, 389–90).

69. 1 Sam 13:19–22; 2 Kgs 1: Ahaziah of Israel inquires of Ekron's famous god rather than of the (inferior?) Yahweh or Baʿal from Samaria (cf. n. 71).

70. Gen 21:22–34: The petty king Abimelech and Abraham the shepherd negotiate and agree on watering rights. Gen 26: The shepherd Isaac lives in loose symbiosis with urban Gerar. He becomes rich and the town dwellers become jealous (26:14). In fact, the shepherds envy the luxury of city life while the urban population envies the independence and flexibility of the shepherds. Agreement is found after a long dispute, until the next crisis. The Samson narrative (Judg 14–15) is set in the transitional zone between Judah and the coast. Neighborly relations, as in the case of Philistines, Shepheleans, and Judeans, typically oscillate between feasting with each other and quarrelling together. First Kings 17:7–10: When the mountains suffer from drought and hunger, food is still available in the coastal plain. During economic crisis, the dwellers of the (Samarian) mountains migrate to the coast (2 Kgs 8:1–6; see Lipschits 1999 for the migration of Benjam-

The structural (geographic, ecological, and economic) elements that characterized the daily life of the merchants of the (urban) coast, and the shepherds and peasants of the mountains, emerge clearly from our analysis. This picture stands in stark contrast to the tendentious theological portrait of the "Philistine" archenemy in the Bible, especially its tendency to emphasize ethnic and religious separation. The theological aim of the Philistine war narratives from Samuel to David is to attribute to David rather than to the Israelite Saul the final victory over the Philistines (2 Sam 3:18): Davidic-Judean royal ideology *ad maiorem regis gloriam*.

Center and Periphery: Business on the Coast, Theology in the Hills

Taking into account the geographical and economic structures (see Knauf 2001b) helps to distinguish biblical ideology from historical facts in which the biblical redactors had little interest. Deeper understanding of the Philistines as a historical phenomenon cannot spring solely from the biblical text because it is theological. Geography, archaeology, epigraphy, iconography, anthropology, and sociology are important means to recover it. What are the characteristics of the coast–hill country relationship?

The Bible focused on Israel and its world, thus in this theological context, the Philistines are evil just because they are strangers, revering other gods. Ecological and economic structures favor, from the start, the coast more than the hills, and thus explain why the highlanders will always consider the inhabitants of the coast as nasty and greedy. Trade and exchange as the basis of coastal economy is the background for socioeconomic dynamics, connecting the coastal economies with those of the hills (Shephelah) and the mountain areas, and causing social change and development. Both the coast and the mountain area profit from this interaction. Generally, the coast does not wage war against the hill country. The coast requires free and safe roads, and depends on the delivery of produce from its hinterland for its own consumption as well as for trade (1 Kgs 5:15; Ezek 27:17). If necessary, force may be used (1 Sam 13:17–18; 23:1–5), or better, the dirty work may be delegated (1 Sam 25; 27). In order to maintain their technological advantage the coastal polities bar the mountain farmers from the necessary technological know-how to produce the manufactured goods themselves (1 Sam

---

inites to the coastal plain; 1 Chr 8:12–13). 2 Kgs 1: Ekron belonged to the most developed part of the land, with better physicians and a stronger god; understandably, Judah wished to count Ekron as part of its own territory (Jos 15:45; 19:43; Judg 1:18).

13:19–20). Keeping up easy flow of delivery and exchange sometimes requires limited policing interventions (1 Sam 13:17–23; 2 Sam 23:14). In case of serious problems, the region in question can easily be sealed off (1 Sam 29:1–11). These operations may produce "anti-colonial" feelings among the population concerned. In the twelfth to eleventh centuries B.C.E., the hill country was relieved from Bronze Age Egyptian colonialism in Canaan. Now, the pressure from the west was felt anew. Resentment against the wealthy coast was expressed by the designation "Canaan." First expressed among the northern tribes of Israel as a polemical designation during the tenth century B.C.E. (Judg 5), it was later used in Judean texts from the seventh century on, to describe Philistines and Phoenician cities, such as Tyre and Sidon.

Historically, wars with the Philistines were fought mainly in areas north of Jerusalem, such as the territory of Benjamin and in the Jezreel Valley. Judah was spared wars and devastation by the Philistines since it was their agricultural hinterland and developing market, controlled from the Shephelah as a glacis of the coastal region. For such economic and political considerations, David established peace with the Philistines, collaborating with the coastal cities. Lacking such collaborators in the region north of Jerusalem, with its larger population and more promising economic opportunities, a different strategy had to be developed by the Philistines. They chose to open this agricultural region with its market by force. This may explain Philistine "police" actions in the Saulide part of the central mountain range and in the Jezreel Valley during the tenth century B.C.E. The books of Samuel correctly record them, but without mentioning their economic and geographical background. On the contrary, David's Philistine wars are not historical; they were raids ordered by the Philistines or by David himself, but the image of the "aggressive Philistine" is founded historically on Saul's Philistine wars, taken over in David's Judah to shore up dynastic claims. David was thus connected to the famous victories against the Philistines from the very beginning of his career under Saul. The historical vassal of the Philistines was turned into the biblical victor over the Philistines. The royal period is "Philistine silent"; theologically correct since David was supposed to have vanquished them, and historically correct also because in the ninth and partly in the eighth century B.C.E. the Philistines were not enemies. Coast and hill country had found a convenient arrangement, with the Shephelah serving as commercial hub. Between approximately 880 and 750 B.C.E., the political as well as the economic power was in the hands of the Phoenicians, and secondarily in Israel and Damascus (Knauf 2000b, 82–83, figs. 2–3). The sharp ethnic separation as expressed by the books of Samuel does not reflect correctly the historical interaction of the different populations of coast and mountains. That sharp separation is an exilic theological construction and exaggeration that stands at odds with the biblical picture of daily relations between these groups. More important and distressing was the social gap between the poor (Judeans) and the rich (coastal people). The poor had nothing with which to oppose the Philistines, apart from verbal attacks. The negative notion "Canaanites" had its origins in the hostile sentiments towards the Late Bronze Age polities, which were perceived as agents of the Egyptian colonial power in that period. By the late-seventh to sixth centuries B.C.E., the designations for the inhabitants of the coast became rather confused; the notion "Canaanites" is interchangeable with "Philistines" or "Phoenicians," the exilic theology did not differentiate between them. Bad feelings did not arise because Philistines and Tyrians were ethnically or religiously different, but because they were rich and superior.

Phoenicia became innovative and advanced in the ninth to eighth centuries B.C.E. and Philistia was so in the eleventh to tenth centuries B.C.E. and again during the *pax Assyriaca* in the seventh century B.C.E. At Judah's front door stood Ekron, a mighty "industrial" site, with Phoenician luxury goods and famous gods. Its economy was built on the processing of olives from different regions, also from the Judean Mountains. This olive supply was essential for Judean agriculture and welfare. Both Ekron and Judah were Assyrian vassals, but better to be a rich vassal than a poor one. The poor ones may have comforted themselves with the thought that the now superior neighbor was previously vanquished and humiliated by the ancestors (David!) of the losers. Economic inferiority, a structural weakness of the mountains against the coast, would thus be religiously sublimated, and identity would be reinforced through isolation.

In Mediterranean history the coexistence of rich coastal merchants with poorer hill people was the rule, and war was the exception. The long war between the Philistines and Israel described in 1 Sam 4–2 Sam 5 is simply an element of Judean Davidic royal ideology, as is the sudden cessation of all conflicts with the Philistines after David's alleged victory. Historically, the relationships and the borders between Philistines and Israelites were not so sharply defined according to ethnic lines. Everyday life was determined by social and economic differences between coast and plain dwellers on one side, and highland farmers and shepherds on the other as well as by the special position of the Shephelah as intermediary. Biblical duality that distinguishes periods with and without Philistine wars and a clear-cut ethnic division between Philistines and Israelites exaggerate the tensions between Israelites and Philistines, ideologically overloading the geographical and socioeconomic structures that govern the relations of the coast with its mountain hinterland and the Shephelah inbetween.

Chapter Eleven
Aegean-Style Pottery in Syria and Lebanon during Iron Age I

*Gunnar Lehmann**

Understanding and explaining the transition from Late Bronze Age to Iron Age in the Levant with its changes and continuities remains a major challenge for archaeology. Among the new elements appearing during the Iron Age in the Levant are decorated ceramics of the LH IIIC (LH IIIC) tradition. Mycenaean pottery (LH IIIA and IIIB) was imported already during the Late Bronze Age to Syria, but the LH IIIC styles of the Iron Age were mostly locally produced and had a wider distribution, appearing even in smaller, rural sites.[1] Recent archaeological research has significantly increased the amount and the variety of Aegeanizing pottery styles in the northern Levant. This paper is a preliminary summary of Aegean and/or Aegeanizing pottery styles in Syria and Lebanon during Iron Age I and the implications connected with this phenomenon. The sites discussed here are located in Lebanon and Syria, but include also evidence from the ʿAmuq Plain of the Hatay province in southeast Turkey. This paper aims at demonstrating that LH IIIC style ceramics are an integral and frequent part of the decorated early-Iron Age pottery of the northern Levant indicating close and continuous contacts during the twelfth and eleventh centuries B.C.E. between Syria, Lebanon, Cyprus, Cilicia, and the Aegean.

The paper starts with a short survey of the relevant archaeological sites. This overview is followed by a catalogue of the ceramics of Aegeanizing style or pottery with significant relations to the Aegean and the eastern Mediterranean. Then the

---

* Department of Bible, Archaeology and Ancient Near Eastern Studies, Ben-Gurion University, P.O.B. 653, Beer Sheva 84105, Israel. E-mail: gunnar.lehmann@gmail.com.

1. I prefer the notion "Late Helladic IIIC" over other notions such as "Mycenaean IIIC" that are outdated in Aegean archaeology.

relative and absolute chronology of the evidence is discussed and the distribution of the ceramics examined. Finally, the implications of these observations are interpreted and discussed against the background of current research.

The Sites

The first part of this paper presents relevant excavations in Syria, Lebanon, and southeast Turkey with finds of Aegean or Aegeanizing pottery dating to the Late Bronze Bronze Age–Iron Age transition and the Iron Age I in the northern Levant.[2]

Syria

Afis

Tell Afis is as of today the key excavation in northern Syria with a stratigraphic sequence that provides the most important chronological reference for the Iron Age in the region. A significant number of Aegean-style pottery dating to the Syrian[3] Iron Age I was found here in well stratified contexts (Venturi 2000). The relevant levels at Afis are Area E, Levels 9b–6 (Late Bronze Age–Iron Age transition and Iron Age I). Levels 5–3 at Area E date to the Syrian Iron Age IC with Cypro-Geometric imports and imitations. The architecture of Area E is characterized by a large residential building that dates to the Late Bronze Age, after the destruction of Level 9b at the beginning of the Syrian Iron Age IB the remains of this building were reused in Level 9a. The architecture of Area E, Levels 9a–5 was of domestic character. The site seems to have been a village during the later part of the Syrian Iron Age IB (Venturi 2000, 529; cf. Bonatz 1998; Mazzoni and Cecchini 1995; Mazzoni 2002).

'Ayn Dara

This is one of the main settlements in the upper Afrin Valley. The pottery discussed here was found during a survey and in soundings of the lower tell. The lower city was a domestic settlement area (Stone and Zimansky 1999, fig. 27:1, 3, fig. 29). The size of the Iron Age I settlement suggests that the site was an urban center during Iron Age I.

2. For a comprehensive bibliography of the sites, see Gunnar Lehmann 2002.

3. Note that the terminology of the Syrian Iron Age phases is different from the Palestinian Iron Age phases.

Tell Baraghitah

This project includes the finds of the River Qoueiq (Quwayq) survey (Matthers 1981, fig. 236:7=fig. 237a).

Jindiris

This is a large site in the Afrin Valley, east of the 'Amuq Plain. The Iron Age I levels "consist of badly preserved domestic buildings and numerous disposal pits dug into the ancient slope" of the tell (Sürenhagen 1999, 163, the only published relevant sherd is fig. 10). The size of the site during Iron Age I remains unclear.

Kazel

One of the main settlements in the 'Akkar Plain, Tell Kazel may have been the capital of the kingdom of Amurru. The end of the Late Bronze Age is represented by Level 6 "lower floor" in Area II and Level 5 "lower floor" in Area IV with a sanctuary. This phase is followed by an abandonment. The Transitional Late Bronze–Iron Age levels include Level 6 "upper floor" in Area II and Level 5 "upper floor" in Area IV, again with a sanctuary in this area. After a destruction by fire, the Iron Age I strata Level 5 in Area II and Levels 4–3 in Area IV follow, which were eventually destroyed by fire too (Badre 2006 with a comprehensive bibliography of previous excavation reports). While there is settlement continuity between the Late Bronze Age and the transitional Late Bronze–Iron Age levels, there is apparently less continuity with following levels of Iron Age I.

The pottery in the area of the sanctuary and the domestic quarters includes a considerable amount of Mycenaean and Aegean style (Jung 2007). Among these were "many hundreds of sherds and pots from the time span of LB II to Iron Age I [that] can be divided into different categories: 1) imported Mycenaean pottery; 2) presumably locally produced Mycenaean pottery; 3) typologically mixed products showing a combination of Mycenaean and Syrian characteristics; 4) Gray Wares; and 5) Handmade Burnished Ware" (Badre et al. 2005, 16). Imported Mycenaean pottery produced in the Argolis was found in layers of the Late Bronze Age. Mycenaean-style pottery produced in southwest Turkey and/or Cyprus appeared in the destruction layer dated to the transition from Late Bronze Age II to Iron Age I. Local productions of LH IIIC styles and Handmade Burnished Ware commenced with the beginning of Iron Age I. Among the local LH IIIC styles a few groups are conspicuously missing: there are no spiral motifs, no wavy-line motifs, and no monochrome painted ("Granary")-style vessels. The LH IIIC assemblages are best compared with LH IIIB Final and LH IIIC Early in the Aegean—two phases that are even in the Aegean difficult to separate (Jung 2007, 563). According to the excavators more stratigraphic research is necessary before a precise date is possible for the Gray Ware fabrics found in Tell Kazel. It is, however, already clear that this style consists of two fabric groups, one apparently imported from the area of Troy and one that is so far of undetermined provenance (Badre et al. 2005, 36).

Mardikh

The site was a small rural settlement during Iron Age I. Published pottery relevant for this study is scarce (TM.74.E.331/1 with double wavy lines, "Mycenaean IIIC:1C"; Bonatz 1998, 214 n. 11, no illustration).

Ras al-Bassit

This site has a Late Bronze Age administrative structure with some modest dwellings around it that were destroyed at the end of that period. On these destructions, poor domestic structures and silos were built. Pottery found in this level included a fragment of a LH "IIIC1" stirrup (?) jar (Courbin 1990, 505, Inv.C. 4009, no illustration) and local pottery similar to ceramics from Ras Ibn Hani "upper" level, dating to the late-twelfth century B.C.E. The next level at Ras al-Bassit yielded finds corresponding to Cypro-Geometric I in Cyprus (Courbin 1990, 503–5; 1993; cf. Caubet 1992, 127–28). A photograph of a small LH III C Late (?) krater fragment was published without a detailed presentation of the associated levels (Courbin 1986, 187, fig. 10; Leonard 1994, no. 2001).

Ras Ibn Hani

Modest domestic structures at this site were built over a Late Bronze Age palace. There are two subphases. The "lower floor" has material roughly contemporary with the Syrian Iron Age IA, while on the "upper floor" Syrian Iron Age IB pottery was found (Bonatz 1993, 128; Caubet 1992, 124–27).

For relevant Aegeanizing pottery from Ras Ibn Hani, see: Badre 1983, fig. 1a (=Bounni et al. 1979, fig. 19:11), 1b–e, cf. fig. 1g for a local imitation of Proto-White Painted; Bounni et al. 1978, 280, fig. 28:1 (=Leonard 1994, no. 1806), 28:2 (=Leonard 1994, no. 1808), 28:3 (=Leonard 1994, no. 1991), 28:4–12, 28:13 (=Leonard 1994, no. 2078 LH IIIC Middle?), 28:14 (=Leonard 1994, no. 2088 LH IIIC Early–Late), 28:15; Bounni et al. 1979, 240, fig. 19:5 (=Leonard 1994, no. 2057 LH IIIB–C), fig. 19:6 (=Leonard 1994, no. 2097 LH IIIC ?), fig. 19:11–12 (fig. 19:11=Badre 1983, fig. 1a: these sherds are not listed by Leonard [1994] as LH IIIC, there may be more relevant illustrations, but particular stylistic details are difficult to discern on the photograph); Bounni et al. 1998, 35 local Mycenaean IIIC:1 krater, no illustration; Lagarce 1983, Tav. 56 "Mycenaean III C:1," Tav. 57:1:1–2 "Mycenaean III C:1," Tav. 57:2:1–3 Semi-circles motifs, Tav. 58 Rectilinear Painted, "Mycenaean III C:1," Wavy-Line, Tav. 59 "Proto-White Painted" and Cypro-Geometric, according to Iacovou not true Proto-White Painted; and

Lagarce and Lagarce 1998, fig. 5a (=Bounni et al. 1978, fig. 28:2), fig. 5b–c ("Mycenaean III C:1"), fig. 5d (=Badre 1983, fig. 1e), fig. 5e (=Lagarce 1983, Tav. 56:8), fig. 5f–g ("Mycenaean III C:1"), fig. 12a (photograph), fig. 13 (drawing=Lagarce 1983, Tav. 56:7), fig. 12b (=Lagarce 1983, Tav. 56:4), fig. 12c–e ("Mycenaean III C:1"), fig. 13 (drawing)=fig. 12a (photograph=Lagarce 1983, Tav. 56:7], fig. 14a [Proto-White Painted?], fig. 14b (=Bounni et al. 1978, fig. 28:1), fig. 14c–f (Proto-White Painted?/White-Painted I), fig. 14g ("Mycenaean III C:1"), fig. 14h–j (Proto-White Painted?/White-Painted I), fig. 14k (Greek Proto-Geometric), fig. 14l (Proto-White Painted?/White-Painted I), fig. 14m (Greek), fig. 15a–b (Iron Age I Wavy-Line decoration), fig. 15c=Lagarce 1983, Tav. 58:3, fig. 15d–g (Iron Age I Wavy-Line decoration), fig. 15h (=Bounni et al. 1978, fig. 28:5), fig. 15i–k (Iron Age I Wavy-Line decoration), fig. 16 (=Badre 1983, fig. 1g), fig. 17 (=Badre 1983, fig. 2c), fig. 18 (Iron Age I Wavy-Line decoration on closed shapes), fig. 19 (Greek Proto-Geometric), fig. 23a–d (Rectilinear Painted decoration, twelfth–eleventh centuries B.C.E.), fig. 23e (=Lagarce 1983, Tav. 58:10), fig. 23f (=Lagarce 1983, Tav. 58:11), fig. 23g–h (Rectilinear Painted decoration, twelfth–eleventh centuries B.C.E.), fig. 24a (=Bounni et al. 1979, fig. 19:19), fig. 24b–e ("Mycenaean III C:1"), fig. 24f–g (=fig. 23e=Lagarce 1983, Tav. 58:9 and 14), fig. 25a–f (Bichrome twelfth century B.C.E.), fig. 27a–e (Bichrome White-Coated, twelfth–eleventh centuries B.C.E.), fig. 28 (=Badre 1983, fig. 2d).

Sukas

After a partial destruction at the end of the Late Bronze Age (Period J) the settlement was immediately rebuilt in Period H2. The excavated architecture is of domestic character in the Late Bronze Age tradition and the site was apparently a village during Iron Age I (Caubet 1992, 129; Ploug 1973, stirrup jar [7, 10, no. 16, only a photograph, no drawing=Leonard 1994, 871], stirrup jar SH67 [p. 8, not illustrated, from the cemetery at the South Harbor]=Leonard 1994, 689; cf. Riis 1973, 205).

Lebanon

Byblos

The site was an important urban center during the Late Bronze Age. Due to the problematic excavation techniques and lacking publications, it is difficult to understand the character of the settlement during Iron Age I. The historical record indicates that Byblos remained an important city during this period.

Aegeanizing pottery from Byblos includes: Hankey 1967, 107–47, pl. 27c–d (=Leonard 1994, no. 1792); Salles 1980, pl. 11:2 (not listed as Mycenaean IIIC by Salles, but classified as LH IIIC early by Leonard 1994, no. 1775); pl. 11:3 (not listed as Mycenaean IIIC by Salles, but classified as LH IIIB [–C] by Leonard [1994, no. 1756]); pl. 11:4 (=Leonard 1994, no. 1857 "LH IIIB–C"); pl. 11:8 (not listed as Mycenaean IIIC by Salles, but classified as locally produced LH IIIB–C by Leonard [1994, no. 1823]); pl. 12:2 is listed by Salles as Mycenaean IIIC, but classified by Leonard (1994, no. 829) as "LH IIIB"; pl. 12:6 (=Leonard 1994, no. 683 "LH IIIC"); pl. 13:1 (listed by Salles as Mycenaean IIIC, but classified by Leonard [1994, no. 1730] as "LH IIIB [–C?]"); pl. 13:2 (listed by Salles as Mycenaean IIIC, but classified by Leonard [1994, no. 1974] as "LH IIIB–C"); pl. 13:3 (listed by Salles as Mycenaean IIIC, but classified by Leonard [1994, no. 1969] as "LH IIIB–C"); pl. 13:4 (listed by Salles as Mycenaean IIIC, but classified by Leonard [1994, no. 1978] as "LH IIIB"); pl. 13:5–6 (handles listed by Salles as Mycenaean IIIC, but not listed by Leonard [1994]); and pl. 13:7–8 (listed by Salles as Mycenaean IIIC, but classified by Leonard [1994, no. 2094] as "LH IIIB–C").

Qrayya

This is a cemetery near Sidon, Lebanon (Guigues 1939, 59–60, pl. 12a=Hankey 1967, 120=Leonard 1994, no. 1784).

Sarepta

There is no evidence of destruction at the end of the Late Bronze Age. The architecture of the relevant levels is characterized by domestic units and pottery workshops. The Iron Age I strata are:

Area Y (Anderson 1988)	Area X (Khalifeh 1988)
Stratum G (1320/1290–1200/1190 B.C.E.)	Period III–IV
Stratum F (1200/1190–1150/1125 B.C.E.)	Period V
Stratum E (1150/25–1050/25 B.C.E.)	Period VI

Gilboa agrees with Anderson's dates and assigned Stratum E to the "early and late [Palestinian] Iron Age IB" (Gilboa 2001a, 299–334).

Aegeanizing pottery from Sarepta includes: Anderson 1988, 267–74: pl. 24: 28 (=Leonard 1994, no. 1818 locally produced [?] LH IIIB–C?); pl. 26:26 (=Leonard 1994, no. 1822 locally produced [?] LH IIIB); pl. 28:19 (=Leonard 1994, no. 1757 LH IIIC Early); pl. 30:10 (=Leonard 1994, no. 1805 locally produced [?] LH IIIC); and Koehl 1985, 44–45, 118–22, nos. 189–201: no. 189 (=Leonard 1994, no. 1060 LH IIIC?), no. 190 (=Leonard 1994, no. 1061 LH IIIC?), no. 191 (=Leonard 1994, no. 1003 LH IIIC Early), no. 192 (=Leonard 1994, no. 1769 LH IIIB:2), no. 193 (=Leonard 1994, no. 1758 LH IIIC Early), no. 194 (=Leonard 1994, no. 1762 LH IIIC Early), no. 195 (=Leonard 1994, no. 1761 LH IIIC Early [–Middle]), no. 196 (=Leonard 1994, no. 1774 LH III C Early), no. 197 (=Leonard 1994, no. 1759

LH IIIC Early); no. 198, Koehl's "derivative Granary Style" (=Leonard 1994, no. 1820 locally produced [?] LH IIIC).

Tyre

The Iron Age I Strata XIV and XIII were exposed in a very limited area. They are domestic in character. During Stratum XIII parts of the excavation area was turned into a pottery dump. The stratigraphy of the relevant levels at Tyre was extensively discussed by Gilboa (2001a, 267–97). She concludes that the pottery of Stratum XIV comprises Late Bronze Age as well as Palestinian Iron Age IA and possibly early Iron IB vessels. Stratum XIII is assigned to the Palestinian Iron Age IB by Gilboa (regarding the relevant published pottery, see Bikai 1978, pl. 39:20=Leonard 1994, no. 1778 with further references).

Turkey

'Amuq Plain

The Plain of Antioch/Antakya, the modern 'Amuq Plain (or Amık in Turkish), was investigated in a regional project with excavations and surveys conducted by the University of Chicago. "Sub-Mycenaean" pottery is abundant in the Iron Age I levels of the 'Amuq Period N. Although the excavations[4] remain unpublished and the survey publication (Braidwood 1937) of the 1930s did not include pottery drawings, Aegeanizing-style pottery was reported to have been frequent in 'Amuq Phase N (Swift 1958). The renewed investigations by the University of Chicago and the University of Toronto (at Tell Ta'yinat) that are currently underway include again a regional survey. And again Aegeanizing-style pottery was so frequent even in smaller sites of the plain that this style of pottery was one of the main dating criteria even for the surface collections (Yener et al. 2000, 188; Casana and Wilkinson 2005, 37–40, fig. A.15; Janeway 2006–2007).

Kinet Höyük

This small Bronze and Iron Age harbor was identified with ancient Issos and is excavated since 1992 by Marie-Henriette Gates. Kinet Höyük is located in the northeasternmost corner of the Mediterranean, on the east side of the Gulf of İskenderun (Hatay province, Turkey). Locally produced vessels in Aegeanizing-style were recorded in the Iron Age I levels (Gates, this volume).

4. The excavated sites relevant here are Tell Ta'yinat, Çatal Höyük, and Tell Judaidah (or Cudeyde in Turkish).

Sabuni (Sabuniye)

This site, near modern Samandağ (Suweidiya) and close to the outlet of the Orontes River, was excavated by Woolley in 1936. These excavations were never adequately published (Woolley [1953, 159] mentioned "Mycenaean" sherds of the thirteenth and twelfth century B.C.E., cf. Hankey 1967, 112). The site was identified again by Pamir in her survey of the Orontes Delta. During the survey a number of vessels of Iron Age I in Aegeanizing-style were found (Pamir and Nishiyama 2002; Pamir 2005, 89, fig. 3.11:1–2).

The Pottery

The following part of this paper will summarize LH IIIC imports and the "Aegeanizing" pottery in Iron Age I Syria and Lebanon. "Aegeanizing" pottery is defined here as imports or local productions that reflect LH IIIC traditions. The decorated pottery presented here consists mainly of bowls and kraters and was probably used for wine consumption. The catalogue includes also some of the pottery that appears with LH IIIC styles, but is itself of a different tradition such as Handmade Burnished or Gray Ware. The catalogue of the pottery is not arranged chronologically, but according to types such as bowls, kraters, etc. After the catalogue, the repertoire of the pottery, its chronology, and its distribution will be discussed. Finally, there will be an outlook on the implications of these ceramics in early Iron Age Syria.

1. Bell-Shaped Bowls (FS 284) with a Linear Decoration of Painted Bands (fig. 1.1)[5]

There is a group of bowls that are decorated solely with horizontal lines and bands (Leonard 1994, 119, nos. 1774–77). The interior of the bowls is either monochrome or painted with narrow bands. The matte-painted decoration would place them later than LH IIIB and within the LH IIIC tradition. Most of the bowls found in the Levant were apparently produced locally.

Two early examples were found in Palestine, in Tell Abu Hawam (Leonard 1994, 119, nos. 1776–77). In Philistia such locally produced bowls appear in large quantities and are part of the so-called Philistine Monochrome or Philistine Mycenaean IIIC ceramics. In LH IIIC Early assemblages in Greece such bowls

5. FS numbers (Furumark shape numbers) and FM numbers (Furumark motif numbers) are explained in Furumark 1941a, 583–643 and 236–434 respectively.

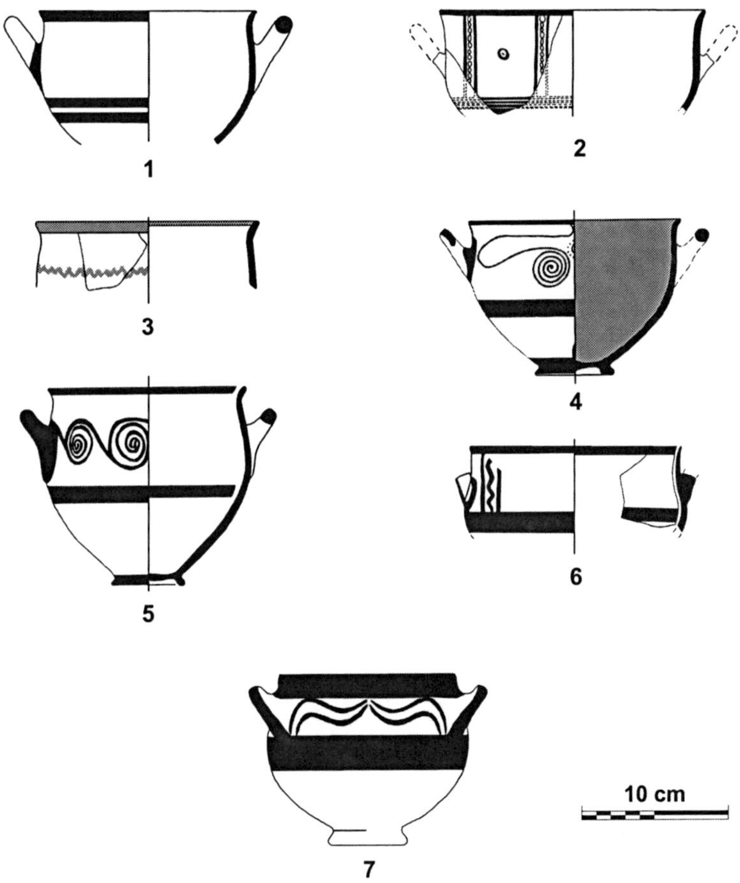

Fig. 1: Syrian Iron Age IA.

Key to fig. 1:

1) Byblos Necropolis K: Salles 1980, pl. 11:2.
2) Byblos Necropolis K: Salles 1980, pl. 11:3.
3) Sarafand (Sarepta) Stratum J/H Deposit: Anderson 1988, 272, fig. 24:28.
4) Sarafand (Sarepta) Stratum G1: Anderson 1988, 273, 612, pl. 28:19.
5) Sarafand (Sarepta) II-A-9 Level 10-1: Koehl 1985, 119–20, no. 193.
6) Sarafand (Sarepta) II-B-6/7 Level 13-1: Koehl 1985, 120, no. 194.
7) Tell Judaidah H-7 surface (Z192): Swift 1958, fig. 21.

appear for example in Korakou,[6] Lefkandi,[7] and Mycenae.[8] In Cyprus this type of minimal decoration on bowls of type FS 284 is somewhat rare (Kling 1989, 94–107, especially 106–7). There are a number of parallels from Maa-Palaeokastro Floor II (Karageorghis and Demas 1988, pl. 50:60/3, pl. 59:82/1, pl. 183: Room 82), Maa-Palaeokastro Floors I–II (Karageorghis and Demas 1988, pl. 210:473), and Maa-Palaeokastro Floor I (Karageorghis and Demas 1988, pl. 243: Room 75A/7), Enkomi Level IIIA (Dikaios 1969–1971, pl. 74:9 [1343/1]), or Kition Area I, Floors IIIA–IV (Karageorghis and Demas 1985, pl. 40:927). In Cilicia this group occurs more frequently, there are numerous, yet unstratified parallels at Tarsus.[9] Examples of this type were also found at Tarsus (Mountjoy 2005, fig. 12), Soli Höyük (Yağci 2003), and Kilise Tepe (Hansen and Postgate 1999, 112), some recently published examples from Kilise Tepe are on exhibit in the Silifke Museum (French 2007a).

- Sarafand (Sarepta) II-C-9 Level 6: Koehl 1985, 120–21, no. 196, LH IIIC Early; cf. Paphos Evreti TE III.11 of uncertain date: Maier 1973, fig. 1; Enkomi Level IIIA: Dikaios 1969–1971, pl. 74:8–9; cf. also Ashdod Area C, Pit L.2001: M. Dothan and Freedman 1967, fig. 28:5=pl. 17:4, Leonard 1994, no. 1774.
- Fig. 1.1: Byblos Necropolis K: Salles 1980, pl. 11:2 (not listed as "Mycenaean" IIIC), Leonard 1994, no. 1775 (listed as LH IIIC Early).
- Tell Afis Area E, Level 9b: Venturi 2002, fig. 21:2, local imitation of LH IIIC Early bowls; cf. Tarsus: French 1975, figs. 13, 17–18:12.
- Tell Afis Area E, Level 9: Mazzoni and Cecchini 1995, fig. 29:3 local product.
- Tell Afis Area E, Level 8: Mazzoni et al. 1999–2000, fig. 12:3.
- Tell Afis Area G: Mazzoni et al. 1999–2000, 20, fig. 17:1–2.
- Sarafand (Sarepta) Stratum G2: Anderson 1988, 272, fig. 26:26. Anderson assigned the bowl to "Mycenaean" IIIB, being either a "Levanto-Mycenaean form or a good local imitation." The fabric is sandy and moderately well levigated, the surface color is light and the

6. Korakou Trench P, Levels V–VI: Rutter 1977, fig. 5 "LH IIIC Early Phase 1"; Korakou House P, Floor 2: Rutter 1977, fig. 10 "LH IIIC Early Phase 3."

7. A similar bowl with a wide band beneath the rim: Lefkandi Phase 1b (Popham and Milburn 1971, 335, fig. 1).

8. Mycenae Causeway Deposit (Wardle 1973, 335, fig. 21:227–38=Rutter 1977, fig. 9, Rutter's LH IIIB2/IIIC Early).

9. Tarsus: French 1975, fig. 13:17–18; Mountjoy 2005b, figs. 11, 14; cf. Goldman 1956, fig. 331:1259–60, 1262; fig. 361:1261 (cf. Sherratt and Crouwel 1987, 341–42). Goldman (1956, 206) states that "there was no stratification with the Tarsus Mycenaean pottery."

paint in matte red. Leonard (1994, no. 1822) included the bowl in his discussion of LH IIIC locally produced bowls of FS 284–285, but dated the vessel also LH IIIB.

- Byblos Necropolis K: Salles 1980, pl. 11:8, not listed as "Mycenaean" IIIC), Leonard 1994, no. 1823 (listed as LH IIIB–C). The bowl seems to be locally produced.
- Tell Kazel Area II, Level 5, Room L–M: Capet 2003, fig. 37b, unpainted.
- Tell Kazel Area II, Level 5, Room N: Capet 2003, fig. 40m, cf. also the painted bowl in fig. 40k.
- Tell Kazel Area II, Level 5, Room O: Capet 2003, fig. 46a, unpainted.
- Tell Kazel Area II, Level 5: Jung 2007, fig. 10:7.

2. Bell-Shaped Bowls (FS 284) with a "Sea Anemone" as Fill in a Panelled Pattern (FM 75) Composed of a Quirk (FM 48:16; fig. 1.2)

This is an uncommon composition in Cyprus during LC III. Parallels in Greece were found, e.g., in Mycenae Causeway Deposit and were dated by Rutter to LH IIIB2/IIIC Early (Rutter 1977, 1).

- Fig. 1.2: Byblos Necropolis K: Salles 1980, pl. 11:3 (not listed as "Mycenaean" IIIC)=Leonard 1994, no. 1756 (identified by him as LH IIIB[–C]; cf. Maa-Palaeokastro Floor II: Karageorghis and Demas 1988, pl. 43: 155A, 238; cf. Mycenae Causeway Deposit: Rutter 1977, fig. 1, Rutter's LH IIIB2/IIIC Early).

3. Bell-Shaped Bowls (FS 284) with a Linear Decoration of Painted Bands and a Compressed Wavy or Zigzag Line (FM 61; Mountjoy 1986, fig. 166:21; fig. 1.3)

These were popular throughout the Aegean during LH IIIB and LH IIIC Early (Kling 1989, 101 with references). Bowls with a narrow painted band at the rim and a compressed zigzag line occur as early as LH IIIB. In Cyprus they occur in LC IIIA and IIIB in almost equal numbers (Kling 1989, 101, fig. 21e). They occur, however, especially frequently in an early context at Maa-Palaeokastro.[10]

A number of parallels were found at Tarsus (Goldman 1956, fig. 334:1322 b, e–f; Mountjoy 2005b, fig. 11:274). A LH IIIC Early example was found in Phyla-

10. Floor II: Karageorghis and Demas 1988, pl. 59:79D/6: Floor I–II; pl. 88: Room 7/1; pl. 97: Area 24A/4; pl. 101: Pit L/6; pl. 114: Room 77/3; Floor I: pl. 107: Courtyard A/16; pl. 116: Room 9/1; pl. 122: Room 20A/2; pl. 124: east of Building I/1; pl. 133: Pit 19A/7; pl. 149: Room 73A/3; cf. also pl. 164: 1954/xii.

kopi (Mountjoy 1986, fig. 189:15). In Çatal Höyük and Tell Judaidah compressed zigzag lines occur in Phase N-Early (unpublished, cf. below plain bell-shaped bowls with thin horizontal lines).

- Fig. 1.3: Sarafand (Sarepta) Stratum J/H Deposit: Anderson (1988, 272, fig. 24:28) assigned this bowl to "Mycenaean" IIIB, while Leonard (1994, no. 1818) dates it "LH IIIB–C (?)." The vessel could be a local product. It is LH IIIB in style and shape, but different in fabric and surface treatment. The paint is reddish and matte.

Some bell-shaped bowls have a horizontal band and a single wavy line that is less compressed. Examples at Enkomi Level IIIA (Dikaios 1969–1971, 319, pl. 98:36 [5862/5]) and Kition Area II, Well 1 (Karageorghis 1985, pl. 238:2227A) have a number of exact, but unpublished parallels at Çatal Höyük and Tell Judaidah, all from Phase N-Early.

4. Bell-Shaped Bowls (FS 284) with a Curve-Stemmed Antithetic Spiral (FM 50; fig. 1.4)

These bowls were one of the most popular pottery types in Cyprus during LC IIIA and in the transition to LC IIIB, in LC IIIB they disappear (fig. 1.4; Kling 1989, 95–98). Interestingly, in Syria and Lebanon during Iron Age I, this motif is relatively rare on bowls and kraters (see below). I was unable to find more than nine fragments with curve-stemmed antithetic spirals.

Upright antithetic stemmed spirals with vertical rows of chevrons, as on a LC IIIA bowl from Kouklia Evreti Well TEIII.23 (Maier 1973, pl. 14:6) occur also in the 'Amuq Plain (Swift 1958, fig. 27g; cf. also Maa-Palaeokastro Floor I: Karageorghis and Demas 1988, pl. 143:690 and 235:690; Tarsus: Mountjoy 2005b, fig. 9; Enkomi IIIB destruction and Level IIIC: Dikaios 1969–1971, pl. 96:13 [5395/2] and pl. 100:9 [5878/1]). Further examples of curve-stemmed antithetic spirals were found in the 'Amuq Plain in Tell Ta'yinat in Phase Ob (evidently out of its original context) and in Tell Judaidah in Phase N-Early (for two more 'Amuq fragments of Phase N, see Swift 1958, fig. 27h–i which may have a curve-stemmed antithetic spiral of the curtailed type, cf. a kylix from Pyla-Verghi, Dikaios 1969–1971, pl. 236:2 [27]).

- Sarafand (Sarepta) II-A-4 Level 8: Koehl 1985, 121, no. 197 (with parallels); Leonard 1994, no. 1759 LH IIIC Early; the line painted on this body sherd may be from an antithetic spiral.
- Fig. 1.4: Sarafand (Sarepta) Stratum G1 (Anderson 1988, 273, 612, pl. 28:19=Herscher 1975, 90–91, fig. 26:4 and 52: 1); matte slip, matte monochrome paint. Note the "sea anemone" (FM 27: 31 or 32) between

the spirals. Anderson assigned this bowl to "early Mycenaean IIIC:1," Leonard (1994, no. 1757) to LH IIIC Early. Bowls with similar spirals were found at Maa-Palaeokastro Floor I–II: pl. 72: Bothros 1/2 and pl. 95: Area 24/7. From Maa-Palaeokastro Floors I–II also comes an exact parallel to the bowl from Sarafand (Karageorghis and Demas 1988, pl. 103: Pit L/24).

- Sarafand (Sarepta) II-A-9 Level 6: Koehl 1985, 119, no. 192, Leonard 1994, no. 1769 LH IIIB:2; curve-stemmed antithetic spirals with a panel were popular in LH IIIB and IIIC (Furumark 1941a, 362–65; Sherratt 1981, 574; cf. Perati Γ: Iakovidis 1969–1970, pl. 112b.462 and Enkomi Level IIIA: Dikaios 1969–1971, pl. 75:7 [4364/3]).
- Sarafand (Sarepta) Stratum F: Anderson 1988, 273, 617, pl. 30:10 "Mycenaean" IIIC:1, Leonard 1994, no. 1805 LH IIIC. The bowl is probably locally produced, the paint is dark red.

5. Bell-Shaped Bowls (FS 284) with a Running Spiral, Simple Line Type (FM 46; fig. 1.5)

These occurred throughout the history of Mycenaean pottery and were popular and widely distributed during LH IIIB and IIIC (Kling 1989, 98). In the Aegean, the running spiral was one of the most popular motifs during LH IIIC Early (Mountjoy 1986, 135). During LC III, the motif occurred in Cyprus mostly in phase LC IIIA; during LC IIIB it became less frequent. In Cilicia the motif appeared in Tarsus (Mountjoy 2005b, figs. 175–177).

- Fig. 1.5: Sarafand (Sarepta) II-A-9 Level 10-1: Koehl 1985, 119–20, no. 193; Leonard 1994, no. 1758 LH IIIC Early; cf. Maa-Palaeokastro Floors I–II: Karageorghis and Demas 1988, pl. 103: Pit L/24, pl. 110:575 and 210:575, pl. 114: Room 75/13 and Area 95/5; Maa-Palaeokastro Floor II: Karageorghis and Demas 1988, pl. 170:106; Enkomi Level IIIA: Dikaios 1969–1971, 81:4; Kouklia Evreti Well TEIII.11 and 18; Maier 1973, fig. 1–2; Tarsus: Goldman 1956, fig. 334:1306.

6. Bell-Shaped Bowls (FS 284) with a Stemmed Spiral (FM 51:6–8)

These appeared in Mycenaean pottery throughout LH IIIB and IIIC, in Cyprus they occurred since LC II and were popular in LC IIIA, they disappear in LC IIIB (Kling 1989, 98 with references). In Cilicia the motif appeared in Tarsus (Mountjoy 2005b, fig. 10:245–50).

- Sarafand (Sarepta) II-C-9 Level 6, Kiln G: Koehl 1985, 120, no. 195; Leonard 1994, no. 1761 LH IIIC Early [–Middle]; cf. Pyla-

Kokkinokremos Area II, Room 4 (LC IIC/LC IIIA): Dikaios 1969–1971, pl. 238:7; Kouklia: Maier 1973, pl. 14:1.

7. Bell-Shaped Bowls (FS 284) with a Panel of Vertical Straight and Wavy Lines (FM 53:38; fig. 1.6)

This motif appears already in LH IIIB. In Cyprus most panels of vertical straight and wavy lines occur in LC IIIA, but the motif is still painted in LC IIIB (Kling 1989, 95–96 with references).

- Fig. 1.6: Sarafand (Sarepta) II-B-6/7 Level 13-1: Koehl 1985, 120, no. 194; Leonard 1994, no. 1762 LH IIIC Early. It is possible that there was also a spiral motif on this fragment. Cf. Maa-Palaeokastro Floors I–II: Karageorghis and Demas 1988, pl. 95: Area 24/10.

8. Bell-Shaped Bowls (FS 284) with an Antithetic Tricurved Arch (fig. 1.7)

Mountjoy dated the motif to LH IIIC Early (1986, 136, fig. 166:22; Kling 1989, 105 with references). The motifs in Greece, however, are more elaborate than the Syrian ones. The particular variation of this motif that is rather popular in Syria (five fragments) has its closest parallels on Cyprus. All these examples on Cyprus are from Enkomi and date to LC IIIA (Kling 1989, 105). Unpublished parallels from the ʿAmuq Plain have been dated to Phase N-Middle (cf. Swift 1958, fig. 28N).

- Fig. 1.7: Tell Judaidah H-7 surface (Z192) (Swift 1958, fig. 21).
- Tell Afis Area E, Level 9a: Pedrazzi 2002, 36, fig. 24:2.
- Tell Afis Area E, Level 9a; Mazzoni et al. 1999–2000, fig. 12:2.
- ʿAyn Dara Trench 1, Level 2: Stone and Zimansky 1999, fig. 27:3.
- Dağılbaz, İskenderun Bay, Turkey, found during a survey by A. E. Killebrew, M.-H. Gates, and the author in 2006 (Lehmann, Killebrew, and Gates 2008).
- Tell Uzunarab surface find, ʿAmuq Plain, Turkey: Nishiyama, personal communication.

9. Plain Bell-Shaped bowls (FS 284) with Thin Horizontal Lines in Dark Brown or Black Paint

These occur in Cyprus and Cilicia in contexts of LC IIIA–IIIB (cf. Enkomi destruction of Level IIIB: Dikaios 1969–1971, pl. 100:1 [876/1]; Kition Area I,

Floor III–IIIA: Karageorghis and Demas 1985, pl. 44:764/2; Kition Area I, Floor III: Karageorghis and Demas 1985, pl. 44:912/1 and 896/2 [?]; Tarsus: French 1975, fig. 17:11–12; fig. 18:3). Unpublished bowls from the ʿAmuq Plain have been dated to all sub-phases of Phase N, Early, Middle, and Late.

10. Bowls with Flaring Rims and a Conical Base (fig. 2.8)

The bowl from Ras Ibn Hani has been compared with "Granary Style" (Badre 1983, 208). The vessel shapes are, however different from form FS 285, the typical skyphos shape of "Granary Style." Unpublished bowls of this type, found in the ʿAmuq Plain, have been dated to Phase N-Middle. Comparable bowls in the Aegean date to LH IIIC Late (Mountjoy 1986, fig. 254:10).

- Fig. 4.8: Ras Ibn Hani Iron Age I "upper floor": Badre 1983, fig. 1g. Similar, but unpublished examples were found in the ʿAmuq Plain, Turkey, at Tell Wuzwuz as a surface find (Nishiyama, personal communication) and at Tell Taʿyinat (T3160).

"Granary Style"

This particular style appears first during LH IIIC Middle (Mountjoy 1986, 156). In Greece and the Aegean, this style is employed on the hydriae, jugs, amphorae, and on cups, kraters, and deep bowls. Open shapes may be decorated with wavy lines, but are more generally linear or monochrome with reserved lines and dotted rims. In contrast to the Aegean, wavy lines characterize the Cypriot repertoire of "Granary Style." In Cyprus, this style is the hallmark of LC IIIB, although a few examples are already present in Enkomi Level IIIA.

Susan Sherratt suggested that wavy-line decoration was not introduced in Cyprus from the Aegean, but originated in the eastern Mediterranean, possibly at Cyprus itself, and spread from there westward to the Aegean (Sherratt 1981, 236; 1994a, 40–42, cf. Kling 1989, 172). In any case, the "Granary Style" in Cyprus is a local production of the island. Thus, the appearance of "Granary Style" in Syria may reflect a Cypriot influence and it might be misleading, both in terms of stylistic development and chronology, to relate this style in Syria to the Aegean LH IIIC styles. In fact, the Syrian pottery decorated in "Granary Style" resembles more closely the Cypriot assemblages than the Aegean ones, especially in its emphasis on wavy line motifs.

Another problem arises from the relationship between "Granary Style" and Proto-White Painted. Both styles seem to be contemporary and both employ wavy line motifs (see above). This has lead to some confusion and "Granary Style" is sometimes not distinguished from Proto-White Painted (for a summary, see Iacovou 1988, 6, cf. Kling 1989, 174). In this paper, I will follow Iacovou's

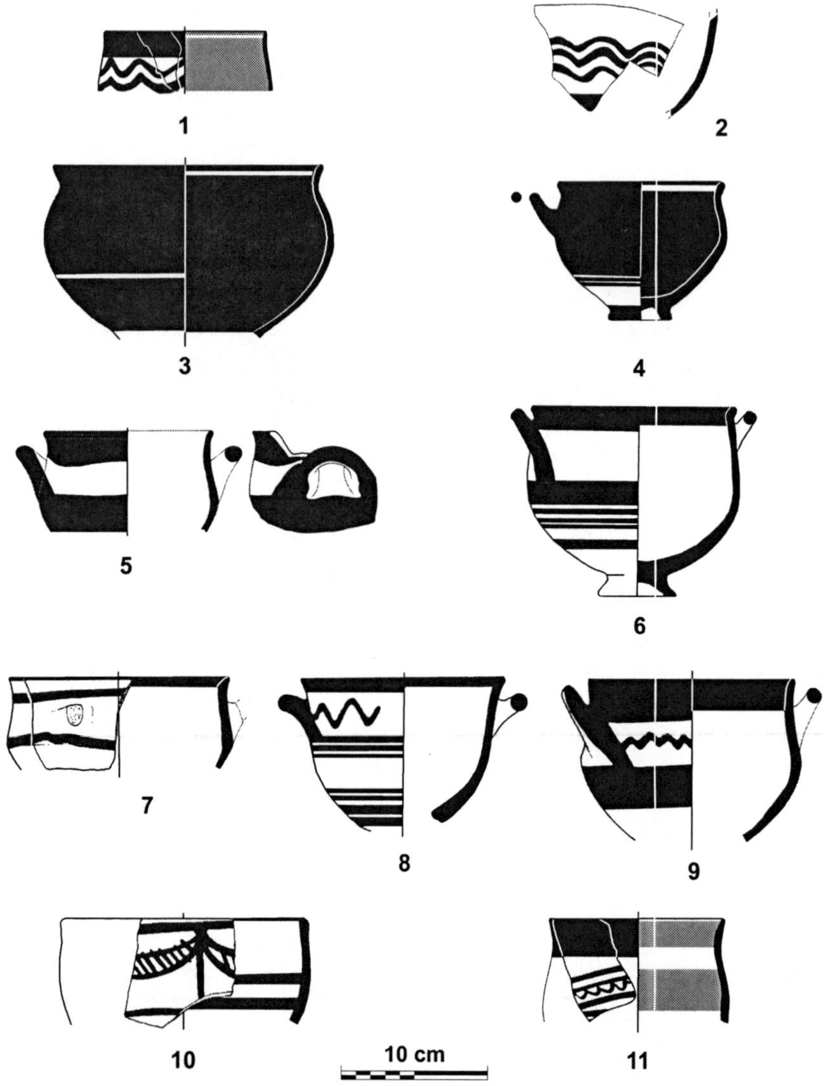

Fig. 2: Syrian Iron Age IB.

definition of Proto-White Painted and her distinction from "Granary Style" (Iacovou 1988, 1). Both styles are distinguished from each other mainly by an analysis of their fabric. Photographs or drawings of ceramics are often not sufficient for this distinction. Certainly, some bowls found in Syria seem to be almost identical to Proto-White Painted bowls like Alaas T.13/6 (Karageorghis 1975, pl. 52, cf. an example from Tell Afis, Bonatz 1998, fig. 2:1). In a personal communication, how-

Key to fig. 2:
1) Tell Afis Area E1, Level 8: Bonatz 1998, 214–15, fig. 2:4.
2) Sarafand (Sarepta) II-A-9 Level 6: Koehl 1985, 121, no. 198.
3) Tell Afis Area E, Level 9a: Pedrazzi 2002, 36, fig. 23.
4) Çatal Höyük N13-2nd b (Phase N-Middle–Late): Swift 1958, fig. 19:A2542.
5) Tell Afis Area C, Level 3: Bonatz 1998, 212, 215, fig. 2:1.
6) Çatal Höyük P4 clearing 2nd (Phase N-Late): Swift 1958, fig. 20:B2361.
7) Tell Afis Area E, Level 9a: Pedrazzi 2002, 35, fig. 23:6.
8) Ras Ibn Hani Iron I "upper floor": Badre 1983, fig. 1g.
9) Tell Afis Area N US4464, 4452: Cecchini 2002, 49, fig. 32:2.
10) Tell Afis Area E, Level 9a: Pedrazzi 2002, 35, fig. 23:3.
11) Tell Afis Area E, Level 7c: Bonatz 1998, 214–15, fig. 3:7.

ever, Iacovou, one of the leading experts in the field of LC III pottery, stated that there is no Proto-White Painted or White-Painted I at Tell Afis (Gilboa 2001a, 345).

11. Bell-Shaped Bowls (FS 285) with a Single Wavy Line or Multiple Wavy Lines (figs. 2.1–2)

These are a subtype of "Granary Style" (Kling 1989, 107–8 with references). Wavy-line decoration appeared first during LH IIIC Middle and continued through Submycenaean (Kling 1989, 107).

- Tell Afis Area E1, Silo 1794, Level 9a: Venturi 2000, fig. 9:2.
- Fig. 2.1: Tell Afis Area E1, Level 8: Bonatz 1998, 214–15, fig. 2:4, greenish gray fabric, fine texture, and hard fired, with a single matte black painted wavy line; multiple wavy-line decoration?
- Tell Afis Area E1, Level 8: Bonatz 1998, 214–15, fig. 2:3, same fabric and colors as Cat. 20; multiple wavy-line decoration?
- Fig. 2.2: Sarafand (Sarepta) II-A-9 Level 6: Koehl 1985, 121, no. 198; Leonard 1994, no. 1820 LH IIIC, locally produced?
- Tell Mardikh TM.74.E.331/1 with double wavy lines, "Mycenaean IIIC:1c": unpublished, cf. Bonatz 1998, 214 n. 11, no illustration.
- Sabuni (Sabuniye, Turkey): Pamir 2005, fig. 3.11:2, cf. fig. 3.11:1.
- Tell Salihiyya surface find, 'Amuq Plain, Turkey: Nishiyama, personal communication; uncertain whether there were indeed multiple wavy lines on this vessel, cf. Enkomi Level IIIA: Dikaios 1969–1971, pl. 76:14 (4660/1).

Some handle fragments with dots may have belonged to bell-shaped bowls with wavy-line decoration. Similar handles at Enkomi were all found in Level

IIIB (Dikaios 1969–1971, pls. 79:26 = 124:8 [232]; 113:5923/2 and 5912/3; 124:6 [107]).

- Tyre Stratum 14: Bikai 1978, pl. 39:14.
- Tell Afis Area E, Level 8: Bonatz 1998, 215, fig. 3:2.

12. Bell-Shaped Bowls (FS 285) with Monochrome Matte Black Paint Completely Covering the Vessel Body ("Granary Style")

In the Aegean, monochrome painted skyphoi appear in contexts that are dated as early as LH IIIB. But most bowls of this style date to LH IIIC (Sherratt 1981, 43; Kling 1989, 107 with references). Bonatz (1998, 214) compares the monochrome bowls, found in Tell Afis, with skyphoi from Enkomi Level IIIB (Dikaios 1969–1971, pls. 79: 29 [5223/1]; 80: 4 = 105: 1 = 124: 2 [233]).

- Tell Afis Area E1, Level 8: Bonatz 1998, 212, 214, fig. 3:3, greenish gray fabric.
- Tell Afis Area E1, Level 9a: Bonatz 1998, 212, 214, fig. 3:4, gray fabric.

13. Bell-Shaped Bowls (FS 285) Monochrome with Reserved Lower Body ("Granary Style"; fig. 2.3–4)

This vessel type began in the Aegean during LH IIIC Middle and continued through Submycenaean. Monochrome-painted bowls without reserved zones in the outer lower body were found already during LH IIIC Early (Mountjoy 1986, 151, fig. 191, 178, fig. 230:1–2, 200, fig. 269:1–2; Kling 1989, 108 with references). Unpublished bowls from the 'Amuq Plain were noted in all sections of Phase N, Early through Late, and are still present in Phase Oa. It is of particular significance for the dating of Phase N at 'Amuq to note that while this group appeared in Phase N Early, in Cyprus it occurred only at the end of LC IIIA and is the *fossil directeur* of LC IIIB. The examples found at Tell Afis, as well as those from the 'Amuq Plain, were found all in levels of the Syrian Iron Age IB and are of buff or buff-pinkish fabric with matte red or reddish brown paint (Munsell 10R4/4).

- Fig. 2.3: Tell Afis Area E, Level 9a: Pedrazzi 2002, 36, fig. 23 ("LH IIIC Middle–Late or Submycenaean"); for parallels in the Aegean, see Mountjoy (1999b, fig. 80:230, fig. 230:1, fig. 238:601, fig. 276:89, fig. 473:13; Enkomi Level IIIB: Dikaios 1969–1971, pl. 124:2 [233], pl. 124: 7 [726] and unstratified: Dikaios 1969–1971, pl. 122:8 [870]).
- Fig. 2.4: Çatal Höyük N13-2nd b (Phase N-Middle–Late): Swift 1958, fig. 19:A2542.
- Tell Afis Area E, Level 9a: Mazzoni et al. 1999–2000, fig. 12:1.
- Tell Afis Area E, Level 8: Bonatz 1998, 212, 215, fig. 3:6.

- Tell Afis Area E, Level 8: Bonatz 1998, 212, fig. 3:8.
- Tell Afis Area E, Level 8: Bonatz 1998, 212, 215, fig. 3:5.
- Tell Afis Area E, Level 8: Bonatz 1998, 212, 214–15, fig. 4:6.
- Tell Afis Area E: Mazzoni and Cecchini 1995, fig. 29:17.

14. Bell-Shaped Bowls (FS 285), Monochrome with Reserved Handle Zone and Reserved Base ("Granary Style"; fig. 2.5–6)

These appear in Cyprus apparently earlier than in the Aegean (Kling 1989, 108, fig. 26d). Examples have been noted at Atheniou Level II in a LC IIIA/IIIB context (T. Dothan and Ben-Tor 1983, 115–17, fig. 53:5, cf. Kling 1989, 108 for date and references). In the Aegean they seem to appear in the LH IIIC Late phase (Mountjoy 1986, 191–92, fig. 254:6). Unpublished skyphoi from the 'Amuq Plain are from Phases N-Middle and Late. A skyphos from the Enkomi wells with uncertain date (Dikaios 1969–1971, pl. 109:20 [6359/1]) has a close unpublished parallel in Çatal Höyük. Only the upper part of the vessel preserved:

- Fig. 2.5: Tell Afis Area C, Level 3: Bonatz 1998, 212, 215, fig. 2:1, greenish fabric with a gray core, white and black grits, and matte black paint.
- Tell Afis Area E, Level 7: Bonatz 1998, 214, fig. 2:2, buff or buff-pinkish fabric with matte red or reddish brown paint.

Handle fragments that may belong to this group:

- 'Ayn Dara Trench 1, Level 2 pit: Stone and Zimansky 1999, fig. 29.
- Çatal Höyük surface find: Nishiyama, personal communication.
- Tell Afis Area E, Level 8: Bonatz 1998, fig. 3:1. Buff or buff-pinkish fabric with matte red or reddish brown paint.

Bowl with the same motif, but with reserved lines in lower body (Kling 1989, 108, fig. 26b):

- Fig. 2.6: Çatal Höyük P4 clearing 2nd (Phase N-Late): Swift 1958, fig. 20 (B2361).
- Tell Afis Area E, Level 9: Bonatz 1998, 4:5. Buff or buff-pinkish fabric with matte red or reddish brown paint.
- Not illustrated: Tell Afis Area E, Level 9: Bonatz 1998, 213, fig. 4:8, a low conical foot of a deep bell-shaped bowl.

Body sherds:

- Tell Afis Area E, Level 9a: Mazzoni and Cecchini 1995, fig. 20:3.

15. Related Bowls (fig. 2.7)

There are a number of bowls that are similar to the preceding group, but have a different bowl shape with flaring rims, a carination under the horizontal handles, and a conical base. Unpublished skyphoi from the ʿAmuq Plain were found in Phase N-Early.

- Çatal Höyük surface find: Nishiyama, personal communication.
- Fig. 2.7: Tell Afis Area E, Level 9a: Pedrazzi 2002, 35, fig. 23:6, "local production."

16. Bell-Shaped Bowls (FS 285), Monochrome with Reserved Handle Zone Filled with Wavy Line ("Granary Style"; fig. 2.9)

In Cyprus these skyphoi were all dated exclusively to LC IIIB (Kling 1989, 108 with references). S. Sherratt regarded this decoration as typical of the latest phase of LH IIIC at Mycenae (Sherratt 1981, 79; cf. Mountjoy 1986: LH III Late: fig. 254:4, 5; [FS 285]; "Submycenaean" fig. 269:3 [FS 286]).

- Fig. 2.9: Tell Afis Area N US4464, 4452 (Cecchini 2002, 49, fig. 32:2), "Sub-Mycenaean White-Painted I, end of eleventh century through first half of the tenth century" B.C.E.
- Tyre Stratum 14: Bikai 1978, pl. 39:20; Leonard 1994, no. 1778, FS 285, FM 53 wavy line, LH III C (late?); Gilboa (2001a, 346) identifies this bowl as a late "Mycenaean IIIC" skyphos that "may be Cypriot."
- Tell Afis Area E, Level 9a: Pedrazzi 2002, 35, imported or locally produced? The painted band at the rim is narrower than on the other examples in this group, for the motif of FM 61, see Mountjoy (1986, fig. 258:6). For parallels in the Aegean, see Mountjoy (1999b, figs. 94:164; 375:167; 317:320); for parallels from Crete, see Kanta (1980, fig. 5:7, fig. 6: 11, fig. 89:1 right).
- Tell Afis Area E, Level 9: Mazzoni and Cecchini 1995, fig. 29:2.
- Tell Afis Area E, Levels 9a–8: Venturi 2000, fig. 7:3.
- Tell Afis Area E, Level 8: Mazzoni et al. 1999–2000, fig. 12:4.
- Tell Afis Area E, Level 7c: Mazzoni et al. 1999–2000, fig. 12:5.

17. Bell-Shaped Bowls with a "Hanging Ladder" or Hatched Motif (fig. 2.10)

These were apparently common in Syria. In Cyprus they were quite uncommon, the motif occurs in a LC IIIA context at Kition in the upper burial layer of Tomb 9 No. 138 (Karageorghis 1974, 70, pls. 72 and 157; Karageorghis 1976, fig. 21). But this "ladder" motif is an antithetic tongue or tricurved arch painted as a hatched band. It is painted in arches with a different orientation than skyphoi discussed here (cf. Kling 1989, 105 with references). Another example was found at Enkomi

Level IIIB (Dikaios 1969–1971, pl. 80:38 [3394/13]). None of the parallels quoted by Bonatz (1998, 216) really match the motif of this group; most of them are vertical "ladder" motifs, rather than horizontal. For more parallels in the Aegean, see Mountjoy 1999b, fig. 120:109 and 116.

- Tell Kazel TK 97 4479.106 (Iron Age I context), unpublished.
- Fig. 2.10: Tell Afis Area E, Level 9a: Pedrazzi 2002, 35, fig. 23:3.
- Tell Afis Area E, Level 9a: Pedrazzi 2002, 35, fig. 23:4.
- Tell Afis Area E, Level 9a: Pedrazzi 2002, 35, fig. 23:5.
- Tell Afis Area E, Level 8: Bonatz 1998, 216, fig. 4:1, greenish gray fabric, slightly smoothed, with thin walls and in matte black paint.
- Tell Afis Area E: Mazzoni and Cecchini 1995, fig. 29:16.
- Çatal Höyük surface find: Nishiyama, personal communication.

18. Bell-shaped bowls with a reserved zone under the rim, filled with a scribbled zigzag and bordered by two or four encircling lines resemble skyphoi from the Argolid (Bonatz 1998, 215 with references; fig. 2.11)

Two other examples, almost identical to the bowl from Tell Afis, were found at Lefkandi and are considered to be Argive imports (Popham, Sackett, and Themelis 1979–1980, 23, pl. 49:166–167). While the technique of monochrome paint with reserved zones still resembles "Granary Style," the motif is already early Proto-Geometric. Note also the appropriate late stratigraphic position of the vessel in the Iron Age I stratigraphy at Tell Afis. There seem to be no exact parallels in Cyprus.

- Fig. 2.11: Tell Afis Area E, Level 7c: Bonatz 1998, 214–15, fig. 3:7, greenish gray fabric, fine texture and hard fired, with a matte black paint.

19. Globular bell-shaped bowls with horizontal bands in dark brown or black paint, with one or two horizontal handles

On the outside, horizontal bands occur in pairs of two or three bands between open zones, the rim is usually painted. There are no additional motifs. The diameter of these vessels at the rim is 16 centimeters or more. In Enkomi an example was found in Level IIIA (Dikaios 1969–1971, pl. 590, pl. 76:3 [4457/3]). Unpublished bowls from the ʿAmuq Plain have been dated to Phase N-Middle and Late.

20. Bell-Shaped Bowls with Multiple Horizontal Bands, the Open Zones between the Single or Multiple Bands are Filled with Wavy Lines or Hanging Semi-Circles (fig. 3.1–3)

The bowls usually have horizontal handles and the rim is painted. Horizontal bands occur also inside the vessel on the rim zone and at the base. The color of the paint is black or matte reddish (10R4/4). I was unable to find exact parallels to this type of decoration in Cyprus that occurred frequently in Syria and in the ʿAmuq Plain. Unpublished bowls from the ʿAmuq Plain date to Phase N-Middle and Late, and they are still present in Phase Oa. Thus, it might be suggested that this is a local Syrian style employing Aegeanizing motifs.

- Fig. 3.1: ʿAyn Dara Trench 1, Level 2 pit: Stone and Zimansky 1999, fig. 27:1=fig. 29 lower left.
- Fig. 3.2: ʿAyn Dara Trench 1, Level 2 pit: Stone and Zimansky 1999, fig. 29 lower right.
- Fig. 3.3: Tell Afis Area E, Level 9a–8: Venturi 2000, fig. 7:1.

21. Local Production Aegeanizing Bell-Shaped Bowls (fig. 3.4–8)

The popularity of Aegeanizing bell-shaped bowls during Iron Age I in Syria and Lebanon finds another expression in a number of various locally produced bell-shaped bowls that resemble the LH IIIC models to varying degrees. The following list attempts to give an impression of the wide range of local productions that were apparently inspired by Aegean and Cypriot ceramics.

- ʿAyn Dara Trench 1, Level 2: Stone and Zimansky 1999, fig. 27:6, the painted motif is unclear, or are the black lines an indication of the joined breaks?
- Fig. 3.4: Tell Baraghita surface find: Matthers 1981, fig. 236:7 and fig. 237A.
- Fig. 3.5: Kazel Area II, Level 6, Building I, Room J on floors of a destruction (late Late Bronze; Badre et al. 1994, 332, fig. 55e).
- Fig. 3.6: Kazel Area II, Level 6, Building I, Room J, on floors of a destruction (late Late Bronze; Badre et al. 1994, 332, fig. 55d, horizontal red bands, compared with "Levanto Mycenaean").
- Kazel Area II, Level 5, Room F (early Iron Age; Badre et al. 1994, 308, fig. 39f, red painted bands. Compare a White-Painted Wheelmade III bowl from Alassa-Pano Mandilaris, Cyprus, T.3/71: Hadjisavvas 1991, fig. 17.7, LC IIIA).

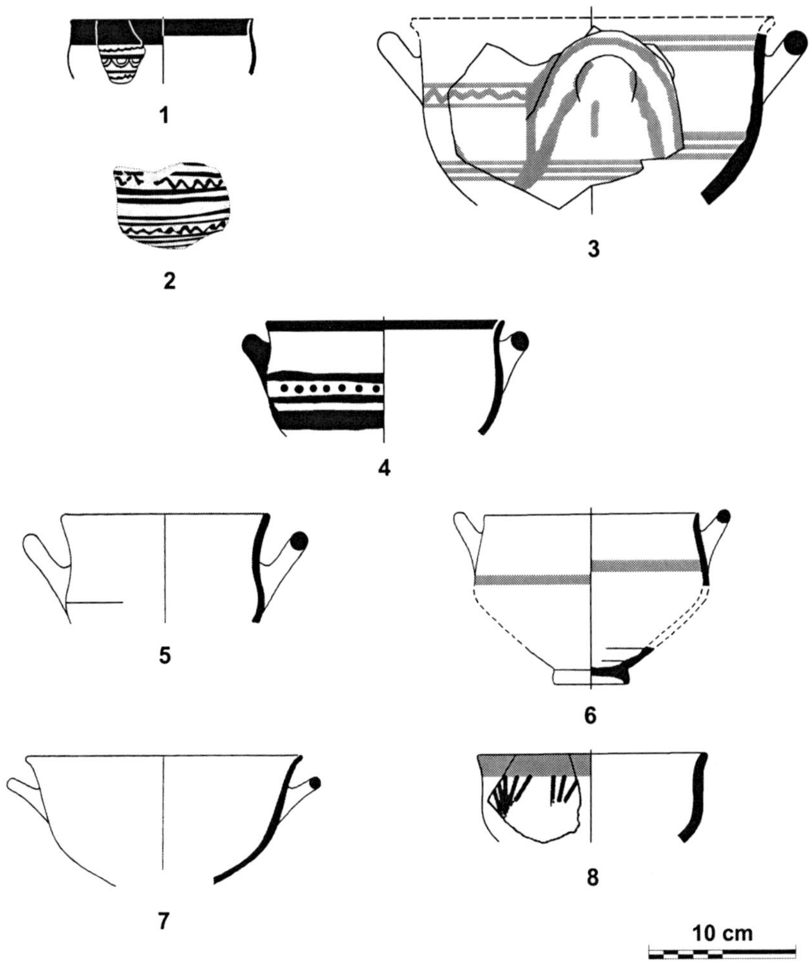

Fig. 3: Syrian Iron Age I.

Key to fig. 3:

1) ʿAyn Dara Trench 1, Level 2 pit: Stone and Zimansky 1999, fig. 27:1=fig. 29 lower left.
2) ʿAyn Dara Trench 1, Level 2 pit: Stone and Zimansky 1999, fig. 27:1=fig. 29 lower right.
3) Tell Afis Area E, Levels 9a–8: Venturi 2000, fig. 7:1.
4) Tell Baraghita surface find: Matthers 1981, fig. 236:7 and fig. 237A.
5) Kazel Area II, Level 6: Badre et al. 1994, 332, fig. 55e.
6) Kazel Area II, Level 6: Badre et al. 1994, 332, fig. 55d.
7) Kazel Area II, Level 5: Badre et al. 1994, 304, fig. 39b.
8) Tyre Stratum 13-2: Bikai 1978, pl. 37:10.

- Fig. 3.7: Kazel Area II, Level 5, Room C (early Iron Age; Badre et al. 1994, 304, fig. 39b, cf. Dor D2-10/9 [late Iron Ib]: Gilboa 2001a, pl. 5.47:1 with a painted spiral [?] decoration).
- Fig. 3.8: Tyre Stratum 13-2: Bikai 1978, pl. 37:10, whether this bell-shaped bowl is a Cypriot import or a Phoenician product, is hard to say without an analysis of the fabric. Stylized tree motifs as on this bowl appear on Proto-White Painted vessels of LC IIIB (cf. Iacovou 1988, fig. 53) as well as on Phoenician ceramics.

22. Bell-Shaped Bowls in Proto-White Painted and Cypro-Geometric I Styles

As already stated, there seem to be only a few Proto-White Painted skyphoi in Syria (Gilboa 2001a, 343–53). Although Proto-White Painted was reported from Ras Ibn Hani (Lagarce 1983, 224–25, pl. 59) and from Tell Afis (Bonatz 1998, 213, 215), according to Maria Iacovou at both sites this identification is erroneous (Gilboa 2001a, 349). Only from the drawings and photographs published and without an analysis of the fabric, it is in some cases almost impossible to say whether a vessel is an imported Cypriot Proto-White Painted or a locally produced imitation.

Most of the skyphoi discussed here have been identified as White-Painted I. Since the White-Painted I style is already beyond the scope of this paper, the few examples illustrated here should serve the purpose of defining the end of the typical LC III skyphos in Syria and Lebanon (for a full treatment of early Cypro-Geometric I imports, see Gilboa 2001a, esp. 350–53).

In the ʿAmuq Plain, Cypro-Geometric I was reported, but not published, from Phases N and Oa (Swift 1958, 121–22, 198, cf. 151–52). My own observations confirm this assessment.

- A White-Painted I skyphos similar to one from Kition Area II, Floor I (Karageorghis and Demas 1985, 217, pl. 224:4829) was found in Çatal Höyük in Phase N.
- A White-Painted I bowl similar to one from Kition Area I, Floor I (Karageorghis and Demas 1985, 70, pl. 33:616=55:616) was found in Çatal Höyük Phase N-Middle.
- Another White-Painted I (?) skyphos from Çatal Höyük Phase N-Middle has parallels in Kition Area II, Floors II–III (LC IIIB, Karageorghis and Demas 1985, 161, pl. 208:5104) and Floor I (Karageorghis and Demas 1985, 220, pl. 224:2495).

Since the material is unpublished, it is difficult to be more precise, but White-Painted I apparently began in Phase N, probably N-Late.

White-Painted I skyphoi also appear in the following sites:

- Tell Afis Area E, Level 8: Bonatz 1998, 214, fig. 4:9, a stemmed foot, from a White-Painted I skyphos (?); cf. Enkomi Level IIIC: Dikaios 1969–1971, pl. 100:25 (5955/1).
- Tell Afis Area E, Levels 7–6: Venturi 2000, fig. 11:2–7.
- Tell Afis Area E, Level 6: Mazzoni and Cecchini 1995, 270, fig. 26:13.
- Tyre Stratum 13-2: Bikai 1978, pl. 37:7.
- Tyre Stratum 13-1: Bikai 1978, 53–55, pl. 34:3.
- Tyre Stratum 13-1: Bikai 1978, 53–55, pl. 34:2.
- Tyre Stratum 10-2: Bikai 1978, 53–55, pl. 28:7.
- Tyre Stratum 10-2: Bikai 1978, 53–55, pl. 28:3
- Tyre Stratum 9: Bikai 1978, 53–55, pl. 22:17.

23. Stemmed Cups Similar to Cypro-Geometric I Skyphoi (fig. 4.1–2)

The petrographic analysis of the cup from Dor showed that the vessel was produced at the coast of either Philistia or the Sharon (Gilboa 2001a, 403).

- Fig. 4.1: Hama Cemetery Period III (Riis 1948, fig. 90).
- Fig. 4.2: Dor G-7 (?; Gilboa 2001a, pl. 5.49:15).

24. Wide Conical Bowl (FS 295) with Two Horizontal Strap Handles and a Carinated Rim (fig. 5.1)

These occur in Enkomi mostly in Level IIIA, a few last examples were found also in IIIB (Kling 1989, 134–35, fig. 5c, with references). The bowl is usually unpainted or linear decorated with horizontal painted bands; Kling listed only one example with a patterned decoration (Kling 1989, 135). Rutter (1977, 2) placed this type in his LH IIIC Phase 2, while Mountjoy dated FS 295 LH III Early–Middle (Mountjoy 1986, 153–54, 180, figs. 197; 233). In the Levant this bowl is especially common in Tarsus (Goldman 1956, pl. 332:1266; French 1975, figs. 16–17; Mountjoy 2005b, fig. 17:420–22), and Ashdod Area G, Stratum XIII (T. Dothan 1982, 105). An unpublished bowl from Çatal Höyük was found in Phase N-Middle.

- Fig. 5.1: ʿAyn Dara Trench I, Level 2 (Stone and Zimansky 1999, fig. 27:7).

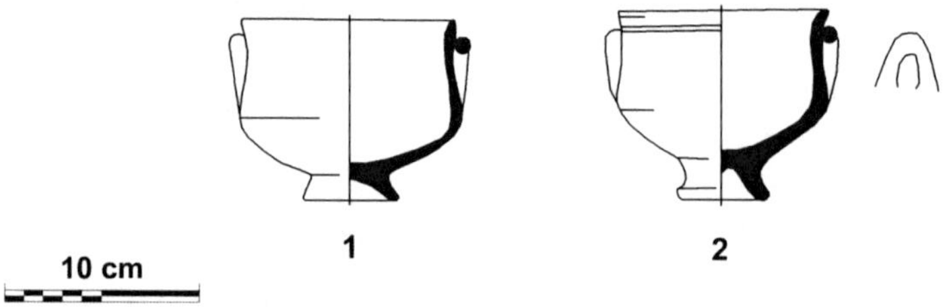

Fig. 4: Late Syrian Iron Age IB–IC.

Key to fig. 4:
1) Hama Cemetery Period III: Riis 1948, fig. 90.
2) Dor G-7: Gilboa 2001a, pl. 5.49:15.

25. Wide Conical or Rounded Bowls with Two Horizontal Strap Handles and a Carinated Rim (fig. 5.2)

These are present in Cyprus already in LC IIC contexts, but become most common in LC IIIA and in LC IIIB they disappear (Kling 1989, 132, fig. 5b, with references).

- Fig. 5.2: Ras Ibn Hani "lower floor" (Badre 1983, fig. 1c, the "lower floor" is the first floor above the Late Bronze destruction).

26. Wide Shallow Bowls with Wavy-Line Decoration and a Round, Symmetrical Design in the Inside and Outside

These features characterize some of the White-Painted I bowls, which also occur with a somewhat stemmed base and strokes painted on the rim (cf. Gjerstad 1948, fig. 1:4–6). Similar bowls were found in Çatal Höyük in Phase N-Middle and Late.

27. Deep Bowl or "Mug" that is Apparently not an Aegean or Cypriot Form (fig. 6.3)

It resembles, however, to some extent the deep semiglobular cups with one vertical handle of LC IIIB (cf. Kling 1989, 141). Similar are also FS 230 and 231, although these shapes do not have the characteristic tall stem. A number of Aegeanizing motifs are employed: the wavy-line decoration, the many horizontal bands, and the scale pattern. The composition of these many rows of decora-

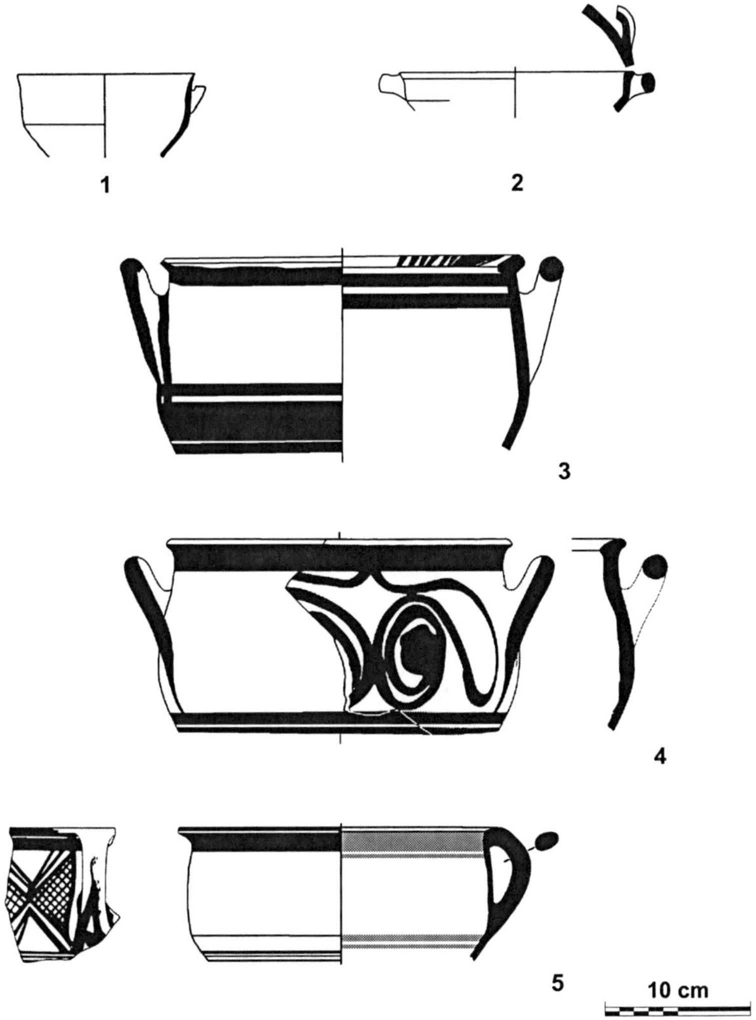

Fig. 5: Syrian Iron Age IA.

Key to fig. 5:

1) ʿAyn Dara Trench I, Level 2: Stone and Zimansky 1999, fig. 27:7.
2) Ras Ibn Hani "lower floor": Badre 1983, fig. 1c.
3) Ras Ibn Hani "lower floor": Badre 1983, fig. 1a.
4) Tell Afis Area E, Level 9b: Bonatz 1998, 217, fig. 5:1.
5) Tell Afis Area E, Level 10: Bonatz 1998, 218, fig. 5:2.

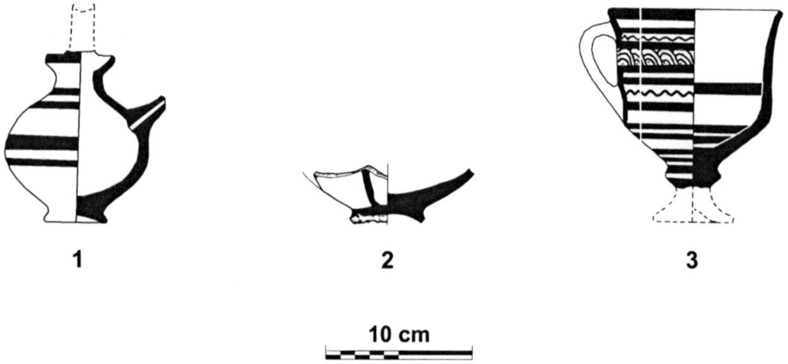

Fig. 6: Syrian Iron Age I.

Key to fig. 6:
1) Çatal Höyük N-Middle (A2688): Swift 1958, fig. 25.
2) Tell Afis Area E, Level 9: Bonatz 1998, 216–17, fig. 4:7.
3) Çatal Höyük unstratified ("outside the north fortifications"): Swift 1958, 67, 73, fig. 22.

tion resembles that of Group 20 (see above). An unpublished beaker from Çatal Höyük was found in the levels between Phases N and O.

- Fig. 6.3: Çatal Höyük unstratified ("outside the north fortifications"): Swift 1958, 67, 73, fig. 22.

Similar mugs:

- Tell Afis Area G: Mazzoni et al. 1999–2000, fig. 17:3.
- Tell Afis Area E, Level 7: Venturi 2000, fig. 11:12 (cf. Mazzoni et al. 1999–2000, 20 n. 48).
- Kinet Höyük Phase 12A: Gates, this volume.

28. Bell-Shaped Krater (FS 281–282) with Geometric Motifs (fig. 5.3)

These occurred in Cyprus mostly in LC IIIA (Kling 1989, 109–26, fig. 3c). They first appear in LC IIC and disappear during LC IIIB.

- Qrayya Cemetery: Guigues 1939, 59–60, pl. 12a; Leonard 1994, no. 1784: FS 284–285, FM 53: 38 wavy line, FM 75 variant panelled pattern, LH IIIB–C, locally produced? Although vertical straight and wavy lines occur on Mycenaean and Aegeanizing pottery, this decoration is rare in the Levant; I am not aware of any parallels to this krater.
- Fig. 5.3: Ras Ibn Hani "lower floor": Badre 1983, fig. 1a, the "lower floor" is the first floor above the Late Bronze destruction. In Cyprus, most LC

III kraters are decorated with some principal motif in addition to horizontal painted bands, such as spirals and/or panels. This krater has no such other principal motifs. The only decoration on these vessels seems to be horizontal painted bands and strokes on the rim. Its findspot dates the krater after the Late Bronze settlement at Ras Ibn Hani and early in Iron Age I. Unpublished bell-shaped kraters with horizontal painted bands from Çatal Höyük and Tell Judaidah were found in Phase N-Middle and Late, but these fragments are small and there might have been additional motifs on the vessels.

29. Bell-shaped krater (FS 281–282) with spiral motifs (fig. 5.4)

These kraters occurred in Cyprus mostly in LC IIIA (Kling 1989, 109–13). They first appear in LC IIC and disappear during LC IIIB.

- Fig. 5.4: Tell Afis Area E, Level 9b: Bonatz 1998, 217, fig. 5:1, buff clay with white and black grits and matte red paint. There is no interior decoration. Kraters with a curve-stemmed antithetic spiral and without panels are rare in Cyprus and appear usually on skyphoi only (cf. Enkomi Level IIIA: Dikaios 1969–1971, pl. 306:125; Enkomi Level IIIB: Dikaios 1969–1971, pl. 308:219; Enkomi Level IIIC: Dikaios 1969–1971, pl. 309:296; and Kition Area I, Floor III: Karageorghis and Demas 1985, pl. 19:896/1, 9016/1; pl. 20:896/2, 931/2). At Enkomi on skyphoi, the antithetic spiral motif with central panel overlaps with the spiral motif without panel, but it has been claimed that the variant without panel between the spirals is generally later (Furumark 1941a, 364; cf. French 1975, 69–70 and Bonatz 1998, 217). This assumption is not supported by Kling's list of skyphoi without a panel between the spirals (Kling 1989, 97 with references). There are only a few bell-shaped kraters without a panel between the spirals in Kling's list (Kling 1989, 245, 264, 283, 302, 340).
- Ras Ibn Hani "lower floor": Badre 1983, fig. 1b, without panel between the spirals?
- Ras Ibn Hani "lower floor": Badre 1983, fig. 1c.
- Ras Ibn Hani (no further information): Lagarce and Lagarce 1988, fig. 13, bell-shaped krater with curve-stemmed antithetic spirals with zigzag motif in a vertical panel. Most parallels to this krater were found in Cyprus in LC IIIA, only one example dates to LC IIIA–IIIB; in the Aegean, the motif appears already in LH IIIB (Kling 1989, 95 with references).

- Byblos Necropolis K: Salles 1980, pl. 13:1, bell-shaped krater with stemmed spiral, a vertical chain lozenge in a panel filled with arcs, a vertical panel with zigzag lines and a "Maltese" cross. The motifs of the vessel were typical for both LH IIIB and LH IIIC. The lozenge (FM 73) appeared in the Aegean in LH IIIB and was popular throughout LH IIIC (Mountjoy 1986, 95–96, 123, 135, 158, 160, 182, 184). In Cyprus this variant of the lozenge is rare and occurs on kraters mainly in LC IIIA. The "Maltese" cross appears in Cyprus since the beginning of the Late Bronze Age; it is present in LC IIB, LC IIIA, and LC IIIB (Kling 1989, 100). The only somewhat similar stemmed spiral in Cyprus was painted on a bell-shaped krater from Kourion Area D: A B1088 (LC IIIA; Benson 1972, 115, pl. 31, cf. Kling 1989, 111). Leonard dated the vessel to "LH IIIB (–C?)" (Leonard 1994, no. 1730) and considers a local production of the krater in Lebanon. The Cypriot evidence supports this assessment; a date to the Late Bronze Age is probable, but early Iron Age I is, however, also possible.

Possible krater fragment:

- Tell Afis Area E, Level 8: Bonatz 1998, 216–17, fig. 4:4, is a tiny fragment with concentric semicircles/arcs in a panel. A bell-shaped krater from Enkomi Level IIIC (Dikaios 1969–1971, pl. 85:20=pl. 309:297 [3612/11]) has the same motif.
- Byblos Necropolis K: Salles 1980, pl. 13:7.
- Byblos Necropolis K: Salles 1980, pl. 13:8, Leonard 1994, no. 2094, the shape of both vessels is unidentifiable, the panel pattern (FM 50 variant) appears in both LH IIIB and IIIC; Salles identified both motifs as "Mycenaean" IIIC; in Cyprus it is difficult to find exact parallels to the two fragments, cf. Enkomi Level IIIA (Dikaios 1969–1971, pl. 74:28=307:193 [3629/18]) and Hala Sultan Teke Room 2, Layer 5, F1103(E; Hult 1978, 62, 79, fig. 132i) both parallels date to LC IIIA.
- Byblos Necropolis K: Salles 1980, pl. 13:2, Leonard 1994, no. 1974, and
- Byblos Necropolis K: Salles 1980, pl. 13:3, Leonard 1994, no. 1969; the motifs appear in both LH IIIB and IIIC. At Cyprus the bird motif filled with dots and the fish filled with wavy lines appear in LC IIC, IIIA, and IIIB (for the bird, cf. T. Dothan 1982, figs. 61–63; for the fish, cf. Maa-Palaeokastro Floor II: Karageorghis and Demas 1988, pl. 43:91, 167; T. Dothan 1982, fig. 64; Tarsus: Goldman 1956, fig. 335:1330), although the animals look different from the examples discussed here (Kling 1989, 118–19 with references). While Salles (1980) dates the vessels to "Mycenaean" IIIC, Leonard (1994) dates them to LH IIIB–IIIC.

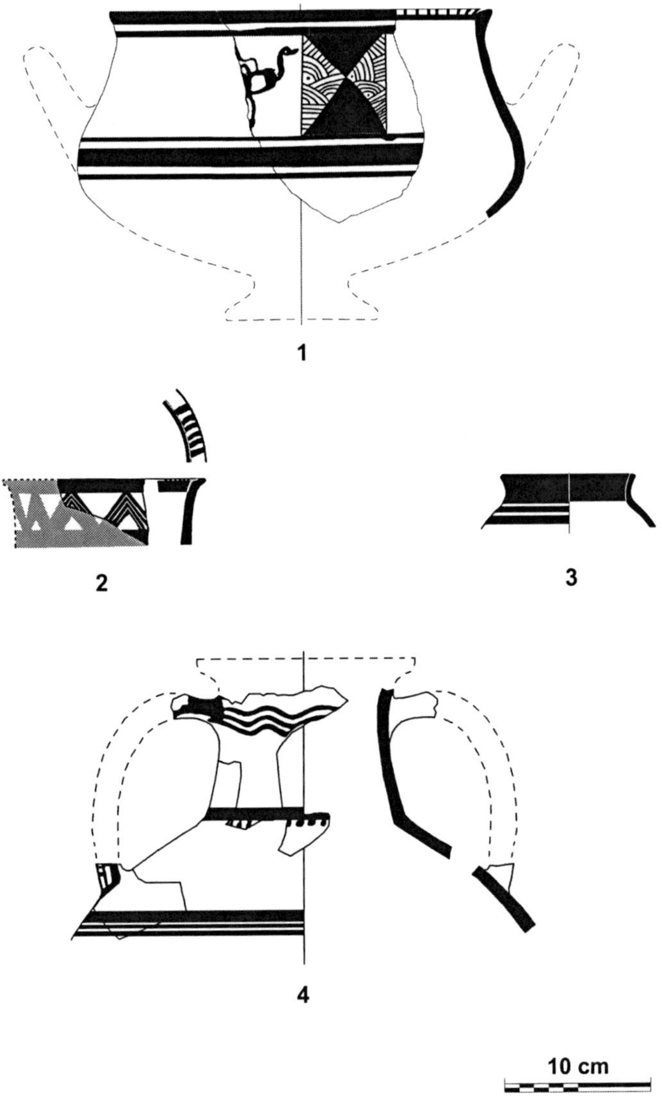

Fig. 7: Syrian Iron Age IB, Proto-White Painted Style.

Key to fig. 7:

1) Çatal Höyük N-Middle (N13-IIb): Swift 1958, fig. 27.
2) Tell Afis Area E, Level 9a: Pedrazzi 2002, 36, fig. 23:7.
3) Tell Afis Area E, Level 9a: Pedrazzi 2002, 36, fig. 23:8.
4) Tell Afis Area E: Venturi (2000, 523, fig. 11:1) assigned this vessel to Levels 7–6, while in Mazzoni and Cecchini (1995, 261, fig. 20:1) it is assigned to Level 9a.

30. Kraters in Syria Resembling Proto-White Painted or White-Painted I Vessels in Cyprus (fig. 7.1)

Vessels such as one in the Hadjiprodromou collection (Karageorghis 1975, pl. 76:H1) or another White-Painted I example (Gjerstad 1948, fig. 3:6) have a parallel in Tell Judaidah Phase N-Middle.

- Fig. 7.1: Çatal Höyük N-Middle (N13-IIb): Swift 1958, fig. 27, the pictorial decoration resembles Proto-White Painted kraters (cf. Iacovou 1988, figs. 46, 55, 58, 62); with more unpublished kraters from the Çatal Höyük, Phase N-Middle.
- Tell Afis Area J: Mazzoni et al. 1999–2000, 31, fig. 25:1, a small fragment with a painted bird head.
- Another type of a Proto-White Painted krater from Cyprus (Iacovou 1988, fig. 44) has a parallel in Syria.
- Tell Afis Area E, Level 9b: Venturi 2000, fig. 6:1 (although this level seems to be too early for a vessel in the Proto-White Painted tradition).

31. Kraters with Geometrical Painted Decoration (fig. 5.5)

Fig. 5.5: Tell Afis Area E, Level 10: Bonatz 1998, 218, fig. 5:2, greenish fabric, gray core with matte black paint. This is a unique example. The same motif, a hatched double-axe appears on a Bichrome Wheelmade open krater at Kition Area II, Floors III–IIIA: Karageorghis and Demas 1985, 122, pls. 115, 194: 2633. The double-axe motif occurs a few times in LC III, but almost always as a solid painted double-axe, not hatched as in this case. Bonatz (1998) assumes that this is a derivative motif of cross-hatched triangles not unusual in Late Cypriot and Syrian pottery of the Late Bronze Age.

32. Krater with a straight neck and thickened rim (fig. 8.1–3)

These kraters appear frequently in the Iron Age I pottery repertoire in north Syria and the ʿAmuq Plain. They are decorated with painted horizontal bands and wavy lines. This decoration may be influenced by the wavy line motifs of the Aegeanizing pottery of LC III Cyprus. Unpublished parallels from Çatal Höyük were found in all phases of N (Early–Late).

- Fig. 8.1: ʿAyn Dara, Trench 1, Level 4: Stone and Zimansky 1999, fig. 27:9.
- Fig. 8.2: ʿAyn Dara, Trench 1, Level 5: Stone and Zimansky 1999, fig. 27:12.
- Fig. 8.3: Jindaris (without further information): Sürenhagen 1999, fig. 10.

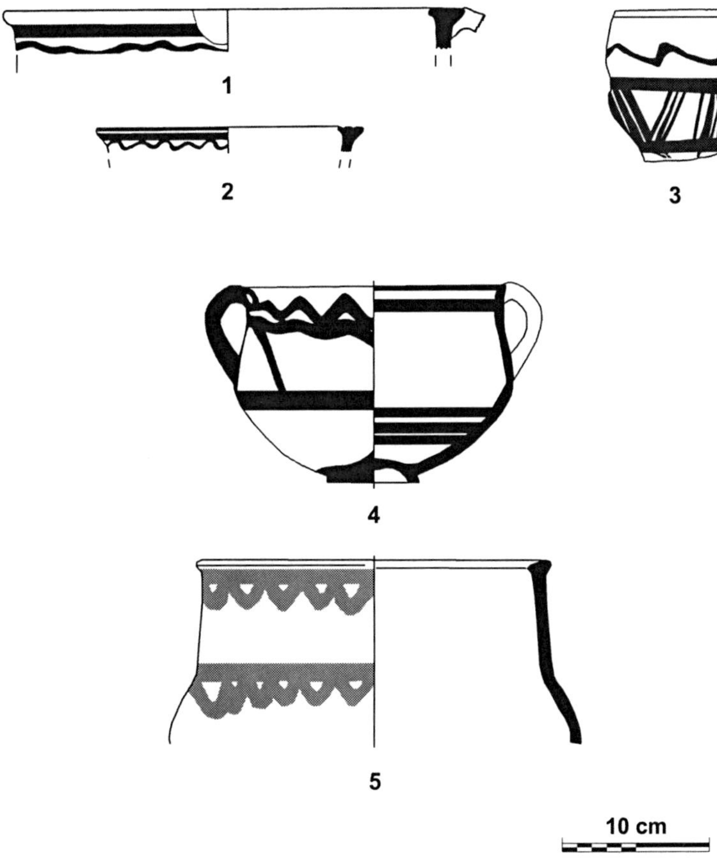

Fig. 8: Syrian Iron Age I.

Key to fig. 8:

1) ʿAyn Dara Trench 1, Level 4: Stone and Zimansky 1999, fig. 27:9.
2) ʿAyn Dara Trench 1, Level 5: Stone and Zimansky 1999, fig. 27:12.
3) Jindaris (without further information): Sürenhagen 1999, fig. 10.
4) Tyre Stratum 14: Bikai 1978, pl. 41:4.
5) Kazel Area II, Level 5: Badre et al. 1994, fig. 35c.

33. Small amphoroid kraters or amphoriskoi (fig. 7.2)

These vessels are common during LC IIIB and the Cypro-Geometric period in Cyprus (for the vessel form, see Karageorghis [1975, 48, pl. 59:8 T17: 8]). The motif, a concentric triangle motif (FM 61A), in this large variation usually on a shoulder or a neck, was employed on Cypriot pottery during LC IIIB and the Cypro-Geometric period (e.g., White-Painted I; Kourion: Benson 1972, pl. 63:Bryn Mawr P68; Kaloriziki: Benson 1973, pl. 44:K113; cf. Kition Area II, Bothros 20: Karageorghis and Demas 1985, pl. 175:4110 with a similar triangle on the shoulder, for the appearance of this motif in LH III Late and Submycenaean, see Mountjoy [1986, 183, fig. 235:18; 195, fig. 258:7]).

- Fig. 7.2: Tell Afis Area E, Level 9a: Pedrazzi 2002, 36, fig. 23:7 (cf. Knossos "Sub-Minoan": Kanta 1980, fig. 113:11; Hama Cemetery Period II: Riis 1948, fig. 130A:23).

34. Iron Age I vessels in Syria and Lebanon decorated with thick and carelessly fast-painted bands that resemble Mycenaean motifs, such as the hanging semicircles (or festoons) and wavy lines (fig. 8.4–5)

The ceramic shapes are difficult to compare with Cypriot or Greek models, but they certainly look "foreign" in their Syrian and Lebanese contexts. Thin wavy-line decoration on kraters in a local Syrian form tradition were observed by Bonatz (1993, 134–35, figs. 1, 3).

- Fig. 8.4: Tyre Stratum 14: Bikai 1978, pl. 41:4, the shape resembles bell-shaped forms, but the vertical handles are hard to find on bell-shaped bowls or kraters in Cyprus. The decoration, a wavy line and horizontal bands, are painted in thick and simple bands. For somewhat similar forms, see Enkomi IIIB: Dikaios 1969–1971, pls. 79:10 (731/6), 14 (347; 83: 24 [4096/7]); Tarsus: Goldman 1956, fig. 336:1353; Kaloriziki T.20:6 [B]; and Benson 1973, 81, pls. 23, 57:K288 (White-Painted I); a similar decoration appears on pieces from Enkomi IIIB: Dikaios 1969–1971, pl. 1969: 95:13 (5330/1); Kition Area II, Floors II–III: Karageorghis and Demas 1985, pl. 139:5068A.
- Fig. 8.5: Kazel Area II, Level 5, Room B: Badre et al. 1994, fig. 35c is a large krater with a straight neck, painted red with hanging semi-circles (or festoons) in thick and simple bands. For parallels, see Ras Ibn Hani: Bounni et al. 1979, fig. 27; Enkomi IIIA: Dikaios 1969–1971, pl. 74:3 (1767) a bowl with a similar decoration; Enkomi IIIB: Dikaios 1969–1971, pls. 95:10a (260/1) and 13 (5330/1); 100:20 (5932/1).

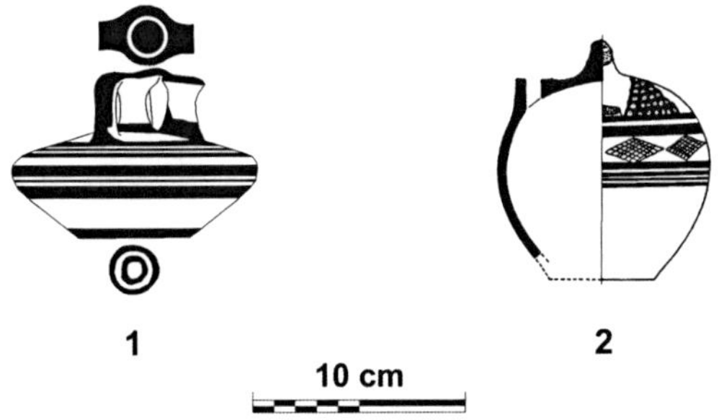

Fig. 9: Syrian Iron Age IA.

Key to fig. 9:
1) Byblos Necropolis K: Salles 1980, pl. 12:2.
2) Byblos Necropolis K: Salles 1980, pl. 12:6.

35. Conical Stirrup Jars (FS 183; fig. 9.1)

These are dated to LH IIIB (Leonard 1994, no. 829). Salles, however, assigned the stirrup jar from Byblos to LH IIIC.

- Fig. 9.1: Byblos Necropolis K: Salles 1980, pl. 12:2.

36. Globular stirrup jars of shape FS 175/176 (fig. 9.2)

These are considered the "mainstream" LH IIIC stirrup jars (Leonard 1994, 57–58 with references). In Cyprus they are dated to LC IIIA (Kling 1989, 161). Sherratt and Mazar (this volume) connect the stirrup jars of this type from Beth Shean to the Egyptian Twentieth Dynasty. They compare the vessels with parallels from Cyprus and Tarsus and date the stirrup jars to the "later stages of Enkomi IIIA and possibly perhaps to the early stages of level IIIB." Thus, Sherratt and Mazar conclude that the transition from Enkomi Level IIIA to IIIB is roughly contemporary with the later years of Ramesses III, i.e., ca. 1150 B.C.E. Mountjoy compares the stirrup jars with vessels in the Aegean and dates the examples discussed here to LH III Early Phase 2 (Mountjoy 2007b). She thinks they do not need to be LH IIIC Middle contra Warren and Hankey (1989, 164–65). For comparisons in Tarsus, see Mountjoy (2005b: fig. 4:44, 48–50).

- Fig. 9.2: Byblos Necropolis K: Salles 1980, pl. 12:6, Leonard 1994, no. 683, triangular patch of joined semicircles in scale pattern, horizontal row of lozenges, cross-hatched.

37. Several top-disc fragments of stirrup jars

These have been dated to LH IIIC. Such fragments are hard to date precisely (cf. Kling 1989, 165).

- Sarafand (Sarepta) II-B-5 Level 5-2: Koehl 1985, 119, figs. 8, 20, no. 190; Leonard 1994, no. 1061 LH IIIC, cf. Tarsus: Goldman 1956, fig. 333:1279.
- Sarafand (Sarepta) II-A-9 Level 10: Koehl 1985, 118, fig. 8, no. 189; Leonard 1994, no. 1060 LH IIIC (?), cf. Enkomi Level IIIA: Dikaios 1969–1971, pl. 82:17–18.
- Sarafand (Sarepta) II-B-9 Level 6: Koehl 1985, 119, fig. 8, no. 191; Leonard 1994, no. 1003 LH IIIC Early, cf. Ashdod Area B, Stratum 2 (M. Dothan and Freedman 1967, pl. 14:18).

38. Jugs with a Tubular Spout (figs. 6.1–2; 10.1)

- Fig. 6.1: Çatal Höyük N-Middle (A2688): Swift 1958, fig. 25, tall ovoid type with basket-handle at right angle to spout. The four Cypriot examples from LC IIIA and IIIB contexts were noted by Kling (1989, 160 with detailed discussion, references, and comparisons). A Proto-White Painted jug has a very similar shape (Alaas Pit A: Karageorghis 1975, pl. 66:A/1). A jug from Submycenaean Skoubris (Mountjoy 1986, 199, fig. 266) has the same arrangement of the handle.
- Spouted jugs with horizontal painted bands and one (or two) wavy lines on the shoulder, most of them of Proto-White Painted style, resemble an unpublished vessel from Tell Ta'yinat (cf. Karageorghis 1975, 52). The jugs are similar to Kling's ovoid type with basket-handle in line with the spout, but lack the vertical bands on the body (Kling 1989, 161–62, fig. 17d). Comparisons were found in Perati NM 9171: Mountjoy 1986, 188, fig. 246 (LH IIIC Late); Alaas T.12/1: Karageorghis 1975, 52, pl. 52 Proto-White Painted; Alaas Pit A: Karageorghis 1975, pl. 66:A/2; Kition Areas I–II, Floor II: Karageorghis and Demas 1985, pls. 48:650; 212: 5352 Proto-White Painted; Kaloriziki T.26: 23 (A): Benson 1973, 76, pl. 59:K163 identified by Benson as Proto-White Painted. This type does not appear before LC IIIB and seems to develop into the White-Painted I style.
- Fig. 6.2: Tell Afis Area E, Level 9: Bonatz 1998, 216–17, fig. 4:7, greenish gray, coarse fabric with matte black paint. This is apparently a jug with a tubular spout, originally with horizontal and vertical bands on the body (cf. Enkomi Level IIIC: Dikaios 1969–1971, pl. 84:11 [5775/3]; Enkomi

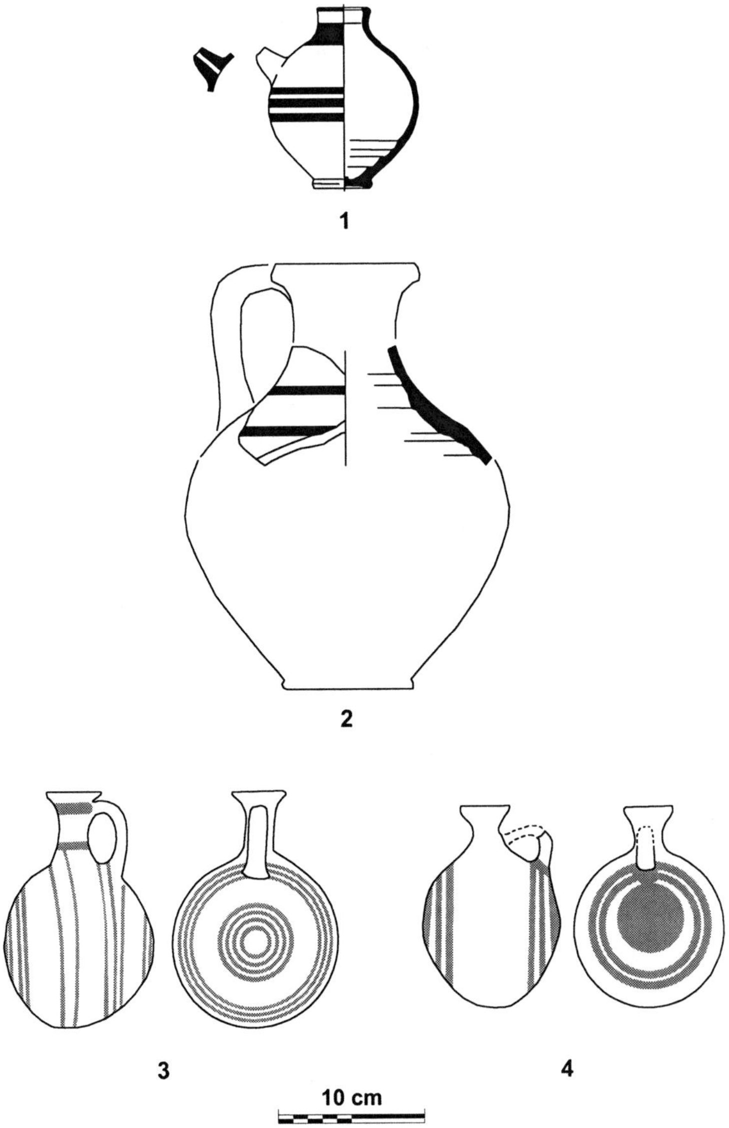

Fig. 10: Syrian Iron Age I.

Key to fig. 10:

1) Tell Kazel Area II, Level 5: Badre et al. 1994, fig. 33c.
2) Tell Afis Area E, Level 9b: Venturi 2000, fig. 6:6.
3) Alaas Tomb 15: Karageorghis 1975, pl. 55:T.15/13.
4) Alaas Tomb 17: Karageorghis 1975, pl. 60:T.17/26.

destruction level of IIIA: Dikaios 1969–1971, pl. 98:17 [129/6]; Enkomi early Level IIIB: Dikaios 1969–1971, pl. 99:31 [5867/10], 49 [5868/18]; Enkomi Level IIIB: Dikaios 1969–1971, pl. 96:8=123:11 [162]; cf. Kling 1989, 160–61).

- Fig. 10.1: Tell Kazel Area II, Level 5, Room A: Badre et al. 1994, fig. 33c, this local jug with bichrome horizontal black and red bands seems to be influenced by Aegeanizing pottery.
- Tell Kazel Area II, Level 5, Room N: Capet 2003, fig. 40j.

39. Hydriae (fig. 10.2)

These are rare in Cyprus and the Levant (cf. Kling 1989, 148–49) and have no prior history on the island and may have been introduced from Greece into Cyprus during LC IIIA. Hydriae appear in Cyprus in LC IIIA and IIIB. An unpublished hydria was found in Tell Ta'yinat, in the 'Amuq Plain. Close comparisons to this vessel were found in LH IIIC Greece (Mountjoy 1986, 203, fig. 212:1 [LH IIIC Middle] and figs. 240, 243 [LH IIIC Late]).

- (Fig. 10.2) Tell Afis Area E, Level 9b: Venturi 2000, fig. 6:6.

40. "Pilgrim bottle" or lentoid flask with one vertical handle from below the rim transversally to one of the flattened sides of the body (fig. 10.3–4)

Usually these vessels are decorated with concentric circles on the two flattened sides. Other unpublished vessels were found in Çatal Höyük Phase N-Middle. In the Aegean, there are similar vessels in LH III Middle and Late (Mountjoy 2001, figs. 272, 317).

- Tell Afis Area E, Silo 1794, Level 9a: Venturi 2000, fig. 9:1.
- Çatal Höyük Phase N: Swift 1958, fig. 26 (a2313), cf. Alaas Tomb 15: Karageorghis 1975, pl. 55:T.15/13 (fig. 10.3); Alaas Tomb 17: Karageorghis 1975, pl. 60:T.17/26 (fig. 10.4).
- Hama Cemetery Period I (G VIII 402, 5 B 304): Riis 1948, fig. 81.
- Tell Kazel Area II, Level 5, Room F: Badre et al. 1994, fig. 39e.
- Tell Kazel Area II, Level 5, Room I: Capet 2003, fig. 36k.

41. Strainer Jug with ovoid body and open trough-shaped spout

An unpublished strainer jug from Çatal Höyük, typical for LC IIIB, has an ovoid body and an open, trough-shaped spout on the shoulder and small holes punctured in the shoulder at the spout (Kling 1989, 153–57, fig. 16a). The tall neck is tapering toward a spreading rim. There is usually a vertical handle from rim to shoulder at right angles to the spout. Some of these jugs have a concentric triangle on the shoulder and horizontal bands (Kling 1989, 154; Enkomi Level IIIB, Dikaios 1969–1971, pl. 83:15 [3031/3]; Enkomi wells with uncertain date: Dikaios 1969–1971, 866, pl. 109:17 [6323/1]; Kaloriziki T.25: 48 [K161]: Benson 1973, 76, pl. 19). The unpublished jug from Çatal Höyük was found in Phase N. Jugs with a goat motif, similar to the pictorial style of Proto-White Painted (Iacovou 1988, figs. 2, 26, although these are not strainer jugs), were found in Çatal Höyük Phase N-Middle.

42. Amphoriskoi with two horizontal loop handles

These appear in northern Syria. The best comparisons are Proto-White Painted (Alaas: Karageorghis 1975, 47–48; Kaloriziki K101, K111, K109: Benson 1973, pls. 18, 44; Kition Area I wells: Karageorghis and Demas 1985, 37:273) or White-Painted I (Gjerstad 1948, fig. 5:11) amphoriskoi from Cyprus. Parallels were found in Çatal Höyük (Phase N) and Tell Ta'yinat.

43. Proto-White Painted amphoriskoi with horizontal lines and/or wavy lines under the lip (fig. 7.3–4)

These are common in Cyprus, but rare in Syria (unpublished amphoriskoi in Syria have parallels in Kaloriziki: Benson 1973, pl. 18:K131; Kition Area I, Floors I–II and Area II, Floor II: Karageorghis and Demas 1985, pl. 51:332/1 and pl. 212:5484; for further comparisons, see Mazzoni and Cecchini [1995, 261 n. 73]). A parallel to Proto-White Painted amphoriskoi at Kition and Kaloriziki was found in Tell Ta'yinat (Kition Area I wells: Karageorghis and Demas 1985, pl. 37:273; Kaloriziki: Benson 1973, pl. 18:K111 and pl. 44:K109; Tell Ta'yinat T3641).

- Tell Kazel Area II pit cutting into Level 5: Jung 2007, fig. 11. A squat amphoriskos with a wider diameter at the rim was found at Tell Afis.
- Fig. 7.3: Tell Afis Area E, Level 9a: Pedrazzi 2002, fig. 23:8; cf. Mountjoy 1999d, fig. 275:78 (LH IIIC Middle) and fig. 50:372 (LH IIIC Late); Alaas: Karageorghis 1975, pl. 59:T.17: 12, 15, 18, 23; pl. 68:A10 (Proto-White Painted, but the rim diameter of the Tell Afis amphoriskos is wider); Gjerstad 1948, fig. 5:9 (White-Painted I).
- Fig. 7.4: Tell Afis Area E: Venturi 2000, 523, fig. 11:1 assigned this vessel to Levels 7–6, while in Mazzoni and Cecchini (1995, 261, fig. 20:1) it is assigned to Level 9a.

Cypro-Geometric I pottery is reported from Çatal Höyük (White-Painted I: A2437, N13 Level 9, Phase N-Late; White-Painted I: E383, J9 Level 4, Phase Oa; Black Slip I: E436, V13 Level 8, Phase N-Middle; Swift 1958, 121–22).

44. Handmade Burnished Ware (fig. 11)

Handmade Burnished Ware or "Barbarian Ware" was first identified in the Aegean at Mycenae in 1964 within early LH IIIC contexts (French and Rutter 1977). After that identification, this type of ceramics was noted at other LH IIIC sites in the Aegean. The excavators were convinced that Handmade Burnished Ware was intrusive, since there is no precedent in earlier Mycenaean ware. The pottery is handmade, at a time when the wheel was in full use, made of a coarse fabric containing large inclusions, dark in color, although the color may vary, and burnished (Pilides 1991, 139). Only years after its identification in the Aegean, Handmade Burnished Ware was also noted in Cyprus (Pilides 1991, 141; 1994; Karageorghis and Demas 1985, part II, 434–37; Karageorghis 1986).

While this pottery occurs in Greece for the first time in LH IIIB: 2 (Rutter 1975, 31; for Troy VIIB, see Bloedow 1985). In Cyprus Handmade Burnished Ware appears first during the transition of LC IIB/IIIA (Pilides 1991, 144). In Greece, this pottery went out of use after the early phases of LH IIIC. In Cyprus, however, Handmade Burnished Ware continues to be found, always in small numbers, down to the end of LC III and the beginning of the Cypro-Geometric period. Handmade Burnished Ware was also found in Syria. Its appearance at Tell Kazel, Syria, could indicate that this pottery may have been previously overlooked in Lebanon and Syria (Badre 2006, 89–92). Handmade Burnished Ware occurs also in Ugarit, Ras Ibn Hani, Ras al-Bassit, and Beirut (Badre 2006, 92). As far as I know none of this material is published. It is also reported from Tell Qasile Strata XI and X (Mazar 1985b, 43–44, fig. 18:16–17, fig. 29:20–22, fig. 34:12–13), Israel, where the vessel forms are different from Tell Kazel and Cyprus.

Handmade Burnished Ware is often associated with ethnic movements that are supposed to have caused the end of Mycenaean LH IIIB (Pilides 1991, 139–41; Rutter 1975, 1990; Deger-Jalkotzy 1977, 1983); others have argued for a local origin of this pottery (Walberg 1976; Small 1990; cf. Rutter 1990). The appearance of this ceramic style in Cyprus and Syria adds to the increasing complexity of the archaeological record of this period.

- Fig. 11.2: Tell Kazel Area II, Niveau 6 (latest occupation of the Late Bronze Age residency): Capet and Gubel 2000, 436 n. 24, fig. 7, TK 95.172; Capet 2003, figs. 24, 31m). The authors understand the occurrence of this pottery style as evidence for a temporal presence of Sea Peoples in Tell Kazel, ancient Sumur. Further examples (fig. 11.1, 3–4)

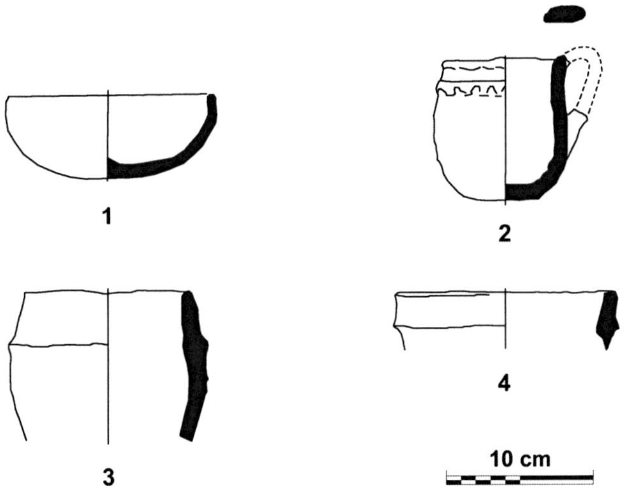

Fig. 11: Syrian Iron Age I, Handmade Burnished Pottery.

Key to fig. 11:

1) Tell Kazel Area II, Niveau 6: Capet 2003, fig. 24b.
2) Tell Kazel Area II, Niveau 6: Capet and Gubel 2000, 436 n. 24, fig. 7, TK 95.172.
3) Tell Kazel Area II, Niveau 6: Capet 2003, fig. 24d.
4) Tell Kazel Area II, Niveau 6: Capet 2003, fig. 24e.

have been published by Capet (2003, fig. 24) and Badre et al. (2005, fig. 9). Analyses of the fabrics indicate that these vessels were locally produced.

45. Gray Ware

This class of pottery is characterized by its gray burnished surface. Gray Ware appears in two variations at Tell Kazel (Badre et al. 2005, 31–32; Badre 2006, 87). The first one shows a burnished surface and white inclusions. Although the fabric of this group was analyzed, its provenance could not yet be determined (Badre et al. 2005, fig. 7:1–2). The second variation has a thick polished slip and silver and gold mica inclusions (Badre et al. 2005, fig. 7:3–4). Not only the shape and the incised decoration of this group resemble parallels in Troy, the chemical analysis of the fabric also points to an origin in northwestern Asia Minor.

Gray Ware appears rather suddenly during the thirteenth century B.C.E. in the Levant and continues to be in use during the twelfth century B.C.E. In Palestine, Gray Ware was found at Tell Abu Hawam, Lachish Stratum VI, and at Tel Miqne

Stratum VIIIA. It was also found at Ugarit, Minet el-Beida, and at several sites in southeastern Cyprus (Buchholz 1973; Heuck-Allen 1990, 1994 with a map of the distribution of Gray Ware in the Levant; Na'aman 2000).

The Relative Chronology

Aegeanizing ceramic styles resembling or imitating LH IIIC vessels were found in Syria during the first two phases of the Iron Age, the Syrian Iron Age IA and IB according to the terminology of Mazzoni that is adopted here (Mazzoni 2000; Venturi 2007). This chronological terminology is referring specifically to Syria and is not to be confused with similar notions in Palestinian archaeology (tables 1–2).

As for the terminology of Aegeanizing pottery there is some confusion, especially with the notion "Mycenaean IIIC:1" (Leonard 1994, 9–10). Still much work has to be done to define the styles involved here in more detail. For a summary of the research, see Buchholz (1999, 390–429 with further literature). It seems to me most useful to refer to Killebrew's reconstruction of phases in the appearance of Mycenaean pottery styles in the Levant (Killebrew 1998b; see also table 1 below). Killebrew's "phases" are here translated into assemblages or groups of pottery styles. While Killebrew dates her phases in a chronological sequence, I interpret the "phases" as stylistic groups that may overlap to some extent.

Group 1 includes LH IIIA2 and IIIB wares that were imported mainly from the Argolid to the eastern Mediterranean during the Late Bronze Age, the fourteenth and thirteenth century B.C.E. (Killebrew 1998b, 160–61). Chemical analyses confirmed that Argive imports in Tell Kazel, Syria, include Hellado-Mycenaean and Levanto-Mycenaean classes of pottery. This confirms the observation that an export-oriented pottery industry controlled by Mycenae produced specifically for Cyprus and the Levant (Badre et al. 2005, 36).

Group 2 is characterized by the appearance of "Derivative Mycenaean" styles that were produced at new and multiple manufacturing centers outside the Argolid (Killebrew 1998b, 161–62). These workshops have not been identified with certainty, but are sought in the eastern Mediterranean, especially in southwest Asia Minor and Cyprus (see provenience studies by Koehl and Yellin [1982, 273]). Among the different styles of this "Derivative Mycenaean" pottery are "Simple Style" ("Mycenaean IIIB late")[11] and "Rude Style" ("Pastoral Style"; Leonard 1994, 8–9; Buchholz 1999, 424–25).

11. Leonard 1994, 7–8; for the provenance, see Badre et al. 2005, 15.

Table 1: Aegean/Aegeanizing Pottery Styles in Syria and Lebanon.

<table>
<tr><th></th><th colspan="3">Aegean/Aegeanizing Pottery Styles in Syria and Lebanon</th><th>Cyprus</th><th>Syria</th><th>Palestine</th><th>Aegean</th></tr>
<tr><td>Group 1</td><td colspan="3">Late Helladic IIIA2 and IIIB</td><td>LC IIB–IIC</td><td>LB</td><td>LB</td><td>LH IIIA2–IIIB</td></tr>
<tr><td>Group 2</td><td colspan="3">White-Painted Wheelmade III
(Simple Style or "Mycenaean" IIIB Late)
(Rude Style or Pastoral Style)</td><td>LC IIC</td><td>LB</td><td>LB</td><td>LH IIIB Late</td></tr>
<tr><td rowspan="2">Group 3</td><td rowspan="2">imported White-Painted Wheelmade III ("Mycenaean" IIIC:1b)</td><td rowspan="2">Group 4</td><td rowspan="2">locally produced White-Painted Wheelmade III ("Mycenaean" IIIC:1b)</td><td rowspan="2">LC IIIA</td><td rowspan="2">Iron IA</td><td rowspan="2">Iron IA</td><td>LH IIIC Early</td></tr>
<tr><td>LH IIIC Middle</td></tr>
<tr><td>Group 5</td><td colspan="3">Wavy-Line Style (Granary Style)
Proto White-Painted</td><td>LC IIIB</td><td>Iron IB</td><td>Iron IB</td><td>LH IIIC Late Submycenaean</td></tr>
</table>

To simplify the confusing multitude of different styles and terms, Kling proposes to call all matte-painted, wheelmade pottery of Mycenaean appearance, but not produced in the Aegean, White-Painted Wheelmade III (Kling 1991). The pottery is usually decorated in a dark matte paint on a light-colored surface. According to scientific analyses of the fabric, the ceramics found on Cyprus were produced on the island (Kling 1989, 91–94). This group includes matte-painted Levanto-Helladic Ware, Decorated LC IIIC, Rude or Pastoral Style, LH IIIB Late (or Simple Style), LH IIIB:2, LH IIIC (including "Mycenaean IIIC:1" and "IIIC:1b"), Submycenaean or Debased Levanto-Helladic, later renamed Decorated LC III Ware (Kling 1984b, 1991). White-Painted Wheelmade III occurs in Cyprus during LC IIC and IIIA.

In Cyprus, the earliest appearance of White-Painted Wheelmade III predates the assumed arrival of Mycenaean settlers on the island (Mountjoy 2001, 174). In Syria, these ceramic styles were found in the latest Late Bronze Age layer of Ugarit (Yon et al. 2000). Killebrew (1998b) dates these styles to the end of the thirteenth and the beginning of the twelfth century B.C.E.

Group 3 is defined by a group of mostly closed vessels, usually stirrup jars, and occasionally bowls (cf. fig. 3:2; for a summary, see Buchholz [1999, 425–29, 456–58). This style is part of Killebrew's Phase 2 (1998b, 162). They are characterized by their more elaborate decoration. This group is part of Kling's White-Painted Wheelmade III and is also called "Mycenaean IIIC:1." It was imported to Syria, Lebanon, and Palestine and follows chronologically the

"Derivative Mycenaean" styles. The petrographic analyses of sherds from Beth Shean and Tell Keisan point to a Cypriot origin of this style.[12] Sherratt and Mazar (in this volume) argue that the style is most closely related to Cypriot parallels. It should be, thus, discussed in the context of the Cypriot stratigraphic sequence and pottery development, and is less related to the Aegean Late Helladic sequence. Although this style has been labeled "LH IIIC Middle" (Warren and Hankey 1989, 164–67, cf. Mountjoy 1986, 168–69), according to Sherratt and Mazar (this volume) this is "essentially meaningless," since the style began earlier in Cyprus and reached the Aegean only later. The closest parallels were found in the later part of Enkomi Level IIIa and the earlier stages of Level IIIb. The vessels at Beth Shean are assigned to Stratum S4, dated by A. Mazar to the Palestinian Iron Age IA, that is, the first half of the Twentieth Dynasty (Setnakht to Ramesses VI, 1186–1136 B.C.E.; cf. Mazar 1985a).

Group 4 is marked by the appearance of a locally produced Aegean-inspired ceramic style in Syria and Palestine, often called "Mycenaean IIIC:1b" (Killebrew 1998b, 162–65). The repertoire of pottery forms includes mainly tablewares such as bell-shaped bowls or skyphoi; carinated bowls with strap-handles; shallow, straight-sided open bowls; bell-shaped kraters; kalathoi; and very small numbers of jugs, spouted jugs, and a few stirrup jars (Killebrew 1998b, pl. 16). Again, the term "Mycenaean IIIC:1b" is misleading. This style has its closest parallels in Cyprus, in Enkomi, Sinda, and Kition. It is not simply a foreign product of Mycenaean settlers, but shares features of fabric, technique, shape, and decoration with White-Painted Wheelmade III wares. Its origins, thus, seem to be Cypriot, a fact that blurs the chronological significance of its stylistic relationships with LH IIIC Middle in the Aegean. Since this style imitates the style of Group 3, its beginnings should be at least overlapping with that group.

Thus, "Mycenaean IIIC:1" (Group 3) and "Mycenaean IIIC:1b" (Group 4) are distinguished in Syria, Lebanon, and Palestine mainly by their place of production. Chronologically they overlap and are, at least to some extent, contemporary. "Mycenaean IIIC:1" seems to have been produced in Cyprus, while "IIIC:1b" as found in Palestine, Lebanon, and Syria was locally made.[13] With the "Derivative," "Mycenaean IIIC:1," and finally the "IIIC:1b" styles the produc-

12. Beth Shean: For the petrographic analysis, see A. Cohen-Weinberger, this volume; for the style, see Sherratt and Mazar, this volume. The vessel from Tell Keisan was found in Stratum 13 (Balensi 1981; Burdajewicz 1994, pl. 13:18, cf. Gilboa 2001a, 227).

13. For more literature, see Finkelstein 1995, 224–25, cf. Killebrew 1998b, 162, but note that the provenience of the Mycenaean IIIC:1 pottery in Palestine was not always identified with certainty. Leonard discussed the terminology of Mycenaean IIIC:1b briefly, noting the confusion in the use of this term. For a detailed discussion, see Kling 1989.

tion of Aegean-style pottery shifted eastwards from Greece to Cyprus and finally to Syria-Palestine.[14] For Cyprus, Kling defined both Groups 3 and 4 as White-Painted Wheelmade III, spanning LC IIC and IIIA periods, encompassing all matte-painted wheelmade pottery in use on the island at this time (Kling 1991).

Group 5 is characterized by styles such as "Granary Style" and "Proto-White Painted Style." "Granary Style" is employed on closed and open vessels. In addition to linear decoration, there are wavy lines and monochrome-covered vessels, sometimes with reserved lines and dotted rims. Aegean vessels of this style appear in the LH IIIC Middle, IIIC Late, and in the Submycenaean phase (Mountjoy 1986, 156, figs. 230–31, 254, 268–69). In Cyprus locally produced "Granary Style" appears in Enkomi first at the end of Level IIIA. The style is, however, most characteristic for Enkomi Levels IIIB and IIIC (Kling 1989, 107–8, 173–74).

Table 2: The stratigraphy of Enkomi in the discussion of Kling 1989 and Iacovou 1988.

Period	Kling		Iacovou	
LC IIIA	Enkomi IIIA	White Painted Wheelmade III	Enkomi IIIA	White-Painted Wheelmade III
			Enkomi IIIB–IIIC	Granary-style (Wavy-line style)
LC IIIB	Enkomi IIIB–IIIC and Sanctuary of the Ingot God, floors I–IV	Granary style (Wavy-line style) and Proto White-Painted	Enkomi Sanctuary of the Ingot God, floors I–III	Proto White-Painted

Was Proto-White Painted-style contemporary with "Granary Style," or did Proto-White Painted replace it? While Kling (1989, 174 n. 2) assumes that both were contemporary, Iacovou argues for a chronological sequence (Iacovou 1988, 1991). Their different views are summarized in table 2 (Vanschoonwinkel 1994). I consider Kling's arguments concerning the date of this style as more convincing than Iacovou's. Kling noted that Proto-White Painted may have had a special function in Cyprus, appearing mostly in religious or funerary contexts (Kling 1989, 174 n. 1, quoting Anita Yannai-James). She further stressed that "fragmentary examples of shapes and motifs which are typical of Proto-White Painted ware as known from other contexts have been found throughout the LC IIIB levels at Enkomi" (Kling 1989, 174).

14. Killebrew 1998b, 166 explicitly states that these styles are Cypriot, rather than Aegean. For similar views, see Galling 1970, 92 and Weippert 1988, 380, who explain the distribution of Mycenaean IIIC:1b pottery in Palestine as a migration of potters, rather than populations.

Absolute Chronology

There seem to be only two chronological "anchors" for the early appearance of LH IIIC pottery in the Iron Age I Levant. The first one is Ugarit (Singer 1999, 713–15, 730). A few "Mycenaean IIIC" sherds were found in the latest habitation level of Ugarit representing the earliest examples of LH IIIC.[15] One of the last historical persons mentioned in Ugaritic letters is Bay, a vizier of the Egyptian pharaoh Siptah (1194–1188 B.C.E.; RS 86.2230, cf. Freu 1988). This evidence leads Yon to conclude that Ugarit was destroyed between 1195 and 1185 B.C.E. (Yon 1992, 120). Independently, one can date the end of Ugarit with Dietrich and Loretz (2002) to 1192 or shortly after.[16]

The second chronological anchor is Stratum VI (S3) at Beth Shean that should date to ca. 1190–1130 B.C.E. according to the Egyptian evidence at the site. LH IIIC Middle vessels found in this level "seem to fit best in a horizon which covers the later part of Level IIIa at Enkomi and perhaps also the early stages of Level IIIb" (Sherratt and Mazar, this volume). These dates are in accordance with radiocarbon dates from Cyprus from the end of LC IIC to ca. 1200 B.C.E. (Manning et al. 2001).

Unlike Susan Sherratt, Penelope Mountjoy insists on the significance of comparisons between LH IIIC styles in the Levant with those of the Aegean. Comparing the stirrup jars from Beth Shean (cf. fig. 3.2) to those in the Aegean, she dates them to LH IIIC Early Phase 2. That is the phase immediately before LH IIIC Middle (Mountjoy 2007b, 587–90). This comparison would provide evidence for dating LH IIIC Early traditions as late as ca. 1150 B.C.E.

Except for these two cornerstones of Iron Age I chronology, there is no consensus as for the date of the evidence. It might be surprising that after a century of archaeology in the Levant, and despite a unique concentration of research in the area, there is yet a major debate about the chronology of the Iron Age. While much of the focus of this debate is on the tenth century B.C.E.,[17] the controversy includes a Low Chronology option for the Philistine material culture as well (Fin-

15. LH IIIC appears in Ugarit in its earliest examples (Yon et al. 2000, 15–18; Courtois 1973; Courtois and Courtois 1987, 210ff., fig. 66a.b; Monchambert 1996; cf. Singer 1999, 730 n. 429; Buchholz 1999, 457–58, Abb. 96a).

16. Even if one does not agree with all the interpretations of Dietrich and Loretz, it is probable that the city witnessed the solar eclipse of January 21, 1192 B.C.E. The destruction of Ugarit would thus be later than this date. For an even later date at 1175 B.C.E., see de Jong and van Soldt (1987–1988, 71).

17. For a comprehensive summary of the Iron Age IIA debate, see the contributions in Levy and Higham 2005.

kelstein 1995, 1998; Ussishkin 1985, 223). The current views are outlined in table 3. In the center of the debate stands the question, whether there was a phase without LH IIIC (="Mycenaean IIIC:1b" pottery=Philistine Monochrome). According to the "Middle Philistine Chronology" (Mazar 1985a; Singer 1985), LH IIIB pottery in Palestine was immediately replaced by LH IIIC after 1180 B.C.E. Contrary to this view, the fact that LH IIIC pottery does not appear in layers of important sites such as Lachish VI, Megiddo VIIA, Sera' IX, and, most of all, in Miqne VIII, is explained by followers of the "Low Philistine Chronology" with an intermediate chronological phase without such LH IIIC ceramics.

Level VIII at Miqne, ancient Ekron, is an important and significant stratum with four sub-phases, in which LH IIIB and IIIC pottery was absent. The level is embedded in an uninterrupted stratigraphic sequence from the Late Bronze Age through Iron Age I. Level VIII was followed by another one (Level VII), in which LH IIIC pottery appeared suddenly and in large quantities. In addition, this type of "Mycenaean" pottery was manufactured locally (Killebrew 1996b). Thus, a "Low Philistine Chronology" seems reasonable, which has important implications for the early Iron Age, re-dating the archaeological evidence some 50 years lower than the previous or traditional chronology (table 1; Killebrew 1998b).

Other scholars, however, have emphasized that there might be other non-chronological reasons for a phenomenon such as a missing ceramic style (Bunimovitz and Faust 2001). Indeed, the "Low Philistine Chronology" also creates some additional problems. It dates the first appearance of "Mycenaean IIIC" at 1130 B.C.E., much later than the eighth year of Ramesses III (1177 B.C.E.). What then characterizes the initial settlement of the Philistines in the archaeological record of Palestine? The Low Chronology has also difficulties to explain the occurrence of LH IIIC Middle ceramics in the well-dated Stratum VI (S3) at Beth Shean that should date to ca. 1190–1133 B.C.E. (cf. Finkelstein 1996b, 172–80; Sherratt and Mazar, this volume).

There is also a debate over a Low Chronology framework at the end of the Palestinian Iron Age I. The debate was started by Israel Finkelstein, who wants to lower the Palestinian Iron Age IIA some 80 years. Amihai Mazar, Finkelstein's opponent in this debate, has in the meantime proposed a modified High Chronology that maintains a beginning of the Palestinian Iron Age in the early tenth century B.C.E., but dates the end of the period to the late-ninth century B.C.E. (table 3a).[18]

18. For a summary of the Iron Age I debate, see the contributions of Finkelstein and Mazar in Levy and Higham 2005 and the relevant contributions in Bietak and Czerny 2007.

Table 3a: Chronology of the early Iron Age in the northern Levant. All dates are B.C.E.

<table>
<tr><td>Palestine[1]</td><td colspan="2">Iron IA
1200–1140/1130</td><td colspan="3">Iron IB
1140/1130–980</td><td colspan="3">Iron IIA
980–840/830</td></tr>
<tr><td>Palestine[2]</td><td>1180–1130</td><td>1130–1080</td><td colspan="2">1080–980</td><td>980–900</td><td colspan="3">900–835</td></tr>
<tr><td>Syrian Periods[3]</td><td colspan="2">Iron IA
1190–1150/1125</td><td colspan="3">Iron IB
1150/1125–1050 1050–950</td><td colspan="2">Iron IC
950–850[4]</td><td>Iron IIA
850–800?</td></tr>
<tr><td>Cypriot Periods</td><td colspan="2">LC IIIA</td><td colspan="2">LC IIIB
(+ early CG IA?)</td><td>CG IA–
mid-CG I</td><td colspan="2">CG IB–CG II</td><td>CG IIIA</td></tr>
<tr><td>Megiddo</td><td colspan="2">VIIA</td><td colspan="2">gap? VIB</td><td>VIA</td><td>gap?</td><td>VB</td><td>VA–IVB</td></tr>
<tr><td>Low Chronology[5]</td><td colspan="2">Transitional Late Bronze–Iron Ages</td><td>Iron 1a</td><td>Iron 1a/b
975–</td><td>Iron 1b
–880</td><td colspan="2">Iron 1/2
880–850</td><td>Iron 2a
850–?</td></tr>
<tr><td>Dor[3]</td><td colspan="2">B-14?
G-Late 11?</td><td>B-13–12
G-10–9</td><td>B-11–10?
D2-12
G-8?</td><td>B-10?–9b
D2-11–9
G-7</td><td colspan="2">B-9a
D2-8c
G-6b</td><td>B-8
D2-8b
G-6b</td></tr>
<tr><td>Tell Keisan</td><td colspan="2">?–13</td><td>12–10</td><td>9c</td><td>9b–9a</td><td colspan="2">8c?</td><td>8b–8a</td></tr>
<tr><td>Tyre</td><td colspan="4">XIV</td><td>XIII-2–XIII-1</td><td colspan="2">XII–XI–X?</td><td>X?–IX</td></tr>
<tr><td>Sarepta II/Y</td><td colspan="4">Late G F</td><td>E</td><td colspan="2">gap?</td><td>D2</td></tr>
<tr><td>Ras Ibn Hani</td><td colspan="2">"Lower Floor"</td><td colspan="2">"Upper Floor"</td><td colspan="4"></td></tr>
<tr><td>Kition (Areas I & III)</td><td colspan="2">Floors IV–IIIA–III</td><td colspan="2">Floor II</td><td>Floor I</td><td colspan="3"></td></tr>
<tr><td>Enkomi (Kling)</td><td colspan="2">IIIA</td><td colspan="2">IIIB–C</td><td colspan="4"></td></tr>
<tr><td>Enkomi (Iacovou)</td><td colspan="2">IIIA–B-C</td><td colspan="6"></td></tr>
<tr><td>'Amuq</td><td>N Early</td><td colspan="2">N Middle</td><td colspan="2">N Late</td><td colspan="2">Oa</td><td>Ob</td></tr>
<tr><td>Tell Afis (Area E)[4]</td><td colspan="2">9b</td><td colspan="2">9a 8</td><td>7–6</td><td colspan="2">5–3</td><td>2–1</td></tr>
<tr><td>Hama</td><td colspan="2">←G1</td><td colspan="3">Cimetières I
F2</td><td colspan="2">Cimetières II
F1
Gate I</td><td>Cimetières III
E2
Buildings II–III</td></tr>
<tr><td>Tarsus</td><td colspan="2">Unstratified Pottery</td><td colspan="5">"Early Iron Age"</td><td>"Middle Iron"→</td></tr>
</table>

Table 3b: Chronology of relevant pottery in relation to the Syrian and Cypriot periods.

<table>
<tr><th>Syrian Periods</th><th>Iron IA
1190–1150/1125 B.C.E.</th><th colspan="2">Iron IB
1150/1125–1050</th><th>1050–950 B.C.E.</th><th>Iron IC
950–850 B.C.E.</th><th>Iron IIA
850–800 B.C.E.?</th></tr>
<tr><td>Cypriot Periods</td><td>LC IIIA</td><td colspan="2">LC IIIB
(+ early CG IA?)</td><td>CG IA–mid-CG I</td><td>CG IB–CG II</td><td>CG IIIA</td></tr>
<tr><td>Pottery
(Aegean)</td><td>Groups 3 & 4 (see text)
LH IIIC Early & Middle</td><td colspan="2">Group 5 (see text)
LH IIC Middle & Late
Submycenaean</td><td></td><td>Euboean Middle–
Late Proto-
Geometric (PG)</td><td>Euboean
Sub-PG I
Sub-PG II–III</td></tr>
<tr><td>Pottery
(Cypriot)</td><td>White-Painted Wheelmade III
(Mycenaean IIIC:1b)</td><td colspan="2">“Granary Style”
Proto-White Painted (end)–
first White Painted I</td><td>White Painted I</td><td>White Painted I–II</td><td>White Painted III
first Black-on-Red</td></tr>
<tr><td rowspan="4">Pottery
(Levant)</td><td colspan="4">Collared-Rim Jars in Palestine</td><td colspan="2"></td></tr>
<tr><td></td><td colspan="2">Wavy Band Pithoi</td><td colspan="3"></td></tr>
<tr><td rowspan="2"></td><td>Early Philistine
Bichrome</td><td>Philistine
Bichrome</td><td>Late Philistine
Bichrome?</td><td colspan="2"></td></tr>
<tr><td colspan="2">Containers Decorated with
Monochrome Red Circles</td><td>Phoenician
Monochrome &
early Phoenician
Bichrome</td><td>Phoenician
Bichrome
dominates</td><td>Phoenician
Bichrome &
first Red Slip in
Phoenicia</td></tr>
<tr><td></td><td></td><td></td><td></td><td colspan="2">‘Amuq Oa: first Red Slip hand
burnished</td><td>‘Amuq Ob:
Red Slip hand
burnished & first
wheel burnished</td></tr>
</table>

1. See A. Mazar 2008; Bruins, van der Plicht, and Mazar 2003.
2. See Finkelstein 1995; 1996; Finkelstein and Silberman 2001.
3. Mazzoni 2000; personal communication; Venturi 2000.
4. Mazzoni dates the end of Iron IC to c. 900 B.C.E. I propose dating it to c. 925 B.C.E.
5. Gilboa 2001; Gilboa and Sharon 2001; 2003; Sharon et al. 2005.

Another key contribution to this debate is the research of Gilboa, Sharon, and Boaretto. Their studies, too, imply that archaeological strata of the eleventh through ninth centuries B.C.E. have to be re-dated (Gilboa and Sharon 2001; Sharon et al. 2005). With their research, they hope to find a solution for the chronology debate using radiocarbon dating. They analyzed hundreds of samples from most relevant sites in Israel, applying charcoal characterization with Raman Spectroscopy and inter-comparisons between three laboratories and different measuring techniques.

The first results of their research support a Low Chronology approach at least for the eleventh–ninth centuries B.C.E. (Sharon et al. 2007). In addition, Gilboa analyzed the pottery typology of Iron Age I ceramics from northern Israel and Lebanon (Gilboa and Sharon 2001; 2003; Sharon et al. 2005). Their research thus provides a comprehensive study of the pottery, the stratigraphy, and the absolute dates of the coastal region in the southern Levant. The results are included in table 3a–b, where they are correlated to the Syrian Iron Age chronology as established by Mazzoni (2000; see also Venturi 1998; 2007 and Bonatz 1998).

Although emphasizing their differences, the leading protagonists, Mazar and Finkelstein, find themselves now within a margin of difference so small that one can actually talk now about one chronological system. Finkelstein and Mazar still disagree about some fifty years for the transition from Iron Age IB to Iron Age IIA. Mazar dates this transition into the first half of the tenth century B.C.E. (Mazar 2008), while Finkelstein dates it to the second half of that century (personal communication). Given the lack of precise resolution in ceramic chronology, the difference of fifty years between Mazar and Finkelstein can be integrated into one new scheme. In no other period would archaeologists argue so fiercely about fifty years and one may assume that they do it in this case only because this period is considered to be the time of David and Solomon.

The controversy is essentially over a transitional phase around 950 B.C.E. This transition from Iron Age I to IIA took place at some sites somewhat earlier and occurred at others later. Thus, the transition was a process of several decades before and after ca. 950 B.C.E. and it is impossible to pinpoint it more precisely with the techniques available today such as pottery chronology and radiocarbon dating (Sharon et al. 2007).

Except for the major changes in the dating of the eleventh and tenth centuries, there would be also some minor changes in the relative chronology. Tell Afis Area E, Stratum 9a contains a number of LC IIIA sherds. If these were not just survivors of the preceding level, that level may have started as early as late LC IIIA. And if the level at Afis (Area E, Stratum 7) indeed contains Proto-White Painted sherds (Mazzoni 2000, 35), a slightly earlier date for that level might be as well necessary. Afis Area E, Stratum 7, and thus also the phase Syrian Iron Age

IB, could have started in LC IIIB. If, however, Iacovou is right in denying any occurrences of Proto-White Painted at Afis at all, then those ceramics are probably best explained as White-Painted I—without any necessity to push Afis Area E, Stratum 7 closer to LC IIIB.

To summarize the chronological discussion, there are two main phases in the LH IIIC traditions of the early Iron Age in the northern Levant:

The first one is the Syrian Iron Age IA. The ceramics of this phase are labeled LH IIIC Early in the Aegean. In addition, some LH IIIC Middle already appeared in this first phase. This phase is contemporary with LC IIIA in Cyprus with the relevant ceramic styles called "Mycenaean IIIC:1b" or White-Painted Wheelmade III.

The second phase is the Syrian Iron Age IB characterized by Wavy-Line Style ("Granary Style") and Proto-White Painted. This phase is the equivalent of Iron Age IB in the southern Levant. In the Aegean these styles are identified as LH IIIC Middle and Late/Submycenaean. This phase is contemporary with LC IIIB in Cyprus.

The Distribution Pattern of the Pottery

The distribution of Aegeanizing LH IIIA2/IIIB and IIIC styles in Syria is illustrated here in figs. 12–14. Figure 12 shows the distribution of LH IIIB and IIIB/C transitional pottery. Figure 13 presents the distribution of ceramics of LH IIIC styles that have parallels in Cyprus LC IIIA, contemporary with the Syrian Iron Age IA in Syria. Figure 14 shows the distribution of pottery of LH IIIC styles with parallels in Cyprus LC IIIB, contemporary with the Iron Age IB in Syria.

Although future publications of material already excavated will doubtlessly change the picture, some major trends are emerging. In Cilicia and the ʿAmuq Plain, locally made imitations of LH IIIC ceramics of Iron Age I have a wider distribution than imported LH IIIB vessels of the Late Bronze Age. While LH IIIB ceramics were found mainly in political centers, elite tombs, or harbors (fig. 1), LH IIIC was found in Cilicia and the ʿAmuq Plain not only in larger settlements, but also in village sites and was observed during archaeological surface surveys, a fact that reflects the quantity of this material in contrast to the earlier LH IIIB that was mostly found in excavations. During the ʿAmuq Plain surveys by Braidwood, Yener, and others[19] the occurrence of Aegeanizing LH IIIC style pottery was the main criterion for assigning a site to Iron Age I.

19. For the surveys in the ʿAmuq Plain, see Braidwood 1937; Yener et al. 2000; 2005.

The earlier Aegeanizing styles of the Syrian Iron Age IA (LC IIIA) with locally made imitations of LH IIIC Early and Middle occur all over northern Syria. They appeared, however, in limited numbers in both large and small settlements. Only at Tell Kazel and Ras Ibn Hani, Aegeanizing pottery of the earlier Syrian Iron Age IA phase seems to occur in larger quantities.

Table 4: Typological groups discussed in this paper and their date. The numbers refer to the typological groups in the chapter.

Syrian Periods	Typological Groups in this Chapter		
	Bowls and Cups	Krater	Other forms
Syrian Iron Age IA	1–8	24–25, 28–29, 31	35–36
Syrian Iron Age IB	10–17, 20, 22, 26–27	30, 33, 34?	40–43

In a second phase, contemporary with the Syrian Iron Age IB (LC IIIB), Aegeanizing ceramics were found in larger quantities with a wide distribution that again includes villages as well as larger settlements. In this later phase the wavy line and reserved slip "Granary Style" of LH IIIC Middle has a remarkable concentration in northern Syria and the 'Amuq Plain. While the white dots on figs. 2 and 3 indicate sites where the distinction of the subphase (Syrian Iron IA or Iron IB) of the Aegeanizing LH IIIC pottery is uncertain, there is reason to believe that in most of these sites styles of the Syrian Iron Age IB phase were found.[20] Thus, during the Syrian Iron Age IB the sites of Cilicia and the 'Amuq Plain were apparently in close exchange with Cyprus. The occurrence of Aegeanizing pottery in inner northern Syria during the Syrian Iron Age IA and IB in sites such as Tell Afis, Tell Mardikh, 'Ayn Dara, etc. may have been directly influenced by the developments in the 'Amuq Plain.

An Interpretation of the Evidence

The appearance of Aegeanizing pottery styles in the Levant during the beginning of the Iron Age is often explained with migrating populations at the end of the Late Bronze Age and the beginning of the Iron Age. While this argument

20. This assumption is based on personal observations in the field, personal communications with the surveyors and excavators in the 'Amuq, and the appearance of "Hellado-Cilician" (Gjerstad 1934, 171–72, 174–75, 195) or "Submycenaean" (Seton-Williams 1954, 134–35) ceramics in surveys in Cilicia.

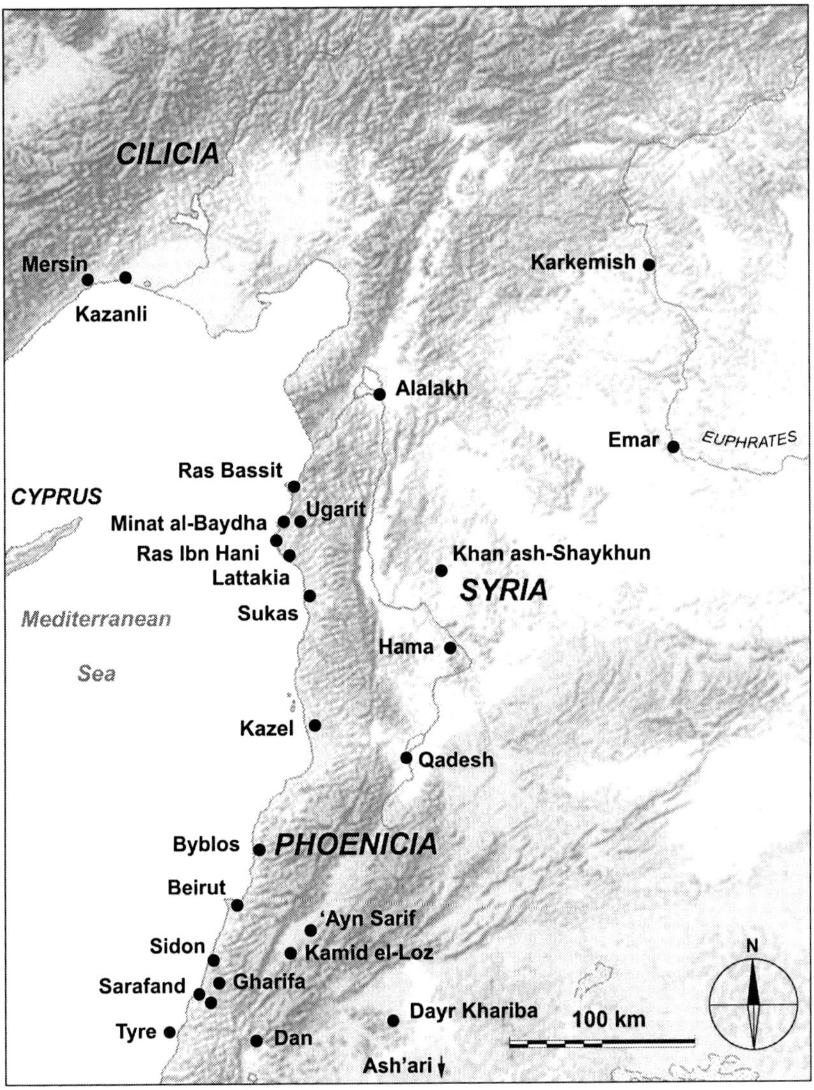

Fig. 12: Distribution of LH IIIB and LH IIIB/C transitional pottery in the northern Levant.

was popular among archaeologists working in the Levant, migration as a general explanatory concept was widely rejected by the New Archaeology (or Processual Archaeology) due to the inadequate methodological and theoretical basis of the traditional archaeology of the 1960s. Today there is a renewed interest in

Fig. 13: Distribution of Aegeanizing LH IIIC-style pottery in the northern Levant during the Syrian Iron Age IA. The white dots indicate sites with Aegeanizing pottery that cannot be assigned to one of the two subphases within the twelfth and early-eleventh centuries B.C.E.

Fig. 14: Distribution of Aegeanizing LH IIIC-style pottery in the northern Levant during the Syrian Iron Age IB. The white dots indicate sites with Aegeanizing pottery that cannot be assigned to one of the two subphases within the twelfth and early-eleventh centuries B.C.E.

migrations that reflects the methodological and theoretical discussions in the social sciences since the 1960s.[21]

The appearance of locally produced Aegean style pottery ("Mycenaean IIIC") in the Levant has been usually interpreted as evidence for migrations from the Aegean to the Levant. The history of research on "Mycenaean" or Aegean style pottery found in one area, Philistia, was recently summarized by Sharon (2001a) and Killebrew (2005). No such comprehensive critique exists for the locally made Aegean-style pottery found in early Iron Age contexts in Syria and Lebanon.[22] Some scholars interpret these finds, too, as evidence for migrations of Sea Peoples (Badre 1983; Lagarce and Lagarce 1988; for more literature, cf. Mazzoni 2000, 34 n. 11; cf. also Sharon 2001a, 576–79). Other scholars, however, are skeptical about the identification of Sea Peoples in Syria and Lebanon (i.e., Caubet 1992; Bonatz 1993, 125–26, 134–35; Venturi 1998, 135 and Mazzoni 2000, 34).

An adequate approach in this direction should be based on an accurate ethnic identification of who the Sea Peoples are (cf. Sharon 2001a, 597–600; Killebrew 2005, 197–230) and how the assumed migration processes are to be analyzed. Burmeister (2000), for example, proposes an explicit model for investigations of migrations, something that has not been attempted in the discussion of the Sea Peoples with the exception of Yasur-Landau (2007). For example, Burmeister examines the role of pioneers in migration processes that initiate social contacts at the forefront of a major migratory movement. He observed that first immigrants usually settle in their own centers and that the connection between those who have already immigrated and those who stayed at home often remained intact over a considerable period of time. A central function of the social network between the emigration and the immigration area is to facilitate the integration in the latter. A conspicuous consequence of these connections is the spatial concentration of migrants of the same origin in the new immigration area (Burmeister 2000, 548–49).

Burmeister also noted that migration processes are often accompanied in their individual phases by return migrations. Returning emigrants supply the home society with additional information and sometimes take an active part in the transformation of the society in the emigration area. Because the society usually does not emigrate as a whole, migrations are selective. The selection cri-

21. A summary on material culture and ethnicity during the Late Bronze and early Iron Age in the southern Levant was recently published by Killebrew (2005). Another book, written by Avraham Faust, on the ethnogenesis of Israel was published in 2006. On recent migrations studies in general, see Burmeister 2000 with extensive literature.

22. Venturi's recent study (2007) became available to me only after the manuscript of this paper was completed.

teria may change in the course of the migration process. If emigration does not occur abruptly but instead covers a longer period of time, it can be expected to have an archaeologically tangible effect on demographic structures (Burmeister 2000, 549–50). Migrations that depend primarily upon gender and age selectivity can result in noticeable demographic changes in the emigration area. Economic, social, and cultural transformations are likewise elicited by emigration (Burmeister 2000, 551).

These "processual" elements of Burmeister's model are complemented by considerations of the causes and reasons for migrations. Such more "post-processual" attempts to reconstruct motivations would include personal attitudes as well as causes perceived as existential threats. "Case studies show that migrations are usually not monocausal and cannot be attributed to single events" (Burmeister 2000, 550). The reasons for historical migrations were not restricted to simple scenarios of overpopulation and famine, as is often assumed for the migrations at the end of the Late Bronze Age. Observed historical migrations usually include a complex pattern of decision making that includes ideological and symbolical considerations. Adequate approaches to ethnicity and migrations only begin to take ground in the archaeology of the Levant. The assumed migration of the Sea Peoples appears to be a complex, long-term historical process that had a number of parallels in other periods such as the Phoenician and Greek colonization or the migrations during the Hellenistic period.

Summarizing the still limited archaeological evidence for Syria and Lebanon during the early Iron Age, it is hard to isolate clear evidence for a massive migration of the Sea Peoples in the region. It has been argued that, rather than relying on a single category of material culture such as Aegeanizing pottery, the researcher must employ a careful, multivariate approach to interpret the identity and the links between material data and past social processes (Dietler and Herbich 1998).

In the case of the Philistines in southwest Palestine, there seems to be evidence for a migration at the beginning of the Iron Age (as emphasized by Barako 2000). An increasing number of scholars interpret monochrome "Mycenaean IIIC:1b" pottery as evidence of the initial Philistine settlement during the twelfth century B.C.E. In their view, its later development, the bichrome "Philistine pottery," reflects a concentrated Philistine presence in southwest Palestine in the eleventh century B.C.E.[23] This would thus constitute a strong case for the pots

23. Contra Trude Dothan, who holds that only the bichrome "Philistine pottery" is an indicator for Philistine presence in Palestine (T. Dothan 1982, 94; T. Dothan and M. Dothan 1992, 29–42, 159–70; cf. Stager 1995). However, in recent years T. Dothan has revised her initial opinion and now considers "Myceanaean IIIC" pottery an indicator of early Philistine settlement

representing the presence of people. Indeed, Bunimovitz and Yasur-Landau have argued in favor of this case of ethnic identification (Bunimovitz and Yasur-Landau 1996). In addition to fine ware such as "Mycenaean IIIC" or the bichrome "Philistine pottery," which account for a significant percentage of the pottery assemblage in the early Iron Age southwest Palestine,[24] there are also one-handled cooking pots/jugs, which are very different from the contemporary local tradition of cooking pots (Killebrew 1999b). This interpretation is strengthened by other categories of material culture that appeared for the first time in southwest Palestine at the beginning of the Iron Age. Among these finds are hearths, unperforated cylindrical loom weights, and an increasing preference for pig and cattle in husbandry.[25] Killebrew was able to show that not only stylistic elements characterize the changes in the pottery, especially "Mycenaean IIIC:1b," but also technological innovations (Killebrew 1998b, 165). Still one can notice a certain lack in other categories of material evidence for the Philistines. For example, specific burials are missing and the mixed, "eclectic" style of the later post-"Mycenaean IIIC" bichrome "Philistine pottery" is actually evidence of a synthesis of Aegean and local "Canaanite" traditions (Stone 1995; Sharon 2001a).

In Syria and Lebanon there is less clear material evidence for ethnic migrations during the early Iron Age. Shortly after ca. 1200 B.C.E. matte-painted Aegeanizing pottery appears in Syria and Lebanon that is generally related to LH IIIC traditions in the Aegean and is especially close to contemporary pottery in Cyprus. The appearance of Aegeanizing pottery during the Syrian Iron Age IA is contemporary with LC IIIA in Cyprus, ca. 1190–1150/25 B.C.E. While some of this Aegeanizing pottery is imported, most probably from Cyprus, many of these vessels are locally produced in Lebanon, Syria, and Cilicia. It has been argued that Aegeanizing pottery styles in the Levant originated in Cyprus rather than in the Aegean. Thus, in their stylistic development they mainly parallel developments in Cyprus and the Dodecanese and to a lesser degree developments in the Aegean. If the Aegeanizing ceramics in Syria and Lebanon are more closely linked with Cyprus and less with the Aegean, then the chronological development of the Aegean LH IIIC is less relevant for the Levant and the terminology of "Late Helladic" styles is essentially misleading. The pottery in the Levant should rather

(e.g., see T. Dothan and Ben-Shlomo, this volume). Most scholars, however, interpret LH IIIC (Mycenaean IIIC:1b) as the first kind of pottery produced by the Philistines during their initial stage of settlement in Palestine (Mazar 1985b, 101–7; 1988, 252–53; Singer 1985, 112; Stager 1985, 62*; 1995, 334–35; cf. the summary at Killebrew 2005, 232).

24. There are pottery assemblages in Tel Miqne-Ekron with more than 50% of this style.

25. There are a number of studies on the specific character of Philistine material culture (Bunimovitz 1990; Karageorghis 1990b, 28; 1992, 80–81; Stager 1991, 33–37 n. 12; Hesse 1986).

be compared with the Cypriot pottery development and chronology during LC IIIA and IIIB (Kling 1989, 170; Sherratt 1981, 196–97; Sherratt 1994b; Killebrew 1998b, 165 and Sherratt and Mazar, this volume).

The majority of the Aegeanizing LH IIIC vessels in Syria and Lebanon are bowls and cups that are probably related to wine consumption. During the Syrian Iron Age IA Aegeanizing pottery appears nowhere in Syria in large numbers and never in the same quantities as in Enkomi for example. The only exceptions are Tell Kazel and Ras Ibn Hani, where there seem to be relatively many Aegeanizing vessels in this phase. Significant amounts of early Aegeanizing LH IIIC pottery, contemporary to LC IIIA, were found also at Tarsus and Kazanli in Cilicia. More recently—and still unpublished—there were finds of Aegeanizing ceramics of this phase at Misis-Mopsuhestia and at Dağılbaz Höyük near İskenderun.[26] Unfortunately, Ras Ibn Hani, Ras al-Bassit, and other sites at the Syrian coast remain unpublished and the true proportion and absolute numbers of Aegeanizing pottery are difficult to estimate.

This early phase of Aegeanizing Iron Age pottery in Syria and Lebanon is followed by a second one, during the Syrian Iron Age IB, contemporary with LC IIIB, ca. 1150/25–1050 B.C.E. This later phase is characterized by ceramic styles similar to the "Granary Style" of LH IIIC Middle (or Wavy-Line Style) and pottery that reflects Proto-White Painted. This phase of Aegeanizing pottery is mainly influenced by Cypriot LC IIIB ceramics. The majority of Wavy-Line Style in Syria and Lebanon was locally produced and occurred in the ʿAmuq Plain and northwest Syria in large numbers. Beyond this core area, Wavy-Line Style still appeared, but was found in smaller quantities in north Syria and southeast Anatolia (see, for example, Tille Höyük Levels I–III, Blaylock 1999, fig. 1:5–6). Towards the end of Iron Age I, this group of Aegeanizing pottery is increasingly replaced by imported Cypro-Geometric I pottery.

Aegeanizing pottery forms a significant part of the early Iron Age pottery repertoire in Syria and Lebanon. It is, however, only one among other styles of painted ceramics in the region during this period (Bonatz 1993, 138–40; Venturi 1998; Mazzoni 2000, 33, 35–36). Is this ceramic evidence sufficient to assume a settlement of Sea Peoples in Syria and Lebanon? Does this evidence support the traditional explanatory paradigm that identified the Sea Peoples as the protagonists and decisive factor for the changes from the Late Bronze Age to the Iron Age at the Levantine coast? Bonatz has stressed the local pottery traditions of cooking pots and transport jars along the Syrian coast during the early Iron

26. Misis (Mopsuhestia) is investigated by G. Salmeri and A. L. D'Agata as part of their Cilicia Survey Project. The Bay of İskenderun is currently studied in an archaeological survey directed by A. E. Killebrew, M.-H. Gates, and G. Lehmann.

Age (1993, 135). In the ʿAmuq Plain and the Afrin Valley there were particular cooking pots with a shell temper that distinguish them from the preceding Late Bronze Age (Swift 1958, 65; Stone and Zimansky 1999, 65, figs. 70:200, 203, 74:8), but the cooking pot forms are clearly a continuation of earlier Late Bronze ones. Aegeanizing cooking jars were recently found in Iron Age I levels at Tell Ta'yinat (Timothy Harrison, personal communication). As pointed out above, such one-handled cooking pots/jugs have been interpreted as evidence for immigrations in the case of the Philistines, introducing new habits of food preparation in the Levant (Killebrew 1999b; Barako 2001, fig. 15).

The domestic architecture follows the Late Bronze Age tradition, its continuation in the Iron Age is well attested along the coast (Bonatz 1993, 125–28). Cult architecture for example was built in the Syrian tradition of a rectangular temple-plan that was longitudinally divided into three parts. Built hearths have not been found in Syria so far, but they appear in Cyprus and Tarsus (Bonatz 1993, 131–34; Barako 2001, fig. 12).

Another important item that plays a role in the distinction of Philistine material culture in Palestine is the cylindrical unperforated loom weight. These loom weights occur during the early Iron Age in Cyprus, the Aegean, and in Israel/Palestine (Bunimovitz 1998, 105; Barako 2001, fig. 14). Such loom weights appeared now in Iron Age I levels at Tell Ta'yinat (Timothy Harrison, personal communication). They were also found in Iron Age II contexts at ʿAyn Dara, Levels XVII–I (Stone and Zimansky 1999, fig. 92:8–13) and in Çatal Höyük Area VI, Level 5b, Room T8-1 in the ʿAmuq Plain (Haines 1971, pl. 16b).

Although at Tell Afis some increase of cattle and pig in the faunal remains is reported (Wachter-Sarkady 1998, 434), there are no significant new trends in husbandry following the transition from Late Bronze Age to Iron Age. However, the available material is very limited (Wachter-Sarkady 1998; Frey and Marean 1999) and the faunal remains of key sites along the Syrian coast such as Ras Ibn Hani are unpublished.

There is an increasing use of cremation burials in Syria and Lebanon, but this type of burial appears first in the Late Bronze Age. It is not clear whether it is associated with Sea Peoples (Bienkowski 1982; Mazzoni 2000, 34–35 with further references).

Thus, it must be noted that most of the artifacts that serve as evidence for the immigration of the Philistines into Palestine appear also in north Syria, especially in the ʿAmuq Plain, during the Iron Age I.

Additional artifacts that link early Iron Age Syria with the Mediterranean seem to be closely connected to industries and crafts in Cyprus and are not products of the post-palatial and rather underdeveloped Aegean (fig. 15).

Two recent studies analyzed the typology, chronology, and distribution of fibulae in the ancient Near East (Pedde 2000) and on Cyprus (Giesen 2001). Mapping the occurrences of fibulae during these periods in the Levant, they seem to appear in some kind of "halo" around Cyprus (cf. Buchholz 1999, 513–14).

Another phenomenon is the occurrence of iron in the Levant during the twelfth and eleventh centuries B.C.E. These finds were listed by Sherratt (1994a).[27] Again, the finds cluster around Cyprus. Note that some of the finds point to a connection with Anatolia in the north, i.e., Lidar Höyük, while there are only few finds recorded in Phoenicia.

The Cypriot bronze stands of the late-thirteenth through early-eleventh centuries B.C.E. are another specialized metallurgical innovation of the island with a wide distribution in the Mediterranean (Papasavvas 2001).

These finds that are linked especially with Cyprus are, in my view, an indication of the importance of Cyprus and the continuation of sea trade after the end of the Late Bronze Age (contra Barako 2000; cf. Bell 2005, 40–41). The distributions in fig. 15 illustrate the close connection between Cyprus and the coastal plains of Cilicia and the 'Amuq. Between the late-thirteenth and early-eleventh centuries B.C.E., the island must have been a center of Levantine trade and industry. According to Papasavvas, there was an explicit Cypriot commercial strategy to create exports such as pottery, and bronze and "utilitarian" iron objects, using specialized technologies that filled vacuums caused by various disruptions in previously established material culture practices (Papasavvas 2001; cf. Tsipopoulou 2003, 86).

Were the Aegeanizing pottery styles of the Syrian Iron Age IA–B in Syria part of such an exchange? The diversity of Aegeanizing ceramic styles of this period and its distribution pattern can be interpreted in that way. Susan Sherratt has shown that during the twelfth until the mid-eleveth century B.C.E. there was a decentralized and multidirectional exchange pattern in the Aegean and the Levant. Some of the contact centers that included Cyprus, the Dodecanese Islands, Crete, Naxos, and the Greek Mainland were in close direct contact, while others were probably connected only indirectly. The studies of S. Sherratt, Jung, and others have demonstrated that contact points in Syria were part of this multidirectional network (Sherratt 1994b; Jung 2005; Badre et al. 2005).[28]

I find it especially important that the link between Syrian and Cypriot pottery styles continued after ca. 1150/25 B.C.E. While in the land of the Philistines Cypriot stylistic influence on pottery production ceased after that time,

27. For a summary on early iron in the Levant, see also Buchholz 1999, 283–93.

28. For the role of Crete and other Aegean areas in this network, see Buchholz 1999, 731–32.

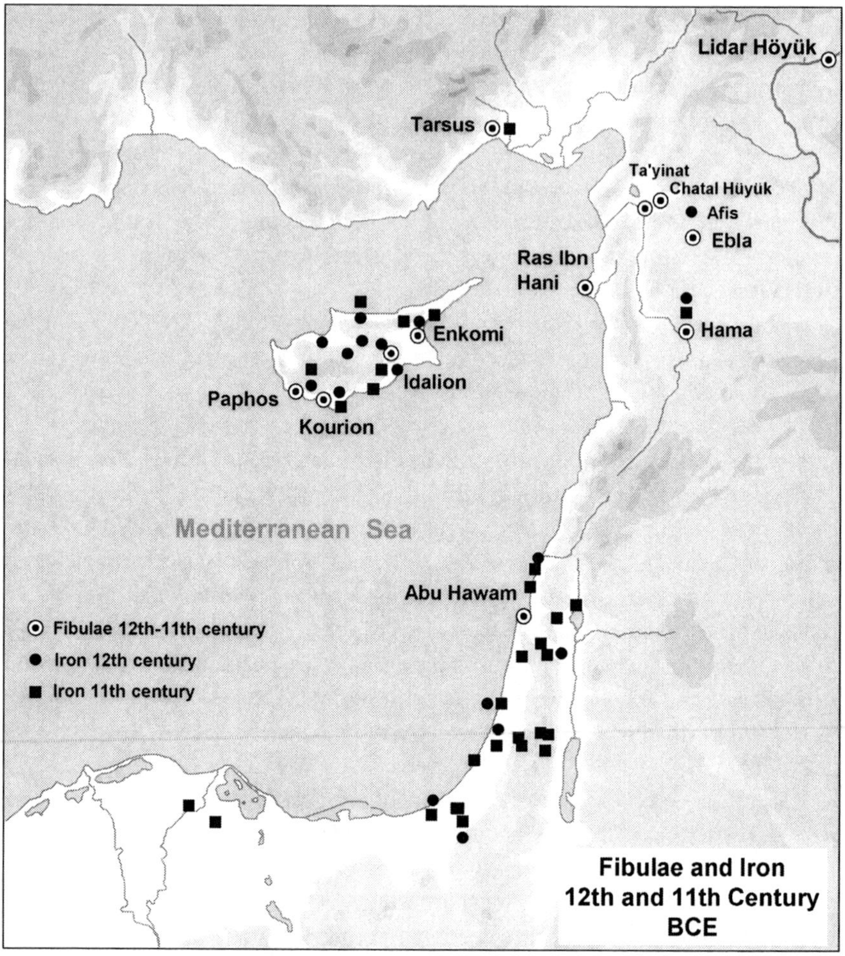

Fig. 15: Distribution of fibulae and iron objects in the Levant during the twelfth and eleventh centuries B.C.E. (from Sherratt 1994a).

the majority of Aegeanizing ceramics in Syria only began at this point with the "Granary Style" of LH IIIC Middle (or Wavy-Line Style) and pottery that reflects Proto-White Painted.[29] And even later, after the Syrian Iron Age IB, Cypriot ceramic styles did not come to an end with LH IIIC styles, but continued to influence Syria with imports and local imitations of Cypro-Geometric styles. This

29. Already Albright (1950, 166) has emphasized that "Granary Style" does not appear in Iron Age I sites in Palestine.

continuing influence of Aegeanizing LH IIIC styles on Syria in the late-twelfth and early-eleventh centuries B.C.E. can hardly be explained with the traditional model of Sea People migrations.

Around 1100 B.C.E., there are indications of a larger political integration of north Syria under the rule of King Taitas of Patasatini (Gonnella, Khayyata, and Kohlmeyer 2005, 92–93). The inscriptions and the monuments of this king are in Luwian hieroglyphs and his reliefs follow Neo-Hittite traditions. The center of the kingdom of Patasatini was apparently situated in the ʿAmuq Plain, where most of the Aegeanizing pottery styles of the eleventh century B.C.E. contemporary with King Taitas was found. Nothing in the epigraphical and artistical evidence of this king ruling in northern Syria indicates a direct Aegean influence.

During the 6th International Congress on the Archaeology of the Ancient Near East at Rome in May 2008, John David Hawkins announced that the country of King Taitas, Patasatini, should be read "Palasatini/Palastini." This new reading is based on the re-interpretation of one Luwian hieroglyphic sign and should be evaluated with great caution. Only further research will show whether there is indeed a connection with the biblical Philistines. Even if this is the case, one has probably to evaluate the meaning of "Palastini/Philistines," a task that might prove much more difficult than it seems at first glance.

It is also difficult to draw conclusive evidence for Greek and Aegean migrations during the late-second millennium from ancient Greek literature and mythology. Among the relevant legends is the Argive Kasos, son of Inachos and brother of Io. After his participation at the siege of Troy, he went to Cyprus and married Kitia-Amyke (cf. Unqi/ʾAmuq), the daughter of King Salaminos. Other traditions relate to Amphilochos and Mopsos as Greek founding fathers of Cilician cities. While some scholars interpret these traditions as reminiscences of Sea People migrations in the early-twelfth century B.C.E. (Lagarce and Lagarce 1988, 150–53), most historians that dedicated detailed discussions to the subject reject the possibility that these legends provide any reliable information in regards to Greek contacts with Cilicia and Syria during the late-second millennium.[30]

To summarize, the transition from the Late Bronze to the Iron Age does not mark a distinct break in the material culture of western Syria and Lebanon (Bonatz 1993, 154; Mazzoni 2000, 31–37). There is a general continuation of local developments. This continuation is apparent in the pottery, architecture, and burials. In the ʿAmuq Plain, discontinuity is discernible, but it is gradual. Most

30. In most studies, historians have rejected the idea that these Classical and Hellenistic narratives contain Bronze Age traditions (Salmeri 2004; Scheer 1993; Vanschoonwinkel 1990; Saliou 1999–2000; Blumenthal 1963, 82–83, 106; Laroche 1958, 275).

drastic is the destruction and abandonment of urban centers such as Ugarit and Alalakh, events that mark dramatic political, but not cultural, changes.

In general, "down sizing" characterizes the early-Iron Age in Syria. The political map of Syria changed, some of the larger regional states dissolved. With that some urban centers and their palace economy disappeared. At the Syrian coast small-scale regional political and economic systems—with towns rather than with cities—flourished during the twelfth and the early-eleventh centuries B.C.E. In northern Syria, political centers like Karkemish continued to exist and ruled apparently the region during the twelfth century B.C.E., eventually being replaced by rulers such as Taitas of Patasatini (Palasatini?). Finally, during the Syrian Iron Age IB, Syria witnessed a process of reurbanization (Mazzoni 2000, 35).

Little change characterizes the long-term developments of most of the material culture. But notable new elements of material culture did appear during the Iron Age I, among them decorated Aegeanizing ceramics, cooking jars, cylindrical loom weights, fibulae, etc. These finds, even when they were locally produced, link northern Syria with a decentralized and multi-directional exchange network that included Cilicia, Cyprus, the Dodecanese Islands, and the Aegean. Limited immigrations from the Mediterranean may have created pockets of Sea People settlements along the Cilician and Syrian coast. But these groups—from the Aegean, western Anatolia and/or Cyprus—were probably not the one major factor in the long-term changes—and continuities—during Iron I. They were only one phenomenon among others such as the continuation of Hittite traditions and the appearance of the Aramaean culture.

The Aegeanizing trends in the material culture of Iron Age I Syria appear to be less the result of a short-term invasion of the Sea Peoples at the beginning of the twelfth century B.C.E. and more of a witness for a continuing cultural exchange with Cyprus and the eastern Mediterranean during the twelfth and eleventh centuries B.C.E.

Chapter Twelve
On the Other "Sea Peoples"

*Michal Artzy**

Unlike the Philistines, who are well documented in both the archaeological and textual evidence, our understanding of the other groups usually associated with the "Sea Peoples" and their material culture has been elusive largely due to the patchy nature of this evidence.[1] The utilization of ancient written records intermingled with archaeological data is an obvious, yet problematic practice given the dearth and disjointed nature of data from the period and the varied circumstances, time, and geographical areas which tend to be pooled in any discussion (for a comprehensive summary of textual references to the Philistines and other "Sea Peoples," see Adams and Cohen, this volume). Although the Philistines appear prominently in the Hebrew Bible, the biblical narrative poses difficulties to the readers and interpreters. Why are the Sikila or Shardana not mentioned in biblical texts? Is it because they were not in direct contact with those who left us the scriptures (Machinist 2000, 66) or is it that by the seventh century B.C.E., during the time of the Deuteronomistic compilation, the biblical texts reflect a later reality (see e.g. Finkelstein 2002a, 133)?

One of the main sources for the "Sea Peoples" often cited by archaeologists is the Onomasticon of Amenope, a document beset by problems mainly associated with modern interpretations. It is dated to the eleventh century B.C.E. and lists the regions settled by the Philistines in the southern coastal plain. This same

---

* Head, Hatter Laboratory, Recanati Institute for Maritime Studies, University of Haifa, Haifa 31905, Israel. E-mail: martzy@research.haifa.ac.il.

1. See Artzy 2006c. See also J. Green's recent publications on the Late Bronze/Iron I cemetery at Tell es-Sa'idiyeh (2009; 2010) and C. Bell's publication on Late Bronze/Iron I Age trade relations in the northern Levant (2005). I have included a few general remarks, especially regarding Tell Abu Hawam and Tel Nami, based on current research being conducted on the ceramic assemblages from these sites, now in preparation.

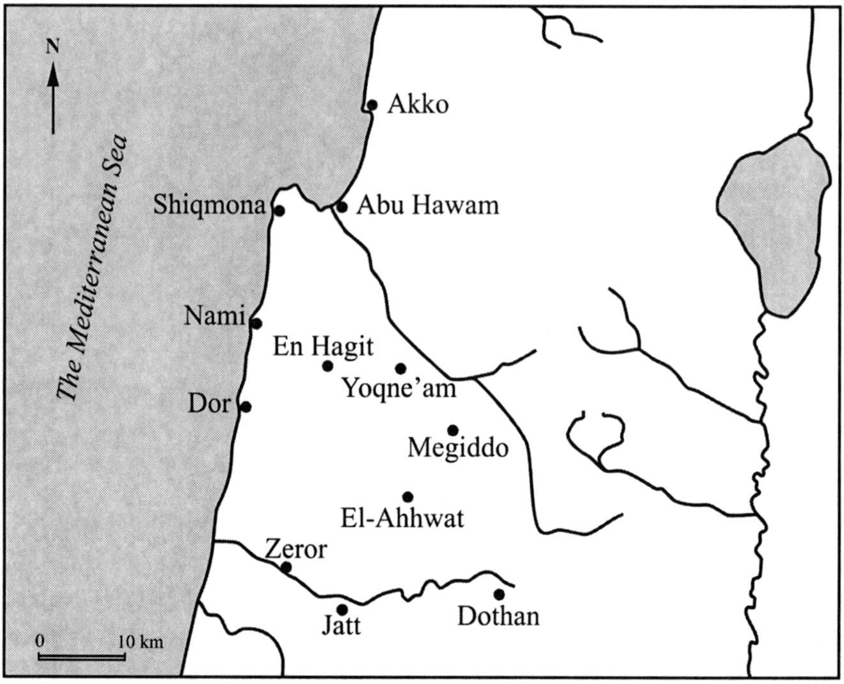

Fig. 1: General map including sites mentioned in this chapter.

document places the SKL/TKR at Dor (because of the mention of their leader in yet another document [Wenamun]) and its vicinity (Stern 2000a, 39–41), and the SRDN who settled further north (Gardiner 1947, I, 190–204). In the 1970s Moshe Dothan, following Albright, utilized the Onomasticon in arriving at the understandable conclusion that some decorated ceramics from Tel Akko, in Level 7 or thereabouts, were to be associated with the Shardana. Among other elements, Dothan used the decorated sherds from Akko to show the similarities and differences from other Mycenaean IIIC ceramics and concluded that the Shardana settled in the Akko area (M. Dothan 1989, 63–64). To the archaeological community this identification made sense because the rather large site of Tel Akko is situated near the sea and abounds with evidence of maritime activities.

Since then another interpretation of the Onomasticon has been put forth suggesting the Shardana were bordering the Sikila to the east at el-Ahhawat (Zertal 2002). Adam Zertal did not use the "pots and people" argument, but relied on, what he felt, were special architectural phenomena, which he compared to the Sardinian Nouraghi culture. He used the Onomasticon of Amenope just as Dothan did, despite the fact that the site is situated east or even southeast of Dor.

This proposition, citing the biblical narrative as evidence, was recently questioned methodically on archaeological grounds (Finkelstein 2002b). Even if we accept the similarities of the architectural elements, it is hard to imagine that the small outlying site on the edge of a hill was either the center of the Shardana (which Zertal identifies by its Semitic name, Haroshet ha-Goyim, as a possible explanation for the lack of a biblical name for the other Sea Peoples) or the city in which the Canaanites kept their chariots, as Zertal would have it. The maritime nature of the Shardana mentioned in other texts is not factored into Zertal's conclusion. As for the biblical reference, it is hard to accept the argument that Sisera, a commander of chariots, was Shardana, despite the fact that his name is similar to the name of the Sardinian city of Sassari (Zertal 2002, 60). I think more caution should be taken when making such an assertion, if only for the reason of linguistics.

The Shardana appear in various ancient texts earlier than the Philistines and are not limited to the period of Ramesses III (see also Adams and Cohen, this volume). They are mentioned in the Amarna letters and in Ugarit as they make their appearance as pirates in Egypt during the first years of Ramesses II's reign. In the Tanis Stele, published by Petrie (1889, pl. 2), a possible sea battle is mentioned. The Egyptologist Jean Yoyotte published the same stela, but found an additional section, which matched and added data to the Shardana question, among others: "Quant aux Shardanes au coeur rebelle … sur le vaisseaux combattants au milieu de la mer …" (Yoyotte 1949, 43). The Shardana come with their war boats and it seems from the text that they had appeared in previous times, but in this particular battle, according to Ramesses II, they were vanquished (Artzy 1987, 82–83).

Thus, the Shardana, if one can identify them in any way and trust the Onomasticon of Amenope, should be looked for in the northern part of modern Israel and if we accept that the Sikila settled in the Dor area, there are plenty of sites north of Dor, which could be considered such as: Tel Shiqmona, on the "nose" of the Carmel; Tell Abu Hawam and Tel Akko in the Bay of Haifa/Akko; and the slightly inland site of Tell Keisan. Ephraim Stern has equated a phase in Dor to the Sikila, which he in turn compares to ceramics found in a pit at Tell Keisan (Stratum 9c or 10) (Stern 2000a, 198–99; Humbert 1993, 864).

Thus, my emphasis is centered on two parameters namely that of time and geography. The period as mentioned is that of the thirteenth to the eleventh centuries (according to traditional chronological frameworks) in the area that extends from the Bay of Akko towards Megiddo and Beth Shean in the north and the Nahal Hadera, Jatt, Dothan Valley, and Wadi Farah at its southern edge (fig. 1). There are sites that are not included in this chapter, such as Dor (Sharon and Gilboa, this volume) and others, including 'En Hagit (Wolff 1998b) and Tel Zeror (Ohata 1970; Kochavi 1993), which are discussed elsewhere. These are all sites that I feel are part of that east–west connection in the period I am discussing. I wish to add that major and secondary routes were flexible in this area leading to changes over time. Events from beyond the sea, in Egypt, Syria, Anatolia, or Cyprus were often the catalysts for change and development.

The thirteenth to eleventh centuries B.C.E. are a lengthy period which saw the conclusion of the Bronze Age and the beginning of the Iron Age and its consolidation, a period of transition where geopolitical and possibly ecological changes amplified the economic ones. Social and economic networks were not necessarily dependent solely on geographical proximity. Regionalism in the small area of northern Israel, Lebanon, and Syria was fluid and maritime connections along with available routes should be considered. For instance, a coastal site such as Ras Ibn Hani, which shows close affinities to contemporary coastal sites in the southern Levant, would under normal circumstances greatly benefit the archaeological community in identifying the possible appearance of the Sea Peoples in the Syro-Lebanese coast. Unfortunately, the excavators of Ras Ibn Hani did not utilize data from sites in modern Israel (Lagarce and Lagarce 1988).

Attempts to decipher the changes and incorporate them into a coherent picture are not simple, during the last few years new data on the coastal sites fortunately supplied partial answers. The strength of these sites in the area under discussion was not only their position on the maritime route, but a combination of the maritime and terrestrial routes from the west to the east and vice-versa. The narrow (ca. 70–80 kilometers) coastal plain between the Mediterranean Sea and the Jordan River, especially the area from the Bay of Akko to the southern confines of the Carmel Ridge, was very tempting to the ancient settlers.

In particular, the coastal plain experienced changes during the period of transition, between the thirteenth and the eleventh centuries B.C.E., or as it is traditionally known, the Late Bronze (LB) IIB and Iron I. However, these changes were neither abrupt nor concurrent. A case of study for this are three sites—Tell Abu Hawam, Tel Akko, and Tel Nami—all located in the Carmel coastal area and to the north. These three show a very different history of settlement during this period. The earliest site, which was also settled for the longest, is Tel Akko, where written sources and archaeological finds indicate habitation from, at least, the MB IIA to the Hellenisitic period. Tell Abu Hawam appears to have been settled in LB IIA and gone through a break, at least, in its maritime activities until the second part of Iron I. Tel Nami was active in the MB IIA and the later part of LB IIB into the earliest part of the Iron I period (late thirteenth–early twelfth century B.C.E.), a period of time which should be renamed LB III.

Tell Abu Hawam was a major harbor/entrepôt during the fourteenth–thirteenth centuries B.C.E. It is a surprisingly small site, which was located directly at the outlet of the Qishon River or the confluence of the Qishon, the Salman, and the sea. It probably served concurrently and alongside the anchorage at Tel

Akko. Numerous varied ceramic imports were noted by Hamilton and Balensi, who conducted extensive excavations at the site (Hamilton 1934; 1935; Balensi 1985; Balensi, Herrera, and Artzy 1993). Mycenaean wares found in the various excavations of the site are often emphasized and these obscure the importance of imports from many other sources, at least in terms of ceramics. If we use ceramics as a guide, Tell Abu Hawam should be noted for the extensive presence of Cypriot ware already in the fourteenth century, but especially in the first half of the thirteenth century B.C.E. The quantities of clearly identifiable Cypriot imports far outweigh the Mycenaean ones. They include: White Slip II, Base Ring II (although there are a few pieces of Base Ring I), White Shave juglets, Red and White Lustrous Ware, and Plain White and Painted Wheelmade Wares (fig. 2). During the 2001 and 2002 excavations, the ratio of Cypriot imports to Mycenaean was larger than fifty to one! In what is now seen as a northern anchorage area, the Mycenaean imports to Tell Abu Hawam are Mycenaean IIIA2–B1, with no later Mycenaean IIIB of Cypriot manufacture, simple style, or Mycenaean IIIC, imported or locally produced examples, which is in direct contrast to Tel Akko. The Mycenaean wares at Tell Abu Hawam are reminiscent of those from Kamid el-Loz and Ayios Dhimitrios, as are many other ceramics. The abandonment of Maroni-Vournes, and parts of Ayios Dhimitrios (South, Russell, and Keswani 1989) seems to have coincided chronologically with the abandonment of the northern anchorages of Tell Abu Hawam sometime in the middle of the thirteenth century or slightly later, well before the assumed total destruction associated with the Sea Peoples. Tell Abu Hawam has additional imports, some from the western Anatolian coast, and these agree well in date with the Mycenaean imports, as does a cartouche of Ramesses II. The changes in life at the harbor of Tell Abu Hawam should not be viewed as necessarily caused by human catastrophe. Such changes could be attributed to geomorphological and geopolitical ones (Artzy 2003a; 2006c). These, besides the local ramifications, could well have been part of a wider occurrence related to events in Cyprus and the Syro-Lebanese coast. Could all these be attributed to an earthquake noticed in some parts of Ugarit (Callot 1994, 204–5)? A few years of interruption in the trade network would have caused havoc in the smaller peripheral and economically interdependent sites, such as Tell Abu Hawam.

Tel Nami presents a different picture, situated on or in the vicinity of the Me'arot River with an alternate route via the Carmel Ridge; it could have been used as a partial replacement for the major entrepôt of Tell Abu Hawam for contacts with Megiddo (Artzy 1998). No Mycenaean IIIA2/B1 sherds were found and surprisingly only a few were Mycenaean IIIB examples. The majority of the Aegean-type pieces are of the shapes associated with Mycenaean ware such as small stirrup jars painted with horizontal bands and decorated pixides. The

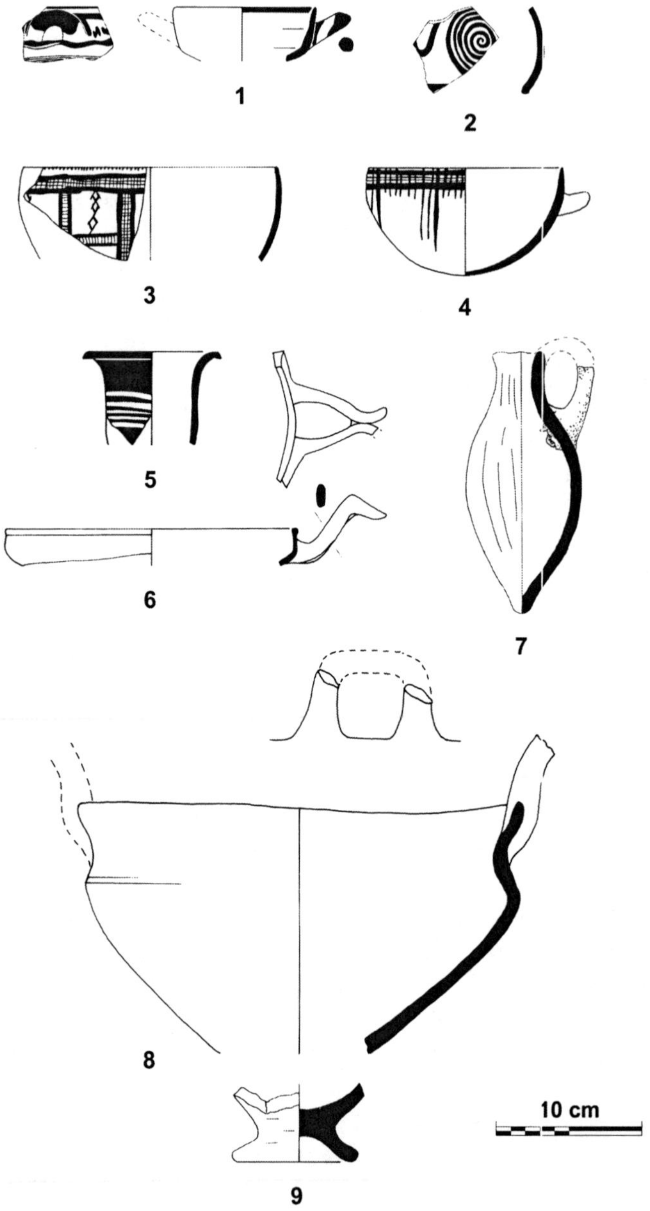

Fig. 2: Tell Abu Hawam Mycenaean, Cypriot, and coastal Anatolian imports (2001 excavations). **1–3)** Mycenaean imports; **4–7)** Cypriot imports; and **8–9)** coastal Anatolian imports found in the Tell Abu Hawam anchorage.

neutron activation analyses were inconclusive as to the provenance of the majority of these vessels. Yet, thin-section petrography carried out on the same vessels indicates a Cypriot origin, although further studies would have to be made. While the majority of the Mycenaean types are still being studied, there are imported Mycenaean type vessels which are clearly produced in Cyprus, of eastern Cypriot clay. They include stirrup jars and kraters.[2] There are other Cypriot imports, few Base Ring II jugs, White Slip II or even III bowls mostly of the latest imports, bearing only line decoration (Artzy 2001; 2006c), similar and likely imports from Enkomi (Pieridou in Dikaios 1969–1971, pl. 193:21, 195:37–38 as well as Todd and Pilides 2001, fig. 19). There are a few White Shaved juglets, some clearly of Cypriot origin and others, which share the problems associated with the stirrup jars mentioned above. Tel Nami seems to have undergone a period of destruction in the early years of the twelfth century B.C.E. It was not resettled after its destruction, thus suffering the same fate as Ugarit.

The largest of the sites is Tel Akko (M. Dothan 1976; 1983; 1985), which shares the same bay as Tell Abu Hawam. While the exact identification of the other two sites mentioned is problematic, Akko, situated on the Na'aman (or Belos River), was mentioned in Egyptian execration texts of the Middle Bronze Age as well as the fourteenth-century Amarna letters and has preserved its ancient name. It is highly fortified with a MB II rampart, the flat top of the rampart's summit appears to have been uninhabited during a majority of the Middle Bronze and LB I–IIa (Artzy 2006a). In the later part of the thirteenth and early-twelfth centuries, these areas were settled. Considered here are Area H, in which an altar with boat incisions was located; Area AB, in which metal recycling and possibly a limited industrial work area was noted; and Area PH (Zagorski 2004), on the southern edge, possibly near a renewed harbor on the Na'aman/Belos Estuary in which ceramics straddling the period mentioned above were found. The imported ceramics, Cypriot White Slip II, White Shave Ware, Base Ring Ware, and Plain White Wheelmade Ware, abound; Mycenaean IIIB and IIIC seem to be mostly of Cypriot manufacture (fig. 3). The ceramics mentioned by Dothan as Shardan at Tel Akko resemble Cypriot types of the period and were, most likely, produced in the general area of Akko (M. Dothan 1989). If there were imports, they were from Cyprus (D'Agata et al. 2005, 375). There is no sign so far of any destruction at the site of Tel Akko that could be assigned to the Sea Peoples. On the contrary, in Area PH, which was inhabited during the transitional period from the Late Bronze to the Iron Age, there is absolutely no sign of destruction (Zagorski 2004). The area is situated on the southern side of the tell near the river, where an anchorage was assumed to have been in the Late Bronze Age.

2. See Artzy and Zagorski 2012.

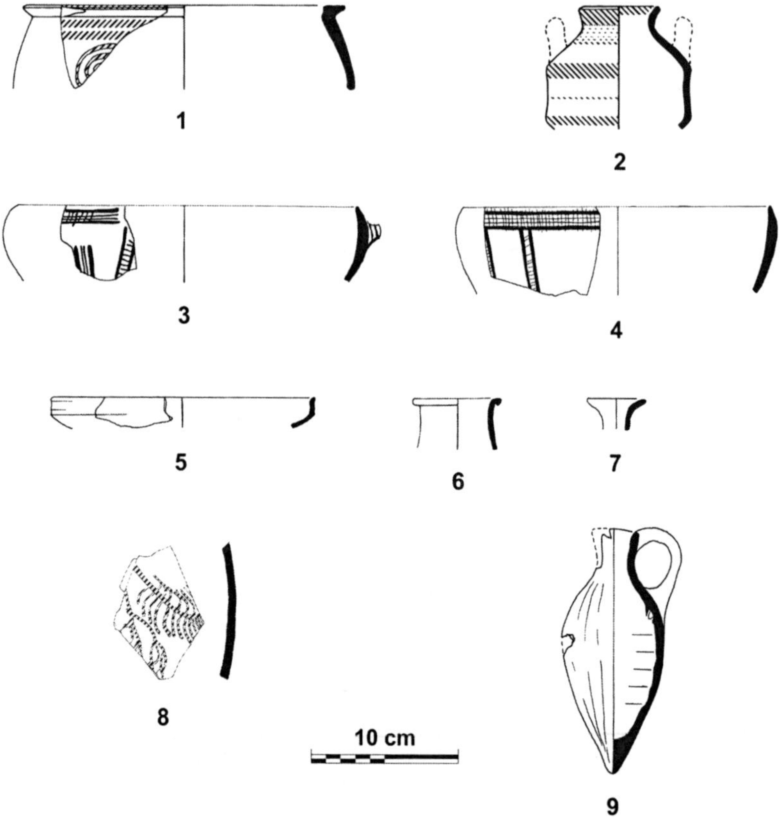

Fig. 3: Tel Akko Cypriot imports found in Area PH.

New elements had already appeared in the fourteenth century B.C.E., but were augmented during the thirteenth, especially its last years, and those of the early twelfth by the following:

1. Incised boats. This practice should probably be associated with "ex-voto" cultic practice. The boats on the altar from Tel Akko were published before (Artzy 1984; 1987) as was their association with these particular shapes found on the altar in Temple IV and the orthostat wall of Temple I in Kition-Kathari (Basch and Artzy 1985). There are also similarities with the incised boats on the cliffs above Me'arot River, barely four kilometers from the site of Tel Nami, whose inhabitants used the river's estuary (Artzy 1997; 1998). No such practice was noted in previous periods. Most of the boat incisions could well be placed in the period we are discussing, namely the thirteenth to the eleventh centuries B.C.E. (Artzy 2003c) and can be attributed to various milieus in the eastern Mediterranean (fig. 4).

2. Burial of adults in pithoi/storejars. The first example was found in Kefar Yehoshua and compared to Hittite or central Anatolian burial practices of double jar burial (Druks 1966) by quoting work done there (Mellink 1988, 102). Since that time, burials in pithoi were noted at Tell es-Sa'idiyeh (Tubb 1988a, 60–61; 1988b, 257; 1990, 29); Sahab, where several such burials were found as well (Ibrahim 1978, 122–23); Tel Nami (Artzy 1995, 26); Megiddo (Esse 1991, 88); and Tel Zeror (Ohata 1970, 70–71). There remains a question as to whether the deceased at Zeror were young adults or children because when the space in a single jar was not sufficient, such as in some of the collared-rim jars, a second jar was added (i.e., a burial that comprised two jars with rims and necks removed with the two vessels placed shoulder to shoulder and the deceased placed inside). The Anatolian equation is still viable although we would prefer not to accept the stipulation that these jars represent burials of Hittite refugees who brought the tradition from central Anatolia (Gonen 1992). Pithoi burials, and not necessarily double pithoi burials, of the period with which we are dealing are now known from several coastal sites in Turkey, namely, Panaztepe (Erkanal 1986, 253–61; Gates 1994, 259) and Beşik Tepe (Korfmann 1986, 311–29; Basedow 2000, 14–35). The fact that the burials at Zeror were usually not in double vessels may simply be for the reason that western Anatolian tradition jars were much larger than the ones in our area.

3. Increase in small-scale metal industrial installations along the coast. At Tell Abu Hawam, several pieces of tuyere were found in the excavations of what is assumed to have been an anchorage at the site during its Level V existence. At Tel Akko, a furnace was excavated by M. Dothan in Area AB (1981a, 111). On a work bench near this furnace two crucibles were found with remnants of bronze in them. The area with the furnace is comparable to that in which the boat altar was found (Artzy 2006a). Tel Nami had, towards the end of the thirteenth century, a budding recycling industry and the scrap metal and finished goods found in the confines of the site were very much part of the Levantine milieu with a clear connection to Cyprus. Some pieces of scrap metal found at Nami are closely related to Cypriot ones (Artzy 2000a; Papasavvas 2001, 234, 338). These installations were well suited for recycling of metals which became available to larger segments of society; they fit well with the small trade (i.e., 'sailor's trade'; Artzy 1985, 95; 2001, 113) and the socioeconomic cast (i.e., 'Nomads of the Sea'; Artzy 1997). Braudel referred to this as trade 'tramping,' a concept then adopted by others in their consideration, especially of Mediterranean trade (Braudel 1972, 103–8; Muhly, Wheeler, and Maddin 1977, 333).

Where the production of the finished metal objects, especially those that were not necessarily utilitarian in nature (e.g., stands, incense burners, jugs, and bowls), took place is difficult to pinpoint. The possibility that during the

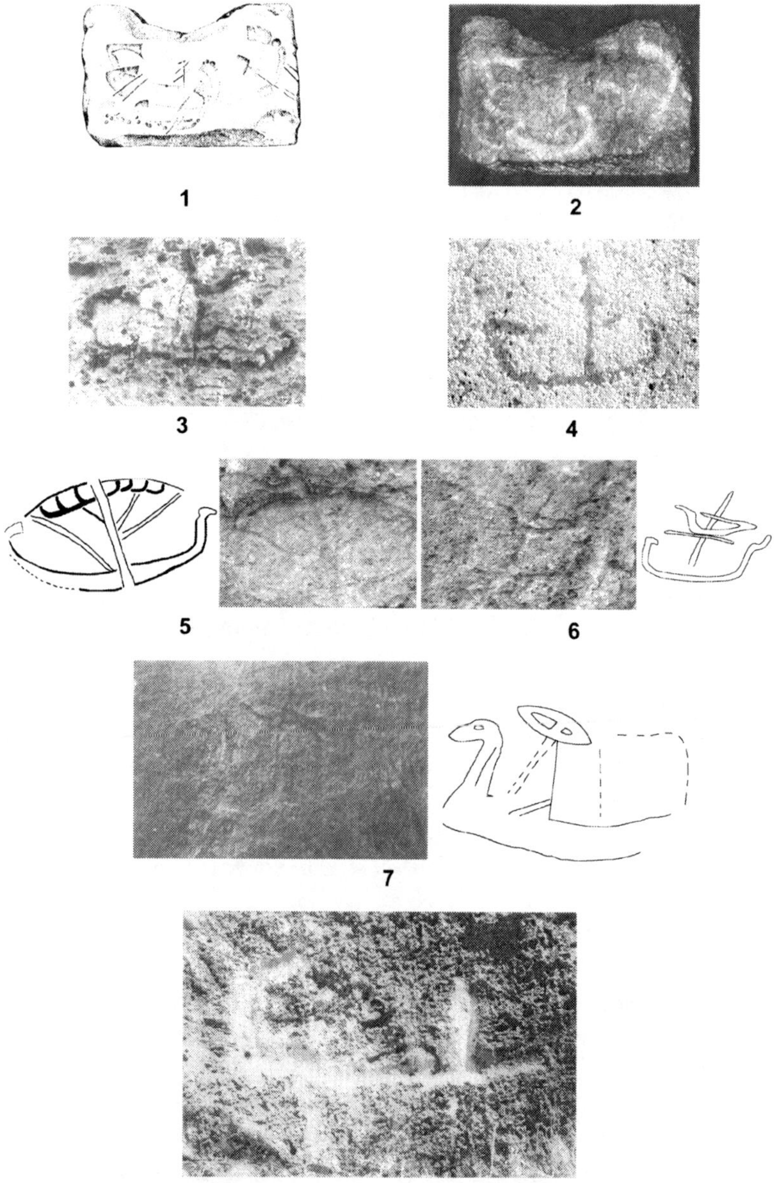

Fig. 4: Compilation of boats found in the Carmel Coast and Cyprus (not to scale). **1–2)** "Fan" boats from altar, Tel Akko; **3)** "Fan" boat from Nahal Me'arot; **4)** "Fan" boat from altar, Temple IV, Kition; **5)** "Birdhead" boat from Nahal Me'arot; **6)** "Birdhead" boat from Nahal Me'arot; **7)** "Birdhead" boat from Nahal Oren; **8)** "Aegean type" boat from Nahal Me'arot.

thirteenth century, especially its latter part, a metal smiths' *koiné* existed in the triangle of Cyprus and the Syro-Lebanese coast, should be entertained. We have already seen that the Cypriots and the coastal Canaanites were producing their own "Mycenaean wares" (Artzy 2005, 357–58). Given the abundance of raw materials in Cyprus and the technological abilities that existed there, one does not have to go either to the Aegean world or the Egyptian to find capable smiths. As for the distinction between Cyprus and the northern Levantine coast, both the geographical proximity (only a day's sail from Cyprus to Ras Shamra or Sidon and Tyre) and the active maritime trade kept the connections strong. The Egyptians, for instance, show "Canaanites" or "Syrians" bearing the ox-hide ingots and along with its large metal cargo of these ingots, the Uluburun wreck carried goods in "Canaanite" store jars, glass ingots, and incense alongside Cypriot ceramics (Pulak 1997, 233–63), now assumed to have originated in the Carmel Coast (Artzy 2006c). There is even an Ugaritic text (*KTU* 4.394) that states a ship bearing metal, probably copper, was lost at sea (Dietrich, Loretz, and Sanmartín 1995). While there are those who still feel that the Syrian states could not have conducted the trade since they were under the domination of the Egyptians and the Hittites (Wachsmann 1989, 35), the intricate relationship between the Egyptians and their coastal vassals, or their even closer neighbors, should be considered in lieu of the Amarna texts. We venture to suggest the possibility that the production of copper, which was done in two stages, was not necessarily carried out in the same place. The first was the smelting of bun ingots in the general area of the mines in Cyprus and at least some of these were shipped to other centers, such as the ones on the Syrian coast to be further remelted and refined. Some ox-hide ingots were also produced. Strangely, the actual ox-hide ingots were found east and west, but not in any quantity on Cyprus. A cargo of more than eighty bun ingots was found in the sea in the vicinity of Tel Nami and although we cannot date them conclusively, they might well be part of this particular trade (Galili and Sharvit 1997, 143–44). The Syrian coast would have thus contributed some of the wood for the energy needed for the ingots' production. Muhly suggested that Cypriot copper might have reached Egypt through Ugarit (1982, 254); could it have undergone some refining there? This, of course, does not mean that sites, such as Enkomi, Hala Sultan Teke, Kition, and others in Cyprus were not part of the production chain, whether in the final melting or the finished products.

It should be borne in mind, as Papasavvas has pointed out, that several expert craftsmen contributed their expertise in the production of the complex bronze items such as the stands (Papasavvas 2001, 262–63). For instance, he mentions seal cutters, who might have been involved in the production of the molds. Moorey, while dealing with the transfer of technology, suggests that could be applied to ceramics or other material goods: "... courts were central to technological developments" (2001, 4). He further states that exchange of skilled craftsmen was, in his opinion, a matter of diplomacy in times of peace.

Something did happen, especially following the weakening and eventual demise of Ras Shamra (Singer 1999), which was, no doubt, a major investor in the trade network. The change, however, in this area was not abrupt. Other sites, such as Enkomi and Hala Sultan Tekke on Cyprus, sites on the coast of Syria and especially Lebanon such as Byblos, Sidon, and Tyre, filled in the void caused by this change and while waiting for their opportunity, moved to procure the trade for themselves. Sidon, towards the end of the thirteenth century B.C.E., already equated itself with Ugarit as a state, rather than just a city (Arnaud 1992, 182); and although Tyre is identified only as a city, earlier, in the Amarna letters, Rib Addi of Byblos exults its wealth and equates Tyre's palace with Ugarit's (EA 89; Moran 1992, 162). Tyre and Sidon as well as Sarepta exhibit no evidence of destruction in their levels during the "Crisis Years" and neither do Akko or Dor. Nami ceased to exist and while there are signs that it was destroyed, there is nothing to indicate that the destruction was not carried out by its own neighbors, such as those to the south in Dor.

Nami's metal industry was based mainly on recycling, and finished objects found there, such as the incense burners, which resemble objects found at Ras Shamra (Schaeffer 1952, 65, fig. 18). It is at this juncture that the time parameter should be considered. During the late-thirteenth and early-twelfth centuries B.C.E., production of finished metal goods found in this area are usually associated with Cypriot metal production, even if the objects were locally produced. By the eleventh century, objects, while still bearing motifs associated with Cyprus and the *koiné*, were locally produced using Feinan copper (Artzy 2006b). Cypriot production of metals, as seen in the Palaepaphos Skales graves (Karageorghis 1983), differs from the Syro-Canaanite. Branching into at least two distinct production lines with lesser contact than in the previous period took place. The reason might well be that there were separate sources of the main component, copper. The Feinan region was producing copper again (Levy et al. 2002; Artzy 2006a). The situation in Cyprus during this period was discussed in the past (Iacovou 1998; this volume); suffice it to say that the metal production is well ensconced in the general trading milieu of the second millennium B.C.E. and especially the last part of it (Sherratt 1994a; 1998, 294–95; Sherratt and Sherratt 1991).

The example of Tell es-Sa'idyeh can convey the situation of archaeological data and arguable interpretations. Tubb (1988a), following Pritchard (1980), felt that there were elements of Aegean immigrants (Sea Peoples) buried in the graves at Tell es-Sa'idiyeh, a suggestion that is completely dismissed by Negbi, who thought that new ethnic elements were not needed to explain metal production in the general area (Negbi 1991; for a response, see Tubb 1995). Negbi argued that most of these areas show clear signs of Egyptian presence, and that there was no need to invoke the "Sea Peoples" as an explanation for the importance of metal work in the area, as claimed by Tubb (Negbi 1991; contra Tubb 1988b). Negbi saw the development as a part of the Canaanite tradition influenced by the Egyptians. I cannot see that the Egyptians in the second part of the thirteenth century played a major role in the coastal area of the Carmel Ridge (Tel Nami) and Bay of Akko (Tell Abu Hawam and Tel Akko), at least not as far as the metal industry is concerned. As stated previously, the material goods found in these sites point towards the Syro-Lebanese coast, the western coast of Anatolia, and especially Cyprus. Take the example of Tel Zeror, where a metal industry, whether recycling or primary production, seems to have flourished in the thirteenth–twelfth centuries (Kochavi 1965, 254–55). Although these installations have not yet been published fully, Kochavi notes that there is an abundance of Cypriot wares in the vicinity. Cypriot wares, such as Base Ring and White Slip, are very common in the later part of the thirteenth-century coast and hinterland, so we should be careful in blindly attributing these to Cypriot metal smiths alone, which certainly is tempting. I would argue that the northern coastal Canaanites, eventually identified as the Phoenicians, from Sidon, Tyre, or both, played an important role in the trade and especially that of metals and their finished products (Artzy 2006b).

The case of Beth Shean is interesting since it is assumed to be the center of Egyptian control over the area. Bienkowski (1989, 60) pointed out that there is negligible evidence for metal working at the site (Negbi 1991, 216–17). It would not be surprising should the present excavations at Tel Rehov, under the direction of A. Mazar, unearth evidence of metal production. According to the excavator at Tell Deir Alla, paraphernalia associated with metal production in the twelfth–eleventh centuries B.C.E. were found (Franken 1969, 21–22). At Tell es-Saʿidiyeh, again in the central Jordan Valley on the eastern side, a considerable number of bronze goods were found. In Megiddo, in Stratum VIa, usually dated to the second part of the eleventh century B.C.E., bronzes were found in the excavations by Schumacher, the University of Chicago (T. Harrison 2004), and the Yadin excavation in the 1960s (1970, 77–78). Some of the pieces in the hoard could well be compared to finds from Cyprus, especially Enkomi and Ugarit, although Ugarit was no longer in existence by that time to supply the actual artifacts.

In the last few years yet another hoard, this time from the site of Jatt, recently identified as Ginti-Kirmil of the Amarna texts (Goren, Finkelstein, and Naʾaman 2004, 256–59), was found. The hoard from an illicit excavation includes numerous pieces, which could well be compared to Cyprus and Ras Shamra, yet it should be dated later, probably to the eleventh century B.C.E. (Artzy 2006b). While, at first, we assumed that some of the pieces might have originated in Cyprus, possibly from robbed tombs (Artzy 2000c, 448), now that the hoard has been seen in its entirety, it seems more likely that most of it, if not all, was actually produced locally. Some of the pieces are much like ones from the Megiddo hoard, such as animal weights, including a monkey. Others, yet not all by any means, are similar to pieces found at Tell es-Saʿidiyeh. Incense burners of types found at Ugarit and Tel Nami were also found, yet when one compares them side-by-side, the differences between the two groups are obvious. Those from Jatt are similar to the ones found at Megiddo in Schumacher's excavation and from Beth Shean during the University of Pennsylvania excavations (fig. 5). A few ceramic pieces found alongside the metal hoard point towards Megiddo Stratum VIa and other Iron IB sites. Yet at the same time, among other things, an iron knife, a rod incense stand, and a possible scepter, similar to ones described by Kourou (1994, 217), resemble pieces that are usually associated with the Cypriot tradition (Artzy 2006b).

There was no shortage of copper sources in the area, especially in the Transjordan. The utilization of copper sources shifted gradually from Cyprus to the Feinan area. The available amount of copper in Transjordan increased and aroused the interest of those who had the experience and expertise. The availability of copper in this region is well documented (Hauptmann 1989; Levy et al. 2002). This measured transformation started in the thirteenth century or even a bit earlier and, as political situations dictated, rose to a heightened utilization of the copper mines in the twelfth and eleventh centuries B.C.E. Local production centers were not far behind. The origin of the tin is still a problem, as it is in previous periods. However, the expanded recycling in sites nearer to the mines might have supplied some of the necessary tin for the alloy.

Yes, there were changes even within this area, but they do not seem to be abrupt, at least according to our present knowledge. Some of the changes mentioned here have already been considered previously (Artzy 1994; 1997; 2003a; 2003b) and will be explored here only in a cursory manner. These include the metal recycling industry, burial practices, appearance of boat incisions on rocks and cultic areas, and new settlement on outlaying areas in the coast. Another topic previously dealt with is the pottery. A quick look at the ware of the time, which is referred to as Mycenaean, reveals that it transforms gradually. What started as imports, mostly from the Aegean, Mycenaean IIIA/B slowly gives way to Mycenaean IIIB, some of which originated in Cyprus. This ware, in turn, was replaced again gradually by locally (along the coast) produced Mycenaean IIIB2, which usually comprised small stirrup jars and small pilgrim flasks. It is only when the wares are coarse, contain large grits, and are undecorated that we assign them to be "local imitation," whatever that means. The changes of imports from Cyprus, those, which are known to be of Cypriot manufacture, are also gradual. They are noted not only in the appearance or cessation of certain wares, such as Lustrous

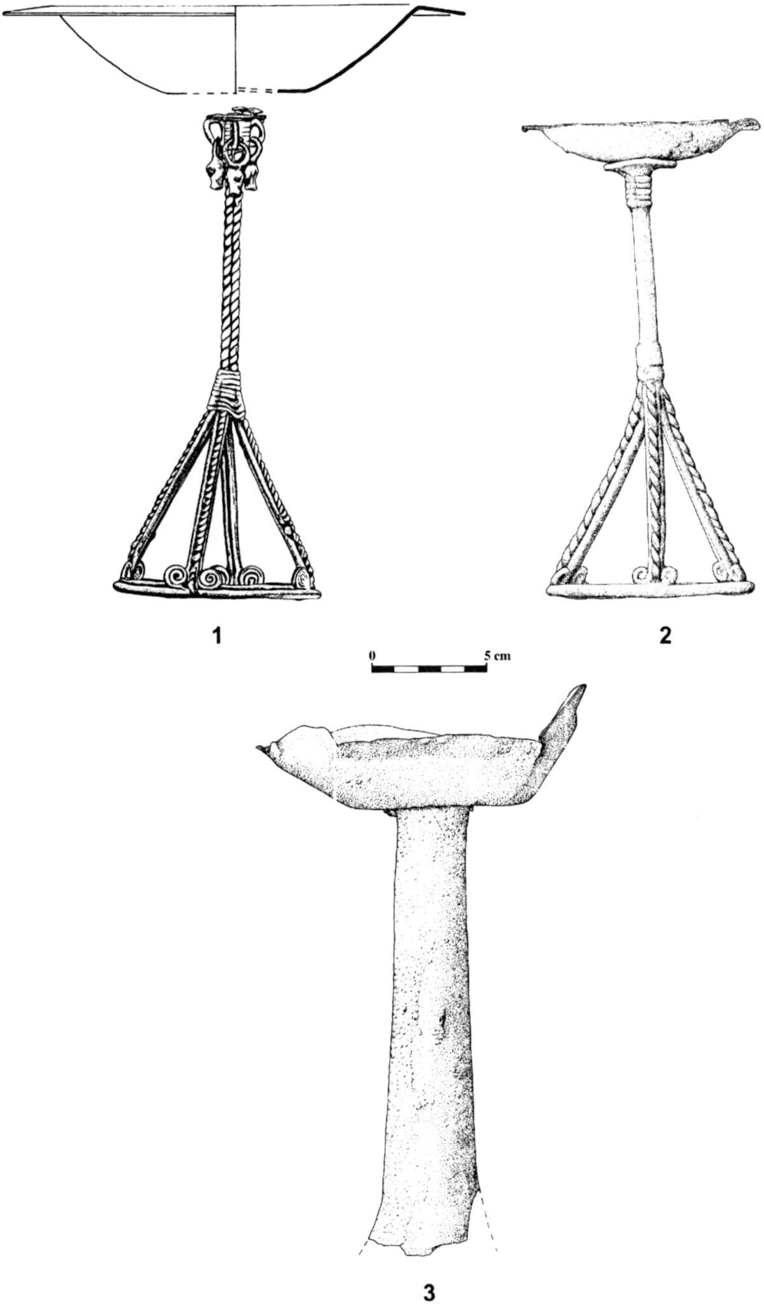

Fig. 5: Incense burners from **1)** Tel Nami and **2–3)** Tell Jatt.

Ware, but also in the changes of the manufacture of some other wares. White Slip II is a case in point. While most of the bowls are grouped as one family, there are clear differences, which should be noted, not only in a regional manner, but in time as well. For instance, the Tell Abu Hawam assemblage differs from that of Tel Nami and of Akko (Area PH), where the later type of White Slip Ware continues into the first years of the twelfth century B.C.E. So far, Akko has not supplied a good Iron I stratigraphy equaling that of Tell Keisan, in the plain just a few kilometers east of Akko, or Dor for that matter (Sharon and Gilboa, this volume).

The Carmel Coast anchorages, Tell Abu Hawam, Tel Akko, and Tel Nami, present a picture of the geopolitical situation of the period extending from the end of the fourteenth through the thirteenth into the early-twelfth centuries B.C.E. A study of the correlation with other sites in the Mediterranean, such as Troy, Kommos, Ras Shamra, Maroni, Ayios Dhimitrios, Enkomi, and Hala Sultan Teke, among others, could well contribute to better understanding the changes and continuity in this area. The coincidence of the major changes or even demise of sites such as Troy VIh, Maroni, Ayios Dhimitios, Kommos, and Tell Abu Hawam should be addressed, as is the case of the demise of Tel Nami and Ras Shamra, approximately forty to fifty years later. The attribution of these changes to migration alone does not take into account the gradual developments. The dearth of what is now named Philistine Monochrome or Bichrome Wares in this area cannot be attributed only to limited excavations. The period of the end of the thirteenth to eleventh centuries in the Carmel Coast and its economic hinterland is plainly different than that of Philistia and the two should not be lumped together haphazardly. Wherever and whenever the original impetus originated, by the twelfth and eleventh centuries differences, even in a small area such as ours, should be taken into consideration.

The people involved in the changes could have been from as far away as western Anatolia, the Aegean, or much closer, such as Cilicia, the Syro-Lebanese coast, and Cyprus. The thirteenth century saw them serving the palaces, acting as economic mercenaries, secondary and tertiary contractors, and intermediaries. They brought some of their own traditions to the anchorages and economic hinterland. They engaged in small trade, which benefited them as well. When the economic and geopolitical situations changed, they either reverted to marauding practices and the "Sea Peoples" surfaced; or as it now emerges, filled the commercial void in a constructive manner. The cultural and commercial debt to Cyprus and the Syro-Lebanese coast should not be underestimated. The northern coastal Canaanites, eventually grouped (by the archaeologists) as Phoenicians, are, no doubt, a major element among the "Other 'Sea Peoples.'"

Chapter Thirteen
The Origin and Date of Aegean-Type Pottery in the Levant

*Elizabeth French**

During the course of the 2001 workshop on the Philistines and other "Sea Peoples" and its many useful presentations and discussions, I came to the conclusion that, as I had previously suspected,[1] there was only one point in the pottery development of the twelfth century to which *on present evidence* we can assign first impetus for the phenomenon that we had met to study. It is self-evident that a phenomenon such as this is most unlikely to have occurred independently in several regions at approximately the same time; there must be an impetus.

The evidence from both Cilicia and Philistia is clear: certain Aegean-type wares are new and appear after a major disruption. Prior to this disruption in each area there had been longstanding sporadic contact with the Aegean and exotica were imported, mainly some commodities (scented oil and flavorings) in small closed vessels. A few sites served as emporia, some possibly with closer connections to the Aegean world.[2] After the disruption, the emphasis changed to a

* British School at Athens, 26 Millington Road, Cambridge CB3 9HP. E-mail: lisacamb@aol.com.

1. French 1998; 1999; now published in detail French 2007b with further definitions of terminology in French and Stockhammer 2009. This paper, which originated at the meeting in 2001, has been updated in spring 2009. The importance of the presence of those currently working in the Aegean at both this meeting (2001) and at Vienna (2003) cannot be overemphasized. Several recent studies have suffered from lack of appreciation of the latest Aegean results (e.g., Yakar 2006).

2. The situation at Ugarit is quite different and distinct not only in the range of dates but also in the type of material imported. This has recently been set out and discussed by two sets of scholars working independently (van Wijngaarden 1999b; Yon, Karageorghis, and Hirschfeld 2000).

wide range of settlement-type pottery on several sites with even the humblest and most remote possessing a rather hodgepodge drinking set.

From the Argolid on the mainland of Greece we now possess a series of stratified building levels covering a period of time, which is conventionally assigned to the first half or two-thirds of the twelfth century B.C.E. This consists of building strata from Mycenae[3] followed by a series of structures from Tiryns[4] where the actual material of the earlier phases excavated so far were only stray sherds.[5] This sequence makes clear not only the length of time covered by these phases, but also how careful we must be not to make assumptions from negative evidence. The recent work at Tiryns also makes clear the relationship of that site to the Levant as there are several imports and related items even in the relatively small area excavated.

It must be emphasized that this is evidence recently established and that none of it is published yet in more than outline. The character of the "Early" material at Mycenae is so simple and basic[6] that were it not stratified clearly above a heavily burnt destruction (which ends Phase VIII) and *in situ* on the floors of five buildings, it could not be identified stylistically as LH IIIC. It is only as a corpus of stratified pottery that the overall style can be distinguished. It will never be possible with certain shapes to assign close stylistic dates.

It is in the horizons immediately following the destruction of the "Early I" phase at Mycenae[7] that all the features which distinguish the first Aegean-type material can be found. That destruction, marked by quantities of pottery on the floors, seems to have been the result of an earthquake and was followed by a subsequent building phase (the "Tower" phase) possibly somewhat short-lived. These buildings were not destroyed but were allowed to decay (thus there is no pottery

3. French 1999; 2007b; 2011. It should be noted that my article (French 1969) has become misleading. In attempting to emphasize the new pre-"Granary Class" material, which we had identified, I listed all the earlier features that I could at that time isolate. It is now clear that these, though often present as sherds in one level, are not all contemporary. Most of these features belong to the second half of LH IIIC Early as defined by Mountjoy (1986).

4. Professor Joseph Maran at the Mycenaean Seminar in London on February 13, 2002. These excavations have now been studied in detail by Stockhammer (2008b).

5. Professor Maran, personal communication.

6. The whole effect is of "utility wares" perhaps suitable to a period of reconstruction after a debacle. The material includes much unpainted as always, but also a very high proportion of vessels with only linear decoration. If we are to make comparisons, the study and publication of these wares from sites in Cyprus and the Levant are quite essential.

7. See Mountjoy 1986, 133 for a diagram of comparative phases (though she has now adjusted the position of Lefkandi in this scheme). As can be seen, both the LH IIIC Early and LH IIIC Middle phases were long and comprise a very marked development of shape and pattern within them.

in situ) and are not overbuilt for many years. But at this juncture we have the evidence from the 2001 excavations at Tiryns where a series of five phases covers the whole of LH IIIC Middle from its earliest beginnings to its end. Phase 2 was destroyed by fire and there is plentiful pottery *in situ* on the floors.

It seems reasonable therefore to propose that the initial impetus of the new pottery found in the Levant comes following the earthquake disaster in the Argolid during LH IIIC Early (but well into the period as defined in Mountjoy 1986). Contacts were established; there was perhaps some emigration or loan of craftsmen as new settlements or trading posts were established. The contacts continued and allowed the development of the style in Philistia (and in some sites in Cilicia) into a full-blown "pleonastic" one. The imports at Tiryns (which, in my view, always took a lead in such affairs) show that the contacts were reciprocal.

Much has been made of the connections among the Levant, Cyprus, and the west Anatolian interface. In both the latter there are clear signs of Cretan influences. But in all—Crete, Cyprus, and the west Anatolian interface—there are as yet no well-dated or extensively stratified sites of the relevant periods. We do not know exactly where any of the evidence we have from them fits in to the overall picture. We cannot therefore be sure that these regions are the origin rather than receiver of the various features. In due time, we may be able to say more when sites with good sequences are found and excavated. In the meantime on the evidence that we have now, all that we may safely assert is that the impetus for the Aegean-type wares in Cilicia and Philistia cannot originate before well into the twelfth century B.C.E.

Chapter Fourteen
"Mycenaean IIIC" and Related Pottery from Beth Shean

*Susan Sherratt and Amihai Mazar**

A restorable stirrup jar and fragments of two other stirrup jars from Level VI of the University of Pennsylvania excavations at Beth Shean were published over thirty years ago by V. Hankey and have since continued to provide the only direct link between imported Late Helladic (LH) IIIC pottery and Egyptian historical chronology (Hankey 1966; 1967, 127–28; James 1966, fig. 49:4). In 1989 Warren and Hankey classified these sherds as "LH IIIC Middle" (Warren and Hankey 1989, 164–65). Since Beth Shean Level VI is dated to the Twentieth Dynasty (James 1966, 149–51; Ward in James 1966, 161–79), and probably continued until the end of the Egyptian domination of Canaan, perhaps during the reign of Ramesses V or VI, the implication of this was that "LH IIIC Middle" had begun by at least the beginning of the reign of Ramesses VI in 1143 B.C.E. The generally accepted date of ca. 1190 B.C.E. for the destruction of Ugarit, where the latest datable Mycenaean pottery of Aegean origin appears to be

* Department of Archaeology, University of Sheffield, Northgate House, West Street, Sheffield S1 4ET; e-mail: s.sherratt@sheffield.ac.uk; and Institute of Archaeology, Hebrew University of Jerusalem, Israel 91905; e-mail: mazar@huji.ac.il. A. Mazar assembled the data for this paper and described the stratigraphic and chronological context; he is also responsible for the descriptions of "MycIIIC" sherds nos. 11, 16, 18, 20, 22–27 and of the locally made sherds. S. Sherratt is responsible for the description of "MycIIIC" sherds nos. 1–10, 12–15, 17, 19, 21, 28, for the analysis of decorative motifs, and for the discussion of the parallels and chronological context. The drawings were prepared by M. Zeltser and the photographs by G. Laron.

LH IIIB (Yon 1992),[1] left a span of roughly a generation, in Warren and Hankey's view, from ca. 1185/1180 to ca. 1150 B.C.E. for "LH IIIC Early" (Warren and Hankey 1989, 165).

In this paper, we publish a group of additional sherds from the Hebrew University of Jerusalem excavations at Beth Shean, which show similarities in several respects to those from the Philadelphia excavations. As we argue below, the detailed context of this pottery has to be reconsidered in light of this new information. At the same time, consideration of its stylistic character suggests a probable origin for most, if not all, of this imported pottery, which in turn contributes to our ability to place it more precisely within a regional chronological sequence. In addition, we also publish four sherds of local Levantine manufacture, which may be classed in broad terms as "MycIIIC"-derivative or related pottery.

The Hebrew University of Jerusalem excavations at Beth Shean, conducted from 1990–1996 under the direction of A. Mazar, revealed an additional residential area of Level VI (Mazar 1993b; Panitz-Cohen and Mazar 2009; see fig. 1 for topography of the tell and excavation areas).[2] This area, Area S, adjoins the northeastern corner of the University Museum excavations (their Squares R–S–7–8). In this area the following stratigraphic sequence was defined:

Stratum S-1: Iron Age IIA (tenth–ninth centuries B.C.E.). Fragmentary public structures.

1. A tiny handful of what are termed "Myc. IIIC:1b" sherds from Ugarit, the precise contexts of which are unknown, seem likely to be either Cypriot products or locally made at Ugarit (Yon, Karageorghis, and Hirschfeld 2000, 64–65, 159–60, fig. 32, pl. 9). These include a few deep bowl fragments. Stylistically, these sherds are decorated in a LH IIIB manner (though some have been overenthusiastically reconstructed to look rather odd) and the designation "Myc. IIIC:1b" seems to derive primarily from the appearance of the fabric, which suggests that they are not Aegean imports, rather than from considerations of shape or decorative style. In Cypriot terms, none of them need be later than Late Cypriot (LC) IIC or the LC IIC/IIIA transition (cf., e.g., Yon, Karageorghis and Hirschfeld 2000, 65 no. 70, 159 no. 486, fig. 32:no. 486 with Karageorghis and Demas 1984, pl. XXXV:152/22–23 from Pyla-Kokkinokremos; and for other deep bowls from LC IIC or IIC/IIIA transitional contexts, see Sherratt 1990b with references). They thus have no significant implications for the relative chronology of the destruction of Ugarit, since the historical, text-derived date of ca. 1190 B.C.E. for the destruction fits very well with the date of ca. 1200 B.C.E. for the LC IIC/IIIA transition indicated by evidence from radiocarbon determinations from Cypriot sites (Manning et al. 2001).

2. These excavations were directed by A. Mazar on behalf of the Institute of Archaeology of The Hebrew University of Jerusalem and within the framework of the Beth-Shean Archaeological Expedition sponsored by the Israel Ministry of Tourism through the Israel Antiquities Authority and the Beth-Shean Tourist Development Authority.

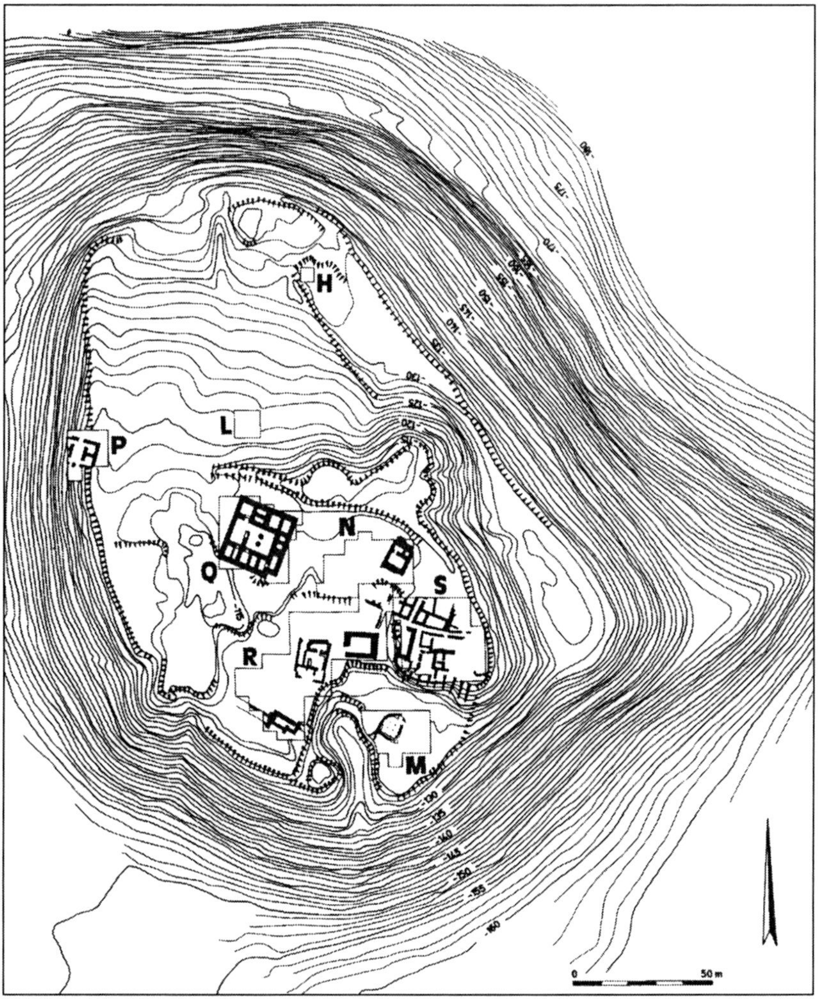

Fig. 1: Topographic map of Tel Beth Shean with the Hebrew University of Jerusalem excavation areas (1989–1996).

Stratum S-2:	Iron Age IB (eleventh century B.C.E.). Canaanite city, post-Egyptian period (probably equivalent to James [1966] Late Level VI and part of Lower Level V).
Stratum S-3a–b:	Iron Age IA (Egyptian Twentieth Dynasty, late phase).
Stratum S-4:	Iron Age IA (Egyptian Twentieth Dynasty, early phase).
Stratum S-5:	End of Late Bronze Age (late Nineteenth Dynasty).

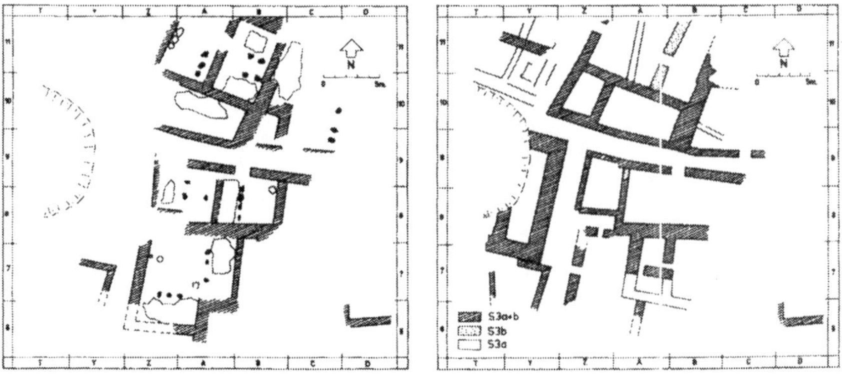

Fig. 2: Schematic plans of Strata S-4 and S-3 in Area S (twelfth century B.C.E.).

Strata S-3a, S-3b, and S-4 parallel Lower Level VI of the previous excavations.[3] Thus the new excavations have been able to define a more precise stratigraphy for this period.

The residential quarter included two streets at right angles to one another. The streets continued in use throughout Strata S-4 and S-3 with a build up of occupation debris more than 1 meter deep (see fig. 2 for schematic plans). The buildings bordering the streets were destroyed at the end of Stratum S-4 (two human skeletons from this level may hint at destruction by earthquake). The area was rebuilt with substantial architectural changes in Stratum S-3, two subphases of which were detected in several rooms. Stratum S-3 came to an end in a fierce fire, which caused a thick destruction layer in which many restorable pottery vessels and other objects were found. This violent destruction marks the end of the Egyptian presence at Beth Shean, probably during the reign of Ramesses IV, V, or VI.

The catalogue that follows includes at least seventeen recognizable sherds or groups of joining sherds and eight additional small body sherds, all except one from Area S. One sherd comes from nearby Area N. Table 1 summarizes the distribution of these sherds by vessel types and strata. All four Levantine "Myc. IIIC"-related fragments (not shown in table 1) were found in Stratum S-3, three of them in the earlier phase of this stratum (S-3b).[4]

3. Though Stratum S-4 could also be correlated with "Late Level VII," a stratigraphic phase defined by James and McGovern in a few small parts of the previously excavated areas, this seems less plausible. See James and McGovern 1993, plan 1.

4. Since the submission of this paper the following publications have appeared relating to the same material: Mazar 2007, a summary of the subject of this paper and chronological discus-

"MycIIIC" sherds from Tel Beth Shean (Group I)

Area S

Stirrup Jars

I:1. 187050/1–4 (Locus 10728b; Level 92.85 m; Stratum S-4) + 10703 (Locus 10711; Level 92.26 m; Stratum S-4) (figs. 3; 10.1)

Five sherds from part of the shoulder and body of a stirrup jar. Four joining fragments (187050/1–4) come from a layer of brick debris and ash under Stratum S-3b Surface 10728a in Square Y/7. Another fragment (consisting of two joining sherds) of this same vessel came from Locus 10711, a striated ashy floor surface in Square Z/7 that is part of the courtyard of Stratum S-4 Building SF. This locus is sealed by Locus 88714, a plaster floor of Stratum S-3b. The connection between these two baskets is surprising since they were found about seven meters apart in two different buildings with a street and two walls separating the two loci. However, both belong to the same stratigraphic horizon and the dispersion was most likely post-depositional.

Description. Buff clay, the same color throughout the section.[5] Exterior surface well smoothed.[6] Fairly glossy reddish-brown paint. Globular stirrup jar. Part of lower shoulder (including the root of one handle) and body down to just below maximum diameter. Preserved shoulder decoration of concentric semicircle group with solid center and dot fringe. A fringe of single semicircles with dot centers runs below the handle root at the bottom edge of the shoulder. Below this are three thin horizontal bands (the central one slightly thicker than the others), followed by a zone of alternating vertical lines and opposed solid triangles (or "double axe") motif, and another group of three thin–thick–thin bands. A further group of three thin–thick–thin bands surrounds the maximum diameter, the upper band fringed by a line of single semicircles with dot centers.

---

sion; Sherratt 2009, the final publication of the first part of this article (relating to the imported MycIIIC sherds); Zukerman 2009, the final publication of the second part of this article (relating to local "Aegean related pottery"); Mommsen, D'Agata, and Yasur-Landau 2009, a neutron activation analysis of 22 samples of the MycIIIC sherds published in the present paper (for a preliminary publication, see D'Agata et al. 2005). These studies show that most of the sherds are of vessels originating in Cyprus, and many of them can be located in eastern Cyprus, near or at Milia, not far from Enkomi.

5. For the Munsell Soil Chart readings of these and the other sherds, see table 2 (p. 368).

6. There is no slip. However, the surface may have been "self-slipped" or "wet-hand finished," in other words, dampened before or during smoothing (cf., e.g., Hodges 1964, 33).

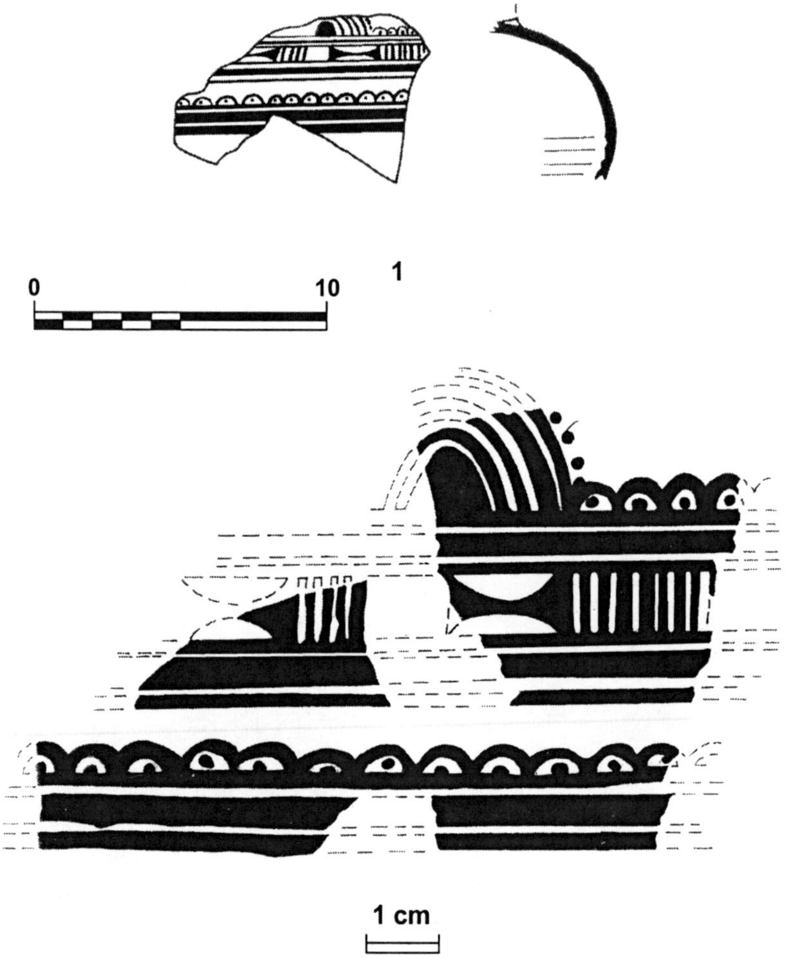

Fig. 3: Drawings of MycIIIC sherd no. I:1.

I:2. 187113 (Locus 18712, Stratum S-4, Square A–6, Level 92.62 m) + 187146 (Wall 78729, Stratum S-3b?, Square Y–7, Level 94.10 m) (figs. 4.2; 10.2; Cohen-Weinberger, appendix, table 1).

Two joining sherds from a stirrup jar, one (187113) from a deep accumulation attributed to Stratum S-4 at the southern end of Area S. The other (187146) comes from cleaning the western face of Wall 78729 of Stratum S-2, about nine meters to the west of the location of the first sherd and at a much higher level. It was presumably displaced from its original context during the Stratum S-2 building operations.

Table 1: Stratigraphic distribution of MycIIIC sherds in Areas S and N at Beth Shean.

	Stratum S-4	Stratum S-3b	Stratum S-3a	Stratum S-3/N3 general	Unstratified	Total
Stirrup jars	nos. I:1–2,[1] I:4, I:6–7	nos. I:2,[1] I:5, I:8–9, I:10[2]–11		no. I:10[2]	no. I:3[3]	11[4]
Jugs	nos. I:12–13					2
Deep bowls (skyphoi)		no. I:15	nos. I:14, 16	no. I:28		4
Misc.	nos. I:21–22, I:27	no. I:23	nos. I:25–26	nos. I:17–20	no. I:24	11
Total	10	8	4	6	2	28

[1] Joining sherds
[2] Joining sherds
[3] Possibly from same stirrup jar as no. 2
[4] Not including the two joining sherds noted in n. 1 above

Description. Fine dark buff, slightly purplish clay, the same color throughout the section. Exterior surface self-slipped pale buff and quite well smoothed; interior surface unsmoothed. Rather faded matte-brown paint. Part of the lower body of a globular stirrup jar, probably similar in shape to nos. I:1 above and I:10 below. The fabric is very similar to that of no. I:3 below, which may possibly be the base of the same stirrup jar. Decorated with a relatively broad body zone of cross-hatched lozenges (cf. no. I:6 below), with a group of three thin bands immediately below this, and another group of three thin bands on the lower body.

I:3. 788040/14 (Locus 78802, topsoil in Square Z–9, Level 93.94 m) (figs. 4.2, 3; 10.2).

Description. Part of the base of a closed vessel, possibly the same stirrup jar as no. I:2 above (both fabric and paint very similar). Dark buff fabric, the same color throughout the section; exterior surface self-slipped pale buff. Matte dark-brown paint. Ring base, diameter ca. four centimeters. Band around base and three thin bands immediately above.

I:4. 888179/1 (Locus 88854, Stratum S-4, Square Z–9, Level 92.87 m) (fig. 5.4; 11.4; Cohen-Weinberger, appendix, table 1).

Four joining sherds from the upper part of a stirrup jar from the top of a deep layer of debris above Floor 88866, a Stratum S-4 floor in Square Z–9. The layer is sealed by Floor 88820 and Oven 78826 of Stratum S-3b at Level 93.15 m.

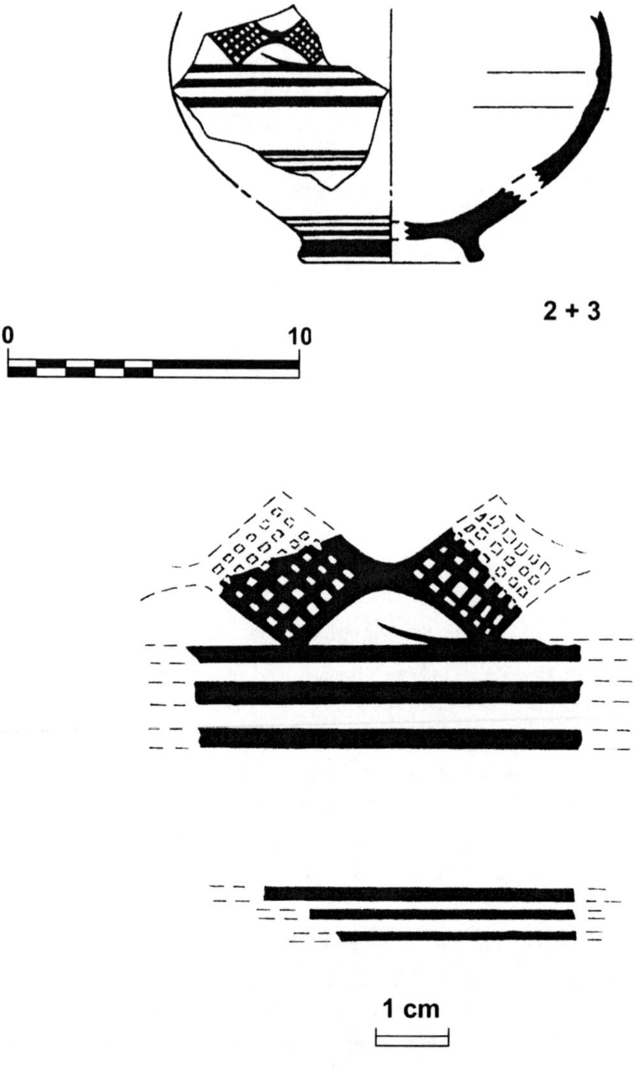

Fig. 4: Drawings of MycIIIC sherds nos. I:2–3.

Description. False neck, handles, and part of the shoulder of a stirrup jar (spout not preserved). Very worn coarsish, sandy fabric of yellowish buff color with visible calcareous-looking inclusions; the same color throughout the section; surfaces unsmoothed. Matte dark-brown paint, very badly worn. Flat top disc, relatively short, squat false neck (made separately and plugged into the

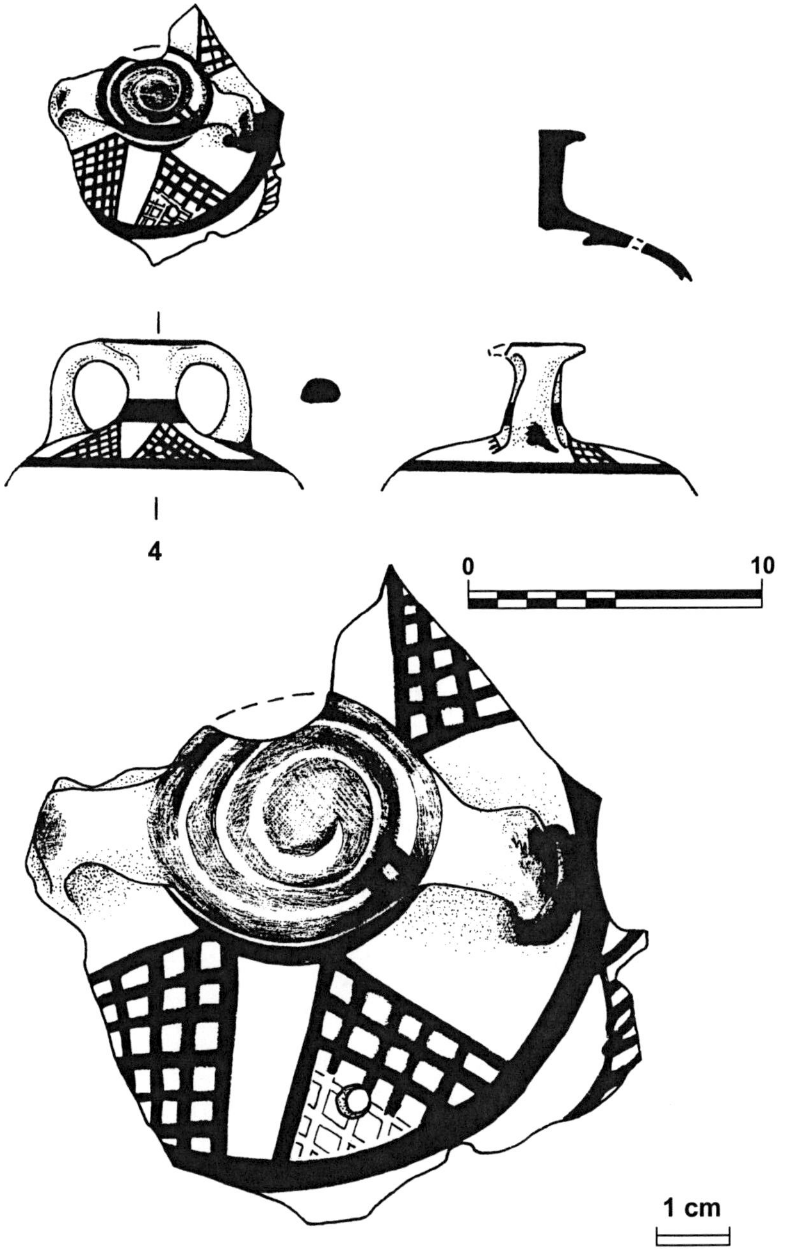

Fig. 5: Drawing of MycIIIC sherd no. I:4.

shoulder).[7] A neat round airhole on the side of the shoulder opposite the spout seems to have been cut out after firing, probably to facilitate smooth pouring. The decoration of the top of the disc is uncertain, but may have taken the form of a spiral. The backs of the handles may have been solid painted, but the paint is almost entirely worn away. The shoulder decoration appears to have consisted of circumcurrent cross-hatched triangles (two of these are visible on the side opposite the spout and part of one to the side of the missing spout). Immediately below the shoulder zone and separated from it by a single band is what looks like a horizontal zone of lozenges, possibly hatched or cross-hatched.

I:5. 188206 (Locus 18824, Stratum S-3b, Square Z–9, Level 92.78 m) (fig. 6.5).

Body sherd, from the top of accumulation in street.

Description. Body sherd of closed vessel, probably from the lower part of a stirrup jar, near the base. Coarsish buff fabric, the same color throughout the section. The fabric seems somewhat like that of no. I:4 above and it is just possible (though not certain) that it is from the same or a similar stirrup jar. Matte-brown paint. Decorated with three broadish bands.

I:6. 988265/1 (Locus 98846, Stratum S-4 or S-3b, Square B–10, Level 91.15 m) (figs. 6.6; 10.6); Cohen-Weinberger, appendix, table 1).

Body sherd of a stirrup jar from occupation debris at Level 91.15 m. This level is almost the same as that of Stratum S-4 found nearby (Locus 10845) with a floor of Stratum S-3b above it at Level 91.30 m. However, at this particular spot, the floors were missing. Attribution to Stratum S-4 is nevertheless plausible.

Description. Sherd from part of the body of a stirrup jar. Fine fawnish buff clay, the same color throughout the section, though the interior surface has a slightly purplish tinge. Exterior surface quite well polished. Very matte light-brown paint. A group of horizontal bands framing fine lines probably just below the shoulder; a horizontal body zone of cross-hatched lozenges (cf. no. I:2 above); a thin band followed by three thinner bands below this.

I:7. 988265/2 (Locus 98846, Stratum S-4 or S-3b, Square B–10–11, Level 91.11 m) (figs. 6.7; 11.7).

Handle fragment, said to be from the same debris as no. I:6 above. For context, see previous item.

7. For the techniques of making or attaching false necks on stirrup jars, see Leonard et al. 1993, 17, 20. This can be done in one piece by drawing up the clay rotationally from the

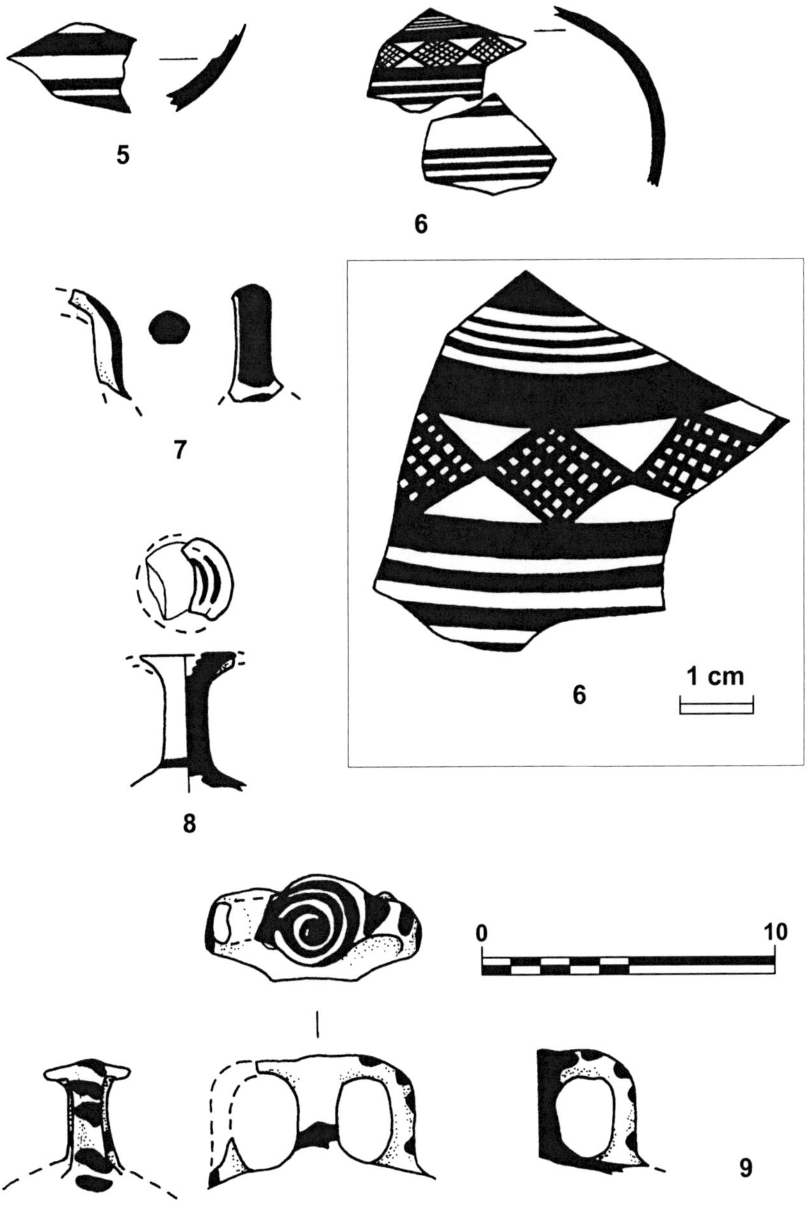

Fig. 6: Drawings of MycIIIC sherds nos. I:5–9.

Description. Stirrup jar handle fragment. Buff clay. Dark brown paint, slightly glossy but very worn. Back of handle solid painted. Trace of band below base of handle.

I:8. 188305 (Locus 18811, Stratum S-3b, Square B–9, Level 92.38 m) (figs. 6.8; 11.8).

False neck of a stirrup jar from an accumulation in a street.

Description. Very worn stirrup jar false neck, the top almost completely flaked away. Buff sandyish clay; very worn paint. Trace of a band around the base of the neck.

I:9. 188033/1 (Locus 10731, Stratum S-3b, Square A–9, Level 92.45 m) (figs. 6.9; 11.9).

The upper part of a stirrup jar from an accumulation in a street.

Description. Disc, false neck, one handle and lower part of the other handle, and part of the shoulder of a stirrup jar. Pale buff clay, the same color throughout the section. Flat disc; false neck formed in one piece with the rest of the vessel by rotational upwards pulling from center of shoulder (compare no. I:4 above). Dark-brown to black matte paint. Spiral on disc; horizontal bars in the form of thick "blobs" down the back of the handle (cf. probably also no. I:10 below). Band around base of false neck.

I:10. 787338/1–5 (Locus 78737, Stratum S-3 destruction layer above the floor of Room 88700, Square A–8, Level 93.25 m) + 107135 (Locus 10731, street surface in Squares Z–09–10, north of Room 88700, attributed to Stratum S-3b, Level 92.33 m) (figs. 7.10; 10.10; Cohen-Weinberger, appendix, table 1).

Six fragments of a stirrup jar, restored. Five of these (787338/1–5) come from Locus 78737, a deep layer of Stratum S-3 destruction debris above a plaster floor

---

shoulder of the vessel (as seen on no. I:9 below), or the false neck can be made separately and either applied over a central hole in the shoulder or plugged into it (as here). Both of the basic methods are found on stirrup jars made in the Aegean and those assumed to have been made in the eastern Mediterranean, without any discernible pattern being visible, though three examples from Tell es-Saʿidiyeh, which neutron activation analysis suggests were made locally, have false necks drawn up from the shoulder. Among the small sample studied by Leonard et al. (1993), no examples on which a separately made false neck was plugged into the shoulder, as opposed to luted onto it, seem to have been observed. However, this appears to have been the method normally used for Philistine stirrup jars (T. Dothan 1982, 123). The method of plugging handles into the bodies of closed vessels has a particularly long and continuous history on Cyprus, from the Red Polished Ware of the Early Bronze Age right down to the Base Ring jugs and juglets of the Late Cypriot period.

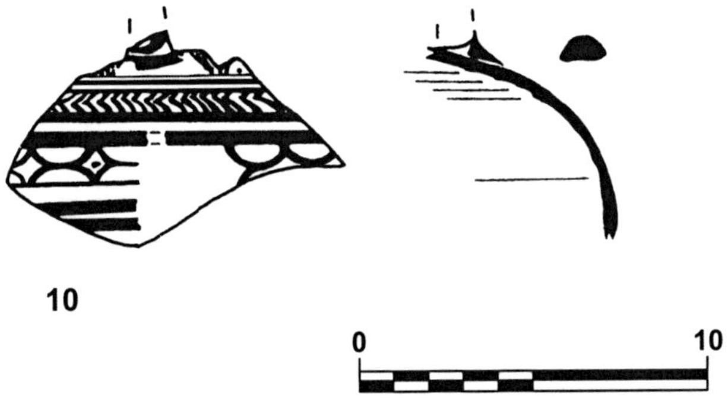

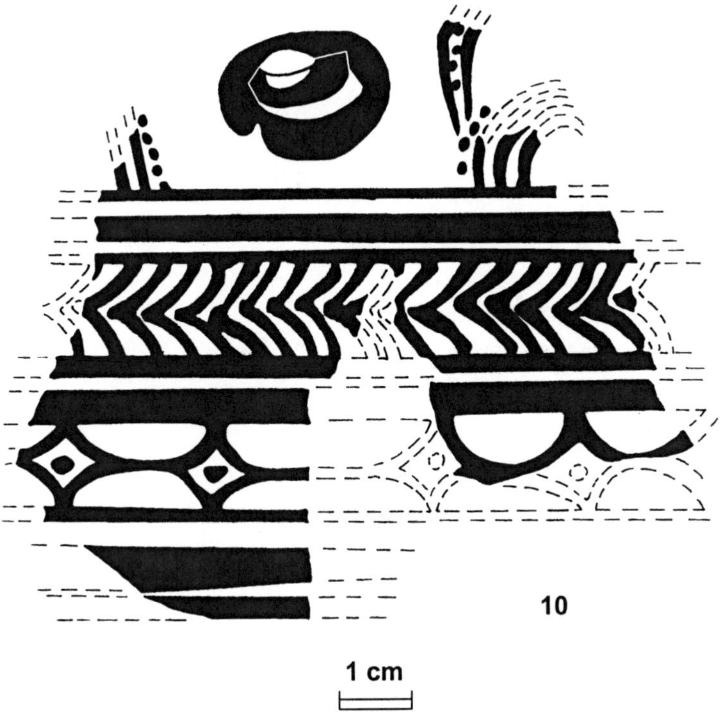

Fig. 7: Drawings of MycIIIC sherd no. I:10.

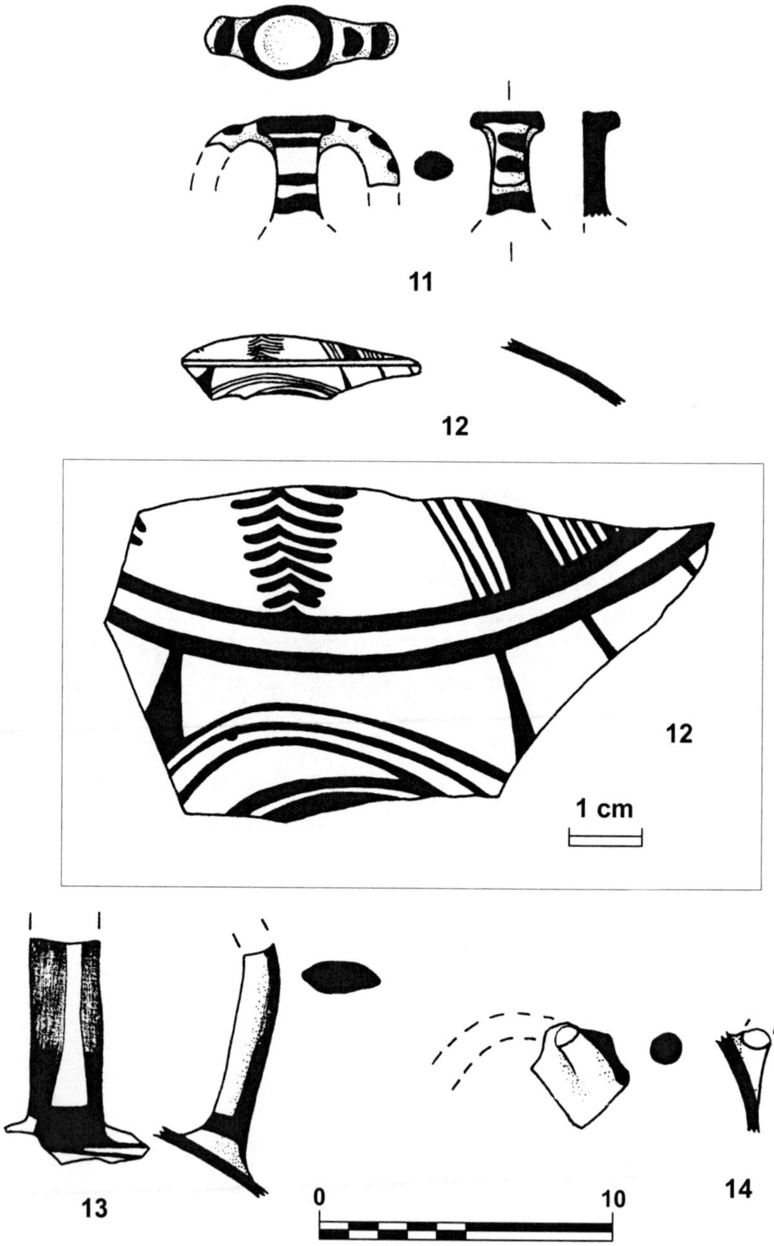

Fig. 8: Drawings of MycIIIC sherds no. I:11–14.

(Locus 88700, Level 92.30 m) in Squares A–8–9.[8] The floor belongs to a large room with walls preserved to a height of more than 1 meter. The destruction layer in this room was thick and undisturbed. The fragments were found almost 1 meter above the floor. The sixth fragment (107135), which has been burnt and warped by fire, was found in Locus 10731, a street accumulation in Square A–9 at Level 92.33 m (cf. no. I:9 above).

Description. Part of shoulder and body of stirrup jar to just below maximum diameter, including the lower part of one handle. Fine buff clay, the same color throughout the section; smoothed exterior surface; pale- to dark-brown fairly matte paint, rather worn (burnt to gray-brown on fragment 107135). The remains of dot-fringed concentric semicircles on the shoulder to the left of the handle with a similar pattern probably also to the right (possibly arranged on top of one another, akin to Hankey 1967, pl. 29:c–d?). Circle of paint around the root of the handle, with what may be the remains of horizontal bars or "blobs" on the back of the handle above this (cf. perhaps no. I:9 above). Horizontal zone of parallel chevrons immediately below the shoulder, separated from it by three thin bands or lines (the central one slightly thicker than the others); two bands below this, followed by a horizontal zone of linked lozenges with dot centers; further bands below.

I:11. 388216 (Locus 38846, Stratum S-3b, Square Y–12, Level 93.30 m) (figs. 8.11; 11.11).[9]

Found in floor build-up layers of Stratum S-3b. Two joining fragments, which make up the disc, false neck, and parts of the handles of a stirrup jar. Very worn. Slender false neck, with narrow concave disc. Matte black paint. Band around outer edge of disc and two bands around false neck; transverse bars on handles.

Jugs

I:12. 188296 (Locus 18832, Stratum S-4, Square Z–9, Level 92.20 m) (figs. 8.12; 10.12)

Fragment of closed vessel, from accumulation of debris in a street.

---

8. This floor is part of a large space mostly excavated by Yadin and Geva as part of their Stratum 4, which corresponds to our Stratum S-3a (Yadin and Geva 1986, 40, fig. 13, Loci 2530 and 2567). Yadin and Geva also describe a thick destruction layer in this space. The continuation of the same destruction was excavated in the new excavations and marks the end of Stratum S-3a.

9. Not seen by S. Sherratt.

Description. Fragment from part of the shoulder and body of a jug (possibly a strainer jug). Buff clay, the same color throughout the section. Fairly well-smoothed exterior surface. Mattish paint, dark-brown and pale-brown (the latter characteristic of the thin lines). Decorated in "Sinda Style" (cf. Schachermeyr 1979, 209–10, figs. 2–3, pl. XXVII). The upper zone preserves a group of parallel chevrons, flanked by a vertical band and thin lines that probably loop above and around the chevrons in the manner of the multiple outlined, curved motifs in Buchholz and Karageorghis (1973, no. 1646). The lower zone, separated from the upper by two thin horizontal bands, has some sort of similar curving looped motif (also with multiple outlines) with tall, thin solid-painted triangles arranged vertically to either side of this.

I:13. 188314 (Locus 18832, Stratum S-4, Square Z–9, Level 92.10 m) (figs. 8.13; 11.13).

Handle fragment, from accumulation of debris in a street (cf. no. I:12 above).

Description. Vertical strap handle and small part of shoulder of a jug (probably similar in shape to no. I:12 above). Fine, even, sandyish buff fabric. Dark-brown to black mattish paint. Paint around handle root and elongated splodge up one side of the handle; two thin bands below the base of the handle, probably demarcating the lower edge of the shoulder zone.

Deep Bowls (skyphoi) (see also no. I:28 below)

I:14. 188147/1 (Locus 18804, Stratum S-3a, Square B–9, Level 92.45 m) (figs. 8.14; 11.14).

Handle fragment, found on a street surface.

Description. Tiny scrap of body sherd of deep bowl (skyphos) with part of horizontal loop handle. Sandy fabric of dirty buff color (similar on the exterior and interior). Trace of matte dark-brown paint at handle root.

I:15. 887221/1 (Locus 78743, Stratum S-3b, Square B–7, Level 92.57 m) (fig. 9.15; Cohen-Weinberger, appendix, table 1).

Two joining fragments from context sealed by Stratum S-3a floor (Locus 68703).

Description. Part of rim and handle root of deep bowl (skyphos). Sandy buff fabric. Matte reddish-brown to brown paint. Paint at root of handle. Line on rim; band below rim on interior.

I:16. 788207/1 (Locus 78849, Stratum S-3a, Square Z/3, Level 93.37 m) (fig. 11.16).[10]

A small fragment of a deep bowl (skyphos) with part of a spiral painted in black.

Vessels of Miscellaneous or Uncertain Shape

I:17. 987271/30 (Locus 88700, floor surface of Stratum S-3, Square A–B–8–9, Level 92.30 m) (fig. 9.17; Cohen-Weinberger, appendix, table 1).

Description. Part of shoulder of closed vessel, possibly pyxis (alabastron), with small horizontal loop handle. Orangeish buff fabric. Pale-yellowish buff exterior surface with a sandy feel. The vessel probably had a relatively wide and short neck (the clay is very thin at the point where the Fragment 987271/30 begins to turn upwards into the neck); fairly pronounced angle between shoulder and body, at the point where the handle is placed, with what appears to be a straight-sided body profile below this. Mattish dark-brown paint. Trace of band at the base of the neck; two lines on the shoulder, above the handle; vertical bars along the back of the handle.

I:18. 887192/86 (Locus 78737, Stratum S-3, Square Z-9 floor, Level 92.5 m, destruction debris above Floor 88700, Square A–8) + 887146/10 (Locus 88700, Stratum S-3, Square A–B–8–9; cf. Locus of nos. I:10 and I:17 above) + 987297 (Locus 98740, dismantling of Stratum S-3 floor) (figs. 9.18; 10.18).[11]

Five joining body sherds from lower body of closed vessel near base. Two relatively thin horizontal bands in brown-red to black paint.

I:19. 787277/33 (Locus 78737, Stratum S-3, Square A–B–8–9, Level 93.30 m) (figs. 9.19; 11.19).

Handle fragment, from baulk cleaning.

Description. Lower part of vertical handle of closed vessel, possibly a stirrup jar. Buff fabric; brown to dark-brown matte paint. Band down center of handle; two bands below.

I:20. 987284/7 (Locus 98740; Stratum S-4 or S-3, Square A–B–8, Level 92.41 m) (not illustrated).[12]

10. Fragment was not seen by S. Sherratt.

11. Fragments were not seen by S. Sherratt.

12. Fragment was not seen by S. Sherratt.

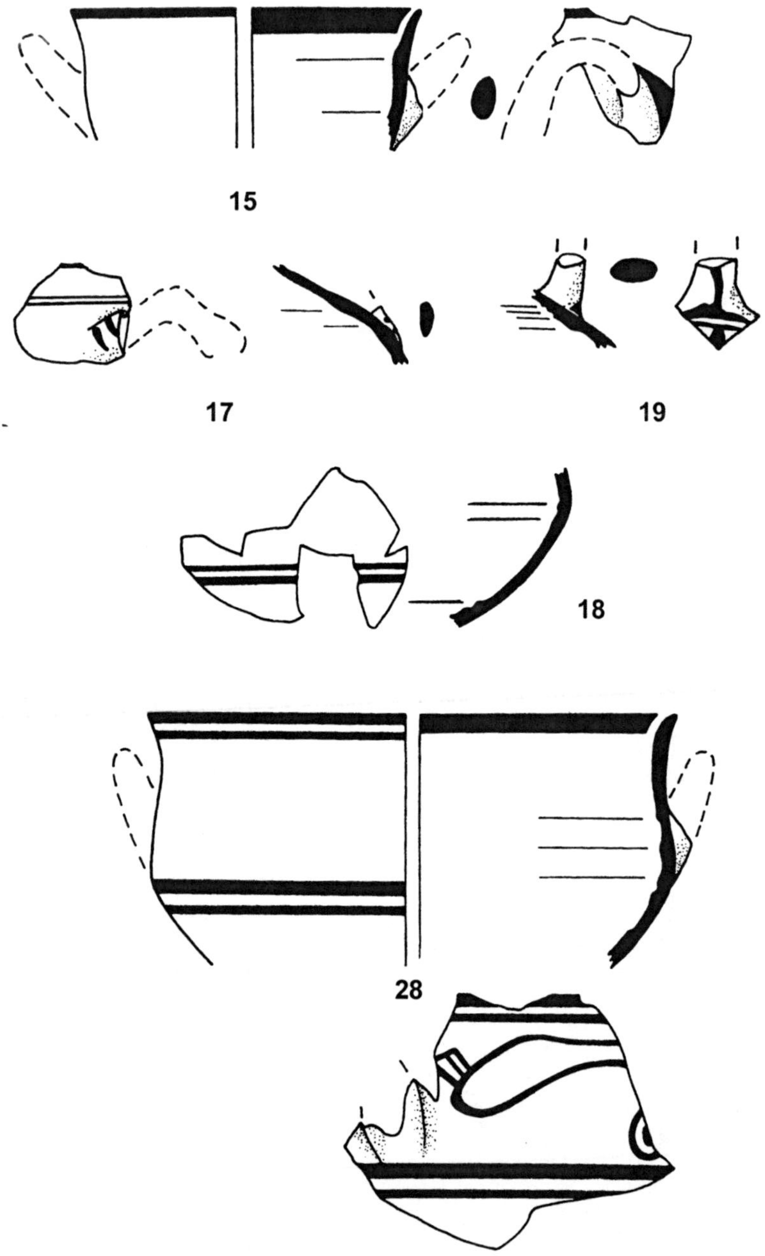

Fig. 9: Drawings of MycIIIC sherds nos. I:15, 17–19, 28.

Small undecorated body sherd from closed vessel, with slight carination (possibly at angle of flat base?).

I:21. 987133 (Locus 98718, Stratum S-4, Square C–10, Level 91.66 m) (not illustrated; Cohen-Weinberger, appendix, table 1).

Small body sherd, from accumulation above Surface 98732.

Description. Body sherd of closed vessel, possibly from the lower body of a jug? Buff clay, the same color throughout the section. Smoothed exterior surface. Pale-brown matte paint. Two thin bands with a further group of three thin bands below.

I:22. 108197/8 (Locus 10841, Stratum S-4, Square C–9, Level 91.15 m) (not illustrated).[13]

Two joining body sherds, unknown whether from closed or open vessel. Broad band in dark-brown paint (very worn) and trace of another band.

I:23. 188197/2 (Locus 18824, Stratum S-3b, street, Square Z–9, Level 92.73 m) (not illustrated; table 2).[14]

From the top of accumulation in street. Very small body sherd, undecorated.

I:24. 988016/3 (Locus 98807, pit in Stratum S-1a, Level 93.35 m) (not illustrated).[15]

Small body sherd; remains of broad bands painted in black.

I:25. 288256 (Locus 78740, Stratum S-3a, street, Level 93.98 m) (not illustrated).[16]

Ring base of stirrup jar? Band painted in black above the base.

I:26. 888157/2 (Locus 88820, Stratum S-3a, Level 93.02 m) (not illustrated).[17]

Small body sherd; remains of decoration in black.

I:27. 188061 (Locus 10809, Stratum S-4, Level 92.25 m) (not illustrated; table 2).[18]

Body sherd; remains of decoration in black paint.

13. Not seen by S. Sherratt.
14. Cf. locus of no. I:5 above; fragment was not seen by S. Sherratt.
15. Fragment was not seen by S. Sherratt.
16. Fragment was not seen by S. Sherratt.
17. Fragment was not seen by S. Sherratt.
18. Fragment was not seen by S. Sherratt.

Table 2: Munsell color chart definitions (compiled by N. Panitz-Cohen).

	Clay Inside	Clay Outside	Decoration
I:1 (187050/1)	10YR8/3	10YR8/3	5YR4/4
I:2 (187113)	7.5YR7/2	7.5YR7/4	10YR3/1, 4/4
I:2 (187146)	7.5YR7/4	10YR7/3	too faded
I:3 (788040/14)	5YR7/3	10YR8/2	10YR3/1(faded)
I:4 (888179/1)	10YR8/3	10YR8/3	10YR4/1(faded) +5YR5/4
I:5 (188206)	10YR8/3	10YR8/3	5YR4/4+5YR3/1 (faded)
I:6 (988265/1)	10YR8/2	10YR8/1	10YR4/2(faded)
I:7 (988265/2)	10YR8/2	10YR8/2	10YR4/1(faded)
I:8 (188305)	10YR8/3	10YR8/3	10YR4/1(faint)
I:9 (188033/1)	10YR8/1	10YR8/1	10YR4/1(faded)
I:10 (787338/5)	10YR8/2	10YR8/2	10YR4/1(faded)
I:12 (188296)	7.5YR8/2	7.5YR8/2	10YR3/1(faded)
I:13 (188314)	10YR8/3	10YR8/3	10YR3/1
I:14 (188147/1)	10YR7/4?	10YR8/3	10YR4/1(faded)
I:15 (887221/1)	10YR7/4	10YR7/4	5YR4/4
I:17 (987271/30)	5YR7/6	10YR7/4?	10YR4/1 to 4/3
I:18 (887192/86)	5YR7/4	7.5YR7/4(lighter)	10YR3/1
I:18 (887146/10)	7.5YR7/4(encrusted)	5YR7/6(light)	10YR4/3-4/1
I:19 (787277/33)	10YR8/2	10YR8/2	10YR4/1(faded)
I:21 (987133)	10YR8/1	10YR8/1	10YR4/2
I:23 (188197/2)	10YR8/3	10YR8/3	none
I:27 (188061)	10YR8/1	10YR8/3	10YR3/1(faded)
I:28 (104026/1)	10YR8/2	10YR8/2	10YR3/2
I:28 (104026/2)	10YR8/2	10YR8/2	10YR4/1(faded)

Area N

I:28. 104026/1 + 104026/2 (Locus 10413, Stratum N3?, Squares Q–R–15–16, Level 92.26 m) (fig. 9.28; Cohen-Weinberger, appendix, table 1).

Two joining fragments of deep bowl (skyphos) from cleaning debris that accumulated after the end of the University of Pennsylvania excavations in this area. Probably to be attributed to Stratum N3 (= Level VI).

Description. Deep bowl (skyphos) rim and body fragments with part of what seems to be the thickening for a handle root. Pale buff clay with slightly sandy surface, the same color throughout the section. Very worn dark-brown paint. The bowl appears to have a rim diameter of about 16 centimeters. Two thin bands at the rim on the exterior and one slightly thicker one on the interior; paint at root of handle. Part of the loop of what appears to be an antithetic spiral without a central panel, or disintegrated spiral (cf., e.g., Kling 1989, 97; Schachermeyr 1976, figs. 66:c–d, 71, pl. 68),[19] with the trace of a parallel chevron group at the outer edge of the loop, apparently close to the handle.

Discussion

Fabric and Paint[20]

Most of these pieces seem likely, on grounds of style, as well as fabric, to be LC IIIA products (cf. Hankey 1993, 104; Mazar 1997b, 159). As far as the visual appearance of the fabric is concerned, most of the stirrup jar fragments (with the possible exception of no. I:4 and perhaps no. I:5), the jug fragments (nos. I:12–13), probably the deep bowl fragments (nos. I:14–15, I:28), and some at least of the miscellaneous fragments seem to fall quite comfortably within the range of variations encountered in LC IIIA pottery of Mycenaean type (cf., e.g., Sherratt 1990a). The clay is mostly relatively fine and well fired, with little in the way of large or obvious grit inclusions, though sometimes somewhat soft and sandy in texture (cf., e.g., nos. I:8, I:13).[21] Fabric color ranges between various shades of lighter or darker buff and is the same throughout the section. There is a variety of surface treatments. On a few (nos. I:2–3), a somewhat paler exterior surface color seems to have been achieved by means of a self-slip (rather than a distinct slip of different composition). On most fragments the exterior surface is well or

19. The existence of the spiral shown at the bottom right is not absolutely certain.

20. For the results of petrographic analysis of nos. I:1–2, I:4, I:6, I:10, I:15–17, I:21, and I:28, see the appendix by Cohen-Weinberger, this volume.

21. This relatively soft, sandyish texture is particularly evident on no. I:8 and may have helped to contribute to its very worn state.

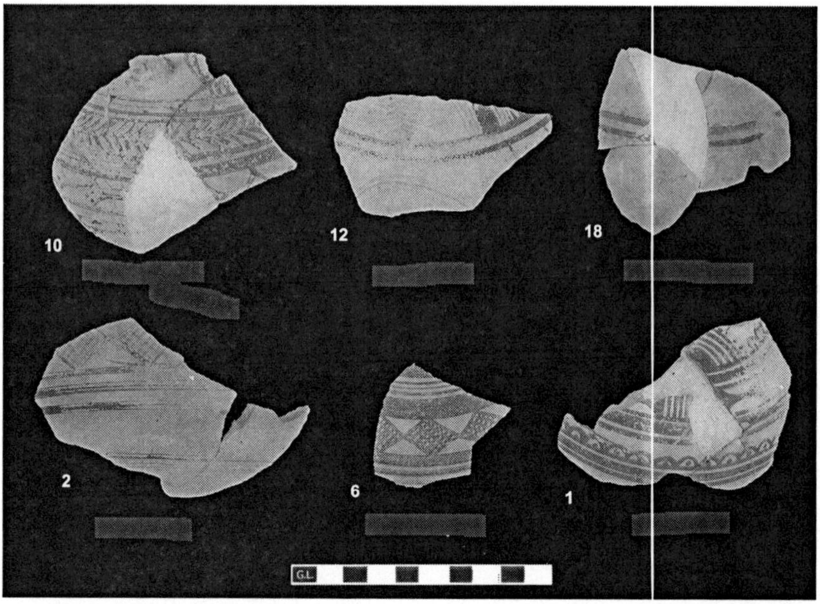

Fig. 10: Photo of selected MycIIIC sherds from Tel Beth Shean (Group I).

quite well smoothed (nos. I:1–2, I:10, I:12) and in one case polished (no. I:6). On one or two others (e.g., nos. I:8, I:13), the surface is left unsmoothed or only rudimentarily smoothed so that the sandy texture of the clay can still be felt on the surface. The paint on these sherds is generally matte or fairly matte, though in a couple of cases slightly or even fairly glossy (nos. I:1, I:7).[22] Its color varies between reddish brown and various shades of pale to dark-brown, sometimes depending on the thickness of the paint as applied. On no. I:12, in particular, the two-tone contrast created by the pale brown of the thin lines and the dark brown of the broader areas of paint may be at least partly deliberate.[23]

The deep bowl fragments (nos. I:14–16, I:28) probably also fall into this category. However, although their fabric and surface treatment (as well as their general design, insofar as it is discernible) fall well within the range of variety known from Cyprus, it is perhaps worth noting that the clay of some at least of these seems more consistently sandy in texture than that of most of the stirrup

22. Although a matte paint finish is more usual on LC IIIA pottery of Mycenaean type (White-Painted Wheelmade III), varying degrees of glossiness are not unknown (cf. Sherratt 1990a, 109–11).

23. Cf. also possibly the apparent two-tone effect of the bands on no. I:18.

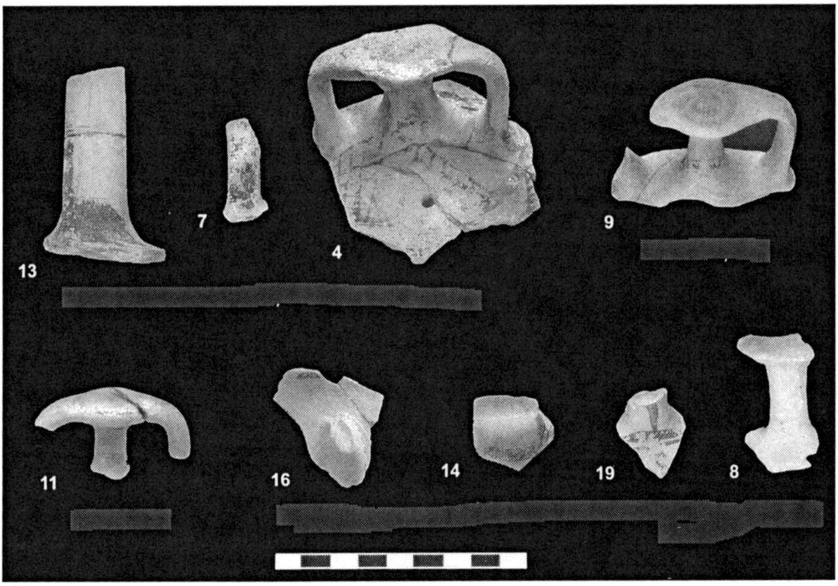

Fig. 11: Photo of selected MycIIIC sherds from Tel Beth Shean (Group I).

jar and jug fragments, and in no case is there any sign of much attempt to create a smooth surface finish. In this connection, it is interesting that the shape itself is one that was also produced on the Levantine mainland from at least the early-twelfth century (Oren 1973, 112, and for an example from one of the Beth Shean tombs, see Oren 1973, figs. 47:7, 74:3), though the results of petrographic analysis of three of them (see Cohen-Weinberger, appendix, table 1, nos. I:15, I:16, and I:28) seem to preclude the possibility that our fragments were produced in the southern Levant (see also below, n. 36). Similar sorts of observations may be made in the case of no. I:17, which is distinguished by its orangish buff clay and pale-yellowish buff surface, which also has a distinctly sandy feel (see also Cohen-Weinberger, appendix, table 1, no. I:12). If this is a pyxis, it is a shape which, though not unknown in the Cypriot repertoire, is relatively rare there, particularly in LC III (cf. Kling 1989, 167, fig. 19:a–b; for examples, see Dikaios 1969–1971, pls. 73:1, 101:4). However, it is a shape that was produced on the Levantine mainland from at least the thirteenth century B.C.E. onwards (Oren 1973, 112 with references).[24]

24. For examples from Lachish and Ain Shems, some with linear decoration, see Hankey 1967, pl. 36:d, cf. also pl. 37:a. See also Cooley and Pratico 1995, figs. 19, 24, 28, 32:1–7, 35:1–6 (especially perhaps fig. 35:1) from the Western Cemetery at Tel Dothan. Cf. in general Leonard

Of the remaining sherds, the visual appearance of the fabric of no. I:4 (and just possibly no. I:5) seems noticeably distinct from that of the others and it is therefore possible that it has a different origin, perhaps somewhere on the Levantine mainland. It is made of relatively coarse clay, with visible white inclusions. The surfaces are unsmoothed, which probably accounts for the very matte and fugitive nature of the paint.

Shapes and Decorations

Stirrup jars. The pattern-decorated stirrup jars, with the exception of no. I:4, fit well into the series of four fragmentary stirrup jars recovered from or attributed to Level VI of the University of Philadelphia excavations (Hankey 1966; 1967, 127–28, pl. 29; James 1966, figs. 49:4, 54:3; Warren and Hankey 1989, 164–65) and with another from Tell Keisan, which neutron activation analysis has suggested was made in the Palaepaphos region on Cyprus (Balensi 1981; Gunneweg and Perlman 1994). As far as one can tell, they appear to be of a broadly similar globular shape (cf. Furumark 1941a, 613–14 no. 176, fig. 6:176) to some, and possibly, all of the examples from the University of Philadelphia excavations and that from Tell Keisan. The banding arrangements on nos. I:1, I:2, I:6, and I:10 (including the alternations between thick and thin lines) also seem highly comparable to those on the stirrup jars from the University of Philadelphia excavations and Tell Keisan,[25] while the transverse bands on the handles of nos. I:9–10 are also found on the Tell Keisan example and PAM 32.304+305 from Beth Shean (Hankey 1967, pl. 29:b bottom left).[26] Transverse bands on the handles of stirrup jars, like those from Beth Shean and Tell Keisan, are also found in Cyprus (Dikaios 1969–1971, 323, pl. 101:24 for an example from early Level IIIb at Enkomi) and are a more or less standard feature of Philistine stirrup jars (T. Dothan 1982, 116–23). As for their decorations, the concentric semicircle groups on the shoulder of no. I:1 are similar to those on the shoulder of PAM 32.305 from the University of Philadelphia excavations (Hankey 1967, pl. 29:b)[27]

1994, 9. For similar shapes in locally made painted ware from the Cemetery 900 tombs at Tell el Far ʿah, see Laemmel 1998, 44, pls. 58–63 and this volume.

25. The fine lines framed by bands above the cross-hatched lozenges on no. I:6 are particularly similar to those immediately below the shoulder zone of PAM 32.36 (Hankey 1967, pl. 29:c–d).

26. Since the separate description of this fragment of false neck and handle in Hankey 1966 (170, pl. 45: fig. 3b) and Hankey 1967 (128, pl. 29:b), it has been found to join the fragment illustrated in Hankey 1967, pl. 29:a (information kindly supplied by the late Vronwy Hankey; and cf. remarks by Hankey 1966, 170).

27. Though the concentric semicircle groups on PAM 32.305 (Hankey 1967, pl. 29:b) are not fringed with dots, unlike those on no. I:1; dot-fringed concentric semicircles (though without

and the zones of cross-hatched lozenges on nos. I:2 and I:6 match those of PAM 32.36 and the Tell Keisan stirrup jar (Balensi 1981, pl. XI). Both of these patterns are well represented in LC IIIA pottery of Mycenaean type and it may indeed be no coincidence that both are prominent among those adopted by Philistine potters (cf. Furumark 1941b, 118–20 with refs.; T. Dothan 1982, 209–12 and 118 fig. 16:4; M. Dothan 1971, figs. 3:1, 87:6, pl. IX:3).[28] On Cyprus, concentric semicircles, both with and without solid centers and/or dot fringes, are one of the motifs quite regularly found on stirrup jars at sites in the east of the island (Kling 1989, 162–63; cf., e.g., Dikaios 1969–1971, pls. 75:16, 82:23–25, 307:155, 309:261–62; Karageorghis and Demas 1985 I, pl. XVIII:872 lower right; Kling 1985, 352; Hult 1981, fig. 80:b; Öbrink 1979, fig. 133:a). At the same time, chains of straight-sided cross-hatched lozenges of the type represented on nos. I:2 and I:6 seem much more characteristic of Cyprus (and of the eastern Mediterranean generally) than of the contemporary Aegean, occurring as elements of different styles of decoration (including the peculiarly Cypriot "Levantine Style")[29] and on a variety of different shapes from LC IIC onwards (cf. Kling 1989, 102; Pieridou 1973, 80; Karageorghis 1976, pl. II).[30] There are several examples of this pattern in the form of horizontal chains on the bodies of stirrup jars, again particularly from sites in eastern Cyprus (e.g., Dikaios 1969–1971, pls. 72:1, 308:214; Hult 1981, fig. 85; Niklasson 1983, fig. 487). It is also found in the same form at Tarsus (Goldman 1956, fig. 333:1281–82).

Of the auxiliary patterns on nos. I:1 and I:10, the zone of horizontal chevrons (no. I:10) and the dot-filled semicircle fringe (on the shoulder and lower body zone of no. I:1) both find parallels on LC IIIA stirrup jars (cf., e.g., Dikaios

---

the solid centers of no. I:1 and PAM 32.305) are found on the shoulder of PAM 32.36 (Hankey 1967, pl. 29:c–d) and possibly beside the spout of UMUP 34.20.18 (James 1966, fig. 54:3).

It is possible that the shoulder of no. I:10 carried some arrangement similar to that on PAM 32.36 (Hankey 1967, pl. 29:c–d), in which the semicircle groups form two alternately spaced tiers, the upper ones linked with the shoulder band by rows of vertical dots. This itself is quite closely paralleled on a fragmentary stirrup jar from Tarsus, which has been described as owing something to earlier (LH IIIA–B) floral patterns (Goldman 1956, fig. 333:1282; cf. French 1975, 69).

28. A cross-hatched lozenge chain also appears on what is probably a stirrup jar fragment from Akko (T. Dothan 1989, 60, fig. 3.1:d) as well as on a small sherd found in a later context at Tel Rehov.

29. On this, see Schachermeyr 1979, 211–13, figs. 4, 6; Kling 1989, 124–25; 2000, 286.

30. The frequency of the motif on LC IIC–IIIA pottery of Mycenaean type may well owe something to the fact that chains of cross-hatched lozenges are a favorite motif on White Slip pottery (cf., e.g., Karageorghis and Demas 1988, pl. LXXXIX:Courtyard A/32 for White Slip II examples from Maa; see also Kling 1989, 102). These remain a frequent pattern on Cypriot Proto-White-Painted pottery.

1969–1971, pls. 75:38, 82:22; Maier 1973, fig. 3; and cf. also M. Dothan 1989, fig. 3.1:f from Akko; and T. Dothan 1982, 119, fig. 17:3–5, 212, 216 fig. 71:2–3 for its occurrence on Philistine stirrup jars). The first of these is a pattern with a long history in LH IIIA–C pottery, which first appears in Cyprus on imported LH IIIA2–B stirrup jars (cf. Furumark 1941a, 379–84). The second, in a version without the dots, is also a frequent motif on imported LH IIIB vessels (Furumark 1941a, 337–40). The dotted variant occurs sporadically on both LC IIIA and LH IIIC pottery. We know of no precise parallels on Cypriot stirrup jars for the two remaining auxiliary patterns, though the dot-centered lozenge chain of no. I:10 occurs on a fragment (possibly of a stirrup jar) from Akko (M. Dothan 1989, fig. 3.2:c). This is a variant of another very common pattern on LH IIIB–C stirrup jars that also finds its way to Cyprus on imported LH IIIB vessels.[31] Much the same may be said of the panelled body zone on no. I:1, which looks like a variant of the kind of zonal pattern seen on an imported LH IIIA2–B stirrup jar from Enkomi (A. Smith 1925, IICb, pl. 3:18; cf. Furumark 1941a, 401), though the solid triangles placed tip-to-tip on their sides (or "double axe") also have counterparts in the contemporary "Sinda" and "Levantine" styles (cf., e.g., Schachermeyr 1979, figs. 2, 4, 6; Kling 1989, 110).

As far as its decoration is concerned, stirrup jar no. I:4 has similarities to that of the stirrup jar from Tell Keisan (Balensi 1981), though the execution seems considerably cruder. The cross-hatched triangles on the shoulder (which might perhaps be seen as a simplified version of the scale triangles on the Tell Keisan stirrup jar) are also found on Cypriot stirrup jars from the equivalent of Enkomi Level IIIa onwards, and, like hatched and cross-hatched lozenges, are a relatively common motif on LC III pottery in general (Kling 1989, 102, 162, 171). However, while we would hesitate to state categorically that this stirrup jar could not have been made on Cyprus, the comparative coarseness of its fabric and the simple and rather crude nature of its decoration provide a noticeable contrast to the other stirrup jars discussed here and suggest that its origin may have been different. The shape of the vessel, with its short, dumpy false neck and thickset handles placed relatively high on the sloping shoulders (fig. 5.4), seems reminiscent of some locally made Late Bronze (LB) II stirrup jars (cf., e.g., Oren 1973, figs. 41:9–

31. For a similar dot-centered example on an imported LH IIIB stirrup jar from Enkomi, see A. Smith 1925, IICb, pl. 3:38. In general, there is also a certain suggestive similarity between the particular form of the motif on no. I:10 and the widely spaced chains of relatively small lozenges frequently seen on White Slip II pottery (cf., e.g., Bailey 1976, pls. XXVI:c, XXVII:a–b).

10, 42b:24 from Beth Shean; Hankey 1967, fig. 5:c from Deir Alla) and it seems possible that this too was made somewhere on the Levantine mainland.[32]

Number I:11 also raises some interesting questions. As shown in the drawing (fig. 8.11), it has a distinctly concave disc. This feature is much more characteristic of Philistine stirrup jars than stirrup jars in either the Aegean or Cyprus, and, together with the comparatively slender and slightly concave false neck profile and narrow disc diameter, gives this piece a suggestively "Philistine" appearance which contrasts with that of nos. I:8–9 (cf. T. Dothan 1982, 115, 117–21). The fragments are particularly badly worn, though there seems to be nothing about the fabric that clearly distinguishes it from the other sherds discussed here.

Jugs. There is no doubt whatsoever about the origin of the jug fragments, nos. I:12 and I:13. Number I:12, which may well come from a strainer jug, is decorated in the highly distinctive "Sinda style" peculiar to eastern Cyprus. (For a strainer jug decorated in this style that seems to provide a particularly close parallel, see Buchholz and Karageorghis 1973, no. 1646 of unknown provenance in the Cyprus Museum; and for other similar pieces see Schachermeyr 1979, pl. XXVII; Dikaios 1969–1971, pls. 71:23, 306:149). This is a style whose influence can be discerned on Philistine pottery of the later Monochrome and Bichrome phases, particularly in the use of quatrefoil-filled spirals, solid triangles and multiple outlining (cf., e.g., Killebrew 1998a, fig. 7:11; M. Dothan 1971, figs. 7:11, 101:11, 13, 102:4; Stager 1995, 339, fig. 3:33–34; T. Dothan and M. Dothan 1992, 163; M. Dothan and Porath 1993, pl. 35:2; T. Dothan 1982, 217).

Deep bowls. Little can be said about the very fragmentary pieces nos. I:14–16 and I:28, except to point out that the deep bowl (skyphos) shape is one that, from at least the beginning of the twelfth century (if not before), was produced both on Cyprus and in the Levant.[33] Despite the impression given by the reconstructed drawing of no. I:15 (fig. 9.15), there is no way of knowing whether either it or no. I:14 originally carried some patterned decoration. The remains of the pattern on no. I:28, however, suggest an antithetic spiral without a central panel or some form of disintegrated spiral, while no. I:16 also appears to have some sort of spiral decoration. Similar types of pattern are, in general, well represented both on LC IIIA and Philistine Monochrome deep bowls (cf., e.g., Schachermeyr 1976, fig. 71; Dikaios 1969–1971, pls. 70:19, 74:34, 109:6; T. Dothan 1998b, figs. 4, 5:6, 8;

32. In some of these respects (particularly the sloping shoulders) it is also not unlike some Philistine stirrup jars (cf., e.g., T. Dothan 1982, 119, fig. 17:3–4, 6).

33. For the production of deep bowls on Cyprus (where they appear already in small numbers in a LC IIC context in Kition Floor IV), see Sherratt 1990b; cf. Kling 1985, 360–61. It seems possible that production in the Levant (for example at Ashdod Stratum XIIIb) may start similarly early.

Stager 1995, fig. 3; T. Dothan and M. Dothan 1992, 163), though it has to be said that the small group of parallel chevrons on the outer edge of the spiral loop, and apparently right next to the handle on no. I:28, seems to be in an unusual position. A deep bowl fragment, decorated with what seems to be an untidy antithetic spiral without a central panel, was also recovered from the University of Philadelphia excavations at Beth Shean (James 1966, 250, fig. 54:4; cf., e.g., Dikaios 1969–1971, 850–52, pls. 74:29, 32, 81:3, 99:16, 109:10; Schachermeyr 1976, 288, fig. 66:c).[34] It may be no coincidence that a locally made deep bowl was recovered from Tomb 221 of the Northern Cemetery (Oren 1973, figs. 47:7, 74:3; see above).

Context and Chronology

The very fragmentary nature of the pieces (including those from the University of Philadelphia excavations)[35] and the fact that in some cases fragments of the same pot were found quite widely scattered (see nos. I:1–2 [possibly also I:3] and I:10 above; and the joining stirrup jar fragments in Hankey 1967, pl. 29:a–b [handle fragment]) strongly suggest that most of these sherds are the result of secondary deposition. This is supported by the contexts, which consist almost entirely of accumulations and debris above streets and floors or fills below floors. Several fragments are badly worn, and one of the pieces of no. I:10 has been burnt, which again suggests that they were subject to considerable movement after the pots to which they originally belonged had been broken. Ten of the pieces come from Stratum S-4 contexts;[36] and, since there is no reason to believe that these are in any way stylistically earlier than those from Stratum S-3 contexts, it seems quite likely that all of them originally derive from Stratum S-4.

34. 33-10-1019, Locus 1733 (UMUP 34.20.24). The fabric of this fragment (which comes from a deep bowl, from near the rim which is missing) is described (James 1966, 250) as fine and of greenish buff color with a smooth creamy surface and black paint. According to Hankey (personal communication), the wheel marks are clearly visible and the dark-brown to black paint is cracked in a manner that suggests that it may originally have been lustrous. The interior of the rim is banded. The suggestion of lustrous paint in this case might seem to point more readily to a Cypriot product, which may, indeed, also be the case with nos. I:14–16, and I:28.

35. PAM 32.36, supposedly a complete stirrup jar from Building 1500 (the Governor's Residence of Level VI), is in fact far from complete, as Hankey 1967, pl. 29:c–d and a slide taken by the late Vronwy Hankey together make clear. It has been heavily restored with plaster and at least two-thirds of the body below the shoulder, the false neck and disc, most of one handle and the spout of the original are missing.

36. Nos. I:1–2, I:4, I:6–7, I:12–13, I:21–22, and I:27.

Particularly crucial in this respect are nos. I:1–2, I:12, and probably also I:6 from Stratum S-4, which clearly relate not only to the ceramic sequence of eastern Cyprus but also to the stirrup jar fragments recovered from the Pennsylvania excavations. In terms of the sequence from Dikaios' excavations at Enkomi, these as a whole would seem most at home in the later stages of Enkomi Level IIIa and possibly perhaps the early stages of Level IIIb. The earliest occurrences of the "Sinda style," of which no. I:12 is a clear example, are found in a middle stage of Level IIIa and continue to be found (though often in tighter, "busier" compositions) down to the end of Level IIIb (Dikaios 1969–1971, pls. 306:145, 147, 149 [middle stage of Level IIIA], 307:157–58, 190, 195 [late stage of Level IIIA; destruction layer of Level IIIA], 308:210, 221, 244, 246 [transitional between Levels IIIA and IIIB; early Level IIIB; destruction layer of Level IIIB], 309:263–265, 268–69 [destruction layer of Level IIIB]; cf. Kling 1989, 125, 171–73, table 59–18). At Kition this style first appears on Floor IIIa, the earliest LC IIIA floor (Karageorghis 1981, 9–10, nos. 38–39, pl. VI:38–39). The concentric semicircle groups of no. I:1, which also has references to the "Sinda style" in its conjoined solid triangles (or "double axe") motif (as well as in the multiple outlining effect of the semicircles themselves), follow much the same chronological pattern, first appearing in the later stages of Enkomi Level IIIa and continuing to be found on stirrup jar fragments in Enkomi Level IIIb (Dikaios 1969–1971, pls. 307:155 [late stage of Level IIIA], 308:229 [early Level IIIB], 309:261–62 [destruction layer of Level IIIB]). The cross-hatched lozenges of nos. I:2 and I:6 are also found on a stirrup jar at Enkomi from a context associated with a late stage of Level IIIa (Dikaios 1969–1971, pl. 308:214 [transitional between Levels IIIA and IIIB]), though the motif itself appears earlier on other shapes, and may indeed have a continuous history from the end of LC II onwards (Dikaios 1969–1971, pls. 306:150 [middle stage of Level IIIA], 307:153, 187, 205–6 [late stage of Level IIIA; destruction layer of Level IIIA]; cf. Kling 1989, table 59–5).

Stylistically, none of the other fragments can easily be regarded as later than these four, though some could conceivably be earlier. Since three (and most probably all) of the four come from Stratum S-4 contexts, it thus seems very likely that all of the pots to which the sherds listed above originally belonged, and, including those represented by the fragments from the University of Philadelphia excavations, reached Beth Shean no later than the end of this stratum or its equivalent.

Stratum S-4 is dated to an early phase of the Twentieth Dynasty, more specifically perhaps to the reign of Ramesses III (1194–1163 B.C.E. on a traditional higher chronology; 1184–1153 B.C.E. on the most recent low chronology (Kitchen 2000, 49), while Stratum S-3 is assigned to the time of Ramesses IV–VI (1163–1143 or 1153–1136 B.C.E.). In view of the recent series of radiocarbon determinations from a number of well-defined LC IIC–IIIA contexts at several Cypriot sites, which confirm the conventional Cypriot chronology by placing the end of LC IIC at roughly around 1200 B.C.E. (Manning et al. 2001), a date corresponding with the later years of Ramesses III's reign (on either chronology) seems, on the face of it, perfectly reasonable for the later phases of Enkomi Level IIIa and the early part of Level IIIb. This is not significantly different from the absolute date suggested for the stirrup jar fragments from the University of Philadelphia excavations by Warren and Hankey (1989, 164–65), who proposed for them a *terminus ante quem* of ca. 1143 B.C.E. on the grounds that they probably arrived at Beth Shean no later than the beginning of Ramesses VI's reign.[37]

A number of quite unnecessary problems and misunderstandings have been caused by the designation "LH IIIC Middle" given by Warren and Hankey not only to the fragments from the Philadelphia excavations at Beth Shean but also to Philistine Monochrome pottery at sites such as Ashdod and Tel Miqne (Warren and Hankey 1989, 164–67). These have arisen for several reasons: in the first place, from the tendency to normalize stylistic classifications drawn up on the basis of twelfth-century Mycenaean pottery, above all from sites in the Argolid such as Mycenae, and to extend these in blanket fashion not only to the whole of the Aegean but also to Cyprus; and, in the second place, from a confusion of stylistic or typological classification with chronological phase (cf. Furumark 1941a, 5–6). A further complication arises from the adoption by Dikaios (1969–1971), on somewhat arbitrary and decidedly tenuous grounds, of Furumark's term "Myc. IIIC:1b" (Furumark 1944) to apply to the earliest pottery of Mycenaean type from LC IIIA contexts at Enkomi and elsewhere (see on this Kling 1989, 64–68, 79–82). This label, which has not been used in the Aegean for some time and has in recent years also been largely discarded on Cyprus (Kling 1991; 2000),[38] was subsequently borrowed directly from Cypriot terminology to apply to the pot-

37. Radiocarbon dates from Beth Shean itself are also consistent with this chronology. Three samples of charred grain found in a public structure in Area N, Stratum N4, which corresponds to Level VII or Late Level VII of the University of Pennsylvania excavations, were dated to 1210–1040, 1270–1130, and 1210–1000 B.C.E. (all calibrated at 1 sigma confidence). This building is one stratigraphic phase earlier than Stratum S-4. Seeds from a silo of Stratum S-3a were dated to 1190–1000 B.C.E. (an additional three dates have a broader date range) (Mazar and Carmi 2001, 1334–36). Despite their wide calibrated ranges, these dates are consistent with the chronology based on correlation with well-dated Egyptian finds at Beth Shean.

38. Following the practice of the excavators of Hala Sultan Tekke, the term White-Painted Wheelmade III is now increasingly used to refer to all painted wheelmade pottery of broadly Aegean type produced on Cyprus in LC IIC–IIIA. This includes pottery previously categorized variously as "Rude (or Pastoral) Style," "Late Myc. IIIB," "Myc. IIIC:1(b)," and "Decorated LC III." All these categories are part of the same ware and the distinctions between them, originally based on certain historically driven assumptions about their relative dates or cultural origins, can now be seen in many cases to be essentially arbitrary and frequently not at all clear in practice. On this, see Kling 1991.

tery also called Philistine Monochrome, which shows clear and sustained stylistic links with pottery produced on Cyprus.

The majority of the pottery fragments from Beth Shean discussed here, as well as those from the University of Philadelphia excavations, have the closest and most consistent parallels on Cyprus rather than on the Greek Mainland or in the Aegean area generally and should be assessed in terms of the Cypriot sequence rather than forced into some blanket LH IIIC typological-stylistic chronology ironed out to cover the whole of the Aegean and Cyprus. A number of aspects of the Cypriot sequence have now become reasonably clear. First, an approximate correlation can be drawn between the conventional transitions from LC IIC to LC IIIA on Cyprus and LH IIIB to LH IIIC on the Greek Mainland with the implication that both transitions may be given a notional rounded date of ca. 1200 B.C.E. (Kling 1989, 170–73; Sherratt 1990a, 117–18; Manning et al. 2001). Second, it seems evident that elaborate types of decoration, which seem to appear relatively suddenly at sites on the Greek Mainland where they are seen as characteristic of a middle stage of LH IIIC (Mountjoy 1986, 155–56), develop gradually over the course of LC IIIA, particularly in the east of Cyprus, where they often take distinctively Cypriot forms (Kling 1989, 173; Sherratt 1990a, 117–18). Examples of these are already present in Enkomi Level IIIa, where they are associated with a general LH/Minoan IIIB or sub-LH/Minoan IIIB style of decoration, which echoes that found in LH/Minoan IIIB and early LH/Minoan IIIC contexts in Greece, Crete, and the Aegean. It is the subsequent Level IIIb which, according to Dikaios (1969–1971, 270), coincides with the height of elaborate development, showing perhaps the greatest degree of overall similarity in a number of features to an elaborate middle stage of LH IIIC in Greece and the Aegean. Indeed, there may be some argument for Cyprus itself having made a direct contribution to the development of elaborate styles of decoration in the Aegean (Kling 1989, 172; Sherratt 1991, 195). Thus the use of the term "LH IIIC Middle," when applied to the pottery recovered at Beth Shean, is essentially meaningless. Though it may well have a "LH IIIC Middle" look about it, in the sense that some of its decoration is relatively elaborate and that it includes some motifs which, in certain parts of the Aegean, would normally be classified as "LH IIIC Middle," the use of this label represents an ultra-normative form of classification based on general stylistic considerations alone, which of itself says nothing about the relative or absolute chronology of the Beth Shean fragments. Nor, for that matter, does it of itself allow us to conclude that "LH IIIC Middle" in the Aegean had begun by 1153 B.C.E. (though, insofar as a broad stylistic classification can be thought of as having such a precisely dated "beginning," it may well have done). In terms of Cyprus, however, the Beth Shean pottery is easier to pin down. Taken as a whole, the most easily datable (and arguably latest) pieces in Cypriot terms, most and probably all of which arrived at the site before the end of Stratum S-4, seem to fit best in a horizon which covers the later part of Level IIIa at Enkomi and perhaps also the early stages of Level IIIb. There seems to be no reason why this horizon should not therefore be considered as roughly contemporary with the later years of the reign of Ramesses III, as the contexts of the Beth Shean pieces seem to suggest. The question of the effect this may have on the dating of LH IIIC pottery in the Aegean is quite a separate one, depending as it does on specific correlations between the sequence on Cyprus and those in different parts of the Aegean. Nevertheless, it seems likely that some of what is conventionally called "LH IIIC Middle" at various places in the Aegean at least partly overlaps the date range of the Beth Shean fragments from Stratum S-4.

Locally Made "MycIIIC-Inspired" Pottery (Group II)[39]

II:1. 787356/1 (Locus 78743, Stratum S-3b, Square B–7, Level 93.14 m) (figs. 12:II:1; 14:II:1; Cohen-Weinberger, appendix, table 1).

Rim fragment from context sealed by Stratum S-3a floor (Locus 68703). Small bowl with distinct out-turned lip (rim diameter: 13.6 cm). Of red-brown fabric with numerous large and small white inclusions and with an off-white slip on both the exterior and interior surfaces. Very matte, washy brown-red paint. Paint on the exterior lip and band inside the rim; antithetic spiral decoration.

II:2. 108012 (Locus 98843, Stratum S-3b, Square A–11, Level 92.11 m) (figs. 12:II:2; 14:II:2; Cohen-Weinberger, appendix, table 1).

From a patchy clay surface. Body sherd of relatively large vessel, unclear whether closed or open, but probably the latter. Light brown (buff) fabric with many black grit inclusions (basalt);[40] unslipped. Purple-red paint. Part of antithetic looped spiral with band below. Possible trace of paint close to horizontal loop handle root on righthand edge. If so, this is probably a fragment from a large bowl or krater.

II:3. 988255/3 (Locus 98843, Stratum S-3b, Square A–11, Level 92.2 m) (figs. 13:II.3; 14:II:3; Cohen-Weinberger, appendix, table 1).

From a patchy clay surface (cf. no. II:2 above). Two joining body sherds, apparently of an open vessel (large bowl or krater). Buff fabric with numerous

39. None of the locally made fragments (nos. II:1–4) were seen by S. Sherratt.

40. Cf. accompanying petrographic report (Cohen-Weinberger, appendix, no. II:2).

small white inclusions; gray core; unslipped. Dark red paint. Spiral with solid center.

II:4. 187230/1 (Locus 18736, Stratum S-3?, Square C–8, Level 92.92 m) (figs. 13:II:4; 14:II:4; Cohen-Weinberger, appendix, table 1).

From destruction debris probably related to Stratum S-3 in a disturbed area at the edge of the mound. A body sherd of what appears to be a large vessel (in view of the two zones of decoration, a closed vessel—perhaps a large jar—seems most likely). Buff fabric; interior rough and unfinished; brown-red paint. Some sort of panel and spiral (?) pattern on the upper zone; three relatively thin horizontal bands; panel with checkerboard center on lower zone, with to left of it a schematic bird with head turned back (long neck in the form of a narrow line, small circular head in outline) and solid, boat-shaped body with possibly the remains of legs below; to left of this upper part of "tree of life" or "date palm" motif?

Discussion

Fabric and Paint

These four sherds seem unlikely for various reasons to be Cypriot products and were probably made somewhere (or perhaps in a variety of places) in the Levant (cf. accompanying petrographic report). The fabric of nos. II:1–2 may perhaps be compared with a fragment from the University of Philadelphia excavations (Level VI; James 1966, fig. 49:15), which is described as a gritty light-brown ware with a cream wash and purple-painted decoration.[41] All four are made of relatively coarse clay, with visible white inclusions in the case of nos. II:1 and II:3, and black inclusions in the case of no. II:2 (also identified in petrographic analysis of no. II:3). The identification of the latter as basalt suggests that these pieces could have been manufactured in the Jordan Valley, perhaps close to Beth Shean, though other locations are also possible (cf. Cohen-Weinberger 1998, 409; Killebrew 1999b, 102–3; Elliott, Xenophontos, and Malpas 1986, fig. 2). The surfaces are unsmoothed, which probably accounts for the very matte (and sometimes washy) nature of the paint, while no. II:1 has been covered on both the interior and exterior with a relatively powdery white slip of the sort often seen on "Philistine monochrome" pottery at sites such as Tel Miqne. The relatively dense matte red paint on no. II:3 seems somewhat reminiscent of that on the fragments

41. For a description of the ware of "locally" made stirrup jars in the Northern Cemetery at Beth Shean, see Oren 1973, 112.

of a possibly locally made amphoroid krater from Area G, Phase 11 at Dor also decorated with running spirals, though the fabric of the Dor krater is rather more orange in color (Stern 2000a, pl. IX:a right).[42]

Shapes and Decorations

Numbers II:1 and II:4, and possibly also the other apparently related fragments, fall into a category which might be described as "para-Philistine" or "Philistine-related." The decoration on no. II:1, which is perhaps the most "Philistine"-looking of all these sherds, recalls that frequently found on Philistine bowls and kraters of the Bichrome phase (cf., e.g., T. Dothan 1982, 99, fig. 2; Killebrew 1998a, fig. 12:7; M. Dothan 1971, figs. 2:5, 73:6–7, 85:7–8, 101:7–8, pls. IX:6, LXXVII:4, XCII:1), though examples that belong to the Monochrome phase are also known (e.g., M. Dothan and Porath 1993, fig. 16:8). Numbers II:2 (also perhaps from a krater or large deep bowl) and II:3 (on which see above), probably decorated respectively with an antithetic and running spiral, seem closer to types of spiral patterns normally associated with the Monochrome phase (cf., e.g., T. Dothan 1989, fig. 1.2) as well as in the earlier stages of LC IIIA on Cyprus, where both motifs are very common (cf. Kling 1989, 95–98). Number II:4 with its two zones of decoration would appear to belong to a closed vessel. It is decorated in a style that recalls that of Philistine pottery,[43] though the bird with its solid boat-shaped body, differs from Philistine birds.[44] A very similar bird occurs on a bichrome krater from Tel Dan Stratum VI, which may be described as Philistine-related (Ilan 1999, pl. 59:1); and, although not in itself very similar, this bird may also represent an identical phenomenon to that represented by a Philistine-related (but non-Philistine) krater fragment from Akko (M. Dothan 1989, 60, fig. 3.2:d).

Context and Chronology

These sherds can be dated to the period of the Twentieth Dynasty, before the end of the Egyptian presence at Beth Shean. While there are no good inde-

---

42. It too appears to have visible white inclusions and a grayish core. I am grateful to Ayelet Gilboa for information about the results of petrographic analysis of this krater, which seems to indicate it is neither Aegean nor Cypriot. The analysis itself was carried out by Y. Goren and A. Cohen-Weinberger.

43. For the panel and spiral(?) pattern on the upper zone, cf. perhaps M. Dothan and Porath 1993, fig. 17:10 from Ashdod Stratum XIIIb. For the checkerboard panel on the lower zone, cf., e.g., Killebrew 1998a, fig. 6:27. For the "tree of life" (or "date palm") motif, e.g., T. Dothan 1982, 108, fig. 10:3, 110, pl. 12, 206, fig. 66:12, 215 (and for Cypriot versions: Hult 1978, fig. 23; Courtois, Lagarce, and Lagarce 1986, pl. XVI:5).

44. It is also quite different from Cypriot and Aegean birds.

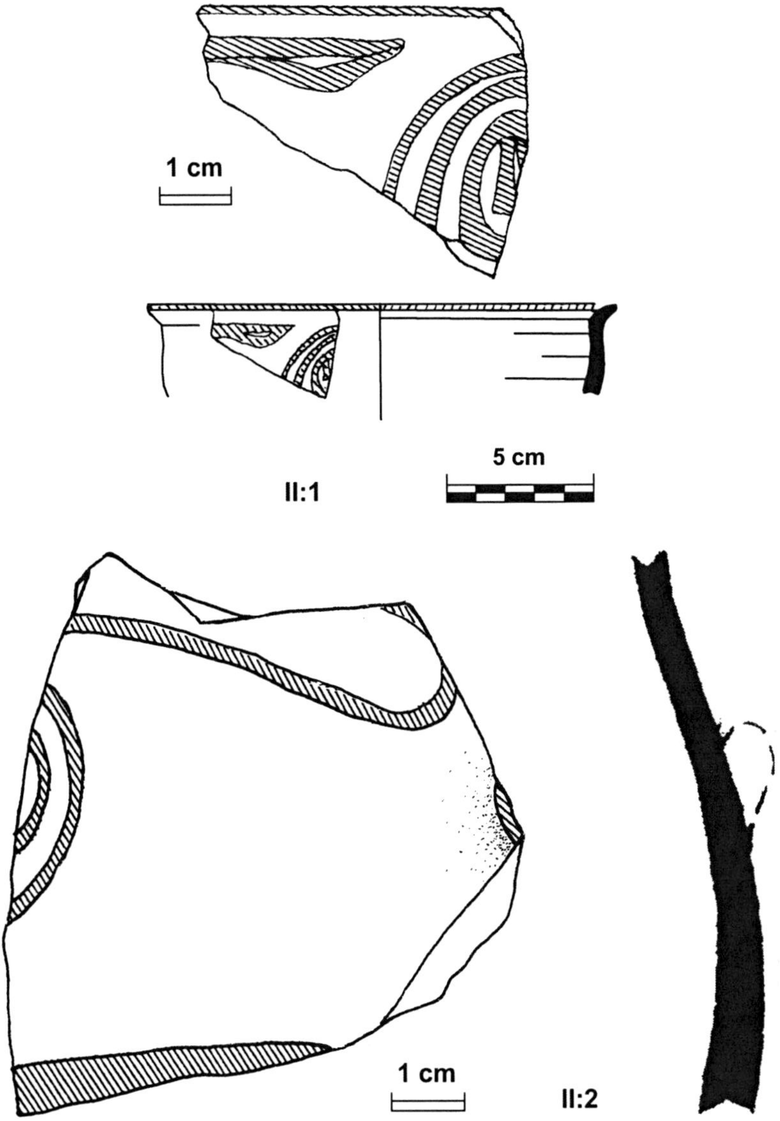

Fig. 12: Drawings of sherds nos. II:1–2.

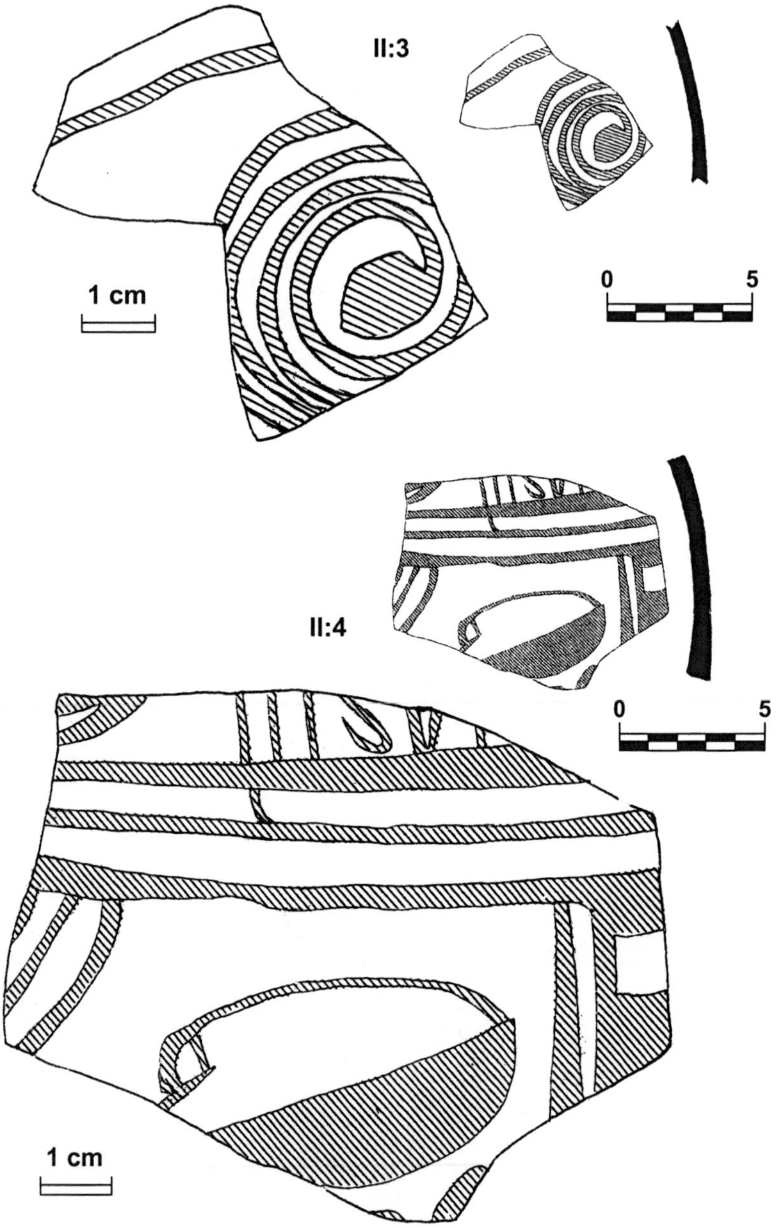

Fig. 13: Drawings of sherds nos. II:3–4.

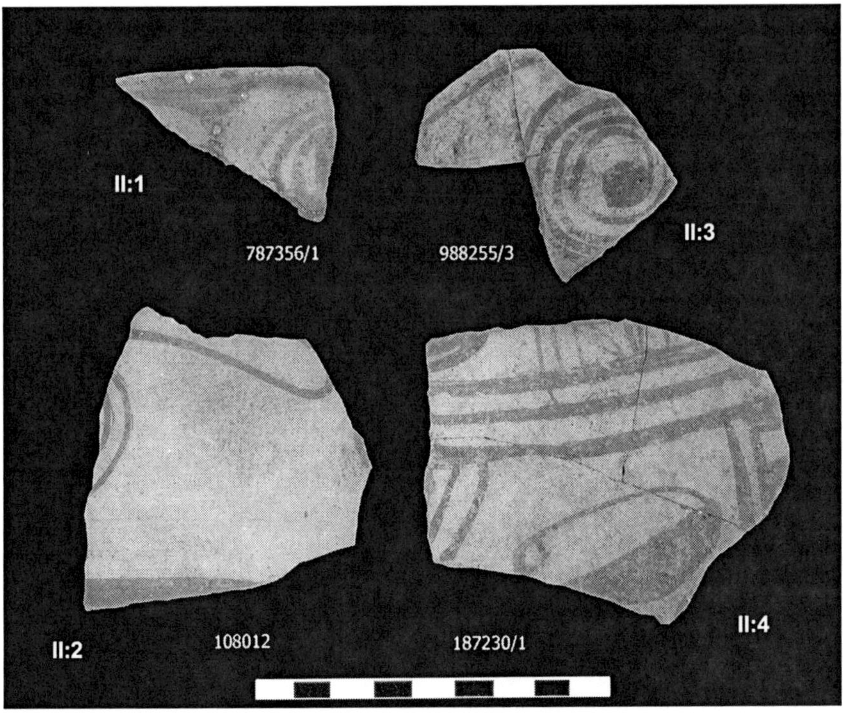

Fig. 14: Photograph of sherds nos. II.1–4.

pendent grounds for the more precise dating of these fragments (all of which were found in Stratum S-3 contexts), it should be noted that they are just as fragmentary as the sherds discussed in the previous section and could therefore equally well be suspected of being residual in Stratum S-3. The similarity between no. II:1 and bowls and kraters of the Philistine Bichrome phase (equivalent, for instance, to Tel Miqne Stratum VI) and the later stages of the Monochrome phase suggest that it, too, probably belongs to much the same horizon as the Cypriot-derived pieces discussed above. A general stylistic relationship between Philistine Bichrome and pottery from Sinda and Enkomi (particularly Sinda Level III and Enkomi Level IIIb and the later phases of Level IIIa) has long been recognized (Albright 1954; Desborough 1964, 211; T. Dothan 1982, 217).

Concluding Remarks

The conclusion that relatively small quantities of imported "MycIIIC" pottery, probably mainly of Cypriot origin and consisting of a limited number of shapes of which stirrup jars form the majority, reached Beth Shean before the end of Ramesses III's reign raises the question of the circumstances in which this pottery arrived there. The question is particularly pertinent in view of the relative scarcity of clear evidence, so far, for the importation of similar pottery on a significant scale to other sites in the southern Levant during Iron Age IA.[45] We are thus not dealing with any sort of large-scale trade in Aegean and (especially) Cypriot pottery and/or its contents, as may be argued for the LB II period. Nevertheless, the presence of an imported Cypriot stirrup jar of similar style and probably also similar date at Tell Keisan in the Akko Plain and of a few sherds of similar pottery at the coastal site of Akko (Balensi 1981; M. Dothan 1989) not only shows that the Beth Shean imports are not a totally isolated phenomenon, but also suggests the route by which they reached the site. Further up the coast from Akko, there is the probability of similar imported pottery from sites such as Sarepta, Tyre, Byblos, Tell Sukas, and Ras Ibn Hani (Warren and Hankey 1989, 162–63), though at most of these sites the extent to which individual pieces can be regarded as imports or as the result of local manufacture is still very far from clear.

Trade or the presence of foreign mercenaries serving in the Egyptian army have been suggested as possible alternative explanations for the Beth Shean imports (Mazar 1997b, 159). However, it is not clear that these suggestions need in any way be mutually exclusive, and there is no inherent reason why both should not apply. The question of who used the imported pottery at Beth Shean and in what context(s) is quite a different one from the question of how they got there and these two questions ought to be addressed separately. As for the first question, most of the imported fragments were found in secondary depositional contexts in rubbish accumulations and debris in what appears to be a residential area, which included overwhelming quantities of locally made Egyptian pottery and other finds of an Egyptian nature, including razors, pendants, and the like. This underlines the essentially Egyptian character of their context and suggests that whoever discarded these pots was well integrated into the structure of the Egyptian garrison, probably at a relatively high level. Furthermore, the association of PAM 32.36 from the University of Philadelphia excavations with

45. It has to be pointed out, however, that we know less than we should like about certain key sites in northern Israel in this period. Next to nothing is known about Dor at this time, apart from the minimal information very recently recovered from Area G, Phase 11, while it is still unclear whether Tell Abu Hawam was functioning in this period (Balensi 1985, 68). Moreover, the results of excavations at both Akko and Tell Abu Hawam are still incompletely published. The absence of imported pottery at Megiddo (Stratum VIIA) might conceivably have some bearing on the status (Egyptian-controlled or otherwise) of the site during this phase (cf. Mazar 2002, 268–71).

Building 1500 (the Governor's Residence) suggests that at least this stirrup jar (or its contents) may have found some use right at the heart of the official Egyptian component of the garrison.

The use of mercenaries by the Egyptian army is well attested, so that the presence of troops of various origins in the garrison at Beth Shean is not improbable. The phenomenon of the Late Bronze and early Iron Age anthropoid clay coffins, found not only at Beth Shean but also at Deir el-Balah, Tell el-Far ʿah South, and Lachish, has often in the past been associated with such mercenaries—though the coffins themselves can tell us nothing specific about the geographical origins or ethnic backgrounds of those buried within (for various views on the users of these coffins, see Oren 1973, 146–50; T. Dothan 1979, 101–4; Stager 1995, 341–42). However, even if we assume that the small collection of imported pots, with its apparently very limited range of shapes, was used primarily by foreign mercenaries serving in the garrison at Beth Shean, it still seems likely that it reached Beth Shean by means of some form of trade. The alternative is to suppose that the pots arrived from Cyprus along with such mercenaries as an inalienable component of their personal baggage, which itself raises a number of questions. In particular, we might wonder why they brought such an idiosyncratically limited selection of types with them, and why stirrup jars figured so prominently among them. We might further wonder why similar types also turn up at Tell Keisan and Akko, where the question of Egyptian strongholds manned by foreign mercenaries does not arise. The fact that the single imported type best represented at Beth Shean is the stirrup jar, which is a form most likely to have travelled on account of its contents, also makes it more likely that some form of trade (however limited in scale) was involved, since the kinds of specialized oils which such stirrup jars probably contained were highly prized by Egyptians and others in the Near East, particularly for ritual use.[46] There is no reason to suppose that only foreign mercenaries could have had a use for such oils at Beth Shean. Even if the pots that contained them did arrive in the baggage of foreign mercenaries, they would still have the potential to be highly tradable items. Mercenaries, too, may have found ways of supplementing their pay on the side.

As it is, the choice with which we are often presented, between a large-scale ubiquitous trade in imported ceramics and the absence of any trade whatsoever, seems something of an unnecessary one. There is plenty of hard evidence on Cyprus for continuing contacts with the Levant and Egypt during the twelfth century, in the form not only of imported Canaanite jars, but also of other goods

46. Cf. the "good" (or "sweet") oil sent from Alasia to the pharaoh "to pour upon thy head whilst thou sittest upon the throne of thy kingdom" (EA 34.50–53; cf. also Hellbing 1979, 24).

and materials, such as ivory, stone vessels, and items of jewelry and amulets in stone, faience, and precious metal. As far as the imported pottery at Beth Shean is concerned, the pattern sketched by the current state of evidence suggests trade of some sort on a limited scale, probably through the port of Akko. It could either have been directed from sources specifically at the garrison at Beth Shean, or (perhaps more likely) arrived on the coast in small quantities as an item of largely incidental, casual trade, and found its way up the Jezreel Valley along traditional supply routes between Beth Shean and the Bay of Akko. What it suggests, at any rate, is that Beth Shean in the period of the Twentieth Dynasty retained some sort of link with the coast, probably vital to the continued presence of an Egyptian garrison.

The four sherds of local manufacture published here may be compared with a few other broadly comparable pieces recovered by the University of Philadelphia excavations and with a few pots (also regarded as of local manufacture) from the Northern Cemetery. Although their precise place or places of manufacture remains unknown, it seems unlikely that this is Beth Shean itself in view of the small numbers involved. While there are similarities to Philistine pottery in some of the decorative motifs used, they may perhaps relate more closely to pottery (as yet poorly known, but probably of local manufacture) from sites such as Dor and Akko and perhaps further north in the coastal Levant. More generally, they fit into a wide spectrum of pottery manufactured in the Levant which shows the influence of pottery of Aegean type, either in terms of shapes or decorative elements or both, of which Philistine pottery is just one manifestation. Such local production begins already in LB II, with the manufacture of container shapes such as stirrup jars and pyxides, and expands to include drinking-related vessels, such as kraters, smaller bowls (or skyphoi), and strainer jugs from somewhere around the transition to the early Iron Age.

Appendix
Petrographic Analysis of MycIIIC pottery from Tel Beth Shean

*Anat Cohen-Weinberger**

Fourteen samples of MycIIIC vessels from Tel Beth Shean were examined under a petrographic (polarizing) microscope. The aims of the petrographic analysis are to identify the raw materials used, describe their variability, determine the geological sources of the raw materials, and assess the possible geographic region where the vessels were manufactured. The local raw materials that have been used over time at Tel Beth Shean are well known (Cohen-Weinberger 1998; Mazar, Ziv-Asudri, and Cohen-Weinberger 2000).

The paste of ten samples (I:1–2, 4, 6, 10, 15–17, 21, 28; table 1) consists of clay matrices and very low percentages of non-plastic components (less than 5 percent of the paste). The clay is either isotropic, indicating high firing temperatures, or unisotropic. The clay of some samples is optically active (i.e., the clay exhibits optical features). Abundant silty mica (mainly biotite) and opaque laths oriented parallel to vessel surfaces appear in most cases. Silty feldspar grains appear as well. The non-plastic components consist of mainly angular quartz grains and, rarely, fragments of igneous and calcareous rocks of fine sand size. The mineralogical assemblage identified herein rules out Israel as a possible clay source. The high firing temperature of the clay well suits the technological tradition of the Aegean world. The petrographic and archaeological considerations (see Sherratt and Mazar, this volume) suggest the Aegean, Cyprus, Cilicia, and northwestern Syria as possible provenance. Previous petrographic studies (e.g., Whitbread 1995; Vaughan 1991; Goren, Finkelstein, and Na'aman 2004), based on geological studies of these areas (e.g., Gass et al. 1994; Juteau 1980; Dubertret 1955) provide a wide range of data that may help to distinguish between these areas. Nevertheless, the clays of the present vessels are well levigated and highly fired, hampering identification of a more specific provenance for the MycIIIC from Tel Beth Shean.

Four samples have a different composition than the above ten samples. Samples II:2 and II:3 are characterized by carbonatic clay, containing few biotite laths. The firing temperature is less then 750°C according to the carbonate condition. The non-plastic components contain basalt and travertine fragments. The relatively low firing temperature and the non-plastic components assemblage suggest

* Israel Antiquities Authority. Email: cohen@israntique.org.il.

Table 1. Inventory and results of the petrographically examined vessels.

Catalog	Basket	Type	Clay	Non-plastic components	Provenance
I:1	187050/1	Stirrup Jar	Carbonatic, silty. Rich in mica laths.	Feldspar, mica grains, angular quartz.	Aegean/Cyprus/Cilicia/ northwestern Syria
I:2	187146	Stirrup Jar	Carbonatic, contains silty mica laths. Rich in rounded and lath opaque grains. Few silty feldspar.	Fine quartz, unidentifiable fine igneous rock fragment. Carbonatic rock fragments.	Aegean/Cyprus/Cilicia/ northwestern Syria
I:4	888179/1	Stirrup Jar	Micaceous, Carbonatic silt, some silty chert.	Some subangular quartz. carbonatic rock fragments. Rarely fine unidentifiable igneous rock fragments.	Aegean/Cyprus/Cilicia/ northwestern Syria
I:6	988265/1	Body Sherd Stirrup Jar	Micaceous, isotropic. Silty quartz, mica laths in clay, rich in silty opaque laths.	Decomposed limestone.	Aegean/Cyprus/Cilicia/ northwestern Syria
I:10	787338/5	Stirrup Jar	Isotropic. Silty mica and plagioclase grains. Abundant silty opaque laths in clay.	Levigated clay with no inclusions except a single quartzite grain.	Aegean/Cyprus/Cilicia/ northwestern Syria
I:15	887221/1	Skyphos	Micaceous, optically active.	Fine quartz, feldspar, chert, siltstone, decomposed carbonate, an angular grain of an opaque angular green-blue mineral.	Aegean/Cyprus/Cilicia/ northwestern Syria

I:16	788207/1	Skyphos	Micaceous, high firing temperature, silty plagioclase and quartz. Silty apatite grains.	Fine angular quartz. Sandstone with silicified cement.	Aegean/Cyprus/Cilicia/ northwestern Syria
I:17	987271/30	Body Sherd, Closed Vessel	Micaceous, optically active. Silty carbonate, quartz and plagioclase.	Decomposed limestone.	Aegean/Cyprus/Cilicia/ northwestern Syria
I:21	987133	Body Sherd	Isotropic, silty quartz, opaque grains, and rarely chert. Some mica grains and abundant of opaque laths fragments.	Well-levigated clay with no inclusions.	Aegean/Cyprus/Cilicia/ northwestern Syria
I:28	104026/1	Skyphos	Isotropic and micaceous.	Angular quartz, unidentifiable fine igneous rock fragment, feldspar.	Aegean/Cyprus/Cilicia/ northwestern Syria
II:1	787356/1	Bowl	Carbonatic/ ferruginous, few mica laths in clay. Rich in silty quartz.	Coarse rounded to angular limestone.	Unknown provenance. Probably local to the Levant.
II:2	108012	Body Sherd	Carbonatic, silty, few mica laths and silty quartz in clay.	Travertine, basalt dolomite, chalk.	Levant, possibly local to Beth Shean.
II:3	988255/3	Body Sherd	Carbonatic, some mica laths glauconite pellet in clay. Silty quartz and plagioclase.	Travertine, highly weathered basalt fragments, chalk, foraminifer, oxihornblande.	Local to the Levant, possibly local to Beth Shean.
II:4	187230/1 (Bird Decoration)	Body Sherd	Carbonatic, few mica laths in clay, silty plagioclase and quartz.	Coarse rounded to angular limestone, fine quartz.	Unknown provenance. Probably local to the Levant.

the Levant as a possible source. The appearance of basalt and travertine in the Beth Shean region may indicate it as a provenance for these vessels (Sneh, Bartov, and Rosensaft 1998).

Samples II:1 and II:4 have a similar composition, consist of carbonatic clay with few mica laths. They were fired at low temperature, contain a high percentage (approximately 20 percent) of coarse rounded to angular limestone. These petrographic affinities give no clue to a specific geographic region.

Chapter Fifteen

The *SKL* Town: Dor in the Early Iron Age

*Ilan Sharon and Ayelet Gilboa**

Dor is a crucial site for the evaluation of a "northern Sea Peoples" phenomenon. It is the only site specifically associated with a non-Philistine "Sea People" by an ancient source—the *TKR/SKL* according to the Egyptian Tale of Wenamun (e.g., *ANET*, 25–29; Goedicke 1975). The latter, however, is of disputed historical validity and context (cf. recently Sass 2002 and references to earlier treatments therein; for the *SKL* and Dor, see, e.g., Scheepers 1991 and references in Stern 2000b, 198).

The association of the *SKL* with other sites, like Tel Zeror (e.g., Kochavi 1993, 1526), and of other groups with other places (as *SHRDN* with Akko [M. Dothan 1984; 1989] or conversely el-Ahwat [lately Zertal 2002] and *DNN* with Dan [Yadin 1968]) is even more tentative and depends on reconstructing place and direction in the associative thought-pattern of Amenope, as he was compiling his enigmatic Onomasticon (Gardiner 1947, 24–63), as well as on the abovementioned association of Dor with the *SKL* as a known compass point. If a clear "Sea People" culture (of one sort of another) cannot be clearly demonstrated at Dor, it bodes ill for the aspirations to recognize such at any other place.

Dj-r of Wenamun is usually identified with biblical דור or דאר and classical Roman Δώρα/Δῶρος. The latter is almost certainly located, according to periploi and onomastica of late antiquity as well as modern archaeological research, at Khirbet el-Burj (Tel Dor in modern Hebrew appellation) on the Mediterranean coast about 45 kilometers north of Tel Aviv and 30 kilometers south of Haifa (fig. 1). Some preliminary investigation of the site took place in the beginning of the twentieth century (Dahl 1915; Garstang 1924), followed by several narrow-scoped problem-oriented probes in the 1950s–1970s, pertaining chiefly to the Roman–

* Institute of Archaeology, Hebrew University of Jerusalem and Department of Archaeology, University of Haifa, respectively.

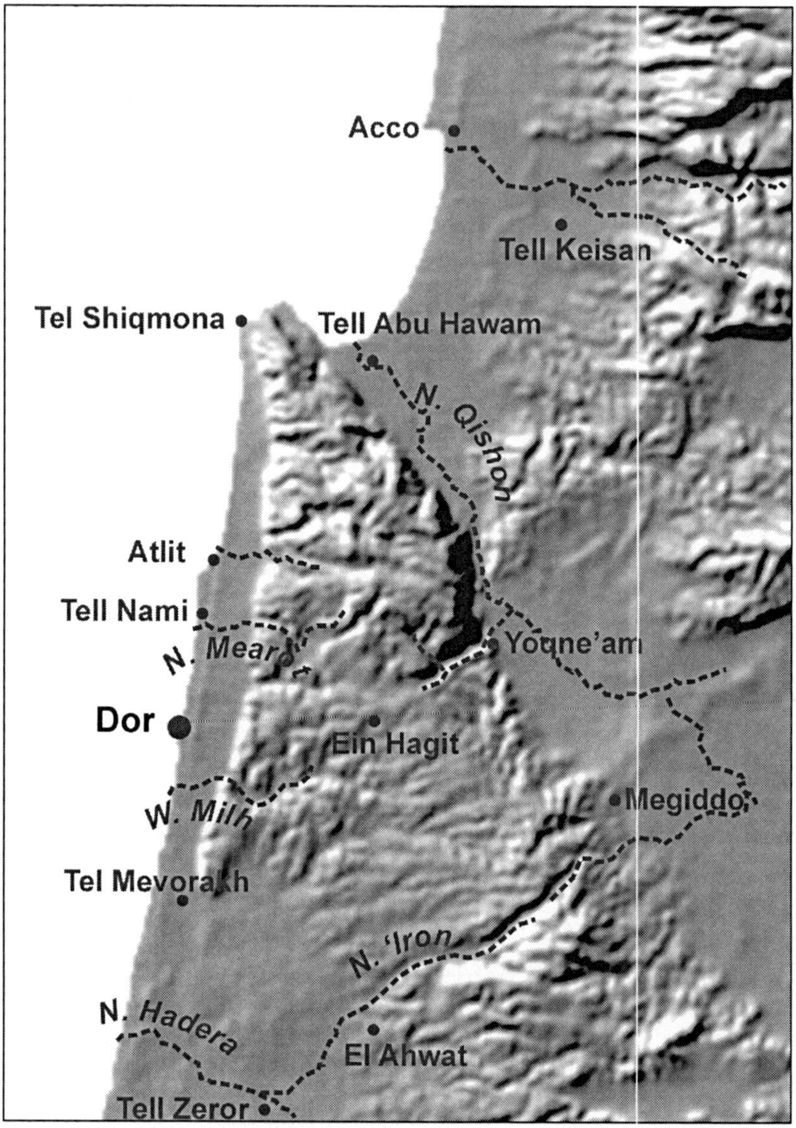

Fig. 1: Topographic map of northern Sharon Plain and Carmel Coast/Mount Carmel.

Byzantine periods (see summary and references in Stern 1993a, 357). Excavations of chiefly maritime installations were conducted in the early 1980s (see below) and a major excavation on the mound was conducted in the last two decades of the century by an international team headed by Professor E. Stern of the Hebrew University of Jerusalem (see Stern 2000a and bibliography therein). The authors spent most of their professional lives on this project and resumed excavations at the site in 2003.[1]

The "*SKL* question" has been a subject of debate among the Dor team ever since early Iron Age remains began to be found in the mid-1980s. Pros and cons of various views were endlessly hashed out in the almost-nightly "kiosk-seminars" at the expedition's camp in Pardes-Hanna.

One reading of the archaeological record of the site in this respect, put forward and argued for by the first director of the project (e.g., Stern 1990; 1991; 1995; and most decisively 2000b) is that the aggregate of Aegean, Aegean-looking, and Philistine-looking objects and attributes found at Dor in the Iron I should be identified as representing "Sikilian" material culture and consequently that similar phenomena in other sites in northern Israel should be interpreted as the material manifestations of other "non-Philistine Sea Peoples." More specifically, this hypothesis posits the existence of four distinct cultural/ethnic/political periods and three cultural transformations within the terminal Late Bronze Age–early Iron Age at Dor. At the end of the Bronze Age the Canaanite town is taken over and the population supplanted by (or at least augmented with and ruled by) "Sikils." Sometime after Wenamun's ostensible visit to Dor, Phoenicians destroy and take over the "Sikil" town. Later on Israelites, under David, capture the Phoenician town and make it their own. Dor is "re-Phoenicianized," according to this view, only in the Persian period and that event is recorded in Eshmunʿazar's inscription (for an extensive exposition, see, e.g., Stern 1993b).

A different version, argued by Raban (see below), sees only a "tripartite" (Canaanite/Sea People/Israelite) cultural division, omitting the early Phoenician interlude altogether.

This essay will argue for yet another reading of the same record—that the cultural sequence at Dor in the early Iron Age is characterized by continuity rather than upheavals, and it essentially documents the gradual transformation of the Late Bronze Canaanite culture into the Iron Age Phoenician one (see Gilboa 1998; 2005) and that the foreign "Sea Peoples" impact on the local material culture should be understood differently than hitherto proposed.

1. Excavations are currently conducted on behalf of the Institute of Archaeology of the Hebrew University of Jerusalem and the Zinman Institute of Archaeology at the University of Haifa. This report, however, was only partially updated and does not take into account later studies and the results of the new excavations (2003–2010). The main studies related to early Iron Age Dor published since 2003 are: Gilboa 2005; Shahack-Gross et al. 2005; Sharon et al. 2005; Gilboa, Cohen-Weinberger, and Goren 2006; Gilboa 2006–2007; Berna et al. 2007; Zorn and Brill 2007; Albert et al. 2008; Gilboa and Sharon 2008; Raban-Gerstel et al. 2008; and Gilboa, Sharon, and Boaretto 2009. Preliminary reports of the field seasons since 2003 may be found at http://dor.huji.ac.il/reports.html. Regarding ^{14}C dating at Dor and elsewhere, see also Sharon et al. 2007.

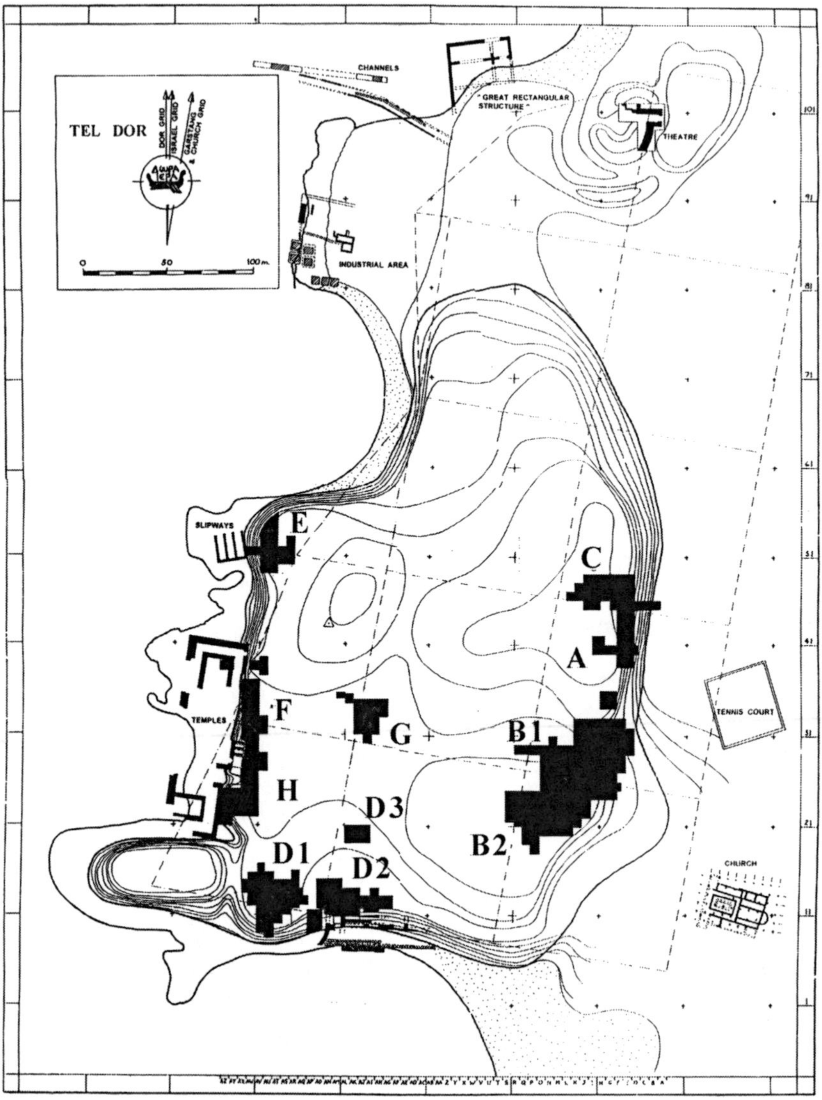

Fig. 2: Plan of Tel Dor and excavation areas.

No evaluation of these conflicting views can be accomplished, however, without an orderly presentation of the findings of the excavation that relate to the question at hand. The two volumes of the final report published to date (Stern et al. 1995) cover areas in which few remains of the early Iron Age were found.

Stern's (1994a) popular overview was written when the exploration of the relevant strata at Dor was just beginning. In the second edition of that book, Stern added a chapter summarizing the results of the second decade of excavation (Stern 2000a, 345–89). The space that could be allotted to the Iron I remains and their integration with those presented in the main body of the book was perforce limited. The facts can be laboriously gleaned from the yearly preliminary reports,[2] condensed from [unpublished] masters' theses and doctoral dissertations (Vansteenhuyse 1998–1999; Lisk 1999; Gilboa 2001a; Matskevich 2003) and sifted from the many articles written (some on other subjects and some in Hebrew) by the various Dor excavators (a full bibliography is available at http://dor.huji.ac.il/bibliography.html). This paper, first and foremost, purposes to summarize these data and present them in an accessible venue (for a more concise and recent summary, see also Gilboa and Sharon 2008).

The fact that the participants in the 2001 workshop on the Philistines and other "Sea Peoples" were accommodated at Kibbuz Nahsholim, located adjacent to the site of Tel Dor, has enabled an orderly exposition of the material culture at early Iron Age Dor, both on-site and at the museum and expedition workrooms. The first part of this essay will attempt to do the same in print. Readers not interested in the detailed Dor-specific report but only in the authors' arguments as to the early Iron Age sequence at Dor may proceed directly to the discussion. Before proceeding with the exposition, however, we must recognize our debt of gratitude to Ephraim Stern, the former project director, to the sponsoring institutions (The Philip and Muriel Berman Center for Biblical Archaeology and Israel Science Foundation of The Israel Academy of Sciences and Humanities [Grant Nos. 812/97, 778/00]), and to the many excavators of Dor over the years—those who agree with our interpretation and those who do not—for providing the arena, the data, and the intellectual stimulus that make scholarly discussions such as this possible.

Location and Environment

In the periods under discussion, Dor was the major harbor town of the northern Sharon/Carmel regions (fig. 1). This is a triangular section of the Levantine coast,

2. A nonexhaustive list includes, in chronological order, Stern, Gilboa, and Sharon 1989; Stern, Sharon, and Gilboa 1988–1989; Stern, Berg, and Sharon 1991; Stern, Gilboa, and Sharon 1992; Stern and Sharon 1993; 1994; 1995; Stern, Gilboa, and Berg 1997; Stern et al. 1997; Stern et al. 1998; Stern, Gilboa, and Sharon 2000; Stern, Gilboa, et al. 2000; Stern, Sharon, et al. 2000; Sharon et al. 2009a–b.

hemmed in between the Mediterranean Sea and Mount Carmel. It is delimited by the Nahal Hadera stream at its wide southern base and narrows to a virtual point at the north—where the Carmel touches the coastline at the southern tip of the Haifa Bay. It is this area and the Carmel itself that forms the natural hinterland of Dor. In the Late Bronze and early Iron Ages Dor shared this area with several smaller sites, the most substantial of which are Tel Nami (e.g., Artzy 1993; 1995), ʿAtlit (e.g., Johns 1938; 1993), and Tel Shiqmona (Elgavish 1993; 1994) to the north; Tel Mevorakh (Stern 1978; 1984) on the coast to the south; and Tel Zomera (Neeman, Sender, and Oren 2000, Hadera site no. 28) and Tel Zeror on the Hadera stream (Neeman, Sender, and Oren 2000, no. 80; Ohata and Kochavi 1967–1970; Kochavi 1993), farther inland.

The Sharon Plain is cut by three north–south calcareous sandstone (locally named *kurkar*) ridges. On the Carmel coast, north of Nahal Taninim, only two *kurkar* ridges exist. The eastern one is now known as the Highway Ridge (under the present Tel Aviv–Haifa Highway) and the western one is the Coastal Ridge. The Coastal Ridge is now partly submerged and parts of it appear as islets and reefs off Dor and Maʿagan Michael, protecting the coast from the onslaught of the waves. Dor itself (figs. 1–2) is located on that ridge, at a point where it skirts the present-day shoreline. Moving sand, originating in the Sahara and pushed northwards by the Nile, Mediterranean currents, and prevailing winds, accumulates on the narrow coastal zone, thus forming a series of bays and lagoons, perfect for the protection and beaching of shallow-keeled boats.

The western part of Tel Dor is situated on the Coastal Ridge, while its eastern part is on a sand spit. Two bays flank it on the north and south. During the time in which the tell was first clearly inhabited, Middle Bronze II, the sea may have been slightly lower than at present. There was almost no sand along the coast (most of the sand along the coast of Israel is younger than 4000–4500 years BP) and environmental conditions were different than those prevailing today (Sivan, Eliyahu, and Raban 2004). Previous research suggested that in ancient times the tell may have been further protected (and cut off from its hinterlands) by a shallow lagoon and swamps on the east—thus making it a peninsula, virtually an island (Raban 1995, 350).

The landscape now covered by sand was previously a wetland, even along the present coast, and only the ingression of the sea during the last thousand years or so brought in the sands. Unlike the coastal swamps that dried up at around ± 8000 years ago, the swamps between the Coastal Ridge and the Highway Ridge survived until the twentieth century C.E., when they were artificially dried up. Thus today's landscape of bountiful agriculture may be misleading. As recently as the beginning of this century, the Kebara swamps, just southeast of Dor, impeded habitation, cultivation, and travel in the Sharon Plain. Some readings of the ancient written sources (e.g., Aharoni 1979, 24, 50) infer a similar situation in the Late Bronze and Iron Ages. Archaeozoological findings from the relevant strata at Dor (see below) lend credence to this view.

Previous Excavations Pertaining to the Iron Age

The first excavator of Dor, John Garstang (1924) dug two trenches on the western and southern slopes of the tell. In his southern trench (Cut I; presently between Areas D1 and D2, see figs. 2–3), above the site's southern bay, the earliest deposits uncovered by him, on bedrock, were dated to the Late Bronze (his Steps G and F). Above these, Step E comprised both Late Bronze and early Iron Age pottery. This step also held a layer of ash, in which, according to Garstang, early Iron Age pottery was found (Garstang 1924, 42). This ash layer might be a candidate for a Late Bronze destruction level—though this cannot be ascertained. As the step seemed to include early Iron Age pottery, it is more plausible to correlate it with the major mid–early Iron Age destruction uncovered in the later excavations in other excavation areas (see below). The most typical ceramic form of Step E and the subsequent D, were sharply carinated jars, which, according to his description (they were not illustrated), may be recognized as the late versions of "Canaanite jars" typifying in this area the Iron 1b horizon (see below). But it is unknown where exactly they were found in relation to Garstang's ash layer. Within Step E, seemingly above and later than the ash layer (the exact stratigraphic association cannot be assessed), a massive boulder wall was constructed, of which Garstang uncovered the western face (Garstang 1924, fig. 1); the same wall was later excavated both by Raban and by Stern (the Bastion, see below).

Between 1980–1984 Avner Raban dug several probes (his Areas A–G) on the beach at the southern bay and on the south slope of the tell—to the south of Garstang's trench, east of Garstang's massive wall, which he numbered W69 (for a final report, see Raban 1995; for a general plan, see fig. 9.12; here figs. 4–5). He divided the features uncovered into several phases: The earliest of these consist primarily of the remains of a quay (E) flanked by structures/surfaces composed of large flat ashlars, all laid as rows of headers, sloping into the bay (these structures underwent a few constructional alterations corresponding to a rise in sea level), further built quays, an ashlar-built well (L62) on the very western fringes of the excavation area, near W69, and possibly some hewn beach-rock plates. Raban dated this earliest phase to the thirteenth–mid-twelfth centuries B.C.E. (i.e., what we would call the "transitional Late Bronze/Iron horizon"; see below). To the second main phase, dated to the mid-twelfth century, were attributed the construction of the massive W69, which Raban interpreted as a retaining wall, and

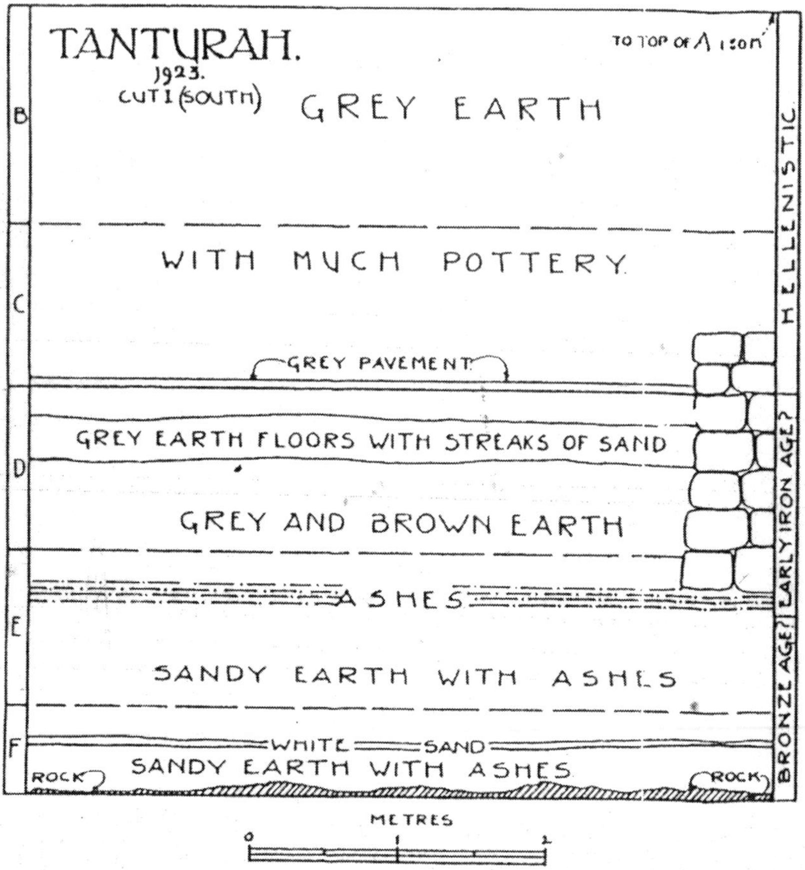

Fig. 3: Garstang's schematic section of his southern trench. (Garstang 1924, pl. 2).

an elevation in both the well and at least one of the quays (A). In a third phase, dated ca. 1100 B.C.E., Quay A was partly dismantled and a higher platform was constructed in its stead. A retaining sea wall is postulated to have protected structures on the lee side of the area, which included, *inter alia*, a slab-built drainage channel (L65) uncovered just east of the well, and the well itself (its last phase of use). These alterations, according to Raban, were a response to topographical changes, which exposed Dor's southern beach and installations to the surge.

Above these was built a massive wall, Wall H, a long retaining wall running east–west along the southern slope of the tell, also constructed to protect the settlement's southern margins. No other meaningful architectural remains related to this wall, and Raban suggested that the harbor, and in fact possibly the entire

Fig. 4: The southern slope of the tell during Raban's excavations. The protruding wall on the left is W69 (our Bastion), adjacent to it is the well, and on the right is Raban's Wall M, the western wall of our Monumental Stone Building.

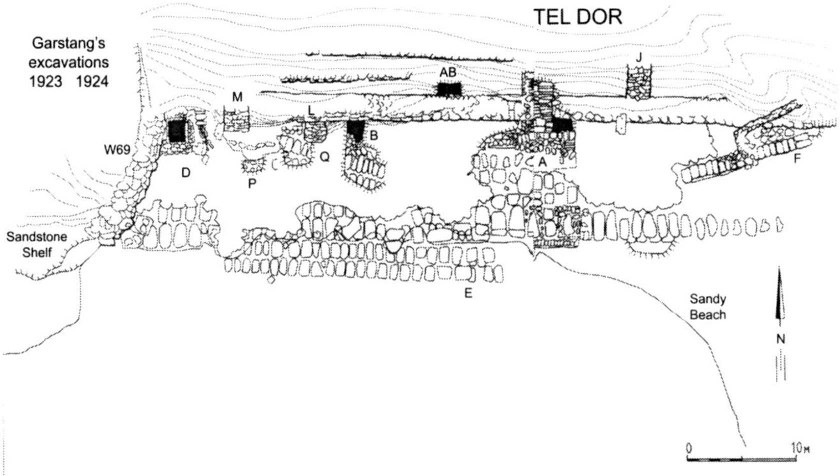

Fig. 5: Plan of Raban's excavations along the mound's southern bay (after Raban 1995, fig. 9:12).

southern waterfront, may have been abandoned then. This wall, in turn, was later replaced by a massive structure constructed of huge limestone boulders—consisting of Raban's Walls M (fig. 4 on right), L, and J, and dated to the early-tenth century B.C.E.

Raban attributed all the early constructional phases in this area, culminating in Wall H, to the "Sea People" occupation at Dor. The quays were compared by him chiefly to the Kition "bastions," which according to him are in fact harbor installations (e.g., Raban 1987; 1988). The later limestone building was associated with the Israelite newcomers under the united monarchy (e.g., Raban 1995, 339), who, lacking any maritime tradition and resisting the potential of the immediate environment, literally turned their back on the sea and constructed their building relatively high up the slope, of huge limestones carried all the way from the Carmel (instead of employing the *kurkar* abundantly available on site). During this period, the sea level may have subsided (Raban 1995, 339). In contrast to both Garstang's and Raban's excavations, Stern's excavations in Area D2, which unearthed further remains of the very same structures uncovered by them (other than the harbor installations), did not uncover any remains that predate the early Iron Age, though they were carried down to bedrock (see below). It should be noted in this context that, though Raban explicitly mentioned Late Bronze Age ceramics (including imports) in association with the southern "harbor installations," nothing in the pottery published by him unequivocally belongs to the Late Bronze Age. Most of the pottery is not earlier than the late Iron I (our Ir1b, see below), with a few Middle Bronze fragments. It seems that the date of the "Sea People harbor" should be reconsidered.

The Hebrew University of Jerusalem Excavations—Stratigraphy

Deposits relevant to the questions at hand were reached in eight disjoint excavation areas (B1, B2, C, D1, D2, E, F, and G, see fig. 2) by several excavators. The following will recap the evidence chiefly from three areas in which the exposures of the relevant deposits were the most extensive (Areas G, B1, and D2). It should be stressed at the outset that no correlation of finds from these areas is possible on stratigraphic grounds alone and the suggested correlations are mostly based on artifactual considerations (which will be spelled out in the next section). Thus the stratigraphy will be described by area—using local phases, each of which denotes a significant change in the architectural layout of the area. Most of these phases are further divisible into subphases (denoted by adding lowercase letters to the phase designation) marking minor changes within the lifecycle of the "phase" (the raising of floor levels, construction of installations, shifting of partition walls, etc.). Phase designations in separate areas do not necessarily coincide, thus Phase 9a in G and 9a in B1 have nothing in common (save the fact that in each area they mark the highest floor-level within the ninth rebuild, counting from the surface).

Furthermore, we do not necessarily subscribe to a naïve "locus-to-stratum" model. Punctuative events (such as a general destruction or a site-wide building scheme), by which strictly contemporaneous "strata" in different parts of the town may be articulated, are the exception rather than the rule—at least at this site. Hence we use the much looser horizon terminology (see below). Phases in different areas assigned to the same "horizon" are held to be broadly contemporary, but not necessarily to have begun and/or ended at the same time, other than in very specific cases. We attribute each stratigraphic phase to a chronological horizon. The ceramic compositions and dating of these horizons are discussed below.

Area G

The most complete stratigraphic sequence spanning the periods under discussion was found in Phases 12–6 of Area G. One factor, which needs to be taken into consideration in this area as well as in others, is the depth of the Iron Age remains at Dor—due to the buildup of Classical and post-Classical cities on top of it, as well as the thickness of accumulation within the Iron Age sequence itself. This limits the exposure of lower strata and hence the completeness of the record for these earlier eras. In Area G, the uppermost levels of the early Iron Age were reached at a depth of 2 meters below surface and were located in almost all the units of the 85 square meter area. The earlier part of the Iron Age (our early Ir1a horizon—see below) is about 4.5 meters below surface and a much smaller exposure, ca. 34 square meters was achieved. Only two probes (about 13 square meters) reached Late Bronze deposits at a depth of 5.5 meters.

Phase G/12 (LB II), found in the aforementioned probes, consists of thick (over 2 meters) deposits of ash, sand, and brick debris, mostly sloping from northeast to the south and to the west. No clear living surfaces were located as well as no architecture. The deposits and the rather small fragments of pottery and copper/bronze slag indicate that these are industrial middens—whether in-town or outside is unclear (Stern et al. 2000, 33*).

Phase G/11 (LB II) also consists of what is apparently metallurgic activity—the main difference being that several superimposed floors/installations were located here, rather than merely waste piles. A number of bronze objects, as well as more extensive potsherd concentrations (though nothing quite *in situ*), were found on these surfaces. The "floors" were extremely uneven, though, and there is no evidence of any walls (Stern, Gilboa et al. 2000, 29*; 2000, 33*).

Phase G/10 (Ir1a early) marks the first appearance of architecture in Area G (figs. 6–7). This is also the first phase in which several definite *in situ* installations appear (Stern, Gilboa et al. 2000, 29*). The center area appears to have been an open (or perhaps semi-open) courtyard, floored by a densely packed series of white ash surfaces sloping from north to south. Over thirty-five layers of this material were counted in one section—which is altogether only 30 centimeters in depth (fig. 8). Among the thin surfaces were occasional shallow depressions with denser concentrations of ashy material. The clay at the bottom of some of these depressions was baked-through by intense heat. In the courtyard and surrounding rooms were found one kiln (fig. 9; Stern, Gilboa et al. 2000, fig. 53)—with an opening to insert a *tuyère* in its wall; one complete ceramic pot bellows; a big flat stone which may have been used for an anvil (or may simply have supported a post), fragments of crucibles, and chunks of copper—from tiny droplets to almost fist-sized. X-ray fluorescence analysis indicated the existence of burnt copper in this phase (Sariel Shalev, personal communication). It seems that in Phase 10 this area was primarily used as a smithy for the (re)melting of bronze. Also found were several enigmatic features: some sort of pen or stilt-supported installations consisting of a semi-circle of nine small post-holes, a stone-lined installation next to the "anvil" with smooth rounded pebbles in it; and a small room attic full of bones, including several cow-skulls (Lisk 1999, fig. 5). What (or whether) these have to do with copper/bronze industry remains to be seen.

Phase G/9 (Ir1a late; fig. 10) witnesses a continuous use of the Phase 10 structure, reusing most of its walls. The building, again, has a central courtyard and rooms on at least three of its sides (its eastern part lies outside the excavation area). Its function, however, has changed; no traces of metallurgy are evident anymore. It was apparently used now for storage and household industry, and probably habitation as well. A fiery destruction (see below) had left quite a lot of evidence *in situ* and so the functions of individual rooms may be reconstructed. The building was entered from the north, through an entrance room equipped with a plaster floor, which opened upon the courtyard and upon the two rooms in the northern row which flank the entrance space. The courtyard, which is the main space excavated, is situated above the Phase 10 "forge" and was partly roofed and partly stone-paved (fig. 11). In its center was a mud-brick installation (Stern, Gilboa, and Berg 1997, 65, fig. 67; Stern et al. 1997, fig. 11; see also Stern, Gilboa, et al. 2000, 28*)—consisting of a 4.6 by 0.8 by 0.65-meter platform with a trough-like top, sloping from both ends towards the center. In the courtyard around it were found mainly storage jars and several basalt grinding stones. One proposal as to the use of this installation was that it was employed for large-scale bread-making (or, rather, dough-kneading; see Stern 2000a, 348, figs. 246–47). It is hardly likely, however, that such an activity would take place on an unbaked mud surface. Another suggestion is that it was indeed a trough, and the space was used as a stable or barn. This, again, does not explain the drainage or the association with grinding-stones. Perhaps the best option is that it was

Fig. 6: General view of Area G, showing mainly walls of Phases G/10 and G/9 (Ir1a), looking north.

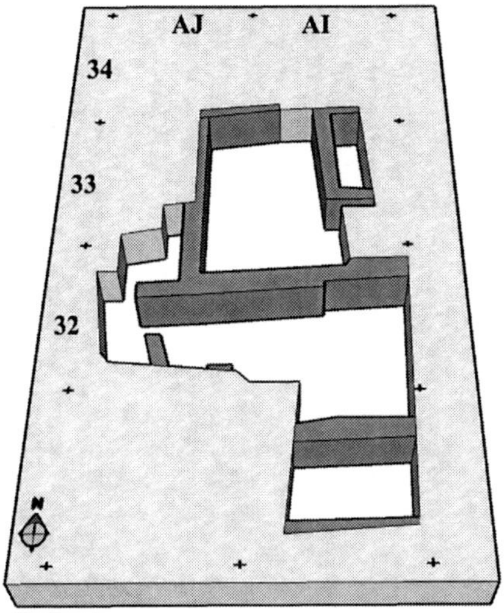

Fig. 7: Schematic reconstruction of Area G, Phase G/10 (early Ir1a).

a grinding installation—used to support a row of lower grinding-stones. Other rooms in the same complex were used for other purposes. Among the northern rooms, one room had a concentration of bones—including several intact skeletons of fish—and must have been used for some fishing-related activity and a

Fig. 8: Accumulation of white and gray ashy surfaces in Area G, Phase G/10 (early Ir1a), looking east.

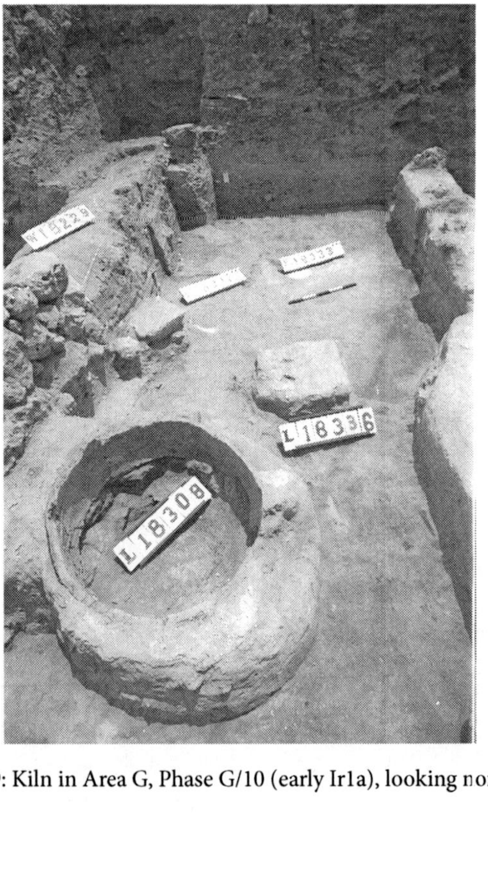

Fig. 9: Kiln in Area G, Phase G/10 (early Ir1a), looking north.

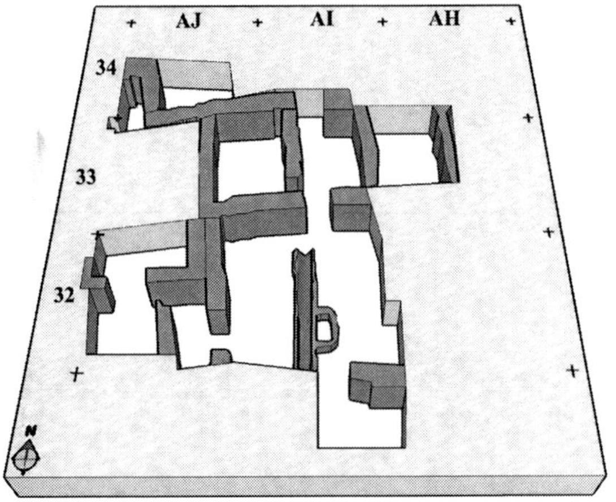

Fig. 10: Schematic reconstruction of Area G, Phase G/9 (late Ir1a).

Fig. 11: The slab-paved courtyard of the Area G structure in Phase G/9 (late Ir1a) with a clay installation, looking north.

Fig. 12: General view of Area G, showing mainly walls of Phases G/8–6, looking north.

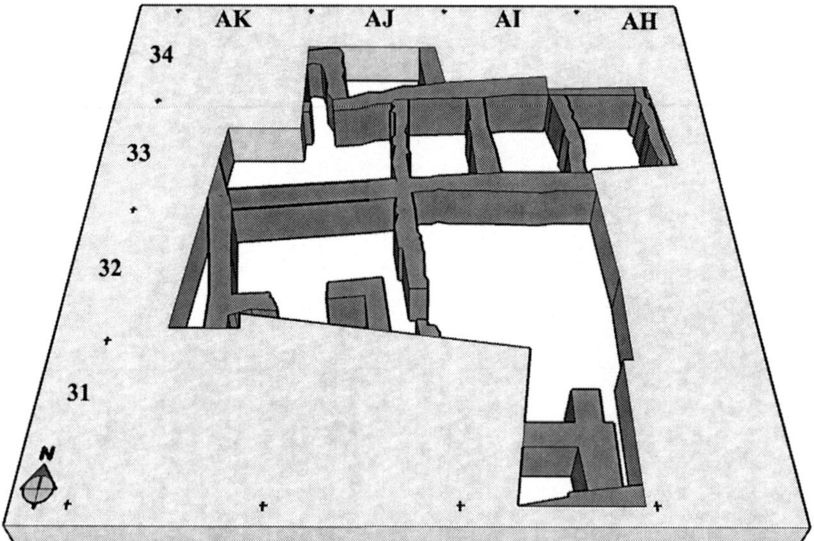

Fig. 13: Schematic reconstruction of Area G, Phase G/8 (Ir1a|b).

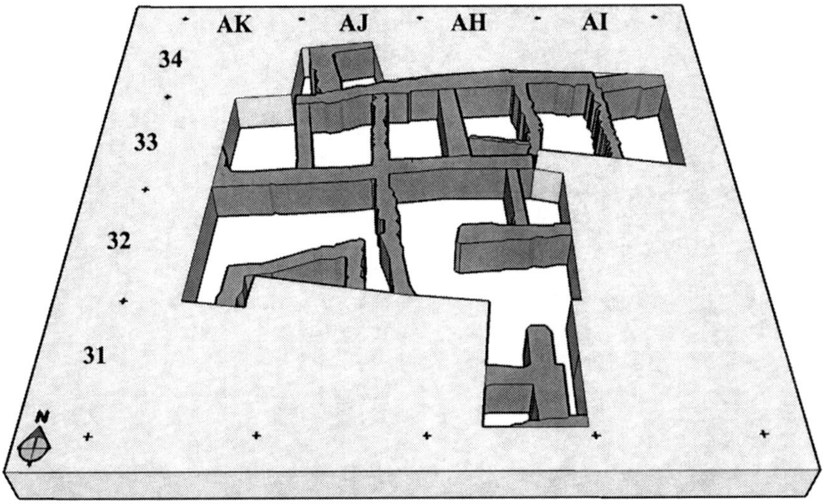

Fig. 14: Schematic reconstruction of Area G, Phase G/7 (mainly Ir1b).

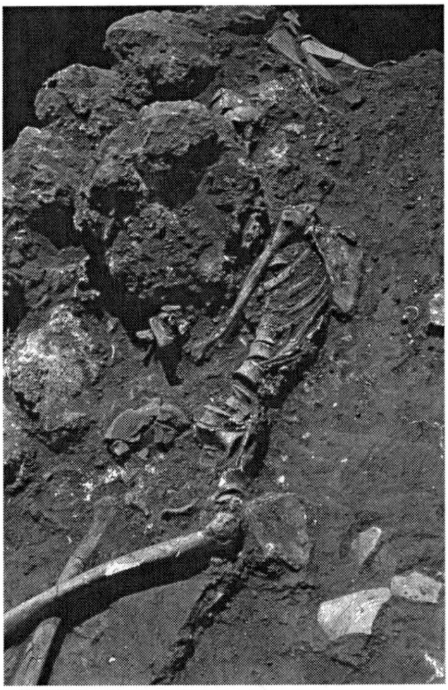

Fig. 15: Crushed female skeleton in Area G, Phase G/7a or G/6b (Ir1|2).

Fig. 16: Cultic ceramic assemblage from Area G, including figurative chalice and skyphos (for stratigraphy, see text).

second room housed two or three large Cypriot-style pithoi (for which see below). On the southern side of the courtyard/grinding installation, one space was full of collared-rim pithoi and storage jars—both of local manufacture and Egyptian imports (Stern, Gilboa, and Berg 1997, 65; Stern, Gilboa et al. 2000, 28*; Stern 2000a, figs. 249, 250; Gilboa 2001a, pl. 5.5–10). The whole complex thus appears to be related to food production—probably aimed at mass consumption at higher than household level.

Stern attributes a cache of vessels, apparently cultic in nature, to Phase 9 (see below, fig. 16; see Stern 2000a, 347, fig. 47; Gilboa 2001a, pl. 5.49–51), but the stratigraphic association for this assemblage should be reconsidered (see below).

Phase 9 ended with a massive fire (e.g., Stern and Sharon 1993, 149–50; Stern et al. 1997, 52–55; Stern 2000a, 352–53). Baked-through bricks and completely calcified limestone blocks attest to the extreme temperatures of the blaze. The debris was thickest and the fire apparently fiercest in the southeastern part of the area—the "pantry" and the south side of the grinding installation—it is this fire that baked the installation and ensured its survival. The destruction level markedly slopes towards the west and north—and virtually no trace of it was found in the edge-units of the area on these sides, though in these spots too, *in situ* artifacts and crushed pottery attest to a traumatic end. This is a fact perhaps worth noting for the ensuing discussion of site-wide destructions and perhaps, in general, discussions of such phenomena. A few other observations relating to the "micro-stratigraphy" of the destruction are perhaps relevant: Sections of roofing-material—a grid of wooden beams covered by reeds/matting material and compacted *pisée*—had collapsed on the "grinding installation" and floors of the central space of the building. Most of the ash and all of the broken jars were found below these roof sections, but most of the burnt-brick collapse was on top. This indicates that the roof fell after the beginning of the fire, and the walls collapsed somewhat later. When the pottery from the Phase 9 rooms was restored, it became evident that in quite a few vessels burnt pieces joined unburnt ones in no apparent pattern. This means that these pots were broken and scattered on the floor before the fire started. What all this reveals about the means of destruction is moot—vandalism (looting and subsequent torching) is our favored explanation, though earthquake (dropping the shelves in the pantry, weakening but not collapsing the structure) and a subsequent firestorm remain a possibility.

Phases G/8 and G/7 (respectively Ir1a–b; Ir1b and Ir1|2 transition). Following the fire, the Phase 9 house was quickly rebuilt on top of the destruction debris, reusing some of the Phase 9 walls and wall stubs, and constructing most new ones on practically the same lines. Phases 8 and 7 (figs. 12–14) are similar and distinguishable only in some of the rooms, differentiated mainly by the raising of floor levels and the shifting of some walls. They are more easily discerned in the courtyard, which was subdivided in Phase 7 into subspaces by new walls (Stern and Sharon 1993, 145–46; 1994, 69).

No destruction phenomena are evident in these phases (but see below) so a functional division of the rooms is difficult. It is significant, however, that above the semi-paved "bread-making" court in Phase 9 a new stone paving was constructed in the later phases (in all these phases, this is one of only two spots which were thus paved). No similar installations were noted in them, however (but then the one in Phase 9 may only have been preserved due to the remarkable circumstances of its destruction).

One dramatic event may have marked the end of Phase 7 (see Stern and Sharon 1993, 147): One of the rooms (the one above the entrance room of Phase 9) was found full of large rocks. Upon the removal of these, a skeleton and several smashed storage jars and other pots were found beneath them (fig. 15; Stern and Sharon 1993, 146–47; Stewart 1993, 35, upper fig.; Stern 1993b, part II: fig. on p. 30). Anthropological study indicates that it was an adult female (nicknamed Doreen), who lay facing the wall with her hands in front of her face (Patricia Smith, personal communication). Several of the fracture marks on her bones were apparently made when the bone was fresh—but had not started healing, i.e., immediately before and/or a short time after death. The evidence is consistent, therefore, with the collapse of the wall having been the cause of death. No similar evidence of collapse or destruction was found in other parts of the area, however. There is thus no evidence that this isolated find can be connected to some wide catastrophe—such as an earthquake (as suggested by Stewart). If this was a purely local structural collapse, why had no one bothered to try and dig the poor woman out? It is perhaps significant that no floors were found in this particular space in subsequent strata—and that the top of the stone collapse is actually higher than where such later floors would have been expected. Perhaps this particular space had not been reused subsequent to this mishap. This points to another possibility—that Doreen should be disassociated from Phase 7 and actually perished later in a *cellar* of the subsequent phase (6b). In fact, the *in situ* ceramic assemblage that accompanied Doreen may be more compatible with Phase 6b than with 7. If Doreen indeed belongs to Phase 6b and not to 7, this may lend some support to the earthquake theory, as some floors of this latter horizon across the tell were abandoned with *in situ* artifacts (but no evidence of trauma beyond that, see below).

During the very last stage of Phase G/7 (7a), someone lost a bracelet or necklace in the southern part of the courtyard of the building. Four scarabs and a seal were found scattered about (see Gilboa, Sharon, and Zorn 2004; cf. Münger 2003). Could this be another indication that Phase 7 did not end peacefully?

A short discussion is in order concerning another discovery perhaps related to these phases. A small cache of apparently cult-related vessels was found in the northwesternmost room of the area (see Stern et al. 1997, 52; Stern 2000a, fig. 47 lower; here fig. 16). It comprises, *inter alia,* a chalice on a square four-hoofed foot, fenestrated with dancing (?) figures in *crèpe schnitt* technique. With it were a painted goblet, a skyphos, a series of small to tiny bowls, possibly votive, chunks of pumice, and other artifacts. The stratigraphic attribution of this cache is not straightforward. For one thing, the tell-tale burnt layer of Phase 9, which serves as a benchmark to correlate the different architectural spaces in Area G, had dwindled to nothing before reaching this room. The immediate stratigraphy of the assemblage is not clear either—it was never established if it was in a pit (which was not delineated), cut from above into a brick wall, or if the objects were lying on a surface (never observed) on top of a mud-brick "bench"—in the manner of contemporary temples and cult-rooms. We maintain, on both stratigraphic and typological grounds (see below) that this group should be attributed to Phase 8, but one should note the alternative, espoused by Stern, that it belongs to Phase 9.

Phase G/6b

The following phase (Ir1|2) is again a rebuilding and elaboration of the same structure as in all previous phases (fig. 17; Stern and Sharon 1993, fig. 13). Floors belonging to this phase were located in almost every excavation unit, but one of

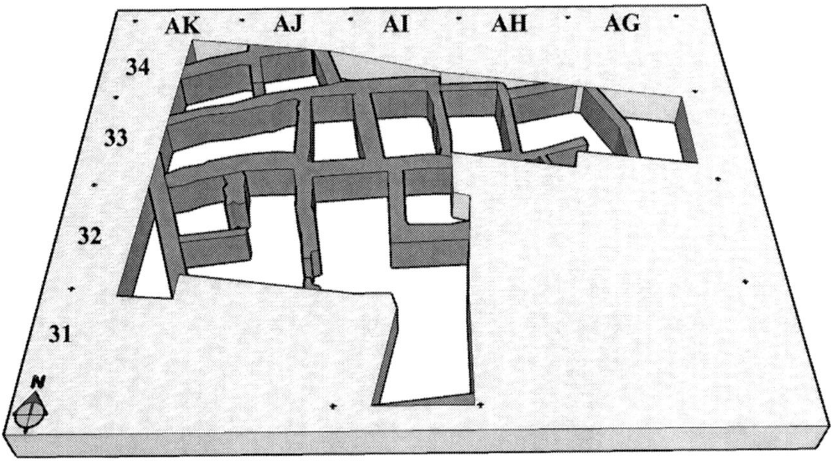

Fig. 17: Schematic reconstruction of Area G, Phases G/6b-a (Ir1|2 and Ir2a).

them, in the northeast extension of the area, was most proliferate in artifacts (and the major one with finds in primary deposition; see Gilboa 2001a, pl. 5.54–58)—it was nicknamed "Cheryl's famous floor" after its excavator (Stern and Sharon 1993, fig. 11; Stern et al. 1997, 51). The cause of destruction (or otherwise abandonment of vessels *in situ*) on "Cheryl's famous floor" is unclear, as is why the rest of the rooms had been swept clean of finds. As mentioned above (Phase G/7), it is possible that Doreen, alongside the collapse on top of her (and the accompanying *in situ* artifacts) actually belongs to this phase, which would add some more traumatic flavor to its end.

Phase G/6a (Ir2a)

This phase concludes our discussion of Area G. It (and all subsequent Iron Age phases in G) was badly riddled with late (Persian and Hellenistic periods) pits—precluding the reconstruction of a coherent plan. Floors of this phase (where found) seem to reach the same walls as the earlier (Phase 6b) floors and so it should essentially be regarded as a reflooring of existing structures (Stern, Gilboa, and Sharon 1992, 45). The chronological horizon of the finds on these floors, however, is later (see below). One remarkable find of this period—from a room adjacent (but stratigraphically later than) the "cultic assemblage" described above, is a floor on which were lying a long, thin ashlar and a stone "table" with four legs (or a roughly hewn horned altar—depending on which way you look at it; Stern 2000a, fig. 54A). They were accompanied, among other finds, by a unique Phoenician Bichrome jar (Stern 2000a, pl. I:4), and a fine Cypriot Bichrome bowl (Gilboa 1999b, fig. 7:1).

Area B1

Area B1, on the east slope of the tell, was one of the areas where the excavation was initiated in 1980 and the first one in which pristine soil was hit, some 14 meters beneath the surface. Exposure of the lowermost levels was perforce extremely limited.

Phase B1/14

This is the deepest level in this area, consisting of a layer of sandy deposit above the pristine dune—about 0.5 meters above present-day mean sea level. No real occupation remains were found in the sounding made into this layer and the potsherds in it, probably of mixed Middle and Late Bronze date, were all small and worn—giving the appearance of beach deposits outside the settled area (Stern, Berg, and Sharon 1991, 60).

Phases B1/13 and B1/12 (Ir1a; Ir1a late)

These are thus the earliest actual occupation levels in B1. The main architectural feature in both is a huge wall oriented north–south, parallel to the tell's perimeter, 2–3 meters thick and preserved 4 meters high (figs. 18–19; see Stern, Berg, and Sharon 1991, 58–60, fig. 5; Stern 2000a, 92–93, fig. 40 and fig. on p. 89). It is constructed with a socle of "cyclopean" limestone boulders and a mud-brick superstructure. Outside (east) of the wall was a thick loose fill of haphazardly thrown layers of sand and mud-brick material—covered with a thick coating of mud and sloping gently eastwards. The whole appears, therefore, to be a fortification wall with a glacis outside it. The difference between Phase 13 and Phase 12 appears only in the narrow strip excavated inside (west) of the "cyclopean" wall: Phase 13 consists of a floor-level reaching the wall—without any further evidence of architecture, whereas in Phase 12 a structure (at least a wall and two rooms) are abutted to the same fortification (Stern 2000a, fig. 39).

Phase B1/12

This phase was destroyed in a catastrophic fire. Thick deposits of ash and burnt bricks crushed the contents of the rooms (mainly storage vessels of various sorts, including a "wavy-band" pithos; see Stern and Gilboa 1989–1990, 114–15; Stern 2000a, figs. 39, 41; Gilboa 2001a, pl. 5.15–17). The destruction accumulation is at times 2 meters high, the bricks in the walls baked red right through and some of the lime-stones are calcified. For all appearances, this destruction of B1/12 is the same as G/9 (see also artifactual considerations, below) possibly making this a (rare—at least for Dor) case of total, site-wide destruction.

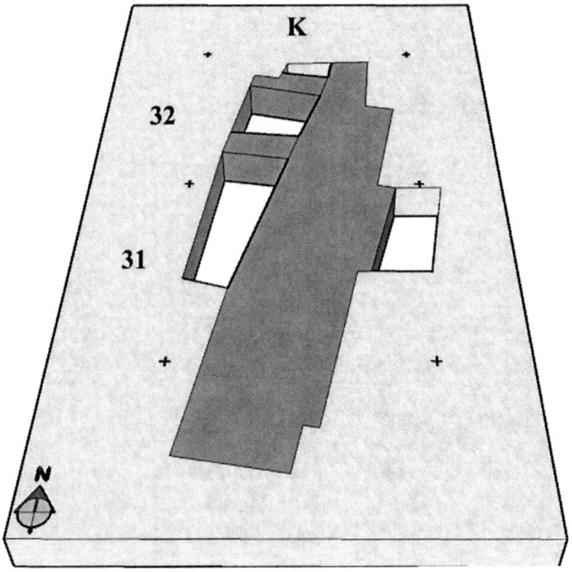

Fig. 18: Schematic reconstruction of Area B1, Phase B1/12 (late Ir1a).

Fig. 19: View of the Phases B1/13–12 city wall in Area B1 (Ir1a), looking south.

Phases B1/11 and B1/10 (Ir1a|b and Ir1b)

Following the destruction, the layout of the area changed (figs. 20–21). These two local phases were discerned at times during the excavation, but the division between them—and allocation of walls and floors to either one—proved difficult. The implications were made that Phase 11 is merely a leveling operation for the construction of Phase 10 and that the span of both phases was brief (Stern, Sharon and Gilboa 1988–1989, 45). A new study (Matskevich 2003) has clarified the situation: There are indeed two different phases and each has its own architecture. In Phase 11 some stub of the now-defunct "cyclopean" city wall was still visible—and the eastern one-third thickness of its mud-brick superstructure was reused (or a new, narrower mud-brick wall built along the same line) as the outer edge of the houses. In Phase 10 new structures were built, somewhat offset from the previous ones, and a new set of floors laid about 0.3–0.4 meter higher. The town expanded in this phase about 15 meters to the east and a new mud-brick city wall was constructed. The nature of both phases was similar, though—modest mud-brick structures with no stone foundation (though a thin layer of cobbles was sometimes used to line the foundation trenches).

Phases B1/9b and B1/9a (Ir1b and Ir1|2)

The following phases are also of similar character and still use the same fortification line (figs. 22–24). Some floors of Phase 9a seemed to bear (a few) artifacts in primary deposition. An alley traverses the area from north to south and it is very difficult to correlate stratigraphically the structures on both sides of it. In fact, we are not sure that the (rubble) building adjacent to the city wall was indeed constructed in Phase 9a (as indicated in fig. 24), or only in Phase 8. The stratigraphy of this area is currently under study.

Phase B1/8 (Ir2a)

This is the last phase of B1 to concern us here, as it already dates to Iron II (see below, fig. 25). In this phase, the row of mostly rubble houses east of the alley definitely existed, but the city wall apparently went out of use. Thus, Phase 8 is the only phase in the Iron Age continuum of Area B for which we do not have evidence of fortification, though there is no telling whether such a fortification may be buried under later constructions that were not dismantled. In Phase 7 of late Ir2a or Ir2ba new stone wall was constructed with a four-chambered gate (see Stern, Berg, and Sharon 1991, 56–57).

Area D2

The most extensive remains of the early Iron Age at Dor were found in this area, which was opened in 1984 on the south edge of the tell just north of Raban's

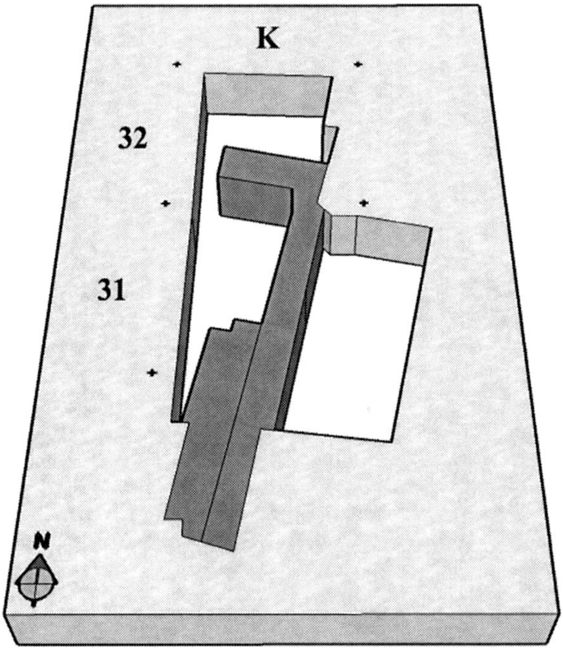

Fig. 20: Schematic reconstruction of Area B1, Phase B1/11 (Ir1a|b).

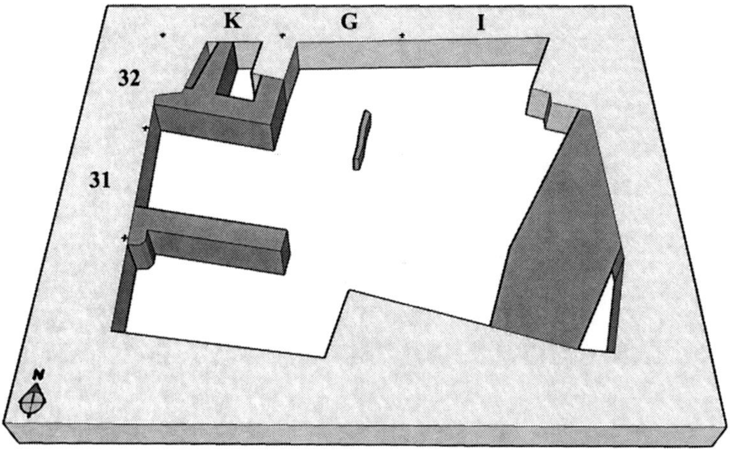

Fig. 21: Schematic reconstruction of Area B1, Phase B1/10 (Ir1b).

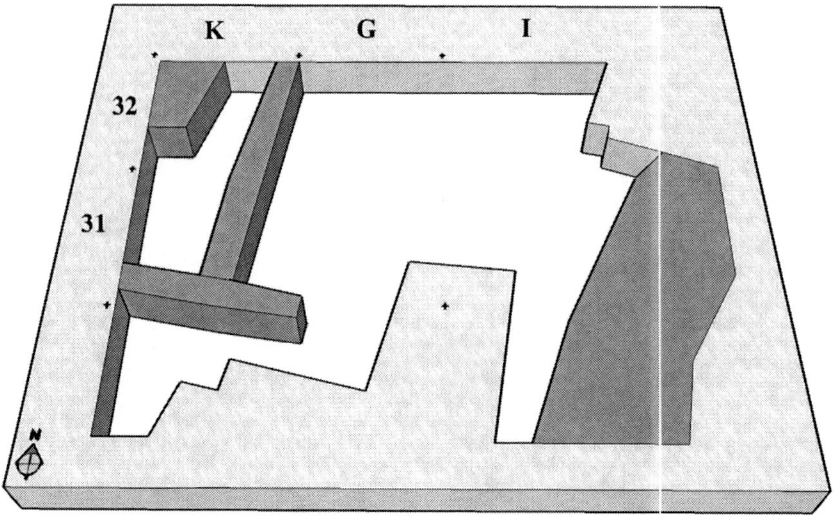

Fig. 22: Schematic reconstruction of Area B1, Phase B1/9b (Ir1b).

Fig. 23: Area B1, view of later Ir I and Ir A phases, looking south. The mud-brick structures on the right are of Phases B1/10–9. The rubble house on the extreme left belongs to Phase B1/8 and possibly to Phase 9a as well, and the long fieldstone wall to its right, forming an alley, belongs to Phase B1/8.

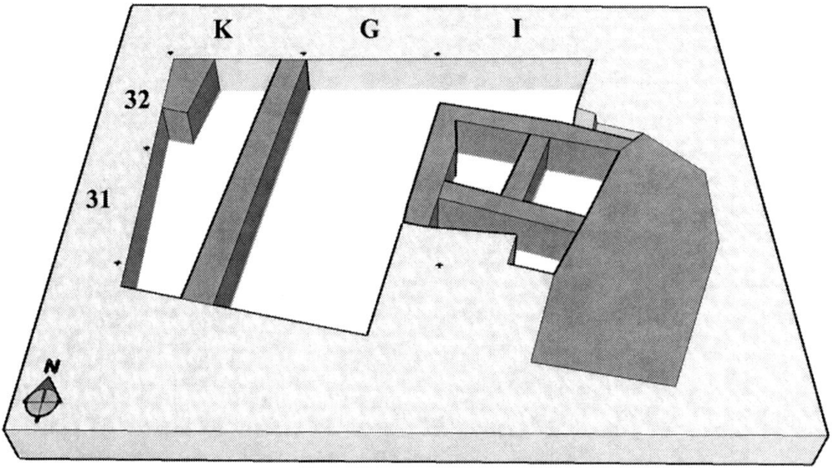

Fig. 24: Schematic reconstruction of Area B1, Phase B1/9a (Ir1|2).

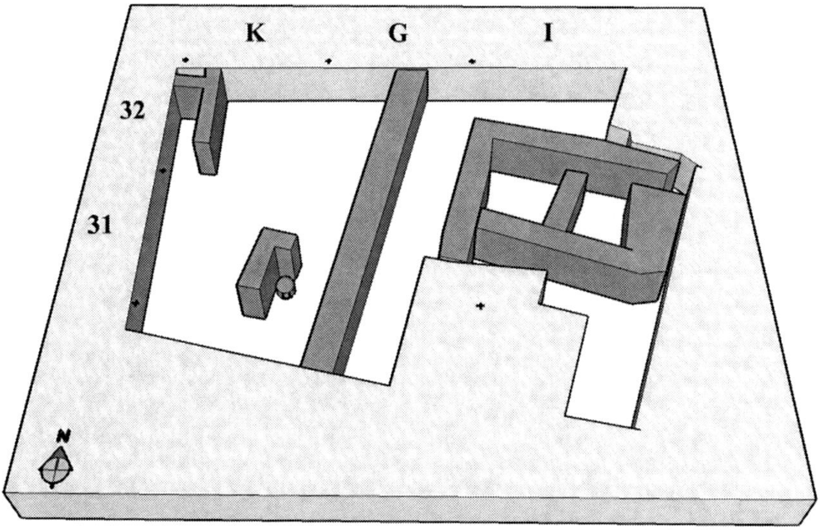

Fig. 25: Schematic reconstruction of Area B1, Phase B1/8 (Ir2a).

probes on the beach of the south bay (above). It was later extended westward all the way to Garstang's south trench of 1923. The area is defined (in the Iron Age) by several massive structures, each of which may have had a different history. These need to be introduced at the outset—with their colloquial names. The stratigraphy will be discussed by reference to this terminology.[3] Coming in towards the tell along the southern bay in which the early harbor installations investigated by Raban are located, one is dwarfed by the stubs of massive walls (Raban's Walls M, L, and J; see figs. 4–5)—visible where eroded by the sea even before excavations. These belong to a limestone-boulder structure dubbed by us the Monumental Stone Building (see below, figs. 30–31; e.g., Stern et al. 1997, 37–38; Stern, Gilboa, and Sharon 2000, 31*). It is over 18 meters wide (the extent of its west wall, our W5340, Raban's Wall M, from the northwest corner to the point where it got cut by the sea) and perhaps 40 meters long (if Raban's Wall J farther to the east is indeed the east wall of the same edifice). Its 1.75 meter-wide walls are preserved almost 5 meters high at its northwestern corner, which is composed of large ashlars (Stern 2000a, fig. 253 on left). These dimensions alone place this structure within the group of the largest Iron Age public buildings in this country. The fact that its construction predates most of these corollaries (below) renders it unique. It certainly ranks among the most massive Iron I structures known around the Mediterranean (for the date, see below).

Only a small part of this building (about 10 by 10 meters) was thus far excavated. Although parts of it (especially the northwestern corner) appear to be a single construction, evidence of filled-in foundation trenches and truncated internal walls indicate that the building was rebuilt (at least partially) at least once (Stern et al. 2000, 31*). The outside walls were rebuilt directly but internal partitions were moved (below, fig. 31). Several superimposed floors were related to each of the construction phases during an obviously long period of use, but artifacts on them were scant and fragmentary. Outside the building several architecturally different strata were identified to co-exist with it (local Phases 10, 9, 8 [c, b, and a], and possibly also 7—see below). It would be elegant to equate the main rebuilding, if not even actual reflooring operations, with the architecturally defined transitions outside the Monumental Stone Building (see below), but we have no evidence that that was the case.

About 10 meters west of the Monumental Stone Building is another imposing structure—only the east wall of which is currently exposed (below, figs. 32, 36 on extreme right). That wall is at least 24 meters long and is preserved to some

3. For a general description of these remains, see, e.g., Stern, Gilboa, et al. 2000, 25*; Stern, Sharon, et al. 2000, 31*; for general views of the area, see Stern 2000a, figs. 252, 253, 255; for a general plan, see Stern, Gilboa, et al. 2000, 33*, fig. 49 of Hebrew text.

4.5 meters at its highest point (Stern 2000a, fig. 252 right, fig. 255 right). The southern part of this wall, long exposed by the sea, curves westwards—following the contours of the *kurkar* ridge exposed at this point. This semicircular appearance has earned the structure its nickname, the Bastion, or the Acropolis Wall. This is the wall whose very southern stretch was uncovered by Garstang (western face only), equaling Raban's retaining W69 (figs. 4–5). Garstang's south trench is actually contained within the Bastion and the lower 1.5 meters above bedrock and below the wall was, according to him, a Late Bronze and possibly also early Iron Age accumulation capped by a layer of ashes. From the thin strip dug by us between the Bastion wall and Garstang's trench, it appears that floor levels inside (west of) the Bastion were considerably higher (perhaps as much as 2 meters) than the corresponding (ceramic) horizons adjacent to the Bastion wall on its outer (eastern) face. This, plus the fact that the base of the wall appears to follow the *kurkar* ridge and that early (Late Bronze Age) deposits that were reported inside it were not located outside (see below), do enhance the notion that this wall had a retaining purpose and separated a higher, older tell on the *kurkar* ridge on the west, from a lower perhaps newer town on the sandy beach. This to date is the only clue to the location of the still elusive, but surely existing Late Bronze town of Dor. Whether the higher part did serve as an independently fortified bastion or an acropolis in the early Iron Age is moot at this point (though early Iron Age deposits, the date of which have not been pinpointed yet, definitely exist in this area, reached while digging the southern part of Area D1).

The Bastion is connected to the Monumental Stone Building by yet another 4-meter-high boulder wall, which we nicknamed the Sea Wall (below, figs. 32, 36 in background; Stern 2000a, fig. 252: wall in background, fig. 253: wall on right, fig. 255: wall with person on it; which is not the same as Raban's postulated sea wall). The Sea Wall abuts both the Monumental Stone Building and Bastion, and hence is structurally later than both. However, the Monumental Stone Building is bound on the west with a deep, slab-covered drainage channel, which is structurally later than (at least the initial phase of) this building (see below fig. 34; Stern 2000a, fig. 254). This observation contradicts Raban's assertion (above) that the drain is significantly earlier than the building (his Wall M). The drain passes under the Sea Wall, and the point at which it drains into the bay was discovered by Raban (above). This means that the Sea Wall, the drainage channel, and the Monumental Stone Building must all have been in use together.

The clearest early Iron Age stratigraphic sequence in D2 is its west sector—bounded by the Sea Wall on the south, the Bastion on the west, and the Monumental Stone Building and drainage channel on the east. Only for this section will we detail the phasing within Iron I. *Grosso modo* the remains can be divided into those that precede the Monumental Stone Building and the Sea Wall (local Phases D2/14–11) and those that are contemporary with these structures (Phases D2/10–8 and possibly D2/7). This distinction is easily made by the fact that the foundation trench of the Sea Wall and the drainage channel cut all the preceding strata. The capstones of the drainage channel mark the lowermost floor level(s), which could possibly relate to the Monumental Stone Building on its outer, western face.

PhaseD2/14

These are fills above bedrock (which was reached in 2000 at a depth of 8.3 meters below present-day surface) and some installations and occupation surfaces directly above it and under any architecture. These remains are quite meager and by no means represent a single occupational (or chronological) episode. Rather, they comprise all activities on the bare *kurkar* ridge and sand beach east of the acropolis before this particular area became part of the urban infrastructure. The scant pottery, however, is definitely of early Iron Age date, though nothing more specific than that may be stated at the moment.

Phases D2/13 and D2/12 (Ir1a late[?] and Ir1a|b)

These two earliest building phases in Area D2, mark the first expansion of the town eastward beyond the acropolis and constitute two constructional episodes within, basically, the same building, nicknamed Natti's Rubble Structure after its excavator (figs. 26–28; Stern et al. 2000, 32*). The main feature is a 1.5-meter wide rubble wall, running east–west some 5 meters north of (and lower than) the Sea Wall. It apparently marks the southern extent of the inhabited area at this point in time. If it served as a fortification it was a fairly insubstantial one (but possibly the town may not have needed a very thick protective wall from this direction). The wall was rebuilt at least once (and hence the two different phases in accord with it). The earlier phase of this wall appears to abut the Bastion on the west (and both phases are cut by the drainage channel on the east). Natti's Rubble Structure extends northward (only partially excavated, its known part consisting of at least four rooms). The end of its lower phase (13) seems to have been abrupt, as *in situ* artifacts were left on at least one of its floors. Following this (in Phase 12), part of the walls continued in use and others were newly rebuilt along similar lines, and the general plan, at least of the excavated part, remained unaltered. This upper phase seems to have ended, at least partially, in destruction. One of its rooms, as well as the area south of the building, was covered with a deep layer of ash.

The question, of course, is whether any of the two mishaps the building underwent correlate with the great fire in Areas B1 and G. Though the pottery assemblage from these contexts has not yet been processed, a preliminary investi-

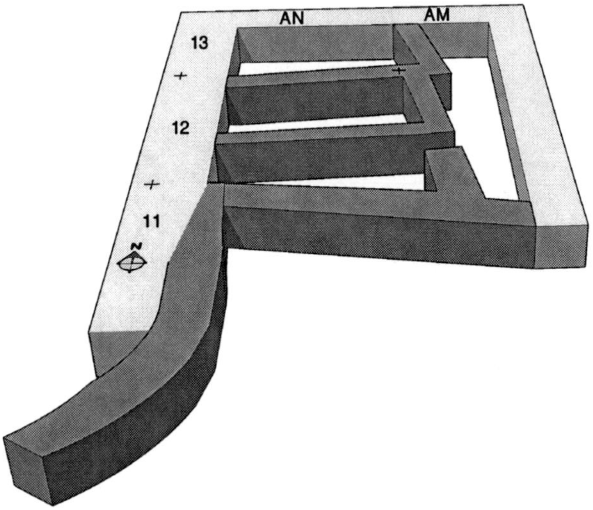

Fig. 26: Schematic reconstruction of Area D2, Phase D2/13 (late Ir1a).

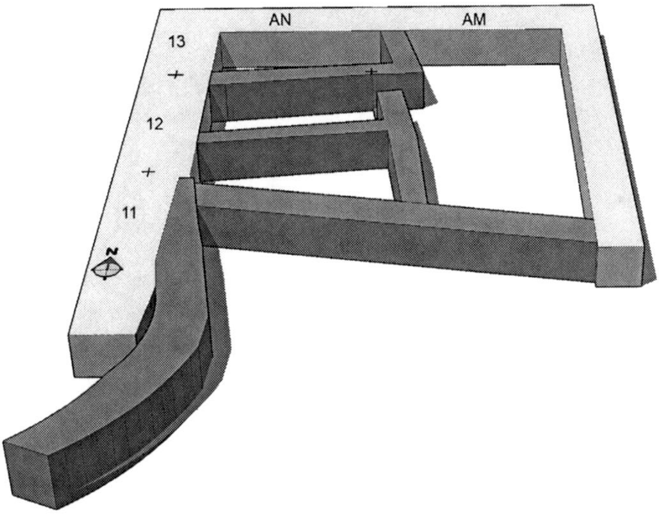

Fig. 27: Schematic reconstruction of Area D2, Phase D2/12 (Ir1a|b).

gation seems to indicate that the assemblage from the early phase (D2/13) may fit that of the "destruction horizon" and that of Phase D2/12 is slightly, but definitely later (Gilboa 2001a, 95–96).

Fig. 28: Area D2, general view of Natti's Rubble Structure (Phases D2/13–12), looking east.

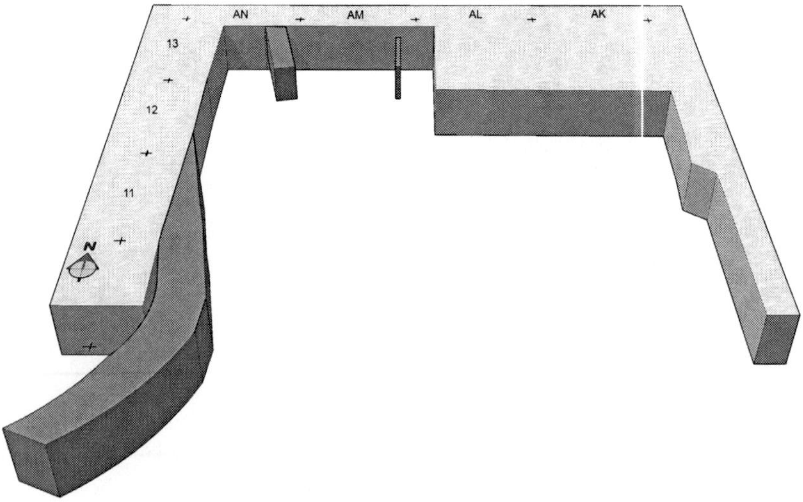

Fig. 29: Schematic reconstruction of Area D2, Phase D2/11 (Ir1b).

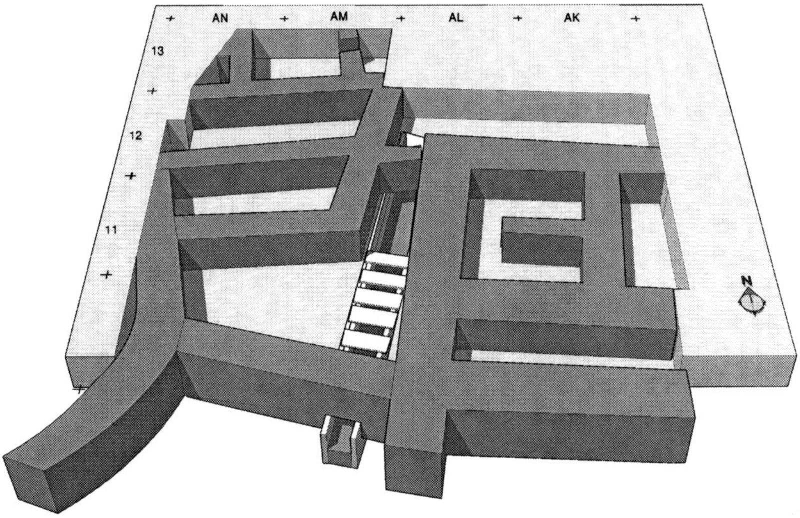

Fig. 30: Schematic reconstruction of Area D2, Phase D2/10 (Ir1b).

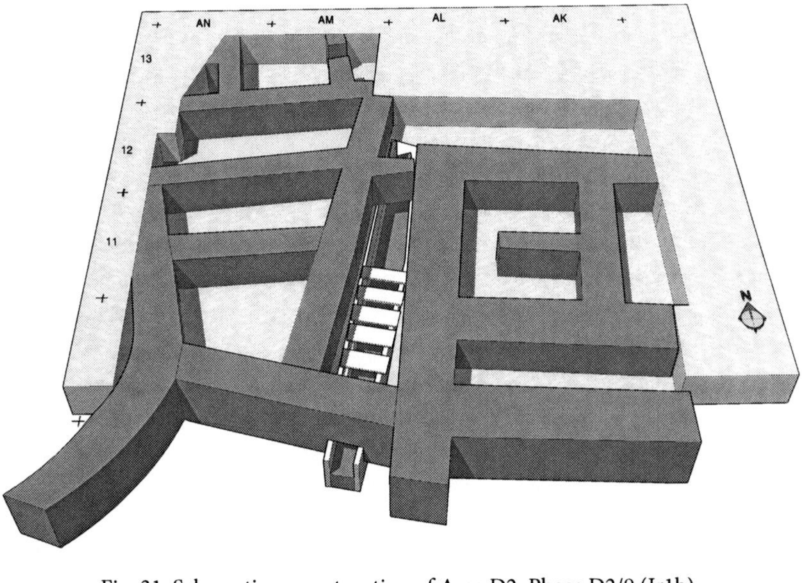

Fig. 31: Schematic reconstruction of Area D2, Phase D2/9 (Ir1b).

Phase D2/11 (Ir1b)

This is a transitional phase, whose remains were found mainly in the northern part of the area above the burnt Phase 12, but still below any structure clearly relatable to the Monumental Stone Building or the drainage channel adjoining it (fig. 29). It comprises merely a few modest and ill-preserved rubble walls and beaten earth floors. A feature relatable to Phase D2/11 in the southern part of the area are some much disturbed and fragmentary human skeletal remains—well above the remains of the Phases 13–12 outer wall, but sealed by the monumental construction of Phase 10 (see below) and not related to any architecture or habitation level. Either this area was outside the Phase D2/11 town and served for burials (which were then disturbed by the building of the Sea Wall and other structures) or the remains were brought here from elsewhere with constructional fill material to raise the floor-levels for the large structures built later.

Phase D2/10 (Ir1b)

This phase (fig. 30) and the subsequent Phase D2/9 of the same horizon mark a dramatic change in the character of the entire area. A system of monumental stone constructions (the Monumental Stone Building, the Sea Wall, and the drainage channel) now crowned the southwest slope of the tell, overlooking the southern bay (figs. 30–36). On the other (west) side of the channel a large building was built, constructed of mud-brick walls, some with and others without fieldstone foundations (the Brick Building; figs. 32, 35–36; e.g., Stern, Gilboa, and Sharon 2000, 31*; Stern, Gilboa et al. 2000, 26*, fig. 252 on right, figs. 251 and 253 in foreground). Only the southern part of this building has been excavated, with walls some 1.8 meters thick, preserved 4.5 meters high. In Phase 10 this part consists of two long, narrow hallways oriented east–west, probably (by form and contents) store rooms. On the west, the walls of the Brick Building were abutted against the Bastion wall, filling the entire trapezoid area defined by the drain, the Monumental Stone Building, and the Sea Wall. None of the well-preserved narrow halls had an entrance to it (though they had fine plaster floors, which were raised and repaved several times) and thus must have been cellars to some superstructure which was not preserved, possibly reached by ladders from upstairs. This building extends to the north, beyond the two narrow halls, but its exact plan in this area is unclear (see Stern, Gilboa et al. 2000, 26*). Its northernmost excavated space, however, was not used for storage, but as some, probably open, working area.

Phase D2/9 (Ir1b)

This is a development of Phase 10 (fig. 31). The same public/commercial character was retained and the Brick Building was renovated. Some of the

Fig. 32: View of main early Iron Age structures in Area D2, looking south. The stone wall along the right edge of the excavated area is the Bastion. Along the left edge is the western wall of the Monumental Stone Building. The Sea Wall is in the background. Inbetween and abutting all of these is the Phases D2/10–9 Brick Building—shown here at the level of the Phase D2/10 floors and the Phases D2/10–9 drain.

Fig. 33: Area D2, the inside of the Monumental Stone Building, looking south. To the right is the west wall of the structure, W5340 (Raban's Wall M), with two constructional stages. Note two sets of inner walls—stone above mud brick.

Fig. 34: Area D2, stone-covered drainage channel between the ashlar corner of the Monumental Stone Building (bottom right) and the Brick Building (left), looking north. Note how the covering slab of the drain has been carefully cut to fit the corner of the Monumental Stone Building (and hence is structurally later than the building). The brick wall on the left, of the Phases D2/10–9 Brick Building, slightly straddles the drain, indicating that it is structurally later.

previous walls were reused (or rebuilt on the same lines), while others were shifted and floors were raised. *Inter alia,* the building was extended now to the south, abutting the Sea Wall, and thus a third east–west long hall was added to the south of the two previous ones. All three boulder structures around it (the Monumental Stone Building, the Bastion, and the Sea Wall) remained in use. We already mentioned the restructuring of the Monumental Stone Building—whether that coincided with the shift from Phase 10 to 9 in the Brick Building cannot be established on present evidence.

Other than the pottery (see below), two finds from the Brick Building are worth mentioning here, namely, a bull-shaped bronze weight (Stern et al. 2000, 36, fig. 47 of Hebrew text), and a small anthropomorphic pottery vessel (Stern

Fig. 35: View of main early Iron Age structures in Area D2, looking east. The Monumental Stone Building at top right (note ashlar corner, top center). The Sea Wall is on the right edge of the picture. In between and abutting these is the Phases D2/10–9 Brick Building—shown here at the level of the Phase D2/9 floors. The stone wall to the left is the south wall of Benni's House (Phases 8c–8a), straddling the Brick Building. (The left wall in the background belongs to the late Roman period.)

2000a, fig. 245). Among the meager finds in the Monumental Stone Building was a probably Cypriot golden pendant in the shape of a bull's head (fig. 37).

Phase D2/8c (Ir1|2)

This phase annihilates the Brick Building, unaccompanied, however, by any signs of destruction (fig. 38). The uppermost floors of the Brick Building, though found intact, were almost devoid of finds, implying that the building was abandoned in an orderly fashion. Why this would have occurred is a mystery. Over the northern part of the structure (over the 'working area') a new building was constructed (figs. 39–40) of an as-yet-unclear function (nicknamed Benni's House; e.g., Stern, Gilboa, and Sharon 2000, 31*; Stern, Gilboa et al. 2000, 26*; Stern, Sharon et al. 2000, 32*). Only two of its rooms were excavated and the building continues northward and westward, beyond the excavated area. In turn, the southern part of the Brick Building (the long and narrow halls) was filled in, plastered over, and at a certain point sealed by a sandwich of two (and not three as

Fig. 36: View of main early Iron Age structures in Area D2, looking south. The stone wall along the right edge of the excavated area is the Bastion. Along the left edge is the western wall of the stone Monumental Stone Building. The Sea Wall is in the background. In between and abutting all of these is the Phases D2/10–9 Brick Building—shown here at the level of the Phase D2/10 floors. The rubble wall (and corner) in the foreground is the southern wall of Benni's House (Phases D2/8c–8a), straddling the Brick Building.

previously supposed) thick *pisée* platforms with an earthen fill in between, which abut Benni's House on the north, the Monumental Stone Building on the west, the Sea Wall on the south, and the Bastion on the east, all of which remain in use (see Stern et al. 1997, 41; Stern, Gilboa, and Sharon 2000, 31*). The function of this construction is unclear; possibly it served some retaining capacity for either the Monumental Stone Building or Benni's House, or both. Likewise, we cannot rule out that the "platform" system was actually laid somewhat later, concurrently with Phase 8b (below). The floor associated with the "platform" system (immediately under it) yielded an important assemblage of apparently *in situ* Cypro-Geometric (CG IB–II) vessels (mainly bowls; e.g., Gilboa 1999b, fig. 4:1–8) and a Euboean mid-/late Proto-Geometric fragment (Gilboa and Sharon 2003, fig. 11:19).

Benni's House—built of rubble, though its one extant external corner was constructed of carefully drafted ashlars in headers and stretchers construction

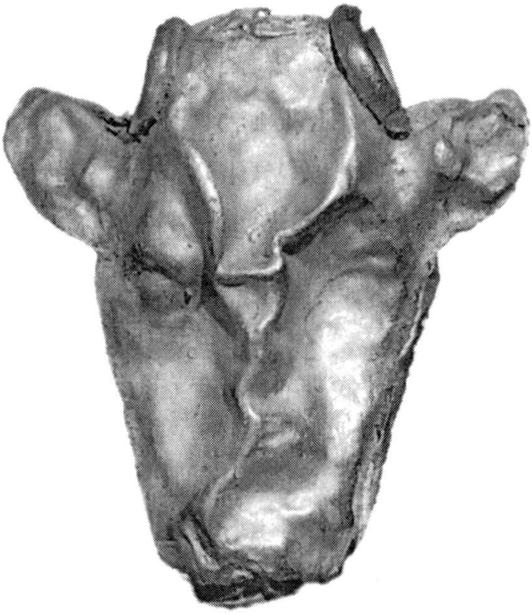

Fig. 37: Cypriot bull-shaped gold pendent from the Monumental Stone Building.

(fig. 40)—collapsed, burying on its floors (nicknamed "Benni's lower floors") an extensive *in situ* assemblage (part of which may be seen in Stern 2000a, fig. 260; Gilboa 2001a, pl. 5.59–66).

Southwest of this house, dug into the debris of the Phase 9 large Brick Building and sealed by the lowest *pisée* platform, a jug was found (fig. 41), carefully covered by a bowl and plastered over, containing a hoard of 8.5 kilograms of silver, packed in linen bags of ca. 490 grams each and sealed by stamped bullae (Stern, Gilboa, and Sharon 2000, 31*; Stern 1998b; 2001a).

Phase D2/8b (Ir2a)

This phase by and large continues the layout of Phase 8c (fig. 38). Benni's House was swiftly repaired after its destruction, but within a very short period of time collapsed again, once more sealing on its floors ("Benni's upper floors") a rich, mainly ceramic assemblage (Gilboa 2001a, pl. 5.73–76). We are unable to tell whether any changes were introduced to the retaining *pisée* system in this phase (and, as stated below, possibly they were initially constructed only in this phase). Phase D2/8b of Ir2a (see below) concludes our presentation of this area. Benni's

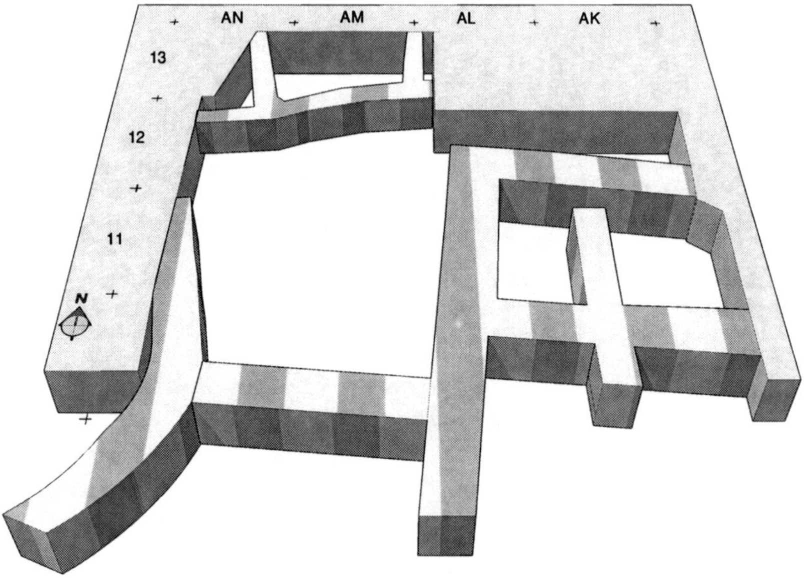

Fig. 38: Schematic reconstruction of Area D2, Phase D2/8c–8b (Ir1|2 and Ir2a).

Fig. 39: Area D2, looking southwest. In foreground, rubble walls of Phase D2/8, Benni's House with later (Iron II and Persian period) constructions on top of it (behind). The installations "in" the house belong to the earlier "working area" of the Phases D2/10–9 Brick Building.

Fig. 40: Area D2, Phase D2/8. Ashlar southeast corner of Benni's House. Note *kurkar*-filled foundation trench on right, cutting into a mud-brick wall of the Brick Building, looking north.

Fig. 41: Area D2, Phase D2/8c, jug with silver hoard found under lower mud-brick platform.

House was rebuilt yet again after its second collapse. Its final floor level (8a) already reflects an IA IIb horizon and it (as well as subsequent Iron Age phases in the area) is therefore out of the purview of this discussion.

Iron Age I Remains in Other Excavation Areas

This concludes the survey of the major Iron Age areas at Tel Dor. However, some finds—and sometimes whole contexts—pertinent to our subject did originate in other areas where Iron Age levels were hit by accident or design.

Area C1

In this area, a deep section was cut through the fortification systems at the eastern side of the tell. The earliest city wall here was a modest mud-brick affair dated to the early Iron II (see Stern, Berg, and Sharon 1991, 57; Sharon 1995, 143–44, fig. 5.25 [the lower mud-brick wall]). Underneath it, however, several superimposed slogging surfaces with early Iron Age materials were found (Stern, Gilboa, and Sharon 1989, 34, fig. 1; Gilboa 1995, fig. 1:10); the latest pieces among these should date to our Ir1b horizon or just slightly later). Whether these constitute a glacis outside a fortification system or just the natural slope of the mound (as we thought at the time) is impossible to tell.

Area E

This area is a much-disturbed and ill-understood section in the northwestern corner of the tell. Here, massive Roman structures (a bathhouse and perhaps other buildings) had been cut into the slope of the mound, leaving earlier strata a jumble of disassociated wall stubs and deposits. One of the latter was the remains of a burnt level, located in several spots within the area (Stern and Gilboa 1989–1990, 115; Stern, Berg, and Sharon 1991, 60). While these burnt deposits definitely belong to the early Iron Age, a more precise designation is impossible. One remarkable find from this area is a fragment of a lioness-head drinking vessel (see fig. 51 below; Stern 2000a, fig. 48 left; Meiberg, this volume) found not in one of the burnt spots but in a mixed context nearby.

Area F

This area on the west side of the mound is the location of the northern of the two temenoi initially excavated by Garstang (see also Area H below). In an effort to verify the redating of the temples to the Roman period, a deep probe was sunk against the southeastern corner of the temenos to see how deep the wall penetrates and obtain pottery from the foundation trench and under the wall. While doing so, earlier strata cut by that foundation trench were reached. At the bottom of that probe a massive boulder wall was encountered which has been badly burnt (Stern, Gilboa, and Sharon 1989; Stern, Gilboa, and Sharon 1992, 45). Both the construction and the (very limited amount of) finds are reminiscent of the massive burnt wall in B1 (the conflagration there belonging to Phase B1/12).

Area H

In this area, cut by the foundation of the southern temenos, the remains of a fine Roman residence were excavated. Among other things, this house featured several deep cellars, dug under the floors of the first-story rooms (presumably) into previous occupation levels (Stern 2000a, fig. 282). Following the dictum of obtaining material sealed underneath each floor, early Iron Age deposits were hit directly under the cellars—though exposure was insufficient to say more than that.

Finally, one significant find from Area B2 needs to be mentioned: an incised bovine scapula, of a type usually ascribed to Cyprus and Philistia at the turn of the Bronze Age/early Iron Age (below fig. 50).

Ceramics, Relative Sequence, and the Correlation of Phases between Areas

In this next stage, we attempt to collate the separate stratigraphic sequences of the different areas at Dor, grouping together phases of similar artifactual (mainly ceramic) attributes into broadly contemporaneous chronological horizons. In the following sections, we will list each of these horizons, specifying each phase(s) within, and briefly characterizing each. Since an exhaustive analysis of the pottery of each phase cannot be accomplished in this venue, we will focus mainly on three groups—the development of the decorated "Canaanite/Phoenician" wares, Cypriot and Cypriot-style pottery and "Aegeanized" wares (to employ the loosest possible designation). This expands on the development of these wares as presented in Gilboa 1998; 1999a; 1999b, as the assemblages are better known now and the stratigraphy is significantly more detailed. However, while this contribution was awaiting publication, several other articles came out in which these ceramics are further elaborated, cf. especially Gilboa 2005; 2006–2007; Gilboa, Sharon, and Boaretto 2009. For the best contexts of this sequence, see

Table 1: Comparative stratigraphies of Areas G, D2, and B1.

Horizon	*Area G (Phase)*	*Area D2 (Phase)*	*Area B1 (Phase)*
Late Bronze	12 (and most of 11)	Missing	14?/Missing?
Late Bronze|Ir1	Missing	Missing	Missing?
Ir1a *early*	10	Missing?	13?
Ir1a *late*	9	13	12
Ir1a|b	8	12	11
Ir1b	7d–c	11, 10, 9	10, 9b
Ir1|2	7b–a, 6b	8c	9a
Ir2a	6a	8b	8

provisionally Gilboa 2001a; Gilboa and Sharon 2003. Table 1 summarizes the collation of the stratigraphic sequences.

One note of caution must precede our discussion: In earlier publications (Gilboa 1989; 1998), the transitional horizon here termed Ir1|2 (see below) was equated with the Megiddo VIA horizon. Subsequently, after the excavation of the extensive Ir1b assemblages, it became clear that the latter are the ones to be chronologically associated with Megiddo VIA and that Ir1|2 is somewhat later.

A short note on nomenclature: The internal divisions we propose for the Dor material do not conform exactly to any of the current periodization schemes for the early Iron Age in the Levant. To avoid confusion, we have used our internal computer codes for the horizon designations and they are coded differently than usual—Ir1a and Ir2b instead of Iron Age IA or Iron Age IIB. When we use in this work the latter designations (e.g., Iron Age I and Iron Age II) we refer to the conventional periodization and not [necessarily] our own horizons. Our Ir1 and Ir2 are roughly the same as Aharoni and Amiran's (1958) IRA I and IRA II (but note our Ir1|2!), but the internal divisions within the Ir1 do not conform to any published attempt to subdivide the Iron Age I (e.g., G. E. Wright 1961, 115–17, 119 chart 8; Mazar 1990, 296). Note also that unlike most periodization schemes, the one we propose is intentionally open-ended, continuous, and non-determinative. The "|" symbol indicates transitional, thus Ir1a|b or Ir1|2. The object is to seriate assemblages and not to agglomerate them. We also try to eschew any historical, much less cultural or ethnic correlations in our period designations (for a detailed discussion, see Gilboa and Sharon 2003, 7–11).

The Late Bronze Age Horizon

Late Bronze Age assemblages *in situ* have yet to be found. Late Bronze II deposits, preliminarily datable to the thirteenth century B.C.E. (R. Stidsing and Y. Salmon, personal communication), were excavated in Area G (Phases G/12 and 11) and perhaps B1/14. Late Bronze Age finds have also surfaced in later contexts all over the tell. Thus any description of Late Bronze artifacts is of necessity provisional and no division or refinement of dating has even been attempted. The standard "Canaanite" repertoire is attested and the only remarkable phenomenon is the abundance of Late Cypriot (LC) II and Late Helladic IIIB imports (e.g., Stern and Sharon 1993, 142; see, e.g., Stern 2000a, pl. I:1)—of all the well-known ceramic families. This is perhaps to be expected in a sea port.

The Late Bronze–Iron I Transition (Late Bronze|Ir1)

This transition is very ill-defined, possibly represented only within the uppermost surfaces of G/11 (Gilboa 2001a, 89–90), and perhaps not at all. These surfaces contained an extremely meager amount of tiny Late Bronze-looking pottery, with (accidentally or not is impossible to tell) no imports. Also, decorated pieces in the Late Bronze painted tradition seem to be few and simplified in style—but this might be due to the utilitarian nature of the single deposit excavated. There are indeed a few unmistakably Iron shapes, like in-turned triangular-rimmed cooking pots, but the assemblage is very small and unsealed and it is highly likely that such pieces are actually associated with the building activities of the next phase in G (10), definitely of early Iron Age date. The argument could be made then that what we are observing is not a gradual transition but merely that the fills beneath the Iron Age Phase 10 already contain Iron Age pieces and that decreasing amounts of Late Bronze Age redepositions give the appearance of a gradual transition. After preliminary processing of the Bronze Age pottery of Phases G/12 and G/11, it seems that the very end of the Late Bronze Age (the late-thirteenth and early-twelfth centuries B.C.E.) is not represented there.

Only two vessels of "western flavor" were found, together, in Phase 11 (or rather, under the floors of Phase 10). One is a fragmentary amphoroid krater (of which several pieces were found; fig. 42) and the other the very top of a stirrup-jar, both of orange-pink well-levigated and well-fired clay, decorated with lustrous orange spirals on buff background; Stern 2000a, pl. IX:1). Thin section petrography suggests that these vessels were locally made, but whether specifically on the Carmel Coast is not yet clear (A. Cohen-Weinberger and Y. Goren, personal communication). Stylistically, the krater most resembles amphoroid kraters found in LC IIC–IIIA horizons (S. Sherratt and M. Iacovou, personal communication; Sherratt, this volume). A slide of a similarly adorned krater from the destruction level of Ugarit was shown by A. Caubet in a lecture held at Ben-Gurion University on May 4th, 2000. (For another similar krater from Ugarit, see de Contenson et al. 1972, fig. 14.)

Most of the Phase 11 surfaces in G (except, as mentioned, the very upper ones) contain "Late Bronze Age imports," and on the other hand Phase 10 (see below) produced (very few) Philistine Bichrome pieces made in Philistia (two of these fragments may in fact belong to Phase 11 but this cannot be ascertained). We thus lack here at present a horizon that, chronologically speaking, parallels the "local Myc IIIC-bearing strata" in Philistia. This horizon is either subsumed in the uppermost surfaces of Phase 11, or else a chronological gap between G/11 and G/10 must be postulated. This crucial horizon in the town's history is still shrouded in darkness.

The Ir1a Horizon (Early and Late)

The division of Ir1a into early and late horizons is based on the clear segregation of these two assemblages in Area G, where Phase 10 defines early Ir1a and 9, ending with the major destruction—late Ir1a. Phase 13 in B1 may belong to early Ir1a (there is not enough pottery to ascertain this) and Phase 12 (the major destruction there) definitely belongs to late Ir1a. In Area D2, the earliest substantial construction, the first phase of Natti's Rubble Structure (Phase D2/13), probably belongs to late Ir1a, but an attribution to the earlier horizon cannot yet be ruled out (Gilboa 2001a, 443). The ceramic assemblages of these two horizons are very similar to each other and must be very close in time, and though they differ in minutiae of formal attributes, only the much better known late Ir1a assemblage is referred to here. The early Ir1a horizon produced the stratigraphically earliest Philistine Bichrome fragments at Dor (see below).

The local undecorated ceramic assemblage is typically "Canaanite" in form (e.g., Gilboa 1998, figs. 1, 3, 6; 2001a, pl. 5.1–18; Gilboa and Sharon 2003, figs. 2–5). Tell-tale types include carinated bowls with short upper walls and sharply shaped flat rims—often with a red band on the rim (the most typical form of this horizon); open, shallow rounded bowls of clear Bronze Age tradition; and a few bell-shaped bowls (see further below). The predominant kraters (from the Late Bronze and through the Ir2a horizon at Dor) are varieties of the handleless open krater, with high "rounded" carination, short vertical upper walls and thickened rim, though kraters with more elaborately shaped rims occur as well, alongside some amphoroid kraters with vertical flat rims. Cooking pots in this horizon are varieties of the in-turned rim ("early shallow" type), with delicately shaped triangular rims, either relatively long or short—but not thick or protrud-

Fig. 42: Painted krater from Area G/11 (LB|Ir).

ing (and "Late Bronze Age types" with out-turned rims are very few). Late types of "Canaanite" storage jars are abundant, both of the triangular profiled, straight shouldered with thickened base and the pear-shaped with thin base varieties—together with "wavy band" and collar-rimmed pithoi (e.g., Stern 2000a, figs. 41, 249; Gilboa and Sharon 2003, fig. 3:4–5; for the pithoi, see Gilboa 2001b; Cohen-Weinberger and Wolff 2001) as well as imported Egyptian jars made of Nilotic clays (e.g., Stern 2000a, fig. 250). Other typical containers include dipper juglets with pointed bases and lentoid flasks (both small and oversized; and strainer-jugs, most apparently of the carinated-with-basket-handle Late Bronze tradition).

Decoration is almost exclusively confined to the smaller containers (small storage jars, strainer jugs, flasks; fig. 43) and only very occasionally is it found on bowls (other than the red band on the rim) or other open forms. The most common type of decoration consists of concentric red bands—on the shoulders of jars, and (vertically) on the bodies of flasks. The same type of bands, but in black, is rarer, though even rarer are alternate red-and-black lines. This sort of decoration is clearly of local Canaanite derivation and indeed exemplifies its swan song (to be revived differently, see below). Other than the containers, the only vessel type that is frequently painted is the amphoroid krater (for one example, see below).

"Western" types or decorations are rather rare in this horizon and seem to fall into two general groups:

1. "Philistine Bichrome," of the usual styles (T. Dothan 1982, ch. 3). Very few such fragments were uncovered at Dor (e.g., fig. 44:1) and points further north in Phoenicia. This type of decoration seems to be almost confined to closed vessels and most of the ones petrographically analyzed at Dor were indeed made on the southern coast/Shephelah (Gilboa, Cohen-Weinberger, and Goren 2006). Thus, they seem to indicate a limited amount of trade between Philistia and the north. While "Philistine" ware is indeed rare at Dor, most of the examples do seem to cluster in the early Ir1a horizon. A few fragments are attested in later Ir1a late,

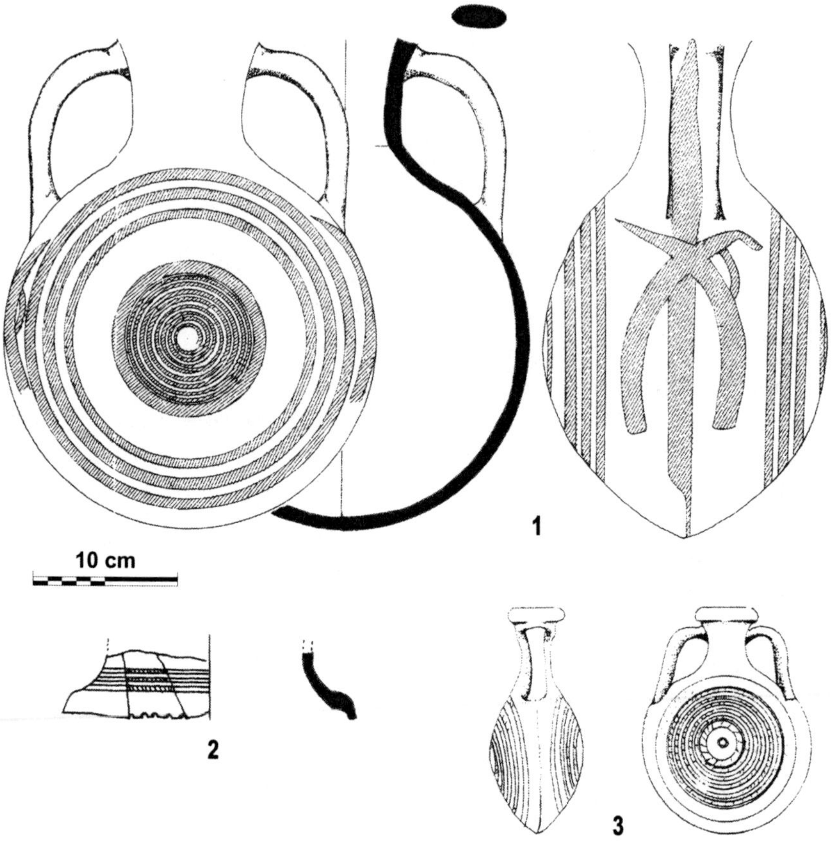

Fig. 43: Red-painted containers in late Canaanite style from Area B1/12 and Area G/9 (late Ir1a).

Ir1a|b, and Ir1b contexts and may or may not be redeposited; clear residuals occur in Ir2 contexts and even later. Thus the Ir1a horizon should, in our opinion, be the horizon equated with the first Philistine Bichrome phase manifested at such contexts as Tell Qasile XII and XI.

2. A one-colored (red/orange/brown/black) decoration, primarily on (quite rare) bell-shaped skyphoi of a variety of fabrics (fig. 44:2–13), the decoration consisting of simple whorls and/or even simpler red bands or striations on the rim. Most of the sherds of this type appear to be of local (Carmel range or northern coast) manufacture (A. Cohen-Weinberger and Y. Goren, personal communication). In addition, some skyphoi are clear imports from sites further south and north along the coast, but no overseas products are attested.

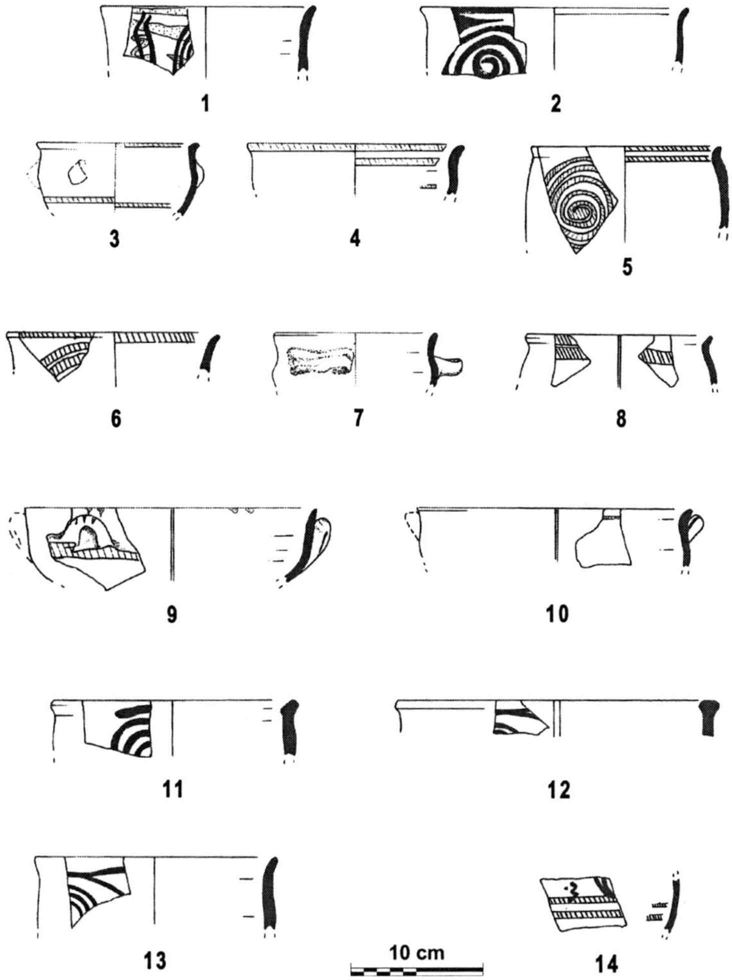

Fig. 44: Locally produced and imported skyphoi, mainly Ir1a.

	Reg. No.	Locus	Area/ Phase	Period	Description	Provenience*
1.	184048	18320	G/10c or 11(?)	Early Ir 1a	Brown fabric; many tiny inclusions. White slip, black decoration.	Southern Shephelah
2.	184529	18337	G/10c or 11(?)	Early Ir1a	Light fabric; white inclusions. White slip, gray/black decoration.	Northwestern Negev

3.	184000	18313	G/10c or 10b	Early Ir1a	Gray fabric, orange core, gray surface. White decoration.	Carmel Coast or Haifa Bay
4.	183968, 183972	18316	G/10b	Early Ir1a	Sandy brown fabric, matte dark red decoration.	Carmel Coast or Haifa Bay
5.	183749/ 22	18316	G/10b	Early Ir1a	Brittle dark orange fabric, many protruding inclusions. Matte dark red decoration.	Not sampled
6.	188441	18570	G/9	Late Ir1a	Dark orange fabric; brown core. Brown-red decoration.	Carmel Coast or Haifa Bay
7.	180995/1	18063	G/ 7	Ir1b	Orange fabric, light surface. Red-orange decoration.	Carmel Coast
8.	183555/5	18302	G/10b or 10a	Early Ir1a	Thin, orange fabric.	Not sampled
9.	306740	19753	D2/14 or 13	Ir1a or Ir 1a|b	Orange fabric, imprints of vegetal matter. Dark red decoration.	Northwestern Negev
10.	194002	19244	D2/13 or 12	Ir1a or Ir1a|b	Brown sandy fabric, light brown core. Dark red decoration.	Not sampled
11.	182155/1	18257	G/10	Early Ir1a	Reddish sandy fabric, brown core, many tiny inclusions.	Not sampled
12.	26082/6	2624	B	Redeposited in Persian-period context	Compact orange fabric, yellow core. White slip, black decoration.	Not sampled
13.	--	Surface	--	?	Orange fabric, wet-smoothed, black decoration.	Not sampled
14.	306047	19750	D2/12	Ir1a|b	Orange fabric. Orange, gray and black decoration.	Lebanese Coast

* Gilboa, Cohen-Weinberger, and Goren 2006 and Cohen-Weinberger and Goren, personal communication. This list updates the one in Gilboa 2001a, 411.

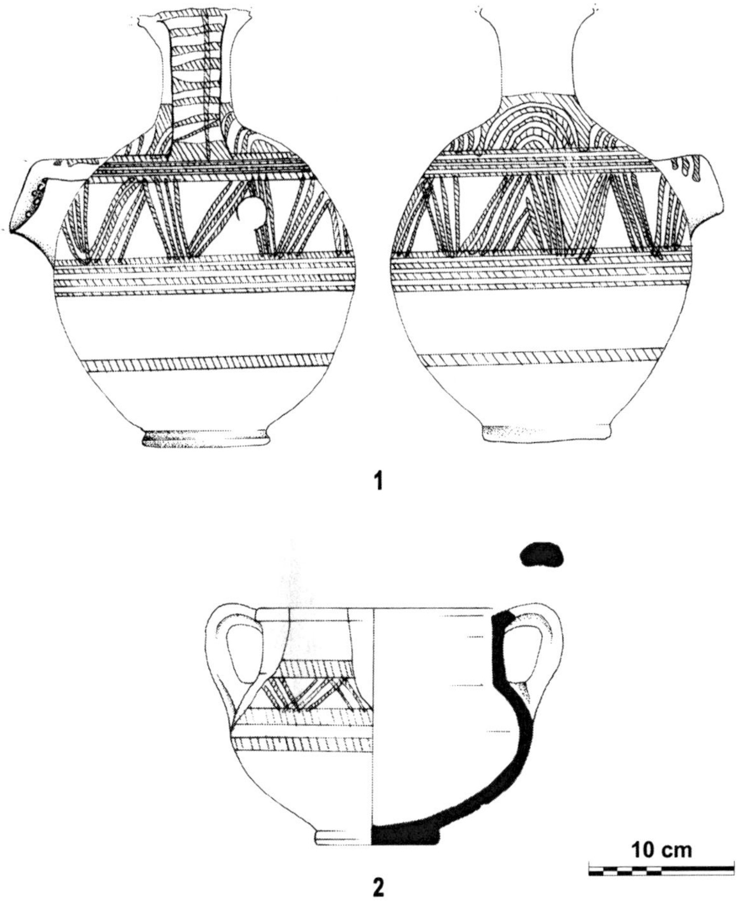

Fig. 45: Orange-painted strainer jug and painted amphoroid krater from Area G/9 (late Ir1a).

3. One remarkable vase—a strainer jug with orange upright concentric semi-ellipsoids on the shoulder and line groups forming a "zigzag" pattern below (fig. 45:1; Stern 2000a, pl. IX:6). It is the only vessel of its kind at Dor, and for that matter, the only complete vessel of any of the presumed "Aegeanized" types ever found at Dor, and thus was duly dubbed "*the* Sikil pot." As regards the execution of the decoration there is a sense of imperfection about this vessel. Some of the groups of diagonal lines in the lower frieze overlap and some do not. At one spot, extra, short diagonal lines were added in the triangle formed by the larger lines. Two of the triangles formed by those lines were painted solid, but the rest

were not. On the handle as well, the one vertical line, conspicuously, is not in the middle. Whether all these "mishaps" are intentional, or the product of an inexperienced painter is, for the time being, impossible to assess.

The orange fabric of the vessel, to the eye, looks similar to those of other painted vessels at Dor. Both "Philistine experts" (T. Dothan and A. Mazar), and "Cypriot" ones (M. Iacovou and S. Sherratt) dismissed the possibility that the vessel may have originated in one of these latter regions. Indeed, both fabric and pigments seem, to the naked eye, different. Likewise, pertrographic analysis indicates that this too is a local product (Gilboa 2001a, 148, courtesy of A. Cohen-Weinberger and Y. Goren).

The decorative scheme on this vessel especially brings to mind Philistine pottery and Cypriot (mainly LC IIIB) ceramics. In Cyprus, a Proto-White Painted (PWP) belly-handled amphora uncovered at Enkomi on *Sol* II of the Ingot God Sanctuary provides an interesting parallel to the design (Courtois 1971, fig. 140:826). Its shoulder is painted with a zigzag pattern composed of groups of four to six lines, irregularly executed, and at least part of the triangles formed by them were painted solid. (In this case, as far as can be gleaned from the published illustrations, this was executed systematically—in all the triangles whose apexes point up.) Interestingly, a very similar zigzag design also occurs on a PWP kalathos uncovered just north of this sanctuary at Enkomi (Courtois 1971, fig. 107:1220). Inside, among other decorations, there is a multiple "zigzag" design and some of the triangles formed by it are painted solid, as on the Dor vessel.

A somewhat more remote parallel to the "zigzag" motif occurs on a Bichrome I amphora from Tomb I at Salamis (Yon 1971, pl. 22:65). There, the triangles formed by the zigzag are filled in by additional, smaller triangles (but as on our jug—not all of them). For another example of a multiple zigzag motif with solid triangles, see Iacovou 1988, fig. 34, cat. no. 15, a PWP pyxis in the Cyprus Museum.

The multiple zigzag motif *per se* has a wider distribution, both regional and temporal. In Syria and southern Anatolia it was common at least from the Late Bronze Age (see below, the discussion of this motif on the amphoroid krater and especially the reference to the Ugarit krater in Courtois and Courtois 1978, fig. 16:10, with a triple zigzag motif with solid-painted triangles).

However, despite the association of this unique vessel with the above-mentioned ceramics in Cyprus, it seems that its decoration owes much more to Syrian than to Cypriot traditions (Gilboa 2006–2007, also reevaluating the amphoroid krater discussed below).

4. An amphoroid krater, manufactured of what seems to be local fabric (it has not been analyzed), also adorned with orange groups of diagonal lines on the upper part of its belly (fig. 45:2; a few other fragments at Dor belong to simi-

larly painted kraters). A nearly identical parallel, both morphologically and in its decoration, was uncovered at Tell Afis, in Level 7 of Area E on the acropolis, dated around the second half of the eleventh–early-tenth centuries B.C.E. (Mazzoni 1998, fig. 16:8). A fragment of an apparently similar krater was uncovered in Level 9a of the same area, dated ca. the late-twelfth and first half of the eleventh centuries (Venturi 1998, fig. 4:2). The triple zigzag motif was considered by these scholars an Aegean-derived motif, but one that had already been adopted in the Levant in the Late Bronze Age. On the other hand, a Cypriot (CG I) association has also been suggested (Venturi 1998, 129, 130 and references; Mazzoni 1998, 166).

Indeed, the Late Bronze and early Iron Levantine parallels cited by the Tell Afis excavators (Mazzoni 1998, 166; from Alalakh, Ugarit, and Hama) are convincing, to which may be added for example Courtois and Courtois 1978, fig. 16:3, 6, 10, from Ugarit (on no. 10 the inner space of the triangles is painted solid, as on the strainer-spouted jug discussed above) and Courtois and Courtois 1978, fig. 17:2–3. Also, as suggested by the Tell Afis team, there are indeed comparable motifs on Mycenaean pottery, and the same design has also been painted on a somewhat similar, though less-elegantly shaped krater at Tarsus, from a very late Late Bronze or early Iron Age context (Goldman 1950, 228, no. 1352).

In Cyprus, in Tomb 521 at Amathus (CG Ib), an anthropomorphic vase in the shape of a woman was found, carrying exactly such a krater with a very similar design on her head (Karageorghis and Iacovou 1990, pl. VII:83). A (PWP or White Painted [WP] I?) amphora from Kouklia Tomb 6 also bears an identical design (Myres and Ohnefalsch-Richter 1899, pl. III:439) and likewise—a PWP bowl from Tomb 132 at Kouklia-Xylino (Flourentzos 1997, pl. XXX:20; for a WP I bowl from the same tomb with a similar design, see Flourentzos 1997, pl. XXIX:12). However, both in shape and decoration, the best parallel in Cyprus to the Dor krater (but with a trumpet base and a painted neck) is an unprovenanced PWP amphoroid krater published by Karageorghis (1985, 826, fig. 5).

The difference between all these mostly single-colored painted vessels and the so-called local Mycenaean IIIC or Philistine Monochrome of the southern coast should be stressed. To begin with—they cannot be considered a "group." They consist of different classes of pots, each with a different style of decoration (and function) and of different antecedents. Also, "western derived" vessels and decorations among them are quite rare. None of them is of anything that may be dubbed "fine ware." Indeed, they are usually characterized by a coarse fabric, lack of slip, and careless decoration. In addition, quantities have to be considered. Other than the "red-circled" jugs, flasks and strainer-jugs in Canaanite style, we are dealing with rare specimens. Also, they are later than the "Monochrome horizon" in Philistia, paralleling the Philistine Bichrome phenomenon.

Finally, a concluding word about imports and foreign influences on pottery: Actual imports are rare in this horizon at Dor. We mentioned Egyptian storage jars made of Nile clay and Philistine Bichrome containers (in as much as they may be called "imports"). The "wavy band" pithoi, ubiquitous in this horizon, are inspired by Cypriot ones, but mostly produced on the mainland and only one of those tested thus far is actually imported from Cyprus (Gilboa 2001b; Cohen-Weinberger and Wolff 2001, table 32.3). The unique strainer jug and the painted amphoroid krater, though local, bear close affinity to the Cypriot LC IIIB horizon, perhaps also to early CG I.

Note again that this horizon, our Ir1a, is later than that termed by Mazar and Wright (on historical grounds) "Iron Age IA" and corresponds better with the first part of what they call "Iron Age IB."

The Ir1a|b Horizon

This horizon is best defined in Area D2, Phase 12 (the upper stage of Natti's Rubble Structure). Other contexts that belong to the same horizon are G/8 and B1/11, that is the levels immediately following the major destruction (see Gilboa 2001a, table on p. 102, termed there early Ir1b). The assemblages of these phases are poorly known to date and thus will not be discussed here, other than the following comments: 1) Typologically, the ceramic assemblage as a whole is intermediate between the earlier (late Ir1a) and subsequent one (Ir1b; see Gilboa 2001a, 150–53, pl. 5.19–20). This is most obvious in the bowl types ubiquitous now: cyma-shaped profiles with only slightly molded rims (e.g., Gilboa 1998, fig. 2:3–4; 2001a, pl. 5.19:6–19; Gilboa and Sharon 2003, fig. 6). These form an evolutionary link between the heavier and more sharply carinated bowls with more elaborate rim treatments of the previous horizon (e.g., Gilboa and Sharon 2003, fig. 2:4–7) and the simple carinated bowls with no rim treatment at all (e.g., Gilboa and Sharon 2003, fig. 7:4–11), which typify the next, but they are clearly distinct from both. 2) This latter fact indicates that this typological phase should be allotted some chronological space, that is, that we have to allow for at least some decades between the late Ir1a and Ir1b horizons. 3) As yet, no Phoenician Bichrome Ware, nor Cypriot table wares (both clearly making their appearance in the next horizon) could be allotted to Ir1a|b, but it should be taken into account that the assemblages of this horizon are quite restricted.

The Ir1b Horizon

The most prolific assemblages of this horizon are the ones in Area D2, Phases 11–9 (the deposits above Natti's Rubble Structure and below the Brick Building, and especially those within the two major constructional stages of the Brick Building itself; see Gilboa 2001a, pl. 5.29–48; Gilboa and Sharon 2003, figs. 7–9). By this definition a significant stretch of time should be allotted to this horizon. Other contexts of this horizon are most of G/7 and B1/10-9b.

The undecorated assemblage is characterized by further deterioration of Late Bronze prototypes. The carinated bowls and cyma-shaped bowls with molded rims of the previous horizons are nearly completely replaced by simple shallow carinated bowls with no rim treatment at all, which are still occasionally painted, with either striations on the rim, or concentric bands, usually in red and sometimes in two colors, or both. Bell-shaped skyphoi and shallow open bowls of the Late Bronze tradition are still in evidence, but rare. The open, handleless, gently carinated krater is still prevalent, though specific subtypes of it—with delicate and careful rim treatments—become dominant. Cooking pots are undistinguishable from those of the previous horizon, but the array of cooking utensils is now enhanced by the first clear appearance of cooking-jugs, usually rounded and one-handled, but rarely also carinated and two-handled. There is an increase in the relative amounts of the straight-shouldered "Canaanite" storage jar, and its neck gets progressively shorter (to the point of disappearing altogether) and the shoulder and rim get thicker; earlier types of this jar with tall cylindrical necks/rims are also still in evidence. Likewise, other aforementioned types (piriform and occasionally painted jars, collar-rimmed pithoi, "wavy band" pithoi, and Egyptian containers) are still in evidence. Undecorated jugs (and other small containers) are few, and their shapes continue previous traditions—for decorated ones see below. Dipper juglets still have pointed bases.

One of the most significant developments within the Ir1b horizon is in the realm of decoration—the initial appearance of the "Phoenician Bichrome" tradition and related wares (figs. 46–48; Gilboa 1999a). Two points must be stressed at the outset of the discussion: 1) Though we use the conventional appellation "Bichrome," the color of the decoration is but one of a host of attributes defining this ceramic "family" (indeed, we already mentioned that two-colored decoration is definitely present in the previous horizons too). 2) The "Bichrome" pottery gradually develops (only) from two of the (mostly) single-painted (mostly red-painted) groups of the previous horizons—the flasks and strainer jugs. This is evident in the following respects (see Gilboa 1999a): a) Morphologically strainer jugs: from carinated, often with a basket handle to rounded with a vertical handle; flasks: from Late Bronze-derived lentoid two-handled shapes to rounded or asymmetric two-handled, to rounded one-handled. b) Color-wise: from single-colored, or occasionally two-colored decoration usually composed of alternating red and black circles of the same width to the conspicuous syntax of two narrow bands enclosing a wide one, either in one color (figs. 46, 48 upper) or in two (figs.

47–48 lower). As the conventional (justified, see below) designation for the latter is "Phoenician Bichrome," the only possible designation for the former is "Phoenician Monochrome," with a capital M. Chronologically it parallels the (first stages of) "Phoenician Bichrome," comprises the same array of vessels, with the same decorative syntax and designs (for the latter, see below). c) Other parallel developments between Phoenician Monochrome and Bichrome, like the adoption of Cypriot decorative motifs. d) A considerable temporal overlap between all these variations (a phenomenon that will drastically change in the next horizon).

The concentric decorations on both Phoenician Monochrome and Bichrome are instrumentally applied, in contrast with "Philistine Bichrome" (and "Philistine Monochrome"), which is usually painted freehand. As mentioned, unlike the completely linear decorative constituents of the previous horizons (as well as both the Canaanite and the Philistine decorative grammars as a whole), an intentional play with the width of the painted bands becomes evident in the "Phoenician Monochrome"—the most conspicuous syntactic element being the enclosed band—a wide band flanked by one or two thin stripes on either side. This (in the form of a wide red band flanked by thin black or black-and-white stripes) would grow to be the characteristic icon of the "Phoenician Bichrome" style. Other motifs evident in both the "Monochrome" and the "Bichrome" styles include: alternating "ladder" patterns and either schematic vegetal motifs or vertical undulating lines; friezes of groups of intersecting diagonal lines; friezes of cross-hatched triangles and lozenges in various compositions, often alternating with other motifs; and composite cross-hatched lozenges and triangles. Many of the decorative motifs, like the decorative syntax as a whole, are of clear Cypriot derivation (Gilboa 1999a). Other motifs (such as Maltese crosses) seem restricted to the Bichrome variants.

Other local vessels of "western character" are all but non-existent in the Ir1b assemblage, though we have noted already that skyphoi with (or without) spiral decoration continue to appear, but are rare.

Another major innovation of the Ir1b at Dor is the reappearance of imported fine wares, in addition to the Egyptian jars, and possibly some of the "wavy band" pithoi (but this will have to be confirmed by clay analysis and does not seem to be very likely, as the production of oversized pithoi in Cyprus in CG I has drastically dwindled at best and was possibly extinct; e.g., Pilides 2000, 109–12). We thus find now the first Cypriot WP I vessels at Dor, mostly open shapes, including skyphoi, and a few Black Slip jugs (e.g., Gilboa 1999b, figs. 2–3; 2001a, pls. 5.39:1–5; 5.46:1–10; 5.48:13–20; no. 15 is possibly of local manufacture; Gilboa and Sharon 2003, fig. 9:15–19). Alongside Cypriot vessels from Tyre, these are the earliest Cypriot fine-ware imports in Iron Age Phoenicia. They reflect a CG IA horizon, possibly also mid-CG I.

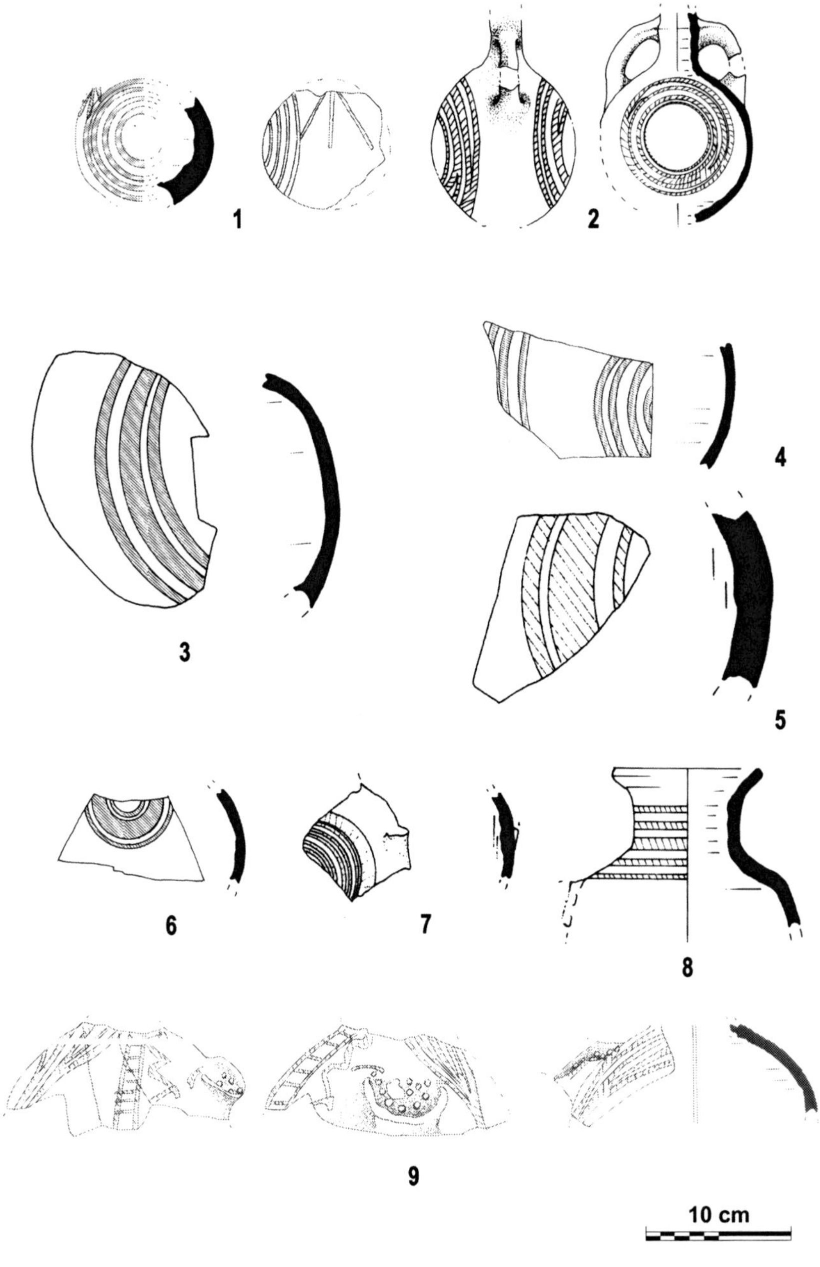

Fig. 46: Early development of "Phoenician Monochrome" containers (Ir1a|b and Ir1b).

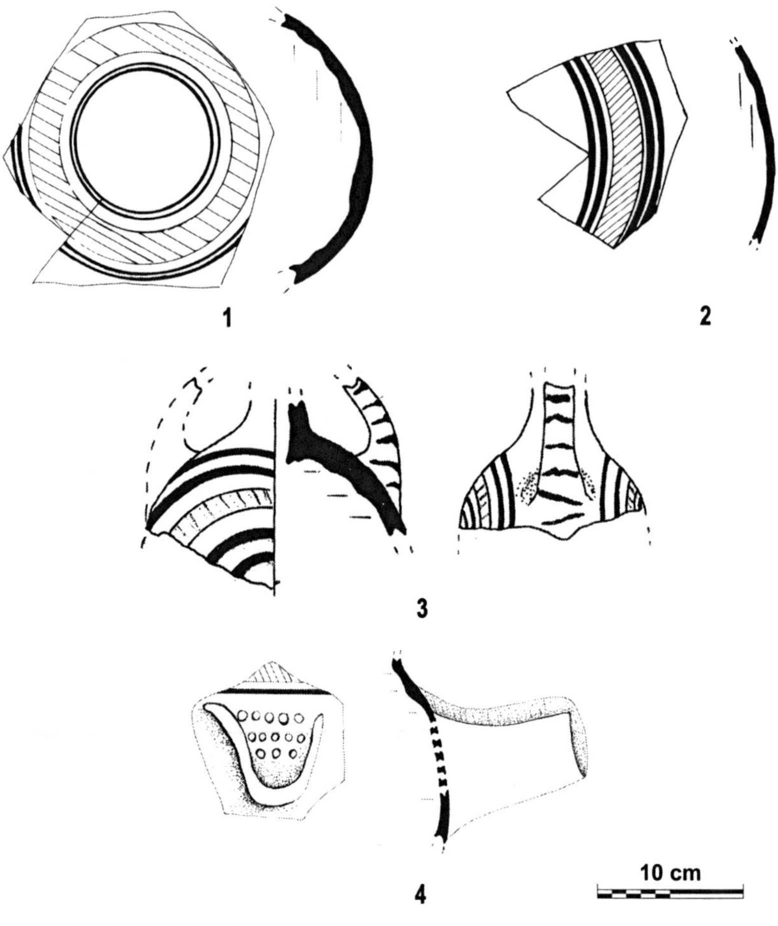

Fig. 47: Early development of "Phoenician Bichrome" containers (Ir1b).

The general ceramic assemblage of this horizon, as well as the tell-tale appearance of Phoenician Bichrome, would place it roughly parallel with Megiddo VIA, i.e., the latter part of Mazar's Iron Age IB (see Mazar 1990, 301, table 6).

The Intermediate Ir1|2 Horizon

Contexts of this horizon are abundant and stratigraphically clearly defined in the three excavation areas presented here: Phase 9a in B1, Phase 6b in G, and Phase 8c in D2. As this horizon lies already on the chronological fringes of Iron I, it

Fig. 48: Cypriot-derived designs on "Phoenician Monochrome" (above) and "Phoenician Bichrome" (below) containers (Ir1b).

is described below only in a general manner. Assemblages of this horizon (e.g., Gilboa 1989, figs. 1–4; 2001a, pl. 5.54–69b; Gilboa and Sharon 2003, figs. 10–11) exhibit late Iron I (in the conventional terminology) as well as incipient Iron II characteristics, but do not yet possess the *fossils directeurs* that typify Iron II in Phoenicia, such as Phoenician red slip (which, however is also rare later on), black-slip wares, or the so-called Cypro-Phoenician (but in fact Cypriot only) Black-on-Red. (For explicit discussions of this horizon, see Gilboa and Sharon 2003; Gilboa, Sharon, and Zorn 2004.) The local undecorated table wares characteristic of this horizon (bowls and kraters) exhibit an uninterrupted evolution of those of the previous horizon and are characterized by still less effort invested in their shaping and none at all in their decoration (both paint and red slip are extremely rare on them). Amphoroid kraters have by now disappeared, as well as most other krater shapes, other than the simple, slightly carinated ones with simple thickened rims. There is a drastic change in the cooking-pot repertoire, though—while we are still within the "early shallow type"—a coarse protruding rim variety is now dominant, the pots are significantly smaller, and for the first time systematically provided with handles. Likewise, the jar repertoire has transformed—the most typical type of storage jar is oblong, with a vertical neck and thick upright rim, sloping shoulders, and pointed base. This type is as yet rarely attested before this horizon at Dor (but on the other hand continues in Ir2a) and heralds the oblong jars typifying Iron Age II. Another type that makes its first appearance in this horizon are swollen, bag-shaped, rounded base storage jars (Gilboa and Sharon 2003, fig. 11:3). Both forms of "Canaanite" jars, the pear-shaped and the straight-shouldered, are present and both collar-rimmed and "wavy-band" pithoi have disappeared by now.

In the realm of decorated wares this is the horizon par excellence of the mature "Phoenician Bichrome" style, which, however is canonized and debased, but still clearly includes Cypriot-derived motifs (see Gilboa 1999a; Gilboa and Sharon 2003, fig. 11:5–11). Monochrome has all but disappeared. A notable change in the globular jar/flask repertoire of this horizon is that the "enclosed band" decoration is now applied to it horizontally as well as vertically (in the strainer jugs the decoration has been horizontal from the very beginning) and that many jugs are provided with ring bases. Also, the Bichrome style is now occasionally evident on vessels other than small containers.

Cypriot imports are by this time numerous at Dor (Gilboa 1989; 1999b) and reflect a CG IB/II horizon. The earliest Greek imports of the Iron Age (two certain fragments; see Stern 2000a, pl. IX:4) of Euboean mid-to-late Proto-Geometric manufacture, are found at Dor in this horizon.

Absolute Dates

The dating of the Dor sequence is discussed in detail elsewhere (Gilboa and Sharon 2001; 2003; Sharon et al. 2005),[4] but this subject cannot be escaped altogether. As is well known, there are no absolute historically derived dates for the Levant between the beginning of the twelfth century (the Twentieth Dynasty in Egypt) and the contexts (almost) unanimously associated with the late eighth-century B.C.E. Assyrian destructions (see Finkelstein 1996a). Failing that, the conventional dating depends on correlating the general archaeological scenario with biblical narratives. If the historical credibility of the latter is doubted, as indeed has been a significant trend lately (see, e.g., the recent summaries in Dever 2001; Finkelstein and Silberman 2001), the absolute-dating framework collapses. This merely underscores the importance of establishing a robust relative sequence and using that, rather than absolute dates, pending the resolution of the absolute chronology problem.

Therefore, we resorted to a strategy of systematic collection and collation of multiple radiocarbon dates from the different horizons. This program has brought up serious discrepancies between the radiometric dates and the biblically derived conventional ones and these are now in the process of being investigated in a wider study. The last word is still far from being said. Thus we shall not offer the ^{14}C-derived dates as a binding framework here. Lacking any other framework that we feel can safely be advocated at this time, we will merely note the options.

Based on conventional Palestinian ceramic chronology, the following dates may be offered: We tentatively suggested some sort of loose contemporaneity between our "Late Bronze|Ir1" horizon and Mycenaean IIIC-bearing strata elsewhere in the Levant. To go any further than that on the present meager evidence would be overreaching. While consensus is that (the different manifestations of) Mycenaean IIIC do not make their debut in the Levant before ca. 1200 B.C.E., there is considerable diversity of opinion as to how late in the twelfth century they do. (For the beginning of *imported* Mycenaean IIIC no earlier than 1185, possibly some decades later, see summary in Gilboa and Sharon 2003, 39, 57.) The locally produced Mycenaean IIIC of Philistia has been dated by some to about 1200, or to the first half of the twelfth century, or to the latter part (respectively, e.g., T. Dothan 1998b, 151; Mazar 1985a; Finkelstein 2000, 164) and the arguments and counter-arguments are well known. The end of the Mycenaean IIIC-like phenomenon would thus get pushed around correspondingly. The ^{14}C program at Dor has not yet extended back to the Late Bronze|Ir1 horizon—and the prospects for resolving this particular controversy using radiocarbon dating

4. Not updated beyond 2006.

are bleak at the outset, due to several sharp peaks in the calibration curve at ca. 1200 B.C.E.

The Ir1a horizon at Dor and in Phoenicia can be (again, loosely) correlated with the flourishing of "Philistine Bichrome" in Philistia, and it *precedes* the appearance of "Phoenician Bichrome." For the parameters of dating the beginning of our Ir1a see above for the end of the Late Bronze|Ir1—that is, any date from the mid-twelfth to the mid-eleventh century B.C.E. might do according to some. As is well known, the dates suggested for Philistine Bichrome in Philistia vary, like those for their Mycenaean IIIC predecessors: the first half of the twelfth century, its second half, or the eleventh century (see summary in Finkelstein 2000). For the end of the Ir1a, the appearance of Phoenician Bichrome is usually relegated to the mid-eleventh century B.C.E. according to the conventional chronology (e.g., Mazar 1990, 537). Thus, a date ca. 1050 B.C.E. for the end of Ir1a (the massive destruction) has been offered (which is in accord with the high and middle chronologies for Philistine Bichrome, but difficult to reconcile with the low one, which places its beginning ca. 1100 or even later). Also, if one assumes a historical scenario by which the *SKL* town visited by Wenamun is represented (only) by the Ir1a levels (e.g., Stern 2000b, table on p. 201) *and* accepts the conventional date for this document (ca. 1075 B.C.E.; see summary and counterarguments in Sass 2002), this would mean that the Ir1a at Dor must have ended after ca. 1075 B.C.E. Radiocarbon dates from Dor for the destruction that terminated the [late] Ir1a destruction were significantly lower than expected and place it and the Ir1a|b transition ca. 1000 B.C.E.)

The Ir1b horizon, possibly paralleling the very last occurrences of Philistine Bichrome in the south, and certainly equaling the first appearance of Phoenician Bichrome in many late Iron Age I contexts across the country, would conventionally date to the second half of the eleventh century B.C.E., possibly also the early tenth. At other sites, the end of this horizon has usually been attributed to the Davidic conquests (ca. 980 B.C.E.), while the "low chronology" ascribes the same destruction layers to Sheshonq's campaign (925 B.C.E.). Current radiocarbon dates from Dor push the terminal date of this horizon, the Ir1b | Ir1|2 transition, all the way to the late-tenth/early-ninth centuries B.C.E.

Our Ir1|2 is probably a short episode which should be more or less equivalent to "Davidic" strata according to the conventional view and thus dated to the beginning of the tenth century B.C.E. According to the "low" historical reading such strata should be relegated to the "gap" between destruction levels imputed to Sheshonq and the establishment of a strong monarchical state by the (according to this view) Omrid dynasty—thus ca. 925–875 B.C.E. Our preliminary radiocarbon dates, again, place this horizon in the early ninth century B.C.E.

Other Finds of Possibly "Western" or "Sea People" Nature

A long-time argument against the "Philistine pottery" phenomenon, as an indication for transhumance of any sort (e.g., lately Sherratt 1998), has been that the "Philistine culture" consists of nothing but decorated tableware. Proponents of the "Aegeans on the move" hypothesis, though, enumerate other phenomena, including other types of artifacts, which are, according to this view, typically Aegean and may be argued to characterize "Sea Peoples" settlements. Some of these do appear at Dor and have indeed been used to supplement the meager (by any account) amount of Aegeanizing ceramics found at the site. They are listed below, alongside other artifacts at Dor that have been brought forward as embodying the association of the material culture of Dor and that of Philistia.

Bi-Metallic Knives (fig. 49)

Slightly curved bronze knives, with iron studs connecting their butts to typically ring-shaped bone handles, have been found for example at Tell Qasile and Ekron in Philistia (Mazar 1985b, 6–7, listing other examples from Israel; T. Dothan 1998b, 158, with references), and attributed to a "Sea Peoples" origin. A ring-shaped handle of this type was found in Area G, just above the Phase 9 destruction debris. The abundant comparanda for these knives, however, are not from the Aegean but from Cyprus (see Sherratt 1994a, 68–71 and Appendix I). In and of itself, the knife handle from Dor indicates nothing but a Cypriot connection—these are amply found at Dor in other objects as well. (For such objects in Crete, Perati in Attica, and possibly Hama and Sarepta, see, e.g., Hoffman 1997, 102–5.) Note also that the object was found above the destruction that, according to Stern, terminates the Sikila town.

Notched Cow Scapulae (fig. 50)

The same is true for notched cow scapulae for the use of which several completely different and equally improbable suggestions have been offered (see summary in Webb 1985; for scapulae at Dor, see Stern 2000b, 199). An almost complete notched scapula was found at Dor, in a mixed (Persian–Roman periods) context in Area B2, and fragments of at least two other such scapulae were found in ill-stratified contexts. Scapulae of this kind have been found at Ekron (e.g., T. Dothan 1998b, 155) and they are ubiquitous in Cyprus. Webb, in her painstaking study of these bones, concluded that they are Levantine in origin (1985, 323).

Clay Lion- and Lioness-Shaped Cups (fig. 51).

In the early Iron Age Levant they have been found in Ekron, Tell eṣ-Ṣafi/Gath, Ashdod, Tell Qasile, Tel Zeror, and Megiddo (see Mazar 1985b, 101–2). A fragment of one was found in a mixed context in Area E at Dor. Though in general lion-shaped cups and rytha *in precious metals* were definitely part of the Aegean (Minoan?) trade of goods, it is clear that these vessels played a pivotal role in the Late Bronze Age "gift exchange," and this apparently was not their sole region of manufacture. Instead of delving into the "who is bringing what and from where" debate, regarding their representations in Egyptian tombs (e.g., Wachsmann 1987, 58–59; Zevulun 1987, 99), it would be more instrumental to trace their parallels in clay, which are certainly more closely related to them functionally and symbolically. As summarized by Zevulun (1987) the best (and indeed very close) stylistic counterparts for the early Iron Age cups in the southern Levant are those from Ugarit. Not only can the very tradition be traced locally to the third millennium B.C.E., but the stylistic attributes of these vessels link them to the east and not to the west (Zevulun 1987, 96) and the only inscription on such a vessel (from Ugarit) associates it with Resheph. Thus the significance of these vessels, once they entered, in the early Iron Age, the cultic ensemble of sites in Philistia and other neighboring regions, is problematic, certainly not *a priori* Aegean, and most plausibly associated with Syria. (But Mazar [2000, 225] associates the Late Bronze Age specimens at Ugarit with Aegean settlers there.) For an in depth discussion of these cups, see Meiberg, this volume.

Small Decorated Chalice/Cult Stand (fig. 16)

This stand, found with other, apparently votive, vessels in Area G has been compared to stands from Tell Qasile X, and, more loosely, Ashdod (Stern 2000b, 201), and a Sea People attribution was sought for it on the basis of its similarity to these "Philistine" cultic vessels. As mentioned above, there is disagreement whether the cultic assemblage of which it forms part belongs stratigraphically to either a pre- or post-major destruction context. The ordinary pottery in this assemblage (especially the bowls) fits a post-destruction (i.e., post-"Sikil") date for it. The stand itself is unique. The Tell Qasile stand is indeed comparable, both in technique and artistic concept, but it should be borne in mind that there is nothing specifically "Philistine" about this stand (which is true for most of the Tell Qasile cult paraphernalia); on the contrary, as stated by Mazar (1980, 89) this type of stand is rather a coastal and Jezreel Valley phenomenon. Very similar fragmentary chalices were found at Tell Abu Hawam (e.g., Balensi 1980, pl. 20:8–10, esp.

Fig. 49: Bone handle of bi-metallic knife from Area G, Phase 8 (Ir1a|b).

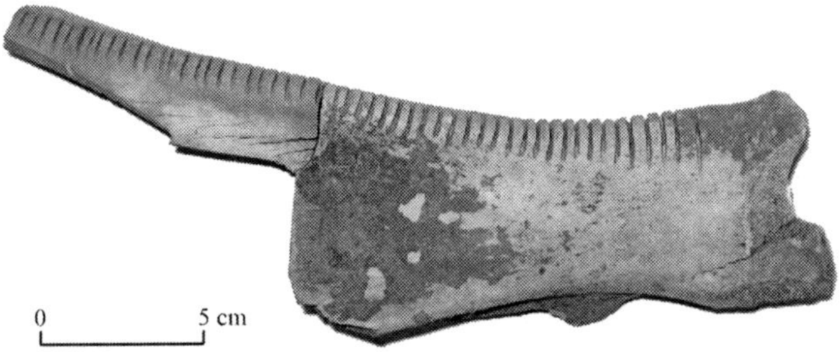

Fig. 50: Notched cow scapula from mixed context in Area B2.

Fig. 51: Unstratified lioness-shaped cup from Area E.

no. 10; see also Hamilton 1935, pl. XVII, no. 276, photographed upside down). Also, the shaping of the rim of the bowl finds its parallels at sites in the Akko Plain and the Jezreel Valley, both on bowls and on chalices (e.g., at Tell Keisan: Burdajewicz 1994, pls. 12:15–15a, 17:3–4, 19:18–19, 34:21; at Yoqneʿam: Zarzeki-Peleg 1997, fig. 12:7).

Miscellaneous

A miniature anthropomorphic vessel (Stern 2000a, fig. 245 left) was found in the Mud-brick Building in Area D2 (Ir1b; the Phoencian city according to Stern) and compared (Stern 2000a, fig. 245 right) to a similar juglet from Tell Qasile XII. The two vessels are indeed similar, but stylistically owe nothing to the west.

Archaeozoological Evidence

Foodways have recently been singled out as a decisive means of establishing ethnicity in early Iron Age Palestine (e.g., Finkelstein 1997). Cuisine, it is argued, is a persistent element in many cultures and tends to change less with passing styles than do pottery styles or art forms, and dietary taboos can give clues as to religion and belief system. In particular, it is argued (Hesse 1986; Hesse and Wapnish 1997; see also discussions in Hesse 1990; 1995, 217–32) that Philistine strata on the southern Levantine coast are distinguishable from previous and subsequent horizons of the same region by an increase in the incidence of pig bones.

The osteological assemblage of the Iron I strata in Area G and D2 at Dor were the focus of a detailed study (Lisk 1999; Raban-Gerstel et al. 2008). These studies compared the Iron Age I horizons in Area G on the basis of animal populations (species composition, domesticated vs. hunted/fished animals, and animals killed for food vs. other uses), livestock administration (culling by age and sex, fitting of herd composition to the environment), and exploitation techniques of meat and secondary products (body-part priority, butchering practices, and bone-size analysis).

The most significant findings of the archaeozoological study were a marked continuity between the Ir1a and Ir1b, as well as the Ir1|2 horizons (the Ir2a sample was not large enough for statistically significant results to be drawn). On the other hand, consumption patterns at Dor seem to be different from those of Philistine sites. One aspect by which Dor is singled out is an extremely high proportion of remains of fish (both fresh and salt water varieties) and other seafood. In this respect all the inhabitants of Dor, at whatever period, were "sea people" and at no time was Dor populated by inhabitants who did not make full use of the sea. Evidence regarding fish remains in Philistine sites has not been forthcoming yet. Another significant difference between Philistia and Dor is the absence of domesticated pigs at Dor. It seems that the inhabitants did occasionally hunt wild pigs, so dietary taboos were not the reason for this preference. Yet another anomaly of Dor is a preference for goats over sheep—somewhat strange in Mediterranean climate conditions.

A second factor underscored by the archaeozoological analysis is that the environment around Dor in the early Iron Age seems swampy. A large number of the wild species are pond brackish water or dense-brush species, including freshwater fish, freshwater turtles, waterfowl, hippopotami, and wild pigs. The preference for goat herding may be a result of brackish drinking water for the flocks.

The archaeozoological findings, therefore, do not support the introduction of a new food technology or habits at any of the periods under discussion, and suggest a difference in food consumption patterns between Philistines and the inhabitants of Dor.

Discussion

Architecture and Urbanism

The first point we need to note is that to date Late Bronze Dor has not been located. To be sure, thick Late Bronze Age deposits were excavated in Area G, approximately the center of the mound, but we do not even know if these are intra- or extramural. As no Late Bronze Age occupation was found either in Area B1 or D2 (in both, pristine sand or bedrock were reached, albeit in small probes) we may minimally say that the Late Bronze town was significantly smaller than those of the Iron Age, though how much smaller is moot. As mentioned, the two lowermost steps in Garstang's trench on the tell's southern slope (just west of Area D2, within the acropolis on the westernmost *kurkar* ridge) bore Late Bronze pottery. This, and topographical considerations, are the basis for the current assumption that the Late Bronze town (and possibly that of the Middle Bronze Age too) must have comprised at least the southwestern part of the tell. Raban's attribution of the earliest quays along the tell's southern slope to the late thirteenth century B.C.E., as mentioned, should be investigated anew.

As indicated above, Garstang's layer of ashes, overlying the Late Bronze deposits, contained, according to him, early Iron Age pottery. Thus, to date there is no support whatsoever for the contention that the Late Bronze settlement was violently destroyed (e.g., Stager 1995, 338). As mentioned above, we cannot support or refute the possibility of a (short) occupational gap after the Late Bronze Age.

The significant spread of the town eastward, to the sand spit, is entirely of Iron I date. This would mean that the area of the Bronze Age settlement was tripled in the Iron I. The crucial question, of course, is when exactly did this outstanding phenomenon occur and whether it was sudden or gradual. The evidence is as follows: in Area G, the earliest (and substantive) architecture (Phase G/10) is of the early Ir1a horizon. The earliest in D2 (Phase D2/13), probably of the late Ir1a, but a slightly earlier date cannot be refuted (a later date is not probable). In B1 (Phase B1/13), architecture (alongside a city wall) is also definitely attested as of late Ir1a, possibly slightly earlier. Thus the town's first extension eastward can be assigned to the early–late Ir1a horizons. As discussed above, chronologically, in familiar terms, this is the early "Philistine Bichrome" period in Philistia, roughly paralleling Tell Qasile XII and XI (Philistine Bichrome ware is present on the very earliest floors of Phase 10 in Area G, possibly even in 11). This means that on present evidence this extension seems to have occurred *later* than at Mycenaean IIIC Ekron (and possibly also Ashkelon). Once the town reached its maximum extent, in the Ir1|2 or Ir2a, it was not enlarged further until the Roman period.

Another significant fact is that the Iron I occupation, wherever it was found, was urban. In the very earliest horizons (early and late Ir1a) a massive fortification wall was built in Area B1, and monumental structures of clearly public nature were built in Area D2 in Ir1b, Phases D2/10–9 (there is no telling whether the earlier Natti's Rubble Structure in D2/13–12 is of a public nature, though its wide southern wall may indeed indicate that). The urban nature of the early Iron Age at Dor is all the more remarkable in an era otherwise characterized by urban decline and by the establishment of societies lacking in urban institutions. While some Canaanite centers (e.g., Megiddo) still maintained the urban organization and reused structures established in the Late Bronze Age, it is only in "Sea Peoples" cities (Ekron, Ashdod, and Ashkelon) where the Iron I is considered a peak of urbanization and where there is evidence for enlargement of the town (which is apparently not true for Ashdod; see, e.g., Finkelstein and Singer-Avitz 2001, 235, 239) and large-scale construction of fortifications and public buildings. In this respect, Dor certainly conforms to the "Sea People" phenomenon, though, as discussed above, on present evidence here this is somewhat later. Of course the case for a similar development in Phoenicia can be hypothesized (and indeed has been), but until very recently could not be substantiated or refuted for lack of large-scale excavations in the major Phoenician centers. Recent excavations at Beirut, however (e.g., Badre 1997; Karam 1997; Finkbeiner and Sader 1997) demonstrated that the (fortified) Late Bronze town expanded and was heavily refortified at an as yet unknown date between the late Late Bronze Age and the early tenth century B.C.E. (see esp. Badre 1997, 50–66).

Continuity of Settlement and Material Culture

One criterion upon which the "cultural succession" hypothesis at Dor might be tested is destruction(s) of the town and disruption(s) of the material culture. The "four culture" sequence proposed by Stern entails three such upheavals (Canaanite to "Sikil" at the end of the Bronze Age, Sikil to Phoenician in mid-Ir1, and later Phoenician to Israelite), while Raban's "tripartite" scheme assumes two (one at the end of the Bronze Age and one sometime in the early tenth century). In a similar vein, Halpern (1996, n. 8) attributes the major destruction at Dor to an Israelite takeover (by Saul or Ishbaal) of the Tjekker (*SKL*) town.

As mentioned, thus far no clue to any destruction of the Late Bronze town has been found in the Hebrew University of Jerusalem excavation (and Garstang's "layer" of ashes is most plausibly later). Of course, the valid objection might be made that [extra mural?] industrial dumps are hardly the place where one would find evidence for war and devastation.

There definitely is evidence for large-scale destruction at the site at the end of late Ir1a and this destruction has indeed been cited (Stern 1990; 1991; 2000b, 203) as evidence for a Phoenician takeover of the *SKL* town. To what extent, though, did this destruction mark a significant break in the local material culture? The stratigraphic/architectural evidence is ambivalent: In one area (B1), the settlement, rebuilt after the destruction, is at least much larger than the destroyed one, expanding beyond the destroyed city wall, although even here the most recent study (Matskevich 2003) indicates reuse of the old fortification wall, after a fashion. In Area G, on the other hand, there is remarkable continuity in architecture, plan, and even the function of individual rooms—between the pre-destruction and post-destruction phases, inconsistent with the moving-in of new inhabitants. In Area D2, if our reconstruction holds, the first stage of Natti's Rubble Structure is apparently also destroyed during the same event, but afterwards reconstructed (as stated, however, the attribution of the first stage to late Ir1a still needs further corroboration).

The appearance of "Phoenician Bichrome" pottery in post-destruction levels has been cited as proof for a cultural change coincident with this destruction (e.g., Stern 1990, 30–32). We have argued here, though, that phases immediately succeeding the destruction (the Ir1a|b) do not yet possess "Phoenician Bichrome" Ware and that the latter appears only some time later (in Ir1b). Moreover, we maintain that "Phoenician Bichrome" develops locally, from local antecedents, and that that evolution can be followed step-by-step. It is thus unnecessary to invoke some foreign invasion to explain the appearance of that pottery group.

Lastly, there is no evidence for any site-wide destruction between the Ir1b and the Ir1|2, nor between Ir1|2 and the Ir2a—such as would be posited (under conventional chronology and historiography) for a "Davidic" takeover of Dor. Above, however, we described some rooms of the Ir1|2 horizon in Areas D2 and G which were abandoned with seemingly their entire equipment. These could theoretically be associated with such an event—for those who would seek to trace it, and such an association could be strengthened if the woman under the collapsed wall in Area G could belong to the same horizon (see above). This indeed is the scenario proposed by Stern (1993b, pt. II, 20). The pottery sequence does not show any sudden "Israelization" in any of these horizons.

Regional Affinities

Another facet upon which a "northern Sea People" cultural phenomenon might be argued for is geographical differentiation. Again, two different hypotheses are possible and have been argued for: Either that the assumed "northern Sea People" culture at Dor (and at other sites of supposed "northern Sea Peoples" settlement) is identical (or at least highly similar) to that of the Philistines—and hence different from the one found inland and in Phoenicia proper; or that the *SKL* possess a distinct set of material attributes—different from both that of Philistia and of other surrounding cultural units. Other "Sea Peoples" would presumably, in such a case, also display distinct material cultures of their own.

Throughout the periods under consideration (with the possible exception of the Late Bronze Age proper, for which currently we do not possess enough data), there is marked similarity between the ceramic assemblage of Dor and its evolution to sites further north along the coast, and a marked difference from the highlands to the east and Philistia to the south. In particular, some of the most indicative attributes defining the ceramic sequence in both Philistia and Israel–Judah, such as the prevalence of hand-burnishing on tableware and its gradual transformation to wheel-burnishing (e.g., Holladay 1990), are almost completely missing at Dor and at other sites along the northern coast. With respect to the northern valleys, chiefly the Jezreel, the situation is somewhat more complicated—the beginning of the sequence, the early Iron Age, is very similar, but toward its end, differences start to multiply. In particular, the conversion to red-slipped and wheel-burnished wares at the onset of the Ir2 is far less noticeable on the coast than at sites such as Yoqneʿam, Megiddo, or Tel Rehov.

The observations above should not be taken as assertion of the insularity of the northern littoral. There is (limited) exchange up-and-down the coast as well as between highland and lowland. Some "Philistine Bichrome" vessels made in Philistia did make their way to Dor and some "Phoenician Bichrome" is found in Philistia as well as inland and even at Negev sites. The fact that these are almost exclusively closed vessels indicates that it was probably contents, rather than the vessels themselves, which was being exchanged.

In the same vein we are not making a case of uniformity within the "Phoenician" littoral. Indeed, as far as the local coarse wares are concerned, each site in Phoenicia is a case unto itself and naturally, the similarities to Dor diminish as one moves northwards along the coast (see Gilboa 2001a, ch. 15; Gilboa and Sharon 2003). The exception to this are the different classes of painted wares (mainly containers), which are very similar (and develop in a similar way through time) at all Phoenician sites. The variety of wares, as well as the results of petrographic studies (A. Cohen-Weinberger and Y. Goren, personal communication) preclude the easy way out—that they were all manufactured and distributed from one center. The surprising uniformity in form and style underlines the special place of these particular types of containers as commercial (and from a certain point in time also ethnic) markers (Gilboa 1999a).

Local "Aegeanizing" Wares

We have noted above that even when one discounts vessels actually made in Philistia (or Cyprus or Greece) there still is a small but persistent number of objects locally made, with Philistine, or Philistine-like, or Cypriot, or other "western" forms, motifs, or affinities (see above). Would these represent the illusive *SKL* material culture?

The counterargument is a quantitative one. After twenty seasons of work—at least ten of which were spent in large-scale excavation of Iron Age I remains in several areas—we have only one complete vessel and a mere handful of additional sherds to show for the entire production of "*SKL* ware" workshops ostensibly active for a hundred years or more. The "quest for the *SKL*" has thrust this meager bounty continuously into the limelight (as does even the present discussion) overshadowing thousands upon thousands of other sherds and objects that are given short shrift.

Foreign Contacts and Influence

One name recurs time and time again in these pages—Cyprus. The dialog between Phoenicia and Cyprus, as it is manifested at Dor, is mild, but multifaceted, durative, and bidirectional. The "Cypro-Phoenician" phenomenon is not overwhelming: At no point is the similarity between these cultures such that one might mistake an assemblage from the Phoenician littoral with a Cypriot one or vice versa. The duration of this dialog is from the very beginning of the Iron

Age and it continues with few disruptions (if any at all) and grows in volume to the Ir2a (and revives later—but that does not concern us here). Its complexity is displayed in the various forms it takes: direct importation of Cypriot vessels to Phoenicia and vice-versa, local production of Cypriot-like wares (some of which may actually be by Cypriot craftsmen working on the mainland—see also Yellin 1989), and the mutual use of a common "symbolic vocabulary" on clearly differentiable local wares in each of the two littorals. We have purposefully used the word "dialog" for this type of "symbolic conversation" to underline that stylistic developments on the island are echoed shortly thereafter on the mainland shore and vice versa. As in the case of nonrandom transmissions from outer space, we may never know the contents of the messages, but we are able to record that a conversation has taken place.

Again, the differences between this phenomenon and what is taking place on the southern plains should be stressed. "Western" influence (whether directly Aegean or Cypriot brokered) on Philistia at the very beginning of the Iron Age is overwhelming, but it is unidirectional (west to east) and after the initial foreign impulses the stylistic development is mostly local and idiosyncratic—and it quickly decays (whether that decay marks "assimilation" or "acculturation" [see Stone 1995] is immaterial for the present discussion).

In addition to Cyprus, and to a certain extent Philistia (as exemplified by the few Philistine Bichrome sherds), the Ramat Menashe area to the east (collar-rimmed pithoi), and, at the end of the period, Euboea (two sherds), extensive, probably maritime relations are attested with Egypt. Egyptian-made jars are abundant throughout the early Iron Age sequence, surely shipped here as containers for some commodity.

Conclusions

Our contention that the local material culture at Dor in the early Iron Age is a single cultural sequence and that the essential process it marks is a gradual transition from Late Bronze Age "Canaanite" to Iron Age "Phoenician" is clear.

We must at this point try to justify why we think the term "Phoenician" is justifiable for describing the phenomena we observe at Dor. Valid objections might be raised on two grounds: The first is geographical. Most regional definitions of the term "Phoenicia" draw the southern border of that district at the tip of the Carmel, that is, just north of the hinterlands of Dor, or even further to the north, north of the Akko Plain. We have noted, however, that culturally, the clear-cut boundary of a single material-culture zone lies south of Dor. The results of the provenience analysis show that all the diagnostic Phoenician wares were indeed manufactured [also] at Dor. Thus, if we deny "Phoenician-ness" to the material culture at Dor, we undermine the ability to identify any early Iron Age material culture attributes as "Phoenician." Another objection might apply to chronology: When is it justified to identify a "Phoenician" material culture (as distinct from "Canaanite")? Needless to say, at this early date, ethnic, linguistic, or religious definitions for "Phoenicianism" will not appear, as we have few clues as to the language and cultic (or any other type of) behavior, much less self-ascription of either the inhabitants of Dor or of parts further north for the beginning of the Iron Age.

Even had we been able to stop an Ir1a Dorite (or Doreen) and ask her "what are you really?," our guess is that her answer would have been less than enlightening. For we are dealing with a formative period in which the new units, which may later on have crystallized to territorial or even ethnic polities, are still in a state of flux.

Another possibility is to avoid the issue altogether by insisting on a *terminus technicus*: By definition, any Iron Age Canaanite is "Phoenician" to modern scholarship, end of story. Such a definition is a bit too arbitrary and avoids the issue in our opinion.

We propose the following mental experiment to try to delineate "Phoenician" from "Canaanite": Let us start at a period where we may all agree that the material culture of the northern littoral is "Phoenician," and then work our way backwards, step by step, to a period where we can all agree that the local material culture is "Canaanite." Is there any stage at which it would be appropriate to stop and declare that from this point it would be appropriate to call the material culture henceforward "Phoenician"? We hold that if any one period may claim that distinction then the Ir1a forms the end of processes we usually associate with Canaanite culture and the root of new ones which will come to fruition in the Phoenician realm.

Given that we do recognize some foreign influences on the local material culture, and that we claim that these "conversations" were essential to the very definition of that material culture—could not that be what the Egyptian author of the Tale of Wenamun meant when he designated Dor as a town of the *SKL*? Perhaps. Why then, this reluctance to bring in the "*SKL* settlement" and the inhabitants of Dor under the "Sea People" umbrella?

One does not need to go to extreme Foucault-ism to admit that the names that scholars give to phenomena are important! Examples abound and the present workshop is a case in point. For thirty years or more, we have lived under the tyranny of Mycenaean IIIC:1b early and so forth. We have all known, since the 1970s, that wares bearing this name were independently manufactured in Mycenae, the Aegean islands, Cyprus, Anatolia, the southern Levantine shores, and in other regions as well. And yet the very use of the same term was asserting unity for these phenomena as well as pinpointing a very precise geographical and temporal origin for them. To pretend that the terminology that seems to have achieved the status of consensus in this workshop, "Aegeanizing pottery," is any less loaded or more theoretically liberating would be naive.

In seeking foreign influences at Dor there is no reason to go any further than the neighboring island. The implication of a homeland further west, much less some "Sicilian connection" or the like which is imputed by this particular transliteration of the Egyptian consonants, is simply not warranted by the finds in the ground.

We do not think that large-scale transhumance or settlement is the correct explanation for the bilittoral dialog we think we can identify in the material culture. We also tried to emphasize the differences that we perceive between what is happening at Dor and in Phoenicia and what is happening in the southern coastal plain. In as much as a word like migration (in the sense of a transference *in toto* of people and culture from one place to a distant one) is applicable to any phenomena in the eastern Mediterranean at the beginning of the Iron Age, that term should be reserved to the process evident in Philistia and under no circumstances can that and the "Cypro-Phoenician dialog" be subsumed under the same term, although a good case can be made for some Cypriot, and probably also Syrian, presence at Dor.

Lastly, if—on Wenamun's say-so—we reserve the term "*SKL* settlement" for what we observe at Dor in the early Iron Age, we have no alternative but to call the material culture of Dor a different name as soon as the term *SKL/TKR* disappears from Egyptian literature, and the Ir2 culture "Israelite" as soon as the kingdom of Israel obtains political control of the area (if we are to take the biblical writer at his word), etc. Thus, not only would we be *a priori* subjugating our professional judgment to that of the philologists and political historians, but our very terminology would be denying our main empirical findings, which indicate continuity rather than disruption, and contiguity to the north, rather than east or south, throughout the early Iron Age.

We have proposed herein a reading of early Iron Age material culture at Dor, which is very different from the one espoused by Stern for many years (1990; 1991; 1995; 2000b). Theoretical polemics upon the valence of the Pots equal People equation notwithstanding, it is disconcerting to find that long-time associates may form rather different interpretations of a basic characterization of the site that they have all been excavating for twenty years. Therein may lie the predicament in which archaeology finds itself at the beginning of the third millennium.

We would like to suggest that at least part of the difference stems from the way basic questions are phrased and the way archaeologists view the role of their discipline within the historical sciences. If the question that is posed is: Given that there was a "Sea Peoples" migration to the Levant, and that Dor is the capital of the *SKL*, how would one define "*SKL*" material culture? Stern's answer—monochrome pottery with spirals, bi-metallic knives, notched scapulae, etc.—might indeed be appropriate. If, however, the question is phrased: If it were not for the serendipity of Mr. Golenischeff acquiring a papyrus in Cairo one fine day 120 years ago, would anyone have even suspected that some hitherto unknown peoples inhabited Dor in the early Iron Age? We say: "No way." Perhaps, then, what is needed is a new understanding of the phenomena that the ancient Egyptian writers might have subsumed under the label "*SKL*."[5]

Acknowledgements

First and foremost we are indebted to Ephraim Stern, the former director of the Tel Dor project, for his generosity in allowing us to present this material and for the intellectual integrity that does not recoil from perspectives that at times differ from his own. We are grateful to Michal Artzy, Ann E. Killebrew, and Gunnar Lehmann and the other participants for the opportunity to participate in this stimulating workshop. The preservation of such a detailed early Iron stratigraphy at Dor was perhaps a lucky break, but the realization of its potential was entirely a matter of the proficiency of its excavators: The early Iron levels in Area B1 were excavated between 1980–1987 under the supervision of the late H. Neil Richardson of Boston University and in 1988 and 1989 respectively by Alon De Groot and John Berg, on behalf of the Hebrew University of Jerusalem. The stratigraphy and pottery sequence was established by Svetlana Matskevich. The Iron Age of Area G was excavated between 1986–1999 by Andrew Stewart of the University of California at Berkeley and by Jeffrey R. Zorn of Cornell University, and in 2000 by Elizabeth Bloch-Smith, New York University and Willem Boshoff with a group from the University of South Africa. The stratigraphy of this area was analyzed by Berg, Bloch-Smith, Sharon, Zorn, and Alan Estes, and the pottery sequence by Gilboa. The early Iron Age horizons of Area D2 were excavated between 1994–2000 by Shira Buchwald, Benni Har-Even, Natti Kranot, and Orna Nagar-Hilman, under the supervision of Gilboa with students from the Hebrew University of Jerusalem and a large group of volunteers from Germany, under Walter and Erica Haury. Talia Goldman and Svetlana Matskevich rendered

5. Such a reinterpretation was presented in Gilboa 2005; 2006–2007, which were meant as sequels to the present paper but ended up being published earlier. The conclusions reached there are not repeated here.

invaluable assistance in checking contexts, supplying stratigraphic and typological details, and preparing the manuscript. Dorit Sivan of the Recanati Institute for Maritime Studies at the University of Haifa advised us on the geological issues. The ceramics presented here were restored by Vered Rosen and Ruthy Gross, and drawn by Rosen and Michal Ben-Gal. The pottery plates were arranged by Goldman and the photographs taken by Zev Radovan, Israel Hirschberg, and Gabi Laron. The plans were drawn by Berg and Matskevich and the computerized reconstructions of the architecture were prepared by Yiftah Shalev then of the Hebrew University of Jerusalem.

Chapter Sixteen

"No land could stand before their arms, from Hatti ... on ..."? New Light on the End of the Hittite Empire and the Early Iron Age in Central Anatolia

*Hermann Genz**

According to the inscription of Ramesses III at Medinet Habu (see Adams and Cohen, this volume), the end of the Hittite Empire is attributed to the actions of the Sea Peoples. Although no foreign elements in the Hittite heartlands point to invading foreigners, at least the apparently violent destruction of the capital Hattuša and many other Hittite settlements seemed to confirm the Egyptian texts. Continuing research at Boğazköy/Hattuša, however, casts doubt on the idea that the city met its end in a sudden catastrophe. The evidence points to a rather slow decline. Moreover, with the end of the Hittite Empire, Hattuša was not totally abandoned. The discovery of a small early Iron Age settlement on Büyükkaya not only fills a gap in the settlement history of central Anatolia, hitherto rightly referred to as a "Dark Age," but also allows interesting observations on the origins of Iron Age cultures in this region.

The cultural unity that characterized the Hittite Empire, most noticeable in the very homogenous pottery throughout the empire, disintegrated with the

* American University of Beirut.

I would like to thank the organizers, A. E. Killebrew, G. Lehmann, and M. Artzy for inviting me to take part in this workshop. For a number of aspects concerning this paper, comments were kindly provided by E. French, P. Mountjoy, and J. Seeher. M. Özsait generously showed me the early Iron Age pottery from his surveys in the Merzifon and Amasya regions during a visit to Istanbul in March 2002; while A. Müller-Karpe showed me the pottery from Level 1b during a visit to Kuşaklı in the summer of 2002.

beginning of the Iron Age. Instead, a number of pottery groups restricted to smaller regions appear. It is only in the coastal regions such as Cilicia or northern Syria that the LH IIIC pottery styles, usually associated with the Sea Peoples, show up. On the central Anatolian Plateau at the end of the Bronze Age, no Aegean-style influences are visible, thus indicating that this area was not directly affected by the movements of the Sea Peoples.

The period of unrest in the eastern Mediterranean along with many other regions at the turn of the thirteenth to the twelfth centuries B.C.E. also greatly affected Anatolia. The last-attested Hittite king, Šuppiluliuma II, reigned until the first years of the twelfth century B.C.E. (Bryce 1998, 361–66), but the Hittite sources do not enable us to date the end of the Hittite Empire more precisely.

The end of the Late Bronze Age at many Anatolian sites is marked by a destruction layer (Bittel 1983, 31–34) and this evidence seemed to be in accordance with the inscription of Ramesses III at Medinet Habu, mentioning Hatti being destroyed by the Sea Peoples (Edel 1985). Until a few years ago our understanding of the process of collapse for the Hittite Empire was greatly hampered by the fact that no remains directly postdating its end were known in central Anatolia.

This situation has changed considerably in recent years. Not only have new Hittite sources shedding light on the end of the Hittite Empire been found, but also a number of sites in central Anatolia have started to produce material remains dating to the early Iron Age.

The view that the Hittite capital of Boğazköy/Hattuša (fig. 1) fell victim to invading foreign hordes cannot be upheld any more. Already Bittel (1983, 27) pointed out in 1983 that according to the finds, no evidence suggested any kind of foreign involvement in the end of Hattuša. Instead, newly discovered documents such as the Bronze Tablet (Otten 1988), the Südburg Inscription (Hawkins 1995c), and seals bearing the name of a hitherto unknown great-king called Kurunta (Neve 1987, 403; Otten 1988, 4–5) instead suggest internal problems during the last years of the Hittite Empire being at least partly responsible for its end (Hoffner 1992, 47–48; Sürenhagen 1996, 287–92). Kurunta belonged to the Hittite royal family and was the ruler of the vassal kingdom of Tarhuntašša.[1] His seals, mentioning the title of a great king, suggest that he managed to usurp the Hittite throne, though he was apparently not officially recognized as king, since he is not mentioned in the genealogy of Šuppiluliuma II (Sürenhagen 1996, 287). This situation of rivalry between Hattuša and Tarhuntašša, which is also confirmed by the

1. For a recent discussion of the borders of Tarhuntašša, see Dinçol et al. 2000.

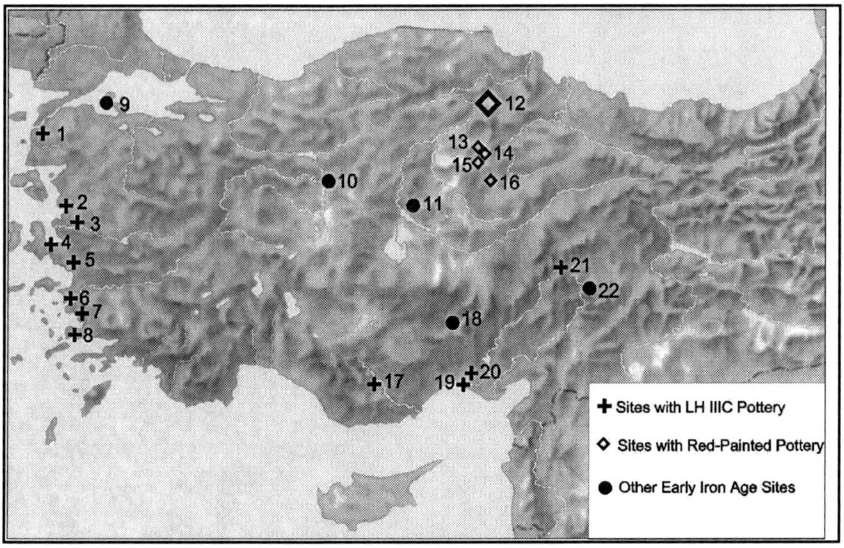

Fig. 1: Early Iron Age Sites in Western and Central Anatolia: 1) Troia; 2) Pitane; 3) Larisa; 4) Klazomenai; 5) Kolophon; 6) Milet; 7) Iasos; 8) Müsgebi; 9) Manastır Mevkii; 10) Gordion; 11) Kaman-Kalehöyük; 12) several sites in the Merzifon Region; 13) Alaca Höyük; 14) Eskiyapar; 15) Boğazköy; 16) Çadır Höyük; 17) Kilise Tepe; 18) Porsuk; 19) Tarsus; 20) Kazanlı; 21) Kuşaklı; and 22) Fıraktın.

Bronze Tablet and the Südburg Inscription, certainly led to internal unrest and very likely to civil war, and must have at least considerably weakened the empire.[2]

The end of the capital Hattuša did not come unexpectedly or suddenly; there are clear indications that speak of a certain decline and a feeling of insecurity that befell its inhabitants during the last years, as has been observed by Seeher (1998b; 2001). Several of the city gates were blocked by hastily erected additions to the fortifications, such as at the northern gate on Büyükkaya and the Sphinx Gate

2. A different interpretation is favored by Singer (1996; 2000b), who sees the campaigns of Šuppiluliuma II against Cyprus and Tarhuntašša as being directed against the Sea Peoples who had already occupied Cyprus and parts of the Anatolian mainland. While it is admittedly not clear who Šuppiluliuma's opponent in the Cyprus campaign was, it is quite unlikely that he would have referred to the Sea Peoples having occupied the kingdom of Tarhuntašša simply as "Tarhuntašša," as he does in the Südburg inscription (Hawkins 1995c, 61–63). Furthermore, we do not know the chronological order of the events during Šuppiluliuma's reign. Singer's proposal to date the campaign against Cyprus before the events recorded in the Südburg inscription is not yet proven beyond any doubt.

on Yerkapı. In the Upper City, fifteen of the twenty-five temples went out of use before the end of the city, and were used as quarries for the building of small houses and workshops (Parzinger and Sanz 1992, 99; Neve 1999, 157).

Even the evidence of the destruction of Hattuša is not without its problems. While it is true that many of the buildings show evidence of burning (Bittel 1983, 26), the traces of destruction by fire are restricted to public buildings such as the palace, the temples, and several city gates. Neither the habitation quarters in the Lower City show any evidence of violent destruction (Bittel 1957, 22–25), nor do the domestic buildings in the Upper City (Neve 1999, 157). Moreover, all buildings that do show traces of burning were found empty. Except for the large pithoi in the magazines of the Great Temple, no traces of any inventory remained. Even if heavy looting is taken into consideration, at least some smashed pottery vessels are to be expected. Since this is not the case, and also no traces of fighting such as weapons or remains of victims are found, it rather looks as if the buildings were carefully cleaned out before they were put to the torch. The interpretation of these observations opens a wide field for speculation. Possibly Šuppiluliuma II considered Hattuša to not be secure anymore and transferred the capital to another location (Seeher 1998b, 519–20).[3] If he did so, he must have chosen a site in the south or southeast of Anatolia, where evidence for the continuation of Hittite culture into the Iron Age is very strong (Hawkins 1988; Güterbock 1992).

For a long time no material remains that could be attributed to the early Iron Age, that is, the centuries following the collapse of the Hittite Empire were known from central Anatolia. This picture has changed considerably during the last few years, with early Iron Age material having been discovered at Boğazköy, Gordion, Kaman-Kalehöyük, Alaca Höyük, Eskiyapar, and Çadır Höyük.

At Boğazköy, excavations on the hill of Büyükkaya produced remains of a small early Iron Age village (Seeher 1997, 327–30; 1998a, 235–39; Genz 2000, 36–37, Abb. 3–5; 2004, 7–10). The building remains uncovered are restricted to postholes, pits, and foundation walls of small rectangular houses made of undressed stones. A stratified sequence suggests a tripartite division of the early Iron Age into early, middle, and late phases. The pottery from the early phase is restricted to simple utilitarian forms like bowls, holemouth-cooking pots, jugs, and jars. Two basic wares can be distinguished: a finer buff one and a coarse ware, ranging in color from brown to black. While the majority of the pottery is handmade, still about a third is wheelmade. Most noteworthy is a clear Hittite tradition, attested not only in the continuing use of the potter's wheel, but also in

3. A transfer of the capital is not without parallel in Hittite history. During the war with Egypt, Muwatalli II made Tarhuntašša his new capital, see Bryce 1998, 251–55.

the shapes of several vessels. Those showing these Hittite traditions cannot simply be residual sherds from the Hittite levels below, since the early Iron Age pottery is generally defined by a better surface treatment like burnishing, which is very rare on Hittite pottery from the late Empire period (Genz 2004, 24).

The pottery from the middle and late phases in general shows a strong continuity with the one of the early phase. Several outstanding differences, however, are the disappearance of Hittite traditions and the almost complete cessation of wheelmade pottery. At the same time, new shapes and decorations do appear. Typical are faceted rims, found on bowls, holemouth pots, pots with a flaring rim, and jugs. Red-painted decoration, restricted to the finer buff ware, is one of the hallmarks of the middle and late phases of the early Iron Age, although only less than 5 percent of the assemblage is painted. The repertoire of the painted motifs is strictly geometric, most typical are dot-filled triangles. Incised decoration, although present, is remarkably rare on Büyükkaya. Other typical features of the pottery of the middle and late phases consist of a variety of knobs and horseshoe-shaped handles on coarse ware pots (Genz 2004, 24–26). A series of radiocarbon dates generally places the early Iron Age levels from Büyükkaya between the beginning of the twelfth and the tenth centuries B.C.E. (Seeher 2000, 373; Genz 2004, 15–16).

The well-stratified pottery found on Büyükkaya enables us to attribute non- or poorly stratified material from Temple 7 in the Upper City of Boğazköy (Parzinger and Sanz 1992, 33–36, Taf. 7–8), Alaca Höyük (Koşay 1944, Taf. V:5–6, VI:3+7; Koşay and Akok 1973, pl. XCIV), Eskiyapar (Bayburtluoğlu 1979, Res. 1–7), and Çadır Höyük (Genz 2001, fig. 1) to the early Iron Age as well. Identical red-painted pottery was found during surveys at a number of sites in the Merzifon region (Özsait and Özsait 2002a; 2002b). The presence of red-painted decoration dates these assemblages to the middle and late phases of the Büyükkaya sequence.

At Kaman-Kalehöyük in the Kırşehir province, excavations have been conducted since 1986. With the exception of the Hellenistic period, the entire second and first millennia B.C.E. are represented at the site. So far, the transition from the Late Bronze to the Iron Age is not clear. Although the Hittite Empire period is attested by finds of pottery and seals, no secure architectural remains have been uncovered so far. The early Iron Age (Level IId) can be subdivided into six different phases (Matsumura 2008, 41). During the later three phases, the settlement was encircled by a fortification wall (Mori and Omura 1995, 10; Matsumura 2008, 41). Buildings are represented by single-room structures, many of them showing postholes for wooden pillars. Although a few fragments of handmade ware with dark burnished surface and incised decoration are attested (Omura 1991, Res. 8:1), the typical pottery of Level IId is buff, wheelmade, and painted with simple geometric patterns, mainly horizontal bands, in black and red (Matsumura 2000, 126–27; 2008).

Early Iron Age pottery is also found at Porsuk in Niveau IV (Dupré 1983, 57–75). The nature of this level is not entirely clear, however. While Dupré postulates a destruction layer at the end of this level (1983, 70), Pelon explicitly states that no architectural remains could be attributed to Niveau IV (1994, 158). The pottery from this level resembles that from early Iron Age levels at Tarsus and from Kaman-Kalehöyük IId (Dupré 1983, pls. 44–59).

A continuity of Late Bronze Age pottery traditions into the early Iron Age is also found at Kilise Tepe in Levels IIa–d, which are dated to the first half of the twelfth century B.C.E. Level IId contained LH IIIC pottery as well (Hansen and Postgate 1999, 113; Symington 2001, 169–72). Red-painted pottery is also present (Hansen and Postgate 1999, figs. 1–25; Symington 2001, fig. 11), but neither the shapes of the vessels nor the painted motifs bear any closer resemblance to early Iron Age red-painted pottery from Büyükkaya and the other sites in the central Kızılırmak Basin.

Karahöyük in Elbistan also shows evidence of the continuity of Hittite pottery into the Iron Age. The presence of a large stele in Level II, inscribed with Luwian hieroglyphs, clearly shows that this site belonged to the Neo-Hittite cultural sphere (Özgüç and Özgüç 1949, 66–83).

In Gordion the early Iron Age levels (YHSS Phases 7B–7A) seem to be separated from the Late Bronze Age (YHSS Phase 8) by a hiatus. However, no traces of destruction were noted at the end of the Late Bronze Age levels. YHSS 7B is tentatively assigned to the eleventh century B.C.E. (Voigt 1994, 267–68; Henrickson 1994, 106–8; Voigt and Henrickson 2000, 333–51). Two different building stages could be distinguished and buildings consisted of semi-subterranean single-room structures, the walls being constructed of wood and mudplaster. The pottery of this phase consists entirely of early Iron Age Handmade Ware. As the name implies, this pottery is handmade, not very-well fired, and has a dark, burnished surface. Incised or impressed decoration occurs quite often and is mainly restricted to rows of impressed dots or incised lines, but in one case a stag is represented as well (Henrickson 1993, 115–17; 1994, 106–8, fig. 10.3; Voigt and Henrickson 2000, 342–49). This pottery marks a complete break to the preceding pottery of the Late Bronze Age. Phase YHSS 7A, tentatively dated to the first half of the tenth century B.C.E., is also represented by two building stages. Again semi-subterranean single-room structures were found, this time constructed of wattle and daub. In the later stage the use of stone slabs as orthostats is attested (Voigt 1994, 269). Among the pottery of phase YHSS 7A early Iron Age Handmade Ware is hardly attested any more. Instead, the predominant pottery is now early Iron Age Buff Ware, which differs markedly from the preceding early Iron Age

Handmade Ware. While still handmade, this pottery was generally finished on a tournette and was much better fired in an oxidizing atmosphere. The shapes of this ware differ substantially from the early Iron Age Handmade Ware and mark the beginning of a new tradition that continues into the Early Phrygian pottery of the following YHSS 6 phase (Henrickson 1993, 117–23; 1994, 108–10, fig. 10.4–6; Voigt and Henrickson 2000, 349–51).

Only at Büyükkaya in Boğazköy, Kaman-Kalehöyük, Kilise Tepe, and Karahöyük in Elbistan has undoubted evidence of settlement continuity at the transition from the Late Bronze into the Iron Age been observed. At all four sites a continuation of Hittite pottery traditions into the Iron Age has been noted, although this Hittite influence seems to last only a short time. At Büyükkaya the Hittite traditions disappear with the end of the early phase of the early Iron Age (Genz 2004, 26). The short-lived continuation of Hittite pottery traditions is best explained by the assumption that parts of the Hittite population remained at the site. At all other sites, where early Iron Age settlement is attested, the transition is either not yet clear, or, as at Gordion, the Late Bronze and early Iron Ages seem to be separated by a hiatus. Except for the short-lived continuation of Hittite pottery traditions at some sites, there is no other evidence for a continuation of Hittite traditions in central Anatolia into the early Iron Age. Large public buildings, monumental stone sculpture, evidence of administrative processes, and the art of writing all disappear in the former heartland of the Hittite Empire. In contrast, these elements continue in the Neo-Hittite kingdoms of southern and southeastern Anatolia, and moreover, the Neo-Hittite kings even link themselves genealogically to the Hittite Dynasty (Hawkins 1988; Güterbock 1992, 54–55).

In Central Anatolia the differences between the Hittite Empire period and the early Iron Age can also be illustrated by the pottery. While in Hittite times throughout the empire, from Gordion in the west to the regions beyond the Euphrates in the east, the pottery is absolutely identical, this vast area split up into smaller ceramic zones in the early Iron Age. The red-painted pottery is restricted to the central area of the Kızılırmak Basin. The wheelmade, painted pottery attested at Kaman-Kalehöyük is also found at Porsuk (Dupré 1983, 57–75, pls. 44–59) and might have its origin in Cilicia, where similar pottery is known from Tarsus (Goldman 1963, 92–107, pls. 55–61). Early Iron Age Handmade Ware seems to be represented mainly to the west of the Kızılırmak River, as the finds from Gordion indicate. However, these smaller ceramic zones were not completely isolated. A limited amount of interaction must have taken place between the different ceramic zones, as indicated by isolated sherds of early Iron Age Handmade Ware inside the Kızılırmak bend at Kaman-Kalehöyük (Omura 1991, Res. 8:1), Çadır Höyük (Gorny et al. 1995, fig. 19F; Genz 2001, fig. 1), and Büyükkaya in Boğazköy (Genz 2004, Taf. 17:3). Connections to the area east of the Euphrates are exemplified by single sherds of grooved ware at Kuşaklı (Müller-Karpe 1996, Abb. 14)[4] and Büyükkaya (Genz 2004, Taf. 28:13).

According to the accounts of Herodotus (7.73) and Strabo (14.5.29), around 1200 B.C.E., the Phrygians migrated from the Balkans to Anatolia, and quite often researchers tried to verify this historical tradition with the help of archaeological material. Certainly neither do the red-painted pottery nor the other early Iron Age pottery found inside the Kızılırmak bend show any relations to Balkanic material. Instead, a number of parallels between early Iron Age pottery from the Kızılırmak Basin and Early and Middle Bronze Age pottery from central Anatolia point to a local, pre-Hittite origin for the early Iron Age pottery traditions (Genz 2005).

The early Iron Age Handmade Ware from Gordion is often compared to the Knobbed Ware from Troy VIIb2 and thus seen as reflecting the immigration of Balkanic peoples (Sams 1992, 58–59; 1994, 20; Voigt 1994, 277; Muscarella 1995, 94; Voigt and Henrickson 2000, 332). The parallels between early Iron Age Handmade Ware and Knobbed Ware, however, are only of a very general nature and thus are of limited value. The same is true for the alleged Balkanic parallels, and thus the early Iron Age Handmade Ware in Gordion cannot be used to prove Balkanic incursions into Anatolia at the beginning of the Iron Age.[5] Only the Knobbed Ware found at Troy VIIb2 (Blegen et al. 1958, 158–81) can be taken as secure evidence of Balkanic influences in northwestern Anatolia, due to its numerous comparisons found in Turkish Thrace, Romania, and Bulgaria (Bloedow 1985; Özdoğan 1993, 162). Apart from Troy, Knobbed Ware was only found south of the Sea of Marmara at the site of Manastır Mevkii on the island of Avşa (Özdoğan 1993, 162), thus indicating that the Balkanic influences were restricted to the northwesternmost parts of Anatolia.

The activities attributed to the Sea Peoples in the eastern Mediterranean have often been connected to the appearance of LH IIIC pottery. In many parts of the eastern Mediterranean this pottery appears immediately following the destruction layers that brought to an end many of the Late Bronze Age settlements (Hankey 1982; Kling 1989).

LH IIIC pottery is also found in Anatolia, but there it is restricted to the coastal regions along the Mediterranean. The southern part of the west coast is certainly to be counted as part of the Mycenaean settlement territory (Niemeier

4. The nature of Layer 1b at Kuşaklı is not entirely clear. While reported as belonging to the early Iron Age (Müller-Karpe 1996, 79), the pottery looks entirely Hittite with the exception of one possible sherd of the East Anatolian Grooved Ware.

5. See Henrickson 1993, 117: "Parallels for simple handmade shapes can be easy to find and thus have limited usefulness."

1998, 25–41; Mountjoy 1998, 53–63). Outside this region, from Troy in the north (Mountjoy 1999b) to Cilicia in the southeast (French 1975; Sherratt and Crouwel 1987), however, the appearance of LH IIIC pottery is accompanied by destruction layers that might be attributed to the Sea Peoples. However, with the exception of one stirrup jar at Fıraktın (N. Özgüç 1955, 303; Mee 1978, 128; Bittel 1983, 34)[6] up to now no LH IIIC pottery has been found on the Anatolian Plateau. While it is reasonable to assume that Cilicia and the Syrian coast were affected by the actions of the Sea Peoples, so far neither historical nor archaeological evidence for any kind of activity of the Sea Peoples in the Hittite heartlands is attested. Surely a threat to the Hittite areas in Cilicia, north Syria, and Cyprus as well as attacks by the Kaška from the Pontic Mountains must have put additional pressure on the already weakened empire, but the real causes for the collapse of the Hittite state seem to be internal rather than external.

6. In addition to the Mycenaean pottery, an Aegean-style bronze knife was found at the site (N. Özgüç 1955, 303–4, fig. 23). The attribution of the Mycenaean pottery from Fıraktın to LH IIIB, as proposed by Özgünel 1996, 119, is unfounded (E. French, personal communication).

Chapter Seventeen
Cilicia

*Elizabeth French**

Cilicia, the name of a Roman province, is used as a convenient designation for the area between the Taurus Mountains and the northeastern corner of the Mediterranean during various periods of its history. The plain is called the Çukurova in Turkish and comprises the provinces (*iller*) of Mersin (formerly Içel) and Adana (formerly Seyhan) of the modern state of Turkey. The open plain at the east is watered by the river valleys of the Seyhan and Ceyhan and is divided from the 'Amuq Plain by the Amanos Range. The Ceyhan forms a route (certainly used at least in Roman times) to the plain of Maraş, passing Tarsus, another valley runs more directly north through the Gülek Boğazı (the Cilician Gates). The western boundary of the area (beyond what Strabo termed *Cilicia Trachaia* or "Rough Cilicia") is marked by the Göksu and a well-travelled route to the Konya Plain.

Serious archaeological exploration of the earlier periods in the area began in 1930 when Gjerstad conducted a survey (from Anamur to Misis) looking for parallels to what he found in Cyprus. His account with some illustrations was published, but for many years the material he had collected could not be found (Gjerstad 1934). It was relocated in the Medelhavsmuseet in Stockholm[1] during spring 2001 and I have been sent a series of photographs of selected sherds. I am hopeful that a detailed study of the material can be carried out in the near future.

Both survey and excavations were carried out by Garstang, mainly in the late 1930s with a little further work after World War II. His excavation at Mersin was

* British School at Athens, 26 Millington Road, Cambridge CB3 9HP. Email: lisacamb@aol.com. I took the opportunity in spring 2009 to update this paper to some extent from the original version.

1. My thanks to the authorities of the Medelhavsmuseet and to Dr. Marie Louise Winbladh for sending me this information.

published (1939; 1953) and some part of the survey material, though more of the important finds from Kazanlı remained unpublished in the Adana Museum.

In the late 1930s (and again after World War II) an excavation was conducted by Hetty Goldman at Tarsus and copious amounts of Aegean-type material were found in the post-Hittite levels. The situation to this point (when only preliminary accounts of the Tarsus excavation were available) was briefly but very competently discussed by Stubbings in his thesis (work completed 1947, published with some additions in 1951).

There followed an extensive survey by Veronica Seton-Williams in 1951 when she collected a considerable amount of surface material and identified eight new sites. The conclusions of this were published, but they cannot be checked as the whereabouts of the material collected are not known. More recent surveys and other work in the immediate area have concentrated on later periods though a new expedition under Turkish colleagues began work in the summer of 2001.[2]

In 1974 Christopher Mee and I undertook a new study of the material stored in the Adana Museum.[3] Our intention was to check the Tarsus material in order to assess it in the light of recently discovered stratified material of the twelfth century B.C.E. on the Greek Mainland, and to see if its local context could be more precisely determined thanks to recent work in Turkey. The latter proved impossible as the Aegean-type wares were dissociated from the local ones, but the former provided substantial new information because large sections of the total corpus were not covered in the original publications (French 1975).

Between 1994 and 1998 Professor Nicolas Postgate excavated the site of Kilise Tepe near Mut, halfway along the Göksu Valley. The full study of the small amount of Aegean-type material found there appeared in the site's final publication (French 2007a).

The results of this work give a relatively clear and comprehensible picture that can be expanded into a generalized view. Gjerstad (1934) identified two classes of Aegean-type material: true Helladic, which he found only on the site of Kazanlı; and what he called "Hellado-Cilician," which he found at seven sites (the most at Kazanlı). At Mersin, his main excavation, Garstang (1953) found two Aegean-type pieces in Levels V–VI and five more in Level IV. This pottery was used to assign dates to the excavation levels but, as both Stubbings (1951) and Mee (1978) point out, this is stretching the evidence as these levels were not well preserved. If these are reconsidered in the light of our present knowledge of Aegean wares

2. In particular, Mountjoy has studied and redrawn all the patterned sherds from the earlier Tarsus excavation in the Adana collection (Özyar 2005, 83–134).

3. We were given much help by the then director of the museum, Dr. Aytuğ Taşyurek, and his assistants. We owe them many thanks.

and using the excellent photograph (Garstang 1939, pl. LXXXIa) rather than the drawing, it is clear that both sherds from Levels VI–V are LH IIIA2[4] and one from Level IV is LH IIIA2/B1. The remaining sherds from Level IV are perfectly acceptable as Hellado-Cilician and can be compared with the Tarsus material. All sherds would thus fit the pattern outlined below. At Kazanlı, on the other hand, in both survey and a small test excavation, Garstang (1937; 1938) found not only Helladic and Hellado-Cilician wares of the twelfth century but some earlier Helladic material, including a possible piece of LH IIA (ca. 1525–1450 B.C.E.).

The preliminary assessment of the Aegean-type material from Tarsus by Daniel (in Goldman 1937) caused considerable confusion as he thought the sherds orginated in the Argolid and compared them to the "Granary Class"—statements that exemplify the misunderstanding which has dogged the study of twelfth-century pottery until recently.[5] In our restudy of 1974, we examined all the material in the Adana Museum. Following washing, we drew and photographed all we could. Later I was able to examine the sherds held by Bryn Mawr College.[6] This fuller corpus had a high proportion of linear wares in a variety of shapes, which showed clear links to the material from Greek sites, particularly Mycenae (Mountjoy 1998), Lefkandi (Euboea; Popham and Sackett 1968; Popham and Milburn 1971), and Emborio (Chios; Hood 1982) though no single site in Greece has yet produced all the shapes together.

Seton-Williams called Gjerstad's "Hellado-Cilician" material Submycenaean but, as this term is now widely and specifically used on the Greek Mainland for something quite different, it is preferable to retain the former term which is both clear and expressive. As explained above, it has not been possible to check any of Seton-Williams results and any use of her data is subject to the errors of misidentification. For this reason I ignore her distinction between Mycenaean and Submycenaean.

Recent excavations at Kilise Tepe had hoped to achieve a reciprocal chronological check for both the Hittite region and the Aegean, but this did not happen. All the Aegean-type material came from clearly post-Hittite levels (without a close date) though eight of the nineteen sherds are probably of earlier manufacture

4. Mee (1978) was misled by the poor drawing. It is clear from the photograph that this is not a jug but a flask.

5. Daniel did however make one observation that has generally escaped notice: what he called the "Granary Class" had one phase, the earliest, which was plainer than the subsequent two phases. He realized that much of the Tarsus material related to this earliest phase.

6. My thanks to Bryn Mawr College for sending me a complete set of color photographs of these sherds with detailed notes on the fabric. My colleague, Carol Bell, has also kindly photographed those held in the Peabody Museum at Harvard University. Neither of these groups is included by Mountjoy (in Özyar 2005, 83–134).

and come from closed vessels (five stirrup jars and three small, closed vessels); only one of the stirrup jar sherds can be called Levanto-Helladic. In addition to these small closed vessels of earlier date, there is a drinking set comprising a jug or amphora, a large bowl, and six (or more) very assorted deep bowls all from a single context (Postgate and Thomas 2007).

If we combine the evidence so far known, we can hypothesize a situation in which there are sporadic imports, mainly of small, closed vessels from various parts of the Aegean and perhaps from Cyprus during the period of the Hittite Empire. The relatively narrow trade may have been the result of positive restriction by authorities. A similar situation seems to have occurred in western Anatolia (Mee 1998). It may be noted that at Tarsus, the capital of the Hittite province of Kizzuwatna, there are only six sherds (all closed), which may belong to this earlier horizon (Mountjoy in Özyar 2005, 87). The only site to have produced increasingly varied Helladic pottery is Kazanlı. In addition to Kazanlı, the only open sherds known to me are two cups, one from Mersin and another of a different shape with spiral decoration from Tanriverdi,[7] both of which are possibly Helladic.

After the end of the Hittite Empire, a completely different scenario can be deduced. There is a widespread but minor presence of Hellado-Cilician material, which is derived from Aegean prototypes of some kind but apparently no actual Aegean imports.[8] At Tarsus the material is plentiful and diverse in range of shape, particularly open shapes formerly so rare. At Kazanlı as well there is plentiful material of this phase. The patterns are distinctive and clearly belong to the Cypro-Levantine horizon. At Kilise Tepe we have a mixed drinking set from an obviously provincial setting. It seems clear that either the destruction marking the end of Hittite control or the political fall-out from it had a notable effect.

There remain problems and perhaps the most intriguing is the exact source (or sources) of the Hellado-Cilician material. It is assumed that it is to some extent "local." The pottery from Tarsus has a generally sandy feel and appearance. This type of ware occurs also at Kazanlı and in one case at Kilise Tepe. Petrological analysis has been carried out at Kilise Tepe but with no firm identifications to date. The pieces from Kilise Tepe have also been tested by Neutron Activation Analysis (NAA) but the results offer no good matches with the corpus of known

7. Thanks to information from Stockholm we can now correct the suggestion by Mee (quoted by Sherratt and Crouwel 1987, n. 3) that the sherd illustrated in fig. 18A right is from Kazanlı rather than Tanriverdi as it is listed in museum records by Gjerstad's own hand.

8. Earlier pieces in these levels (including those of Helladic origin) can be considered residual as at Kilise Tepe.

pottery.[9] This is unfortunate as the ware of these sherds (with one exception) is thus far completely unparalleled. It is extremely thin and very hard—surprising characteristics in what seems to be a "provincial" output.

Complete recording of the material collected by Gjerstad will yield more information, but the most useful project would be further work at Kazanlı. The site is not built over and was visited in the summer of 2001 by the Turkish team working on the Tarsus material. Good sherds, I am told, may still be collected on the surface; how much more could be learned from an excavation on what, at present seems, to be a unique site in Cilicia, is yet to be seen.

9. Samples were taken from Tarsus in the 1970s for NAA in Edinburgh, but no data are available.

Chapter Eighteen
Early Iron Age Newcomers at Kinet Höyük, Eastern Cilicia

*Marie-Henriette Gates**

Over the course of a sixteen-year field project, the Kinet Höyük excavations succeeded in investigating an instructive sample of Late Bronze and early Iron Age phases at this ancient seaport in the Mediterranean's northeasternmost corner. While the exposure of these levels was moderate in size (320 m^2) and restricted to the mound's west side, the results showed such highly characterized features that they may well apply to the site as a whole. They document a sharp break at the end of LB II, and resettlement of the site in the following century by a different population. This report presents a brief assessment of the completed fieldwork and research that is still in progress.

Kinet's Location and Cultural Setting

Kinet Höyük is a 3.3-hectare mound at the very back of the Gulf of İskenderun, on the shore of a narrow coastal corridor known in classical antiquity as the Issos Plain (fig. 1). Until the end of the Hellenistic period, the site owed its existence to two harbors: a modest natural bay on its north side and an estuary along its south flank. Access to the site was certainly more convenient by sea than overland: even today, despite transformations brought by erosion and alluviation, the mound projects like a high and visible promontory towards the bay. Kinet's livelihood must have depended mainly on maritime traffic, although its somewhat remote

* Department of Archaeology, Bilkent University, Faculty of Humanities and Letters, 06800 Bilkent, Ankara, Turkey. Email: mgates@bilkent.edu.tr.

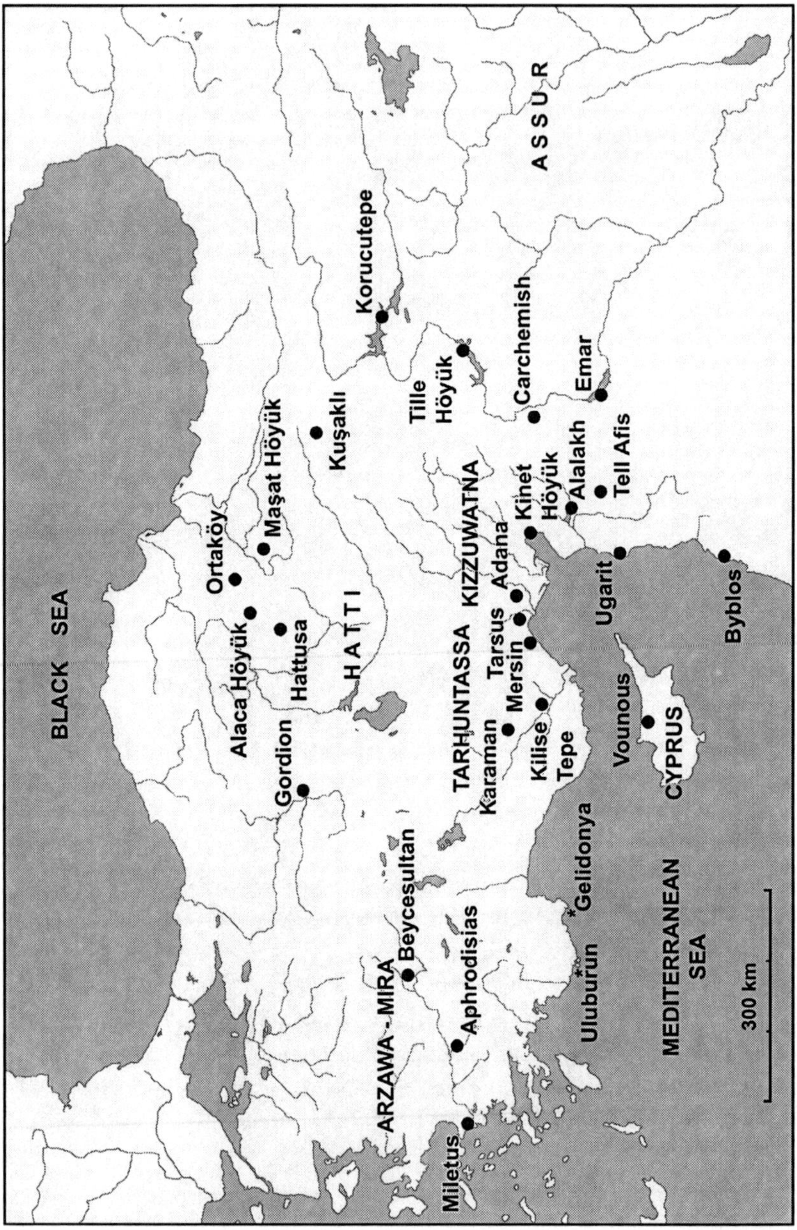

Fig. 1: Map of the Hittite Empire (after Neve 1993, fig. 5 and Hawkins 1998, fig. 11).

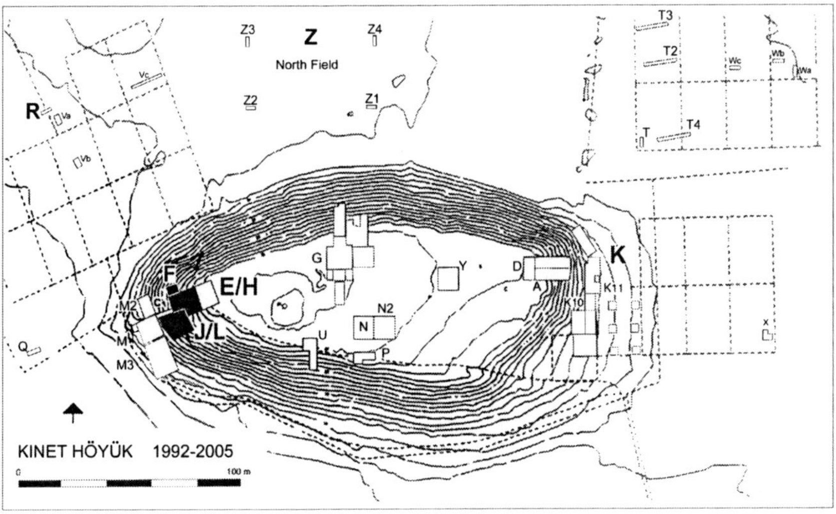

Fig. 2: Kinet Höyük, topographic plan with West Slope trenches marked.

location invites additional justifications, for instance that, on occasion, it served as a frontier post.

In ancient terms, this seaport was situated on Cilicia's eastern border against mountainous terrain that formed a passable but nonetheless significant land barrier from regions to the east and south, the ʿAmuq and western Syria.[1] The Kinet area was understood, from the perspective of classical geographers, to have belonged to the broad Cilician Plain extending to its west. This was certainly the case for its cultural affiliations. Our excavations indicate that during much of its long settlement history, Kinet conformed especially to the trends known from Tarsus and Mersin, its excavated Cilician neighbors. Like them, Kinet was incorporated into the Hittite Empire's territory in ca. 1500 B.C.E. and its final LB II, thirteenth-century B.C.E. phase ended in sudden destruction (Gates 2001a, 137; 2006). However, Kinet's succeeding early Iron Age settlement does not follow events at the other two Cilician sites: 1) unlike Tarsus (but like Mersin),

1. Kinet Höyük has long been considered the likeliest candidate for classical Issos, a thriving port in Xenophon's time (*Anab.* 1.4), landmark for Alexander's defeat of the Persians (333 B.C.E.), and for Septimius Severus's conclusive victory against his main rival to the imperial throne (194 C.E.; Hellenkemper 1984; Bing 1985 [1993]; Gates 1999a, 303–4). Our excavations have found no epigraphical confirmation for Kinet's ancient name(s), but the site's settlement phases match the historical descriptions well.

there was no reoccupation characterized by LH IIIC pottery (cf. Goldman 1950, 205–9; French 1975; Garstang 1953, 242–43); 2) unlike both Tarsus (Hanfmann 1963, 3–5, 95–97) and Mersin (Garstang 1953, 253–54), Kinet's early Iron Age deposits are reasonably thick; and 3) although the post-LB II, Early Iron population at Kinet was intrusive, it was rural and cannot have arrived by sea. By the late-eleventh or early-tenth century, Kinet reacquired an urban format and was reintegrated into a common Cypro-Cilician culture that marked the onset of the Middle Iron Age in this region. On a larger scale, a comparable pattern of reurbanization in the Middle Iron Age can be documented for the Aramaean kingdoms in western Syria (Sader 2000, 72–75), for the eastern Mediterranean in general, and for the Anatolian Plateau. Kinet did participate in the general ebb and flow of successive civilizations, despite its small size and apparent isolation, and can be considered a fair reflection of larger cultural and economic issues.

Late Bronze Stratigraphy

As excavated, Kinet's Late Bronze phases consist of four architectural levels spanning the late-sixteenth/early-fifteenth to thirteenth centuries B.C.E. They have been uncovered on the mound's West Slope, in OPs. J/L and E/H (fig. 2). The earliest LB I (Period 15) level, Kinet Phase IV:2, is represented by part of a large-scale building that remained in use for some time through three distinct subphases before its eventual abandonment (Gates 2001b, 206–7; 2006, 295–99). It was succeeded by three separate levels of LB II domestic architecture (Kinet Phase IV:1) (Gates 2006, 299–304). The earliest (Period 14 with two subphases) was violently destroyed by human agents, since arrowheads, spearheads, and other weapons were found strewn about the burned debris. The next (Period 13.1 housing) was built soon thereafter along the same orientation and architectural principles as its predecessor (fig. 3). It too was destroyed by fire, preserving furnishings *in situ* but no evidence for why the building burned (Gates 2000, 194–95). A final LB II level, designated Period 13.2 and recovered only in OP. E/H (2005 season) except for a single pit in OP. L, showed an impoverishment in building techniques and layout of its housing, and an overall decline in living standards. It was levelled by an earthquake (Gates 2006, 302–4).

Ceramic types date Period 15 to the late-sixteenth–fifteenth centuries B.C.E. and Periods 14–13.2 to the fourteenth and thirteenth centuries (Gates 2006). There is no visible difference between the material culture of Periods 14 and 13.1; their predecessor, Period 15, illustrates an earlier version of the same Hittite cultural horizon. Period 13.2, when changes in manufacturing quality maintained but debased the Hittite tradition, represents Kinet's final Late Bronze occupation. Its end can be placed ca. 1200 B.C.E. on circumstantial criteria only.

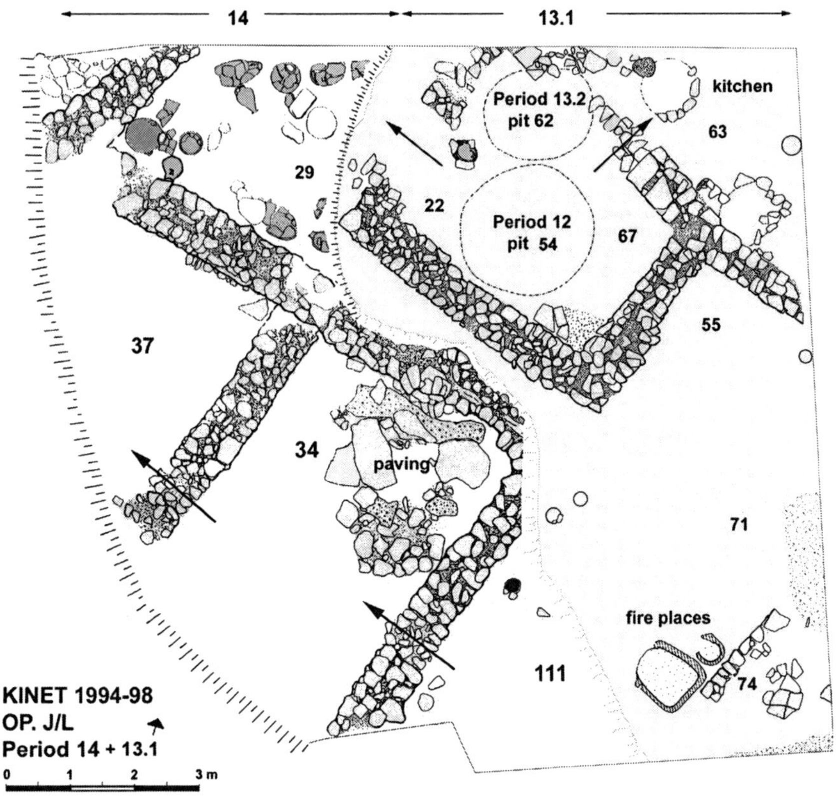

Fig. 3: Kinet LB II building plans in OP. J/L: Periods 14 and 13.1 (shaded).

Late Bronze Age Pottery

The pottery from Periods 15–13.1 illustrates production standards that were applied throughout the Hittite Empire, when Kinet was perhaps named *Izziya* (Forlanini 1984, 147; 2001, 553–57; Gates 2001a, 138; 2006, 305–7). This central Anatolian repertoire became standardized during the fourteenth and thirteenth centuries B.C.E. into a mass-produced industry characterized by well-fired buff, somewhat gritty fabrics; occasional burnished red bands on bowl rims; brown- or red-slipped and burnished potstands and pitchers; the frequent use of potmarks, incised before firing on the exteriors of vessels (Gates 2001a, 156–57, figs. 8–9); and a narrow range of shapes—essentially limited to small plates/bowls, cooking platters, and craters (Gates 2001a, 138–39, 150–53, figs. 2–5). At Kinet, all pottery was manufactured on a wheel, except for the coarse-ware cooking platters, which look coilmade. The only local vessels from Late Bronze Kinet that did

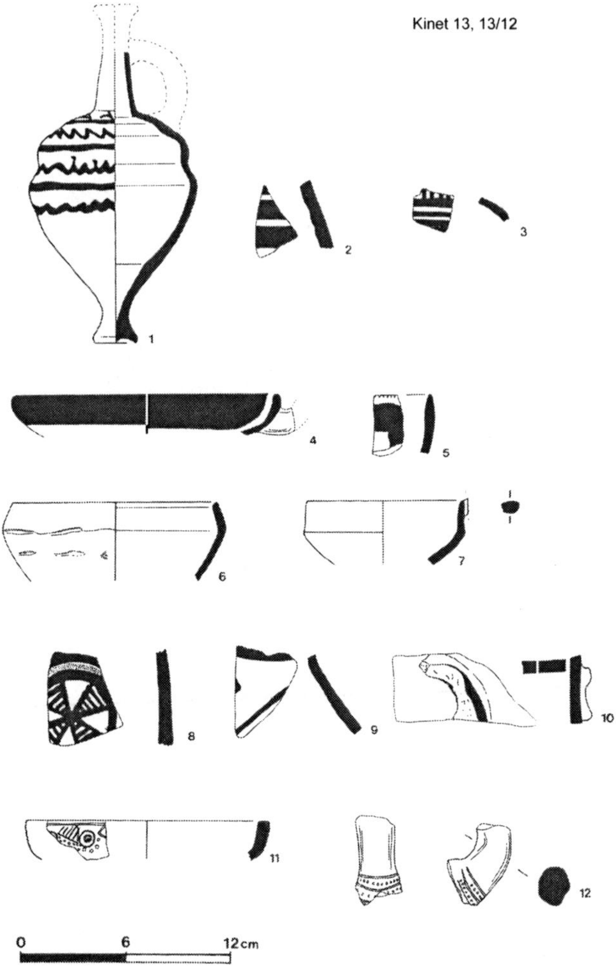

Fig. 4: Painted and imported pottery from Kinet Periods 13 and 13/12.

Key to fig. 4:

1. KT 4209 + 3934 ['94 J 23 L. 73 + 24 L. 69]. Pres. h = 16.2 cm. Fine buff fabric; very dense sand and fine lime inclusions, some vegetal temper; well fired. Pale buff slip, thickly applied and wiped/scraped to form narrow, overlapping horizontal bands. Fair surface polish. Matte brown paint, casually applied. Wheelmade. Period 13.1. Cf. T. Dothan 1982, 158, pl. 72, Type 8 juglet, Cyprus (Cesnola Collection).

2. KT 4296 ['94 J 29 L. 107]. Max. pres. h = 4.0 cm, th = 0.8 cm. Very fine orange fabric; negligeable inclusions; well fired. Exterior surface painted with brown bands, and fired to

a high gloss (sintered); interior unfinished (closed vessel). Wheelmade. Mycenaean. Period 13.1.

3. KT 7893 ['97 L 48 L. 239]. Max. pres. h = 2.5 cm, th = 0.5 cm. Very fine cream fabric; no inclusions. Exterior surface painted with brown to black bands (color varying according to paint thickness) and fired to a high gloss (sintered); interior seems slipped. Wheelmade. Mycenaean. Period 12b (pit fill).

4. KT 8740 ['97 L 60 L. 311]. Max. pres. h = 3.2 cm, th = 0.4 cm. Fine red fabric with gray core; dense fine lime inclusions; well fired. Surface wet-smoothed, mottled red to brown. Handmade. Cypriot Base-Ring II bowl (exceptionally poor manufacture). Period 13.1 destruction debris.

5. KT 8740 ['97 L 60 L. 311]. Max. pres. h = 3.4 cm, th = 0.5 cm. Fine red-brown fabric with thin gray core; dense fine quartz-like inclusions; brittle. Surface white-slipped, with slight polish; painted with fine brown dashes on rim and to outline the thick black band on exterior. Handmade. Cypriot White Slip II bowl (exceptionally poor manufacture). Period 13.1 destruction debris.

6. KT 8836 ['97 L 71 L. 323]. Max. pres. h = 4.5 cm, th = 0.5 cm. Fine red-brown fabric; rare lime inclusions, some fine vegetal temper; well fired. Surface irregular, exterior scraped; streaky slip, mottled red-brown to brown. Handmade. Cypriot Monochrome. Period 13.1.

7. KT 8748 ['97 L 60 L. 311]. Max. pres. h = 3.4 cm, th = 0.5 cm. Fine gray fabric/core; fine sand, lime and micaceous inclusions; hard fired. Surface irregular; thick wet-smoothed/slipped, pinkish buff color, matte. Handmade. Cypriot Monochrome (?). Period 13.1.

8. KT 4304 ['94 J 29 L. 110]. Max. pres. h = 5.3 cm, th = 0.8 cm. Fine pale cream fabric; fine to large lime inclusions; fine vegetal temper; well fired. Exterior surface wet-smoothed/self-slipped, and decorated with matte black and dark, purplish-red paint. Wheelmade. Philistine Bichrome. Period 13.1/12 wash over Period 14.

9. KT 4296 ['94 J 29 L. 107]. Max. pres. h = 5.1 cm, th = 0.7 cm. Fine pale buff fabric; rare lime inclusions; well fired. Exterior surface polished, decorated with brown to black (sintered) paint; interior unfinished. Wheelmade. Myc IIIC. Period 13.1/12 wash over Period 14.

10. KT 7066 ['97 L 42 L. 199]. Max. pres. h = 3.8 cm, th = 0.7 cm. Medium fine buff fabric; fine sand and some larger lime inclusions, rare specks of mica; hard fired. Interior and exterior cream-slipped/wet-smoothed; matte black paint on handle and interior stripe. Wheelmade. Myc IIIC. Period 12c.

11. KT 4463 ['94 J 34 L. 116]. Max. pres. h = 2.4 cm, th = 0.8 cm. Medium coarse red-brown fabric; dense sand and lime inclusions, some fine mica; hard fired. Dull red slip with slight polish. Exterior decorated with deep sharp incisions, and irregular punctate pattern. Handmade? East Thracian? Period 13.1/12 wash over Period 14. Cf. Özdoğan 1998, 34, fig. 2a–b, survey pottery, eastern Thrace; Koppenhöfer 1997, 324, fig. 16:1–3, Buckelkeramik, Troy VIIb.

12. KT 8635 ['97 L 55 L. 304]. Max. pres. h = 5.1 cm, av. diam = 2.1 cm. Medium coarse gray fabric (core); dense sand and white (shell?) inclusions, rare mica specks; hard fired. Surface brown with gray mottling, burnished. Deep incised and punctate decoration at base. East Thracian? Period 12a. For shape and decoration technique, cf. Koppenhöfer 1997, 322, fig. 14:4–5, 325, fig. 17:5, Troy VIIb.

Fig. 5: Kinet early Iron Age, Period 12 in OP. L and OP. E/H: OP. L Phase 12b at lower left, 12c at lower right.

not belong to the Hittite repertoire of shapes were "Canaanite" jars, occurring in both collared and collarless varieties (Gates 2001a, 152, fig. 4:1). These storage and transport amphorae, while sharing the standard fabric of the other types, are the only indication that Kinet was located in the eastern Mediterranean, rather than on the Anatolian Plateau.

Kinet, like other sites in the Hittite provinces, produced few exceptions to this remarkably uniform and restricted repertoire. Painted pottery is rare and monochrome. One of the few complete examples is a Period 13.1 "juglet with a pinched-in girth," made in a fine, possibly local, fabric, but with a distinctive surface finish (fig. 4.1). It was carelessly painted with straight and wavy bands, and hook motifs at the base of the neck (for a discussion of this type and its Philistine derivatives, see T. Dothan 1982, 157–60). Clearly imported pottery is also rare, the number of sherds (ca. 40) too small to calculate a meaningful percentage of the assemblage. It is also worth noting that no imported vessels were preserved except as small sherds, in contrast to the excellent collections of complete local wares from the Period 14 and 13.1 floors. Best represented in the thirteenth-century sample are standard Cypriot export types: Base-Ring II (fig. 4.4), White Slip II (fig. 4.5), and Monochrome (fig. 4.6–7). Only a handful of Mycenaean sherds, all from poor contexts, can be identified with certainty (fig. 4.2–3). Whatever the foreign goods making their way into thirteenth-century B.C.E. Kinet, they do not seem to have included many ceramic products.

An even smaller number of exotic sherds from Periods 13.1 and 13.2, and their early Iron Age successor, Period 12, gives a rough chronological index for the transition into the twelfth century B.C.E. These consist, on the one hand, of a Philistine Bichrome pinwheel sherd from a (probably) open vessel (fig. 4.8) and two other Myc IIIC types—one, with a spiral, from the shoulder of a closed vessel (fig. 4.9), the second, from a large, handled bowl or crater (fig. 4.10). A second pair, a carinated bowl rim and a handle, belongs to a completely different family (fig. 4.11–12). With their fairly coarse, slipped, and burnished fabric, and incised and punctuated decoration, these two recall the Balkan-related Early Iron handmade industry of Troy VIIb's "Buckelkeramik" (Koppenhöfer 1997, 337–41, 324, fig. 16) and eastern Thrace (Özdoğan 1998, 33–35 and 34, fig. 2b). Although none of these sherds has an impeccable context, the handle at least does come from an early Period 12 deposit. More significant than context is that these imports attest to occupation at the site soon after the official collapse of the Hittite Empire.

Early Iron Age Stratigraphy

Kinet's earliest Iron Age (Kinet Phase III:3) occupation, designated Period 12, was excavated on the mound's West Slope to its fullest sequence in OP. L (1997 season: 50 m^2; see fig. 2), where it directly overlies the destruction debris of the LB II, Period 13.1 Hittite level. This exposure was later expanded to the northeast into OP. E/H (2004 season), but the sharply sloping and eroded deposits here added little to OP. L's results, except to confirm this period's general character. Period 12 was also reached further north in 1998 in OP. F, where it was not excavated beyond the uppermost surface but exhibited similar features. An assessment of Kinet's early Iron Age settlement is thus based essentially on the small sector in OP. L, although for reasons developed further below, they appear to provide a valid sample for the whole.

In every one of its aspects, the Period 12 deposit represented a complete change from the preceding levels. It consisted in OP. L of three successive stages of outdoor activities (fig. 5). In the earliest (12a), trash and burned debris accumulated gradually to a height of ca. 1.2 meters. These garbage pits contained exceptional quantities of animal bones, often preserved as large pieces and sometimes partly articulated. In a second stage (12b), eight contemporary pits were cut down from the top of the trash layers into this 5-by-10-meter area. They range in diameter from 0.8 to 2 meters and in depth from 0.2 to 1 meters. The large, deep pits were lined with fine organic matter, and evidently intended for storage; others contained ashes and lime. Three were later used for garbage disposal, mostly animal bones; but on average the pits produced little pottery and four were "empty." In a final stage (12c), the pits were filled in with soil and sealed with large stones, and a group of flat, roughly circular features, made of pebbles coated with a thick layer of pisé, was installed. One of them was eventually replaced with a later version in the same spot. These features—the largest is 1.6 meters wide—have been tentatively labelled "work platforms" because of slight burning around their edges. The soil around them was littered with animal bones (including elephant) and had a distinctive greasy texture. The trash layers, pits, and work platforms extended into E/H, but in compressed deposits that could not be articulated with the same clarity. In 1998 OP. F, the final phase of this sequence was announced by similar concentrations of animal bones, fragments of stone and pisé features, and the outline of large pits. In all three trenches, Period 12c's surfaces were eroded and capped by the stone foundations of buildings representing Kinet Period 11.

Kinet's Period 12 Pottery

The pottery recovered from the Period 12a trash layers (figs. 6–10), the initial reoccupation in the excavated area, differs from the LB II repertoire in every respect: clay preparation, fabric, surface treatment, and vessel shapes.[2] Fabrics included dense and coarse mineral inclusions and vegetal temper; they were

2. T. M. Cross, who supervised the 1997 OP. L excavations, undertook the study of its pottery with R. Schneider during the Kinet 2001 season, at my request. I did not read the report that she had prepared until after her death, however, and was therefore unable to discuss it with her. The summary I am giving here is based, in its detail, on this excellent study, but my assessment remains different from what was concluded in her report. Cross proposed that the LB II ceramic industry was maintained throughout Period 12, since she favored residual "drab ware" plates as the diagnostic index of the Period 12 assemblage. This was also the preliminary conclusion summarized in the 1997 season's report (Gates 1999b, 264–65), written before the faunal sample had been analyzed. In light of the faunal remains, I have re-examined all of the pottery that Cross referred to for her report and am again struck (as indeed we both were when these deposits were being excavated) by how radically different the Period 12 ceramic assemblage seems as a

sometimes chaff-faced and overfired in colors ranging from red and orange to brown and dull black. Manufacture was mostly on the wheel, sometimes by hand, and in either case produced irregular results that cannot be fully appreciated from the profile drawings. Surface treatment, such as slips and wet-smoothing, was poor. Slight burnishing is common on slipped and unslipped surfaces. Horizontal "pattern" burnishing occurs on a very coarse fabric, especially used for large storage containers (fig. 9.9).

A small, but steady percentage was painted with clumsy geometric designs (straight or wavy bands, crosshatching, and hatched triangles) in monochrome purple, brown, or black paint (figs. 7; 10). Included in this group is a spout in the shape of a bovine head, from the top of a 12b pit (fig. 8.8). This painted component, which is both hand- and wheelmade, begins with the earliest Period 12 deposits (12a) and continues throughout the phase. Bichrome decoration does not make an appearance until the very end in 12c (fig. 10.2–3), heralding the start of this popular decorative style in the Middle Iron Age.

Much of the Period 12 sample consisted of weathered, non-diagnostic sherds that give only partial shapes, but enough to illustrate that they answered needs different from the standard Hittite plates and bowls, craters, and cooking platters. Coarse-ware cooking vessels and storage containers (figs. 6.10–12; 9.7–9) and wide-necked pitchers and flasks seem especially common (fig. 8.1, 3–6). Bowls (figs. 6.1–5; 9.1–2, 5), a less-frequent type, tend towards deeper shapes than previously, another trait that continued into the Middle Iron Age. Most noticeable is the non-homogeneous character of this repertoire, where fabrics and shapes varied without adhering to any evident standard.

Kinet's Period 12 pottery suggests a small-scale household industry that can be related to the Iron I tradition found in inland western Syria, for instance at Hama's cremation cemetery and contemporary settlement (Riis 1948) and Tell Afis VII (Venturi 2000); or in the western Cilician highlands, at Kilise Tepe, in the transitional LB II–Early Iron Levels IIa–e (Hansen and Postgate 1999). But precise parallels are difficult to pinpoint and should not be expected. Collections from the two upper phases were moreover mixed, since the 12b pits in OP. L cut down into the LB II, Period 13.1 deposits where complete vessels had been abandoned on floors. As a result, it is not possible to determine from the ceramics alone whether the LB II Hittite tradition lingered on throughout Period 12, alongside the new elements.

---

whole. The intrusion of Period 13 types is readily explained by the untidy nature of the Period 12 deposits and pit-digging down to Period 13 floors.

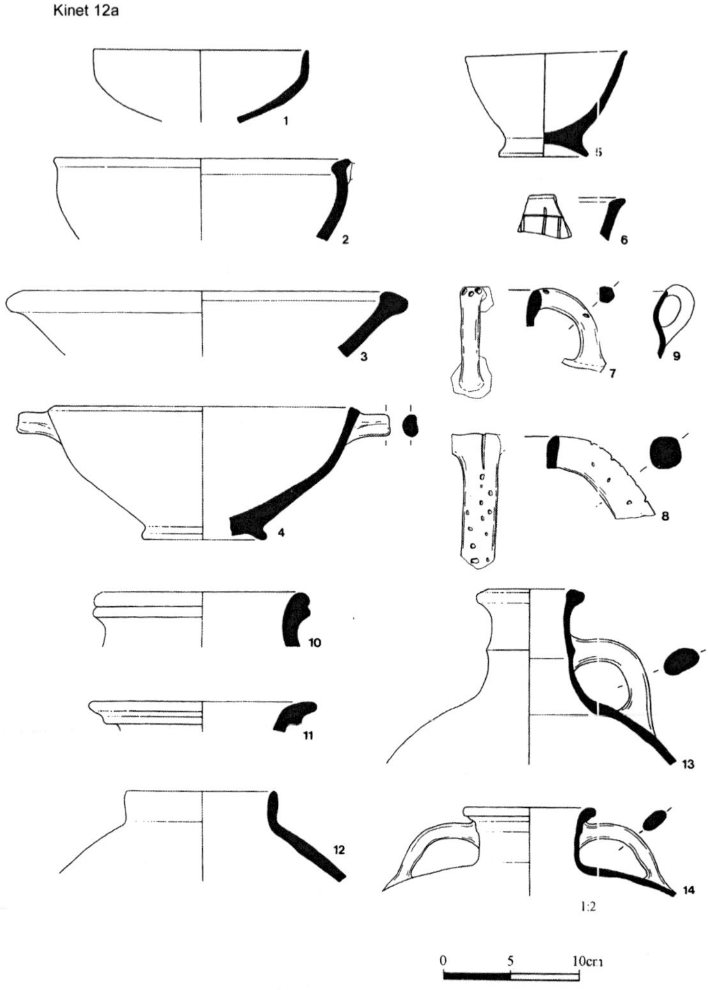

Fig. 6: Pottery from Kinet Period 12a (* = earliest deposits).

Key to fig. 6:

*1. KT 8400 ['97 L 53 L. 286]. Max. pres. w = 15.1 cm, th = 0.6 cm. Medium coarse dark buff with orange core; dense small to larger sand and lime inclusions; fine to larger vegetal temper. Brittle. Surface scraped and vaguely wet-smoothed, light buff with red mottling. Shape irregular, somewhat warped. Wheelmade. Period 12a.
*2. KT 8400 ['97 L 53 L. 286]. Max. pres. h = 6.2 cm, th = 0.9 cm. Medium coarse buff; dense sand and white (quartz and shell) inclusions; fine vegetal temper. Hard fired. Surface wet-smoothed/self-slipped, light buff. Ridge of handle at base of rim. Wheelmade. Period 12a. For shape, cf. Postgate 1998, 223, fig. 4, Kilise Tepe Level II, D1246.

3. KT 7893 ['97 L 48 L. 239]. Max. pres. h = 5.8 cm, th = 1.1 cm. Medium coarse brown with gray core; dense fine to larger sand and shell inclusions, fine mica; fine vegetal temper. Surface wet-smoothed, brown. Wheelmade. Period 12a. For shape, cf. Postgate 1998, 223, fig. 4, Kilise Tepe Level II, D986.

4. KT 7795 ['97 L 48 L. 235]. H = 9.6 cm, diam = 23 cm. Medium fine reddish-brown fabric; dense, fine to medium ground shell and lime inclusions, mica specks; some vegetal temper. Hard fired. Surface scraped, handle crudely applied (excess clay left rough on bowl wall). Interior and exterior wet-smoothed, and partially burnished with horizontal strokes (deliberate pattern-burnish?). Wheelmade. Period 12a. For shape, cf. Killebrew 1998a, 390, fig. 7:4, Tel Miqne-Ekron VII (Phase 9A).

5. KT 7789 ['97 L 48 L. 232]. H = 8.1 cm, diam = 12.9 cm. Coarse brown fabric; dense medium to large black, ground shell and lime inclusions, some mica specks; dense vegetal temper. Hard fired. Surface irregular. Interior and exterior coated with red-brown wash, irregularly wiped. Handmade, irregular in shape. Period 12a.

6. KT 7789 ['97 L 48 L. 232]. Max. pres. h = 3.4 cm, th = 0.7 cm. Medium coarse buff to brown fabric; dense fine to larger black and ground shell inclusions, fine mica specks; vegetal temper. Hard fired. Surface slightly wet-smoothed, buff to light brown. Incised before firing (shallow incisions). Wheelmade. Period 12a.

*7. KT 8386 ['97 L 60 L. 279]. Max. pres. h = 7.0 cm, av. diam = 1.3 cm. Fine orange fabric; fine to larger dark, ground shell and lime inclusions; fine vegetal temper. Well fired. No visible surface finish (very worn). Handle irregularly shaped, somewhat twisted; top decorated with three punched dots, at juncture with rim [of juglet]. Period 12a.

*8. KT 8386 ['97 L 60 L. 279]. Max. pres. l = 9.4 cm, av. diam = 2.6 cm. Same fabric as no. 7. Surface wet-smoothed, slight burnish, orange to buff. Handle somewhat irregular; decorated with deep vertical incision at top (starting at pitcher rim), deep and irregular punches down length of handle. Period 12a.

9. KT 8282 ['97 L 55 L. 260]. Max. pres. h = 6.1 cm, th = 0.5 cm. Coarse buff fabric with dark gray core; very dense fine to larger dark quartz and ground shell inclusions; coarse vegetal temper. Brittle. Surface slightly wet-smoothed. Shape irregular. Handmade. Period 12a.

*10. KT 8758 ['97 L 72 L. 319]. Max. pres. h = 4.4 cm, wall th = 1.1 cm. Medium coarse buff fabric with gray core; exceptionally dense fine to larger sand and ground shell inclusions, fine to larger mica specks; fine vegetal temper. Surface wet-smoothed, buff. Wheelmade. Period 12a.

11. KT 8177 ['97 L 48 L. 256]. Max. pres. h = 2.6 cm, rim diam = 17.1 cm. Medium coarse buff fabric with gray core; dense fine sand and fine to medium ground shell and lime inclusions, some fine mica specks; fine vegetal temper. Hard fired. Surface wet-smoothed, buff to gray with slight polish on rim. Wheelmade. Period 12a.

12. KT 7991 ['97 L 48 L. 248]. Max. pres. h = 7.4 cm, th = 1.0 cm. Same fabric as no. 1. Same exterior surface treatment as no. 5. Wheel- or coilmade. Period 12a.

*13. KT 8294 ['97 L 55 L. 264]. Max. pres. h = 12.9 cm, rim diam = 7.9 cm. Medium fine dark orange fabric; dense sand and fine to large lime inclusions; some vegetal temper. Surface wet-smoothed/self-slipped, light buff. Wheelmade. Period 12a.

*14. KT 8347 ['97 L 55 L. 269]. Max. pres. h = 13 cm, max. pres. diam = 43.6 cm. Same fabric as no. 13. Surface preserves thicker slip, pale yellow. Wheelmade. Period 12a.

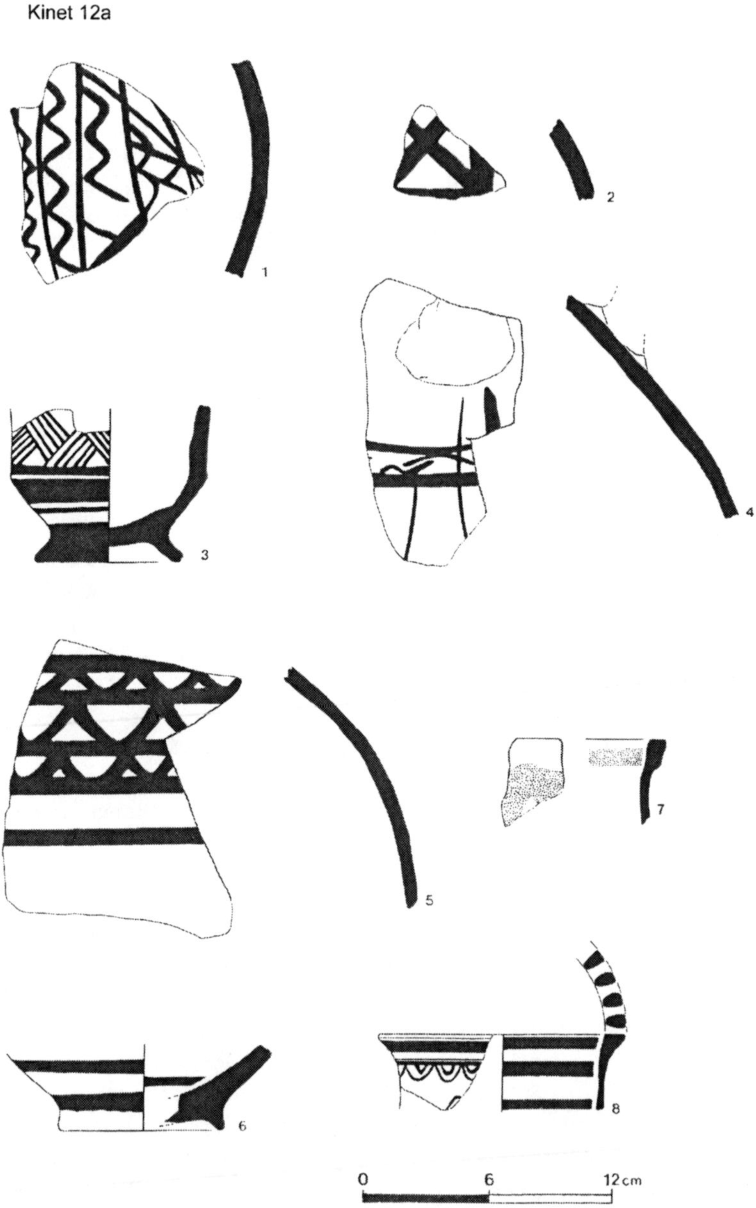

Fig. 7: Painted pottery from Kinet Period 12a (* = earliest deposits).

Key to fig. 7:

1. KT 8278 ['97 L 53 L. 258]. Max. pres. h = 9.2 cm, th = 0.7 cm. Medium coarse dark buff; dense small to larger sand and lime inclusions; fine to larger vegetal temper. Well fired. Exterior surface wet-smoothed and burnished, light brown; untidily decorated with light to dark brown paint (depending on thickness), some crackling. Shape and surface somewhat uneven. Coilmade. Body sherd for a spherical vessel or pilgrim flask. Period 12a. Cf. Riis 1948, 93, fig. 129, Hama cemetery G VII (a) [Period I = Hama F].

*2. KT 8834 ['97 L 65 L. 322]. Max. pres. h = 4.5 cm, th = 1.0 cm. Medium coarse dark buff with gray core; dense small to larger sand and ground shell inclusions, fine mica specks; dense vegetal temper. Well fired. Exterior surface burnished, dark buff; casually decorated with red-brown paint. General effect is coarse. Closed vessel. Wheelmade. Period 12a.

3. KT 8834 ['97 L 65 L. 322]. Max. pres. h = 4.5 cm, th = 1.0 cm. Same fabric as no. 3, also chaff-faced. Hard fired. Exterior surface wet-smoothed; decorated in dark purple paint, with slight polish. General effect is coarse. Closed vessel. Wheelmade. Period 12a.

For chevrons replacing crosshatched designs in the later phase of Early Iron Kilise Tepe, cf. Hansen and Postgate 1999, 113, Kilise Tepe Level IIe.

*4. KT 8358 ['97 L 55 L. 275]. Max. pres. h = 14 cm, th = 0.8 cm. Medium coarse buff with orange to gray core; dense, fine to large dark and ground shell inclusions, much fine to larger mica specks; fine vegetal temper. Well fired. Exterior surface smoothed and polished; decorated with yellow-brown paint, sintered. Wheelmade. Period 12a.

5. KT 7777 ['97 L 48 L. 222]. Max. pres. h = 13.5 cm, th = 0.8 cm. Orange version of fabric no. 1, but with denser vegetal temper, and chaff-faced. Hard fired. Exterior surface wet-smoothed; decorated in red-brown to black paint (depending on thickness), some crackling. Closed vessel. Wheelmade. Period 12a. Cf. Riis 1948, 54, fig. 43, Hama cemetery G IV 168 [Period I = Hama F].

6. KT 7795 ['97 L 48 L. 232]. Max. pres. h = 4.4 cm, wall th = 1.1 cm. Medium coarse grayish buff fabric with orange interior; dense fine to large dark inclusions, rare mica specks; vegetal temper. Hard fired. Exterior surface smooth and cream-slipped, decorated with black bands (crackled); interior very worn, painted with concentric black band. Imitation of Myc IIIC? Period 12a.

7. KT 7795 ['97 L 48 L. 232]. Max. pres. h = 5.0 cm, wall th = 0.5 cm. Medium coarse dark buff fabric; large black and fine lime inclusions; dense vegetal temper; and chaff-faced. Hard fired. Interior and exterior wet-smoothed (very worn); casually decorated with matte purple-brown paint (crackled). Wall thickness irregular, perhaps handmade. Period 12a.

8. KT 7777 ['97 L 48 L. 227]. Max. pres. h = 3.7 cm, wall th = 0.4 cm. Medium fine pale gray-buff fabric, inclusions negligeable. Well fired, somewhat porous. Surface wet-smoothed, light to darker buff; decorated with a fine brush in dark brown to black paint, crackled. Wheelmade. Period 12a. For shape, cf. Postgate 1998, 223, fig. 3, Kilise Tepe Level II, D753.

Kinet 12b (pits)

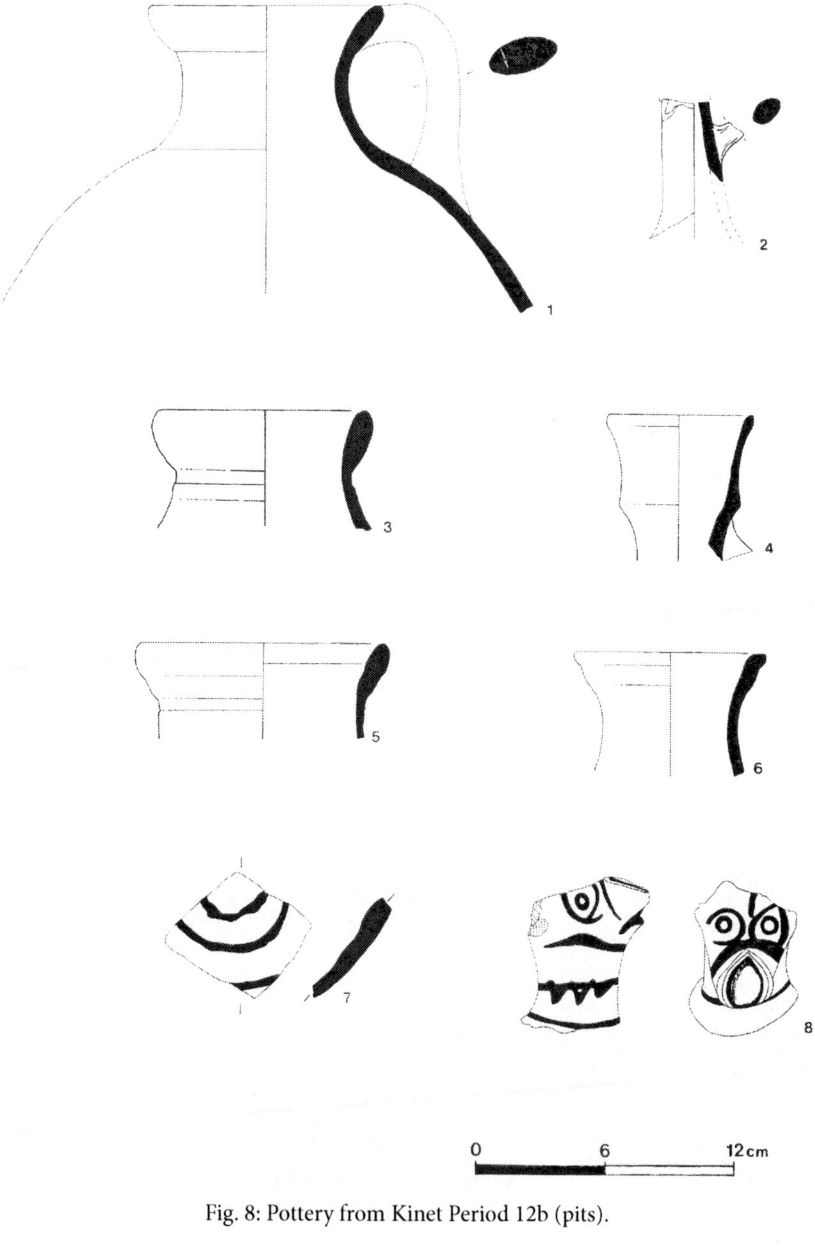

Fig. 8: Pottery from Kinet Period 12b (pits).

Key to fig. 8:

1. KT 8571 ['97 L 62 L. 295]. Max. pres. h = 13.0 cm, max. pres. diam = 24.4 cm. Medium fine dark orange fabric; dense sand and fine to large lime inclusions; some vegetal temper. Well fired. Surface wet-smoothed/self-slipped, light buff. Wheelmade. Period 12b.

2. KT 8571 ['97 L 62 L. 295]. Max. pres. h = 6.5 cm, max. pres. diam = ca. 4.8 cm. Medium fine orange to dark buff fabric; fine to larger dark and lime inclusions, some mica specks. Well fired. Exterior slipped and burnished, buff. Period 12b (or residual Period 13.1).

3. KT 8435 ['97 L 62 L. 289]. Max. pres. h = 6.2 cm, rim diam = 11.3 cm. Medium coarse orange-buff fabric with gray core; dense sand inclusions. Well fired. Surface wet-smoothed, cream to pale orange. Wheelmade. Period 12b.

4. KT 8571 ['97 L 62 L. 295]. Max. pres. h = 7.5 cm, rim diam = 7.8 cm. Medium coarse pale orange fabric; dense fine to large ground shell inclusions, fine dark specks, some mica; fine vegetal temper. Well fired. Surface self-slipped/slipped, pale buff; broad groove at top of neck. Wheelmade. Period 12b.

5. KT 8571 ['97 L 62 L. 295]. Max. pres. h = 4.9 cm, rim diam = 13.2 cm. Medium coarse gray fabric; dense fine to large sand and ground shell inclusions; fine vegetal temper. Overfired (surface cracked). Surface wet-smoothed, light brown; fine sharp groove at top of neck. Wheelmade. Period 12b.

6. KT 8289 ['97 L 54 L. 262]. Max. pres. h = 6.5 cm, rim diam = 10.0 cm. Medium coarse orange fabric; dense large dark and ground shell inclusions; dense coarse vegetal temper; and chaff-faced. Brittle/overfired. No visible surface finish (worn), mottled orange to dark orange. Wheelmade, irregular. Period 12b.

7. KT 8280 ['97 L 54 L. 259]. Max. pres. h = 6.3 cm, th = 1.0 cm. Medium fine orange buff fabric; dense fine to large sand and ground shell inclusions; dense vegetal temper. Well fired. Surface burnished, buff; decorated with light to dark brown paint (depending on thickness), somewhat sintered. Hand or coilmade (surfaces lumpy). Body sherd for pilgrim flask. Period 12b.

8. KNH 616 ['97 L 52 L. 255]. Max. pres. h = 6.7 cm, max. pres. w = 4.4 cm. Medium coarse buff fabric; dense dark sand inclusions; vegetal temper. Surface thickly slipped, and painted in matte red to brown. Deep fine incisions outlining eyes; mouth and ears applied separately, as were (missing) horns. Spout in shape of bull's head, with channel for pouring liquids through open mouth. Anciently broken at base of neck. Period 12b.

For bull-headed spouts on kernoi, see T. Dothan 1982, 224, 225, pl. 6–8.

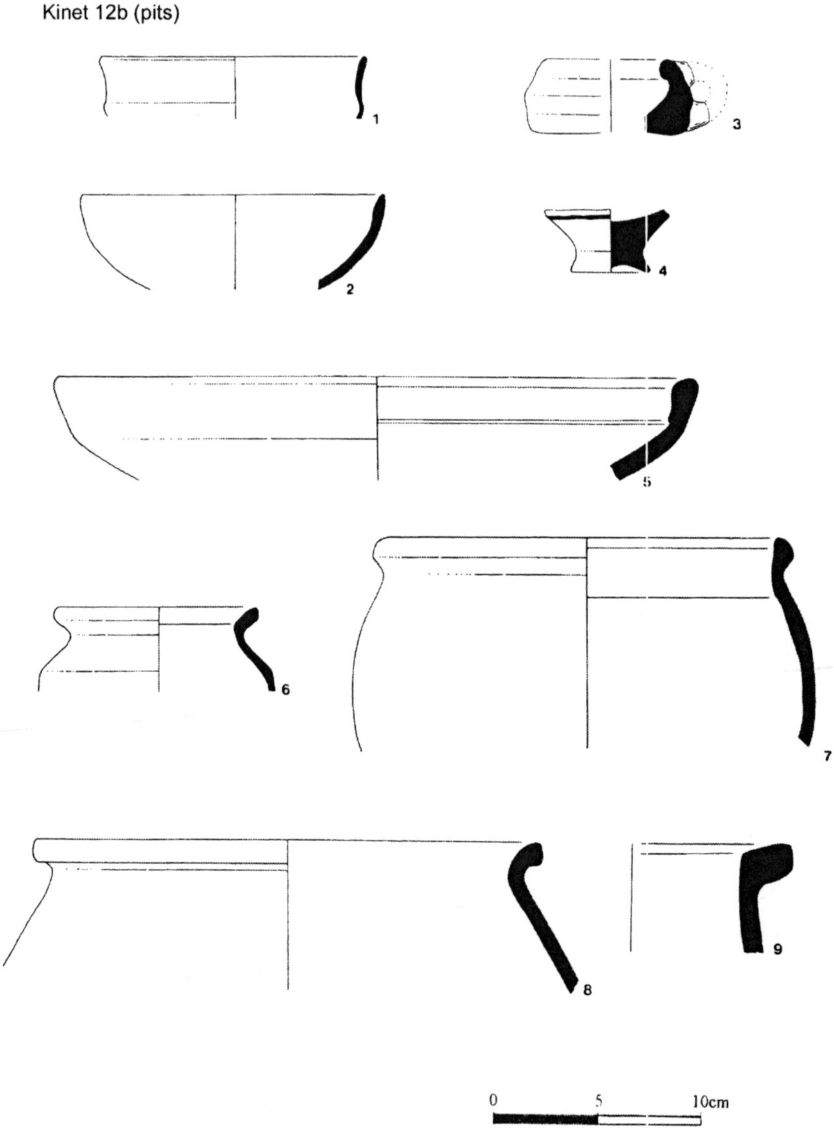

Fig. 9: Pottery from Kinet Period 12b (pits).

Key to fig. 9:

1. KT 8571 [‘97 L 62 L. 295]. Max. pres. h = 3.4 cm, rim diam = 15.2 cm. Medium coarse light buff fabric with gray core; very dense fine to larger dark (sand), some fine ground shell inclusions; fine vegetal temper. Brittle. Wet-smoothed/slipped on exterior and interior lip, light pinkish buff. Wheelmade. Period 12b.

Cf. Killebrew 1998a, 388, fig. 6:20–21, Tel Miqne-Ekron VII (Phase 9B).

2. KT 8442 [‘97 L 62 L. 292]. Max. pres. h = 6.1 cm, rim diam = 17.0 cm. Medium fine buff fabric; dense fine to larger sand and ground shell inclusions; some coarse vegetal temper. Hard fired, somewhat porous. Interior and exterior wet-smoothed/self-slipped, cream. Coilmade (?), surface irregular. Period 12b.

3. KT 8571 [‘97 L 62 L. 295]. H = 4.0 cm, max. diam = 9.6 cm. Medium coarse buff fabric; medium to large dark inclusions, some fine mica specks. Poorly or secondarily fired. Handmade, misshapen. Period 12b.

4. KT 8571 [‘97 L 62 L. 295]. Max. pres. h = 3.5 cm, base diam = 4.5 cm. Medium coarse orange fabric; dense fine to large dark inclusions, some mica specks; vegetal temper. Hard fired. Exterior surface smooth and cream-slipped, decorated with black band; interior unfinished. Similar to KT 7795 from Period 12A (fig. 3.6). Imitation of Myc IIIC? Period 12b.

5. KT 8442 [‘97 L 62 L. 292]. Max. pres. h = 5.7 cm, rim diam = 36.0 cm. Medium coarse buff-gray fabric (secondarily burnt); dense fine to larger dark and ground shell inclusions, some mica specks; vegetal temper. Well fired. Interior wet-smoothed, exterior has no surface finish. Wheelmade. Period 12b.

6. KT 8571 [‘97 L 62 L. 295]. Max. pres. h = 4.6 cm, max. diam = 13.0 cm. Medium fine orange-buff fabric; dense fine sand and fine to larger ground shell inclusions, rare mica specks; fine vegetal temper. Well fired. Interior and exterior self-slipped, orange-buff. Wheelmade. Period 12b.

7. KT 8571 [‘97 L 62 L. 295]. Max. pres. h = 10.2 cm, rim diam = 20.0 cm. Coarse dark brown to black fabric (exterior smoke-blackened); very dense large crushed quartz and ground shell inclusions, large mica flecks; some coarse vegetal temper. Hard fired. Exterior surface scraped, wet-smoothed. Coilmade. Cooking ware. Period 12b.

8. KT 8571 [‘97 L 62 L. 295]. Max. pres. h = 8.1 cm, rim diam = 28.3 cm. Coarse brown fabric with dark gray core; dense medium to large crushed quartz and some ground shell inclusions; coarse vegetal temper. Hard fired. Interior and exterior wet-smoothed, brown. Wheelmade. Period 12b.

9. KT 8571 [‘97 L 62 L. 295]. Max. pres. h = 5.1 cm, th = 1.3 rim, rim diam cannot be estimated (very large vessel). Coarse brown fabric with black core; dense medium to large ground quartz and shell inclusions; some coarse vegetal temper. Brittle (surface crackled). Interior and exterior thickly wet-smoothed, light brown; pattern-burnished in narrow horizontal bands, widely spaced. Wheelmade? Period 12b. (A thinner-walled, less coarse, reddish-brown version of this ware with vertical pattern-burnishing also occurs. It is wheelmade.)

Fig. 10: Pottery from Kinet Period 12c ("work platforms").

Key to fig. 10:

1. KT 7953 ['97 L 48 L. 251]. Max. pres. h = 4.4 cm, rim diam cannot be estimated (deep bowl). Gritty dark-orange fabric. Painted on exterior and interior with dull, red paint. Wheelmade. Period 12c.

2. KT 7581 ['97 L 50 L. 222]. Max. pres. h = 8.1 cm, rim diam = 28.2 cm. Medium fine dark orange fabric; dense fine dark (sand) and fine to larger ground shell inclusions, slight mica; vegetal temper. Well fired. Surfaces slightly wet-smoothed; decorated in matte black and dark-red paint. Wheelmade. Period 12c.

3. KT 7110 ['97 L 42 L. 203]. Max. pres. h = 1.1 cm, base diam ca. 10 cm. Same as no. 2 (could belong to same vessel). Period 12c.

4. KT 7891 ['97 L 50 L. 238]. Max. pres. h = 5.0 cm, th = 1.0 cm. Medium coarse light brown fabric with gray core; fine to larger sand and lime inclusions, some fine mica; dense coarse vegetal temper, chaff-faced. Hard fired. Exterior surface smoothed, decorated in thick brown paint. Coilmade. General effect is coarse (same type as fig. 3.2). Period 12c.

5. KT 4333 ['94 CII 38 L. 89]. Max. pres. h = 9.1 cm, max. diam = 17.9 cm. Medium-coarse orange fabric; dense fine to larger sand and ground-shell inclusions; dense vegetal temper. Well fired. Surface smoothed (very worn); careless decoration in brown to black paint, somewhat crackled. Wheel- or coilmade. From a Middle Iron Age context on the West Slope.

6. KT 7891 ['97 L 50 L. 238]. Max. pres. h = 6.8 cm, th = 0.9 cm. Fine cream fabric; negligible inclusions; fine vegetal temper. Well fired. Interior and exterior surface thickly wet-smoothed and wiped, cream; decorated with matte dark-brown paint. Wheelmade. Fragment of large, high-necked vessel. Period 12c.

7. KT 4847 ['95 L 6 L. 9]. Max. pres. h = 6.1 cm, wall th = 0.6 cm. Medium fine pinkish-buff fabric; dense fine sand inclusions. Hard fired, porous. Exterior surface slightly wet-smoothed, pale cream/white; casually decorated in matte brown paint. Wheelmade. Technique of decoration similar to no. 5. From a Middle Iron Age context. For style of decoration, cf. Hansen and Postgate 1999, 115, figs. 11–12, Kilise Tepe Level IIb.

8. KT 7583 ['97 L 50 L. 223]. Max. pres. h = 3.4 cm, th = 0.6 cm. Overfired (greenish) version of no. 7. Period 12c.

9. KT 7581 ['97 L 50 L. 222]. Max. pres. h = 14.4 cm, rim diam = 12.2 cm. Medium coarse orange fabric; fine sand, very dense fine to large crushed shell inclusions; very dense coarse vegetal temper, chaff-faced. Brittle. Exterior surface wet-smoothed, trace of burnishing inside rim. Wheelmade. Warped, irregular, rim cracked in firing. Period 12c. For shape, cf. Venturi 2000, 515, fig. 7:13, Tell Afis VII [9a/b].

It is only with Period 11 and the reappearance of architecture in the West Slope trenches, that the professionally painted component assigned at Tarsus to the early Iron Age was introduced (e.g., White Painted, Bichrome, and Black-on-Red; Hanfmann 1963, 92–95; see Gates 2000, 196, 205, fig. 6).[3] This repertoire would give an upper limit of 1050/950 B.C.E. for the end of Kinet Period 12 and its start some time after 1200.

Faunal Evidence for Newcomers to Kinet

It could be concluded that Kinet Period 12's poor potting skills resulted from socioeconomic changes only, such as a gradual breakdown in the established workshop production, or farmers from the local countryside moving into the ruins of the coastal town (e.g., Dever 1992, 107–8). However, the rich sample of animal bones also shows a radical transformation, involving both a shift from the LB II diet and unfamiliarity with the area's food resources. S. Ikram, the Kinet project's zooarchaeologist, considers the sample sufficiently large to be representative: NISP 5,971 bones, well over 100 per m^3 since the 12b pits were mostly empty (2003, 286). She found that the most common Period 12 domesticates were still ovicaprids, but that herding strategies had changed: sheep and goats were evenly balanced in numbers (sheep were much preferred in LB II) with larger percentages of older animals than before (Ikram 2003, 288). Butchering techniques were different (Ikram 2003, 291–92). Also striking was the disappearance of deep-sea fishing and hunting, an important supplement for Kinet's LB II inhabitants (Ikram 2003, 289). Notable exceptions were five elephant bones—a molar, rib, and parts of one foot (Ikram 2003, 290), but these too point to experience with another, less-populated environment, and the exploitation of resources foreign to Kinet's maritime landscape (on elephants and seminomadic populations in early Iron Age northwest Syria, see Miller 1986, 29–34).[4]

The faunal remains reflect a pastoralist or agro-pastoralist economy, practiced by people with a reluctance to fish, especially by boat, or to hunt in Kinet's

3. With Kinet Period 11 and its Iron Age successors, the proportion of painted to plain wares becomes 25–30 percent. This is still very far from the figures claimed for Iron I in the 'Amuq and at Tell Afis (Venturi 2000, 534), but a pronounced increase from Period 12, when painted sherds make up less than 5 percent of the assemblage.

4. Elephant bones (and tusks) are well represented at second-millennium B.C.E. Syrian sites (Miller 1986, 30–31), but the only ones at Kinet are these five from Period 12. At nearby Sirkeli, an elephant foot bone was also found in the recent excavations; its context (unspecified) would be either MB II or Middle Iron Age (von den Driesch in Hrouda 1997, 132).

neighboring mountains. They did not maintain the LB II inhabitants' dietary customs and must thus be considered an entirely non-local, perhaps even seasonal population.[5] The change moreover is radical enough that it may reasonably be extrapolated from the West Slope sample to the entire site.

Conclusions

From every perspective, the cultural assemblage for Kinet's initial Iron Age settlement indicates a departure from its Late Bronze urban structure, which was oriented around harbors and maritime business. Instead, the site was newly occupied by a population for whom animal processing was a major activity, pottery manufacture was casual, and permanent architecture was unnecessary. It should be added that their lifestyle was not enhanced by much in the way of metal or other non-perishable possessions, although these did include an iron knife handle with rivets (from 12c), the earliest iron object from Kinet.[6]

The arrival of Kinet's Period 12 pastoralists can be linked, as argued by Sader (2000) and others, to the breakdown of formal territorial boundaries along the Hittite Empire's southeast periphery after 1200 B.C.E. They must represent one of the many small-scale population shifts behind the scenes, while Sea Peoples were claiming more flamboyant roles in the archaeological record.

Acknowledgements

It is a great pleasure to thank M. Artzy, A. E. Killebrew, and G. Lehmann for organizing the stimulating conference and workshop on the Philistines and other "Sea Peoples"; for inviting me to participate; and for introducing outsiders like me to the many archaeologists who generously showed us the Sea Peoples "at home."

This paper is in large part based on the superb fieldwork and analytical skills of T. M. Cross, whose death in April 2002 left her many friends, colleagues, and the Kinet project bereft of a most precious associate. I much regret that the two of us will no longer be able to debate its questions, and the many others that enlivened our discussions over the past thirty-three years. She has my deepest thanks,

5. For a comparable change in diet at Iron I Tel Miqne-Ekron, see Hesse 1986.

6. Metalwork being common at Kinet in all other periods, it is significant that so little was recovered from Period 12 deposits. Besides the iron knife, the following were found: a bronze needle point (12a); two crescent-shaped lead pendants, a pair of bronze loops or earrings, and a bronze knife blade (12b pits); and a fine bronze spearpoint or arrowhead (12c).

as does R. Schneider for working on Kinet pottery with her. Illustrations were prepared by N. Yılmaz. The Late Bronze and Early Iron excavations reported here were carried out by Bilkent University's Kinet Höyük project with funding from the Institute for Aegean Prehistory, the Tarbell Family Foundation, British Petroleum-Turkey, Bilkent and Georgetown Universities, and several private donors.

Chapter Nineteen
The Southeast Aegean in the Age of the Sea Peoples

*Mario Benzi**

Since the beginning of Late Bronze (LB) III, the southeast Aegean islands as well as some sites on the west coast of Asia Minor (Miletus, Iasos, and Müskebi) came under Mycenaean control and throughout the Mycenaean palace period their inhabitants adopted many aspects of the Mycenaean culture, such as burial customs, pottery, weapons, and jewelry. Like the islands of the central Aegean and other marginal areas, the southeast Aegean may be regarded as a province of the so-called Mycenaean Periphery, although there is still much discussion on the nature of the Mycenaean presence and involvement there.[1]

Unfortunately, the lack of settlement evidence and the state of research and/or publication at the few excavated sites prevent, for the moment, any assessment of the events that took place in the area from the late-thirteenth century B.C.E. to the disappearance of the Mycenaean culture. In fact, after more than a century of archaeological research, the settlement at Troy is still the only Bronze Age east Aegean site which has been extensively excavated and adequately published.

In spite of a number of obvious common traits and their close geographic proximity, the history of the two main islands of the Dodecanese as well as that of the Mycenaeanized centers on the west coast of Anatolia were different in many respects, such as pottery production, wealth, involvement in long-distance trade, and population fluctuations.

---

* Università di Pisa, DPT Scienze Archeologiche, Via Galvani 1, 56100 Pisa. Email: benzi@arch.unipi.it; mario.domenico.benzi@alice.it.

1. On this much-debated problem, see, e.g., French 1978; Mee 1988; Melas 1988; Bryce 1989b; French 1993; Cline 1995; Gates 1995; Benzi 1996; Mountjoy 1998; and Niemeier 1998; 2007b.

The difference in the number of tombs in use and arguably in population at Ialysos on Rhodes and Seraglio on Kos is particularly striking. Statistics of the number of tombs in use at the Eleona-Langada cemetery show that at the Seraglio there was a steady growth in population from a minimum 13.4 percent in Late Helladic (LH) IIB–IIIA:1 through 15.7 percent in LH IIIA:2, 28 percent in LH IIIB to a maximum 42.7 percent in LH IIIC. At Ialysos the corresponding figures are as follows: 18 percent in LH IIB–IIIA:1; 36.5 percent in LH IIIA:2; 14.5 percent in LH IIIB; and 31 percent in LH IIIC (Macdonald 1986, 126–29; Benzi 1996, 949–50; Deger-Jalkotzy 1998, 110). The dearth of exotica and objects in gold and silver in the LH IIIA:2–B tombs at the Eleona-Langada cemetery indicates that Seraglio was much less involved in the international trade than Ialysos, where such objects are relatively common and are still found during the critical LH IIIB period (Benzi 1992, 216). The high proportion of imported pottery further evidences that Ialysos and Rhodes were much involved in the international trading network. Clay analyses of LH IIIA–B vessels from Ialysos and the cemetery at Pylona-Aspropilia show that large amounts of imported pottery reached not only the major site but also the many minor cemeteries scattered all over the island (Jones and Mee 1978; Jones 1986a, 501–7; Karantzali and Ponting 2000, 232–38; Ponting and Karantzali in Karantzali 2001, 105–7).

There is no doubt that throughout the Late Bronze Age Miletus was the main trading center and the most prominent site in southwest Anatolia, while Iasos was a settlement on a much more modest scale. This is perhaps explained, at least in part, by the fact that Miletus was situated on the southern side of the then large Latmic Gulf and had a ready access to the mouth of the Meander Valley on an important trade route leading from the Aegean to central Anatolia,[2] while Iasos, being virtually cut off from the Anatolian hinterland, did not enjoy the advantageous location for trade of its northern neighbor.

2. Hawkins 1998, 25–26 and fig. 10 (followed by Mountjoy 1998, 47) has recently suggested that there was no direct overland route from the interior of Anatolia to Miletus. Hawkins' argument is based on the route (reported in the Tawagalawa Letter) the Hittite king Hattusili III followed in order to bring help to the men of Lukka against Piyamaradu. We must, however, bear in mind that a heavy army moving overland had to follow different routes from those suitable to merchants. Although Miletus is located on the unfavorable side of the old Latmic Gulf, this should not have prevented the light Bronze Age merchant boats from sailing from and to the mouth of the Meander, which in the Bronze Age was most likely navigable (W.-D. Niemeier, personal communication).

RHODES

In spite of hundreds of chamber tombs, very little settlement evidence has been as yet discovered on Rhodes. A handful of LH IIIB–C sherds come from the Acropolis of Lindos. This was most likely a site of some importance but the Bronze Age layers were destroyed by extensive later building activity (Hope Simpson and Lazenby 1973, 151 with relevant bibliography). LH IIIA:2–B sherds and remains of buildings have come to light in the old as well as in the new excavations at Trianda (Benzi 1988a; Marketou 1988, 31).[3] Marketou's ongoing excavations have definitely disproved the earlier suggestion that from LH IIIA:2 onward "the main Mycenaean centre in the Ialysos area was elsewhere, probably further inland and nearer to the Mycenaean cemeteries" (Hope Simpson and Lazenby 1973, 135). Now there is substantial evidence showing that there was a settlement at Trianda in LH IIIA:2–B, although the problem of the settlement to be connected with the extensive LH IIIC cemetery is still unsolved.[4] It is, however, possible that the uppermost and latest levels of the Mycenaean settlement were removed by floods, erosion, and agricultural activity (Benzi 1988a, 53; Karantzali 1999b).

In LH IIIB the cemeteries at Ialysos and other sites on the northwest coast suffered a severe setback evidenced by the massive decrease in the number of tombs in use.[5] However, there were still wealthy tombs at Ialysos in LH IIIB and nine out of the fourteen LH IIIB chambers excavated by the Italians seem to be new foundations. Elsewhere the population pattern remained basically unchanged, but at almost every site—except some cemeteries in the southeast part of the island, notably those at Passia and Vathy-Apsaktiras (Benzi 1988b, 64–66; Benzi 1992, 215; 1988a, 56–77)—LH IIIB pottery appears in smaller proportion to that of LH IIIA:2. If there was a decline on Rhodes during LH IIIB, the cause should perhaps be sought in some event(s) taking place at the beginning of the period or in the transitional LH IIIA:2/B1 phase (about 1325–1290 B.C.E.). At that time there was much trouble in west Anatolia due to the showdown of Hit-

---

3. A handful of sherds from three plots of the new excavations are illustrated by Karantzali and Ponting (2000, 238, pl. 42a–b). Almost all of them are dated LH IIIA:2 or IIIA:2–B and B1; only a krater sherd (it is not stated which one of those illustrated) is assigned to LH IIIB2–C Early, but Karantzali kindly informs me that the find context suggests a dating not later than IIIB. For a thorough discussion of the new finds, see Karantzali 1999b. I warmly thank Karantzali for giving me the opportunity to read her paper in advance of publication.

4. A handful of LH IIIC sherds (to be published by the present writer) from the votive deposit of the Athena Temple on the Acropolis of Ialysos can hardly support the hypothesis of the presence of a Mycenaean settlement there.

5. As I have pointed out (Benzi 1988b, 65) the evidence for the sites on the northwest coast must be taken with some caution because most of the material from the area is missing.

tites and Arzawans and the appearance of a man called Piyamaradu, who was to cause much trouble for the whole coastal area of Asia Minor throughout the first half of the thirteenth century.[6] However, there is no evidence in Hittite sources that the islands of the Dodecanese were involved in such conflicts. In fact there is no evidence supporting Mee's view (1982, 88) that Ialysos and other sites in the area were destroyed. According to Marketou, who is carrying on extensive excavations at Trianda, the decline of Ialysos in the thirteenth century was the consequence of difficult environmental conditions following the collapse of the flood control system (Marketou 1998, 61–63; Karantzali 1999b). As to Furumark's suggestion that LH IIIA:2 pottery continued to be produced in Rhodes, this seems extremely unlikely since there is much canonical LH IIIB1 pottery both imported and locally made (Furumark 1941a, 541; Benzi 1992, 216; Mountjoy 1999b, 284–85). Likewise, the suggestion that the scarcity of LH IIIB pottery may be due to the fact that in this period there was the custom of putting little pottery in tombs (Mountjoy 1998, 35) does not seem a convincing explanation since in some LH IIIB tombs there was much pottery.[7] The only sign of stagnation is the absence of LH IIIB2 pottery. However, since that style had a very limited impact outside the Argolid, its absence in the east Aegean does not have any other implication but the breakdown of trade with the Mainland in the last decades of the thirteenth century. Clay analyses of vases from Ialysos and Pylona-Aspropilia have shown that a good deal of LH IIIA:2–B1 pottery was imported from the Argolid and other Mainland areas, while in LH IIIC most of the pottery deposited in tombs was made locally.[8] In LH IIIA:2 a highly peculiar, possibly Minoan-inspired style, was developed in south Rhodes (Mountjoy 1995a; 1998). The lack of settlement evidence precludes any speculation on what happened at Ialysos at the end of LH IIIB, but continuous habitation is indicated by the appearance of LH IIIC Early pottery in tombs and by the sudden increase of the cemetery in the first phase of LH IIIC (Benzi 1988b, 67; 1992, 216–18). At both Ialysos and Kameiros several earlier tombs were reused (on the reuse of earlier tombs in LH IIIC, see Cavanagh and Mee 1978; Benzi 1982; 1988c, 261; 1992, 221–22). At Ialysos, quite surprisingly, only three of the fourteen LH IIIB tombs continued in use (Benzi 1992, 222 [NT 38, NT 64, NT 66]). In the rest of the island only Maritsa, Siana, and Kariones were apparently deserted; elsewhere habitation continued though on

6. On the remarkable role of Piyamaradu in western Anatolian affairs and relevant bibliography, cf. Starke 1997, 453–54.

7. Good examples are provided by Ialysos NT 53 and Kariones T 2 (Benzi 1992, 343–47, 421–22).

8. See Jones and Mee 1978; Jones 1986a, 501–7; Karantzali and Ponting 2000, 232–38; and Ponting and Karantzali in Karantzali 2001, 105–7.

a considerably smaller scale.[9] At most sites the occupation came to an end in LH IIIC Early, but at few sites continued on until LH IIIC Middle/Late.[10] Mee suggested that refugees arrived on Rhodes from the Mainland at the beginning of LH IIIC (Mee 1982, 89–90; see also Dietz 1984, 115; Macdonald 1986, 149; Deger-Jalkotzy 1998, 110). He believes that the reuse of chamber tombs cannot

9. Benzi 1988c, 261; 1992, 223–24 and tables I–III, but Mountjoy's redating to LH IIIA:2 of a number of south Rhodian vases previously assigned to LHIIIC implies an even more extensive desertion of south Rhodes than previously suggested (Mountjoy 1995a, 33).

10. Kameiros (Benzi 1992, 412–19): Kalavarda-Aniforo LH IIIA:2–C Advanced to Late from Tombs 46–48, 50 (figs. 8, 23–25); Kaminaki Lures-Tzitzo LH IIIA:2–C Middle (Advanced) a single vase (fig. 6.22). Apollakia LH IIIA:2–C Early (11%; Benzi 1992, 434) only an amphoriskos can be assigned to LH IIIC Middle (Mountjoy 1999c, fig. 423:145; Benzi 1992, 434). Lelos LH IIIA:2–C Early (Benzi 1992, 422–31). A few LH IIIC Early vases come from two of the seven tombs excavated by the Italians. Kattavia-Granto LH IIIA:1–B (Benzi 1992, 434–35): The linear jug (Blinkenberg and Johansen 1924, pl. 45:5) with pinched rim and wavy band down the handle could be LH IIIC Early. Lachania LH IIIA:1–C Early (Benzi 1992, 435–37): The deep bowls (Benzi 1992, pls. 139f–l, 171f) are assigned to LH IIIB or transitional to LH IIIC by Benzi, to LH IIIB by Mountjoy (1999c, 1025 nn. 466–447). The stemmed spiral bowl pl. 171f (fig. 1.5) is assigned to LH IIIC Early by Benzi (1992, 150, 437). Deger-Jalkotzy (1998, 109–10, 120) points out that the decoration of this bowl "resembles that of two much debated bowls from Pyla-Kokkinokremos on Cyprus," which was founded and abandoned during the transitional LC IIA/IIIA. The deep bowls (Benzi 1992, 437, pl. 139m–n; Mountjoy 1999c, 1062, fig. 435:238–39) are LH IIIC Early. Vathy-Apsaktiras LH IIIA:1–C Early (12%; Benzi 1992, 437–39): From an extensive chamber tombs cemetery plundered by villagers were recovered about 280 vases. Eighty-nine are in Copenhagen and many others in the Akavi Collection in Rhodes. Most of the pottery is LH IIIC Early; two vases in the Akavi Collection (M. L. Morricone 1979–1980, figs. 23–24) and some surface sherds (Dietz 1984, fig. 73:7–7a) may be later. Passia LH IIIA:2–C Early/Middle (Dietz 1984; Benzi 1992, 440): Dietz's dating of two stirrup jars and a deep bowl to LH IIIC Middle/Late (Dietz 1984, 98 nos. 11–13, followed by Benzi 1992, 440) is rejected by Mountjoy, who assigns all the LH IIIC pottery from Passia to LH IIIC Early (1999c, 982). Gennadi LH IIIB–C:A chamber tomb has been recently reported; the finds are unpublished. Lardos LH IIIA:1–C Early (Benzi 1992, 440–45): A monochrome deep bowl with strong flaring lip could be later (Benzi 1992, 441, pls. 143f, 171l). Pylona-Ambelia LH III(A:2–)B–C Middle (Developed; Benzi 1992, 445–48): All the LH IIIC pottery is dated by Mountjoy to LH IIIC Early. I have assigned three vases to LH IIIC Middle (Benzi 1992, pls. 145a, e–f, g–h). Pylona-Aspropilia LH IIIA:2–C Middle/Late (Karantzali 2001): LH IIIC pottery has been found in two (T 4 and T 5B) of the six chamber tombs excavated at this site. Almost all the twenty-six vases from T 4 are LH IIIC Early and Middle, three are dated by the excavator to LH IIIC Middle/Late and two are assigned to LH IIIC Late (Karantzali 2001, 18–19, 21), namely, a wavy-line amphoriskos and a composite vessel with very simple linear decoration (Karantzali 2001, 61–63, fig. 41, pls. 43f, 44d 16791 and 16785). None, however, shows unequivocal LH IIIC Late traits. From Chamber B of double-chamber Tomb 5—which was in use from LH IIIA:2 on—come ten LH IIIC vessels. Five of them are dated by the excavator to LH IIIC Middle/Late. They include a linear conical bowl (Karantzali 2001, 56, fig. 39, pl. 39d 18638), an amphoriskos with tassel pattern,

be ascribed but to displaced individuals.[11] It must, however, be underlined that this unusual burial habit is attested in some areas of the Mainland, including the Argolid, where there is no question of refugees (Cavanagh and Mee 1978, 32–36). Likewise, the increase in the number of clay figurines deposited in LH IIIC tombs has perhaps been overrated. After all, the eleven LH IIIC figurines found at Ialysos are not so impressive as to be attributed to refugees from the Mainland.[12] Therefore, I have suggested that the increase of the population at Ialysos, being contemporary with growing depopulation in the rest of the island as well as with a strong survival of earlier local motifs in LH IIIC pottery (which implies continuity of population), is better explained by a process of synoecism than migration (Benzi 1988b, 70; 1988c, 261–62; 1992, 224–25). In any case, the LH IIIC pottery shows that the influence from Crete is now stronger than that from the Mainland and an influx of Minoan settlers has also been suggested (Kanta 1980, 306; Deger-Jalkotzy 1998, 119).

The LH IIIC pottery of Ialysos is a peculiar blend of local tradition and influences coming from Crete and the Mainland with the first two components exhibiting much more evidence than the latter. This peculiar style sets Ialysos apart from the east Aegean *koiné* (including Kos, Kalymnos, Chios, and Miletus) as defined by Mountjoy (1998, 53–63), and is the main reason for the various ways such pottery has been dealt with by different scholars. When studying LH IIIC Rhodes, my first concern was to fit this highly peculiar material into an established chronological system, therefore my approach was largely based on Mainland contexts and my attention was focused on vases betraying Mainland influence. By contrast Mountjoy's recent study is largely based on Minoan materials. She traces back to Minoan prototypes a substantial part of the Rhodian LH IIIC repertoire. Since LM IIIC pottery may have been ahead of the Mainland, the result is that in a number of cases my dating is later than that suggested by Mountjoy. Our different approaches also result in a different phasing of the Rhodian material. I adopted a three-phase chronological scheme: Early, Advanced (corresponding by and large to LH IIIC Middle), and Advanced-to-Late (includ-

---

a monochrome amphoriskos (Karantzali 2001, 62–63, fig. 41, pl. 44b–c 18662 and 18663), and a monochrome flask with plastic knobs on the shoulder (Karantzali 2001, 64, fig. 41, pl. 45d 18663). However, only the tassel pattern amphoriskos and the flask have some LH IIIC Late traits. The late phase of the period does not seem really represented at that site. Archangelos LH IIIA:2–C Early (Benzi 1992, 449–50). Koskinou LH IIIA:1–C Early (Benzi 1992, 449–50): only one vessel may be LH IIIC.

11. It must be emphasized that such tombs were not reused at the same time yet in different phases of LH IIIC (cf. Benzi 1992, 222, 224).

12. For the distribution of clay figurines on Rhodes and the eastern Aegean, see Mee 1982, 20, 44; Benzi 1992; 1999.

ing vessels with characteristics which are LH IIIC Middle [Advanced] as well as LH IIIC Late in Mainland terms; Benzi 1988c; 1992, 216–17). Mountjoy distinguishes only two phases—a comprehensive LH IIIC Early–LH IIIC Middle (Developed) phase and a LH IIIC Middle (Advanced) phase. Mountjoy's argument is based on the assumption that a number of Minoan motifs were adapted from imported Minoan octopus stirrup jars onto their local counterparts and then onto other shapes, and that LH IIIC Early and LH IIIC Middle (Developed) cannot be separated stylistically partly because there is much conservatism and partly because there is an influx of LM IIIC Early motifs which are not seen on the Mainland before LH IIIC Middle (Mountjoy 1999c, 985–86, 1045–53). Nearly all the Rhodian octopus stirrup jars have more or less distinctive Minoan features; ten or so are actual Minoan imports (Mee 1982, 32–34; Macdonald 1986, 135–38; Benzi 1992, 86–91). Mountjoy assigns all the imported pieces to LM IIIC Early (Mountjoy 1999c, 1045, pls. 6e–8). Kanta had already dated some octopus stirrup jars from Crete and Rhodes to an early, though not clearly defined, stage of LM IIIC (Kanta 1980, 255–56, 305), but in a recent paper dealing with the LM IIIB–C Early deposit from Trench B at Kastelli Chanion, she makes a statement which seems to cast some doubt on her previous dating. She states:

> The IIIC Octopus Stirrup Jar style present in Crete and Rhodes does not exist among the Trench B material. The developed Octopus Stirrup Jar on the Mainland and the islands dates from LH IIIC Middle. The absence of such sherds or their Minoan equivalents at Kastelli provides a chronological frame for the material ... together with the absence of elaborate IIIC Middle kraters. (Kanta 1997, 96)

The impression one gets reading the papers presented at the 1994 LM III Pottery Conference is that there is still much disagreement among specialists about the beginning, development, and phasing of LM IIIC. As to octopus stirrup jars, no new evidence was produced at the conference. Some octopus stirrup jars from Ialysos are very similar to LM IIIB examples and may well date from LM IIIC Early,[13] but I still believe that the most baroque examples with much elaborate filling motifs (not necessarily the Pictorial ones only) should belong to a later stage of LH IIIC. Since all such arguments are based on style, this remains an open question, which cannot be definitely settled until stratified evidence is found on Crete. Unfortunately, such vases do rarely occur in stratified levels. Spare yet interesting evidence is provided by the excavations at Kastelli Chanion. Here a

13. NT 15/2; NT 32/2, 17; NT 35/1; NT 84/6 (commonly regarded as the earliest in the series); and NT 87/3.

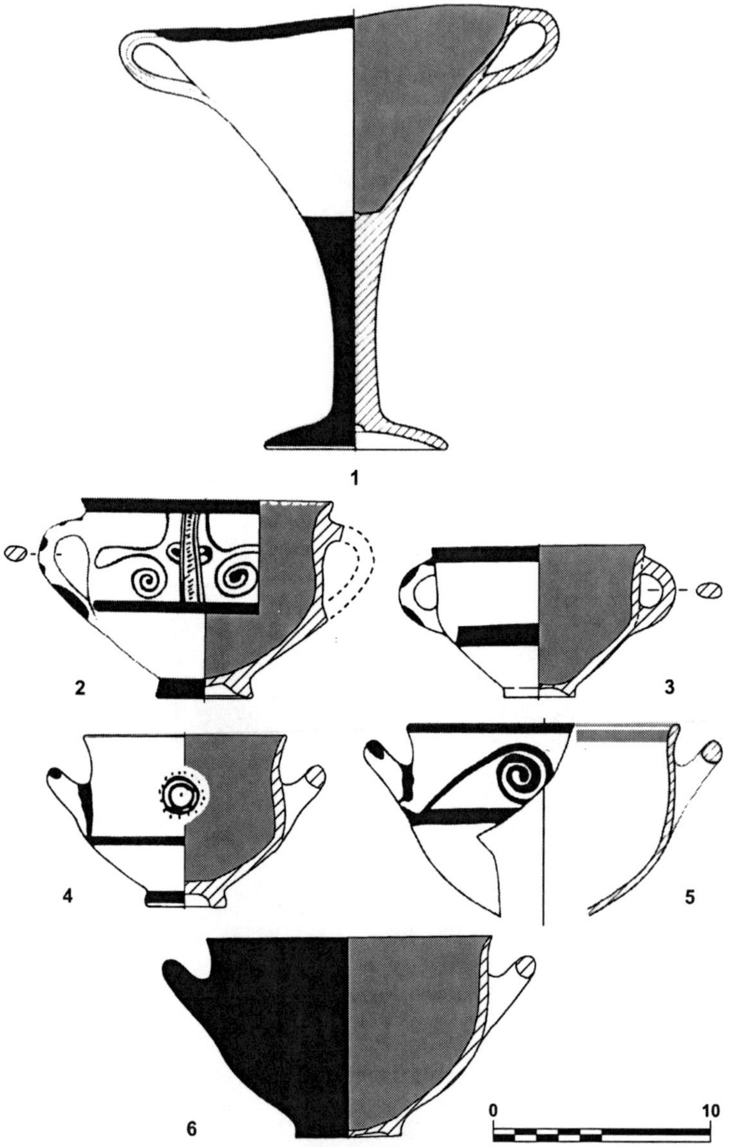

Fig. 1: **1)** LH IIIC kylix from Ialysos NT 38 (after Benzi 1992, pl. 175e); **2)** LH IIIC deep bowl from Ialysos NT 21 (after Benzi 1992, pl. 171a); **3)** LH IIIC deep bowl from Ialysos NT 21 (after Benzi 1992, pl. 171b); **4)** LH IIIC Early rosette bowl from Ialysos NT 72 (after Benzi 1992, pl. 171e); **5)** LH IIIC Early deep bowl from Lachania (Rhodes; after Benzi 1992, pl. 171f); **6)** LH IIIC monochrome deep bowl from Ialysos NT 12 (after Benzi 1992, pl. 171h).

fringed octopus of a very simple type is depicted on a stirrup jar coming from a LM IIIC Early deposit. By contrast, elaborate filling motifs of types which are often found on developed octopus stirrup jars are painted on a fragmentary closed vessel coming from one of the latest LM IIIC pits (Hallager and Hallager 2000, 144–45, pls. 38, 59e:1, 69a:10).

A few parallels with pottery of LH IIIC Early and Middle from the Mainland and Lefkandi indicate that contacts with the West were resumed after the LH IIIB2 gap. The shapes include kylikes (fig. 1.1), various types of deep bowls (figs. 1.2–6), conical bowls from Ialysos T 64 (fig. 2.7), and Pylona-Asprospilia (Benzi 1992, 129, pl. 162d; Karantzali 2001, 56, fig. 39, pl. 39d 18638),[14] semiglobular cups (fig. 2.8), and shallow angular bowls with dots on rim and carination (fig. 2.9). As stated above, the number of vases inspired by Mainland models is far from impressive, yet we have to bear in mind that our conclusions are mainly based on open shapes, which are very well attested in settlement deposits but are rarely found in burial contexts. The LH IIIC Pictorial Style is much less common than on Kos. On Kos, however, most of the Pictorial material comes from the settlement. Some of the Rhodian Pictorial vases may be imports from Kos (fig. 2.10).[15] LH IIIC Early to Middle was a period of recovery and prosperity on Rhodes. After the LH IIIB crisis, Ialysos was apparently able to resume its outstanding trading role. There is evidence for a wide range of trading connections, including Crete, the central and western Aegean, the Mainland as well as Cyprus and the eastern Mediterranean[16] while the recent find of a bronze fibula at Pylona-Aspropilia has at last provided unequivocal evidence for contacts with Europe (see below).

Mountjoy assigns almost all the vases I dated to my Advanced-to-Late period to LH IIIC Middle (Advanced). Several of them are dark ground with reserved decoration, a feature of LH IIIC Middle (Advanced) and Late on the Mainland (figs. 4.15–18; 5.19–20). In this group Mountjoy assigns to IIIC Early–IIIC Middle (Developed) all the vessels decorated with earlier motifs (figs. 2.11–13; 3.13–14). This seems a question of personal view. Indeed, I think the dark-ground decoration is chronologically more diagnostic than the survival of earlier motifs. Only

---

14. Another conical bowl in the Florence Museum is likely to come from a site in southern Rhodes (Benzi 1988c, 254, pl. 14a).

15. Cf. a very similar stirrup jar from Langada (L. Morricone 1965–1966, fig. 335). A LH IIIC Middle Pictorial jar from Ialysos NT 80 (Benzi 1992, pl. 106c; Mountjoy 1999c, 1066, fig. 436:255) may also be an import from Kos.

16. Some Cypriot bronze mirrors and stone mortars are of particular interest since they were no doubt produced during the twelfth century B.C.E. (Macdonald 1986, 140–41; Benzi 1992, 182, 206).

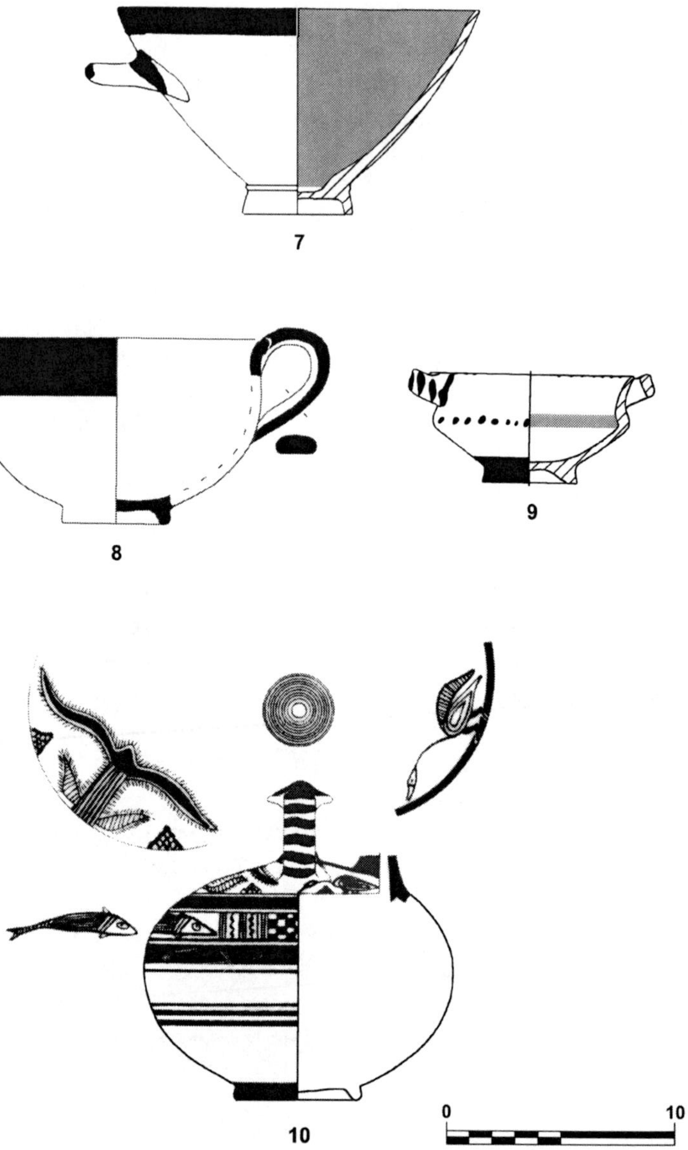

Fig. 2: **7)** LH IIIC conical bowl from Ialysos NT 64 (after Benzi 1992, pl. 162d); **8)** LH IIIC semiglobular cup from Kameiros-Kalavarda T 46 (after Mountjoy 1999a, fig. 434:224); **9)** LH IIIC shallow angular bowl from Ialysos NT 40 (after Benzi 1992, pl. 170e); **10)** LH IIIC Middle Pictorial stirrup jar from Ialysos NT 87 (after Mountjoy 1999c, fig. 440:275).

two stirrup jars from Ialysos (one missing) are definitely dated to LH IIIC Late by Mountjoy and these are assigned as Minoan (fig. 5.20), while I dated twenty-four vessels to LH IIIC (Advanced-to-) Late, notably some Wavy Line amphoriskoi (figs. 4.17–18) and some vessels with necklace pattern (fig. 4.15; Mountjoy 1999c, 989, 1074, fig. 444:281; Benzi 1992, 220–21, 224).[17] In the rest of the island pottery dating to LH IIIC Middle (Advanced) has been found at Phanes (a single vase; fig. 5.21), Kameiros (fig. 6.22–23),[18] and in the recently discovered cemetery at Pylona-Aspropilia in the Lindos area.[19] The Close Style stirrup jars from Kameiros and Phanes could be imports from the Argolid.[20] In conclusion, only a very few vessels from Ialysos and perhaps Kameiros (figs. 6.24; 7.25) may be LH IIIC Late.[21] The process of depopulation was evidently increasing as the period progressed. The island was no doubt deserted before the end of LH IIIC Late.

Kos

Unlike Rhodes, excavations on Kos have been concentrated on the major settlement at the Seraglio and the related cemeteries at Eleona and Langada.[22] Although the stratigraphy at the Seraglio was notoriously much disturbed and the excavation records were lost during the war, Morricone was able to distinguish four cities (1972–1973, 388–96). A deposit of carbonized figs found on a third city floor in association with LH IIIB vessels provides some evidence for a LH IIIB destruction (L. Morricone 1972–1973, 227–29, figs. 154–158; Mee 1982, 88; Mountjoy 1999c, 1075).[23] However, neither the extent of such destruction is known nor is there any evidence that it marked the transition to the fourth and

17. The Subminoan stirrup jar NT 87/8e (Benzi 1992, 95, 396, 397, pls. 112d, 167b assigned to LH IIIC Late; fig. 5.20) is the only vessel from Rhodes dated to LH IIIC Late by Mountjoy. She, however, suggests that another stirrup jar from the same tomb (Benzi 1992, 95, 99, 396, 397, pl. 112a–b NT 87/8a assigned to LH IIIC Advanced) and the missing stirrup jar NT 73/5 (Benzi 1992, 381, 382 assigned to LH IIIC Advanced) could be LM IIIC Late but possibly contemporary with LH IIIC Middle in Mainland terms (cf. also below n. 64).

18. See also Mountjoy (1999c, fig. 439:272, 274) from Kameiros-Kalavarda T 47 and T 50.

19. See above n. 10.

20. Mountjoy (1999c, 1068, fig. 439:269–271) points out that fig. 271 is made of orange clay with mica and may be a local east Aegean product.

21. Some vases from Kameiros assigned by the present writer to his Advanced-to-Late phase (Benzi 1992, 224) are obviously dated by Mountjoy to LH IIIC Middle (Advanced), see above n. 11.

22. Elsewhere on Kos very few Mycenaean sites have been discovered so far; LH IIIC sherds are reported from Kardamaina on the south coast (cf. Alevra et al. 1985, 18).

23. Of the four vases found on the floor two can hardly be dated, but a flask with flowers on

11

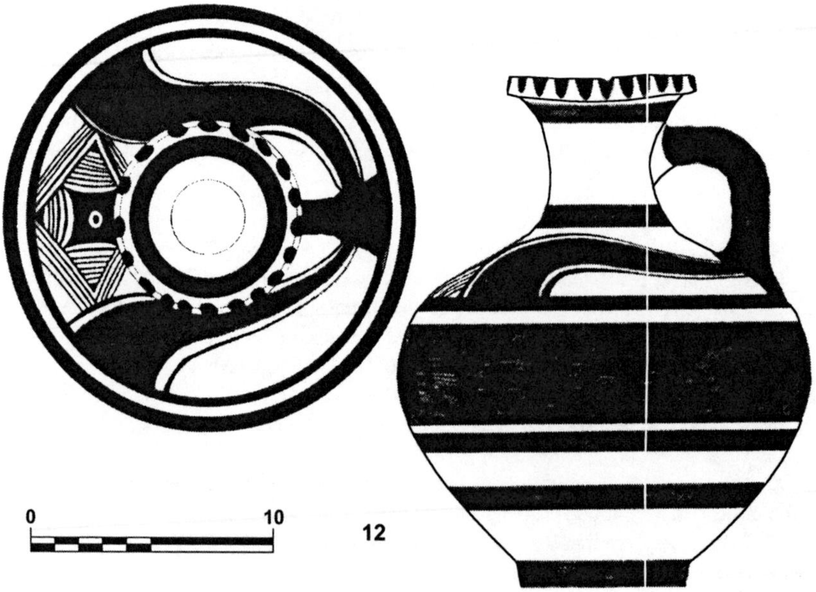

12

Fig. 3: **11)** LH IIIC Advanced-to-Late stirrup jar from Ialysos NT 15 (after Mountjoy 1999c, fig. 433:217); **12)** LH IIIC Advanced-to-Late jug from Ialysos NT 17 (after Benzi 1992, pl. 163a)

last city. This city was even more disturbed and it is impossible to say whether it was deserted or destroyed. The cemetery was in continuous use during LH IIIC Early to Middle (Advanced). The hallmark of LH IIIC Middle on Kos is the large number of vases decorated in Pictorial Style. They include amphoroid and ring-based kraters, stirrup jars, strainer jugs, deep bowls, and kalathoi (Mountjoy 1999c, 1106–10, fig. 452–453). Krater sherds from Seraglio and Bademgediği on the coast of Anatolia are of particular interest. They show warriors and rowers with unusual headgear, which are quite different from Mycenaean helmets (fig. 7.26; L. Morricone 1972–1973, 359–60, figs. 356–358; Mountjoy 1999c, fig. 452:102–104, 460:170; 2005a). Some of them bear a vague resemblance to the "feathered" helmets of the Philistines. The evidence is obviously too scanty to allow any conclusion on whether or not such grotesque figures depict the Sea Peoples. In any case, nothing resembling such warriors had ever been depicted before in the east Aegean.[24] Two krater sherds with wavy line decoration are among the latest examples of a local east Aegean class of pottery produced from LH IIIA:2 onwards, which will be discussed below (see Iasos; fig. 8.27). Only four vases have features of LH IIIC Late, suggesting to Mountjoy that "that this phase is not really represented" at Seraglio. According to Karantzali, however, the recent Greek excavations at Seraglio have provided evidence that the settlement lasted until the end of the period (Mountjoy 1999c, 1081, figs. 455:129, 132; 460:168–69; Karantzali 1999b).[25] The site was not reoccupied until the Proto-Geometric period when it became a cemetery.

---

the shoulder and a linear mug with strongly concave sides are LH IIIB, the latter possibly suggesting a LH IIIB Late dating. See Vitale 2005, 87, fig. 14.

24. Although there is no evidence for a western Anatolian presence in the southern Levant, where the Peleset/Philistines settled, the southwestern coast of Anatolia has been regarded by some scholars as the area where at least some of the Sea Peoples assembled before moving east towards Cyprus and the Levant. Deger-Jalkotzy (1998, 112) suggests that raids from pirates based in southwestern Anatolia may have played an important role in the depopulation of the Dodecanese in LH IIIC. The west Anatolian origin of the Sea Peoples has been strongly opposed by Niemeier (1998, 45–49). Discussing the much-debated problem of the origin of the Sea Peoples goes far beyond the scope of this paper; the number of articles and special studies dealing with this question defies listing, see, e.g., Sandars 1985; Bunnens 1985; Vanschoonwinkel 1991, 466–94; Niemeier 1998.

25. No LH IIIC Late pottery from the Greek excavations has been published as yet.

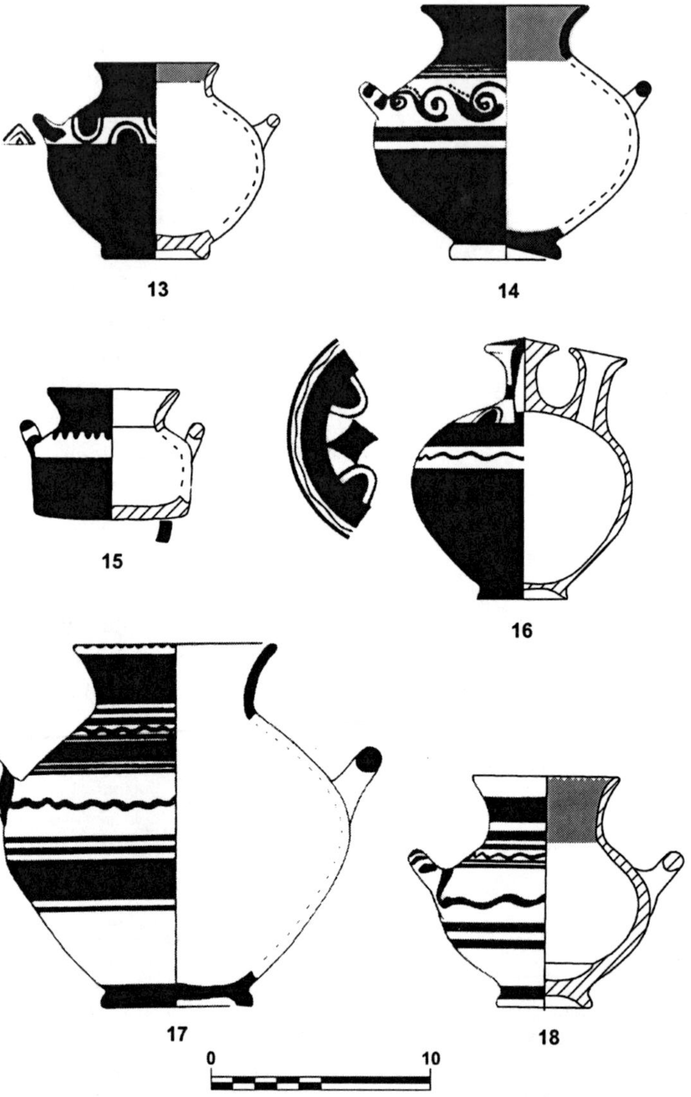

Fig. 4: **13)** LH IIIC Advanced-to-Late amphoriskos from Ialysos NT 70 (after Mountjoy 1999c, fig. 423:137); **14)** LH IIIC Advanced(-to-Late) amphoriskos from Ialysos NT 32 (after Mountjoy 1999c, fig. 423:138); **15)** LH IIIC (Advanced-to-) Late pyxis from Ialysos NT 13 (after Mountjoy 1999c, fig. 425:167); **16)** LH IIIC (Advanced-to-) Late stirrup jar from Ialysos NT 16 (after Benzi 1992, pl. 166g); **17)** LH IIIC (Advanced-to-) Late amphoriskos from Ialysos NT 42 (after Mountjoy 1999c, fig. 437:256); **18)** LH IIIC (Advanced-to-) Late amphoriskos from Ialysos NT 87 (after Benzi 1992, pl. 167g).

Rhodes and Kos LH IIIC Trading Connections

Whereas eastern Mediterranean objects are relatively common at Ialysos, objects of European origin are relatively more common on Kos. The well-known Naue II sword (which had been ritually "killed") and the "northern" spearhead from the LH IIIB Langada T 21 are of outstanding importance being two of the earliest European-type bronzes found in the Aegean (L. Morricone 1965–1966, 137–39, figs. 123–125; see also Kilian-Dirlmeier 1993, 94–95, pl. 34:228; Avila 1983, 60–61, pl. 18:129). According to Catling, the Kos sword reflects an early stage (most likely going back to the thirteenth century) in the development of the Naue II type, which accords with its LH IIIB find context (Catling 1961).[26] Nevertheless, Deger-Jalkotzy has recently objected to the LH IIIB dating pointing out that some vases in the tomb could be LH IIIC Early (Deger-Jalkotzy 1998, 111). None of the vases from this tomb can be later than LH IIIB with the sole exception of a stemmed bowl with darkground decoration. Though this type of decoration is a feature of LH IIIC Advanced and Late on the Mainland, the homogeneous LH IIIB context suggests this vase is a local oddity (cf. Mountjoy 1999c, 1097, fig. 448:61). Since they were the usual equipment of the European warrior, the Kos weapons cannot be regarded as mere imports, yet it is impossible to say whether they belonged to an European mercenary fighting in the service of the local community, as Catling would suggest, or were adopted by a Mycenaean warrior very well acquainted with the most recent developments in fighting tactics, as other scholars would prefer.[27] Also the way through which such objects reached the Aegean has not yet been clarified. Sandars suggested the weapons from Langada as well as a spearhead from Seraglio (L. Morricone 1972–1973, fig. 231) may originate from Romania, while Harding has emphasized the Italian connection of many European bronzes found in the Aegean suggesting an Adriatic route, which would be supported by the distribution of amber in LH IIIC contexts (Sandars 1983, 53–57; Harding 1984, 279–81).[28] Nonmilitary objects of European type found on Kos include a violin-bow fibula from Langada T 10, a leaf-shaped fibula

26. The sword has been dated to LH IIIB by Snodgrass (1971, 307), Hooker (1976, 145), and Sandars (1978, 93), to LH IIIB–C1 by Kilian-Dirlmeier (1993, 95), and to LH IIIC Early by Courtois (1972, 25). A LH IIIB2 Late dating is suggested by Vitale (2009, 1236).

27. For a recent discussion of this type of sword and relevant bibliography, see Vanschoonwinkel 1991, 260–64. For recent discussions of the Kos weapons, see Macdonald 1986, 145–46; Deger-Jalkotzy 1998, 111–12. For recent discussions of the Naue II swords and updated bibliography, see Jung and Mehofer 2005–2006 and Jung 2009.

28. The burial gifts from Langada T 10 included amber, cf. L. Morricone 1965–1966, 102, fig. 82.

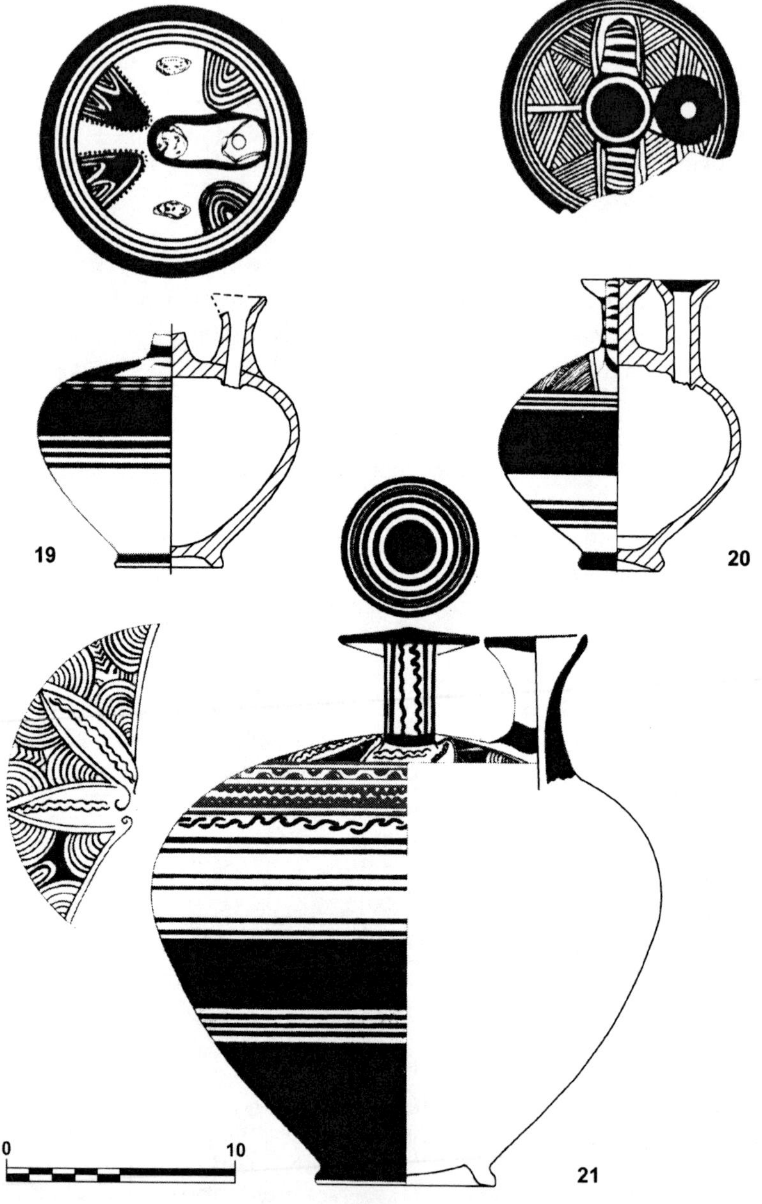

Fig. 5: **19)** LH IIIC Advanced-to-Late stirrup jar from Ialysos NT 87 (after Benzi 1992, pl. 167c); **20)** LH IIIC (Advanced-to-) Late stirrup jar from Ialysos NT 87 (after Benzi 1992, pl. 167b); **21)** LH IIIC Advanced Close Style stirrup jar from Phanes (after Mountjoy 1999c, fig. 439:269).

from Langada T 20, and a knife of the Scoglio del Tonno type from Seraglio (L. Morricone 1965–1966, 102–3, fig. 84; 134, fig. 119; Macdonald 1986, 146, fig. 9a; L. Morricone 1972–1973, fig. 239 left; knives of this type have been discussed by Harding 1975, 197–99; for a recent study of the knife, see Benzi 2009, 163, fig. 5). From Langada T 34 comes a razor which is of Aegean type but bears a geometric decoration of central European type (Macdonald 1986, 146, fig. 9b), which is paralleled on a spearhead and a knife of the so-called Siana type from the cemetery at Menemen/Panaztepe in the Izmir area (Ersoy 1988, 67–68, fig. 3:2–3). Until recently there was little evidence for connections between Europe and Rhodes and the "European" ancestry of the few objects in question is still a matter of debate. The origin of the ring-handled knife from Ialysos NT 15 has always been disputed by specialists (Benzi 1992, 177, pl. 179h);[29] the "drop-shaped" spearhead from Pylona-Ambelia betrays some "northern" influence yet its split socket is of Aegean type (Benzi 1988c, 260, pl. 16e; 1992, 175, pl. 179d). Only a knife from Rhodes in Florence was unequivocally attributed by Bouzek to a European type (Bouzek 1985, 145–47, 4.1.1B:4; Benzi 1988c, 260, pl. 16d). Amber is far from common in Rhodes as well as in the whole east Aegean. It occurs in one LH IIIB tomb (NT 53) and in two LH IIIC tombs at Ialysos (OT 13 and NT 20). The beads from OT 13 are of the LH IIIC Tiryns type (Benzi 1992, 194; Harding and Hughes-Brock 1974, 155, 160, fig. 6:16–17). The absence of characteristic European type bronzes on Rhodes has always been difficult to explain since there is substantial evidence that Rhodes had trading connections with areas which were in touch with Italy and Europe, and clay analyses have shown that Rhodian LH IIIC pottery was exported, though in very small quantities, as far away as Scoglio del Tonno.[30] This picture has now been changed by the discovery of an arched fibula in the LH IIIC Chamber Tomb 4 at Pylona-Aspropilia. The Pylona Fibula belongs to the relatively late type with plastic knots, which was in use from LH IIIC Middle/Late to Proto-Geometric (Karantzali 1999a, 295, fig. 35; 2001, 70–71, fig. 42, pl. 47a). From the same tomb come some LH IIIC Middle (Advanced) vessels.[31] This unexpected find seems to suggest that the dearth of European objects on Rhodes may be merely due to the chance of preservation and discovery. European-type bronzes have been recently found at Troy. Although their find contexts are not always clear, they are likely to come from Troy VIIb contexts. They include a leaf-shaped fibula with incised decora-

29. According to Macdonald (1986, 140, fig. 7) the use of rivets "may indicate that this is an Aegean adaptation of a European type"; contra Harding 1984, 133–34.

30. The Rhodian provenance of the well-known octopus stirrup jar suggested by Taylor on stylistic grounds has been confirmed by clay analysis (Jones 1986a, 208).

31. See above n. 10.

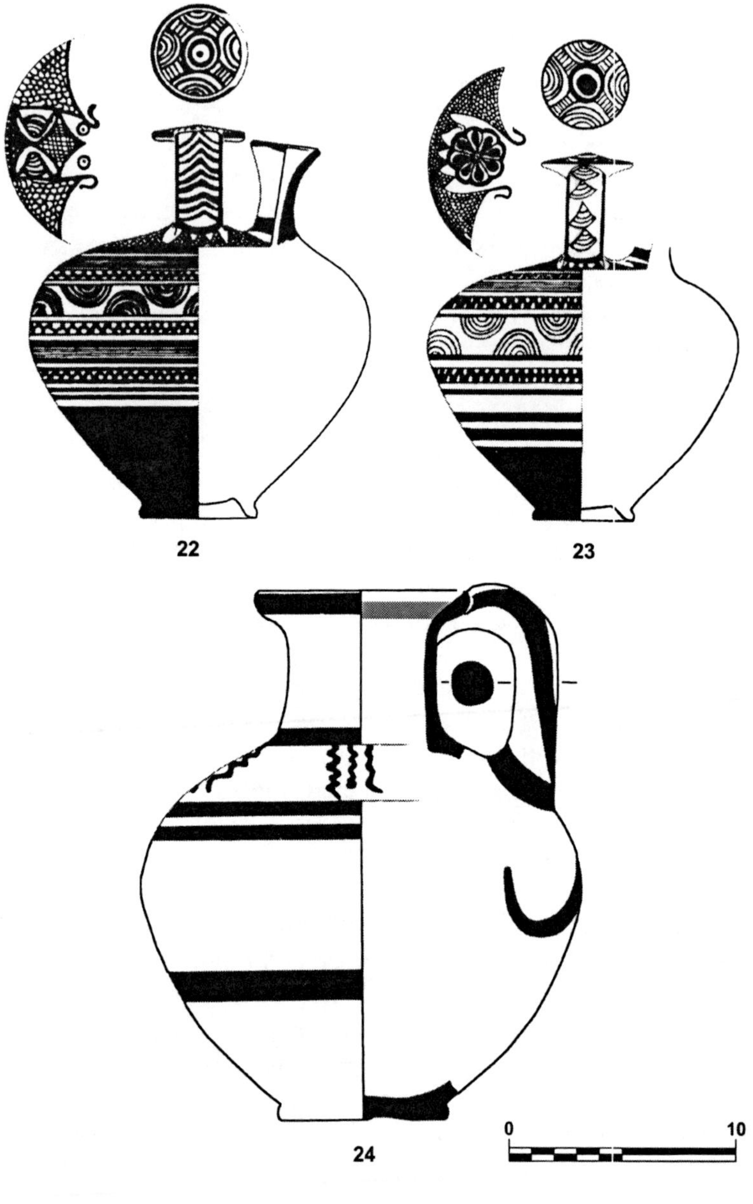

Fig. 6: **22)** LH IIIC Advanced Close Style stirrup jar from Kameiros-Tzitzo (after Mountjoy 1999c, fig. 439:270); **23)** LH IIIC Advanced Close Style stirrup jar from Kameiros-Kalavarda T 48 (after Mountjoy 1999c, fig. 439:271); **24)** LH IIIC (Advanced-to-) Late jug from Kameiros-Kalavarda T 50 (after Mountjoy 1999c, fig. 437:263).

tion, two violin-bow fibulae—one of which with twisted bow (Koppenhöfer 1997, 310, fig. 5:1–3)—and a unique double spiral head pin of a type which is extremely rare in the Aegean (Koppenhöfer 1997, 312, fig. 6:1).[32] Apparently such objects found their way into Troy at the same time as the so-called Barbarian Ware (Troy VIIb1) and the Buckelkeramik (Troy VIIb2; Mountjoy 1999c, 324, 334), which were perhaps brought to Troy by newcomers from the Balkans. Though found in LH IIIC contexts and then later than the objects from Kos, the Troy finds as well as those from Menemen/Panaztepe lend further support to Sandars' view that European objects and influence reached the east Aegean straight from the eastern Balkans. With the sole exception of Troy VIIb, the much discussed handmade burnished pottery usually referred to as Barbarian Ware is conspicuously absent in the whole east Aegean as it is in the Cyclades.[33]

Astypaleia

Four Mycenaean chamber tombs were excavated at Armenochori and Synkairos. Though none of them has been fully published, enough material is published to suggest that the island was culturally more akin to the Dodecanese than the Cyclades. The pottery is a mixture of Mycenaean, Rhodian, Minoan, and Anatolian elements. Two three-handled stemmed kraters with sharply inslanting upper body are very similar to the Trojan Shape C82. A large carinated bowl with two basket handles on rim corresponds to Troy Shapes A59 and A60, which occur in Troy VIh and VIIa.[34] Bowls of this type have also been found at Vathy Cave on Kalymnos, Passia, and Lachania in south Rhodes (Benzi 1993, 282, fig. 5d; Dietz 1984, 23, fig. 5; Benzi 1992, pl. 140a). The earliest Mycenaean pottery is LH IIIA:2. In LH IIIC shapes and decoration are characteristic of the east Aegean *koiné*, which includes Astypaleia itself, Kos, Kalymnos, and Miletus. None of the published vessels is later than LH IIIC Early (Mountjoy 1999c, 1138–45).[35]

32. On spiral head pins and their rarity in Greece and the Aegean, see Jacobstahl 1956, 126–27; Harding 1984, 137; Bouzek 1985, 166.

33. For a recent survey of the finds, see Pilides 1994 with previous bibliography.

34. On Anatolian influence on east Aegean pottery, see Benzi 1996, 954–67; Mountjoy 1998, 37–45; 1999c, 1138.

35. Mountjoy's is the most recent and authoritative assessment of the material from Astypaleia.

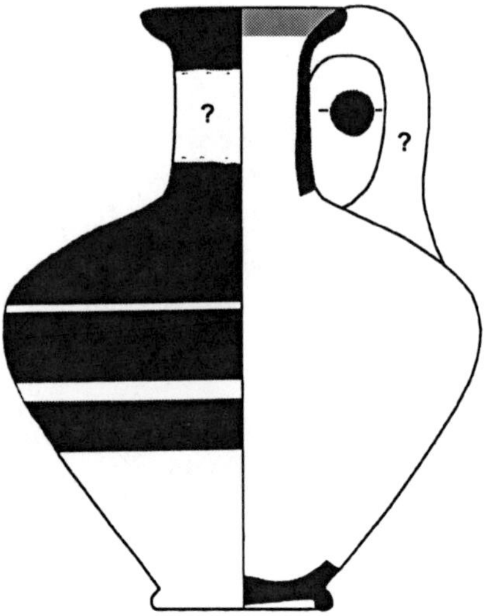

25

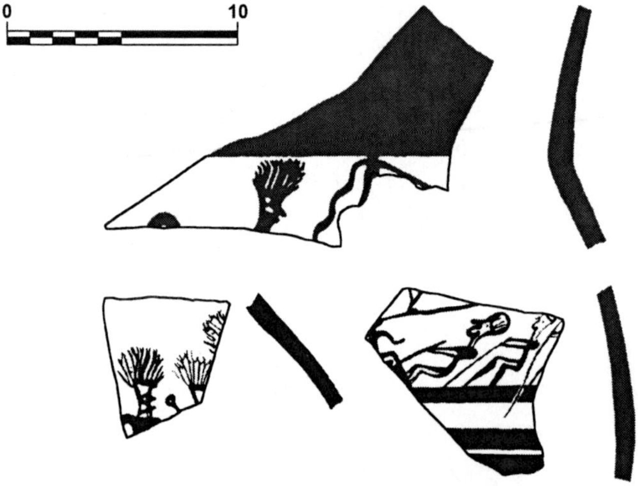

26

Fig. 7: **25)** LH IIIC (Advanced-to-) Late trefoil-mouthed jug from Kameiros-Kalavarda T 46 (after Mountjoy 1999c, fig. 437:265); **26)** LH IIIC Middle Pictorial krater sherds from the Seraglio, Kos (after Mountjoy 1999c, fig. 452:102–104, 460:170).

Kalymnos

Unstratified sherds dating from LH IIIA1 to LH IIIC have been found in the Vathy Cave on the east coast (Benzi 1993, 281–87). The latest pottery is LH IIIC Middle (Advanced). A sherd with a deep rim band and monochrome interior comes from a LH IIIB2 Group B deep bowl and is likely to represent the only occurrence of canonical LH IIIB2 pottery in the southeast Aegean (Mountjoy 1999c, 1129; Benzi 1993, 286, fig. 6d). Alongside the canonical Mycenaean pottery, the cave yielded a number of sherds made in a very distinctive southeastern Aegean micaceous fabric, which is discussed below (see Iasos). Sherds dating to LH IIIA2–B were found on the slopes of the Perakastro hill close to the modern town of Pothia (Hope Simpson and Lazenby 1962, 172–73). From chamber tombs in the bed of the river running into the harbor to the east of Perakastro comes a group of LH IIIB–C vases now in the British Museum.[36] There is little diagnostic LH IIIC Early pottery in this tomb material.[37] Two linear deep bowls from Vathy should date from this period, although such bowls are still found in later contexts (Benzi 1993, 286, fig. 6b–c; Mountjoy 1999c, 1131).[38] Most of the LH IIIC pottery belongs to LH IIIC Middle (Advanced) and shares many characteristics with that of Kos and Astypaleia, as Mountjoy has pointed out (1999c, 1126–27). Pictorial pottery is represented by a collar-necked jar, two Octopus Stirrup Jars, and a kalathos. One stirrup jar has Minoan filling motifs and could be an import from Crete (Mountjoy 1999c, 1127, 1134, fig. 464:18). The other belongs to a well-known group of LH IIIC Advanced octopus stirrup jars, whose main feature is the extensive use of pictorial fill motifs.[39] A neck-handled amphora with wavy line decoration, a stirrup jar with a high cone to false mouth, and a monochrome mug with reserved unpatterned zone have features which might be regarded as LH IIIC Late on the Mainland (Mountjoy 1999c, 1126–27, 1136–37, figs. 463:15, 465:21, 466:28).

36. Other vases said to be from Kalymnos are to be found in Oxford, Amsterdam, and Würzburg (Mountjoy 1999c, 1126–38). Two fragmentary Octopus Stirrup Jars in Amsterdam and Oxford most likely belong to the same pot (Mountjoy 1997–1998).

37. Mountjoy (1999a, 1126, figs. 462:5–9, 463:10–11) regards as borderline LH IIIB/C some vases with stylistic features belonging to both phases.

38. For discussion of the type and of a linear deep bowl from Ialysos T 21, cf. Benzi 1992, 152, pls. 37c, 171b. A LH IIIC Middle linear bowl from Emporio is a good example of the later development of the type (Mountjoy 1999c, 1153, fig. 473:12).

39. Vases of this type painted in a variety of local styles come from Pitane, Kos, Rhodes, Naxos, and Perati (Mee 1982, 34; Macdonald 1986, 143).

27

Fig. 8: LH IIIC Middle krater sherds from the Seraglio, Kos (after Mountjoy 1999c, fig. 460:175–176).

Miletus

At Miletus a new settlement (Miletus VI) was built early in LH IIIB1, following the destruction of the preceding settlement (Miletus V).[40] According to Niemeier, such destruction occurred in the transitional LH IIIA:2/B:1 phase or at the end of LH IIIA:2 and is connected by several scholars with the Hittite expedition against the city of Millawanda in the third year of the reign of Mursili II, which is dated 1319–1318 or 1315–1314 B.C.E.[41] Somewhere during the thirteenth century a fortification wall of Anatolian/Hittite type was built around Miletus VI.[42] Apparently Miletus VI was not affected by the wave of destruction at the end of LH IIIB but was destroyed in LH IIIC (Schiering 1959–1960, 5). The latest pottery from the old excavations has been dated to LH IIIC Late by Schachermeyr but to IIIC Early by Mountjoy (Schachermeyr 1980, 338–39; Mountjoy 2004). Unfortunately, although much unstratified LH IIIB:1 and C sherds have been found in the new excavations, no undisturbed Miletus VI levels have been discovered so far (Niemeier and Niemeier 1997, 218, fig. 29b–c; cf. Mountjoy 1999c, 1122, fig.

40. The Niemeiers' ongoing excavations in the area of the Athena Temple have shown that the three Bauphasen of the old excavations were not the early phases of occupation at the site, but the fourth, fifth, and sixth (see Greaves and Helwing 2001, 505–6).

41. Cf., e.g., Wilhelm and Boese 1987, 108; Bryce 1989a, 299.

42. There has been much discussion on the character of the poorly preserved wall of Miletus. For a thorough discussion and full references, cf. Niemeier and Niemeier 1997, 196–97; Niemeier 1998, 38.

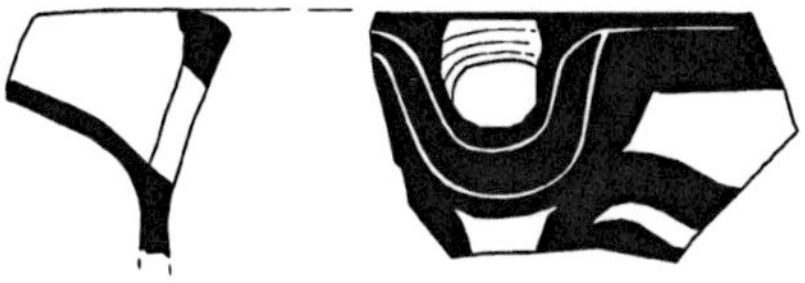

28

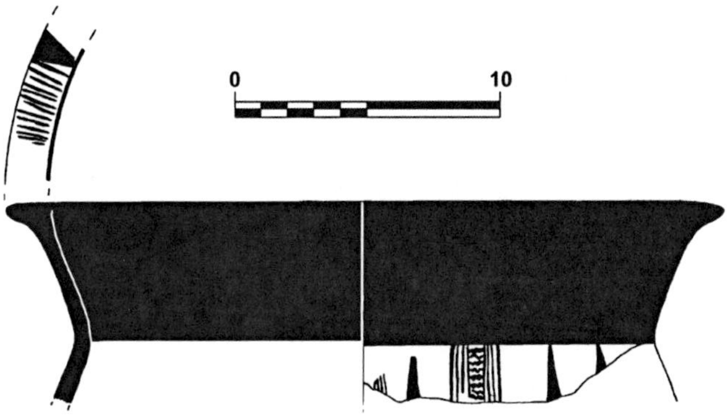

29

30

Fig. 9: **28)** LH IIIA:2 local krater sherd from Iasos (East Basilica); **29)** LH III(B–)C Early local amphoroid krater from Iasos (East Basilica); **30)** LH IIIC Early deep bowl from Iasos (Agora). Not to scale.

461:182; for comprehensive accounts of the new excavations, see Niemeier 2005; 2007a; 2009). There is, however, evidence suggesting that the site suffered a major destruction towards the end of LH IIIB or at the beginning of LH IIIC. According to the excavator, Miletus VI was followed by another settlement labelled Miletus VII, which was inhabited until a late phase of LH IIIC (Niemeier 2009, 19, 21). The end of Miletus VII and the transition to the "Dark Ages" are not yet clear. After the end of the Bronze Age settlement Miletus was not apparently reoccupied until the appearance of locally produced early Proto-Geometric pottery, but a few pieces could be Submycenaean.

Iasos

Substantial traces of LB III occupation have been discovered at Iasos beneath the Roman Imperial Agora, the sanctuary of Artemis Astias, and the so-called East Basilica, an impressive Late Roman building near the East Gate (Benzi 1986; 2005). Unfortunately the LB III layers were much disturbed by later building activity and are virtually unstratified. The LB III pottery consists of two main groups: a) a little group of canonical Mycenaean vases; and b) an overwhelming quantity of local pottery, which also includes pieces most likely imported from other sites in the southeast Aegean, notably Miletus and Kos. All the local pottery is produced in the highly micaceous (rich in gold mica) fabric which is characteristic of southeast Anatolia and is also found in the Dodecanese. Quite surprisingly, flakes of gold mica are to be found in all the sherds ascribed to the canonical Mycenaean class. This seems to indicate that they were not imported from the Greek Mainland and thus arises the problem of their place of manufacture. Clay analyses have shown that a large amount of canonical Mycenaean pottery from Miletus and Troy was produced locally (Gödeken 1988; Mountjoy 1997a; Mommsen, Hertel, and Mountjoy 2001); recent clay analyses of pottery from the Pylona-Aspropilia cemetery on Rhodes have identified a group of imported material quite different from the Argolid and other known control groups, which seems to suggest a non-Mainland, possibly southeast Aegean origin for this material (Karantzali and Ponting 2000, 229; Ponting and Karantzali in Karantzali 2001). In the absence of clay analyses the utmost caution is required, but it seems very likely that the canonical Mycenaean pottery from Iasos was also produced locally or imported from other centers in the southeast Aegean. The earliest canonical Mycenaean pottery is LH IIIA:1.[43] LH IIIA:2 and IIIB are well

43. It consists of a dozen or so sherds (Benzi 1986, 30, figs. 1–3a; 2005, 207, pl. L:a–j).

represented by characteristic shapes such as kylikes (FS 257 and FS 258) and deep bowls (FS 284; Benzi 1986, 30–31, figs. 4–6; 2005, 207–9, pls. L:k, LI–LII:a). Other open shapes include krater, mug, and stemmed bowl (Benzi 2005, 209, pl. LII:b–e). Monochrome and plain wares are scarcely represented. Though made locally, they seem to imitate the corresponding Mycenaean classes.[44] The few preserved shapes include kylikes, handleless cups, and shallow angular bowls (Benzi 2005, 211, pls. L:j, LII:j–n, LIII:b). It is not clear whether this lack of monochrome and plain wares is due to the selection made by the excavators or to the fact that local painted pottery was used instead.

The local pottery produced in the characteristic east Aegean red micaceous fabric with matte paint falls into three classes: a) light red paint on white-to-pale yellow slip; b) brown-to-black paint on white- to pale-yellow slip; and c) red-to-brown/black paint on the more or less smoothed ground. At its best the slip of the first class has a much attractive milky appearance. The decoration consists of more or less accurate versions of canonical Mycenaean motifs—often combined in uncanonical ways—and of a number of odd motifs, some of which are difficult to trace back to Mycenaean models. The wavy line—single, double, and multiple, either framed or unframed—is by far the most common motif (Benzi 2005, 210–14, pls. LIII–LVI). Its popularity is difficult to explain. The wavy line is scarcely attested in Mycenaean pottery before LH IIIC. In LM III pottery the wavy line is more common but an influence or inspiration from Crete seems unlikely for there is no evidence supporting it. Likewise, an influence of the incised Grey and Tan Ware from Troy seems unlikely as well. As Mountjoy and the present writer have suggested, the popularity of the wavy line most likely reflects a local tradition going back to the LB I Light-on-Dark pottery where such a motif is extremely common (Mountjoy 1998; Benzi 2005, 206; Momigliano 2007). Local wares of similar or closely related fabrics and decoration have been found all over the east Aegean from Troy[45] to Kalymnos (Benzi 1993, 282–85, figs. 4–5), Kos (fig. 8.27; Mountjoy 1999c, 1077–8), Astypaleia (Mountjoy 1999c, 1138), Rhodes,[46]

---

44. Given the extremely fragmentary condition and the bad preservation of the material, it is not always easy to distinguish monochrome ware imitating the corresponding Mycenaean class from the red wash pottery of Anatolian tradition like that found at Miletus (Niemeier and Niemeier 1997, 228, fig. 53).

45. LH IIIA:2 (Troy VIh): Mountjoy 1999a, 256, 257, 263, fig. 2:10; 274, fig. 8:51; 256, 286, fig. 12:107; 257, 287, fig. 12:117; LH IIIB (Troy VIh IIIB contaminations): Mountjoy 1999a, 268 (Blegen, Caskey, and Rawson 1953, fig. 419:7); 275, fig. 8:53, 55; and LH IIIB (Troy VIIa): Mountjoy 1999d, 304, fig. 2:4, 9; 321, fig. 11:48–49.

46. On Rhodes this pottery is much less common than on Kos. A few sherds come from LH IIIA:2–B settlement contexts at Trianda (Benzi 1988a, 53, fig. 52; Karantzali 1999b, fig. 7:13269, 19099b). Examples from tombs include a spouted krater from Ialysos NT 4 (Mee 1982, pl. 17:1;

Müskebi,[47] and Miletus[48] and were also exported to Tiryns (Voigtländer 1986, 21, fig. 5).[49] Though occasionally found in tombs, this is a mainly domestic pottery. At Iasos several shapes produced in these fabrics are close imitations of standard Mycenaean types such as kraters, kylikes, kalathoi, mugs, deep bowls, and basins. Basins are particularly common and were produced in a wide range of shapes and sizes.[50] There are, however, other shapes whose derivation from standard Mycenaean types seems less obvious. The earliest datable examples of such fabrics come from LH IIIA:2 contexts at Troy VIh and Rhodes,[51] the latest from LH IIIC (Advanced and perhaps later) contexts. Since there is very little stratigraphical evidence, the stylistic development of this pottery is extremely uncertain and pieces lacking a context cannot be closely dated. Mountjoy has recently suggested that flowing wavy lines were mainly used in LH IIIA:2, tight wavy lines in LH IIIB, wiggly, multiple, and framed wavy lines in LH IIIC (Mountjoy 1998, 39, 56; 1999d, 275)[52] but such criteria cannot be taken for certain and there were no

---

Benzi 1992, 8, 115, pl. 2b; Mountjoy 1998, fig. 5:2; Mountjoy 1999c, 1009, fig. 410:71), a straight-sided alabastron FS 94 from Lelos T 7 (Benzi 1992, 8, 41, 430, pl. 137m) coming from LH IIIA:2 contexts, and a mug from Pylona-Aspropilia T 3 (Karantzali 2001, 33, fig. 29, pl. 25b 16508) coming from a LH IIIA:2–IIIA:21/B1 context. There are other examples lacking context.

47. LH IIIB two-handled bowl from T 3 (Boysal 1969, 16, pl. 20:3; Özgünel 1996, 140, pl. 24:1; Mee 1978, 141–42); LH IIIB–C Early ovoid jar FS 37 from T 13 (Boysal 1969, 7, pl. 6:4; Özgünel 1996, 129, 145, pl. 18:5; Mee 1978, 139); LH IIIA:2 small piriform jar FS 45 from T 22 (Boysal 1969, 6, pl. 5:1; Özgünel 1996, 43; Mee 1978, 138); LH IIIA:2–B shallow cup and conical cup from T 33 (Boysal 1969, 18–19, pl. 22:1, 4; Özgünel 1996, 112, 113; Mee 1978, 142), etc.

48. A two-handled bowl, a conical cup, and some krater sherds come from LH IIIB–C Bauphase III contexts (Miletus VI; Weickert 1957, 119, 121 pls. 32:3–4, 34:3); a basin comes from the destruction level of Bauphase II (Miletus V) dating to the end of LH IIIA:2 or LH IIIA:2/B transition (Hommel 1959–1960, 50, pl. 43:3–4). Voigtländer (1986, 21–22, figs. 6–8) assigned on stylistic grounds a number of sherds from basins, craters, and deep bowls with wavy line decoration from the old excavations to the transitional phase at the end of thirteenth century, though suggesting that some pieces may be later.

49. Knell and Voigtländer (1980, 132–33, pl. 63.2) assign them to LH IIIC Early.

50. Cf. Benzi 2005, 213, pl. LV:a–d; Mountjoy 1986, 131–33, fig. 163 FS 294 and fig. 164 Small Bowl. Bowls of this type come from LH IIIB:1 contexts at Korakou and Tiryns (Rutter 1974, 281–82, 385, figs. 6:20, 13:20; Schönfeld 1988, 169 and n. 66, fig. 1:11 and table 1:27, 35–37). At Nichoria and Ayios Stephanos linear as well as monochrome and patterned basins of very similar shape do appear as early as LH IIIA:2 (Shelmerdine 1992, 498, figs. 9-44–9-45 P3694–P3697; Mountjoy 1999c, 275, fig. 92:136–139). (I thank P. Mountjoy for calling to my attention the basins from Ayios Stephanos.) An example comes from the destruction level of Miletus V, see n. 48.

51. See nn. 45–46.

52. But Mountjoy (1999b, 316, fig. 8:38) remarks that a jug with double wavy line of flowing type from a LH IIIB Troy VIIa context "is difficult to date since it has the wavy lines found

doubt exceptions to the rule. The earliest datable example from Iasos is likely to be a krater sherd from the East Basilica (fig. 9.28), decorated with three wavy lines, which are closely paralleled by those on a spouted krater from Ialysos found in a LH IIIA:2 context.[53]

The evidence for LH IIIC is poor because the upper Bronze Age levels were much disturbed by later building activity and because local LH IIIC pottery is difficult to identify. Very little canonical LH IIIC pottery was found. The stump of a kylix (perhaps with swollen stem) from the Agora has the handle stripe continuing down below the handle (Benzi 2005, 212, pl. LIV:e). Similar handle stripes are found on some LH IIIC painted kylikes from Ialysos (Benzi 1992, 142, pls. 150c, 175e; Mountjoy 1999c, fig. 434:234). From the East Basilica come sherds of two outstanding amphoroid kraters of a characteristic southeast Aegean type. Kraters of this shape have been found at Chios, Kos, Rhodes, and Miletus, and were also exported as far away as Cyprus and Ugarit.[54] Astypaleia, Kos, and Miletus have been suggested as the most likely places of production for these highly characteristic vessels, which were apparently produced from a late phase of LH IIIB to LH IIIC Middle (Advanced; Mountjoy 1999c, 1144). A large neck and shoulder sherd preserves the upper parts of whorl-shells alternating with panelled patterns (fig. 9.29). The heads of these shells are abbreviated to triangles in full paint and to triangle-shaped groups of vertical lines, which seem to be a distinctive feature of local southeast Aegean pottery.[55] This krater cannot be later than the LH IIIC Early. From the East Basilica come large fragments of another amphoroid krater

---

from LHIIIA:2 onwards. It is assigned to this phase, but could be later." Mountjoy (1999c, 1080, fig. 441:h–i Kos) further comments: "A common motif in this phase (IIIC Middle) is the wavy line which appears in a tight or flowing version; it may be depicted singly or as several parallel lines or in framed version; the latter version of the motif is not found on the Mainland until its appearance in the Protogeometric phase."

53. See n. 46.

54. Chios (Mountjoy 1999c, 1149, fig. 472:1–2); Astypaleia (Mountjoy 1999c, 1142, 1144, fig. 469:6–7); Kos (Mountjoy 1999c, 1078–79, 1080, 1097, 1099, figs. 448:65–67, 452–54 [L. Morricone 1972–1973, 188, 239, 289, 370–71, figs. 73, 176, 255–56, 369–70]); Rhodes (Benzi 1992, pls. 150–151; Mountjoy 1999c, fig. 421:130); Miletus (Weickert 1957, 120, pls. 32:2, 33–34:1; Schiering 1959–1960, 23, pl. 14:2; Mountjoy 1998, fig. 11); and were also exported to Cyprus (Mountjoy 2009) and Ugarit (Courtois 1973, 141–61; Leonard 1994, 27–33, Groups B–C; Yon, Karageorghis, and Hirschfeld 2000, 13).

Courtois was the first to suggest that such vases were imports from the southeastern Aegean, namely from Kos or Miletus. More recently the island of Astypaleia has also been indicated as a possible place of manufacture (Mountjoy 1999c, 1142).

55. Other examples are to be found on amphoroid kraters from Miletus and Astypaleia as well as on vessels of other shapes (cf. Mountjoy 1999c, 1142, 1144, fig. 469:6–7; Weickert 1957, 120, pls. 33–34:1 Miletus VI; Mountjoy 1998, figs. 11, 17:6 from the Degirmentepe cemetery).

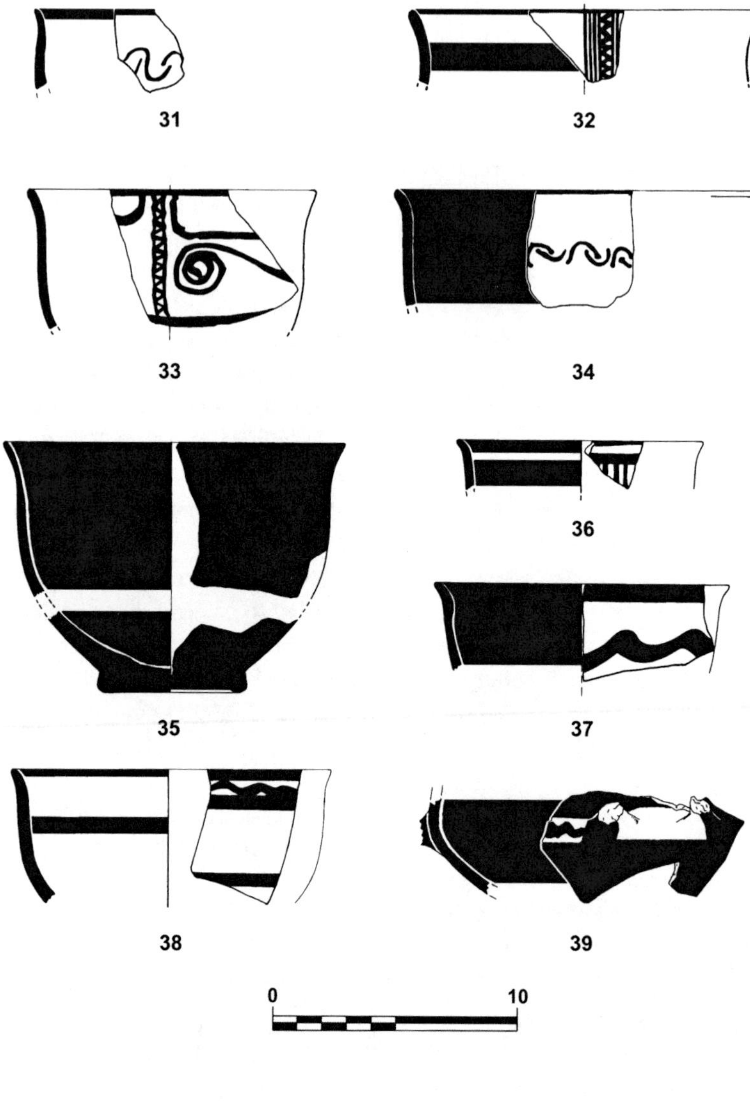

Fig. 10: **31)** LH IIIC Early deep bowl from Iasos (East Basilica); **32)** LH IIIC Early deep bowl from Iasos (East Basilica); **33)** LH IIIC Early deep bowl from Iasos (East Basilica); **34)** LH IIIC Developed deep bowl from Iasos (East Basilica); **35)** LH IIIC Middle deep bowl from Iasos (Agora); **36)** LH IIIC east Aegean deep bowl from Iasos (East Basilica); **37)** LH IIIC east Aegean deep bowl from Iasos (East Basilica); **38)** LH IIIC east Aegean deep bowl from Iasos (Agora); and **39)** LH IIIC collar-necked jar from Iasos (Agora).

of the same type (fig. 9.30; Levi 1969–1970, 484, fig. 27).[56] The decoration of extended running spirals with concentric arcs and semicircles fill is apparently unique, but running spirals with similar fill appear on some east Aegean vessels dating to LH IIIC Middle (Mountjoy 1999c, figs. 461:180, 467:30, 473:7 from Kos, Kalymnos, and Emporio Chios). The large band connecting the spirals recalls some disintegrated versions of the octopus found on LH IIIC Middle stirrup jars from Crete (notably the one from Erganos [Benzi 1986, 32]),[57] Perati, and the east Aegean (Iakovides 1969–1970, 197, fig. 75, pl. 43a:1088 Perati; Forsdyke 1925, A 931; Benzi 1992, 94, pl. 108b Ialysos; L. Morricone 1972–1973, 271, fig. 226 from Kos; Crouwel 1984, 64, figs. 3–4 from Kalymnos).[58]

In comparison with other settlement deposits, there are very few canonical deep bowls at Iasos. It seems likely that here the most common drinking vessels were the small bowls and cups massively produced in local fabrics. From what can be inferred from sherds, all the deep bowls have a deep semiglobular shape with more-or-less flaring rims. The decoration is generally panelled, sometimes with antithetic spiral pattern. Some small-sized examples with bell-shaped profile can hardly be later than LH IIIC Early (fig. 10.31–33). Another deep bowl with monochrome interior is decorated with a narrow Quirk motif. Similar narrow zonal motifs are often found on LH IIIC Early deep bowls (fig. 10.33; Benzi 1992, pl. 148i Rodi; Mountjoy 1999c, 1105, fig. 451:91–92, 94–95 [L. Morricone 1972–1973, 352, fig. 345b, d–e] Seraglio). A monochrome example with strongly flaring rim should be LH IIIC Middle (Developed; fig. 10.35; Benzi 1992, 152, pls. 143f, 171l Lardos; Mountjoy 1999c, 1122, fig. 461:188 [L. Morricone 1965–1966, 210, fig. 220] Kos-Langada). The stylistically latest example found so far at Iasos has uncanonical lip banding and a narrow reserved interior band below rim (fig. 10.36).[59] Three Wavy Line deep bowls with monochrome interior, framed Wavy Line and Wavy Line encased in a reserved zone respectively are among the few local vessels that may be assigned to LH IIIC with some degree of certainty (fig. 10.37–39). Closed shapes are scarcely documented. From the East Basilica come a clumsy amphoriskos with very faint traces of linear decoration and a baseless flask (FS 186) with concentric circles (Levi 1969–1970, fig. 27). This is a charac-

56. The sherd on the right comes from a flask.

57. Cf. Kanta 1980, 256, figs. 24:1; 134:7 from Erganos and Kritsa; Betancourt 1985, 131 from Mouliana.

58. Schachermeyr (1980, 151, pls. 26e, 27d) suggested that the spirals on the Iasos krater recall the tentacles of the octopus depicted on a stirrup jar from Ialysos T 17 (Benzi 1992, pl. 21c–d).

59. Cf. Voigtländer 1986, 21, fig. 6D from Miletus. For the earlier appearance of such feature on Crete and perhaps Rhodes, see Mountjoy 1999c, 988.

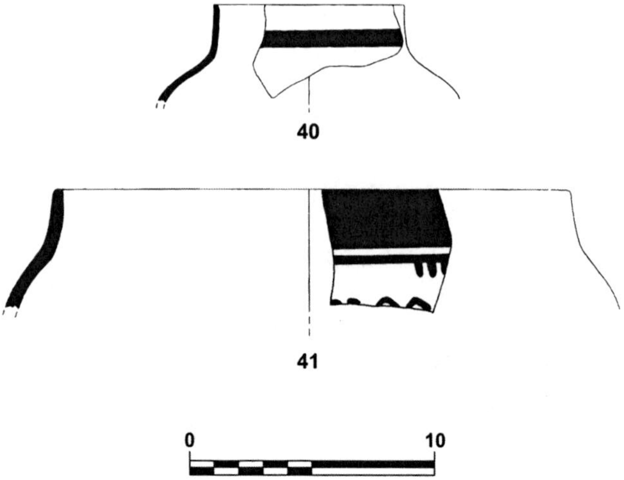

Fig. 11: **40–41)** LH IIIC collar-necked jars from Iasos (Agora).

teristic east Aegean shape, which most likely developed from an earlier Anatolian type (Benzi 1992, 105–6; Mountjoy 1998, 39, 56, fig. 20:1; Mountjoy 1999c, 1021, 1074, figs. 416:98, 440:278).[60] Fragments of two collar-necked jars were found in the Agora (fig. 11.40–41). The Necklace Pattern round the base of neck of fig. 11.41 suggests this vessel could date from LH IIIC Middle (Advanced?). Iasos was apparently deserted before the end of LH IIIC Middle. It cannot be said whether it was destroyed or abandoned.

Müskebi

The large chamber tomb cemetery at Müskebi on the Alikarnassos Peninsula was most likely founded in LH IIIA:1. LH IIIA:2 marked the peak of its use while in LH IIIB there was a conspicuous decline in the number of burials. According to Özgünel's recent reassessment of the material, ten of the thirty-nine datable tombs were in use in LH IIIC, but only three or four of them yielded pottery safely dating to that period; none of the published vases need be later than LH IIIC Early.[61] Mee suggested strong Rhodian connections as two Rhodian shapes

60. Cf. also Boysal 1969, pl. 33:2 and Özgünel 1996, 137, pl. 22:1 from Müskebi.

61. According to Özgünel (1996, 153–56), ten tombs were in use in LH IIIC, but only three

never found anywhere else in the east Aegean (the basket vase and the brazier) are attested at Müskebi (Mee 1982, 78, 89). He also compared the decline of the cemetery in LH IIIB to the similar situation at Ialysos. Mee's view has been criticized by Mountjoy, who underlines instead the strong connections of Müskebi with Miletus and other sites of east Aegean *koiné* (Mountjoy 1998, 36). Most of the pottery with clay described as "ziegelrot" and with "creme-bis beigefarbiger Überzug" or "hellbeigefarbiger Überzug" is likely to fall into Class A and B of local east Aegean pottery as described above (see Iasos).

---

or four of them have yielded pottery safely assignable to that period. According to Mountjoy (1998, 53) two tombs (T 13, T 29) certainly have LH IIIC pottery and two possibly (T 35, T 42).

T 3: the only vessel dated to LH IIIC is an east Aegean two-handled bowl with wavy line decoration, which is likely to be earlier (Boysal 1969, 16, pl. 20:3; Özgünel 1996, 140, pl. 24:1; Mee 1978, 141–42 assigned it to LH IIIB).

T 13: The ovoid jar FS 37 and the baseless flask (Boysal 1969, pls. 6:4, 33:2a–b; Özgünel 1996, 129, 137, 145, pls. 18:5, 22:1; Mee 1978, 139, 140) are no doubt LH IIIC; the small sized jars (Boysal 1969, pl. 7:1, 3; Özgünel 1996, 98; Mee 1978, 139), which are a cross between the LH IIIB FS 48 and the amphoriskos, are likely to date from a late phase of LH IIIB or LH IIIC Early.

T 18: The only vessel assigned to LH IIIC is an undiagnostic juglet with panelled decoration, which could well be earlier (Boysal 1969, pl. 17:2; Özgünel 1996, 134; Mee 1978, 139).

T 23: None of the three vases from this tomb can be LH IIIC (Boysal 1969, pls. 13:1a–b, 19:6, 31:4).

T 28: Only a linear juglet may be LH IIIC (Boysal 1969, pl. 18:7; Özgünel 1996, 134; Mee 1978, 139 assigns it to LH IIIB).

T 29: Both the vases from this tomb—a stirrup jar and a juglet (Boysal 1969, pls.16:2, 18:9)—are late LH IIIB or early LH IIIC.

T 32: All the pottery is LH IIIA:2 and B.

T 33: No vessel from this tomb can be later than LH IIIB; the large conical-piriform jar (Boysal 1969, pl. 4:2; Özgünel 1996, 129; Mee 1978, 138) with multiple zigzag set in the handles zone could be an import from southern Rhodes where similar patterns appear on local LH IIIA:2 vases, cf. Mountjoy 1995a, 26, fig. 7:2–3; the carinated conical cup with tight wavy line is an east Aegean product, which can hardly be later than LH IIIB (Boysal 1969, pl. 22:1; Özgünel 1996, 113 LH IIIB; Mee 1978, 142).

T 34: All the pottery is LH IIIA:2 and B.

T 35: All the pottery is likely to be LH IIIA:2.

T 42: The kylix (Boysal 1969, pl. 29:5; Özgünel 1996, 139; Mee 1978, 141) is no doubt LH IIIC Early; the juglet (Boysal 1969, pl. 17:6; Mee 1978, 139) is difficult to date closely but could be contemporary.

T 45: No vase is unequivocally LH IIIC.

Conclusions

The above survey of the southeast Aegean in LH IIIC dramatically underlines our basic ignorance of the events that took place there during that critical period. The absence of excavated settlement sites proves once again a stumbling block, which cannot be overcome. The wave of destruction that struck many Mainland sites at the end of LH IIIB can hardly be perceived on the southeast Aegean islands. Only Seraglio on Kos has produced scanty evidence for destruction in the course of LH IIIB. On the Anatolian coast Miletus VI was destroyed towards the end of LH IIIB or at the beginning of LH IIIC. In the whole east Aegean only Troy VIIa was destroyed towards the end of LH IIIB. In a recent paper Mountjoy suggested that Troy VIIa was destroyed in late LH IIIB or in Transitional LH IIIB:2–C Early, but she now thinks that the destruction occurred in the Transitional Phase (Mountjoy 1998, 46, table I; 1999b, 297–301 and table I).[62] The settlement at Bademgediği Tepe lasted until LH IIIC (Middle; Meriç and Mountjoy 2002; Meriç 2007, 32, 35).

The suggested abandonment or destruction of Ialysos and other sites on the northwest coast of Rhodes early in LH IIIB is mere speculation. Few as they are, the LH IIIB tombs at Ialysos indicate that the site was still inhabited. In any case, the causes for such decline must be sought in some event(s) taking place at the beginning or in the course of the period rather than at its end. The situation at Ialysos is similar to the one at Müskebi, where very few tombs were in use in LH IIIB, but at other sites in the southeastern Aegean such as Kos, Astypaleia, south Rhodes, and Miletus this was a flourishing period. Little can be said about the transition from LH IIIB to LH IIIC. It must, however, be underlined that in comparison with many areas of the Mainland very few minor sites on Rhodes were deserted at the end of LH IIIB. If all that implies that the southeast Aegean, like the Cyclades, was spared by the first wave of destruction at the end of LH IIIB remains to be seen. In any case, the fact that the general situation in the early phase of LH IIIC is different in many respects from that of the previous phase suggests that something happened. At Ialysos the major change is the sudden increase of population evidenced by the number of tombs in use in the cemetery. On the grounds of the contemporary decrease of population in the rest of the island and of the strong local component in the LH IIIC pottery style of Rhodes, I suggest that the inhabitants of the minor sites moved for security reasons to the main center. Other scholars have suggested an influx of immigrants

62. I warmly thank Mountjoy for informing me of her most recent dating of Troy VIIa destruction.

from the Mainland or Crete. Contacts with both areas are easily detectable in the LH IIIC pottery of Rhodes, but the influence from Crete is stronger. In light of the present evidence it is impossible to say which explanation is right, while it cannot be excluded that the recovery of Ialysos was the result of many factors. As Mountjoy has pointed out, another difference from LH IIIB is that Rhodes developed its own pottery style, which is quite different from that of the east Aegean *koiné* as defined by the same scholar. Several sites—notably on Rhodes but also on Astypaleia and Müskebi—were abandoned at the end of LH IIIC Early. It is impossible to say if the abandonment of such sites is to be connected with the new wave of destruction that affected a number of sites on the Mainland (for instance Tiryns) as well as on the islands (Phylakopi, Koukounaries, and possibly Ayios Andreas) at the end of LH IIIC Early and/or in LH IIIC Developed. In any case, LH IIIC Middle is a flourishing period on Rhodes and Kos alike. On Rhodes the abandonment of several minor sites in the countryside is, at least in part, counterbalanced by the increase of the population at Ialysos. The richly furnished tombs, the resumption of wide-ranging trading connections as well as the development of very elaborate classes of pottery, such as the Octopus Style and the Pictorial Style, indicate that on the major islands of the Dodecanese as well as in other parts of the Aegean the central phase of LH IIIC was much more than the Indian summer of the Mycenaean culture. Nevertheless, LH IIIC Late is very poorly represented. Mountjoy assigns to LH IIIC Late no more than two or three vessels from Ialysos (from NT 73 and NT 87). However, pottery possibly dating to LH IIIC Late comes from eight (NT 13, NT 15, NT 17, NT 20, NT 21, NT 40, NT 42, and NT 87) of the forty tombs in use in LH IIIC. In five of them such phase is represented by no more than two vessels, while NT 17, NT 21, and NT 87, which are among the most richly furnished tombs in the cemetery, yielded five to six LH IIIC Late vessels each (Benzi 1992, 226, table II, 256, 275, 396).[63] As I said above, most of such vessels have stylistic traits which are to be found in LH IIIC Advanced and Late alike. At Kameiros no more than three or four vessels may be LH IIIC Late. The whole island was apparently deserted before the end of LH IIIC. By contrast, Mountjoy's dating of the Rhodes materials suggests that the extant Mycenaean settlements came to an end at the close of LH IIIC Middle (Advanced). According to Mountjoy the settlement at Seraglio and the related cemeteries were abandoned at the end of LH IIIC Middle, but Karantzali has recently stated that the Greek excavations—which are still unpublished—have provided evidence that the settlement was still inhabited in the final phase of the period. Even if there were still a few people living on Kos and Rhodes during LH

63. They account for 6.5%, 11%, and 17% respectively of the pottery found in each tomb.

IIIC Late, it is however evident that both Ialysos and Seraglio suffered a severe setback at or immediately after the end of LH IIIC Middle. Unfortunately, on the grounds of burial evidence only it is impossible to say whether Ialysos and Seraglio were destroyed or abandoned.

Chapter Twenty

Aegean Elements in the Earliest Philistine Ceramic Assemblage: A View From The West

*Jeremy B. Rutter**

Ann Killebrew's publication in some detail of the pottery from the earliest Iron Age levels isolated in Field INE at Tel Miqne-Ekron has sharply defined the nature of the change in locally produced ceramics at the interface between the end of the LB II era and the initial Iron I period (1998a; 1998b).[1] Her subsequent analysis of what appear to be intrusive features in the earliest Iron I assemblage at that site (2000) has established what the nature and range of the Aegean elements are in the pottery that has been persuasively associated with the initial Philistine occupation of Tel Miqne-Ekron. My purpose in the paper that follows is to comment upon Killebrew's findings from the perspective of a ceramic analyst with thirty years of experience working on contemporary assemblages from both the Greek Mainland and the island of Crete.[2] As will become clear, there is almost as much

* Department of Classics, Dartmouth College, Hanover, New Hampshire 03755. Email: jeremy.rutter@dartmouth.edu.

The following analysis is based on a paper delivered in May 2001. A number of relevant scholarship on the subject of the earliest Philistine ceramic assemblage has since appeared, none of which is cited in my chapter below but much of which is referred to in various other chapters and appears in the bibliography of this volume. The most pertinent of these titles are: Badre, Boileau et al. 2005; Bell 2006; Ben-Shlomo 2006; Ben-Shlomo et al. 2008; Capet 2006–2007; D'Agata et al. 2005; M. Dothan and Ben-Shlomo 2005; T. Dothan and Zukerman 2004; T. Dothan, Gitin, and Zukerman 2006; French and Stockhammer 2009; Gilboa 2006–2007; Janeway 2006–2007; Jung 2006b; 2006c; Killebrew 2006–2007; 2010; Mazow 2005; Mountjoy 2005b; 2006; du Piêd 2006–2007; Sherratt 2006; Stockhammer 2008; and Yasur-Landau 2002; 2005; 2007; 2010.

1. I have unfortunately not seen the fuller treatment accorded to this transition in Killebrew 1998b and so am relying in what follows on Killebrew 1998a.

2. Most of the issues addressed here have been tackled previously by S. Sherratt, whose ceramic as well as wider spheres of expertise span both the Aegean and Cyprus. Her assessment of

to be learned from what is not present among the Aegean features of Miqne's earliest Philistine pottery as there is from what is. Moreover, comparison of the early Philistine assemblage from Tel Miqne with that so far published from the ostensibly contemporary Stratum XIIIb at Ashdod (M. Dothan and Porath 1993) offers a couple of additional insights of potential interest.

A review of the Aegeanizing assemblage of Strata VII and VI at Tel Miqne as this has so far been presented by Killebrew can be brief (table 1a–b; figs. 1–2). The most common open vessel forms are deep bowls and larger kraters on the one hand, both outfitted with a pair of horizontal loop handles, and shallow rounded or carinated bowls and larger rounded basins on the other, all featuring horizontal strap handles. Only the kraters and deep bowls are decorated with patterns. By far the most common decorative treatment is simple banding, attested on all shapes including the krater.[3] Solid coatings of paint do not occur, whether over the whole vessel or just on the interior. The only unpainted forms are shallow angular bowls (which may also be banded) and large, conical, horizontal-handled lekanai or kalathoi (which are invariably undecorated). The sole additional Mycenaeanizing open shape represented in these early Iron I levels at Miqne is a shallow tray with a conical wall profile that is topped by a distinctive double horizontal loop handle, a seemingly very rare shape and once again one decorated with purely linear ornament.

As might be expected in a domestic as opposed to a funerary assemblage, at least in the Aegean, the number of closed vessel types represented is far less abundant, though not necessarily more limited typologically. Distinctive spout and neck fragments among the extremely fragmentary sherd material provide unambiguous evidence for the trefoil-mouthed jug, the basket-handled and tubular-spouted feeding bottle, and the stirrup jar. Substantial numbers of rim and neck fragments could belong to either one-handled jugs, two-handled amphorae, or three-handled hydriae.[4] None of the closed fragments so far illustrated by Killebrew bear patterns, so all of these closed vessel types were presumably decorated

the Aegeanizing elements in the early Philistine assemblages at Tel Miqne and Ashdod, written before the publication of Killebrew's two studies, is very similar to my own (1998, 303–5).

3. Although Killebrew does not illustrate or mention any linear kraters from Field INE, a large fragment of one from a Stratum VII context in Field IV has been published by T. Dothan (2000, fig. 7.7:6).

4. No large horizontal handles from closed shapes are reported by Killebrew, so it is uncertain whether such shapes as hydriae (FS 128; Mountjoy 1986, 143–44, 166–67, figs. 178, 212), belly-handled amphorae (FS 58; Mountjoy 1986, 160–61, fig. 202), or collar-necked jars (FS 63–64; Mountjoy 1986, 138–40, 161–62, figs. 169–70, 204–5) may be represented in Tel Miqne Strata VII–VI.

simply with bands. Finally,[5] Miqne's earliest Iron I ceramics include fairly numerous examples of a wide-mouthed cooking jug that lacks any local antecedents in the preceding Late Bronze Canaanite repertoire but has a well-established Aegean pedigree.

Killebrew's overall assessment of this Aegeanizing component as one which is closely related to contemporary Mycenaeanizing assemblages of the LC IIIA phase on Cyprus and the LB IIB period in Cilicia, but quite different from those characteristic of the contemporary Greek Mainland, Crete, or various Aegean island groups such as the Cyclades or the Dodecanese is right on the mark (table 1). Killebrew concludes: "Thus the appearance of Mycenaean IIIC:1b pottery at several of the major cities in Iron I Philistia, such as Tel Miqne-Ekron and Ashdod, does seem to indicate a transference of material culture via large-scale immigration from Cyprus and/or Cilicia to the southern coast of Canaan. However, it is not yet clear whether the producers of White Painted Wheelmade wares on Cyprus and Cilicia were 'Aegeanized' eastern Mediterraneans or 'eastern Mediterranean' Aegeans ..." (1998a, 402).

A more detailed examination of what differentiates the initial Philistine and related Cypriot and Cilician assemblages from Aegean assemblages may be a worthwhile first step in an attempt to tackle this problem.[6] From an Aegeanist's perspective, perhaps the most striking difference is the total absence at Miqne of drinking vessels with vertical handles—semiglobular cups of FS 215, carinated cups of FS 240, or kylikes of the carinated FS 267 or the conical FS 274 and 275 (fig. 3). These are precisely the forms that, along with the prevalence of exclusively linear decoration on the deep bowl, have been used to define the earliest stages of LH IIIC pottery on the Greek Mainland (Rutter 1977; Mountjoy 1986, 134–54; 1999b, *passim*), and consequently their routine absence from twelfth-century assemblages in Cilicia, Philistia, and most Cypriot sites—Maa-Palaeokastro being a notable exception (Kling 1988)—has not surprisingly made

5. Killebrew illustrates at least one oddity that cannot be connected readily with any well-established Aegean form: a loop-handled cup rim that she identifies as a "mug" (Killebrew 1998a, 397, fig. 10:7). This piece has no connection with the Mycenaean shape conventionally described with that term (FS 226; Mountjoy 1986, 112, 128, 147), nor is it readily identifiable as a fragment of any other common Mycenaean vessel type.

6. Obviously it would also be worthwhile to make as much use of the information relevant to this problem from the excavation of Strata XIII and XII at Ashdod (T. Dothan 1982, 36–41; M. Dothan and Porath 1993), from the earliest Iron I levels so far exposed at Ashkelon, and from contexts attributable to Strata VII–VI in other sectors at Tel Miqne itself (e.g., Fields IV and X; see T. Dothan 2000), but the ceramic assemblages from these other locales have yet to be analyzed as thoroughly and holistically as have those from Tel Miqne Field INE.

Table 1a: Tablewares (open shapes).

Shape: DECORATION	Tel Miqne [Killebrew 1998a, figure (stratum/phase)]	Tel Miqne [Killebrew 2000]
Krater FS 281–282: PATTERNED	fig. 6:27 (VII/9B), fig. 7:14–15 (VII/9A), fig. 12:9,13 (VI/8A)	Form AS-5: figs. 12.1.12, 12.2.5
Krater FS 281–282, carinated body: PATTERNED	fig. 10:17 (VI/8B–C)	Form AS-5: fig. 12.1.13
Deep Bowl FS 284: LINEAR	fig. 7:8–10 (VII/9A)	Form AS-4: figs. 12.1.8, 12.2.4
Deep Bowl FS 284: PATTERNED	fig. 6:23 (VII/9B), fig. 10:6 (VI/8B–C), fig. 12:7,8,10 (VI/8A)	Form AS-4: figs. 12.1.9–10, 12.2.4
Deep Bowl FS 284, carinated body: PATTERNED	fig. 7:11–13 (VII/9A)	Form AS-4: fig. 12.1.11
Basin FS 294: LINEAR	fig. 6:26 (VII/9B), fig. 7:3 (VII/9A), fig. 10:9 (VI/8B–C)	Form AS-2: figs. 12.1.3, 12.2.2
Shallow Angular Bowl FS 295: UNPAINTED	fig. 6:20–21 (VII/9B), fig. 7:4–5,7 (VII/9A), fig. 10:4 (VI/8B–C), fig. 12:4 (VI/8A)	Form AS-3: figs.12.1.4–6, 12.2.3
Shallow Angular Bowl FS 295: LINEAR	fig. 6:19 (VII/9B), fig. 7:6 (VII/9A), fig. 10:3 (VI/8B–C), fig. 12:5 (VI/8A)	Form AS-3: figs.12.1.7, 12.2.3
Shallow Rounded Bowl FS 296: LINEAR	fig. 6:22 (VII/9B), fig. 7:2 (VII/9A), fig. 12:6 (VI/8A)	Form AS-1: figs. 12.1.1–2, 12.2.1
Tray FS 322: LINEAR	fig. 7:16 (VII/9A)	Form AS-7: figs. 12.2.7, 12.3.2

Cyprus [Kling 1989]	**Maa-Palaeokastro [Kling 1988; Karageorghis and Demas 1988]**	**Tarsus [French 1975]**
Bell Krater: 108–26, fig. 3c	327; pl. CCX: West of Building II/2, Room 79C/2	fig. 6:1–3
Carinated Ring-Based Krater: 127, fig. 3d	<not present>	<not present>
<no equivalent>	326–27; pls. CX, CCX no. 473; pls. LXXVII, CXCII no. 592; pls. L, CLXXV: Room 60/3; pls. LIX, CLXXXIII: Room 82/1	figs. 17:5–13, 18:1–17
Skyphos: 94–107, fig. 3a	317–27; *passim*	figs.8:1–5, 9:1–4, 10:1–15, 11:1, 13:1–29
<no equivalent>	325–27; pls. LXXVII, CXCII no. 353	<not present>
<no equivalent>	329 [Spouted Form FS 302]; pls. CXXV, CCXXIV no. 137; pls. CIII, CCX Pit L/24; pl. CCXXX Pit 15/33; pl. CXLIX south of Room 80/2	fig. 19:6 (?) [Spouted Form FS 302]
Mycenaean IIIC Carinated Bowl: 134–35, fig. 5c	329; *passim* (e.g., pls. CLV, CCXLVII no.703)	72
Mycenaean IIIC Carinated Bowl: 134–35, fig. 5c	329; *passim* (e.g., pls. XLVIII, CLXXV no. 292)	figs. 16:1–24, 17:1–4
Wide Conical or Rounded Bowl with Plain or Out-Turned Rim: 131–34, figs. 5a, d	<not present; place taken by linear one-handled conical bowl FS 242 (?)>	<not present; replaced by linear one-handled conical bowl FS 242 (?)>
<no equivalent>	<not present>	<not present>

Table 1b: Tablewares (closed shapes), domestic industrial shapes, and cooking vessels.

Shape: DECORATION	Tel Miqne [Killebrew 1998a, figure (stratum/phase)]	Tel Miqne [Killebrew 2000]
Wide-Mouthed Amphora/ Jug/Hydria FS 69/106, 110/128: LINEAR	fig. 6:28–29 (VII/9B)	Form AS-9: fig. 12.3.8
Narrow-Necked Jug FS 121: LINEAR	fig. 7:20 (VII/9A)	Form AS-9: fig. 12.3.9
Trefoil-Mouthed Jug FS 137: LINEAR	fig. 6:30 (VII/9B)	Form AS-9: figs. 12.2.9, 12.3.7
Feeding Bottle FS 162: LINEAR	fig. 6:31 (VII/9B), fig. 10:20, 22 (VI/8B–C)	Form AS-8a: figs. 12.2.8, 12.3.3–4
Stirrup Jar FS 174–176: PATTERNED	fig. 10:21 (VI/8B-C)	Form AS-11: figs. 12.2.11, 12.3.10
Kalathos/Tub FS 291: UNPAINTED	fig. 6:25 (VII/9B), fig. 7:17-18 (VII/9A), fig. 10:11 (VI/8B–C), fig. 12:14 (VI/8A)	Form AS-6: figs. 12.2.6, 12.3.1
Cooking Jug or Amphora FS 65–66	fig. 7:19 (VII/9A), fig. 10:13–14 (VI/8B–C), fig. 12:15 (VI/8A)	Form AS-10: figs. 12.2.10, 12.3.11–14

Cyprus [Kling 1989]	**Maa-Palaeokastro [Kling 1988; Karageorghis and Demas 1988]**	**Tarsus [French 1975]**
Amphora with Tall Neck, Rim Handles: 148, fig. 12b; Globular Jug with Tall Neck: 149, fig. 13b; Hydria: 148–49, fig. 13a	333 [FS 106]; 333 [FS 128]; pl. LI no. 297; pl. CXCIII no. 502; pl. CCXXXV no. 322 [FS 106]; pls. LXXIX, CXCIII no. 498; pl. CCXXX no. 236; pl. CCXXXV no. 382; pls. CLI, CCXLV nos. 346, 348, 605	figs. 2:12 [linear], 3:1346 [patterned]
Neck-Handled Jug: 151–52, fig. 14c	<not present>	<not present>
Jug with Trefoil Spout: 150–51, fig. 14a	<not present>	<not present>
Tubular-Spouted Jug with Basket Handle: 158–61, fig. 17c–d	331–32; pl. XCVIII no. 138; pl. CXLIX Room 73A/3; pl. L west of Room 60/7	<not present>
Stirrup Jar: 161–65, fig. 18a–b	330–31; *passim* (e.g., pl. CXLIX Room 80/10, 11, Room 73A/1)	56, fig. 4
Plain White Handmade Basin (rather than Flat-based Kalathos: 145–47, fig. 10c)	<not present in Aegean form, FS 291>; 129 no. 599, pls. LXXX, CXCV	fig. 19:11 (?) <Aegean form>
<cooking vessels not surveyed>	<cooking vessels not surveyed>; 115 nos. 578, 692, pls. LX, CLXXXIII; 122 no. 425, pls. LXXX, CXCIII; 127 no. 374, pls. LXXX, CXCIII; 148 no. 387, pls. CIX, CCXI; 201 no. 350, pls. CLIII, CCXLIV	[Goldman 1950, 217 nos. 1220–1221, figs. 324, 389]

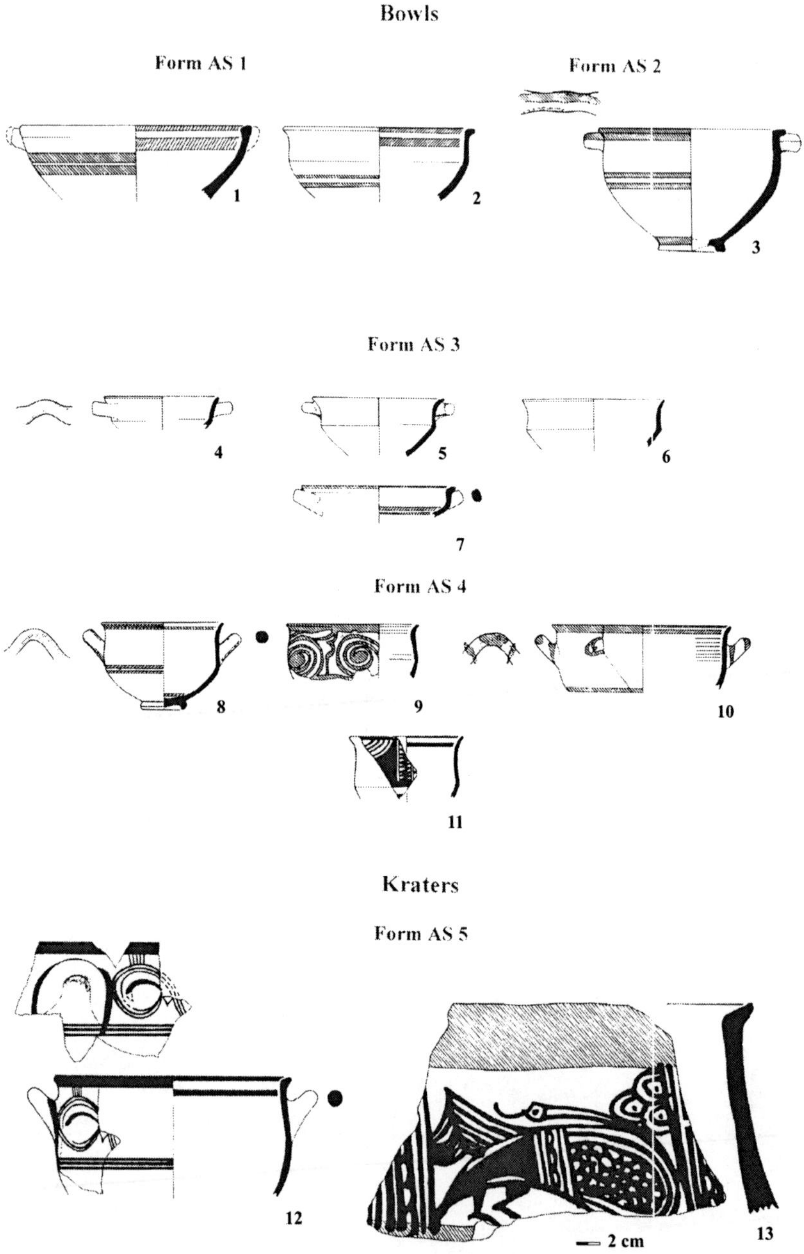

Fig. 1: Aegean-inspired ceramic types from Tel Miqne-Ekron Strata VII–VI (after Killebrew 2000, 237).

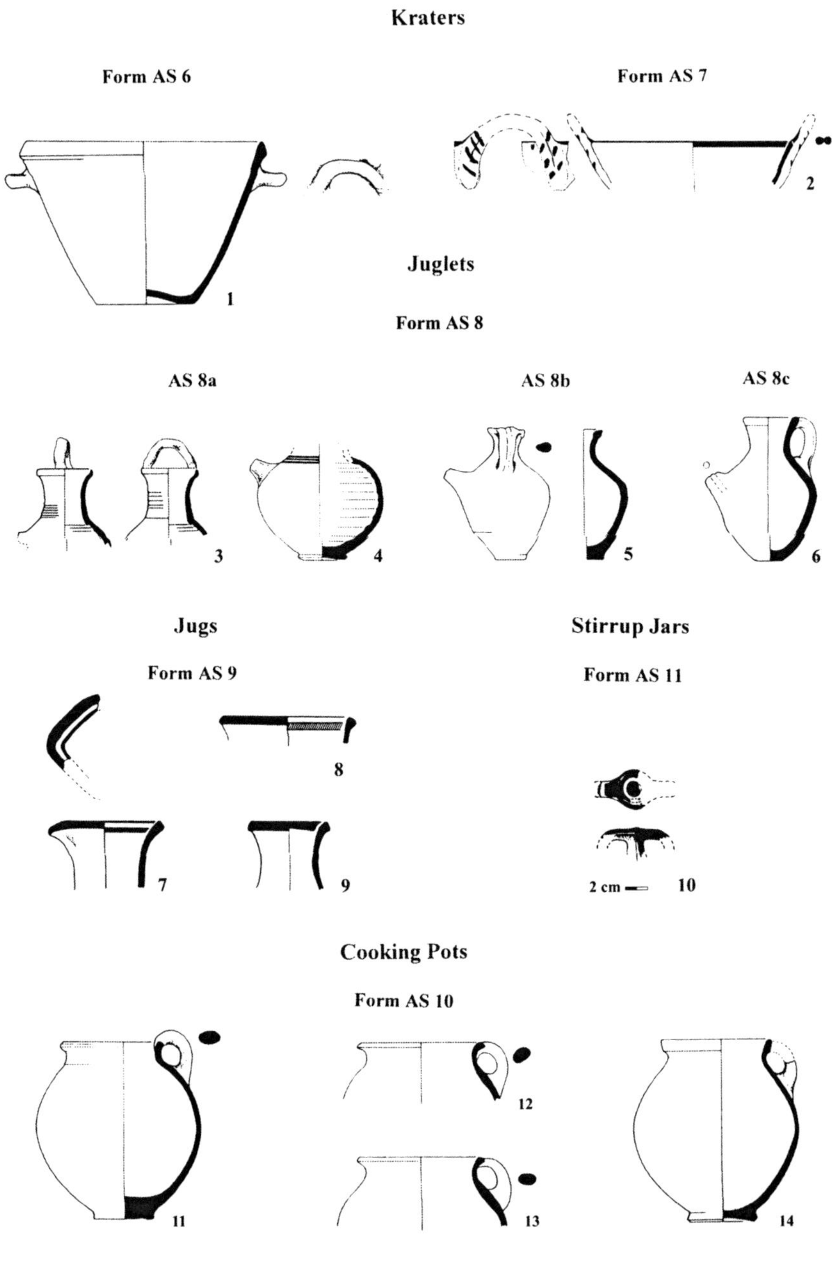

Fig. 2: Aegean-inspired ceramic types from Tel Miqne-Ekron Strata VII–VI (after Killebrew 2000, 241).

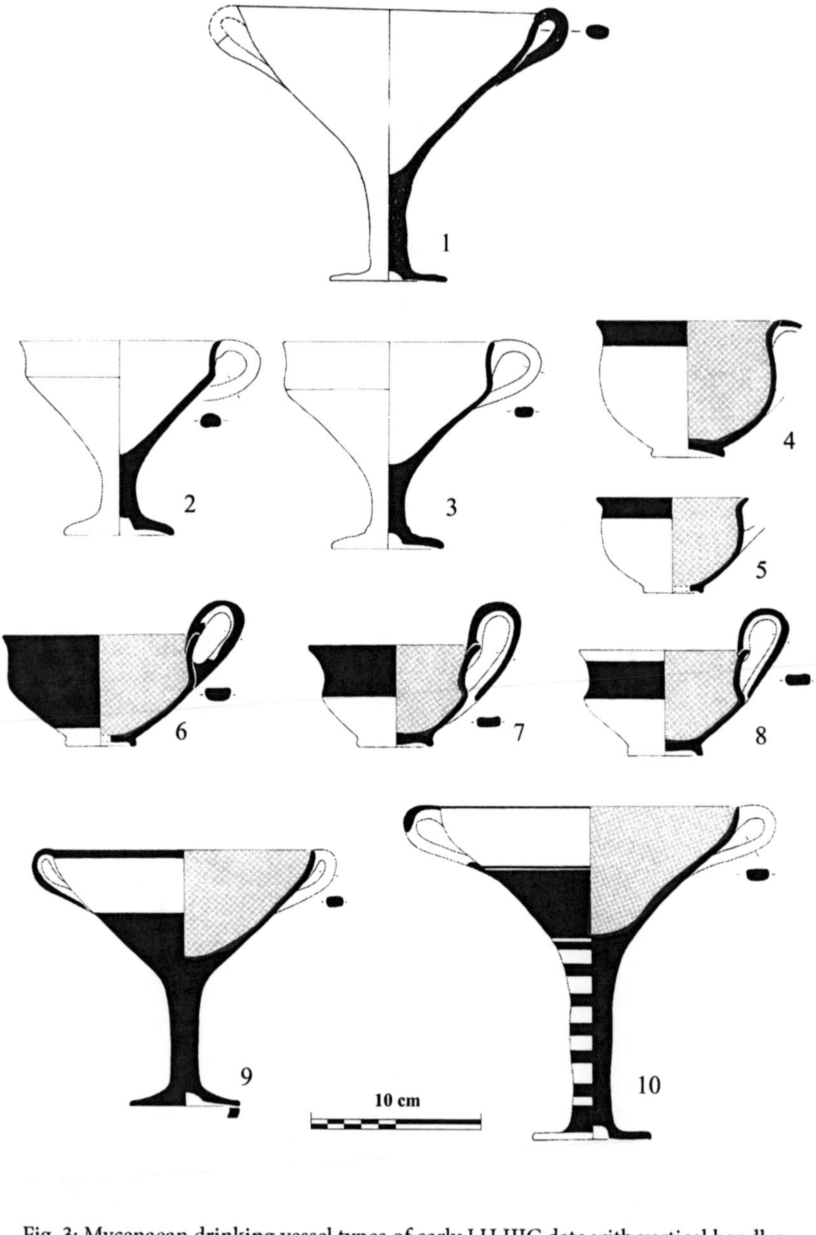

Fig. 3: Mycenaean drinking vessel types of early LH IIIC date with vertical handles: **1)** conical kylix FS 274; **2–3)** carinated kylixes FS 267; **4–5)** semiglobular cups FS 215; **6–8)** carinated cups FS 240; **9–10)** conical kylixes FS 275; after Koehl 1984, 212 (I); Mountjoy 1995b, 220 (2–3); 1999b, 231 (4–10).

correlation of mainland Greek and coastal Levantine ceramic assemblages during the first half of the twelfth century rather problematic.

Equally striking to an Aegeanist are the radically skewed percentages of decorative syntaxes at Miqne and elsewhere in the Levant relative to those current in the Aegean. As already noted, true patterns are restricted to deep bowls and kraters among open shapes at Miqne, and this is broadly speaking also the case elsewhere in the east. Solidly coated vessels and even solidly coated interiors are virtually non-existent, again with the exception of western Cypriot sites such as Maa-Palaeokastro and Palaepaphos-Evreti. Aside from the large conical lekanai or kalathoi (about which there will be more to say shortly), fine unpainted Mycenaeanizing vessels at Miqne as well as on Cyprus and in Cilicia appear to be restricted to a single shape, the shallow angular bowl that is Furumark's Shape 295. The popularity of simple linear ornament on Aegeanizing vessel forms in the coastal Levant at this time is overwhelming. A similar tendency does, to be sure, characterize the earliest phases of LH IIIC on the Greek Mainland, but it is nowhere nearly as pronounced. Yet the simple fact that purely linear décor does enjoy a relatively short-term spike in frequency during the early LH IIIC era, especially on the relatively few specific vessel forms that are common to and frequent in both regions—the deep bowl and the shallow rounded as well as angular bowls—allows us to align this period in the Aegean chronologically with the period of initial Philistine settlement in coastal Canaan.[7] In other words, what has routinely been described for decades in the literature as "Mycenaean IIIC:1b" pottery would actually be more accurately characterized as "LH IIIC:1a" if one were to continue to use Furumark's terminology for this era.[8]

7. In view of the increasingly important roles played by Cypriot traders and Cypriot producers of Mycenaeanizing pottery in the course of the thirteenth and twelfth centuries B.C.E. (Sherratt 1998), one wonders whether the increasing popularity of purely linear ornament on miscellaneous bowl types in the later LH IIIB period (Mountjoy 1986, 133; 1999b, 152) and especially the dramatic increase in simple linear décor on a much wider array of shapes during the LH IIIC Early period (Mountjoy 1986, 135) might not be due to Cypriot influence on Aegean ceramics (Sherratt 1991, 195). For the possible Cypriot impact on LH IIIC Middle pottery, see Sherratt 1998, 304 n. 22.

8. The argument from the popularity of linear decoration in the two regions is happily confirmed by the evidence furnished by the fairly narrow range of motifs on the decorated pottery of Stratum VII at Tel Miqne: stemmed and antithetic spirals, vertical strings of zigzag and joining semicircles framed in panels, isolated semicircle groups, lozenges, checkerboard, antithetic streamers, and occasional birds and fish (Killebrew 1998a, 397, figs. 6:23, 27; 7:11–15; T. Dothan 2000, fig. 7.7–8). Compare the pattern range for the LH IIIC Early phase at the site of Korakou in Corinthia, in particular the one represented on deep bowls and kraters: Mountjoy 1999c, 228–37, figs. 73–78.

A third category of differences between the Miqne assemblage and early LH IIIC assemblages within the Aegean involves absences at Miqne that may be less immediately striking than the dearth of vertical-handled drinking vessels to which I have already drawn attention but that cumulatively become rather impressive. As noted already by both Sherratt (1991, 193–95, citing Catling and Jones 1986, 595) and Killebrew (1998a, 397), small closed containers with comparatively wide mouths—that is, the rounded as well as straight-sided alabastra and piriform jars that had formed such a substantial percentage of the Mycenaean imports to the Levant in the palatial era (Leonard 1981; van Wijngaarden 1999b, esp. 135–55, 231–58)—virtually disappear in the twelfth century from Cypriot assemblages, not being represented there even by such LH IIIC functional equivalents as amphoriskoi and small collar-necked jars. Perhaps significantly, these shapes, though rare on Cyprus and non-existent at Miqne,[9] are well enough represented at Tarsus in Cilicia and thus provide at least one significant difference between Philistine and Cilician Aegeanizing ceramics (French 1975, 56, figs. 2, 5). A second such difference is the complete absence at Miqne of the one-handled, lipless, and linearly decorated bowl of Furumark's Shape 242, dozens of examples of which have been reported from Tarsus. This shape is very popular in the Cyclades and Dodecanese, at Lefkandi on Euboea, and at mainland Greek sites in Attica, but is rare at Mycenaean centers in the Peloponnese and equally rare on Cyprus, being attested to my knowledge only at Maa-Palaeokastro (Kling 1988, 328–29). It seems likely that the distributions of the lipless FS 242 with a single loop handle and the typically lipped and often somewhat shallower FS 296 with two strap handles[10] may be complementary. The latter shape, termed a shallow rounded bowl in table 1a, is extremely common on Cyprus and at Miqne, and likewise shows up at a number of Peloponnesian sites in the early LH IIIC period, whereas it is seemingly rare to non-existent at Tarsus and in the Aegean islands where the one-handled functional variant is most at home. Another void in Miqne's Aegeanizing repertoire is any evidence for the large transport stirrup jar, Furumark's Shape 164, or indeed for any Aegeanizing vessel form that could have been used to transport either liquid or solid produce in bulk.[11] This absence is simply explained by the fact that this function was performed entirely by the Canaanite or storage jar, a ceramic

9. These forms appear to be rare anywhere in Philistia; for amphoriskoi and pyxides at sites other than Tel Miqne, see T. Dothan 1982, 125–31 Type 4, figs. 18–19, pls. 36–45.

10. Although I refer to this bowl form here and in table 1 as Furumark's Shape 296, Mountjoy prefers to identify it as FS 295 Type B (1986, 153–54; 1999c, 159, 236, figs. 41:321–22, 78:204).

11. For a brief survey of some different choices for this function made by various groups within the Aegean and an investigation of the rationale lying behind at least one such choice, see Rutter 2000.

form with a very long local history that was one of the principal survivals in the Philistine assemblage from the preceding Late Bronze Canaanite repertoire. Even as far north and west as Cyprus, jars of this type are preferred to the Aegean transport stirrup jar during the thirteenth and twelfth centuries, as they also were by the operators of the ship wrecked off Uluburun at the end of the fourteenth century.[12]

The restricted range of Aegean cooking vessel types is likewise a distinctive feature of the Miqne assemblage. As emphasized by Killebrew (1998a, 242; 2000, 397), tripod vessels, whether pots of Furumark's Shape 320 or the trays peculiar to Crete (Hallager and Hallager 2000, 158–61, fig. 32:1–2, 6), are missing at Miqne. But the Mycenaeanizing cooking jars at Miqne, as at Ashdod, on Cyprus, and in Cilicia, probably consisted both of one-handled "jugs" and two-handled "amphoras," both long-established types on the Greek Mainland (Furumark's Shapes 65 and 66, respectively), where the advent of a strap handle from shoulder to rim rather than the earlier loop handle appears to coincide roughly with the transition from LH IIIB to LH IIIC.[13]

The unpainted conical lekanai or kalathoi from Miqne likewise constitute a restricted range of functionally specific vessels, in this case what might best be termed "domestic industrial" as opposed to table service, transport and/or storage, or cooking.[14] These plain tubs, like the cooking vessels just mentioned,

12. The Uluburun wreck of shortly before 1300 B.C.E. has yielded over 150 Canaanite amphorae, the vast majority of them "filled collectively with over a ton of resin" (Mills and White 1989; Serpico and White 2000). By contrast, the wreck contained just ten examples of the large transport stirrup jar, Furumark's Shape 164.

13. Rutter 1974, 123–24 (FS 65), 294–95 (FS 66); Mountjoy 1995b, 223, 227, fig. 21. For the loop-handled types especially characteristic of the LH IIIB era, see the color illustrations of a pair of vessels from Thebes in Tzedakis and Martlew 1999, 185–86 nos. 175–76. Loop-handled versions of these two shapes are among the latest products of the long-lived, large-scale ceramics industry that flourished on the island of Aegina throughout the Middle Bronze Age and for most of the Late Bronze Age (Lindblom 2001, 26–31, figs. 4:15–16, 6:19, 8:18, 37–38, 84 no. 970, 85 no. 994, 86 no. 1028, 90 no. 1104). One feature that distinguishes all Aegean examples of these wide-mouthed cooking jugs and amphorae from their southern Levantine derivatives at Tel Miqne and other Philistine sites (Killebrew 2000, 242) is the red to reddish-brown fracture and surface color and extremely sandy texture of the Aegean cooking ware. The Philistine cooking pots likewise have sandier and coarser textures than the tablewares with which they are found (Killebrew 2000, 243), but they lack the significantly darker fractures and surfaces that differentiate almost all Aegean cooking fabrics from typically paler-firing storage and serving vessels. The analogous Cypriot cooking pots have the darker surfaces characteristic of the Aegean prototypes.

14. Killebrew has compared these plain tubs with the Mycenaean kalathos (Furumark's Shape 291), but the latter are almost invariably decorated, sparingly in LH IIIC Early but often quite lavishly in LH IIIC Middle and frequently with pictorial motifs, especially fish (Mount-

are remarkably standardized in their dimensions at Miqne, with rim diameters measuring consistently just under 30 centimeters. Although they have both simply decorated as well as plain analogues on Crete and the Greek Mainland, they resemble most closely a series of Plain White Handmade LC IIC–IIIA basins from Cyprus, except that the Cypriot basins have vertical rather than horizontal handles.[15]

Finally, there is no hint in the Miqne assemblage of the dark-surfaced, handmade, and burnished class of pottery—sometimes referred to as Barbarian Ware—often reported from early LH IIIC domestic assemblages on the Greek Mainland, common at Troy in City VIIb, and occasionally found even on Cyprus and in Syria (Pilides 1994; Bankoff, Meyer, and Stefanovich 1996; Koppenhöfer 1997; Badre 2006; Jung 2006a, 21–27; Strack 2007).

The degree of standardization exhibited by the earliest Philistine ceramic assemblage at Miqne is striking and manifests itself at a number of different levels. Homogeneity in shape and size has already been noted with respect to the cooking pots and undecorated conical lekanai. Decorative standardization seems to be typical of a surprising number of the deep bowls insofar as their banding is concerned, especially in Stratum VII. These bowls routinely feature a band at the rim, two bands below the handle zone, and three splashes at the roots and apex of each handle, while on the interior a single band below the painted rim is the rule. By contrast, the linear treatments of early LH IIIC bowls in the Aegean, as well as on most LC IIIA bowls on Cyprus, whether they be patterned or linear, is nowhere nearly as regular, even within individual sites or regions. Might such regularities be due to a highly specialized labor force, a virtual caste of potters whose kilns have been uncovered in some numbers at Miqne (Killebrew 1996a)?[16]

---

joy 1986, 118, 152, 179–80; Mountjoy 1999b, 158, 174, 578–79, 602). Furthermore, Mycenaean kalathoi typically have flaring body profiles rather than the strictly conical bodies of the tubs from Miqne and their Plain White Handmade analogues from Cyprus. It is for precisely these reasons that Sherratt, too, has seen in the Miqne vessels a vessel form that served an industrial purpose, possibly in the context of the textile industry (1998, 303–5 and n. 26). The term lekane for this shape, as used by T. Dothan (2000, fig. 7.8:4), is thus preferable to kalathos.

15. For both plain and simply decorated analogues from Crete, see Watrous 1992, 144, figs. 53:1418, 58:1592, 63:1660; Hallager and Hallager 2000, 159, fig. 32:8; 161; for plain ovoid, medium coarse tubs with similar profiles from a very early LH IIIC context at Iria, see Döhl 1973, 175 A41, 177 H14, 193, fig. 21, pl. 77:3–4; for the plain version with vertical handles from Cyprus, aside from the example from Maa-Palaeokastro cited in table 1a, see Karageorghis and Demas 1984, 34 no. 18, 41, no. 103, pls. XXI, XXXVI.

16. For the notion that the early Iron Age settlers at Tel Miqne and other Philistine sites were specialized artisans particularly focused in the production of value-added commodities

Another feature present in the Aegeanizing repertoire at Miqne that seems a little odd from an Aegeanist's perspective is the popularity of feeding bottles in a settlement assemblage. In the Aegean, comparatively few examples of this form come from contexts other than tombs. Perhaps significantly, however, I have noticed a substantial number of feeding bottle fragments from later LM IIIB settlement deposits at Kommos (Watrous 1992, 78 no. 1354, 81 no. 1390, 90 no. 1580, 143, fig. 53, pls. 33, 35, 39, plus several additional unpublished specimens), although their rarity in LM IIIC levels at Chania (Hallager and Hallager 2000, 154 and n. 186) makes clear that their popularity at Kommos is by no means a regular feature of thirteenth through twelfth-century Minoan settlement debris.

Yet another peculiarity of the Miqne Aegeanizing pottery is the presence of several deep bowls with unmistakably carinated body profiles. This feature appears to be very rare on Cyprus, but can be paralleled in the early twelfth century in the Aegean at sites in the southern Peloponnese such as Ayios Stephanos in Laconia and Pylos in Messenia (Mountjoy 1999b, 279, 352, figs. 95:176–79; 120:110, 112). Both the decoration and the shape of these bowls in turn suggest a connection with Crete. Recent publications of stratified LM IIIC assemblages make clear that carinated deep bowls can be extremely popular at some sites—for example, at Chania in the west (Hallager and Hallager 2000, 139–43, figs. 30:8; 31; pl. 35)—and essentially unknown at others—Kavousi in the east, for example (Mook and Coulson 1997). But the comparanda from Chania have flat bases and straight-sided profiles above the carination rather than being ring-based and concave-flaring in their upper body as at Miqne—and of course Cretan bowls also have solidly coated interiors, so the Minoan parallel is not at all a close one. My point here is simply to note that these carinated deep bowls once again distinguish the Aegeanizing component at Miqne from what one would expect to see on Cyprus or in Cilicia.

Finally, no one who has ever studied Philistine pottery can fail to be struck by the astonishing popularity of the bird motif, the fish also being reasonably common but far less frequent overall (T. Dothan 1982, 198–203). For an Aegeanist, one particularly striking aspect of this phenomenon is the simple fact that virtually no other representational form appears on earlier Philistine pottery. Birds and fish are, to be sure, among the most popular of LH IIIC (Vermeule and Karageorghis 1982; Sakellarakis 1992; Güntner 2000) and LC IIIA (Kling

such as ceramics, metalwork produced largely from scrap, and textiles, see Sherratt 1998, esp. 301–7. Standardized linear decoration is also a feature of the deep bowls, shallow angular bowls, and convex-bodied handleless cups recovered in Stratum XIIIb at Ashdod, especially (and not surprisingly) among the numerous complete vessels found in piles in what has been identified as a potter's shop at that site (M. Dothan and Porath 1993, 11–13, fig. 14, pls. XII; XIII:1–2).

1984a; 1989, 106, 118–22, 130, 156, 410–13, tables 59–14 through 59–17) pictorial motifs as well, but they are by no means the only ones. Does this distinctive iconographic focus have any particular significance? For example, might the omission of such terrestrial animals as horses, bulls, dogs, and deer indicate a lack of interest in hunting or agriculture, the frequency of birds and fish revealing, by contrast, an absorption with fauna seen primarily at sea? That is, might the Philistines' predilection for birds and fish on their crockery reflect a predominantly maritime orientation of Philistine culture? Might the complete absence of scenes of the hunt and of warfare on both land and sea, subject matter that plays a predominant role on contemporary and slightly later Mycenaean pottery in the Argolid, Locris, Euboea, and the Dodecanese (Dakoronia 1987; 1999; Rutter 1992; Sherratt 1992, 331), further indicate that the Philistines may have been more interested in marine mercantile activities than in piracy and raiding? Most authorities would probably argue that this is inferring far too much from far too little, in addition to giving unusual weight to negative evidence. So let us stick to the hard facts and itemize what most would agree are legitimate conclusions from the preceding rehearsal of the basic data.

First, the Aegeanizing component in the ceramic assemblage of Miqne Stratum VII (and seemingly also Ashdod Stratum XIIIb) is not restricted to tablewares, but includes cooking vessels and a domestic industrial item. As argued by Killebrew, Sherratt, and others, this Aegeanizing component has its closest parallels in LC IIIA strata on Cyprus, especially in the eastern part of that island. Indeed, one may legitimately view the domestic industrial lekanai (or kalathoi) as more Cypriot than Aegean, while the vessels employed at Miqne for transport and storage have no Aegean connection at all and have as much of a claim to be considered Cypriot as they do Canaanite. In terms of Aegean relative chronology, Miqne VII matches up well with what is currently termed LH IIIC Early (or Phases 2–3) in the Aegean. The presence of a single painted tray fragment and of trefoil-mouthed linear jugs in the upper levels of Stratum VII may be used as evidence for a relatively late date within LH IIIC Early for its lower levels, since both of these types make their initial appearance in the Aegean, on present evidence, in LH IIIC Middle (Mountjoy 1986, 167, fig. 213; 180, fig. 234).[17]

This much seems unobjectionable. Let us conclude with some more provocative suggestions intended as possible points of departure for future debates on the lifeways of the twelfth-century settlers in the southern Levant whom we

17. Similar indicators of a relatively advanced date within LH IIIC Early for the earliest Philistine pottery at Ashdod are the pronounced cone at the top of stirrup jar false necks (M. Dothan and Porath 1993, fig. 17:9) and perhaps also the strainer-jug decorated with a bird (M. Dothan and Porath 1993, fig. 17:10).

identify as the Philistines. The total absence of vertical-handled drinking vessels of Aegean types from Miqne Strata VII and VI, like their rarity in Cypriot contexts, speaks for a fundamentally different approach to communal drinking activities between the Greek Mainland and islands on the one hand and most of Cyprus and Cilicia, and all of Philistia, on the other.[18] Specific Mycenaean decorative complexes such as the Ephyraean style of LH IIB and the Zygouries style of early LH IIIB make clear that the Mycenaean drinking assemblage in palatial times consisted, in declining order of frequency, of stemmed goblets or kylikes, jugs, kraters, and one-handled ladles or dippers (Wright 1996; 2004). In the early LH IIIC period, dippers evidently change from a round-bodied (FS 236) to a carinated (FS 240) form, but otherwise the collapse of the palatial system does not seem to have entailed any major, immediate impact on this traditional drinking assemblage.[19] On Cyprus, by contrast, the standard drinking assemblage appears to have consisted only of kraters and shallow horizontal-handled bowls (South 1988).[20] It is clearly this latter assemblage that is represented in both Cilicia and Philistia, where kraters and shallow linear bowls are common but stemmed cups and high-handled dippers are missing. One presumes that this difference is an ethnic one, but could it equally well, or even alternatively, represent a difference in the nature of the beverage being consumed? In this connection, the popularity of the side-spouted strainer-jug in Philistia (T. Dothan 1982, 132–55 Type 6; M. Dothan and Porath 1993, fig. 17:10), as well as in Cyprus (Kling 1989, 153–58) and portions of the eastern Aegean (Mountjoy 1999c, 1040–43 nos. 182–186 [Rhodes], 1146 no. 1 [Ikaria]), suggests that beer was a far more common beverage in the east than within the Aegean basin, particularly west of Naxos. Perhaps the popularity of the feeding bottle in Philistine settlement assemblages remarked upon earlier is likewise the result of a need for pouring vessels that incorporate a coarse filtering function to be connected with beer drinking.

---

18. A single short-stemmed kylix fragment, preserving only linear decoration, was found in Stratum XIIIb at Ashdod (M. Dothan and Porath 1993, 178–79, fig. 17:7). The singularity of this piece, when contrasted with the abundance of this form in Aegean contexts throughout the thirteenth and twelfth centuries B.C.E., suggests that it may have served a special purpose in a Philistine context, perhaps one connected with cult. I am grateful to T. Dothan for having drawn my attention to this piece in the course of the workshop in May 2001.

19. For the tendency of the latest examples of the traditional Mycenaean dipper of FS 236 to develop a carinated profile, see Mountjoy 1999b, 285 no. 193, 916–18 no. 142 (LH IIIC Early).

20. Thus the finds from Maa-Palaeokastro, which include a substantial number of vertical-handled drinking vessels in the form of both conical and carinated kylikes, would appear to represent a more typically Aegean drinking assemblage (Karageorghis and Demas 1988; Kling 1988).

Comparison of the earliest Philistine pottery from Tel Miqne with that from Ashdod, at the same time as it shows how similar the two assemblages are, nevertheless also reveals some minor differences that may be worth exploring. For example, a series of handleless, convex-sided bowls decorated with a single band at the rim from Ashdod (M. Dothan and Porath 1993, fig. 14:1–7) lack published equivalents at Tel Miqne. Were it not for their ring bases, one might be tempted to connect them with the linear pulled-rim bowls and bell cups that are so popular a feature of the LM IIIA2–B ceramic repertoire of eastern Crete (Bosanquet and Dawkins 1923, 85–86, fig. 68:2; Kanta 1980, pl. 59:1; MacGillivray 1997, 197–98, fig. 2a–b [bell cup], 200, fig. 4b [pulled-rim bowl]). Sherratt has suggested that the Ashdod bowls are more likely to be versions of a Mycenaeanizing vessel type peculiar to Cyprus (2000, 303 and n. 20). A series of tiny deep bowls (rim diameter between eight and ten centimeters) often featuring paint only at the rim (M. Dothan and Porath 1993, fig. 14:9–15, 17–18, 20) suggests that the deep bowl as a form may have been produced at Ashdod in two distinct sizes, a practice that is not well paralleled either at Tel Miqne or in the Aegean but that again may have a precedent on Cyprus in later LC IIC or early LC IIIA (Sherratt 1990b, esp. 161; 2000, 303 and n. 20). Thus, features that may prove to be indicative of minor regional differences within Philistine Aegeanizing ceramics can perhaps be explained by invoking parallels that are peculiar to Cyprus.

Something else that seems to have emerged from the preceding review of the available data is that, notwithstanding the many similarities linking the earliest Mycenaeanizing pottery of Philistia with that of both Cilicia and Cyprus, there are also a number of important differences, especially insofar as Cilicia is concerned. What appears to distinguish the material from Miqne and Ashdod principally from that of southeastern Cyprus,[21] to which it is otherwise closest, is its typological standardization. This fact suggests that this earliest Philistine pottery may have been produced by a far more tightly knit group of artisans than were responsible for this kind of activity not only back in the Aegean but even on Cyprus. Killebrew has already drawn attention to the distinctive choices of clay sources, paste preparation, vessel formation techniques, and firing processes made by the earliest Iron Age potters at Miqne. It might prove interesting to see such technological studies extended to encompass quantitative analyses of morphological, dimensional, and decorative standardization. Killebrew's studies suggest that some of the technical features of Philistine ceramic production at Miqne—for example, specific choices of clay sources and paste recipes—begin to

21. For the existence of significant ceramic regionalism within Cyprus early in the LC IIIA period, see Kling 1988 (for Maa-Palaeokastro); 2000, 288–91 (for the Kouris River drainage sites of Alassa and Kourion).

change as early as Stratum VI, at which time bichrome decoration also makes its initial appearance. Might the strict standardization that appears to characterize the Aegeanizing pottery of the initial Philistine settlement likewise have fallen by the wayside in the course of the later twelfth century?

The functionally restricted nature of the Aegeanizing vessels in the earliest Philistine assemblages from Tel Miqne and Ashdod is very difficult to explain within an interpretative framework that conceives of these forms as marking an Aegean ethnic element within the Philistine population that occupied these two sites at some point in the first half of the twelfth century B.C.E. The peculiar and distinctive mixture of Aegeanizing tableware and cooking forms can be duplicated only on Cyprus, and for that matter only within certain subregions within Cyprus.[22] A more compelling interpretative approach to the Aegeanizing component in the earliest Philistine ceramic repertoire is therefore to view it as an extension of the Cypriot practice of large-scale production of substitutes for genuine Mycenaean imports that began roughly a century earlier (Sherratt 1998; 1999). One question that immediately springs to mind is, of course, if these earliest Philistine assemblages are to be viewed as derived wholly from Cyprus rather than even partially from the Aegean, what elements of the Cypriot repertoire have dropped out in the migration of this assemblage from southeastern Cyprus to Philistia and why—but that is a topic for a Levantine specialist, not an Aegeanist!

22. For a culture that clearly participated extensively in interregional exchange, the Philistine utilization of a single type of container for bulk transport and storage, namely, the Canaanite jar, rather than some mixture of large Aegean stirrup jars, Cypriot pithoi (Pilides 2000), and Canaanite jars as on the Uluburun ship, or even the combination of pithoi and Canaanite jars that is characteristic of major Cypriot settlements of the late LC IIC and LC IIIA periods, is also distinctive.

Chapter Twenty-One
The Late LH IIIB and LH IIIC Early Pottery of the East Aegean–West Anatolian Interface

*Penelope A. Mountjoy**

This paper discusses some of the characteristic ceramic features of the East Aegean–West Anatolian Interface (see Mountjoy 1998, 33–67) in the late LH IIIB and LH IIIC Early phases. This is the period of the collapse of the Mycenaean palatial centers on the Greek Mainland, the fall of the Hittite Empire, and the activities of the so-called Sea Peoples. A brief overview of the characteristic ceramic features of the Interface in these phases has already been presented;[1] it is enlarged here with particular reference to the Rhodian Style. Even though the ceramic corpus from the Interface in these phases is not large, since only a few key sites have been excavated, it is worth paying attention to the pottery from this area in these phases as it has features which are quite distinct from the pottery of Mainland Greece; moreover, elements from it are reflected in the contemporary Mycenaean pottery found in Cyprus and the Levant, which might allow for some cross-dating. To illustrate this phenomenon, some parallels from Cyprus and Ugarit are also included here.

The LH IIIC Rhodian Style

I have suggested that there was an east Aegean pottery *koiné* in LH IIIC Early and Middle, which had its roots in LH IIIB and extended up the Interface as far as Chios; it may even have extended as far as Troy, but too little pottery of these

* British School at Athens, Souedias 52, 10676 Athens, Greece.

1. For the primary definition with illustrations, one should consult Mountjoy 1998, 43–45, 53–67.

phases is known for conclusions to be drawn (Mountjoy 1998, 53–67; 1999c, 45, 967–69). Rhodes, however, was not part of this *koiné*. In LH IIIC Early–Middle (Developed) it had its own pottery style derived from Crete, based on motifs adapted from imported Minoan octopus stirrup jars (Mountjoy 1999c, 46–47, 985–88, 1045). This style is best represented in the numerous graves in the cemetery at Ialysos. The floruit of this style occurred after the destructions on the Greek Mainland and the collapse of the Hittite Empire.

I date a very large number of Rhodian vases to LH IIIC Early–Middle (Developed) since there is no obvious development in the decoration and no stratigraphy is available, which would enable the pottery definitely to be separated into LH IIIC Early and LH IIIC Middle (Developed). The main Minoan contribution probably occurred in LH IIIC Early when the style evolved. Benzi prefers to see most of these vases as belonging to LH IIIC Middle (Developed and Advanced).[2] In support of this dating, he quotes A. Kanta as implying that octopus stirrup jars did not begin on Crete in LM IIIC Early, but in LM IIIC Middle at the same time as they appear on the Greek Mainland and in the Aegean islands. The reason for this is that they are not present in the LM IIIC Early phase of Chania: Kastelli Trench B (Kanta 1997, 96); this applies, too, to the elaborately decorated kraters, which are also lacking in Kastelli Trench B in this phase. On the other hand, in her publication of the LM IIIC pottery from Kastelli, B. Hallager makes the position quite clear: "the so-called closed style." This decorative style is usually found on vessels with large surfaces to be decorated (mainly kraters and stirrup jars) and, as seen here, it is found on these vessels from the very beginning of the LM IIIC period, thus ruling out speculations about this "style" being a characteristic of a developed phase of LM IIIC" (Hallager and Hallager 2000, 147; see also Rethemiotakis 1997, 331). More stratified LM IIIC Early and Middle material is obviously needed from Crete to clarify this problem. It may be that further LM IIIC Early deposits might reveal subphases that have not yet been isolated. However, it should be borne in mind that features do not always appear simultaneously in Crete and on Mainland Greece (Mountjoy 1999b, 511–16); the fact that this decorative style, which I would call "pleonastic" (see Mountjoy 1999b, 513 for a discussion of the terminology), seems to begin on the Mainland and Aegean islands in LH IIIC Middle is not necessarily a criterion for dating its appearance on Cretan material to this phase.

Long before the east Aegean LH IIIC pottery *koiné* came into being, a regional style had already developed in south Rhodes in LH IIIA2 that combined Anatolian and Minoan shapes and motifs (see Mountjoy 1995a, 21–35 for a discussion of this style). Furumark dated the vases belonging to the style of various stages of

2. I thank M. Benzi for allowing me to read his paper prior to publication.

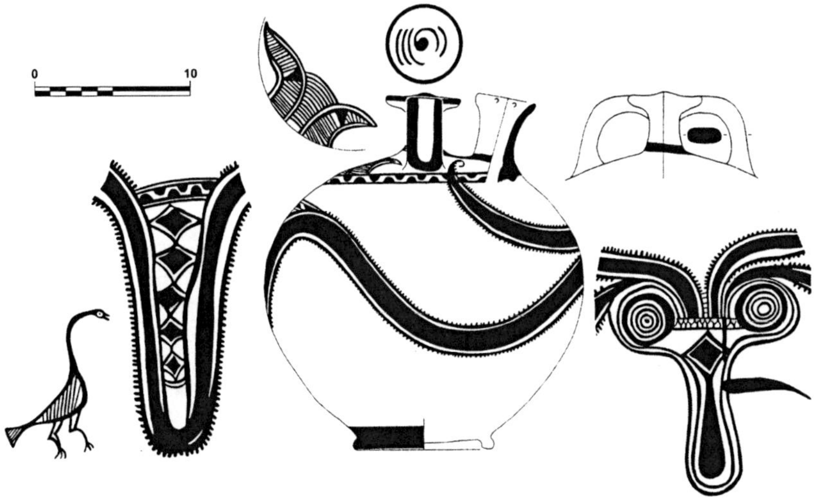

Fig. 1: Ialysos, octopus stirrup jar with horns FS 176 (Forsdyke 1925, pl. 13, fig. 231; Mountjoy 1999b, Rhodes no. 189).

LH IIIC using Mainland criteria, but their decoration comprises Minoan elements which appeared much earlier on Crete than on the Mainland (i.e., LM IIIA not LM IIIC). The vases can also be dated to LH IIIA2 from imported examples in LH IIIA2 context in north Rhodes at Ialysos (Benzi 1992, 163 Ts. 48.12, 62.1). The stacked triangle and the cross-hatched triangle, two of the most frequent motifs of this style, thus appeared in the Interface and on Crete in LH/LM IIIA2 and not in LH IIIC Middle Advanced as on the Greek Mainland. The stacked triangle later becomes one of the characteristic motifs of the LH IIIC Rhodian Style.

A number of motifs are characteristic of the LH IIIC Rhodian Style. One of the main motifs is horns (figs. 1–4). Horns develop from the tongue motif Furumark Motif (FM) 19 (Furumark 1941a, fig. 47:40–48) and have the wide base of this motif; they are often used antithetically. They should not be confused with streamers, also used antithetically, which develop from the tricurved arch motif on FM 62 (Furumark 1941a, fig. 68:31–35), and have a very narrow base. Horns are used on many shapes, but especially on octopus stirrup jar shoulders (fig. 1). Horns are outlined with a single line and may have a simple hatched fill (figs. 2.2; 3.1, 3) or have a hatched fill with a solid painted triangle in the middle (figs. 2.1, 3, 4; 3.2). The motif comes from Crete; fig. 4 is an imported Minoan stirrup jar with horns. An example of horns found on Crete itself can be seen on a stirrup jar from Palaikastro, but here the horns are not hatched (Sackett and Popham 1965, 289, fig. 10e). When placed antithetically, horns often have a lozenge between them (fig. 2.1, 4; fig. 3.1, 3). The lozenge is painted solid in a similar manner to the

Fig. 2: Ialysos, horns and half-moon spirals: **1–2)** amphoriskos FS 61 (Ialysos T.61.1. Benzi 1992, pl. 94a; Mountjoy 1999c, Rhodes no. 154 and Ialysos T.85.2. Benzi 1992, pl. 109d; Mountjoy 1999c, Rhodes no. 152); **3)** alabastron FS 99 (Ialysos T.32.27. Benzi 1992, pl. 60a; Mountjoy 1999c, Rhodes no. 172); and **4)** strainer jug FS 155 (Ialysos T.17.46. Benzi 1992, pl. 29c–d; Mountjoy 1999c, Rhodes no. 183). Scale 1:3.

triangle in the horns and then outlined with a single line. Outlined solid lozenge is also used in other compositions (fig. 1). This variant of the lozenge may come originally from Crete where it can be seen on LM IIIB larnakes (Watrous 1991, pl. 91a).

Another motif used with horns is the half-moon spiral (figs. 2.2, 4; 3.2, 4; 5). It may have been adapted from the half moons found on the false mouths of Minoan stirrup jars (Mountjoy 1999d, pl. 8d, f). There seem to be no Minoan parallels to the half-moon spirals themselves.

Stacked triangles (figs. 5; 7.1–3) are another Minoan feature used in the LH IIIC Rhodian Style; they were already in use on Crete in LM IIIA and were taken over to form one of the elements in the local LH IIIA2 South Rhodian style (see above; e.g., Mountjoy 1995a, 24, fig. 4a shoulder). Another type of triangle, the outlined solid triangle, can be seen on a Minoan import (fig. 6). This motif too was adapted into the Rhodian Style in the LH IIIC Early phase (figs. 7.4; 9.3).

Outlined solid semicircles (fig. 7.3; 8) are also used in this style. They may derive from outlined rock pattern as used on Crete, for example, on LM IIIB larnakes from Kavrochori, Gazi, and Armenoi (Watrous 1991, pls. 89c, e, 90d–f, 92a).

A Rhodian development, which does not seem to be found on Crete, is the use of a foliate band abbreviated to droplets (fig. 9). It is placed either horizontally as a main motif (figs. 9.1; 10.1) or vertically as a triglyph filler (fig. 9.2–4). It may also be found acting as a triglyph between horns (fig. 3.2), often with a lozenge on top (figs. 2.4; 3.1, 3). Two particularly interesting parallels to the use of droplets as triglyph fillers come from Tarsus (Goldman 1950, fig. 330:1299, 1288b + 1289); one of these parallels (fig. 330:1288b + 1299 [see French 1975, 60, fig. 10:1289 for the join]) also has a lozenge above the droplets in the Rhodian fashion, but the lozenge is not the Rhodian type. The hatched fill of horns can also be adapted to act as a triglyph (fig. 10.1–3).

The horn triglyph, that is a horn with a fill generally found in triglyphs (fig. 11, a Minoan import), and ladder triglyphs (fig. 12) are found on octopus stirrup jars but not on other shapes; they are used to link the tentacles.

These are the main motifs of the LH IIIC Early Rhodian Style. Of these motifs, stacked and cross-hatched triangles do not appear on the Greek Mainland until LH IIIC Middle (Furumark 1941a, fig. 68 FM 61A); solid semicircles, triangles, and lozenges, outlined with a single line, are rare, if extant there[3]; half-moon

3. Furumark gives no examples of this type of triangle, one example of a lozenge (1941a, fig. 71 FM 73aa; no provenance given, but probably Rhodian) and one example of semicircles (1941a, fig. 58 FM 43b from Asine). The remaining examples are from the Interface.

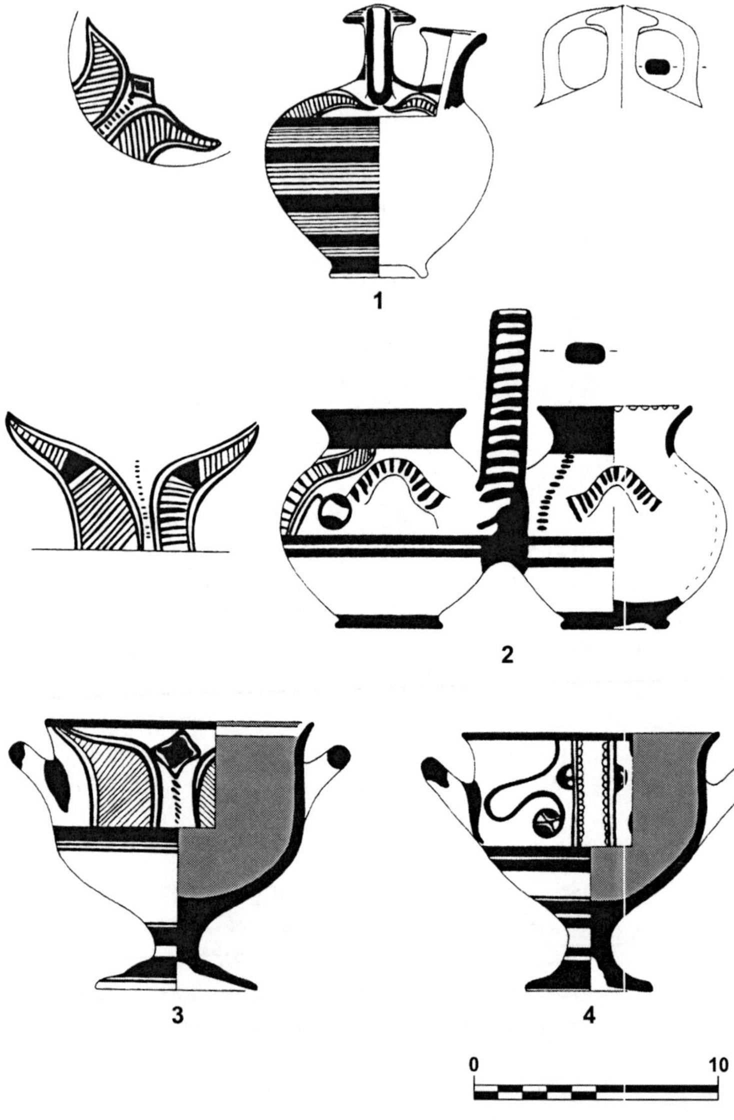

Fig. 3: Ialysos, horns and half-moon spirals: **1)** stirrup jar FS 176 (Ialysos T.38.9. Benzi 1992, pl. 69e, h; Mountjoy 1999c, Rhodes no. 201); **2)** double vase FS 325 (Ialysos T.21.38. Benzi 1992, pl. 39a; Mountjoy 1999c, Rhodes no. 222); and **3–4)** stemmed bowl FS 306 (Ialysos T.21.9. Benzi 1992, pl. 36p; Mountjoy 1999c, Rhodes no. 248 and Ialysos T.21.10. Benzi 1992, pl. 36q; Mountjoy 1999c, Rhodes no. 251). Scale 1:3.

Fig. 4: Ialysos, Minoan octopus stirrup jar with horns FS 176 (Ialysos T.15.2. Benzi 1992, pl. 15c).

Fig. 5: Ialysos, octopus stirrup jar with half-moon spiral and stacked triangles FS 176 (Ialysos T.17.2. Benzi 1992, pl. 21c).

Fig. 6: Ialysos, Minoan octopus stirrup jar with outlined solid triangles FS 176 (Ialysos T.87.4. Benzi 1992, pl. 110d–e).

spirals and horns of the hatched Rhodian type do not appear there at all. Nor, so far, are these last two motifs found in the rest of the Interface.[4]

Interface Vessel Shapes

A number of vessel shapes are peculiar to the Interface in late LH IIIB–LH IIIC; they are rare or not present at all on the Greek Mainland.

Piriform jar

The large ovoid east Aegean piriform jar FS 37, 38 appears in LH IIIB and continues in use in LH IIIC Early, except on Rhodes, where it is rare in the latter phase.

4. A possible exception is an octopus stirrup jar from Ialysos (T.21.1 Benzi 1992, pl. 36a–d), which depicts birds with wings consisting of hatched horns and the body of one bird composed of a half-moon spiral variant; a row of droplets is also present and a single hatched horn with a long tail at the tip (Benzi 1992, pl. 36b). The fabric of this vase suggests it may be an import from Kos (Mountjoy 1999c, 1048).

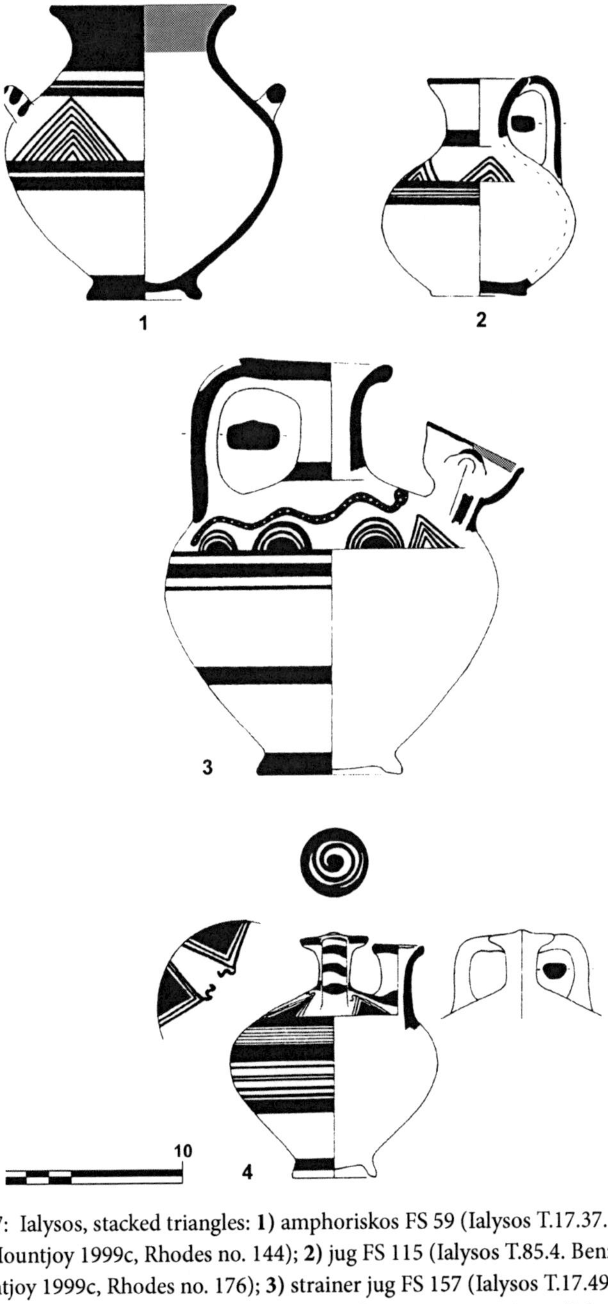

Fig. 7: Ialysos, stacked triangles: **1)** amphoriskos FS 59 (Ialysos T.17.37. Benzi 1992, pl. 26i; Mountjoy 1999c, Rhodes no. 144); **2)** jug FS 115 (Ialysos T.85.4. Benzi 1992, pl. 109f; Mountjoy 1999c, Rhodes no. 176); **3)** strainer jug FS 157 (Ialysos T.17.49. Benzi 1992, pl. 29g–h; Mountjoy 1999c, Rhodes no. 186); and **4)** stirrup jar FS 176 (Ialysos T.68.1. Benzi 1992, pl. 98a–b; Mountjoy 1999c, Rhodes no. 214). Scale 1:3.

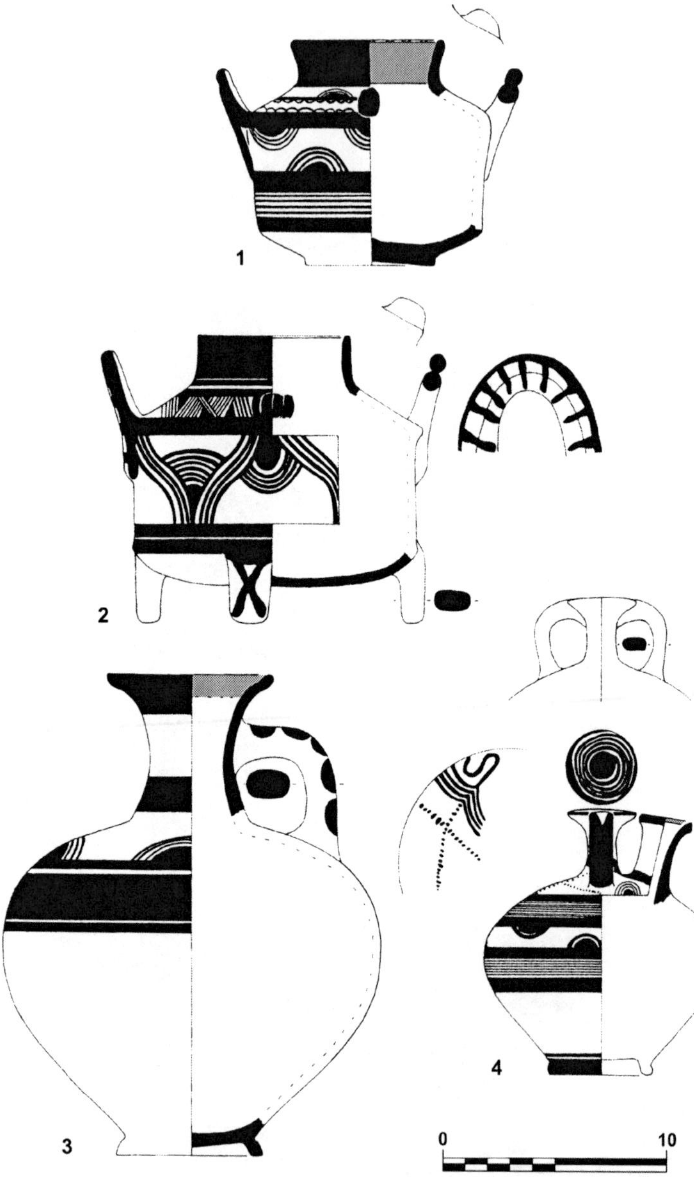

Fig. 8: Ialysos, semicircles: **1)** alabastron FS 97 (Ialysos T.32.8. Benzi 1992, pl. 60b; Mountjoy 1999c, Rhodes no. 168); **2)** alabastron FS 99 (Ialysos T.85.3. Benzi 1992, pl. 109e; Mountjoy 1999c, Rhodes no. 173); **3)** narrow-necked jug FS 121 (Ialysos T.32.19. Benzi 1992, pl. 59a; Mountjoy 1999c, Rhodes no. 178); and **4)** stirrup jar FS 176 (Ialysos T.83.6B. Benzi 1992, pl. 107g; Mountjoy 1999c, Rhodes no. 196). Scale 1:3.

Fig. 9: Ialysos, droplets 1–4: **1, 3)** amphoriskos FS 59 (Ialysos T.17.27. Benzi 1992, pl. 26g; Mountjoy 1999c, Rhodes no. 146 and Ialysos T.17.34. Benzi 1992, pl. 26f; Mountjoy 1999c, Rhodes no. 150); **2)** amphoriskos FS 61 (Ialysos T.17.6. Benzi 1992, pl. 25g; Mountjoy 1999c, Rhodes no. 160); and **4)** deep bowl FS 284 (Ialysos T.17.55. Benzi 1992, pl. 30b; Mountjoy 1999c, Rhodes no. 240). Scale 1:3.

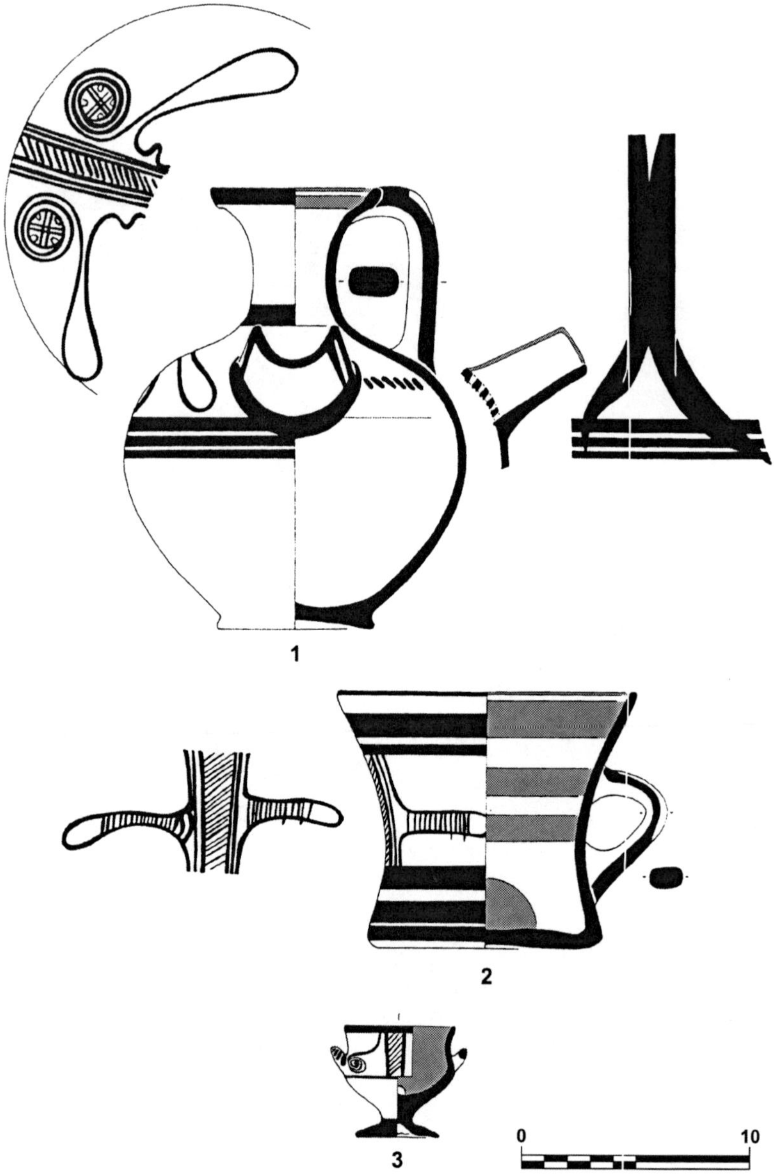

Fig. 10: Ialysos, droplets 1 and triglyphs with hatched fill adapted from horns 1–3: **1)** strainer jug FS 155 (Ialysos T.17.43. Benzi 1992, pl. 28e; Mountjoy 1999c, Rhodes no. 185); **2)** mug FS 226 (Ialysos T.21.36. Benzi 1992, pl. 38o; Mountjoy 1999c, Rhodes no. 227); and **3)** stemmed bowl FS 306 (Ialysos T.21.12. Benzi 1992, pl. 36s; Mountjoy 1999c, Rhodes no. 250). Scale 1:3.

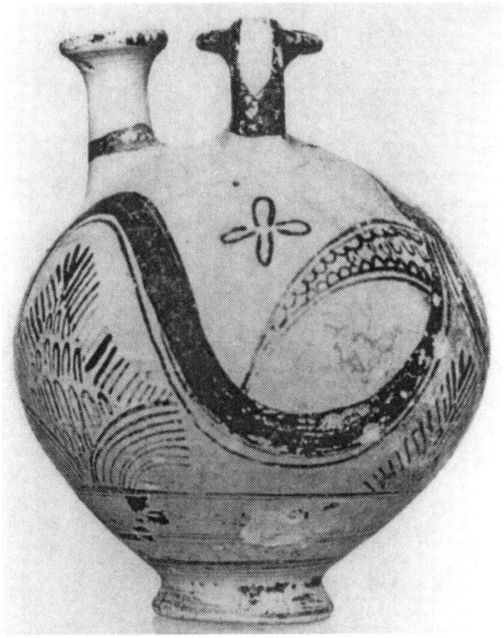

Fig. 11: Ialysos, Minoan octopus stirrup jar with horn triglyph FS 176 (Ialysos T.32.17. Benzi 1992, pl. 58m–n).

On the Greek Mainland the piriform jar is not common after LH IIIB (Mountjoy 1998, 54 and fig. 10).

Based Shapes

Some Interface shapes may have a carinated lower body and a ring base instead of the flat base found on their counterparts on the Greek Mainland (Mountjoy 1998, 55–56 and figs. 17–18). Based mugs are found all along the Interface from Troy down to Kos, but they do not seem to be present on Rhodes. On the other hand, the based kalathos is found on Rhodes (e.g., Benzi 1992, pl. 144b Lartos 36) as well as at other Interface sites. The same applies to the straight-sided alabastron FS 97. This shape does appear on the Greek Mainland, but, although widely spread, is not very common (Mountjoy 1999c, Argolid no. 331, Laconia no. 232, Attica no. 333).

Fig. 12: Ialysos, octopus stirrup jar with ladder triglyph FS 176 (Ialysos T.32.2. Benzi 1992, pl. 56c–f).

Tall Narrow Mug

In contrast to the usual large mug, which is nearly as wide as it is high (Mountjoy 1986, fig. 101), a tall narrow mug appears in the Interface (Mountjoy 1998, 55 and fig. 16). Its earliest appearance seems to date to LH IIIA2. This tall type does not seem to have been used on the Greek Mainland. A vessel from Lartos seems to be the only Rhodian example (Mountjoy 1998, fig. 16:4). It may be an import from elsewhere in the Interface. A mug very similar to it has been found at Ugarit (Yon et al. 2000, fig. 24 no. 385); it is dated to Late Ugarit 3 (Schaeffer 1949, 52).

Strainer Jug

Strainer jugs are common on Rhodes at Ialysos, but they seem to be rare in the rest of the Interface (Mountjoy 1999c, 1113). Strainer jugs often depict horns and half-moon spirals (see above).

Amphoroid Krater and Stand

The amphoroid krater (Mountjoy 1998, 54 and figs. 11–13) is popular in the east Aegean *koiné* but rare on Rhodes.[5] The shape has close affinities to the Minoan version rather than to those exported from the Greek Mainland (cf. Betancourt 1985, pl. 30A with Mountjoy 1993, 73 no. 153). It has a short, straight neck, a large globular body, and a very small pedestal base. The decoration of these kraters is idiosyncratic in as much as the handle ring has its back to the handle and thus frames the decorative zone instead of the handle; the handle ring, the band down each edge of the handle, and the wavy line down the center of the handle may all continue onto the lower body giving the appearance of tails. These amphoroid kraters were exported to Ugarit,[6] where Courtois (1973, 149–50) notes that there were very many sherds belonging to this shape and that all the examples were found in the last period of the settlement (1973, 150). A number were analyzed chemically and petrographically and proved to have a provenance compatible with southwestern Anatolia and the offshore islands (the Dodecanese and Caria) (1973, 151–52), that is Miletos–Kos–Kalymnos (the east Aegean *koiné*). Courtois lists many comparisons between the kraters from Ugarit and those from Miletos (1973, 149–64), but export from Astypalaia, Kos, and Kalymnos cannot be ruled out (Mountjoy 1999c, 1078; also Courtois and Courtois 1987, 210). Courtois also points out that there are some iconographic differences with the material from Miletos; he suggests that the vases were presumably ordered by clients and that the differences are the result of local taste (1973, 153).

These kraters were supported on large cylindrical stands. This type is a feature of the Interface in late LH IIIB–IIIC Early; a version of it is already extant in LH IIIA2 (Mountjoy 1998, fig. 2.2). Other examples come from Miletos and Baklatepe.[7] A variant at Troy is fenestrated; it dates to Troy VIIa that is LH IIIB (Mountjoy 1999d, 303, fig. 2). The cylindrical stand is usually linear, but the Trojan fenestrated type generally carries spiral-form decoration.

---

5. The single published example may be an import (Mountjoy 1999c, 1030–31).

6. E.g., Yon, Karageorghis, and Hirschfeld 2000, cat. nos. 68–69. These two vases have gold and silver mica and dark orange and purple grits similar to the clay from the Kos–Kalymnos–Miletos area. I thank A. Caubet and N. Hirschfeld for allowing me to handle this material.

7. Miletos: Schiering 1959–1960, pl. 15 and two others unpublished Schiering 1959–1960, 23; also new finds from the recent excavations displayed by W.-D. Niemeier at the Panionion Congress in September 1999; Baklatepe: Özkan, Erkanal, and Kale 1999, 186, pl. 11.

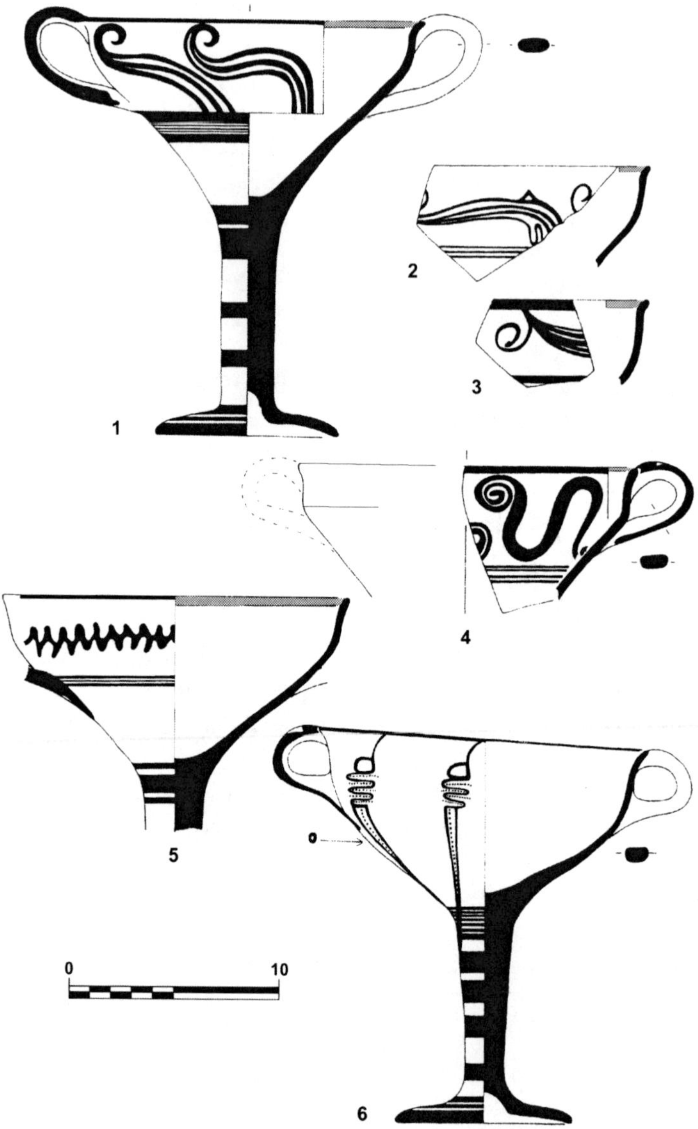

Fig. 13: Carinated kylix: **1)** Degirmentepe (Heilmeyer et al. 1988, 25 no. 9); **2–4)** Troy (Blegen, Caskey, and Rawson 1953, fig. 418.3; Mountjoy 1999a, fig. 10.79; Blegen, Caskey, and Rawson 1953, fig. 416.7; Mountjoy 1999a, fig. 10.80; and Schmidt 1902, 165 no. 3400; Mommsen, Hertel, and Mountjoy 2001, fig. 16.32); **5)** Hala Sultan Tekke (T.1. Åström, Bailey, and Karageorghis 1976, pl. 67.79); and **6)** LH IIIB1 Kopreza (Mountjoy 1986, fig. 141.12). Scale 1:3.

Kylix with Slight Carination

An east Aegean type of kylix has a short upper body with a very slight carination instead of the usual rounded body of the Greek Mainland type (fig. 13; cf. fig. 13.1–5 with the Mainland example fig. 13.6). The carinated shape originated in LM IIIB on Crete (Popham 1984, pl. 180.4, 9) and became more sharply carinated in LM IIIC (Rethemiotakis 1997, 315, fig. 23g–h, Mook and Coulson 1997, 346, fig. 11.31). The shape travelled to Cyprus (fig. 13.5). A feature of this type is the banding at the level of the handle base. This is a LH IIIA2 Early feature on the Greek Mainland (Mountjoy 1986, 88), after which the banding moves down to the lower body or to the top of the stem (fig. 13.6). However, the LH IIIA2 Early type continued at Troy into LH IIIA2 Late (Mountjoy 1999a, 277, 279) and a variant of it was in use all down the Interface in LH IIIB.

Paint

During LH IIIB–IIIC Early in the Interface and the Levant, the paint may have changed from lustrous to matte. In the Interface at Troy, matte paint took over from lustrous paint in LH IIIB (i.e., Troy VIIa;[8] Mountjoy 1997a, 262; 1999d, 301, Mommsen, Hertel, and Mountjoy 2001, 171); it varies in color from orange to red and even to purple. At Bakla Tepe (Izmir Museum vitrina) and at Miletos (Degirmentepe) the paint may be matte or semilustrous in LH IIIB–IIIC Early. However, on Kos, Kalymnos, and Astypalaia the paint remains lustrous. On Cyprus matte paint first seems to occur in the LH IIIB2 Rude or Pastoral Style (Furumark 1941a, 465); some of the LH IIIB–IIIC vases from Ugarit are also decorated in matte paint (Yon et al. 2000, cat. nos. 69, 385, 434) or matte/semilustrous paint (Yon et al. 2000, cat. nos. 68, 429, 474).

8. For the revised dating of Troy, see Mountjoy 1997a, 275–94; 1999d. The Phase VIh destruction is dated to LH IIIA2, as almost all its stratified Mycenaean pottery belongs to this phase. The few LH IIIB sherds found in the Phase VIh levels (most likely being Phase VIIa intrusions) came in when Phase VIIa pithoi were inserted. The Phase VIh levels were greatly disturbed as these huge pithoi were set one to two meters below the Phase VIh floors. Phase VIIa was LH IIIB. The latest pieces in it date to the Transitional LH IIIB2–IIIC Early phase.

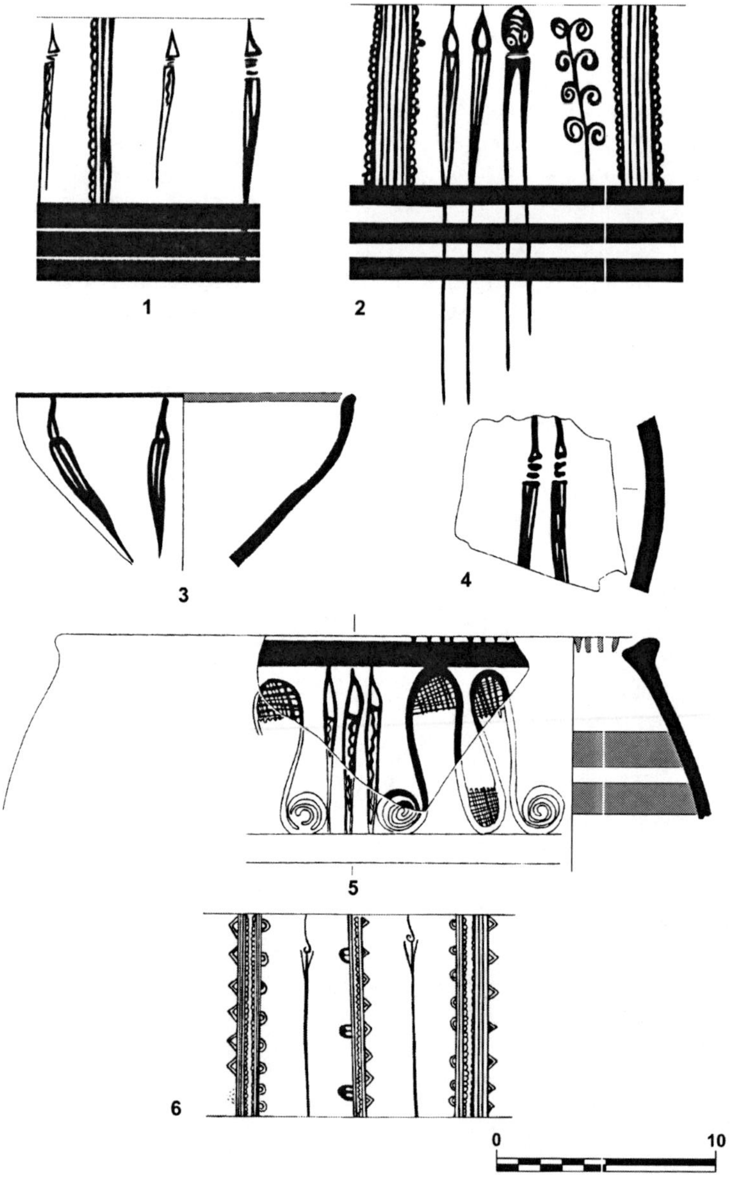

Fig. 14: Whorl-shell: Type I: **1)** Astypalaia: Armenochori (Mountjoy 1998, fig. 12.1; 1999c, Astypalaia no. 7); **2)** Degirmentepe (Mountjoy 1998, fig. 11); and **3–4**) Ugarit (after Yon et al. 2000, fig. 25 cat. 404 and Courtois and Courtois 1978, fig. 42.25); **5)** Kition: Bamboula (after Yon and Caubet 1985, fig. 54.259); and Type II: **6)** Miletos (after Weickert 1957, pl. 34). Various scales.

Fig. 15: Whorl-shell: Type II: **1)** Degirmentepe (Rohde 1981, fig. 85; Mountjoy 1998, fig. 17.6); and **2)** Baklatepe (after Özkan, Erkanal, and Kale 1999, cover photograph). Various scales.

Interface Vessel Decoration

Pictorial Style

The pictorial style (Mountjoy 1998, figs. 13, 15.3) is very common in the settlement material on Kos, but less common elsewhere in the east Aegean *koiné*, perhaps because no settlement contexts of this date have been excavated with the result that most of the corpus comes from tombs. The style seems not to be present on Rhodes; instead pictorial motifs are used as filling motifs on octopus stirrup jars or in isolation on other vessels (Mountjoy 1999c, Rhodes Nos. 184, 189, 192).

Octopus stirrup jars

Octopus stirrup jars are common on Rhodes at Ialysos, but rare in the rest of the Interface. The Rhodian octopus stirrup jar has drooping tentacles framing the body of the octopus, bands separating the shoulder zone from the body zone, and very little filling ornament (fig. 5; Mountjoy 1999c, 1045–83).

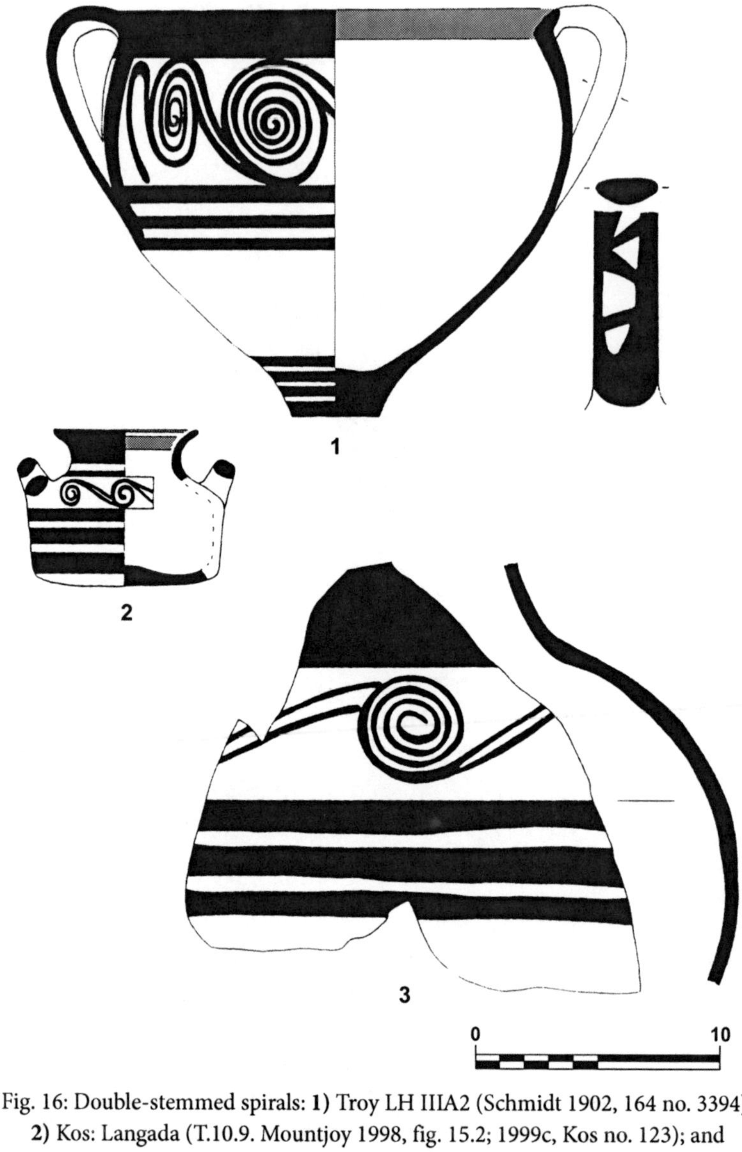

Fig. 16: Double-stemmed spirals: **1**) Troy LH IIIA2 (Schmidt 1902, 164 no. 3394); **2**) Kos: Langada (T.10.9. Mountjoy 1998, fig. 15.2; 1999c, Kos no. 123); and **3**) Ugarit, Sud Acropole (after Courtois and Courtois 1978, fig. 46.4). Scale 1:3.

Kalathoi

Kalathoi with three knobs on the interior corresponding to each handle attachment and with elaborate interior decoration are found in the east Aegean *koiné* but not, so far, on Rhodes (Mountjoy 1998, 56 and fig. 15.3).

Wavy line

This motif (Mountjoy 1998, fig. 19) has a long history in the east Aegean. Parallel wavy lines are already popular in LH IIIA2 (Mountjoy 1998, 39 and figs. 4.2, 5), whereas on the Greek Mainland they are not popular until LH IIIC Late (Mountjoy 1986, figs. 253, 254.10). They continue to be popular in the east Aegean *koiné* (Kos, Kalymnos, Chios, Miletos, and Iasos) and may be framed (Mountjoy 1998, fig. 19.1, 5–7).

Heavy paneled style

Paneled decoration with antithetic spiral is elaborated (Mountjoy 1998, 54, fig. 14): the stems of the spirals may have several tiers of loops, sometimes joined by chevrons, with a lozenge in each loop; the lozenge is also elaborated with multiple semicircles in each corner. This decoration is found at Troy, Chios: Emporio, Kos: Seraglio, Miletos, and Tarsus (Mountjoy 1998, fig. 14; Miletos: Weickert 1957, pl. 32.1; Tarsus: French 1975, 59, fig. 6.3).

Whorl-shells

Two distinct types of whorl-shell are found in the Interface in the Transitional LH IIIB–IIIC Early and LH IIIC Early phases (figs. 14–15). The first Interface type has vertical or wavy lines down the body (fig. 14.1–2) instead of the usual dots and a triangular head instead of an oval one (compare with the LH IIIB example [fig. 13.6]). This type is also found at Ugarit (fig. 14.3–4) and on Cyprus (fig. 14.5).[9]

The second Interface whorl-shell type has a head consisting of a hook (fig. 14.6), which may have a thickened end (fig. 15.1 and Weickert 1957, pl. 32.1 top right), or a hook with a spiral (fig. 15.2).

These types of whorl-shell are not found on the Greek Mainland, although the bodies of the whorl-shells on a LH IIIB2 krater from Tiryns have a zigzag line down them (Mountjoy 1986, fig. 156.1).[10]

Long multiple-stemmed spirals

These spirals (Mountjoy 1998, fig. 15.1) are found so far on Kos (Mountjoy 1999c, Kos Nos. 99, 111 (variation), 164 [?Kos]) and at Miletos (Weickert 1957, pl. 32.2). They are portrayed against an open ground.

---

9. For the complete vessels from which fig. 12.1–2 is taken, see Mountjoy 1998, figs. 11, 12.1. A second krater from Astypalaia has whorl-shells with the usual oval head but a wavy/zigzag line down the body (Mountjoy 1999c, Astypalaia no. 6).

10. For the complete vessels from which fig. 12.6–7 is taken, see Weickert 1957, pl. 34 and Mountjoy 1998, fig. 17.6.

Double-stemmed spirals

Double-stemmed spirals (fig. 16.2; Mountjoy 1998, 54, figs. 14.2, 15.2–3) are another Interface feature. The spirals are not technically running spirals, but isolated spirals with double stems just touching the back of the adjacent spiral. They may have developed from a LH IIIA2 variant in the Interface consisting of a double-stemmed running spiral. It can be seen on a LH IIIA2 kylix from Troy (fig. 16.1). These spirals are found as a main decoration on stirrup jars from Miletos (Schiering 1959–1960, pl. 14.3 left [burnt in the final destruction, p. 23]) and from the nearby cemetery at Degirmentepe (Heilmeyer et al. 1988, 25 no. 3 inv. 316901). They also appear on an amphoroid krater found at Ugarit (fig. 16.3) (Courtois and Courtois 1978, 333, fig. 46.4). The piece is assigned by Courtois and Courtois to a Carian provenance (1978, 332). This type of spiral continues in use in LH IIIC Middle; it is also used as subsidiary decoration as, for example, on a kalathos from Kalymnos and an amphoroid krater from Chios (Mountjoy 1998, 60, fig. 15; 59, fig. 14.2).

At the moment comparisons between the Interface and Cyprus and the Levant (especially Philistia) are limited partly owing to the difference in find contexts, which result in different assemblages, and partly owing to lack of publication. In the Interface the cemeteries of Kos: Langada and Kos: Eleona, Astypalaia: Armenochori, and Ialysos furnish much material belonging to the phases under discussion, but settlement material is needed to go with it in order to draw parallels with that, for example, from Enkomi and Ekron. Troy, Miletos, Iasos, and Kos: Seraglio are the only large Interface settlements excavated, but none have good stratigraphy for these phases and none are fully published. A much larger and more evenly distributed sample from the Interface should give rise to many more comparisons with Cyprus and the Levant.

Chapter Twenty-Two

Aegean-Style Material Culture in Late Cypriot III: Minimal Evidence, Maximal Interpretation

*Maria Iacovou**

My assignment is to contribute the Cyprus piece of the jigsaw puzzle. I intend to devote the first part of this paper to provide a Cyprocentric perspective to the Workshop's primary theme: "In light of recent discoveries and written texts, how do we understand the social, economic, and political structure at the end of the Late Bronze Age and the transition to the Iron Age in the eastern Mediterranean?"[1] My response will focus on the potentials and the shortcomings of the relevant material evidence.

Written Texts

It is a well-known fact that there are no new or, for that matter, old readable texts from Bronze Age Cyprus written in a local script. Despite the fact that the island claims its own share to literacy from the beginning of the Late Cypriot era (ca. 1600 B.C.E.), as long as the locally developed Cypro-Minoan script con-

* Professor, Archaeological Research Unit, Department of History and Archaeology, University of Cyprus. Email: mariai@ucy.ac.cy.

Following the workshop, this paper was slightly updated in 2008, but the text has not been updated. Readers are therefore kindly asked to consider that the paper was expected to have been published before Iacovou 2007, in which it is (inadvertently) cited as 2007a.

1. To Ann E. Killebrew, Gunnar Lehmann, and Michal Artzy, the organizers of the Workshop on Philistines and Other Sea Peoples, which took place in the Spring of 2001, I express sincere thanks for the invitation to participate in a lively international debate, as well as for their Mediterranean hospitality. I thank in particular Ann Killebrew for her readiness to be of assistance while this paper was being prepared for submission. My gratitude goes to Jennifer Webb,

tinues to defy decipherment, Cyprus will continue to be textually silent and, in this respect, "prehistoric" to the very end of the second millennium B.C.E. This constitutes my main objection to a new chronological scheme, which defines the Late Cypriot period as "protohistoric."[2] The first readable text from Cyprus to be written in a local script is post-Bronze Age. It is an inscription in the Greek language (Masson and Masson 1983) and its archaeological context dates it to the Cypro-Geometric I period (Karageorghis 1983, 60–61). Known as the Cypriot syllabary, this local script, which developed from the Cypro-Minoan (cf. Palaima 1991), became the established system for conveying the Greek language on Cyprus during the first millennium B.C.E. (cf. Baurain 1991; Bazemore 1998).

Recent Discoveries

As a result of the Cyprus Department of Antiquities' implementation of a new policy that discourages excavation, especially wherever long-term projects remain unpublished (cf. Hadjisavvas 2000), no truly recent discoveries pertaining to the end of the Late Bronze Age (I mean specifically the twelfth century B.C.E.) have been forthcoming from controlled—as opposed to rescue—excavations.[3] In view of this, a critical evaluation of the published remains, which constitute factual evidence regarding the twelfth century B.C.E. in Cyprus, is in order before we attempt to respond to the Workshop's second theme: "What is the context, nature and distribution of locally produced Aegean-style material culture?" It is therefore imperative to rediscover the skeleton of the twelfth century B.C.E. in Cyprus and proceed from there to see to what extent it can be fleshed out with empirical evidence, which may or may not be Aegean in style.

---

steadfast friend and colleague, who read, corrected, and discussed with me a pre-final version of this paper; she should not, however, be held responsible for any mistakes that may appear in the revised version, nor for the views herein expressed.

2. Cf. Knapp 1994, 282, and more recently, Knapp 1997, 35, table 1, on the Bronze Age periods of Cyprus assigned to a "Protohistoric Bronze Age."

3. Following the publication of Pyla-Kokkinokremmos in 1984 (Karageorghis and Demas 1984), Kition in 1985 (Karageorghis and Demas 1985), and Maa-Palaeokastro in 1988 (Karageorghis and Demas 1988), fieldwork pertaining to the twelfth-century B.C.E. horizon came to an almost complete standstill. Of the "old" field projects the only one that continues to be excavated, albeit intermittently, is the twelfth-century B.C.E. settlement stratum of Hala Sultan Tekke-Vizakia under Professor Emeritus Paul Åström (cf. Åström 2001, 65). Of the "new" field-projects the one which holds some promise for the twelfth century B.C.E. is the reinvestigation of the site of Episkopi-Bamboula, currently conducted by Professor Gisela Walberg (University of Cincinnati).

Part I

Settlement History and the Inadequacy of "Single-Factor Explanations"[4]

In Cypriot archaeology, the twelfth century B.C.E. is represented by LC IIIA. Its absolute age range covers the best part of the twelfth century, from ca. 1200 (see Manning et al. 2001, 328) to ca. 1125/1100 B.C.E. (a frequently used, but weak and unsubstantiated, absolute date). LC IIIA ought to be regarded as the last phase of the island's Late Bronze culture. LC IIIB, in spite of its name,[5] is much better suited as the initial phase of a fully blown Early Iron culture than as the ultimate phase of the Late Bronze in Cyprus (cf. Iacovou 1988, 84; 2001, 87, 89; Sherratt 2000, 82).

Our assessment of the island's twelfth-century B.C.E. archaeological landscape should not be biased by the preconception that "events" in Cyprus are, or ought to be, associated to any considerable degree with events in the Levant or in the Aegean (*pace* Karageorghis 1992, 85; Bunimovitz 1998, 105). Let us also be reminded of Sandars' words of wisdom that "it is even more hazardous to attempt to bring Cyprus into line with the Egyptian record of events" (1985, 174). The grand event itself, if by that term we agree to describe the "collapse" or "systems-failure"—and not simply "decline" or "destruction" (Dever 1992, 106)—of the Late Bronze empires and urban city-states, was certainly the same; quite naturally, however, it triggered different processes in the geopolitical entity of the island of Cyprus more so than it did in the Levant or the Aegean. In other words, that is why we do not have in twelfth-century B.C.E. Cyprus either a Philistine or a LH IIIC, post-palatial Mycenaean cultural phenomenon of the sort that archaeology traces in Palestine and Aegean Greece respectively. According to Dever, "the changes that ushered in the new era at the end of the Bronze Age were gradual, lasting ca. 1250–1150 B.C.E. These were so varied from site to site that a regional approach is necessary to comprehend the overall shift from the Bronze to the Iron Age" (1992, 92).

In order to comprehend the island's response to the main, Mediterranean-wide event, we have to take into consideration its individual history. In summary, this would be Cyprus's comparatively late development of an urban culture (cf. Coleman et al. 1996, xi–xii; Herscher 1996, 6–7) and the fact that to the very end of the Late Bronze Age it does not seem to have grown into a unitary state

4. Dever 1992, 92.

5. There is no unanimity as to what may constitute the cultural context of LC IIIB. The argument over its definition will not be resolved without a significant increase of ceramic material

(cf. Merrillees 1992; Keswani 1993, 74; 1996, 234). Even Enkomi, the presumed archaic or earliest state (Peltenburg 1996, 27), which was founded at the beginning of LC I (ca. 1600 B.C.E.) and maintained control over the export of copper for the better part of the Late Bronze Age, did not establish an island-wide authority (Iacovou 2007, 16). The emergence of regionally based polities by the late-fourteenth century B.C.E. (cf. Muhly 1989, 303; Knapp 1997, 66) implies that an island-wide administrative system failed to be imposed (reviewed by Webb 1999, 305).

Unlike the Canaanite states, geographically their closest neighbors and culturally nearest kin, the newly urbanized Late Cypriot polities did not suffer Egyptian or any other foreign control (cf. Dever 1992, 101–2; Bunimovitz 1998, 104–5). Cyprus remained politically independent from Egypt and the Hittite Empire (Cadogan 1998, 12–13).[6] The island's phenomenal immunity from direct political interference by the second-millennium land-based superpowers becomes a historically approachable factor in the first millennium B.C.E., when the evidence renders viable an assessment of the relation of the Iron Age polities (the city-kingdoms) to the Neo-Assyrian Empire. In this instance, we can see how and why the Cypriot rulers were able to retain a presumptuous political independence (Stylianou 1989, 390; Yon and Malbran-Labat 1995, 173).

Let us now concentrate on the following dictum, similar versions of which are still encountered in the literature—and since this workshop is dedicated to the memory of Moshe Dothan let me quote from his and Trude Dothan's monograph: "The sudden appearance of Mycenaean IIIC1b pottery there [Cyprus], apparently in association with the destruction and rebuilding of the major Cypriot cities, had led the archaeologists working there to associate it with the arrival of Aegean immigrants from the Greek mainland after the destruction of the Mycenaean palaces" (T. Dothan and M. Dothan 1992, 162). In reverse order we should examine: a) how truly sudden was the appearance of Aegean-style pottery; and b) the validity of the destruction and rebuilding scenario. I start with the latter.

The LC IIC/LC IIIA Juncture: Closures without Destruction

In a generic description of the late thirteenth-century B.C.E. human environment of Cyprus, neither extensive natural catastrophes, nor island-wide human-gener-

---

from different sites, which can be stratigraphically associated with an interim—post-LC IIIA, pre-Cypro-Geometric I—phase.

6. "The claimed Hittite control of Cyprus (if Alassiya is Cyprus) is unidentifiable in the archaeological record" (Cadogan 1998, 12). "No archaeological evidence has been uncovered as yet to corroborate the Hittite claims of their sovereignty over the island" (Bunimovitz 1998, 104).

ated destruction constitute a determining factor. The archaeologically tangible "historical" phenomenon, which determines the end of the thirteenth century and equally the transition to the twelfth century, is the closure of numerous Late Cypriot settlements: primary as well as secondary and tertiary centers were abandoned but the excavation record does not support the assumption that these sites suffered massive, deliberate destruction prior to their abandonment.

In each case the "abandonment event" is dated either shortly before the end of LC IIC or soon after the inception of LC IIIA. Why? The chronology of a Late Cypriot site's abandonment does not depend on strict cross-island comparisons of stratified settlement deposits, but rather on the types and the relative quantities of Aegean-style pottery recovered from the respective site. The abandonment is assigned to the one or other end of the LC IIC/IIIA juncture depending primarily on the presence or absence of "Mycenaean IIIC1b" pottery. It is important to remember why this Aegean-style pottery has been diagnosed for so long as the earliest LH IIIC-style pottery of local (Cypriot) manufacture: The term "Mycenaean IIIC1b" was established by Furumark who wished to underline that, stylistically as well as chronologically, the introduction of LH IIIC-style pottery in Cyprus had missed the early phase, namely [Furumark's] "Mycenaean IIIC1a" (Furumark 1944, 261; 1965, 115). It was this view on the stylistic correlation of locally made LH IIIC to Aegean-made LH IIIC pottery that determined the sequence of events (therefore also their relative chronology) at Enkomi. Dikaios associated the (presumed) absence of "Mycenaean IIIC1a" with a "short break" between Enkomi Level IIB, which was destroyed in LC IIC, and Enkomi Level IIIA, Enkomi's earliest LC IIIA level (1969–1971, 487).[7]

Although this interpretation was meant to refer exclusively to Enkomi, and could also accommodate Sinda (below), it acquired a formulaic potency: "Mycenaean IIIC1b" was *de facto* expected to mark the reconstruction that followed the destruction of a LC IIC level at the end of the thirteenth century B.C.E.[8] This in its turn amplified the destructions (natural or man-made) and propagated the view that the Late Cypriot settlement structure suffered greatly at the end of the thirteenth century (during the LC IIC/IIIA transition), either by natural catastrophes

7. There is a difference of opinion between Iacovou (1988, 10–11) and Kling (1989, 32–33) as to the relative chronology of Dikaios' Enkomi Levels IIIA–C, which stems from the definition of LC IIIA and LC IIIB respectively (cf. Iacovou 1989, 52).

8. Hence, the preliminary assessment of "events" at Kition (cf. Karageorghis 1976, 58–59) differs from the final interpretation: "We cannot therefore attribute the rebuilding in Area II to a destruction, natural or otherwise, of the earlier structures" (Karageorghis and Demas 1985, 92; also Karageorghis 1990b, 20).

or by the Sea Peoples' activity.[9] Thus "a major episode of disruption followed by cultural change" (Sherratt 1991, 186) was identified throughout the island.

Today this notion is almost entirely behind us since the increasing number of sites, which were closed and abandoned without evidence of destruction during LC IIC/IIIA, require that we propose alternative historical interpretations to account for their demise, and that we classify the case of Enkomi in a different category: that of Late Cypriot settlements that were not abandoned. "Despite the setback of the abandonments and destructions at the end of LC IIC, the Cypriots continued doing what they had been doing in the 13th century" (Cadogan 1998, 13), and therefore Enkomi, along with Hala Sultan Tekke, Kition, and Palaepaphos thrived as the urban centers of twelfth-century B.C.E. Cyprus (below).

In her review of Cypriot sites and the scholarship pertaining to pottery classification and relative chronology, Barbara Kling prudently remarks that, in order to parallel the cultural break associated with the destruction of the Mycenaean palatial system in the Aegean—inherent in the LH IIIB to LH IIIC transition—"the definition of the LCIIC/IIIA transition, in fact, evolved from the ceramic one to the stratigraphic and historical one" (Kling 1989, 79). Thus a dramatic ceramic change had to be borne by this seemingly momentous passage from LC IIC to LC IIIA.

Kling herself advocates as a temporary working principle "the quantitative ceramic definition to distinguish these periods" (Kling 1989, 80–81; criticized by Sherratt 1991, 190). Based on this principle, the abandoned Late Cypriot sites fall into two groups. The first (early?) group is formed by those sites where none of the stylistic ceramic features regarded as characteristic of "Mycenaean IIIC1b" elsewhere in Cyprus have been noted (Kling 1989, 60). Prime type sites of this group are Kalavassos-Ayios Dhimitrios (South 1989; 1995; 1996) and Maroni-Vournes (Cadogan 1989; 1996) in the Vasilikos Valley. The abandonment of these two settlements—where readily distinguishable industrial production (mainly for olive oil) and storage complexes of ashlar masonry have been excavated—is assigned to LC IIC because no "Mycenaean IIIC1b" pottery considered diagnostic of the next phase, namely LC IIIA, had appeared prior to their abandonment.[10]

9. Notice how often "patterns of destruction and settlement" in Cyprus become *a priori* related to newcomers (cf. Bunimovitz 1998, 103).

10. In the West, Myrtou-Pigadhes, considered to have been the most extensive Late Cypriot settlement in the region (of which Joan du Plat Taylor excavated a relatively small area with an early LC IIA–IIB intramural cult place), was an abandoned town in LC IIIA; only a cult site may have been functioning (cf. Webb 1999, 35–37, 44–53). For short reviews on the history of other Late Cypriot settlements, consult Karageorghis 1990b.

Then there is the more complex and less well-defined case of the second (later?) group of abandoned Late Cypriot sites: Those believed to have survived a while longer into the next phase. Their abandonment is assigned to an early stage of LC IIIA on the evidence of Aegean-style ceramic features that are not categorized as "Mycenaean IIIC1b" because they are considered of less pure "Mycenaean" origin (Sherratt 1998, 303). Besides the fact that the repertory of shapes for these ceramics can vary from site to site, they are neither consistently nor unanimously described in the same ceramic terms. In the end, the same shape may be classified either as Late Mycenaean IIIB or as Decorated Late Cypriot III while both can fit under the umbrella term White Painted Wheelmade III (cf. Kling 1989, 1–2; Sherratt 1991, 186 nn. 2–3).

Irrespective of the controversy over ceramic definitions, what these Late Cypriot sites seem to have in common is that neither the transition to LC IIIA, nor their eventual demise and abandonment is marked by whole-scale destruction. Prime sites of this category are Kourion-Bamboula (Weinberg 1983, 1–3, fig. 1; Benson 1972, 3–9; Kling 1989, 17–23) and Alassa, ten kilometers to the north, up the river Kouris (Hadjisavvas 1989)—the inland settlement with the impressive ashlar buildings that came as a shock to Cypriot archaeology when its discovery in the early 1980s shattered the pattern of coastal-only urban polities (cf. Herscher 1996, 6).[11] Both sites were inhabited since LC I.[12] Following a destruction-free transition to LC IIIA, burial customs remain unchanged (cf. Kling 1989, 23; Hadjisavvas 1989, 34–41). Then, "at the close of the Bronze Age and more precisely during LC IIIA the settlement [Alassa] was abandoned. There is no evidence of violent destruction or fire" (Hadjisavvas 1989, 41).[13]

---

11. Alassa-Paliotaverna, the site of the ashlar buildings, is at an altitude of 260 meters; the area excavated is 1,410 square meters. Alassa-Pano Mandilaris (a small part of the LC IIC–IIIA settlement) is at an altitude of 240 meters; the excavated area of 1,000 square meters includes eight tombs of which seven were found sealed under the hard surface of the square and the street (Hadjisavvas 1989, 34–41).

12. The earliest settlement remains at Bamboula date to LC IA; a major architectural reorganization and expansion took place in LC IIC/IIIA. "Although the LCIIIA levels in which the Decorated Late Cypriot III ware predominated represented a major reconstruction effort on the site, the excavators regarded this phase to be continuous from LCIIC" (Kling 1989, 23). "Alassa preserves no traces of violent destruction, abandonment or reoccupation. The site was continuously inhabited from LCIB to LCIIIA" (Hadjisavvas 1991, 173).

13. In the West, Myrtou-Pigadhes, which is considered to have been the most extensive Late Cypriot settlement in the region, was an abandoned town in LC IIIA; only a cult site may have been functioning at the site where Joan du Plat Taylor had excavated a relatively small area with an early LC IIA–IIB intramural cult place (cf. Webb 1999, 35–37, 44–53).

Bamboula and Alassa are assumed to have lasted into LC IIIA on the basis of such Aegean-style (fast-wheel) pottery shapes as the shallow bowl and jug (cf. Hadjisavvas 1991, fig. 17.4–7). To the extent that they have been excavated, however, Bamboula and Alassa share the phenomenal absence of an Aegean shape that in Cyprus and the Levant has acquired a degree of notoriety: the LH IIIC skyphos (Kling 1989, 86; Hadjisavvas 1991, 179). Is this a chronological indicator or a regional phenomenon (cf. Sherratt 1991, 190)?

The difficulty is readily brought to the foreground as soon as we compare the LC IIIA abandonment horizon of Bamboula and Alassa to that of Athienou, excavated in 1971–1972 by Trude Dothan and Amnon Ben-Tor. Situated inland, close to twenty kilometers southeast of Nicosia, Athienou-Bamboulari tis Koukkouninas, a 2,500-square meter extramural "cultic site connected with metal working" (T. Dothan and Ben-Tor 1983, 140), was abandoned in LC IIIA, following a destruction-free transition from LC IIC to LC IIIA (cf. Webb 1999, 21–29). At Athienou, twelve vases constitute the diagnostic Aegean-style ceramic group of LC IIIA and half of these are skyphoi (T. Dothan and Ben-Tor 1983, 116, fig. 53; Kling 1989, 47, 84, 227, 359).[14]

In conclusion, many Late Cypriot sites suffered abandonment in LC IIC/IIIA but they do not provide indication for wide-scale destruction caused either by a devastating natural catastrophe—that is, the earthquakes at Mycenae (cf. French 1998, 4)—or a violent enemy action, as was the case at Ras Shamra-Ugarit which, due to the severity of the destruction it suffered at the very beginning of the twelfth century B.C.E., was never reinhabited (cf. Yon 1992, 117). This is particularly well exemplified in the case of the primary settlement of Kalavassos-Ayios Dhimitrios where "most of the town appears to have been peacefully yet thoroughly deserted but, a fire in Building X [the ashlar-built administrative and storage center] at or shortly after the abandonment may be connected with the more widespread destructions at some other sites" (South 1989, 322–23). Below we will try to find out which these undefined "other sites" may be.

Eventually, the "impasse" reached in the process of trying to anchor a Late Cypriot site's closure to LC IIC or LC IIIA on the basis of Aegean-style ceramics, highlighted the fact that ceramic developments in Cyprus during the thirteenth and twelfth centuries were altogether distinct from the regional events that caused the demise and abandonment of a whole hierarchy of settlements in Late Bronze

---

14. Originally a LC II cult complex with a bronze-working facility (Stratum III), Athienou was subsequently (in LC IIIA) given over to the secondary processing and refining of copper ore and the storage of agricultural commodities. The ceramic assemblage in LC IIIA (Stratum II) no longer suggests ritual activity; it is in keeping with the industrial character of the site (Webb 1999, 29).

Cyprus. This was first emphasized by Susan Sherratt (1981). At that point, she was concerned with Enkomi and pointed out that the development of Aegean-style ceramics was independent from the periodic episodes of destruction and rebuilding of the Enkomi levels (reference in Iacovou 1988, 11 n. 166).[15] Once a rigid ceramological distinction between LC IIC and LC IIIA was removed—and was replaced instead by "ceramic fluidity" (Sherratt 1991, 187)—the way was opened to acknowledge the striking cultural continuities that define the transition to LC IIIA. These continuities—for instance, the use of ashlar masonry, the employment of Cypro-Minoan signs, the traditional burial custom of inhumation in intramural chamber tombs—transcend the passage to the twelfth century B.C.E. and, together with some novel aspects, characterize the settlements, which survived in LC IIIA.

In fact, if it were feasible to record from stratified deposits the temporal stylistic evolution of Aegean-style ceramics in Cyprus, then the LC IIC/IIIA site abandonment could be "measured" as an episode of some duration: A horizon of settlement closures, which reached a peak during the LC IIC/IIIA juncture but did not bring the Late Cypriot culture (or the island's Late Bronze Age) to an end; not for another century.

The Twelfth-Century B.C.E. Settlement Landscape of Cyprus

Cultural continuities are identified and can be studied at some length in the twelfth-century B.C.E. strata of the few primary sites, which were not abandoned either at the end of LC IIC or after the transition to LC IIIA. These sites traverse the full length of LC IIIA; on them rests our knowledge of the island's twelfth-century landscape. They are Enkomi and Sinda in the east; Kition and Hala Sultan Tekke in the south; and Palaepaphos in the southwest. Sinda had been abandoned in LC IIIA (Furumark 1965, 115–16; Furumark and Adelman 2003, 46, 64–65, 73). Enkomi and Hala Sultan Tekke were completely abandoned (never again to be resettled) during the transition to LC IIIB. Kition and Palaepaphos survived well beyond the twelfth century B.C.E. In the long run, they became the capitals of Iron Age polities. To this date, however, Late Bronze to Early Iron continuity of occupation has been recorded stratigraphically only in Kition. In Area II of the temple precinct, the earliest architectural remains date to LC IIC and occu-

15. Sherratt rejected the notion that "a neat line" could be drawn between LC IIC and LC IIIA either on ceramic grounds or on grounds of a break in cultural continuity; she pleaded that "ceramic developments on the one hand, and the chequered fortunes of individual sites on the other" should be viewed "as two quite separate continua whose relationship to one another is no more than incidental" (Sherratt 1991, 191).

pation lasts uninterruptedly until the Cypro-Geometric I period (Karageorghis 1985, 24).

I briefly wish to mention here and thus add (though with caution) a sixth site to the above list, Idalion-Ambeleri, a fortified inland settlement that seems to have been established on the summit of the Ambeleri Hill in LC IIIA (Gjerstad et al. 1934, 460, Plan V; Ălin 1978). The Late Bronze remains, excavated in the 1930s by the Swedish-Cyprus Expedition, contain Aegean-style pottery (cf. Kling 1989, 11, 59). Like Sinda, Idalion was not a primary urban center (reviewed by Webb 1999, 84–91); unlike Sinda, however, it may represent the inaugural phase of a long and successful establishment on Ambeleri. In the Iron Age, the site held the administrative center of the kingdom of Idalion, but the interim periods have yet to be clearly documented stratigraphically (consult Hadjicosti 1997; 1999).

The above-mentioned sites provide as much as 90 percent of the published ceramic data that justify use of the term locally produced LH IIIC in twelfth-century B.C.E. Cyprus. As a result of this overstated qualification, however, the extent, the character and the function of their excavated sectors have received insufficient consideration. To begin with, it should be noted that none of the five sites is in any way a "new" LC IIIA settlement. Having been founded as early as MC III/LC I, Enkomi may be the oldest settlement though evidence from tombs suggests that Hala Sultan Tekke had also been founded in MC III/LC I and Palaepaphos in LC I (cf. Karageorghis 1990a). Kition was not established long before LC IIC and the same seems to be true of the walled town of Sinda (cf. Kling 1989, 35; Furumark and Adelman 2003, 65). Do these five sites provide evidence for a settlement-wide destruction of their LC IIC strata before the transition to LC IIIA? To answer this we need to review the extent of their investigation as well as their publication record individually.

Enkomi-Ayios Iakovos

Everybody knows Enkomi, yet not many realize that the "archaic state" of Cyprus and the settlement where Aegean-style ceramic material was identified to such an impressive extent as early as the 1950s (Coche de la Ferté 1951) remains to this date the only Late Cypriot settlement in the island that can be considered adequately excavated (fig. 1). The total area (400 meters north-to-south by 350 meters east-to-west) enclosed within its late thirteenth-century B.C.E. monumental rampart—and it is the only primary urban center where the line of a city-wall has been traced almost in its entirety—is 140,000/150,000 square meters. Nearly one sixth of the walled town has been excavated by the combined efforts of two missions: the French mission under Claude Schaeffer and the Cyprus mission of the Department of Antiquities under Porphyrios Dikaios. For as long as a decade (between the years 1948–1958), the two worked in parallel in separate sectors

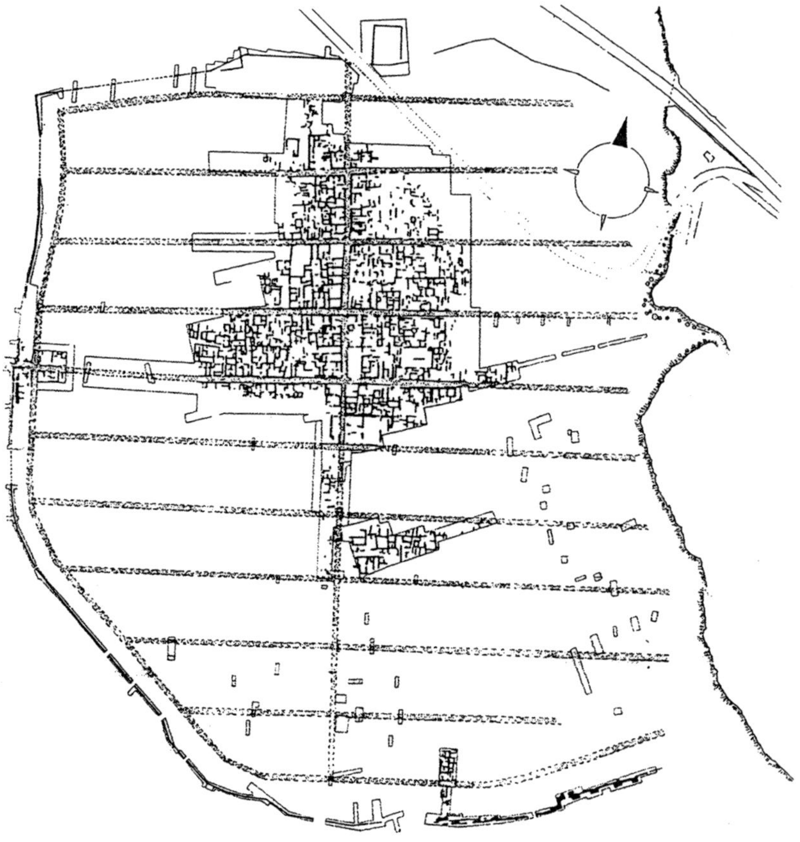

Fig. 1: Ground plan of Enkomi (modified from Courtois, Lagarce, and Lagarce 1986, fig. 1).

of the site (cf. Courtois, Lagarce, and Lagarce 1986, 1–2; Lagarce 1993, 91–103). Half a century later, the vertical and horizontal extent of Enkomi's investigation is unique as regards the archaeology of Cyprus. It is the only Late Cypriot site where excavation has established the settlement's continuity stratigraphically (as opposed to indirectly, through the evidence of scattered tombs and trial trenches) from its foundation in MC III/LC I to its (gradual) abandonment at the end of the twelfth century B.C.E., during the transition from LC IIIA to LC IIIB, when it began to shift to the nearby site of Salamis. Furthermore, within the "cyclopean" rampart the excavated sectors have established households and sanctuaries, and industrial production areas and workshops for specialized crafts, all within an impressive urban grid system commanded by two main communication arteries, one running north–south, the other east–west, in alignment with city-gates (cf. Courtois, Lagarce, and Lagarce 1986, 2–7).

In the opinion of the late Dikaios, the rich and prosperous LC IIC level (Level IIB) was violently destroyed (Dikaios 1969–1971, 485); the construction of the "cyclopean" fortification wall, however, predated the destruction (Dikaios 1969–1971, 512); ashlar-built constructions, on the other hand, appeared as a novelty of the post-destruction horizon (Level IIIA) simultaneously with local "Mycenaean IIIC1b" pottery which became, from then on, the prevailing pottery in the town. Thus, the transition from LC IIC to LC IIIA was identified as the single most crucial moment in Enkomi's five-hundred-year-long settlement history. It may have been so but only as far as the site's individual history is concerned.

Sinda-Sira Tas

Located on a rock plateau in the heart of the vast eastern plain of Mesaoria and only fifteen kilometers from Enkomi, Sinda was not chosen because of its naturally defensible topography. It was rather established as a fortress in order to guard the copper-route and protect this rich agricultural region, which is Enkomi's hinterland. Karageorghis, who had suggested earlier that Sinda may have been built by newcomers whose ultimate aim was the occupation of nearby Enkomi, later on admitted to the idea that "Sinda was built and fortified in order to guard the route through which copper ore from the Troodos copper mines reached Enkomi" (Karageorghis 1990b, 12–13; also Åström in Furumark and Adelman 2003, 71).

A Late Cypriot walled settlement (250 meters east-to-west by 200 meters north-to-south) with an 800-meter long "cyclopean" rampart (mostly robbed of its stone construction), which encloses an area of 46,500 square meters, Sinda-Sira Tas[16] is Furumark's own site (Furumark and Adelman 2003, 26, 69). Generations of Cypriot archaeology students come to stare in disbelief at Sinda's ground plan (Furumark 1965, 103, fig. 3) when, after years of reading about the significance of the Aegean-style ceramics of Sinda, they are confronted with the reality of the settlement's excavation record. Besides exposing the city-gate, Furumark's excavation of this walled town amounted to sinking a series of trenches in the northern corner and in the southwest part of the site.[17] Under the circumstances it was a lot

16. Sira Tas means "row of stones" and refers to the remains of the city wall. "The area within the City Wall forms an irregular polygon with an extension of approximately 46.500 square meters" (Furumark and Adelman 2003, 26).

17. Inside the wall, great parts were bare rock; excavation work was consequently concentrated in three main areas: the northwest corner of the town, the main gate, and an area in the southwest part (Furumark and Adelman 2003, 20); in his preface to the recently published vol-

of work for a field project that did not last more than a month: from December 1947 to January 1948.

There is evidence for a settlement that must have preceded the construction of the circuit wall, but Sinda Period I was founded from the start as a fortified town with massive walls (Furumark 1965, 105; Dikaios 1969–1971, 486). It suffered a violent catastrophe contemporary with Enkomi's Level IIB but its "cyclopean" wall survived the destruction (Furumark and Adelman 2003, 65). In accord with Enkomi Level IIIA, Sinda Period II, the LC IIIA rebuilding, was characterized by the use of "Mycenaean IIIC1b" ceramics (Kling 1989, 34–35). Period II also met with destruction but the diagnostic pottery in the final town period (Period III) was still "Mycenaean IIIC1b" in style (Furumark 1965, 107) and it was in use when Sinda was finally abandoned sometime in the twelfth century B.C.E. (Furumark 1965, 115). According to Furumark and Adelman, "the site was abandoned by its inhabitants, apparently without any archaeologically discernible disaster. This abandonment took place before the so-called Proto-White Painted and related fabrics of Myc.IIIC1c date had appeared" (2003, 64).

Hala Sultan Tekke-Vizakia

The Late Bronze Age town of Hala Sultan Tekke (fig. 2), by the Larnaca salt lake, is estimated to have extended over an area of 276,000 square meters (Åström 1986, 8; elsewhere 240,000 square meters: Åström 1996, 10).[18] It appears at first sight to have been considerably larger than Enkomi but the estimated extent in hectares or square meters of the two may not be directly comparable since the criteria for a size-estimate for Tekke are nebulous: There is, according to its excavator, no trace of a town wall to contain the urban center (Åström 1996, 10). It is considered to have probably been inhabited from as early as Enkomi, namely from MC III/LC I (Åström 1985a, 174), but again this rests entirely on the evidence provided by tombs and surface collection of sherd material; it has not been traced stratigraphically in the town's levels (Karageorghis 1990b, 16). Vertical soundings below the LC IIIA settlement levels have established that a LC II-period settlement is in fact buried underneath (Åström 1986, 15). The character and extent of this thirteenth-century B.C.E. settlement are unknown and there is

ume of Sinda, Adelman explains that Furumark was not able to carry out the control excavations he planned (Furumark and Adelman 2003, 9).

18. Around twenty-seven hectares according to Swiny (1981, 78) while Kling thinks that "the Bronze Age settlement site covers an extensive area, estimated at 20–40 hectares" (Kling 1989, 55).

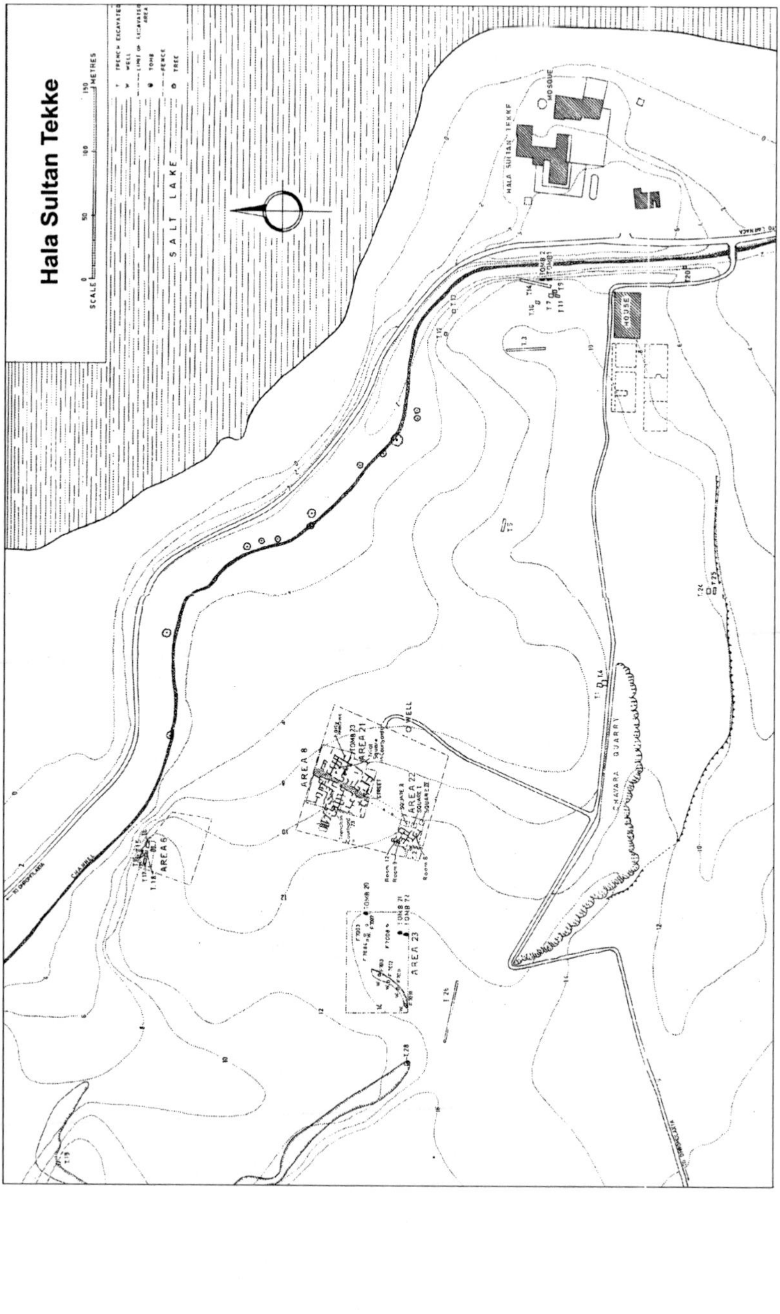

Fig. 2: Hala Sultan Tekke (from Åström 1989 by kind permission of Paul Åström).

to this date no substantial evidence to support a destruction that may have preceded the establishment of the LC IIIA urban center.[19]

Horizontal investigation of the LC IIIA town within these twenty-five hectares is minimal by comparison to Enkomi. Nevertheless, it was laid out in a roughly rectilinear, grid system, "a so-called 'Hippodamic' town plan with streets at right angles" (Åström 1996, 10). It is appropriate to note here that the same principles of urban planning—with domestic quarters laid out "on sound principles of town planning along long straight streets provided with good drains" (South 1996, 41)—were identified in Kalavassos-Ayios Dhimitrios (estimated settlement size: 11.5 hectares), which, like Tekke, has no evidence of a defensive wall. Kalavassos-Ayios Dhimitrios, however, was already abandoned in LC IIC (above). Urban planning does not, therefore, count as a novelty exclusively associated with the twelfth-century B.C.E. horizon of Cyprus.

Hala Sultan Tekke, like Enkomi, was eventually abandoned towards the end of the twelfth century B.C.E. The silting of their respective harbors, rather than any violent attack, must have played a decisive role (Lagarce 1993, 91; Gifford 1980). In fact, Åström maintains that "the lagoon before the site [of Tekke] silted up and became a salt-lake about 1000 B.C." (Åström 1985a, 175). Neither Tekke nor Enkomi were ever resettled, nor were they ever disturbed by anything other than agricultural activities. I am only stressing this in order to underline the completely different settlement history of Kition and Palaepaphos (below).

Kition

Situated on a low plateau (600 meters by 1,500 meters), less than ten meters above sea level, Kition is not as old as Enkomi or Tekke (fig. 3): Its earliest settlement remains (namely Kition Floor IV) date to LC II (Karageorghis and Demas 1985, 3–4). The excavated area of the Late Cypriot settlement is nearly 6,000 square meters and is almost entirely concentrated in the temple precinct (Area II), where 5,265 square meters of the sacred quarter were excavated; in Area I the extent of the excavated sector is only 22 meters by 17 meters. The excavators state in the definitive publication of the Bronze Age levels of Kition: "There is no evidence from floor IV to indicate that it was violently destroyed or abandoned" (Karageorghis and Demas 1985, 92). Thus, the LC IIIA period (Kition Floors IIIA–III) is described as a prosperous "new era" with a grand-scale rebuilding plan (Karageorghis and Demas 1985, 38). The great Temple 1 (28 meters by 18.5 meters) with its finely worked drafted ashlar monoliths—one of two unsur-

19. The excavator believes he has evidence for a destruction that affected the LC IIIA levels (Åström 1985b, 9; 1986, 11).

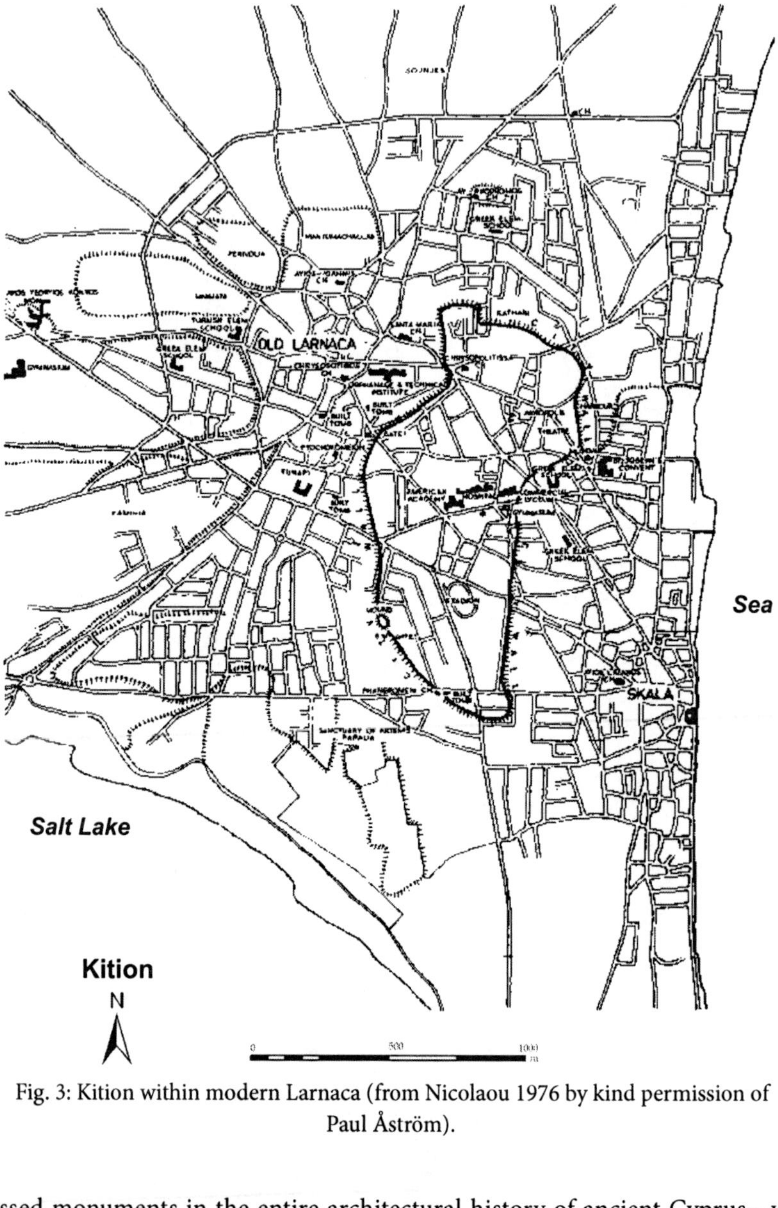

Fig. 3: Kition within modern Larnaca (from Nicolaou 1976 by kind permission of Paul Åström).

passed monuments in the entire architectural history of ancient Cyprus—was constructed for the LC IIIA floor.

Kition possessed a mud-brick rampart in LC IIC that was replaced by a "cyclopean" wall of conglomerate blocks in LC IIIA; a 125-meter long stretch of this wall was excavated in Area II and another 15 meters in Area IV (Karageorghis and Demas 1985, 86). The rest of the line of the city-wall is believed to follow the irregular perimeter of the plateau (Karageorghis and Demas 1985, 4). It has been traced and subsequently documented by Nicolaou (1976) around a huge area estimated at 700,000 square meters. This may in fact represent the maximum growth of the Iron Age urban center during the age of the Cypro-Phoenician kingdom but it is highly unlikely that it "constitutes the Late Bronze Age town of Kition" (Karageorghis and Demas 1985, 86).[20] Even if all the population of the old site of Tekke had been absorbed in LC IIIA by the newly founded (in LC IIC) and rapidly expanding Kition settlement, I have serious reservations that in the course of the twelfth-century B.C.E. Kition could have grown into an urban nucleus six times larger than the maximum size achieved by Enkomi after half a millennium of continuous habitation.[21]

It is time to acknowledge that we have no substantial evidence by which to defend the actual extent of the walled urban nucleus of Kition in the twelfth century. However, scholars working in Cyprus have taken it for granted that Kition grew overnight into a walled mega-site of 70 hectares in LC IIIA (cf. Swiny 1981, 78; Merrillees 1992, 328; Knapp 1996, 80). This belief has contributed to the dissemination of a construct regarding the relative size of LC IIC and LC IIIA settlements. Hence colleagues from abroad have been misled to consider Enkomi, at about 15 hectares, as one of the smaller coastal towns of Cyprus because "Kition is estimated to cover 70 hectares" (Bunimovitz 1998, 104). The problem is further accentuated by a second similar construct that presents Palaepaphos as a 65-hectare urban center (Knapp 1996, 80 repeated in Knapp 1997, 53, fig. 5).

Palaepaphos

Palaepaphos possesses the second of the two monumental temene (cf. Webb 1999, 58–84) constructed in the island during the LC IIC/IIIA juncture (fig. 4). The history of the settlement is beset by many more unanswered problems than Kition. Karageorghis underlined them in his handy monograph on *The End of the Late Bronze Age in Cyprus*: "The city site of Late Bronze Age Palaepaphos still awaits excavation. Not until then will we be able to study the stratigraphy of the

20. "Kition was a walled city from the Late Bronze Age down to the end of the Classical period and the boundaries of its fortifications have been traced more or less throughout their perimeter. A large portion of the northernmost part of the City Wall has been exposed during regular excavations, other small parts have been uncovered during building operations and the rest has been traced hypothetically through surface survey" (Karageorghis and Demas 1985, 3).

21. Alison South (2002, 70) has in fact pledged in print an article entitled, "The Size of Bronze Age Kition: A Factoid" (to appear in *Report of the Department of Antiquities, Cyprus*).

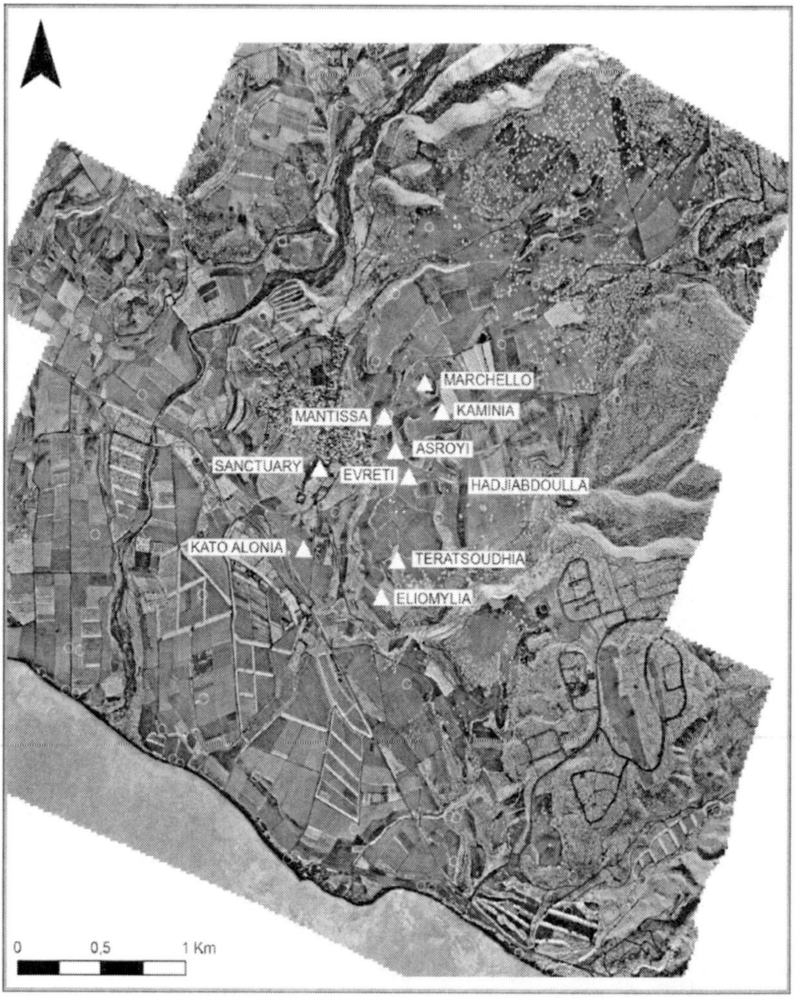

Fig. 4: Orthophotomap of Palaepaphos with Late Cypriot burial and settlement clusters in relation to the Sanctuary of Aphrodite (courtesy of The Palaepaphos Urban Landscape Project 2010).

site and the succession of events in the city's history—in particular what happened during the crucial periods LCIIC and LCIIIA" (1990b, 15).

After a century of cautious work at Palaepaphos, the temenos with its megalithic ashlar blocks and orthostats remains the sole architectural evidence from the Late Bronze Age (Maier 1984, 8–15; Maier and von Wartburg 1985, 146–52, with bibliography). The topographical extent of the Late Cypriot urban center of Palaepaphos is much harder to estimate than that of Kition since, like Tekke, it has not been established whether it was contained within a city rampart in LC IIC/IIIA. With the exception of a small number of vases and other items recovered from the temenos—which are associated with the LC IIC/IIIA transition—Aegean-style material has been recovered in appreciable quantities from settlement debris found in wells (refuse pits) in the terrain to the east (localities of Asproyi and Evreti) and northeast (localities of Kaminia, Mantissa, and Marcello) of the temenos (cf. Kling 1989, 44–46). In the characteristically Late Cypriot custom, tombs were constructed within the settlement (Maier and Karageorghis 1984, 80). Thus the localities of Asproyi and Evreti in particular "were at least partly covered by living quarters of the period" (Maier 1997, 101). It should be noted, however, that only a handful of vases from the tombs are described as "Mycenaean IIIC"; the majority of Aegean-style ceramics from mortuary context belong to the "Decorated Late Cypriot III" variety (Maier 1973, 72; Kling 1989, 46).

The settlements of Kition and Palaepaphos were not abandoned either during the transition to the first millennium B.C.E., or to this date. Kition is the ancient equivalent of modern-day Larnaca. Thus, it is highly unlikely that a domestic quarter of Late Cypriot Kition, large enough to allow comparisons with the urban schemes of contemporary Enkomi and Tekke, could be recovered in the future.[22] Palaepaphos, on the other hand, despite the fact that it was densely inhabited during the Iron Age, is still today a promising, largely agricultural landscape (outside the modern village of Kouklia), one that with a carefully designed approach could be made to render a few of the much sought-after answers to the archaeology of twelfth-century B.C.E. Cyprus (Iacovou 2008b).[23]

New and Short-Lived LC IIC and/or LC IIIA Sites

The review of Cyprus's twelfth-century B.C.E. settlement landscape is completed with the third group of Late Cypriot sites, those that have neither a past nor a

22. The excavated plot in Kition Area I is too small (22 meters by 17 meters) to allow for speculations as to urban planning (Karageorghis and Demas 1985, 5–18).

23. Following the transfer of the kingdom's capital to Nea Paphos sometime in the fourth century B.C.E., Palaepaphos was never again to regain the status of an urban polity. After the closure of the "pagan" activities at the temenos in late antiquity, alternatively in the Early Christian era, it became a small agricultural community that, during the medieval period, belonged to the royal estate of the Lusignans. The area of the temenos was accorded a relatively high degree of protection by the Department of Antiquities fairly early on (cf. Maier 1984; Maier and Karageorghis 1984; Maier and von Wartburg 1985).

future: They are as new as they are short-lived establishments (Karageorghis 2001, 1). This category is at the moment represented by two sites: Pyla-Kokkinokremos and Maa-Palaeokastro. The former bears the mark of a singularly short-lived site that was founded "a few decades prior to its abandonment, namely at the end of the 13th century B.C." (Karageorghis 1990b, 10). The latter is an exclusively twelfth-century B.C.E. settlement to the extent that it was founded "at the very end of LCIIC" and abandoned before the appearance of Aegean-style ceramics "which herald the LCIIIB period" (Karageorghis 1990b, 26). If, in accord with Karageorghis (1990b, 9–10, 26), we allocate Maa-Palaeokastro a fifty-year lifespan and thus an even shorter one for Kokkinokremos, both sites become veritable "time capsules."

Pyla-Kokkinokremos

Only 800 meters from the south coast, the rocky plateau of Kokkinokremos rises steeply from the low land at 63 meters above sea-level and commands a superb view of the sea and fertile plain. The area excavated on Kokkinokremos is barely 1,006 square meters with 106 square meters (Area I) excavated by Dikaios and 900 square meters (Area II) by Karageorghis (Karageorghis and Demas 1984, 6, 20). Although excavations were confined to these two sectors, it is stated categorically that "a surface survey has shown that the entire plateau was inhabited" (Karageorghis and Demas 1984, 4–5). If so, based on the plateau's maximum dimensions (600 meters by 450 meters: Karageorghis and Demas 1984, 3), Kokkinokremos must have been a settlement ranging between 200,000–270,000 square meters, therefore not only a considerably larger site than Enkomi, but as extensive as Hala Sultan Tekke is believed to have been.

Reservations as to its actual urban extent in LC IIC and LC IIIA notwithstanding, Hala Sultan Tekke was an old settlement (founded in MC III/LC I), which had every opportunity to grow into a 24–27 hectare town (though this has not been confirmed). Can we envision the growth of an equal-size settlement on top of Kokkinokremos when it did not last as long as fifty years? The architectural scheme of the excavated units suggests that the settlement did not undergo gradual growth: The whole operation was planned and executed at one time as a highly organized communal endeavor (Karageorghis and Demas 1984, 26).

Furthermore, the domestic nature of the structures estimated to have numbered at least two hundred units, indicates that it sheltered a stable community (Karageorghis and Demas 1984, 24). Geologically, however, there is no possibility for the plateau to have had water wells. Therefore water supplies for the needs of such an extensive settlement (and population) had to come from the plain below. There must have been a very good reason for the abandonment of the cluster of earlier Late Cypriot settlements-cum-cemeteries, e.g., Pyla-Verghi, Pyla-Steno, situated on fertile agricultural land on either side of the steep hill of Kokkinokremos (Karageorghis and Demas 1984, 5, nn. 5–6 and fig. 2). I do not necessarily wish to imply a direct relation between the inhabitants of these sites (they have not been thoroughly investigated; see Karageorghis 2001, 3) and the foundation or the founders of Kokkinokremos. I wish to underline, however, that the plain and the waterless cliff both presented options and that a conscious decision was made in favor of the latter, which was a naturally defensible site. This gives additional strength to the suggestion that Kokkinokremos was a refuge settlement founded under duress or during a crisis of insecurity. The area of Pyla is neither "remote" (*pace* Karageorghis 2001, 1), nor isolated from other contemporary urban centers: Its distance from Kition is hardly ten kilometers. Whoever was managing this one-phase, rapidly implemented building program on top of the plateau had a firm control over the human resources of Kokkinokremos. Could it not have been established by Kition itself?

At the end of the day, this one-floor settlement was abandoned in haste. Those who fled did not return to claim the hoards they had hidden and, besides scrap metal, a pair of silver bun-ingots was also left behind, an imported commodity of great value and of utmost rarity in Cyprus (Karageorghis and Demas 1984, 60–65). All the above features render Kokkinokremos a unique Late Cypriot settlement. It certainly affords little to no comparison with the location, function, and domestic and military architecture of the other new and short-lived site, Maa-Palaeokastro.

Maa-Palaeokastro

At a distance of 26 kilometers from the primary urban center of Palaepaphos, Maa-Palaeokastro, a long and narrow promontory isolated in the far west of the island, encompasses a considerably smaller area (maximum length of 450 meters by maximum width of 150 meters) than Kokkinokremos. Its 46,000 square meters (Karageorghis and Demas 1988, 1) were easily rendered defensible by the construction of a fifty-meter stretch of "cyclopean" wall on the landward side—its seaward equivalent is barely distinguishable (Karageorghis and Demas 1988, 51). The total area protected by this truly monumental rampart is of equal size to the settlement of Sinda (46,500 square meters), whose defensive architecture is of the same type and date. At Maa, however, the area excavated is adequate compared to Sinda's and it was furthermore promptly published upon completion of the excavation.

The foundation of Maa and the construction of its fortification, which like Sinda's had a dog-leg entrance, involved "a considerable organization of human resources" (Karageorghis and Demas 1988, 51–52). Maa is an austere and waterless site (Karageorghis and Demas 1988, 51 and fig. 1) with communal cooking facilities—it may have functioned as a fortified garrison camp—but it did employ ashlar blocks of poor quality in the construction of some of its first period (Floor II) units (Karageorghis and Demas 1988, 99). The destruction, which Maa Floor II is believed to have endured during the LC IIC/IIIA transition, had a distinctly different outcome compared to Enkomi's contemporary destruction: It was neither followed by a major reconstruction, nor did it promote Maa to an urban settlement. It resulted in the much poorer LC IIIA establishment of its second period (Floor I), which was shortly afterwards completely abandoned in the course of the twelfth century B.C.E.

It is worth noting that from Maa Floor II, which suffered destruction, a considerable number of used weapons such as daggers, arrowheads, and sling bullets of bronze were collected, which did not belong to hoards of scrap metal.[24] At Kokkinokremos, on the other hand, no weapons were found—except for fifty-five pebbles, which were perhaps used as sling bullets (Karageorghis and Demas 1984, 41, 110, 59).

The number of Aegean-style vases recovered from Kokkinokremos is eight—two skyphoi, two bell-craters, two amphoroid craters, one shallow bowl, and one jug (cf. Kling 1989, 225)—but, according to the excavators, not one sherd from the site belongs to the "Mycenaean IIIC1b" category (Karageorghis and Demas 1984, 66; see also Kling 1989, 63–64). This creates a quantitative and qualitative contrast with the Aegean-style ceramics of Maa-Palaeokastro where the inhabitants of Floor II were already using "Mycenaean IIIC1b" pottery "in fairly large quantities when their settlement was destroyed" (Karageorghis and Demas 1988, 256). In Floor I "Mycenaean IIIC1b" pottery predominates "at the expense of LCIIC wares" but its increase is not accompanied "by a discernible stylistic development" (Karageorghis and Demas 1988, 260).

Part II

Widespread Destructions?

Following the review in Part I, it has hopefully become clear that Cyprus has been erroneously described in the past as a land devastated by the nearly simultaneous destruction of its Late Bronze urban centers. As the evidence stands today—back in the 1980s I myself placed greater emphasis on settlement-wide destruction

---

24. Daggers: Karageorghis and Demas 1988, 232 no. 309 [pl. LXXXIII]; 235 no. 87 [pl. XCIII]; no. 451 [pl. LXIII]; arrowheads: Karageorghis and Demas 1988, 220 no.152; nos. 178, 180, 511 [pl. LXIII]; sling bullets: Karageorghis and Demas 1988, 223 nos. 262, 646.

(see Iacovou 1989)—destruction seems to have been regional and episodic. Of the primary urban centers only Enkomi may have suffered (always according to Dikaios) a whole-scale destruction during the LC IIC/IIIA juncture. Sinda, a secondary inland town and Enkomi's protégé, appears to have shared Enkomi's fate (Furumark and Adelman 2003, 65), while Maa-Palaeokastro, a garrison camp for all we know, was "violently destroyed by fire" at the beginning of LC IIIA (Karageorghis 1990b, 26). These contemporary, or near contemporary, destructions, as they have been identified in the material record of three very different (a primary coastal town, a secondary inland establishment, and a military outpost), albeit strongly fortified, settlements did not cause the permanent departure of their respective populations. All three sites continued to be inhabited and were eventually abandoned at different moments in the late-twelfth century B.C.E. without evidence of widespread violence. Further support regarding the non-violent or catastrophic abandonment of Enkomi is provided by a "new reading" of the sanctuary of the Ingot God by Jennifer Webb. Webb argues that the cult images of the Ingot God and the Horned God were not abandoned in the face of a hostile attack (*pace* Dikaios 1969–1971, 534); they were purposefully "cached" in the process of a ritual associated with the formal closure of their respective sanctuaries (Webb 2000, 77).

Consequently, extensive destruction, as claimed for Enkomi at the LC IIC/IIIA juncture, or extensive urban reorganization, as claimed for Kition, are not directly related to, nor responsible for, the appearance of Aegean-style material culture in the island.[25] Chronologically, the introduction of Aegean-style pottery precedes settlement abandonment (e.g., Kokkinokremos) or settlement disturbances (e.g., Enkomi) as much as it precedes urban enhancement (e.g., Kition). With this remark we can begin to address the Workshop's second theme, that is, "What is the context, nature and distribution of locally-produced Aegean-style material culture during the twelfth century?"

A Locally Produced Aegean-Style Pottery in Context

Aegean Late Helladic III-type pottery began to be imitated in Cyprus no later than the thirteenth century B.C.E. The LC IIC "Aegeanizing" ceramics were inspired to a considerable degree by the presence of imported Peloponnesian [Mycenaean] and Minoan pottery and local ceramic traditions (Kling 1989, 170; 2000, 281–82; Sherratt 1991, 193). In fact, the Pastoral Style is one of the ear-

25. On destruction and/or urban reorganization at this juncture, one should not fail to consult the extensive analysis in Karageorghis and Demas 1985, 267–77.

liest pictorial expressions of this ceramic phenomenon (Iacovou 2006a), which can be duly appreciated in the wider context of the introduction of wheelmade wares in the Late Cypriot pottery production. "Cyprus is apparently unique in its adoption of the fast potters' wheel as not only does the specialised production of handmade wares continue throughout the Late Cypriot but the wares for which the wheel was adopted continue to be manufactured in both handmade and wheelmade forms, with the same fabric and vessel types" (Crewe 2004, 2). This describes a phenomenal situation, which lasted from the beginning of LC I, when wheelmade pottery was first introduced to Cyprus as a Levantine innovation, until LC IIC. Not only did the pre-thirteenth century B.C.E. wheelmade types fail to replace the handmade wares, it was the two highly distinct handmade fine wares of Base-Ring and White Slip that were the prime export ceramics of Cyprus.

In the course of LC IIC and LC IIIA, however, settlement strata reveal a fascinating process through which both the handmade and wheelmade forms began to be integrated into a new single-category, fast-wheel production, which was largely Aegean in style (Sherratt 1991, 192–93). Consequently, the Cypriot phenomenon of an Aegean-style pottery production lies in the eventual substitution of the centuries-old handmade and (since LC I) also wheelmade manufacture of a vast range of Late Cypriot wares by a fast-wheel ceramic industry which was only barely of a Cypriot tradition. Thus, the fast-wheel painted pottery, which was industrially mass produced (for the first time) during the island's Late Bronze urban horizon in the thirteenth and twelfth centuries B.C.E., was Aegean in style.

Nevertheless, at the end of the day, when fast-wheel ceramic production had finally led to the complete eclipse of handmade and/or wheelmade Cypriot wares, the Aegean-style ceramics of Cyprus had not been "faithful" either to a LH IIIB or LH IIIC repertory of shapes. From the start, the local Aegeanizing ceramic industry had behaved in an eclectic manner (Sherratt 1991, 193–94): From the wide-ranging repertory of its Aegean prototype, it had adopted only a limited number of shapes. Susan Sherratt's thesis (1981) and, not long afterwards, Barbara Kling's (1989) were the first substantial efforts to approach the internal stylistic development of the Cypriot production of Aegeanizing pottery in the thirteenth and twelfth centuries. Before the 1980s an array of terms, coined in the course of the twentieth century to describe the local manufacture of Aegean-style pottery, was charged with historical determinism. Almost all of them were meant to indicate whether a fast-wheel decorated ware had been produced either before or after that specific moment in time when Aegean immigrants were believed to have settled in Cyprus (i.e., the twelfth century B.C.E.) and to denote simultaneously the ware's relative closeness to, or distance from, the Late Helladic prototype. It is interesting to note that Kling has catalogued specimens which had been classified in their respective site publication under the following terms: Rude Style, Decorated Late Cypriot III, Late Mycenaean IIIB, Cypro-Mycenaean, Mycenaean IIIC:1b, Mycenaean IIIC:1c, Granary Style, Submycenaean, White Painted Wheelmade III, even "inferior Mycenaean ware" (1989, 177–236).

After half a century of struggling with these overlapping terms (recently, Kling 2000, 282), Cypriot archaeology had to admit that most of these supposedly chronologically diagnostic wares were in fact produced on either side of the "great divide." Ceramic forms such as the skyphos and the shallow bowl (cf. Maier 1985, 122–25) are identical in LC IIC and LC IIIA. This is "a strong indicator of cultural continuity rather than change" (Kling 1989, 80). At the same time however there are shapes that "clearly derive from Aegean ceramics," such as the kalathos, the pyxis, or the amphoriskos (Kling 1989, 171), which are not attested in LC IIC. They were added to the local repertoire in LC IIIA (Sherratt 1991, 192). If these new twelfth-century B.C.E. additions to the Aegean-style repertory of Cyprus were all found to belong to a particular LH IIIC regional production, one would be allowed to associate their reproduction in Cyprus with an influx of people from a specific region of the Aegean. This however is negated by the multi-regional provenance of the new LC IIIA Aegeanizing shapes; they range from the Cyclades to Crete and the Dodecanese (Sherratt 1991, 195; Kling 2000, 282).

Consequently, in Cyprus, the earliest Aegean-style pottery is manifested well before the site abandonment horizon of LC IIC/IIIA. It is, for instance, attested at Kalavassos-Ayios Dhimitrios where the local imitations of Aegean pottery (predominantly shallow bowls) are classified under the umbrella term "White Painted Wheelmade III" (cf. Kling 1989, 60). There is, however, a certain unique aspect in the Cypriot phenomenon, which does not characterize any of the other east Mediterranean industries of Aegean-style pottery production, and to this we need to direct our attention. The fast-wheel pottery industry and the Aegean ceramic prototype remained inextricably linked in the ceramic production of Cyprus for much longer than anywhere else in the Mediterranean. In fact, the Aegean-style pottery of Cyprus reached its finest quality production and its widest range of utilitarian as well as exuberant shapes not in the thirteenth or twelfth centuries B.C.E., but in the eleventh (Iacovou 1991, 199–204) in the repertory of Proto-White Painted (LC IIIB) and of White Painted I (Cypro-Geometric IA). It was not before the early-tenth century B.C.E. (Cypro-Geometric IB) that the mass-produced White Painted/Bichrome Wares incorporated into their repertory a Phoenician shape, the globular jug, and a new local shape, the shallow dish (Iacovou 1988, 36, 39).

None of the other east Mediterranean centers of Aegean-style pottery production can claim a continuous and steady output from as early on as the thirteenth century B.C.E. as do the Cypriot workshops; nor did they last as long since they acquired a distance from the Late Helladic III Aegean prototype very early on. The establishment of an Aegean-style ceramic industry on the Levantine and Syrian coast, and in the Philistine urban centers, seems to have been a short-lived phenomenon confined to the twelfth century B.C.E.

Cultural Continuities and Cultural Novelties in LC IIC–LC IIIA

Besides pottery, other aspects of the twelfth-century B.C.E. material culture of Cyprus have been claimed as diagnostic features of an exclusively Aegean-oriented cultural influence. Dikaios, Furumark, and Karageorghis ascribe the construction of the megalithic fortifications of Enkomi, Sinda, and Maa to the end of LC IIC, that is, the crisis years around 1200 B.C.E., and consider them products of a period of general unease and insecurity. It is a fact that there are no monumentally fortified settlements in the island before the end of the thirteenth century B.C.E. Despite the fact that Dikaios used the term "cyclopean" to describe the rampart constructed around Enkomi shortly before the destruction of the town's LC IIC Level IIB, he never intended to identify it with Mycenaean citadels: "The method of construction is in no way that of the Cyclopean walls of the Greek Mainland" (Dikaios 1969–1971, 512).

Karageorghis, though he attributes the construction of the "cyclopean" city-rampart of Kition to urban enhancement (Karageorghis and Demas 1985, 86), maintains that the prototype is to be found in Hittite Anatolia. From there it was adopted by the Mycenaeans, who in turn introduced it to Cyprus (Karageorghis 1992, 81). "The introduction of 'Cyclopean'-type walls at the very beginning of the LC IIIA period at Enkomi, Kition, Sinda and Maa-Palaeokastro was due to the arrival of Mycenaean settlers in Cyprus" (Karageorghis 2000a, 259).

Ashlar architecture has been abundantly attested in sites that were abandoned at the end of the thirteenth century B.C.E., before LC IIIA (e.g., Kalavassos-Ayios Dhimitrios and Maroni-Vournes), or shortly after the inception of LC IIIA (e.g., Alassa). Consequently, the use of ashlars for the construction of large civic and cultic edifices was introduced to Cyprus no later than LC IIC. It is unanimously recognized as a prime material marker for the climax of urban development on the island (Negbi 1986; Webb 1999, 4). In fact, in the publication of Kition, where one comes across an impressive acknowledgment regarding the substance of the cultural continuities which characterize the transition from LC IIC–IIIA, ashlar masonry plays a pivotal role: "There is far more continuity to be read into the transition from floor IV to floor IIIA than is at first apparent in the total reconstruction of and reorganization of the temple precinct. The essence of this change may be summed up in the notion of monumentality and the use of ashlar masonry" (Karageorghis and Demas 1985, 92). Furthermore, though this monumental architectural style is believed to have been inspired from abroad, the "inspiration was not the result of an invasion and an installation in the island of foreign elements" (Karageorghis and Demas 1985, 277).

In addition to "cyclopean" fortifications and ashlar architecture, horns of consecration, central hearths, bath-tubs, Handmade Burnished Ware, and shaft graves have also been singled out as evidence pointing to the establishment of Aegean immigrants in twelfth-century B.C.E. Cyprus (cf. Karageorghis 1992, 1994, 1998, 2000a). Two issues need to be kept in mind here: First, that most of these aspects have been claimed as salient characteristics of LC IIC material culture (e.g., ashlar architecture, horns of consecration, and bath-tubs), therefore they are not truly novel aspects in LC IIIA, since they have been reported from sites which were abandoned before the twelfth century B.C.E.; second, the association of some of these novel aspects (i.e., ashlar architecture, "cyclopean" fortifications, and Handmade Burnished Ware) with the Mycenaean heartland and Late Helladic culture is to say the least, indirect: Hittite Anatolia is credited as their origin, yet their implantation in Cyprus is ascribed to Aegean people.

I am fully prepared to admit the viability of this and many other scenarios which attempt to create an interpretative frame for the appearance of the above novelties but the crux of the issue as far as Late Bronze Cyprus is concerned, lies elsewhere. Genuine LC IIC and/or LC IIIA novelties all of these may be, but they are not homogeneously or invariably present in twelfth-century B.C.E. settlements (reviewed above), nor do they have a lasting impact in Cypriot culture. They create a considerable degree of diversity amongst contemporary sites and a short-term lack of cultural balance (Iacovou 2005a). Take, for instance, ashlar constructions and "cyclopean" ramparts; why did they altogether vanish from the island's built environment before the transition to the eleventh century B.C.E., never to reappear in the Iron Age?

Only one novelty of Aegean origin, which has been attested throughout the island in the thirteenth and twelfth centuries, had a more lasting impact: The Aegeanizing ceramic industry, which reached full maturity in the eleventh century B.C.E. Of all the novel aspects, Aegeanizing pottery alone had undergone evolution and had its own insular development. This cannot be claimed for the "cyclopean" forts, the Handmade Burnished Ware, or the shaft graves in Cyprus. As for ashlar architecture, the more we advance from the late-thirteenth into the twelfth century B.C.E., one "senses" a shortage of man-power and/or technical skills in some places (e.g., Enkomi) and an abundance, or concentration of them, in others (i.e., Palaepaphos and Kition).

The significance of the LC IIIA reorganization of the temple precinct in Kition and its rebuilding with ashlars are defined as "a cosmetic change" and a deliberate decision geared towards the notion of monumentality: "The source of Kition's new wealth and prestige in LCIIIA" (Karageorghis and Demas 1985, 275), which may parallel that of Palaepaphos where an equally impressive temenos was constructed at the same time, suggests that the historical episode defining the LC IIC/IIIA transition was a crisis that worked in favor of some centers in as much as it worked against others. Nonetheless, the LC IIIA nucleated sites are indigenous, pre-existing establishments; they were not founded afresh by Aegean immigrants in the twelfth century B.C.E. and they did not introduce a new settlement pattern.

The "Time Capsules" in Their Cultural Milieu

Kokkinokremos and Maa, on the other hand, are newly founded establishments. They are undoubtedly two distinctly different expressions of the "crisis years" in Cyprus but at the same time they have no lasting impact in the island's Late Bronze or early Iron Age history. They do not even introduce a new settlement pattern as far as the twelfth century B.C.E. is concerned. They drop out of the island's settlement geography as quickly and as suddenly as they had appeared. Since they were never reoccupied, they are valuable "time capsules" of the LC IIC/IIIA critical juncture.

Kokkinokremos and Maa-Palaeokastro have no time depth. Thus, one could hope to identify there an Aegean cultural kit, namely cultural novelties exclusively associated with the introduction of Aegean-style material culture or the arrival and establishment of Aegean people. Furthermore, since the short duration of their existence is contemporary with specific levels from long-term settlements, such as Kition and Enkomi, and had a distinctly different material culture been introduced in these short-lived sites, one ought to have been able to identify it. With the exception of bath-tubs and hearths, features which have been attested at sites such as Kalavasos-Ayios Dhimitrios and Alassa (cf. Karageorghis 2000a, 260–4) before the LC IIC/IIIA abandonment phase, Kokkinokremos and Maa-Palaeokastro are altogether missing vital cultural indicators such as: a) texts, b) burials, and c) cult centers, which might have determined an immigrant population's "cultural baggage."

Texts

With the exception of the usual Cypro-Minoan signs inscribed as a rule on pottery, neither Kokkinokremos nor Maa-Palaeokastro have produced epigraphic evidence. They were not venues for the introduction of a new language or a new system of writing in Cyprus. The transfer of a script of Aegean origin has not been attested anywhere in the eastern Mediterranean. The establishment, therefore, of Aegean people in Cyprus and equally in the Levant in the twelfth century

B.C.E. is not supported by epigraphic evidence. Considering, however, that the Mycenaean-Greek language had lost its system of writing (i.e., Linear B) after the collapse of the palace economy at the end of the thirteenth century B.C.E., this should not surprise us in the least (Chadwick 1975).[26]

The only twelfth-century B.C.E. textual novelty in Cyprus is found on a silver bowl from the LC IIIA urban center of Hala Sultan Tekke. It bears a Semitic inscription rendered in an Ugaritic cuneiform script that reads, "made by Aky son of Yiptahaddou" (Åström and Masson 1982). Like so many other unique or short-lived phenomena, which characterize the twelfth century of Cyprus and find no continuity in the eleventh century B.C.E. or in the early Iron Age in general, the Hala Sultan Tekke Semitic inscription is unique: It does not introduce a new script or language in Cyprus. The same could have been true of a syllabic inscription on an obelos from an eleventh- or tenth-century B.C.E. chamber tomb with a dromos from the Iron Age necropolis of Palaepaphos-Skales, which discloses in the Cypro-Arcadian dialect a Greek proper name (Masson and Masson 1983); but it is not. This early Greek inscription is today unique only as far as the Cypro-Geometric period is concerned. The epigraphic record of Iron Age Cyprus proves that it is currently the earliest evidence of a script (Cypriot syllabary) and a language (Cypro-Arcadian Greek), which became the island's predominant system of writing and majority language during the era of the Iron Age Cypriot kingdoms when, besides Greek, two more languages were used in the island: the indecipherable Eteocypriot language, which was also written in the syllabary, and Phoenician, which was written alphabetically (cf. Masson 1983; Collombier 1991).

If we compare the Cypriot and the Philistine phenomenon on the basis of script and language, we see that in both cases the twelfth century B.C.E. fails to disclose either a new script or a new language. As far as the early Iron Age is concerned it is a fact that Greek did not become a written or for that matter a spoken language in Philistia or anywhere else in the Levant. In Cyprus, on the other hand, Greek did become the island's predominant language and eventually (following the abolition of the kingdoms at the end of the fourth century B.C.E. and the incorporation of Cyprus to the Ptolemaic kingdom of Egypt), the island's only language (Iacovou 2006b). Moreover, the syllabic scribal system— the exclusive tool of the Cypro-Arcadian Greek dialect—managed to survive to the end of

26. To this day, Linear B has not been attested outside the Aegean; it never left the palace/administrative centers of Crete and mainland Greece. Linear B illustrates a fascinating phenomenon of the rapid extinction of a scribal system not supported by anything other than a palatial administration.

the first millennium B.C.E., despite the officially imposed use of the Greek alphabet (cf. Michaelidou-Nicolaou 1993; Bazemore 2002, 158).

Burials

Not one grave of any type has been located at Kokkinokremos or Maa. The absence of *intra muros* burials is an oddity, which alienates the two new sites from all the other twelfth-century B.C.E. centers where tombs continue to be found intramurally in accordance with the Late Cypriot tradition. For example, no fewer than eight tombs were excavated in the settlement of Alassa-Pano Mandilaris (Hadjisavvas 1989, 34–41). This site, which survived the transition to early LC IIIA (see above), was in its final phase largely contemporary with Kokkinokremos and also with the early period of Maa. The situation at Sinda is far from conclusive (due to its limited investigation) but no twelfth-century B.C.E. graves have been reported from Furumark's excavation. The construction of the notorious Sinda Tomb 1, a kidney-shaped chamber with a dromos, found within the city rampart, is said to antedate the foundation of the walled town (Furumark and Adelman 2003, 35, 38, 69).[27] In LC IIC the chamber was emptied and put to another use, probably as a sanctuary (but see also Webb 1999, 143–44).

The truth is that the Late Cypriot *intra muros* burial custom of inhumations in chamber tombs that were meant to be accessible for repeated use did not come out unscathed following the transition to LC IIIA. Very few of these Late Cypriot (family?) chambers can be said to have continued in use after LC IIC; they were being closed (cf. Dikaios 1969–1971, 518) and it is not unusual to find settlement structures built over them. Urban expansion could fit as an explanation in some cases, but the fact remains that we do not find new burial chambers constructed elsewhere within the settlement to replace them.

Thus, an unequivocally indigenous cultural marker, that is, the Late Cypriot funerary custom *par excellence*, was dying out in the course of LC IIIA. This could only be initiated by the social groups living within the twelfth-century B.C.E. settlements. When the demise of a type of tomb constructed for long-term use is temporally (in the twelfth century B.C.E.) and spatially (intramurally) accentuated by the contemporary appearance of a type of tomb meant for single use, i.e., the shaft grave, it becomes easier to acknowledge that major social transformations must have been taking place within the urban limits of the LC IIIA settlements. These shaft graves are small, shallow cuttings and though their use was

27. It is worth pointing out that to the southeast of the walled town lies an extensive Bronze Age necropolis of plundered tombs (hence the locality's name, Cukurluk, "the place full of holes"), whose chronological relation to the LC IIC–IIIA town of Sinda has not been discussed by Furumark and Adelman (2003, 26).

not restricted to low-status individuals (Niklasson 1983; Keswani 1989, 55–56), they could not have served as the funerary monuments of established and secure social groups. They are not many, so they do not actually serve as an alternative or a substitute to the standard Cypriot grave, but they seem to be exclusively associated with twelfth-century B.C.E. settlement strata at Enkomi, Hala Sultan Tekke, Palaepaphos, and Kition (cf. Niklasson-Sönnerby 1987; Karageorghis 2000a, 257–59). This is currently the strongest material evidence pointing to the social and political transformations, which were taking place in Cyprus at the end of the Late Bronze Age.

The use of *intra muros* graves of any kind, however, does not survive the transition to the early Iron Age. The final stage of this dramatic change takes place in the eleventh century B.C.E., during LC IIIB, when the island finally turns to extramural, community-organized burial grounds where a previously unattested type of grave is being constructed: the chamber tomb with the long dromos (cf. Catling 1994, 134). The earliest such necropolis is found at Gastria-Alaas, on the east coast north of Enkomi (Karageorghis 1975). From then on it becomes the established burial pattern of Iron Age Cyprus. Dikaios, who was deeply concerned with the unsolved problem of the "disposal of the dead" in twelfth-century B.C.E. Enkomi (Level IIIA)—since "the rock-cut chamber tombs" (read, Late Cypriot chamber tombs) had been abandoned, suggested that a separate area either inside or *outside* the periphery of the town had begun to be used "as a grave yard" (Dikaios 1969–1971, 518). The complete absence of tombs from the excavated sectors of Kokkinokremos and Maa, and the island-wide dearth of newly constructed twelfth-century B.C.E. graves allows us to put forward (in the name of future investigation) the idea that separate burial grounds, beyond settlement limits, may have been inaugurated before the end of LC IIIA.

Cult buildings: Cypriot religious organization

Kokkinokremos and Maa-Palaeokastro, to the extent that they have been excavated, did not reveal domestic cult centers, nor public sanctuaries of any kind (see Webb 1999, 144). Regarding Late Cypriot cult practice in general, Keswani maintains that there is no coherent system of symbols that would suggest a state-sponsored religion in Late Bronze Cyprus and no iconographic evidence of subordination to a common central authority (Keswani 1993, 74). In some respects she is right, though her arguments have been contradicted by Webb (1999, 307). Nevertheless, it was the traditional Cypriot cult practice, which was glorified with the ashlar temene erected at Kition and Palaepaphos during the LC IIC/IIIA juncture, and not an Aegean cultic tradition.

The organization of the open-air temene in LC IIIA does not introduce specifically Aegean or Mycenaean characteristics in cult practice. Moreover, unlike other architectural novelties, such as the use of ashlars for civic buildings or the construction of "cyclopean" city-walls (above), the two megalithic temene were not short-term expressions of either the climax of urban development associated with LC IIC, or of the "crisis years" associated with the transition to the twelfth century B.C.E. The twelfth century was only the inaugural phase in their amazingly long, successful, and continuous function throughout the Iron Age. In fact, in the absence of archaeologically recognizable "palaces" at Kition and Palaepaphos (the Iron Age public building at Kouklia-Hadjiabdullah is the only reliable candidate; see Maier and von Wartburg 1985, 155), the two LC IIIA temene remain in command of the sacred as well as the secular landscape of their respective polities to the end of the age of the kingdoms (ca. 310 B.C.E.) almost a millennium later (Iacovou 2005b).

Consequently, the LC IIC material culture was nowhere suddenly, totally, or violently replaced by a new LC IIIA culture of Aegean origin. The relocation of people from the Aegean to Cyprus can no longer be defended by the production of Aegean-style pottery alone and "previous arguments [which] suggested an incursion of a dominant population from the Mycenaean mainland in LC IIIA have been undermined in favor of an increased emphasis on the continuity of local cultural traditions" (Webb 1999, 6).

Whither Twelfth-Century B.C.E. Archaeology?

In view of the sweeping historical interpretations that the twelfth-century B.C.E. Aegean-type material culture generated within Cyprus (e.g., the island's Aegean colonization) and beyond (e.g., the Philistines' ethnic identity), its twelfth-century excavation record is embarrassingly limited.[28] The number of sites where substantial twelfth-century B.C.E. settlement strata have been located are a handful, and though the total in square meters of excavated/exposed LC IIIA settlement strata may seem adequate, about half of that area belongs to Enkomi. In most of the other sites, the extent of the excavated area is insufficient: the ratio between excavated and non-excavated area is less than the absolute minimum required to render identifiable basic settlement functions, namely administrative, cultic, industrial, craft specialization, and funerary areas. Consequently, valiant interpretations aside, the cultural landscape of the island, from the end of the

28. Almost two decades ago, when the generalization of evidence from comparatively small excavated areas was criticized by F. G. Maier, it was Sinda that was used as a case in point: "The conclusions drawn from this site loom large in the reconstruction of the history of the twelfth century in Cyprus" (Maier 1986, 316).

thirteenth century (the LC IIC/IIIA transition) to the eleventh century B.C.E. (the LC IIIA/IIIB transition), remains a complex puzzle of highly diverse, non-matching settlement histories.

It is probably time to admit that what has elevated Enkomi to the status of the Late Bronze metropolis of Cyprus is the fact that it was adequately excavated in depth and width: We have an exact record of the duration of occupation in time and the maximum extent of occupation in space. Within its "cyclopean" rampart, twelfth-century B.C.E. Enkomi may have been a medium-size urban settlement by comparison to Kition, Palaepaphos, or Hala Sultan Tekke, but this is only a hypothesis, which lacks tangible archaeological proof (Iacovou 2007). For the time being, with an excavation record as limited and fragmentary as that of the other LC IIIA urban centers, the reconstruction of Cyprus's social and political history at the end of the Late Bronze Age is riddled with problems. The twelfth century B.C.E. of Cyprus is not a horizon which has been adequately investigated, and this is a fact one should not try to conceal in one's interpretation.

The Early Iron Age Sequel or Cyprus's Response to Aegean-Style Material culture

We may continue to suspect—and justifiably so—that Aegean people were the prime makers, users, and consumers of the material culture that created a twelfth-century B.C.E. Aegeanizing horizon in the eastern Mediterranean. The physical presence of this people, however, cannot be proven, certainly not by the industrially-successful Late Helladic III-style pottery production which, international acclaim notwithstanding, dissipated at the end of the twelfth century B.C.E. A much longer view into the Iron Age is required before one can reach some tentative conclusions.

Relocations, migrations, and colonizations are, as a rule, slow processes with long-term consequences to the human environment, which has to absorb them. As such, they cannot be properly studied on the evidence of the material culture of one short cultural horizon alone, or by comparing the thirteenth to the twelfth century B.C.E. Even if we could prove that each and every one of the so-called "Sea Peoples" who reached the Levant at the end of the Late Bronze Age, was a Mycenaean-Greek speaker and a carrier of an Aegean cultural "kit," the fact is that their purported establishment in the eastern Mediterranean, in the land of Philistia for example, had little to no lasting impact upon the subsequent periods (Iacovou 1998). Eventually, whether they had come, whether they had produced themselves and for themselves "Mycenaean IIIC1b" pottery, meant very little to the social and political history of Syria and Palestine in the early Iron Age: The material culture of the region was not Aegeanized beyond the degree that it was—

mainly through the manufacture of Aegean-style pottery—during a very short period in the twelfth century B.C.E. With this statement, I do not by any means wish to ignore the truly touching evidence provided by the seventh-century B.C.E. royal dedicatory inscription of Ekron, of a king who, after four hundred years of Philistine acculturation, was named Achish, the "Achaean"(?) (Gitin, T. Dothan, and Naveh 1997; Gitin 1998, 173–74).

I mean to stress, however, that a similar contemporary event had a completely different outcome in the island of Cyprus. But, in order to appreciate the sequel, a much longer view is required—from the thirteenth to the eleventh centuries B.C.E. and into the Iron Age. Of all the eastern Mediterranean coasts that present us with a shorter or longer twelfth-century B.C.E. Aegeanizing ceramic horizon that may or may not conceal a contemporary influx of people, the suspected but hardly visible Aegean infiltration acquired a lasting impact and a linguistically and epigraphically established physical presence only in Cyprus. It caused the island to undergo a language change and that became the Aegean peoples' indelible imprint.

Chapter Twenty-Three
The Ceramic Phenomenon of the "Sea Peoples": An Overview

*Susan Sherratt**

The act of crystallizing in print the proceedings of a successful workshop, like the 2001 workshop on the Philistines and other Sea Peoples, which gave rise to this volume, is always a tricky business. This is because the best workshops invariably have an interim, contingent character, marked by a strong sense of "work in progress," by the free exchange of new (and often raw) information, spontaneous *ad hoc* (and usually half-digested) responses, and the uninhibited interchange of different approaches and different points of view in as cooperative, open-minded, and exploratory a fashion as possible. A really good workshop is an important part of a means to an end rather than an end in itself. It provides the "cooking pot" in which the ingredients of a good, nutritious stew are assembled and begin to blend together. However, it is only after a considerable period of subsequent slow cooking, the continued breaking down and blending of the original ingredients and the addition of further ones, along with much trial-tasting and some carefully adjusted seasoning, that one can hope to end up with a complete and satisfying dish.

The task that I was originally set by the organizers of the workshop and the editors of this volume was to present a "summing up," and in particular to address the "big picture" of how we should see the whole phenomenon of Aegean-style

* Department of Archaeology, University of Sheffield, Northgate House, West Street, Sheffield S1 4ET. E-mail: s.sherratt@sheffield.ac.uk.

This paper was completed in 2002, and, while a few updates to the bibliography have since been made, it has not been possible to take full account of relevant material that has been published in recent years. This includes pottery from sites such as Tell Ta'yinat (Janeway 2006–2007; 2011), Ras Ibn Hani (du Piêd 2006–2007; 2011), Tell Kazel (Jung 2006a; 2012), Tell Tweini (Jung 2010), and the very valuable survey by Gunnar Lehmann (2007).

material culture in the east. This seemed to me at the time (and still seems) something of a tall order, not least since I have had the feeling for some while now that the "big picture" is very big indeed, extending from the Levant in the east to the central Mediterranean in the west, and going back in time at least as far as the beginning of the thirteenth century B.C.E. (Sherratt 1998; 2003). Instead, therefore, I will confine myself to what might be called a "medium picture" and attempt a survey of the geography and chronology of the most prominent archaeological element of the phenomenon as I see it. Bear in mind, however, that at this stage even this "medium picture" is only very hazily delineated, with many of the elements still poorly focused and some missing altogether. It is also, inevitably, tinted with my own prejudices.

One of the most important achievements of the workshop and this resulting volume, for which I would like to thank the organizers and editors, has been to extend a discussion hitherto focused almost exclusively on what might be called the "Philistine phenomenon" to what appears to be the same (or at least very similar) phenomena in other coastal regions of the eastern Mediterranean. This widening of the context of discussion is greatly welcomed. For perhaps the first time, the workshop enabled people with first-hand familiarity with relevant material in regions such as Cyprus, Cilicia, the 'Amuq, and the southern Levant to get together and compare notes on all its down-to-earth and detailed aspects. If there are regrets, one of them is perhaps that, given the nature of national antiquities legislation in many of the regions concerned, more of the material could not actually have been brought together in one place, so that the workshop's participants could have compared more than merely notes. The other regret is that, unavoidably in the circumstances, some of those with greatest first-hand familiarity with the phenomenon as encountered in places like coastal Syria and the Lebanon were unable to take part. What is quite certain is that, if we are to begin really to understand this phenomenon, we cannot afford to be regionally selective, confining ourselves neatly within modern political boundaries or within regional archaeological specialties or traditions of interpretation and interpreting the phenomenon in a piecemeal manner according to these traditions. We have to look at it in its entirety, in its specific details and local contexts wherever it occurs, as well as in its wider regional and Mediterranean contexts.

What?

We can start by addressing three simple questions. What archaeological form does the phenomenon of Aegean-style material culture in the east take? Where do we find it? And when does it occur? In answer to the first of these questions,

I should point out that the title I finally settled on for this paper ("The Ceramic Phenomenon of the 'Sea Peoples'") is quite deliberate. This is because what we are essentially talking about under the rubric of "Aegean-style material culture" in the eastern Mediterranean is the production and use, in a number of coastal or island regions and at an as yet unknown number of sites, of a type of painted pottery that we are accustomed by long-standing convention to thinking of as particularly characteristic of the Aegean. It is, above all, pottery that has been the linchpin of the traditional culture-historical narratives of this period, originally written by archaeologists trained in the Classics, and effectively determined by an imaginative confection of nineteenth- and early twentieth-century Classical mythology whose outlines as they affect the Philistines have been traced by T. Dothan and M. Dothan (1992) and critically discussed by Sharon (2001a, 557–67), while some aspects of its formative context have been analyzed by Silberman (1998). And despite the somewhat contentious (particularly from an Aegean viewpoint) claims based from time to time on a variety of other aspects of material culture—from ashlar masonry to hearthed megara, or from metalwork to seated goddesses—it is still, it seems to me, first and foremost a question of pottery.[1] Take away the pottery and I very much doubt if anyone would have thought of organizing an archaeological workshop to discuss the problem of Aegean-style material culture in the early twelfth-century eastern Mediterranean, let alone under the heading of "Sea Peoples." If it were not for the pottery, it would be almost impossible to imagine that the question of Aegean-style material culture in any region of the eastern Mediterranean would seriously have arisen in the first place, at least once archaeology had begun to gain even a modicum of independence from complete and unquestioning subservience to a nineteenth-century form of pseudo-textual "history."

The phenomenon is, then, first and foremost, a question of the taking into local production of what we think of as an Aegean type of painted pottery at various places in the eastern Mediterranean. It is a phenomenon which, under various labels—ranging from the comparatively value-laden "imitation" to the more economically biased "import substitution"—is not altogether unknown in the second millennium in this part of the world when it comes to other types of pottery, from the occasional Egyptian versions of Kamares Ware in the earlier centuries of the millennium (Kemp and Merrillees 1980, 57) through the Bichrome pottery manufactured in the area of Megiddo and the White Shaved juglets and Base

1. This emerges particularly clearly from an excellent paper by Amihai Mazar (2000) on the temples and cult of the early Philistines, which documents the diversity of cultural relations and influences appearing to underlie these and the, at best, ambiguous and, at worst, exiguous nature of Aegean connections which they display.

Ring bowls produced by Levantine potters later on (Artzy 1985). Exactly where our particular phenomenon occurs is another question—one that this volume has begun to address, but has by no means yet fully answered (fig. 1).

Where?

Cyprus is one area that is reasonably well documented (Kling 1989; see also Iacovou, this volume). The pottery we are talking about occurs at a number of sites on the island—though it is necessary to bear in mind the still limited number and range of Cypriot Late Bronze Age settlements that have been excavated—and the curious observation that (as far as we can tell) the most "Aegean"-looking pottery in terms of shapes and decorations seems only rarely to have been deposited in LC IIIA tombs (Maier 1986, 313). It also seems to have been produced in different parts of the island, since there are some observable stylistic differences between east and west (Kling 1989, 172; 2000). In precisely how many places and where exactly it was made remains unclear, though the combination of its distribution and the results of analytical work carried out so far suggests that the greater part of its production (and probably also its greatest concentration of use) was mainly in the urban coastal centers or sites closely tied to them (Knapp and Cherry 1994, 61–62). While in general the fabric has a soft, sandy surface feel and the paint is usually matte or very matte, this generalization also masks a degree of variation (Kling 1989, 91; Sherratt 1990a, 111). Though I am prepared to stick my neck out and say that the kind of hard, beautifully smooth surface and deep glossy paint that is characteristic of imported Argive LH IIIA and IIIB pottery at its best[2] is probably never seen on this pottery, some surfaces are much smoother and more compact than others and the paint can sometimes be slightly glossy or even occasionally quite glossy. What is also interesting about it is that, though it has its own distinct character and the details of style are different, it displays a certain parallelism with the Aegean in several of the broad trends of development during the twelfth century (Kling 1989; 2000). Moreover, some of us have argued that it is even possible to detect certain specifically Cypriot developments travelling westward to influence LH IIIC pottery in various areas of the Aegean, as well as probably the other way round (Kling 1989, 172–73; Sherratt 1991, 195; Deger-Jalkotzy 1994, 19). The other thing that particularly needs emphasizing is that what Dikaios (1969–1971), basing himself on Furumark (1944), called "Myc. IIIC:1b" pottery is only a selective part of a single coherent ware, White Painted

2. Often recognizable in the way the light catches it even in black-and-white photographs (see, e.g., Jones 1986b, pl. 7.14 and cf. 563 [Argive LH IIIA–B imports at Tell Abu Hawam]).

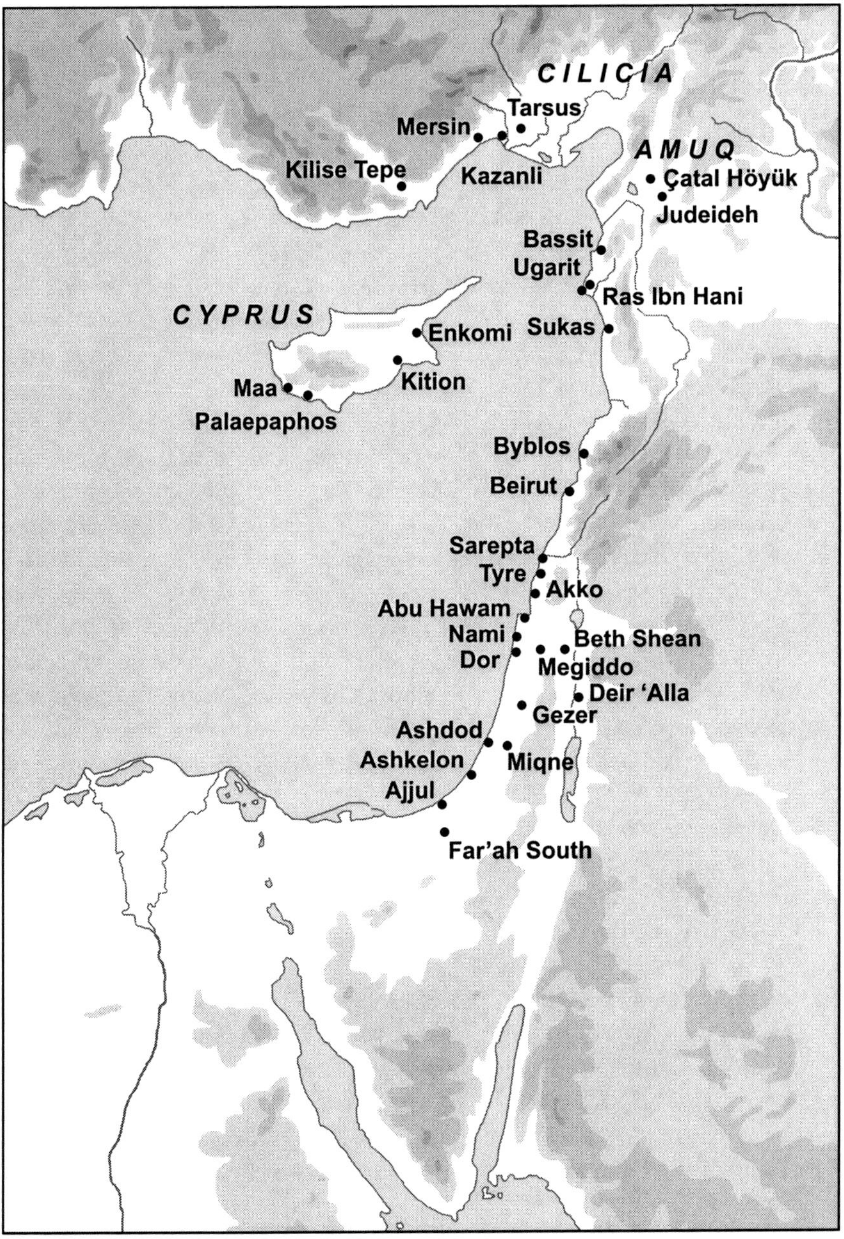

Fig. 1: Map of the eastern Mediterranean, showing sites mentioned in the text.

Wheelmade III—that is, a wheelmade painted ware, broadly similar in fabric and treatment to Aegean Late Bronze Age painted ware, which also encompasses what Dikaios called "Late Myc. IIIB," "Rude Style,"[3] and "Decorated LC III," and includes a number of shapes and decorations for which an "Aegean" label seems wholly inappropriate (Kling 1991; 2000, 281–82 with n. 3). In the earlier part of LC IIIA this ware makes up an average of 68 percent of the fine and decorated pottery from Enkomi Level IIIa and an average of 38 percent of the total pottery from Kition Floors IIIA and III (Dikaios 1969–1971, 458; Kling 1985, tables 4–5). The rest of the pottery is made up of plain wares (especially Plain White Wheelmade/Plain Wheelmade) and varied forms of coarse wares (including Wheelmade cooking pots, pithoi, and Canaanite jars as well as others), two or three varieties of handmade wares, such as White Slip, Base Ring, and White Shaved, whose proportions diminish steadily from the end of LC IIC onwards (though some of their shapes are still produced in Plain or Painted Wheelmade Ware), and increasing quantities of wheelmade Bucchero (Dikaios 1969–1971, 258–59, 574–94; Karageorghis and Demas 1985, II, 19–36, 103–55). The distinction within this single White Painted Wheelmade III Ware (initially particularly by Dikaios) of the separate categories I have already mentioned, which has done much to contribute to the nightmare of Cypriot Late Bronze Age ceramic terminology, is—as Kling (1987; 1991) has pointed out—not a question of a difference in wares, but largely a function of assumptions about the cultural origins and relative chronology of certain selected shapes and decorations, which themselves rest on assumptions concerning certain postulated large-scale "historical events" and their effects on the island.

The phenomenon in Cilicia has been relatively well known since the surveys of Gjerstad (1934) and Seton-Williams (1954), Garstang's soundings at sites such as Kazanli and Mersin (1937; 1938; 1939), and Goldman's excavations at Tarsus (1950), though again the various terminologies used at different times by different people have probably contributed more to confusion than enlightenment. The recent excavations at Kilise Tepe confirm that it is not confined to eastern Cilicia but also turns up in the form of a few examples of "Mycenaean" shapes decorated with simple banding at a particularly significant spot where the western edge of the narrow coastal plain meets an important access route through the Taurus (French, this volume; Hansen and Postgate 1999, 112; cf. also Gjerstad 1934, 176–77, fig. 19). At Tarsus and Kazanli, it has been guessed that this type of pottery perhaps made up roughly between a quarter and a third of the total ceramic range in LB IIB levels (cf. Mee 1978, 131, 145). At Kilise Tepe the handful of bowls

3. Also, since the early 1980s, called "Pastoral Style" (cf. Vermeule and Karageorghis 1982, 60).

and perhaps a jug or amphora (French, this volume) stand out against the decidedly non-Aegean appearance of the rest of the pottery likely to be of similar date (Hansen and Postgate 1999, 113, cf. figs. 1–5, 11–13; see also Ünlü 2005 from Tarsus). We do not yet know where this pottery was made, or in how many places, though the differences in fabric noted between the few pieces recovered so far from Kilise Tepe and those from Tarsus and Kazanli (French, this volume) suggest a variety of sources of supply. We cannot even yet be sure how much of it, if any, was actually made in Cilicia.[4] Stylistically, there are some very close similarities, long ago noted by French (1975, 73–74; cf. Mee 1978, 150; Mountjoy 2005b, 86), between the Tarsus pottery and that produced in Cyprus, including most of the range of shapes and types of decoration. The general appearance of the fabrics and range of surface finishes (at least from Tarsus and Kazanli) also looks very much like that found on Cyprus (French 1975, 55, 74; Mee 1978, 131–32, 145; Sherratt and Crouwel 1987, 331–32). However, the Tarsus and Kazanli material also shows a few similarities to that of the eastern Aegean (particularly perhaps the Dodecanese) that do not seem to be shared with Cyprus: the presence of one or two octopus stirrup jars at Tarsus, for instance (Goldman 1950, fig. 333:1338; French 1975, 62); or certain distinctive types of spiral and lozenge composition which occur at Kazanli and Tarsus as well as on Kos, Chios, and at Troy (Gjerstad 1934, fig. 18:A; French 1975, fig. 6:3; Sherratt and Crouwel 1987, 335, 340, fig. 4:3; L. Morricone 1972–1973: figs. 374–75; Hood 1982, pl. 119:d; Blegen et al. 1958, fig. 279:14). What we do not know, of course, is whether those pots with a particularly eastern Aegean appearance were made in Cilicia or imported from the eastern Aegean. At the same time, a certain distinctive type of bird bowl, decorated with a single bird on each side, turns up at Tarsus, at Kition, Palaepaphos, and Maa-Palaeokastro on Cyprus, and on Kos (Kling 1984a, 48 with references; Karageorghis and Demas 1988, pl. CCXLIII:250; L. Morricone 1972–1973, fig. 361b). My guess is that these were probably made in southern or southwest Cyprus—but who knows?

Since the University of Chicago expedition in the 1930s, we have heard reports of what appear to be locally made versions of Aegean-type painted pottery of Late Bronze Age/early Iron Age date in the ʿAmuq, particularly from the sites of Çatal Höyük and Tell el-Judeideh. Braidwood (1937, 6) characterized this pottery, associated with his Period V (later called ʿAmuq N) which he dated to between 1200 and 1000 B.C.E., as "Sub-Mycenaean or Late Helladic IV wares, perhaps Cypriote in origin."[5] The only published description and discussion we have

4. See Jones 1986b, 607 for the suggestion of a compositional similarity between "Myc. IIIC" from Kition and similar pottery from Tarsus and Mersin.

5. Later, Haines (1971, 2) called it "Levanto-Helladic IV (Sub-Mycenaean)."

had of this pottery hitherto (before 2002) is that of Swift (1958, 63–123) who, however, illustrated very little of it (though see now Janeway 2011 for material from Tall Ta'yinat). Swift gives an account of an amalgam of local Syro-Palestinian traditions with a relatively restricted element of Mycenaean-derived shapes and decorative ideas, apparently within one painted ware (Swift 1958, 65, 72). The ware itself is described as varying between pink, buff, and green in color without a separate slip and with red or black paint, which is sometimes faintly lustrous in appearance (Swift 1958, table 7). The shapes of clear Mycenaean derivation are severely limited, consisting mainly of deep bowls (skyphoi) with a lesser number of neck-handled amphorae and perhaps a couple of other shapes (Swift 1958, 73–74, 119). Particularly notable is the absence of stirrup jars. Decorative elements are also restricted with the main emphasis on banding, areas of monochrome, and a limited number of motifs, chief among which are wavy lines, concentric semicircles, and spirals of various sorts (Swift 1958, figs. 19–21, 24–26, 27:D–I, 28). Swift's conclusion is that this pottery is later in date than that of LB IIB Tarsus, and that its closest parallels lie rather in the LB IIB/Iron Age "transitional" period at Tarsus and with the latest "Decorated LC III" pottery from Enkomi (the equivalent of Dikaios' Enkomi Level IIIC; Swift 1958, 120). The fact that it is accompanied, in Phase N at Çatal Höyük, by a number of Cypro-Geometric imports tends to support the idea of its late start and suggest to Swift that its chronological range probably lay between 1150 and 950 rather than between 1200 and 1000 (Swift 1958, 117).[6] Swift's conclusions as to the Cypriot charac-

---

6. Cf. now Janeway 2011. The only glimpse I have ever caught of any of the 'Amuq pottery "in the flesh" was when Jan Verstraete kindly showed me a couple of sherds in the University of Cincinnati Classics Study Collection (see Κειμηλια: *The UC Classics Study Collection Database*. Online: http://classics.uc.edu/index.php/research/63-studycollection). At the time, as far as I remember, these reminded me of a fragment of what looks like a relatively late Philistine bowl from the LB IIB/Iron Age transitional levels at Tarsus (Goldman 1950, fig. 336:1354). In the same transitional levels at Tarsus is a bowl or krater fragment with wavy line decoration (Goldman 1950, fig. 336:1356; cf. Dikaios 1969–1971, pl. 310:321a, c, e [from Enkomi late Level IIIB and Level IIIC]).

As far as comparisons between the 'Amuq pottery and the Enkomi sequence are concerned, deep bowls decorated in solid paint with reserved lines (Swift 1958, 77, fig. 19) which, according to Swift, are among the commonest types of deep bowl decoration at Çatal Höyük, first appear at Enkomi at the end of Level IIIB and in Level IIIC, at the same time as the neck-handled amphora (cf. Swift 1958, fig. 24). Another of the three deep bowls illustrated by Swift (1958, fig. 20) also resembles one from the end of Enkomi Level IIIB (cf., e.g., Dikaios 1969–1971, 597, pl. 124:9). The particular forms of concentric semicircle motifs illustrated by Swift (1958, fig. 27:E–F) find good parallels in Enkomi Level IIIC (cf., e.g., Dikaios 1969–1971, pl. 84:14). At the other end of the chronological spectrum, I am particularly struck by the shape of the third deep bowl illustrated by Swift (1958, fig. 21) which, despite its "Myc. IIIC" decoration, has an offset lip,

ter of the "Aegean" element in the 'Amuq pottery and its relatively late date do not appear to be contradicted by more recent studies (see Lehmann, this volume; Janeway 2011). Much of it seems very Cypriot in character and may include some Cypriot and/or Cilician imports. Stylistically, it gives an impression of being relatively late in Cypriot terms with similarities particularly to the pottery of Enkomi from the end of Level IIIB and Level IIIC and to Proto-White Painted. The range also appears to continue well down into Cypro-Geometric. In this latter respect, it resembles the picture from early Iron Age levels at Tarsus, Mersin, and Kilise Tepe, where Cilician "white-painted" and "bichrome" pottery of the eleventh and later centuries bears more than a passing resemblance to its Cypriot equivalents (Goldman 1963, 93; Garstang 1953, 253–54; Hansen and Postgate 1999, 117).

Further south is Ras Ibn Hani, which survived (or revived) after the destruction of its royal palace and of its immediate neighbors, Ugarit and Minet el-Beida. There are also reports of the phenomenon at Ras el-Bassit and Tell Sukas (Caubet 1992, 127–28; Hankey 1967, 114). Though these have not so far been substantiated convincingly at Sukas (Riis et al. 1996), the excavator at Ras el-Bassit has expressed the view that contacts with Cyprus were apparently never interrupted (Courbin 1983, 120). For illustrations of what was found in the early Iron Age levels at Ras Ibn Hani,[7] we are dependent on a series of preliminary reports (Bounni et al. 1978; 1979; Lagarce and Lagarce 1978; Caubet 1992, 123–27; see also now du Piêd 2011, 225). Without knowing precisely what it consists of, what sort of proportions it comes in, exactly what it looks and feels like, and how much it varies, we are still somewhat in the dark. The excavators, however, seem to single out three categories (Bounni et al. 1978, 280–82; 1979, 251–57): What they call fine wares, whose resemblance to those in Cyprus, for example at Enkomi, is said to be remarkable (Bounni et al. 1978, 280, fig. 28:1, 3–4, 14; cf. Lagarce and Lagarce 1978, 59); what they call a more rustic type of kraters and bowls of which

---

which seems rather more akin to those of some Cypro-Geometric or Greek Proto-Geometric or sub-Proto-Geometric skyphoi (cf., e.g., Kearsley 1989, fig. 1:6 [Al Mina]; Popham, Sackett and Themelis 1979–1980, pl. 125:Tomb 2 [Lefkandi]; Gjerstad 1948, fig. XVIII:5 [Cypriot White Painted III]). This, combined with several of the imported Cypriot and Greek vessels listed by Swift (1958, 120–23), suggests that the date range of 'Amuq N may extend down into the ninth century, possibly to a time contemporary with Al Mina Level X. A somewhat similar range of pottery, also with Cypriot connections, is now known from across the Orontes at Tell Afis (Levels 9a–8 and 7–6) and dated between the end of the twelfth and the ninth centuries (Venturi 1998, 129–37; Lehmann, this volume). It is associated, in Levels 9a–7 with pottery regarded by the excavators as Cypriot imports (Bonatz 1998). Stratified below these, in Level 9b, is a krater with resemblances both to kraters from Ras Ibn Hani and from the Philistine region (Bonatz 1998, 217–18, figs. 1:1, 3, 5:1).

7. Fer I, sol inférieur (cf. Bounni et al. 1979, 245–55).

it is said that their many resemblances to pottery from more southerly sites, such as Afula and Ashdod, are apparent from the particularities of execution (Bounni et al. 1978, 280, fig. 28:2, 6; 1979, 251–52, fig. 25);[8] and pieces of bichrome kraters which are said to closely resemble Philistine bichrome pottery (Bounni et al. 1978, 280–82, fig. 28:11, 15; Lagarce and Lagarce 1978, 61). The obvious stylistic similarities to Cyprus in this case look as though they cover a considerable span, from at least the beginning of LC IIIA (or earlier) down to its end or even later, and including bowls with the kind of wavy line decoration which is particularly characteristic of Enkomi Level IIIC (Bounni et al. 1978, fig. 28:10, 13). At the other end of the spectrum, we have a few shallow bowls (called "cups" by the excavators), which seem generally very similar to those found at Minet el-Beida and Ugarit before its destruction, as well as in Cyprus in LC IIC or transitional LC IIC/IIIA, and whose claim to be regarded as peculiarly "Mycenaean" seems highly debatable (Bounni et al. 1979, 251–52 with references, fig. 25:3–6; cf., e.g., Schaeffer 1949, figs. 55:13, 57:15, 58:5; 1978, figs. 33:20, 22, 52:2). The relatively large number of kraters is particularly stressed by the excavators and seems interesting in view of the number of imported kraters (of both Aegean and Cypriot manufacture) found in Late Bronze Ugarit (Bounni et al. 1979, 251; cf. Leonard 1994, 207–9; van Wijngaarden 1999, 89; 2002, 331–40).[9] This pottery is also accompanied by other types of wares that continue those found at Late Bronze Ugarit and Ras Ibn Hani, and by masses of Canaanite jars (Bounni et al. 1979, 252–55, fig. 26). The excavators themselves believe that all this pottery was made at Ras Ibn Hani and though I do not doubt that much of it was, I am not sure, in view of the excavators' own descriptions, that we can necessarily exclude the possibility that at least some of it was imported, possibly from Cyprus itself and probably also from further south on the Levantine coast (see du Piêd 2011, 225, 227). Before leaving Ras Ibn Hani, it seems worth quoting the conclusions drawn by A. Caubet at the end of her survey of twelfth-century occupation on the Syrian coast: "As for the occupants of the Syrian coastal sites following the destructions at the end of the Bronze Age, at present no material or historical argument permits their identification as 'Sea Peoples.' The archaeological evidence that bears witness to any reoccupation is essentially the pottery, the significance of which is more chronological than cultural. Nothing suggests connections between the pottery discovered at Ras Bassit and Ras ibn Hani with foreign populations … The Mycenaean IIIC:1 imported or locally imitated ceramics were simply the

8. This also includes pilgrim or lentoid flasks (Bounni et al. 1979, 252 n. 5).

9. Kraters of one sort or another make up over 15 percent of the imported Aegean or Aegean-type pottery published from Ugarit and Minet el-Beida before 1978 (figures from van Wijngaarden 1990).

type of ware being made for everyday use at this time" (1992, 130). From what one can see of ceramic continuity between Late Bronze and Early Iron at Ras Ibn Hani and at the southern harbor site at Tell Sukas (where round-bottomed pyxides are singled out as the clearest examples of Mycenaean "imitations" [Riis et al. 1996, 55–56, fig. 37:3455/1,3441/1,3766/1; see further below]), Caubet's remarks seem entirely justified.

Further down the coast is Sarepta and almost certainly also other coastal sites—if and when we learn enough about them in this period.[10] At Sarepta, where the phenomenon is classified under the headings of "Late Helladic IIIC early 'Eastern Mediterranean Style,'" "Derivative Mycenaean," and probably also (at least partly) "Simple Style" (Koehl 1985, 42, 44),[11] the absolute quantities seem

10. The deep sounding at Tyre (Bikai 1976) has not, as far as I can see, produced any clear indications of this ceramic phenomenon. The often-mentioned "derivative Granary Style" deep bowl or cup from Stratum XIV (Bikai 1976, pl. XXXIX:20; cf. Koehl 1985, 61 n. 145; Coldstream and Bikai 1988, 38) seems to me, on the grounds of its profile, size, and the description of its paint (which is characterized as "blue-black metallic"), much more likely to be an Early Proto-Geometric (perhaps late-eleventh century) import from Greece (cf., e.g., Desborough 1952, pls. 27:Tomb P.G.25, 29:B; Popham and Sackett 1968, fig. 53; Wells 1983, fig. 77). If so, it should probably count as one of the earliest early Iron Age Greek imports to the Levant, possibly roughly contemporary with the Levantine juglet from Skoubris Tomb 46 at Lefkandi (Popham, Sackett, and Themelis 1979–1980, 126, pls. 106:46.3, 270:b). It is perhaps not without significance that it should be found at Tyre, which has otherwise produced by far the largest number of Middle Proto-Geometric (tenth-century) imports in the eastern Mediterranean (Coldstream and Bikai 1988; Coldstream 1989; 1998). See now also Maeir, Fantalkin and Zukerman 2009 for a deep bowl fragment from a late Iron Age I context at Tell eṣ-Ṣafi, claimed to be an import from the Argolid, which is probably of a roughly similar date to the Tyre cup.

11. The basis of the distinction between these categories is not entirely clear, but seems to be partly one of fabric appearance, partly one of the shapes involved, and partly one of presumed date. The fabric of the first of these categories ("Late Helladic IIIC early 'Eastern Mediterranean Style,'" which is not described in general terms) seems to be relatively heterogeneous (cf. Koehl 1985, 118–22). It can sometimes be fairly coarse; it ranges in color from red to very pale brown, and is covered with a matte slip of pale or pinkish color. The paint is matte and varies in color between red, reddish brown, and black. The description of one piece, whose fabric is described as fairly coarse, suggests that it may be decorated in a bichrome technique (Koehl 1985, 120–21 no. 196 [where it is compared to a piece from Ashdod], figs. 8, 20). The shapes listed are confined to stirrup jars and deep and shallow bowls. The fabric of the second category ("Derivative Mycenaean") is described as coarse, gritty, and reddish in color, covered with a matte tan slip and matte red paint, and burnished, usually after painting (Koehl 1985, 42), and seems to be used mainly for stirrup jars, lentoid (pilgrim) flasks, and shallow bowls. The fabric of the third category, "Simple Style," is also relevant to the phenomenon of Levantine production of an Aegean type of painted pottery. As far as fabric is concerned, it seems to differ little in appearance from that of the "Derivative Mycenaean" category, perhaps the only difference being that it is slightly less gritty (Koehl 1985, 42). Many of the pots placed in this category are also described

small, but the overall impression has some similarities to that glimpsed at Ras Ibn Hani. This includes the impression of a considerable time span in Cypriot terms within the first of these categories, emphasized again by one or two bowls that would seem most at home in Enkomi Level IIIC or Kition Floor II (Koehl 1985, 44, 120–21 nos. 194, 197–98, figs. 8, 20–21), as well as by material that looks earlier (Koehl 1985, 118–22 nos. 189–93, 195–96, 199, figs. 8, 20–21; Pritchard 1975, 91, figs. 26:4, 52:1). The inclusion of the other two categories may well take us back into the later thirteenth century (Koehl 1985, 42–44, 109–10 nos. 154–55, 111–17 nos. 159, 162, 165, 169–71, 175, 177–83, 185–86, figs. 7–8, 18–19; see further below). Here, too, there is the smell—in the description of fabrics—of imports or at least resemblances to pottery from coastal areas further south (Koehl 1985, 42, 44, 109, 111–15, 120–21, 146–47);[12] and we may be dealing with actual imports from both Cyprus and these areas. This type of pottery is accompanied, in the limited areas excavated, by a relentlessly plain or simply banded repertoire of bowls of varying types and sizes and large numbers of storage or transport jars (Pritchard 1975, 64–65, 77–84).

Further south still, there is the cluster of sites around the Bay of Akko and the entrance to the Jezreel Valley (Stern 2000b). The tiny amount of the Akko pottery so far published mainly in line drawings or sketches (M. Dothan 1989, fig. 3.1–2; 1993c, 21) seems for the most part thoroughly Cypriot in terms of its shapes and decorations, though some pieces might equally be thought to have a somewhat "Philistine" appearance (cf., e.g., M. Dothan 1993c, 21 with T. Dothan 1998b, fig. 4). The nature and variety of its fabric(s) remain to be seen, but seem likely on present evidence to be varied and interesting (see below), while the association of at least one deep bowl with a kiln (M. Dothan 1989, 60, fig. 3.1:a) suggests that

---

as having been burnished after painting (Koehl 1985, 109 no. 154, 111 no. 160, 113–15 nos. 169, 172–75). The separate distinction of this rather nebulous category is derived from Furumark (1941b, 116–18), who used it to classify a narrow range of closed vessels (piriform jars, stirrup jars, and lentoid flasks) typically decorated only with simple bands and found in the Levant which he dated on a mixture of stylistic and contextual grounds to late Mycenaean IIIB.

In general, the "Late Helladic IIIC early 'Eastern Mediterranean Style'" category seems to cluster mainly in the levels assigned to Periods IV–V in Area II.X at Sarepta, while sherds of the "Derivative Mycenaean" and "Simple Style" categories seem to cluster in the levels immediately below these (Period III) (cf. Koehl 1985, table 2).

12. This includes one apparently bichrome fragment (Koehl 1985, 120–21 no. 196; see preceding note). Notable also are those pieces classified in Koehl's "Simple Style" and "Derivative Mycenaean" style that have surfaces burnished after painting (see also preceding note). For this as one of the more striking characteristics of apparently locally made "Mycenaean" ware from Akko which the participants were fortunate enough to be shown during the workshop, see further below.

some of it was probably made there. At Akko, as at Sarepta, there is no evidence for a clear stratigraphic break between the late-thirteenth and twelfth centuries (M. Dothan 1993c, 21; Artzy 2001, 108), which is the time span associated with the installation of industrial workshops on top of the ramparts, involving such activities as pottery manufacture, metalworking, and textile dyeing (Artzy, this volume).

Neutron activation analysis of a stirrup jar from nearby Tell Keisan suggests that it comes from the Palaepaphos area in Cyprus—a suggestion that seems consonant with its appearance (Balensi 1981, 400, pl. XI; Gunneweg and Perlman 1994). Carrying on up the Jezreel Valley to the Egyptian fortress at Beth Shean, a handful of sherds from that site—the majority from stirrup jars or other closed vessels—also seem very likely to be genuine Cypriot products (Mazar 1993b, 216; 1997b, 159; Sherratt 2009; Cohen-Weinberger 2009; Mommsen, D'Agata, and Yasur-Landau 2009), though peppered among them are fragments of what appear to be "local," or more generally Levantine coastal, manufacture (Sherratt and Mazar, this volume; see now also Zukerman 2009; Cohen-Weinberger 2009, 526–28, table 8.4). Back on the coast, from Dor, in the murky depths of Area G Phase 11 (but without any real context, either architectural or ceramic), comes part of an amphoroid krater with spiral decoration that petrographic analysis suggests was locally made. The combination of its shape and decoration would suggest a comparative date in Cypriot terms of either late in LC IIC or early in LC IIIA (Stern 2000a, pl. IX:a right; for Dor, see also Sharon and Gilboa, this volume).[13]

We then come to the Philistine area, particularly the sites of Ashdod, Tel Miqne-Ekron, Ashkelon, and most recently Tell eṣ-Ṣafi. In the context of this volume (see especially the contributions by Killebrew, Mountjoy, Dothan and Ben-Shlomo, and Maeir), I need not say much about the phenomenon at these sites, except to note that the precise proportions of the so-called Mycenaean IIIC:1b (or "Philistine monochrome"), in Field INE at Tel Miqne-Ekron at least, according to Killebrew (1998a), seem to have been fairly insignificant in the first two phases of Stratum VII, becoming noticeable in Phase 9B when the kilns appear, and first appearing in large quantities in Phase 9A, the final phase

---

13. For the position at Dor (especially Area G), see Stern 2000b, 199–201; Sharon and Gilboa, this volume, with further references. I am grateful to Ilan Sharon for sending me a color photo of the amphoroid krater fragment, to Maria Iacovou (who saw it in person) for discussing her impressions of it with me, and to Ayelet Gilboa for the information that it appears to be of local manufacture on the basis of petrographic analysis carried out by Y. Goren and A. Cohen-Weinberger (see now Sharon and Gilboa, this volume, and fig. 42). Along with it was found a fragment of a stirrup jar in the same ware. For another fragment from Dor, also distinctly Cypriot-looking, but probably of somewhat later date, see Wolff 1998a, 778 fig. 14.

of the stratum. As far as the shapes and decorations are concerned, these seem to represent a somewhat selective and streamlined (and probably functionally determined) range of the types produced in contemporary Cyprus, predominantly drinking bowls (especially deep bowls), kraters, stirrup jars, and side-spouted jugs (Killebrew 1998a; 2000; Rutter, this volume). The decoration for the most part represents a thoroughly characteristic sample of that found on Cypriot White Painted Wheelmade III, though it also has some peculiarities of its own. At Tel Miqne-Ekron at least, to judge by the chronological sequence of illustrations presented by Killebrew (1998a, figs. 6–7, 10; cf. also Stager 1995, fig. 3:11–49), we can see a parallel stylistic development to that seen on Cyprus, with rather more elaborate forms of decoration, very comparable, for instance, to some of those from Enkomi Level IIIB, appearing in the latest phase of Stratum VII and the early phases of Stratum VI. Stratum VI also sees the beginning of Philistine Bichrome, consisting of much the same repertoire in terms of shapes, which by Stratum V has apparently replaced the "Myc. IIIC:1b" pottery completely. Stylistically, the earlier Bichrome also shows recognizable similarities in style to the kind of relatively elaborate style associated, for instance, with Enkomi Level IIIB or Sinda III. Thereafter, in the later part of the twelfth century, pottery in Cyprus and at the Philistine sites continues along separate lines in each of these respective areas.

I would like to raise one more issue concerning this pottery before I leave it. This is that, having been used to seeing it illustrated mainly in line drawings, I have often been quite puzzled as to how one could be quite certain in any given instance that an individual sherd or pot was indeed made in the area and not imported from Cyprus. Having had an opportunity in 2000 to see a little of the Miqne pottery up close, and having had the opportunity to examine some "Philistine monochrome" sherds from Garstang's excavations at Ashkelon in the Ashmolean Museum[14] together with Sabine Laemmel, I find I am less puzzled

14. Ashmolean Museum No. 1927.2100 from the North Cutting (Stratum 2, Bag 3), dug for stratification purposes by J. Garstang, Palestine Exploration Fund excavations, 1921 (see Phythian-Adams 1921; and for similar sherds, see Phythian-Adams 1923, 71–72, 80–81, pl. II). This includes fragments of linear decorated deep bowls (1927.2100.6–9) (fig. 2), shallow bowls (1927.2100.10 [a shallow conical bowl, probably handleless; cf. M. Dothan and Porath 1993, fig. 14:1–7] and 1927.2100.18 [a very shallow bowl with decoration of zigzags between straight lines on the interior]), a side-spouted jug (1927.2100.17) (fig. 2), a fragment of what is possibly a strainer jug with decoration of birds flanking a cross-hatched panel (1927.2100.19) (fig. 2), and other closed vessels with banded decoration (1927.2100.11–14) (fig. 2), all decorated in monochrome paint, as well as a fragment of a cooking pot (1927.2100.20; for shape, cf., e.g., Killebrew 1998a, figs. 7:19, 10:13–14). Two other sherds (1927.2100.4 [a krater] and 1927.2100.15 [the neck of a large jar or amphora]), otherwise of the same ware, are decorated in bichrome. Since, as

Fig. 2: Selected "monochrome" sherds from Garstang's excavations at Ashkelon, 1921. From top left: Ashmolean Museum 1927.2100.8, 7, 6, 12, 11, 9, 19, 17. Reproduced courtesy of the Department of Antiquities, Ashmolean Museum.

---

it turned out, there was no stratigraphy worth speaking of in the North Cutting, it is not known whether these "Philistine monochrome" sherds from Ashkelon should be regarded as contemporary with "Philistine bichrome" pottery or whether they belong to a pre-bichrome phase, evidence for which is said to exist in Grid 38 of the recent excavations (Stager 1995, fig. 3:38–49). Certainly, as far as the shapes and decoration are concerned, they would fit very comfortably in what is known of the latter. The fabric of the cooking pot bears little resemblance to the typical "sandy" Mycenaean wheelmade cooking pot ware (see, e.g., Döhl 1973, 186–91), and instead is more like Cypriot Plain Wheelmade Ware in appearance and texture.

in some respects and still puzzled in others (fig. 2). The fabrics of the Ashkelon sherds differ widely in color, ranging from greenish or grayish buff, through buff, pink, orangey-red to brick red. Some have no distinct slip,[15] though most of them are covered (sometimes on the exterior surface only) with a pale slip, which is often powdery in consistency.[16] The paint is thoroughly matte in finish and ranges in color from light brown to dark magenta-red. What is perhaps most noticeable about all these sherds, however, is that the surfaces, particularly in the interiors, have a very distinctive gritty feel, quite unlike anything I have yet encountered on any Mycenaean or Minoan pottery in the Aegean and also unlike anything I have yet encountered in the White Painted Wheelmade III of Cyprus, though it occurs to me that it is not totally unlike some of the Cypriot plain wheelmade wares in this respect. It is perhaps possible to get some slight sense of this grittiness from color photographs, for example, of one of the "Philistine monochrome" sherds from Ashkelon published by Stager (1991, 33) and another of pots from Ashdod Stratum XIIIb (M. Dothan and Porath 1993, color pls.), though it is something that I suspect is unmistakable only when one can actually feel it with one's fingers. This sense of grittiness is hinted at in Koehl's description of at least some of the "Derivative Mycenaean" and "Eastern Mediterranean Style" pottery from Sarepta (Koehl 1985, 42, and especially 120–21 no. 196), and in the excavators' account of some of the pottery (including the bichrome sherds) at Ras Ibn Hani (Bounni et al. 1978, 280).

On the other hand, the Tel Miqne pottery seems in general less obviously gritty, though it is characterized by what seems to be variation in fabric texture, color, and surface finish (Killebrew, this volume; Mountjoy, this volume). At the same time, it appears as though the paint is invariably very matte, as on the Ashkelon (and apparently also the Ashdod) pottery. As at Ashkelon, one of the more striking features is a powdery surface finish, the result of the application of a powdery slip, probably to give a pale surface color, but this does not seem to be invariable (cf. T. Dothan and M. Dothan 1992, pl. 22). Some at least of the variations seem visually indistinguishable from among the range of variations encountered on Cyprus, so to some extent my puzzlement continues; and I suspect that, if one were to put some of the Miqne sherds in a Cypriot con-

15. 1927.2100.8-9, 12, 15. Of these, 1927.2100.12 (part of a closed vessel) is of a bright orangey-red colored fabric.

16. A distinct white or pale slip can be seen on 1927.2100.4, 6–7, 10–11, 13–14, 17–18. On 1927.2100.10 (a shallow conical bowl) a white slip is applied to the exterior only; the interior surface retains the brick-red color of the clay fabric. The slip is distinctly powdery on 1927.2100.4 (a bichrome krater), 1927.2100.7 (a deep bowl), 1927.2100.11, 14 (closed vessels), and 1927.2100.17 (a side-spouted jug).

text, one would be hard put to tell the difference (cf. Bikai 1994, 31). However, something else that struck me about just one or two of the Miqne deep bowls that I was kindly permitted to examine was the difficulty of telling whether they were wheelmade or handmade. This was either because they were handmade or because the interior and exterior surfaces had been heavily smoothed off the wheel in vertical or diagonal directions so that no trace of wheelmarks remained. While this is something frequently encountered, for instance, on Cycladic Middle Bronze Age pottery, I have never seen this either on Aegean Late Bronze Age pottery or on Cypriot White Painted Wheelmade III where any smoothing is done on the wheel and the wheelmade (or at least wheel-finished) nature of the pot is rarely in doubt. It occurs to me that this may be an indication that these bowls were made by potters more accustomed to making handmade pots, or who (perhaps less probably) for one reason or another wanted their finished products to look handmade. Another thing that struck me were some signs of what seemed to be a merging of local "Canaanite" and "Myc. IIIC:1b" features, such as the addition of a painted band round the neck of a large jug with cylindrical neck, vertical handle, and pinched spout, a normal "Canaanite" type (cf., e.g., Killebrew 1998a, 389, fig. 3:10). This kind of merging has analogies in Cyprus, where one comes across such hybrids as White Painted Wheelmade III versions of Base Ring bowls and White Slip milkbowls, slipped or painted to look like the handmade versions. These are little details and for all I know may be extremely unusual at Tel Miqne-Ekron, but they are the sort of thing we need to be alert to if we are really to get to grips with the nature of the phenomenon that interests us. At the very least, they suggest that there may be risks involved in normalizing our ceramic classifications too readily and thus creating categories with unnecessarily distinct and rigidly drawn boundaries between them.

I have two more observations before I leave the "where?" question. The first is that there is quite an impressive correlation between the general areas of the eastern Mediterranean (and in many cases the actual sites) where this ceramic phenomenon can be seen and the places where imported pottery of Late Helladic (or Late Minoan) IIIA and IIIB turns up, though the imported pottery penetrates in small quantities rather further inland.[17] The same applies to imports of Cypriot pottery in the Late Bronze Age Levant, whose general distribution has recently been plotted by Nicola Schreiber (2003, map 16); and the sheer quantity of White Slip bowls which reached coastal sites like Akko in the fourteenth–

17. See, e.g., the distribution maps compiled by Gregori and Palumbo (1986, figs. 3–4). If one were to take into account absolute quantities rather than overall distributions of imported Aegean pottery, the correlation would seem even more striking.

thirteenth centuries is something that we are only now beginning to appreciate (Artzy 2001; this volume).

There is no need here to rehearse the reasons for believing that much of the imported Aegean pottery that reached the Levant in the fourteenth–thirteenth centuries was actually carried and marketed by Cypriots (Hankey 1981a, 44–45; 1993, 103; Hirschfeld 1992; Sherratt 1999). What is also interesting, however, are the geographical locations of those regions and sites where *both* Cypriot and Mycenaean imported pottery *and* the ceramic phenomenon in which we are interested are found in the eastern Mediterranean mainland, particularly in relation to conjunctions of maritime and overland routes. The only exceptions to the pattern of correlation lie in the north, particularly in Cilicia which lay under full Hittite imperial control during the later-fourteenth and thirteenth centuries, where both Mycenaean and Cypriot imports seem to have been severely (and probably deliberately) restricted down to the end of the period of Hittite control (Sherratt and Crouwel 1987, 345). This probably gives us a clue to another important factor that determined the locations of our ceramic phenomenon—that is, their relationship to general political configurations in the late-thirteenth and twelfth centuries, from roughly around the death of Ramesses II. The loosening up or disappearance of Egyptian and Hittite imperial control in some regions, and associated switches in supply routes in others, together offered a variety of opportunities of differing character for opportunistic interstitial growth in increasingly diversified forms of decentralized trade and the establishment of new trading patterns and partnerships. It seems to me no coincidence, for example, that it is only after it ceased to be a Hittite imperial province that we see the signs of Cilicia reverting once more to an outlook that reflected its natural, geographical position facing towards the eastern Mediterranean, and engaging in the sort of informal, maritime interchange that the trade in Aegean and Cypriot pottery seems to have represented (Sherratt and Crouwel 1987, 345; Artzy 1997, 3; cf. Sherratt 1999). Cyprus almost certainly had a central and increasingly diversified role as player and stimulus in this general process of opportunistic and interstitial trade in the later-thirteenth and early-twelfth centuries, and an element of import substitution of pottery, in places where local markets not only for Cypriot pottery but also for Cypriot-carried and Cypriot-produced Aegean pottery already existed, is quite likely to have played a part in it.

Finally, still on the "where?" question, it seems worth remembering that the eastern Mediterranean is not the only area outside the Minoan-Mycenaean cultural sphere (whatever we think we mean by that) in which a painted ware of "Aegean" type is taken into production in a local context during the second millennium. It happens at Troy and elsewhere in coastal Anatolia, probably as early as the fourteenth century or perhaps even earlier (Mountjoy 1997a; 1998, 34). It happens in southern Italy at least by the early-thirteenth century and possibly also in Sicily and Sardinia a little later (Vagnetti 1999; 2000, 312–13). It happens in Macedonia from early in the twelfth century or perhaps a little earlier (Kiriatzi et al. 1997). At least on the face of it, these are examples of a very similar ceramic phenomenon, though the particulars of the contexts may be rather different. I leave you to consider the logical implications of extending to these the traditional "migration/invasion" interpretation of this phenomenon in the eastern Mediterranean. At the very least, it would result in a picture of a massive and prolonged diaspora of Aegeans of no clearly identifiable origin, who perceived pottery as the most important (and indeed sole) focus and material symbol of their self-identity, and among whom—one would have to conclude—potters were disproportionately represented.

When?

The traditional account has it that the appearance of this ceramic phenomenon in the eastern Mediterranean dates to the years around and following 1200 B.C.E., and is a direct effect of the collapse of the Mycenaean palaces in the Aegean, the fall of Ugarit, and the events of the eighth regnal year of Ramesses III in the Levant; and that it is something that appears suddenly after a simultaneous horizon of destruction and mayhem. On Cyprus at least, however, it has been clear for more than thirty years now that this is not actually the case.[18] Cypriot production of an Aegean type of pottery begins well back in the thirteenth century, starting probably with the so-called Rude Style kraters, and increases steadily in quantity and repertoire during the course of the century (Kling 1989, 170; 1991; Sherratt 1990b; 1991). By the time we get to what is conventionally thought of as the start of LC IIIA (that is, around Enkomi Level IIIA or Kition Floor IIIa), there is already a wide repertoire of shapes based variously, and fluidly, on Aegean, local Cypriot and probably also metallic models (Sherratt 1990b). Thereafter, although there may be a certain amount of streamlining and "thinning down," we continue to see the occasional periodic introduction of new shapes, and the gradual development of new types of decoration throughout LC IIIA (Kling 1991).

18. Indeed, this is the problem that Dikaios' convoluted terminology, which is referred to above, was designed to get round. By drawing an almost entirely spurious distinction between "Late Myc. IIIB" and "Myc. IIIC:1b" he succeeded in disguising the fact that the local production of a Mycenaean type of pottery, which he felt compelled to associate exclusively with the LC IIIA constructions that followed the destruction of Enkomi Level IIB (which he associated with Achaean/Mycenaean invaders), was already taking place in LC II (see Kling 1985; 1987; 1989, 28–32, 170; 2000, 287).

Well before the end of LC IIC, Cyprus was exporting the products of this White Painted Wheelmade III production to the adjacent mainland. This can be seen in the "Rude Style" kraters at Ugarit, Byblos, Beirut, Megiddo, Gezer, and elsewhere (Leonard 1994, 9; cf. Anson 1980a; 1980b), as well as in a considerable number of pots of various types (notably from Ugarit, but also at other sites, such as Sarepta, Tell el-Ajjul, and Tell el-Far'ah South among others) whose general appearance and/or the appearance of their fabric[19] suggests that they were probably made on Cyprus rather than imported from the Aegean itself (Stubbings 1951, 82–83; Koehl 1985, 146; Laemmel, this volume).

Nor is this process of local production before the twelfth century confined to Cyprus. Over the years, what have been called local "imitations" or locally made "copies" of Mycenaean pottery have been noted from a wide variety of sites in Syria and the Levant, dating to the thirteenth and even the fourteenth centuries. These consist mainly of stirrup jars, straight-sided alabastra (pyxides), lentoid (pilgrim) flasks, and piriform jars, sometimes unpainted but more often decorated with simple bands and occasionally with some additional ornament which may or may not resemble "Aegean" decoration.[20] They are regarded as "imitation" because of what is seen as their "inferior" fabric and imitations of "Mycenaean" pottery, mainly on account of the particular shapes, which are regarded as primarily "Mycenaean"—though it seems to me that they are no more or less "imitations" (if one insists on using that somewhat value-laden term) than is the "Myc. IIIC:1b" pottery from Miqne, Ashdod, or Ashkelon. Indeed, it might be asked in what sense, once such shapes can be seen to form part of local ceramic repertoires, the application of the label "Mycenaean" has any useful meaning at all.[21] The distinction drawn by Hankey (1982, 170) between locally made "imitations" and the equally locally made "Myc. IIIC" "real thing" dissolves into a state of particular fuzziness in the later thirteenth century[22] when not only do such "imitations" increase in number (at some sites arguably displacing Aegean

19. And in a few cases, actual fabric analysis: cf. Gunneweg et al. 1986, 14; Perlman, Asaro, and Dothan 1973, 151.

20. Albright 1930–1931, 44–45; Guy 1938, 157–58; Hamilton 1935, 39 no. 240; Woolley 1955, 371; Schaeffer 1949, fig. 73:2–3, 7, 12–13; Stubbings 1951, 63, 67, 74–78, 81, 83–85; Hankey 1967, 112, 132, 142, 145, fig. 5:c, pl. 36:d; 1977; 1981b, 113–15, fig. 3; 1982, 170; 1993, 103, 105; 1995, 183; M. Dothan 1971, 155, fig. 81:12, pl. LXXV:4; Baramki 1973; Leonard 1994, 9; Laemmel 1998; 2009, 171–78.

21. The designation "imitation Mycenaean" seems particularly odd in the case of the lentoid or pilgrim flask, since the shape in Mycenaean pottery is often regarded as an Aegean "imitation" of an eastern one (Furumark 1941a, 32; Leonard 1994, 80).

22. Oren's "terminal Bronze Age," as described by him at the 2001 workshop.

imports altogether),[23] but also appear to include some widening of the range of shapes beyond closed containers. At Ugarit, for example, Monchambert has argued for the local manufacture or "imitation" of "Mycenaean" kraters, jugs and bowls, as well as stirrup jars, flasks, and jars (Monchambert 1983, 27–28, fig. 1:1–4; cf. Yon 1992, 117, fig. 14.5:c).[24] This seems of particular interest in view of the evident element of ceramic continuity between predestruction Ugarit and early Iron Age Ras Ibn Hani (Bounni et al. 1979, 252–55; cf. Caubet 1992, 127–28).

There seems to be considerable variety in the fabrics involved in such thirteenth-century local production (insofar as it can be distinguished), which suggests that it was probably taking place in a number of workshops in a wide range of different places. There are also wide variations in the degree to which these resemble their supposed Mycenaean "prototypes," in terms of fabric, technology, surface finish, shape, decoration, and varied combinations of these (Leonard 1994, 51, 80; Laemmel 1998; this volume). Most would appear to be wheel-turned, but a few are apparently handmade (Hamilton 1935, 39 no. 240). In the far south, at Haruba in northern Sinai, the fabric of a number of stirrup jars decorated with simple bands is described as soft, low-fired, and of a creamy pink color (E. Oren, personal communication); in other cases fabrics are described as brick- or orange-red, brown or buff in color; sometimes (as at Gharifeh and Sarepta) a soft or relatively coarse red fabric is covered with a white or light-colored slip (Stubbings 1951, 77; Baramki 1973, 194; Koehl 1985, 42; Monchambert 1983, 28, fig. 1:2–3; Hamilton 1935, 39 no. 240). The paint, as on the "Philistine monochrome" pottery, is invariably matte and can vary between a range of shades from orange-red through purple to black; in some cases (as perhaps at Ugarit) a deliberate bichrome technique may be used.[25] However, on one of the most striking varieties, the outer surface has been intensively burnished after painting, giving the whole surface of the pot (including the paint) an unusual kind of burnished gloss. I have not seen a technique anything like this on any Aegean or Cypriot pottery and can only conclude that it represents an attempt by an

23. Thus at the late thirteenth-century site of Tel Nami neutron activation suggests that none of the stirrup jars was produced in the Aegean. While at least one appears to have been made in Cyprus, several others were probably manufactured in the Levant (Artzy 1993, 1097; 1994, 130; personal communication; this volume). See also Koehl's remarks on the later Mycenaean IIIB pottery at Sarepta (Koehl 1985, 146).

24. Some of these (including a stirrup jar) are said to be decorated in a bichrome technique (Monchambert 1983, 28). For locally made kraters at Megiddo, supposedly also derived from Mycenaean types, see also Guy 1938, 157–58.

25. An apparently deliberate use of two colors is also occasionally found on LC IIC pottery of Mycenaean type (cf., e.g., Karageorghis 1974, 87; Sherratt 1990a, 111 n.4).

unorthodox (and extraordinarily laborious) means to replicate the lustrous paint characteristic of imported Mycenaean pottery, particularly that manufactured in the Argolid.[26] This fabric is found at Akko, Beth Shean, and apparently also at Sarepta, and seems to be used mainly for closed containers, such as stirrup jars and lentoid flasks.[27] Where it was made and in how many places remains to be seen. Its precise chronological contexts are still not entirely clear, but at Akko it appears to be associated mainly with the later-thirteenth century, while at Sarepta it seems to cluster mainly in the period immediately preceding the pottery categorized as "Myc. IIIC Early" (Koehl 1985, table 2). In view of the stratigraphical continuity evident at both sites, it may have persisted into the early-twelfth century—though it seems unlikely that it continued for long. Given the labor involved in burnishing the entire surface in this way, it is improbable that the practice long outlived the memory of the regular importation of Aegean (particularly Argive) pottery that is likely to have inspired it.

By contrast, it is interesting that, more or less without exception, the so-called "Myc. IIIC" pottery (which relates most closely and consistently to that of Cyprus) appears to be characterized by paint with a matte surface finish. The replication of a lustrous effect (by whatever means) does not seem to have been something that the producers of this pottery either desired or thought important. This would not be surprising if (as the repertoires of shape and decoration suggest) Cypriot pottery of this type formed their main models, since, though a degree of lustrousness in the paint of the Cypriot output is certainly not unknown (cf. Sherratt 1990a, 111), the generality is a much more consistently matte effect than is encountered in the Aegean, even in LH IIIC. As it is, Stratum XIIIb at

26. For the technology behind the lustrous paint on Late Bronze Age Aegean pottery, see Jones 1986b, 788–92. It is curious that, though Cypriot potters sometimes produced something approaching this lustrous effect, apparently by the use of a similar technique to that used in the Aegean, Levantine potters (including the potters responsible for "Philistine monochrome" pottery) never seem to have done so. It would appear that either they did not know how to, or (perhaps particularly in the case of the "Philistine monochrome" potters) lustrous paint was not one of the "Aegean" ceramic effects they were aware of or desired to achieve.

27. Participants at the workshop were able to see examples of this striking pottery from Akko with their own eyes, thanks to the kindness of the organizers and those working with the Akko ceramic material (among them, Ezra Marcus). Its presence at Sarepta is inferred from Koehl's descriptions of the fabrics of pots categorized by him as "Derivative Mycenaean" and "Simple Style." For a clear description of lentoid flasks with this surface treatment from Beth Shean Strata N-4, S-4, S-3b, and S-3a (late-thirteenth to twelfth centuries), see Panitz-Cohen 2009, 256–58 (FL 71a), photo 5.47. Petrographic analysis suggests that these may have been made in western Galilee (Cohen-Weinberger 2009, 521 table 8.1 no. 75, 523 table 8.2 no. 75). These are described as "burnished after painting" (Koehl 1985, 42, 109–15 nos. 154–55, 160–61, 165, 169, 171–75, 178, figs. 7, 18–19).

Ashdod provides some reasons for thinking that even this directly Cypriot-inspired production may have started before the end of the thirteenth century. Not only do the apparently locally produced contents of the "potters' shop" (M. Dothan and Porath 1993, 12, 55–58, figs. 14–15, pls. 35:9–16, 36, 37:1–4, color pls.; T. Dothan and M. Dothan 1992, 167) seem to correlate best with White Painted Wheelmade III from LC IIC or LC IIC/IIIA transitional contexts (including types, like handleless conical bowls, squat carinated bowls, and side-spouted jugs, for which an Aegean origin can convincingly be ruled out [cf. Kling 1989, 170]),[28] but the same stratum also produces a fragment of a kylix described as covered with an off-white slip of the "Myc. IIIC:1" class (M. Dothan and Porath 1993, 58, fig. 17:7). This is most readily comparable to LC IIC kylikes from the lower burial of Kition Tomb 9, and, if not of local manufacture, may be a Cypriot import (Sherratt 2006).[29] At the same time, a kylix identical to one from the lower burial of Kition Tomb 9 is also known from Ugarit, providing a neat three-way linkage, which suggests that the beginning of Ashdod Stratum XIIIb and its locally made "Myc. IIIC:1b" pottery may predate (if only by a short while) both the end of LC IIC and the destruction of Ugarit.

Epilogue

Having attempted to address the questions I raised at the beginning concerning the ceramic phenomenon commonly attributed to "Sea Peoples," I should probably stop there. However, it seems worth emphasizing that it is difficult to avoid seeing this phenomenon in all the regions that we have looked at, with the pos-

---

28. The side-spouted jugs from the "potters' shop," with their large, clumsy flared spouts, do not even look Cypriot either. In this respect, the spouts seem somewhat reminiscent of those on some of the Late Bronze stirrup jars from the Levant regarded as local "imitations" (cf., e.g., Franken 1992, figs. 4–3:19, 4–6:9, pl. 6:a from Deir 'Alla). Though the shape as a whole may be new in the early Iron Age, flasks of very similar shape with basket handles (though without spouts) occur already in the Levant in the Late Bronze Age (cf. Metzger 1993, pls. 122, 158 from Kamid el-Loz), while there is also a Late Bronze Age tradition of jugs and other vessels with sometimes large side spouts (cf., e.g., Tufnell 1958, pl. 82:936–38 from Lachish). Similarly, it seems doubtful whether there is any very good reason to regard the simple handleless bowl shapes as necessarily derived from any specific foreign (as opposed to a generalized eastern Mediterranean) tradition.

29. Kylikes are not normally noted as part of the "Myc. IIIC:1b" ("Philistine monochrome") repertoire, for example at Tel Miqne, so the latter might be thought more likely. However, it appears that kylikes have now also been recovered from among the Stratum XII material in Area H at Ashdod (Dothan and Ben-Shlomo, this volume).

sible partial exception of Cilicia, as mediated primarily through Cyprus and, in the case of pottery commonly classified as "Myc. IIIC" and dated from the early-twelfth century onwards, almost certainly exclusively so. The production and/or consumption of Aegean-type pottery in the twelfth century seems for the most part directly relatable in terms of repertoire, style, and even in some aspects of surface appearance (particularly the matte nature of the paint) to that produced on Cyprus, and to that extent Cyprus (which earlier seems to have been instrumental in marketing genuinely imported Aegean pottery in the eastern Mediterranean) appears as both a central focus and major stimulus for the phenomenon. The role of Cyprus in the changing economic structure not only of the eastern Mediterranean but of the whole eastern half of the Mediterranean in the later-thirteenth and twelfth centuries is therefore crucial to understanding it. This forms part of a much bigger picture than can possibly be outlined within the limits of this relatively small-scale canvas, but one which I have attempted to delineate elsewhere (Sherratt 1998; 2003).

At the same time, there are subtleties in the eastern Mediterranean picture. Local production on the Levantine mainland of what may loosely be called (on one criterion or another) an Aegean-type pottery starts well before the end of the thirteenth century, and seems to be quite widespread and varied both in its appearance and its technology. Some of it is "Aegean" only by virtue of the shapes and use of painted decoration; in other cases (as at Akko and possibly also Sarepta) an attempt also seems to be made, by means of determined burnishing, to replicate the lustrous paint of genuine Mycenaean (particularly perhaps Argive) imports. While it starts with the closed package containers that form 60–70 percent of imported Mycenaean pottery, by the end of the century (as apparently at Ugarit and possibly at Ashdod) it has expanded to include production of the kinds of open or non-packaging shapes whose models arrive either as imports of genuinely Aegean pottery or as imports of Cypriot-produced pottery of Aegean type (White Painted Wheelmade III). While in most areas close links in repertoire, style, and general appearance with Cypriot White Painted Wheelmade III of the late-thirteenth and early-twelfth centuries can be seen, in some areas these purely ceramic stylistic links appear to be maintained down to the end of the twelfth century while in others (e.g., the Philistine region) they do not. In the ʿAmuq, on the other hand, it looks as though such links may only *begin* to appear in the twelfth century. In most areas, the picture is bedevilled by the difficulty of not knowing for certain what was made where: How much of it (and which pieces) were made on the spot, and how much brought in from somewhere else (and how many other places) in the eastern Mediterranean generally. The answers to these questions seem likely to emphasize both the complexity and variety within the overall picture, with some of the apparent differences in pattern between different sites or regions perhaps ultimately explicable in terms of differential patterns of interaction determined both by the configuration of relatively complex route and exchange networks and by different local or regional sociopolitical and economic conditions.

There is still a great deal we need to learn if we are to fully understand the ceramic phenomenon in the eastern Mediterranean as a whole. One way we could start is by freeing ourselves from what Bunimovitz (1995, 328) has called "the tyranny of historical context," which has led to pottery of this sort from selected regions or sites being incorporated into a traditional culture-historical, event-based (and text-led) narrative, while leaving it effectively unexplained (or at least conveniently ignored) elsewhere. We need instead to begin to examine it on its own terms, both as a generalized phenomenon and within its specific local or regional contexts, and to consider all the possible factors that may have a bearing on where it is found, what determines its distribution, and the timing of its appearance. We also need to examine our use of terminology and the way in which our classifications may be determined by preconceptions about the cultural or ethno-historical significance of particular groups of pottery in particular contexts, which may lead us to draw unnecessarily rigid boundaries within an overall class or general type of pottery, which, in terms of more objective descriptive criteria, has more in common than not. We need to ask ourselves to what extent it makes sense, or is appropriate, to put distinct "ethnic" or "ethno-geographical" labels on pottery at all, either on specific wares (where we can isolate or identify these) or on specific shapes or decorative styles, let alone on individual decorative motifs. While a comparative study of pottery may illuminate general patterns of interaction between different geographical areas, it tells us nothing about the perceived "identity" of who made or used particular pots, notwithstanding the convenient archaeological labels we apply to these. Once a particular type of pottery or shape of pot or style of decoration becomes a regular aspect of local ceramic production (for whatever reason), it becomes, in Caubet's words, "simply the type of ware being made for everyday use at this time" (1992, 130)—no more and no less. Dramatic "events" such as the migration of "ethnic" groups are not the only possible reason for the taking into local production of an Aegean type of painted pottery in the eastern Mediterranean, particularly since there is good reason to believe that, in both Cyprus and the Levant, this process had already started well before these "events" are presumed to have taken place.

Finally, and at a more basic level, we need the kind of information that can only be obtained from fully illustrated publication (with photographs, not only scaled-down line drawings)[30] and from regular intercommunication between

30. The potential of new technologies seems to me quite revolutionary when it comes to the dissemination or publication of crucial information about pottery at the most basic level.

those familiar with such pottery in different parts of the eastern Mediterranean. We need to know precisely where and when such pottery is found, in what quantities, and in what kinds of ceramic (as well as more general) contexts. We need to know what it looks and feels like: In other words, not only the details of shapes and decoration involved, but also of fabric consistencies, surface treatments and techniques of construction, and the extent to which these vary both within and between sites, within and between regions, and over time. Eventually, we need to figure out exactly where such pottery is made and in how many different production centers or units within centers, so that we can begin to track the movement (or lack of movement) of individual pots more precisely both within and between regions. The 2001 workshop and this resulting volume have begun to provide answers to some of the more general and at least a few of the more basic of these questions as far as some parts of the eastern Mediterranean are concerned. We are perhaps a little further along the way to gaining some wider insights into the range and nature of "the ceramic phenomenon of the 'Sea Peoples'" as a whole.[31]

Scanned images of actual sherds (rather than drawings or photographs of sherds) even at a relatively low resolution can provide many of the kinds of information that can only otherwise be gained from seeing or handling the pottery itself. Internet publication of pottery in this form—or even the publication of conventional black-and-white photographs—can do much to obviate the problems of identification and interpretation caused by the practice of publishing two-dimensional line drawings, which are not only incapable of conveying any information about texture and color but also tend to produce preinterpreted, "sanitized" versions of pots as substitutes for the generally much messier realities of pottery.

31. I am grateful to Ann Killebrew, Michal Artzy, and Gunnar Lehmann, who conceived and organized the Sea Peoples workshop to such excellent effect, for the opportunity to be present at it, and to these and the other participants for a wealth of information and stimulating points of view. My thanks, too, to Professor Trude Dothan for the chance to attend one of her "hands-on" seminars on the Miqne pottery in May 2000. I owe particular debts to Michal Artzy, Maria Iacovou, Ann Killebrew, Barbara Kling, and Sabine Laemmel for their patience (in some cases over many years) in chewing over with me the problems of the "ceramic phenomenon of the 'Sea Peoples'" in both Cyprus and the Levant.

Appendix
The "Sea Peoples" in Primary Sources

*Matthew J. Adams and Margaret E. Cohen**

This appendix collects the textual references to the "Sea Peoples" that occur in Egyptian, Ugaritic, Hittite, and other Late Bronze to early Iron Age sources. The "Sea Peoples" included here are those peoples listed in Ramesses II's Kadesh Inscriptions (Kitchen 1979, 2–147), Merenptah's Great Karnak Inscription (Kitchen 1982a, 2–12), and, perhaps most famously, those named in the "confederation of peoples" (Kitchen 1983, 40.3–4) at Ramesses III's mortuary temple, Medinet Habu (Redford 1992, 243, n. 14). Every effort has been made to produce a comprehensive listing of the mentions of these particular peoples. We have not, however, attempted to provide a complete bibliography for the various texts, and therefore the references that we provide are intended to point the researcher to, in most cases, easily available translations, transcriptions, and/or transliterations. When a citation is given for a text of transcribed hieroglyphs, the first Arabic numeral refers to the page and the second to the line number of that page.

We have tried to limit the scope of primary materials to the Late Bronze Age/early Iron Age horizon. We have done this primarily to minimize the amount of interpretation required to evaluate whether a text should be included or excluded as reliable, primary data. Thus we have not dealt here with later first-millennium B.C.E. materials, including, for example, the biblical material on the Philistines or references to alleged Sea Peoples in classical Greek sources.

---

* Matthew J. Adams, Bucknell University; e-mail: mja198@gmail.com. Margaret E. Cohen, The Pennsylvania State University; e-mail: mec243@psu.edu.

We wish to express our gratitude to Ann E. Killebrew and Gunnar Lehmann for putting together this book and inviting our participation. Thank you also to Baruch Halpern, Donald B. Redford, and Itamar Singer† for their kind comments and suggestions. Of course, any mistakes or omissions are the authors' alone. Thank you also to Megaera Lorenz for supplying some important bibliography.

The compilation is arranged in a numerical hierarchy according to the following pattern:

Name of Sea People
Type of Source (i.e., Egyptian, Ugaritic,[1] Hittite, Other)
Name of Specific Source (e.g., Papyrus Harris)
Brief description of specific mention within the text followed by select bibliographic information

1. LUKKA[2]

1.1 Egyptian

1.1.1 Ramesses II: Kadesh Inscription(s)

a) Ramesses II claims a victory in the Lukka land (Kitchen 1979, 4.1–4; Davies 1997, 56.4; Gardiner 1960).
b) The countries allied with Khatti against the Egyptians are Naharin, Arzawa, Dardany, Keshkesh, Masa, Pidasa, Arwen, Karkiša, **Lukka**, Kizzuwadna, Carchemish, Ugarit, Qode, Nuhasse, Mushanet, and Qadesh (Kitchen 1979, 17.15; Davies 1997, 60.45; *ARE*, III:§309; Gardiner 1960).
c) The countries allied with Khatti against the Egyptians are Arzawa, Masa, Pidasa, Keshkesh, Arwen, Kizzuwadna, Aleppo, Aketeri, Kadesh, and **Lukka** (Kitchen 1979, 32.5; *ARE*, III:§312; Gardiner 1960).
d) The chiefs of the lands assembled with Khatti against Ramesses II are Arzawa, Masa, Arwen, **Lukka**, Dardany, Carchemish, Karkiša, and Aleppo (Kitchen 1979, 50.12–15; Davies 1997, 68.150; Gardiner 1960).
e) The countries allied with Khatti against the Egyptians are Dardany, Naharin, Keshkesh, Masa, Pidasa, Karkiša, **Lukka**, Carchemish, Arzawa, Ugarit, Arwen, Inesa, Mushanet, Qadesh, Aleppo, and Qode (Kitchen 1979, 111.13–14; Davies 1997, 88.45; Gardiner 1960).
f) Lukka are counted in a list of prisoners taken by Ramesses II (Kitchen 1979, 143.15; Gardiner 1960).
g) Lukka is one of the countries in league with Khatti against the Egyptians (Kitchen 1979, 927.13).

---

1. The "Ugaritic" source category includes texts from Ugarit written in Akkadian.

2. General references: del Monte and Tischler 1978, 249–50; del Monte 1992, 96; Bryce 1979 and 1992. The Lukka are associated with the "Sea Peoples" primarily because of the reference to them in Merenptah's Great Karnak Inscription (see 1.1.2 below). They, unlike most of the others in this catalog, are much better known thanks to Hittite texts. For this reason, we have included all of the Lukka mentioned outside of Khatti, but only the more historically important attestations from Khatti itself. For the minor references that are missing, see del Monte and Tischler 1978 and del Monte 1992.

1.1.2 Merenptah: Great Karnak Inscription

a) The northerners allied with the Libyans are Eqwesh, Teresh, **Lukka**, Sherden, and Shekelesh (lacuna distorts exact context) (Kitchen 1982a, 2.13; Davies 1997, 152.1; *ARE*, III:§574).

b) List of allies of the Libyans: Sherden, Shekelesh, Eqwesh, **Lukka**, and Teresh (others in lacuna?) (Kitchen 1982a, 4.2; Davies 1997, 154.14; *ARE*, III:§579).

1.1.3 Onomasticon of Amenope

a) The Lukka appear in the sequence: … Libu, Qeheq, Keshkesh, Denyen, Khatti, […], **Lukka**, Pidasa, Arzawa, Carchemish… (*AEO*, I:#247; for commentary, see *AEO*, I:127–28).

1.2 Ugaritic

1.2.1 RS 20.238

a) In a letter from the king of Ugarit to the king of Alashiya, the king of Ugarit is left defenseless against the "enemy" because "all of [his] ships are in the land of Lukka"[3] (Nougayrol et al. 1968, 24.23; Beckman 1996, 27).

1.3 Hittite

1.3.1 The Annals of Tudhaliya I/II (*CTH* 142)

a) [L]ukka is a member of a west Anatolian rebellion (Assuwan Confederacy) against Hatti (*KUB* XXIII:11 and 13; Garstang and Gurney 1959, 121–23; Bryce 1979, 3; see del Monte and Tischler 1978, 6:40 for alternative restoration).

1.3.2 The Plague Prayer of Mursili II to the Sun-goddess of Arinna (*CTH* 376)

a) Lukka is listed as a land which once gave tribute to Hatti but now revolts (*KUB* XXIV:3; *ANET*, 396; Singer 2002, 49–54; Bryce 1979, 5).

1.3.3 Treaty of Muwattalli II and Alaksandu (*CTH* 76)

a) In the offensive agreement of this treaty, Muwattali enlists Alaksandu's aid should the former campaign against the city of Lukka (Beckman 1999, #13, §11; Garstang and Gurney 1959, 111–14).

---

3. This letter has traditionally been interpreted as a response to R.S.L. 1 (Nougayrol et al. 1968, 23), which indicates the name of its sender only as king (*šarri-ma*, line 1). It has been argued convincingly, however, that the king in question must be the king of Carchemish (Singer 1999, 720 n. 394). Thus, this text should not necessarily be read in context of R.S.L. 1 as traditionally done.

1.3.4 The Tawagalawa Letter (*CTH* 181)

a) "The men of Lukka" turn for help to both Ahhiyawa and to the Hittite king, after being attacked by Piyamaradu[4] (*KUB* XIV:3; Garstang and Gurney 1959; Sommer 1932).

1.3.5 Annals of Hattusili (*CTH* 82)

a) Lukka is included in what appears to be a list of rebel groups (*KUB* XXI:6 + 6a; Gurney 1997, 128–29; for commentary, see Bryce 1979, 8).

b) The Lukka are mentioned three additional times, but the context is unclear in each case (*KUB* XXI:6 + 6a; Gurney 1997, 130–31).

1.3.6 Südburg Inscription

a) In this inscription Šuppiluliuma II's conquest and annexation of the Lukka and their neighbors is described (Neve 1989; Hawkins 1990; 1995c; for a different interpretation, see Singer 2000b, 27–28).

1.3.7 Yalburt (Ilgin) Inscription

a) Tudhaliya conducts military operations against the Lukka lands. (Hawkins 1995b, Appendix I; Özgüç 1988, 172–74 and pls. 85–95).

1.3.8 Instruction of Tudhaliya IV to His Stewards (*CTH* 255.1)

a) Lukka is an enemy of Tudhaliya IV (*KUB* XXVI:12; see also Bryce 1998, 337, n. 44).

1.4 Other

1.4.1 EA 38

a) In this letter to Akhenaten, the king of Alashiya complains that the Lukka are seizing his villages (Knudtzon 1964, 292–95, line 10; Moran 1992, 111).

2. Sherden[5]

2.1 Egyptian

2.1.1 Ramesses II: Kadesh Inscription(s)

a) Ramesses II prepares his troops for battle; included are the Sherden "who he had brought back by victory of his strong arm," (i.e., captured troops from another campaign that are pressed into military service) (Kitchen 1979, 11.6–10; Davies 1997, 58.25; *ARE*, III:§307; Gardiner 1960).

2.1.2 Ramesses II: Tanis Stele

a) Ramesses II repels a Sherden attack on Egypt (Kitchen 1979, 290.14; *ARE*, III:§491; Kitchen 1982b, 40–41).

---

4. Although the text does not explicitly say by whom the men of Lukka are attacked, we follow Itamar Singer's view that Piyamaradu is the culprit. (I. Singer, personal communication; Singer 1983b).

5. General references: Loretz 1995; Kahl 1995; Dietrich and Loretz 1972; *AEO*, 1:#194–99.

2.1.3 Ramesses II: Papyrus Anastasi I

a) Ramesses II sends a raiding party into Canaan comprising **Sherden**, Kehek, Meshwesh, and Nubian troops (Gardiner 1964, 19* and 29.4; Fischer-Elfert 1986, 264; Wente 1990, 106).

2.1.4 Merenptah: Great Karnak Inscription

a) The northerners allied with the Libyans are Eqwesh, Teresh, Lukka, **Sherden**, and Shekelesh (lacuna distorts exact context) (Kitchen 1982a, 2.13–14; Davies 1997, 152.1; *ARE*, III:§574).

b) A list of allies of the Libyans are **Sherden**, Shekelesh, Eqwesh, Lukka, and Teresh (others in lacuna?) (Kitchen 1982a, 4.1; Davies 1997, 154.14; *ARE*, III:§579).

c) Numbers of Sherden captives and slain are enumerated (Kitchen 1982a, 8.8 and 8.11; Davies 1997, 162.52–53; *ARE*, III:§588).

2.1.5 Merenptah: Athribis Stele

a) Libyans, Eqwesh of the sea, Shekelesh, Teresh, and **Sherden** are included in the list of captured peoples from the Libyan campaign (Kitchen 1982a, 22.10; *ARE*, III:§601).

2.1.6 Merenptah: Papyrus Anastasi II

a) Sherden are included in pharaoh's army (Gardiner 1937, 15.1–2; Caminos 1954, 45).

b) Pharaoh equips the conquered "Sherden of the sea" for use in his army (Gardiner 1937, 20.2; Caminos 1954, 64).

2.1.7 Stele of Setemhebu

a) A fortress of the Sherden is mentioned in Setemhebu's titulary (Petrie 1904, 22 and pl. XXVII:1; see also Loretz 1995, 138 and Kahl 1995).

2.1.8 Ramesses III: Medinet Habu

a) Ramesses III distributes weapons to the Sherden and Nubians (Kitchen 1983a, 28.15–16; The Epigraphic Survey 1930, pl. 29, lines 39–40; Edgerton and Wilson 1936, 36).

b) Ramesses III captures the chief of the "Sherden of the sea" (Kitchen 1983a, 104.13; The Epigraphic Survey 1970, pl. 600B, line 5; *ARE*, IV:§129).

2.1.9 Ramesses III: Papyrus Harris

a) Sherden troops serve in Ramesses III's army (Erichsen 1933, 91.2; Peden 1994, 213; *ARE*, IV:§397).

b) Sherden troops serve in Ramesses' army (Erichsen 1933, 92.15; Peden 1994, 215; *ARE*, IV:§402).

c) Ramesses III defeats the Sherden and Weshesh, brings them as captives into Egypt, and settles them in his "strongholds" (Erichsen 1933, 93.1; Peden 1994, 215; *ARE*, IV:§403).

d) Sherden serve in Ramesses III's army (Erichsen 1933, 96.2; Peden 1994, 219; *ARE*, IV:§410).

2.1.10 Papyrus Amiens

a) Sherden manage a domain of Ramesses III (Gardiner 1948, 7.13).

b) Sherden deliver grain (Gardiner 1948, 11.9).

2.1.11 Papyrus Wilbour

a) Forty-two Sherden landowners/settlers are mentioned by name. Additionally, the titles *šmsw nꜣ šrdn ꜥnd ṯꜣy sryt šrdn* are also present. (Gardiner 1941–1948; Faulkner 1952, 52–54).

2.1.12 The Adoption Papyrus (P. Ashmolean Museum 1945.96)

a) In this will, which was drafted in Middle Egypt, the witnesses include: "Pkamen, the Sherden" and "Satameniu, the Sherden, and his wife 'Adjed'o" (Gardiner 1940, 23–24; Cruz-Uribe 1988).

2.1.13 Papyrus Moscow 169 (Onomasticon Golénischeff)

a) Sherden are listed as a type of people (Papyrus Moscow 169, 4.5; *AEO*, I:25, 28; Kahl 1995, 140).

2.1.14 Papyrus BM 10326

a) The sender of this letter claims to have requested a policeman to be sent to him "through the Sherden Hori" (Černý 1939, 19.12; Wente 1967, 37–42 [#9]; Wente 1990, 192).

2.1.15 Papyrus Turin 2026

a) This letter mentions a Sherden named Hori who once delivered spears to the sender (Černý 1939, 72.14; Wente 1967, 83–85 [#50]; Wente 1990, 190).

2.1.16 Papyrus BM 10375

a) A Sherden named Hori hand-delivered a letter to Butehamon, the scribe (Černý 1939, 45.2; Wente 1967, 59–65 [#28]; Wente 1990, 194).

2.1.17 Onomasticon of Amenope

a) The Sherden appear in the sequence: … Ashkelon, Ashdod, Gaza, Assyria, Shubaru, […], **Sherden**, Tjekker, Peleset, Khurma, […], … (*AEO*, I:#268; for commentary, *AEO*, I:194–99)

2.1.18 Osorkon II: Donation Stele

a) A prophet named Hora is in possession of a piece of Sherden land (Daressy 1915, 141–42).

2.1.19 Stele of Padjesef (Nineteenth–Twenty-Second Dynasty)

a) Padjesef is described as a Sherden of the fortress, Usermaatre (Petrie 1904, 22 and pl. XXVII, 2; cf. Loretz 1995, 138 and Kahl 1995).

2.2 Ugaritic[6]

2.2.1 RS 17.112

a) This text is a lawsuit between two citizens of Ugarit: Iluwa and Amar-^{d}U, the son of Mut-^{d}U, the *šerdanu* (*PRU*, IV:234.6).

2.2.2 RS 19.011

a) This text contains a possible use of Sherden as personal name (*Ḏrdn*). (*KTU*, 2.61; *PRU*, V:114; see suggestion by Singer 1999, 726 n. 416).

2.2.3 RS 15.167+163

a) In this contract, the unnamed son of a Sherden has sold an estate to one Kurwanu (*PRU*, III:124.13).

2.2.4 RS 15.118

a) In this document one Ibshalu received the property of a man named ^{M}*še-er-ta-an-ni* as a royal gift from Ammistamru II (*PRU*, III:131.5).

2.2.5 RS 8.145

a) Context unknown (see *PRU*, III:257.27).

2.2.6 RS 15.073

a) Four Sherden are counted in a record of persons (guards?) in the palace along with *ṯnnm*, *ḫsnm*, *mrum*, *mrynm*, *mkrm*, *hbṭnm*, and *mḏrġlm* (*KTU*, 4.163, line 9).

2.2.7 RS 15.015 + RS 15.025

a) Five Sherden are counted in a record of persons (guards?) in the palace along with *ṯnnm*, *ḫsnm*, *mrynm*, *mkrm*, *hbṭnm*, *mrum*, and *mḏrġlm* (*KTU*, 4.137, line 3).

2.2.8 RS 15.094

a) Five Sherden are counted in a record of personnel along with *ṯnnm*, *ḫsnm*, *mrynm*, *mkrm*, *mrum*, *mḏrġlm*, *hbṭnm* (*KTU*, 4.173, line 4).

2.2.9 RS 15.095

a) Five Sherden are counted in a record of personnel along with *ṯnnm*, *ḫsnm*, *mrum*, *mkrm*, *mrynm*, *hbṭnm*, and *mḏrġlm* (*KTU*, 4.174, line 8).

2.2.10 RS 15.103

a) Five Sherden are counted in a record of personnel along with *ṯnnm*, *ḫsnm*, *mrynm*, *mrum*, *mkrm*, *hbṭnm*, and *mḏrġlm* (*KTU*, 4.179, line 5).

2.2.11 RS 16.165

a) Sherden occur as recipients in this list of wine rations along with *hršm*, *mštt*[ ], *mḏrġlm*, *mlm*, *ḫzrm*, *mrynm*, *ḫty*, and *ʿṯtr* (*KTU*, 4.216, line 7).

2.2.12 RS 16.251

a) The ethnic Sherden occurs in the name of a man: ^{I}*al-la-an-še-ri-da-ni* (*PRU*, III:109–110.5).

6. For the equation of Ugaritic *ṯrtnm* with *šerdanū*, see Loretz 1995.

2.3 Hittite

(no attestations found)

2.4 Other

2.4.1 EA 81

a) A Sherden man defects from Rib-Hadda of Byblos to ʿAbdi-Aširta (Knudtzon 1964, 392–97, line 16; Moran 1992, 150).

2.4.2 EA 122

a) The text mentions Sherden people living under the suzerainty of Rib-Hadda of Byblos (Knudtzon 1964, 526–29, line 35; Moran 1992, 201).

2.4.3 EA 123

a) The text mentions Sherden people living under the suzerainty of Rib-Hadda of Byblos (Knudtzon 1964, 528–33, line 15; Moran 1992, 202).

3. Eqwesh[7]

3.1 Egyptian

3.1.1 Merenptah: Great Karnak Inscription

a) The northerners allied with the Libyans are **Eqwesh**, Teresh, Lukka, Sherden, and Shekelesh (lacuna distorts exact context) (Kitchen 1982a, 2.13; Davies 1997, 152.1; *ARE*, III:§574).

b) List of allies of the Libyans are Sherden, Shekelesh, **Eqwesh**, Lukka, and Teresh (others in lacuna?) (Kitchen 1982a, 4.1; Davies 1997, 154.14; *ARE*, III:§579).

c) Eqwesh captives and slain are enumerated and noted as having no foreskins (Kitchen 1982a, 8.9 and 8.12; Davies 1997, 162.52–54; *ARE*, III:§588).

3.1.2 Merenptah: Athribis Stele

a) The Libyans, **Eqwesh of the sea**, Shekelesh, Teresh, and Sherden are included in the list of captured peoples from the Libyan campaign (Kitchen 1982a, 22.8; *ARE*, III:§601).

3.2 Ugaritic

(no attestations found)

3.3 Hittite

3.3.1 The Indictment of Madduwatta (*CTH* 147)

a) In this letter from Arnuwanda I to Madduwatta, the Hittite king recalls that Attarissiya, the "ruler of Ahhiya," had chased Madduwatta out of his own land and that it was Arnuwanda's father, Tudhaliya I/II, who

7. General references: del Monte and Tischler 1978, 1–2; del Monte 1992, 1; see del Monte and Tischler 1978, 1–2 for miscellaneous fragmentary attestations not given here.

rescued him by getting rid of Attarissiya (*KUB* XIV:1 + *KBo* XIX:38; Goetze 1928; Beckman 1999, #27, §§1–4).

b) At the end of this letter, Arnuwanda accuses Madduwatta of joining up with Attarissiya and the ruler of Piggaya in raiding the Hittite vassal, Alashiya (*KUB* XIV:1 + *KBo* XIX:38; Goetze 1928; Beckman 1999, #27, §30).

3.3.2 An Oracle Text (*CTH* 571.2)

a) This text is one question in a series put to an oracle, which mentions a deity of Ahhiyawa and a deity of Lazpa (Lesbos) who were to be brought to an ailing Mursilis (*KUB* V:6; *KBo* XVI:97; Güterbock 1983, 134; Sommer 1932, 282–83).

3.3.3 The Offences of the Šeha River Land (*CTH* 211)

a) Broken context. Güterbock suggests a translation that indicates that someone made war on someone else "and relied on the king of Ahhiyawa" (*KUB* XXIII:13; Güterbock 1983, 137; 1992; Sommer 1932, 314–19; see also Singer 1983b, 207 for interpretation).

3.3.4 Annals of Mursili (*CTH* 61)

a) In the beginning of the third year, Uhhazitis of Arzawa and the city of Millawanda joined the king of the Ahhiyawa (*KBo* III:4 + *KUB* XXIII:125 + *KBo* III:3; Güterbock 1983, 134–35; Goetze 1933; for other interpretations of the text, see references in Güterbock 1983).

b) The context is broken. For year four the text mentions "the sons of Uhhazitis," "the sea," "king of the Ahhiyawa," and a sending by ship (Goetze 1933, 66–67; for a summary of and references to various restorations and interpretations, see Güterbock 1983, 135).

3.3.5 The Tawagalawa Letter of Hattusili III (*CTH* 181)

a) In this letter from a Hittite king to the king of Ahhiyawa, who is addressed as "my brother," arrangements are discussed for the return of Piyamaradu to the Hittite king. Piyamaradu, who had caused some trouble for the Hittite king, fled by boat from Millawanda to the king of Ahhiyawa, and was apparently residing there when this letter was composed. Also mentioned in the text is the brother of the king of Ahhiyawa, Tawagalawas (*KUB* XIV:3; Garstang and Gurney 1959; Sommer 1932, 2–19; see Güterbock 1983, 136 for interpretation of the text adopted here; see also Singer 1983b, 210–13; Bryce 2003, 199–212; Hawkins 1998, 17 n. 73).

3.3.6 Treaty of Tudhaliya IV and Shaushgamuwa (*CTH* 105)

a) In the alliance clause of this treaty, the kings of Egypt, Babylonia, Assyria, and Ahhiyawa are noted as equals to the king of Khatti. However, "Ahhiyawa" has been crossed out (*KUB* XXIII:1; Beckman 1999,

#17, §11; Kühne and Otten 1971; Sommer 1932, 320–21; for summary of views and references to interpretations of this passage, see Güterbock 1983, 136).

b) Also in the alliance clause, a blockade is established against Ahhiyawan ships bound for Assyria(?) (*KUB* XXIII:1; Beckman 1999, #17, §13; Kühne and Otten 1971; Sommer 1932, 320–21).

3.3.7 Letter of a Hittite King to a King of Ahhiyawa (*CTH* 183)

a) (*KUB* XXVI:91; Sommer 1932, 268–74)

3.3.8 Miscellaneous Fragments (*CTH* 214)

a) Miscellaneous fragments (*KUB* XXXI:29; *KUB* XXVI:76; *KBo* XVI:22; *KUB* XXI:34).

b) Broken context (*KUB* XIV:2; Güterbock 1983, 134; Sommer 1932, 298–306).

3.3.9 Hittite Letter Fragments (*CTH* 209)

a) Hittite letter fragments (*KBo* II:11; *KUB* XXIII:98; *KUB* XIII:95).

3.3.10 Lot Oracle Text (*CTH* 572)

a) A lot oracle text mentions Ahhiyawa (*KUB* XVIII:58).

3.3.11 Liver Oracle Texts (*CTH* 570)

a) A liver oracle text mentions Ahhiyawa (*KUB* XXII:56; *KUB* V:6; Sommer 1932, 282–90).

3.4 Others

(no attestations found)

4. Teresh

4.1 Egyptian

4.1.1 Merenptah: Great Karnak Inscription

a) The northerners allied with the Libyans are Eqwesh, **Teresh**, Lukka, Sherden, and Shekelesh (lacuna distorts exact context) (Kitchen 1982a, 2.13; Davies 1997, 152.1; *ARE*, III:§574).

b) List of allies of the Libyans are Sherden, Shekelesh, Eqwesh, Lukka, and **Teresh** (others in lacuna?) (Kitchen 1982a, 4.2; Davies 1997, 154.14; *ARE*, III:§579).

c) Numbers of Teresh captives and slain are enumerated (Kitchen 1982a, 8.11; Davies 1997, 162.52–54; *ARE*, III:§588).

4.1.2 Merenptah: Athribis Stele

a) Libyans, Eqwesh of the sea, Shekelesh, **Teresh**, and Sherden are included in the list of captured peoples from the Libyan campaign (Kitchen 1982a, 22.9; *ARE*, III:§601).

4.1.3 Ramesses III: Medinet Habu Inscription

a) A chief of the "Teresh of the sea" captured by Ramesses III (Kitchen

1983a, 104.14; The Epigraphic Survey 1970, pl. 600B, line 7; *ARE*, IV:§129).

4.1.4 Ramesses III: Rhetorical Stele (Chapel C at Deir el-Medina)

a) The Peleset and Teresh have sailed(?) "in the midst of the sea" (Kitchen 1983a, 91.11–12; Peden 1994, 64.8).

4.2 Ugaritic

(no attestations found)

4.3 Hittite

(no attestations found)

4.4 Other

(no attestations found)

5. SHEKELESH[8]

5.1 Egyptian

5.1.1 Merenptah: Great Karnak Inscription

a) The northerners allied with the Libyans are Eqwesh, Teresh, Lukka, Sherden, and **Shekelesh** (lacuna distorts exact context) (Kitchen 1982a, 2.13; Davies 1997, 152.1; *ARE*, III:§574).

b) List of allies of the Libyans are Sherden, **Shekelesh**, Eqwesh, Lukka, and Teresh (others in lacuna?) (Kitchen 1982a, 4.2–3; Davies 1997, 154.14; *ARE*, III:§579).

c) The Shekelesh are included in a list of captives and slain (Kitchen 1982a, 8.8–16; Davies 1997, 162.52–4; *ARE*, III:§588).

5.1.2 Merenptah: Cairo Column

a) The Shekelesh are mentioned together with invading Libyans (lacunae distort context) (Kitchen 1982a, 23.6; *ARE*, III:§595).

5.1.3 Merenptah: Athribis Stele

a) Libyans, Eqwesh of the sea, **Shekelesh**, Teresh, and Sherden are included in the list of captured peoples from the Libyan campaign (Kitchen 1982a, 22.5–16; *ARE*, III: §601).

5.1.4 Ramesses III: Medinet Habu

a) Peleset, Denyen, and **Shekelesh** are overthrown by Ramesses III (Kitchen 1983a, 36.7–8; The Epigraphic Survey 1930, pl. 44, lines 14–15; Edgerton and Wilson 1936, 47; *ARE*, IV:§81).

b) Peleset, Tjekker, **Shekelesh**, Denyen, and Weshesh are in a confederation against Egypt (Kitchen 1983a, 40.3–4; The Epigraphic Survey 1930,

8. Wente 1963; Wainwright 1939.

pl. 46, line 18; Edgerton and Wilson 1936, 53; Peden 1994, 28.18; Edel 1985, 225; *ARE*, IV:§64).

c) Tjekker, the land of the Peleset, Denyen, Weshesh, and **Shekelesh** overthrown by Ramesses (Kitchen 1983a, 73.9–10; The Epigraphic Survey 1932, pl. 107, lines 7–8; Edgerton and Wilson 1936, 130–31).

5.2 Ugaritic

5.2.1 RS 34.129

a) A Hittite king requests from Ugarit the extradition of a man who was once a prisoner of the Shekelesh (or Tjekker depending on who exactly the ^{URU}*šikalaiu* are, see Singer 1999, 722), whom, he notes, live on boats (Bordreuil 1991, no. 12; Dietrich and Loretz 1978).[9]

5.3 Hittite

(no attestations found)

5.4 Other

5.4.1 Tiglath-pileser III (Annals text 13)

a) In a northern and western campaign, Tiglath-pileser plunders a fortress, whose commandant is a man named Shiqila (^{m}*Ši-qi-la-a*). This reference is uncertain as it is a personal name. However, reference 5.2.1 above, which is localized in the same general area, may offer support here (*ARAB*, I:§771; Tadmor 1994, 66–67).[10]

6. Karkiša

6.1 Egyptian

6.1.1 Ramesses II: Kadesh Inscription(s)

a) Ramesses II claims a victory in the land of Karkiša (Kitchen 1979, 4.6–11; Davies 1997, 56.4; Gardiner 1960; *ARE*, III:§306).

b) The countries allied with Khatti against the Egyptians are Naharin, Arzawa, Dardany, Keshkesh, Masa, Pidasa, Arwen, **Karkiša**, Lukka, Kizzuwadna, Carchemish, Ugarit, Qode, Nuhasse, Mushanet, and Qadesh (Kitchen 1979, 17.15–18.5; Davies 1997, 60.45; Gardiner 1960; *ARE*, III:§309).

c) The chiefs of the lands assembled with Khatti against Ramesses II are Arzawa, Masa, Arwen, Lukka, Dardany, Carchemish, **Karkiša**, and Aleppo (Kitchen 1979, 51.1–6; Davies 1997, 68.150; Gardiner 1960).

d) The countries allied with Khatti against the Egyptians are Dardany, Naharin, Keshkesh, Masa, Pidasa, **Karkiša**, Lukka, Carchemish, Arzawa,

9. See also 9.2.1 below.

10. See also 9.4.1 below.

Ugarit, Arwen, Inesa, Mushanet, Qadesh, Aleppo, and Qode (Kitchen 1979, 111.13–14; Davies 1997, 88.45; Gardiner 1960).

e) Ramesses II presents chiefs of Khatti to Amun, one of whom is a Karkiša (*ARE*, III:§349).

6.2 Ugaritic

(no attestations found)

6.3 Hittite

6.3.1 The Annals of Tudhaliya I/II (*CTH* 142)

a) The Karkiša are listed as a member of the west Anatolian rebellion (Assuwan Confederacy) against Hatti (*KUB* XXIII:11 and 13; Garstang and Gurney 1959, 121–23).

6.3.2 The Annals of Mursili II (*CTH* 61)

a) Mursili II allows a refugee, Manapa-Tarhunta, to hide from his brothers in the land of Karkiša (*KBo* III:4 + *KUB* XXIII:125 + *KBo* III:3; Güterbock 1983, 134–35; Goetze 1933).

6.3.3 Treaty of Mursili II and Manapa-Tarhunta of the land of the Seha River (*CTH* 69)

a) Mursili II reminds Manapa-Tarhunta that he is responsible for Manapa-Tarhunta's survival in the land of Karkiša (Beckman 1999, 82–86, #12; Friedrich 1930, 1–41).

6.3.4 Treaty of Muwattalli II and Alaksandu (*CTH* 76)

a) In the offensive agreement of this treaty, Alaksandu must aid Muwattalli II if he campaigns against Karkiša (Beckman 1999, 90, #13; Garstang and Gurney 1959; Friedrich 1930, 42–102).

6.4 Other

6.4.1 An02 [292] from Pylos

a) This tablet mentions *Ko-ro-ki-ja* women. Ventris and Chadwick suspect this term to be an ethnonym. Though a dubious reference, we include this possibility here to encourage the consideration of the Linear B onomasticon in studies of Late Bronze Age interrelations (Ventris and Chadwick 1974, 166).

7. Weshesh

7.1 Egyptian

7.1.1 Ramesses III: Medinet Habu

a) Peleset, Tjekker, Shekelesh, Denyen, and **Weshesh** are named in a confederation against Egypt (Kitchen 1983a, 40.3–4; The Epigraphic Survey 1930, pl. 46, line 18; Peden 1994, 28.18; Edgerton and Wilson 1936, 53; Edel 1985, 225; *ARE*, IV:§64).

b) Tjekker, the land of the Peleset, Denyen, **Weshesh**, and Shekelesh are overthrown by Ramesses (Kitchen 1983a, 73.9–10; The Epigraphic Survey 1932, pl. 107, lines 7–8; Edgerton and Wilson 1936, 130–31).

7.1.2 Ramesses III: Papyrus Harris

a) Ramesses III defeats the Sherden and Weshesh, brings them as captives into Egypt, and settles them in his "strongholds" (Erichsen 1933, 93.1; Grandet 1994; Peden 1994, 215; *ARE*, IV:§403; *ANET*, 260–62).

7.2 Ugaritic

(no attestations found)

7.3 Hittite

(no attestations found)

7.4 Other

(no attestations found)

8. Denyen[11]

8.1 Egyptian

8.1.1 Ramesses III: Medinet Habu

a) Peleset, **Denyen,** and Shekelesh are overthrown by Ramesses III (Kitchen 1983a, 36.7–8; The Epigraphic Survey 1930, pl. 44, lines 14–15; Edgerton and Wilson 1936, 47; *ARE*, IV:§81).

b) Denyen beg for mercy from Rameses III (Kitchen 1983a, 37.1–2; The Epigraphic Survey 1930, pl. 44, line 23; Edgerton and Wilson 1936, 48; *ARE*, IV:§82).

c) Peleset, Tjekker, Shekelesh, **Denyen**, and Weshesh are named in a confederation against Egypt (Kitchen 1983a, 40.3–4; The Epigraphic Survey 1930, pl. 46, line 18; Edgerton and Wilson 1936, 53; Peden 1994, 28.18; Edel 1985, 225; *ARE*, IV:§64).

11. The normalization of the Egyptian group writing: *d3-ỉn-ỉw-n3* (*dnỉn*) is variously rendered as Danuna and Denyen. We have chosen the latter here. Further, although it can only be speculation given the state of the evidence, some scholars have equated the Denyen with Δαναοί. This equation would open up a large number of references to Danaoi to this catalog; however we have chosen to compile this list with as little interpretation as possible. It is worth noting here the occurrence of (*tỉ-n3-y-w*) *Tnj* in the Aegean place name list on the Amenhotep III statue bases from Kom el-Hetan. W. Helck (1971) and others (see Cline 1987, 3 n. 13) have equated *Tnj* with the Danaoi. The group writing on the statue bases, though separated from the Medinet Habu spelling by some two hundred years, is significantly different from that of the Denyen at Medinet Habu. While not impossible, this evidence may suggest that Denyen and *Tnj* do not refer to the same entity.

d) Tjekker, the land of the Peleset, **Denyen**, Weshesh, and Shekelesh are overthrown by Ramesses III (Kitchen 1983a, 73.9–10; The Epigraphic Survey 1932, pl. 107, lines 7–8; Edgerton and Wilson 1936, 130–31).

8.1.2 Ramesses III: Papyrus Harris

a) The Denyen, "in their isles," are defeated by Ramesses III (Erichsen 1933, 92.17–18; Grandet 1994; Peden 1994, 215; *ARE*, IV:§403; *ANET*, 260–62).

8.1.3 Onomasticon of Amenope

a) The Denyen occur in the sequence: … Libu, Qeheq, Keshkesh, **Denyen**, Khatti, […], Lukka, Pidasa, Arzawa, Carchemish … (*AEO*, I:#244; for commentary, see *AEO*, I:124–27).

8.2 Ugaritic

(no attestations found)

8.3 Hittite

8.3.1 Letter from Ramesses II to Hattusili III

a) Broken context (Edel 1994, I:#31 and II:139; *KBo* XXVIII:25).

8.3.2 Karatepe Inscription[12]

a) This is a semi-autobiographical building inscription of Azitawadda of Adana, king of Danunites, found in West Anatolia. This text exists in Phoenician and Hittite versions and dates to the early-first millennium B.C.E. (*KAI*, 26; *ANET*, 653–64; see also references of discussions of the text in *ANET*, 653).

8.3.3 Çineköy Inscription[13]

a) This eighth-century hieroglyphic Luwian and Phoenician bilingual inscription of one Wariyka of Adana in the Cilician plain in Anatolia is sometimes cited as attesting the Denyen. In this Inscription, Wariyka indicates that his people became a vassal of Assyria saying: "…all the house of Ashur became for me like a father [and like] a mother, and Danunians (*dnnym*) and Assyrians became like one house (Tekoğlu and Lemaire 2000; Lipiński 2004, 127–28).

---

12. Both the Karatepe Inscription here and the Çineköy Inscription below are sometimes cited in reference to the Denyen. This equation is problematic because both inscriptions date to around the eighth century, significantly later than the Ramesside inscriptions and other sources mentioned here. In both inscriptions, the ethnicon *dnnym* appears to be derived from the name of the city: *dnnym* are those who are from Adana. Additionally, the city of Adana is already mentioned in Hittite texts of the Late Bronze Age. Therefore, any attempt to connect Adana and the *dnnym* with the Denyen of the Medinet Habu inscription is also an attempt to imply that the "Sea People's" Denyen originated in Cilicia. In our opinion, this goes beyond the current state of the evidence.

13. See previous note.

8.4 Other

8.4.1 EA 151

a) In a letter to pharaoh, Abi-Milku, king of Tyre, indicates that the king of Danuna has died. The Danuna here may or may not refer to the same Denyen of the other Sea Peoples sources. A possible inference to be gained with this letter is that Danuna is located in Canaan (Redford 1992, 252, n. 55) (Knudtzon 1964, 622–27, line 52; Moran 1992, 238).[14]

9. Tjekker/Sikila(?)[15]

9.1 Egyptian

9.1.1 Ramesses III: Medinet Habu

a) The Peleset and Tjekker "quiver in their bodies" (Kitchen 1983a, 25.5; The Epigraphic Survey 1930, pls. 27–28, lines 51–52; Edgerton and Wilson 1936, 30; Peden 1994, 16.51; *ARE*, IV:§44).

b) Defeated Tjekker chiefs speak to Ramesses III (Kitchen 1983a, 34.11–12; The Epigraphic Survey 1930, pl. 43, line 18–20; Edgerton and Wilson 1936, 45; *ARE*, IV:§77).

c) The Peleset, **Tjekker**, Shekelesh, Denyen, and Weshesh are named in a confederation against Egypt (Kitchen 1983a, 40.3–4; The Epigraphic Survey 1930, pl. 46, line 18; Edgerton and Wilson 1936, 53; Edel 1985, 225; Peden 1994, 28.18; *ARE*, IV:§64).

d) Defeated Tjekker prisoners praise Ramesses III (The Epigraphic Survey 1932, pl. 99; *ARE*, IV:§§78–79).

e) **Tjekker**, the land of the Peleset, Denyen, Weshesh, and Shekelesh are overthrown by Ramesses III (Kitchen 1983a, 73.9–10; The Epigraphic Survey 1932, pl. 107, lines 7–8; Edgerton and Wilson 1936, 130–31).

---

14. Though the reference has come to our attention too late to incorporate here, the reader is directed to Tammuz 2001.

15. The traditional reading of "Tjekker" for the group writing *ṯ3-k3-rw* (*ṯkr*) has been challenged by Rainey 1982 and Edel 1984. They suggest a reading of "skl"–*Sikil (ultimately complementing their connection with Sicily). While their arguments have some convincing elements, we are still hesitant to adopt this equation. The ethnic *Sikil in this form is not attested in Near Eastern texts (excluding the possibility of the Egyptian texts here if Tjekker is to be equated). Despite their insistence (see especially Edel 1984, 8), an equation of *Sikil (Tjekker) with URUšikalaiu seems out of the range of possibilities as the Egyptians would be more likely to represent /š/ with their own /š/ (group writing, *š3*); there are no examples of Egyptian scribes representing Semitic /š/ with their own /ṯ/ (see Hoch 1994, 422 and 432). Thus the URUšikalaiu are more likely to be equated with the Shekelesh of Egyptian inscriptions. If the Tjekker of the Egyptian texts are Semitic speakers, there are many more possibilities (see Hoch 1994, 436 for the different correlations between Egyptian *ṯ* and Semitic phonemes).

f) A chief of the Tjekker is captured by Ramesses III (Kitchen 1983a, 104.12; The Epigraphic Survey 1970, pl. 600B, line 4; *ARE*, IV:§129).

9.1.2 Ramesses III: Papyrus Harris

a) Tjekker are defeated by Ramesses III and "reduced to ashes" (Erichsen 1933, 92.18; Grandet 1994; Peden 1994, 215; *ARE*, IV:§403; *ANET*, 260–62).

9.1.3 Onomasticon of Amenope

a) The Tjekker occur in the sequence: … Ashkelon, Ashdod, Gaza, Asher, Shubaru, […], Sherden, **Tjekker**, Peleset, Khurma, […], … (*AEO*, I:#269, for commentary, see *AEO*, I:199–200).

9.1.4 The Report of Wenamun[16]

a) Dor is described as a city of the Tjekker (Gardiner 1932, 61.11; Goedicke 1975; *ANET*, 25–29; *AEL*, II:224–230; *ARE*, IV:§565).

b) A [Tjekker] is the thief who stole Wenamun's goods (*ARE*, IV:§568).

c) Eleven Tjekker ships arrive at Byblos to arrest Wenamun (Gardiner 1932, 73.11; Goedicke 1975; *ANET*, 25–29; *AEL*, II:224–30; *ARE*, IV:§588).

d) Zekker-Ba'al interviews the Tjekker who seek Wenamun (Gardiner 1932, 74.10; Goedicke 1975; *ANET*, 25–29; *AEL*, II:224–30; *ARE*, IV:§590).

9.2 Ugaritic

9.2.1 RS 34.129

a) A Hittite king requests from Ugarit the extradition of a man who was once a prisoner of the Tjekker (or Shekelesh depending on who exactly the ^{URU}*šikalaiu* are, see Singer 1999, 722), who, he notes, live on boats (Bordreuil 1991, no. 12; Dietrich and Loretz 1978; Singer 1999, 722).[17]

9.3 Hittite

(no attestations found)

16. While some scholars continue to use The Report of Wenamun as an historical document (e.g., Stern 2006, 386), it is becoming increasingly more common to view the piece as a work of literature (e.g., Baines 1999). In our opinion, the tale has much more in common with Homer's *Odyssey* than with an official report and should be used cautiously in "Sea Peoples" studies. In any case, note the chronological problems with dating the text, the events therein, and the historical geography as presented, e.g., by Egberts (1991; 1998) and Sass (2002).

17. We mention this here because of a certain degree of doubt on the identification of the ^{URU}*šikalaiu*, however, see also 5.2.1 above, which we believe is a much more convincing equation.

9.4 Other

9.4.1 Tiglath-pileser III (Annals text 13)

a) In a northern and western campaign, Tiglath-pileser plunders a fortress, whose commandant is a man named Shiqila ([m]*Ši-qi-la-a*). This reference is uncertain as it is a personal name (*ARAB*, I:§771; Tadmor 1994, 66–67).[18]

10. Peleset[19]

10.1 Egyptian

10.1.1 Ramesses III: Medinet Habu

a) The Peleset and Tjekker "quiver in their bodies" (Kitchen 1983a, 25.5; The Epigraphic Survey 1930, pls. 27–28, lines 51–52; Edgerton and Wilson 1936, 30; Peden 1994, 16.51; *ARE*, IV:§44).

---

18. We mention this here because of a certain degree of doubt on the identification of the [URU]*šikalaiu*, however, see also 5.4.1 above, which we believe is a much more convincing equation.

19. The newly discovered inscription of King Taita of Padasatini at Aleppo has now entered the discussion of the "Sea Peoples" and the Philistines. Hawkins' recent and tentative proposal that the name of the kingdom should be amended to Palistin and connected to the better-known Philistines (2009, 171–72) has been adopted zealously by several scholars (Kohlmeyer 2009; T. Harrison 2009; Sass 2010). The similarity of this name to that of the Philistines has even sparked commentary on remote topics such as the kingdom of Solomon (!; Sass 2010, 173). The inscriptional evidence is as follows: On two stelae of Taita and his wife (the Meharde Stele and the Sheizar Stele; Hawkins 2000, 415–19), the ethnocon Walistin is used in reference to Taita. The new Aleppo temple inscription of Taita (Aleppo 6; Hawkins 2009, 169) has the variant Palistin. A fourth inscription, from Tell Ta'yinat, mentions one Halparuntiyas of Walistin (Tell Ta'yinat Inscription 1; Hawkins 2000, 365–67).

A few comments should be made here in order to explain why we do not include these inscriptions in our list of "Sea Peoples," if not to assuage the enthusiasm for the discovery of a Philistine "empire" (Sass 2010) in Syria. While we have no basis to doubt the emendation of the Taita ethnicon to Palistin on the basis of a revised understanding of the Luwian sign TA_4 (Hawkins 2009, 171), two elements of the word remain unresolved. First, the *-in* ending is not present in the transcription in the Medinet Habu reliefs, Assyrian inscriptions, or even in the biblical texts (the *-ine* ending that we use today in English derives from the Greek toponymic suffix). Hawkins suggests that the Taita *-in* may have been incorporated by adoption of the masc. pl. Aramaic ending analogous to the biblical Hebrew pluralization, *plštym* < *plšty* (Hawkins 2009, 171). One wonders however, if Aramaic is the appropriate comparison (especially given the early date assigned to the inscription); in Phoenician or Ugaritic, a mem would be expected in the construction of the plural (note that the bilingual Karatepe inscription and the Çinekoy statue inscription are Luwian/Phoenician). Second, the Meharde and Sheizer inscriptions of Taita and the Halparuntiyas inscription preserve the ethnicon Walistin—i.e., the variant Palistin is a hapax). There is no clear explanation for the Wa- and Pa- alternation. Hawkins offers that there may have been some hesitancy over how to represent the initial consonant in

b) Peleset are hiding in their towns in fear of Ramesses III (Kitchen 1983a, 28.4; The Epigraphic Survey 1930, pl. 29, lines 20–22; Edgerton and Wilson 1936, 35; *ARE*, IV:§71).
c) **Peleset**, Denyen, and Shekelesh are overthrown by Ramesses III (Kitchen 1983a, 36.7–8; The Epigraphic Survey 1930, pl. 44, lines 14–15; Edgerton and Wilson 1936, 47; *ARE*, IV:§81).
d) Peleset beg for mercy from Ramesses III (Kitchen 1983a, 37.2–3; The Epigraphic Survey 1930, pl. 44, line 24; Edgerton and Wilson 1936, 48; *ARE*, IV:§82).
e) **Peleset**, Tjekker, Shekelesh, Denyen, and Weshesh are named in a confederation against Egypt (Kitchen 1983a, 40.3–4; The Epigraphic Survey 1930, pl. 46, line 18; Edgerton and Wilson 1936, 53; Peden 1994, 28.18; Edel 1985, 225; *ARE*, IV:§64).
f) Tjekker, the land of the **Peleset**, Denyen, Weshesh, and Shekelesh are overthrown by Ramesses III (Kitchen 1983a, 73.9–10; The Epigraphic Survey 1932, pl. 107, line 7f.; Edgerton and Wilson 1936, 130–31).
g) Countries of the Peleset are "slain" by Ramesses III (Kitchen 1983a, 102.8; The Epigraphic Survey 1932, pl. 118c; Edgerton and Wilson 1936, 146).
h) A chief of Peleset is captured by Ramesses III (*ARE*, IV:§129).[20]
i) A captured chief of the P[eleset] depicted (Kitchen 1983a, 104.14; The Epigraphic Survey 1970, pl. 600B, line 8).

Hieroglyphic Luwian (Hawkins 2009, 171). What vocalization would warrant hesitancy between Pa- and Wa- in Luwian and still be rendered with a /p/ in Egyptian and later Hebrew (and also Assyrian, Patinayya, if Yamada is correct in equating this term with Walistin; Yamada 2000, 96; Hawkins 2009, 171 and references)? Alternatively, it may be worth observing that the Luwian Hieroglyphic signs L.334 (pa) and L.439 (wa) have a similar overall shape that might explain the single example of the variant writing of Palistin in the Aleppo temple inscription as an error. Third, the phenomenon of locally made Mycenaean IIIC pottery present in great quantities at sites in the ʿAmuq (T. Harrison 2009, 181–83; given as evidence in Hawkins 2009, 171–72), does not necessarily support the identification of Taita and his kingdom as "Philistine"—this ceramic tradition with local variation is a feature of most coastal regions of the Levant and Cyprus in the early Iron Age where it is variously identified with whatever "Sea People" group is geographically preferred by any given author.

In short, while Taita may have been descended from immigrants who arrived in the ʿAmuq as a consequence of the period of mass migration at the end of the Bronze Age, the identification of his ethnic group with that which settled the coastal plain of the southern Levant is premature. Until the phonetic and historical difficulties are resolved and more evidence comes to light, we reserve judgment on Taita's ethnic origins.

20. We had difficulty reconciling this reference with the Epigraphic Survey's Medinet Habu volumes.

10.1.2 Ramesses III: Papyrus Harris

a) Peleset are defeated by Ramesses III and "reduced to ashes" (Erichsen 1933, 92.18; Grandet 1994; Peden 1994, 215; *ARE*, IV:§403; *ANET*, 260–62).

10.1.3 Ramesses III Rhetorical Stele (Chapel C at Deir el-Medina)

a) The Peleset and Teresh have sailed(?) "in the midst of the sea" (Kitchen 1983a, 91.11–12; Peden 1994, 64.8).

10.1.4 The Onomasticon of Amenope

a) The Peleset occur in the sequence: ... Ashkelon, Ashdod, Gaza, Assyria, Shubaru, [...], Sherden, Tjekker, **Peleset**, Khurma, [...], ... (*AEO*, I:#270, for commentary, see *AEO*, I:200–205).

10.1.5 Pedeset Inscription

a) This Third Intermediate Period[21] inscription on a Middle Kingdom statue bears the name: *P3-di-3st s3 'py* whose title is *wpwty n p3-Kn'n n Pršt* ("Envoy to the Canaan of Philistines") (Steindorff 1939; Singer 1994, 330).

10.2 Ugaritic

(no attestations found)

10.3 Hittite

(no attestations found)

10.4 Other

(no attestations found)

21. *P3-di-3st* is attested from the Third Intermediate period through the Ptolemaic period (Ranke 1935, 121.18).

Bibliography

Ackermann, Oren, Hendrik J. Bruins, and Aren M. Maeir. 2005. A Unique Human-Made Trench at Tell es-Safi/Gath: Anthropogenic Impact and Landscape Response. *Geoarchaeology* 20:303–28.

Adams, William Y., Dennis P. Van Gerven, and Richard S. Levy. 1978. The Retreat from Migrationism. *Annual Review of Anthropology* 7:483–532.

Aharoni, Yohanan. 1979. *The Land of the Bible: A Historical Geography.* 2nd rev. ed. Translated by A. F. Rainey. London: Burns & Oates.

Aharoni, Yohanan, and Ruth Amiran. 1958. A New Scheme for the Subdivision of the Iron Age in Palestine. *IEJ* 8:171–84.

Albert, Rosa Maria, Ruth Shahack-Gross, Dan Cabanes, Ayelet Gilboa, Simcha Lev-Yadun, Martha Portillo, Ilan Sharon, Elisabetta Boaretto, and Steve Weiner. 2008. Phytolith-Rich Layers from the Late Bronze and Iron Ages at Tel Dor (Israel): Mode of Formation and Archaeological Significance. *Journal of Archaeological Science* 35:57–75.

Albright, William F. 1929. Progress in Palestinian Archaeology During the Year 1928. *BASOR* 33:1–10.

———. 1930–1931. *The Pottery of the First Three Campaigns.* Vol. 1 of *The Excavation of Tell Beit Mirsim in Palestine.* AASOR 12. New Haven, Conn.: Yale University Press.

———. 1932a. An Anthropoid Clay Coffin from Sahab in Transjordan. *AJA* 36:295–306.

———. 1932b. *The Pottery of the First Three Campaigns.* Vol. 1 of *The Excavations at Tel Beth Mirsim.* AASOR 12. New Haven: Yale University Press.

———. 1950. Some Oriental Glosses on the Homeric Problem. *AJA* 54:162–76.

———. 1954. *The Archaeology of Palestine.* The Pelican Archaeology Series. Harmondsworth, Middlesex: Penguin.

Alevra, Georgia, Sofia Kalopisi, Nota Kourou, Anna Laimou, and Maria-Afroditi Panagiotidi. 1985. Anaskafe sten Kardamaina (Archaia Alasarna) tes Kos. *Archaiologike Ephemeris: Chronika* 124:1–18.

Ålin, Per. 1978. Idalion Pottery from the Excavations of the Swedish-Cyprus Expedition. *Opuscula Atheniensia* 12:91–109.

Allen, Susan H. 1994. Trojan Grey Ware at Tel Miqne-Ekron. *BASOR* 293:39–51.

Alt, Albrecht. 1953. Ägyptische Tempel in Palästina und die Landnahme der Philister. Pages 216–30 in *Kleine Schriften zur Geschichte des Volkes Israel, Band I.* Edited by A. Alt. 2 vols. Munich: Beck. *ZDPV* 67:1–20.

Amiran, Ruth. 1969. *Ancient Pottery from the Holy Land: From Its Beginnings in the Neolithic Period to the End of the Iron Age.* Jerusalem: Massada Press.

Anderson, William P. 1988. *Sarepta I: The Late Bronze and Iron Age Strata of Area II, Y. The*

University Museum of the University of Pennsylvania Excavations at Sarafand, Lebanon. Beirut: Publications de l'Université libanaise.

———. 1989. The Pottery Industry at Phoenician Sarepta (Sarafand, Lebanon), with Parallels to Kilns from Other East Mediterranean Sites. Pages 197–215 in *Cross-Craft and Cross-Cultural Interactions in Ceramics.* Edited by P. E. McGovern, M. D. Notis, and W. D. Kingery. Ceramics and Civilisations 4. Westerville, Ohio: American Ceramic Society.

Anson, Dimitri. 1980a. Composition and Provenance of Rude Style and Related Wares. *RDAC* 1980:109–23.

———. 1980b. The Rude Style Late Cypriot IIC–III Pottery: An Analytical Typology. *Opuscula Atheniensia* 13:1–18.

Anthony, David W. 1990. Migration in Archaeology: The Baby and the Bathwater. *American Anthropologist* 92:895–914.

Archäologisches Landesmuseum Baden-Württemberg, ed. 2001. *Troia: Traum und Wirklichkeit.* Stuttgart: Theiss.

Arnaud, Daniel. 1992. Les ports de la 'Phénicie' à la fin d'âge du Bronze récent (XIV–XII siècles) d'après les texts cunéiformes de Syrie. *SMEA* 30:179–94.

Arnold, Dean. 1985. *Ceramic Theory and Cultural Process.* New Studies in Archaeology. Cambridge: Cambridge University Press.

Artzy, Michal. 1975. "The Origin of the Palestinian Bichrome Ware." Ph.D. diss., Brandeis University.

———. 1984. Unusual Late Bronze Ship Representations from Tel Akko. *Mariner's Mirror* 70:59–64.

———. 1985. Supply and Demand: A Study of Second Millennium Cypriote Pottery in the Levant. Pages 93–99 in *Prehistoric Production and Exchange: The Aegean and Eastern Mediterranean.* Edited by A. B. Knapp and T. Stech. University of California at Los Angeles Institute of Archaeology Monographs 25. Los Angeles: Institute of Archaeology, University of California, Los Angeles.

———. 1987. On Boats and Sea Peoples. *BASOR* 266:75–85.

———. 1993. Nami, Tel. *NEAEHL* 3:1095–98.

———. 1994. Incense, Camels and Collared Rim Jars: Desert Trade Routes and Maritime Outlets in the Second Millennium. *OJA* 13:121–47.

———. 1995. Nami: A Second Millennium International Maritime Trading Center in the Mediterranean. Pages 17–41 in *Recent Discoveries in Israel: A View to the West.* Edited by S. Gitin and W. Dever. New York: Archaeological Institute of America.

———. 1997. Nomads of the Sea. Pages 1–16 in Swiny, Hohlfelder, and Swiny 1997.

———. 1998. Routes, Trade, Boats and "Nomads of the Sea." Pages 439–48 in Gitin, Mazar, and Stern 1998.

———. 2000a. Cult and Recycling of Metal at the End of the Late Bronze Age. Pages 27–32 in *Festschrift für Hans-Günter Buchholz zu seinem achtzigsten Geburtstag am 24. Dezember 1999.* Edited by P. Åström and D. Sürenhagen. SIMA 127. Jonsered: Åströms.

———. 2000b. The Continuation of Cypriote "Sea-Desert" Trade Involvement in the 12th Century BC. Pages 445–52 in *Proceedings of the Third International Congress of Cypriot Studies, April 16–20, 1996.* Edited by G. K. Ioannide and S. A. Chatzestylle. Leukosia: Hetaireia Kypriakon Spoudon.

———. 2001. White Slip Ware for Export? The Economics of Production. Pages 107–15 in *The White Slip Ware of Late Bronze Age Cyprus: Proceedings of an International Conference Organized by the Anastasios G. Leventis Foundation, Nicosia in Honour of Malcolm Wiener, Nicosia 29th–30th October 1998*. Edited by V. Karageorghis. Denkschriften der Gesamtakademie 20; Contributions to the Chronology of the Eastern Mediterranean 2. Vienna: Österreichische Akademie der Wissenschaften.

———. 2002. The Aegean, Cyprus, the Levant and Bichrome Ware: Eastern Mediterranean Middle Bronze Age Koine? Pages 1–20 in Oren and Ahituv 2002.

———. 2003a. Bronze Trade in the Late Bronze–Early Iron Period: Tel Masos and Tel Kinrot in Eastern Mediterranean Context. Pages 15–23 *Saxa Loquentur: Studien zur Archäologie Palästinas/Israels: Festschrift für Volkmar Fritz zum 65. Geburtstag*. Edited by C. den Hertog, U. Hübner, and S. Münger. AOAT 302. Münster: Ugarit-Verlag.

———. 2003b. Mariners and Their Boats at the End of the Late Bronze and the Beginning of the Iron Age in the Eastern Mediterranean. *TA* 30:232–46.

———. 2005. *Emporia* on the Carmel Coast? Tel Akko, Tell Abu Hawam and Tel Nami of the Late Bronze Age. Pages 355–62 in Laffineur and Greco 2005.

———. 2006a. "Filling in" the Void: Observations on Habitation Pattern at the End of the Late Bronze at Tel Akko. Pages 115–22 in Maeir and de Miroschedji 2006.

———. 2006b. The Carmel Coast During the Second Part of the Late Bronze Age: A Center for Eastern Mediterranean Transshipping. *BASOR* 343:45–64.

———. 2006c. *The Jatt Metal Hoard in Northern Canaanite/Phoenician and Cypriote Context*. Cuadernos de Arqueología Mediterranea 10. Barcelona: Laboratorio de Arqueología de la Universidad Pompeu Fabra de Barcelona.

Artzy, Michal, and Svetlana Zagorski. 2012. Cypriot "Mycenaean" IIIB Imported to the Levant. Pages 1–12 in *All the Wisdom of the East: Studies in Near Eastern Archaeology and History in Honor of Eliezer D. Oren*. Edited by M. Gruber, S. Aḥituv, G. Lehmann, and Z. Talshir. OBO 255. Fribourg: Academic Press; Göttingen: Vandenhoeck & Ruprecht.

Asaro, Frank, Iz Perlman, and Moshe Dothan. 1971. An Introductory Study of Mycenaean IIIC:1 Ware from Tel Ashdod. *Archaeometry* 13:169–75.

Assmann, Jan. 1992. *Das kulturelle Gedächtnis: Schrift, Erinnerung und politische Identität in frühen Hochkulturen*. Munich: Beck.

Aston, David. 1989. Qantir/Piramesse-Nord–Pottery Report 1988. *Göttinger Miszelle: Beiträge zur ägyptologischen Diskussion* 113:7–32.

———. 1996. *Egyptian Pottery of the Late New Kingdom and Third Intermediate Period (Twelfth–Seventh Centuries BC): Tentative Footsteps in a Forbidding Terrain*. Studien zur Archäologie und Geschichte Altägyptens 13. Heidelberg: Heidelberger Orientverlag.

Åström, Paul. 1972. *The Late Cypriot Bronze Age: Architecture and Pottery*. Vol. 4, Part 1C of *The Swedish Cyprus Expedition*. Lund: Swedish Cyprus Expedition.

———. 1977. *The Chamber Tombs*. Part I of *The Cuirass Tomb and Other Finds at Dendra*. SIMA 4. Göteborg: Åströms.

———. 1985a. Hala Sultan Tekke. Pages 173–81 in Karageorghis (ed.) 1985.

———. 1985b. The Sea Peoples in the Light of New Excavations. *Centre d'Études Chypriotes, Cahier* 3:3–18.

———. 1986. Hala Sultan Tekke: An International Harbour Town of the Late Cypriot Bronze Age. *Opuscula Atheniensia* 16:7–17.

———. 1989. *Hala Sultan Tekke 9: Trenches 1972–1987 with an Index for Volumes 1–9.* SIMA 45: 9. Göteborg: Åströms.

———. 1993. Late Cypriot Bronze Age Pottery in Palestine. Pages 307–13 in Biran and Aviram 1993.

———. 1996. Hala Sultan Tekke—A Late Cypriot Harbour Town. Pages 9–14 in Åström and Herscher 1996.

———. 1998. *Hala Sultan Tekke 10: The Wells.* SIMA 45:10. Jonsered: Åströms.

———. 2001. *Hala Sultan Tekke 11.* SIMA 45:11. Jonsered: Åströms.

———, ed. 1987. *High, Middle or Low? Acts of an International Colloquium on Absolute Chronology Held at the University of Gothenburg 20–22 August 1987.* 2 vols. Göteborg: Åströms.

Åström, Paul, Donald M. Bailey, and Vassos Karageorghis. 1976. *Hala Sultan Tekke* I: *Excavations 1897–1971.* Studies in Mediterranean Archaeology 45/1. Göteborg: Åströms.

Åström, Paul, and Ellen Herscher, eds. 1996. *Late Bronze Age Settlement in Cyprus: Function and Relationship.* SIMA Pocket-Book 126. Jonsered: Åströms.

Åström, Paul, and Emilia Masson. 1982. A Silver Bowl with Canaanite Inscription from Hala Sultan Tekké. *RDAC* 1982:72–76.

Avila, Robert A. J. 1983. *Bronzene Lanzen- und Pfeilspitzen der griechischen Spätbronzezeit.* Prähistorische Bronzefunde 5:1. Munich: Beck.

Bachhuber, Christoph, and R. Gareth Roberts, eds. 2009. *Forces of Transformation: The End of the Bronze Age in the Mediterranean. Proceedings of an International Symposium Held at St. John's College, University of Oxford 25–6th March, 2006.* Themes from the Ancient Near East BANEA Publication 1. Oxford: Oxbow.

Badre, Leila. 1983. Les peuples de la mer à Ibn Hani. Pages 203–9 in Bartolini and Bondi 1983.

———. 1997. Bey 003 Preliminary Report. *Bulletin d'archéologie et d'architecture libanaises* 2:6–94.

———. 2006. Tell Kazel—Simyra: A Contribution to a Relative Chronological History in the Eastern Mediterranean During the Late Bronze Age. *BASOR* 343:65–95.

Badre, Leila, Marie-Claude Boileau, Reinhard Jung, Hans Mommsen, and Michael Kerschner. 2005. The Provenance of Aegean- and Syrian-Type Pottery Found at Tell Kazel. *Ägypten und Levante* 15:15–47.

Badre, Leila, Eric Gubel, Emmanuelle Capet, and Nadine Panayot. 1994. Tell Kazel (Syrie). Rapport préliminaire sur les 4e–8e campagnes de fouilles (1988–1992). *Syria* 71:259–346.

Bailey, Donald M. 1976. The British Museum Excavations at Hala Sultan Tekke in 1897 and 1898: The Material in the British Museum. Pages 1–32 in Åström, Bailey, and Karageorghis 1976.

Baines, John. 1996. Contextualizing Egyptian Representations of Society and Ethnicity. Pages 339–84 in *The Study of the Ancient Near East in the Twenty-First Century: The William Foxwell Albright Centennial Conference.* Edited by J. S. Cooper and G. M. Schwartz. Winona Lake, Ind.: Eisenbrauns.

———. 1999. On Wenamun as a Literary Text. Pages 209–33 in *Literatur und Politik im pharaonischen und ptolemäischen Ägypten: Vorträge der Tagung zum Gedenken an Georges Posener 5.–10. September 1996 in Leipzig.* Edited by J. Assmann and E. Blumenthal. Bibliothèque d'étude 127; Publications de l'Institut français d'archéologie orientale du Caire 832. Cairo: Institut français d'archéologie orientale du Caire.

Balensi, Jacqueline. 1980. "Les fouilles de R.W. Hamilton à Tell Abu Hawam: Niveaux IV et V." Ph.D. diss., Université de Strasbourg.
———. 1981. Tell Keisan, témoin original de l'apparition du "Mycénien IIIC 1a" au Proche-Orient. *RB* 88:399–401.
———. 1985. Revising Tell Abu Hawam. *BASOR* 257:65–74.
Balensi, Jacqueline, Maria Herrera, and Michal Artzy. 1993. Abu Hawam, Tell. *NEAEHL* 1:7–14.
Baly, Denis. 1957. *The Geography of the Bible: A Study in Historical Geography.* New York: Harper.
Bankoff, H. Arthur, Nathan Meyer, and Mark Stefanovich. 1996. Handmade Burnished Ware and the Late Bronze Age of the Balkans. *Journal of Mediterranean Archaeology* 9:193–209.
Barako, Tristan. 2000. The Philistine Settlement as Mercantile Phenomenon? *AJA* 104: 513–30.
———. 2001. "The Seaborne Migration of the Philistines." Ph.D. diss., Harvard University.
———. 2003. One if by Sea ... Two if by Land: How Did the Philistines Get to Canaan? One: By Sea. *BAR* 29, no. 2 (March/April):26–33, 64, 66.
———. 2007a. *Tel Mor: The Moshe Dothan Excavations, 1959–1960.* Israel Antiquities Authority Reports 32. Jerusalem: Israel Antiquities Authority.
———. 2007b. Coexistence and Impermeability: Egyptians and Philistines in Southern Canaan During the Twelfth Century BCE. Pages 509–16 in *The Synchronisation of Civilisations in the Eastern Mediterranean in the Second Millennium B.C. II: Proceedings of the Second EuroConference of SCIEM 2000 at the Austrian Academy, Vienna, May 28 to June 1 2003.* Edited by M. Bietak and E. Czerny. Österreichische Akademie der Wissenschaften, Denkschriften der Gesamtakademie 29; Contributions to the Chronology of the Eastern Mediterranean 4. Vienna: Österreichische Akademie der Wissenschaften.
Baramki, Dimitri. 1973. The Impact of the Mycenaeans on Ancient Phoenicia. Pages 193–97 in Dikaios 1973.
Barkay, Gabriel. 1992. A Group of Stamped Handles from Judah. *ErIsr* 23:113–28. [Hebrew]
Barkay, Gabriel, and Andrew Vaughn. 1996. *Lmlk* and Official Seal Impressions from Tel Lachish. *TA* 23:61–74.
Barlow, Jane Atwood, Diane R. Bolger, and Barbara Kling. 1991. *Cypriot Ceramics: Reading the Prehistoric Record.* University Museum Monograph 74; University Museum Symposium Series 2. Philadelphia: University Museum of Archaeology and Anthropology, University of Pennsylvania.
Bartolini, Piero, and Sandro Filippo Bondi, eds. 1983. *Atti del 1 Congresso internazionale di studi fenici e punici, Roma, 5–10 novembre 1979.* Rome: Consiglo Nationale delle Richerche.
Basch, Lucien, and Michal Artzy. 1985. Ship Graffiti at Kition. Pages 322–36 in Karageorghis and Demas 1985.
Basedow, Maureen. 2000. *Besik-Tepe: Das spätbronzezeitliche Gräberfeld.* Studia Troica Monographien 1. Mainz: Zabern.
Bass, George F. 1967. *Cape Gelidonya: A Bronze Age Shipwreck.* Transactions of the American Philosophical Society, new ser. 57:8. Philadelphia: American Philosophical Society.

———. 1986. A Shipwreck at Ulu Burun (Kas): 1984 Campaign. *AJA* 90:269–96.

Bauer, Alexander. 1998. Cities of the Sea: Maritime Trade and the Origin of the Philistine Settlement in the Early Iron Age Southern Levant. *OJA* 17:149–68.

Baurain, Claude. 1991. L'écriture syllabique à Chypre. Pages 389–424 in Baurain, Bonnet and Krings 1991.

Baurain, Claude, Corinne Bonnet, and Véronique Krings, eds. 1991. *Phoinikeia Grammata: lire et écrire en Méditerranée. Actes du colloque de Liège, 15–18 novembre 1989.* Collection d'études classiques 6; Studia Phoenicia; Travaux du Groupe de contact interuniversitaire d'études phéniciennes et puniques. Namur: Société des études classiques.

Bayburtluoğlu, Inci. 1979. Eskiyapar „Phryg Çağı." Pages 293–303 in *VIII. Türk Tarih Kongresi, Ankara, 11–15 Ekim 1976: Kongreye sunulan bildiriler.* Ankara: Türk Tarih Kurumu Basimevi.

Bazemore, Georgia B. 1998. "The Role of Script in Ancient Society: The Cypriote Syllabic Inscriptions. A Study in Grammatology." Ph.D. diss., University of Chicago.

———. 2002. The Display and Viewing of the Syllabic Inscriptions of Rantidi Sanctuary. Pages 155–212 in *Script and Seal Use on Cyprus in the Bronze and Iron Ages*. Edited by J. S. Smith. Colloquia and Conference Papers 4. Boston: Archaeological Institute of America.

Beckman, Gary, trans. 1996. Akkadian Documents from Ugarit. Pages 26–28 in *Near Eastern and Aegean Texts from the Third to the First Millennia BC.* Edited by A. B. Knapp. Vol. 2 of *Sources for the History of Cyprus.* Edited by P. W. Wallace and A. G. Orphanides. Altamont, N.Y.: Greece and Cyprus Research Center.

———. 1999. *Hittite Diplomatic Texts.* 2nd ed. SBL Writings from the Ancient World Series 7. Atlanta: Scholars Press.

Bell, Carol. 2005. "The Influence of Economic Factors on Settlement Continuity Across the LBA/Iron Age Transition on the Northern Levantine Littoral." Ph.D. diss., University College, London.

———. 2006. *The Evolution of Long Distance Trading Relationships across the LBA/Iron Age Transition on the Northern Levantine Coast: Crisis, Continuity and Change. A Study Based on Imported Ceramics, Bronze and Its Constituent Metals.* BAR International Series 1574. Oxford: Archaeopress.

Ben-Dov, Meir. 1976. Napa: A Geographical Term of Possible "Sea People" Origin. *TA* 3:70–73.

Ben-Shlomo, David. 2006. *Decorated Philistine Pottery: An Archaeological and Archaeometric Study.* BAR International Series 1541. Oxford: Archaeopress.

Ben-Shlomo, David, Itzhaq Shai, and Aren M. Maeir. 2004. Late Philistine Decorated Ware ("Ashdod Ware"): Typology, Chronology, and Production Centers. *BASOR* 335:1–34.

Ben-Shlomo, David, Itzhaq Shai, Alexander Zukerman, and Aren M. Maeir. 2008. Cooking Identities: Aegean-Style Cooking Jugs and Cultural Interaction in Iron Age Philistia and Neighboring Regions. *AJA* 112:225–46.

Benson, Jack L. 1972. *Bamboula at Kourion: The Necropolis and the Finds Excavated by J. F. Daniel.* Museum Monograph of the University Museum; The Haney Foundation Series, University of Pennsylvania 12. Philadelphia: University Museum of Archaeology and Anthropology, University of Pennsylvania.

———. 1973. *The Necropolis of Kaloriziki: Excavated by J. F. Daniel and G.H. McFadden for*

the University Museum, University of Pennsylvania, Philadelphia. SIMA 36; Museum Monographs. Göteborg: Åströms.
Ben-Tor, Amnon, and Doron Ben-Ami. 1998. Hazor and the Archaeology of the Tenth Century B.C.E. *IEJ* 48/1-2:1-37.
Benzi, Mario. 1982. Tombe micenee di Rodi riutilizzate nel TEIIIC. *SMEA* 23:323-36.
———. 1986. I Micenei a Iasos. Pages 29-34 in *Studi su Iasos di Caria*. Bollettino d'Arte suppl. to vols. 31-32, 1985. Rome: Istituto Poligrafico e Zecca dello Stato.
———. 1988a. Mycenaean Pottery Later than LH IIIA:1 from the Italian Excavations at Trianda on Rhodes. Pages 39-55 in Dietz and Papachristodoulou 1988.
———. 1988b. Mycenaean Rhodes: A Summary. Pages 59-72 in Dietz and Papachristodoulou 1988.
———. 1988c. Rhodes in the LH IIIC Period. Pages 253-62 in French and Wardle 1988.
———. 1992. *Rodi e la civiltà micenea*. Incunabula Graeca 94. Rome: Gruppo editoriale internazionale.
———. 1993. The Late Bronze Age Pottery from Vathy Cave, Kalymnos. Pages 275-88 in Zerner, Zerner, and Winder 1993.
———. 1996. Problems of the Mycenaean Expansion in the South-Eastern Aegean. Pages 947-78 in *Atti e Memorie del II Congresso Internazionale di Micenologia* III. Edited by E. De Miro, L. Godart, and A. Sacconi. Rome: Gruppo editoriale internazionale.
———. 1999. Mycenaean Figurines from Iasos. *Parola del Passato* 54:269-82.
———. 2005. Mycenaeans at Iasos? A Reassessment of Doro Levi's Excavations. Pages 205-15 in Laffineur and Greco 2005.
———. 2009. LB III Trade in the Dodecanese: An Overview. Pages 47-62 in Borgna and Càssola Guida 2009.
Berna, Francesco, Adi Behar, Ruth Shahack-Gross, John Berg, Elisabetta Boaretto, Ayelet Gilboa, Ilan Sharon, Sariel Shalev, Sana Shilstein, Naama Yahalom-Mack, Jeffrey R. Zorn, and Steve Weiner. 2007. Sediments Exposed to High Temperatures: Reconstructing Pyrotechnological Processes in Late Bronze and Iron Age Strata at Tel Dor (Israel). *Journal of Archaeological Science* 34:358-73.
Betancourt, Philip. 1985. *The History of Minoan Pottery*. Princeton: Princeton University Press.
Bienkowski, Piotr. 1982. Some Remarks on the Practice of Cremation in the Levant. *Levant* 14:80-89.
———. 1989. Prosperity and Decline. *BASOR* 275:59-63.
———. 2007. Landscape, Identity, and Reciprocal Relations: The Wadi Arabah as Relationship and Discourse. Pages 407-22 in Crawford et al. 2007.
Bierling, Neal. 1998. *Tel Miqne-Ekron Excavations, 1995-1996, Field XNW, Areas 77, 78, 79, 89, 90, 101, 102: Iron Age I*. Tel Miqne-Ekron Limited Edition Series 7. Jerusalem: W. F. Albright Institute of Archaeological Research.
Bietak, Manfred. 1984. Ramsesstadt. Pages 128-46 in *Pyramidenbau-Steingefäße*. Vol. 5 of *Lexikon der Ägyptologie*. Edited by W. Helck and W. Westendorf. Wiesbaden: Harrassowitz.
———. 1991. Zur Landnahme Palästinas durch die Seevölker und zum Ende der ägyptischen Provinz Kana'an. *MDAIK* 47:35-50.
———. 1993. The Sea Peoples and the End of the Egyptian Administration of Canaan. Pages 292-306 in Biran and Aviram 1993.
Bietak, Manfred, and Ernst Czerny, eds. 2007. *The Synchronisation of Civilisations in the*

Eastern Mediterranean in the Second Millennium B.C. III: Proceedings of the SCIEM 2000–2nd EuroConference Vienna, 28th of May–1st of June 2003. Contributions to the Chronology of the Eastern Mediterranean 9; Denkschriften der Gesamtakademie, Österreichische Akademie der Wissenschaften 37. Vienna: Österreichische Akademie der Wissenschaften.

Bikai, Patricia. 1976. "Tyre: Report of an Excavation 1973–1974." Ph.D. diss., Graduate Theological Union.

———. 1978. *The Pottery of Tyre: Excavations for the Department of Antiquities, Lebanon, 1973–4*. Warminster: Aris & Phillips.

———. 1987. *The Phoenician Pottery of Cyprus*. Nicosia: A. G. Leventis Foundation.

———. 1994. The Phoenicians and Cyprus. Pages 31–37 in Karageorghis (ed.) 1994.

Bing, John D. 1985 [1993]. Sissu/Issus, and Phoenicians in Cilicia. *American Journal of Ancient History* 10:97–123.

Biran, Avraham, and Joseph Aviram, eds. 1993. *Biblical Archaeology Today, 1990: Proceedings of the Second International Congress on Biblical Archaeology, Jerusalem, June–July 1990*. Jerusalem: Israel Exploration Society: Israel Academy of Sciences and Humanities.

Biran, Avraham, and Ora Negbi. 1966. The Stratigraphical Sequence at Tel Sippor. *IEJ* 16:160–73.

Bittel, Kurt. 1957. Vorläufiger Bericht über die Ausgrabungen in Boghazköy im Jahre 1956: Untersuchungen in der Altstadt. *MDOG* 89:6–25.

———. 1958. *Troy IV: Settlements VIIa, VIIb and VIII*. Princeton: Princeton University Press.

———. 1983. Die archäologische Situation in Kleinasien um 1200 v. Chr. und während der nachfolgenden vier Jahrhunderte. Pages 25–47 in Deger-Jalkotzy 1983.

Blaylock, Stuart R. 1999. Iron Age Pottery from Tille Höyük, South-Eastern Turkey. Pages 263–86 in *Iron Age Pottery in Northern Mesopotamia, Northern Syria, and South-Eastern Anatolia: Papers Presented at the Meetings of the International "table ronde" at Heidelberg (1995) and Nieborów (1997) and Other Contributions*. Edited by A. Hausleiter and A. Reiche. Münster: Ugarit-Verlag.

Blegen, Carl, Catherine Boulter, John Caskey, and Marion Rawson. 1958. *Settlements VIIa, VIIb and VIII*. Vol. 4 of *Troy: Excavations Conducted by the University of Cincinnati, 1932–1938*. Princeton: Princeton University Press.

Blegen, Carl, John Caskey, and Marion Rawson. 1953. *The Sixth Settlement*. Vol. 3 of *Troy: Excavations Conducted by the University of Cincinnati, 1932–1938*. Princeton: Princeton University Press.

Blinkenberg, Christian, and Knud Friis Johansen. 1924. *Corpus Vasorum Antiquorum Danemark 2: Musée National 1*. Copenhagen: Champion and Branner.

Bliss, Frederick J., and R. A. Stewart Macalister. 1902. *Excavations in Palestine During the Years 1898–1900*. London: Palestine Exploration Fund.

Bloedow, Edmund. 1985. Handmade Burnished Ware or Barbarian Pottery and Troy VIIb. *La Parola del Passato* 222:161–99.

Blumenthal, Ekkehard. 1963. *Die altgriechische Siedlungskolonisation unter besonderer Berücksichtigung der Südküste Kleinasiens*. Tübingen: Geographisches Institut der Universität Tübingen.

Boas, Adrian, Aren M. Maeir, and Tammi Schneider. 2000. Tel Zafit. *Explorations and Surveys in Israel* 20:114–15. [Hebrew]

Bonatz, Dominik. 1993. Some Considerations on the Material Culture of Coastal Syria in the Iron Age. *Egitto e Vicino Oriente* 16:123–58.

———. 1998. Imported Pottery. Pages 211–29 in Cecchini and Mazzoni 1998.

Bordreuil, Pierre, ed. 1991. *Une bibliothèque au sud de la ville: les textes de la 34e campagne (1973)*. Ras Shamra-Ougarit 7. Paris: Éditions Recherche sur les civilisations.

Borgna, Elisabetta, and Paola Càssola Guida. 2009. *Dall'Egeo all'Adriatico: Organizzazioni sociali, modi di scambio e interazione in età postpalaziale (XII–XI sec. a.C). Atti del seminario internazionale (Udine, 1–2 dicembre 2006)*. Studi e ricerche di protostoria mediterranea 8. Rome: Quasar.

Bosanquet, Robert C., and Richard Dawkins. 1923. *The Unpublished Objects from the Palaikastro Excavations 1902–1906*. British School at Athens Supplementary Paper 1. London: British School at Athens.

Bounni, Adnan, and Jacques Lagarce. 1989. Ras Ibn-Hani (mission franco-syrienne). Pages 91–97 in *Contribution française à l'archéologie syrienne (1969–1989)*. Beirut: Institut français d'archéologie du Proche Orient.

Bounni, Adnan, Elisabeth Lagarce, and Jacques Lagarce. 1998. *Ras Ibn Hani, I: le palais nord du Bronze Récent. Fouilles 1979–1995: synthèse préliminaire*. Paris: Geuthner.

Bounni, Adnan, Elisabeth Lagarce, Jacques Lagarce, and Nassib Saliby. 1978. Rapport préliminaire sur la deuxième campagne de fouilles (1976) à Ibn Hani (Syrie). *Syria* 55:233–301.

Bounni, Adnan, Elisabeth Lagarce, Jacques Lagarce, Nassib Saliby, and Leila Badre. 1979. Rapport préliminaire sur la troisième campagne de fouilles (1977) à Ibn Hani (Syrie). *Syria* 56:217–91.

Bourke, Stephen, and Jean-Paul Descoeudres, eds. 1995. *Trade, Contact, and the Movement of Peoples in the Eastern Mediterranean: Studies in Honor of Basil Hennessy*. Mediterranean Archaeology, Suppl. 3. Sydney: Meditarch.

Bouzek, Jan. 1985. *The Aegean, Anatolia and Europe: Cultural Interrelations in the Second Millennium B.C.* SIMA 29. Göteborg: Åströms.

Boysal, Yusuf. 1969. *Katalog der Vasen im Museum in Bodrum I: mykenisch-protogeometrisch*. Ankara: Türk Tarih Kurumu Basımevi.

Braidwood, Robert. 1937. *Mounds in the Plain of Antioch: An Archaeological Survey*. OIP 48. Chicago: University of Chicago Press.

Braudel, Fernand. 1972. *The Mediterranean and the Mediterranean World in the Age of Philip II*. New York: Perennial Library.

Breasted, James Henry. 1905–1907. *Ancient Records of Egypt*. 5 vols. Chicago: University of Chicago Press. Reprint, New York: Russell & Russel, 1962.

Briend, Jacques, and Jean-Baptiste Humbert. 1980. *Tell Keisan (1971–1976): une cité phénicienne en Galilée*. OBO, Series Archaeologica 1. Fribourg: Éditions Universitaires.

Brug, John F. 1985. *A Literary and Archaeological Study of the Philistines*. BAR International Series 265. Oxford: BAR.

Bruins, Hendrik J., Johannes van der Plicht, and Amihai Mazar. 2003. 14C Dates from Tel Rehov: Iron-Age Chronology, Pharaohs, and Hebrew Kings. *Science* 300:315–18.

Brunton, Guy, and Reginald Engelbach. 1927. *Gurob*. British School of Archaeology in Egypt and Egyptian Research Account, Twenty-Fourth Year 41. London: British School of Archaeology in Egypt: B. Quaritch.

Bryce, Trevor. 1979. The Role of the Lukka People in Late Bronze Age Anatolia. *Antichthon* 13:1–11.

———. 1989a. Ahhiyawans and Mycenaeans: An Anatolian Viewpoint. *OJA* 8:297–310.
———. 1989b. The Nature of Mycenaean Involvement in Western Anatolia. *Historia* 38:1–21.
———. 1992. Lukka Revisited. *JNES* 51:121–30.
———. 1998. *The Kingdom of the Hittites*. Oxford: Clarendon.
———. 2003. *Letters of the Great Kings of the Ancient Near East: The Royal Correspondence of the Late Bronze Age*. London: Routledge.
Buchbinder, Binyamin. 1969. *Geological Map of HaShephela Region, Israel*. 1:20,000 Scale. 5 Sheets. Report of the Geological Survey of Israel OD/1/68; Report of the Institute for Petroleum Research and Geophysics 1030. Jerusalem: Geological Survey of Israel [Hebrew].
Buchholz, Hans-Günter. 1973. Grey Troian Ware in Cyprus and Northern Syria. Pages 179–87 in *Bronze Age Migrations in the Aegean: Archaeological and Linguistic Problems in Greek Prehistory. Proceedings of the First International Colloquium on Aegean Prehistory, Sheffield*. Edited by R. A. Crossland and A. Birchall. London: Duckworth.
———. 1999. *Ugarit, Zypern und Ägäis: Kulturbeziehungen im zweiten Jahrtausend v.Chr.* AOAT 261. Münster: Ugarit-Verlag.
Buchholz, Hans Günter, and Vassos Karageorghis. 1973. *Prehistoric Greece and Cyprus: An Archaeological Handbook*. London: Phaidon.
Bunimovitz, Shlomo. 1986. Is the "Philistine Material Culture" Really Philistine? Methodological Problems in the Study of the Philistine Culture. *Archeologia* 1:11–21. [Hebrew]
———. 1989. "The Land of Israel in the Late Bronze Age: A Case Study of Socio-Cultural Change in a Complex Society." Ph.D. diss., Tel Aviv University.
———. 1990. Problems in the "Ethnic" Identification of the Philistine Culture. *TA* 17:210–22.
———. 1994. The Problem of Human Resources in Late Bronze Age Palestine and Its Socioeconomic Implications. *UF* 26:1–20.
———. 1995. On the Edge of Empires—Late Bronze Age (1500–1200 BCE). Pages 320–31 in Levy 1995.
———. 1998. Sea Peoples in Cyprus and Israel: A Comparative Study of Immigration Processes. Pages 103–13 in Gitin, Mazar, and Stern 1998.
Bunimovitz, Shlomo, and Avraham Faust. 2001. Chronological Separation, Geographical Segregation, or Ethnic Demarcation? Ethnography and the Iron Age Low Chronology. *BASOR* 322:1–10.
Bunimovitz, Shlomo, and Zvi Lederman. 1997. Beth-Shemesh: Culture Conflict on Judah's Frontier. *BAR* 23, no. 1 (January/February):42–49, 75–77.
———. 1998. Tel Beth-Shemesh, 1991–1996. *Excavations and Surveys in Israel* 20:143–48.
———. 2000. Tel Beth-Shemesh, 1997–2000—Excavations and Surveys. *IEJ* 50:254–58.
———. 2001. The Iron Age Fortifications of Tel Beth Shemesh: A 1990–2000 Perspective. *IEJ* 51:121–47.
———. 2003. The Final Destruction of Beth Shemesh and the *Pax Assyriaca* in the Judean Shephelah. *TA* 30:3–26.
Bunimovitz, Shlomo, and Assaf Yasur-Landau. 1996. Philistine and Israelite Pottery: A Comparative Approach to the Question of Pots and People. *TA* 23:88–101.
Bunimovitz, Shlomo, and Orna Zimhoni. 1990. "Lamp and Bowl" Foundation Deposits

from the End of the Late Bronze Age—Beginning of the Iron Age in Eretz-Israel. *ErIsr* 21:41–55. [Hebrew]
———. 1993. "Lamp-and-Bowl" Foundation Deposits in Canaan. *IEJ* 43:99–125.
Bunnens, Guy. 1985. I Filistei e le invasioni dei Popoli del Mare. Pages 227–56 in *Le origini dei Greci: Dori e mondo egeo.* Edited by D. Musti. Rome: Laterza.
———, ed. 2000. *Essays on Syria in the Iron Age.* Ancient Near Eastern Studies Supplement 7. Louvain: Peeters.
Burdajewicz, Mariucz. 1994. "La céramique palestinienne du Fer I: la contribution de Tell Keisan, site de la Galilée maritime." Ph.D. diss., Warsaw University.
Burmeister, Stefan. 2000. Archaeology and Migration: Approaches to an Archaeological Proof of Migration. *Current Anthropology* 41:539–68.
Cadogan, Gerald. 1989. Maroni and the Monuments. Pages 43–51 in Peltenburg 1989.
———. 1996. Change in Late Bronze Age Cyprus. Pages 15–22 in Åström and Herscher 1996.
———. 1998. The Thirteenth-Century Changes in Cyprus in Their East Mediterranean Context. Pages 6–16 in Gitin, Mazar, and Stern 1998.
Cahill, Jane. 1995. Rosette Stamp Seal Impressions from Ancient Judah. *IEJ* 45:230–52.
Callot, Olivier. 1994. *La trancheé "ville sud": études d'architecture domestique.* Ras Shamra Ougarit 10; Publications de la Mission archéologique française de Ras Shamra-Ougarit. Paris: Éditions Recherche sur les civilisations; Lyon: Maison de l'Orient.
Çambel, Halet. 1999. *Karatepe-Arslantaş: The Inscriptions. Facsimile Edition.* Vol. 2 of *Corpus of Hieroglyphic Luwian Inscriptions.* Untersuchungen zur indogermanischen Sprach- und Kulturwissenschaft, n. F. 8. Berlin: de Gruyter.
Caminos, Ricardo A. 1954. *Late-Egyptian Miscellanies.* Brown Egyptological Studies 1. Oxford: Oxford University Press.
Capet, Emmanuelle. 2003. Tell Kazel (Syrie): Rapport préliminaire sur les 9e–17e campagnes de fouilles (1993–2001) du Musée de l'Université Américaine de Beyrouth, chantier II. *Berytus* 47:63–121.
———. 2006–2007. Les peuples des céramiques "barbares" à Tell Kazel (Syrie). *Scripta Mediterranea* 27–28:187–207.
Capet, Emmanuelle, and Eric Gubel. 2000. Tell Kazel: Six Centuries of Iron Age Occupation (c. 1200–612 B.C.). Pages 425–57 in Bunnens 2000.
Carr, David. 2005. *Writing on the Tablet of the Heart: Origins of Scripture and Literature.* Oxford: Oxford University Press.
Carter, Charles. 1999. *The Emergence of Yehud in the Persian Period: A Social and Demographic Study.* JSOTSup 294. Sheffield: Sheffield Academic Press.
Casana, Jesse J. 2003. "From Alalakh to Antioch: Settlement, Land Use, and Environmental Change in the Amuq Valley of Southern Turkey." Ph.D. diss., University of Chicago.
Casana, Jesse J., and Tony J. Wilkinson. 2005. Settlement and Landscapes in the Amuq Region. Pages 25–65 in *Surveys in the Plain of Antioch and Orontes Delta, Turkey, 1995–2002.* Vol. 1 of *The Amuq Valley Regional Projects.* Edited by K. A. Yener. OIP 131. Chicago: Oriental Institute of the University of Chicago.
Catling, Hector. 1961. A New Bronze Sword from Cyprus. *Antiquity* 35:115–22.
———. 1964. *Cypriote Bronzework in the Mycenaean World.* Oxford: Clarendon.
———. 1994. Cyprus in the 11th Century B.C.—An End or a Beginning? Pages 133–40 in Karageorghis (ed.) 1994.

Catling, Hector, and Richard E. Jones. 1986. Cyprus 2500–500 BC: The Aegean and the Near East, 1500–1050 BC. Pages 523–65 in Jones 1986b.

Caubet, Annie. 1992. The Reoccupation of the Syrian Coast After the Destruction of the "Crisis Years." Pages 123–31 in Ward and Joukowsky 1992.

Cavanagh, William G., and Christopher B. Mee. 1978. The Re-Use of Earlier Tombs in the LH IIIC Period. *Annual of the British School at Athens* 73:31–44.

Cecchini, Serena. 2000. The Textile Industry in Northern Syria During the Iron Age According to the Evidence of the Tell Afis Excavation. Pages 211–33 in Bunnens 2000.

———. 2002. Area N: Presentazione e cronologia. Pages 47–53 in *Tell Afis, Siria: 2000–2001*. Edited by S. Mazzoni. Pisa: Università degli Studi di Pisa.

Cecchini, Serena, and Stefania Mazzoni, eds. 1998. *Tell Afis (Syria): scavi sull'acropoli 1988–1992*. Ricerche di archeologia del Vicino Oriente 1; Tell Afis 1. Pisa: Edizioni ETS.

Černý, Jaroslav. 1939. *Late Ramesside Letters*. Bibliotheca Aegyptiaca 9. Brussels: Fondation égyptologique Reine Élisabeth.

Chadwick, John. 1975. The Prehistory of the Greek Language. Pages 805–19 in *The Cambridge Ancient History, Vol. 2, Part 2*. Edited by I. Edwards. Cambridge: Cambridge University Press.

Chapman, John, and Helena Hamerow, eds. 1997. *Migrations and Invasions in Archaeological Explanation*. BAR International Series 664. Oxford: Archaeopress.

Cifola, Barbara. 1994. The Role of the Sea Peoples at the End of the Late Bronze Age: A Reassessment of Textual and Archaeological Evidence. *Orientis Antiqui Miscellanea* 1:1–23.

Çilingiroğlu, Altan, and David H. French, eds. 1994. *Anatolian Iron Ages 3: The Proceedings of the Third Anatolian Iron Ages Colloquium Held at Van, 6–12 August 1990*. Ankara: British Institute of Archaeology.

Cline, Eric. 1987. Amenhotep III and the Aegean: A Reassessment of Egypto-Aegean Relations in the 14th Century BC. *Or* 56:1–36.

———. 1995. Tinker, Tailor, Soldier, Sailor: Minoans and Mycenaeans Abroad. Pages 265–87 in Laffineur and Niemeier 1995.

Cline, Eric, and Diane Harris-Cline, eds. 1998. *The Aegean and the Orient in the Second Millennium: Proceedings of the 50th Anniversary Symposium, Cincinnati, 18–20 April 1997*. Aegaeum 18. Liège: Université de Liège, Histoire de l'art et archéologie de la Grèce antique; Austin, Tex.: University of Texas at Austin, Program in Aegean Scripts and Prehistory.

Cobet, Justus, Volkmar von Graeve, Wolf-Dietrich Niemeier, and Konrad Zimmerman, eds. 2007. Frühes Ionien—eine Bestandsaufnahme: Panionion-Symposion Güzelçamli 26. September–1. Oktober 1999. Milesische Forschungen 5. Mainz: Zabern.

Coche de la Ferté, Étienne. 1951. *Essai de classification de la céramique mycénienne d'Enkomi (campagnes 1946 et 1947)*. Bibliothèque archéologique et historique 54. Paris: Geuthner.

Cohen-Weinberger, Anat. 1998. Petrographic Analysis of the Egyptian Forms from Stratum VI at Tel Beth-Sehan. Pages 406–12 in Gitin, Mazar, and Stern 1998.

———. 2009. Petrographic Studies. Pages 519–29 in Panitz-Cohen and Mazar 2009.

Cohen-Weinberger, Anat, and Sam R. Wolff. 2001. Production Centers of Collared-Rim

Pithoi from Sites in the Carmel Coast and Ramat Menashe Regions. Pages 639–57 in Wolff 2001.

Coldstream, John N. 1989. Early Greek Visitors to Cyprus and the Eastern Mediterranean. Pages 90–96 in *Cyprus and the East Mediterranean in the Iron Age: Proceedings of the Seventh British Museum Classical Colloquium*. Edited by V. Tatton-Brown. London: British Museum.

———. 1998. The First Exchanges between Euboeans and Phoenicians: Who Took the Initiative? Pages 353–60 in Gitin, Mazar, and Stern 1998.

Coldstream, John N., and Patricia Bikai. 1988. Early Greek Pottery in Tyre and Cyprus: Some Preliminary Comparisons. *RDAC* 1988:35–43.

Coleman, John E., Jane A. Barlow, Marcia K. Mogelonsky, and Kenneth W. Schaar. 1996. *Alambra: A Middle Bronze Age Settlement in Cyprus. Archaeological Investigations by Cornell University 1974–1985*. SIMA 118. Jonsered: Åströms.

Collombier, Marie. 1991. Écritures et sociétés à Chypre à l'âge du Fer. Pages 425–47 in Baurain, Bonnet, and Krings 1991.

Conrad, Diethelm. 1985. A Note on an Astarte Plaque from Tel Akko. *Michmanim* 2:19–24.

Contenson, Henri de, Elisabeth Lagarce, Jacques Lagarce, and Rolf Stucki. 1972. Rapport préliminaire sur la XXXII0 campagne de fouilles a Ras Shamra. *Annales archéologiques arabes syriennes* 22:25–43.

Cook, Robert. 1997. Greek Painted Pottery. 3rd ed. *Methuen's Handbooks of Archaeology Series*. London: Routledge.

Cooley, Robert, and Gary Pratico. 1995. Tell Dothan: The Western Cemetery with Comments on Joseph Free's Excavations, 1953 to 1964. Pages 147–90 in *Preliminary Excavation Reports: Sardis, Bir umm Fawakhir, Tell el-'Umeiri, the Combined Caesarea Expeditions and Tell Dothan*. Edited by W. G. Dever. AASOR 52. Ann Arbor, Mich.: American Schools of Oriental Research.

Cotelle-Michel, Laurence. 2004. *Les sarcophages en terre cuite en Égypte et en Nubie de l'époque prédynastique à l'époque romaine*. Dijon: Faton.

Courbin, Paul. 1983. Bassit. *Annales archéologiques arabes syriennes* 33:119–27.

———. 1986. Bassit. *Syria* 63:175–220.

———. 1986–1987. Rapport sur la Xe et dernière campagne de fouilles a Ras el-Bassit. *Annales archéologiques arabes syriennes* 36–37:107–20.

———. 1990. Bassit-Posidaion in the Early Iron Age. Pages 503–9 in *Greek Colonists and Native Populations: Proceedings of the First Australian Congress of Classical Archaeology Held in Honour of Emeritus Professor A. D. Trendall*. Edited by J. P. Descoeudres. Canberra: Humanities Research Centre; Oxford: Clarendon.

———. 1993. Fragments d'amphores protogéometriques grecques à Bassit (Syrie). *Hesperia* 62:95–113.

Courtois, Jacques-Claude. 1971. Le sanctuaire du dieu au l'ingot d'Enkomi-Alasia. Pages 151–362 in *Alasia I*. Edited by C. F.-A. Schaeffer. Mission d'Alasia 4. Paris: Mission archéologique d'Alasia, Collège de France.

———. 1972. Chypre et l'Europe préhistorique à la fin de l'âge du Bronze: données nouvelles sur le monde mycénien finissant. Pages 23–33 in *Praktika tou protou Diethnous Kypriologikou Synedriou, Leukosia, 14–19 Apriliou 1969*. Edited by V. Karageorghis and A. Christodoulou. Nicosia: Hetaireia Kypriakon Spoudon.

———. 1973. Sur divers groupes de vases mycéniens en Méditerranée orientale (1250–1150 av.J-C). Pages 137–65 in Dikaios 1973.

Courtois, Jacques-Claude, and Louis Courtois. 1978. Corpus céramique de Ras Shamra-Ugarit, niveau historique deuxième partie. Pages 191–370 in *Ugaritica VII: mission de Ras Shamra, Tome 18*. Edited C. F.-A. Schaeffer. Bibliothèque archéologique et historique 99. Leiden: Brill.

———. 1987. Enkomi und Ras Shamra, zwei Außenposten der mykenischen Kultur. Pages 182–217 in *Ägäische Bronzezeit*. Edited by H.-G. Buchholz. Darmstadt: Wissenschaftliche Buchgesellschaft.

Courtois, Jacques-Claude, Jacques Lagarce, and Elisabeth Lagarce. 1986. *Enkomi et le Bronze Récent à Chypre*. Nicosia: A. G. Leventis Foundation.

Crawford, Sidnie White, Amnon Ben-Tor, J. P. Dessel, William G. Dever, Amihai Mazar, and Joseph Aviram. 2007. *"Up to the Gates of Ekron": Essays on the Archaeology and History of the Eastern Mediterranean in Honor of Seymour Gitin*. Jerusalem: W. F. Albright Institute of Archaeological Research: Israel Exploration Society.

Crewe, Lindy. 2004. "Social Complexity and Ceramic Technology on Late Bronze Age Cyprus: The New Evidence from Enkomi." Ph.D. diss., University of Edinburgh.

Crouwel, Joost. 1984. Fragments of Another Octopus Stirrup Jar from Kalymnos in Amsterdam. *Bulletin Antieke Beschaving* 59:63–68.

Cruz-Uribe, Eugene. 1988. A New Look at the Adoption Papyrus. *JEA* 74:220–23.

Cusick, James, ed. 1998. *Studies in Culture Contact: Interaction, Culture Change, and Archaeology*. Center for Archaeological Investigations, Southern Illinois University, Carbondale Occasional Paper 25. Carbondale: Center for Archaeological Investigations, Southern Illinois University.

Dagan, Yehuda. 1982. Survey of the Southern Part of Hulda Map 13-13. Pages 20–25 in *Shephelat Yehuda, Selected Articles*. Tel Aviv: Ha-Mador liYedi'at ha-Aretz shel ha-Tenu'a ha-Kibbutzit. [Hebrew]

———. 1992. "The Shephelah During the Period of the Monarchy in Light of Archaeological Excavations and Survey." MA thesis, Tel Aviv University.

D'Agata, Anna Lucia. 2000. Interactions Between Aegean Groups and Local Communities in Sicily in the Bronze Age: The Evidence from Pottery. *SMEA* 42/1:61–83.

D'Agata, Anna Lucia, Yuval Goren, Hans Mommsen, Alexander Schwedt, and Assaf Yassur-Landau. 2005. Imported Pottery of LHIIIC Style from Israel: Style, Provenance and Chronology. Pages 371–79 in Laffineur and Greco 2005.

Dahl, George. 1915. The Materials for the History of Dor. *Transactions of the Connecticut Academy of Sciences* 20:1–181.

Dakoronia, Phanouria. 1987. War-Ships on Sherds of LH IIIC Kraters from Kynos. Pages 117–21 in *Tropis II: Proceedings of the 2nd International Symposium on Ship Construction in Antiquity*. Edited by H. Tzalas. Athens: Hellenic Institute for the Preservation of Nautical Tradition.

———. 1999. Representations of Sea-Battles on Mycenaean Sherds from Kynos. Pages 119–28 in *Tropis V: Proceedings of the 5th International Symposium on Ship Construction in Antiquity*. Edited by H. Tzalas. Athens: Hellenic Institute for the Preservation of Nautical Tradition.

Daniel, John F. 1937. Two Late Cypriote III Tombs from Kourion. *AJA* 41:56–85.

Daressy, Georges. 1915. Trois stèles de la période bubastide. *ASAE* 15:140–47.

Davies, Benedict G. 1997. *Egyptian Historical Inscriptions of the Nineteenth Dynasty*. Documenta Mundi Aegyptiaca 2. Jonsered: Åströms.

Deger-Jalkotzy, Sigrid. 1977. *Fremde Zuwanderer im spätmykenischen Griechenland: Zu einer Gruppe handgemachter Keramik aus den Mykenisch III C Siedlungsschichten von Aigeira*. Vienna: Österreichische Akademie der Wissenschaften.

———. 1994. The Post-Palatial Period of Greece: An Aegean Prelude to the 11th Century B.C. in Cyprus. Pages 30–31 in Karageorghis (ed.) 1994.

———. 1998. The Aegean Islands and the Breakdown of the Mycenaean Palaces around 1200 B.C. Pages 105–20 in *Eastern Mediterranean: Cyprus–Dodecanese–Crete 16th–6th Cent. B.C. Proceedings of the International Symposium Held at Rethymnon–Crete in May 1997*. Edited by V. Karageorghis and N. C. Stampolidis. Athens: University of Crete and The A. G. Leventis Foundation.

———, ed. 1983. *Griechenland, die Ägäis und die Levante während der "Dark Ages" vom 12. bis zum 9. Jh. v. Chr.: Akten des Symposions von Stift Zwettl, 11.–14. Oktober 1980*. Vienna: Österreichische Akademie der Wissenschaften.

Deger-Jalkotzy, Sigrid, and Anna Elisabeth Bächle, eds. 2009. *LH III C Chronology and Synchronisms III: LH III C Late and the Transition to the Early Iron Age. Proceedings of the International Workshop Held at the Austrian Academy of Sciences at Vienna, February 23rd and 24th, 2007*. Philosophisch-Historische Klasse Denkschriften 384; Veröffentlichungen der mykenischen Kommission 30. Vienna: Österreichische Akademie der Wissenschaften.

Deger-Jalkotzy, Sigrid, and Michaela Zavadil, eds. 2007. *LH III C Chronology and Synchronisms II, LH III C Middle: Proceedings of the International Workshop Held at the Austrian Academy of Sciences at Vienna, October 29th and 30th, 2004*. Philosophisch-Historische Klasse Denkschriften 362; Veröffentlichungen der mykenischen Kommission 28. Vienna: Österreichische Akademie der Wissenschaften.

Demsky, Aaron. 1997. The Name of the Goddess of Ekron—A New Reading. *Journal of the Ancient Near Eastern Society of Columbia University* 25:1–5.

Desborough, Vincent. 1952. *Protogeometric Pottery*. Oxford Monographs on Classical Archaeology 2. Oxford: Clarendon.

———. 1964. *The Last Mycenaeans and Their Successors: An Archaeological Survey, c. 1200–c. 1000 B.C.* Oxford: Clarendon.

Dever, William. 1986. *Gezer IV: The 1969–1971 Seasons in Field VI, the "Acropolis."* Annual of the Nelson Glueck School of Biblical Archaeology 4. Jerusalem: Nelson Glueck School of Biblical Archaeology.

———. 1992. The Late Bronze Age–Early Iron I Horizon in Syria-Palestine: Egyptians, Canaanites, "Sea Peoples," and Proto-Israelites. Pages 99–110 in Ward and Joukowsky 1992.

———. 2001. *What Did the Biblical Writers Know & When Did They Know It?* Grand Rapids, Mich.: Eerdmans.

Dickinson, Oliver. 2006. *The Aegean from Bronze Age to Iron Age: Continuity and Change Between the Twelfth and Eighth Centuries BC*. New York: Routledge.

Dietler, Michael, and Ingrid Herbich. 1998. Habitus, Techniques, Style: An Integrated Approach to the Social Understanding of Material Culture and Boundaries. Pages 232–63 in *The Archaeology of Social Boundaries*. Edited by M. Stark. Washington, D.C.: Smithsonian Institution Press.

Dietrich, Manfried, and Oswald Loretz. 1972. Die Schardana in den Texten von Ugarit.

Pages 39–42 in *Antike und Universalgeschichte: Festschrift Hans Erich Stier zum 70. Geburtstag am 25. Mai 1972*. Edited by R Stiehl and G. A. Lehmann. Münster: Aschendorff.

———. 1978. Das "seefahrende Volk" von šikila (RS 4.129). *UF* 10:53–56.

———. 2002. Der Untergang von Ugarit am 21. Januar 1192 v.Chr.? Der astronomisch-hepatoskopische Bericht KTU 1.78 (= RS 12.061). *UF* 34:53–74.

Dietrich, Manfried, Oswald Loretz, and Joaquín Sanmartín, eds. 1976. *Die keilalphabetischen Texte aus Ugarit*. AOAT 24. Kevelaer: Butzon & Bercker; Neukirchen-Vluyn: Neukirchener.

Dietrich, Manfried, Oswald Loretz, and Joaquín Sanmartín, eds. 1995. *KTU: The Cuneiform Alphabetic Texts from Ugarit, Ras Ibn Hani and Other Places*. Abhandlungen zur Literatur Alt-Syrien-Palästinas und Mesopotamiens 8. Münster: Ugarit-Verlag.

Dietz, Søren. 1984. *Excavations and Surveys in Southern Rhodes: The Mycenaean Period*. Vol. 4, Part 1 of *Lindos: Results of the Carlsberg Foundation Excavations in Rhodes 1902–1914*. Publications of the National Museum, Archaeological-Historical Series 22:1. Copenhagen: National Museum of Denmark.

Dietz, Søren, and Ioannis Papachristodoulou, eds. 1988. *Archaeology in the Dodecanese*. Copenhagen: National Museum of Denmark, Dept. of Near Eastern and Classical Antiquities.

Dikaios, Porphyrios. 1969–1971. *Enkomi: Excavations 1948–1958*. 3 vols. Mainz: Zabern.

———, ed. 1973. *Acts of the International Archaeological Symposium "The Mycenaeans in the Eastern Mediterranean," Nicosia 27th March–2nd April 1972*. Cyprus: Ministry of Communications and Works, Dept. of Antiquities.

Dinçol, Ali M., and Belkıs Dinçol. forthcoming. Two New Inscribed Storm-God Stelae from Arsuz (İskenderun). In *Across the Border: The Relations between Syria and Anatolia in the Late Bronze Age and Iron Ages*. Edited by K. A. Yener. Leuven: Peeters.

Dinçol, Ali M., Jak Yakar, Belkıs Dinçol, and Avai Taffet. 2000. The Borders of the Appanage Kingdom of Tarhuntašša—A Geographical and Archaeological Assessment. *Anatolica* 26:1–29.

Döhl, Hartmut. 1973. Iria: Die Ergebnisse der Ausgrabungen 1939. Pages 127–94 in *Frühhelladische Keramik auf der Unterburg von Tiryns*. Vol. 6 of *Tiryns: Forschungen und Berichte*. Edited by U. Jantzen. Mainz: Zabern.

Dommelen, Peter van. 2006. The Orientalizing Phenomenon: Hybridity and Material Culture in the Western Mediterranean. Pages 135–52 in *Debating Orientalization: Multidisciplinary Approaches to Change in the Ancient Mediterranean*. Edited by C. Riva and N. C. Vella. Monographs in Mediterranean Archaeology 10. London: Equinox.

Donner, Herbert, and Wolfgang Röllig. 1966–1969. *Kanaanäische und aramäische Inschriften*. 2nd ed. Wiesbaden: Harrassowitz.

Dorsey, David. 1991. *The Roads and Highways of Ancient Israel*. Baltimore: Johns Hopkins University Press.

Dothan, Moshe. 1960a. Excavations at Tel Mor, 1959. *BIES* 24:120–32. [Hebrew]

———. 1960b. The Ancient Harbour of Ashdod. *Christian News from Israel* 11/1:16–19.

———. 1971. *Ashdod II–III: The Second and Third Seasons of Excavations, 1963, 1965, Soundings in 1967*. Atiqot English Series 9–10. Jerusalem: Dept. of Antiquities and Museums in the Ministry of Education and Culture.

———. 1972. Relations Between Cyprus and the Philistine Coast in the Late Bronze Age.

Pages 51–56 in *Praktika tou Protou Diethnous Kypriologikou Synedriou*. Nicosia: Hetaireia Kypriakon Spoudon.
———. 1976. Akko: Interim Excavation Report First Season 1973/74. *BASOR* 224:1–48.
———. 1979. Ashdod at the End of the late Bronze Age and the Beginning of the Iron Age. Pages 125–34 in *Symposia Celebrating the Seventy-Fifth Anniversary of the Founding of the American Schools of Oriental Research (1900–1975)*. Edited by F. M. Cross. Occasional Publication of the Zion Research Foundation 1–2. Cambridge, Mass.: American Schools of Oriental Research.
———. 1981a. ʿAkko 1980. *IEJ* 31:110–12.
———. 1981b. The Beginning and End of Archaeological Periods at Adjacent Sites. *ErIsr* 15:151–53. [Hebrew]
———. 1983. Reshita shel Akko ve-hachafirot ba. *Qardom* 24–25:9–18. [Hebrew]
———. 1984. Šardina at Akko? Pages 105–15 in *Sardinia in the Mediterranean*. Vol. 2 of *Studies in Sardinian Archaeology*. Edited by M. S. Balmuth. Ann Arbor, Mich.: University of Michigan Press.
———. 1985. Ten Seasons of Excavations in Ancient Akko. *Qad* 18:2–24. [Hebrew]
———. 1986. Šardina at Akko? Pages 105–15 in *Studies in Sardianian Archaeology*. Vol. 2 of *Sardinia in the Mediterranean*. Edited by M. S. Balmuth. Ann Arbor, Mich.: University of Michigan Press.
———. 1989. Archaeological Evidence for Movements of the Early "Sea Peoples" in Canaan. Pages 59–70 in Gitin and Dever 1989.
———. 1992. Ashdod. *ABD* 1:477–82.
———. 1993a. Ashdod. *NEAEHL* 1:93–102.
———. 1993b. Mor, Tel. *NEAEHL* 3:1073–74.
———. 1993c. Tel Acco. *NEAEHL* 1:17–24.
———. 1995. Tel Miqne-Ekron: The Aegean Affinities of the Sea Peoples. Pages 41–59 in Gitin (ed.) 1995.
Dothan, Moshe, and David Ben-Shlomo. 2005. *Ashdod VI: The Excavations of Areas H and K (1968–1969)*. Israel Antiquities Authority Reports 24. Jerusalem: Israel Antiquities Authority.
Dothan, Moshe, and David N. Freedman. 1967. *Ashdod I: The First Season of Excavations 1962*. Atiqot English Series 7. Jerusalem: Israel Department of Antiquities and Museums.
Dothan, Moshe, and Yosef Porath. 1982. *Ashdod IV: Excavations of Area M*. Atiqot English Series 15. Jerusalem: Israel Department of Antiquities and Museums.
———, eds. 1993. *Ashdod V: Excavations of Area G. The Fourth–Sixth Seasons of Excavations 1968–1970*. Atiqot English Series 23. Jerusalem: Israel Antiquities Authority.
Dothan, Trude. 1979. *Excavations at the Cemetery of Deir el-Balah*. Qedem 10. Jerusalem: Institute of Archaeology, Hebrew University of Jerusalem.
———. 1982. *The Philistines and Their Material Culture*. Jerusalem: Israel Exploration Society.
———. 1989. The Arrival of the Sea Peoples: Cultural Diversity in Early Iron Age Canaan. Pages 1–14 in Gitin and Dever 1989.
———. 1994. The Philistine as Other: Biblical Rhetoric and Archaeological Reality. Pages 61–73 in *The Other in Jewish Thought and History: Constructions of Jewish Culture and Identity*. Edited by L. Silberstein and R. Cohn. New Perspectives on Jewish Studies. New York: New York University Press.

———. 1995. Tel Miqne-Ekron: The Aegean Affinities of the Sea Peoples' (Philistines') Settlement in Canaan in Iron Age I. Pages 41–56 in Gitin (ed.) 1995.
———. 1996. An Early Phoenician Cache from Tel Miqne-Ekron. *ErIsr* 25: 145–50, 93*. [Hebrew]
———. 1998a. The Pottery. Pages 20–49 in *Tel Miqne-Ekron: Report on the 1995–1996 Excavations in Field XNW. Areas 77,78,79,89,90,101,102. Iron Age I: Text and Data Base (Plates, Sections, Plans).* Edited by N. Bierling. The Tel Miqne-Ekron Limited Edition Series 7. Jerusalem: Tel Miqne-Ekron Project Office: W. F. Albright Institute of Archaeological Research.
———. 1998b. Initial Philistine Settlement: From Migration to Coexistence. Pages 148–61 in Gitin, Mazar, and Stern 1998.
———. 2000. Reflections on the Initial Phase of Philistine Settlement. Pages 145–58 in Oren 2000.
———. 2002. Bronze and Iron Objects with Cultic Connotations from Philistine Temple Building 350 at Ekron. *IEJ* 52:1–27.
Dothan, Trude, and Amnon Ben-Tor. 1983. *Excavations at Athienou, Cyprus 1971–1972.* Qedem 16. Jerusalem: Hebrew University of Jerusalem.
Dothan, Trude, and Moshe Dothan. 1992. *People of the Sea: The Search for the Philistines.* New York: Macmillan.
Dothan, Trude, and Seymour Gitin. 1990. Ekron of the Philistines: How They Lived, Worked and Worshiped for Five Hundred Years. *BAR* 16, no. 1 (January/February):20–36.
———. 1993. Miqne, Tel (Ekron). *NEAEHL* 3:1051–59.
———. 2008. Miqne, Tel (Ekron). *NEAEHL* 5:1952–58.
Dothan, Trude, Seymour Gitin, and Alexander Zukerman. 2006. The Pottery: Canaanite and Philistine Traditions and Cypriote and Aegean Imports. Pages 71–175 in *Tel Miqne-Ekron Excavations 1995–1996: Field INE East Slope—Iron Age I (Early Philistine Period)*, ed. M. W. Meehl, T. Dothan, and S. Gitin. Tel Miqne-Ekron Final Field Report Series 8. Jerusalem: W. F. Albright Institute of Archaeological Research and Institute of Archaeology, Hebrew University of Jerusalem.
Dothan, Trude, and Alexander Zukerman. 2004. A Preliminary Study of the Mycenaean IIIC:1b Pottery Assemblages from Tel Miqne-Ekron and Ashdod. *BASOR* 333:1–54.
Drews, Robert. 1993. *The End of the Bronze Age: Changes in Warfare and the Catastrophe ca. 1200 B.C.* Princeton: Princeton University Press.
———. 1998. Canaanites and Philistines. *JSOT* 81:39–61.
———. 2000. Oxcarts, Ships and Migration Theories. *JNES* 59:161–90.
Druks, Adam. 1966. A "Hittite" Burial Near Kefar Yehoshua. *Yediot* 30:213–20. [Hebrew]
Dubertret, Louis. 1955. Géologie des roches vertes du nord-ouest de la Syrie et du Hatay Turquie). *Notes et Mémoires sur le Moyen-Orient* 6:170.
Dupré, Sylvestre. 1983. *La céramique de l'âge du Bronze et de l'âge du Fer.* Vol. 1 of *Porsuk.* Éditions Recherche sur les civilisations Mémoire 20. Paris: Éditions Recherche sur les civilisations.
Edel, Elmar. 1983. Bemerkungen zu Helcks Philisterartikel in *BN* 21. *BN* 22:7–8.
———. 1984. Sikeloi in den ägyptischen Seevölkertexten und in Keilschrifturkunden. *BN* 23:7–8.
———. 1985. Der Seevölkerbericht aus dem 8. Jahre Ramses' III. (MH II, pl. 46, 15–18):

Übersetzung und Struktur. Pages 223–37 in *Mélanges Gamal Eddin Mokhtar* 1. Edited by P. Posener-Kriéger. Cairo: Institut français d'archéologie orientale.

———. 1994. *Die ägyptisch-hethitische Korrespondenz aus Boghazköi in babylonischer und hethitischer Sprache*. 2 vols. Abhandlungen der Rheinisch-Westfälischen Akademie der Wissenschaften 77. Opladen: Westdeutscher Verlag.

Edelstein, Gershon, and Jonathan Glass. 1973. The Origin of Philistine Pottery in Light of Petrographic Analysis. Pages 125–32 in *Excavations and Studies in Honor of Shmuel Yeivin*. Edited by Y. Aharoni. Tel Aviv: Carta. [Hebrew]

Edelstein, Gershon, and Nicola Schreiber. 2000. Two Decorated Iron Age Bronze Belts from Tell 'Eitun. *Atiqot* 39:113–19.

Edgerton, William, and John Wilson. 1936. *Historical Records of Ramses III: The Texts in Medinet Habu Volumes I and II, Translated with Explanatory Notes*. SAOC 12. Chicago: University of Chicago Press.

Egberts, Arno. 1991. The Chronology of the Report of Wenamun. *JEA* 77:57–67.

_____. 1998. Hard Times: The Chronology of 'The Report of Wenamun' Revised. *ZÄS* 125:93–108.

Elgavish, Joseph. 1993. Shiqmona. *NEAEHL* 4:1373–78.

———. 1994. *Shiqmona: On the Coast of Mt. Carmel*. Tel Aviv: Hakkibutz Hameuchad and the Israel Exploration Society. [Hebrew]

Elliott, Carolyn, Costas Xenophontos, and John G. Malpas. 1986. Petrographic and Mineral Analyses Used in Tracing the Provenance of Late Bronze Age and Roman Basalt Artefacts from Cyprus. *RDAC* 1986: 80–96.

Emberling, Geoff. 1997. Ethnicity in Complex Societies: Archaeological Perspectives. *Journal of Archaeological Research* 5:295–344.

Engelbach, Reginald. 1915. *Riqqeh and Memphis* VI. British School of Archaeology in Egypt and Egyptian Research Account, Nineteenth Year 26. London: British School of Archaeology in Egypt.

Eph'al, Israel. 1997. The Philistine Entity and the Origin of the Name "Palestine." Pages 31*–35* in *Tehillah le-Moshe: Biblical and Judaic Studies in Honor of Moshe Greenberg*. Edited by M. Cogan, B. Eichler, and J. Tigay. Winona Lake, Ind.: Eisenbrauns. [Hebrew]

The Epigraphic Survey. 1930. *Earlier Historical Records of Ramses III*. Vol. 1 of *Medinet Habu: Field Director, Harold Hayden Nelson*. OIP 8. Chicago: University of Chicago Press.

———. 1932. *Later Historical Records of Ramses III*. Vol. 2 of *Medinet Habu: Field Director, Harold Hayden Nelson*. OIP 9. Chicago: University of Chicago Press.

———. 1934. *The Calendar, the "Slaughter House," and Minor Records of Ramses III*. Vol. 3 of *Medinet Habu: Field Director, Harold Hayden Nelson*. OIP 23. Chicago: University of Chicago Press.

———. 1940. *Festival Scenes of Ramses III*. Vol. 4 of *Medinet Habu: Field Director, Harold Hayden Nelson*. OIP 51. Chicago: University of Chicago Press.

———. 1957. *The Temple Proper, Part 1*. Vol. 5 of *Medinet Habu: Field Director, Harold Hayden Nelson*. OIP 83. Chicago: University of Chicago Press.

———. 1963. *The Temple Proper, Part 2*. Vol. 6 of *Medinet Habu: Field Director, Harold Hayden Nelson*. OIP 84. Chicago: University of Chicago Press.

———. 1964. *The Temple Proper, Part 3*. Vol. 7 of *Medinet Habu: Field Director, Harold Hayden Nelson*. OIP 93. Chicago: University of Chicago Press.

———. 1970. *The Eastern High Gate*. Vol. 8 of *Medinet Habu: Field Director, Harold Hayden Nelson*. OIP 94. Chicago: University of Chicago Press.

Epstein, Claire. 1966. *Palestinian Bichrome Ware*. Documenta et Monumenta Orientis Antiqui 12. Leiden: Brill.

Erichsen, Wolja. 1933. *Hieroglyphische Transkription*. Vol. 1 of *Papyrus Harris*. Bibliotheca Aegyptiaca 5. Brussels: Fondation égyptologique Reine Élisabeth.

Erkanal, Armagan. 1986. Panaztepe Kazisin, 1985 Yili Sonuclari. *Kazı Sunucları Toplantısı* 11:255–64.

Ersoy, Yaşar E. 1988. Finds from Menemen/Panaztepe in the Manisa Museum. *Annual of the British School at Athens* 83:55–82.

Esse, Douglas. 1991. The Collared Rim Pithos at Megiddo: Ceramic Distribution and Ethnicity. *JNES* 51:81–103.

Fantalkin, Alexander. 2004. The Final Destruction of Beth Shemesh and the *Pax Assyriaca* in the Judean Shephelah: An Alternative View. *TA* 31:245–61.

Faulkner, Raymond O. 1952. *Index*. Vol. 4 of *The Wilbour Papyrus*. Edited by A. H. Gardiner. Oxford: Oxford University Press.

Faust, Avraham. 2006. *Irael's Ethnogenesis: Settlement, Interaction, Expansion, and Resistance*. London: Equinox.

Finkbeiner, Uwe, and Hélène Sader. 1997. Bey 020 Preliminary Report of the Excavations 1995. *Bulletin d'archéologie et d'architecture libanaises* 2:114–205.

Finkelberg, Margalit. 1988. From *Ahhiyawa* to 'Αχαιοί. *Glotta* 66:127–34.

———. 2005a. Greece in the Eighth Century B.C.E. and the Renaissance Phenomenon. Pages 62–76 in *Genesis and Regeneration: Essays on Conceptions of Origins*. Edited by Sh. Shaked. Jerusalem: Israel Academy of Sciences and Humanities.

———. 2005b. *Greeks and Pre-Greeks: Aegean Prehistory and Greek Heroic Tradition*. Cambridge: Cambridge University Press.

Finkelstein, Israel. 1994. The Archaeology of the Days of Manasseh. Pages 169–87 in *Scripture and Other Artifacts: Essays on the Bible and Archaeology in Honor of Philip J. King*. Edited by M. D. Coogan, J. C. Exum, and L. E. Stager. Louisville, Ky.: Westminster/John Knox.

———. 1995. The Date of the Settlement of the Philistines in Canaan. *TA* 22:213–39.

———. 1996a. The Archaeology of the United Monarchy: An Alternative View. *Levant* 28:177–87.

———. 1996b. The Stratigraphy and Chronology of Megiddo and Beth-Shan in the 12th–11th Centuries BCE. *TA* 23:170–84.

———. 1996c. The Territorial-Political System of Canaan in the Late Bronze Age. *UF* 28:221–55.

———. 1997. Pots and People Revised: Ethnic Boundaries in the Iron Age I. Pages 216–37 in Silberman and Small 1997.

———. 1998. Philistine Chronology: High, Middle or Low? Pages 140–47 in Gitin, Mazar, and Stern 1998.

———. 2000. The Philistine Settlements: When, Where and How Many? Pages 159–80 in Oren 2000.

———. 2001. The Rise of Jerusalem and Judah: The Missing Link. *Levant* 32:105–15.

———. 2002a. El-Ahwat: A Fortified Sea People City? *IEJ* 52:187–99.

———. 2002b. The Philistines in the Bible: A Late-Monarchic Perspective. *JSOT* 27:131–67.

Finkelstein, Israel, and Nadav Na'aman. 2004. The Judahite Shephelah in the Late 8th and Early 7th Centuries BCE. *TA* 31:60–79.

Finkelstein, Israel, and Neil A. Silberman. 2001. *The Bible Unearthed: Archaeology's New Vision of Ancient Israel and the Origin of Its Sacred Texts*. New York: Free Press.

Finkelstein, Israel, and Lily Singer-Avitz. 2001. Ashdod Revisited. *TA* 28:231–59.

Fischer, Bettina, Hermann Genz, Éric Jean, and Kemalettin Köroglu. 2003. *Identifying Changes: The Transition from Bronze to Iron Ages in Anatolia and Its Neighbouring Regions. Proceedings of the International Workshop, Istanbul, November 8–9, 2002*. Istanbul: Türk Eskiçag Bilimleri Enstitüsü.

Fischer, Robert. 2010. *Die Ahhijawa-Frage: Mit einer kommentierten Bibliographie*. Dresdner Beiträge zur Hethitologie 26. Wiesbaden: Harrassowitz.

Fischer-Elfert, Hans-Werner. 1986. *Die satirische Streitschrift des Papyrus Anastasi I: Übersetzung und Kommentar*. Ägyptologische Abhandlungen 44. Wiesbaden: Harrassowitz.

Flourentzos, Pavlos. 1997. The Early Geometric Tomb No. 132 from Palaepaphos. *RDAC* 1997:205–18.

Foley, John M. 1997. Oral Tradition and Its Implications. Pages 146–73 in *A New Companion to Homer*. Edited by I. Morris and B. Powell. Mnemosyne Suppl. 163. Leiden: Brill.

Forlanini, Massimo. 1984. La regione del Tauro nei testi hittiti. *Vicino Oriente* 7:129–69.

———. 2001. Quelques notes sur la géographie historique de la Cilicie. Pages 553–63 in Jean, Dinçol, and Durugönül 2001.

Forsdyke, Edgar J. 1925. *Prehistoric Aegean Pottery*. Vol. I, part I of *Catalogue of the Greek and Etruscan Vases in the British Museum*. London: British Museum.

Fox, Nili S. 2000. *In the Service of the King: Officialdom in Ancient Israel and Judah*. Monographs of the Hebrew Union College 23. Cincinnati: Hebrew Union Press.

Franken, Hendricus J. 1961. The Excavations at Deir 'Alla in Jordan. *VT* 11:361–72.

———. 1964a. The Excavations at Deir 'Alla—1964. *VT* 14:417–22.

———. 1964b. Clay Tablets from Deir 'Alla, Jordan. *VT* 14:377–79.

———. 1969. *Excavations at Tell Deir 'Alla*. Documenta et Monumenta Orientis Antiqui 16. Leiden: Brill.

———. 1992. *Excavations at Tell Deir 'Alla: The Late Bronze Age Sanctuary*. Documenta et Monumenta Orientis Antiqui 16. Louvain: Peeters.

French, Elizabeth. 1969. The First Phase of Late Helladic IIIC. *AA* 1969:133–36.

———. 1975. A Reassessment of the Mycenaean Pottery at Tarsus. *AnSt* 25:53–75.

———. 1978. Who Were the Mycenaeans in Anatolia? Pages 165–68 in *The Proceedings of the Xth International Congress of Classical Archaeology I*. Ankara: Türk Tarih Kurumu Basimevi.

———. 1993. Turkey and the East Aegean. Pages 155–58 in Zerner, Zerner, and Winder 1993.

———. 1998. The Ups and Downs of Mycenae: 1250–1150 BC. Pages 1–5 in Gitin, Mazar, and Stern 1998.

———. 1999. "The Postpalatial Levels at Mycenae, an Up-Date," Mycenaean Seminar 17/3/99. *Bulletin of the Institute of Classical Studies of the University of London* 43:222–23.

———. 2000. Poster Presentation at *Lighten Our Darkness: Cutural Transformations at the*

Beginning of the First Millennium BC—From the Alps to Anatolia, Birmingham, 6–9 January.

———. 2007a. The Mycenaean Pottery. Pages 373–76 in vol. 1 of *Excavations at Kilise Tepe, 1994–98: From Bronze Age to Byzantine in Western Cilicia*. Edited by J. N. Postgate and D. Thomas. McDonald Institute Monographs; British Institute of Archaeology at Ankara Monograph 30. 2 vols. London: British Institute at Ankara; Cambridge: McDonald Institute for Archaeological Research.

———. 2007b. The Impact on Correlations to the Levant of the Recent Stratigraphic Evidence from the Argolid. Pages 525–36 in Bietak and Czerny 2007.

———. 2011. *The Post-Palatial Levels*. Well Built Mycenae 16/17. Oxford: Oxbow Books.

———. forthcoming. Minoans and Mycenaeans in Anatolia. In *The Archaeology of Anatolia: An Encyclopedia*. Edited by G. K. Sams. Ankara: Bilkent University.

French, Elizabeth, and Paul Åström. 1980. A Colloquium on Late Cypriote III Sites. *RDAC* 1980:267–69.

French, Elizabeth, and Jeremy Rutter. 1977. The Handmade Burnished Ware of the Late Helladic IIIC Period: Its Modern Historical Context. *AJA* 81:111–12.

French, Elizabeth, and Philipp Stockhammer. 2009. Mycenae and Tiryns: The Pottery of the Second Half of the 13th Century B.C.: Contexts and Definitions. *Annual of the British School at Athens* 104:175–232.

French, Elizabeth, and Kenneth A. Wardle, eds. 1988. *Problems in Greek Prehistory: Papers Presented at the Centenary Conference of the British School of Archaeology at Athens, Manchester, April 1986*. Bristol: Bristol Classical.

Freu, Jacques. 1988. La tablette RS 96.2233 et la phase finale du royaume d'Ugarit. *Syria* 65:395–98.

Frey, Carol J., and Curtis W. Marean. 1999. Mammal Remains. Pages 123–37 in Stone and Zimansky 1999.

Friedrich, Johannes. 1930. *Staatsverträge des Hatti-Reiches in hethitischer Sprache II*. MVAG 34/1. Leipzig: Hinrichs.

Friend, Glenda. 1998. The Loom Weights. Vol. 3, Part 2 of *Tell Taannek 1963–1968*. Publications of the Palestinian Institute of Archaeology, Excavations and Surveys. Birzeit: Birzeit University.

Fritz, Volkmar, and Aharon Kempinski. 1983. *Ergebnisse der Ausgrabungen auf der Ḥirbet el-Mšāš (Tệl Māśôś) 1972–1975*. 3 vols. Abhandlungen des Deutschen Palästinavereins. Wiesbaden: Harrassowitz.

Furumark, Arne. 1941a. *Mycenaean Pottery: Analysis and Classification*. Skrifter Utgivna av Svenska Institutet i Athen 20. Stockholm: Kungl. Vitterhets, historie och Antikvitets Akademien.

———. 1941b. *The Chronology of Mycenaean Pottery*. Stockholm: Kungl. Vitterhets Historie och Antikvitets Akademien.

———. 1944. The Mycenaean IIIC Pottery and Its Relation to Cypriote Fabrics. *Opuscula Archaeologica* 3:194–265.

———. 1965. The Excavations at Sinda: Some Historical Results. *Opuscula Atheniensia* 6:99–116.

Furumark, Arne, and Charles Adelman. 2003. *Swedish Excavations at Sinda, Cyprus: Excavations Conducted by Arne Furumark 1947–1948*. Skrifter Utgivna av Svenska Institutet i Athen Series Prima in 4:0; 50. Stockholm: Åströms.

Galil, Gershon. 1995. A New Look at the "Azekah Incription." *RB* 102:321–29.

Galili, Ehud, and Yaakov Sharvit. 1997. Seker tat-Yami ba-Yam ha-Tichon 1992–1996. *Hadashot Arkheologiyot* 97:143–44. [Hebrew]

Galili, Ehud, Mina Weinstein-Evron, Israel Hershkovitz, Avi Gopher, Mordecai Kislev, Omri Lernau, Liora Kolska-Horwitz, and Hanan Lernau. 1993. Atlit-Yam: A Prehistoric Site on the Sea Floor off the Israeli Coast. *Journal of Field Archaeology* 20:133–57.

Galling, Kurt. 1965. Goliath und seine Rüstung. *VTSup* 15:150–69.

———. 1970. Besprechung "Kenyon, K.M., Archäologie im Heiligen Land": Neukirchen 1967. *ZDPV* 86:90–92.

———, ed. 1979. *Textbuch zur Geschichte Israels*. 3rd ed. Tübingen: Mohr.

Gans, Herbert J. 1994. Symbolic Ethnicity and Symbolic Religiosity: Towards a Comparison of Ethnic and Religious Acculturation. *Ethnic and Racial Studies* 17:577–92.

Garbini, Giovanni. 1991. On the Origin of the Hebrew-Philistine Word *seren*. Pages 516–19 in *Semitic Studies in Honor of Wolf Leslau on the Occasion of His Eighty-Fifth Birthday, November 14th, 1991*. Edited by A. S. Kaye. Wiesbaden: Harrassowitz.

Gardiner, Alan H. 1932. *Late-Egyptian Stories*. Bibliotheca Aegyptiaca 15. Brussels: Fondation égyptologique Reine Élisabeth.

———. 1937. *Late-Egyptian Miscellanies*. Bibliotheca Aegyptiaca 7. Brussels: Fondation égyptologique Reine Élisabeth.

———. 1940. Adoption Extraordinary. *JEA* 26:23–29.

———. 1941–1948. *The Wilbour Papyrus*. 3 vols. Oxford: Oxford University Press.

———. 1947. *Ancient Egyptian Onomastica*. 3 vols. Oxford: Oxford University Press.

———. 1948. *Ramesside Administrative Documents*. Oxford: Oxford University Press.

———. 1960. *The Kadesh Inscriptions of Ramesses II*. Oxford: Printed for the Griffith Institute.

———. 1964. *Egyptian Hieratic Texts: Literary Texts of the New Kingdom I*. Hildesheim: Olms.

Garfinkel, Yosef. 2007. Dynamic Settlement History of Philistine Ekron: A Case Study of Central Place Theory. Pages 17–24 in Crawford et al. 2007.

Garfinkel, Yosef, Trude Dothan, and Seymour Gitin, eds. forthcoming. *Tel Miqne-Ekron Excavations, 1985–1988, 1990, 1992–1995, Field IV Lower, the Elite Zone: The Iron Age I Early Philistine City*. Tel Miqne-Ekron Final Field Report Series 9. Jerusalem: W. F. Albright Institute of Archaeological Research.

Garsiel, Moshe. 2000. David's Warfare against the Philistines in the Vicinity of Jerusalem. Pages 150–64 in *Studies in Historical Geography and Biblical Historiography Presented to Zecharia Kallai*. VTSup 81. Edited by G. Galil and M. Weinfeld. Leiden: Brill.

Garstang, John. 1924. Tanturah (Dora), Parts I and II. *Bulletin of the British School of Archaeology in Jerusalem* 4:35–36; 6:65–75.

———. 1937. Explorations in Cilicia: The Neilson Expedition. Preliminary Report. *Liverpool Annals of Archaeology and Anthropology* 24:52–68.

———. 1938. Explorations in Cilicia: The Neilson Expedition. Preliminary Report II (Concluded). *Liverpool Annals of Archaeology and Anthropology* 25:12–23.

———. 1939. Explorations in Cilicia: The Neilson Expedition. Fifth Interim Report. Parts III and IV: Exploration at Mersin: 1938–39. *Liverpool Annals of Archaeology and Anthropology* 26:89–158.

———. 1953. *Prehistoric Mersin, Yümük Tepe in Southern Turkey: The Neilson Expedition in Cilicia*. Oxford: Clarendon.

Garstang, John, and Oliver R. Gurney, 1959. *The Geography of the Hittite Empire*. London: British Institute of Archaeology at Ankara.

Gass, Ian, C. J. MacLeod, B. J. Murton, Andreas Panayiotou, K. O. Simoniak, and Costas Xenophontos. 1994. *The Geology of the Southern Troodos Transform Fault Zone*. Memoir Geological Survey Department, Ministry of Agriculture, Natural Resources and Environment, Nicosia 9. Nicosia: Cyprus Geological Survey Department.

Gates, Charles W. 1995. Defining Boundaries of a State: The Mycenaeans and Their Anatolian Frontier. Pages 289–97 in Laffineur and Niemeier 1995.

Gates, Marie-Henriette. 1994. Archaeology in Turkey. *AJA* 92:249–78.

———. 1999a. Kinet Höyük in Eastern Cilicia: A Case Study for Acculturation in Ancient Harbors. *Olba* 2:303–12.

———. 1999b. 1997 Archaeological Excavations at Kinet Höyük (Yeşil-Dörtyol, Hatay). *Kazı Sonuçları Toplantısı* 20:259–81.

———. 2000. 1998 Excavations at Kinet Höyük (Yeşil-Dörtyol, Hatay). *Kazı Sonuçları Toplantısı* 21:193–208.

———. 2001a. Potmarks at Kinet Höyük and the Hittite Ceramic Industry. Pages 137–57 in Jean, Dinçol, and Durugönül 2001.

———. 2001b. 1999 Excavations at Kinet Höyük (Yeşil-Dörtyol, Hatay). *Kazı Sonuçları Toplantısı* 22: 203–22.

———. 2006. Dating the Hittite Levels at Kinet Höyük: A Revised Chronology. Pages 293–309 in Mielke, Schoop, and Seeher 2006.

______. 2011. Southern and Southeastern Anatolia in the Late Bronze Age. Pages 393–412 in *The Oxford Handbook of Ancient Anatolia (10,000–323 B.C.E.)*. Edited by S. R. Steadman and J. G. McMahon. Oxford: Oxford University Press.

Gazit, Dan. 1996. *Map of Urim (125)*. Pirsume Rashut ha-'atikot; Seker arkheologi shel Yisrael. Jerusalem: Israel Antiquities Authority. [Hebrew]

Genz, Hermann. 2000. Die Eisenzeit in Zentralanatolien im Lichte der keramischen Funde vom Büyükkaya in Boğazköy/Hattuša. *Türkiye Bilimler Akademisi Arkeoloji Dergisi* 3:35–54.

———. 2001. Iron Age Pottery from Çadır-Höyük. *Anatolica* 27:159–70.

———. 2004. *Büyükkaya I: Die Keramik der Eisenzeit*. Boğazköy-Hattuša, Ergebnisse der Ausgrabungen 21. Mainz: Zabern.

———. 2005. Thoughts on the Origin of the Iron Age Pottery Traditions in Central Anatolia. Pages 75–84 in *Anatolian Iron Ages 5: Proceedings of the Fifth Anatolian Iron Ages Colloquium Held at Van, 6–10 August 2001*, ed. A. Çilingiroğlu and G. Darbyshire. Monograph of the British Institute of Archaeology at Ankara 31. London: British Institute of Archaeology.

Gershuny, Lily. 1985. *Bronze Vessels from Israel and Jordan*. Prähistorische Bronzefunde 2, 6/7. München: Beck.

Gerstel-Raban, Noa. 2005. "Faunal Remains from Tel Dor: An Early Iron Age Port City," MA thesis, University of Haifa. [Hebrew]

Giesen, Katharina. 2001. *Zyprische Fibeln: Typologie und Chronologie*. Jonsered: Åströms.

Gifford, John. 1980. "Paleography of Archaeological Sites of the Larnaca Lowlands, Southeastern Cyprus." Ph.D. diss., University of Michigan.

Gilboa, Ayelet. 1989. New Finds at Tel Dor and the Beginnings of Cypro-Geometric Pottery Import to Palestine. *IEJ* 39:204–18.

———. 1995. The Typology and Chronology of Iron Age Pottery and the Chronology of

Iron Age Assemblages. Pages 1–50 in *Areas A and C: The Finds*. Vol. 1, part B of *Excavations at Dor: Final Report*. Edited by E. Stern, J. Berg, A. Gilboa, B. Guz-Zilberstein, A. Raban, R. Rosenthal-Heginbottom, and I. Sharon. Qedem Reports 2; Publications of the Institute of Archaeology, Hebrew University of Jerusalem. Jerusalem: Institute of Archaeology, Hebrew University of Jerusalem in Cooperation with The Israel Exploration Society.

———. 1998. Iron I–IIA Pottery Evolution at Dor—Regional Contexts and the Cypriot Connection. Pages 413–25 in Gitin, Mazar, and Stern 1998.

———. 1999a. The Dynamics of Phoenician Bichrome Pottery: A View from Tel Dor. *BASOR* 316:1–21.

———. 1999b. The View from the East—Tel Dor and the Earliest Cypro-Geometric Exports to the Levant. Pages 119–39 in Iacovou and Michaelides 1999.

———. 2001a. "Southern Phoenicia During Iron Age I–IIA in the Light of the Tel Dor Excavations: The Evidence of Pottery." Ph.D. diss., Hebrew University of Jerusalem.

———. 2001b. The Significance of Iron Age "Wavy Band" Pithoi along the Syro-Palestinian Littoral. Pages 163–73 in Wolff 2001.

———. 2005. Sea Peoples and Phoenicians along the Southern Phoenician Coast—A Reconciliation: An Interpretation of *Šikila* (*SKL*) Material Culture. *BASOR* 337:47–78.

———. 2006–2007. Fragmenting the Sea Peoples, with an Emphasis on Cyprus, Syria and Egypt: A Tel Dor Perspective. *Scripta Mediterranea* 27–28:209–44.

Gilboa, Ayelet, Anat Cohen-Weinberger, and Yuval Goren. 2006. Philistine Bichrome Pottery—The View from the Northern Canaanite Coast: Notes on Provenience and Symbolic Properties. Pages 303–35 in Maeir and de Miroschedji 2006.

Gilboa, Ayelet, Avshalom Karasik, Ilan Sharon, and Uzy Smilansky. 2004. Towards Computerized Typology and Classification of Ceramics. *Journal of Archaeological Science* 31:681–94.

Gilboa, Ayelet, and Ilan Sharon. 2001. Early Iron Age Radiometric Dates from Tel Dor: Preliminary Implications for Phoenicia, and Beyond. *Radiocarbon* 43:1343–51.

———. 2003. An Archaeological Contribution to the Early Iron Age Chronological Debate: Alternative Chronologies for Phoenicia and Their Effects on the Levant, Cyprus and Greece. *BASOR* 332:7–80.

———. 2008. Between the Carmel and the Sea: Tel Dor's Iron Age Reconsidered. *NEA* 71:146–70.

Gilboa, Ayelet, Ilan Sharon, and Elisabetta Boaretto. 2009. Tel Dor and the Chronology of Phoenician "Pre-colonization" Stages. Pages 113–204 in *Beyond the Homeland: Markers in Phoenician Chronology*. Edited by C. Sagona. Monograph Series of Ancient Near Eastern Studies 28. Louvain: Peeters.

Gilboa, Ayelet, Ilan Sharon, and Jeffrey R. Zorn. 2004. Dor and Iron Age Chronology: Scarabs, Ceramic Sequence and 14C. *TA* 31:32–59.

Gilula, Mordechai. 1976. An Inscription in Egyptian Hieratic from Lachish. *TA* 3:107–8.

Gitin, Seymour. 1989. Tel Miqne-Ekron: A Type Site for the Inner Coastal Plain in the Iron Age II Period. Pages 23–50 in Gitin and Dever 1989.

———. 1995. Tel Miqne-Ekron in the 7th Century B.C.E.: The Impact of Economic Innovation and Foreign Cultural Influences on a Neo-Assyrian Vassal City-State. Pages 61–79 in Gitin (ed.) 1995.

———. 1997. The Neo-Assyrian Empire and Its Western Periphery: The Levant, with a Focus on Philistine Ekron. Pages 77–103 in *Assyria 1995: Proceedings of the 10th Anni-*

versary Symposium of the Neo-Assyrian Text Corpus Project Helsinki, September 7–11, 1995. Edited by S. Parpola and R. Whiting. Helsinki: The Neo-Assyrian Text Corpus Project.

———. 1998. Philistia in Transition: The Tenth Century BCE and Beyond. Pages 162–83 in Gitin, Mazar, and Stern 1998.

———, ed. 1995. *Recent Excavations in Israel: A View to the West: Reports on Kabri, Nami, Miqne-Eqron, Dor, and Ashkelon*. Archaeological Institute of America, Colloquia and Conference Papers 1. Dubuque, Iowa: Kendall Hunt.

Gitin, Seymour, and William G. Dever, eds. 1989. *Recent Excavations in Israel: Studies in Iron Age Archaeology*. AASOR 49. Winona Lake, Ind.: Eisenbrauns.

Gitin, Seymour, Trude Dothan, and Joseph Naveh. 1997. A Royal Dedicatory Inscription from Ekron. *IEJ* 47:1–16.

Gitin, Seymour, Amihai Mazar, and Ephraim Stern, eds. 1998. *Mediterranean Peoples in Transition: Thirteenth to Early Tenth Centuries B.C.E. In Honor of Professor Trude Dothan*. Jerusalem: Israel Exploration Society.

Gittlen, Barry M. 1992. The Late Bronze Age 'City' at Tel Miqne/Ekron. *ErIsr* 23:50*–53*.

Giveon, Raphael. 1985. *Egyptian Scarabs from Western Asia from the Collections of the British Museum*. OBO, Series Archaeologica 3. Freiburg: Universitätsverlag; Göttingen: Vandenhoeck & Ruprecht.

Gjerstad, Einar. 1934. Cilician Studies. *RAr* 3:155–203.

———. 1948. *The Cypro-Geometric, Cypro-Archaic and Cypro-Classical Period*. The Swedish Cyprus Expedition 4/2. Stockholm: Swedish Cyprus Expedition.

Gjerstad, Einar, John Lindros, Erik Sjöqvist, and Alfred Westholm. 1934. *The Swedish Cyprus Expedition II: Finds and Results of the Excavations in 1927–1931*. Stockholm: Swedish Cyprus Expedition.

Gödeken, Karin B. 1988. A Contribution to the Early History of Miletus: The Settlement in Mycenaean Times and Its Connections Overseas. Pages 307–15 in French and Wardle 1988.

Goedicke, Hans. 1975. *The Report of Wenamun*. Johns Hopkins Near Eastern Studies. Baltimore: Johns Hopkins University Press.

Goetze, Albrecht. 1928. Madduwattas. *MVAG* 32/1.

———. 1933. Die Annalen des Mursilis. *MVAG* 38.

———. 1947. A New Letter from Ramesses to Hattusilis. *JCS* 1:241–52.

Golani, Amir. 1996. "The Jewelry and the Jeweler's Craft at Tel Miqne-Ekron During the Iron Age." MA thesis, Hebrew University of Jerusalem.

Goldman, Hetty. 1937. Excavations at Gözlü Kule, Tarsus, 1936. *AJA* 41:262–86.

———, ed. 1950. *The Hellenistic and Roman Periods*. Vol. 1 of *Excavations at Gözlü Kule, Tarsus*. 2 vols. Princeton: Princeton University Press.

———, ed. 1956. *From the Neolithic through the Bronze Age*. Vol. 2 of *Excavations at Gözlü Kule, Tarsus*. 2 vols. Princeton: Princeton University Press.

———, ed. 1963. *The Iron Age*. Vol. 3 of *Excavations at Gözlü Küle, Tarsus*. 2 vols. Princeton: Princeton University Press.

Goldwasser, Orly. 1982. The Lachish Hieratic Bowl Once Again. *TA* 9:137–38.

———. 1984. Hieratic Inscriptions from Tel Sera' in Southern Canaan. *TA* 11:77–93.

Gonen, Rivka. 1984. Urban Canaan in the Late Bronze Period. *BASOR* 253:61–73.

———. 1992. *Burial Patterns and Cultural Diversity in Late Bronze Age Canaan*. ASOR Dissertation Series 7. Winona Lake, Ind.: Eisenbrauns.

Gonnella, Julia, Walid Khayyata, and Kay Kohlmeyer. 2005. *Die Zitadelle von Aleppo und der Tempel des Wettergottes: Neue Forschungen und Entdeckungen*. Münster: Rhema.

Goody, Jack. 2000. *The Power of the Written Tradition*. Smithsonian Series in Ehnographic Inquiry. Washington, D.C.: Smithsonian Institution Press.

Goren, Yuval. 1995. Shrines and Ceramics in Chalcolithic Israel: The View through the Petrographic Microscope. *Archaeometry* 37:287–305.

———. 1996. The Southern Levant in the Early Bronze Age IV: The Petrographic Perspective. *BASOR* 303:33–72.

———. 2000. "Petrographic Characteristics of Several Key Southern Levantine Ceramic Materials." No pages. Cited 14 June 2012. Online: http://intarch.ac.uk/journal/issue9/goren/sect4.html.

Goren, Yuval, Israel Finkelstein, and Nadav Na'aman. 2004. *Inscribed in Clay: Provenance Study of the Amarna Letters and Other Ancient Near Eastern Texts*. Monograph Series of the Institute of Archaeology 23. Tel Aviv: Tel Aviv University.

Gorny, Ronald, Gregory McMahon, Samuel Paley, and Lisa Kealhofer. 1995. The Alişar Regional Project: 1994 Season. *Anatolica* 21:68–100.

Grandet, Pierre. 1994. *Le Papyrus Harris I (BM 9999)*. 2 vols. Bibliothèque d'étude. Cairo: Institut français d'archéologie orientale.

Greaves, Alan M., and Barbara Helwing. 2001. Archaeology in Turkey: The Stone, Bronze, and Iron Ages, 1997–1999. *AJA* 105:463–511.

Green, John. 2009. Forces of Transformation in Death: The Cemetery at Tell es-Sa'idiyeh Jordan. Pages 80–91 in Bachhuber and Roberts 2009.

———. 2010. Creating Prestige in the Jordan Valley: A Reconstruction of Ritual and Social Dynamics from the Late Bronze–Early Iron Age Cemetery at Tell es-Sa'idiyeh. Pages 765–79 in *Near Eastern Archaeology in the Past, Present and Future*. Vol. 1 of *Proceedings of the 6th International Congress of the Archaeology of the Ancient Near East, 5 May–10 May 2009, "Sapienza", Università di Roma*. Edited by P. Matthiae, F. Pinnock, L. Nigro, and N. Marchetti. Wiesbaden: Harrassowitz.

Gregori, Barbara, and Gaetano Palumbo. 1986. Presenze micenee in Siria-Palestina. Pages 365–89 in Marazzi, Tusa, and Vagnetti 1986.

Guichard, Michael. 1993. Flotte crétoise sur l'Euphrate? *NABU* 1993:44–45.

Guigues, Paul-Emile. 1939. *Lébé'a, Kafer Garra, Qrayé: nécropoles de la région sidonienne*. Bulletin du Musée de Beyrouth 1:35–76.

Gunneweg, Jan, Trude Dothan, Isadore Perlman, and Seymour Gitin. 1986. On the Origin of the Pottery from Tel Miqne-Ekron. *BASOR* 264:3–16.

Gunneweg, Jan, and Isadore Perlman. 1994. The Origin of a Mycenaean IIIC:1 Stirrup-Jar from Tell Keisan. *RB* 101:559–61.

Güntner, Wolfgang. 2000. *Tiryns XII: Figürlich bemalte mykenische Keramik aus Tiryns*. Mainz: Zabern.

Gurney, Oliver R. 1997. The Annals of Hattusilis III. *AnSt* 47:127–39.

Güterbock, Hans G. 1983. The Hittites and the Aegean World: Part 1. The Ahhiyawa Problem Reconsidered. *AJA* 87:133–38.

———. 1986. Troy in Hittite Texts? Wilusa, Ahhiyawa, and Hittite History. Pages 33–44 in *Troy and the Trojan War: A Symposium Held at Bryn Mawr College, October 1984*. Edited by M. J. Mellink. Bryn Mawr, Penn.: Bryn Mawr College.

———. 1992. Survival of the Hittite Dynasty. Pages 53–55 in Ward and Joukowsky 1992.

Guy, Philip L. O. 1938. *Megiddo Tombs*. OIP 33. Chicago: University of Chicago Press.

Gvirtzman, Gdaliahu. 1969. Maps. Vol. 2 of *The Saqiye Group (Late Eocene to Early Pleistocene) in the Coastal Plain and Hashephela Regions, Israel.* Bulletin of the Geological Survey of Israel 51; Report of the Institute for Petroleum Research and Geophysics 1022. Jerusalem: Geological Survey of Israel.

Gvirtzman, Gdaliahu, Moshe Wider, Ofer Marder, Hamudi Khalaily, Rivka Rabinovich, and Hagai Ron. 1999. Geological and Pedological Aspects of an Early-Paleolithic Site: Revadim, Central Coastal Plain, Israel. *Geoarchaeology* 41:101–26.

Hadjicosti, Maria. 1997. The Kingdom of Idalion in the Light of New Evidence. *BASOR* 308:49–63.

———. 1999. Idalion before the Phoenicians: The Archaeological Evidence and Its Topographical Distribution. Pages 35–54 in Iacovou and Michaelides 1999.

Hadjisavvas, Sophokles. 1989. A Late Cypriot Community at Alassa. Pages 32–42 in Peltenburg 1989.

———. 1991. LC IIC to LC IIIA without Intruders: The Case of Alassa-*Pano Mandilaris*. Pages 173–80 in Barlow, Bolger, and Kling 1991.

———. 1996. Alassa: A Regional Centre of Alasia? Pages 6–8 in Åström and Herscher 1996.

———. 2000. Unpublished Excavations: The Case of Cyprus. Pages 5–10 in *The Problem of Unpublished Excavations: Proceedings of a Conference Organized by the Department of Antiquities and the Anastasios G. Leventis Foundation, Nicosia, 25th–26th November, 1999.* Edited by S. Hadjisavvas and V. Karageorghis. Nicosia: Dept. of Antiquities, Cyprus: A. G. Leventis Foundation.

Haines, Richard. 1971. *Explorations in the Plain of Antioch II: The Structural Remains of the Later Phases. Chatal Hüyük, Tell al-Judaidah, and Tell Ta'yinat.* Chicago: University of Chicago Press.

Halbwachs, Maurice. 1950. *La mémoire collective.* Paris: Presses Universitaires de France.

———. 1992. *On Collective Memory.* Heritage of Sociology. Chicago: University of Chicago Press.

Hallager, Birgit P. 1997. LM III Pottery Terminology: Goblets, Kylix and the Footed Cup. Pages 15–55 in Hallager and Hallager 1997.

Hallager, Erik, and Birgit P. Hallager. 2000. *The Late Minoan IIIC Settlement.* Vol. 2 of *The Greek-Swedish Excavations at the Agia Aikaterini Square Kastelli, Khania 1970–1987.* Skrifter Utgivna av Svenska Institutet i Athen 47:2. Jonsered: Åströms.

———, eds. 1997. *Late Minoan III Pottery: Chronology and Terminology. Acts of a Meeting Held at the Danish Institute at Athens, August 12–14, 1994.* Monographs of the Danish Institute at Athens 1. Athens: Danish Institute at Athens.

Halpern, Baruch. 1991. Jerusalem and the Lineages in the Seventh Century BCE: Kinship and the Rise of Individual Moral Liability. Pages 11–107 in *Law and Ideology in Monarchic Israel.* Edited by B. Halpern and D. Hobson. JSOTSup 124. Sheffield: Sheffield Academic Press.

———. 1996. The Construction of the Davidic State: An Exercise in Historiography. Pages 44–75 in *The Origins of the Early Israelite States.* Edited by V. Fritz and P. R. Davies. JSOTSup 228. Sheffield: Sheffield Academic Press.

———. 2001. *David's Secret Demons: Messiah, Murderer, Traitor, King.* The Bible in Its World. Grand Rapids. Mich.: Eerdmans.

Hamilakis, Yannis. 1999. La trahison des archéologues? Archaeological Practice as Intellectual Activity in Postmodernity. *Journal of Mediterranean Archaeology* 12:60–79.

Hamilton, Robert W. 1934. Tell Abu Hawam: Interim Report. *QDAP* 3:78–80.
———. 1935. Excavations at Tell Abu Hawam. *QDAP* 4:1–69.
Hanfmann, George M. 1963. The Iron Age Pottery of Tarsus. Pages 18–332 in Goldman 1963.
Hankey, Vronwy. 1966. Late Mycenaean Pottery at Beth-Shan. *AJA* 70:169–71.
———. 1967. Mycenaean Pottery in the Middle East: Notes on Finds Since 1951. *Annual of the British School at Athens* 62:107–48.
———. 1977. The Aegean Pottery. Pages 45–51 in *Akko: Tombs near the Persian Garden*. Edited by S. Ben Arieh and G. Edelstein. Atiqot English Series 12. Jerusalem: Dept. of Antiquities and Museums.
———. 1981a. The Aegean Interest in El Amarna. *Journal of Mediterranean Anthropology and Archaeology* 1:38–49.
———. 1981b. Imported Vessels of the Late Bronze Age at High Places. Pages 108–17 in *Temples and High Places in Biblical Times: Proceedings of the Colloquium in Honor of the Centennial of Hebrew Union College–Jewish Institute of Religion, Jerusalem 14–16 March 1977*. Edited by A. Biran. Jerusalem: Nelson Glueck School of Biblical Archaeology of Hebrew Union College.
———. 1982. Pottery and Peoples of the Mycenaean IIIC Period in the Levant. Pages 167–71 in *Archéologie au Levant: recueil à la mémoire de Roger Saidah*. Collection de la Maison de l'Orient méditerranéen 12. Lyons: Maison de l'Orient méditerranéen.
———. 1993. Pottery as Evidence for Trade: The Levant from the Mouth of the River Orontes to the Egyptian Border. Pages 101–8 in Zerner, Zerner, and Winder 1993.
———. 1995. A Late Bronze Age Temple at Amman Airport: Small Finds and Pottery Discovered in 1955. Pages 169–85 in Bourke and Descoeudres 1995.
Hansen, Connie K., and J. Nicholas Postgate. 1999. The Bronze to Iron Age Transition at Kilise Tepe. *AnSt* 49:111–21.
Harding, Anthony F. 1975. Mycenaean Greece and Europe: The Evidence of Bronze Tools. *Proceedings of the Prehistoric Society* 41:183–202.
———. 1984. *The Mycenaeans and Europe*. London: Academic Press.
Harding, Anthony F., and Helen Hughes-Brock. 1974. Amber in the Mycenaean World. *Annual of the British School at Athens* 69:145–72.
Harrison, Roland K. 1988. Philistine Origins: A Repraisal. Pages 11–19 in *Ascribe to the Lord: Biblical and Other Studies in Memory of Peter C. Craigie*. Edited by L. Eslinger and G. Taylor. JSOTSup 67. Sheffield: Sheffield Academic Press.
Harrison, Timothy P. 2004. *Megiddo III: Final Report of the Stratum VI Excavations*. OIP 127. Chicago: University of Chicago Press.
———. 2009. Neo-Hittites in the "Land of Palistin": Renewed Investigations at Tell Ta'yinat on the Plain of Antioch. *NEA* 72:174–89.
Hauptmann, Andreas. 1989. The Earliest Periods of Cooper Metallurgy in Feinan, Wadi Araba, Jordan. Pages 119–35 in *Old World Archaeometallurgy: Proceedings of the International Symposium "Old World Archaeometallurgy," Heidelberg 1987*. Edited by A. Hauptmann, E. Pernicka, and G. A. Wagner. Der Anschnitt, 7; Veröffentlichungen aus dem Deutsches Bergbau-Museum Bochum 44. Bochum: Deutschen Bergbau-Museum.
Hawkins, J. David. 1982. The Neo-Hittite States in Syria and Anatolia. Pages 372–441 in *The Cambridge Ancient History*, Vol. 3, Part 1. Edited by J. Boardman, I. E. S.

Edwards, N. G. L. Hammond, and E. Sollberger. Cambridge: Cambridge University Press.

———. 1988. Kuzi-Tešub and the "Great Kings" of Karkamiš. *AnSt* 38:99–108.

———. 1990. The New Inscription from the Südburg of Boğazköy-Hattuša. *AA* 3:305–14.

———. 1995a. "Great Kings" and "Country-Lords" at Malatya and Karkamiš. Pages 73–85 in *Studio Historiae Ardens: Ancient Near Eastern Studies Presented to Ph. H. J. Houwink ten Cate on the Occasion of His 65th Birthday*. Edited by Th. P. J. van den Hout and J. de Roos. Uitgaven van het Nederlands Historisch-Archaeologisch Instituut te Istanbul 74. Istanbul: Nederlands Historisch-Archaeologisch Instituut.

———. 1995b. Karkamish and Karatepe: Neo-Hittite City-States in North Syria. *CANE* 2:1295–1307.

———. 1995c. *The Hieroglyphic Inscription of the Sacred Pool Complex at Hattusa (Südburg)*. Studien zu den Boğazköy-Texten Beiheft 3. Wiesbaden: Harrassowitz.

———. 1998. Tarkasnawa King of Mira: "Tarkondemos," Boğazköy Sealings and Karabel. *AnSt* 48:1–31.

———. 2000. *Inscriptions of the Iron Age*. Vol. 1 of *Corpus of Hieroglyphic Luwian Inscriptions*. 3 vols. Studies in Indo-European Language and Culture n.s. 8. Berlin: de Gruyter.

———. 2009. Cilicia, the Amuq, and Aleppo: New Light in a Dark Age. *NEA* 72:164–73.

Heilmeyer, Wolf-Dieter, Elke Goemann, Luca Giulianai, Gertrud Platz, and Gerhard Zimmer. 1988. *Antikenmuseum Berlin: Die ausgestellten Werke*. Berlin: Staatliche Museen Preussischer Kulturbesitz.

Helck, Wolfgang. 1971. *Die Beziehungen Ägyptens zu Vorderasien im 3. und 2. Jahrtausend v. Chr.* 2nd ed. Ägyptologische Abhandlungen 5. Wiesbaden: Harrassowitz.

Hellbing, Lennart. 1979. *Alasia Problems*. SIMA 57. Göteborg: Åströms.

Hellenkemper, Hansgerd. 1984. Das wiedergefundene Issos. Pages 43–50 in *Aus dem Osten des Alexanderreiches: Völker und Kulturen zwischen Orient und Okzident. Iran, Afghanistian, Pakistan, Indien*. Edited by J. Ozols and V. Thewalt. DuMont Dokumente. Cologne: DuMont.

Heltzer, Michael. 1976. *The Rural Community in Ancient Ugarit*. Wiesbaden: Reichert.

Heltzer, Michael, and Edward Lipiński, eds. 1988. *Society and Economy in the Eastern Mediterranean (c. 1500–1000 B.C.): Proceedings of the International Symposium Held at the University of Haifa, April–May 1985*. OLA 23. Leuven: Peeters.

Henrickson, Robert. 1993. Politics, Economics, and Ceramic Continuity at Gordion in the Late Second and First Millennia B.C. Pages 88–176 in *The Social and Cultural Contexts of New Ceramic Technologies*. Edited by W. D. Kingery. Ceramics and Civilization 6. Westerville, Ohio: American Ceramic Society.

———. 1994. Continuity and Discontinuity in the Ceramic Tradition of Gordion During the Iron Age. Pages 95–129 in Çilingiroğlu and French 1994.

Herrmann, Christian. 1994. *Ägyptische Amulette aus Palästina/Israel: Mit einem Ausblick auf ihre Rezeption durch das Alte Testament*. OBO 138. Freiburg: Universitätsverlag; Göttingen: Vandenhoeck & Ruprecht.

Herscher, Ellen. 1975. The Imported Pottery. Pages 85–96 in Pritchard 1975.

———. 1996. Introduction. Pages 6–8 in Åström and Herscher 1996.

Herzog, Zeev. 1993. Gerisa, Tel. *NEAEHL* 2:480–84.

———. 1997. *Archaeology of the City: Urban Planning in Ancient Israel and Its Social Impli-*

cations. Tel Aviv Monograph Series 13. Tel Aviv: Emery and Claire Yass Publications in Archaeology.

———. 2003. The Canaanite City between Ideology and Archaeological Reality. Pages 85–100 in *Saxa loquentur: Studien zur Archäologie Palästinas/Israels. Festschrift für Volkmar Fritz zum 65. Geburtstag*. Edited by C. G. den Hertog, U. Hübner, and S. Münger. AOAT 302. Münster: Ugarit-Verlag.

Hesse, Brian. 1986. Animal Use at Tel Miqne Ekron in the Bronze Age and Iron Age. *BASOR* 264:17–27.

———. 1990. Pig Lovers and Pig Haters: Patterns of Palestinian Pork Production. *Journal of Ethnobiology* 10:195–225.

———. 1995. Husbandry, Dietary Taboos and the Bones of the Ancient Near East: Zooarchaeology in the Post-Processual World. Pages 197–232 in *Methods in the Mediterranean: Historical and Archaeological Views on Texts and Archaeology*. Edited by D. B. Small. Leiden: Brill.

Hesse, Brian, and Paula Wapnish. 1997. Can Pig Remains Be Used for Ethnic Diagnosis in the Ancient Near East? Pages 238–70 in Silberman and Small 1997.

Heuck-Allen, Susan. 1990. "Northwest Anatolian Grey Wares in the Late Bronze Age: Analysis and Distribution in the Eastern Mediterranean." Ph.D. diss., Brown University.

———. 1994. Trojan Grey Ware at Tel Miqne-Ekron. *BASOR* 293:39–51.

Heurtley, Walter A. 1938. A Palestinian Vase-Painter of the Sixteenth Century B.C. *QDAP* 8:21–34.

Higginbotham, Carolyn R. 2000. *Egyptianization and Elite Emulation in Ramesside Palestine: Governance and Accommodation on the Imperial Periphery*. Culture and History of the Ancient Near East 2. Leiden: Brill.

Hill, Jane. 1999. Syncretism. *Journal of Linguistic Anthropology* 9:244–46.

Hirschfeld, Nicolle. 1992. Cypriot Marks on Mycenaean Pottery. Pages 315–19 in *Mykenaïka: actes du IXe Colloque international sur les textes mycéniens et égéens. Organisé par le Centre de l'Antiquité grecque et romaine de la Fondation hellénique des recherches scientifiques et l'École française d'Athènes, octobre 1990*. Edited by J.-P. Olivier. Bulletin de correspondance hellénique supplément 25. Paris: Boccard.

Hitchcock, Louise A. 2011. "Transculturalism" as a Model for Examining Migration to Cyprus and Philistia at the End of the Bronze Age. *Ancient West and East* 10:267–80.

Hobbs, T. Raymond. 1985. *2 Kings*. Word Biblical Commentary 13. Waco, Tex.: Word Books.

Hoch, James E. 1994. *Semitic Words in Egyptian Texts of the New Kingdom and Third Intermediate Period*. Princeton: Princeton University Press.

Hodder, Ian. 1999. *The Archaeological Process: An Introduction*. Oxford: Blackwell.

Hodges, Henry. 1964. *Artifacts*. New York: Praeger.

Hoffman, Gail L. 1997. *Imports and Immigrants: Near Eastern Contacts with Iron Age Crete*. Ann Arbor: University of Michigan Press.

Hoffner, Harry A., Jr. 1992. The Last Days of Khattusha. Pages 46–52 in Ward and Joukowsky 1992.

Holladay, Jack S. 1990. Red Slip, Burnish and the Solomonic Gateway at Gezer. *BASOR* 277/278:23–70.

Hommel, P. 1959–1960. Die Ausgrabungen beim Athena-Tempel in Milet 1957. II. Der Abschnitt östlich des Athena-Tempels. *IstMitt* 9–10:31–62.

Hood, Sinclair. 1982. *Excavations in Chios, 1938–1955: Prehistoric Emporio and Ayio Gala II*. Supplementary Volume of the British School of Archaeology at Athens 16. London: British School of Archaeology at Athens: Thames & Hudson.

Hood, Sinclair, Juliet Clutton-Brock, Perry G. Bialor, and John Boardman. 1982. *Excavations in Chios, 1938–1955: Prehistoric Emporio and Ayio Gala II*. Supplementary Volume of the British School of Archaeology at Athens 15. London: British School at Athens.

Hooker, James T. 1976. *Mycenaean Greece*. London: Routledge & Kegan Paul.

Hope Simpson, Richard, and John F. Lazenby. 1962. Notes from the Dodecanese I. *Annual of the British School at Athens* 57:154–75.

———. 1973. Notes from the Dodecanese III. *Annual of the British School at Athens* 68:127–79.

Hrouda, Barthel. 1997. Vorläufiger Bericht über die Ausgrabungsergebnisse auf dem Sirkeli Höyük/Südtürkei von 1992–1996. *IstMitt* 47:91–150.

Hult, Gunnel. 1978. Area 8: The 1974 Campaign. Pages 1–15 in *Hala Sultan Tekke 4*. SIMA 45:4. Göteborg: Åströms.

———. 1981. *Hala Sultan Tekke 7: Excavations in Area 8 in 1977*. SIMA 45:7. Göteborg: Åströms.

Humbert, Jean-Baptiste. 1993. Keisan, Tell. *NEAEHL* 3:862–67.

Iacovou, Maria. 1988. *The Pictorial Pottery of Eleventh Century B.C. Cyprus*. SIMA 79. Göteborg: Åströms.

———. 1989. Society and Settlements in LCIII. Pages 52–59 in Peltenburg 1989.

———. 1991. Proto-White Painted Pottery: A Classification of the Ware. Pages 199–205 in Barlow, Bolger, and Kling 1991.

———. 1998. Philistia and Cyprus in the 11th Century. Pages 332–44 in Gitin, Mazar, and Stern 1998.

———. 2001. Cyprus from Alashiya to Iatnana—The Protohistoric Interim. Pages 85–92 in *Ithake: Festschrift für Jörg Schäfer zum 75. Geburtstag am 25. April 2001*. Edited by S. Böhm and K.-V. von Eickstedt. Würzburg: Ergon.

———. 2005a. Cyprus at the Dawn of the First Millennium B.C.E.: Cultural Homogenization versus the Tyranny of Ethnic Identifications. Pages 125–36 in *Archaeological Perspectives on the Transmission and Transformation of Culture in the Eastern Mediterranean*. Edited by J. Clarke. Levant Supplementary Series 2. Oxford: Oxbow.

———. 2005b. The Early Iron Age Urban Forms of Cyprus. Pages 17–43 in *Mediterranean Urbanization, 800–600 BC*. Edited by B. W. Cunliffe and R. Osborne. Proceedings of the British Academy 126. Oxford: Oxford University Press for the British Academy.

———. 2006a. *À contretemps*: The Late Helladic IIIC Syntax and Context of Early Iron Age Pictorial Pottery in Cyprus. Pages 191–204 in *Pictorial Pursuits: Figurative Painting on Mycenaean and Geometric Pottery. Papers from Two Seminars at the Swedish Institute at Athens in 1999 and 2001*. Edited by E. Rystedt and B. Wells. Skrifter Utgivna av Svenska Institutet i Athen 4, 53. Stockholm: Svenska Institutet i Athen.

———. 2006b. "Greeks," "Phoenicians" and "Eteocypriots": Ethnic Identities in the Cypriote Kingdoms. Pages 24–59 in *"Sweet Land—": Lectures on the History and Culture of Cyprus*. Edited by J. Chrysostomides and C. Dendrinos. Camberley: Porphyrogenitus.

———. 2007. Site Size Estimates and the Diversity Factor in Late Cypriote Settlement Histories. *BASOR* 348:1–23.

———. 2008a. Cultural and Political Configurations in Iron Age Cyprus: The Sequel to a Protohistoric Episode. *AJA* 112:625–57.

———. 2008b. The Palaepaphos Urban Landscape Project: Theoretical Background and Preliminary Report 2006–2007. *RDAC* 2008:263–89.

Iacovou, Maria, and Demetres Michaelides, eds. 1999. *Cyprus: The Historicity of the Geometric Horizon. Proceedings of an Archaeological Workshop, University of Cyprus, Nicosia, 11th October 1998*. Nicosia: Archaeological Research Unit, University of Cyprus.

Iakovidis, Spyros E. 1969–1970. *Perati: to Nekrotapheion*. 3 vols. Vivliotheke tes en Athenais Archaiologikes Hetaireias 67. Athens: Athens Archaeological Society.

Ibrahim, Moawiyeh M. 1978. The Collared-Rim Jar of the Early Iron Age. Pages 116–26 in *Archaeology in the Levant: Essays for Kathleen Kenyon*. Edited by R. Moorey and P. Parr. London: Warminster.

Ikram, Salima. 2003. A Preliminary Study of Zooarchaeological Changes Between the Bronze and Iron Ages at Kinet Höyük, Hatay. Pages 283–93 in Fischer et al. 2003.

Ilan, David. 1999. "Northeastern Israel in the Iron Age I: Cultural, Socioeconomic and Political Perspectives." Ph.D. diss., Tel Aviv University.

Iliffe, John H. 1935. A Tell Far'a Tomb Group Reconsidered: Silver Vessels of the Persian Period. *QDAP* 4:182–86.

Jacobsthal, Paul. 1956. *Greek Pins and Their Connections with Europe and Asia*. Oxford: Clarendon.

James, Frances. 1966. *The Iron Age at Beth Shan: A Study of Levels VI–IV*. University Museum Monograph. Philadelphia: University Museum of Archaeology and Anthropology, University of Pennsylvania.

James, Frances, and Patrick McGovern. 1993. *The Late Bronze Age Egyptian Garrison at Beth Shan: A Study of Levels VII and VIII*. Philadelphia: University Museum of Archaeology and Anthropology, University of Pennsylvania.

Janeway, Brian. 2006–2007. The Nature and Extent of Aegean Contact at Tell Ta'yinat and Vicinity in the Early Iron Age: Evidence of the Sea Peoples? *Scripta Mediterranea* 27–28:123–46.

———. 2011. Mycenaean Bowls at 12th/11th Century BC Tell Tayinat (Amuq Valley). Pages 167–85 in Karageorghis and Kouka 2011.

Jasink, Anna Margherita, and Mauro Marino. 2007. The West Anatolian Origins of the Que Kingdom Dynasty. *SMEA* 49:407–26.

Jean, Éric. 2003. From Bronze to Iron Ages in Cilicia: The Pottery in Its Stratigraphic Context. Pages 79–91 in *Identifying Changes: The Transition from Bronze to Iron Ages in Anatolia and Its Neighbouring Regions: Proceedings of the International Workshop, Istanbul, November 8–9, 2002*. Edited by B. Fischer, H. Genz, É. Jean, and K. Köroglu. Istanbul: Türk Eskiçag Bilimleri Enstitüsü.

Jean, Éric, Ali M. Dinçol, and Serra Durugönül, eds. 2001. *La Cilicie: espaces et pouvoirs locaux (2e millénaire av. J.-C.–4e siècle ap. J.-C.). Actes de la table ronde internationale d'Istanbul, 2–5 novembre 1999*. Varia Anatolica 13. Istanbul: Institut français d'études anatoliennes Georges Dumézil; Paris: Boccard.

Jennings, Anne. 1991. A Nubian "Zikr": An Example of African/Islamic Syncretism in Southern Egypt. *Anthropos* 86:545–52.

Joffe, Alexander. 1999. Ethnicity in the Iron I Southern Levant: Marginal Notes. *Akkadica* 112:27–33.

Johns, Cedric N. 1938. Excavations at Pilgrim's Castle, Atlit (1933): Cremated Burials of Phoenician Origin. *QDAP* 6:121–52.

———. 1993. ʿAtlit. *NEAEHL* 1:112–17.

Jones, Richard E. 1986a. Chemical Analysis of Aegean-Type Late Bronze Age Pottery Found in Italy. Pages 205–14 in Marazzi, Tusa, and Vagnetti 1986.

———, ed. 1986b. *Greek and Cypriot Pottery: A Review of Scientific Studies*. Fitch Laboratory Occasional Paper 1. Athens: British School at Athens.

Jones, Richard E., and Christopher B. Mee. 1978. Spectrographic Analyses of Mycenaean Pottery from Ialysos on Rhodes: Results and Implications. *Journal of Field Archaeology* 5:461–70.

Jong, Teive de, and Wilfred H. van Soldt. 1987–1988. Redating an Early Solar Eclipse of the Sun Record (KTU 1.78): Implications for the Ugaritic Calendar and for the Secular Accelerations of the Earth and Moon. *JEOL* 30:65–77.

Joppke, Christian. 1999. How Immigration Is Changing Citizenship: A Comparative View. *Ethnic and Racial Studies* 22:629–52.

Jung, Reinhard. 2005. Aspekte des mykenischen Handels und Produktaustauschs. Pages 45–70 in *Interpretationsraum Bronzezeit: Bernard Hänsel von seinen Schülern gewidmet*. Edited by B. Horejs, R. Jung, E. Kaiser, and B. Terzan. Universitätsforschungen zur prähistorischen Archäologie 121. Bonn: Habelt.

———. 2006a. *Chronologia comparata: Vergleichende Chronologie von Südgriechenland und Süditalien von ca. 1700/1600 bis 1000 v. u. Z.* Veröffentlichungen der mykenischen Kommission 26; Österreichische Akademie der Wissenschaften, Philosophisch-Historische Klasse, Denkschriften 348. Vienna: Österreichische Akademie der Wissenschaften.

———. 2006b. Εὔποτον Ποτέριον: Mykenische Keramik und mykenische Trinksitten in der Ägäis, in Syrien, Makedonien und Italien. Pages 407–23 in *Studi in protostoria in onore di Renato Peroni*. Florence: Insegna del Giglio.

———. 2007. Tell Kazel and the Mycenaean Contacts with Amurru (Syria). Pages 551–70 in Bietak and Czerny 2007.

———. 2009. I "bronzi internazionali" ed il loro contesto sociale fra Adriatico, Penisola balcanica e coste Levantine. Pages 129–57 in Borgna and Càssola Guida 2009.

———. 2010. La céramique de typologie mycénienne. Pages 115–21 in *Tell Tweini: Onze campagnes de fouilles syro-belges (1999–2010)*. Edited by M. al-Maqdissi, K. van Lerberghe, J. Bretschneider, and M. Badawi. Damascus: Ministère de Culture, Direction Générale des Antiquités et des Musées.

———. 2012. Can We Say, What's Behind All Those Sherds? Ceramic Innovations in the Eastern Mediterranean at the End of the Second Millennium. Pages 104–20 in *Materiality and Social Practice: Transformative Capacities of Intercultural Encounters*. Edited by J. Maran and P. W. Stockhammer. Oxford: Oxbow.

Jung, Reinhard, and Mathias Mehofer. 2005–2006. A Sword of Naue II Type from Ugarit and the Historical Significance of Italian-Type Weaponry in the Eastern Mediterranean. *Aegean Archaeology* 8:111–35.

Juteau, Thierry. 1980. Ophiolites of Turkey. *Ofioliti* 2:199–237.

Kahl, Jochem. 1995. Les témoignages textuels égyptiens sur les Shardana. Pages 137–40 in Yon, Sznycer, and Bordreuil 1995.

Kaiser, Otto. 1985. *Rechts- und Wirtschaftsurkunden, historisch-chronologische Texte*. Vol. 1 of *Texte aus der Umwelt des Alten Testaments*. Gütersloh: Mohn.

Kalsbeek, Jan, and Gloria London. 1978. A Late Second Millennium B.C. Potting Puzzle. *BASOR* 232:47–56.
Kaniewski, David, Etienne Paulissen, Elise Van Campo, Harvey Weiss, Thierry Otto, Joachim Bretschneider, and Karel Van Lerberghe. 2010. Late Second–Early First Millennium BC Abrupt Climate Changes in Coastal Syria and Their Possible Significance for the History of the Eastern Mediterranean. *Quaternary Research* 74:207–15.
Kaniewski, David, Elise Van Campo, Karel Van Lerberghe, Tom Boiy, Klaas Vansteenhuyse, Greta Jans, Karin Nys, Harvey Weiss, Christophe Morhange, Thierry Otto, and Joachim Bretschneider. 2011. The Sea Peoples, from Cuneiform Tablets to Carbon Dating. *PLoS ONE* 6. No pages. Cited 13 August 2012. Online: http://www.plosone.org/article/info%3Adoi/10.1371/journal.pone.0020232.
Kanta, Athanasia. 1980. *The Late Minoan III Period in Crete: A Survey of Sites, Pottery and Their Distribution.* SIMA 58. Göteborg: Åströms.
———. 1997. LM IIIB and LM IIIC Pottery Phases: Some Problems of Definition. Pages 83–110 in Hallager and Hallager 1997.
Karageorghis, Vassos. 1974. *The Tombs.* Vol. 1 of *Excavations at Kition.* Nicosia: Department of Antiquities, Cyprus.
———. 1975. *Alaas: A Protogeometric Necropolis in Cyprus.* Nicosia: Department of Antiquities, Cyprus.
———. 1976. *Kition: Mycenaean and Phoenician Discoveries in Cyprus.* New Aspects of Antiquity. London: Thames & Hudson.
———. 1981. *The Non-Cypriote Pottery.* Vol. 4 of *Excavations at Kition.* Nicosia: Department of Antiquities, Cyprus.
———. 1983. *Palaepaphos-Skales: An Iron Age Cemetery in Cyprus.* 2 vols. Ausgrabungen in Alt-Paphos auf Cypern 3. Konstanz: Universitätsverlag Konstanz.
———. 1985. Chronique des fouilles et découvertes archéologiques à Chypre en 1985. *Bulletin de correspondance hellénique* 110:823–80.
———. 1986. "Barbarian" Ware in Cyprus. Pages 246–53 in Karageorghis (ed.) 1986.
———. 1990a. *Tombs at Palaepaphos.* Nicosia: A. G. Leventis Foundation.
———. 1990b. *The End of the Late Bronze Age in Cyprus.* Nicosia: Pierides Foundation.
———. 1992. The Crisis Years: Cyprus. Pages 79–86 in Ward and Joukowsky 1992.
———. 1994. The Prehistory of Ethnogenesis. Pages 1–10 in Karageorghis (ed.) 1994.
———. 1998. Hearths and Bathtubs in Cyprus: A "Sea Peoples" Innovation? Pages 276–82 in Gitin, Mazar, and Stern 1998.
———. 2000a. Cultural Innovations in Cyprus Relating to the Sea Peoples. Pages 255–79 in Oren 2000.
———. 2000b. Some Thoughts on the Late Bronze Age in Cyprus. *Cahiers du Centre d'Études Chypriotes* 30:9–15.
———. 2001. Patterns of Fortified Settlements in the Aegean and Cyprus c. 1200 B.C. Pages 1–12 in *Defensive Settlements of the Aegean and the Eastern Mediterranean after c.1200 B.C.: Proceedings of an International Workshop Held at Trinity College Dublin, 7th–9th May, 1999.* Edited by V. Karageorghis and C. Morris. Nicosia: A. G. Leventis Foundation; Dublin: Trinity College.
———, ed. 1983. *Palaepaphos-Skales: An Iron Age Cemetery in Cyprus.* Ausgrabungen in Alt-Paphos auf Cypern 3. Konstanz: Universitätsverlag Konstanz.
———, ed. 1985. *Archaeology in Cyprus 1960–1985.* Nicosia: A. G. Leventis Foundation.
———, ed. 1986. *Acts of the International Archaeological Symposium "Cyprus Between*

the Orient and the Occident," Nicosia, 8–14 September 1985. Nicosia: Department of Antiquities, Cyprus.

———, ed. 1994. *Cyprus in the 11th Century B.C.: Proceedings of the International Symposium Organized by the Archaeological Research Unit of the University of Cyprus and the Anastasios G. Leventis Foundation, Nicosia, 30–31 October 1993*. Nicosia: A. G. Leventis Foundation.

Karageorghis, Vassos, and Martha Demas. 1984. *Pyla-Kokkinokremos: A Late 13th–Century B.C. Fortified Settlement in Cyprus*. Nicosia: Department of Antiquities, Cyprus.

———, eds. 1985. *The Pre-Phoenician Levels: Areas I and II*. Vol. 5 of *Excavations at Kition*. 4 vols. Edited by V. Karageorghis and M. Demas. Nicosia: Department of Antiquities, Cyprus.

———, eds. 1988. *Excavations at Maa-Palaeokastro 1979–1986*. Nicosia: Department of Antiquities, Cyprus.

Karageorghis, Vassos, and Maria Iacovou. 1990. Amathus Tomb 521: A Cypro-Geometric I Group. *RDAC* 1990:75–100.

Karageorghis, Vassos, and Ourania Kouka, eds. 2011. *On Cooking Pots, Drinking Cups, Loomweights and Ethnicity in Bronze Age Cyprus and Neighbouring Regions: An International Archaeological Symposium Held in Nicosia, November 6th–7th 2010*. Nicosia: A. G. Leventis Foundation.

Karam, Nadim. 1997. Bey 013: Rapport préliminaire. *Bulletin d'archéologie et d'architecture libanaises* 2:95–113.

Karantzali, Efi. 1999a. Neoi mykenaïko taphoi Rodou. Pages 285–300 in *Acts of the First International Interdisciplinary Colloquium "The Periphery of the Mycenaean World" Lamia, 25–29 September 1994*. Lamia: Greek Ministry of Culture.

———. 1999b. I Mykinaïki Enkatastasi sta Dodekanisa. Paper presented at the second international interdisciplinary colloquium "The Periphery of the Mycenaean World," Lamia, Greece, September 26–30, 1999.

———. 2001 *The Mycenaean Cemetery at Pylona on Rhodes*. BAR International Series 988. Oxford: Archaeopress.

Karantzali, Efi, and Matthew J. Ponting. 2000. ICP-AES Analysis of Some Mycenaean Vases from Pylona, Rhodes. *Annual of the British School at Athens* 95:219–38.

Karmon, Yehuda. 1983. *Israel: Eine geographische Landeskunde*. Wissenschaftliche Länderkunden 22. Darmstadt: Wissenschaftliche Buchgesellschaft.

Kearsley, Rosalinde. 1989. *The Pendent Semi-Circle Skyphos: A Study of Its Development and Chronology and an Examination of It as Evidence for Euboean Activity at Al Mina*. Bulletin Supplement 44. London: University of London, Institute of Classical Studies.

Keel, Othmar. 1990. Früheisenzeitliche Glyptik in Palästina/Israel, mit einem Beitrag von H. Keel-Leu. Pages 331–421 in *Die frühe Eisenzeit, ein Workshop*. Vol. 3 of *Studien zu dem Stempelsiegeln aus Palästina/Israel*. Edited by O. Keel, M. Shuval, and C. Uehlinger. OBO 100. Freiburg: Universitätsverlag.

———. 1994. Philistine "Anchor" Seals. *IEJ* 44:21–35.

———. 1995. *Corpus der Stempelsiegel-Amulette aus Palästina/Israel: Von den Anfängen bis zur Perserzeit. Einleitung*. OBO 10, Series Archaeologica. Freiburg: Universitätsverlag; Göttingen: Vandenhoeck & Ruprecht.

Keel, Othmar, and Max Küchler. 1982. *Der Süden*. Vol. 2 of *Orte und Landschaften der Bibel*. Göttingen: Vandenhoeck & Ruprecht.

Keesing, Felix M. 1973. *Culture Change: An Analysis and Bibliography of Anthropological*

Sources to 1952. Stanford Anthropological Series 1. Stanford: Stanford University Press.
Kelm, George, and Amihai Mazar. 1995. *Timnah: A Biblical City in the Sorek Valley*. Winona Lake, Ind.: Eisenbrauns.
Kemp, Barry, and Robert Merrillees. 1980. *Minoan Pottery in Second Millennium Egypt*. Mainz: Zabern.
Kempinski, Aharon. 1986. Philological Evidence for the Problem of the Philistine Assimilation. *Archeologia* 1:28–30. [Hebrew]
———. 1993. Masos, Tel. *NEAEHL* 3:986–89.
Kessler, Dieter. 1975. Eine Landschenkung Ramses' III. zugunsten eines "Großen der thrw" aus mr-mš'.f". *Studien zur altägyptischen Kultur* 2:103–34.
Keswani, Priscilla S. 1985. *Excavations at Kition V: The Pre-Phoenician Levels: Areas I and II*. Nicosia: Department of Antiquities, Cyprus.
———. 1989. Dimensions of Social Hierarchy in Late Bronze Age Cyprus: An Analysis of the Mortuary Data from Enkomi. *Journal of Mediterranean Archaeology* 2:49–86.
———. 1993. Models of Local Exchange in Late Bronze Age Cyprus. *BASOR* 292:73–83.
———. 1996. Hierarchies, Heterarchies, and Urbanization Processes: The View from Bronze Age Cyprus. *Journal of Mediterranean Archaeology* 9:211–50.
Khalifeh, Issam A. 1988. *Sarepta 2: A Stratigraphic and Ceramic Analysis of the Late Bronze and Iron Age Periods from Area II, Sounding X, A/B-8/9, at Sarepta (Modern Sarafand)*. Beirut: Publications de l'Université libanaise.
Kilian-Dirlmeier, Imma. 1993. *Die Schwerter in Griechenland (außerhalb der Peloponnes), Bulgarien und Albanien*. Prähistorische Bronzefunde, Abteilung IV, 12. Stuttgart: Steiner.
Killebrew, Ann E. 1996a. Pottery Kilns from Deir el-Balah and Tel Miqne-Ekron. Pages 135–62 in *Retrieving the Past: Essays on Archaeological Research and Methodology in Honor of Gus W. Van Beek*. Edited by J. D. Seger. Winona Lake, Ind.: Eisenbrauns.
———. 1996b. *Tel Miqne-Ekron: Report of the 1985–1987 Excavations in Field INE. Areas 5, 6, 7: The Bronze and Iron Ages. Text and Data Base*. Jerusalem: W. F. Albright Institute of Archaeological Research.
———. 1998a. Ceramic Typology and Technology of Late Bronze II and Iron I Assemblages from Tel Miqne-Ekron: The Transition from Canaanite to Philistine Culture. Pages 379–405 in Gitin, Mazar, and Stern 1998.
———. 1998b. Mycenaean and Aegean-Style Pottery in Canaan During the 14th–12th Centuries B.C. Pages 159–69 in Cline and Harris-Cline 1998.
———. 1999a. "Ceramic Craft and Technology During the Late Bronze and Iron I Ages: The Relationship between Pottery Technology, Style, and Cultural Diversity." Ph.D. diss., Hebrew University of Jerusalem.
———. 1999b. Late Bronze and Iron I Cooking Pots in Canaan: A Typological, Technological, and Functional Study. Pages 83–126 in *Archaeology, History and Culture in Palestine and the Near East: Essays in Memory of Albert E. Glock*. Edited by T. Kapitan. ASOR Books 3. Atlanta: Scholars Press.
———. 2000. Aegean-Style Early Philistine Pottery in Canaan During the Iron I Age: A Stylistic Analysis of Mycenaean IIIC:1b Pottery and Its Associated Wares. Pages 236–53 in Oren 2000.
———. 2005. *Biblical Peoples and Ethnicity: An Archaeological Study of Egyptians, Canaanites, Philistines, and Early Israel, 1300–1100 B.C.E.* Atlanta: SBL.

———. 2006. The Emergence of Ancient Israel: The Social Boundaries of a "Mixed Multitude" in Canaan. Pages 555–72 in Maeir and de Miroschedji 2006.
———. 2006–2007. The Philistines in Context: The Transmission and Appropriation of Mycenaean-Style Culture in the East Aegean, Southeastern Coastal Anatolia and the Levant. *Scripta Mediterranea* 27–28:245–66.
———. 2007. The Canaanite Storage Jar Revisited. Pages 166–88 in Crawford et al. 2007.
———. 2010. The Philistines and Their Material Culture in Context: Future Directions of Historical Biblical Archaeology for the Study of Cultural Transmission. Pages 156–67 in *Historical Biblical Archaeology and the Future: The New Pragmatism*. Edited by T. E. Levy. London: Equinox.
———. forthcoming a. Introduction to the Levant during the Transitional Late Bronze Age/Iron I and Iron Age I Periods. In *The Oxford Handbook of the Archaeology of the Levant*. Edited by M. Steiner and A. E. Killebrew. Oxford: Oxford University Press.
———. forthcoming b. *Tel Miqne-Ekron Excavations, 1985–88, Field INE Report: Iron I*. Edited by S. Gitin. Jerusalem: W. F. Albright Institute of Archaeological Research.
Killebrew, Ann E., and Justin S. E. Lev-Tov. 2008. Early Iron Age Feasting and Cuisine: An Indicator of Philistine-Aegean Connectivity. Pages 339–46 in *Dais, the Aegean Feast: Proceedings of the 12th International Aegean Conference, University of Melbourne, Centre for Classics and Archaeology, 25–29 March 2008*. Edited by L. A. Hitchcock, R. Laffineur, and J. Crowley. Aegaeum 29. Liège: Université de Liège, Histoire de l'art et archéologie de la Grèce antique; Austin, Tex.: University of Texas at Austin, Program in Aegean Scripts and Prehistory.
King, Philip J., and Lawrence E. Stager. 2001. *Life in Biblical Israel*. Louisville: Westminster John Knox Press.
Kiriatzi, Evangelina, Stelios Andreou, Sarantis Dimitriades, and Kostas Kotsakis. 1997. Co-Existing Traditions: Handmade and Wheelmade Pottery in Late Bronze Age Central Macedonia. Pages 361–67 in *Technē: Craftsmen, Craftswomen and Craftsmanship in the Aegean Bronze Age. Proceedings of the 6th International Aegean Conference, Philadelphia, Temple University, 18–21 April 1996*. Edited by R. Laffineur and P. P. Betancourt. Aegaeum 16. Liège: Université de Liège, Histoire de l'art et archéologie de la Grèce antique.
Kirkpatrick, Patricia G. 1988. *The Old Testament and Folklore Study*. JSOTSup 62. Sheffield: Sheffield Academic.
Kislev, Michael, and Maria Hopf. 1985. Food Remains from Tell Qasile. Pages 1401–47 in *Excavations at Tell Qasile, Part II*. Edited by A. Mazar. Qedem 20. Jerusalem: Institute of Archaeology.
Kitchen, Kenneth A. 1975. *Ramesside Inscriptions Historical and Biographical I*. Oxford: Blackwells.
———. 1979. *Ramesside Inscriptions Historical and Biographical II*. Oxford: Blackwells.
———. 1980. *Ramesside Inscriptions Historical and Biographical III*. Oxford: Blackwells.
———. 1982a. *Ramesside Inscriptions Historical and Biographical IV*. Oxford: Blackwells.
———. 1982b. *Pharaoh Triumphant: The Life and Times of Ramesses II*. Warminster, England: Aris & Phillips.
———. 1983a. *Ramesside Inscriptions Historical and Biographical V*. Oxford: Blackwells.
———. 1983b. *Ramesside Inscriptions Historical and Biographical VI*. Oxford: Blackwells.
———. 1987. The Basics of Egyptian Chronology in Relation to the Bronze Age. Pages 37–55 in Åström 1987.

———. 1989. *Ramesside Inscriptions Historical and Biographical VII*. Oxford: Blackwells.

———. 1990. *Ramesside Inscriptions Historical and Biographical VIII*. Oxford: Blackwells.

———. 1993. A "Fanbearer on the King's Right Hand" from Ashdod. Pages 109–10 in M. Dothan and Porath 1993.

———. 2000. Regnal and Genealogical Data of Ancient Egypt (Absolute Chronology I): The Historical Chronology of Ancient Egypt, A Current Assessment. Pages 39–52 in *The Synchronisation of Civilisations in the Eastern Mediterranean in the Second Millennium B.C.: Proceedings of an International Symposium at Schloß Haindorf, 15th–17th of November 1996 and at the Austrian Academy, Vienna, 11th–12th of May 1998*. Edited by M. Bietak. Österreichische Akademie der Wissenschaften, Denkschriften der Gesamtakademie 19. Vienna: Österreichische Akademie der Wissenschaften.

———. forthcoming. *Tel Miqne-Ekron Excavations, 1985–88, Field INE Report, Iron Age I*. Edited by S. Gitin. Jerusalem: W. F. Albright Institute and the Hebrew University.

Kletter, Raz. 1996. *The Judean Pillar-Figurines and the Archaeology of Asherah*. BAR International Series 636. Oxford: Tempus Reparatum.

Kling, Barbara. 1984a. The Bird Motif in the Mycenaean IIIC:1b Pottery of Cyprus. Pages 46–57 in *The Scope and Extent of the Mycenaean Empire: Temple University Aegean Symposium 9, April 1984*. Philadelphia: Department of Art History, Temple University.

———. 1984b. Mycenaean IIIC:1b Pottery in Cyprus: Principal Characteristics and Historical Context. Pages 29–38 in *Cyprus at the Close of the Late Bronze Age*. Edited by V. Karageorghis and J. D. Muhly. Nicosia: A. G. Leventis Foundation.

———. 1985. Comments on the Mycenaean IIIC:1b Pottery from Kition Areas I and II. Pages 337–74 in Karageorghis and Demas 1985, Vol. 1.

———. 1987. Pottery Classification and Relative Chronology of the LCIIC–LCIIIA Periods. Pages 97–114 in *Western Cyprus: Connections—An Archaeological Symposium Held at Brock University, St. Catharines, Ontario, Canada, March 21–22, 1986*. SIMA 77. Edited by D. Rupp. Göteborg: Åströms.

———. 1988. Appendix III: Some Stylistic Remarks on the Pottery of Mycenaean IIIC:1 Style from Maa-Palaeokastro. Pages 317–39 in Karageorghis and Demas 1988.

———. 1989. *Mycenaean IIIC:1b and Related Pottery in Cyprus*. SIMA 87. Göteborg: Åströms.

———. 1991. A Terminology for the Matte-Painted, Wheelmade Pottery of Late Cypriot IIC–IIIA. Pages 181–84 in Barlow, Bolger, and Kling 1991.

———. 2000. Mycenaean IIIC:1b and Related Pottery in Cyprus: Comments on the Current State of Research. Pages 281–95 in Oren 2000.

Knapp, A. Bernard. 1994. Emergence, Development and Decline in Bronze Age Cyprus. Pages 271–304 in *Development and Decline in the Mediterranean Bronze Age*. Edited by C. Mathers and S. Stoddart. Sheffield Archaeological Monographs 8. Sheffield: J. R. Collis.

———. 1996. Settlement and Society on Late Bronze Age Cyprus: Dynamics and Development. Pages 54–80 in Åström and Herscher 1996.

———. 1997. *The Archaeology of Late Bronze Age Cypriot Society: The Study of Settlement, Survey and Landscape*. Glasgow: Department of Archaeology, University of Glasgow.

______. 2008. *Prehistoric and Protohistoric Cyprus: Identity, Insularity, and Connectivity*. Oxford: Oxford University Press.

Knapp, A. Bernard, and John Cherry. 1994. *Provenience Studies and Bronze Age Cyprus:*

Production, Exchange and Politico-Economic Change. Monographs in World Archaeology 21. Madison, Wis.: Prehistory Press.

Knauf, Ernst A. 1991. King Solomon's Copper Supply. Pages 167–86 in Lipiński 1991.

———. 2000a. The "Low Chronology" and How Not to Deal With It. *BN* 101:56–63.

———. 2000b. Jerusalem in the Late Bronze and Early Iron Ages: A Proposal. *TA* 27:75–90.

———. 2001a. History, Archaeology, and the Bible. *TZ* 57:262–68.

———. 2001b. Saul, David, and the Philistines: From Geography to History. *BN* 109:15–18.

———. 2005. Deborah's Language: Judges ch. 5 in Its Hebrew and Semitic Context. Pages 167–82 in *Studia Semitica et Semitohamitica: Festschrift für Rainer M. Voigt*. Edited by B. Burtea, J. Tropper, and H. Younansardaround. AOAT 317. Münster: Ugarit-Verlag.

Knell, Heiner, and Walter Voigtländer. 1980. Die Ergebnisse in den Quadranten V2 und VI2. Pages 118–52 in *Tiryns IX: Grabungen in der Unterburg 1971*. Edited by J. Ulf. Mainz: Zabern.

Knudtzon, Jørgen Alexander, ed. 1964. *Die El-Amarna-Tafeln mit Einleitung und Erläuterungen*. 2 vols. VAB 2. Leipzig: Hinrichs, 1915. Repr. Aalen: Zeller.

Kochavi, Moshe. 1965. Tel Zeror. *IEJ* 15:253–55.

______. 1993. Zeror, Tel. *NEAEHL* 4:1524–26.

Koehl, Robert. B. 1984. Observations on a Deposit of LC IIIC Pottery from the Koukounaries Acropolis on Paros. Pages 207–24 in *The Prehistoric Cyclades: Contributions to a Workshop on Cycladic Chronology*. Edited by J. A. MacGillivray and R. L. N. Barber. Edinburgh: Department of Classical Archaeology, University of Edinburgh.

———. 1985. *Sarepta III: The Imported Bronze and Iron Age Wares From Area II, X. The University Museum of the University of Pennsylvania Excavations at Sarafand, Lebanon*. Publications de l'Université libanaise; Section des études archéologiques 2. Beirut: Librairie Orientale.

Koehl, Robert B., and Joseph Yellin. 1982. The Origin and Provenience of Mycenaean "Simple Style" Pottery. *AJA* 86:273.

Kohlmeyer, Kay. 2009. The Temple of the Storm God in Aleppo during the Late Bronze and Early Iron Ages. *NEA* 72:190–202.

Kohlmeyer, Kay, and Eva Strommenger. 1982. *Land des Baal: Syrien, Forum der Völker und Kulturen*. Mainz: Zabern.

Koppenhöfer, Dietrich. 1997. Troia VII: Versuch einer Zusammenschau einschließlich der Ergebnisse des Jahres 1995. *Studia Troica* 7:295–353.

Korfmann, Manfred. 1986. Beşik-Tepe: Vorbericht über die Ergebnisse der Grabungen von 1984. *AA* 1986:301–29.

Koşay, Hâmit Zübeyr. 1944. *Ausgrabungen von Alaca Höyük: ein Vorbericht über die im Auftrage der Türkischen Geschichtskommission im Sommer 1936 durchgeführten Forschungen und Entdeckungen*. Veröffentlichungen der Türkischen Geschichtskommission 5. Ankara: Türk Tarih Kurumu Basımevi.

Koşay, Hâmit Zübeyr, and Mahmut Akok. 1973. *Alaca Höyük Kazısı*. Ankara: Türk Tarih Kurumu Basımevi.

Kourou, Nota. 1994. Scepters and Maces in Cyprus Before, During and Immediately After the 11th Century. Pages 203–27 in Karageorghis (ed.) 1994.

Kühne, Cord, and Heinrich Otten. 1971. *Der Šaušgamuwa-Vertrag*. Studien zu den Boğazköy-Texten 16. Wiesbaden: Harrassowitz.

Laemmel, Sabine. 1998. "The Nature of the Ceramic Material from the 900 Cemetery at Tell Far'ah (South)." MPhil diss., Lincoln College.

———. 2009. A Note on the Material from the Late Bronze and Early Iron Age Cemeteries from Tell el-Far'ah South. Pages 170–85 in Bachhuber and Roberts 2009.

Laffineur, Robert, and Emanuele Greco, eds. 2005. *Emporia: Aegeans in the Central and Eastern Mediterranean. Proceedings of the 10th International Aegean Conference, Athens, Italian School of Archaeology, 14–18 April 2004*. Aegaeum 25. Liège: Histoire de l'art et archéologie de la Grèce antique, Université de Liège; Austin: Program in Aegean Scripts and Prehistory, University of Texas at Austin.

Laffineur, Robert, and Wolf-Dietrich Niemeier, eds. 1995. *Politeia: Society and State in the Aegean Bronze Age. Proceedings of the 5th International Conference, Heidelberg, 10–13 April 1994*. Aegaeum 12. Liège: Histoire de l'art et archéologie de la Grèce antique, Université de Liège; Austin: Program in Aegean Scripts and Prehistory, University of Texas at Austin.

Lagarce, Jacques. 1983. Rapports de Ras Ibn Hani avec la Phénicie et la Méditerranée orientale à l'âge du Fer. Pages 223–26 in Bartolini and Bondi 1983.

———. 1993. Enkomi: Fouilles françaises. Pages 91–106 in *Kinyras: l'archéologie française à Chypre: table ronde tenue à Lyon, 5–6 novembre 1991*. Edited by M. Yon. Travaux de la Maison de l'Orient 22. Lyon: Maison de l'Orient; Paris: Boccard.

Lagarce, Jacques, and Elizabeth Lagarce. 1978. Découvertes archéologiques à Ras Ibn Hani, près de Ras Shamra: un palais du roi d'Ugarit, des tablettes inscrites en caractères cunéiformes, un établissement des peuples de la mer et une ville hellénistique. *CRAI* 1978:45–65.

———. 1988. The Intrusion of the Sea Peoples and Their Acculturations: A Parallel Between Palestinian and Ras Ibn Hani Data. Pages 137–69, 310–33 in vol. 3 of *Studies in the History and Archaeology of Palestine. Proceedings of the First International Symposium on Palestine Antiquities*. Edited by S. Sha'ath. Aleppo: Aleppo University Press.

Lambrou-Phillipson, Connie. 1993. The Limitations of the Pottery Model in the Identification of Trading Colonies. Pages 365–68 in Zerner, Zerner and Winder 1993.

Laroche, Emmanuel. 1958. *Études sur les hiéroglyphes hittites 6: Adana et les Danouniens*. Paris: Geuthner.

Lass, Egon H. E. 1994. Quantitative Studies in Flotaton at Ashkelon, 1986 to 1988. *BASOR* 294:23–38.

———. 1971. *Catalogue des texts hittites*. Études et commentaires 75. Paris: Klincksieck.

Latacz, Joachim. 2001. *Troia und Homer: der Weg zur Lösung eines alten Rätsels*. Munich: Koehler & Amelang.

Leclant, Jean. 1971. Fouilles et travaux en Égypte et au Soudan, 1969–1970. *Or* 40:224–66.

Lehmann, Gunnar. 2001a. Phoenicians in Western Galilee: First Results of an Archaeological Survey in the Hinterland of Akko. Pages 65–112 in A. Mazar and Mathias 2001.

———. 2001b. The "Sea People Phenomenon": Migration and Transmission of Culture in the Levant at the End of the Late Bronze Age. Pages 411–26 in *Migration und Kulturtransfer: der Wandel vorder- und zentralasiatischer Kulturen im Umbruch vom 2. zum 1. vorchristlichen Jahrtausend. Akten des Internationalen Kolloquiums, Berlin, November 1999*. Edited by R. Eichmann and H. Parzinger. Kolloquien zur Vor-und Frühgeschichte 6. Bonn: Habelt.

———. 2002. *Bibliographie der archäologischen Fundstellen und Surveys in Syrien und Libanon*. Rahden, Westfalen: Leidorf.

———.2007. Decorated Pottery Styles in the Northern Levant during the Early Iron Age and Their Relationship with Cyprus and the Aegean. *UF* 39:487–550.

Lehmann, Gunnar, Ann E. Killebrew, and Marie-Henriette Gates. 2008. The Mopsos Project: The 2006 Season of Archaeological Survey (Bay of Iskenderun Region). Pages 171–88 in vol. 3 of *25. Araştirma Sonuçlari Toplantisi, 28 Mayis–1 Haziran 2007 Kocaeli 2007.* Edited by F. Bayram, A. Özme, and B. Koral. T. C. Kültür ve Turizm Bakanlığı 3112; Kültür Varliklari ve Müzeler Genel Müdürlüğü 125. Ankara: Kültür ve Turizm Bakanliğı Dösimm Basımevi.

Lehmann, Gustav. 1983. Zum Auftreten von „Seevölker"-Gruppen im östlichen Mittelmeerraum—eine Zwischenbilanz. Pages 79–92 in Deger-Jalkotzy 1983.

Leonard, Albert Jr. 1981. Considerations of Morphological Variation in the Mycenaean Pottery from the South-East Mediterranean. *BASOR* 241:87–101.

———. 1994. *An Index to the Late Bronze Age: Aegean Pottery from Syria-Palestine*. SIMA 114. Jonsered: Åströms.

Leonard, Albert Jr., Michael J. Hughes, Andrew Middleton, and Louise Schofield. 1993. Methods of Making Aegean Stirrup-Jars: Techniques and Tradition. *Annual of the British School at Athens* 88:105–23.

Leriou, Natasha, 2002. Constructing an Archaeological Narrative: The Hellenization of Cyprus. *Stanford Journal of Archaeology* 1. No pages. Online: http://www.stanford.edu/dept/archaeology/journal/newdraft/leriou/paper.pdf. Cited 15 December 2011.

Lev-Tov, Justin S. E. 2000. "Pigs, Philistines, and the Ancient Animal Economy of Ekron from the Late Bronze Age to the Iron Age II." Ph.D. diss., University of Tennessee.

Levi, Doro. 1969–1970. Iasos: le campagne di scavo 1969–70. *Annuario della Scuola Archeologica Italiana di Atene* 47–48(n.s. 31–32):461–532.

Levy, Thomas E., ed. 1995. *The Archaeology of Society in the Holy Land*. London: Leicester University Press.

Levy, Thomas E., Russell Adams, Andreas Hauptmann, Michael Prange, Sigrid Schmitt-Strecker, and Mohammad Najjar. 2002. Early Bronze Age Metallurgy: A Newly Discovered Copper Manufactory in Southern Jordan. *Antiquity* 76:425–37.

Levy, Thomas E., and Thomas Higham, eds. 2005. *The Bible and Radiocarbon Dating: Archaeology, Text and Science*. London: Equinox.

Lichtheim, Miriam. 1973–1980. *Ancient Egyptian Literature*. 3 vols. Berkeley, Calif.: University of California Press.

Lindblom, Michael. 2001. *Marks and Makers: Appearance, Distribution and Function of Middle and Late Helladic Manufacturers' Marks on Aeginetan Pottery*. SIMA 128. Jonsered: Åströms.

Lipiński, Edward. 1999. "Sea Peoples" and Canaan in Transition c. 1200–950 B.C. *OLP* 30:1–35.

———. 2000. *The Aramaeans: Their Ancient History, Culture, Religion*. OLA 100. Leuven: Peeters.

———. 2004. *Itineraria Phoenicia*. OLA 127. Leuven: Peeters

———, ed. 1991. *Phoenicia and the Bible: Proceedings of the Conference Held at the University of Leuven on the 15th and 16th of March 1990*. OLA 44. Leuven: Peeters.

Lipschits, Oded. 1999. The History of the Benjamin Region Under Babylonian Rule. *TA* 26:155–90.

Lisk, Elisha. 1999. "Tel Dor: An Iron Age Port City Zooarchaeological Analysis." MA thesis, Tel Aviv University.

Liverani, Mario. 1987. The Collapse of the Near Eastern Regional System at the End of the Late Bronze Age: The Case of Syria. Pages 66–73 in *Centre and Periphery in the*

Ancient World. New Directions in Archaeology. Edited by M. J. Rowlands, M. T. Larsen, and K. Kristiansen. Cambridge: Cambridge University Press.

———. 1988. *Antico Oriente: Storia, società, economia*. Collezione storica. Rome: Laterza.

———. 2005. *Israel's History and the History of Israel*. Bibleworld. London: Equinox.

Lord, Albert Bates. 1960. *The Singer of Tales: A Study in the Processes of Composition of Yugoslav, Greek, and Germanic Oral Narrative Poetry*. Cambridge, Mass.: Harvard University Press.

———. 1991. *Epic Singers and Oral Tradition*. Myth and Poetics. Ithaca, N.Y.: Cornell University Press.

Loretz, Oswald. 1995. Les Serdanu et la fin d'Ougarit: à propos des documents d'Égypte, de Byblos et d'Ougarit relatifs aux Shardana. Pages 125–36 in Yon, Sznycer, and Bordreuil 1995.

Loud, Gordon. 1948. *Megiddo II: Seasons of 1935–1939*. OIP 62. Chicago: University of Chicago Press.

Lucassen, Jan, and Leo Lucassen, eds. 1999. *Migration, Migration History, History: Old Paradigms and New Perspectives*. International and Comparative Social History 4. Bern: Lang.

Luckenbill, Daniel D. 1926–1927. *Ancient Records of Assyria and Babylonia*. 2 vols. Chicago: University of Chicago Press.

Machinist, Peter. 2000. Biblical Traditions: The Philistines and Israelite History. Pages 53–83 in Oren 2000.

Macdonald, Colin F. 1986. Problems of the Twelfth Century B.C. in the Dodecanese. *Annual of the British School at Athens* 81:125–51.

Mackay, E. Anne, ed. 1999. *Signs of Orality: The Oral Tradition and Its Influence in the Greek and Roman World*. Mnemosyne, Bibliotheca Classica Batava Supplementum 188. Leiden: Brill.

Mackenzie, Duncan. 1913. The Philistine City of Ashkelon. *PEFQS* 40:8–23.

MacGillivray, Joseph. 1997. Late Minoan II and III Pottery and Chronology at Palaikastro: An Introduction. Pages 193–207 in Hallager and Hallager 1997.

Maeir, Aren M. 2000. Tel Zafit—1998. *Hadashot Arkheologiyot* 112:122–23, 97*–98*. [Hebrew]

———. 2001. The Philistine Culture in Transformation: A Current Perspective Based on the Results of the First Seasons of Excavations at Tell-es-Safi/Gath. Pages 111–29 in *Settlement, Civilization and Culture: Proceedings of the Conference in Memory of David Alon*. Edited by A. M. Maeir and E. Baruch. Ramat Gan: Bar Ilan University. [Hebrew]

———. 2003a. A Late Bronze Age, Syrian-Style Figurine from Tell es-Sâfi/Gath. Pages 197–206 in *Shlomo: Studies in Epigraphy, Iconography, History and Archaeology in Honor of Shlomo Moussaieff*. Edited by R. Deutsch. Tel Aviv-Jaffa: Archaeological Center.

———. 2003b. Notes and News: Tell es-Sâfi. *IEJ* 53:237–46.

———. 2006. Philistine "Head Cup" (Rhyton) from Tell es-Sâfi/Gath. Pages 335–45 in Maeir and de Miroschedji 2006.

———. 2008. Ẓafit, Tel. *NEAEHL* 5:2079–81.

Maeir, Aren M., and Adrian Boas. 1998. Archaeology in Israel: Tell es-Safi. *AJA* 102:785–86.

———. 1999. Tel Zafit—1997. *Hadashot Arkheologiyot* 110:88, 68*. [Hebrew]

Maeir, Aren M., and Carl S. Ehrlich. 2000. Tel Zafit—1999. *Hadashot Arkheologiyot* 112:121–22, 96*–97*. [Hebrew]

———. 2001. Excavating Philistine Gath: Have We Found Goliath's Hometown? *BAR* 27, no. 6 (November/December):22–31.

Maeir, Aren M., Alexander Fantalkin, and Alexander Zukerman. 2009. The Earliest Greek Import in the Iron Age Levant: New Evidence from Tell es-Sâfi/Gath, Israel, *Ancient West and East* 8:57–80.

Maeir, Aren M., Mario M. Martin, and Stefan J. Wimmer. 2005. An Incised Hieratic Inscription from Tell es-Sâfi, Israel. *Egypt and the Levant* 14:125–34.

Maeir, Aren M., and Pierre de Miroschedji, eds. 2006. *"I Will Speak the Riddles of Ancient Times": Archaeological and Historical Studies in Honor of Amihai Mazar on the Occasion of His Sixtieth Birthday.* 2 vols. Winona Lake, Ind.: Eisenbrauns.

Maeir, Aren M., and Joe Uziel. 2007. A Tale of Two Tells: A Comparative Perspective on Tel Miqne-Ekron and Tell eṣ-Ṣâfi/Gath in Light of Recent Archaeological Research. Pages 29–42 in Crawford et al. 2007.

Magrill, Pamela, and Andrew Middleton. 1997. A Canaanite Potter's Workshop at Lachish, Israel. Pages 68–73 in *Pottery in the Making: World Ceramic Traditions.* Edited by I. Freestone and D. R. M. Baimster. London: British Museum Press.

———.2004. Late Bronze Age Pottery Technology: Cave 4034 Revisited. Pages 2514–49 in *The Renewed Archaeological Excavations at Lachish (1973–1994).* Edited by D. Ussishkin. Tel Aviv University, Sonia and Marco Nadler Institute of Archaeology Monograph Series 22. Tel Aviv: Emery and Claire Yass Publications in Archaeology.

Maier, Franz Georg. 1973. *Evidence for Mycenaean Settlement at Old Paphos.* Pages 68–78 in Dikaios 1973.

———. 1984. *Alt-Paphos auf Cypern: Ausgrabungen zur Geschichte von Stadt und Heiligtum 1966–1984.* Trierer Winckelmannsprogramme 6. Mainz: Zabern.

———. 1985. Excavations at Kouklia (Palaepaphos): Thirteenth Preliminary Report. Seasons 1983 and 1984. Appendix: A Note on Shallow Bowls. *RDAC* 1985:122–25.

———. 1986. Kinyras and Agapenor. Pages 311–20 in Karageorghis (ed.) 1986.

———. 1997. The Mycenaean Pottery of Palaipaphos Reconsidered. Pages 93–102 in *Cyprus and the Aegean in Antiquity: From the Prehistoric Period to the 7th Century A.D.* Nicosia: Department of Antiquities, Cyprus.

Maier, Franz Georg, and Vassos Karageorghis. 1984. *Paphos: History and Archaeology.* Nicosia: A. G. Leventis Foundation.

Maier, Franz Georg, and Marie-Louise von Wartburg. 1985. Reconstructing History from the Earth, c. 2800 B.C.–1600 A.D.: Archaeology at Palaepaphos, 1960–1985. Pages 142–72 in Karageorghis (ed.) 1985.

Manning, Sturt, Bernhard Weninger, Alison South, Barbara Kling, Peter Kuniholm, James Muhly, Sophokles Hadjisavvas, David Sewel, and Gerald Cadogan. 2001. Absolute Age Range of the Late Cypriot IIC Period on Cyprus. *Antiquity* 75:328–40.

Maqdissi, Michel al-, Heike Dohmann-Pfälzner, Peter Pfälzner, and Antoine Suleiman. 2003. Das königliche Hypogäum von Qaṭna. *MDOG* 135:189–218.

Maran, Joseph. 2004. The Spreading of Objects and Ideas in the Late Bronze Age Eastern Mediterranean: Two Case Examples from the Argolid of the 13th and 12th Centuries B.C. *BASOR* 336:11–30.

Marazzi, Massimiliano, Sebastiano Tusa, and Lucia Vagnetti, eds. 1986. *Traffici Micenei nel Mediterraneo: Problemi storici e documentazione archeologica. Atti del Convegno di*

Palermo (11–12 maggio e 3–6 dicembre 1984). Magna Graecia 3. Taranto: Istituto per la Storia e l'Archeologia della Magna Grecia.

Marder, Ofer, Gedaliya Gvirtzman, Hagai Ron, Hamoudy Khalaily, Moshe Wieder, Rina Bankirer, Rivka Rabinovich, Naomi Porat, and Idit Saragusti. 1999. The Lower Paleolithic Site of Revadim Quarry, Peliminary Finds. *Journal of the Israel Prehistoric Society* 28: 21–53.

Marfoe, Leon. 1979. The Integrative Transformation: Patterns of Socio-Political Organization in Southern Syria. *BASOR* 234:1–42.

———. 1998. *Kamid el-Loz 14: Settlement History of the Biqa' up to the Iron Age*. Saarbrücker Beiträge zur Altertumskunde 53. Bonn: Habelt.

Marketou, Toula. 1988. New Evidence on the Topography and Site History of Prehistoric Ialysos. Pages 27–38 in Dietz and Papachristodoulou 1988.

———. 1998. Excavations at Trianda (Ialysos) on Rhodes: New Evidence for the Late Bronze Age I Period. *Rendiconti Accademia Nazionale dei Lincei Classe di Scienze Morali, Storiche e Filologiche* 9:39–82.

Martin, Mario A. S. 2009. Egyptian Fingerprints at Late Bronze Age Ashkelon: Egyptian-style Beer Jars. Pages 297–304 in *Exploring the Longue Durée: Essays in Honor of Lawrence E. Stager*. Edited by J. D. Schloen. Winona Lake, Ind.: Eisenbrauns.

Martin, Mario A. S., and Tristan J. Barako. 2007. The Egyptian and Egyptianized Pottery. Pages 129–65 in *Tel Mor: The Moshe Dothan Excavations, 1959–1960*. By T. J. Barako. Israel Antiquities Authority Reports 32. Jerusalem: Israel Antiquities Authority.

Maspero, Gaston. 1896. *The Struggle of the Nations: Egypt, Syria and Assyria*. Edited by A. H. Sayce. Translated by M. L. McClure from French. History of the Ancient Peoples of the Classic East 2. New York: Appleton.

Masson, Olivier. 1983. *Les inscriptions chypriotes syllabiques: recueil critique et commenté*. 2nd rev. and enl. ed. École française d'Athènes, Études chypriotes I. Paris: Boccard.

Masson, Olivier, and Emilia Masson. 1983. Les objets inscrits de Palaepaphos-Skales. Pages 411–15 in Karageorghis (ed.) 1983.

Master, Daniel M. 2003. Trade and Politics: Ashkelon's Balancing Act in the Seventh Century B.C.E. *BASOR* 330:47–64.

———. 2005. Iron I Chronology at Ashkelon: Preliminary Results of the Leon Levy Expedition. Pages 337–48 in Levy and Higham 2005.

Matskevich, Svetlana. 2003. "Stratigraphy and Pottery of Early Iron Age Layers of Area B1 at Tel Dor, Israel." MA thesis, Hebrew University of Jerusalem.

Matsumura, Kimiyoshi. 2000. On the Manufacturing Techniques of Iron Age Ceramics from Kaman-Kalehöyük. Pages 119–35 in *Kaman-Kalehöyük 9*. Anatolia Archaeological Studies 9. Tokyo: Middle Eastern Culture Center in Japan.

———. 2008. The Early Iron Age in Kaman-Kalehöyük: The Search for Its Roots. Pages 41–50 in *Fundstellen: Gesammelte Schriften zur Archäologie und Geschichte Altvorderasiens ad honorem Hartmut Kühne*. Edited by D. Bonatz, R. M. Czichon, and F. J. Kreppner. Wiesbaden: Harrassowitz.

Matthäus, Hartmut. 1982. Einheimische, ägäische und nahöstlische Elemente. Pages 185–99 in Muhly, Maddin and Karageorghis 1982.

Matthers, John. 1989. Excavation by the Palestine Exploration Fund at Tell el-Hesi 1890–1892. Pages 37–67 in *Tell el-Hesi: The Site and the Expedition*. Edited by B. T. Dahlberg and K. G. O'Connell. ASOR Excavations Reports. Winona Lake, Ind.: Eisenbrauns.

———, ed. 1981. *The River Qoueiq, Northern Syria, and Its Catchment: Studies Arising from the Tell Rifa'at Survey 1977–79*. BAR International Series 98. Oxford: BAR.

Mazar, Amihai. 1980. *The Philistine Sanctuary: Architecture and Cult Objects*. Part 1 of *Excavations at Tell Qasile*. Qedem 12. Jerusalem: Institute of Archaeology, Hebrew University of Jerusalem.

———. 1985a. The Emergence of Philistine Culture. *IEJ* 35:95–107.

———. 1985b. *The Philistine Sanctuary: Various Finds, the Pottery, Conclusions, Appendixes*. Part 2 of *Excavations at Tell Qasile*. Qedem 20. Jerusalem: Institute of Archaeology, Hebrew University of Jerusalem.

———. 1988. Some Aspects of the "Sea Peoples" Settlement. Pages 251–60 in Heltzer and Lipiński 1988.

———. 1990. *Archaeology of the Land of the Bible: 10,000–586 BCE*. New York: Doubleday.

———. 1991. Comments on the Nature of the Relations Between Cyprus and Palestine During the 12th–11th Centuries B.C. Pages 95–104 in *Proceedings of an International Symposium "The Civilisations of the Aegean and Their Diffusion in Cyprus and the Eastern Mediterranean, 2000–600 B.C.," 18–24 September 1989*. Edited by V. Karageorghis. Larnaca: Pierides Foundation.

———. 1993a. Iron Age Beth Shean in the Light of the Excavations in 1990–1991. *ErIsr* 24:130–47. [Hebrew]

———. 1993b. Beth Shan in the Iron Age: Preliminary Report and Conclusions of the 1990–1991 Excavations. *IEJ* 43:201–29.

———. 1993c. Qasile, Tell. *NEAEHL* 4:1204–12.

———. 1994a. Tel Beth Shean 1992–1993. *Hadashot Arkheologiyot* 101–102:49–52. [Hebrew]

———. 1994b. The Northern Shephelah in the Iron Age: Some Issues in Biblical History and Archaeology. Pages 247–67 in *Scripture and Other Artifacts: Essays on the Bible and Archaeology in Honor of Ph. J. King*. Edited by M. D. Coogan, J. C. Exum, and L. E. Stager. Louisville, Ky.: Westminster John Knox.

———. 1997a. Four Thousand Years of History at Tel Beth-Shan: An Account of the Renewed Excavations. *BA* 60:62–76.

———. 1997b. Iron Age Chronology: A Reply to I. Finkelstein. *Levant* 29:157–67.

———. 1998. On the Appearance of Red Slip in the Iron Age I Period in Israel. Pages 368–78 in Gitin, Mazar, and Stern 1998.

———. 2000. The Temples and Cult of the Philistines. Pages 213–32 in Oren 2000.

———. 2002. Megiddo in the Thirteenth–Eleventh Centuries B.C.E.: A Review of Some Recent Studies. Pages 264–82 in Oren and Ahituv 2002.

———. 2007. Myc IIIC in the Land of Israel: Its Distribution, Date and Significance. Pages 571–83 in Bietak and Czerny 2007.

———. 2008. From 1200 to 850 B.C.E.: Remarks on Some Selected Archaeological Issues. Pages 86–120 in *Israel in Transition: From Late Bronze II to Iron IIa (c. 1250–850 B.C.E.)*. Edited by L. L. Grabbe. New York: T&T Clark.

Mazar, Amihai, and Israel Carmi. 2001. Radiocarbon Dates from Iron Age Strata at Tel Beth Shean and Tel Rehov. *Radiocarbon* 43/3:1333–42.

Mazar, Amihai, and Ginny Mathias, eds. 2001. *Studies in the Archaeology of the Iron Age in Israel and Jordan*. JSOTSup 331. Sheffield: Sheffield Academic Press.

Mazar, Amihai, and Nava Panitz-Cohen. 1997. *Timnah (Tel Batash) Final Reports I: Stra-*

tigraphy and Architecture. QEDEM 37. Jerusalem: Institute of Archaeology, Hebrew University of Jerusalem.
———. 2001. *Timnah (Tel Batash) II: The Finds from the First Millennium BCE*. Qedem 42; Publications of the Institute of Archaeology, Hebrew University of Jerusalem. Jerusalem: Institute of Archaeology, Hebrew University of Jerusalem.
Mazar, Amihai, A. Ziv-Asudri, and Anat Cohen-Weinberger. 2000. The Early Bronze Age II–III at Tel Beth Shean: Preliminary Observations. Pages 255–78 in *Ceramics and Change in the Early Bronze Age of the Southern Levant*. Edited by G. Philip and D. Baird. Levantine Archaeology 2. Sheffield: Sheffield Academic Press.
Mazar, Benjamin. 1975. Dor and Rehov in an Egyptian List of Towns. Pages 154–59 in *Cities and Districts in Eretz-Israel*. Edited by B. Mazar. Jerusalem: Mossad Bialik. [Hebrew]
Mazow, Laura B. 2005. "Competing Material Culture: Philistine Settlement at Tel Miqne-Ekron in the Early Iron Age." Ph.D. diss., University of Arizona.
Mazzoni, Stefania. 1998. The Late Iron I and Early Iron II Levels. Pages 163–200 in Cecchini and Mazzoni 1998.
———. 2000. Syria and the Periodization of the Iron Age: A Cross-Cultural Perspective. Pages 31–60 in Bunnens 2000.
———. ed. 2002. *Tell Afis, Siria, 2000–2001*. Pisa: Universita degli Studi di Pisa.
Mazzoni, Stefania, and Serena M. Cecchini. 1995. Tell Afis (Siria) 1994: Rapporto preliminare. *Egitto e Vicino Oriente* 18:243–306.
Mazzoni, Stefania, Deborah Giannessi, Candida Felli, and Fabrizio Venturi. 1999–2000. Tell Afis, Siria 1999. *Egitto e Vicino Oriente* 22–23:5–103.
McClellan, Thomas L. 1975. "Quantitative Studies in the Iron Age Pottery of Palestine." Ph.D. diss., Philadelphia: University of Pennsylvania.
McGlade, James, and Sander van der Leeuw. 1997. Introduction: Archaeology and Non-linear Dynamics—New Approaches to Long-Term Change. Pages 1–31 in *Time, Process and Structured Transformation in Archaeology*. Edited by J. McGlade and S. E. Van der Leeuw. One World Archaeology. London: Routledge.
McGovern, Patrick. 1986. Ancient Ceramic Technology and Stylistic Change: Contrasting Studies from Southwest and Southeast Asia. Pages 33–52 in *Technology and Style*. Edited by W. D. Kingery. Ceramics and Civilisation 2. Columbus, Ohio: American Ceramic Society.
Mee, Christopher B. 1978. Aegean Trade and Settlement in Anatolia in the Second Millennium B.C. *AnSt* 28:121–56.
———. 1982. *Rhodes in the Bronze Age*. Warminster: Aris & Phillips.
———. 1988. A Mycenaean Thalassocracy in the Eastern Aegean? Pages 301–5 in French and Wardle 1988.
———. 1998. Anatolia and the Aegean in the Late Bronze Age. Pages 137–49 in *The Aegean and the Orient in the Second Millennium. Proceedings of the 50th Anniversary Symposium, Cincinnati, 18–20 April 1997*. Pages 137–49 in Cline and Harris-Cline 1998.
Meehl, Mark W., Trude Dothan, and Seymour Gitin. 2006. *Tel Miqne-Ekron Excavations 1995–1996: Field INE East Slope—Iron Age I (Early Philistine Period)*. Tel Miqne-Ekron Final Field Report Series 8. Jerusalem: W. F. Albright Institute of Archaeological Research and Institute of Archaeology, Hebrew University of Jerusalem.
Melas, Evie M. 1988. The Dodecanese and W. Anatolia in Prehistory: Interrelationships, Ethnicity and Political Geography. *AnSt* 38:109–20.

Mellink, Machteld. 1988. Archaeology in Anatolia. *AJA* 96:19–150.

Meriç, Recep. 2007. Ein Vorbericht über eine spätbronzezeitliche befestigte Höhensiedlung bei Metropolis in Ionien: Die Arzawa Stadt Puranda? Pages 27–36 in Cobet et al. 2007

Meriç, Recep, and Penelope Mountjoy. 2002. Mycenaean Pottery from Bademgediği Tepe (Puranda) in Ionia: A Preliminary Report. *IstMitt* 52: 79–98.

Merrillees, Robert. 1992. The Government of Cyprus in the Late Bronze Age. Pages 310–28 in part 3 of *Acta Cypria: Acts of an International Congress on Cypriote Archaeology Held in Göteborg on 22–24 August, 1991.* Edited by P. Åström. SIMA Pocket-Book 120. Jonsered: Åströms.

Metzger, Martin. 1993. *Kamid el-Loz 8: Die spätbronzezeitliche Tempelanlage. Die Kleinfunde.* Saarbrücker Beiträge zur Altertumskunde 40. Bonn: Habelt.

Michaelidou-Nicolaou, Ino. 1993. Nouveaux documents pour le syllabaire chypriotes. *Bulletin de correspondance hellénique* 117:346–47.

Mielke, Dirk Paul, Ulf-Dietrich Schoop, and Jürgen Seeher. 2006. *Strukturierung und Datierung in der hethitischen Archäologie: Voraussetzungen, Probleme, neue Ansätze, Internationaler Workshop, Istanbul, 26.–27. November 2004.* Byzas 4. Istanbul: Ege Yayinlari.

Miller, Robert. 1986. Elephants, Ivory and Charcoal: An Ecological Perspective. *BASOR* 264:29–43.

Mills, John, and Raymond White. 1989. The Identity of the Resins from the Late Bronze Age Shipwreck at Ulu Burun (Kas). *Archaeometry* 31:37–44.

Momigliano, Nicoletta. 2007. Kamares or Not Kamares? This Is [Not] the Question. Southeast Aegean Light-on-Dark (LOD) and Dark-on-Light (DOL) Pottery: Synchronisms, Production Centres, and Distribution. Pages 257–72 in *Middle Helladic Pottery and Synchronisms. Proceedings of the International Workshop Held at Salzburg, October 31st–November 2nd, 2004.* Edited by F. Felten, W. Gauss, and R. Smetana. Ägina-Kolonna 1; Contributions to the Chronology of the Eastern Mediterranean 14; Denkschriften der Gesamtakademie 42. Vienna: Österreichische Akademie der Wissenschaften.

Mommsen, Hans, Anna D'Agata, and Assaf Yasur-Landau. 2009. Neutron Activation Analysis of Mycenaean IIIC-Style Pottery. Pages 510–18 in Panitz-Cohen and Mazar 2009.

Mommsen, Hans, Dieter Hertel, and Penelope Mountjoy. 2001. Neutron Activation Analysis of the Pottery from Troy in the Berlin Schliemann Collection. *AA* 2001:169–211.

Monchambert, Jean-Yves. 1983. La céramique de fabrication locale à Ougarit à la fin du Bronze Récent. *Syria* 60:25–45.

———. 1996. Du Mycenien IIIC a Ougarit. *Orient-Express* 2:45–46.

Monte, Giuseppe F. del, ed. 1992. *Die Orts- und Gewässernamen der hethitischen Texte, Supplement.* Vol. 6/2 of *Répertoire géographique des textes cunéiformes.* Beihefte zum Tübinger Atlas des Vorderen Orients, Reihe B, Geisteswissenschaften 7/6. Wiesbaden: Reichert.

Monte, Giuseppe F. del, and Johann Tischler, eds. 1978. *Die Orts-und Gewässernamen der hethitischen Texte.* Vol. 6 of *Répertoire géographique des textes cuneiforms.* Beihefte zum Tübinger Atlas des Vorderen Orients, Reihe B, Geisteswissenschaften 7/6. Wiesbaden: Reichert.

Mook, Margaret, and William Coulson. 1997. Late Minoan IIIC Pottery from the Kastro at Kavousi. Pages 337–70 in Hallager and Hallager 1997.

Moorey, Peter R. S. 2001. The Mobility of Artisans and Opportunities for Technological Transfer. Pages 1–13 in *The Social Context of Technological Change*. Edited by A. J. Shortland. Oxford: Oxbow Books.

Moran, William L. 1992. *The Amarna Letters*. Baltimore: Johns Hopkins University Press.

Mori, Masao, and Sachihiro Omura. 1995. A Preliminary Report on the Excavations at Kaman-Kalehöyük in Turkey (1989–1993). Pages 1–42 in *Essays on Ancient Anatolia and Its Surrounding Civilizations*. Bulletin of the Middle Eastern Culture Center in Japan 8. Edited by T. Mikasa. Wiesbaden: Harrassowitz.

Morricone, Luigi. 1965–1966. Eleona e Langada: Sepolcreti della Tarda Età del Bronzo a Coo. *Annuario della Scuola Archeologica Italiana di Atene* 43–44 (n.s. 27–28):5–311.

———. 1972–1973. Coo: scavi e scoperte nel "Serraglio" e in località minori (1935–1943). *Annuario della Scuola Archeologica Italiana di Atene* 50–51 (n.s. 34–35):139–396.

Morricone, Maria Luisa. 1979–1980. Vasi della Collezione Akavi di Rodi. *Annuario della Scuola Archeologica Italiana di Atene* 57–58 (n.s. 41–42):217–342.

Morris, Ellen F. 2005. *The Architecture of Imperialism: Military Bases and the Evolution of Foreign Policy in Egypt's New Kingdom*. Probleme der Ägyptologie 22. Leiden: Brill.

Morris, Ian, and Barry Powell, eds. 1997. *A New Companion to Homer*. Mnemosyne, Bibliotheca Classica Batava Supplementum 163. Leiden: Brill.

Mountjoy, Penelope. 1986. Mycenaean Decorated Pottery: A Guide to Identification. SIMA 73. Göteborg: Åströms.

———. 1993. *Mycenaean Pottery: An Introduction*. Oxford University Committee for Archaeology Monograph 36. Oxford: Oxford University Committee for Archaeology.

———. 1995a. Mycenaean Pottery from South Rhodes. *Proceedings of the Danish Institute at Athens* 1:21–35.

———. 1995b. Thorikos Mine No. 3: The Mycenaean Pottery. *Annual of the British School at Athens Supplement* 90:195–227.

———. 1997a. Local Mycenaean Pottery at Troia. *Studia Troica* 7:259–67.

———. 1997b. The Destruction of the Palace at Pylos Reconsidered. *Annual of the British School at Athens Supplement* 92:109–37.

———. 1997–1998. An Octopus Stirrup Jar from Kalymnos. *Opuscula Atheniensia* 22-23:152–54.

———. 1998. The East Aegean–West Anatolian Interface in the Late Bronze Age: Mycenaeans and the Kingdom of Ahhiyawa. *AnSt* 48:33–67.

———. 1999a. The Destruction of Troy VIh. *Studia Troica* 9:253–93.

———. 1999b. Late Minoan IIIC/Late Helladic IIIC: Chronology and Terminology. Pages 511–16 in *Meletemata: Studies in Aegean Archaeology Presented to Malcolm H. Wiener as He Enters His 65th Year*. Aegaeum 20. Edited by P. Betancourt, V. Karageorghis, R. Laffineur, and W.-D. Niemeier. Liège: Université de Liège.

———. 1999c. *Regional Mycenaean Decorated Pottery*. Rahden, Westfalen: Marie Leidorf.

———. 1999d. Troy VII Reconsidered. *Studia Troica* 9:295–346.

———. 2001. *Mycenaean Pottery: An Introduction*. Oxford University School of Archaeology Monograph 36. Oxford: Oxford University School of Archaeology.

———. 2004. Miletos: A Note. *Annual of the British School at Athens* 99:189–200.

———. 2005a. Mycenaean Connections with the Near East in LH IIIC: Ships and Sea Peoples. Pages 423–27 in Laffineur and Greco 2005.

———. 2005b. The Mycenaean Pottery from the 1934–1939 Excavations at Tarsus. Pages

83–134 in *Field Seasons 2001–2003 of the Tarsus-Gözlükule Interdisciplinary Research Project*. Edited by A. Özyar. Istanbul: Ege Yayinlari.

———. 2006. Mycenaean Pictorial Pottery from Anatolia in the Transitional LH IIIB2–LH IIIC Early and the LH IIIC Phases. Pages 107–22 in *Pictorial Pursuits: Figurative Painting on Mycenaean and Geometric Pottery. Papers from Two Seminars at the Swedish Institute at Athens in 1999 & 2001*. Edited by E. Rystedt and B. Wells. Acta Instituti Atheniensis Regni Sueciase 4:53. Stockholm: Swedish Institute at Athens.

———. 2007a. A Definition of LH IIIC Middle. Pages 221–42 in *LH III Chronology and Synchronisms II: LH III C Middle Proceedings of the International Workshop Held at the Austrian Academy of Sciences at Vienna, October 29th and 30th, 2004*. Edited by S. Deger-Jalkotzy and M. Zavadil. Philosophisch-Historische Klasse Dendschriften 362; Veröffentlichungen der Mykenischen Kommission 28. Vienna: Österreichische Akacemie der Wissenschaften.

———. 2007b. The Dating of the Early LC IIIA Phase at Enkomi. Pages 583–94 in Bietak and Czerny 2007.

———. 2009. Cyprus and the East Aegean: LH IIIC Pottery Connections. Pages 59–71 in *Cyprus and the East Aegean: Intercultural Contacts from 3000 to 500 BC. An International Archaeological Symposium Held at Pythagoreion, Samos, October 17th–18th 2008*. Edited by V. Karageorghis and O. Kouka. Nicosia: A. G. Leventis Foundation.

———. 2010. A Note on the Mixed Origins of Some Philistine Pottery. *BASOR* 359:1–12.

Muhly, James D. 1982. The Nature of Trade in the LBA Eastern Mediterranean. Pages 251–69 in Muhly, Maddin, and Karageorghis 1982.

———. 1989. The Organization of the Copper Industry in Late Bronze Age Cyprus. Pages 298–314 in Peltenburg 1989.

———. 1996. The Significance of Metals in the Late Bronze Age Economy of Cyprus. Pages 45–60 in *The Development of the Cypriot Economy from the Prehistoric Period to the Present Day*. Edited by V. Karageorghis and D. Michaelides. Nicosia: University of Cyprus: Bank of Cyprus.

Muhly, James D., Robert Maddin, and Vassos Karageorghis, eds. 1982. *Early Metallurgy in Cyprus 4000–500 B.C: Acts of the International Archaeological Symposium, Larnaca, Cyprus, 1–6 June 1981*. Nicosia: Pierides Foundation.

Muhly, James D., Tamara S. Wheeler, and Robert Maddin. 1977. The Cape Gelidonya Shipwreck and the Bronze Age Metals Trade in the Eastern Mediterranean. *Journal of Field Archaeology* 4:353–62.

Müller-Karpe, Andreas. 1996. Untersuchungen in Kuşaklı 1995. *MDOG* 128:69–94.

Müller-Scheeßel, Nils. 1998. "Archaeology is nothing if it is not critique"—Zum Archäologieverständnis von Michael Shanks und Christopher Tilley. Pages 243–71 in *Theorie in der Archäologie: Zur englischsprachigen Diskussion*. Edited by M. K. H. Eggert and U. Veit. Münster: Waxmann.

Münger, Stefan. 2003. Egyptian Stamp-Seal Amulets and Their Implications for the Chronology of the Early Iron Age. *TA* 30:66–82.

Muscarella, Oscar W. 1995. The Iron Age Background to the Formation of the Phrygian State. *BASOR* 299/300:91–101.

Myres, John L., and Max Ohnefalsch-Richter. 1899. *A Catalogue of the Cyprus Museum*. Oxford: Clarendon.

Na'aman, Nadav. 1974. Sennacherib's "Letter to God" on His Campaign to Judah. *BASOR* 214:25–39.

———. 1986. Habiru and Hebrews: The Transfer of a Social Term to the Literary Sphere. *JNES* 45:271–88.
———. 1991. The Kingdom of Judah under Josiah. *TA* 18:3–71.
———. 1994. Hezekiah and Kings of Assyria. *TA* 21:235–54.
———. 1996. Sources and Composition in the History of David. Pages 170–86 in *The Origins of the Ancient Israelite States*. Edited by V. Fritz and P. R. Davies. JSOTSup 228. Sheffield: Sheffield Academic Press.
———. 1997. The Network of Canaanite Late Bronze Kingdoms and the City of Ashdod. *UF* 29:599–626.
———. 2000. The Contribution of the Trojan Grey Ware from Lachish and Tel Miqne-Ekron to the Chronology of the Philistine Monochrome Pottery. *BASOR* 317:1–8.
———. 2002. In Search of Reality Behind the Account of David's Wars with Israel's Neighbours. *IEJ* 52:200–24.
Naveh, Joseph. 1985. Writing and Scripts in Seventh Century BCE Philistia: The New Evidence from Tell Jemmeh. *IEJ* 35:8–21.
———. 1998. Achish-Ikausu in the Light of the Ekron Dedication. *BASOR* 310:35–37.
Naville, Edouard, and Francis Griffith. 1890. *The Mound of the Jew and the City of Onias: Belbeis, Samanood, Abusir, Tukh el Karmus, 1887. The Antiquities of Tell el Yahûdîyeh and Miscellaneous Work in Lower Egypt during the Years 1887–1888*. Seventh Memoir of the Egypt Exploration Fund. London: Kegan Paul.
Neeman, Yehudah, Shlomo Sender, and Eldad Oren. 2000. *Archaeological Survey of Israel—Map of Michmoret (52); Map of Hadera (53)*. Archaeological Survey of Israel; Israel Antiquities Authority Publications; Publications of the Archaeological Survey of Israel. Jerusalem: Israel Antiquities Authority.
Negbi, Ora. 1974. The Continuity of the Canaanite Bronzework of the Late Bronze Age into the Early Iron Age. *TA* 1:159–72.
———. 1986. The Climax of Urban Development in Bronze Age Cyprus. *RDAC* 1986:97–121.
———. 1991. Were There Sea Peoples in the Central Jordan Valley at the Transition from the Bronze Age to the Iron Age? *TA* 18:205–43.
Nelson, Janet L. 1999. *Rulers and Ruling Families in Early Medieval Europe: Alfred, Charles the Bald, and Others*. Variorum Collected Studies CS657. Aldershot: Ashgate.
Neve, Peter. 1987. Die Ausgrabungen in Boğazköy-Hattuša 1986. *AA* 1987:381–412.
———. 1989. Die Ausgrabungen in Boğazköy-Hattuša 1988. *AA* 1989:320–32.
———. 1993. *Hattuša—Stadt der Götter und Tempel: Neue Ausgrabungen in der Hauptstadt der Hethiter*. Mainz: Zabern.
———. 1999. *Die Bebauung im zentralen Tempelviertel*. Vol. 1 of *Die Oberstadt von Hattuša: Die Bauwerke*. Boğazköy-Hattuša 16. Berlin: Mann.
Nichols, Johanna. 1998. Modeling Ancient Population Structures and Movement in Linguistics. *Annual Review of Anthropology* 26:359–84.
Nicolaou, Kyriakos. 1976. *The Historical Topography of Kition*. SIMA 43. Göteborg: Åströms.
Niditch, Susan. 1996. *Oral World and Written Word: Ancient Israelite Literature*. Library of Ancient Israel. Louisville, Ky.: Westminster John Knox.
Niemann, Hermann M. 1993. *Herrschaft, Königtum und Staat: Skizzen zur soziokulturellen Entwicklung im monarchischen Israel*. Forschungen zum Alten Testament 6. Tübingen: Mohr.

———. 1997. The Socio-Political Shadow Cast by the Biblical Solomon. Pages 252–99 in *The Age of Solomon: Scholarship at the Turn of the Millennium*. Edited by L. K. Handy. SHCANE 11. Leiden: Brill.

———. 1998. Kein Ende des Büchermachens in Israel und Juda (Koh 12,12)—Wann begann es? *BK* 53:127–34.

———. 1999. Zorah, Eshtaol, Beth Shemesh and Dan's Migration to the South: A Region and Its Traditions in the Late Bronze and Iron Ages. *JSOT* 86:25–48.

———. 2001. Von Oberflächen, Schichten und Strukturen. Was leistet die Archäologie für die Erforschung der Geschichte Israels und Judas? Pages 79–121 in *Steine–Bilder-Texte: Historische Evidenz außerbiblischer und biblischer Quellen*. Edited by C. Hardmeier. Arbeiten zur Bibel und ihrer Geschichte 5. Leipzig: Evangelische Verlagsanstalt.

______. 2003. Pentapolis. Pages 1088–89 in vol. 6 of *Religion in Geschichte und Gegenwart: Handwörterbuch für Theologie und Religionswissenschaft*. Edited by H. G. Betz, D. S. Browning, B. Janowski, and E. Jüngel. 9 vols. 4th ed. Tübingen: Mohr Siebeck.

Niemeier, Barbara, and Wolf-Dietrich Niemeier. 1997. Milet 1994–1995: Projekt "Minoisch-mykenisches bis protogeometrisches Milet". Zielsetzung und Grabungen auf dem Stadionhügel und am Athenatempel. *AA* 1997:189–248.

Niemeier, Wolf-Dietrich. 1998. The Mycenaeans in Western Anatolia and the Problem of the Origins of the Sea Peoples. Pages 17–65 in Gitin, Mazar, and Stern 1998.

______. 2005, Minoans, Mycenaeans, Hittites and Ionians in Western Asia Minor. New Excavations in Bronze Age Miletus-Millawanda. Pages 1–36 in *The Greeks in the East*. Edited by A. Villing. British Museum Research and Publication 157. London: British Museum.

______. 2007a. Milet von den Anfängen menschlicher Besiedlung bis zur Ionischen Wanderung. Pages 3–20 in Cobet et al. 2007.

______. 2007b. Westkleinasien und Ägäis von den Anfängen bis zur Ionischen Wanderung: Topographie, Geschichte und Beziehungen nach dem archäologischen Befund und den hehitischen Quellen. Pages 37–96 in Cobet et al. 2007.

______. 2009. Milet und Karien vom Neolithikum bis zu den 'Dunklen Jahrhunderten.' Mythos und Archäologie. Pages 7–25 in *Die Karer und die Anderen: Internationales Kolloquium an der Freien Universität Berlin, 13. bis 15. Oktober 2005*. Edited by F. Rumscheid. Bonn: Habelt.

Niemeyer, Hans-Georg. 2000. The Early Phoenician City-States on the Mediterranean: Archaeological Elements for Their Description. Pages 89–115 in *A Comparative Study of Thirty City-State Cultures*. Edited by M. H. Hansen. Historik-filosofiske Skrifter 21. Copenhagen: Reitzels.

Niklasson, Karin. 1983. Tomb 23: A Shaft-Grave of the Late Cypriote III Period. Pages 169–213 in *Hala Sultan Tekke 8: Excavations 1971–79*. Edited by P. Åström, E. Åström, A. Hatziantoniou, K. Niklasson, and U. Öbrink. SIMA 45:8. Göteborg: Åströms.

Niklasson-Sönnerby, Karin. 1987. Late Cypriote III Shaft Graves: Burial Customs of the Last Phase of the Bronze Age. Pages 219–25 in *Thanatos: les coutumes funéraires en Égée à l'âge du Bronze. Actes colloque de Liège, 21–23 avril 1986*. Edited by R. Laffineur. Aegaeum 1. Liège: Histoire de l'art et archéologie de la Grèce antique, Université de Liège.

Nissenbaum, Arie, and Ann E. Killebrew. 1995. Stable Isotopes of Carbon and Oxygen as a Possible New Tool for Estimating Firing Temperatures of Ancient Pottery. *Israel Journal of Chemistry* 35:131–36.

Noort, Edward. 1994. *Die Seevölker in Palästina*. Palaestina Antiqua 8. Kampen: Kok Pharos.

Nougayrol, Jean, Emmanuel Laroche, Charles Virolleaud, and Claude F.-A. Schaeffer, eds. 1968. *Ugaritica V*. Mission de Ras Shamra 16. Paris: Geuthner.

Öbrink, Ulla. 1979. *Hala Sultan Tekke 5: Excavations in Area 22, 1971–1973 and 1975–1978*. SIMA 45:5. Göteborg: Åströms.

Ofer, Avi. 2001. The Monarchic Period in the Judaean Highland: A Spatial Overview. Pages 14–37 in A. Mazar and Mathias 2001.

Ohata, Kiyoshi. 1970. *Tel Zeror III: Report of the Excavation, Third Season 1966*. Tokyo: Society for Near Eastern Studies in Japan.

Ohata, Kiyoshi, and Moshe Kochavi. 1967–1970. *Tel Zeror I–III: Preliminary Report of the Excavation, 1st–3rd Seasons 1964–1966*. Tokyo: Society for Near Eastern Studies in Japan.

Omura, Sachihiro. 1991. 1990 Yılı Kaman-Kalehöyük Kazısı. *Kazı Sonuçları Toplantısı* 13:319–36.

———. 1996. A Preliminary Report on the Ninth Excavation at Kaman-Kalehöyük (1994). Pages 86–134 in *Essays on Ancient Anatolia and Syria: Studies in the Second and Third Millennium B.C.* Edited by T. Mikasa. Wiesbaden: Harrassowitz.

Oren, Eliezer. 1973. *The Northern Cemetery of Beth Shan*. Museum Monograph of the University Museum of the University of Pennsylvania. Leiden: Brill.

———. 1993. Haror, Tel. *NEAEHL* 2:580–84.

———, ed. 2000. *The Sea Peoples and Their World: A Reassessment*. University Museum Monograph 108; University Museum Symposium Series 11. Philadelphia: University Museum, University of Pennsylvania.

Oren, Eliezer, and Shmuel Ahituv, eds. 2002. *Aharon Kempinski Memorial Volume: Studies in Archaeology and Related Disciplines*. Beer-Sheva 15. Beersheva: Ben Gurion University of the Negev Press.

Ornan, Tallay. 1986. *A Man and His Land: Highlights from the Moshe Dayan Collection*. Israel Museum Catalogue 270. Jerusalem: Israel Museum.

Orni, Efraim, and Elisha Efrat. 1980. *Geography of Israel*. 3rd ed. Jerusalem: Israel Universities Press.

Otten, Heinrich. 1988. *Die Bronzetafel aus Boğazköy: Ein Staatsvertrag Tuthalijas IV*. Studien zu den Boğazköy Texten 1. Wiesbaden: Harrassowitz.

Özdoğan, Mehmet. 1993. The Second Millennium of the Marmara Region: The Perspective of a Prehistorian on a Controversial Historical Issue. *IstMitt* 43:151–63.

———. 1998. Early Iron Age in Eastern Thrace and the Megalithic Monuments. Pages 29–40 in *Thracians and Phrygians: Problems of Parallelism. Proceedings of an International Symposium on the Archaeology, History and Ancient Languages of Thrace and Phrygia: Ankara, 3–4 June 1995*. Edited by N. Tuna, Z. Aktüre, and M. Lynch. Ankara: Centre for Research and Assessment of the Historic Environment: Faculty of Architecture, Middle East Technical University Press.

Özgüç, Nimet. 1955. Fırakdin Eserleri/Finds at Fırakdin. *Belleten* 19:295–307.

Özgüç, Tahsin. 1988. *İnandıktepe: Eski Hitit Çağında. Önemli Bir Kült Merkezi*. Türk Tarih Kurumu Yayınları 43. Ankara: Türk Tarih Kurumu Basımevi.

———. 2002. *Die Hethiter und ihr Reich: das Volk der 1000 Götter*. Bonn: Theiss.

Özgüç, Tahsin, and Nimet Özgüç. 1949. *Karahöyük Hafriyatı Raporu/Ausgrabungen in Karahöyük*. Ankara: Türk Tarih Kurumu Basımevi.

Özgünel, Coşkun. 1996. *Die mykenische Keramik in Anatolien*. Asia Minor Studien 23. Bonn: Habelt.

Özkan, Turhan, Hayat Erkanal, and Hakan Kale. 1999. *Tahtalı Barajı Kurtarma Kazısı Projesi*. Izmir: T.C. Kültür Bakanlığı.

Özsait, Mehmut, and Nesrin Özsait. 2002a. Amasya'da „Erken Demir Çağ" Keramikleri. *Arkeoloji ve Sanat* 107:17–24.

———. 2002b. Les céramiques du Fer Ancien ("L'âge obscur") dans la région d'Amasya. *Anatolia Antiqua* 10:79–95.

Özyar, Aslı. 2005. *Field Seasons 2001–2003 of the Tarsus-Gözlükule Interdisciplinary Research Project*. Istanbul: Ege Yayınları.

Palaima, Thomas. 1991. The Advent of the Greek Alphabet on Cyprus: A Competition of Scripts. Pages 449–71 in Baurain, Bonnet, and Krings 1991.

Pamir, Hatice. 2005. The Orontes Delta Survey. Pages 67–98 in *Surveys in the Plain of Antioch and Orontes Delta, Turkey, 1995–2002*. Vol. 1 of *The Amuq Valley Regional Projects*. Edited by K. A. Yener. OIP 131. Chicago: Oriental Institute of the University of Chicago.

Pamir, Hatice, and Shin'ichi Nishiyama. 2002. The Orontes Delta Survey: Archaeological Investigation of Ancient Trade Stations/Settlements. *Ancient West and East* 1:294–314.

Panitz-Cohen, Nava. 2009. The Local Canaanite Pottery. Pages 195–433 in Panitz-Cohen and Mazar 2009.

Panitz-Cohen, Nava, and Amihai Mazar, eds. 2009. *The 13th—11th Centuries BCE Strata in Areas N and S*. Vol. 3 of *Excavations at Tel Beth-Shean, 1989–1996*. Jerusalem: Israel Exploration Society: Institute of Archaeology, Hebrew University of Jerusalem.

Papasavvas, Giorios. 2001. *Bronze Stands from Cyprus and the Aegean*. Nicosia: A. G. Leventis Foundation.

Parry, Milton. 1953–1979. *Serbocroatian Heroic Songs*. 3 vols. Cambridge, Mass.: Harvard University Press.

Parzinger, Hermann, and Rosa Sanz. 1992. *Die Oberstadt von Hattuša: Hethitische Keramik aus dem zentralen Tempelviertel. Funde aus den Grabungen 1982–1987*. Boğazköy-Hattuša 15. Berlin: Mann.

Pedde, Friedhelm. 2000. *Vorderasiatische Fibeln: von der Levante bis Iran*. Abhandlungen der Deutschen Orient-Gesellschaft 24. Saarbrücken: Saarbrücker Druckerei und Verlag.

Peden, Alexander J. 1994. *Egyptian Historical Inscriptions of the Twentieth Dynasty*. Documenta Mundi Aegyptiaca 3. Jonsered: Åströms.

Pedrazzi, Tatiana. 2002. Area E: l'occupazione del Bronzo Tardo II–Ferro I: Il settore Nord. Pages 33–38 in *Tell Afis, Siria, 2000–2001*. Edited by S. Mazzoni. Pisa: Università degli Studi di Pisa.

Pelon, Olivier. 1994. The Site of Porsuk and the Beginning of the Iron Age in Southern Cappadocia. Pages 157–62 in Çilingiroğlu and French 1994.

Peltenburg, Edgar J. 1996. From Isolation to State Formation in Cyprus, c. 3500–1500 BC. Pages 17–43 in *The Development of the Cypriot Economy from the Prehistoric Period to the Present Day*. Edited by V. Karageorghis and D. Michaelides. Nicosia: Printed by Lithographica.

———, ed. 1989. *Early Society in Cyprus*. Edinburgh: Edinburgh University Press in Association with The National Museums of Scotland and The A. G. Leventis Foundation.

Perlman, Isadore, Frank Asaro, and Trude Dothan. 1973. Provenance of the Deir el-Balah Coffins. *IEJ* 23:147–51.

Petrie, William M. Flinders. 1889. *Tanis*. Memoir of the Egypt Exploration Fund 2/4. London: Trübner.

———. 1904. *Ehnasya*. Memoir of the Egypt Exploration Fund 26. London: Egypt Exploration Fund.

———. 1907. *Gizeh and Rifeh*. British School of Archaeology in Egypt and Egyptian Research Account, Thirteenth Year 13. London: British School of Archaeology in Egypt.

———. 1930. *Beth Pelet I (Tell Fara)*. Publications of the British School of Archaeology in Egypt and Egyptian Research Account 48. London: British School of Archaeology in Egypt.

Petrie, William M. Flinders, Alexander Murray, and Francis Griffith. 1888. *Nebesheh (Am) and Defenneh (Tahpanhes)*. Memoir of the Egypt Exploration Fund 5. London: Trübner.

Philip, Graham. 1999. Complexity and Diversity in the Southern Levant During the Third Millennium BC: The Evidence of Khirbet Kerak Ware. *Journal of Mediterranean Archaeology* 12:26–57.

Phythian-Adams, William. 1921. Stratigraphical Sections. *PEFQS* 53:163–69.

———. 1923. Report on the Stratification of Askalon. *PEFQS* 55:60–84.

Piêd, Lione du. 2006–2007. The Early Iron Age in the Northern Levant: Continuity and Change in the Pottery Assemblages from Ras el-Bassit and Ras Ibn Hani. *Scripta Mediterranea* 27–28:161–85.

———. 2011. Early Iron Age Society in the Northern Levant: Architecture, Pottery and Finds. Pages 219–36 in Karageorghis and Kouka 2011.

Pieridou, Angelike. 1973. *O protogeometrikos rythmos en Kypro*. Bibliothiki tis en Athinais Archaiologikis Etaireias 77. Athens: Athinais Archaiologikis Etaireias.

Pilides, Despo. 1991. Handmade Burnished Wares of the Late Bronze Age: Toward a Clearer Classification System. Pages 139–50 in Barlow, Bolger, and Kling 1991.

———. 1994. *Handmade Burnished Wares of the Late Bronze Age in Cyprus*. SIMA 105. Jonsered: Åströms.

———. 2000. *Pithoi of the Late Bronze Age in Cyprus: Types from the Major Sites of the Period*. Nicosia: Department of Antiquities, Cyprus.

Ploug, Gunhild. 1973. *Sukas 2: The Aegean, Corinthian and Eastern Greek Pottery and Terracottas*. Copenhagen: Munksgaard.

Popham, Mervyn. 1965. Some Late Minoan Pottery from Crete. *Annual of the British School at Athens* 60:316–42.

———. 1984. *The Minoan Unexplored Mansion at Knossos*. Annual of the British School at Athens Suppl. 17. Athens: British School of Archaeology at Athens.

Popham, Mervyn, and Elizabeth Milburn. 1971. The Late Helladic IIIC Pottery of Xeropolis (Lefkandi): A Summary. *Annual of the British School at Athens* 66:333–52.

Popham, Mervyn R., and L. Hugh Sackett, eds. 1968. *Excavations at Lefkandi, Euboea, 1964–1966: A Preliminary Report*. London: Thames & Hudson.

Popham, Mervyn, L. Hugh Sackett, and Petros G. Themelis, eds. 1979–1980. *Lefkandi I:*

The Iron Age. British School of Archaeology at Athens Suppl. 11. London: Thames & Hudson for the British School of Archaeology at Athens.

Porat, Naomi. 1989. "Composition of Pottery—Application to the Study of the Interrelations between Canaan and Egypt During the Third Millennium B.C." Ph.D. diss., Hebrew University of Jerusalem.

Postgate, J. Nicholas. 1998. Kilise Tepe 1996: A Summary of the Principal Results. *Kazı Sonuçları Toplantısı* 19:209–26.

Postgate, J. Nicholas, and David Thomas. 2007. *Excavations at Kilise Tepe, 1994–98: From Bronze Age to Byzantine in Western Cilicia*. 2 vols. British Institute of Archaeology at Ankara Monograph 30. London: British Institute at Ankara; Cambridge: McDonald Institute for Archaeological Research.

Price Williams, David. 1977. *The Tombs of the Middle Bronze Age II Period from the "500" Cemetery at Tell Fara (South)*. Institute of Archaeology, Occasional Publication 1. London: Institute of Archaeology.

Pritchard, James B. 1969. *Ancient Near Eastern Texts Relating to the Old Testament*. 3rd ed. Princeton: Princeton University Press.

———. 1980. *The Cemetery at Tell es-Saʿidiyeh, Jordan*. University Museum Monograph 41. Philadelphia: University Museum, University of Pennsylvania.

———, ed. 1975. *Sarepta: A Preliminary Report on the Iron Age: Excavations of the University Museum of the University of Pennsylvania, 1970–72*. Museum Monographs. Philadelphia: University Museum, University of Pennsylvania.

Pulak, Cemal. 1997. The Uluburun Shipweck. Pages 233–62 in Swiny, Hohlfelder, and Swiny 1997.

Raban, Avner. 1987. The Harbor of the Sea Peoples at Dor. *BA* 50:118–26.

———. 1988. The Constructive Maritime Role of the Sea Peoples in the Levant. Pages 261–94 in Heltzer and Lipiński 1988.

———. 1995. Dor-Yam: Maritime and Coastal Installations at Dor in Their Geomorphological and Stratigraphic Context. Pages 285–354 in *Areas A and C: Introduction and Stratigraphy*. Vol. 1A of *Excavations at Dor, Final Report*. Edited by E. Stern. Qedem Reports 1. Jerusalem: Institute of Archaeology, Hebrew University of Jerusalem in Cooperation with the Israel Exploration Society.

Raban-Gerstel, Noa, Guy Bar-Oz, Irit Zohar, Ilan Sharon, Ayelet Gilboa. 2008. Early Iron Age Dor (Israel): A Faunal Perspective. *BASOR* 349:25–59.

Rahmstorf, Lorenz. 2003a. Clay Spools from Tiryns and Other Contemporary Sites: An Indication of Foreign Influence in LH III C? Pages 397–415 in *The Periphery of the Mycenaean World: 2nd International Interdisciplinary Colloquium, 26–30 September 1999, Lamia*. Edited by N. Kyparissi-Apostolika and M. Papakonstantinou. Athens: Ministry of Culture.

———. 2003b. The Identification of Early Helladic Weights and Their Wider Implications. *Aegeum* 24:293–99.

———. 2008. *Kleinfunde aus Tiryns: Terrakotten, Stein, Bein und Glas/Fayence vornehmlich der späteren Bronzezeit*. Tiryns 16. Wiesbaden: Reichert.

———. 2011. Handmade Pots and Crumbling Loomweights: "Barbarian" Elements in the Eastern Mediterranean in the Last Quarter of the 2nd Millennium BC. Pages 315–30 in Karageorghis and Kouka 2011.

Rainey, Anson F. 1975. The Identification of Philistine Gath: A Problem in Source Analysis for Historical Geography. *ErIsr* 12:63*–76*.

———. 1978. *El-Amarna Tablets, 359–379*. 2nd rev. ed. Suppl. to *Die El-Amarna-Tafeln mit Einleitung und Erläuterungen*, by. J. A. Knudtzon. AOAT 8. Kevelaer: Butzon und Bercker: Neukirchen-Vluyn: Neukirchener.

———. 1980. The Administrative Division of the Shephelah. *TA* 4:194–202.

———. 1982. Toponymic Problems. *TA* 9:130–36.

———. 1983. The Biblical Shephelah of Judah. *BASOR* 251:1–22.

———. 1995. Unruly Elements in Late Bronze Canaanite Society. Pages 481–96 in *Pomegranates and Golden Bells: Studies in Biblical, Jewish, and Near Eastern Ritual, Law, and Literature in Honor of Jacob Milgrom*. Edited by D. P. Wright, D. N. Freedman, and A. Hurvitz. Winona Lake, Ind.: Eisenbrauns.

Ranke, Hermann. 1935. *Verzeichnis der Namen*. Vol. 1 of *Die Ägyptischen Personennamen*. Glückstadt: Augustin.

Redford, Donald B. 1992. *Egypt, Canaan, and Israel in Ancient Times*. Princeton: Princeton University Press.

———. 2000. Egypt and Western Asia in the Late New Kingdom: An Overview. Pages 1–20 in Oren 2000.

Reed, William L. 1964. *The Excavation at Dibon (Dhibân) in Moab: The Second Campaign, 1952*. AASOR 36–37. New Haven, Conn.: Yale University Press.

Reese, Donald S. 2002. On the Incised Scapulae from the East Mediterranean and the Near East. *Bonner zoologische Beiträge* 50/3:183–98.

Rethemiotakis, George. 1997. Late Minoan III Pottery from Kastelli Pediadha. Pages 305–36 in Hallager and Hallager 1997.

Rice, Prudence. 1984. Change and Conservatism in Pottery-Producing Systems. Pages 231–88 in *The Many Dimensions of Pottery: Ceramics in Archaeology and Anthropology*. Edited by S. E. van der Leeuw and A. C. Pritchard. Amsterdam: University of Amsterdam.

———. 1987. *Pottery Analysis: A Sourcebook*. Chicago: University of Chicago.

Riis, Poul J. 1948. *Hama II.3: Fouilles et recherches de la Fondation Carlsberg, 1931–1938: les cimetières à crémation*. Nationalmuseets skrifter, Større beretninger 2:3. Copenhagen: Nordisk.

———. 1961–1962. L'activité de la mission archéologique danoise sur la côte phénicienne en 1960. *Les Annales archéologiques de Syrie* 11–12:133–44.

———. 1973. The Mycenaean Expansion in the Light of the Danish Excavations at Hama and Sukas. Pages 198–206 in Dikaios 1973.

Riis, Poul J., Jørgen Jensen, Marie-Louise Buhl, and Benedikt Otzen. 1996. *Sukas X: The Bronze and Early Iron Age Remains at the Southern Harbour*. Publications of the Carlsberg Expedition to Phoenicia 12; Historisk-filosofiske skrifter 17. Copenhagen: Kongelige Danske Videnskabernes Selskab.

Rohde, Elisabeth. 1981. Antike Funde mit thrakischen Bezügen. Pages 40–49 in *Troja und Thrakien: Annäherung an eine Kultur. Kleiner Führer durch die Ausstellung Troja und Thrakien. Museum für Ur- und Frühgeschichte, Stattliche Museen zu Berlin, anlässlich der gemeinsamen Ausstellung mit dem Historischen Institut und Museum der Akademie der Wissenschaften der VR Bulgarien*. Edited by E. Hühns. Berlin: Museum für Ur- und Frühgeschichte

Rosen, Arlene M. Unpublished report. Miqne-Ekron Geoarchaeological Report on the 1984, '85, and '86 Seasons.

Rothenberg, Benno. 1972. *Timna: Valley of the Biblical Copper Mines*. New Aspects of Antiquity. London: Thames & Hudson.

———. 1988. *The Egyptian Mining Temple at Timna*. Researches in the Arabah 1; Metal in History 2. London: Institute for Archaeo-Metallurgical Studies and the Institute of Archaeology, University College.

Routledge, Bruce E. 2004. *Moab in the Iron Age: Hegemony, Polity, Archaeology*. Archaeology, Culture, and Society. Philadephia: University of Pennsylvania Press.

Rudolph, Wilhelm. 1974. *Joel, Amos, Obadja, Jona*. Kommentar zum Alten Testament 13.2. Gütersloh: Gütersloher Verlagshaus.

Rutherford, Robert B. 1999. Homer for the New Millennium. *Classical Review* 49:337–41.

Rutter, Jeremy. 1974. "The Late Helladic IIIB and IIIC Periods at Korakou and Gonia in the Corinthia." Ph.D. diss., University of Pennsylvania.

———. 1975. Ceramic Evidence for Northern Intruders in Southern Greece at the Beginning of the Late Helladic IIIC Period. *AJA* 79:17–32.

———. 1977. Late Helladic IIIC Pottery and Some Historical Implications. Pages 1–20 in *Symposium on the Dark Ages in Greece*. Edited by E. N. Davis. New York: Archaeological Institute of America, New York Society: Hunter College.

———. 1990. Some Comments on Interpreting the Dark-Surfaced Handmade Burnished Pottery of the 13th and 12th Century BC Aegean. *Journal of Mediterranean Archaeology* 3:29–49.

———. 1992. Cultural Novelties in the Post-Palatial Aegean World: Indices of Vitality or Decline? Pages 61–78 in Ward and Joukowski 1992.

———. 2000. The Short-Necked Amphora of the Post-Palatial Mesara. Pages 177–88 in *Proceedings of the 8th International Cretological Congress*. Edited by A. Karetsou. Heraklion: Society of Cretan Historical Studies.

Sackett, L. Hugh, and Mervyn Popham. 1965. Excavations at Palaikastro VI. *Annual of the British School at Athens* 60:248–315.

Sader, Hélène. 2000. The Aramaean Kingdoms of Syria: Origins and Formation Processes. Pages 61–76 in Bunnens 2000.

———. 2010. The Aramaeans of Syria: Some Consideratons on Their Origin and Material Culture. Pages 273–300 in*The Books of Kings: Sources, Composition, Historiography and Reception*. VTSup 129; Formation and Interpretation of Old Testament Literature. Edited by A. Lemaire and B. Halpern. Leiden: Brill.

Sakellarakis, Giannes. 1992. *The Mycenaean Pictorial Style in the National Archaeological Museum of Athens*. Athens: Kapon Editions.

Saliou, Catherine. 1999–2000. Les fondations d'Antioche dans l'Antiochikos (Oratio XI) de Libanios. *Aram* 11–12:357–88.

Salles, Jean-François. 1980. *La nécropole "K" de Byblos*. Recherche sur les grandes civilisations Mémoire 2. Boulogne: Association pour la diffusion de la pensée française.

Salmeri, Giovanni. 2004. Hellenism on the Periphery: The Case of Cilicia and an Etymology of Soloikismos. *YCS* 31:181–206.

Sams, G. Kenneth. 1992. Observations on Western Anatolia. Pages 56–60 in Ward and Joukowski 1992.

———. 1994. *The Early Phrygian Pottery*. Vol. 4 of *The Gordion Excavations, 1950–1973: Final Reports*. University Museum Monograph 79. Philadelphia: University Museum, University of Pennsylvania.

Sandars, Nancy K. 1978. *The Sea Peoples: Warriors of the Ancient Mediterranean 1250–1150 B.C.* Ancient Peoples and Places 89. London: Thames & Hudson.

———. 1983. North and South at the End of the Mycenaean Age: Aspects of an Old Problem. *OJA* 2:43–68.

———. 1985. *The Sea Peoples.* London: Thames & Hudson.

Sapir, E. 1936. Hebrew 'argaz, A Philistine Word. *JAOS* 56:272–81.

Sass, Benjamin. 1983. The Revadim Seal and Its Archaic Phoenician Inscription. *AnSt* 33:169–75.

———. 2002. Wenamun and His Levant—1075 B.C. or 925 B.C. *Ägypten und Levante* 12:247–55.

———. 2010. Four Notes on Taita King of Palistin with an Excursus on King Solomon's Empire. *TA* 37:169–74.

Schachermeyr, Fritz. 1976. *Die mykenische Zeit und die Gesittung von Thera.* Vol. 2 of *Die ägäische Frühzeit: Forschungsbericht über die Ausgrabungen im letzten Jahrzehnt und über ihre Ergebnisse für unser Geschichtsbild.* Mykenische Studien 3–4. Vienna: Österreichische Akademie der Wissenschaften.

———. 1979. The Pleonastic Pottery Style of Cretan Middle IIIC and Its Cypriot Relations. Pages 204–14 in *Acts of the International Archaeological Symposium "The Relations between Cyprus and Crete, ca. 2000–500 B.C": Nicosia, 16th April–22nd April 1978.* Nicosia: Department of Antiquities, Cyprus.

———. 1980. *Griechenland im Zeitalter der Wanderungen vom Ende der mykenischen Ära bis auf die Dorier.* Die ägäische Frühzeit 4. Vienna: Österreichische Akademie der Wissenschaften.

Schaeffer, Claude F.-A. 1938. Les fouilles de Ras Shamra-Ugarit, neuvième campagne (printemps 1937). *Syria* 19:193–255.

———. 1949. *Ugaritica II: nouvelles études relatives aux découvertes de Ras Shamra.* Mission de Ras Shamra 5; Bibliothèque archéologique et historique 47. Paris: Geuthner.

———. 1952. *Enkomi-Alasia: Nouvelles Missions en Chypre 1946–1950.* Publications de la mission archéologique française et de la mission du Gouvernement de Chypre à Enkomi 1. Paris: Klincksieck.

———. 1978. *Ugaritica VII.* Mission de Ras Shamra 18; Bibliothèque archéologique et historique 99. Paris: Mission archéologique de Ras Shamra.

———, ed. 1956. *Le Palais Royal d'Ugarit IV.* Mission de Ras Shamra 9. Paris: Geuthner.

Schäfer-Lichtenberger, Christa. 2000. The Goddess of Ekron and the Religious-Cultural Background of the Philistines. *IEJ* 50:82–91.

Scheepers, Anne. 1991. Anthroponymes et toponymes du récit d'Ounamon. Pages 17–83 in Lipiński 1991.

Scheer, Tania S. 1993. *Mythische Vorväter: Zur Bedeutung griechischer Heroenmythen im Selbstverständnis kleinasiatischer Städte.* Munich: Editio Maris.

Schiering, Wolfgang. 1959–1960. Die Ausgrabung beim Athena-Tempel in Milet 1957, I: Südabschnitt. *IstMitt* 9–10:4–30.

Schmidt, Hubert. 1902. *Heinrich Schliemann's Sammlung trojanischer Altertümer.* Berlin: Reimer.

Schniedewind, William. 1998. The Geopolitical History of Philistine Gath. *BASOR* 309:69–77.

Schönfeld, Guntram. 1988. Bericht zur bemalten mykenischen Keramik: Ausgrabungen in Tiryns 1982/83. *AA* 1988:153–211.

Schreiber, Nicola. 2000. "An Archaeological and Historical Investigation into the 'Cypro-Phoenician' Pottery of the Iron Age Levant." Ph.D. diss., New College, University of Oxford.

———. 2001. A Word of Caution: Black-on-Red Pottery at Tel Mevorakh in the "Tenth" Century B.C. *PEQ* 133:132–35.

———. 2003. *The Cypro-Phoenician Pottery of the Iron Age*. Culture and History of the Ancient Near East 13. Leiden: Brill.

Schulman, Alan R. 1993. A Ramesside Queen from Ashdod. Pages 111–14 in M. Dothan and Porath 1993.

Schunck, Klaus-Dietrich. 1963. *Benjamin: Untersuchungen zur Entstehung und Geschichte eines israelitischen Stammes*. Beihefte zur Zeitschrift für die alttestamentliche Wissenschaft 86. Berlin: Töpelmann.

Seeher, Jürgen. 1997. Die Ausgrabungen in Boğazköy-Hattuša 1996. *AA* 1997:317–41.

———. 1998a. Die Ausgrabungen in Boğazköy-Hattuša 1997. *AA* 1998:215–41.

———. 1998b. Neue Befunde zur Endzeit von Hattuša: Ausgrabungen auf Büyükkaya in Boğazköy. Pages 515–23 in *Acts of the IIIrd International Congress of Hittitology, Çorum, September 16–22, 1996*. Edited by S. Alp and A. Süel. Ankara: Uyum Ajans.

———. 2000. Die Ausgrabungen in Boğazköy-Hattuša 1999. *AA* 2000:355–76.

———. 2001. Die Zerstörung der Stadt Hattuša. Pages 623–34 in *Akten des IV. Internationalen Kongresses für Hethitologie, Würzburg, 4.–8. Oktober 1999*. Edited by G. Wilhelm. Studien zu den Boğazköy-Texten 45. Wiesbaden: Harrassowitz.

Serpico, Margaret, and Raymond White. 2000. The Botanical Identity and Transport of Incense During the Egyptian New Kingdom. *Antiquity* 74:884–97.

Seton-Williams, Veronika. 1954. Cilician Survey. *AnSt* 4:121–74.

Shahack-Gross, Ruth, Rosa-Maria Albert, Ayelet Gilboa, Orna Nagar-Hilman, Ilan Sharon, and Steve Weiner. 2005. Geoarchaeology in an Urban Context: The Uses of Space in an Early Iron Age Phoenician Monumental Construction at Tel Dor (Israel). *Journal of Archaeological Science* 32:1417–31.

Shai, Itzhack, and Aren Maeir. 2003. The Pre-LMLK Jars: A New Class of Storage Jars of the Iron Age IIA. *TA* 30:108–23.

Shanks, Michael. 1999. *Art and the Greek State: An Interpretive Archaeology*. New Studies in Archaeology. Cambridge: Cambridge University Press.

Shanks, Michael, and Ian Hodder. 1995. Processual, Postprocessual and Interpretive Archaeologies. Pages 3–29 in *Interpreting Archaeology: Finding Meaning in the Past*. Edited by I. Hodder, M. Shanks, A. Alexandri, V. Buchli, J. Carman, J. Last and G. Lucas. London: Routledge.

Sharon, Ilan. 1995. The Stratigraphy of Areas A and C. Pages 49–234 in *Areas A and C: Introduction and Stratigraphy*. Vol. 1A of *Excavations at Dor, Final Report*. Edited by E. Stern. Qedem Reports 1. Jerusalem: Institute of Archaeology, Hebrew University of Jerusalem in Cooperation with The Israel Exploration Society.

———. 2001a. Philistine Bichrome Painted Pottery: Scholarly Ideology and Ceramic Typology. Pages 555–609 in Wolff 2001.

———. 2001b. "Transition Dating"—A Heuristic Mathematical Approach to the Collation of ^{14}C Dates from Stratified Sequences. *Radiocarbon* 43:345–54.

Sharon, Ilan, Ayelet Gilboa, A. J. Timothy Jull, and Elisabetta Boaretto. 2005. The Early Iron Age Dating Project: Introduction, Methodology, Progress Report and an Update on the Tel Dor Dates. Pages 65–92 in Levy and Higham 2005.

———. 2007. Report on the First Stage of the Iron Age Dating Project in Israel: Supporting a Low Chronology. *Radiocarbon* 49:1–46.

Sharon, Ilan, Ayelet Gilboa, and Avshalom Karasik. 2006. Tel Dor—2004. *Hadashot Arkheologiyot* 118. No pages. Cited 2 June 2009. Online: http://www.hadashot-esi.org.il/report_detail_eng.asp?id=313&mag_id=111.

Sharon, Ilan, Ayelet Gilboa, Andrew Stewart, Elisabeth Bloch-Smith, Ann E. Killebrew, Steve Weiner, Rebecca S. Martin, Heidi Koenig, and Ephraim Stern. 2009a. Tel Dor—2000, 2002, 2003. *Hadashot Arkheologiyot* 121. No pages. Online: http://www.hadashot-esi.org.il/report_detail_eng.asp?id=1290&mag_id=115. Cited 2 June 2009.

Sharon, Ilan, Ayelet Gilboa, Andrew Stewart, Steve Weiner, Elisabeth Bloch-Smith, Ann E. Killebrew, S. Rebecca Martin, Talia Goldman, and Yiftah Shalev. 2009b. Dor 2005—An Account of the 23rd Season of Excavations. *Hadashot Arkheologiyot* 121. No pages. Cited 2 June 2009. Online: http://www.hadashot-esi.org.il/report_detail_eng.asp?search=&id=1252&mag_id=115).

Shavit, Alon. 2000. Settlement Patterns in the Ayalon Valley in the Bronze and Iron Ages. *TA* 27:189–230.

Shelmerdine, Cynthia W. 1992. LH IIIA2–B2 Pottery. Pages 495–617 in *Minnesota Messenia Expedition: Excavations at Nichoria in Southern Greece II. The Bronze Age Occupation.* Edited by W. A. McDonald and N. C. Wilkie. Minneapolis: University of Minnesota Press.

Sherratt, Andrew, and E. Susan Sherratt. 1991. From Luxuries to Commodities: The Nature of Mediterranean Bronze Age Trading Systems. Pages 351–86 in *Bronze Age Trade in the Mediterranean: Papers Presented at the Conference Held at Rewley House, Oxford, in December 1989.* Edited by N. H. Gale. SIMA 90. Jonsered: Åströms.

Sherratt, E. Susan. 1981. "The Pottery of Late Helladic IIIC and Its Significance." Ph.D. diss., University of Oxford.

———. 1990a. Palaepaphos-Teratsoudhia Tomb 105 Chamber B: "Myc. IIIC:1b" Sherds. Pages 108–22 in *Tombs at Palaepaphos: 1. Teratsoudhia 2. Eliomylia.* Edited by V. Karageorghis. Nicosia: A. G. Leventis Foundation.

———. 1990b. Note on Two Pots from Palaepaphos-Eliomylia Tomb 119. Pages 156–63 in *Tombs at Palaepaphos.* Edited by V. Karageorghis. Nicosia: A. G. Leventis Foundation.

———. 1991. Cypriot Pottery of Aegean Type in LC II–III: Problems of Classification, Chronology and Interpretation. Pages 185–98 in Barlow, Bolger, and Kling 1991.

———. 1992. Immigration and Archaeology: Some Indirect Reflections. Pages 316–47 in part 2 of *Acta Cypria: Acts of an International Congress on Cypriote Archaeology Held in Göteborg on 22–24 August 1991.* Edited by P. Åström. SIMA Pocket-Book 117. Jonsered: Åströms.

———. 1994a. Commerce, Iron and Ideology: Metallurgical Innovation in 12th–11th Century Cyprus. Pages 59–107 in Karageorghis (ed.) 1994.

———. 1994b. Patterns of Contact Between the Aegean and Cyprus in the 13th and 12th Centuries B.C. *Archaeologia Cypria* 3:35–46.

———. 1998. "Sea Peoples" and the Economic Structure of the Late Second Millennium in the Eastern Mediterranean. Pages 292–313 in Gitin, Mazar, and Stern 1998.

———. 1999. E pur si muove: Pots, Markets and Values in the Second Millennium Mediterranean. Pages 163–211 in *The Complex Past of Pottery: Production, Circulation and Consumption of Mycenaean and Greek Pottery (Sixteenth to Early Fifth Centuries B.C.). Proceedings of the Archon International Conference, Held in Amsterdam,*

8–9 November 1996. Edited by J.-P. Crielaard, V. Stissi, and G. J. van Wijngaarden. Amsterdam: Gieben.
———. 2000. Circulation of Metals and the End of the Bronze Age in the Eastern Mediterranean. Pages 82–98 in *Metals Make the World Go Round: Supply and Circulation of Metals in Bronze Age Europe*. Edited by C. Pare. Oxford: Oxbow Books.
———. 2003. The Mediterranean Economy: "Globalisation" at the End of the Second Millennium BCE. Pages 37–63 in *Symbiosis, Symbolism and the Power of the Past: Canaan, Ancient Israel and Their Neighbors from the Late Bronze Age through Roman Palestine. Proceedings of the Centennial Symposium, W. F. Albright Institute of Archaeological Research and American Schools of Oriental Research, Jerusalem, May 29–May 31, 2000*. Edited by W. G. Dever and S. Gitin. Winona Lake, Ind.: Eisenbrauns.
———. 2006. The Chronology of the Philistine Monochrome Pottery—An Outsider's View. Pages 361–74 in Maeir and de Miroschedji 2006.
———. 2009. Imported Mycenean IIIC Pottery. Pages 478–99 in Panitz-Cohen and Mazar 2009.
Sherratt, E. Susan, and Joost H. Crouwel. 1987. Mycenaean Pottery from Cilicia in Oxford. *OJA* 6:325–52.
Shuval, Menakem. 1990. A Catalogue of Early Iron Stamp Seals From Israel. Pages 67–161 in *Die Frühe Eisenzeit*. Vol. 3 of *Studien zu den Stempelsiegeln aus Palästina/Israel*. Edited by O. Keel, M. Shuval, and C. Uehlinger. OBO 100. Freiburg: Universitätsverlag.
Silberman, Neil A. 1998. The Sea Peoples, the Victorians, and Us: Modern Social Ideological and Changing Archaeological Interpretations of the Late Bronze Age Collapse. Pages 268–75 in Gitin, Mazar, and Stern 1998.
Silberman, Neil A., and David B. Small, eds. 1997. *The Archaeology of Israel: Constructing the Past, Interpreting the Present*. JSOTSup 239. Sheffield: Sheffield Academic Press.
Simons, Jan. 1937. *Handbook for the Study of Egyptian Topographical Lists Relating to Western Asia*. Leiden: Brill.
Singer, Itamar. 1983a. Inscriptions from Aphek. *Cathedra* 27:19–26. [Hebrew]
———. 1983b. Western Anatolia in the Thirteenth Century B.C. *AnSt* 33:205–17.
———. 1985. The Beginning of Philistine Settlement in Canaan and the Northern Boundary of Philistia. *TA* 12:109–22.
———. 1988. The Origin of the Sea Peoples and Their Settlement on the Coast of Canaan. Pages 239–50 in Heltzer and Lipiński 1988.
———. 1993. The Political Organization of Philistia in Iron Age I. Pages 132–41 in Biran and Aviram 1993.
———. 1994. Egyptians, Canaanites, and Philistines in the Period of the Emergence of Israel. Pages 282–338 in *From Nomadism to Monarchy: Archaeological and Historical Aspects of Early Israel*. Edited by I. Finkelstein and N. Na'aman. Jerusalem: Israel Exploration Society.
———. 1996. Great Kings of Tarhuntašša. *SMEA* 38:63–71.
———. 1999. A Political History of Ugarit. Pages 603–734 in *Handbook of Ugaritic Studies*. Edited by W. G. Watson and N. Wyatt. HO, Erste Abteilung; Der Nahe und Mittlere Osten 39. Leiden: Brill
———. 2000a. Cuneiform, Linear, Alphabetic: The Contest between Writing Systems in the Eastern Mediterranean. Pages 23–32 in *Mediterranean Cultural Interaction*. Edited by

A. Ovadiah. Howard Gilman International Conferences 2. Tel Aviv: Tel Aviv University.
———. 2000b. New Evidence on the End of the Hittite Empire. Pages 21–33 in Oren 2000.
———. 2002. *Hittite Prayers*. SBL Writings from the Ancient World 11. Atlanta: SBL.
———. 2006a. The Philistines in the Bible: A Reflection of the Late-Monarchic Period? *Zmanim* 94:74–82 [Hebrew].
———. 2006b. Ships Bound for Lukka: A New Interpretation of the Companion Letters RS 94.2530 and RS 94.2523. *AoF* 33:242–62.
———. 2009. A Fragmentary Tablet from Tel Aphek with Unknown Script. Pages 403–14 in *Exploring the Longue Durée: Essays in Honor of Lawrence E. Stager*. Edited by J. D. Schloen. Winona Lake, Ind.: Eisenbrauns.
———. forthcoming. "Old Country" Ethnonyms in "New Countries" of the "Sea Peoples" Diaspora. In *The Quest for Excellence: Studies in Honor of Guenter Kopcke*. Edited by R. B. Koehl. Philadelphia: Academic Press.
Sivan, Dorit, Dorit Eliyahu, and Avner Raban. 2004. Late Pleistocene to Holocene Wetlands Now Covered by Sand Along the Carmel Coast of Israel and Their Relation to Human Settlement: An Example from Dor. *Journal of Coastal Research* 20:1035–48.
Slane, Dorothy A. 1987. "Middle and Late Bronze Age Architectue and Pottery in Gözlu Kule, Tarsus: A New Analysis." Ph.D. diss., Bryn Mawr College.
Small, David B. 1990. Handmade Burnished Ware and Prehistoric Aegean Economics: An Argument for Indigenous Appearance. *Journal of Mediterranean Archaeology* 3:3–25.
Smith, Amy. 1925. *Corpus Vasorum Antiquorum: Great Britain I. British Museum 1*. London: British Museum.
Smith, George A. 1931. *The Historical Geography of the Holy Land*. London: Hodder & Stoughton. Repr., New York: Harper & Row, 1966.
Smith, Joanna S. 1994. "Seals for Sealing in the Late Cypriot Period." Ph.D. diss., Bryn Mawr College.
Sneh, Amihai, Yuval Bartov, and Menachem Rosensaft. 1998. *Geological Map of Israel. Scale: 1:200,000*. Sheet I. Jerusalem: Geological Survey of Israel.
Snell, Daniel C. 2001. *Flight and Freedom in the Ancient Near East*. Culture and History of the Ancient Near East 8. Leiden: Brill
Snodgrass, Anthony M. 1971. *The Dark Age of Greece: An Archaeological Survey of the Eleventh to Eighth Centuries BC*. New York: Routledge.
Sommer, Ferdinand. 1932. *Die Ahhijavā-Urkunden*. Abhandlungen der Bayerischen Akademie der Wissenschaften, Philosophisch-historische Abt., n. F. 6. Munich: Bayerische Akademie der Wissenschaften. Repr. Hildesheim: Gerstenberg, 1975.
South, Alison. 1988. Kalavasos-Ayios Dhimitrios 1987: An Important Ceramic Group from Building X. *RDAC* 1988:223–28.
———. 1989. From Copper to Kingship. Pages 315–24 in Peltenburg 1989.
———. 1995. Urbanism and Trade in the Vasilikos Valley in the Late Bronze Age. Pages 187–97 in Bourke and Descoeudres 1995.
———. 1996. Kalavasos-Ayios Dhimitrios and the Organisation of Late Bronze Age Cyprus. Pages 39–49 in Åström and Herscher 1996.
———.2002. Late Bronze Age Settlement Patterns in Southern Cyprus: The First Kingdoms? *Cahiers du Centre d'Études Chypriotes* 32:59–72.
South Alison, Pamela Russell, and Priscilla S. Keswani. 1989. *Vasilikos Valley Project 3:*

Kalavasos-Ayios Dhimitrios II, Ceramics, Objects, Tombs, Specialist Studies. Edited by I. A. Todd. SIMA 71:3. Göteborg: Åströms.

Stager, Lawrence E. 1985. Merenptah, Israel and Sea Peoples: New Light on an Old Relief. *ErIsr* 18:56*–64*.

———. 1991. When Canaanites and Philistines Ruled Ashkelon. *BAR* 17, no. 2 (March/April): 24–43.

———. 1995. The Impact of the Sea Peoples in Canaan (1185–1050 BCE). Pages 332–48 in Levy 1995.

———. 1996. Ashkelon and the Archaeology of Destruction: Kislev 604 BCE. *ErIsr* 25:61*–74*.

———. 2008. Tel Ashkelon. *NEAEHL* 5:1578–86.

Stager, Lawrence E., J. David Schloen, Daniel M. Master, and Michael D. Press. 2008. Stratigraphic Overview. Pages 215–323 in *Ashkelon 1: Introduction and Overview (1985–2006).* Edited by L. E. Stager, J. D. Schloen, and D. M. Master. Harvard Semitic Museum Publications; Final Reports of the Leon Levy Expedition to Ashkelon 1. Winona Lake, Ind.: Eisenbrauns.

Starke, Frank. 1997. Troia im Kontext des historisch-politischen und sprachlichen Umfeldes Kleinasiens im 2. Jahrtausend. *Studia Troica* 7:447–87.

Starkey, Janet, and Lankester Harding. 1932. *Beth Pelet II: Beth Pelet Cemetery*. Publications of the British School of Archaeology in Egypt and Egyptian Research Account 52. London: British School of Archaeology in Egypt.

Steen Eveline van der. 1996. The Central East Jordan Valley in the Late Bronze and Early Iron Ages. *BASOR* 302:51–74.

Steindorff, Georg. 1937. *Aniba: Service des antiquités de l'Égypte, Mission archéologique de Nubie 1929–1934,* Vol. 2. Glückstadt: Augustin.

———. 1939. The Statuette of an Egyptian Commissioner in Syria. *JEA* 25:30–33.

Stern, Ephraim. 1978. *Excavations at Tel Mevorakh, Part One*. Qedem 9. Jerusalem: Hebrew University of Jerusalem.

———. 1981. Achaemenid Tombs at Schechem. *ErIsr* 15:312–30. [Hebrew]

———. 1984. *Excavations at Tel Mevorakh, Part Two*. Qedem 18. Jerusalem: Hebrew University of Jerusalem.

———. 1990. New Evidence from Dor for the First Appearance of the Phoenicians along the Northern Coast of Israel. *BASOR* 279:27–33.

———. 1991. Phoenicians, Sikils and Israelites in the Light of Recent Excavations at Dor. Pages 85–94 in Lipiński 1991.

———. 1993a. Dor. *NEAEHL* 1:357–68.

———. 1993b. The Many Masters of Dor, Parts I–III. *BAR* 19, no. 1 (January/February): 22–31; 19, no. 2 (March/April): 18–29; 19, no. 3 (May/June): 38–49.

———. 1993c. Ẓafit, Tel. *NEAEHL* 4:1522–24.

———. 1994a. *Dor—the Ruler of the Seas: Twelve Years of Excavations at the Israelite-Phoenician Harbor Town on the Carmel Coast.* Jerusalem: Israel Exploration Society. [Hebrew]

———. 1994b. A Phoenician-Cypriote Votive Scapula from Tel Dor: A Maritime Scene. *IEJ* 44:1–12.

———. 1995. Tel Dor: A Phoenician-Israelite Trading Center. Pages 81–93 in *Recent Excavations in Israel: A View to the West.* Edited by S. Gitin. Dubuque, Iowa: Kendall/Hunt.

———. 1998a. The Relations Between the Sea Peoples and the Phoenicians in the Twelfth and Eleventh Centuries BCE. Pages 345–52 in Gitin, Mazar, and Stern 1998.

———. 1998b. Buried Treasure: The Silver Hoard from Dor. *BAR* 24. no. 4 (July/August): 46–51, 62.

———. 2000a. *Dor—Ruler of the Seas: Nineteen Years of Excavations at the Israelite-Phoenician Harbor Town on the Carmel Coast.* Jerusalem: Israel Exploration Society.

———. 2000b. The Settlement of the Sea Peoples in Northern Israel. Pages 197–212 in Oren 2000.

———. 2001a. The Silver Hoard from Tel Dor. Pages 19–26 in *Hacksilber to Coinage: New Insights into the Monetary History of the Near East and Greece.* Edited by M. Balmuth. Numismatic Studies 24. New York: American Numismatic Society.

———. 2001b. *The Assyrian, Babylonian, and Persian Periods (732–332 B.C.E.).* Vol. 2 of *Archaeology of the Land of the Bible.* ABD Reference Library. New York: Doubleday.

———. 2006. The Sea Peoples Cult in Philistia and Northern Israel. Pages 385–98 in Maeir and de Miroschedji 2006.

Stern, Ephraim, John Berg, Ayelet Gilboa, Bracha Guz-Zilberstein, Avner Raban, Renate Rosenthal-Heginbotton, and Ilan Sharon. 1995. *Areas A and C.* Vol. 1 of *Excavations at Dor, Final Report.* Qedem Reports 1–2. Jerusalem: The Institute of Archaeology, Hebrew University of Jerusalem in Cooperation with The Israel Exploration Society.

Stern, Ephraim, John Berg, Ayelet Gilboa, and Ilan Sharon. 1998. Tel Dor—1995. *Hadashot Arkheologiyot* 18:37–40.

Stern, Ephraim, John Berg, Ayelet Gilboa, Ilan Sharon, and Jeffrey R. Zorn. 1997. Tel Dor, 1994–1995: Preliminary Stratigraphic Report. *IEJ* 47:29–56.

Stern, Ephraim, John Berg, and Ilan Sharon. 1991. Tel Dor, 1988–1989: Preliminary Report. *IEJ* 41:46–61.

Stern, Ephraim, and Ayelet Gilboa. 1989–1990. Tel Dor—1989. *Hadashot Arkheologiyot* 9:114–17.

Stern, Ephraim, Ayelet Gilboa, and John Berg. 1997. Tel Dor—1994. *Hadashot Arkheologiyot* 16:64–66.

Stern, Ephraim, Ayelet Gilboa, and Ilan Sharon. 1989. Tel Dor, 1987: Preliminary Report. *IEJ* 39:32–42.

———. 1992. Tel Dor, 1991: Preliminary Report. *IEJ* 42:34–46.

———. 2000. Tel Dor—1996. *Hadashot Arkheologyiot* 20:30–33.

Stern, Ephraim, Ayelet Gilboa, Ilan Sharon, John Berg, Jeffrey R. Zorn, Reiner Mack, Binyamin Har-Even, Natti Kranot, and Svetlana Tzibulsky. 2000. Tel Dor 1997–1998. *Hadashot Arkheologiyot* 111:23–29.

Stern, Ephraim, and Ilan Sharon. 1993. Tel Dor 1992: Preliminary Report. *IEJ* 43:126–50.

———. 1994. Tel Dor 1992/1993. *Hadashot Arkheologiyot* 14:61–72.

———. 1995. Tel Dor 1993: Preliminary Report. *IEJ* 45:26–36.

Stern, Ephraim, Ilan Sharon, Shira Buchwald, Binyamin Har-Even, Natti Kranot, and Ayelet Gilboa. 2000. Tel Dor 1999. *Hadashot Arkheologiyot* 112:29*–23*.

Stern, Ephraim, Ilan Sharon, and Ayelet Gilboa. 1988–1989. Tel Dor—1987. *Hadashot Arkheologiyot* 39:32–47.

Stewart, Andrew. 1993. A Death at Dor. *BAR* 19, no. 2 (March/April): 2:30–37.

Stockhammer, Philipp W. 2008. *'Kontinuität und Wandel—Die Keramik der Nachpalastzeit aus der Unterstadt von Tiryns'* (Heidelberg). No pages. Cited August 2008.Online: http://www.ub.uni-heidelberg.de/archiv/8612/.

———. 2012. Conceptualizing Cultural Hybridization in Archaeology. Pages 43–58 in *Conceptualizing Cultural Hybridization: A Transdisciplinary Approach*. Edited by P. W. Stockhammer. Transcultural Research—Heidelberg Studies on Asia and Europe in a Global Context. Heidelberg: Springer.

Stone, Bryan. 1995. The Philistines and Acculturation: Culture Change and Ethnic Continuity in the Iron Age. *BASOR* 298:7–32.

Stone, Elizabeth C., and Paul Zimansky. 1999. *The Iron Age Settlement at 'Ain Dara, Syria: Survey and Soundings*. BAR International Series 786. Oxford: Archaeopress.

Strack, Sara. 2007. "Regional Dynamics and Social Change in the Late Bronze and Early Iron Age: A Study of Handmade Pottery from Southern and Central Greece." Ph.D. diss., University of Edinburgh.

Strange, James. 2000. The Philistine City-States. Pages 129–39 in *A Comparative Study of Thirty City-State Cultures*. Edited by M. H. Hansen. Historik-filosofiske Skrifter 21. Copenhagen: Reitzels.

Strobel, August. 1976. *Der spätbronzezeitliche Seevölkersturm: Ein Forschungsüberblick mit Folgerungen zur biblischen Exodusthematik*. Beiheft zur Zeitschrift für die alttestamentliche Wissenschaft 145. Berlin: de Gruyter.

Stubbings, Frank. 1951. *Mycenaean Pottery from the Levant*. Cambridge: Cambridge University Press.

Sturtevant, Edgar H. 1928. The Tawagalawaš Text. *The American Journal of Semitic Languages and Literatures* 44.4: 217–31.

Stylianou, Panico. 1989. *The Age of the Kingdoms: A Political History of Cyprus in the Archaic and Classical Periods*. Archbishop Makarios III Foundation, Meletai kai Ypomnemata II. Nicosia: Archbishop Makarios III Foundation.

Sugerman, Michael O. 2000. "Webs of Commerce: The Archaeology of Ordinary Things in Late Bronze Age Israel and Palenstine." Ph.D diss., Harvard University.

Sürenhagen, Dietrich. 1996. Politischer Niedergang und kulturelles Nachleben des hethitischen Großreiches im Lichte neuerer Forschung. Pages 283–93 in *Vom Halys zum Euphrat: Thomas Beran zu Ehren*. Edited by U. Magen and M. Rashad. Altertumskunde des Vorderen Orients 7. Münster: Ugarit-Verlag.

———. 1999. Tell Gindaris and the Western Afrin Valley. *Annales archéologiques arabes syriennes* 43:159–67.

Swanton, Michael. 1996. *The Anglo-Saxon Chronicles*. New ed. Chronicles and Memorials of Great Britain and Ireland During the Middle Ages 23. London: J. M. Dent.

Sweeney, Deborah, and Assaf Yasur-Landau. 1999. Following the Path of the Sea Persons: The Women in the Medinet Habu Reliefs. *TA* 26:116–45.

Swift, Gustavus F., Jr. 1958. "The Pottery of the 'Amuq Phases K to O and Its Historical Relationships." Ph.D. diss., University of Chicago.

Swiny, Stuart. 1981. Bronze Age Settlement Patterns in Southwest Cyprus. *Levant* 13: 51–87.

Swiny, Stuart, Robert L. Hohlfelder, and Helena W. Swiny, eds. 1997. *Res Maritimae: Cyprus and the Eastern Mediterranean from Prehistory to Late Antiquity. Proceedings of the Second International Symposium "Cities on the Sea," Nicosia, Cyprus, October 18–22, 1994*. American Schools of Oriental Research, Archaeological Reports 4; Cyprus American Archaeological Research Institute Monograph 1. Atlanta: Scholars Press.

Symington, D. 2001. Hittites at Kilise Tepe. Pages 167–84 in Jean, Dinçol, and Durugönül 2001.

Tadmor, Hayim. 1966. Philistia Under Assyrian Rule. *BA* 29:86–102.

———. 1994. *The Inscriptions of Tiglath-Pileser III King of Assyria*. Jerusalem: Israel Academy of Sciences and Humanities.

Tadmor, Miriam. 1982. Female Cult Figurines in Late Canaan and Early Israel: Archaeological Evidence. Pages 139–73 in *Studies in the Period of David and Solomon and Other Essays: Papers Read at the International Symposium for Biblical Studies, Tokyo, 5–7 December, 1979*. Edited by T. Ishida. Winona Lake, Ind.: Eisenbrauns.

Tammuz, Oded. 2001. Canaan—A Land Without Limits. *UF* 33:501–43.

Tekoğlu, Recai, and André Lemaire. 2000. La bilingue royale Louvito-Phénicienne de Çineköy. *CRAI* 2000:961–1006.

Todd, Ian A., and Despo Pilides. 2001. The Archaeology of White Slip Production. Pages 27–41 in *The White Slip Ware of Late Bronze Age Cyprus: Proceedings of an International Conference Organized by Anastasios G. Leventis Foundation, Nicosia in Honour of Malcolm Wiener, Nicosia, 29th–30th October 1998*. Edited by V. Karageorghis. Denkschriften der Gesamtakademie 20; Contributions to the Chronology of the Eastern Mediterranean 2. Vienna: Österreichische Akademie der Wissenschaften.

Tonkin, Elizabeth. 1992. *Narrating Our Past: The Social Construction of Oral History*. Cambridge Studies in Oral and Literate Culture 22. Cambridge: Cambridge University Press.

Tsipopoulou, Metaxia. 2003. Review of G. Papasavvas, *Khalkinoi yposates apo ten Kypro kai ten Kretev [Bronze Stands from Cyprus and Crete]*. *BASOR* 330:85–87.

Tubb, Jonathan N. 1988a. Tell es-Sa'idiyeh: Preliminary Report on the First Three Seasons of Renewed Excavations. *Levant* 20:23–88.

———. 1988b. The Role of the Sea Peoples in the Bronze Industry of Palestine/Transjordan in the Late Bronze–Early Iron Age Transition. Pages 99–122 in *Bronzeworking Centres of Western Asia c. 1000–538 BC*. Edited by J. E. Curtis. London: Kegan Paul.

———. 1990. Preliminary Report of the Fourth Season of Excavations at Tell es-Sa'idiyeh in the Jordan Valley. *Levant* 22:21–46.

———. 1995. The Aegean Presence in Egypto-Canaan. Pages 136–45 in *Egypt, the Aegean and the Levant: Interconnections in the Second Millennium BC*. Edited by W. V. Davies and L. Schonfield. London: British Museum.

Tufnell, Olga. 1940. *Lachish II (Tell ed-Duweir): The Fosse Temple*. The Wellcome-Marston Archaeological Research Expedition to the Near East 1. Oxford: Oxford University Press.

———. 1958. *Lachish IV (Tell ed-Duweir): The Bronze Age*. The Wellcome-Marston Research Expedition to the Near East 4. London: Oxford University Press.

Tzedakis, Yanis, and Holley Martlew, eds. 1999. *Minoans and Mycenaeans: Flavours of Their Time. National Archaeological Museum, 12 July–27 November 1999*. Athens: Kapon Editions.

Uehlinger, Christoph. 1998. Ashdod. Pages 807–8 in vol. 1 of *Religion in Geschichte und Gegenwart: Handwörterbuch für Theologie und Religionswissenschaft*. Edited by H. G. Betz, D. S. Browning, B. Janowski, and E. Jüngel. 9 vols. 4th ed. Tübingen: Mohr Siebeck.

———. 2000. Gaza I. Page 481 in vol. 3 of *Religion in Geschichte und Gegenwart: Hand-*

wörterbuch für Theologie und Religionswissenschaft. Edited by H. G. Betz, D. S. Browning, B. Janowski, and E. Jüngel. 9 vols. 4th ed. Tübingen: Mohr Siebeck.

Ulf, Christoph, ed. 2003. *Der neue Streit um Troia: Eine Bilanz*. Munich: Beck.

Ünlü, Elif. 2005. Locally Produced and Painted Late Bronze to Iron Age Transitional Period Pottery of Tarsus-Gözlükule. Pages 145–68 in *Field Seasons 2001–2003 of the Tarsus-Gözlükule Interdisciplinary Project*. Edited by A. Özyar. Istanbul: Ege Yayinlari.

Ussishkin, David. 1985. Levels VII and VI at Tel Lachish and the End of the Late Bronze Age in Canaan. Pages 213–28 in *Palestine in the Bronze and Iron Ages: Papers in Honour of Olga Tufnell*. Edited by J. N. Tubb. University of London, Institute of Archaeology Occasional Publication 11. London: Institute of Archaeology.

Uziel, Joseph. 2003. "The Tell es-Safi Archaeological Survey." MA thesis, Bar-Ilan University.

———. 2007. The Development Process of Philistine Material Culture: Assimilation, Acculturation and Everything in Between. *Levant* 39:165–73.

Uziel, Joseph, and Aren M. Maeir. 2005. Scratching the Surface at Gath: Implications of the Tell eş-Şafi/Gath Surface Survey. *TA* 32:50–75.

Vagnetti, Lucia. 1999. Mycenaean Pottery in the Central Mediterranean: Imports and Local Production in Their Context. Pages 137–61 in *The Complex Past of Pottery: Production, Circulation and Consumption of Mycenaean and Greek Pottery (Sixteenth to Early Fifth Centuries BC). Proceedings of the Archon International Conference, Held in Amsterdam, 8-9 November 1996*. Edited by J.–P. Crielaard, V. Stissi, and G. J. van Wijngaarden. Amsterdam: Gieben.

———. 2000. Western Mediterranean Overview: Peninsular Italy, Sicily and Sardinia at the Time of the Sea Peoples. Pages 305–26 in Oren 2000.

Vanschoonwinkel, Jacques. 1990. Mopsos: légendes et réalité. *Hethitica* 10:185–211.

———. 1991. *L'Égée et la Mediterranée Orientale à la Fin du IIe millénaire: témoignages archéologiques et sources écrites*. Archaeologia Transatlantica 9. Louvain-la-Neuve: Art and Archaeology Publications.

———. 1994. La présence grecque à Chypre au 11e siècle av. J.-C. Pages 109–32 in Karageorghis (ed.) 1994.

Vansina, Jan. 1965. *Oral Tradition: A Study in Historical Methodology*. Chicago: Aldine.

———. 1985. *Oral Tradition as History*. Madison: University of Wisconsin Press.

Vansteenhuyse, Klaas. 1998–1999. "A Critical Review of Archaeological Models for Ethnicity: Case-Study. The Sikil at Tel Dor (Israel)." MA thesis, Katholieke Universiteit Leuven.

Vaughan, Sarah. 1991. Late Cypriot Base Ring Ware: Studies in Raw Materials and Technology. Pages 337–68 in *Recent Developments in Ceramic Petrology*. Edited by A. Middleton and I. Freestone. British Museum Occasional Paper 81. London: British Museum Research Laboratory.

Ventris, Michael, and John Chadwick. 1974. *Documents in Mycenaean Greek*. 2nd ed. Cambridge: Cambridge University Press.

Venturi, Fabrizio. 1998. The Late Bronze II and Early Iron I Levels. Pages 123–62 in Cecchini and Mazzoni 1998.

———. 2000. Le premier âge du Fer à Tell Afis et en Syrie septentrionale. Pages 505–36 in Bunnens 2000.

———. 2002 Area E: l'occupazione del Bronzo Tardo II–Ferro I. Il settore sud. Pages 29–33 in *Tell Afis, Siria: 2000–2001*. Edited by S. Mazzoni. Pisa: Università degli Studi di Pisa.

———. 2007. *La Siria nell'età delle trasformazioni (XIII–X sec. a.C.): Nuovi contributi dallo scavo di Tell Afis*. Studi e Testi Orientali 8, Serie Archeologica. Bologna: CLUEB.

———. 2010. Cultural Breakdown or Evolution? The Impact of Changes in 12th Century BC Tell Afis. Pages 1–28 in *Societies in Transition: Evolutionary Processes in the Northern Levant between Late Bronze Age II and Early Iron Age. Papers Presented on the Occasion of the 20th Anniversary of the New Excavations in Tell Afis, Bologna, 15th November 2007*. Edited by F. Venturi. Studi e testi orientali 9; Serie archeologica 2. Bologna: CLUEB.

Vermeule, Emily. 1974. *Toumba tou Skourou, The Mound of Darkness: A Bronze Age Town on the Morphou Bay in Cyprus*. Boston: Harvard University and the Museum of Fine Arts.

Vermeule, Emily, and Vassos Karageorghis. 1982. *Mycenaean Pictorial Vase Painting*. Cambridge, Mass.: Harvard University Press.

Visser, Edzard. 2001. Die Troianer und ihre Alliierten in der Sicht Homers. Pages 84–87 in *Troia—Traum und Wirklichkeit*. Edited by Archäologisches Landesmuseum Baden-Württemberg. Stuttgart: Theiss.

Vitale, Salvatore. 2005. L'insediamento di 'Serraglio' durante il Tardo Bronzo. *Annuario della Scuola Archeologica Italiana di Atene* 83:71–94.

———. 2006. The LH IIIB–LH IIIC Transition on the Mycenaean Mainland: Ceramic Phases and Terminology. *Hesperia* 75:177–204.

———. 2009. The Serragalio, Eleona, and Langada Archaeological Project (SELAP): Report on the Results of the 2009 and 2010 Study Seasons. *Annuario della Scuola Archeologica Italiana di Atene* 87:1233–52.

Voigt, Mary M. 1994. Excavations at Gordion 1988–89: The Yassihöyük Stratigraphic Sequence. Pages 265–93 in Çilingiroğlu and French 1994.

Voigt, Mary M., and Robert Henrickson. 2000. The Early Iron Age at Gordion: The Evidence from the Yassıhöyük Stratigraphic Sequence. Pages 327–60 in Oren 2000.

Voigtländer, Walter. 1986. Milets Beziehungen zur Argolis in späthelladischer Zeit. Pages 17–34 in *Milet 1899–1980: Ergebnisse, Probleme und Perspektiven einer Ausgrabung. Kolloquium Frankfurt am Main 1980*. Edited by W. Müller-Wiener. IstMitt 31. Tübingen: Wasmuth.

Voskos, Ioannis, and A. Bernard Knapp. 2008. Cyprus at the End of the Late Bronze Age: Crisis and Colonization or Continuity and Hybridization? *AJA* 112:659–84.

Wace, Alan J. B., and Frank H. Stubbings. 1963. *A Companion to Homer*. London: Macmillan.

Wachsmann, Shelley. 1987. *Aegeans in the Theban Tombs*. OLA 20. Leuven: Peeters.

———. 1989. "Seagoing Ships and Seamanship in the Late Bronze Levant." Ph.D. diss., Hebrew University of Jerusalem.

Wachter-Sarkady, Claudia. 1998. Archaeobotanical Investigations. Pages 433–50 in Cecchini and Mazzoni 1998.

Wainwright, Gerald A. 1939. Some Sea-Peoples and Others in the Hittite Archives. *JEA* 25:148–53.

Walberg, Gisela. 1976. Northern Intruders in Mycenaean IIIC? *AJA* 80:186–87.

Ward, William A., and Martha S. Joukowsky, eds. 1992. *The Crisis Years: The 12th Century B.C. From Beyond the Danube to the Tigris*. Dubuque, Iowa: Kendall/Hunt.

Wardle, Kenneth A. 1973. A Group of Late Helladic IIIB 2 Pottery from within the Citadel at Mycenae: The "Causeway Deposit." *Annual of the British School at Athens* 68:297–342.

Warren, Peter, and Vronwy Hankey. 1989. *Aegean Bronze Age Chronology*. Bristol: Bristol Classical Press.

Watrous, L. Vance. 1991. The Origin and Iconography of the Minoan Painted Larnax. *Hesperia* 60:285–307.

———. 1992. *Kommos III: The Late Bronze Age Pottery*. Princeton: Princeton University Press.

Watterson, Barbara. 1991. *Women in Ancient Egypt*. New York: St. Martin's Press.

Way, Kenneth C. 2010. Assessing Sacred Asses: Bronze Age Donkey Burials in the Near East. *Levant* 42:210–25.

Webb, Jennifer M. 1985. The Incised Scapulae. Pages 317–28 in Karageorghis and Demas 1985, Vol. 2.

———. 1999. *Ritual Architecture, Iconography and Practice in the Late Cypriot Bronze Age*. SIMA Pocket-Book 75. Jonsered: Åströms.

———. 2000. The Sanctuary of the Ingot God at Enkomi: A New Reading of Its Construction, Use and Abandonment. Pages 69–82 in *Contributions to the Archaeology and History of the Bronze and Iron Ages in the Eastern Mediterranean: Studies in Honour of Paul Åström*. Edited by P. Fischer. Vienna: Österreichisches Archäologisches Institut.

Webster, Jane. 2001. Creolizing the Roman Provinces. *AJA* 105/2:209–25.

Wees, Hans van. 1997. Homeric Warfare. Pages 668–93 in *A New Companion to Homer*. Edited by I. Morris and B. Powell. Mnemosyne, Bibliotheca Classica Batava Suppl. 163. Leiden: Brill.

Weickert, Carl. 1957. Die Ausgrabungen beim Athena-Tempel in Milet 1955. *IstMitt* 7:102–32.

Weinberg, Saul S. 1983. *Bamboula at Kourion: The Architecture*. University Museum Monograph 42. Philadelphia: University Museum of Archaeology and Anthropology, University of Pennsylvania.

Weinstein, James M. 1981. The Egyptian Empire in Palestine: A Reassessment. *BASOR* 241:1–28.

———. 1992. The Collapse of the Egyptian Empire in the Southern Levant. Pages 142–50 in Ward and Joukowsky 1992.

Weippert, Helga. 1988. *Palästina in vorhellenistischer Zeit*. Handbuch der Archäologie, Vorderasien 2:1. Munich: Beck.

Weiss, Ehud, and Michael Kislev. 2001. The Economic Activity of Iron Age Ashkelon: Plant Remains as Indicators. Pages 75–88 in *Ashkelon: A City on the Seashore*. Edited by A. Sasson, Z. Safrai, and N. Sagiv. Tel Aviv: Eretz. [Hebrew]

Weiss, Harvey, ed. 1985. *Ebla to Damascus: Art and Archaeology of Ancient Syria*. Washington, D.C.: Smithsonian Institute.

Wells, Berit. 1983. *The Protogeometric Period: An Analysis of the Settlement*. Vol. 4, part 2 of *Asine II: Results of the Excavations East of the Acropolis 1970–1974*. Stockholm: Svenska Institutet i Athen.

Welten, Peter. 1973. *Geschichte und Geschichtsdarstellung in den Chronikbüchern*. WMANT 42. Neukirchen-Vluyn: Neukirchener.

Wengrow, David. 1996. Egyptian Taskmasters and Heavy Burdens: Highland Exploitation and the Collared-Rim Pithos of the Bronze/Iron Age Levant. *OJA* 15:307–26.

Wente, Edward F. 1963. Shekelesh or Shasu? *JNES* 22:167–72.

———. 1967. *Late Ramesside Letters*. SAOC 33. Chicago: The University of Chicago Press.

———. 1990. *Letters from Ancient Egypt*. SBL Writings from the Ancient World 1. Atlanta: Scholars Press.

Wente, Edward F., Jr., and Charles van Siclen. 1977. A Chronology of the New Kingdom. Pages 217–61 in *Studies in Honor of George R. Hughs*. Edited by J. Johnson and E. F. Wente, Jr. SAOC 39. Chicago: Oriental Institute, University of Chicago.

Whitbread, Ian. 1995. *Greek Transport Amphorae: A Petrological and Archaeological Study*. Fitch Laboratory Occasional Paper 4. Athens: British School at Athens.

Wijngaarden, Gert J. van. 1990. "Ugarit en het Aegeisch gebied: handelscontacten in de Late Bronstijd." MA thesis, University of Amsterdam.

———. 1999a. An Archaeological Approach to the Concept of Value: Mycenaean Pottery at Ugarit (Syria). *Archaeological Dialogues* 6:2–46.

———. 1999b. "Use and Appreciation of Mycenaean Pottery Outside Greece: Contents of LH I–LH IIIB Finds in the Levant, Cyprus and Italy." Ph.D. diss., University of Amsterdam.

———. 2002. *Use and Appreciation of Myceneaen Pottery in the Levant, Cyprus and Italy (1600–1200 BC)*. Amsterdam Archaeological Studies 8. Amsterdam: Amsterdam University Press.

Wilhelm, Gernot, and Johannes Boese. 1987. Absolute Chronologie und die hethitische Geschichte des 15. und 14. Jahrhunderts v. Chr. Pages 74–117 in Åström 1987.

Wilkie, Laurie A. 2000. Culture Bought: Evidence of Creolization in the Consumer Goods of an Enslaved Bahamaian Family. *Historical Archaeology* 34/3:10–26.

Wolff, Hans Walter. 1977. *Obadja und Jona*. Vol. 3 of *Dodekapropheton*. BKAT 14:3. Neukirchen-Vluyn: Neukirchener Verlag.

Wolff, Samuel R. 1998a. Archaeology in Israel. *AJA* 102:757–807.

———. 1998b. An Iron Age I Site at 'En Hagit (Northern Ramat Menashe). Pages 449–54 in Gitin, Mazar, and Stern 1998.

———, ed. 2001. *Studies in the Archaeology of Israel and Neighboring Lands in Memory of Douglas L. Esse*. SAOC 59; ASOR Books 5. Chicago: Oriental Institute of the University of Chicago; Atlanta: American Schools of Oriental Research.

Wood, Bryant G. 1991. The Philistines Enter Canaan—Were They Egyptian Lackeys or Invading Conquerors? *BAR* 17, no. 6 (November/December): 44–52, 89–90.

Wood, Michael. 1996. *In Search of the Trojan War*. Updated ed. Berkeley: University of California Press.

Woolley, C. Leonard. 1953. *A Forgotten Kingdom: Being a Record of the Results Obtained from the Excavation of Two Mounds, Atchana and Al Mina, in the Turkish Hatay*. London: Penguin.

———. 1955. *Alalakh: An Account of the Excavations at Tell Atchana in the Hatay, 1937–1949*. Reports of the Research Committee of the Society of Antiquaries of London 18. Oxford: University Press for the Society of Antiquaries.

Woudhuizen, Frederik C. 2006. "The Ethnicity of the Sea Peoples." Ph.D. diss., Erasmus Universiteit Rotterdam.

Wright, George E. 1961. The Archaeology of Palestine. Pages 73–112 in *The Bible and the Ancient Near East: Essays in Honor of William Foxwell Albright*. Edited by G. E. Wright. New York: Routledge.

Wright, James C. 1996. Empty Cups and Empty Jugs: The Social Role of Wine in Minoan and Mycenaean Societies. Pages 287–309 in *The Origins and Ancient History of Wine*. Edited by P. E. McGovern, S. J. Fleming, and S. H. Katz. Food and Nutrition in History and Anthropology 11. Amsterdam: Gordon & Breach.

———. 2004. Mycenaean Drinking Services and Standards of Etiquette. Pages 90–104 in *Food, Cuisine and Society in Prehistoric Greece*. Edited by P. Halstead and J. C. Barrett. Sheffield Studies in Aegean Archaeology 5. Oxford: Oxbow.

Yadin, Yigael. 1968. And Dan, Why Did He Remain in Ships? *AJBA* 1:9-23.

———. 1970. The Megiddo of the Kings of Israel. *BA* 33:66–96.

Yadin,Yigael, and Shulamit Geva. 1986. *Investigations at Beth Shean: The Early Iron Age Strata*. Qedem 23. Jerusalem: Hebrew University of Jerusalem.

Yağcı, Remzi. 2003. The Stratigraphy of Cyprus WS II and Mycenaean Cups in Soli Höyük Excavations. Pages 93–106 in Fischer et al. 2003.

Yakar, Jak. 2006. Dating the Sequence of the Final Destruction/Abandonment of LBA Settlements: Towards a Better Understanding of Events that Led to the Collapse of the Hittite Kingdom. Pages 33–51 in Mielke, Schoop, and Seeher 2006.

Yalçin, Serdar. 2005. "Re-evaluation of the Late Bronze to Early Iron Age Transitional Period: Stratigraphic Sequence and Plain Ware of Tarsus-Gözlükule." MA thesis, Boğiçi University.

Yamada, Shigeo. 2000. *The Construction of the Assyrian Empire: A Historical Study of the Inscriptions of Shalmanesar III Relating to His Campaigns in the West*. Culture and History of the Ancient Near East 3. Leiden: Brill.

Yassine, Khair. 1975. Anthropoid Coffins from Raghdan Royal Palace Tomb in Amman. *ADAJ* 20:57–68.

———. 1988. *Archaeology of Jordan: Essays and Reports*. Amman: Department of Archaeology, University of Jordan.

Yasur-Landau, Assaf. 2002. "Social Aspects of Aegean Settlement in the Southern Levant in the End of the 2nd Millennium BCE." Ph.D. diss., Tel Aviv University. [Hebrew]

———. 2005. Old Wine in New Vessels: Intercultural Contact, Innovation and Aegean, Canaanite and Philistine Foodways. *TA* 32:168–91.

———. 2007. Let's Do the Time Warp Again: Migration Processes and the Absolute Chronology of the Philistine Settlement. Pages 609–20 in Bietak and Czerny 2007.

———. 2010. *Philistines and Aegean Migration at the End of the Late Bronze Age*. New York: Cambridge University Press.

Yellin, Joseph. 1989. The Origin of Cypro-Geometric Pottery from Tel Dor. *IEJ* 39:219–27.

———. 2007. Instrumental Neutron Activation Based on Provenance Studies at the Hebrew University of Jerusalem, with a Case Study on Mycenaean Pottery from Cyprus. *Archaeometry* 49:271–88.

Yener, K. Aslihan, ed. 2005. *Surveys in the Plain of Antioch and Orontes Delta, Turkey, 1995–2002*. Vol. 1 of *The Amuq Valley Regional Projects*. Chicago: Oriental Institute, University of Chicago.

Yener, K. Aslihan, Christopher Edens, Timothy P. Harrison, Jan Verstraete, and Tony J. Wilkinson. 2000. The Amuq Valley Regional Project, 1995–1998. *AJA* 104:163–220.

Yisraeli, Yael. 1993. Far'ah, Tell el- (South). *NEAEHL* 2:441–44.

Yon, Marguerite. 1971. *Salamine de Chypre II: la tombe T. I. du XI e S. av. J.-C.* Salamine de Chypre 2. Paris: Boccard.

———. 1992. The End of the Kingdom of Ugarit. Pages 111–22 in Ward and Joukowsky 1992.

———. 1997. *La cité d'Ougarit sur le tell de Ras Shamra*. Paris: Éditions Recherche sur les Civilisations.

Yon, Marguerite, and Annie Caubet. 1985. *Kition-Bamboula III: le sondage L–N 13 (Bronze Récent et Géométrique I)*. Éditions Recherche sur les civilisations Mémoire 56. Paris: Éditions Recherche sur les civilizations.

Yon, Marguerite, and Florence Malbran-Labat. 1995. La stèle de Sargon II à Chypre. Pages 169–79 in *Khorsabad, le palais de Sargon II, roi d'Assyrie: Actes du colloque organisé au Musée du Louvre par le Service culturel les 21 et 22 janvier 1994*. Edited by A. Caubet. Paris: Documentation française.

Yon, Marguerite, Vassos Karageorghis, and Nicolle Hirschfeld. 2000. *Céramiques mycéniennes d'Ougarit*. Ras Shamra-Ougarit 13. Paris: Éditions Recherche sur les civilisations; Nicosia: A. G. Leventis Foundation.

Yon, Marguerite, Vassos Karageorghis, and Nicolle Hirschfeld, and Annie Caubet. 2000. *Ras Shamra-Ougarit XIII: céramiques mycéniennes*. Paris: Association pour la diffusion de la pensée française; Nicosia: A. G. Leventis Foundation.

Yon, Marguerite, Maurice Sznycer, and Pierre Bordreuil, eds. 1995. *Le pays d'Ougarit autour de 1200 av. J.-C.: histoire et archéologie. Actes du colloque international, Paris, 28 juin–1er juillet 1993*. Ras Shamra-Ougarit 11. Paris: Éditions Recherche sur les civilisations.

Yoyotte, Jean. 1949. Les stèles de Ramsès II à Tanis. *Kemi* 10:58–74.

Zagorski, Svetlana. 2004. "Tel Akko (Area PH) from the Late Bronze IIB to the Iron IA Period." MA thesis, University of Haifa. [Hebrew]

Zarzeki-Peleg, Anabel. 1997. Hazor, Jokneam and Megiddo in the Tenth Century B.C.E. *TA* 24:258–88.

Zerner, Carol, Peter Zerner, and John Winder. 1993. *Wace and Blegen: Pottery as Evidence for Trade in the Aegean Bronze Age 1939–1989. Proceedings of the International Conference Held at the American School of Classical Studies at Athens, Athens [sic], December 2–3, 1989*. Amsterdam: Gieben.

Zertal, Adam. 2002. Philistine Kin Found in Early Israel. *BAR* 28, no. 3 (May/June): 18–31, 60–61.

Zevulun, Uza. 1983–1984. Ram-Headed Cup of Late Canaanite Date from the Moosberg Collection. *Israel—People and Land: Haaretz Museum Yearbook* 1/19:41–54. [Hebrew]

———. 1987. A Canaanite Ram-Headed Cup. *IEJ* 37:88–104.

Zimhoni, Orna. 1990. Two Ceramic Assemblages from Lachish Levels III and II. *TA* 17:3–52.

———. 1997. *Studies in the Iron Age Pottery of Israel*. Tel Aviv Occasional Publications 2. Tel Aviv: Institute of Archaeology, Tel Aviv University.

Zorn, Jeffrey, and Robert Brill. 2007. Iron Age I Glass from Tel Dor, Israel. *Journal of Glass Studies* 49:256–59.

Zuckerman, Sharon. 2008. Fit for a (Not-Quite-So-Great) King: A Faience Lion-Headed Cup from Hazor. *Levant* 40:115–25.

Zukerman, Alexander. 2009. Notes on Pottery with Philistine, Cypriot and Aegean Affinities. Pages 500–509 in Panitz-Cohen and Mazar 2009.

Zukerman, Alexander, and Seymour Gitin, forthcoming. In Garfinkel, T. Dothan, and Gitin forthcoming.

Subject Index

CPSIA information can be obtained
at www.ICGtesting.com
Printed in the USA
FFOW03n0537291017
41577FF

9 781589 831292